W9-DGW-025

Families
and Their Social Worlds

Karen Seccombe
Portland State University

Boston • New York • San Francisco
Mexico City • Montreal • Toronto • London • Madrid • Munich • Paris
Hong Kong • Singapore • Tokyo • Cape Town • Sydney

Executive Editor: *Jeff Lasser*
Senior Development Editor: *Leah Strauss*
Series Editorial Assistant: *Lauren Houlihan*
Associate Editor: *Deb Hanlon*
Senior Marketing Manager: *Kelly May*
Production Editor: *Claudine Bellanton*
Editorial Production Service: *Marty Tenney, Modern Graphics, Inc.*
Composition Buyer: *Linda Cox*
Manufacturing Buyer: *Debbie Rossi*
Electronic Composition: *Modern Graphics, Inc.*
Interior Design: *Roy Neuhaus*
Photo Researcher: *Lisa Jelly Smith*
Cover Administrator and Designer: *Joel Gendron*

For related titles and support materials, visit our online catalog at www.ablongman.com

Between the time website information is gathered and then published, it is not unusual for some sites to have closed. Also, the transcription of URLs can result in typographical errors. The publisher would appreciate notification where these errors occur so that they may be corrected in subsequent editions.

Library of Congress Cataloging-in-Publication Data

Seccombe, Karen
Families and their social worlds / Karen Seccombe.
p. cm.
Includes bibliographical references and index.
ISBN-13: 978-0-205-51645-2
ISBN-10: 0-205-51645-9
1. Family. I. Title.
HQ503.S38 2008
306.85—dc22

2007010726

Printed in the United States of America

10 9 8 7 6 5 4 3 2 1 RRD-OH 11 10 9 8 7

Photo credits appear on page 577, which constitutes an extension of the copyright page.

Brief Contents

Contents

CHAPTER 2 Families Throughout the World: Marriage, Family, and Kinship 36

CHAPTER 3 Families Throughout History 66

CHAPTER 4 Sex, Gender, and Families 96

CHAPTER 5 Social Stratification, Social Class, and Families 130

CHAPTER 6 Race, Ethnicity, and Families 168

PART II Negotiating Family Relationships

CHAPTER 7 Courtship, Intimacy, and Partnering 204

CHAPTER 8 Marriage: A Personal Relationship and Social Institution 240

CHAPTER 9 Becoming a Parent 270

CHAPTER 11 Families and the Work They Do 334

CHAPTER 12 Aging Families 366

PART III Social Problems and Families

CHAPTER 13 Violence and Abuse 404

CHAPTER 14 Divorce and Repartnering 436

PART IV What Have We Learned?

Preface

Family courses are popular on college campuses because families themselves are entities of profound interest. We are intensely curious about families, and they are the center of many of our conversations, movies, television shows, songs, news stories, and cartoons. Families can offer some of the most exciting times of our lives: falling in love, getting married, or the birth or adoption of a baby. Families also can offer some of the worst times: disagreements, betrayal, violence, and divorce. What students tend to forget, however, is that families are far more than just personal relationships. Families are a powerful social institution with a set of rules, regulations, and norms (sometimes written, sometimes not) that are situated in a particular culture in a particular historical time.

I hope that you find this an upbeat and high-quality text written for students in both Sociology and Family Studies programs. I envision that students may have likely taken at least an Introduction to Sociology course, and would therefore be familiar with general sociological concepts, e.g., culture, stratification, social structure, socialization, race and ethnicity. I review and build upon these concepts—highlighting the "sociological imagination"—and show how they can be applied to a specific substantive area—the field of families. I want to teach students to think about families beyond their own personal experiences, and even beyond family structure in the United States. I hope to impart a passion for critical thinking as students see that families exist within social worlds. My overarching goal is to show that our conceptions and organizations of families are imbedded within our social structure, and to make the discovery of this fact interesting to students as I showcase how and why family scholars do their work. Moreover, as a sociological imagination reveals that many family concerns are really *social issues* rather than merely private ones, solutions to these concerns must be social in nature as well. Therefore, imbedded in each chapter are important policy considerations to illustrate what is currently being done, and perhaps even more importantly, what *can* be done to strengthen families and intimate relationships. "Social Policy and Family Resilience" identifies social policies that have made a real difference in the lives of millions, in the United States and elsewhere.

Briefly, the text has several key themes: (1) families are both a public social institution and a private personal relationship; (2) social inequality has a powerful influence on family life; (3) family policies reflect historical, cultural, political, and social factors; and (4) understanding families in the United States requires a comparative perspective.

Families are Both a Public Social Institution and a Private Personal Relationship

Families are not isolated entities, but live in larger social worlds affected by other social institutions such as the economy, religious norms, and the political system. Families can best be understood by examining how they interact with (and are influenced by) other social institutions within society. Families cannot merely be separated as "havens" from the rest of society. Patterns of education, religious customs, economic systems, and political systems all shape family patterns, attitudes, behaviors, and the constraints and opportunities experienced by individual members. For example, specific social institutions may influence who is considered an appropriate mate, which family members work outside the home and what kind of work they do, who has the primary responsibility for housework and other domestic labor, how children are raised and disciplined, which children can be schooled, how power and decision-making among family members will be allocated, and the roles that extended family members are expected to play.

To help students realize these interconnections, this text uses numerous cross-cultural and historical examples in each chapter to clearly illustrate the interrelationship between social institutions. For example, I discuss how marriage norms are influenced by economic systems, how conceptions of gender are influenced by political systems, or how fertility is influenced by religion. I then show how the interrelationships exist in our own culture as well. It is important to recognize how our personal choices and behaviors are shaped by larger social structures. For example, how does one's level of education affect the chances of having children? And is the relationship between level of education and the likelihood of having children identical for men and women? Are children viewed as an asset in the United States, and how might views toward children be related to structural conditions, such as capitalism, urbanization, or the distribution of money and other resources?

Social Inequality Has a Powerful Influence on Family Life

Most Americans believe that the United States provides nearly equal opportunities for everyone. However, I show that American society is highly stratified on the basis of economics, power, and social status. Inequality is woven into many of our basic social structures and institutions. These patterns of social inequality filter down and shape all dimensions of family life, e.g., the neighborhood in which you live, your gendered expectations, whether you are legally allowed to marry your partner, the values you are likely to hold for your children, the type of job you are likely to get, your consumption patterns, daily stressors, and your coping mechanisms. Social class, sex, race and ethnicity, and sexual orientation affect the way family members interact with one another and the way that they are responded to.

Conversely, patterns of social inequality are also shaped *by* families. Americans fantasize that they can be anything they want to be, but in reality there is little substantial upward (or downward) social mobility. People usually live out their lives in generally the same social class in which they were born. Families pass on their wealth and social capital (or their lack of it) to their newest members, and this perpetuates social inequality. For example, because of U.S. inheritance laws, affluent parents are able to distribute their wealth to their children upon their death. Consequently, some of the richest people have only marginal employment histories. Yet others work relentlessly, often in the unglamorous but growing service sector, and find no real route to a better life. Their wages are low, they may not receive health insurance or other benefits. And they live on the margin only one paycheck away from impoverishment. My goal is to reveal to students the complexities of social inequality, and its often deleterious effects on families.

Family Policies Reflect a Complex Set of Historical, Cultural, Political, and Social Factors

If families are public social institutions in addition to private personal relationships, then we must recognize the importance of federal, state, and local involvement. The third theme of this text is that government regulates many conditions of families, and these policies reflect historical patterns, cultural values, social conditions, and political viewpoints. This may occur by enacting specific policies targeting certain groups or certain aspects of family life, such as welfare reform, requiring partners to get a blood test before marrying, or passing legislation to prohibit gays and lesbians from marrying.

Conversely, historical, cultural, political, and social factors may also exercise a strong influence backhandedly by the *absence* of specific policies. For example, the U.S. government offers no systematic paid leave to women who have just given birth. This is in sharp contrast to other industrialized nations (and many nonindustrialized ones). Commonly in other countries, women will receive 6 to 12 months off of work, with full or nearly full pay. Why does the United States offer so little to new parents? The United States is far more likely than other countries to believe that family matters are personal issues, reflecting our longstanding belief in rugged individualism. Family policies reflect values about personal responsibility versus collective good, the role of work in our lives, the expectations placed on mothers and fathers to manage the inherent conflicts between their work and family lives, and the level of concern over social inequality.

The text explores the origins of many critical family policies and reveals how they operate today, e.g., social security, welfare, employer-sponsored health insurance, and with what consequences. Drawing upon United States and cross-cultural examples, policy discussions are integrated into each chapter to illustrate how specific policies can be used to strengthen families and make them more resilient, e.g., maternity leave, child care, family allowance, child support, affirmative action, and universal health care.

Understanding Families in the United States Requires a Comparative Perspective

The fourth theme of the text shows that one of the best ways to understand what is happening in the United States today is to examine what has happened in other times and in other places around the world. Learning how other societies structure families, how they collectively think about families, how they encourage members to interact, and how they deal with the challenges families face can provide insight into our own concerns. We cannot ignore what is happening in other places, because societies are becoming increasingly interconnected. New technologies, immigration, commerce across borders, and greater ease in world communication and travel have increased visibility, and the United States can no longer remain isolated. While many problems, such as poverty or HIV/AIDS, are considerably worse in other countries, other problems loom larger in the United States than elsewhere. For example, the U.S. infant mortality rate is among the highest for developing countries, and the life expectancy rate is among the lowest. How can a society as richly endowed as the United States have such poor health statistics? U.S. poverty is rising and is among the highest of developed countries as are teenage pregnancy rates and the likelihood of divorce. What can we learn from other countries to better understand our own?

Likewise, it is easy to ignore history and only focus on the here and now. But many of our current family issues are rooted in the traditions of the past. For example, to truly understand the high rate of divorce in the United States we should be aware of the ways in which the notion of love, which evolved in the eighteenth century, changed the entire basis on which mates were chosen, and thereby increased the likelihood of couples ending an unhappy marriage.

Chapter Overviews

Chapter 1 introduces a sociological imagination, which uses a comparative approach and empirical methods to describe and explain patterns of family structure, family change, and social relationships. As a public social institution, families are not entities isolated from the rest of society, but continually change and adapt to peoples' needs, and to the changes found in other social institutions. This chapter introduces four specific themes that are found within each chapter: (1) the family is a public social institution as well as a private personal relationship; (2) social inequality powerfully shapes virtually all dimensions of family life; (3) family policies reflect historical, cultural, political, and social factors; and (4) a comparative approach can yield insight into family structure and family dynamics.

Chapter 2 examines both the universal functions and variation in structure within marriage, family, and kinship patterns throughout the world, revealed by sources of comparative data. Families are found in every society because they provide functions that other social institutions cannot provide. Yet families are not monolithic or static, but continually adapt to changing circumstances. Two perspectives are presented that contrast the nature of social change upon families: Modernization and World Systems Theory. Although the latter focuses more on the economic and political interdependence, and exploitation found among nations, both agree that processes such as industrialization dramatically transform the culture and the environment, and therefore reshape the form, function, and roles within families.

Chapter 3 suggests that a look at history can provide us with critical insights about families today. Family historians use multiple research methods to piece together the everyday life of families in the past. Historians looking from preindustrial societies to more recent groups reveal that we have unfairly glorified families in the past. We now know that many families suffered hardship, and social problems were widespread. Yet, commonly we compare families today with the idealized version of the "normal" family of the brief 1950s in which we envision that fathers earned the wages, mothers stayed at home to care for children. This chapter provides a historical overview of families. The goal is to show that our current attitudes, behaviors, and public policies relating to such family concerns as courtship, mate selection, cohabitation, marriage, sexuality, children, the elderly, and extended families are intricately connected to the past.

Chapter 4 explores the ways that sex and gender affect us, and shapes family and intimate relationships. Virtually all social institutions, whether political, religious, economic, educational, or familial, distinguish between men and women in fundamental ways that extend far beyond biological sex differences. Gender is largely a social construction; a comparative approach reveals that expected masculine and feminine behaviors vary historically and cross-culturally. Several key agents of socialization are responsible for teaching gender norms, such as families, toys, schools, peer groups, and the mass media. Patriarchy is manifested around the world, although its form is highly variable. Despite our thinking to the contrary, patriarchy persists in western nations, including the United States. The ways in which sex and gender are rooted in our social structure have critical implications for how families are constructed and how family members interact, and these will be revealed in the upcoming chapters.

Chapter 5 introduces the importance of social class to understanding families. Social stratification and social class are important components of C. Wright Mills' claim that our personal experiences are in large part shaped by broad social, historical, and cultural forces. This chapter explores social stratification, social class, poverty, and family resiliency. Persons living in poverty are particularly vulnerable in terms of their health and social well-being. Strong family policies, such as the earned income tax credit or national health insurance, can go a long way in assisting families struggling to make ends meet. It is also important to recognize that social class interacts with other statuses and dimensions of stratification, such as sex, race, or ethnicity. A person is not simply rich, poor, or somewhere in the middle, but a working-class Hispanic woman; a Chinese American upper-class male; a black middle-class female; or a poor white woman; these statuses, together, influence our experiences.

Chapter 6 emphasizes that we all have a race and an ethnicity. Although whites have the privilege of rarely thinking about them, it remains that skin color, physical features, country of origin, culture, and dominant language are associated with family structure and family interaction. This chapter provides an important foundation to upcoming chapters by introducing basic facts about race, ethnicity, and the changing demographic landscape of the United States. I introduce general definitions, and then look at the demographic trends and social characteristics of several racial and ethnic groups. Each race or ethnic group has a rich history and culture associated with it, and draws upon its heritage in meaningful ways to create relevant family structures. These family structures need not be denigrated simply because they differ from others. The purpose of this chapter is to introduce the idea that there is more than one model to family life, and that race and ethnicity (alone, and in conjunction with other statuses such as sex and class) provide unique opportunities and challenges, and are important statuses that frame our family lives.

Chapter 7 introduces several key concepts surrounding the development of intimacy, including mate selection, love, sexual orientation, sexuality, and cohabitation. People become intimate, form partnerships, or marry to improve their economic conditions, for sheer survival, to increase their social standing, or to please their parents and build family alliances. Cultural traditions, the environment, social norms, and religious customs have as much to do with mate selection as love and affection, sexual convenience, or compatibility. Many cultures do not necessarily equate love with marriage, and in fact may see love as dangerous to a good marital relationship. Values also change over time. Today in the United States it is becoming increasingly common for unmarried couples to engage in sexual relationships and to cohabit. However, same-sex marriage continues to be steeped in controversy, unlike Canada's recent court ruling in favor of wider support for civil unions.

Chapter 8 examines marriage as both as social institution and a personal relationship, noting that it is recognized in some form around the world. As a social institution there are rules, rights, and responsibilities surrounding marriage, which is seen as a stabilizing force within societies. Therefore, the government sees this as its business. As a personal relationship, marriage is deeply meaningful to the individuals involved, although "meaningful" is conceptualized differently within social, historical, and cultural locations. Americans are highly committed to marriage. Most claim that they want to marry and consider marriage important to their personal happiness. Nonetheless, there are many changes in marriage underway. For example, people tend to marry later, and many cohabit prior to marriage or in place of marriage. Some propose to legalize same-sex marriages, and spouses are renegotiating terrain such as the division of household labor and other roles. These changes have also inspired a growing and controversial marriage movement designed to preserve, strengthen, and promote traditional marriage.

Chapter 9 focuses on the process of becoming a parent. It reveals that seemingly micro-level personal issues such as whether, when, who, and how to have a baby reflect more than just biology. Values, such as pronatalism, shape our attitudes and behaviors. Political, religious, economic, health care, and other social institutions also shape parenthood, including fertility, pregnancy, adoption, childbirth, and transitioning to parenthood—dimensions of family life that many see as exceedingly personal. China, as the most extreme case, accepts a level of governmental policy and involvement that many around the world deem highly intrusive. Nonetheless, all countries have family policies, either explicit or implicit, that organize fertility and parenthood for their citizens. Family policies in the United States often minimize the connection between social structure (macro) and the lived experience (micro) of individual families. For example, compared to other nations, Americans are often expected to fend for themselves, as is the case with maternity and family leaves.

Chapter 10 points out that although raising children may be universal, the act of *parenting* is highly variable. Parenting attitudes and practices depend to a large extent on the type of tasks or competencies that members of a society (or subgroup) are expected to have. "Mothering" and "fathering" include the emotional, physical, and financial work involved with caring for children, but it is important to keep in mind that these identities take place within specific historical and cultural contexts, and even in the United States today they are framed by structures of sex, race, ethnicity, and class. Parenting contexts are becoming increasingly diverse with more children being raised by single parents, gay and lesbian parents, and grandparents. Teen birth rates are actually declining, but this remains an important parenting environment. These contexts raise new challenges and are of critical policy concern. Many countries directly assist parents with the financial costs of raising children. The United States also does so, but leans toward annual tax credits rather than monthly assistance, such as a family allowance.

Chapter 11 explores the empirical research and theoretical perspectives surrounding the topic of working families. All families do meaningful work inside or outside the home. Home and work used to be "separate spheres," and largely segregated by sex; however, the trend overall has been an increase in mothers working outside the home for pay. The changing nature of the economy has altered the context and meaning of work for many families. Jobs are becoming less secure, with nonstandardized work schedules, and fewer union protections. Many families now need two paychecks to make ends meet. No longer are work and family domains separate; instead, they interact and influence each other in many critical ways. Issues such as work–family conflicts, feelings of time deficits with children, negotiations over the division of household labor, and struggles to find suitable child care are issues that most employed families face today. Family-friendly workplace policies, such as flexible work hours, and national family policies, such as assistance with child care, can help alleviate the stress that many employed families experience.

Chapter 12 shows that the population around the world is aging rapidly, with many implications for families. A comparative perspective is important for understanding these implications because the most rapid growth in the aging population occurs in developing nations, which are often poor, and therefore less equipped to handle the strain on the economic and health care resources that this growth will bring. To complicate these issues even further, the largest increase around the world is among those aged 80 and over. The pronounced effects of these demographic changes will be felt throughout the global economy. In the United States, the elderly population is also rapidly growing, and given its size, the concerns of the elderly become all of our concerns. Concerns include promoting social and economic well-being; supporting intimate relationships; fostering positive bonds with adult children and grandchildren; and coping with retirement, widowhood, health and caregiving.

The focus of **Chapter 13** is gender-based violence, and violence and abuse among intimates. It explores sexual trafficking, definitions and measures of violence, dating aggression, spouse/partner abuse, child abuse, elder abuse, and explanations for violence. The overall goal is to reveal that, even though violence is experienced on a deeply personal level, it is really a *social problem*. Abuse is rooted in complex and longstanding societal- and individual-level traditions that create norms promoting violence and male privilege. However, zero-tolerance movements within our legal and criminal justice systems, along with battered women's shelters, are sprouting up throughout the country to spread awareness and help victims of violence.

Chapter 14 reveals that divorce is not simply a personal issue; it is a social problem with an intricate weaving of structural, historical, cultural, and personal factors that operate to explain attitudes toward divorce, rising and falling divorce rates, divorce policy, and how families cope with a divorce. For example, divorced women in the United States often struggle financially to support their families, given low pay structures and inadequate child support collection. To best understand divorce, I introduce both the macro and micro issues that surround it. This chapter evaluates several different ways to measure the divorce rate, but all find that the United States (alongside Russia) has the highest rate of divorce in the world. Empirical data suggest that children are particularly vulnerable to the hardships associated with divorce, including a greater likelihood of poverty and other behavioral and social problems. Most divorced persons remarry or repartner after the divorce. A stepfamily consists of a remarried or repartnered couple in which at least one spouse has a child from a previous relationship. Stepfamilies have many unique characteristics compared to two-parent biological families, and face a number of specific challenges.

Chapter 15 reviews the contributions that the sociological imagination offers to our understanding of families. The four themes that run throughout the book are reviewed and specific examples from earlier chapters are provided: (1) families are both a public social institution and a private personal relationship; (2) social inequality has a powerful influence on family life; (3) family policies reflect historical, cultural, political, and social factors; and (4) understanding families in the United States requires a comparative perspective. A sociological perspective reveals that families are complex entities. Despite important cultural universals that are found in families throughout the world, family structures and the relationships embedded within families reflect historical, political, and cultural contexts. They also reflect power and social inequality. The goal is to understand such issues as mate selection, marriage rituals, gendered expectations, division of household labor, fertility patterns, parent–child relationships, aging and the care of the elderly, family conflict and violence, and divorce and repartnering within these contexts. Only then can we reveal trends that illuminate both the past (i.e., where we've been) and the future (i.e., where we're going) to build resilient families.

Features

Each chapter begins with a **Chapter Preview** that introduces students to the chapter's main topics. A chapter-opening vignette draws students in to the narrative. Most chapters include a section titled "Social Policy and Family Resilience" highlighting important social policies around the world designed to strengthen families, including world family planning efforts, the Earned Income Tax Credit, family and maternity leaves, early childhood education policies, and family allowances.

Within each chapter, there are several types of features (at least three per chapter) that illustrate important themes and all include critical thinking questions:

- **Eye on the World** presents national and global maps that highlight regional or global differences on relevant topics (e.g., fertility rates, income inequality; the elderly population; infant mortality; status of women) and include several critical-thinking questions per map.

CHAPTER PREVIEW

Every society has the social institution known as family. This chapter reveals both the universal functions and variation in structure within family relationships throughout the world. Families are found in every society because they provide functions that no other social institution can (or wants to) provide. However, there is tremendous diversity because families reflect the environment, historical period, and culture in which they are found, and they continually adapt to changing circumstances. In this chapter you will learn:

- Functions of the family, both universal features and variations
- The types of data available to study families throughout the world
- Variations in marriage patterns, including monogamy and polygamy
- Patterns of power and authority
- Patterns of kinship, descent, and inheritance
- Patterns of residence
- Two specific theories that attempt to explain social change and families: Modernization theory and world systems theory
- Differences in families around the world through contrasts of India, Japan, and Sweden

37

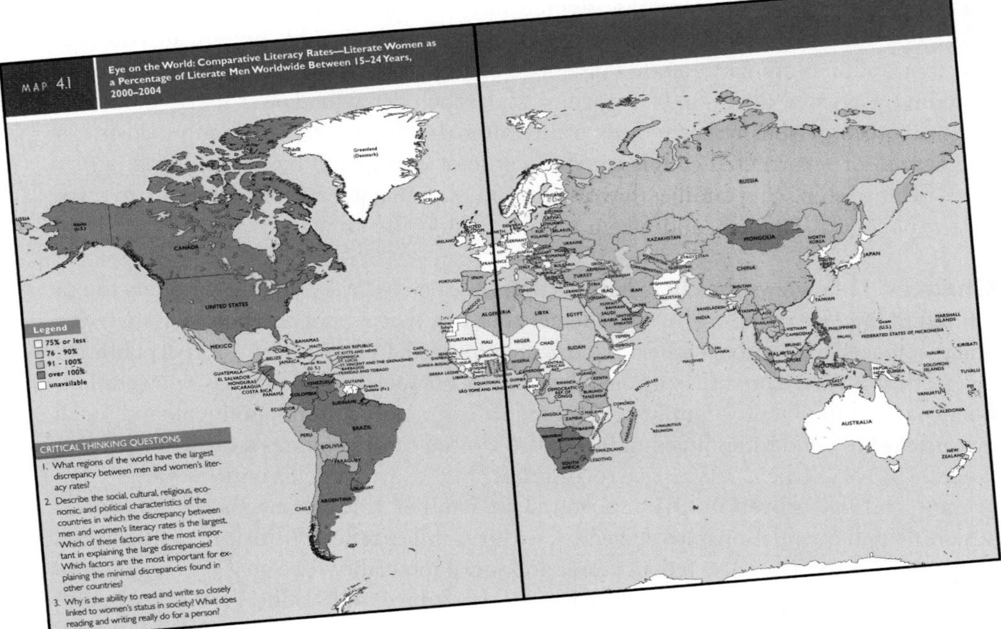

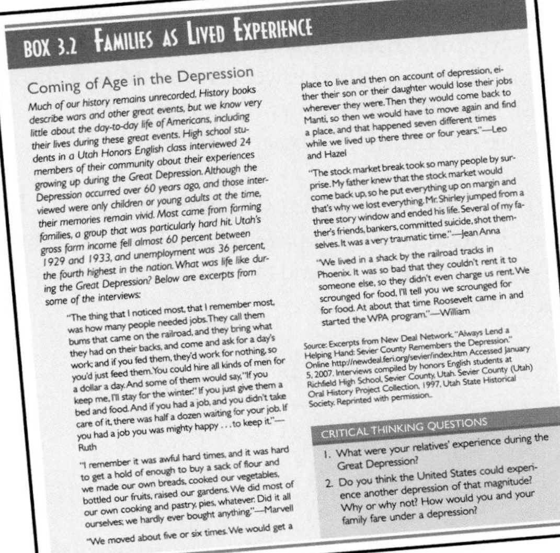

BOX 3.2 Families as Lived Experience

Coming of Age in the Depression

Much of our history remains unrecorded. History books describe wars and other great events, but we know very little about the day-to-day life of Americans, including their lives during these great events. High school students in a Utah Honors English class interviewed 24 members of their community about their experiences growing up during the Great Depression. Although the Depression occurred over 60 years ago, and those interviewed were only children or young adults at the time, their memories remain vivid. Most came from farming families, a group that was particularly hard hit. Utah's gross farm income fell almost 60 percent between 1929 and 1933, and unemployment was 36 percent, the fourth highest in the nation. What was life like during the Great Depression? Below are excerpts from some of the interviews:

> "The thing that I noticed most, that I remember most, was how many people needed jobs. They call them bums that came on the railroad, and they bring what they had on their backs, and come and ask for a day's work; and if you fed them, they'd work for nothing, so you'd just feed them. You could hire all kinds of men for a dollar a day. And some of them would say, "If you keep me, I'll stay for the winter." If you just give them a bed and food. And if you had a job, and you didn't take care of it, there was half a dozen waiting for your job. If you had a job you was mighty happy . . . to keep it."—Ruth

> "I remember it was awful hard times, and it was hard to get a hold of enough to buy a sack of flour and we made our own breads, cooked our vegetables, bottled our fruits, raised our gardens. We did most of our own cooking and pastry, pies, whatever. Did it all ourselves; we hardly ever bought anything."—Marvell

> "We moved about five or six times. We would get a place to live and then on account of depression, either their son or their daughter would lose their jobs wherever they were. Then they would come back to Manti, so then we would have to move again and find a place, and that happened seven different times while we lived up there three or four years."—Leo and Hazel

> "The stock market break took so many people by surprise. My father knew that the stock market would come back up, so he put everything up on margin and that's why we lost everything. Mr. Shirley jumped from a three story window and ended his life. Several of my father's friends, bankers, committed suicide, shot themselves. It was a very traumatic time."—Jean Anna

> "We lived in a shack by the railroad tracks in Phoenix. It was so bad that they couldn't rent it to someone else, so they didn't even charge us rent. We scrounged for food, I'll tell you we scrounged for for food. At about that time Roosevelt came in and started the WPA program."—William

Source: Excerpts from New Deal Network. "Always Lend a Helping Hand: Sevier County Remembers the Depression." Online http://newdeal.feri.org/sevier/index.htm Accessed January 5, 2007. Interviews compiled by honors English students at Richfield High School, Sevier County, Utah. Sevier County (Utah) Oral History Project Collection, 1997, Utah State Historical Society. Reprinted with permission.

CRITICAL THINKING QUESTIONS

1. What were your relatives' experience during the Great Depression?
2. Do you think the United States could experience another depression of that magnitude? Why or why not? How would you and your family fare under a depression?

- **Families as Lived Experience** provides personal stories that clearly illustrate the concepts of that chapter (e.g., transracial adoption; a parent's view of pressure on young girls to wear sexy clothing; a career-oriented woman discusses what it is like to have children; rebuilding a relationship after a divorce; and celebrating a 105th birthday).

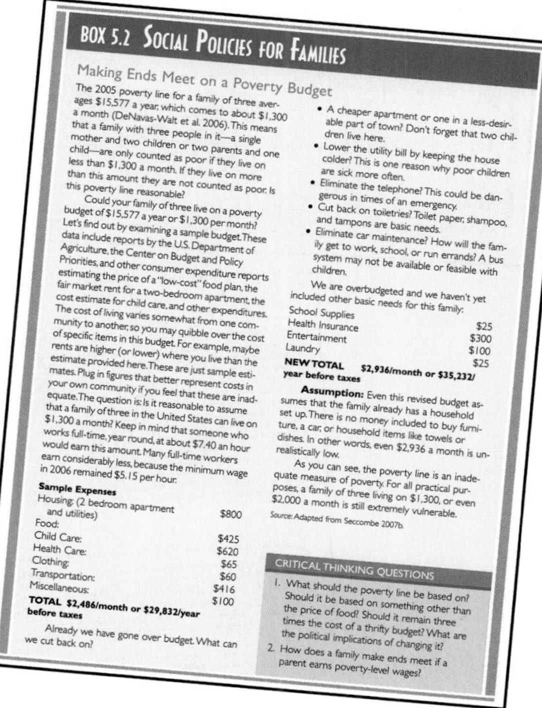

BOX 5.2 Social Policies for Families

Making Ends Meet on a Poverty Budget

The 2005 poverty line for a family of three averages $15,577 a year, which comes to about $1,300 a month (DeNavas-Walt et al. 2006). This means that a family with three people in it—a single mother and two children or two parents and one child—are only counted as poor if they live on less than $1,300 a month. If they live on more than this amount they are not counted as poor. Is this poverty line reasonable?

Could your family of three live on a poverty budget of $15,577 a year or $1,300 per month? Let's find out by examining a sample budget. These data include reports by the U.S. Department of Agriculture, the Center on Budget and Policy Priorities, and other consumer expenditure reports estimating the price of a "low-cost" food plan, the fair market rent for a two-bedroom apartment, the cost estimate for child care, and other expenditures. The cost of living varies somewhat from one community to another, so you may quibble over the cost of specific items in this budget. For example, maybe rents are higher (or lower) where you live than the estimate provided here. These are just sample estimates. Plug in figures that better represent costs in your own community if you feel that these are inadequate. The question is: Is it reasonable to assume that a family of three in the United States can live on $1,300 a month? Keep in mind that someone who works full-time, year round, at about $7.40 an hour would earn this amount. Many full-time workers earn considerably less, because the minimum wage in 2006 remained $5.15 per hour.

Sample Expenses

Housing: (2 bedroom apartment and utilities)	$800
Food:	
Child Care:	$425
Health Care:	$620
Clothing:	$65
Transportation:	$60
Miscellaneous:	$416
TOTAL $2,486/month or $29,832/year before taxes	$100

Already we have gone over budget. What can we cut back on?

- A cheaper apartment or one in a less-desirable part of town? Don't forget that two children live here.
- Lower the utility bill by keeping the house colder? This is one reason why poor children are sick more often.
- Eliminate the telephone? This could be dangerous in times of an emergency.
- Cut back on toiletries? Toilet paper, shampoo, and tampons are basic needs.
- Eliminate car maintenance? How will the family get to work, school, or run errands? A bus system may not be available or feasible with children.

We are overbudgeted and we haven't yet included other basic needs for this family:

School Supplies	
Health Insurance	$25
Entertainment	$300
Laundry	$100
NEW TOTAL $2,936/month or $35,232/year before taxes	$25

Assumption: Even this revised budget assumes that the family already has a household set up. There is no money included to buy furniture, a car, or household items like towels or dishes. In other words, even $2,936 a month is unrealistically low.

As you can see, the poverty line is an inadequate measure of poverty. For all practical purposes, a family of three living on $1,300, or even $2,000 a month is still extremely vulnerable.

Source: Adapted from Seccombe 2007b.

CRITICAL THINKING QUESTIONS

1. What should the poverty line be based on? Should it be based on something other than the price of food? Should it remain three times the cost of a thrifty budget? What are the political implications of changing it?
2. How does a family make ends meet if a parent earns poverty-level wages?

- **Social Policies for Families** highlight specific policies that can be used to support families, including their origin, implementation, and consequences (e.g., Social Security; the poverty line reform; health care; family leave policies; antimiscegenation laws).

- **Our Global Community** provides an in-depth look at family issues in another culture (e.g., trafficking of girls; Japanese divorce and custody laws; transnational families; HIV/AIDS in sub-Saharan Africa; concepts of adolescence in nonindustrialized societies; marriage and nepotism in Iraq).

BOX 6.3 Our Global Community

One Child's Very Special First Fourth of July

An increasing number of families are choosing to adopt children from other countries for infertility or humanitarian reasons. "Cloe" is a recent adoptee from the People's Republic of China. The following is a tribute by a grandmother, famous newspaper columnist Ellen Goodman, that reveals the love and pride she has in her new granddaughter.

It will be her very first parade, her very first Fourth of July. Our granddaughter will be both the newest citizen at the picnic and the newest member of our family.

Cloe, this little girl with shiny black hair and a quiet, curious stare, has come to America and to us. We have embraced her with a loyalty that is all the more tenacious for having not been preordained by biology. We have the sort of attachment that the word "adoption" cannot begin to describe.

Just six weeks ago, Cloe was halfway around the world in an orphanage in China. Six weeks before that, my stepdaughter and her husband got her photograph in the mail. It put a face—her face—on what had been a stack of papers, a mound of red tape, and of course, a hope.

Psychologists, neurologists, "ologists" of every variety may say it's impossible to bond to a photograph. But we connected to Cloe before she was named Cloe. We connected to her before she had any idea we existed or that there was a world outside the orphanage, outside the province, the country, the continent.

Before the travel papers arrived, we waited anxiously, tracking the reports of SARS, worried that Beijing would close down the border before our children became parents, before this child of China could become a child of America. But when the moment came to gather Cloe, it seemed as sudden as the wait had seemed interminable.

After all that time, she was just a plane trip away. In a single moment, a year-old child was transferred from one set of hands to another, and from one fate to another. The entire arc of her short life was transformed from being abandoned to being treasured.

Now we will take her to watch the parade of homemade flats come down the road and cheer the scramble up the greased pole. We will bring a newcomer to the American birthday party, but she has brought us to the wider world. We have made her an American and she has made us a part of the global village.

Our Cloe is one of about 20,000 international adoptions within the last year, one of the 5,000 girls from China. Over many months, we learned to spot them in the grocery store or the street. We learned to wonder what this wave of girls will make of their experience, of the great economic and political winds that changed the course of their lives.

In China, an ancient culture that still sets a higher value on the head of a boy has collided with a government policy that pressures families to have only one child. As a result, hundreds of thousands of girls are growing up in orphanages. As a very different result, thousands of girls are growing up in America, more privileged than brothers left behind.

As for Cloe, we know the joy her story brings to our family. But we can only guess at the loss to the woman who left her day-old daughter on fortune's doorstep.

My stepdaughter tells me about the final medical exam Cloe was given on the way out of China. The pediatrician carefully examined the little patient. Then looking evenly at the new parents, she said directly, "You have a very beautiful, healthy daughter. You are very lucky."

What, we still wonder, did this accomplished, modern Chinese woman make of her own country that gives away so many of its daughters? What did she feel about a culture in which this "beautiful healthy daughter" faced the options of either an orphanage or America? For that matter, what did she think of Americans? Does she think we regard the world's children as a product—made in China—to import because we can afford to?

America is continually made and remade by newcomers. But this daughter of China has reminded us how small our world is and how vast: a village you can traverse in a day and a place of stunning disconnects and differences, haves and have-nots.

Ours was already a global family, brought together with luck of the draw and the pluck of ancestors who came from places as far away as Italy and England, Russia and Germany. On this Fourth of July, we add another continent to our heritage and another child to our list of supreme good fortune. Welcome, Cloe, to America.

Source: Goodman 2003.

CRITICAL THINKING QUESTIONS

1. Why are international adoptions increasing in popularity?
2. Will children adopted from other countries—China, Guatemala, Korea, Russia—retain their own race or ethnic identity if white families raise them? What are the pros and cons of parents promoting a child's race or ethnic identity?
3. Following up on Goodman's questions, what do you think the female physician thinks of China? Of the one-child policy? Of the United States?

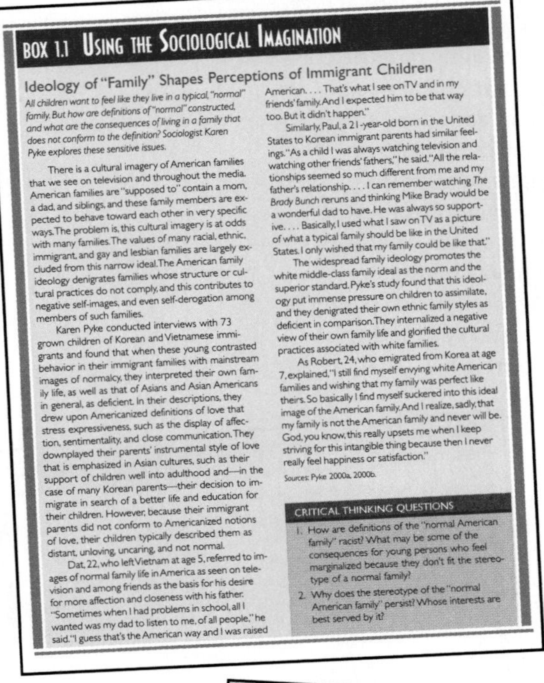

BOX 1.1 USING THE SOCIOLOGICAL IMAGINATION

Ideology of "Family" Shapes Perceptions of Immigrant Children

All children want to feel like they live in a typical, "normal" family. But how are definitions of "normal" constructed, and what are the consequences of living in a family that does not conform to the definition? Sociologist Karen Pyke explores these sensitive issues.

There is a cultural imagery of American families that we see on television and throughout the media. American families are "supposed to" contain a mom, a dad, and siblings, and these family members are expected to behave toward each other in very specific ways. The problem is, this cultural imagery is at odds with many families. The values of many racial, ethnic, immigrant, and gay and lesbian families are largely excluded from this narrow ideal. The American family ideology denigrates families whose structure or cultural practices do not comply, and this contributes to negative self-images, and even self-derogation among members of such families.

Karen Pyke conducted interviews with 73 grown children of Korean and Vietnamese immigrants and found that when these young contrasted behavior in their immigrant families with mainstream images of normalcy, they interpreted their own family life, as well as that of Asians and Asian Americans in general, as deficient. In their descriptions, they drew upon Americanized definitions of love that stress expressiveness, such as the display of affection, sentimentality, and close communication. They downplayed their parents' instrumental style of love that is emphasized in Asian cultures, such as their support of children well into adulthood and—in the case of many Korean parents—their decision to immigrate in search of a better life and education for their children. However, because their immigrant parents did not conform to Americanized notions of love, their children typically described them as distant, unloving, uncaring, and not normal.

Dat, 22, who left Vietnam at age 5, referred to images of normal family life in America as seen on television and among friends as the basis for his desire for more affection and closeness with his father. "Sometimes when I had problems in school, all I wanted was my dad to listen to me, of all people," he said. "I guess that's the American way and I was raised American. . . . That's what I see on TV and in my friends' family. And I expected him to be that way too. But it didn't happen."

Similarly, Paul, a 21-year-old born in the United States to Korean immigrant parents had similar feelings. "As a child I was always watching television and watching other friends' fathers," he said. "All the relationships seemed so much different from me and my father's relationship. . . . I can remember watching *The Brady Bunch* reruns and thinking Mike Brady would be a wonderful dad to have. He was always so supportive. . . . Basically, I used what I saw on TV as a picture of what a typical family should be like in the United States. I only wished that my family could be like that."

The widespread family ideology promotes the white middle-class family ideal as the norm and the superior standard. Pyke's study found that this ideology put immense pressure on children to assimilate, and they denigrated their own ethnic family styles as deficient in comparison. They internalized a negative view of their own family life and glorified the cultural practices associated with white families.

As Robert, 24, who emigrated from Korea at age 7, explained, "I still find myself envying white American families and wishing that my family was perfect like theirs. So basically I find myself suckered into this ideal image of the American family. And I realize, sadly, that my family is not the American family and never will be. God, you know, this really upsets me when I keep striving for this intangible thing because then I never really feel happiness or satisfaction."

Sources: Pyke 2000a, 2000b.

CRITICAL THINKING QUESTIONS

1. How are definitions of the "normal American family" racist? What may be some of the consequences for young persons who feel marginalized because they don't fit the stereotype of a normal family?
2. Why does the stereotype of the "normal American family" persist? Whose interests are best served by it?

- **Using the Sociological Imagination** illustrates the diversity in family experiences (e.g., a personal ad for polygamy; changing Hispanic views of gender; historical relationship between love and marriage; immigrant children's views of American families and the transgendered experience).

Each chapter ends with a **Conclusion**, a list of **Key Terms** with definitions and page references, a **Resources on the Internet** section, and a list of publications for **Further Reading**.

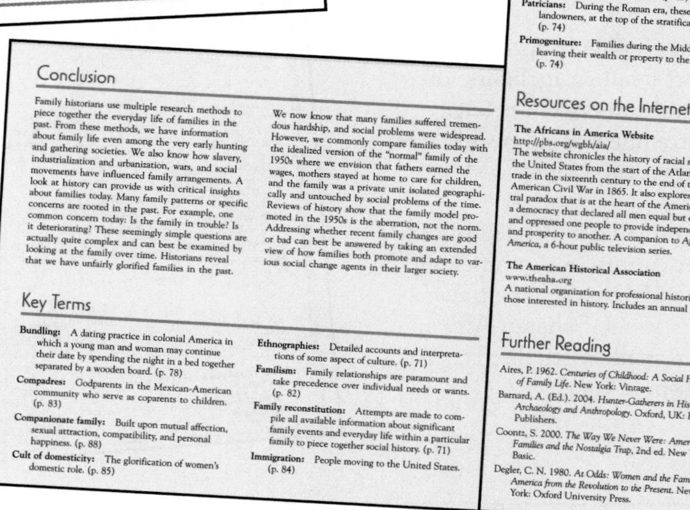

Conclusion

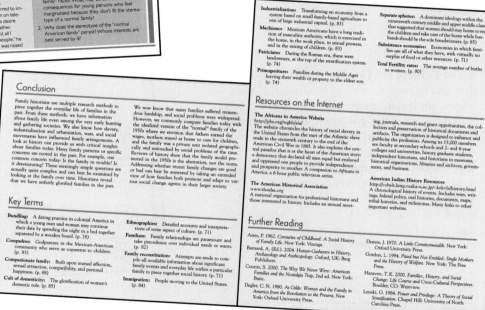

Family historians use multiple research methods to piece together the everyday life of families in the past. From these methods, we have information about family life even among the very early hunting and gathering societies. We also know how slavery, industrialization and urbanization, wars, and social movements have influenced family arrangements. A look at history can provide us with critical insights about families today. Many family patterns or specific concerns are rooted in the past. For example, one common concern today: Is the family in trouble? Is it deteriorating? These seemingly simple questions are actually quite complex and can best be examined by looking at the family over time. Historians reveal that we have unfairly glorified families in the past.

We now know that many families suffered tremendous hardship, and social problems were widespread. However, we commonly compare families today with the idealized version of the "normal" family of the 1950s where we envision that fathers earned the wages, mothers stayed at home to care for children, and the family was a private unit isolated geographically and untouched by social problems of the time. Reviews of history show that the family model promoted in the 1950s is the aberration, not the norm. Addressing whether recent family changes are good or bad can best be answered by taking an extended view of how families both promote and adapt to various social change agents in their larger society.

Key Terms

Bundling: A dating practice in colonial America in which a young man and woman may continue their date by spending the night in a bed together separated by a wooden board. (p. 78)

Compadres: Godparents in the Mexican-American community who serve as coparents to children. (p. 83)

Companionate family: Built upon mutual affection, sexual attraction, compatibility, and personal happiness. (p. 88)

Cult of domesticity: The glorification of women's domestic role. (p. 85)

Ethnographies: Detailed accounts and interpretations of some aspect of culture. (p. 71)

Familism: Family relationships are paramount and take precedence over individual needs or wants. (p. 82)

Family reconstitution: Attempts are made to compile all available information about significant family events and everyday life within a particular family to piece together social history. (p. 71)

Immigration: People moving to the United States. (p. 84)

Industrialization: Transforming an economy from a system based on small family-based agriculture to one of large industrial capital. (p. 83)

Machismo: Mexican Americans have a long tradition of masculine authority, which is exercised in the home, in the work place, in sexual prowess, and in the raising of children. (p. 83)

Patricians: During the Roman era, these were landowners, at the top of the stratification system. (p. 74)

Primogeniture: Families during the Middle Ages leaving their wealth or property to the eldest son. (p. 74)

Separate spheres: A dominant ideology within the nineteenth century middle and upper middle classes that suggested that women should stay home to rear the children and take care of the home while husbands should be the sole breadwinners. (p. 85)

Subsistence economies: Economies in which families use all of what they have, with virtually no surplus of food or other resources. (p. 71)

Total Fertility rates: The average number of births to women. (p. 90)

Resources on the Internet

The Africans in America Website
http://pbs.org/wgbh/aia/
The website chronicles the history of racial slavery in the United States from the start of the Atlantic slave trade in the sixteenth century to the end of the American Civil War in 1865. It also explores the central paradox that is at the heart of the American story: a democracy that declared all men equal but enslaved and oppressed one people to provide independence and prosperity to another. A companion to *Africans in America*, a 6-hour public television series.

The American Historical Association
www.theaha.org
A national organization for professional historians and those interested in history. Includes an annual meeting, journals, research and grant opportunities, the collection and preservation of historical documents and artifacts. The organization is designed to enhance and publicize the profession. Among its 15,000 members are faculty at secondary schools and 2- and 4-year colleges and universities, history graduate students, independent historians, and historians in museums, historical organizations, libraries and archives, government, and business.

American Indian History Resources
http://cobalt.lang.osaka-u.ac.jp/~krkvls/history.html
A chronological history of events. Includes wars, writings, federal policy, oral histories, documents, maps, tribal histories, and milestones. Many links to other important websites.

Further Reading

Aires, P. 1962. *Centuries of Childhood: A Social History of Family Life*. New York: Vintage.

Barnard, A. (Ed.). 2004. *Hunter-Gatherers in History, Archaeology and Anthropology*. Oxford, UK: Berg Publishers.

Coontz, S. 2000. *The Way We Never Were: American Families and the Nostalgia Trap*, 2nd ed. New York: Basic.

Degler, C. N. 1980. *At Odds: Women and the Family in America from the Revolution to the Present*. New York: Oxford University Press.

Demos, J. 1970. *A Little Commonwealth*. New York: Oxford University Press.

Gordon, L. 1994. *Pitied but Not Entitled: Single Mothers and the History of Welfare*. New York: The Free Press.

Haraven, T. K. 2000. *Families, History, and Social Change: Life Course and Cross-Cultural Perspectives*. Boulder, CO: Westview.

Lenski, G. 1984. *Power and Privilege: A Theory of Social Stratification*. Chapel Hill: University of North Carolina Press.

Supplements

We carefully designed a supplements package that supports the aims of *Families and Their Social Worlds* in order to provide students and instructors with a wealth of support materials to ensure success in teaching and in learning.

Instructor's Manual and Test Bank Each chapter in the Instructor's Manual, authored by Susan Cody-Rydzewski of LaGrange College, contains Learning Objectives, Key Terms, Lecture Outlines, Chapter Summary, Discussion Questions, Classroom Activities, and Web Links. Each chapter in the Test Bank, authored by Karen

Seccombe, consists of multiple choice questions, true/false questions, fill-in-the-blank questions, and essay questions.

Computerized Testing Program A computerized version of the Test Bank, authored by Karen Seccombe, is available with Tamarack's easy-to-use TestGen software, which lets you prepare tests for printing as well as for network and online testing. It provides full editing capability for Windows and Macintosh. Each chapter in the Test Bank consists of multiple choice questions, true/false questions, fill-in-the-blank questions, and essay questions. Available in print and electronically through the Allyn & Bacon/Longman Instructor's Resource Center: **www.ablongman.com/irc**.

PowerPoint Lecture Presentations This complete set of chapter-by-chapter PowerPoint lecture presentations, authored by Kathy Greaves of Oregon State University, contains approximately 20 slides per chapter specific to *Families and Their Social Worlds*. The slides provide lecture outlines, include figures and tables from the text, and reinforce the main ideas of each chapter.

MyFamilyLab is a state-of-the-art, interactive and instructive online solution for Marriage and Family courses. Designed to be used as a supplement to a traditional lecture course, or to completely administer an online course, MyFamilyLab combines multimedia, tutorials, videos, self-assessments, news articles, tests and quizzes to make teaching and learning fun.

Acknowledgments

A book is never a solo venture. I would like to thank all of those who had a helping hand in the process of turning my ideas for a family text into reality. The encouragement you gave, the challenging questions you posed, the responses you endured, and the personal and professional backing you offered have made this book one of which I am very proud. Thank you. The School of Community Health at Portland State University offered the ambiance conducive to writing, and the resources to help make it happen. My neighborhood friends provided me with the extracurricular diversions that kept my project humming along at full speed. Other friends who live far away in distance but close in spirit were also invaluable, and I particularly thank Becky Warner, Karen Pyke, J. Elizabeth Miller, and Suzanne Smith, who despite the distance, are always there for me. And I would like to offer a huge thank you to Gary Lee, Kathy Kaiser, Bill Martin, and Manley Johnson, who sparked this intellectual interest in families in the first place. They have each been wonderful mentors to me at various stages of my career, and without their attention and care, who honestly knows where I would be right now?

I would like to thank the following reviewers for their insightful comments and ideas on an early manuscript that laid the groundwork for this text: Carolyn Bond, Boston University; David A. Ford, University of Central Oklahoma; Helen M. Gore-Laird, University of Houston; Edythe Krampe, California State University, Fullerton; Diane Levy, University of North Carolina, Wilmington; Garvey F. Lundy, University of Pennsylvania; Marla A. Perry, Iowa State University; and Ida Harper Simpson, Duke University.

I extend great thanks as well to the following reviewers who offered extensive comments and ideas on this manuscript: Wendy Cook-Mucci, Southern Illinois University;

Cynthia R. Hancock, University of North Carolina, Charlotte; Debra A. Henderson, Ohio University; and Karen S. Joest, State University of New York, Oneonta.

I also appreciate the tremendous help that I received from the folks at Allyn and Bacon who took my words and actually turned them into a beautiful book, including Jeff Lasser, Executive Editor; Leah Strauss, Senior Development Editor; Claudine Bellanton, Production Editor; Marty Tenney, Production Project Manager; Deb Hanlon, Supplements Editor; and Lisa Jelly Smith, Photo Researcher. Few professors want to use a book without supplements, so we all appreciate the work that Kathy Greaves of Oregon State University put into the beautiful PowerPoints and the creativity that Susan Cody-Rydzewski of LaGrange College put into the Instructor's Manual.

And, most naturally, I would like to acknowledge my husband Richard, and daughters Natalie—who is now six years old (and in kindergarten—wow!)—and Olivia, who is four (and rapidly soaking up Mandarin in her immersion preschool). While many authors thank their family members for their sacrifices, I believe that writing this book actually enhanced our lives. What a unique and crazy opportunity to combine theory, methods, and application!

Now, to the readers, if you have questions or comments, please send them my way. I want to hear from you: **seccombek@pdx.edu**.

Karen Seccombe

About the Author

Karen Seccombe is a professor in the School of Community Health at Portland State University, located in Portland, Oregon. She received her B.A. in sociology at California State University, Chico, her M.S.W. in health and social welfare policy from the University of Washington, and her Ph.D. in sociology from Washington State University. Her research focuses on poverty, welfare, access to health care, and the effects of social inequality on families. She is the author of *"So You Think I Drive a Cadillac?": Welfare Recipients' Perspectives on the System and its Reform*, 2nd edition (Allyn and Bacon); *Families in Poverty* (Allyn and Bacon); *Just Don't Get Sick: Access to Health Care in the Aftermath of Welfare Reform* (Rutgers University Press, forthcoming), and *Marriages and Families: Relationships in Social Context*, with Rebecca L. Warner (Wadsworth). She is a National Council on Family Relations fellow, and a member of the American Sociological Association, and the Pacific Sociological Association, where she has held elective offices. Karen lives in Portland with her husband Richard, a health economist, her six-year-old daughter, Natalie Rose, and her four-year-old daughter, Olivia Lin. In her spare time she enjoys hiking near their cabin in the Oregon Cascades, walking the sandy beaches of the Oregon coast, exploring the kid-friendly playgrounds, attractions, and restaurants in Portland and surrounding areas, and traveling just about anywhere—the San Juan Islands are high on her list.

CHAPTER 1

Families and the Sociological Imagination

Chapter Outline

Chapter Preview

This chapter introduces the scientific study of families and shows how a sociological perspective broadens our understanding of personal relationships. However, families are more than just personal relationships; they are also an important social institution, and as such, they are socially constructed to meet human needs. Given their seemingly endless diversity, how do we study families in any systematic way? In this chapter you will learn:

- A definition of families, showing the political reality of why definitions are important
- The importance of a sociological imagination, including the value of a comparative perspective and the use of empirical data
- The changing of families, and the conservative, liberal, and feminist interpretations of these changes
- The role of the state in family policy, highlighting how the U.S. approach to family policy compares with other developed nations
- The four themes of this book: (1) Families are both a public institution and a private personal relationship; (2) Social inequality has a powerful influence on family life; (3) Family policies reflect historical, cultural, political, and social factors; and (4) Understanding families in the United States requires a comparative perspective

Family life is serious business, even in comic strips. The popularity and long lives of comic strip families make them trusted observers and reporters of the public discourse. More than 100 million people read the daily comics, and they come away with a variety of interpretations, including perceptions of ideal families, gender stereotypes, and proper roles for mothers and fathers. A research team headed by Ralph LaRossa, a sociologist at Georgia State University, systematically examined the content of 490 Father's Day and Mother's Day comic strips published from 1940 to 1999. The oldest comic in the study was Gasoline Alley, *first published in 1919. Others such as* Blondie, Bloom County, Cathy, Dennis the Menace, The Family Circus, Garfield, Hi and Lois, Little Orphan Annie, Peanuts, Pogo, *and* Ziggy *were also included.*

Focusing in particular on the roles of fathers, the researchers found that the depiction of fatherhood fluctuated significantly. In the past, fathers were often viewed as incompetent or were mocked as they performed (or tried to perform) parenting duties. Likewise, during the 40-year period from the mid-1950s to the mid-1990s, fathers were rarely shown to be supportive or nurturing. Comic strips today have a greater emphasis on fathers spending quality time with their children. "The fluctuation reflects societal shifts," says LaRossa. "When you look at the figures across six decades, they go up and down in a way understandable with what was happening in larger society."

The researchers also noted that the comics generally portrayed an homogeneous and stereotypical picture of family life. For example, virtually all characters were white. In this sample, only 5 percent of the comics featured an African American parental figure as a main character. Families also tend to be middle class, nuclear in structure, and with two parents in the home. Other family types are largely excluded. (LaRossa et al. 2000)

Families are entities of profound interest. In many ways, what could be more mundane than families—getting up, having breakfast, carpooling the kids, going to work, making dinner, doing homework, watching TV, and putting everyone to bed? At the same time, however, we are intensely curious about families; they are the center of many of our movies, television shows, songs, news stories, and cartoons. Families can offer some of the most exciting times of our lives: falling in love, getting married, or the birth or adoption of a baby. Families can also offer some of the worst times: disagreements, betrayal, violence, and divorce.

Virtually all of us grew up within some type of family, and most of us hope to recreate a new family through marriage or a partnership, and possibly with children. Although we talk about "the family" as though there is only one singular experience, we also know that there are tremendous differences. Some families do not have children while others have many; some have two parents while others have only one; some have grandparents living with them while others do not. Some families celebrate Christmas, while others focus on other traditions during the season, such as Hanukkah or Kwanzaa. Some families are happy, while others are riddled with conflict.

Given the differences among families and given racial, ethnic, class, and cultural diversity, how is it possible to understand families in any systematic way? This text uses a sociological perspective to examine and interpret families. All human behavior, including family life, occurs in a social context. Family scientists across disciplines recognize the need to understand how our personal relationships are shaped by this social context.

What Are Families?

The U.S. Census Bureau defines a family as two or more people living together who are related by birth, marriage, or adoption. This traditional definition remains the basis for the implementation of many social programs and policies, including employee fringe benefits such as health and dental insurance or family and medical leaves.

Nonetheless, most family scientists suggest that this traditional definition be expanded because it does not adequately reflect the reality of the rich diversity of family life in society today (Allen 2004; Scanzoni 2004; Smith 1993). Some propose that if people *feel* that they are a family and *behave* as though they are a family, then they should be recognized as such. The focus should be on being more inclusive of family relationships. In 2001, the family scholarly journal published by the National Council on Family Relations changed its name from *The Journal of Marriage and the Family* to *The Journal of Marriage and Family* (deleting the word "the") to reflect the growing recognition of multiple family forms. This change corresponds to the public's generally changing attitudes toward families. A study based on five large national data sources found increasing tolerance of family diversity since the 1960s (Thornton and Young-Demarco 2001). Americans are more likely to accept divorce, cohabitation, remaining single, and being childfree as legitimate lifestyles, while at the same time also espousing that marriage, children, and a strong family life are important goals toward which they are striving. There is also movement toward more egalitarian relationships (Thornton and Young-DeMarco 2001). Teenagers espouse these views as well, as shown in Table 1.1. Over half of high school seniors agree that having a child without being married is experimenting with a worthwhile lifestyle, and a majority of females and nearly two-thirds of males agree that cohabiting before marriage is a good idea (National Marriage Project 2006).

This book uses a broader and more inclusive definition than that taken from the Census Bureau. **Families** are defined here as *relationships by blood, marriage, or affection, in which members may cooperate economically, may care for any children, and may consider their identity to be intimately connected to the larger group.*

This definition could also include **fictive kin** within its parameters. Fictive kin are nonrelatives whose bonds are strong and intimate, such as the relationships shared among unmarried homosexual or heterosexual partners, or very close friends. In fact, these bonds could be stronger than those between biological relatives. For example, one's favorite "Nana Marge" may not really be a relative at all. Fictive kin can provide important services and care for individuals, including assistance around the holiday season, or through critical life transitions, such as the birth of a child or a divorce. The term "families", as used throughout this book, draws upon these relationships as well as the more traditional ones.

TABLE 1.1 Attitudes of U.S. High School Seniors Toward Marriage and Family

Percentage of High School Seniors Who. . . .

Said Having a Good Marriage and Family Life Is Extremely Important

	Boys	*Girls*
1981–1985	69	81
2001–2004	70	82

Said It Is Very Likely They Will Stay Married to the Same Person for Life

	Boys	*Girls*
1981–1985	56	68
2001–2004	57	64

Agreed or Mostly Agreed that Most People Will Have Fuller and Happier Lives if They Choose Legal Marriage Rather than Staying Single or Just Living with Someone

	Boys	*Girls*
1981–1985	38	36
2001–2004	38	32

Said Having a Child Without Being Married Is Experimenting with a Worthwhile Lifestyle or Not Affecting Anyone Else

	Boys	*Girls*
1981–1985	43	40
2001–2004	56	56

Agreed or Mostly Agreed with the Statement: "It Is Usually a Good Idea for a Couple to Live Together Before Getting Married in Order to Find Out Whether They Really Get Along."

	Boys	*Girls*
1981–1985	47	37
2001–2004	64	57

Source: The National Marriage Project 2006.

The Political Reality: Why Definitions Are Important

Does it really matter how we define the term family? Yes, it matters a great deal. The definition used has important consequences with respect to informal and formal rights. For example, neighbors, schools, and other community groups are likely to interact with family members differently than with other nonrelated groups who live together. Families even get special membership discounts to a wide variety of organizations that roommates

Definitions of "family" have important social, political, and economic consequences; many gays and lesbians ask that the benefits that accrue to married couples also be extended to them.

or friends do not get. You may find that an individual membership to a particular organization that you wish you joined is $25, but a family rate is $30, regardless of family size!

However, even more is at stake than a few dollars. The agreed-upon definition has important formal consequences that are legally recognized. For example, under most employer insurance plans only a worker's spouse and legal children can be covered by a health or dental insurance policy. **Domestic partners**, defined as adults in long-term committed relationships and responsible for each other's financial and emotional well-being, are usually excluded from coverage (Human Rights Campaign Foundation 2006). In most places around the country, domestic partners, either heterosexual or homosexual, have faced a number of obstacles simply because they lack the legal basis of marriage.

Employers are beginning to recognize that denying benefits to partners in committed relationships may not only be unjust, but it may also be bad for business. In 1982, the New York City weekly *The Village Voice* became the first employer to offer domestic partner benefits to its lesbian and gay employees. By 2005, over 7,500 employers offered domestic partner benefits. These employers include 228 *Fortune* 500 companies, along with thousands of private-sector companies; city, county, and state governments; and colleges and universities (Human Rights Campaign Foundation 2006). Documentation of proof of domestic partnership, such as financial statements or written statements by each partner is left up to the discretion of the employer. Most employers that cover domestic partners do so regardless of sexual orientation (Employee Benefit Research Institute 2004). Despite the continued growth in the number of employers who offer domestic partner benefits, the IRS has ruled that domestic partners cannot be considered spouses for tax purposes.

The Sociological Imagination

Many of our personal experiences are not random. They are shaped by **social structure**, which is the organized pattern of social relationships and social institutions that together form the basis of society. For example, how has your sex influenced your life experience? Has being male or being female influenced your choice of a college major, your hobbies, interests, and relationships? Perhaps another way of thinking of this is: How would your life be different if you were the "opposite sex?" Likewise, how has your family structure affected you? You may have grown up with one parent, two parents, or with no parents at all. How did this structure affect your financial well-being, your social capital, and overall opportunities? As another example, how does the U.S. health care system affect your family life? If you are one of the 47 million Americans without health insurance and need health care, you may have some vivid stories of its impact on you or your family (DeNavas-Walt et al. 2006).

Using a **sociological imagination** reveals general patterns in what otherwise might be thought of as simple random events (Mills 1959). C. Wright Mills stressed the importance of understanding the relationship between individuals and the society in which they lived. Family problems such as divorce, unemployment, child abuse, limited access to health care, work-family stress, finding adequate child care, and pay inequities are more than just personal troubles experienced in isolation by a few people. They are issues that affect large numbers of people and originate in the institutional arrangements of society. Individual behavior and outcomes are linked to the social structure.

Peter Berger elaborated on these ideas in his 1963 book *Invitation to Sociology*. Although we like to think of ourselves as individuals, much of our behavior (and others' behavior toward us) is actually patterned on the basis of what social categories we fall into such as age, income, race, ethnicity, sex, and physical appearance. For example, men and women behave differently for reasons that often have nothing to do with biology. Many of these patterns are socially produced. In other words, boys and girls, men and women, are each taught and encouraged to think of themselves differently and to behave in different ways. Society lends a hand in shaping our lives. Why are over 90 percent of students in bachelor of science nursing programs female? This is obviously not the result of some biological imperative, some quirk of the occupation itself, or some random event. Rather, society even has a hand in shaping something as seemingly personal and individual as the choice of a college major (England and Li 2006).

Emile Durkheim conducted an early study on the subject of suicide documenting how social structures in society affect human behavior (Durkheim 1897). At first glance, what could be more private and individualized than the reasons that surround a person's decision to take his or her own life? The loss of a loving relationship, job troubles, financial worries, or low self-esteem are just some of the many reasons that a person may have for attempting suicide. Yet looking through official records and death certificates, Durkheim noted that suicide was not a completely random event, and that there were several important patterns worthy of attention. He found that men were more likely to kill themselves than were women. He noted that Protestants were more likely to take their lives than were Catholics and Jews. He found that wealthy people were more likely to commit suicide than were the poor. Finally, it appeared that unmarried people were more likely to kill themselves than were married people. Although his study was conducted over 100 years ago, recent research indicates that these patterns persist. Suicide today is a major social problem, with nearly 30,000 individuals taking their lives each year. It is the eleventh leading cause of death for all Americans, and the third for youths aged 15–24 (National Center for Injury Prevention and Control 2005).

The sociological imagination draws attention to the fact that seemingly private issues are often public ones (Mills 1959). For example, whenever a child is orphaned because of AIDS, it is a personal tragedy. However, when the number of children throughout the world orphaned because of AIDS runs in the tens of millions (a number roughly equal to every child in the United States under the age of 5)—including 20 percent of the children of Botswana—and more than 2 million children are infected themselves, AIDS is far more than a personal problem (AVERT.org 2007; UNAIDS 2006a, b). It becomes a serious public issue that requires public attention to resolve.

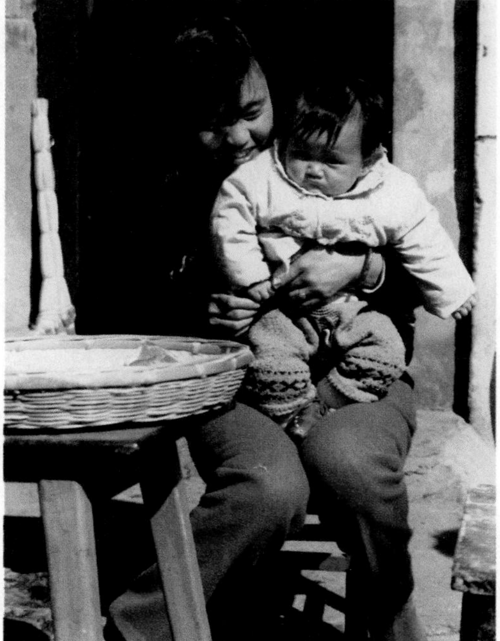

The infant mortality rate (deaths of children in their first year of life) is shockingly high in the United States. Other countries and regions, including Hong Kong, have significantly lower infant mortality rates than the United States.

Comparative Perspective

The sociological imagination uses a **comparative perspective** to studying families. If we want to know what is happening in the United States, it becomes particularly meaningful to compare the country to something else, such as other cultures or to other points in history. For example, an examination of the nature of dating practices or weddings in the United States becomes far more insightful when compared to the practices in other cultures such as India, or at other points in time, such as Colonial America.

It is easy to sit back and assume that our society's way of doing things is always the best way. However, this **ethnocentrism** can have considerable costs. A comparative perspective allows Americans to look at other societies around the world and learn how others organize their social life and respond to its challenges (Ember and Ember 2006). This, in turn, allows us to learn about ourselves.

Perhaps nowhere is a comparative approach more important than in the realm of family life. The structure and dynamics of families affect all of us in substantial and profound ways. Learning how other societies structure families, how they collectively think about families, and how they deal with the challenges families face can provide insight into our own concerns. Many problems that we face in the United States are more serious elsewhere, such as the tremendous poverty among developing nations. Other problems loom larger here. For example, the infant mortality rate in the United States is among the worst of industrial nations, as shown in Map 1.1. The U.S. rate in 2006, at approximately 6.7 deaths per 1,000 live births, was higher than most of western Europe, Canada, Australia, New Zealand, Japan, Iceland, and Hong Kong (Population Reference Bureau 2006). Given the vast wealth in the United States, it is alarming that the infant death rates are comparable to countries that are so much poorer, including Cuba, Croatia, Taiwan, and South Korea. Why is the U.S. infant mortality rate so much higher than peer nations? A comparative perspective examines the organization, values, and policies of those peer nations and evaluates the relevance of these for the country. Obviously, with respect to lowering infant mortality, they are doing something right and the United States could take note.

MAP 1.1 **Eye on the World: Comparative Infant Mortality Rates, 2005**

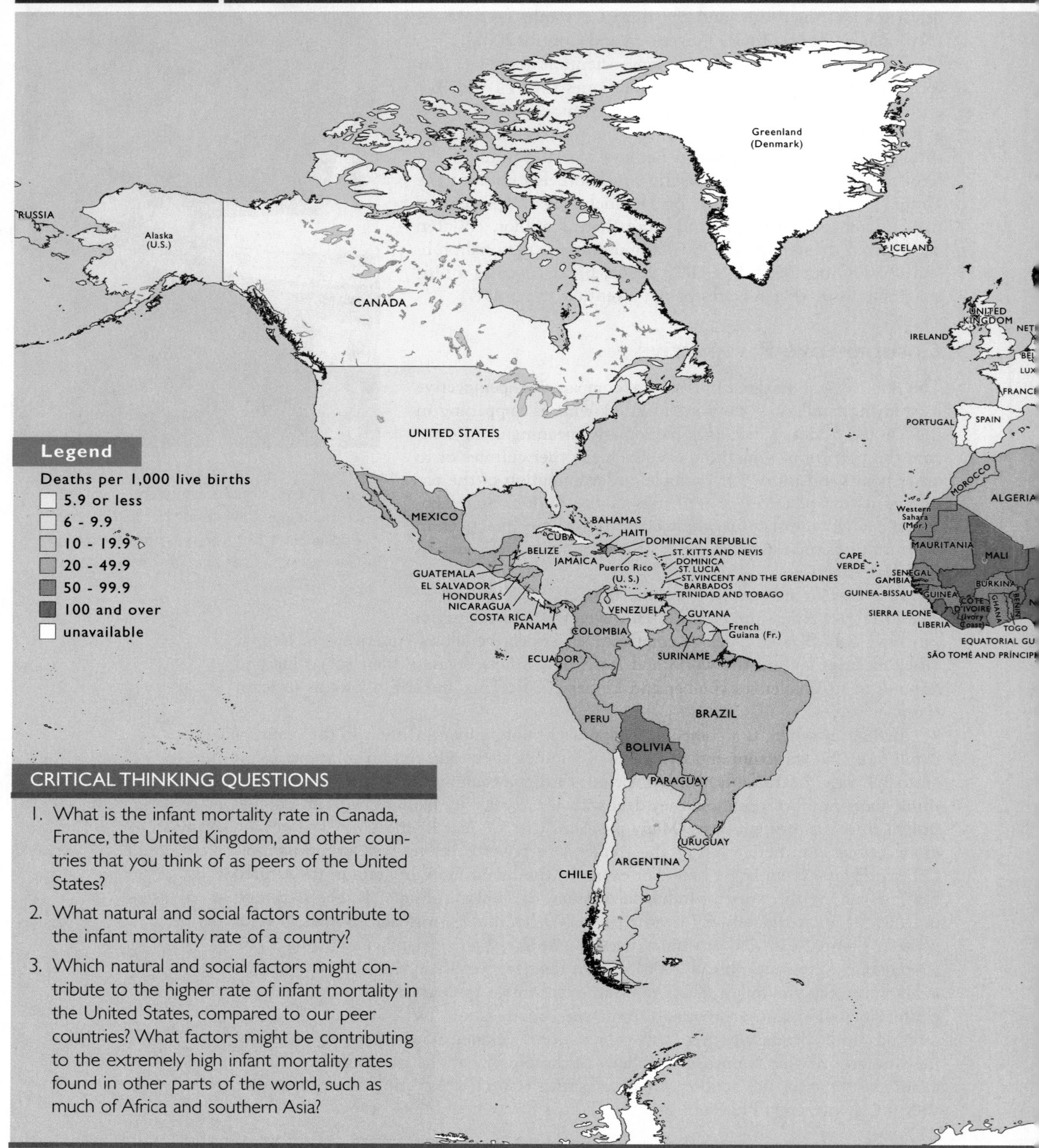

CRITICAL THINKING QUESTIONS

1. What is the infant mortality rate in Canada, France, the United Kingdom, and other countries that you think of as peers of the United States?
2. What natural and social factors contribute to the infant mortality rate of a country?
3. Which natural and social factors might contribute to the higher rate of infant mortality in the United States, compared to our peer countries? What factors might be contributing to the extremely high infant mortality rates found in other parts of the world, such as much of Africa and southern Asia?

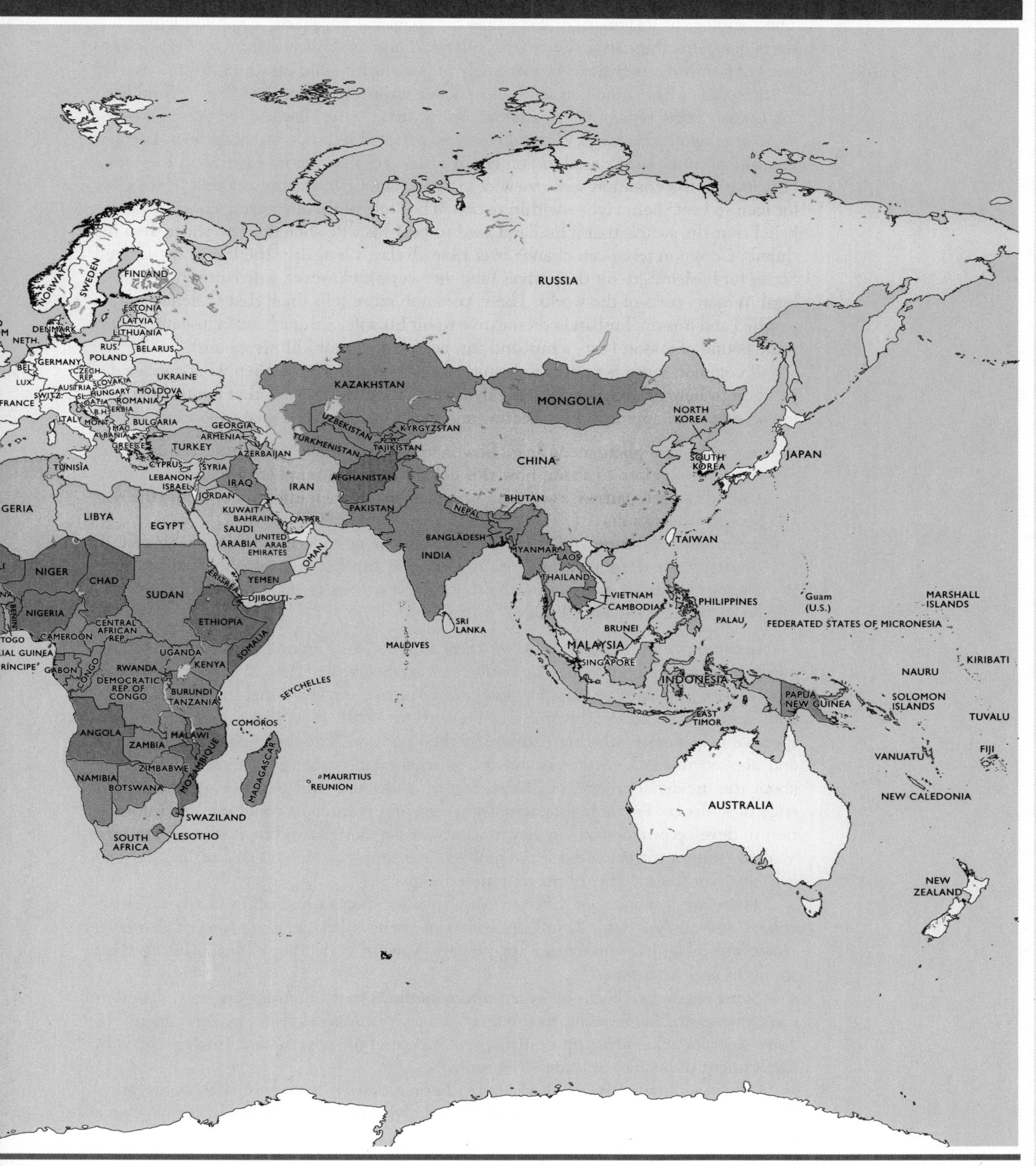

Source: Population Reference Bureau 2005.

An Empirical Approach

The sociological imagination also values an **empirical approach**, a method which answers questions through a systematic collection and analysis of data. Uncovering patterns of family dynamics can be extremely important for building stronger families.

Most of us have common sense ideas about intimacy, domestic violence, child rearing (or any other type of family interaction for that matter) based upon personal experiences, religious teachings, cultural customs, personal habits, or societal laws. Because virtually all of us were raised in families, we may feel that we are experts on the topic. Historically, the common sense view of violence among intimates was that it was okay for men to beat their wives—within reason. The "rule of thumb" saying comes from the belief that the switch that a husband used to beat his wife should be no wider than his thumb. Common sense can change over time. Today it is against the law in the United States for husbands to hit their wives (and vice versa). However, wife battering is not illegal in many parts of the world. There, common sense tells them that violence can be justified and it is the husband's prerogative to hit his wife, although again, usually within some bound of reason (e.g., a husband can beat, but cannot kill his spouse).

If common sense is subject to historical and cultural whims, then what can we depend on to help us understand family dynamics? Sociologists and other family scientists use an empirical approach in collecting and analyzing data. The goal can either be to

- describe some phenomena (e.g., how many women have been physically assaulted by someone close to them; how this compares to the number of men who are assaulted by their partners each year; how women and men interpret or justify the reasons for the assault)
- determine the cause-and-effect relationships or provide insight into why certain events do or do not occur (e.g., the relationship between alcohol and violence among intimates; the relationship between attitudes of male dominance and domestic violence (Kendall 2002)

Because of empirical research, we know that violence among intimates is a serious and pervasive social problem. One nationwide study revealed that 22 percent of women report being physically assaulted by someone close to them (National Institute of Justice and Centers for Disease Control and Prevention 1998). How can a sociological perspective help women who are battered by their partners? Family scholars conduct basic and applied research to understand the phenomenon, striving to reveal information about the incidence, predictors, social factors associated with violence, or the experience of violence. Psychologists, social workers, and politicians could use this information to develop programs to prevent violence, assist victims, and treat the perpetrators. Violence among intimates is a social problem, not simply an individual one, and the goal is to uncover the social patterns that underlie it.

There are a number of different ways that sociologists and other family scientists collect and analyze data. A full discussion of them is beyond the scope of this text. However, Table 1.2 summarizes six primary ways of collecting data, outlining their strengths and weaknesses.

Some researchers focus on **quantitative methods** in which the focus is on data that can be measured numerically. Examples of this may be found in surveys, experiments, or doing a secondary analysis on available statistics from the government (such as the U.S. Department of Justice) or some other source.

Others use **qualitative methods** and focus on narrative description with words rather than numbers to analyze patterns and their underlying meanings. Examples of qualitative

TABLE 1.2 **Six Research Methods: A Summary**

Method	Application	Advantages	Limitations
Survey	For gathering information about issues that are not directly observed, such as values, opinions, and other self-reports. Can be mail, telephone, or administered in person. Useful for descriptive or explanatory purposes; can generate quantitative or qualitative data.	Sampling methods can allow researcher to generalize findings to a larger population. Can provide open-ended questions or a fixed response.	Surveys must be carefully prepared to avoid bias. A potential for a low return or response rate. Can be expensive and time consuming. Self-reports may be biased.
In-depth Interview	For obtaining information about issues that are not directly observed, such as values, opinions, and other self-reports. Useful for getting in-depth information about a topic. Conducted in person, conversation is usually audiotaped and later transcribed. Generates qualitative data.	Can provide detailed and high-quality data. Interviewer can probe or ask follow-up questions for clarification or to encourage the respondent to elaborate. Can establish a genuine rapport with respondent.	Expensive and time consuming to conduct and transcribe. Self-reports may be biased. Respondent may feel uncomfortable revealing personal information.
Experiment	For explanatory research that examines cause-and-effect relationship among variables. Several types: classical experimental design and quasi-experimental designs based on degree of controlling the environment. Generates quantitative data.	Provides greatest opportunity to assess cause and effect. Research design relatively easy to replicate.	The setting may have an artificial quality to it. Unless the experimental and control group are randomly assigned or matched on all relevant variables, and the environment is carefully controlled, bias may result.
Focus Groups	For obtaining information from small groups of people who are brought together to discuss a particular topic. Often exploratory in nature. Particularly useful for studying public perceptions. Facilitator may ask only a few questions; goal is to get group to interact with one another. Generates qualitative data.	Group interaction may produce more valuable insights than individual surveys or in-depth interviews. Research can obtain data quickly and inexpensively. Good at eliciting unanticipated information.	Setting is contrived. Some people may feel uncomfortable speaking in a group and others may dominate.
Observation	For exploratory and descriptive study of people in a natural setting. Researcher can be a participant or nonparticipant. Generates qualitative data.	Allows study of real behavior in a natural setting. Does not rely on self-reports. Researchers can often ask questions and take notes. Usually inexpensive.	Can be time consuming. Could be ethical issues involved in certain types of observation studies, i.e., observing without consent. Researcher must balance roles of participant and observer. Replication of research is difficult.

(continued)

TABLE 1.2 Continued

Method	Application	Advantages	Limitations
Secondary Analysis	For exploratory, descriptive, or explanatory research with data that were collected for some other purpose. Diverse. Can be large data sources based on national samples, e.g., U.S. Census, or can be historical documents or records. Generates quantitative or qualitative data, depending on the source of data used.	Saves the expense and time of original data collection. Can be longitudinal, with data collected at more than one point in time. Good for analyzing national attitudes or trends. Makes historical research possible.	Because data were collected for another purpose, the researcher cannot control what variables were included or excluded. Researcher has no control over sampling or other biases of the data.

research methods include in-depth interviews, focus groups, observation studies, or conducting a secondary analysis using narrative documents (such as letters or diaries).

None of these methods is inherently better or worse than the others. The method used depends on the research questions that are posed. For example, if we want to better understand what family life was like in the nineteenth century, we would not want to conduct a survey. How would people who are alive today best inform us of what happened 150 years ago? Obviously, the best method would be to conduct a secondary analysis of documents that were written during that time period. Diaries, letters, or other lengthy correspondence between people could help us understand the common everyday experiences between families. Likewise, we could analyze historical records to get an aggregate picture about, for example, immigration trends, age at first marriage, or the average length of time between marriage and first birth. Census records; birth, marriage, and death registers; immigration records; slave auctions and other transactions; church records; newspapers and magazine articles; employment ledgers; and tax records can also provide insightful clues into the family lives of large numbers of ordinary people.

Theory

Research is guided by **theory**, which is a general framework, explanation, or tool used to understand and describe the real-life world (Ingoldsby et al. 2003; White and Klein 2002). Theories are important both before and after data have been collected because they help us decide what topics to research, what questions to try to answer, how to best answer them, and how to interpret the research results. Before collecting data, theories can help frame the question. When data have been collected and patterns emerge, theories can help make sense of what was found.

There are many theoretical perspectives that make different assumptions about the nature of society. Figure 1.1 summarizes the most often used theories in studying families. Some are more **macro** in nature and attempt to understand societal patterns. These include structural functionalism, conflict theory, and feminist theory. Other theories are more **micro** in nature and focus on personal dynamics and face-to-face interaction, such as social exchange, symbolic interaction, developmental theory, and family systems theory.

FIGURE 1.1 **Summary of Family Theories**

Source: Adapted from Ingoldsby et al. 2004.

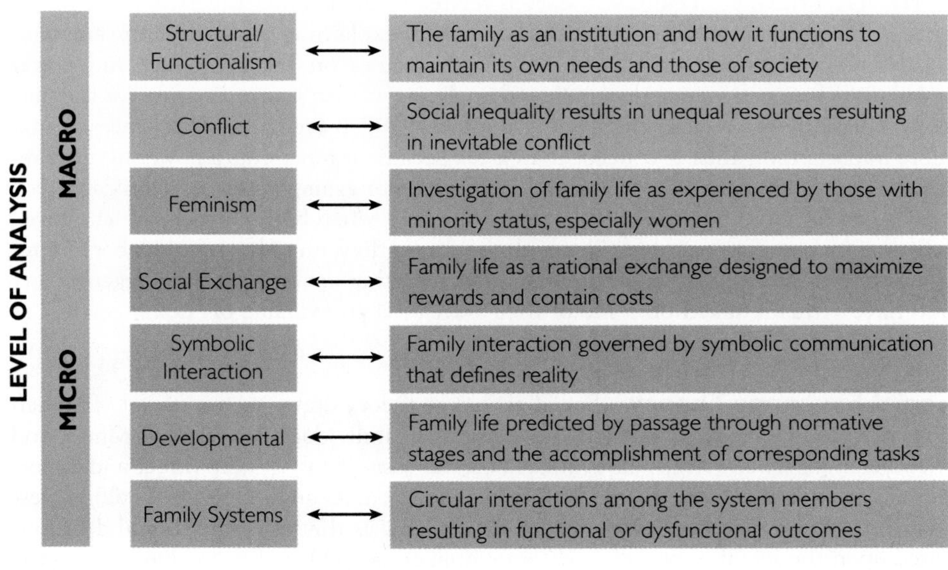

Structural Functionalism **Structural functionalist theory** (often abbreviated to *functionalism*) attempts to determine the structure, systems, functions, and equilibrium of social institutions; in this case, families. A popular theory in the 1940s and 1950s, the focus is on how families are organized, how they interact with other social systems, the functions that families serve, and how they are a stabilizing force in society (Parsons 1937; Parsons 1951). For example, Parsons and Boles (1955) focused on the division of labor in families, noting the ways in which separate spheres for men and women contributed to the stability and functionality of families. The expressive roles and tasks fell to women, whereas the instrumental roles fell to men (Parsons and Boles 1955), which they argued contributed to smooth family functioning. Functionalists rarely note the tensions, conflicts, or the political ideologies behind their ideas, which may explain why this trend has fallen out of fashion in more recent decades.

Conflict Theory **Conflict theory** emphasizes issues surrounding social inequality, power, conflict, and social change; in this case, how these factors influence, or are played out, in families. Those who follow the writings of Karl Marx focus on the consequences of capitalism for families—for example, tensions and inequality generated by the gross distribution of wealth and power associated with capitalism (Marx and Engels 1971). Other conflict theorists focus on a wider set of issues surrounding conflict, inequality, or power differentials. For example, a conflict theorist might ask why virtually all elderly persons regardless of income receive government-subsidized health care that covers many of their health care needs (Medicare) when there is no similar program for children.

Moreover, President George W. Bush extended prescription coverage for the elderly, again offering nothing to children. Is this different treatment due to the fact that the elderly represent a large special interest group and powerful voting block, whereas children are virtually powerless?

Feminist Theory **Feminist theory** is related to the conflict theory, but the difference is that gender is seen as the central concept for explaining family structure and family dynamics (Osmond and Thorne 1993). It focuses on the inequality and power imbalances between men and women and analyzes "women's subordination for the purpose of figuring out how to change it" (Gordon 1979). It recognizes that *gender* is a far more important organizing concept than is *sex* because it represents a powerful set of relations that are fraught with power and inequality. For example, research indicates that women do far more household labor than men even when both partners are employed full-time for pay. Feminist theorists see the gendered division of household labor as a result of power imbalances between men and women that are embedded in larger society and have virtually taken on a life of their own. It is an example of "doing gender" as West and Zimmerman say (1987).

Social Exchange Theory **Social exchange theory** draws upon a model of human behavior used by many economists. It assumes that individuals are rational beings, and their behavior reflects decisions evaluated on the basis of costs—both direct and opportunity costs—and benefits (Nye 1979; Becker 1981). Exchange theorists would suggest that a particular type of family structure or dynamic is the result of rational decisions based upon the social, economic, and emotional costs and benefits, as compared to the alternatives. For example, Becker (1981) argued that a woman often rationally chooses to exchange her household labor for the benefits of a man's income because she understands that men are more "efficient" in the labor market (they usually earn higher wages than women).

Symbolic Interaction Theory **Symbolic interaction theory** emphasizes the symbols we use in everyday interaction—words, gestures, appearances—and how these are interpreted by others (Mead 1935). Our interactions with others are based on how we interpret these symbols. Some symbols are obvious (an engagement ring, a kiss, a smile) and show us how to interact or what roles to play. Others are less obvious and confusing to interpret, thereby causing tension or conflict in a relationship. For example, the symbol of a mother might be straightforward, and we have a general agreement, at least in U.S. culture, about her roles—but what is the role of a stepmother?

Developmental Theory **Developmental theory** suggests that families (and individual family members) go through distinct stages over time, with each stage having its own set of tasks, roles, and responsibilities. These developmental changes include (1) married couple; (2) childbearing; (3) preschool age; (4) school age; (5) teenage; (6) launching center; (7) middle-aged parents; and (8) aging family members (Duvall and Miller 1985). Early development theorists claimed that the stages were inevitable and occurred in a relatively linear fashion, although most now recognize that there is widespread variation. For example, some families never have children. Other families have children later in life, so that parents may be facing tasks associated with middle age (e.g., planning for retirement) before children are launched. The developmental approach uses both micro and macro approaches to describe and explain family relationships and stages over the various family stages (Rodgers and White 1993).

A related perspective, the **life course perspective**, examines how individuals' lives change as they pass through the myriad events in their lives, with the recognition that many changes are socially produced and shared among a cohort of people (Elder Jr. 1998; Schaie and Elder 2005). For example, sociologist Glen Elder's longitudinal study followed a cohort of children throughout the Great Depression and afterwards to see how an historical event of such large proportions affected a cohort of Americans (Elder 1999). Another example of a cohort study would be to track men who served in combat in the Vietnam war to see how a major traumatic event such as war has shaped a cohort of men.

Family Systems Theory A system is more than the sum of its parts. Likewise, the **family systems theory** proposes that a family system—the family members and the roles that they play—is larger than the sum of its individual members (Broderick and Smith 1979). Collectively it becomes a system, but it also includes subsystems within it, such as the married couple subsystem, the sibling subsystem, or the parent-child subsystem. All family systems and subsystems create boundaries between them and the environment with varying degrees of permeability. They also create *rules of transformation* so that families function smoothly and know what to expect from another member. All systems tend toward equilibrium so that families work toward a balancing point in their relationship, and they maintain this equilibrium by feedback or control. Therefore, the family systems theory is particularly useful in studying how the members of the family (or subsystems within the family) communicate with one another and the rippling effects of that communication.

Families and Social Change

Any cursory review of family history will show that families have undergone tremendous changes. That fact is rarely disputed. It is the *meanings* and *implications* of these changes that are under considerable debate. Put simply, do the recent changes in families imply that they are deteriorating, as some suggest?

A Snapshot of American Families Today and How They Have Changed

Without question, a number of changes in families have taken place over the past several decades. Some of the more significant changes include the following, and will be discussed in greater depth in subsequent chapters:

1. *Both men and women are postponing marriage*. Because of expanding opportunities and changing norms, people are marrying at later ages than in the past. Women now marry at an average age of 25, compared to 21 in 1970. Men now marry at an average age of 27, compared to 23 in 1970.
2. *The percentage of persons who have never married has declined slightly*. About 4 percent of elderly women have never married, down from 6 percent in 1980. Among men, the decline in lifelong singlehood is less dramatic, but exists nonetheless: 4 percent of elderly men aged 65 and older have never married, down from 5 percent in 1980. In other words, people now are somewhat more likely to marry, not less likely.
3. *Family size is shrinking*. Fewer people are having three or more children today. Family size is particularly shrinking among black and Hispanic families. Only about

12 percent of black families contain three or more children, compared to 18 percent in 1980. Likewise, 18 percent of Hispanic families have three or more children compared to 23 percent in 1980. White families with three or more children declined from 11 percent to 9 percent.

4. *The divorce rate has declined.* In the 1960s, the divorce rate began to rise rapidly, peaking at approximately 23 divorces per 1,000 married women around 1980. However, since this time, the rate of divorce has declined to just less than 18 per 1,000 married women.
5. *Mothers are increasingly likely to be employed for pay outside the home.* Although single mothers usually have had to work outside the home, more married women with children are in the workplace than ever before. Today nearly 40 percent of married couples with children have both parents working outside the home full time, and another 28 percent contain a full-time and a part-time worker. Only 28 percent of married couples today have just one wage earner, as compared to 55 percent in 1965.
6. *Single-parent households are on the rise, particularly among men.* Since 1970 there has been a 300 percent increase in single-parent households headed by mothers and a 500 percent increase in those headed by fathers. Today, 26 percent of white families are headed by one parent, as are 61 percent of black families and 34 percent of Hispanic families.
7. *Hispanic groups, at over 40 million, are now the largest minority in the United States, comprising 14 percent of the population.* In contrast, blacks constitute 12 percent of the population. Nearly two-thirds of Hispanics are of Mexican origin. Nearly 80 percent of Hispanics live in California, Texas, New York, Florida, Illinois, Arizona, New Jersey, New Mexico, or Colorado, but the number of Hispanics in other states, such as Oregon, Washington, and Georgia is growing rapidly. However, because the birth and immigration rates are higher among Hispanics, it is estimated that their presence in the United States will continue to grow much faster than other groups. Mexican Americans, with a population of over 23 million, comprise 67 percent of all Hispanics. The second-largest Hispanic group is the catchall "other Hispanic" category (about 7 million), while persons of Puerto Rican descent are the third-largest group (about 3.2 million). Cubans make up less than 10 percent of all Hispanics with a population of 1.2 million.
8. *The teenage birthrate is declining.* The birthrate among teenagers has declined by about 20 percent since 1990. This decline is occurring among all racial and ethnic groups, and is particularly pronounced among blacks.
9. *Unmarried couples living together are becoming increasingly common.* The number of unmarried couples has tripled since 1980 to nearly 5 million. A large increase is also seen among the elderly population, virtually doubling from 119,000 to 220,000 since 1980.
10. *The rich have gotten richer, while middle- and low-income groups have lost ground.* If we break households down into five groups based on the size of their income, the richest fifth of the population earns nearly 50 percent of total U.S. income, while the poorest fifth earns only 4 percent. Over the past few decades the earnings of each group have declined, except among the highest earning group. Moreover, the highest 5 percent of earners have made the greatest gains. Their share of income increased from around 15 percent to 20 percent since 1980.
11. *The elderly population has been increasing almost four times as fast as the population as a whole; seniors now constitute one of every eight people (35 million).* In 1900 only a small portion of people—1 in 25—were aged 65 or older. It is likely that many younger people spent long portions of their lives rarely even seeing an elderly person. Today,

persons aged 100 and over—referred to as *centenarians*—are among the most rapidly growing elderly cohort in the United States. They now number about 55,000, but may jump to nearly 1 million in just 50 years.

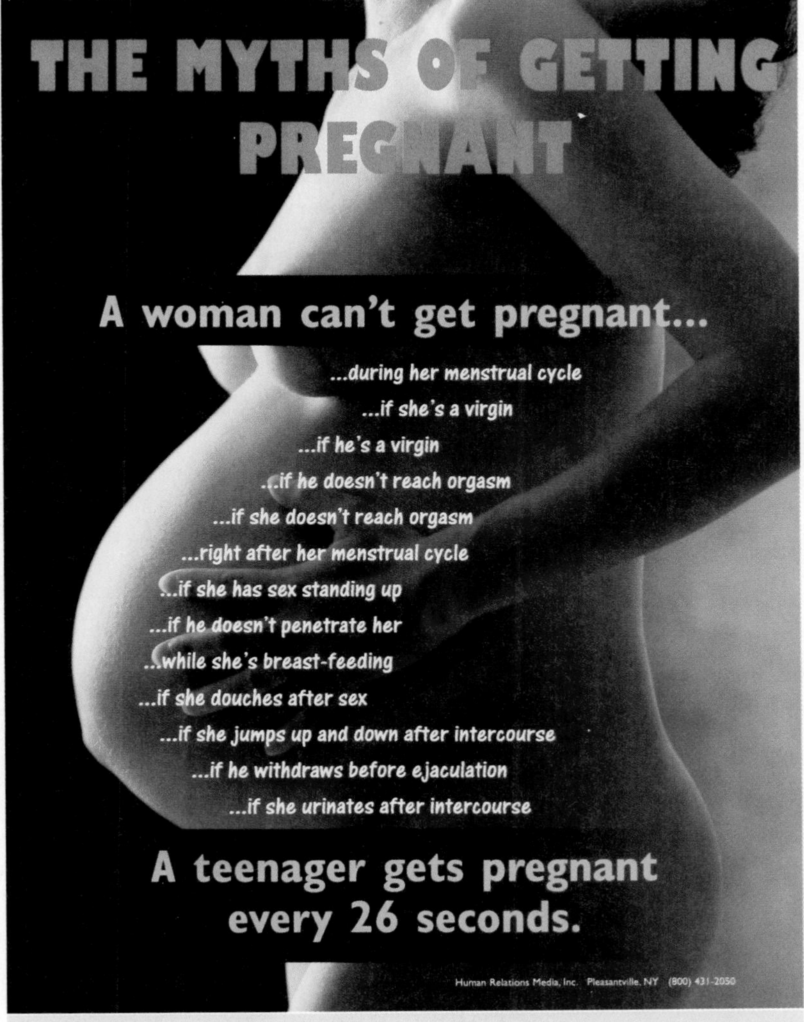

The teenage birthrate has declined among all racial and ethnic groups in the United States over the past 15 years, in part due to explicit advertisements like this one that is designed to inform teenagers about sexuality and pregnancy.

Family Change as a Political Issue

Families are changing in composition, expectations, and roles. What is causing these changes? Are they good or bad? What are the consequences of family change? There is an ongoing debate over the implications of these changes—a debate that is woven into the U.S. political discourse. Janet Giele summarizes three conflicting political viewpoints about the causes and consequences of changes in families (1996), as shown in Figure 1.2 on page 20.

Conservative Perspective

Conservatives express grave concern that many of the changes in family structure put children at risk (Murray 1984; Popenoe 2001; Whitehead and Popenoe 2005). They suggest that many challenges that families face can be linked to gross cultural and moral weakening, which in turn contributes to father absence and family disorganization through divorce or illegitimacy. This ultimately results in greater poverty, crime, drug use, and a host of other social problems that cause struggle for many families. The conservative model is diagrammed in Figure 1.2 and is contrasted with the liberal and feminist perspectives that are also described here.

Conservatives argue that the weakening of the U.S. moral fabric can be traced to the modern secularization of religious practice and the decline of religious affiliation. They suggest that these trends have reshaped our cultural norms so that certain harmful practices are no longer seen as immoral, such as nonmarital sex, cohabitation, or having a child outside of marriage. When this happens, we witness the breakdown of the traditional two-parent family, which conservatives argue is the cornerstone of society. Fathers become increasingly irrelevant in the lives of women and children. Divorce rates and illegitimacy soar. Husbands divorce their wives, leaving their children "behind." They form new unions and have additional children, often without providing financially or emotionally for the children they already have. Conservatives often argue that welfare

FIGURE 1.2 **Models of Family Change**

Source: Giele 1996.

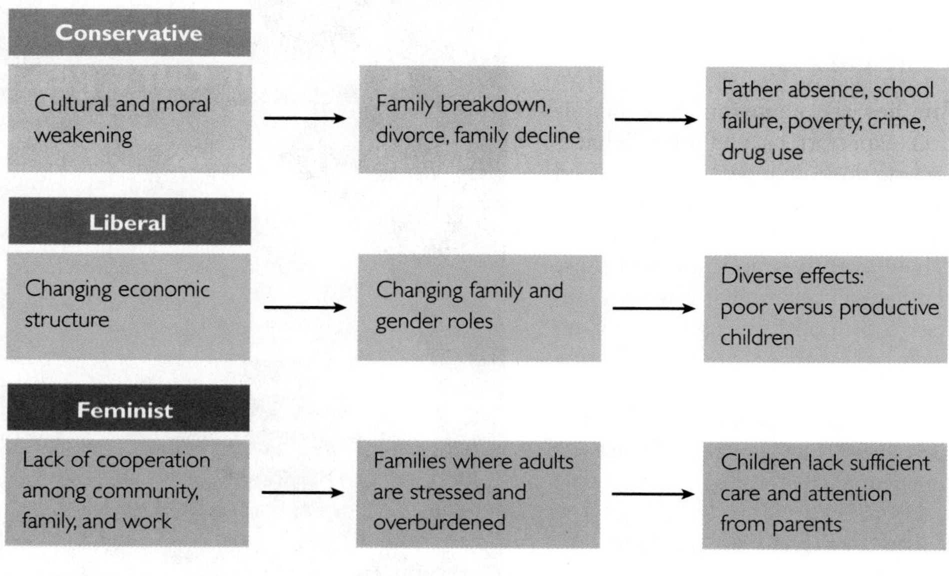

and other social programs actually serve to undermine families, rather than help them because they encourage family breakups.

When families break up and fathers become increasingly marginalized, social problems flourish. Poverty becomes rampant, and children fail to thrive. They do more poorly in school, and possibly turn to alcohol, drugs, and crime to try to alleviate their suffering. Conservatives suggest that the solution to this downward spiral is to strengthen and support traditional marriage. To restore the ideal of the two-parent family, other types of families should be made less attractive. The government should minimize its support of single mothers, and encourage couples to marry and rely upon one another for the care of their children.

Liberal Perspective Liberals also note that families have undergone tremendous change in recent decades, and children face a number of serious challenges because of these changes. However, they suggest that these challenges are the result of economic and structural changes that place new demands on families without offering any additional social supports. The liberal model is also diagrammed in Figure 1.2. These changes include the loss of relatively high-paying manufacturing jobs, an erosion of the minimum wage, a decline in employer-sponsored fringe benefits such as health insurance, and a rise in the number of low-paying service sector jobs. These economic changes have several implications for families, and men and women's relationships within families. First, there is an increasing need for both husbands and wives to work and earn a two-paycheck income. Second, there is less time available for prenatal child care, and therefore a greater need for child care centers. Third, young women may be less inclined to marry men who have few good economic prospects. According to William Julius Wilson, a scholar and former president of the American Sociological Association, it is partly the lack of jobs in the inner city that drives up the rate of out-of-wedlock births because the men are not considered "marriageable" (Wilson 1996).

The result is that an underclass is created. Poor children face extraordinary challenges because they do not have the social supports to weather these changes. Liberals essentially believe in a market economy, but they ask for sufficient social supports to help the families in the bottom tier. These social supports include welfare benefits, job training programs, educational subsidies, expansion of programs like Head Start, and strengthening supports for working families, such as through earned income tax credits (EITCs), or high-quality child care.

Feminist Perspective The feminist perspective (shown in Figure 1.2) blends elements from both conservative and liberal perspectives. With conservatives, they share a heightened respect for the often invisible, but very important caregiving work done in families. With liberals, they share a concern that the changes in economic conditions have had a number of deleterious consequences for families, particularly those that are most vulnerable. Yet, while having some features in common, there are also sharp differences. The feminist perspective criticizes conservatives for exploiting female caregivers to allow men to be more active in the public realm. Meanwhile, liberals perpetuate the notion that the best families are those that are somehow self-sufficient.

Feminists attribute the difficulties children face to a lack of cooperation between the community, family, and employment to improve the quality of life. A sense of individualism permeates U.S. culture and has replaced a collective responsibility for each other's welfare. Comparative research in other countries reveals that where support is generous enough to help all families (not just the most vulnerable), poverty and its associated problems plummet, and health, education, and well-being soar. Instead, in the United States, the lack of collectivism results in families in which adults feel routinely stressed and overburdened. Although poor families may feel these stresses more acutely than the middle class, all families suffer. Children may end up suffering because they lack sufficient care and attention from their parents, who receive so little outside help. Instead, families are expected to fend for themselves.

Feminists critically evaluate the U.S. economic system and ask for alternative policies that place higher value on the quality of human relationships. They work for reforms that build and strengthen neighborhoods and volunteer groups, support caregiving activities, and encourage education and employment among both women and men. Family policies should be enacted to protect and nurture families, including in the areas of child care, maternity benefits, health care, work guarantees, and other economic supports. In sum, feminists judge the strength of a family not by its form (dual parent versus single parent), but by the social well-being that comes from parents knowing that they have the support necessary to be family caregivers and productive workers (Giele 1996).

The State and Family Policy

Compared to many other developed nations, the United States is conspicuously lacking a national family policy (Bergmann 1996; Bogenschneider 1997; Elrod 1999; Kamerman 2003; Warner 2005). Americans are more distrustful of big government. Independence and self-reliance are seen as good virtues, and Americans are uncomfortable with offering "too much" assistance because they fear that it will decrease initiative and encourage dependence. Therefore, families are generally expected to fend for themselves with only minimal assistance. The policies and programs that are in place are usually selective in nature, and available only for a few, often as tax breaks that come once a year. Other developed countries lean more toward offering universal policies and programs that are regularly available to all citizens.

Selective versus Universal

Social policies do not exist in a vacuum; they represent a nation's history, rich cultural traditions, and values. The United States has a long history of rugged individualism and a distrust of government and its programs. Much of colonial America was populated by people trying to flee government controls or what were viewed as government intrusions into their lives. Therefore, it is not surprising that family policies in the United States reflect and promote the concept of individualism and self-sufficiency. U.S. policies reflect our belief that people should be in charge of their own destinies. We acknowledge that some people may need a helping hand, but Americans have little tolerance for people who seem to be unwilling or unable to pull themselves up by "their bootstraps" (Quadagno 1982; Trattner 1999). Borrowing from early English "poor laws," U.S. policies evolved over the seventeenth and eighteenth centuries and make clear distinctions between "worthy" needy people (people who cannot support themselves through no fault of their own, such as the disabled or children) and the "unworthy" (able-bodied men and women).

Not surprisingly then, the United States has a laissez-faire approach in which families are largely left to fend for themselves. Many programs tend to be **selective programs**, meaning that persons need to meet some eligibility requirement to qualify for benefits. Most often this means that persons must meet certain income thresholds; for example, people have to be below a certain income to qualify for Medicaid (health insurance program). This is referred to as **means-tested**. Income thresholds are kept relatively low to limit the number of users of the program and thus control their costs. There is a general fear and distrust that people will take advantage of services and programs if they are made too accessible (Hancock 2004; Seccombe 2007a).

However, not all programs in the United States are means-tested. Police and fire protection and public education are available to all persons, regardless of income. It is not always clear to the observer why some programs are available to everyone and others are not. For example, why is education a "right," but health insurance a "privilege," primarily available to persons with generous employers, to those who are poor enough to qualify for Medicaid (along with other criteria), or to persons over the age of 65? Is education really more important than health care? Or is it simply a result of some historical circumstance, such as early unions fighting for universal education rather than universal health insurance?

When we compare the philosophy of the United States to the philosophies of most of Europe, Canada, and other countries, we see vast differences in approaches. Most developed nations have an interrelated, coordinated set of proactive and **universal programs** available to all persons that are designed to help strengthen all families. Universal programs are not means-tested; rather, they are social and economic programs available to everyone. For example, as shown in Table 1.3, in a 2004 review of developed nations, the United States was the only country without universal health insurance coverage, paid maternal/parental leave at childbirth, or a family allowance/child depend-

TABLE 1.3 **Child Safety Net Policies in 23 Other Developed Countries Compared with the United States**

Country	Universal Health Insurance/ Health Care	Paid Maternal/ Parental Leave at Childbirth	Family Allowance/ Child Dependency Grant
Australia	Yes	Yes	Yes
Austria	Yes	Yes	Yes
Belgium	Yes	Yes	Yes
Canada	Yes	Yes	Yes
Czech Republic	Yes	Yes	Yes
Denmark	Yes	Yes	Yes
Finland	Yes	Yes	Yes
France	Yes	Yes	Yes
Germany	Yes	Yes	Yes
Hungary	Yes	Yes	Yes
Iceland	Yes	Yes	Yes
Italy	Yes	Yes	Yes
Japan	Yes	Yes	Yes
Luxembourg	Yes	Yes	Yes
Netherlands	Yes	Yes	Yes
New Zealand	Yes	Yes	Yes
Norway	Yes	Yes	Yes
Poland	Yes	Yes	Yes
Portugal	Yes	Yes	Yes
Spain	Yes	Yes	Yes
Sweden	Yes	Yes	Yes
Switzerland	Yes	Yes	Yes
United Kingdom	Yes	Yes	Yes
United States	**No**	**No**	**No**

Source: Social Security Online 2004.

ency grant (Social Security Online 2004). While Americans think of these issues in individualistic terms and expect parents largely to figure it out themselves, other countries have specific policies to ensure that all people can receive these benefits. Unfortunately, many parents in the United States are not able to "figure it out themselves." How does one figure out how to get health insurance when an employer does not offer it and the costs of purchasing it yourself far exceed your budget? How do you arrange for a paid maternal leave after the birth of your child when an employer tells you that you will be fired if you don't quickly return to work? How do you find a family allowance, when most people in the United States have never even heard of such a program and the government does not offer one?

In other countries, these programs are financed by **progressive taxation**—those who earn more money pay a higher percentage of their income in taxes. They have adopted these programs because their citizens tend to believe in structural explanations for poverty and inequality, and therefore look for structural solutions. Americans are much more likely to equate poverty and its consequences with individual failure, immorality, lack of thrift, or laziness. For example, when asked "why are there people in this country who live in need?" 39 percent of Americans blamed personal laziness, compared to only 16 percent of Swedes (World Values Survey 1994).

Family Policy and Family Values

Examining specific family policies (or the lack thereof) can tell a great deal about U.S. collective family values. The following example examines recent sweeping welfare reform legislation passed in the late 1990s that continues to have serious consequences for poor families today. It illustrates the individualist orientation common in the United States that generally leaves families on their own.

Example: Welfare Reform Welfare has been one of the most challenging social policy concerns in the United States. Its principal cash program, **Temporary Assistance for Needy Families (TANF)**, formerly called Aid to Families with Dependent Children (AFDC), was originally designed to help protect women and their children from conditions of poverty. It was created in 1935 as Title IV of the Social Security Act, a critical piece of legislation produced during the New Deal when millions of families were suffering financial hardship. The goal was to keep single mothers out of the workforce because the general sentiment at the time was that children who only have one parent would benefit by having that parent at home.

Much has changed in 70 years. Most Americans no longer feel comfortable paying mothers to stay home and take care of their children. In 2005, over two-thirds of married women with dependent children under age 18 were employed outside the home (U.S. Department of Labor 2006a). As the employment of mothers becomes the rule rather than the exception, people question the value of paying poor single mothers to stay home with their children. They ask: Is it necessary to subsidize poor and single mothers so that they do not have to work outside the home when most middle-class mothers are employed? Ignored in the discussions are the differing circumstances between the two groups. Poor single mothers must be both mothers and fathers to their children. They have no one else to rely upon to share the financial and emotional strains that accompany parenting.

Welfare programs have been accused of fostering long-term dependency, family breakups, and illegitimacy (Murray 1984, 1988). Welfare recipients are viewed by many people as lazy and unmotivated, looking for a free ride at the expense of the taxpayer (Hancock 2004; Seccombe 2007a). To ensure that welfare isn't too easy to get, some regions impose rigorous application procedures. For example, New York City's TANF application is among the most complex. It includes requiring applicants to attend two eligibility interviews in two different locations, undergo fingerprinting and photographing for fraud prevention purposes, receive a home visit from an eligibility verification investigator, attend a mandatory workforce orientation, and attend daily job search classes (5 days per week) for the duration of the 30-day eligibility determination period (Holcomb et al. 2003).

For decades, both Republicans and Democrats have tried to reconstruct welfare or end it entirely. In 1997 then-President Clinton implemented sweeping welfare reform legislation known as the Personal Responsibility and Work Opportunity Reconciliation

Act (PRWORA). From this legislation, TANF was created (Coven 2005). The legislation set lifetime welfare payments at a maximum of 5 years, with the majority of adult recipients being required to work after 2 years. Many states have adopted significantly shorter time frames, and some make no allowances for women who have young babies. Moreover, 21 states have also adopted some form of family caps, meaning that benefits will not be increased for a child born while a mother is already receiving TANF (Rowe and Russell 2004).

Since the passage of welfare reform, many people have left welfare, usually for low-wage work. The enforcement of time limits and work requirements, coupled with the expanding economy and low unemployment rate of the 1990s, contributed to a dramatic initial drop in the number of families receiving TANF. From March 1994 to December 2005, national caseloads fell by over 60 percent, declining from 5 million to about 1.9 million families (U.S. Department of Health and Human Services 2006a).

How are these families faring? Unfortunately, families leaving welfare for work are not necessarily better off financially (Acs and Loprest 2004; Edin and Lein 1997; Seccombe 2007a). The median wage for former welfare recipients approximates $7.15 an hour, which leaves many families in poverty (depending on family size) (Loprest 2002). One Oregon study found that only about one-quarter of former welfare recipients were offered insurance from an employer; however, many families could not accept the benefits because they could not afford to pay for them (Seccombe and Hoffman 2007). Only a slightly larger share was offered paid sick leave (U.S. Department of Health and Human Services 2001; Seccombe and Hoffman 2007). The results of a nationwide study reveal that families leaving welfare struggle to make ends meet. Approximately one-third of TANF leavers say they have had to cut the size of a meal or skip meals because they did not have enough food. Sixty percent worried at least sometimes that they would run out of food before having money to buy more. Over half reported that they had often or sometimes run out of food and were without means to buy more. Nearly half reported that they were unable to pay their mortgage, rent, or utility bills in the past year, particularly among those who left TANF most recently. Ten percent had to move in with others because of their inability to pay their bills (Acs and Loprest 2004).

The number of families on cash welfare has declined by about 60 percent since welfare was reformed a decade ago; nonetheless, many families remain poor due to the low wages they receive for the work they do and the lack of critical benefits such as health insurance.

How then do families survive on welfare and low-wage work? One study of 214 welfare and 165 wage-reliant mothers found a number of crafty and deceptive strategies (Edin and Lein 1997). Some strategies were illegal because they were not reported to the welfare agency, but the mothers claimed that without this type of assistance, their families would be completely destitute.

- *Contributions from family, friends, or boyfriends:* "He sometimes gives me money. When I sent her up there to his mother's house, he buy her Pampers and baby food, but all he puts into my hand is a $20 bill. I mean, what does he expect me to buy with $20? I can't even buy but two boxes of Pampers with $20. He's coming over here tonight to bring her back, and I said I needed $40 'cause she need so many things right now. But I don't think he gonna bring it. He always says he's gonna bring money, but he never does because he's never working steady. If he doesn't bring money this time, I am not gonna let her go up there to his mother's house to visit anymore."
- *Reported work:* "Working overtime if I have to, anything to get a few extra dollars. I try to get to work one-half hour early, and leave one-half hour late; that's an extra 5 hours worth of pay each week! It comes in handy."
- *Unreported side jobs:* "I wish I could report my job, I really do. But then I just couldn't make it right now, not until I get a raise or some overtime. I dream about the day when I can go in and tell my caseworker, 'I don't need your assistance, I got a job.' I dream about the day I can kiss welfare good-bye."
- *Underground work:* "Some of our friends will sell drugs. I know some of my friends who have turned tricks. Usually, some people do it for their family, and some people do it for drugs. At one point I did sell drugs in order to keep my family [together]. When my husband left, and I had to make sure I could pay my bills. That's what I did."
- *Agency-based strategies:* "I don't like to beg, but I will for the kids. I go to a church where they give you canned goods: tuna, spaghetti, tomato sauce, eggs. . . . I've been twice in 2 months. They don't like you to show up too often, but if you really need it, they'll give it."

Other countries have a different approach to welfare. For example, in her book *Saving Our Children from Poverty* (1996), economist Barbara Bergmann states that only one-quarter of single mothers in France receive welfare-type benefits, compared to two-thirds of single mothers in the United States. The reason for this difference is not because France is stingy. On the contrary, France has made a successful commitment to enhancing low-tier jobs. They have improved the conditions surrounding low-tier work so that these jobs pay a living wage, and the government does not automatically eliminate an array of benefits that are vital to a family's well-being. A single mother in France who moves from welfare to work retains approximately $6,000 in government cash and housing grants. She continues to receive health insurance and pays only a small amount for child care, as do all French citizens. Therefore, even though France has an unemployment rate that is substantially higher than that in the United States, its poverty rate is considerably lower.

Themes of This Book

Several themes are woven throughout this textbook that draw from the previous discussion. Each of these themes is highlighted here.

Families Are Both a Public Social Institution and a Private Personal Relationship

Families fulfill many of our own personal needs for love, warmth, and intimacy. It is within families that we raise our children and nurture their social, emotional, and physical growth. Nonetheless, we should not forget that families are also a public **social institution**. A social institution is a major sphere of social life, with a set of beliefs and rules that are organized to meet basic human needs. In addition to talking about your specific family, we talk about *the* family. Families are a social institution in much the same way our political, economic, religious, health care, and educational systems are social institutions. As we will see in Chapter 2, in early human civilizations, families were the center of most activities. The earliest hunting and gathering societies were based almost exclusively on kinship. In families we learned and practiced religion, we educated the young, and took care of the sick. This pattern was modified little until recently. With the advent of technology and the industrial revolution, other institutions developed and took on many of these functions. Today, we worship in churches, synagogues, and mosques; children are educated in schools; and we go to hospitals when we are sick.

Families continue to represent a major sphere of social life for most people—and despite their diversity, families still have a surprising organized set of beliefs and rules, and they are organized to meet certain fundamental needs. For example, in virtually every society, families are considered the best place to raise children.

Families can best be understood by examining how they interact with (and are influenced by) other social institutions. Families cannot merely be separated out as "havens" from the rest of society. Patterns of education, religious customs, economic systems, and political systems all shape family patterns, attitudes, behaviors, and the constraints and opportunities experienced by individual members. For example, norms associated with social institutions may influence who is considered an appropriate mate, which family members work outside the home and what kind of work they do, who has the primary responsibility for housework and other domestic labor, how children are raised and disciplined, which children can be schooled, how power and decision making among family members will be allocated, and the roles that extended family members are expected to play.

However, in all likelihood, most people do not reflect very often on families as social institutions. Instead, they focus on the lived day-to-day experience of being in a family, either in their **family of orientation** (defined as the family they were born into) or the **family of procreation** (more broadly used to refer to the family made through partnership, marriage, and/or with children). People tend to think about their families in extremely individualized terms, often without seeing their interconnection to larger social structures. Many aspects of family life, however, including our chances of marrying or being in a committed partnership, of bearing children, of divorcing, the kind of neighborhood we live in, the type of job we are likely to get, the sort of child care we are likely to use, our general health and well-being, and the likelihood of living to see our grandchildren, are affected by broader social structures in which we are embedded.

It is important to recognize how our personal choices and behaviors are shaped by the larger social structures. For example, how does one's level of education affect the chances of having children? Is the relationship between level of education and the likelihood of having children identical for men and women? Are children viewed as an asset, and how might views toward children be related to capitalism, urbanization, or the distribution of money and other resources?

At the same time, being mindful of these social forces does not imply that we are passive recipients of them. **Human agency** is the ability of human beings to create viable lives even when they are constrained or limited by social forces (Baca Zinn and Dill 1994; Baca Zinn and Eitzen 1996). Rich, poor, male, female, young, or old—we are all actively producing our lives, even in light of the social forces that help shape our opportunities. We do have free choice, but it is important to be mindful of the ways that we are influenced by the structure of the society in which we live.

Social Inequality Has a Powerful Influence on Family Life

A second theme of the text is that social inequality is a critical organizing feature in society and has an important influence on family life. Most Americans believe that the United States provides nearly equal opportunities for everyone. However, as will be shown in detail in Chapter 5, U.S. society is highly stratified on the basis of economics, power, and social status. Inequality is woven into many of the basic social structures and social institutions. These patterns of social inequality filter down and shape all components of family life—the neighborhood in which you live, your gendered expectations, the values you are likely to hold for your children, the type of job you are likely to get, your consumption patterns, daily stressors, and your coping mechanisms. Social class, sex, race, and ethnicity affect the way family members interact with one another and the way in which they are responded to.

Conversely, patterns of social inequality are also shaped *by* families. Americans fantasize that they can be anything they want to be, but in reality there is little substantial upward (or downward) social mobility. People usually live out their lives in generally the same social class in which they were born. Families pass on their wealth and social capital (or their lack of it) to their newest members, and this perpetuates social inequality. For example, because of the U.S. inheritance laws, affluent parents are able to distribute their wealth to their children upon their death. Relatively little of the wealth is taxed and redistributed, as is the case in other countries. Consequently, some of the richest people have only marginal employment histories. They do not need to work for a living—yet others who work relentlessly, often in the unglamorous but growing service sector, find no real route to a better life. Their wages are low; they may not receive health insurance or other benefits and live on the margins only one paycheck away from impoverishment. What type of wealth or social capital do these parents have to pass on to their children?

This text examines the assumptions, values, and ideologies that are used to justify or explain social inequality and its shaping of families. We will see that the ideologies of more powerful groups are often presented as "normal" or "common sense" rather than showing their true ideological slant. Box 1.1 shows how U.S. culture tends to define the "normal" American family without regard to the inherent racism in such a definition.

Family Policies Reflect Historical, Cultural, Political, and Social Factors

If families are public social institutions in addition to private personal relationships, then we must recognize the importance of federal, state, and local involvement. The third theme of this text is that government regulates many conditions of families, and these policies reflect historical patterns, cultural values, political viewpoints, and many social conditions, including the distribution of power and inequality in society. This may occur in the passing of specific policies targeting certain groups or certain aspects of family life, such as welfare reform, requiring partners to get a blood test before marrying, or passing legislation to prohibit gays and lesbians from marrying.

Conversely, historical, cultural, political, and social factors may also have great influence backhandedly by the *absence* of specific policies. For example, the U.S.

BOX 1.1 Using the Sociological Imagination

Ideology of "Family" Shapes Perceptions of Immigrant Children

All children want to feel like they live in a typical, "normal" family. But how are definitions of "normal" constructed, and what are the consequences of living in a family that does not conform to the definition? Sociologist Karen Pyke explores these sensitive issues.

There is a cultural imagery of American families that we see on television and throughout the media. American families are "supposed to" contain a mom, a dad, and siblings, and these family members are expected to behave toward each other in very specific ways. The problem is, this cultural imagery is at odds with many families. The values of many racial, ethnic, immigrant, and gay and lesbian families are largely excluded from this narrow ideal. The American family ideology denigrates families whose structure or cultural practices do not comply, and this contributes to negative self-images, and even self-derogation among members of such families.

Karen Pyke conducted interviews with 73 grown children of Korean and Vietnamese immigrants and found that when these young contrasted behavior in their immigrant families with mainstream images of normalcy, they interpreted their own family life, as well as that of Asians and Asian Americans in general, as deficient. In their descriptions, they drew upon Americanized definitions of love that stress expressiveness, such as the display of affection, sentimentality, and close communication. They downplayed their parents' instrumental style of love that is emphasized in Asian cultures, such as their support of children well into adulthood and—in the case of many Korean parents—their decision to immigrate in search of a better life and education for their children. However, because their immigrant parents did not conform to Americanized notions of love, their children typically described them as distant, unloving, uncaring, and not normal.

Dat, 22, who left Vietnam at age 5, referred to images of normal family life in America as seen on television and among friends as the basis for his desire for more affection and closeness with his father. "Sometimes when I had problems in school, all I wanted was my dad to listen to me, of all people," he said. "I guess that's the American way and I was raised American. . . . That's what I see on TV and in my friends' family. And I expected him to be that way too. But it didn't happen."

Similarly, Paul, a 21-year-old born in the United States to Korean immigrant parents had similar feelings. "As a child I was always watching television and watching other friends' fathers," he said. "All the relationships seemed so much different from me and my father's relationship. . . . I can remember watching *The Brady Bunch* reruns and thinking Mike Brady would be a wonderful dad to have. He was always so supportive. . . . Basically, I used what I saw on TV as a picture of what a typical family should be like in the United States. I only wished that my family could be like that."

The widespread family ideology promotes the white middle-class family ideal as the norm and the superior standard. Pyke's study found that this ideology put immense pressure on children to assimilate, and they denigrated their own ethnic family styles as deficient in comparison. They internalized a negative view of their own family life and glorified the cultural practices associated with white families.

As Robert, 24, who emigrated from Korea at age 7, explained, "I still find myself envying white American families and wishing that my family was perfect like theirs. So basically I find myself suckered into this ideal image of the American family. And I realize, sadly, that my family is not the American family and never will be. God, you know, this really upsets me when I keep striving for this intangible thing because then I never really feel happiness or satisfaction."

Sources: Pyke 2000a, 2000b.

CRITICAL THINKING QUESTIONS

1. How are definitions of the "normal American family" racist? What may be some of the consequences for young persons who feel marginalized because they don't fit the stereotype of a normal family?
2. Why does the stereotype of the "normal American family" persist? Whose interests are best served by it?

government offers no systematic paid leave to women who have just given birth. This is in sharp contrast to other developed nations (and many developing ones), as you will learn in Chapter 8. Commonly in other countries, women receive 6 to 12 months off of work, with full or nearly full pay. A recent study comparing attitudes in 31 countries toward family policies reveals that the United States is far more likely to believe that family matters are personal issues than are other countries, reflecting a longstanding belief in rugged individualism. For example, an international survey asking whether women should receive paid maternity leave when they have a baby received a nearly unanimous "yes" in other countries, but in the United States, nearly a quarter of Americans said "no." Why would so many people object to women receiving paid maternity benefits?

Family policies reflect historical, cultural, political, and social factors in every society—values about personal responsibility versus collective good, the role of work in our lives, the expectations placed on mothers and fathers to manage the inherent conflicts between their work and family lives, and the level of concern over social inequality.

Parasuraman and Greenhaus (1997) identify three solutions that can be used when family and work conflict with one another. First, establishing policies that create more family-friendly work environments, such as paid maternity and family leaves, could alter the situation. A second approach is that employees themselves should learn specific techniques for managing their conflicts, such as choosing a one-job family pattern. A third approach would modify the meanings of the situation. It would suggest that people have

For each child under six, you will receive $100 per month.

But you may need to apply.

The Government of Canada's **Universal Child Care Benefit** came into effect on July 1, 2006. It provides Canadian families with $100 per month for each child under six.

If you already receive the Canada Child Tax Benefit (CCTB), you will automatically receive the Universal Child Care Benefit. If you are one of the ten percent of families who do not receive the CCTB, you need to complete the CCTB form.

It's simple to apply

Log on to www.universalchildcare.ca and click on the application links. It's that easy. Or, visit your local Service Canada Centre to obtain the form in person. You can also call 1 800 959-2221.

You can apply anytime

The first benefit cheques have been mailed. You can apply anytime and receive payments retroactively up to 11 months from your date of application.

This initiative is part of Canada's Universal Child Care Plan which will also support the creation of thousands of real child care spaces through the **Child Care Spaces Initiative.**

For more information, visit the website at www.universalchildcare.ca

Government of Canada Gouvernement du Canada

Canada

Other developed countries have a less punitive attitude toward welfare; for example, programs to help with child care costs are universal, rather than means-tested, as they are in the United States. This ad was posted in a Canadian newspaper in 2006 reminding families to apply for benefits.

family and work conflicts simply because they *want* to work more hours or *want* more money. Policies would focus on increasing personal responsibility and commitments (Bogenschneider 2000).

Of these three solutions, the United States most often adopts the second and third approaches. Family issues, whether they are poverty or income insecurity, work-family conflicts, or caring for dependents, are often seen as personal issues or problems. This is in contrast to many other countries that take a more structural view.

The different policy approaches between the United States and other countries will become apparent as we explore each of the topics of each chapter in this text. Social policies, either by their commission or omission, critically influence virtually all aspects of family life, including how families are structured or organized, and the values, attitudes, and behaviors of its members. Therefore, social policy discussions are presented in each chapter, rather than relegating family policy to a concluding chapter at the end of the text.

A comparative perspective is valuable because societies are increasingly interconnected with one another. Oscar-winning actress Angelina Jolie became the first recipient of the Church World Service Immigration and Refugee Program Humanitarian Award, which honored her for her work as Goodwill Ambassador for the United Nations High Commissioner for Refugees (UNHCR).

Understanding Families in the United States Requires a Comparative Perspective

The final theme of this text focuses on the importance of learning about other cultures and other historical periods to better inform us of American families. In the past it was easier to ignore what was happening in the world beyond our borders, but this is no longer the case because societies are becoming increasingly interconnected. New technologies, immigration, commerce across borders, and greater ease in world travel have increased visibility and the United States can no longer remain isolated. Societies see other ways of doing things and sometimes adopt pieces of another's culture. One can now travel to many distant parts of the world and still find American fast food, such as McDonald's or Kentucky Fried Chicken. Likewise, the United States also has adopted other foods and cultural artifacts. Tacos and pizza are staples in our diets today, but were considered exotic or regional ethnic food only a short time ago. How has this changed the rhythm of life in the United States?

Likewise it is easy to ignore history and to only focus on the here and now—but many of our current family issues are rooted in the traditions of the past. For example, to better understand the current and heated debate over abortion, we should be aware that it was once not opposed by religious groups, including the Catholic church. Likewise, to truly understand the high rate of divorce in the United States, we should be aware of the ways in which the current notion of love, which evolved in the eighteenth century, changed the entire basis on which mates were chosen, and thereby increased the likelihood of couples ending an unhappy marriage (Coontz 2005).

A comparative perspective helps us understand our current situation because it informs us of other possibilities. These other possibilities could be in the form of alternative social arrangements, ways to frame an issue, or policy solutions. For example, how can a comparative perspective help us understand the nature and role of

BOX 1.2 Our Global Community

Adolescence Among the Maasai

The conception of adolescence and the way it is experienced are far from universal. An interesting contrast to adolescence in the West is found among the Maasai, an ethnic group living on the savannas of Kenya and Tanzania.

The Maasai are a small tribe in a mosaic of African peoples; they are tall, thin pastoralists who can be spotted miles away by their signature red clothing. Their lives are simple; they depend on their cattle and their families, living closely with the earth. Wealth is measured by the number of cattle and children a man has, and the economy is a family-based one in which all contribute to the family's well-being. The men are in charge, primarily protecting the village and caring for the animals.

For the men, the passage to adulthood is a long and rigorous process. Early on a boy is assigned to a *moran*, the group of warriors with whom he will be associated, his age mates. The moran is divided into junior and senior groups as well as the specific group with whom the boy will be circumcised. Male circumcision takes place between the ages of 13 and 17; some boys do not have younger brothers old enough to take their place caring for the animals, so they stay behind to help with the cattle until a younger brother is ready. When the circumcision takes place, the young man is not allowed to cry or yell; to do so leads to disrespect for his entire family. His parents could be beaten by members of the entire village for raising such a coward.

Once boys are circumcised, they become junior warriors and live with their age mates in a special dwelling set aside for them. The mother accompanies her son, adorning herself with elaborate beaded ear ornaments that show everyone she is the mother of a warrior. She builds a house for him while he roams about freely with his moran, having sex with women, hunting, growing his hair long, and decorating elaborate headdresses. The moran becomes so close that they even urinate together; these men are now brothers and share everything in life, even their wives when they later take them.

When the junior morans age, they become senior warriors and the life of the community is centered on them. They direct the stock, are in charge of defense and security, and occasionally deal with the local government. They are hunters and are allowed to do so by the Kenyan government, although only to a limited extent. Theirs is a most important position in that society, and the young men are now fully adults.

What about women? They build the houses, collect wood, cook, clean, milk the cows, and raise the children. Girls are circumcised by age 13, marking their availability for marriage. They, too, are adults.

From this example, one can see that adolescence as we know it at home in the United States does not exist in all cultures. Instead, being in a moran and being circumcised prepares a young man in the Maasai for his coming role in society. There is no delineation as a teen; the young man is a warrior in training and thus is fully respected and important to his society. He is responsible and his job is crucial to the survival of his society. The young woman may be married by age 13, also deemed an adult.

Source: Adapted from: Leeder 2004.

CRITICAL THINKING QUESTIONS

1. What exactly is the job of an adolescent in the United States? Is it crucial to the survival of society?
2. Are there any American rituals—religious, cultural, academic—that demarcate adolescence? What rituals would you propose?
3. Is there anything in the Maasai cultural traditions that could be useful to the United States?

adolescence in U.S. culture? This is an important concern because it is well known that adolescents commit a disproportionate number of crimes, experience higher-than-average unemployment, and face a host of other social problems such as teen pregnancy or drug use. A comparative perspective reveals that adolescence, as we know it today, is largely a social construction (Leeder 2004; Mintz 2004). It is not a biological imperative. It is a relatively new phenomenon, originating in the West in the late nineteenth century as a result of newly instigated child labor laws and the changing nature of the labor market. Until then, children's labor was needed on farms and dependence was virtually unheard of. Adolescents were considered to be mini-adults. By the late nineteenth century, with industrialization and urbanization and the concern over their effects on children, there was a movement to increase the protection of young people. Social reformers referred to as *child savers* were particularly interested in developing social programs that were age based and targeted toward children. Compulsory education increased the length of time children spent in school until well into their teenage years. Adolescence became a new period of transition between childhood and adulthood, but without clear-cut norms about what to expect during this period. There was little in the way of initiation rites to elevate this status; in many ways, it was a point of limbo. By the twentieth century, the concept of adolescence as a separate stage of life had taken hold, and now is associated with a large component of popular culture, which is highly segregated from adult-oriented culture. Unique clothing, music, and food are directly marketed toward this relatively new consumer group. Nonetheless, it is not completely clear what the developmental tasks of this age group are and how they can best serve the needs of society. Separating adolescents from adults, but giving them an unclear or unknown set of developmental tasks, has not served adolescents well. As historian Steven Mintz (2004) writes, "If there is any lesson that the history of childhood can teach us, it is the error of thinking that we can radically separate the lives of children from those of adults."

How do other cultures construct this age period? How are these social constructions related to the level of technology or wealth in society? Is there anything that we can learn from other cultures, even those that are radically different from our own? Box 1.2 describes a vivid contrast to the concept of adolescence in the West by looking at how a group living in Kenya and Tanzania see this age period.

Conclusion

This chapter introduces a sociological imagination to the study of families and intimate relationships. Rather than seeing families as simply personal and private relationships that operate in a random fashion, we recognize that many seemingly personal family issues are related to social structure and must be examined accordingly. To understand family dynamics, a sociological perspective uses a comparative approach and empirical methods to describe and explain patterns of family structure, family change, and social relationships. As a public social institution, families are not isolated entities from the rest of society, but are continually changing and adapting to peoples' needs and to the changes found in other social institutions in society. Yet policies to help families are notoriously selective or absent in the United States. The upcoming chapters will examine specific family issues through the lens of the sociological imagination. This text has four specific themes that are found within each chapter: (1) the family is a public social institution as well as a private personal relationship; (2) social inequality powerfully shapes virtually all dimensions of family life; (3) family policies reflect historical, cultural, political, and social factors; and (4) a comparative approach can yield insight into family structure and family dynamics.

Key Terms

Comparative perspective: Looking at other societies around the world or looking at a culture historically to see how others organize their social life and respond to its challenges. (p. 9)

Conflict theory: This theoretical perspective emphasizes issues surrounding social inequality, power, conflict, and social change. (p. 15)

Developmental theory: Families and family members go through distinct stages each with its own set of tasks, roles, and responsibilities. (p. 16)

Domestic partners: Heterosexual or homosexual unmarried couples in long-term committed relationships. (p. 7)

Empirical approach: Answers questions through a systematic collection and analysis of data. (p. 12)

Ethnocentrism: The assumption that society's way of doing things is always the best way. (p. 9)

Families: Relationships by blood, marriage, or affection, in which members may cooperate economically, may care for any children, and may consider their identity to be intimately connected to the larger group. (p. 5)

Family of orientation: The family into which you were born. (p. 27)

Family of procreation: The family you make through partnership, marriage, and/or with children. (p. 27)

Family systems theory: Family members, and the roles they play make up a system, and this system is larger than the sum of its individual members. (p. 17)

Feminist theory: Gender is the central concept for explaining family structure and dynamics. (p. 16)

Fictive kin: Nonrelatives whose bonds are strong and intimate. (p. 5)

Human agency: The ability of human beings to create viable lives even when they are constrained or limited by social forces. (p. 28)

Life course perspective: Examines how individuals' lives change as they pass through the events in their lives, recognizing that many changes are socially produced and shared among a cohort of people. (p. 17)

Macro theories: A general framework that attempts to understand societal patterns, such as structural functionalism, conflict theory, and feminist theory. (p. 14)

Means-tested: People have to be below a certain income to qualify for a social program. (p. 22)

Micro theories: A general framework that focuses on personal dynamics and face-to-face interaction, including social exchange, symbolic interaction, developmental, and family systems theories. (p. 14)

Progressive taxation: Those who earn more pay a higher percentage of their income in taxes. (p. 24)

Qualitative methods: The focus is on narrative description with words rather than numbers to analyze patterns and their underlying meanings. (p. 12)

Quantitative methods: The focus is on collecting data that can be measured numerically. (p. 12)

Selective programs: Persons need to meet some eligibility requirement to qualify for benefits. (p. 22)

Social exchange theory: Individuals are rational and their behavior reflects an evaluation of costs and benefits. (p. 16)

Social institution: A major sphere of social life, with a set of beliefs and rules that is organized to meet basic human needs, such as the family, political, or educational systems. (p. 27)

Social structure: The organized pattern of social relationships and social institutions that together form the basis of society. (p. 8)

Sociological imagination: Reveals general patterns in what otherwise might be thought of as simple random events. (p. 8)

Structural functionalist theory: This theoretical perspective suggests that all social institutions, including the family, exist to fill a need in society. (p. 15)

Symbolic interaction theory: This theoretical perspective focuses on the social interaction between family members and other groups, concerned with the meanings and interpretations that people have. (p. 16)

Temporary Assistance for Needy Families (TANF): The principal cash welfare program previously known as Aid to Families with Dependent Children (AFDC). (p. 24)

Theory: A general framework, explanation, or tool to understand and describe the real-life world. (p. 14)

Universal programs: Social and economic programs that are available to all persons or families. (p. 22)

Resources on the Internet

The American Sociological Association
www.asanet.org
The American Sociological Association (ASA), founded in 1905, is a nonprofit membership association dedicated to advancing sociology as a scientific discipline and profession serving the public good. With approximately 13,000 members, the ASA encompasses sociologists who are faculty members at colleges and universities, researchers, practitioners, and students. About 20 percent of its members work in government, business, or nonprofit organizations.

The National Council on Family Relations
www.ncfr.com
The National Council on Family Relations (NCFR) provides a forum for family researchers, educators, and practitioners to share in the development and dissemination of knowledge about families and family relationships, establishes professional standards, and works to promote family well-being. NCFR publishes two scholarly journals, as well as books, audio/video tapes, and learning tools. It sponsors an annual conference of cutting-edge research papers, methods, and practices, including research updates for practitioners.

The American Psychological Association
www.apa.org
The American Psychological Association (APA) is a scientific and professional organization that represents psychology in the United States. With more than 150,000 members, APA is the largest association of psychologists worldwide. The objective of the APA is to advance psychology as a science and profession and as a means of promoting health, education, and human welfare to the public.

Further Reading

Adams, B. N., and J. Trost, (Eds.). 2004. *Handbook of World Families*. Thousand Oaks, CA: Sage.

Amato, P. R., A. Booth, D. R. Johnson, and S. J. Rogers. 2007. *Alone Together: How Marriage in America Is Changing*. Cambridge, MA: Harvard University Press.

Andersen, M. L., and H. F. Taylor. 2007. *Sociology: Understanding a Diverse Society*, 4th ed. Belmont, CA: Wadsworth.

Babbie, E. 2004. *The Practice of Social Research*, 10th ed. Belmont, CA: Wadsworth.

Best, Joel. 2001. *Damned Lies and Statistics: Untangling Numbers From the Media, Politicians, and Activists*. Berkeley: University of California Press.

Coleman, M., and L. H. Ganong (Eds.). 2004. *Handbook of Contemporary Families: Considering the Past, Contemplating the Future*. Thousand Oaks, CA: Sage.

Ingoldsby, B. B., S. R. Smith, and J. E. Miller. 2004. *Exploring Family Theories*. Los Angeles, CA: Roxbury Publishing Company.

Mason, M. A., A. Skolnick, and S. D. Sugarman. 2003. *All Our Families: New Policies for a New Century*, 2nd ed. New York: Oxford University Press.

McKenry, P. C., and S. J. Price (Eds.). 2000. *Families and Change: Coping with Stressful Events and Transitions*. Newbury Park, CA: Sage.

Reeder, E. 2004. *The Family in Global Perspective: A Gendered Journey*. Thousand Oaks, CA: Sage.

Schaie, K. W., and G. L. Elder Jr. (Eds). 2005. *Historical Influence on Lives and Aging*. New York: Springer.

Seccombe, K. 2007. *'So You Think I Drive a Cadillac?': Welfare Recipients' Perspectives of Welfare and Its Reform*, 2nd ed. Boston: Allyn & Bacon.

Strauss, A., and J. Corbin. 1990. *Basics of Qualitative Research: Grounded Theory Procedures and Techniques*. Newbury, Park, CA: Sage.

CHAPTER 2

Families Throughout the World: Marriage, Family, and Kinship

Chapter Outline

CHAPTER PREVIEW

Every society has the social institution known as family. This chapter reveals both the universal functions and variation in structure within family relationships throughout the world. Families are found in every society because they provide functions that no other social institution can (or wants to) provide. However, there is tremendous diversity because families reflect the environment, historical period, and culture in which they are found, and they continually adapt to changing circumstances. In this chapter you will learn:

- Functions of the family, both universal features and variations
- The types of data available to study families throughout the world
- Variations in marriage patterns, including monogamy and polygamy
- Patterns of power and authority
- Patterns of kinship, descent, and inheritance
- Patterns of residence
- Two specific theories that attempt to explain social change and families: Modernization theory and world systems theory
- Differences in families around the world through contrasts of India, Japan, and Sweden

One of the traditional organizing features of the Vietnamese family has been the preference of married couples to coreside with the husband's parents when possible. This custom, based on Confucianism, is referred to as a patrilocal *living arrangement. When a first son marries, he is obliged to move in with his parents, at least until another brother marries and joins the family.*

However, as Vietnam becomes an increasingly modernized nation, has the custom of patrilocality declined? A common theory of family change suggests that as educational and occupational opportunities expand, as adult children become more geographically mobile, and as the country becomes more urbanized, greater independence between family members is likely to emerge. The nuclear family will gradually replace extended families, and support for traditional family obligations, such as patrilocality, will decline.

Sociologists Charles Hirschman and Nguyen Huu Minh analyzed data from the Vietnam Longitudinal Study, which is based on 1,855 households in the largest province in the Red River Delta in northern Vietnam. The survey included a wide range of questions on family relationships, structure, educational and occupational history, siblings, and marriage and children.

The researchers found, somewhat unexpectedly, that the proportion of newly married couples that followed the patrilocal custom actually increased in recent decades rather than declined. Between 1956 and 1965, 72 percent of sons lived with parents after their marriage. However, between 1986 and 1995, the percentage had increased to 83 percent. The researchers did find that the length of time sons and their wives coresided had declined somewhat. After 5 years, fewer than 30 percent of the more recent cohorts still lived with their parents, compared to over 40 percent between 1956 and 1965.

The researchers also found that relatively few aspects of modernization contributed to a lower incidence of living with parents. Adult children who worked in nonagricultural occupations and who married later in life were somewhat less likely to coreside with the groom's parents. However, overall it appears that the underlying cultural preference to live with the groom's parents immediately after marriage remains strong and grows stronger in Vietnam. Hirschman and Minh conclude that not all aspects of the traditional family structure may undergo the same tensions associated with modernization. Joint living arrangements, at least in the son's early part of marriage, may be mutually beneficial, and show no sign of declining. (Hirschman and Minh 2002) ■

Throughout history and throughout the world, people have lived in families. As a social institution, families are at the center of all societies because they fulfill needs that few other institutions can. Yes, societies develop their own variation in how marriage, families, and kinship groups should function and what they are supposed to do, but what is surprising is the amazing similarity from one region of the world to another. What are some of these similarities?

Functions of the Family: Variations and Universals

Drawing upon a theoretical perspective of structural functionalism, sociologists and family scientists often discuss families in terms of the important functions they serve for individuals and for society at large. These functions include marriage, the regulation of sexual behavior, reproduction and the socialization of children, property and inheritance, economic cooperation, assignment of roles and status, and shared intimacy.

Marriage

Marriage is an arrangement that is strictly human. It is an institutional arrangement between persons to publicly recognize social and intimate bonds. Cultural norms specify who is eligible to be married, to whom and to how many people an individual can marry, what the marriage ceremony will consist of, and the norms surrounding how married persons should behave. In his cross-cultural study, anthropologist William Stephens provided a broad definition of marriage: It is (1) a socially legitimate sexual union, begun with (2) a public announcement, (3) undertaken with some idea of performance, and (4) assumed with a more or less explicit marriage contract that spells out reciprocal obligations between spouses, and between spouses and their children (Stephens 1963). The public announcement is often in the form of a wedding, which is a cultural ritual that represents a rite of passage. The wedding rituals are exceedingly diverse in terms of what the bride and groom wear, what they do, and who witnesses the event. Nonetheless, weddings are powerful rituals because they denote movement from one phase of life to another—the transition between being single and being married. Historian Lewis Henry Morgan describes the marriage arrangement and wedding of the Iroquois tribe in early North America (1962):

> Marriage was not founded upon the affections. . . . When the mother considered her son of a suitable age for a marriage, she looked about her for a maiden, whom she judged would accord with him in disposition and temperament. A negotiation between the mothers ensued, and a conclusion was reached. . . . Not the least singular of the transaction was the entire ignorance in which the parties remained of the pending negotiation. Objection on their part was never attempted; they received each other as the gift of their parents. When the fact of marriage had been communicated to the parties, a simple ceremonial completed the transaction. On the day following the announcement, the maiden was conducted by her mother, accompanied by a few friends, to the home of her intended husband. She carried in her hand a few cakes of unleavened corn bread, which she presented on entering the house, to her mother-in-law, as an earnest of her usefulness and of her skill in the domestic arts. After receiving it, the mother of the young warrior returned a present of venison, or other fruit of the chase, to the mother of the bride, as an earnest of his ability to provide for his household. This exchange of presents ratified and concluded the contract, which bound the new pair together in the marriage relations.

Regulation of Sexual Behavior

Every culture regulates sexual behavior. Cultural norms make it clear who can have a sexual relationship with whom and under what circumstances. One virtually universal regulation is the **incest taboo**, which forbids sexual activity (and marriage) among close family members. The definition of "close family members" differs, although it usually involves at least parents and their children, and among siblings. However, sometimes the taboo is extended to one side of the family but not to the other. For example, a person may be forbidden from having a sexual relationship with cousins on the mother's side, but a partner from the father's side of the family would be permitted.

Sexual relations among close relatives increase the chance of inherited genetic abnormalities. However, it is likely that the incest taboo originated not because of biology, but because of social consideration. It is a mechanism to minimize jealousies, competition, and conflict that could undermine smooth family functioning and lead to chaos (Ellis 1963). The incest taboo is also an important mechanism for forging broader alliances by requiring marriage outside of the inner family circle.

Reproduction and Socializing Children

For a society to continue, it must produce new members to replace those who die or move away. Families have the primary responsibility for producing the newest members and for teaching them the culture in which they live. Children learn the language, values, beliefs, interpersonal skills, and general knowledge necessary to adequately function in society primarily from their families (Parsons and Boles 1955). Societies generally encourage that reproduction be done inside established families rather than randomly among unrelated partners so that parents (or some prescribed family member) will be responsible for socializing children.

Property and Inheritance

As families moved from a nomadic lifestyle as hunters and gatherers to one based on agriculture, it became possible for the first time for people to accumulate surplus property beyond what was needed for sheer survival. Friedrich Engels (1884) tied the origin of the family to males' desire to identify heirs so that they could pass down their property to their sons. Monogamy worked in men's favor. Without it, paternity was uncertain. Therefore men sought to strictly control women sexually, economically, and socially through marriage.

Economic Cooperation

Adults and children have physical needs for food, shelter, and clothing. Families are the first line of defense for providing these to its members. Usually there is a gendered division of labor found among societies, with certain tasks primarily performed by men and others by women. However, exactly which tasks are considered masculine or feminine varies from one society to the next.

Families are both productive and consumptive units. In the past, families produced most of their goods and services such as making soap, spinning cloth, and growing food. In industrialized societies today, family members tend to work outside the home for wages and purchase many of the items that they previously produced. Therefore, these families are largely considered consumptive units.

Social Placement, Status, and Roles

All members of society relate in some way to the basic structure of that society, usually in a way that preserves order and minimizes confusion and conflict. We fit in by way of a complex web of **statuses** (positions in a group or society) and **roles** (behaviors that are associated with those positions). By way of our families, we are given an identity and position in society. For example, we are born into a certain social class, ethnic or racial group, religious affiliation, or region of the country. Statuses that we are born into are called **ascribed statuses**. Ones that we achieve on our own are called **achieved statuses**; these include our level of education or the type of job we hold. Our ascribed statuses give us an identity and a way of seeing the world. Likewise, they shape how others respond to us. A Hispanic teenage girl raised by parents who are migrant farm workers has a decidedly different social placement from that of the son of a prominent white family in New York City. Social statuses influence nearly all aspects of our lives. Much of what we think of as our own unique "personality" or our own unique choices really result from our initial social placement with our family.

Care, Warmth, Protection, and Intimacy

In addition to food, shelter, and clothing, research indicates that humans need warmth and affection to survive and thrive. Families are intended to provide the care, warmth, protection, and intimacy that individuals need. However, not all families give equal weight to these features. For example, in many cultures, love and intimacy are not the primary reasons for marriage and in fact may be completely absent. It is common in some cultures for persons to marry without having met prior to their wedding day. Their parents arranged their marriages based on factors other than love, such as economics or the wish to cultivate certain kinship ties. Nonetheless, even in these unions the protection and care of spouses, extended family members, and children are primary functions.

These are some of the functions of families. Nonetheless, how these functions are performed can vary greatly.

Sources of Comparative Family Data

How is information about family structure and patterns of interaction around the world obtained? There are multiple methods that include original data collection by cultural anthropologists, comparative family sociologists, and other family scientists. However, much of our understanding of families around the world comes from information contained in the Human Relations Area Files, Inc. (HRAF), an internationally recognized organization founded at Yale University in 1949. The data in the HRAF facilitate worldwide comparative studies of human behavior, society, and culture. From the North American Hmong's beliefs in the causes and cures of diseases or the Pashtun's religious views, this multicultural database provides in-depth information on all aspects of cultural and social life. The HRAF is unique because each culture or ethnic group contains a variety of source documents (books, articles, and dissertations) that have been indexed and organized according to HRAF's comprehensive culture and subject classification systems (HRAF 2004).

Also of interest to comparative family scholars is George Murdock's *World Ethnographic Atlas*, a database of 1,167 societies, and Standard Cross Cultural Sample (SCCS) (Murdock 1967). The SCCS contains the best-described society in each of 186 cultural provinces throughout the world chosen at a time when cultural independence was maximal; therefore, it is primarily a sample of preindustrial societies. The SCCS variables include those in the *Ethnographic Atlas*, but in a form useful for testing hypotheses because the cases in the sample are independent.

We now turn to some of the disparities found in marriage and family patterns. We begin by examining the norms surrounding how marriage partners are selected.

Variations in Marriage Patterns

How do you intend to choose your mate (or how did you choose your mate)? Would it surprise you to hear that no one really has completely "free rein" in picking a marriage partner? In some countries, the external control is obvious and deeply rooted in cultural traditions. Fathers choose their son or daughter's marriage partner with little or no input from those who will be directly affected. Marriage is viewed as an economic union between two families rather than a relationship between two individuals based on love. Therefore, it may seem perfectly understandable to all parties why a father would orchestrate the marriage of his child rather than leaving it to inexperienced young adults. The prospective bride and groom are often all too happy to give such a big responsibility over to their parents.

In other countries such as the United States, young people shudder at the thought of a parent choosing their future spouse. We prefer to base marriage on romantic love and mutual attraction; parental involvement appears minimal. Yet, external control over mate selection occurs, but it is more subtle. Imagine the possible reactions from family when a person marries someone outside his or her race or ethnicity, wants to marry someone of the same sex, or when the age gap between partners is particularly large with the woman being much older. It is likely that this person would experience sanctions. The sanctions can be minor or as severe as parental rejection.

External control over mate selection, whether in the United States or a country as rigid as Pakistan, operates through norms of endogamy and exogamy. **Endogamy** refers to norms that encourage marriage between people of the same social category. For example, norms may encourage people to marry within their own racial, ethnic, religious, age, or social class background. Although marrying outside of our own social category may or may not be prohibited by law, it is sanctioned to varying degrees.

In contrast, **exogamy** refers to norms that encourage marriage between people of different social categories. For example, a person is required to choose a spouse from outside his or her immediate family or must only select a partner from the other sex. The precise norms fluctuate cross-culturally. For example, in many countries it is illegal for a person to marry a first cousin, while in other countries a first cousin would be seen as an ideal mate.

If marriage is not strictly a private choice, what is it based on? Ethnographic studies by anthropologists and sociologists reveal that most marriage and family patterns reflect social, economic, and political life in a given culture. Some cultures allow men to have more than one wife, while others practice strict monogamy. In some cultures, the newly married couple virtually always resides with the husband's family. They would never consider the possibility of moving to their own household, yet this is the expected practice in the United States. There are cultures that expect brothers to live together and share one wife. These marriage and family practices are not simply random. From her anthropological work, Jean Stockard suggests that they reflect the following cultural practices and conditions (Stockard 2002):

- *The physical environment, material goods, level of technology, and subsistence, and how these have shaped the social organization.* The physical and social environments play key roles in family organization. For example, as agriculture developed, the family system became more extended, and family members were defined by their ability to contribute to the labor of agriculture. In particular, nonmechanized farming

economies create and sustain extended families that are likely to have patriarchal power, patrilocal residence, and patrilineal descent.
- *The significance of descent ideology and structure—the clan, lineage, and descent line*. For example, how does the matrilineal structure in historical Iroquois society (organized around female lines of descent) structure both the organization of households and marriage, shaping the meaning of marriage for bride, groom, and their kin?
- *Social processes, especially residence practices that reproduce and sometimes modify kinship structures across the generations*. For example, how does marriage as the Chinese practice it create families in each generation that continue to focus on sons and the chain of male descendants, and not on daughters?

Box 2.1 addresses some of these specific issues among the !Kung San of Africa.

Different marriage and family patterns have real consequences for the way we experience family life. They reflect the expectations about whom and how we marry, where we should live, who should have power, and how we inherit and trace our lineage. What are some of the specific customs and marriage and family practices throughout the world?

Monogamy

Most readers of this book conceptualize marriage as a relationship between two partners (if not for a lifetime, at least for a period of time). We call this marriage pattern **monogamy**, from Greek meaning "one union." Under monogamy, the law (or custom) does not allow individuals to have multiple spouses. Monogamy is practiced in many parts of the world, especially in developed nations. However, it is not the preferred type of union in much of Africa or the Middle East. In fact, in his comprehensive study of marriage and family patterns, George Murdock found that monogamy was the preferred and exclusive form of marriage for only 15 percent of the 238 societies in his 1949 sample, and 24 percent of 554 societies in the 1957 world ethnographic sample (Murdock 1949, 1957). His research was slanted toward preindustrialized nations, so we would not want to generalize these findings to the world at large, but we do see in Map 2.1 (on pages 46 and 47), that in many parts of the world monogamy is not the expected or preferred form of marriage.

If monogamy is not universal, then what are the alternatives?

Polygamy

Other societies practice **polygamy**, which allows for more than one spouse at a time. It is the preferred norm in many places in the world; however, because of relatively equal sex ratios between men and women, it is unlikely that all the adult members can actually practice polygamy. It is often reserved for those who are the wealthiest or most senior members of society. Having multiple spouses is generally a status symbol, a mark of prestige (Stephens 1963). There are two types of polygamy.

Polygyny

The most common type, **polygyny**, is the practice in which husbands can have more than one wife. Polygyny is allowed in many nonindustrial societies in the world today, although we do not know its exact prevalence. In his nonrepresentative samples, Murdock found that 81 percent of the 238 societies he studied in 1949, and 75 percent of his expanded set of 554 societies in 1957 practiced polygyny. Israeli anthropologist Joseph Ginat suggests that as many as a third of the world's population lives in a region that allows it, although the percentage of men who actually practice it is much smaller (Stack 1998). Polygyny is more likely to be found in developing countries, in-

BOX 2.1 Our Global Community

Marriage Among the !Kung San of Southern Africa

It is easy to fall prey to the belief that everyone in the world practices marriage patterns similar to ours: In early adulthood you meet someone, fall in love with them, and marry them. A closer look around the world reveals patterns that are in striking contrast to ours.

The !Kung San are people now inhabiting territories bordering on the Kalahari Desert, primarily in Botswana, Namibia, and Angola. They are a branch of the San peoples, an indigenous people of Africa, numbering approximately 50,000 that once occupied a vast territory in southern Africa. Given the name "Bushmen" by European colonists, they call themselves the *Ju/'hoansi*, which means "the real people." Until the 1970s, when political and economic change forced an end to their traditional way of life, they were one of the several remaining contemporary populations in the world practicing hunting and gathering, also known as *foraging*. This way of life, or *subsistence adaptation*, is believed to resemble the one characterizing all human populations prior to the development of agriculture about 10,000 years ago.

Marriage among the !Kung San resembles marriage as practiced by people for most of human history. The accounts of ethnographers report that girls were typically married very young, anywhere from age 8 to 12 on average. A new bride protested marriage in general and often her parents' choice of husband in particular. The marriage ceremony itself was, from the outsider's perspective, understated and hardly noticeable. The arrangement of marriage entailed the demonstration of hunting skills by the husband, who was expected to hunt after marriage not just for his wife, but more important, for her father.

New husbands were usually at least 18 to 25 years old, and sometimes as old as 30, creating a disparity in the ages of bride and groom of 10 years or

Even hunting and gathering societies have complex family structures that reinforce many of the same functions that modern families perform.

cluding parts of Africa and South America. Where practiced, it is often supported by religious custom. These societies are also associated with high degrees of male dominance and authority.

Researchers Charles Welch and Paul Glick examined 15 selected African countries and found that, depending on the country, between one in five and one in three married men had more than one wife (1981). They found that those who practiced polygyny tended to have two, or occasionally three, wives and only rarely more than that (Welch and Glick 1981). Polygyny is primarily practiced by the wealthy. Having numerous wives is a sign of family wealth, education, and other dimensions of high status. It is used as a way to increase fertility within a family, because multiple wives increase the number of children born within the family. While Westerners

more. Many if not most girls married before reaching their first menstrual period, but !Kung San feel strongly that marital sexual relations must not be consummated until the young wife is sexually mature. Indeed, they do not permit a husband, older and perhaps more anxious to begin sexual relations, to force himself on his young wife, believing it would make her crazy.

Ethnographic descriptions reveal an apparent connection between a *subsistence adaptation*, in this case hunting, and the practice of marriage. In marrying, a husband assumes an obligation called *brideservice*: He must hunt for his father-in-law for many years not only to establish but also to maintain his marriage to the man's daughter.

Marriage is a relationship involving more than just the couple. There are at least three partners to marriage, including the husband and his young wife, but most important, his father-in-law, for whom the husband must hunt. With a large stake in the outcome, the parents arrange and negotiate the marriage, a matter far too important to be left to the passions and whims of the young people.

With the establishment of a !Kung San marriage, a newly married couple assumes residence in a small house built adjacent to the house of the young bride's parents. Through the distributions of meat from a son-in-law during brideservice, the boundaries of nuclear families are regularly crossed, linking the families of the bride and groom and her parents in an important economic relationship. In addition, gifts of meat that are received by the father-in-law are shared again by him to include his daughter's family.

These patterns identify that !Kung San society has no isolated nuclear families living apart unto themselves. Each is linked in important ways to other families, as the long process of brideservice dramatically emphasizes. Meat is so greatly valued that its distribution is not based on generalized reciprocity, but is shared according to an established protocol. The husband is expected to take the best cut, giving the prime piece to his wife's parents. Following this first-order distribution, waves of further sharing follow, ending in many gifts of meat to people in the band.

The giving of meat in this society in some sense creates a kind of politics: Giving of meat creates personal prestige in receiving a good cut of meat, and redistributing shares to others also creates obligations in them. Such giving is an important part of being male.

Source: Adapted from Stockard 2002.

CRITICAL THINKING QUESTIONS

1. Do you think that the gathering done primarily by women also creates a kind of politics? Why or why not?
2. How do you think this aspect of their culture has changed since the 1970s when tremendous economic and political changes occurred?

may be tempted to assume that multiple wives would be jealous or competitive with one another, a study based in polygynous Nigeria indicated that the wives tend to get along with one another. When asked how they would feel if their husbands took another wife, about 60 percent said they would be pleased to share the housework, care of their husband, and childrearing, and to have someone to share things with (Ware 1979).

It is possible that more than 100,000 American families currently practice polygyny, although it is illegal (Tapestry against Polygamy 2006). It is primarily found in Utah and other western states. In a study of these polygynous families, Altman and Ginat found that, on average, they contained four wives and 27 children (Altman and Ginat 1996). Why would women in the United States submit to the practice of polygyny? What is in

MAP 2.1 Eye on the World: Comparative Marital Patterns

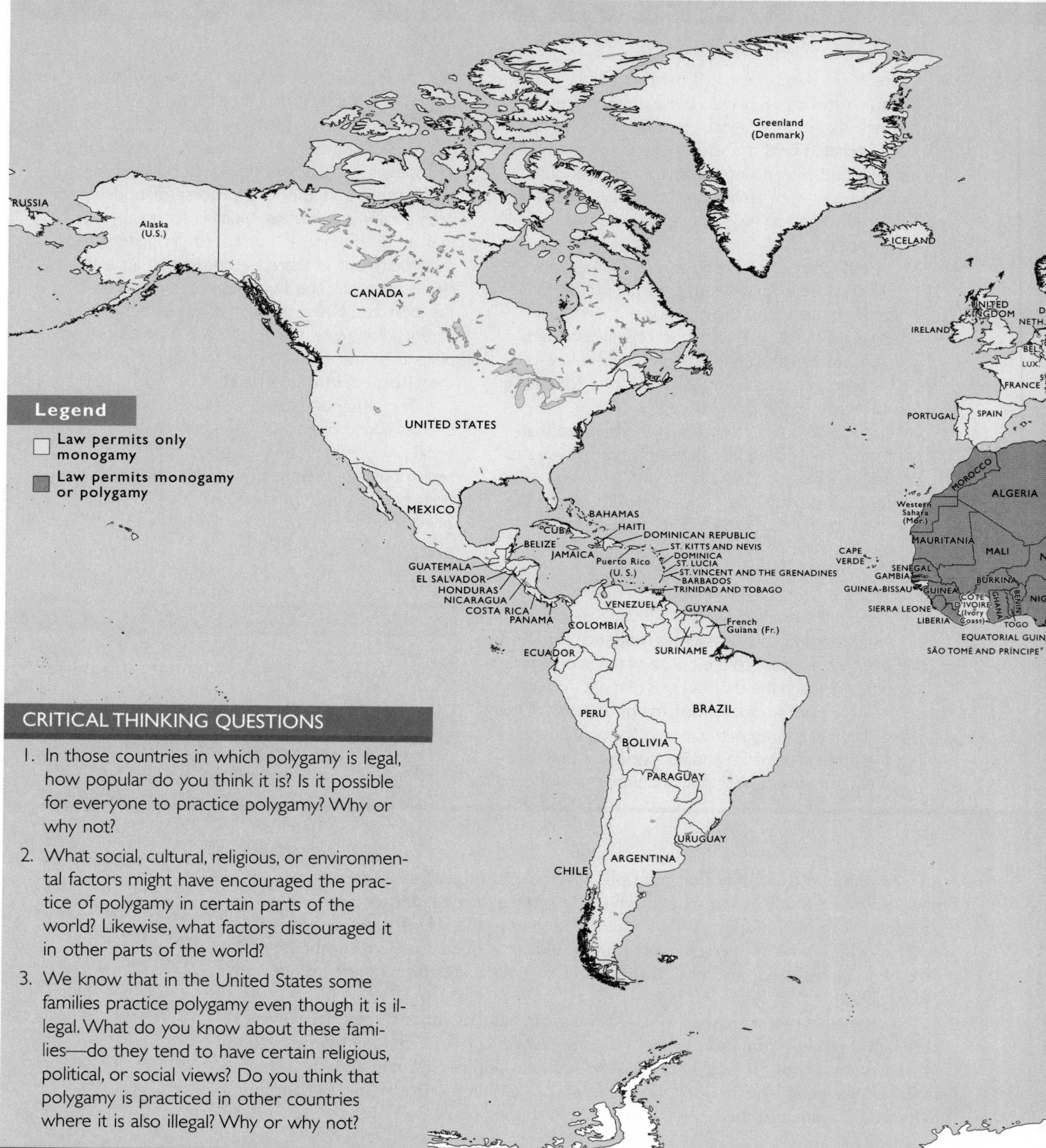

CRITICAL THINKING QUESTIONS

1. In those countries in which polygamy is legal, how popular do you think it is? Is it possible for everyone to practice polygamy? Why or why not?
2. What social, cultural, religious, or environmental factors might have encouraged the practice of polygamy in certain parts of the world? Likewise, what factors discouraged it in other parts of the world?
3. We know that in the United States some families practice polygamy even though it is illegal. What do you know about these families—do they tend to have certain religious, political, or social views? Do you think that polygamy is practiced in other countries where it is also illegal? Why or why not?

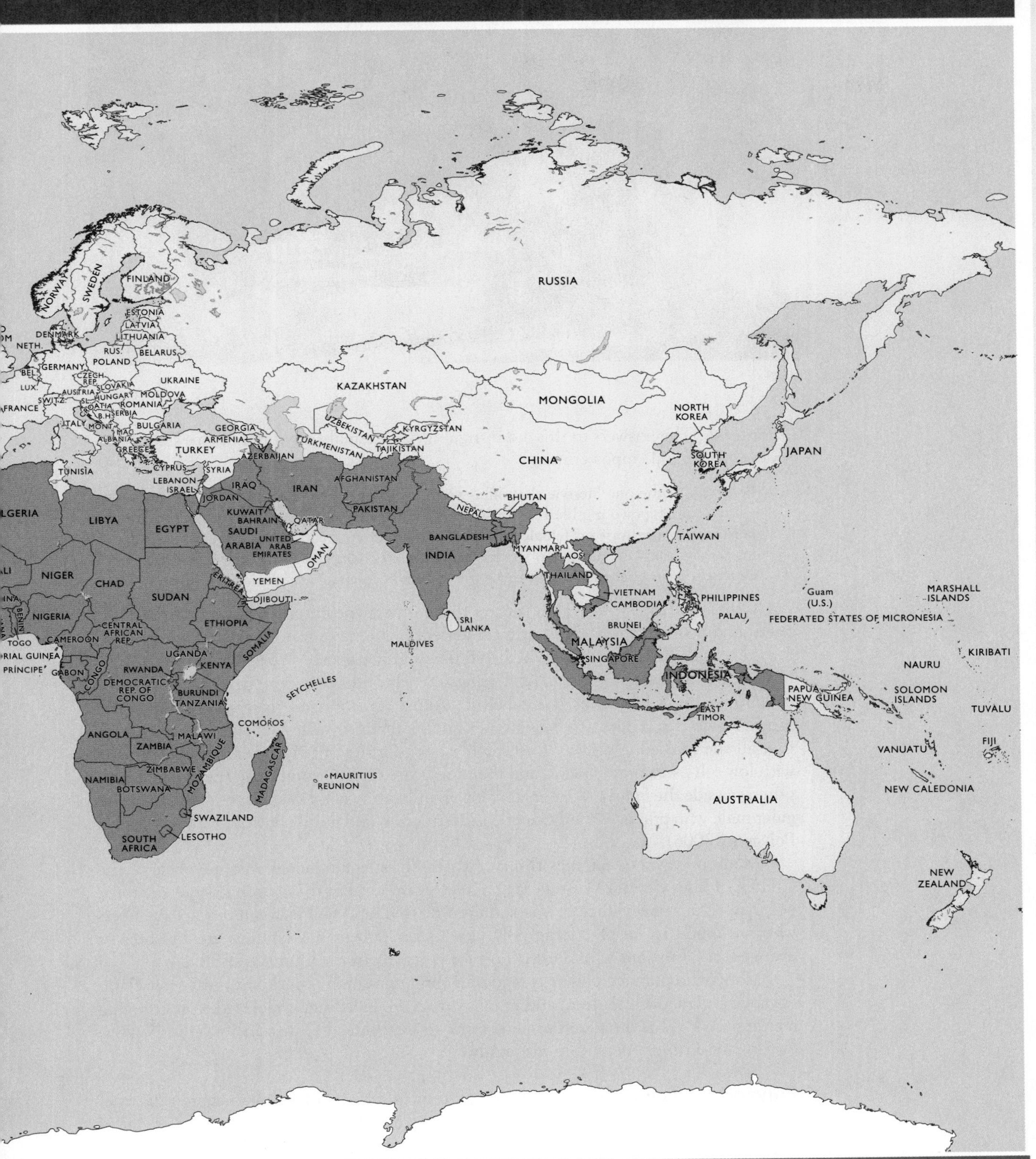
RUSSIA
FINLAND
SWEDEN
NORWAY
ESTONIA
LATVIA
LITHUANIA
DENMARK
NETH.
RUS.
BELARUS
POLAND
GERMANY
BEL.
LUX.
CZECH REP.
SLOVAKIA
UKRAINE
AUSTRIA
HUNGARY
MOLDOVA
SWITZ.
FRANCE
ROMANIA
SERBIA
B.H.
ITALY
MONT.
BULGARIA
ALBANIA
GREECE
GEORGIA
ARMENIA
AZERBAIJAN
TURKEY
CYPRUS
SYRIA
LEBANON
ISRAEL
TUNISIA
KAZAKHSTAN
MONGOLIA
UZBEKISTAN
KYRGYZSTAN
TURKMENISTAN
TAJIKISTAN
NORTH KOREA
SOUTH KOREA
JAPAN
CHINA
IRAQ
IRAN
AFGHANISTAN
JORDAN
KUWAIT
BAHRAIN
QATAR
SAUDI ARABIA
UNITED ARAB EMIRATES
PAKISTAN
NEPAL
BHUTAN
BANGLADESH
INDIA
MYANMAR
LAOS
TAIWAN
THAILAND
VIETNAM
CAMBODIA
PHILIPPINES
OMAN
YEMEN
ERITREA
DJIBOUTI
LGERIA
LIBYA
EGYPT
NIGER
CHAD
SUDAN
ETHIOPIA
NIGERIA
BENIN
TOGO
CAMEROON
CENTRAL AFRICAN REP.
RIAL GUINEA
PRÍNCIPE
GABON
CONGO
UGANDA
KENYA
SOMALIA
RWANDA
DEMOCRATIC REP. OF CONGO
BURUNDI
TANZANIA
SEYCHELLES
COMOROS
ANGOLA
ZAMBIA
MALAWI
ZIMBABWE
MOZAMBIQUE
MADAGASCAR
NAMIBIA
BOTSWANA
MAURITIUS
REUNION
SWAZILAND
LESOTHO
SOUTH AFRICA
SRI LANKA
MALDIVES
BRUNEI
MALAYSIA
SINGAPORE
INDONESIA
EAST TIMOR
PAPUA NEW GUINEA
PALAU
Guam (U.S.)
FEDERATED STATES OF MICRONESIA
MARSHALL ISLANDS
KIRIBATI
NAURU
SOLOMON ISLANDS
TUVALU
VANUATU
FIJI
NEW CALEDONIA
AUSTRALIA
NEW ZEALAND

Source: *Peters World Atlas* 2001.

Although illegal, more than 100,000 American families currently practice polygyny. One study found that, on average, polygynous families contained four wives and 27 children.

it for them? The answers to this are intriguing. One female supporter claims that it provides support and empowerment:

> Polygyny "is the one lifestyle that offers an independent woman a real chance to have it all . . . it is an empowering lifestyle for women. It provides me with the environment and opportunity to maximize my female potential without all the tradeoffs and compromises that attend monogamy. The women in my family are friends. You don't share two decades of experience, and a man, without those friendships becoming very special." (Joseph 1997)

Others feel differently. They suggest that women who enter polygynous unions have been manipulated, threatened, or intimidated. Some have had the marriages arranged for them with little input. One high-profile child abuse case in 1998 involved polygamist and businessman John Daniel Kingston who allegedly whipped his 16-year-old daughter with a belt after she rebelled against an arranged marriage to Kingston's brother. She was ordered to become her uncle's fifteenth wife, but she refused, stating that all she wanted to do was finish high school. Critics of polygyny argue that females with low self-esteem are sought, and then subjugated to male authority and isolated from others outside the family. Women develop an unhealthy emotional dependence on a singular male who practices methods of ego destruction and mind control (Tapestry against Polygamy 2006).

Many polygynous families think of themselves as fundamentalist members of the Church of Jesus Christ of Latter-Day Saints (Mormon), but the church has not tolerated polygynous marriages since it was outlawed in 1890 and will excommunicate members who are found to be practicing polygyny. Other polygynous families are Muslims or evangelical Christians who find support for polygyny in the Quran and Bible.

Many who practice polygyny lead quiet and unassuming lives, shy away from flamboyance and media attention, and in many ways are indistinguishable from other loving families. Box 2.2 is an advertisement from an evangelical Christian living in Nevada looking for a third wife to join his family.

Polyandry **Polyandry** is a marriage pattern in which several men share one wife. This type of marriage pattern is exceedingly rare. Murdock found that only 1 percent of his samples practiced polyandry.

BOX 2.2 Using the Sociological Imagination

A Personal Ad from Adolph, Mary, and Megan

In truth, one does not even have to look around the world to find different marriage patterns. The following is a personal ad found on the Internet, in which a family is looking for a third wife to join them. It is reprinted here, with permission from one of the wives, Mary. While polygamy is not legal in the United States, nonetheless, it is practiced in many families.

Hello, our family consists of my two wives and myself. We are all interested in our family becoming larger—if God blesses me with another wife. We are seeking a Christian lady with a kind spirit, who is levelheaded and has a positive attitude towards the Lord, their own life and towards others.

Let me tell you a little bit about us. . . .

I am 50 years old, blond hair, blue eyes, 6 feet tall, and weigh 200 pounds. I work as a business consultant. My wives are 33 and 22 years old and they both help me in our business. We don't drink, smoke, or take drugs. We don't object to social drinking now and then. However, we do object to smoking.

We are all real home bodies. We enjoy quiet times at home alone and with friends and family. We only have a few friends and we have had them for a long time. We don't need to have a lot of neighbors or non-family around us to be happy. We value our privacy and those close to us. We find our home very enjoyable.

Mary likes to cook which is great because I like gourmet meals, especially when it is all natural and prepared at home. She also has an interest in gardening and really wants to learn to sew. Megan likes to read and discuss ideas. We all have a good sense of humor, sometimes odd, but always fun! We want a large family and plan to have children in the near future.

We are evangelical Christians. We are not legalistic nor do we believe in taboos. We study the Bible from taped classes for about an hour every night. God has given all of us instructions for life in written form, the Bible. An owner's manual for the soul. It only makes sense to learn what our Lord has to tell us. Then, of course, comes the challenging part; practicing what you know you should do. We find that taking in God's word daily and applying what we learn gives us a good basis for a strong spiritual life.

I became interested in plural marriage many years ago. My wives have learned about it since we got together. The Bible is very clear that God ordained marriage, sanctioning polygamy just as He did monogamy. There are many instances in the Bible where men practicing plural marriage were greatly blessed. God blesses people living according to His principles. I consider companionship, talking to one another, sharing thoughts and interests the most important factors in a relationship. I am affectionate, both physically and verbally. I believe mutual respect and relating honestly to others is vital to a permanent relationship.

My priorities in a relationship in order of importance are: Being loved, Companionship, Honesty, Respect, and lastly Sex. The best foundation for a good relationship is friendship. Deep friendships grow in intensity and last forever. Too much emphasis is put on sex today. You can't build a lasting relationship based only on sex. A friendship built on soul rapport is far more important and will last a lifetime. Then, sharing sexual intimacy, as an expression of genuine love, is very meaningful. We believe that marriage is a lifetime commitment. I don't believe in premarital sex and my wives are not interested in a bi-sexual relationship. We believe marriage must have a foundation built on Christian principles.

Communication is of primary importance to us. We like to discuss ideas and share personal feelings. Talking and relating to one another is so very important. We want to know how you feel, what makes you happy and what makes you sad. We don't want you to ever feel alone. We want you to know that you are supported by a family who cares, who will listen to you, who can meet your needs and a husband who cherishes you and our relationship. A good relationship is a long conversation that always seems too short. A lasting relationship depends on what each person can bring to the relationship instead of what they can take out of it. A good relationship is more than finding the right person, it is being the right person.

(continued)

I am affectionate. I like to give hugs in the kitchen or cuddle during a movie. I like a woman to wrap her arms around me for no reason even when I'm busy working. I'm not a macho moron hung up on impressing dimwitted friends by neglecting you. I don't have to treat you like a slave in order to feel like a man. I am very secure in my masculinity. A woman is beautiful and designed to be feminine, responsive and loving. I enjoy a woman's companionship and affection very much.

We are looking for a woman who is positive toward the Bible and has Christian values. A woman who is a lady, gentle, loyal, faithful, and feminine. A woman who wants to wear dresses instead of Levis. A woman who wants to make a career of her husband, children, family, and home. A woman who is proud to be a wife and mother.

If you have children, they will find a home filled with lots of love, acceptance and most of all guidance. Your age is not a major issue. Friendship, honesty and respect are of utmost importance. Where you live, your past, or your economic circumstances are not at issue either. What is important is that we all get along and have the same values and principles to guide our lives and futures.

If you're interested in becoming friends, let's talk. Tell us what is important to you in life. What you like to do. What you're looking for in a relationship. What you want for your life in the future.

Source: Polygamy.com 2003. Available online at **www.polygamy.com/Families/Adolph.htm**

Accessed May 5, 2003. Reprinted by permission.

CRITICAL THINKING QUESTIONS

1. How do Adolph, Mary, and Megan compare to the stereotype of a polygamous family? How are they similar or different?
2. Adolph suggests that the Bible supports polygamy. Do you agree or disagree? On what basis do you agree or disagree?
3. Why do you think the United States outlaws polygamy? Do you think the United States should outlaw it?

There are several unique features associated with it, and it is not the flip side of polygyny (Cassidy and Lee 1989; Stephens 1963). First, polyandry may occur in societies with difficult environmental conditions where poverty is widespread. It is practiced only in agricultural societies where land is severely limited and weather or other conditions are harsh. Second, the multiple husbands are usually brothers or otherwise related. They may, for example, belong to the same clan and be of the same generation. This minimizes jealousy or possessiveness. Third, the marriage often takes place because it is seen to provide economic advantages to the men involved. For example, one husband may recruit his brothers or clan to work on his land with him. Fourth, women's status is often low with a limited role in the productive economy. Girls may be seen as burdensome to families and an economic liability. Female infanticide may be practiced as a way of eliminating the need to care for girls, and therefore a shortage of women and girls for marriage may arise.

Anthropologist Jean Stockard describes the practice of polyandry among the members of the Tibetan Nyinba settlement in Nepal (2002). The villages are established at elevations between 9,000 and 11,000 feet, and the mountainous terrain makes it difficult to support their agrarian lifestyle. Nyinba brothers are raised to cooperate both in marriage and in their labor so that the household can be sustained. Only a household with many sons will thrive in this environment, with at least one needed for agricultural work, others needed for small-scale cattle herding, and others involved in the long-distance salt trade, traveling with pack animals between Tibet and India, trading salt for grain. Marriage cannot break up the family or else they would all be impoverished.

Nyinba males put cooperation above competition and jealousy. Therefore, all brothers share one wife. She marries into the family and moves into their household. As the sole woman, she does not have an elevated status; rather she does the work that wealthier families give to slaves. She plows and weeds the fields, and performs all of the work of grain processing. She is also responsible for all domestic tasks and child care.

All brothers in the household will share the Nyinba wife sexually, rotating her among the men, and she is to show no favoritism. When she becomes pregnant, it is expected that she will have kept track of paternity. The Nyinba do admit that sometimes a wife will apportion paternity to a specific spouse just to make sure that all husbands have at least one offspring. As expected, sons are more highly valued than daughters, who might be denied food if it is in short supply (Stockard 2002).

Polyandry is not sanctioned by any religious groups in the United States, and in fact some that support polygyny denounce the practice of polyandry outright.

Patterns of Power and Authority

Patriarchy

Women and men often receive drastically different treatment throughout the world. The term **patriarchy**, which means rule of the father, refers to a form of social organization in which the norm is that men have a natural right to be in positions of authority over women. It is far more than an individual man controlling an individual woman. Patriarchy is manifested and upheld in a wide variety of social institutions, including legal, educational, religious, family, and economic institutions. For example, the legal system may rule that women must cover their faces or hair in public; the educational system may enforce unequal or no formal education for girls; family norms may prescribe

Patriarchy, as illustrated here, refers to a form of social organization in which men are in positions of authority over women, including within legal, educational, religious, family, and economic institutions. It may be against the law for women to uncover their faces or hair in public.

that women only eat the leftover food after all males have finished their meal; and religious institutions may attribute male dominance to "God's will." Patriarchy is the most dominant form of authority pattern. It is widespread and is found to some degree in virtually every society. Patriarchy is particularly notable in politics, where men predominate. For example, in most of Africa, women hold less than 10 percent of parliamentary seats in government. Even in developed nations, women are grossly underrepresented. In the United States, women hold only about 20 percent of seats in the U.S. House of Representatives and Senate. Only in Sweden do women hold close to half of parliamentary seats (Population Reference Bureau 2005).

Likewise, the ability to read and write is crucial to accessing information and thereby increasing personal and political power. However, literacy rates among women aged 15 to 24 vary significantly, from a low of only about 40 percent in Pakistan and Bangladesh, to a high of virtually 100 percent in most developed nations (Population Reference Bureau 2005).

Matriarchy

A theoretical alternative to patriarchy is **matriarchy**, which is a form of social organization in which the norm or the expectation is that the power and authority in society would be vested in women. I refer to this as a *theoretical alternative* because no known cases of true matriarchies have ever been recorded. It is sometimes confused with matrilineal, a kinship pattern discussed below, but, in fact, matriarchy is a decidedly different concept.

Egalitarian

In between these two extremes are authority patterns that could be best described as **egalitarian**. In these societies the expectation would be that power and authority are equally vested in both men and women; for example, men and women are equally likely to be political leaders, serve in government, or influence public policy. Although the United States and many other countries are headed in this direction, it would be wrong to assume that all vestiges of patriarchy have been eliminated, as we will explore in Chapter 4.

Patterns of Kinship, Descent, and Inheritance

Where did you get your last name? How is property passed down? Who are considered to be your legal relatives? There are different ways in which a family's descent or heritage can be traced. These issues are important to sociologists and other family scientists because rules of kinship, descent, and inheritance can tell us how power is transmitted. It is common for families to pass on their wealth and assets to succeeding generations. At birth, a baby inherits two different bloodlines. We know that these are of equal importance genetically. Are these bloodlines also of equal *social* importance?

Bilateral

Developed nations most commonly use a **bilateral** pattern of descent, in which descent can be traced through both male and female sides of the family. Kin relationships are not restricted to only one parent's lineage, but recognize the lineage of both parents. For example, the United States recognizes that relatives can come from both a mother's side of the family *and* a father's side. Cousins, aunts, uncles, grandparents, and other kin can be traced to both bloodlines, which are of equal importance.

Patrilineal

A bilateral approach may seem common sense to most readers of this book; however, commonly found throughout the world is a **patrilineal** pattern, in which lineage is traced exclusively (or at least primarily) through the man's family line. A patrilineal society would recognize a father's relatives as kin, but minimal (or at least different) connections would be established with a mother's side of the family.

However, it is important to note that vestiges of patrilineal descent can also be seen in the United States, which practices a bilateral model. For example, most women routinely take their husband's last name when they marry (Scheuble and Johnson 1993). When Kate Harris marries Tom Smith, she usually goes by the new name of Kate Smith, or she may be called Mrs. Tom Smith, forfeiting both her first and last name. There are many personal reasons why it may be easier to have only one last name in a family. Nonetheless, sociologists and family scientists are intrigued with patterns, and one glaring pattern is that it is virtually always the wife who changes her last name; husbands rarely do. The changing of wives' names is a carryover from where, upon marriage, a woman became the legal property of her husband, and his lineage was the most important.

Matrilineal

A few societies can be characterized as having **matrilineal** descent patterns, characterized as having the lineage more closely aligned with women's families rather than men's families. This is not the exact opposite of a patrilineal pattern, however. In a matrilineal descent pattern it is not women who are in positions of power to pass on their lineage, but rather women pass it on through their family side via their brothers or other male members of the family. Even in a matrilineal society men retain the control over their lineage. A child raised in a matrilineal society could have little to do with his or her biological father, at least where lineage is concerned. The biological father may retain ties of affection, but it is the child's maternal uncles who are key male figures in the child's life, at least with respect to patterns of kinship, descent, and inheritance.

Patterns of Residence

Much can be learned about the role of marriage, family, and kinship by examining the norms surrounding the residential patterns of a newly married couple. Jean Stockard suggests that the postmarital residence pattern is a cultural practice that is critical to understanding broad marriage, family, and kinship dynamics (2002): "Postmarital residence generates inequalities, which characterize relationships of the genders in societies everywhere. These inequalities are culturally constructed differently from those found in the United States. . . . postmarital residence . . . is at the heart of the analysis of marriage and gender."

Neolocal

In industrial societies like the United States, the expectation is for the couple to live separately from either set of parents. This is referred to **neolocal**, where the newly married couple establishes its own residence and lives there independently. Sometimes a young couple will live with a parent temporarily for financial considerations (Goldscheider and Goldscheider 1994; Savage and Fronczek 1993). For example, a young couple may coreside with either the wife or husband's parents while they go to school or save to buy a house. Nonetheless, the general expectation in the United States and most developed nations is for couples to establish their own residences immediately after marriage.

Patrilocal

However, in other parts of the world **patrilocal** residence is normative. In these countries, it is expected that the newly married couple will live with the husband's family. As shown in the chapter-opening vignette, patrilocal patterns are common in many Asian countries and other places in the world where greater emphasis is placed on extended families and patriarchy. These cultural values may then be brought to the United States as they immigrate. Stockard (2002) describes the consequences of patrilocality for traditional Chinese families:

> The Chinese case provides perhaps one of the clearest examples of the power of residence in reinforcing the position of one spouse over the other, empowering the permanent resident (the husband in this case) and isolating the newcomer (the wife) in a house focused on an exclusive line of descent. Through the regular practice of patrilocal residence across the generations, a family sent daughters off in marriage to the villages and households of their new husbands—in effect dispersing the family females while retaining the males. Not only were daughters dispersed, they became members of households in which their interests were pitted against those of the other in-marrying wives, generation by generation.

Matrilocal

Far less common is a **matrilocal** pattern, in which the expectation is that the newly married couple will live with the family of the wife. Most are based on the subsistence adaptation of horticulture and use simple hoes or digging sticks, and engage in only minimal or distant warfare (Ember and Ember 2006). An example of a matrilocal culture was found among the North American Iroquois.

Modernization Theory: Social Change and Families

As societies are touched by industrialization, they undergo a process that sociologists call **modernization**. Modernization is a process of social and cultural transformation from traditional (or "third-world") societies to modern industrial societies, which touches many aspects of social life. It changes social relationships by increasing social differentiation and alters the division of labor in society. Kinship ties weaken, and nuclear families tend to predominate over extended family forms. Fertility rates decline and life expectancy increases. Some of the changes are positive, such as a higher standard of living for many people, while other changes are problematic, such as increased pollution.

Sociologist Peter Berger (1977) described a number of characteristics associated with the process of modernization, including:

1. *The decline of small cohesive communities in which social interaction occurred within primary groups of family and close friends*
2. *The decline of traditions and expansion of personal choice*

3. *Increasing diversity and change*
4. *A focus on the future*
5. *A decline in the importance of religious institutions*

The Loss of Community: Gemeinschaft and Gesellschaft

German sociologist Ferdinand Tonnies (1963) suggested that modernization represents a progressive loss of **gemeinschaft** or the intimacy found in primary relationships. Prior to industrialization, families lived for generations in or near the same small community or rural village. People identified with one another, and relationships were personal and enduring. A sense of belonging to the group usually outweighed personal differences. Families were the pillars of society, family members were highly dependent on each other, divorce was rare, and patriarchy was the norm.

Tonnies argued that industrialization changed the fabric of social life. Industrialization, and the urbanization that follows, result in a society of largely impersonal secondary relationships, called **gesellschaft**. There is little sense of belonging to a cohesive group, fewer personal ties, and people are more likely to put their own needs above those of others. The role of families is more diffuse, with other secondary relationships taking over many of the functions normally performed within the family.

World Revolution and Family Patterns

Sociologist William J. Goode (1963, 1993) used existing data from several regions of the world including sub-Saharan Africa, India, China, Japan, and several countries in the Middle East to examine how industrialization and modernization affected family patterns, including such issues as mate selection, kinship, marital relationships, and divorce. He argued that industrialization and modernization changed families in radical ways for a number of reasons, including the geographic mobility that occurred in search of factory jobs in the cities; the resulting social mobility that occurred as people were trained into a new class of jobs as managers and supervisors; the changing emphasis from ascribed to achieved status; and the increasing specialized division of labor. Work was something increasingly performed away from the family, and men and women's roles within the family were beginning to be differentiated as never before. What changes in the family resulted from industrialization and modernization, according to Goode? These changes include a shift to the conjugal nuclear family, which entailed the following:

1. *Mate selection became freer*. Goode found that as societies developed, young adults played a greater role in selecting a spouse. Parental control waned. Young adults had greater opportunities to interact with each other without the supervision of parents and other chaperones, and romantic love became an important ingredient for marriage.
2. *A shift away from extended families*. Goode's work revealed that changing family forms accompany industrialization. There was a shift away from extended families, which may have been less practical with geographic mobility, to a nuclear family form. Families became more isolated from their extended kin network and from the community more generally. They increasingly became a private retreat—a "haven in a heartless world." Families also became smaller because children were increasingly viewed as an economic liability, rather than the asset they were on the farm.
3. *Kinship evolved toward bilateral*. Goode reported that when countries undergo industrialization, they tend to move toward a bilateral rule of descent, rather than

remaining patrilineal or matrilineal. With industrialization, fewer people owned extensive property to be handed down to a narrowly defined set of heirs.

4. *Families became more egalitarian*. Goode found that patriarchal norms declined as countries developed. Along with the rise of romantic love as a basis for marriage, spouses emphasized the companionate nature of their relationship. However, a decline in patriarchal norms does not ensure equal treatment. Even with the advent of industrialization, women were (and in some places still are) still denied basic rights such as voting privileges, the right to initiate divorce, or the ability to own property.

World Systems Theory: Social Change and Families

Drawing upon a conflict paradigm, some family scholars see that changes in families can be traced to changing global economic markets and political structures, a perspective called **world systems theory**. Nations, cultures, and family norms do not exist in isolation; rather, every country is inextricably tied to others in the world. Immanual Wallerstein's works *The Modern World System* (1974) and *The Modern World System II* (1980) highlight the linkages, interdependence, and exploitation among economies between nations and how these influence virtually all dimensions of social life, including family structure. The interdependence of nations has resulted in a modern world in which some countries have remained impoverished and debt ridden because they are exploited by other countries that have amassed great wealth at their expense. According to this perspective, the "core" countries, primarily the United States, western Europe, and Japan, use their historical advantages to manipulate countries for their own benefit by extracting resources, profits, and cheap labor; by promoting debt; and by destroying the environment in the poorer countries. Consequently, poorer periphery and semiperiphery nations cannot industrialize or modernize and remain impoverished, in debt, with an environment that is quickly being destroyed, and largely under the control of core nations often through transnational corporations.

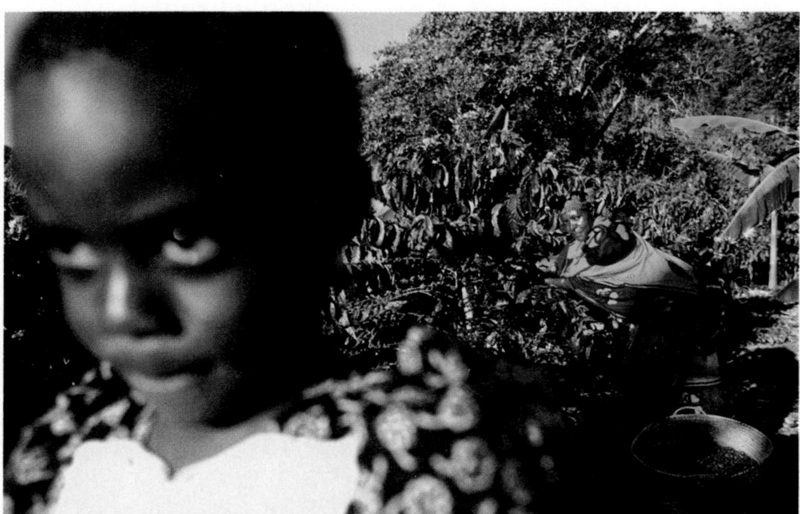

World Systems Theory highlights the economic linkages and exploitation occurring between nations, and how these influence virtually all dimensions of life, such as the child labor shown here.

This economic and political dependence affects family structure and family interaction in poor nations in many ways. For example, rural families in impoverished periphery nations may move from producing food crops that support traditional family structures to cash crops that are regulated by world prices. As a result, men, especially young men, must migrate to cities to find ways to support their families while women stay home and work in agriculture and raise children. This sex-based pattern of segregated migration often keeps families poor and isolated.

Families Around the World

Developing Nations, Example: India

India is one of the world's poorest nations. It is also one of the most populous at approximately 1 billion persons. Although India constitutes just 2.4 percent of the world's land area, it supports about 16 percent of the world's population. It is the second most populous country in the world after China, but because of China's powerful one-child policy that strictly limits the number of births to one child per family (or two births in some circumstances), India could soon overtake China for the number one position.

How poor is India? The United Nations compares the purchasing power parity (PPP) of people in different countries in terms of what the money can buy in a local economy. Wealthy countries such as the United States, Canada, Japan, and Switzerland are very high—the PPP is at least $29,000 per person. In a poor country like India, the PPP hovers around $3,139. This compares to at least $8,000 for most of eastern Europe or $7,642 for China. Poorer countries can be found. The PPP for Ethiopia, for example, is around $53 (U.N. Development Programme 2006). Nonetheless, India is recognized throughout the world as a poor nation, struggling to keep its people fed, clothed, and housed.

India recognized early on that its high fertility rate would impoverish its people further. Therefore, since independence in the 1950s, India has launched an aggressive campaign to reduce its number of births. This has been a difficult process, given the low education and literacy rates of many Indians, yet the family planning programs have had some success. As shown in Figure 2.1, the crude birth rate has fallen from about 45 per 1,000 population in 1951 to about 25 children in 2005 and is expected to fall to 17 per 1,000 by 2025 (UN Development Programme 2005). However, given the high number of young childbearing-age people, the population continues to grow rapidly.

A disturbing result of the quest to reduce the number of children is the growing sex ratio imbalance. In the natural order, slightly fewer females are born than males. Males are more likely to die in infancy (as is the case throughout the life course); therefore, the initial oversupply of males at birth contributes to a more balanced sex ratio in later life. However, in many parts of India, the number of girls born is significantly below what would occur naturally. Overall in India there were 105.2 males for every 100 females in 2005 (UN Development Programme 2005). Data from some Indian states show as many as 123 boys for every 100 girls (Premi 2002). What accounts for the gross imbalance?

A clue can be found in India's practice of patriarchy (Agnes 2001). The custom and laws distinctly favor men over women. Likewise, when parents have children, they have a strong preference for boys over girls because boys are viewed as economic assets, while girls are seen as liabilities. Often, girls are provided with less food, schooling, and medical care when these are in short supply; boys are breastfed longer than girls, and they are more likely to be fully vaccinated (International Institute for Population Sciences and ORC Macro 2000). Families without at least one son are significantly more likely to divorce (Bose and South 2003).

Spending precious family resources on girls is viewed as wasteful because it is assumed that girls will someday marry and leave the family. Marriages are frequently arranged while the daughter is still a young child. Traditionally, women remain responsible for virtually all domestic labor and child care when married. Few women have lucrative careers or jobs in India. Among the women who are employed, few are in professional or managerial positions, most make low wages, and considerable sex discrimination persists (Westley 2002).

FIGURE 2.1 **Crude Birth Rate (per 1,000 population), 1950–2025 (Estimate) for India, Japan, Sweden, and the United States**

Source: United Nations, 2006. Population, Resources, Environment and Development: The 2005 Revision. Online: http://unstats.un.org/pop/dvariables/Dretrieval.aspx Accessed December 7, 2006.

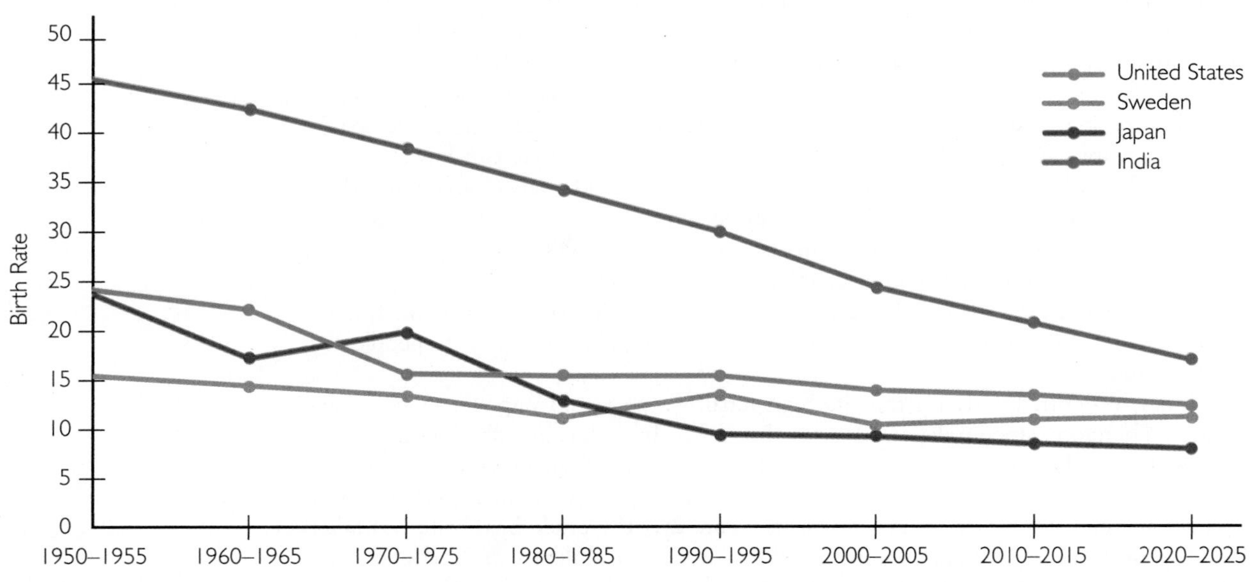

Where did all the girls go? With the push toward smaller families and with patriarchy operating so prominently, it is surmised that some parents who detect through ultrasound or amniocentesis that they are having a girl abort the fetus. Others practice female infanticide after birth (Westley 2002). Still others abandon their daughters and hope that they will be adopted; however, very few are, and most live out their lives in underfunded and understaffed orphanages.

Traditions and customs touch Indian families in other ways as well. The Hindu religion is a prominent feature of Indian life. Hindus recognize and abide by the caste system, even though many of the distinctions made on the basis of caste are now illegal in India. For example, Hindus in India believe that persons in a higher caste will be "polluted" if they are in contact with someone of a lower standing. Therefore segregation is commonplace and has been referred to as *hidden apartheid* (Human Rights Watch 1999). The *untouchables* or Dalits, who number near 40 million, may not enter the higher-caste sections of villages, may not use the same wells, wear shoes in the presence of others, or visit the same temples. Dalit children are frequently made to sit in the back of classrooms, and adults and children work in near slave-like conditions. Men in higher castes often abuse Dalit women, and the police ignore women's complaints (Human Rights Watch 1999):

> In India's southern states, thousands of Dalit girls are forced to become prostitutes for upper-caste patrons and village priests before reaching the age of puberty. Landlords and police use

sexual abuse and other forms of violence against women to inflict political "lessons" and crush dissent within the community. Dalit women have been arrested and tortured in custody to punish their male relatives who are hiding from authorities.

Cultures in Transition, Example: Japan

Unlike India, Japan is a highly developed nation, yet Japan has a tradition steeped in segregated and traditional gendered expectations. Women and men's roles in work, family, and other social institutions are still highly differentiated, although some convergence has been noted in recent decades. For example, fewer mothers are employed full-time outside the home in Japan than in any other developed nation, although the numbers are increasing somewhat. Female labor force participation rivals that in the United States, yet Japanese women's work is typically not on any career path, they hold few managerial or professional positions, and they do the vast majority of the housework and child care (Brinton 1993; Ishii-Kuntz 2004; Kamo 1994).

When mothers are employed, it is still expected that taking care of children is women's work, while earning the family income is men's work. Marital and family roles are more divided in Japan than in many other developed nations, including in the United States (Ishii-Kuntz 1998, 2004). Husbands often have a workday that extends well into the evening and requires them to socialize with coworkers or clients. With husbands' extended absences from home, most childrearing and other domestic tasks fall onto the shoulders of women—but it is not simply that these jobs require long absences from home. Instead, an interplay of sex and the economy is operating; when women hold these jobs, they are still expected to take care of domestic responsibilities.

A number of research studies reveal that fathers in Japan are less involved in their children's lives on a daily basis than are American fathers. They exercise what Ishii-Kuntz (1994) has described as a *weak secondary role* in the home. Using national data, Ishii-Kuntz found that Japanese fathers spend significantly less time with their sons than do their American counterparts, as shown in Figure 2.2. Boys in the United States spend about 1 hour on a weekday and about 2 hours on a weekend with their fathers. In Japan, boys spend only about half that amount of time with their fathers. Both Japanese and American fathers interact with daughters less frequently than with sons, and no significant differences are noted between the two in the amount of time they spend with their daughters.

However, marriage and family life are exceedingly important in the lives of the Japanese. One example of this commitment to the family is the comparatively very low rate of divorce. Divorce is only one-fifth as common in Japan as in the United States. This lower rate is likely due to several features of Japanese culture and family life: (1) Japanese culture stresses conformity and subordination of individual needs to those of the larger group; (2) the loss of income could be devastating to wives who, if employed, likely earn considerably less than husbands; and (3) closeness and coresidence with other family may buffer the effects of problematic marriages, because Japanese marriages are rarely couple-centered (Stack 1992).

Another indicator of their family commitment is the trend for elderly Japanese to coreside with their adult children and grandchildren even if they are in good health and financially stable. Although the proportion of Japanese who prefer to live autonomously is increasing, studies reveal that approximately one-half of married women report that it is either a "good custom" or a "natural duty" to care for elderly parents (Ogawa and Retherford 1993).

Despite the apparent centrality of marriage and family in the heart of Japanese culture, trends show that some tremendous changes are taking place. One important

FIGURE 2.2 **Amount of Time Spent in Father–Child Interaction in the United States and Japan**

Source: Ishii-Kuntz 1994.

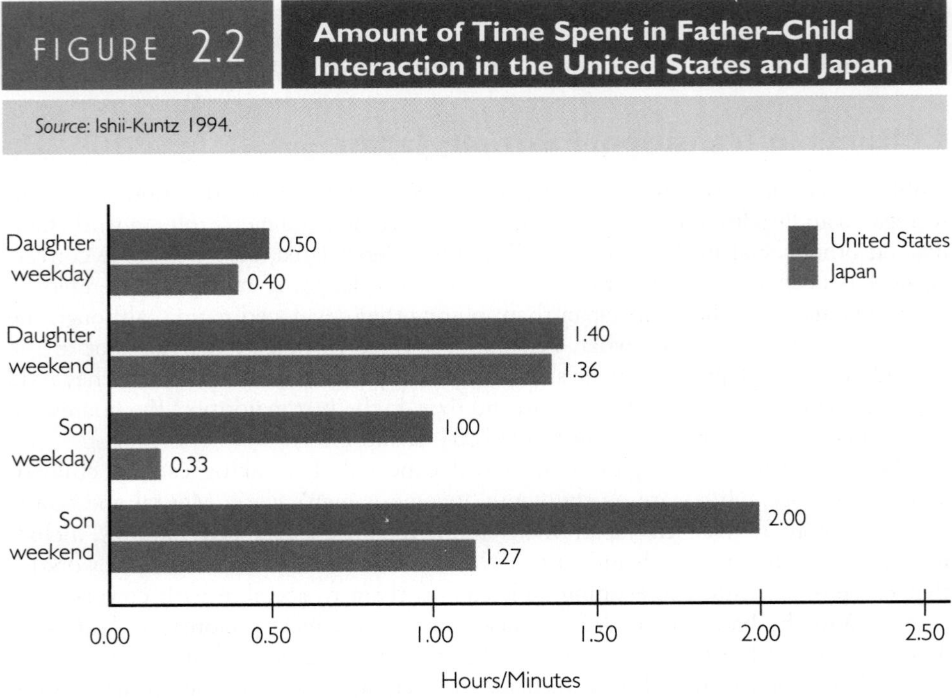

change is that fewer women are marrying, and those that do are marrying much later than ever before (Kashiwase 2002; Raymo 1998). According to national data, the median age at first marriage for women increased from 25 years in 1975 to 27 years in 2000, and its increase is accelerating quickly (Kashiwase 2002). In 1970, fewer than 9 percent of women between the ages of 30 and 34 in Japan were unmarried, but this had increased to 20 percent by 1995 (Raymo 1998). Moreover, fewer women are bearing children, and those who do often have them relatively late in life (Jolivet 1997; Kashiwase 2002). The average age for becoming a mother was 26 in 1975 and 28 in 2000.

Most of this change is a result of delaying rather than forgoing marriage. However, it is also likely that some women who initially only anticipated delaying a marriage will ultimately remain unmarried for life (out of choice or by default). Several reasons for delaying marriage have been noted, including (1) a growing gap in attitudes regarding women's roles in society; (2) increases in women's education and labor force participation; (3) an imbalance in the number of men to women; and (4) the increases in the attractiveness of single life, while at the same time a decrease in the attractiveness of traditional marriages (Atoh 1995; Raymo 1998; Tsuya and Mason 1995). In the 1997 book *Japan: The Childless Society*, Muriel Jolivet outlines the pressures on women that make bearing and raising children unattractive. She suggests that the Japanese government, concerned about a birthrate that is far below replacement level at 1.4, criticizes women who choose not to have children as being selfish. Only recently has the government approved birth control for widespread use, long after the rest of the world considered it safe and approved it—yet Viagra, the pill for male impotence won approval in Japan quickly, further pointing to a double standard (Kageyama 1999).

Some women in Japan are now resisting these social pressures and are limiting their family size. Japan's crude birthrate in 2005 was 9.2 per 1,000 population, compared to over 17 just 30 years earlier, as seen in Figure 2.1. Japan's birthrate is expected to decline even further, to 7.9 by 2025, below replacement level. Meanwhile, the birth rate in the United States has remained virtually unchanged, hovering around 14 per 1,000 population, although it too is expected to decline by 2025 (UN Development Programme 2005). Moreover, Jolivet reports that over 70 percent of women aged 40 to 49 have had abortions (1997). Abortions are estimated at roughly 340,000 per year, fewer than in the United States, but higher than most of Europe (Kageyama 1999).

As this section has shown, Japan is a country that is experiencing tremendous economic and social transitions. Next, to contrast with India and Japan, we will examine the family structure in a country that espouses equality between men and women.

Toward Equality, Example: Sweden

Sweden is an interesting country in which to examine marriage and family patterns. It is one of the world's wealthiest nations and its people enjoy a high standard of living. The birthrate is low, close to that of Japan, but it is unusual in that it is expected to rise by 2025, as shown in Figure 2.1. Swedes are also healthy; life expectancy is at or near the world's highest. The **infant mortality rate**, defined as the number of deaths within the first year of life per 1,000 births in the population, is 2.4 per 1,000, less than half that of the United States, as shown in Figure 2.3 (Population Reference Bureau 2006).

Swedes have sometimes been criticized as antifamily because, compared to their counterparts in the United States, they are less likely to marry and more likely to cohabit and have children outside the confines of legal marriage. Sociologists examining demographic changes in Sweden's families noted that the marriage rate began to decrease significantly in the 1960s and 1970s. Many Swedes were (and are) choosing to marry later or to not marry at all. Sweden has one of the highest average ages at first marriage and one of the lowest marriage rates found anywhere in the world (Popenoe 1986, 1991, 2005). If current trends continue, only about 60 percent of Swedish women today will ever marry, compared to over 85 percent of women in the United States. Instead of marrying, many Swedes prefer cohabitation. Using a snapshot of today, about 28 percent of all couples in Sweden are cohabiting, compared to about 8 percent of Americans (Popenoe 2005). Moreover, many more couples in both countries will cohabit over the course of their lifetime.

FIGURE 2.3 **2006 Infant Mortality Rate per 1,000 Births for India, Japan, Sweden, and the United States**

Source: Population Research Bureau 2006.

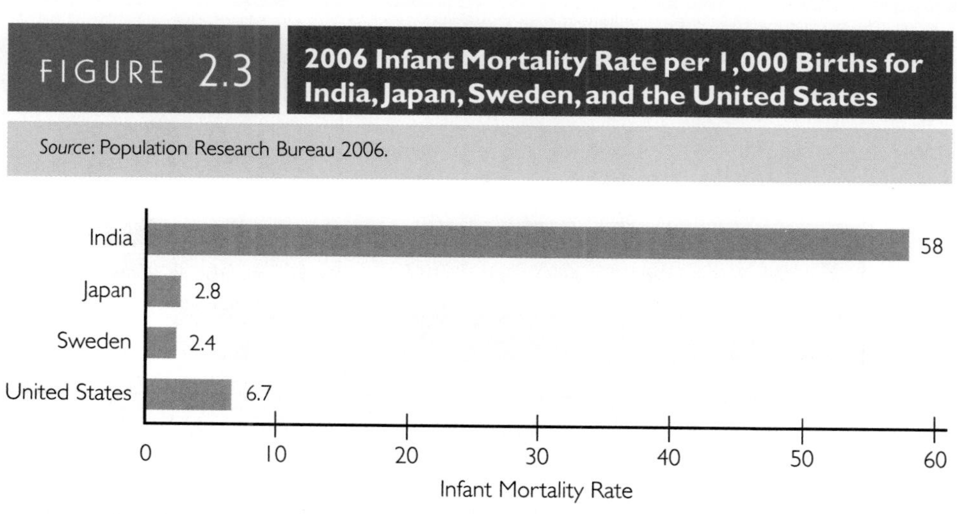

However, these data should not necessarily be interpreted as an antifamily sentiment. Even David Popenoe (2005), a critic of Sweden's seemingly antimarriage attitude writes: "What most Americans don't realize is that, in a strict comparison, Scandinavia is probably preferable to the United States today as a place to raise young children." The Scandinavian concern for children sometimes even smacks of traditional family values. For example, generous maternity and paternity leave policies allow parents of young children to stay at home rather than quickly returning to work after their children's birth. Moreover, all Swedish married couples with children aged 16 and younger, if seeking a divorce, must have a 6-month waiting period before a divorce becomes final. Child poverty is virtually nonexistent.

Family life inside and outside of marriage is valued in Sweden, arguably to an even greater extent than in the United States. In fact, researchers Olah, Bernhardt, and Goldscheider, when comparing national data from the United States and Sweden, found that Swedish men are considerably *more* likely to live in a household with children, including their own biological children, than are American men, as shown in Figure 2.4. Swedish men are less likely to be married; however, they are not necessarily rejecting family life and committed relationships. In Sweden, marriage and cohabitation are virtually equally acceptable lifestyles. Children born within cohabiting relationships are not stigmatized, nor are their unmarried parents.

The vast majority of mothers in Sweden are employed outside the home. A major difference between the United States and Sweden (and much of the rest of western Europe) is the degree of public support provided to children and their families (Olah et al. 2003; Popenoe 2005; Zimmerman 2001). For example, new parents in Sweden have generous maternity and paternity leaves in which they continue to receive pay, benefits, and a job guarantee (Social Security Online 2004). These have been available to fathers since 1974, although fathers are less apt to take advantage of these benefits than are mothers. Nonemployed parents are also eligible for a flat-rate benefit for the same period as the leave for employed parents.

Families also receive a **child allowance**, which is a cash grant from the government for each child. Families having three or more children receive an increase in benefits.

FIGURE 2.4 **Percentage of Families that Include Children (men and women, aged 30–34)**

Source: Adapted from Olah et al. 2003.

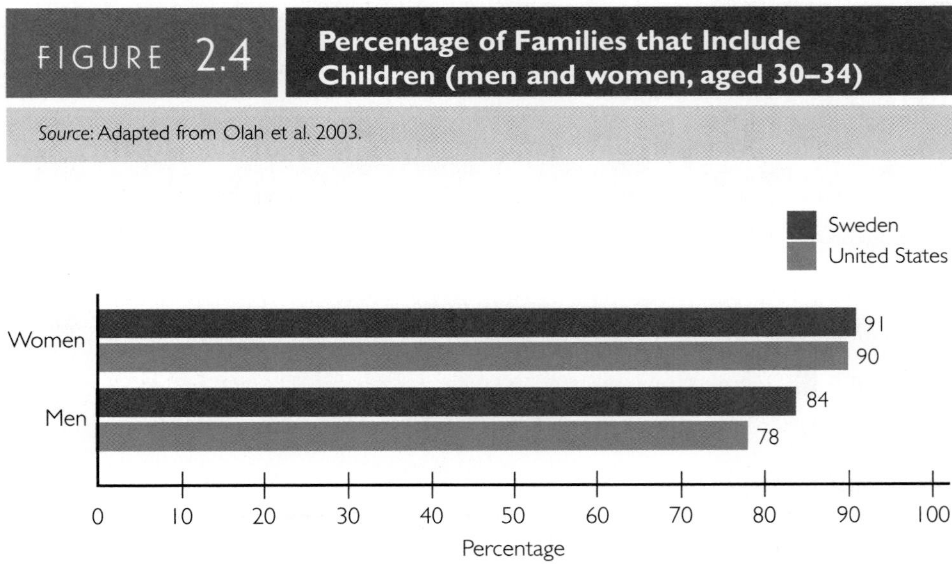

The government provides these grants to help defray the costs of raising children (Social Security Administration 2004; *World's Women 2000 Trends and Statistics* 2000). Generous housing allowances are also available to families with children so that citizens pay no more than 40 percent of their income in rent. "The more children you have the more subsidies you get, so you get housing of the need, not of the wallet," state Gilman and Gilman (1989). Moreover, child care is subsidized by the government if a parent is in school or employed at least 20 hours per week, and parents are charged relatively modest fees based on their income (Gustaffson and Stafford 1994). Married, cohabiting, and single parents are eligible for these benefits. These policies were enacted to (1) encourage more couples to have children, because the birthrate in Sweden was dropping dramatically; (2) encourage more women to work outside the home, because Sweden had the need for additional workers; and (3) keep pace with Sweden's changing conceptions of gender and movement toward greater egalitarianism.

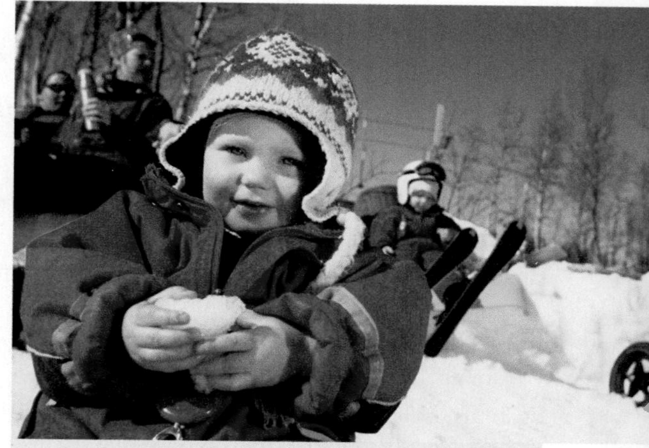

Although Swedes have been criticized as anti-family because they are increasingly likely to cohabit rather than marry, Swedes actually place a very high value on children. The government offers a wide variety of universal family policies and programs to strengthen families, such as child allowances or family leaves for parents.

Gendered expectations in Sweden have moved far beyond age-old traditions (Baxter and Kane 1995). Swedish men spend more time doing household tasks than do men in the United States, Denmark, Norway, Finland, or Hungary (Swanbrow 2002). About half of respondents in a Swedish national survey believed that the ideal family situation with children less than 7 years of age is for "both parents to work, either full-time or part-time and share the responsibility for home and children equally." Almost two-thirds agreed entirely that "in order to make a marriage or a non-marital cohabitation successful, it is important that both have jobs they like" (Olah et al. 2003). However, despite this sentiment and Sweden's public effort to equalize domestic relationships, researchers find that the primary responsibility for household chores and child care continues to fall to women (Haas 1992; Swanbrow 2002).

Conclusion

This chapter reveals both the universal functions and variation in structure within marriage, family, and kinship patterns throughout the world. Families are found in every society because they perform functions that other social institutions cannot perform—yet families are not monolithic. As a social institution they reflect the environment, historical period, and culture in which they are found. Moreover, families are not static, but are continually adapting to changing circumstances. Two perspectives are presented that contrast the nature of social change upon the family: modernization theory and world systems theory. Although the latter focuses more on the economic and political interdependence and exploitation found among nations, both agree that processes such as industrialization dramatically transform the culture and the environment, and therefore reshape the form, function, and roles within families.

Key Terms

Achieved statuses: Statuses achieved on our own. (p. 41)

Ascribed statuses: The statuses a person is born with, such as his or her sex, race and ethnic background, and social class. (p. 41)

Bilateral: Descent can be traced through both male and female sides of the family. (p. 52)

Child allowance: A cash grant from the government for each child. (p. 62)

Egalitarian: The expectation that power and authority are equally vested in men and women. (p. 52)

Endogamy: Norms that encourage marriage between people of the same social category. (p. 42)

Exogamy: Norms that encourage marriage between people of different social categories. (p. 42)

Gemeinschaft: A type of society that emphasizes the intimacy found in primary relationships. (p. 55)

Gesellschaft: A type of society that is based on largely impersonal secondary relationships. (p. 55)

Incest taboo: A rule forbidding sexual activity (and marriage) among close family members. (p. 61)

Infant mortality rate: The number of deaths within the first year of life per 1,000 births in the population. (p. 61)

Matriarchy: A form of social organization in which the norm is that the power and authority in society would be vested in women. (p. 52)

Matrilineal: A descent pattern characterized as having the lineage more closely aligned with women's families rather than men's families. (p. 53)

Matrilocal: The married couple is expected to live with the family of the wife. (p. 54)

Modernization: A process of social and cultural transformation from traditional societies to modern societies that influences all dimensions of social life. (p. 54)

Monogamy: The law or custom that does not allow individuals to have multiple spouses. (p. 43)

Neolocal: The married couple is expected to establish its own residence and live there independently. (p. 53)

Patriarchy: A form of social organization in which the norm is that men have a natural right to be in positions of authority over women. (p. 51)

Patrilineal: A descent pattern in which lineage is traced exclusively (or at least primarily) through the man's family line. (p. 53)

Patrilocal: A married couple will live with the husband's family. (p. 54)

Polyandry: The marriage pattern that involves one woman and several husbands. (p. 48)

Polygamy: A law or custom that allows for more than one spouse at a time (gender unspecified). (p. 43)

Polygyny: The marriage pattern in which husbands can have more than one wife. (p. 43)

Roles: Behaviors associated with social positions in society. (p. 40)

Statuses: Social positions in a group or society. (p. 40)

World systems theory: A perspective that focuses on the economic and political interdependence and exploitation among nations. (p. 56)

Resources on the Internet

Polygamy.com
www.polygamy.com
The purpose of this site is to provide a resource for people who wish to move beyond monogamy. It promotes plural marriage by encouraging "honorable individuals" wishing to pursue polygamy as the marriage structure for their family.

American Anthropology Association
www.aaanet.org
A professional organization designed to further the professional interests of anthropologists and to disseminate anthropological knowledge and its use to address human problems.

Genealogy.com
www.genealogy.com
This website will help you start your family tree, search for ancestors, and share your discoveries with family and friends.

National Geographic Society
www.nationalgeographic.com
This site from the National Geographic Society offers information on world cultures, the environment, kinship, maps, and magazines for children; it also provides links to related topics.

Human Relations Area Files
www.yale.edu/hraf/
An internationally recognized organization in the field of cultural anthropology at Yale University; the mission of Human Relations Area Files (HRAF) is to encourage and facilitate comparative studies.

Further Reading

Berger, P. 1977. *Facing Up to Modernity: Excursions in Society, Politics, and Religion*. New York: Basic Books.

Bumiller, E. 1990. *May You Be the Mother of a Hundred Sons: A Journey Among the Women of India*. New York: Fawcett Columbine.

Cruikshank, M. 2003. *Learning to Be Old: Gender, Culture, and Aging*. Lanham, MD: Rowman & Littlefield.

Fox, R. 1967. *Kinship and Marriage*. Baltimore, MD: Penguin Books.

Goode, W. J. 1993. *World Changes in Divorce Patterns*. New Haven, CT: Yale University Press.

"Human Relations Area Files." New Haven, CT: Yale University. Available online at www.yale.edu/hraf.

Lee, G. R. 1982. *Family Structure and Interaction: A Comparative Analysis*, 2nd ed. Minneapolis: University of Minnesota Press.

Murdock, G. 1949. *Social Structure*. New York: Macmillan.

Murdock, G. 1957. "World Ethnographic Sample." *American Anthropologist* 59:664–687.

Popenoe, D. 1998. *Disturbing the Nest: Family Change and Decline in Modern Society*. New York: Aldine de Gruyter.

Tonnies, F. 1963. [original 1887]. *Community and Society (Gemeinschaft and Gesellschaft)*. New York: Harper and Row.

Trask, B. S. and R. R. Hamon, 2007. *Cultural Diversity and Families: Expanding Perspectives*. Thousand Oaks, CA: Sage.

Wallerstein, J. 1983. "Children of Divorce: The Psychological Tasks of the Child." *American Journal of Orthopsychiatry* 53:230–243.

Wallerstein, J., and S. Blakeslee. 1989. *Second Chances: Men, Women, and Children After Divorce*. New York: Ticknor and Fields.

CHAPTER 3

Families Throughout History

Chapter Outline

Chapter Preview

One of the best ways to understand where families are going is to understand where they have been. We often glorify families of the past, but social historians have taught us that many issues that families face today are not unique and have their roots in the past. Thus, we can learn much from exploring family history. In this chapter you will learn:

- Why we bother to explore family history, and how social historians piece together the history of family life
- How families operated in hunting-gathering, horticultural, and agrarian societies
- How family life varied in the preindustrial United States for Native Americans, European colonists, African Americans in slavery, and Mexicans
- Changes brought by industrialization, urbanization, and immigration
- The "modern" family was shaped by national events, including the two world wars, the Great Depression, and the post-World War II baby boom of the 1950s
- The 1960s and 1970s brought tremendous social changes to families and intimate relationships
- Today's relationship between families and the economy has important social roots

The following narrative describes the life of a young slave girl in nineteenth century America who is forced to have a sexual relationship with a man she detests so that her owner can have more slave children. As heartbreaking as such an account is, what can we learn from history that has relevance today?

"Massa Hawkins am good to he niggers and not force 'em work too hard. Massa Hawkins 'lows he niggers to have reason'ble parties and go fishin', but we'uns am never tooken to church and has no books for larnin'. Dere am no education for de niggers.

Dere am one thing Massa Hawkins does to me when I can't chunt from my mind. I knows he don't do it for meanness, but I allus holds it 'gainst him. What he done am force me to live with dat nigger, Rufus, 'gainst my wants.

After I been at he place 'bout a year de massa come to me and say 'You gwine live with Rufus in dat cabin over yonder. Go fix it for livin'.' I's 'bout sixteen year old. I took charge of de cabin after work am done and fixes supper. Now, I don't like that Rufus, 'cause he a bully.

We'uns has supper, den I goes here and der talkin' till I's ready for sleep and den I gits in de bunk. After I's in, dat nigger come and crawl in de bunk with me 'fore I knows it. I says, 'what you means, you fool nigger?' He say for me to hush de mouth. 'Dis am my bunk, too,' he say.

De nex' day I goes to de missy and tells her what Rufus wants and missy dat am de massa's wishes. She say, "yous am de portly gal and Rufus am de portly man. De massa wants you-uns fer to bring forth portly chillen.

I's thinkin' 'bout what de missy say, but say to myself, 'I's not gwine live with dat Rufus.' Dat night when him come in de cabin, I grabs de poker and sits on de bench and says, 'Git 'way from me, nigger, 'fore I bust yous brains out and stomp on dem. He say nothin' and git out.

De nex' day de massa call me and tell me, 'Woman, I's pay big money for you and I's done date for de cause I wants yous to raise me chillens. I's put you to live with Rufus for dat purpose. Now, if you doesn't want whipping at de stake, yous do what I wants.

I thinks 'bout massa buyin me offen de block and savin' me from bein' sep'rated from my folks and 'bout bein' whipped at de stake. Dere it am. What am I's to do? So I 'cides to do as massa wish ans so I yields." (Adapted from Slave Narrative Collection, Federal Writers Project 1936) ■

An historical perspective shows how social structure affects the ways that families are organized and how it influences the rights, responsibilities, and roles exercised among specific family members. Many "current" family issues have their roots firmly planted in the past, and the more we know about history, the better we can understand families today.

Why Study Family History?

There is widespread concern today that the family is in great trouble (Popenoe and Dafoe Whitehead 2002; Struening 2002; Whitehead and Popenoe 2005). Family researchers David Popenoe and Barbara Dafoe Whitehead, from the National Marriage Project at Rutgers University, voice alarm about what they see as significant changes in the family, including America's relatively high divorce rate; the increasing percentage of single mothers; the large number of people who choose not to marry or choose not to have children; the growing number of children whose parents (i.e., mothers) work full time; and the increasing number of people who choose to cohabit instead of marrying. They see these trends as indications that marriage is being neglected, children are no longer the center of families, and that the importance of fathers is marginalized. Popenoe warns that the "massive erosion of fatherhood contributes mightily to many of the major social problems of our time" (1996). He also stated (1993):

> Like the majority of Americans, I see the family as an institution in decline and I believe that this should be a cause for alarm—especially as regards the consequences for children. In some sense, of course, the family has been declining since the beginning of recorded history—yet we've survived. But often overlooked in the current debate is the fact that recent family decline is unlike historical family change. It is something unique, and much more serious.

The popular media—television shows, newspapers, and magazines—bombard us with stories about the demise of the family. We hear that in the "good old days," there were fewer problems: Life was easier, family bonds were stronger, families had more authority to fulfill its functions, and people were happier. Abortion, divorce, teenage sex and parenthood, homosexuality, juvenile delinquency, and poverty are only some of the consequences attributed to the decline of the family and of "family values."

But is this concern about the well-being of families really new? Other family scholars inform us that these golden years of the past never really existed as we have fantasized them. They suggest that families have always faced issues such as desertion, poverty, children born out of wedlock, cohabitation, alcoholism, unemployment, violence, and child abuse, and there has always been concern about these problems (Abramovitz 1996; Coontz 1997, 2000; Demos 1970, 1986; Gordon 1994). In reviewing historical and cross-cultural variations in family life, we are reminded that the images we have of families in the "good old days" of the past—of a dad at work as the sole breadwinner and mom as a full-time housewife and mother nurturing her children—is largely a myth. This ideal type was popular for only a brief period, primarily in the 1950s. However, even during its height, significant numbers of lower-income and minority families did not maintain this ideal type. In other words, the 1950s' style of family, which is held up and revered as an ideal model of family life today, is not only an aberration historically, but never really existed for millions of Americans even during this brief period (Farrell 1999).

With such conflicting perspectives, how do we evaluate which of these views is correct? Or, in reality, is there truth in both views?

Having an historical perspective can reveal the answers to questions such as these. History can show the ways that families are changing and evolving. In fact, Popenoe, a sociologist, and Whitehead, a social historian, recently noted the possibility of a "family turnaround" that may have begun in the late 1990s (Whitehead and Popenoe 2003).

They point to statistics that hint of this possibility: the percentage of persons age 35–44 who are married has increased, the divorce rate is continuing to decline, there is an upturn in the percentage of married persons who state that their marriages are "very happy," teen out-of-wedlock births are declining, and the likelihood of black children living in a two-parent household has increased. If indeed the United States is witnessing a family turnaround, is it possible that this is simply one of many? Does history repeat itself? Perhaps families are constantly changing and turning around.

For persons interested in the workings of contemporary families, a look at history can provide remarkable insight (Coontz 2005). The historical literature reveals how and why family patterns have evolved as they have. It shows that families are constantly in a state of change, changes that both reflect and initiate alterations in the larger social structure. Families, both as a social institution and as a lived experience, are socially constructed to meet basic human needs. Families are not isolated entities, but rather are embedded in, and reflect, both cultural and historical roots. A look at history shows where we have been, how we came to be how we are, and where we might be headed in the future.

This chapter provides an historical overview of families. It will by necessity be a brief and highly selective synopsis because the literature is extensive. The goal is to show that current attitudes, behaviors, and public policies relating to such family concerns as courtship, mate selection, cohabitation, marriage, sexuality, children, the elderly, and extended families are intricately interwoven with the past.

Piecing Together the History of Family Life

What was family life like within the earliest human groups? What was the structure of kinship systems, and what were the expectations among family members in hunting and gathering societies, in agrarian societies, in colonial America, and during the Industrial Revolution? How did slavery, the colonization of the natives and Mexicans, industrialization, and immigration affect family relationships?

Anthropologists, historians, and family scholars attempt to weave together our "social history" to tell us about daily life, customs, and lifestyles of ordinary citizens. This is a radical departure from the work of most historians who focus on events such as wars, economic downturns, and other large-scale social events. Instead, these scholars are interested in uncovering aspects of everyday family life, including power, the division of labor, relationships between parents and children, and kinship rules (Degler 1980; Schvaneveldt et al. 1993). Because this field is still relatively new, our knowledge about the details of the earliest families, and details about nonwhite or poor families in the United States are more limited. However, recent attempts are being made to learn more about these groups, including African Americans, Latinos, Native Americans, Asian Americans, women, European immigrants, and the elderly.

Historians, anthropologists, and family scholars draw upon a number of written documents, including diaries, letters, or other lengthy correspondence between people to understand the common everyday experiences between families. They analyze historical records to get an aggregate picture about, for example, immigration trends, age at first marriage, or the average length of time between marriage and first birth. Census records; birth, marriage, and death registers; immigration records; slave auctions and other transactions; church records; newspapers and magazine articles; employment ledgers; and tax records can also provide insightful clues into the family lives of large numbers of ordinary people. Researchers also analyze the remains of artwork left behind.

Preindustrial and other societies without a written language are more difficult to study. How can we possibly understand family life among hunters and gatherers? No written records are available—but all is not lost. Although imprecise, researchers may turn to the few such hunting and gathering groups that continue to exist into modern times in remote regions of the world. Anthropologists provide extensive **ethnographies**, which are detailed accounts and interpretations of some aspect of culture.

Finally, scholars may rely upon **family reconstitution**, in which attempts are made to compile all available information about significant family events and everyday life within a particular family. Any members of each generation who are still alive will be interviewed, and they will be asked to reconstruct their family history. A significant responsibility falls on the eldest members to reconstruct the generation that preceded them. Other pertinent documents will be combed as well so that family life and household patterns can be uncovered.

Historical methods are not without their limitations or their criticisms. Historical researchers work as detectives and try to obtain the widest number of sources possible as they reconstruct and interpret the past. Sometimes numerous sources are available, but unfortunately, sometimes clues are few or sketchy. Details of family life outside of white middle classes remain somewhat limited.

Families and Societies

If we examine families over hundreds of thousands of years, from the beginning of recorded human history to the present, we can see that many characteristics of families today are remarkably similar to those found in hunting and gathering societies, as shown in Table 3.1 (Yorburg 2002). Because families throughout time have largely held the same set of functions as outlined in Chapter 2—marriage; the regulation of sexual behavior; reproduction and socializing children; property and inheritance; economic cooperation; social placement, status, and roles; and providing care, warmth, protection, and intimacy—it is perhaps not surprising that they organize themselves in a relatively similar fashion.

However, as societies become more complex, many of the family functions are shared or taken over by outsiders, such as teachers in schools, or doctors in hospitals. Max Weber (1947) suggested that as societies become more complex, the division of labor becomes more specialized for increased efficiency. This includes the job of being a parent; it is more efficient in modern industrialized or postindustrialized societies to pay professionals to do many of the tasks that parents used to do in the past.

Families in Preindustrial Societies

Family Life as a Hunter-Gatherer

Throughout most of human history, humans used hunting and gathering as their mode of production. They wandered in small groups of no more than 50 persons, migrating frequently in pursuit of small animals and gathering edible plants. They made simple tools to assist them in foraging, fishing, or hunting. Possessions were few; everything the group owned had to be carried with them in their frequent moves. These societies had **subsistence economies**; families used all of what they had, and there was virtually no

TABLE 3.1 **Families in Major Types of Societies**

	Hunting and Gathering	Horticultural	Agricultural	Industrial and Postindustrial
Family Functions	All-inclusive: physical care, intellectual development, emotional support	All-inclusive	Some sharing with experts, specialists	Sharing with experts, specialists in all spheres, including emotional support; emotional support becomes most important
Family Structures (Forms)	Nuclear	Extended	Extended and semi-extended	Nuclear and seminuclear
Premarital Sexual Activity	Unrestricted	Mixed, depending on social status; higher-status females restricted	Restricted; double standard for all females	Unrestricted, except for the deeply religious
Marital Choice	Personal preference, free choice, personal qualities	Arranged by family; social background most important	Arranged by family on basis of social status	Romantic love, personal preference, personal qualities, shared interests and values most important
Husband-Wife Relationship				
Power	Egalitarian	Varies, depending on social status	Authoritarian	Egalitarian: senior partner/junior partner roles
Gender Roles	Work and leisure activities shared	Separate work and leisure activities	Physically and emotionally separate	Shared leisure activities, two-earner households, shared child care, less sharing of household chores
Communication	High, talking, confiding, joking	Mixed, depending on social status	Low	High, closeness, sharing, companionship, friendship most highly valued
Parent-Child Relationships	Permissive	Mixed, depending on social status	Authoritarian	Permissive/authoritative (democratic)

Source: Yorburg 2002.

surplus of food or other resources. Consequently, there were few social divisions (Lenski 1984; Nolan and Lenski 1999).

Sex and age were the primary factors guiding the division of labor. There was little division of labor within male or female groups; all men performed similar tasks, as did all women. There was little if any hierarchy within sex categories, and therefore labor was shared equally. However, precisely *what* was defined as men's work or as women's work may have differed from one group to another. Generally speaking, the men's main task was to hunt for food; other tasks reserved for men varied from one group to another. Women's primary task was to care for any offspring. In their ethnographies, anthropologists report that mothers carried their young children with them virtually everywhere and nursed them for several years. Therefore, because women were less mobile than men, their tasks also included finding plants and hunting small animals close to home. Nonetheless, hunters and gatherers likely saw men and women as having equal importance.

Family Life in Horticultural and Agrarian Societies

About 7,000 to 10,000 years ago, humans discovered the advantages of staying in one place where they could plant and cultivate crops to supplement the food obtained by hunting and gathering (Lenski 1984; Nolan and Lenski 1999). They used crude instruments to dig holes in the ground so that seeds could be planted. About 3,000 years ago humans began to use animals to pull plows.

These seemingly simple advances brought widespread change. The size of groups increased dramatically, upwards of a thousand members gathered together. Perhaps even more important, there was at times a surplus of food. These two factors led to the importance of kinship group lineages. Families wanted to ensure that their surplus went only to their own members, rather than be dispersed to the group as a whole. Most lineages were patrilineal, although matrilineal ones existed. Kinship was an important tool for survival; it was the primary form of social organization and social cohesiveness in a world without governments, schools, health care systems, or social welfare programs.

As agrarian societies became more developed and the use of more sophisticated technology in agricultural production became more widespread, social inequality increased significantly. Some kinship groups were more successful; their surpluses, land ownership, and general wealth grew disproportionately. This wealth was then passed on to their children as they became adults. In time, there was very little mobility in social class position; barring the unforeseen natural disaster, the wealthy passed their resources to their children, and children of peasants remained poor. Groups were clearly identified by title, as shown in preindustrial England in Table 3.2, and there was little intermingling between the gentry and others.

Children were socialized by their own kin and learned their skills by observing the adults. They rarely interacted with other families until it was time to marry. Unmarried girls and women were closely supervised. Kin groups strictly controlled mate selection because marriage was seen as an economic transition between two kinship groups. It could not be taken lightly or left to the whim of the young themselves. Most marriages included significant transfer of economic assets from one family to another via a dowry, bride wealth, or some other form of transaction (Murdock 1967). Polygamy was common, particularly polygyny.

Early European Families Social stratification was a central feature of the early European society. Among the Romans, the **patricians**, as landowners, were at the top of the stratification system; slaves were at the bottom. Although life was segregated by sex, women identified far more with their social class than they did their sex. Patrician women were not equals with their male counterparts, but they were considerably more privileged and influential than were persons of the lower classes.

By the middle ages many small farms had been lost. Instead of dividing up parcels among all sons, fathers with any wealth or property often left it to only the eldest son, a practice known as **primogeniture**. Younger sons inherited little or nothing. Over time this resulted in fewer numbers of estates, but those that continued were of greater

TABLE 3.2 Chart of Rank and Status: Preindustrial England

Gentry	Grade	Title	Form of Address	Status Name	Occupational Name
	1. Duke, Archbishop		The Right Honourable, The Honourable		
	2. Marquess		The Lord The Lady		
Nobilitas Major (Greater Nobility) Lords and Ladies	3. Earl	Lord, Lady	My Lord My Lady	Nobleman	None
	4. Viscount		Your Grace (for Grade 1)		
	5. Baron, Bishop		Your Lordship, Your Ladyship, etc.		
Nobilitas Minor (Lesser Nobility) Gentlemen	6. Baronet	Sir			
	7. Knight	Dame[1,2]	The Worshipful, Your Worship, etc.		[Professions] Army Officer, Doctor of Medicine, Doctor of Law, Merchant, etc.
	8. Esquire	Mr.		Gentleman	
	9. Gentlemen	Mrs.[3]			
	Clergyman		Sir[2]		[Your Reverence]
	10. Yeoman	Goodman	Worthy[2]	Yeoman	
	11. Husbandman	Goodwife[3] (Goody)			Husbandman
	12. Craftsman Tradesman Artificer			None	Name of Craft (Carpenter, etc.)
	13. Labourer	None	Name and Surname only		Labourer
	14. Cottager Pauper				None

[1]Often called "Lady" by courtesy
[2]Occasional, obsolescent usage
[3]For unmarried as well as married women

Source: Laslett 1984.

magnitude. The owners thereby became extremely wealthy, and their wealth provided them with tremendous power. They became the political as well as the economic base of society. Although slavery no longer existed formally, serfs worked the land for the wealthy landowners, bought and sold alongside the property in a fashion not too distant from slavery.

Although the ideal type of family in horticultural and agrarian societies leaned toward the extended family, in reality there were few extended families during early Europe, the Middle Ages, or preindustrial Europe. This is due to several reasons. First, mortality rates were high; most people did not live long enough to spend significant time living with their adult children and grandchildren. Moreover, men and women tended to marry in their mid-twenties, or even later, and many women did not marry at all. Because only one male in a family inherited the wealth—and women wanted to marry well—there was a shortage of rich men for their female counterparts.

In one of the first major books in family history, *Centuries of Childhood* (1962), Philippe Aries wrote of family life in the Middle Ages. He pieced together a number of historical artifacts, including art from 1,000 years ago. Perhaps one of his most important findings is that childhood as we tend to think of it today—as a separate stage of life with unique needs—did not really exist during this period. Babies and toddlers were often neglected or ignored because parents did not want to waste time, money, or affection when so many of them died. Aries reports few if any social rituals for dead children or their "grieving" parents, such as headstones to identify their graves. Those children who did survive were treated as miniature adults without child-related toys or games. Usually by age 7, children performed needed work in the fields or in the home. Adults other than biological parents often raised children. Poor children in particular may have been apprenticed out, even as young as age 5. However, not all scholars agree with Aries' conclusions; some believe that childhood was indeed a special time of life, although not to the extent or with the length of time we see it today. What Aries may have been detecting is the common detachment between parents and children because of the high infant mortality rates of the time. Parents may have hesitated to become too emotionally involved with their young children because so many died (Pollock 1983, 1987).

Family Life in Preindustrial United States

Native Americans

Imperialistic European explorers and colonists came to the "new world" to find resources for themselves and their countries; however, they found that the land was already inhabited by people who were much different from themselves. Referred to as "Indians" because of Christopher Columbus' erroneous belief that he had found India, the native people had existed in these lands for perhaps 30,000 years. When European settlers arrived there were nearly 18 million natives with diverse customs and speaking about 300 different languages (John 1988). Lack of understanding, empathy, racism, and ethnocentrism led to numerous conflicts and attempts to virtually obliterate Native American groups. For example, exposure to small pox (deliberately or unwittingly), for which Native Americans had built no immunity, killed millions of adults and children. By the early twentieth century, only an estimated 240,000 Native Americans remained (Wells 1982).

Most Native Americans lived in tribal societies based on lineages, and these ranged from hunting-gathering groups to larger groups using sophisticated horticultural methods. Some groups practiced polygamy, although most were monogamous. About one-quarter of the tribes were based on matrilineal descent. Among the Apache or Hopi, for example, a person traced relatives through the mother's side of the family. It was the mother's relatives, including her brothers, that played key roles in socializing children.

There were nearly 18 million Native Americans living in the area now designated as the United States when Europeans arrived. Most lived in tribal societies based on lineages, and these ranged from simple hunting-gathering groups to larger groups using sophisticated horticultural methods.

Historians have reported that in many native tribes women held higher status than among their white counterparts. Although the image of a second-class "squaw" has been glorified in Hollywood, in many tribes women held considerable power and were involved in political affairs, healing, and even warfare (Braund 1990). Puberty was generally an important life stage, and elaborate rituals were developed to celebrate it for both boys and girls (Szasz 1985). Among girls, some rituals emphasized a taboo; for example, isolating newly menstruating girls and forbidding them to eat certain foods, touch their own bodies, or interact with others. Other girls' rituals surrounding menstruation were more celebratory in nature, with feasting, music, and dance. Young women may have married soon after reaching puberty, around age 12–15, whereas young men were several years older. The parents, along with the mother's brother in matrilineal societies, typically arranged marriage partners. Marriages forged alliances among different groups, creating useful allies in times of warfare. Wedding ceremonies varied, ranging from no formal ceremony to elaborate multiday affairs (Joe et al. 1999). The birth of children was an extremely welcomed event, but given high infant mortality rates, family sizes tended to be small. Most Native American groups were kind, loving, and permissive with their children.

Although Native Americans consisted of diverse groups and conflict or wars sometimes erupted among them, nothing prepared them for the scale of massive destruction they experienced in the nineteenth century. Often under the guise of religion, "progress," or sheer economic greed, Native American groups experienced slaughter and enslavement, and were forcibly removed from their land and put onto reservations. Many of their traditions were difficult or impossible to maintain under these circumstances, and Native Americans suffered extreme poverty and hardship.

Colonial America: European Colonists

Several family historians such as John Demos, author of *A Little Commonwealth* (1970), Steven Mintz and Susan Kellogg, authors of *Domestic Revolution: A Social History of American Family Life* (1989), Nancy Cott, author of *Public Vows: A History of Marriage and the Nation* (2002), and Carl Degler, author of *At Odds: Women and the Family in America from the Revolution to the Present* (1980) have given us some surprising glimpses into colonial family life. They show that the family was the cornerstone of colonial society. It was the primary social institution, helping early immigrants adapt to life in the New World. Families were perceived as an important component of the community

Historians and family scholars draw upon written documents such as diaries or letters; they analyze historical records such as birth or death registers, immigration records, slave auctions, or newspaper articles; and they analyze artwork of a particular era to find insightful clues about ordinary family life in the past.

rather than a private relationship, and therefore the community did not hesitate to get involved in family matters, including monitoring how husbands treated their wives, or how parents treated their children.

The family was, first and foremost, a "community of work" or a *business* because it was the central focus of economic production. Family and work were inseparable. Each household was nearly self-sufficient, and all family members—men, women, and children—worked together at productive tasks to meet their material needs. It raised the food and made most of the clothing, furniture, and household goods that the family used. Men and boys had the primary responsibility for tending the crops, although the women and girls in the family often assisted them. However, women and girls were usually exceedingly busy with household tasks. Cooking, cleaning, taking care of younger children, and making important items such as clothing, soap, or candles took up most of their day. Men and women were highly dependent on one another for survival (Degler 1983; Kulikoff 2000).

The family also served as a *school.* Formal schooling conducted away from home was extremely rare, particularly in early colonial times. Instead, it fell to parents, usually fathers, to educate their children, to teach them how to read and write, and impart to them the vocational and technical skills they would need in their adult life. Fathers were given the responsibility of teaching their children because of their presumed greater intelligence. Formal schools began to appear toward the end of the colonial period, but they were not mandatory, and therefore many children, especially girls, non-Europeans, and poor children, did not attend them.

Moreover, families were *health and social welfare institutions*. There were no hospitals, and there were few doctors during this period. Families, women in particular, took over the role of caring for the sick and infirm. Families also took care of the elderly, the homeless, or orphaned children. These services were not provided by outside social institutions, but by families—one's own, or someone else's (Demos 1970, 1986). Jails were rare. Instead, courts sentenced criminals and so-called "idle" people to live with more respected families in the community. Families were viewed as a natural setting in which to impose discipline, but also to encourage reform.

For both women and men, marriage and family were central events in life. Although marriages were often undertaken because of business or financial interests, love and affection between husbands and wives were expected. But how did men and women meet prospective marriage partners?

Courtship and Partnering Courtship, partnering, and mate selection are particularly interesting family issues. Mate selection is a relatively patterned and predictable activity, heavily influenced by social structure. Many people are initially inclined to believe that love operates spontaneously outside the rules of everyday life; however, factors such as social class or geographic proximity have always played critical roles.

During colonial America, casual dating was frowned upon. Young women were usually not left alone to meet men; parental permission was needed to allow a young man to see a young woman, and the couple was usually chaperoned by friends or relatives. Parents, fathers in particular, exerted considerable influence over whom a son or daughter could date. The mate selection system in the seventeenth and early eighteenth centuries is best described as one that was open to choice, but was also highly regulated (Farrell 1999). Although generally parents did not select their children's mates, as is the case in many parts of the world today, marriage did require parental consent. The courts could punish those who married without obtaining such consent (Wall 1990).

Despite heavy parent involvement, premarital sex and premarital pregnancy occurred with surprising frequency. According to some historians, nearly a third of women were pregnant at the time of their marriage (Demos 1970). Many became pregnant as a result of a dating practice known as **bundling**. Because a young man may have traveled a great distance to see his date or fiancée and people generally went to sleep early, he may have been allowed to stay the night at her house. Space was at a premium, so the young man and woman continued their date by spending the night in bed together, separated by a wooden board. The couple was supposedly under the watchful eye of the other family members who likely shared the bedroom, but apparently sexual relationships sometimes occurred.

Others, including slaves or indentured servants, were vulnerable to rape and bore children out of wedlock. Indentured servants were often young, poor, and came to the United States alone. A family already living in the United States paid their fare on the condition that the indentured servant would work for the family for a period of 7 years. Their treatment was variable; some indentured servants were treated like family members, while others were abused and exploited.

Household Structure Most people in colonial America lived in nuclear families. Because people didn't live very long (average life expectancy at birth was 35 to 45 years in 1650) (Farrell 1999), older adults may have died before their grandchildren were born. Extended families comprised of grandparents or other family members were the exception rather than the rule, and may have occurred for personal reasons, such as to take care of a frail elder.

Families in colonial America were large by today's standards, often containing seven or eight children, as shown in Table 3.3 (Demos 1970). The age differences between children were large, and mortality rates were high. Siblings may have been 25 years apart or more in age. Therefore, some children were married and out of the house while other children were only babies.

It was common for husbands or wives to marry two or three times because of high death rates, often related to childbirth or dangers on the frontier. The surviving spouse remarried very quickly because his or her livelihood often depended upon it. Therefore, children within a household commonly had stepsiblings or half-siblings. Some households also contained servants or slaves, and these were sometimes counted as household

TABLE 3.3 Size of Families in Plymouth Colony

	Average Number of Children Born	Average Number Living to Age 21	Size of Sample
First-Generation Families	7.8	7.2	16
Second-Generation Families	8.6	7.5	47
Third-Generation Families	9.3	7.9	33

Note: The 96 families in this sample were chosen for analysis because the evidence on their membership seemed especially complete and reliable. Also, in all these families both parents lived at least to age 50, or else, if one parent died, the other quickly remarried. Thus in all cases there were parents who lived up to, and past, the prime years for childbearing.

Source: Demos 1970.

family members in statistical records. In his book *The World We Have Lost* (1971), Peter Laslett describes the results of a demographic count of a particular region in 1688. Of the 72 husbands, 21 of them were noted as having been married before: 13 had been married twice, 1 a number of times unspecified, 3 had been married three times, 3 had been married four times, and 1 had been married five times.

Relationships Between Husbands and Wives Husbands and wives worked as a team to ensure that their family survived and thrived. A wife was considered her husband's helpmate, but not his equal; colonial America was highly patriarchal (Cott 2002; Welter 2002). The husband was considered to be the head of the family and it was his wife's duty to obey him. New England clergymen often referred to male authority as "laws" that women must accept, and in the South, husbands denounced assertive wives as "impertinent." Females were thought to be morally weaker, a belief codified by religious institutions and rationalized by the story of Eve, who was responsible for original sin by eating the forbidden fruit from the tree of knowledge. The story promotes the idea that women are a dangerous temptation to men and must therefore be controlled.

At the same time, there was a shortage of women in colonial America, and this sex imbalance tended to enhance the status and position of women somewhat. Compared to their counterparts in England, women in colonial America had more rights on average, including some measure of property rights and the right to make contracts. These rights varied from one colony to another, and sometimes from one community to another, but there is evidence that some women could retain limited ownership of certain property after marriage.

Women's status may have been enhanced somewhat because they had crucial economic roles inside and outside the family. For the most part, wives did the cooking, sewing, cleaning, gardening, certain farm chores, and produced many products for the family. Families needed the labor of women, and their duties were highly valued by society. As historian Carl Degler tells us (1983):

> Over the long term of a lifetime [their tasks] were probably more arduous and demanding than those performed by the men. One traveler in 18th century Carolina reported that "the ordinary women take care of cows, hogs, and other small cattle, make butter and cheese, spin cotton, and flax, help to sow and reap corn, wind silk from the worms, gather Fruit and look after the House." Looking after the house was itself a heavy task since that included not only

> cleaning the physical interior but the washing and mending of the family's clothes, preparing meals under the handicaps of an open fireplace and no running water, preserving various kinds of foods, making all the soap, candles, and most of the medicines used by the family, as well as all the clothes for the family. And then, as the quotation suggests, the women had to be ready at planting or harvest time to help in the fields. On top of this, of course, was the bearing and rearing of children. . . . Unlike the work of the husband-farmer, a woman's work went on after dark and at undiminished pace throughout the year.

Parenting Compared to parents today, some scholars believed that parents in colonial America tended to be relatively strict, emotionally distant, and expected obedience from their children. Some of this detachment may stem from the high infant and child mortality rates during this period; parents were cautious about becoming too close with their children (Corsaro 1997).

Families tended to follow the teachings of the Bible. Parents and children read the Bible together, one of the few readily available books and sources of moral instruction. Children were thought to be born with "original sin" and needed firm discipline and severe religious training to prevent them from going to hell. Discipline was strict to break their innate rebellion and selfishness. Firm guidance was seen as necessary to ensure that children would grow up to be productive members of society. Excessive tenderness could spoil the child.

Children were treated as miniature adults in many ways (Mintz 2004); there was little concept of adolescence, as there is today. As soon as children were old enough to labor on the family farm or in the household, they were put to work. "Once the child had begun to assume an adult role and style, around the age of six or seven, the way ahead was fairly straightforward," writes historian Demos (1970).

There were social class variations in childrearing patterns then, as there are today. Wealthy families tended to be more indulgent with their children than poorer families—yet, child labor of some sort was nearly universal because their labor was needed for family survival. Parents considered a boy to belong under his father's tutelage, while a girl's training was the domain of the mother. Daughters' education included heavy doses of domestic tasks, such as cooking, cleaning, and sewing.

Colonial America: African Americans and Slavery

The first Africans brought over to the United States were enslaved for a specified amount of time, and then were considered "free" and able to marry and purchase their own land. But by 1790, the slave trade was well under way with at least 750,000 Africans captured, brought to the United States against their will, and held as slaves. Thousands more died in the long grueling ship ride to the United States where food, water, and sanitary conditions were abysmal. Slaves were used primarily in the south, where the agrarian economy relied on exploiting their cheap labor. Although not all whites in the south owned slaves, the southern culture supported the importation, selling, breeding, and horrendous living conditions of slaves.

Like free Americans, most slaves lived in separate families centered on a monogamous couple, but the similarities ended there (Gutman 1976). African Americans lived under conditions no other American could imagine; they were property and thus could be bought and sold on a master's whim. There was always the threat and the frequent fact of separation of family members by sale or inheritance (Scott 1982).

Masters and slaves considered slave marriages and stable families to be important. Masters encouraged marriage among slaves for multiple motives, including as a mechanism for social control. Slaves in committed relationships were considered to be better workers and less likely to run away. Married slaves were also more likely to have children, thereby making arranged "breeding" described in the opening vignette less relevant. This became increasingly important by the early 1800s when the United States prohibited the importation of new slaves.

Slaves formed strong family bonds under the constant threat of separation by sale or inheritance. It is likely that at least one-third of slave couples were broken up by selling off one or both partners to another owner.

Yet in colonial America, it was not easy for a slave to find a spouse. In the north, most slaves were not allowed to associate with other slaves. They lived alone or in very small groups with their masters. In the southern states, most slaves lived on small plantations with 10 or fewer other slaves. Nonetheless, marriages did occur, although not recognized legally, and true bonds occurred. A vast array of real and "fictive" kin provided slaves with a loving, supporting, and protective community, as best as they could (Scott 1982).

Slave marriages were fragile; one study conducted in several southern states reveals that over one-third of marriages were terminated by selling off either the husband or wife to another party elsewhere (Gutman 1976). Another study reports that only 14 percent of slave couples said they lived together without some sort of disruption. The master broke up almost one-third of these, but an even higher proportion was due to an early death of one of the spouses (Blassingame 1972). However, even when slavery tore apart families, kinship bonds persisted. Children were often named after lost relatives as a way to preserve family ties.

Prior to the Civil War, there were approximately 150,000 free African Americans living in the south, and another 100,000 living in the northern part of the country (Mintz and Kellogg 1989), yet, even "free" African Americans were not necessarily allowed to vote, attend white schools and churches, or hold certain kinds of jobs, and they were subject to severe prejudice and discrimination. There were few legal protections available. Consequently, many free African Americans were poor, had high levels of unemployment, and were barely literate. Women had an easier time than did men in finding employment because whites sought out women as domestic servants. Moreover, the number of free women outnumbered free men in urban areas. Together, the high rates of poverty and the sex imbalance of free African Americans challenged their ability to marry and raise children. It is therefore not surprising that many children were reared in female-headed households. One study indicated that when property holdings, a key measure of income, are held constant, the higher incidence of one-parent families among African Americans largely disappeared (Mintz and Kellogg 1989). Poverty shapes family life.

One of the key concerns fueling the small but growing abolition movement in the early nineteenth century involved ideas about family. Abolitionists declared an attack against slavery using passionate images of slave families being broken up on the auction block. They condemned slavery as a "system of universal concubinage," which eliminated the possibility of marriage among African American adults, destroyed families, and put women into vulnerable situations with their male masters. Harriet Beecher Stowe's *Uncle Tom's Cabin*, written in the early nineteenth century and considered a classic today, focused on how slavery destroyed opportunities for meaningful family life (Scott 1982). As one historian notes:

> She portrayed the slaves, not as abstract victims or members of an alien and different race and culture, but as husbands and wives and mothers and fathers whose suffering, love, and concern for each other and their children was identical to that of the white mothers and fathers to whom she addressed the novel.

For years slavery has been used to explain current African American family patterns. African American families have been criticized for being matriarchal, assumed to be a carryover from norms established during slavery. In a study of marital power and decision making among families in Detroit over 40 years ago, researchers Blood and Wolfe report that "Negro" wives were twice as likely to be "dominant" in their families as compared to wives who were white (1960). However, historians have begun to revise our conceptions of families under slavery. Instead of seeing slave families as inadequate, incomplete, or emasculated, historians are noting the resiliency of slave families (Sudarkasa 1999; Wilkinson 1997). The popularity of televised programs such as *Roots*, which vividly portrayed the strength of family bonds under some of the most adverse conditions possible, and books such as *The Black Family in Slavery and Freedom* by historian Herbert Gutman (1976), indicates that African American family ties were strong when they were permitted to exist. Historians note the strength of the extended family in caring for kin, and that the relationships created by "blood" were considered more important than those created by marriage (Sudarkasa 1999).

Mexicans

Mexicans had a rich history along the west and southwestern portions of what is now the U.S. border, drawn from the contributions of Native American and Spanish heritage. The Spanish elite owned large tracts of land used for grazing cattle or sheep. Others, often with a combined ancestry of Spanish and Native American, were the laborers or those who had considerably smaller land holdings.

After decades of war with Mexico, the United States annexed Mexican territory in 1848. Although the Treaty of Guadalupe Hidalgo guaranteed Mexicans the retention of their property, most landowners had their land confiscated and old land grants were no longer effective. Consequently, many Mexican families who were secure and had some degree of wealth prior to annexation became laborers on land now owned by others.

Mexican laborers have been crucial to the southwestern economy for the past 160 years. Many Mexicans have been hired to do the physical labor that whites choose not to do. During the nineteenth century employers hired women and children as domestics, laundresses, and cooks, as well as farm laborers alongside their husbands and sons. Men were hired to work in the railroads or in mining, along with farm laboring. Their pay was little, far below what whites typically earned, and consequently multiple family members were often employed—husband, wife, and children—so that they could feed themselves and keep a roof over their heads.

Despite the economic hardships, Mexican Americans have been quite successful at preserving their traditional family structure. Family relationships were paramount and took precedence over individual needs or wants, a characteristic known as **familism** (Williams 1990). Families leaned toward extended models, with several generations living together or near one another and pooling resources (Mindel 1980). Parents chose specific adults as godparents to their children, and these have come to be known as

compadres, or coparents. They were close family friends who adopted a coparenting role with their godchildren. Relationships were warm and loving, and godparents provided special gifts and opportunities to their godchild. They were also authority figures expecting respect and obedience, alongside the biological parents.

Women usually worked outside the home because of economic necessity, but they defined their primary role as wives and mothers. Women were responsible for virtually all of the household labor and hands-on childrearing. When a mother was away at work, other female family members chipped in—grandmothers, aunts, cousins, and older female siblings. Mexican American families have a long tradition of **machismo**, or masculine authority, and it is demonstrated in the home, in the workplace, in sexual prowess, and in the raising of children. There is a clear double standard, with males being afforded greater leeway and sexual freedom and fathering children is a great source of pride. For example, a high premium is placed on women's virginity prior to marriage and sexual faithfulness within marriage, whereas premarital and extramarital affairs among men are expected, or at least tolerated (Del Castillo 1984; Mirande 1985). Likewise, children were socialized according to strict traditions associated with gender. Compared to boys, girls were restricted and heavily supervised in social settings.

American Families in the Nineteenth Century

Family life changed considerably in the nineteenth and early twentieth century because of two primary factors: industrialization and immigration.

The Changing Nature of the Economy: Industrialization and Urbanization

Industrialization transformed an economy from a system based on small family-based agriculture to one of large industrial capital. Small family farms increasingly could not support themselves and folded or else were bought out by large commercial farming companies. There was considerable movement to urban areas in search of jobs. During the early part of the industrial revolution, families were often separated because men moved to urban areas in search of work, leaving the rest of the family behind. "Work" became something that was increasingly being done away from the home. More and more goods and services were produced for profit outside the home, and families purchased these with the wages they earned at outside jobs. The new industries needed large numbers of laborers, so they began to look to women and children to fill jobs alongside men. Industries could pay women and children lower wages and often considered them "better" workers because they were less demanding, more docile, and obedient. Historian Steven Mintz reveals that for many children, childhood was a time of cruelty—grim factory or farm labor, poverty, loneliness, and economic and sexual exploitation. Poor, immigrant and black children suffered disproportionately, working side-by-side with their mothers and fathers (Mintz 2004).

Working conditions in factories could be exceedingly dangerous, unsanitary, and inhumane. Upton Sinclair wrote of the harrowing conditions that crippled or killed many people, as he described a fictional family working in a meatpacking plant in Chicago in the famous book *The Jungle*, which was originally published in 1906:

> Of the butchers and floorsmen, the beef-boners and trimmers, and all those who used knives, you could scarcely find a person who had the use of his thumb; time and time

Industrialization and urbanization fostered a great need for labor in new and growing industries, including factories, mills, and meat packing plants. Immigrants—men, women, and children—often filled these dirty and dangerous jobs.

> again the base of it had been slashed, till it was a mere lump of flesh. . . . The hands of these men would be criss-crossed with cuts, until you could no longer pretend to count them or to trace them. They would have no nails—they had worn them off pulling hides; their knuckles were swollen so that their fingers spread out like a fan. There were men who worked in the cooking rooms, in the midst of steam and sickening odors, by artificial light; in these rooms the germs of tuberculosis might live for two years, but the supply was renewed every hour. There were the beef-luggers, who carried two-hundred pound quarters into the refrigerator cars; a fearful kind of work, that began at four o'clock in the morning, and that wore out the most powerful men in a few years. There were those who worked in the chilling rooms, and whose special disease was rheumatism; the time limit that a man could work in the chilling rooms was said to be five years. There were the wool-pluckers, whose hands went to pieces even sooner than the hands of the pickle men; for the pelts of the sheep had to be painted with acid to loosen the wool, and then the pluckers had to pull out this wool with their bare hands, till the acid had eaten their fingers off. (1981, 98)

Many jobs became categorized and separated by sex. Men did the heavy manual labor. Women toiled in tedious and repetitive factory jobs, and other jobs that corresponded with their domestic skills, such as seamstress. Both men and women's wages were low, and consequently children also often worked full-time, doing dirty and dangerous work as well.

Demographic Changes: Immigration

The large waves of **immigration** of people moving to the United States provided the labor fueling industrialization. Millions of Irish, German, English, Scandinavian, and other northern European immigrants came to the United States in the mid-1800s encouraged by the prospect of a better life. By the late nineteenth and early twentieth century, millions more came from southern and eastern Europe, including Greeks, Poles, Italians, Russians, and other Slavic groups. Other groups from Asia such as the Chinese later immigrated to work in certain industries. Between 1830 and 1930, over 30 million immigrants came to the United States.

Immigrants were an important component of the changing economy and were employed in a number of key industries. A survey of 20 major mining and manufacturing industries found that over half of the workers were foreign born. In clothing factories, the figure was over three-quarters. In packinghouses, steel mills, textile mills, and coal mines, nearly half of the workers were immigrants to the United States (Steinberg 1981).

Most immigrants were poor and vulnerable. In her book *Foreign and Female: Immigrant Women in America, 1840–1930*, Weatherford (1986) describes the appalling conditions in which many immigrant families lived. Housing was crowded, substandard, and often lacked appropriate sanitation facilities. Raw sewage was strewn about causing disease epidemics in the neighborhoods in which immigrants congregated. Upton Sinclair (1981) also describes dreadful conditions of immigrant families' neighborhoods, including the raw sewage and cesspools drawing flies and rodents where children played. Epidemics were rampant among immigrant neighborhoods. For example, a cholera epidemic killed nearly one-fifth of the residents in a crowded New York immigrant neighborhood, but the rest of the city was virtually untouched.

The strain of family life under these abysmal working and living conditions was severe and took its toll. Alcoholism, violence, crime, and other social problems stemming from demoralization plagued many families, yet immigrants continued to crowd the cities in search of work because they hoped that it would lead eventually to a better life. Many immigrants hoped that if they simply worked hard enough, they would soon join the ranks of the middle and upper classes. They were ill prepared for the working conditions, living environments, and prejudice and discrimination they would face.

Class Ideology As poor single women, immigrants, and lower-income families were selling their labor for wages in the city or toiling on a dying breed of family farms, a new ideology began to emerge in the middle and upper classes. According to this ideology known as **separate spheres**, although single women may need to work—and indeed many did in growing fields such as teaching, nursing, or textile work—ideally, married women with children should stay at home. The **cult of domesticity** glorified the domestic role and elevated it to a pinnacle achievement. A wife's primary job was to rear the children and take care of the home while a husband should be the sole breadwinner (Beecher 1869; Cott 1997). Wives and mothers no longer produced goods and services in the home, but consumed them in the process of caring for their family (Welter 1977). Women's proper role was to support their husbands and raise and nurture their children. The world of work was presented as a dangerous and corrupt place, unsuitable for women's delicate nature and naturally higher morals. Women should create safe havens for their husbands so that husbands may have a brief respite from the stress and corruptions of the work environment (Cott 1997). The expectations for being a good wife and mother were explicitly spelled out in self-help books.

This ideology was based on specific assumptions about the nature of men and women. Women's fundamental nature was seen as distinctly different from men's and included the virtues of piety, purity, submissiveness, and domesticity (Welter 1966). Women were supposed to be the guardian of the home and the moral values associated with it. Love was promoted as the basis for her caregiving, and increasingly love became a private emotion, removed from any outside practical action to help others (Cancian 1989). Women were cut off from the outside world; they were considered too delicate to handle its harshness. They were "ladies."

These values became the dominant ideology and also formed the basis of many social policies, such as denying women the rights to own property, to speak in many public settings, or to vote. However, this lifestyle was virtually unattainable for many women, including poor, working class, minority, and immigrant women—yet they too

BOX 3.1 Social Policies for Families

The Nineteenth Amendment Is Ratified

With the ending of the Civil War, the right to vote was given to black men. Although there was widespread difficulty enforcing this right, especially in the South, women of all race and ethnic groups were legally barred from voting until the twentieth century. What is the history behind granting the vote to women? Susan B. Anthony was a leader in this controversial movement.

Susan B. Anthony was instrumental in helping women receive the constitutional right to vote.

The demand for the right to vote of U.S. women was first seriously devised at Seneca Falls, New York, in 1848. In that year, Lucretia Coffin Mott and Elizabeth Cady Stanton organized the Seneca Falls Convention (Flexner 1959) and drafted the Declaration of Sentiments, which was modeled after the Declaration of Independence. The document listed various forms of discrimination against women including the denial of suffrage. Also, they claimed equal rights in universities, professions, and the right to share in all political offices, and demanded equality in marriage, freedom, and various rights that men had (Porter 1971).

In 1872, Susan B. Anthony was arrested along with other women who voted on November 5, in Rochester, New York, for claiming that the provisions of the Fourteenth and Fifteenth Amendments applied to all citizens, male and female, and "she [indirectly] wanted Congress to pass legislation making it possible to exercise that right" (Gurko 1974). Within 2 weeks after the voting incident, the women were arrested on the federal criminal charge of "having voted without the lawful right to vote."

were held up to this ideal, and because they could not meet it, were considered failures. Women who had to work to support their families were looked down upon with contempt and pity and were often viewed as less than true and virtuous women.

During this period, ideas about children and the developmental stages associated with childhood began to change. Childhood and adolescence were increasingly viewed as distinct stages in the life cycle. Children were no longer considered simply miniature adults, perhaps because middle- and upper-class families no longer had to rely upon their labor. They were seen as individuals in their own right, not simply as extensions of their parents. Children were innocent and could be molded into good or bad citizens. There was a marked decline in the use of spanking and other firm disciplinary techniques (Degler 1980).

Women had a critical role within the family teaching children strong moral values. Childrearing books played up the importance of mothers, while making the assumption that fathers would not be around very much. Women's childrearing responsibilities were elevated in importance, and outside work was frowned upon because it would presumably take the woman away from her primary, natural, and most important work of all.

Before a trial was held for Anthony, she was briefly imprisoned for illegally voting, along with other women. Bail was at $500, and all accepted but Anthony. She preferred to go to jail than pay, however, the judge didn't want Susan B. Anthony in jail, so he paid the bail himself.

The trial of the *United States of America v. Susan B. Anthony* opened on June 17, 1873. Anthony's defense was that the Fourteenth Amendment's privileges and immunities clause gave all citizens, including women, naturalized in the United States the right to vote (Dorr 1970). The judge would not allow Anthony to testify for herself. After much contemplation by the judge and the contending arguments by the attorneys, the judge ruled that the Fourteenth Amendment was inapplicable and directed the all-male jury to bring in a guilty verdict. When Anthony's counsel, protesting this clearly unconstitutional procedure, requested that the jury be polled, the judge instead summarily discharged the jurors. All in all, Anthony was charged $100, but never paid it.

On January 10, 1918, the House approved the Nineteenth Amendment, which said that the right of citizens of the United States to vote shall not be denied or abridged by the United States or any other state on account of sex. Many states granted suffrage to women before the actual ratification of the amendment, but finally after a year and a half, the Senate passed the amendment on June 19, 1919. The Nineteenth Amendment became part of the U.S. Constitution on August 26, 1920.

Sources: Adapted from Nemeth 2000; Dorr 1970, Flexner 1959, Gurko 1974, Kraditor 1965, Porter 1971.

CRITICAL THINKING QUESTIONS

1. What arguments were made against letting women vote? How would those arguments stand up to scrutiny today?
2. Do you know any women alive today (a grandmother or a great-grandmother) who remembers when women received the vote? How did they feel about the controversy?

Families in the Twentieth Century: The Rise of the "Modern" Family

The early 1900s contained many social events affecting the structure and dynamics of family life. Box 3.1 chronicles the passage of the Nineteenth Amendment that gave women the right to vote and reveals that the fight was neither quick or easy. There were also two world wars, a depression, and the post-World War II affluence of the 1950s. Technological innovations reduced the amount of time spent on domestic labor. The automobile changed the ways families traveled and made increased distances readily available. New residential patterns—migration to the cities in search of work and the subsequent creation of suburbs and flight from the cities—increased travel and commuting time. Together, these factors decreased the time that fathers spent with their families.

These changes led to new lifestyles, family structures, and views about the family. Dating emerged as a mechanism for those in the newly defined stage of adolescence to meet one another and select mates. Schools brought young men and women together, and peer influence increased. The automobile provided a degree of privacy not found before.

The movement away from parental control and an increase in discretionary income brought a change of power and roles in the couple relationship. Young men were expected to initiate and pay for dates. Women were expected to control the degree of intimacy and sexuality within the date. A study of dating conducted in the 1930s on the campus at Pennsylvania State University found that young men and women would readily evaluate, or rate, others in terms of their dating value. The goal was to be evaluated highly so that you could get the "best" dates. Men received top scores if they had access to an automobile, if they could dance well, and if they had more money. Young women were rated more highly if they dressed well, were good conversationalists, and were popular (Waller 1937).

Because of numerous social, technological, and demographic changes, families moved away from being a more public economic unit to a more private relationship set apart from the community emphasizing the companionship between wives and husbands, into what Ernest Burgess (1945) called the **companionate family**. These are families that are built upon mutual affection, sexual attraction, compatibility, and personal happiness. Young adults placed a greater emphasis on romantic love and attraction in their search for mates than did their parents and grandparents. Married partners had high expectations that the attraction should continue throughout their lives.

National Events: World Wars and the Great Depression

National events and crises such as World War I, the Great Depression, and World War II caused powerful shifts in family life. For example, during the Great Depression of the 1930s, millions of formerly middle-class individuals and families became unemployed and impoverished. An estimated one in four workers was unemployed and searching for work, although even this figure likely discounts seasonal workers (Gordon 1994). Many families were dislocated or members abandoned their families, going from town to town looking for work. Between one and two million were estimated to be homeless, sleeping in rat-infested shelters when they could afford or find them, on park benches, or under bridges. Finding enough food to feed their families, and locating clothing, shelter, and heat were major hurdles during this period (Watkins 1993). Meanwhile, persons who were fortunate enough to continue to keep their jobs often faced large declines in their wages. Box 3.2 describes growing up during the Depression.

The stresses associated with impoverishment of this magnitude affected families in many ways. Some used destructive coping skills, such as alcohol. Children were forced to become more independent and try to supplement family wages when they could. High levels of male unemployment put pressure on women to resign from their jobs because they were seen as taking jobs away from men who had a greater "right" to them. Even the government discriminated against women: approximately half of school districts fired married female teachers, three-quarters would not hire a married woman, and in 1932 a federal order stated that only one spouse could work for the federal government (McElvaine 1993; Milkman 1976). Discrimination against minority groups also increased; their pay was drastically reduced, their unemployment reached nearly 50 percent, and some government positions held unofficial quotas (Watkins 1993).

World War II also contributed to a number of significant changes in families. As men were drafted to join the war effort, industries, factories, and other businesses needed female labor to fill in the gaps. Initially it was not easy to encourage millions of women, often married and with children, to fill the available jobs. The government, in conjunction with larger media efforts, developed a large propaganda effort promoting employment as women's patriotic duty. "Rosie the Riveter" became an im-

BOX 3.2 Families as Lived Experience

Coming of Age in the Depression

Much of our history remains unrecorded. History books describe wars and other great events, but we know very little about the day-to-day life of Americans, including their lives during these great events. High school students in a Utah Honors English class interviewed 24 members of their community about their experiences growing up during the Great Depression. Although the Depression occurred over 60 years ago, and those interviewed were only children or young adults at the time, their memories remain vivid. Most came from farming families, a group that was particularly hard hit. Utah's gross farm income fell almost 60 percent between 1929 and 1933, and unemployment was 36 percent, the fourth highest in the nation. What was life like during the Great Depression? Below are excerpts from some of the interviews:

> "The thing that I noticed most, that I remember most, was how many people needed jobs. They call them bums that came on the railroad, and they bring what they had on their backs, and come and ask for a day's work; and if you fed them, they'd work for nothing, so you'd just feed them. You could hire all kinds of men for a dollar a day. And some of them would say, "If you keep me, I'll stay for the winter." If you just give them a bed and food. And if you had a job, and you didn't take care of it, there was half a dozen waiting for your job. If you had a job you was mighty happy . . . to keep it."—Ruth

> "I remember it was awful hard times, and it was hard to get a hold of enough to buy a sack of flour and we made our own breads, cooked our vegetables, bottled our fruits, raised our gardens. We did most of our own cooking and pastry, pies, whatever. Did it all ourselves; we hardly ever bought anything."—Marvell

> "We moved about five or six times. We would get a place to live and then on account of depression, either their son or their daughter would lose their jobs wherever they were. Then they would come back to Manti, so then we would have to move again and find a place, and that happened seven different times while we lived up there three or four years."—Leo and Hazel

> "The stock market break took so many people by surprise. My father knew that the stock market would come back up, so he put everything up on margin and that's why we lost everything. Mr. Shirley jumped from a three story window and ended his life. Several of my father's friends, bankers, committed suicide, shot themselves. It was a very traumatic time."—Jean Anna

> "We lived in a shack by the railroad tracks in Phoenix. It was so bad that they couldn't rent it to someone else, so they didn't even charge us rent. We scrounged for food, I'll tell you we scrounged for for food. At about that time Roosevelt came in and started the WPA program."—William

Source: Excerpts from New Deal Network. "Always Lend a Helping Hand: Sevier County Remembers the Depression." Online http://newdeal.feri.org/sevier/index.htm Accessed January 5, 2007. Interviews compiled by honors English students at Richfield High School, Sevier County, Utah. Sevier County (Utah) Oral History Project Collection, 1997, Utah State Historical Society. Reprinted with permission.

CRITICAL THINKING QUESTIONS

1. What were your relatives' experiences during the Great Depression?
2. Do you think the United States could experience another depression of that magnitude? Why or why not? How would you and your family fare under a depression?

portant symbol of women's work as a patriotic act. Women were suddenly praised for working outside the home.

Surrounded by the images of strong women employed in defense and manufacturing industries, women flocked to volunteer or to work in paid positions. For the first time, employers provided free or low-cost child care. Working-class jobs such as ditch digging, operating heavy machinery, or factory work were promoted to women as psychologically and emotionally fulfilling. Because of the drastic labor shortage, even racial prejudice and discrimination was less apparent: All women's labor was sorely needed and "color bars" that had previously limited the kinds of jobs minorities could hold were minimized, if only temporarily.

Another important by-product of World War II was an acceleration of the divorce rate. Although the rate of divorce had been slowly but steadily increasing for decades, during the war it rose dramatically, spiking in 1946, a year after the war ended. The war probably caused some people to marry in haste and to make poor choices in a partner, and it also caused considerable strain when families were reunited. Readjustment was difficult for the married couple as well as for their children. From a young child's perspective: Who is this strange man coming into our house and living with us?

Post-World War II: The Unique 1950s

As World War II ended and veterans returned from the war, marketing employment to women ended. Women were now encouraged to give up their positions for the sake of men. Some women gladly did so, while others resisted because they needed the pay and job experience, or enjoyed the work. Some women who refused to quit were fired. Few protective laws prohibited arbitrary firing of women or minority groups.

In the 1950s women were encouraged to find fulfillment primarily as wives and mothers. The media no longer provided women such as Rosie the Riveter, but portrayed images of Betty Crocker instead. Movies and televisions moved away from strong women, and instead pushed softer, sexier women such as Marilyn Monroe or sweet and innocent women such as Doris Day. Women's ultimate goal was to capture a man and live the domestic life. Popular television shows such as *Ozzie and Harriet*, *Leave it To Beaver*, and *Father Knows Best*, provided a glimpse into the idealized American family (Coontz 2000; Pyke 2000a, b).

The media blitz was successful. During the 1950s the average age at first marriage dropped to an all-time low since records had been kept; for women it was 19 years of age. The **total fertility rate**, or the average number of children born to women, climbed upward quickly, and this period has now been labeled the "baby boom." This, in turn, contributed to the privatization of the family. The new larger families craved the spaciousness and privacy of suburbs where they could have their own yards rather than relying on community parks and play spaces for their children. In the suburbs women cared for their children in isolation, volunteered in their children's schools and within the community, and chauffeured their children to various lessons and events. The federal government undertook massive highway construction projects that enabled long commutes from home to work, primarily by individual car rather than public transportation.

Cultural images were strong; however, this type of family was not attainable for many. Working-class and poor women, including many minority women, often worked full or part time because their husbands did not earn enough to support the family; even with their combined wages, they could not afford homes in the growing suburbs. Moreover, with the rising divorce rate after World War II and the rising rate of out-of-wedlock births, many women needed to work because they did not have a husband to support them. Nonetheless, the cultural image was powerful, and many women and men ascribed to this as an ideal, even if it was unlikely to be a part of their day-to-day reality.

Social Change and the 1960s and 1970s

The 1960s marked a time of significant social change on many fronts that affected families. The civil rights movement was picking up steam; the women's movement was bringing renewed attention to the prejudice and discrimination that women experience in the workplace, in the home, and in other social settings; the antiwar movement was posing serious questions about the U.S. involvement in the Vietnam war; the sexual revolution, fueled by the widespread availability of the birth control pill made us question our previous way of thinking about nonmarital sexual behavior; and the environmental movement uncovered the various threats to the environment brought on by the increasing number of automobiles, acid rain, or overpopulation. Together these social movements changed our attitudes and changed the way we lived. For example, job ads in newspapers, including the *Los Angeles Times* had long been segregated into "Jobs—Male" and "Jobs—Female" categories. The jobs for females were restricted to such jobs as bank teller, sales clerk, secretary, and nurse. This changed during the 1960s as the women's movement questioned the practice and argued persuasively that it was prejudicial and discriminatory.

The post-World War II 1950s glorified domesticity, and women were encouraged to leave the workplace to find fulfillment primarily as wives and mothers.

In her influential book, *The Feminine Mystique* (1963), Betty Friedan documented and criticized the push toward domesticity. Her interviews with female college students revealed that their primary reason for attending college was to find a suitable husband. Few women dreamed of jobs or careers. College women who were unattached by their senior year felt like they had failed in their ultimate mission—to get their "MRS." degree. Friedan's content analyses of women's magazines show a similar trend. Magazine articles, short stories, and advertisements glorified domesticity. Few women had jobs or careers; in fact those who did were often portrayed as cold, aloof, and unfeminine. The "normal" or "natural" role for a woman was portrayed as a wife and helpmate to her husband, and as a mother to a large number of children. Yet these roles were not fulfilling for many women, and they led to widespread depression—a problem "that has no name."

What caused the U.S. society to critically question so many dimensions of social life all at once? One explanation for the widespread interest in social change is the sheer number of young adults in the culture. The first wave of children born during the post-World War II baby boom was finishing high school, attending college, or being drafted to fight in the Vietnam war. Historians have suggested that high degrees of social change are correlated with a high number of young adults in society. They are old enough to be cognizant of social and economic injustice, but are too young to be preoccupied with the responsibilities associated with work and family that can detract from activism (Bidwell and Mey 2000).

Recent Family Issues and Their Historical Roots

As we have seen from our look at history, families are never isolated from outside events. Political actions, economic conditions, prominent religious orientations, and the development of new scientific knowledge all shape the way we conceptualize families as a social institution and influence the way we experience family life on a daily basis. Many issues that we are concerned about in the early twenty-first century (teenage pregnancy, quality child care, the division of household labor, high divorce rates) are not new issues, but have a deep and rich history associated with them. We need to know "where we've been" to know "where we are going." One example of how a sense of history shapes our understanding of events today is the way in which the economy affects the family.

An Example: Families and the Changing Economy

Despite a robust economy during the 1990s, the distribution of income and wealth in the United States became increasingly skewed during the early part of the twenty-first century. Data from the U.S. Census Bureau show that the rich have made tremendous gains in income and total wealth during the past few decades, while middle and lower classes have experienced stagnation or a decline in real earnings, adjusted for inflation (Congressional Budget Office 2005; Shapiro 2005). Moreover, the highest 5 percent of earners have made the most tremendous gains.

Less attention has been given to the plight of the middle class that has seen a significant erosion of that lifestyle in recent years. During the past century, relatively high-paying manufacturing jobs were plentiful, with wages and fringe benefits bolstered by unions stressing the importance of paying family living wages. However, since the 1970s, the U.S. economy has shifted to a more service-oriented economy and manufacturing jobs have disappeared (or have been outsourced overseas). Instead of living wages with benefits, the greatest increase in jobs is in the lower-paying ser-vice sector. Approximately three-quarters of workers are now employed in service jobs such as retailing, custodial work, banking, health care, education, or transportation. Moreover, union membership has declined along with job security and the fringe benefits that unions provide for their members. An increasing number cannot find work at all. The national unemployment rate hovered around 4.7 percent in early 2006, with 7 million people looking for work (Bureau of Labor Statistics 2006). However, this figure underestimates the true extent of the problem because it only includes those persons who have actively looked for work in the previous 4 weeks. It fails to include the other 1.5 million persons who are considered "marginally attached" to the labor force—they wanted and looked for a job sometime in the previous 12 months. Many have simply given up.

Increasingly workers are finding that temporary jobs with nonstandardized schedules are the best that they can find, and most are not happy with the arrangement (Presser 2000, 2003). Presser, a social demographer, notes that only 55 percent of workers have a standard full-time, 35–40 hour, Monday through Friday, daytime schedule. Nearly one-half of workers have nonstandard schedules, which include evenings, weekends, or rotating schedules (Presser 2000). Among couples with children, the risk of divorce increases up to six times when one of the spouses works between midnight and 8 A.M., as compared to daytime hours when controlling for such factors as the number of hours worked, the education level of spouses, previous marital experience, age difference, number of children, and the gender role attitudes of both spouses (Presser 2003).

Many families who consider themselves middle class have also noticed that their purchasing power has steadily declined because their incomes have failed to keep up with inflation. This is especially true for younger workers. Housing costs have become unaffordable for many people hoping to buy their first home. Likewise, the cost of a new car has risen faster than incomes over the past several decades. In the mid-1970s the average family spent one-third of its income to purchase an average-priced car, but car prices have risen so dramatically that a family now spends approximately half of its income for the same purchase (Bennet 1995).

Because of this "middle-class slide," many families today not only work longer hours, but an increasing number also have both spouses employed full time outside the home and yet still find themselves in alarming debt. One response to lower wages is to borrow money, which then must be repaid with interest. Credit cards such as Visa, MasterCard, or American Express are tempting to people with economic difficulties. Opportunities for receiving these cards are widespread. Total credit card debt has tripled over a recent 10-year period.

Thus, an understanding of family economics today necessitates that we look at other historical periods—of booms and busts—so that we can place current issues into their appropriate context. We should pay attention, for example, to the historical rise and decline of unions, to the history behind job outsourcing, to the consequences of inflationary or deflationary historical periods, and to the factors associated with periods of poverty and periods of austerity. Only then can we understand what is truly happening to families in the United States and in the world today.

Conclusion

Family historians use multiple research methods to piece together the everyday life of families in the past. From these methods, we have information about family life even among the very early hunting and gathering societies. We also know how slavery, industrialization and urbanization, wars, and social movements have influenced family arrangements. A look at history can provide us with critical insights about families today. Many family patterns or specific concerns are rooted in the past. For example, one common concern today: Is the family in trouble? Is it deteriorating? These seemingly simple questions are actually quite complex and can best be examined by looking at the family over time. Historians reveal that we have unfairly glorified families in the past. We now know that many families suffered tremendous hardship, and social problems were widespread. However, we commonly compare families today with the idealized version of the "normal" family of the 1950s where we envision that fathers earned the wages, mothers stayed at home to care for children, and the family was a private unit isolated geographically and untouched by social problems of the time. Reviews of history show that the family model promoted in the 1950s is the aberration, not the norm. Addressing whether recent family changes are good or bad can best be answered by taking an extended view of how families both promote and adapt to various social change agents in their larger society.

Key Terms

Bundling: A dating practice in colonial America in which a young man and woman may continue their date by spending the night in a bed together separated by a wooden board. (p. 78)

Compadres: Godparents in the Mexican-American community who serve as coparents to children. (p. 83)

Companionate family: Built upon mutual affection, sexual attraction, compatibility, and personal happiness. (p. 88)

Cult of domesticity: The glorification of women's domestic role. (p. 85)

Ethnographies: Detailed accounts and interpretations of some aspect of culture. (p. 71)

Familism: Family relationships are paramount and take precedence over individual needs or wants. (p. 82)

Family reconstitution: Attempts are made to compile all available information about significant family events and everyday life within a particular family to piece together social history. (p. 71)

Immigration: People moving to the United States. (p. 84)

Industrialization: Transforming an economy from a system based on small family-based agriculture to one of large industrial capital. (p. 83)

Machismo: Mexican Americans have a long tradition of masculine authority, which is exercised in the home, in the work place, in sexual prowess, and in the raising of children. (p. 83)

Patricians: During the Roman era, these were landowners, at the top of the stratification system. (p. 74)

Primogeniture: Families during the Middle Ages leaving their wealth or property to the eldest son. (p. 74)

Separate spheres: A dominant ideology within the nineteenth century middle and upper middle classes that suggested that women should stay home to rear the children and take care of the home while husbands should be the sole breadwinners. (p. 85)

Subsistence economies: Economies in which families use all of what they have, with virtually no surplus of food or other resources. (p. 71)

Total fertility rates: The average number of births to women. (p. 90)

Resources on the Internet

The Africans in America Website
http://pbs.org/wgbh/aia/
The website chronicles the history of racial slavery in the United States from the start of the Atlantic slave trade in the sixteenth century to the end of the American Civil War in 1865. It also explores the central paradox that is at the heart of the American story: a democracy that declared all men equal but enslaved and oppressed one people to provide independence and prosperity to another. A companion to *Africans in America*, a 6-hour public television series.

The American Historical Association
www.theaha.org
A national organization for professional historians and those interested in history. Includes an annual meeting, journals, research and grant opportunities, the collection and preservation of historical documents and artifacts. The organization is designed to enhance and publicize the profession. Among its 15,000 members are faculty at secondary schools and 2- and 4-year colleges and universities, history graduate students, independent historians, and historians in museums, historical organizations, libraries and archives, government, and business.

American Indian History Resources
http://cobalt.lang.osaka-u.ac.jp/~krkvls/history.html
A chronological history of events. Includes wars, writings, federal policy, oral histories, documents, maps, tribal histories, and milestones. Many links to other important websites.

Further Reading

Aries, P. 1962. *Centuries of Childhood: A Social History of Family Life*. New York: Vintage.

Barnard, A. (Ed.). 2004. *Hunter-Gatherers in History, Archaeology and Anthropology*. Oxford, UK: Berg Publishers.

Coontz, S. 2000. *The Way We Never Were: American Families and the Nostalgia Trap*, 2nd ed. New York: Basic.

Degler, C. N. 1980. *At Odds: Women and the Family in America from the Revolution to the Present*. New York: Oxford University Press.

Demos, J. 1970. *A Little Commonwealth*. New York: Oxford University Press.

Gordon, L. 1994. *Pitied but Not Entitled: Single Mothers and the History of Welfare*. New York: The Free Press.

Haraven, T. K. 2000. *Families, History, and Social Change: Life Course and Cross-Cultural Perspectives*. Boulder, CO: Westview.

Lenski, G. 1984. *Power and Privilege: A Theory of Social Stratification*. Chapel Hill: University of North Carolina Press.

Lenski, G., and P. Nolan. 2006. *Human Societies*, 10th ed. Boulder, CO: Paradigm Publishers.

Main, G. L. 2001. *Peoples of a Spacious Land: Families and Cultures in Colonial New England*. Boston: Harvard University Press.

Mintz, S. 2004. *Huck's Raft: A History of American Childhood*. Cambridge, MA: Belknap Press.

Mintz, S., and S. Kellogg. 1989. *Domestic Revolution: A Social History of Family Life*. New York: The Free Press.

CHAPTER 4

Sex, Gender, and Families

Chapter Outline

CHAPTER PREVIEW

Sex and gender influence virtually all aspects of families and intimate relationships. For example, they affect what is expected of us and how we behave in dating relationships, as marriage partners, and as parents. This chapter introduces the concepts of sex and gender, including both micro and macro dimensions. Subsequent chapters will examine how sex and gender influence specific family issues. In this chapter you will learn:

- The difference between sex and gender, including biological differences and those that are socially constructed
- How we learn about gender, including family members, toys, schools, peers, and the mass media
- Class, race, and ethnicity influences on gender
- Rigid gender expectations that can harm both males and females
- Examples of patriarchy internationally, including female genital cutting, Sharia, and the power of education
- Examples of patriarchy in western nations, including the origin of last names, double sexual standards, and women's income and earnings
- How family planning policy can build family resilience throughout the world

What do you think of the statement, "If you want to increase your likelihood of staying married, you should have at least one son"? You might feel uncomfortable with such blatant favoritism of sons over daughters, yet all over the world, the presence of boys seems to hold marriages together, according to research by economists Gordon Dahl and Enrico Moretti (2003). In the United States, the parents of a girl are nearly 5 percent more likely to divorce than are the parents of a boy. The more daughters, the bigger the effect: The parents of three girls are almost 10 percent more likely to divorce than the parents of three boys. In Mexico, Colombia, and Kenya the gap is wider. In Vietnam, it is wider still; parents of a girl are 25 percent more likely to divorce than parents of a boy.

Why do fathers apparently stick around for sons when they won't stick around for daughters? Or alternatively, why do mothers stay married if they have sons when they won't do the same for daughters? Do fathers prefer the company of sons to daughters? Do parents think a boy needs a male role model more than girls do? Do they worry that boys cannot cope with the consequences of divorce? Do they believe that a devastated daughter is less of a tragedy than a devastated son?

Dahl and Moretti suggest that explanations fall into one of two categories: Either sons improve the quality of marriage or sons exacerbate the pain of divorce. They suggest that before we decide which explanation to believe, we should look for external evidence on the demand for sons versus daughters. Do most parents prefer a son to a daughter?

In some cases, such as China with its ongoing problems of female infanticide and abandonment, the answer is obvious—but is there a preference in the United States as well? Dahl and Moretti find several clues that indicate a strong preference for sons. First, divorced women with sons are substantially more likely to remarry than divorced women with daughters. Daughters lower the probability of remarriage, and lower the probability that the remarriage will succeed. Second, parents of girls are significantly more likely to try to have another child than are parents of boys. This suggests that having at least one son appears to be more important to parents than having at least one daughter. In the United States, Colombia, and Kenya, a couple with three girls is about 4 percent more likely to try for another child than a couple with three boys; in Mexico it is about 9 percent; in Vietnam it is 18 percent; and in China, prior to the one-child policy imposed in the early 1980s, it was 90 percent. Finally, Dahl and Moretti look at the marriage rates of U.S. parents who conceive out of wedlock. Among unmarried couples who are expecting a child, if an ultrasound reveals that the child is a boy, such couples are more likely to get married than if the child is a girl.

Dahl and Moretti cannot say with certainty what these data represent, or why parents seem to prefer sons to daughters. However, it seems to be a common sentiment throughout the world and leads the authors to suspect that boys preserve marriages by making marriages feel stronger, not by making divorces feel more problematic. (Dahl and Moretti 2003; Landsburg 2003) ■

One of the first questions asked of a pregnant woman is: "Are you having a boy or a girl?" We are annoyed when a baby wears green or yellow and we receive no hints. Why are we so concerned about learning a person's sex?

Everyone knows that men and women, as well as boys and girls, are distinguished by their genitals; however, in most social situations people have their clothes on, so we look for other cues. We rely on secondary sex characteristics such as voice, facial and body hair, breasts, or height. We also rely on cultural cues. Hair length, shoes, clothing, makeup, and jewelry are cultural artifacts to more easily identify a person's sex category. Cultural norms and values decree what males and females are "supposed" to be like. Culture accentuates secondary sex characteristics and exaggerates sex differences (however they are defined) throughout the life course. As early as infancy we decorate boys in blue and girls in pink, and these colors seem to matter a great deal to parents. What parent would dare dress their infant son in a pink layette?

Virtually all common institutions in society, whether political, religious, economic, educational, or familial, distinguish between men and women in profound and fundamental ways. Throughout the world we are virtually obsessed with perceived sex differences, and these differences become the basis on which power is distributed. "Men are rational and therefore best suited to the world of politics; women are emotional and therefore better suited for the world of home" is a creed echoed by many people around the world. Perceptions about differences between men and women are sometimes used to deny women equal rights under the law or equal opportunities in work or education. Society seems to value the contributions of boys, girls, men, and women differently.

This chapter introduces the concepts of sex and gender and explores the ways that being male or female affects us and shapes family and intimate relationships. Subsequent chapters will examine how sex and gender influence specific topics such as developing intimacy, marriage, having and raising children, work and family, aging, domestic violence, divorce, and repartnering. Here we introduce the micro and macro dimensions of sex and gender and examine how they may influence one another. For example, seemingly personal gendered features of families such as a mother's decision to work outside the home for pay; how household labor is divided up; power; and decision making are often rooted in general ideas about sex and gender, so it is important to have a basic understanding of these before we move to subsequent chapters.

Sex and Gender: What's the Difference?

The term **sex** refers to biological differences and one's role in reproduction. Typically people think of sex based on genitalia: male and female. However, anatomical categories are not always easily identifiable, as is the case with **intersexed** individuals. The ambiguity is often the result of chromosomal or hormonal imbalances during the prenatal stage. **Hermaphrodites** are those born with both male and female genitals. The rate of hermaphroditism is approximately .012 per 1,000 live births (Blackless et al. 2000). The genitals are usually surgically reconstructed to adhere to the child's genetic chromosomes, either XX for a female or XY for a male.

In contrast to sex, which is rooted in biology, **gender** refers to the culturally and socially constructed differences between males and females found in the meanings, beliefs, and practices associated with femininity and masculinity. These are learned attitudes and behaviors, not biological or physical qualities. Gender is **socially constructed**. We are born male or female, but we learn the culturally and socially prescribed traits associated with masculine or feminine patterns of behavior.

Gender Is Socially Constructed

In most societies throughout the world today, and certainly throughout history, men and women have been viewed as far more different than alike. We even refer to one another as "the opposite sex." For example, men are often assumed to be more aggressive, sexual, unemotional, rational, and task oriented than women, whereas women are assumed to be more nurturing, passive, and dependent. Many social roles played out in families every day reflect these presumed characteristics. For example, research shows that mothers spend far more time than do fathers on child care, even when both work outside the home for pay, because women are thought to be more innately nurturing.

However, the suggestion that men and women are opposite from one another is seriously flawed. Modern social science and biological researchers note that men and women are far more alike than different (Lips 1997). Both men and women express aggression, passivity, nurturance, rationality, instrumentality, and other gender-typed behaviors. We all possess both masculine and feminine traits.

Gendered expectations are in large part socially constructed. They are variable across and within cultures, are historically situated, and reflect broad social patterns within society (Coltrane 1998). Gender is not completely innate or instinctive. Rather, much of it is socially and culturally produced.

Sex Differences

Nonetheless, it is important to note that men and women are not identical; their biological differences extend beyond the ones necessary for reproduction (Deaux 1984; Hyde and Linn 1988; Kimura 2002; Maccoby and Jacklin 1974; Wharton 2005). Although using human subjects in this line of research presents a set of particular challenges, many studies suggest that males are generally stronger, more active, and more aggressive than females. However, in other ways males are more fragile. For example, infant mortality rates are higher among males and their life expectancy is shorter in almost all countries, including the United States (Population Reference Bureau 2006). Males are affected with more genetic disorders and suffer from accidents at a higher rate than do females. Depression, however, is far more common among women.

There is also scientific evidence that males and females may solve intellectual problems differently. Although most research points to no overall differences in levels of intelligence (measured with IQ tests), there appear to be differences in patterns of problem solving. On average, men perform better than women at certain spatial tasks, having an advantage in some tests that require the subject to imagine rotating an object or manipulating it. Men also tend to score better in mathematical reasoning tests. In contrast, women on average outperform men in terms of their precision with certain manual tasks. Women also tend to excel on tests that measure recall of words or matching items. One study used a map to measure how men and women performed in learning a specific route. Men learned the route in fewer trials and with fewer errors, but women remembered more of the landmarks.

What is the cause of these differences? For many years it was popular to attribute sex differences exclusively, or nearly so, to social learning. The argument was that men and women are treated differently because of gender typing, and therefore they come to behave differently and develop different skill sets. However, the accumulating evidence now suggests that some cognitive and skill differences are present at very early ages. Moreover, research conducted with nonhumans show surprisingly similar patterns. For example, a Duke University study has shown that female rats have a greater tendency to use landmarks in spatial learning tasks, just as it appears that women do (Kimura 2002).

These differences may result from hormones such as women's higher levels of estrogen and progesterone, and men's higher levels of androgens, including testosterone. Exposure to different hormones begins in the uterus and may have implications for the way the brain is "wired." Studies of female fetuses who have been exposed to abnormally large quantities of androgens because of a genetic defect called congenital adrenal hyperplasia (CAH) showed that the CAH girls as children were more likely to prefer playing with more typical masculine toys, such as construction or transportation toys, as compared to the other girls who preferred more typically feminine toys (Kimura 2002).

Although brain research is still in its infancy because of its complexity, there is some evidence that the size, shape, and use of the brain may differ somewhat by sex (Hines 2005). Some studies suggest that women may use more parts of their brain at once while men are more inclined to have focused responses (Onion 2005). One study conducted with mice has shown that as mammals develop in the womb, testosterone and related hormones trigger cell death in some regions of the male brain and foster cell development in other regions (Forger et al. 2004). Removing or adding testosterone to mice shortly after birth causes their brains to develop according to the presence of the hormone, regardless of their sex.

Given these intriguing studies, what is the role of nature versus nurture, and how would this play out in families? Social scientists suggest that most sex differences that we see in a given society are probably a result of both biological and social influences, with social factors powerfully shaping biological ones. This process becomes clear as we examine the wide variety of sex and gendered expectations cross-culturally. What one culture defines as distinctly feminine behavior or activities, another may see as quite masculine, as the research by the famous anthropologist George Murdock has shown (Murdock 1949, 1957). Are females more emotional—or are males? Answers to questions like this are not universal; they vary across different cultures.

Although we may all possess both masculine and feminine traits, most of us display primarily the gendered traits that are associated with our sex. Females are indeed usually more "feminine" and tend to behave in culturally prescribed feminine ways and males are more "masculine." This is likely due to the strong cultural messages received throughout our lives as well as biological forces.

Incongruence Between Sex and Gender

Most (but certainly not all) cultures have a binary view of sex and gender; you are either male and behave in masculine ways or female and behave in feminine ways. Exceptions to this include the Berdache in Native American culture, in which some men assume a woman's social roles in virtually every respect. They are considered a third gender and not necessarily gay or lesbian.

However, about one in 50,000 individuals over the age of 15 in the United States has discordant sex and gendered identities (Cloud 1998). **Transgendered** individuals are those who feel most natural and comfortable expressing gendered traits that are associated with the other sex. A man may feel "normal" engaging in "feminine" traits such as wearing certain clothing (e.g., dresses), engaging in particular grooming practices (e.g., painting nails), or in having "feminine" hobbies. Likewise, some women are also transgendered, although transgendered women are not usually as obvious because we allow women more leeway to behave in traditionally masculine ways (e.g., wearing men's clothing or participating in sports).

A small number of transgendered individuals harbor a deep sense of discomfort about their sex and wish to live fully as members of the other sex. Usually referred to as **transsexuals**, these individuals may undergo sex reassignment surgery and hormone treatments, either male-to-female or female-to-male. Surgery can produce the likeness

BOX 4.1 Using the Sociological Imagination

Transgendered Experience Leads Scientist to Critique Sex and Gender Differences

Are sex and gender differences due to biology, or to the social environment? While we may never know the exact amount that each of these factors plays, Dr. Ben Barres, an MD, PhD, neurobiologist and professor at Stanford University, has a unique perspective. He has lived both as a woman and as a man. Dr. Barres, who used to be known as Barbara, underwent a sex change operation at the age of 42. He has now, happily, lived as a man for the past 10 years.

Dr. Barres is one of many transgendered men and women in the United States. What propelled him into the public light was his written response rebuking the assertion by the president of Harvard that biological differences play a major role in explaining why so few women work in the upper echelons of science, making up only 10 percent of tenured faculty. Dr. Barres firmly disagrees, and argues that women and men are treated very differently, that men have considerable privileges, and discrimination against women is rampant.

Dr. Barres explained that most men and women are unaware of the discriminatory way that women are treated because they have no basis on which to compare that treatment. "By far, the main difference I have noticed is that people who don't know I am transgendered treat me with much more respect," compared to when he was a woman. He describes numerous incidents in his own life. For example, after giving a lecture he overheard a colleague say, "Ben Barres gave a great seminar today, but then his work is much better than his sister's," unknowingly referring to him prior to his sex change operation when he was named Barbara (Vendantam 2006). As an undergraduate at MIT Barbara Barres solved a difficult math problem that stumped her mostly male classmates, and was ridiculed by her professor, "your boyfriend must have solved it for you."

Dr. Barres describes how, as a man, he is interrupted less often, is afforded greater respect for his work, and has far greater access to other physician and science colleagues. "I can even finish a whole sentence without being interrupted by a man" (Vendantam 2006).

His personal experience is bolstered by a range of studies showing bias in science. For example, when a panel of scientists evaluated grant proposals in which no names were attached, men and women scored equally well. However, when the names of the authors were included and therefore the sex revealed, women applying for research grants

of external genitals, but it cannot alter the internal reproductive organs. About 25,000 Americans have felt so strongly that their sex does not really represent who they are that they have undergone sex reassignment surgery, despite the fact that it is expensive, time consuming, and can be emotionally taxing. In Box 4.1 we meet one of these individuals, Dr. Ben Barres, formerly known as Barbara.

Where Do We Learn Gender?

If much of gendered behavior is socially constructed and learned, where do we learn it? Through a process called **gender socialization**, we are taught the norms associated with being male or female in our particular culture (Kramer 2004; Wharton 2005). Gender socialization may be a conscious effort, such as a teacher criticizing a young girl for being rowdy and "unladylike" in the classroom or scolding a young boy for displaying his emo-

needed to be three times more productive than men to be considered equally competent (*Science Daily* 2006).

Critics dismiss women who complain of discrimination as being irrational and emotional, but Barres insists that it is very real. In 2004, the National Institutes of Health (NIH) had 60 men (out of 64 evaluators) reviewing applications for one of its prestigious scientific awards. All nine grants were awarded to men. The next year, Dr. Barres convinced the NIH to have a more balanced set of evaluators. This time, 6 of the 13 grants went to women. His goal is to bring discrimination to light to empower women because he reveals most do not even recognize that they are being treated differently.

Sources: Adapted from *Science Daily*. 2006. "Transgender Experience Led Stanford Scientist to Critique Gender Differences." Online: **www.sciencedaily.com/releases/2006/07/060714174545.htm** Accessed November 21, 2006; Vedantam, Shankar, 2006. "Male Scientist Writes of Life as Female Scientist." Washingtonpost.com. Online: **www.washingtonpost.com.** July 13. Accessed November 21, 2006.

Dr. Ben Barres, a Stanford professor who underwent a sex change from female to male, has been outspoken on the issue of women's rights. He has the unique perspective of having been both sexes, and claims that women are routinely discriminated against.

CRITICAL THINKING QUESTIONS

1. How does the experience of Dr. Ben Barres add a unique perspective on the causes of sex and gender differences?
2. Can you devise a study that might help us further understand what sex and gender differences are biological, and which ones are socially produced by our environment?
3. Have you ever experienced sex discrimination, or received a privilege because of your sex?

tions because "big boys don't cry." It also may occur on a less-conscious level, such as parents providing different toys for their children—dress-up clothes for their daughters and war toys for their sons. Who teaches young boys and girls about expected masculine and feminine behaviors?

Family Members

Parents and other family members have the primary responsibility for introducing the gendered norms and expectations in their culture. They teach a child about what to wear, how to behave, what toys to play with, what the child's status is, and what the overall expectations are for the child (Bem 1993; Leaper 2002; Lips 1997; Maccoby 1998; Pollack 1999). For example, Elisabeth Bumiller, in her book, *May You Be the Mother of a Hundred Sons*—a title taken from a well-known blessing given to a Hindu woman at the time of her wedding—describes the subordinate lives of typical women in

India. Women are socialized first by their families to feel inferior to the boys they go to school with, and eventually, to the men that they marry (1990):

> The "typical" Indian woman, representing about 75 percent of the 400 million women and female children in India, lives in a village. She comes from a small peasant family that owns less than an acre of land, or from a landless family that depends on the whims of big farmers for sporadic work and wages. . . . A woman like this may begin producing babies as early as the age of fourteen. She delivers them on the floor of her hut, usually with the help of her mother-in-law or a dai, an untrained village midwife. . . . One in ten children in India will not live to be a year old. If the child is a girl, there is an even smaller chance that she will survive, even though girls are biologically stronger at birth than boys. This is because the girl will often be given less food and care than her brother. Assuming she lives, she may go, erratically, to a one-room village school but will be pulled out whenever her mother needs help with the other children and the chores in the house. Her education is over when she is married off as a teenager to a young man she has never met: from then on, she will begin a new life with her husband's family as a virtual beast of burden. "I am like an animal," Phula, the forty-year-old wife of a farmer, told me in a village in India's northern plains.

Many parents in developed countries also believe that girls and boys are supposed to be different and therefore treat them differently early on. Baby girls are held more gently and cuddled more than boys are, and infant girls are described as more dainty and delicate than infant boys. Clothing usually fits these stereotypes (Coltrane 1998; Maccoby 1998; Maccoby and Jacklin 1974; Rubin et al. 1974; Stern and Karraker 1989). An analysis of child care books and parenting websites reveals that gender nonconformity is viewed as problematic, and is linked implicitly and explicitly to homosexuality (Martin 2005).

Differential treatment continues throughout childhood, repeating itself over and over and creating a self-fulfilling prophecy far beyond any true existing biological differences. Parents, solely on the basis of sex, may assign rules, toys, expected behavior, chores, hobbies, and a multitude of other cultural values or artifacts differently. For example, girls may be required by their parents to do the dishes daily, while their brothers mow the lawn weekly; parents may allow more rough play from their sons than their daughters; teenage girls may have an earlier curfew than their brothers. When girls and boys are treated differently it is not surprising that they become more different. This then is seen by many parents as only natural, and therefore it becomes reinforced.

Fathers in particular tend to encourage their children to behave in different ways because of their sex. They emphasize achievement for their sons, while focusing more on interpersonal issues with their daughters (Gurian 1999; Maccoby and Jacklin 1974). Fathers are more involved in families that have boys, and as seen in the opening vignette, families with boys are more stable and parents may be less likely to divorce (Katzev et al. 1994; Landsburg 2003).

Toys

Children's toys and games are also differentiated on the basis of sex, and girls as young as 18 months of age have shown a preference for dolls over trucks (although boys showed no preference) (Serbin et al. 2001). Toys for boys often emphasize rough-and-tumble play (e.g., sports, guns, vehicles, action figures), whereas toys for girls often focus on quiet or nurturing activities (e.g., dolls, arts and crafts, kitchens, and cooking). An analysis of virtually any children's toy store will reveal that pink aisles specialize in girl toys whereas others are reserved for toys for boys. A toy as seemingly gender-neutral as a bicycle takes on great gender significance by its color: pink for girls.

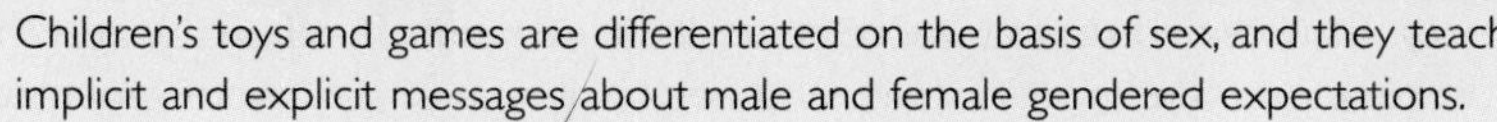

Children's toys and games are differentiated on the basis of sex, and they teach implicit and explicit messages about male and female gendered expectations.

While both boys and girls play with dolls, the types of dolls they play with are distinctive and reinforce traditional stereotypes. Baby dolls are popular and often come with a bottle so girls can practice feeding skills. In addition, 99 percent of girls between the ages of 3 and 10 in the United States own at least one Barbie doll (Greenwald 1996), which also reinforces stereotypes about adult women and their bodies. Barbie clothing and furniture accessories constitute a near billion-dollar business for Mattel. In contrast, dolls for boys are referred to as action figures and are often rugged and warlike.

Children's books give a lopsided view of the world and reinforce traditional stereotypes about males and females. One study examined the words and illustrations from 60 randomly selected children's books from a public library in a medium-sized city in the Midwest, 20 each from the 1970s, 1980s, and 1990s (Etaugh 2003). The researchers went through the books page by page and counted how many times girls and women displayed traditionally feminine traits (e.g., sympathetic, domestic, warm, emotional, dependent) and how many times they were shown with traditionally masculine traits (e.g., strong, clever, powerful, competent, independent, assertive). If the traditionally feminine traits outnumbered the traditionally masculine traits by at least two to one, the book was classified as being feminine stereotyped. On this basis, 85 percent of the books in each decade were feminine stereotyped.

Etaugh (2003) did find a greater balance in some aspects within the more recent books. In some of these books, girls were shown combining both traditional feminine traits and masculine ones; girls were adventurous, bold, and clever, while also soft, warm, and nurturing. However, when the girls grow up, there is much more pressure to conform to traditional stereotypes. Adult women in the children's books were portrayed in diametrically opposed ways—either as full-time homemakers who were not shown in any other role outside the home or as masculine women who were virtually never shown to have families. While homemakers were usually shown to be warm and caring and portrayed in a positive light, the masculinized unmarried women were often cast in a negative light. Of all 60 books there was only one instance of an employed mother despite the fact that most mothers work outside the home (2003).

Even a study of children's books evaluated as "nonsexist" by a group of independent raters still portrays housework as women's work. Although the nonsexist books were more likely than other books to show women and girls at work or playing in active and nonstereotypical ways, they also portrayed women and girls doing domestic chores, unlike the boys and men who were never portrayed doing housework (Dickman and Murnen 2004).

Schools

Day care centers, preschools, elementary schools, secondary schools, and even college classrooms are other important arenas in which gender socialization occurs. Educators have noted that teachers call on boys to answer questions more often than girls, and boys are given more public praise by teachers. Teachers appear to have lower expectations for girls than boys; they solve the problem or give girls answers more quickly, whereas they expect boys to solve the problem themselves.

Children of all ages are increasingly exposed to educational technology in schools. One study conducted a content analysis of educational software that was created for preschoolers. The results revealed that far more characters are male than female, and the male characters were more likely to display characteristics such as assertiveness or achievement (Sheldon 2004).

Gender socialization is part of the **hidden curriculum** that informally teaches girls that academic achievement could mean forfeiting popularity (Orenstein 1994; Sadker and Sadker 1994; Wellhousen and Yin 1997). A survey of over 3,000 boys and girls between the ages of 9 and 15 conducted by the American Association of University Women (AAUW) found that during adolescence, girls' self-esteem and self-confidence (including academically) drop at an alarming rate, while boys' do not (1992). The survey also found that teenage girls are much more likely than boys to say they are "not smart enough" or "not good enough" to achieve their dreams. This is particularly troublesome for Latina girls, where the number who respond that they are "happy with the way I am" plunges 38 points between the ages of 9 and 15, as compared to 33 percent for white girls, and 7 percent for African American girls (AAUW 1992).

As is the case with other children's books, textbooks and readers in circulation predominately tell stories of boys or men as main characters, showing girls sidelined in a limited number of roles or occupations (Crabb and Bielawski 1994). Girls and women are particularly invisible in science and math textbooks (Sadker and Sadker 1994). Even a study focusing on college textbooks reveals gender stereotyping (Yanowitz and Weathers 2004).

Peers

Young children are socialized by their same-sex peers to conform to traditional gender expectations. Martin and Fabes (2001) observed play behavior of 28 boys and 33 girls aged 3 to 6 over a 6-month period at a university day-care facility. Although the boys and girls were not very different in most of their behaviors at the beginning of the school year, differences intensified by the spring. The more time boys spent playing with other boys, the greater the likelihood that they were observed to be rougher, more aggressive, dominance oriented, and more active in their play the following spring. For girls, exposure to same-sex peers lowered their aggression and activity levels by the spring. The authors suggest that peers may play the role of gender "enforcers," who monitor and maintain gendered behavior by conveying the acceptable norms and the consequences if those norms are violated (Partenheimer 2001).

Psychologist Eleanor Maccoby examined children's play groups and found that children between the ages of 2 and 3 tend to prefer same-sex peer play groups when provided with the opportunity to do so (Maccoby 1998). She also noted that when girls were playing with other girls, they were as active as were boys playing with other boys. However, when girls were playing with boys, they frequently stood back and let the boys dominate the toys or games. Maccoby speculated that the boys' rougher play and greater focus on competition was unattractive to girls, and girls responded by pulling back rather than by trying to exert their own play style. Maccoby suggests that these peer groups reinforce different interaction styles that carry over into adulthood: boys' groups reinforce a more competitive, dominance-oriented style of interaction, which carries over into adult male communication patterns that include greater interrupting, contradicting, or boasting. Girls' cooperative groups reinforce a style that contributes to adult female communication patterns that include expressing agreement and acknowledging the comments of others and asking questions rather than making bold pronouncements (1998). A study in Texas reveals that children who engage in more same-sex play were better liked by peers and were viewed by teachers as being socially competent (Colwell and Lindsey 2005).

It is not only young children who succumb to gendered expectations. As Box 4.2 on page 108 indicates, the pressure for girls to conform to sexualized gendered expectations is fierce. Girls aged 13 to 17 spent $152 million on thong underwear—why? Moreover, even girls aged 7 to 12 are drawn to these undergarments. Peer pressure to be seen as sexual beings begins early.

The Mass Media

Television is an increasingly important mechanism for socializing children. During the past several years, there has been an explosion of television shows aimed at babies and toddlers, including an extensive Baby Einstein series. A recent study by the Henry J. Kaiser Foundation, based on a national sample of over 1,000 parents, reports that 59 percent of children between the ages of 6 months and 2 years watch television for more

Peer groups are powerful agents of socialization at all ages, but particularly during the teenage years. Peers play the role of gender "enforcers" who monitor and maintain gendered behavior by conveying acceptable norms and the consequences if those norms are violated.

BOX 4.2 Families as Lived Experience

The Thing About Thongs

The sexualization of young girls is a vivid reminder about the power of marketing, as shown in this essay in a newsmagazine.

All in all, I had thought I was doing pretty well in bridging the "generation gap"—though my kids would say even this outmoded phrase betrays a certain cluelessness. In any case, my teenagers and I can readily agree on playing Radiohead and Coldplay during car trips. We laugh together at *Queer Eye* and John Steward. Then there's Johnny Depp. My 14-year-old daughter and I are totally eye to eye on that one (as long as I don't remind her that he's closer to my age than hers). Luckily we've been able to skirt such deal breakers as tattooing and body piercing. So far. But my self-image as a relatively cool mom unraveled like a cheap slip last month in the lingerie department of Lord & Taylor, where we were doing some back-to-school shopping. The bottom-line point of contention: underwear.

My daughter made it very clear that I just didn't get it. Why did I not grasp that one couldn't be seen in the girls' locker room sporting those packaged bikini underpants from Jockey or Hanes? Granny pants is what some kids call them. "Mom," my daughter wearily explained, "basically, every girl at school is wearing a thong." The only viable alternative, one that my daughter favored, was an item called boyshorts, a low-riding pair of short shorts loosely, or should I say tightly, based on Britney's stagewear. Either way, it was going to be 8 to 20 bucks apiece, not three for $9. "But who sees them?" I sputtered. My daughter explained that besides the locker-room scene, girls liked to wear their overpriced thongs with a silky strap showing—not unlike the way they wear their bras.

She was right about my not getting it. How did a risqué item popularized as a tool of seduction by Monica Lewinsky become the de rigueur fashion for eighth- and ninth-graders? Yet the trend is undeniable. Sales of thongs to tweens (a market now defined ridiculously broadly as ages 7 to 12) have quadrupled since 2000, from a modest $400,000 to $1.6 million, according to NPD Fashionworld, a market-tracking firm. And there's nothing skimpy about what girls ages 13 to 17 spent on thongs last year: $152 million, or 40 percent of their overall spending on underpants. Do their mothers know?

Where this thing for thongs comes from is obvious: Britney, Beyoncé, *The Real World*, even PG movies like *Freaky Friday*. When a 12-year-old wears a thong, "it's not about rebellion against adults," says child therapist Ron Taffel. In Taffel's view, the adult establishment has become too weak and weary to inspire rebellion. Getting thongs or tattoos, or body piercings, he argues, is actually a "statement to other kids that they are part of this very, very intense, powerful sec-

than 2 hours daily. In fact, more than one-quarter of children under 2 have a television in their room.

Boys, especially middle-class white boys, are usually at the center of most television programming enjoying the most roles and showing the most activity (Barcas 1983; Seiter 1993; Spicher and Hudak 1997). There are four times as many male characters as female in the Saturday morning cartoon lineup, according to one study of 118 cartoon characters in the Saturday morning shows (Spicher and Hudak 1997). Even commercials depict men and women differently, with females far more likely to be working or playing inside the house rather than outside with the males (Kaufman 1999).

Class, Race and Ethnicity, and Gender

Although gender in and of itself is a powerful construct in society and shapes many aspects of family relationships, there are significant class, race, and ethnic variations in the

ond family of peer group and pop culture that is shaping kids' wants, needs and feelings." This phenomenon is gripping kids at ever-earlier ages. Peer pressure is at its most intense between fifth and eighth grade, says Taffel, "but it can begin in first and second grade."

Adult forces—parents, schools, and churches—find it hard to compete with pop culture. Some schools have dress codes that outlaw visible underwear, but enforcing a ban on something as subtle as a thong isn't easy, as a vice principal at a San Diego high school learned to the detriment of her career last year. Her methodology left something to be desired: she was demoted after she lifted skirts for an undies inspection before allowing girls into a school dance.

Is the underwear battle worth picking? Those who think so are worried that the thong is a blatant sexual advertisement or, at least, a tempting tease for the opposite sex. This may not be so, according to developmental psychologist Deborah Tolman. "Kids are engaged with their sexuality at younger ages, but they're not necessarily sexually active," she says. The tween thong is, in a sense, the perfect symbol for the schizoid way that girls' sexual role has evolved. On one hand, Tolman observes, girls are expected, as always, to be the "gatekeepers" to sex. (God forbid that boys should be held responsible.) And, yet, she says, nowadays even young tweens feel social pressure to look sexy—without crossing over the murky line into seemingly slutty. In short, says Tolman, "the good-girl, bad-girl thing has grown much more complicated."

Which is exactly what troubled me in the lingerie department. It wasn't until we got to the parking lot that I did what psychologists say a perplexed parent should do: I asked why the underwear mattered and listened hard to the answer. Tolman calls this the "authentic ask." My daughter's answer reflected her sense of style. But for many girls who want thongs, it may be pragmatism: What else works under tight low-rider jeans? I gave the O.K. to boyshorts at $8.50 a pair. She's delighted. "Mom," she said the other day, "you really ought to try them."

Source: Adapted from Claudia Wallis, "The Thing About Thongs," *TIME*, 6 October 2003, p. 94.

CRITICAL THINKING QUESTIONS

1. Why is there so much social pressure on girls to look sexy, whether they are sexually active or not?
2. What are some consequences for the sexualization of "tweens," girls aged 7–12?
3. Why would girls and women wear clothing that is uncomfortable for the sake of fashion? Can you provide any other examples of girls and women forgoing comfort for fashion?

gender socialization process. For example, Hale-Benson (1986) found that African American girls are more likely than their white counterparts to be encouraged by their parents to be independent and self-reliant and have higher self-esteem. Women play strong roles in African American households. Consequently, African American children appear to hold fewer gender stereotypes than do white children (Bardwell et al. 1986).

As revealed in Box 4.3, gendered expectations are rapidly changing among Hispanics. Older Hispanics—both men and women—tend to be more patriarchal in their attitudes and behaviors than younger Hispanics. Older Hispanic women believed traditional gendered expectations granted them a form of respect and protection, and they were critical of young women who want to share power with their husbands (Hirsch 2003).

Like contours of race, gender socialization is also shaped by the nuances of social class. For example, parents who have higher levels of education appear to be less traditional than are parents who have less education (Bardwell et al. 1986). Working class families often push for heightened gender segregation. Children are strongly encouraged to conform to the culturally valued gender ideals and are praised for and reinforced

BOX 4.3 Using the Sociological Imagination

Modernization and Changing Latino Conceptions of Gender

Jennifer Hirsch, in her 2003 book A Courtship After Marriage, *documents how the shift to modernity has changed the face of Latino conceptions of gender within intimate relationships, including love, sexuality, and the meaning and practice of marriage.*

Are gendered expectations changing among Hispanics? What are the consequences of this change? The 2003 book, *A Courtship After Marriage*, addresses these questions, and is based on a study of transnational families who are connected to both Atlanta, Georgia, and one of two neighboring communities in Mexico. Some families own property in both countries; others do not, but move from one country to the other for work. Thus, Hirsch focused on a group of migrants who feel and act both Mexican and American, which challenges earlier research over simplistic notions about identity and assimilation.

Hirsch developed extensive life histories from 13 women in each location, organized into six topical interviews: (1) childhood and family life; (2) social networks, migration, and differences between life in the United States and Mexico; (3) gender, earning and spending money, and the household division of labor; (4) menstruation, reproduction, and fertility control; (5) reproductive health, sexually transmitted diseases, and infidelity; and (6) dating, marriage, and sexuality.

Her initial intention was to interview each woman's husband, but the sex segregation among Mexicans made this virtually impossible. Unrelated men and women typically do not interact with one another; private interviews violated the tradition of separate spheres and made both Hirsch and the respondents highly uncomfortable. Consequently, Hirsch was forced to make a significant, but understandable compromise: to gain the trust of married women she could interact little with men. Therefore, her analysis of men in family relationships, including their attitudes, behaviors, and norms, are most often filtered through the lens of the women in their lives.

Her book is a story of social change. There are clear differences in "ideal" relationships between older and younger women. For older women, marriage was often not a union based on companionship, mutual affection, or gender equality. The following is a typical response to the query: "What did you think you would have to do to be a good wife?"

> Well to obey all of his—I did all the things I had to do. . . . In the past women were very submissive, they did what their husband said, whether it was right or wrong, you just had to do it. Now I see that things are different. (Hirsch 2003, 115)

The older women defined, and defended traditional gender differences. They expected their husbands to decide when they could leave the house, what they could wear, and when they would have sex. Their jobs were to cook,

toward "correct" gender behavior. For example, boys are pressured not to cry or to express their feelings lest they be labeled "sissies," whereas girls are taught to pay attention to the feelings of others (Adams and Coltrane 2003; Maccoby 1998).

The Pitfalls of Masculinity

Much of the early gender literature focused on the way that girls' and women's lives have been affected by rigid conceptions of gender. More recently, some have argued that although both boys and girls receive gender messages, perhaps boys experience even more pressure to conform to culturally valued ideals (Adams and Coltrane 2003; Kane 2006; Messner 2002). Girls are allowed more leeway. They can behave in ways that have been

clean, run the household efficiently, raise the children, and provide sex for their husbands. The older women believed that complying with these expectations granted them a form of protection. It gave them respect that could be used in the community, at church, with their families, with their husbands' families, and with other women. In fact, older women were critical of young women who want to share power with their husbands.

Nonetheless, younger women proudly voiced different expectations for marriage, sexuality, and love. Young people repeatedly claimed that they are not like their parents. They are striving to "reinvent intimate relations as a way of expressing that they are modern people" (Hirsch 2003, 12). The term *modern* was frequently used to indicate that their lives are not only different from their parents', but that their lives are supposedly *better*; more pleasurable, satisfying, and even more prestigious. Younger women emphasized companionate marriages—ones based on mutual attraction, affection, and a more equitable division of labor and shared marital power. A typical respondent (Hirsch 2003) said:

> From the beginning—and maybe it is that I do not like for him to tell me what to do, that he should be the one to give orders—I told him here we are both in charge. He asked me why, and I said to him that when just the man gives the orders, they get really bossy with their wives. So [I told him] that here we are going to do what both of us say. Yes, in terms of being the boss, the man is the boss, but I do not let myself get pushed round. We both are the boss. (p. 123)

Social change, however, does not come easily and without reservation. When the respondent was asked if she ever just says he is the boss because it sounds better, she answered, "well, yes" (Hirsch 2003). Women and men are struggling with changing gender expectations, and their struggle is exacerbated by their transnationalism and differing gender expectations within their two countries. Hirsch provides a penetrating analysis of how this struggle is manifested and negotiated. Younger Mexican women and men are not blindly adopting U.S.-based notions about love, sex, and marriage; rather, their desires are based on a unique set of circumstances associated with migration intertwined with longstanding cultural traditions, and a quest to be seen as modern.

Source: Hirsch 2003.

CRITICAL THINKING QUESTIONS

1. "Social change does not come easily and without reservation." What types of conflicts do you expect between mothers and daughters?
2. Whose life is easier: mother's or daughter's? Why?
3. How do race, class, and gender interact in this example?

considered masculine; for example, there is little social stigma in being a "tomboy," whereas boys are not allowed to behave in ways that are deemed feminine. To be told that "you throw like a girl" or to be labeled a "sissy" (which is the opposite of a tomboy) is tantamount to social suicide. Likewise, women have moved into many occupations traditionally held by men (such as doctor or lawyer) while few men find the occupations of nurse or legal secretary attractive. In the home, despite women's increasing likelihood to be employed, men have not increased their time in domestic tasks at the same rate. Adams and Coltrane (2003) suggest:

> Paradoxically, masculine gender identity is also considered to be more fragile than feminine gender identity . . . and takes more psychic effort because it requires suppressing human feelings of vulnerability and denying emotional connection. . . . Boys, therefore, are given less gender latitude than girls, and fathers are more intent than mothers on making sure that their

sons do not become sissies. Later, as a result, these boys turned men will be predisposed to spend considerable amounts of time and energy maintaining gender boundaries and denigrating women and gays.

The result of suppressing emotions is well noted. Problem behaviors of young boys, including use of alcohol and drugs, police detainment, fighting and other acts of aggression against their peers, school suspension, or forcing someone to have sex against her will are all associated with heightened traditional masculine ideals (Christopher and Sprecher 2000).

Institutional Sex Discrimination: Patriarchy

Historical and cross-cultural research reveals that masculinity and femininity have been defined and evaluated quite differently, and many intimate and family relationships are rooted in these fundamental conceptions about gender. The term *patriarchy*, which was introduced in previous chapters, means rule of the father. It refers to a form of social organization in which the norm or expectation is that men have a natural right to be in control of women. Patriarchy is manifested and upheld in a wide variety of social institutions including legal, educational, religious, and economic ones.

Patriarchy is widespread and is found in virtually every society; however, it is obviously more pronounced in some societies than in others. There are many places in the world today where women cannot drive, vote, divorce, or own property in their own name. In virtually every society women's activities and jobs carry less prestige and pay than those that are primarily held by men. Even when men and women work in identical or comparable jobs, women are paid significantly less for their effort overall. Moreover, women are underrepresented in public office and it is men who primarily make the laws that women must follow, including on issues that affect women in particular, such as abortion, birth control, or guaranteed family leave. These inequities are justified on the basis of biology ("it's human nature"), religion ("it's God's will"), or cultural customs ("that's the way we do things here").

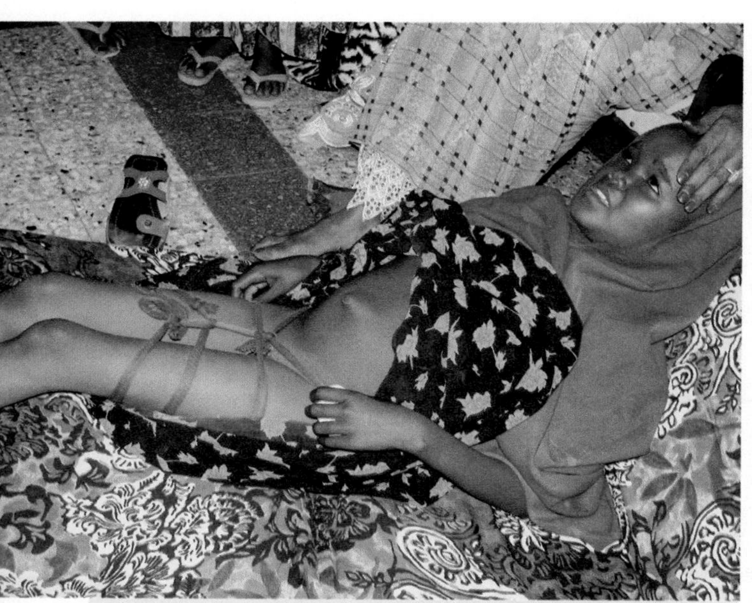

This young girl, like 100 million others, suffers as she tries to recover from the dangerous practice of "female genital cutting" or "mutilation." In an excruciatingly painful procedure, often without anesthesia, her clitoris, and possibly part of her vagina as well, is cut and removed with a knife, razor blade, or broken glass. She is then sewn up to ensure virginity.

We begin this discussion by illustrating two extreme examples of patriarchy that are experienced in the world today. Sometimes it is easier to see how patriarchy operates by examining the most glaring examples. We will then turn to gendered experiences in the United States and other developed nations: Does patriarchy operate here as well?

Female Genital Cutting

> I was genitally mutilated at the age of ten. I was told by my late grandmother that they were taking me down to the river to perform a certain ceremony, and afterwards I would be given a lot of food to eat. As an innocent child, I was led like a sheep to be slaughtered.
>
> Once I entered the secret bush, I was taken to a very dark room and undressed. I was blindfolded and

> stripped naked. I was then carried by two strong women to the site for the operation. I was forced to lie flat on my back by four strong women, two holding tight to each leg. Another woman sat on my chest to prevent my upper body from moving. A piece of cloth was forced in my mouth to stop me screaming. I was then shaved.
>
> When the operation began, I put up a big fight. The pain was terrible and unbearable. During this fight, I was badly cut and lost blood. All those who took part in the operation were half-drunk with alcohol. Others were dancing and singing, and worst of all, had stripped naked.
>
> I was genitally mutilated with a blunt penknife. After the operation, no one was allowed to aid me to walk. The stuff they put on my wound stank and was painful. These were terrible times for me. Each time I wanted to urinate, I was forced to stand upright. The urine would spread over the wound and would cause fresh pain all over again. Sometimes I had to force myself not to urinate for fear of the terrible pain. I was not given any anesthetic in the operation to reduce my pain, nor any antibiotics to fight against infection. Afterwards, I hemorrhaged and became anemic. This was attributed to witchcraft. I suffered for a long time from acute vaginal infections.

This is the story of Hannah Koroma of Sierra Leone from Amnesty International (2004).

This woman, like nearly 100 million other women and girls living in over two dozen countries in Africa and the Middle East, has experienced the painful and dangerous practice of what is described as *female genital cutting* or *mutilation* (Mackie 1996, 2000; Yount 2002). Among countries with adequate national data, Egypt has the highest prevalence; in 1995, 97 percent of ever-married women aged 15–49 have had their genitals cut (El-Zanaty et al. 1996).

In one form of genital cutting, **clitoridectomy**, the clitoris is cut out of the body. In the more extreme form, **infibulation**, the vaginal lips are also cut or scraped away, and the outer portion of the vagina is stitched together, leaving only a miniscule opening for menstrual blood and urine to escape the body. The procedure is done crudely; a layperson rather than a physician usually conducts it. One study of nearly 2,000 women living in Egypt who had their genitals cut reports that only 14 percent of the cutting was performed by a doctor (Yount 2002). In an excruciatingly painful procedure, often without anesthesia, the girl is tied or held down and the instrument used may be a knife, razor blade, or broken glass. Often the girl's body is stitched together with thorn or catgut, and her knees are bound together for several weeks for the incision to heal itself and not tear open again when she walks.

The health consequences of genital mutilation are swift, long lasting, and severe, and include much more than a loss of sexual pleasure. Immediate consequences include possible shock, hemorrhaging, or bleeding to death. Soon afterwards, women face possible pelvic infection, dangerous scarring, and internal pain from urination and menstrual fluids that cannot properly escape the body. As they mature, they may experience infertility, a greater likelihood of miscarriage, recurrent urinary tract infections, anal incontinence and fissures. Intercourse will be painful, childbirth will be prolonged and obstructed, it is likely that the perineal area will be lacerated, and there is a greater chance of stillborn births.

In those countries where female genital cutting is practiced, it has widespread support; in fact, most women intend to continue the practice with their own daughters (Williams and Sobieszczyk 1997; Yount 2002). One national study in Sudan revealed that close to 90 percent of all women surveyed either had the procedure performed on their daughters or planned to do so. Nearly one-half of women in support of cutting favored infibulation, the most extreme form (Williams and Sobieszczyk 1997). Failure to do so will make their daughters "different" or "promiscuous" and perhaps unmarriageable (Leonard 2000; Mackie 2000).

Why is this practice so popular, and why has it continued for so many years? It is deeply rooted in the patriarchal traditions (rather than religious teachings) in these societies. It has been described as "one of the most severe . . . means of 'educating' women about their subordinate status" (Abd el Salam 1998). Women are expected to be subject to the social and sexual control of men at all times. They are expected to be virgins at the time of marriage and must remain sexually faithful thereafter. Removing the clitoris, the source of women's sexual pleasure, ensures that they will not experience orgasm, and thus the likelihood of engaging in or enjoying sexual relationships outside of marriage is lessened. Among women whose entire external genital area has been removed, the opening that remains is so small as to forbid penetration. Husbands are virtually guaranteed that their wives are virgins.

Female genital cutting persists, and is endorsed, perpetuated, and often conducted by other women because their status is low and their options are few. Marriage and motherhood are the primary ways in which women receive recognition. Without marriage, they bring shame to themselves and to their families. Virginity is highly valued, and this procedure helps to ensure that women's sexuality will be muted. Mothers believe that if they do not have their daughter's clitoris removed or have her infibulated, her chances of finding a husband will be reduced considerably and the daughter will bear considerable shame.

Sharia

> *"She deserves to be stoned to death," the prosecutor declared, "because pregnancy in a woman who is not known to be married is clear evidence of extramarital sex."* (Jerome et al. 2003)

Amina Lawal, a 32-year-old Nigerian single mother sits in an Islamic Sharia court in northern Nigeria and nursed her 2-year-old daughter, as she listens to her fate. Her crime? Sex outside of marriage, indicated by the birth of her daughter. Amina testified that she had been raped. However, to convict a man of rape, Nigeria's Sharia courts usually require that there be four male Muslim witnesses, or possibly eight male non-Muslim witnesses, or 16 female non-Muslim witnesses. Amina, as with most other rape victims, could not provide these witnesses and was therefore being charged with adultery. She was tried and convicted. Her punishment? She will be buried up to her chest, and the surrounding crowd will throw stones at her until she is dead. The stones must be of the correct size, large enough to inflict pain, but not too large as to kill her quickly. She must die slowly and painfully in front of the large crowd.

Fortunately for Amina, her sentence was overturned one month later. According to her defense lawyer, she was freed on the grounds that neither the conviction nor the confession was legally valid. Were they valid, she would likely have been tortured to death.

Amina's plight is a symptom of a much larger problem in Nigeria and other parts of Africa. Radical interpretations of Islamic law, or **Sharia**, are being used to establish extreme and punitive rules by which Muslims are governed. It is argued that these rules form the basis for relations between man and God, and between individuals, whether Muslim or non-Muslim. The Sharia contains the rules by which a Muslim society is organized and governed, and it provides the means to resolve conflicts among individuals and between the individual and the state. Extremists maintain that their laws and punishments are authorized directly by God; therefore any opposition is seen as blasphemy. Questioning the practice is equated with questioning God.

In practice, the new Sharia courts in Nigeria have most often meant the reintroduction of spectacular and gruesome punishments, such as amputation of one or both hands for theft or stoning for adultery with little respect for the much tougher rules of evidence. Some observers say the expansion of the system and its stricter enforcement have helped reduce social problems, such as public drinking and prostitution—although even supporters of Sharia acknowledge that powerful men are able to drink and sleep with women in private while poor people, particularly poor women, are prosecuted. The application of Sharia is found in both criminal and civil matters, including divorce.

In the minds of many observers, the new Sharia punishments are seen as particularly stark and brutal manifestations of the huge inequalities and abuses of power that exist throughout Nigerian society. Unless that changes, analysts warn, Amina Lawal is unlikely to be the last poor person to be threatened with a punishment that causes an international outcry. Amnesty International (2003) estimates that 10,000 people have died in Nigeria under Sharia law.

The Power of Education

Women's status throughout the world is highly variable, and it appears that one key determinant of women's status in society is their average level of education. In countries where women's average level of education is lower, they have little social or political power. This changes as women's average level of education begins to rise. Education offers women a new viewpoint of the world, the ability to read and access information, the potential to increase their economic status, improved self-esteem, and the ability to engage in public debates and to bargain effectively for their rights, all of which increase their level of power in society. It also tends to lower their fertility, critical to granting women greater freedoms. Policies to improve the status of women in the world must take into consideration the importance of educating women.

Although the gender gap in primary and secondary schooling is closing somewhat, women still lag significantly behind men in many countries, especially parts of Africa and southern Asia (Ashford and Clifton 2005). Furthermore, it remains that two-thirds of the world's nearly 900 million illiterate persons are women (United Nations 2000). In virtually every country where illiteracy is high, women are less likely to be able to read and write than men. Map 4.1 indicates the percentage of literate women as a percentage of literate men between the ages of 15 and 24.

Does Patriarchy Exist in Western Nations?

Despite the high number of highly educated women in western countries, these countries also contain many patriarchal norms and customs. Although not on par with the basic human rights violations just described, several important vestiges of patriarchy continue to flourish.

In countries like the United States, the roles of women are changing quickly. Young women today have many more opportunities than did their grandmothers. They can marry or not; they can have a career or not; they can have children or not; they can live alone, travel, or have sex outside of marriage. Nonetheless, despite these changes in behavior, attitudes across the population change more slowly. What is, or should be, the role of women today? Table 4.1 shows the difference in gender expectations in 24 westernized nations. It reveals the percentage of the surveyed population in each country that agrees with the following statements: "Being a housewife is fulfilling"; "A job is the best way for women to be independent"; "The husband should work and the wife should stay home"; and "Women really want a home and children." As you can see, there is over a 60 percent spread in opinion on some of these issues.

Recent newspaper headlines reveal vestiges of patriarchy close to home.

Women Who Get Pregnant Find Jobs Can Be at Risk

Wal-Mart Gender Bias Lawsuit Faces Key Class-Action Hearing

MAP 4.1

Eye on the World: Comparative Literacy Rates—Literate Women as a Percentage of Literate Men Worldwide Between 15–24 Years, 2000–2004

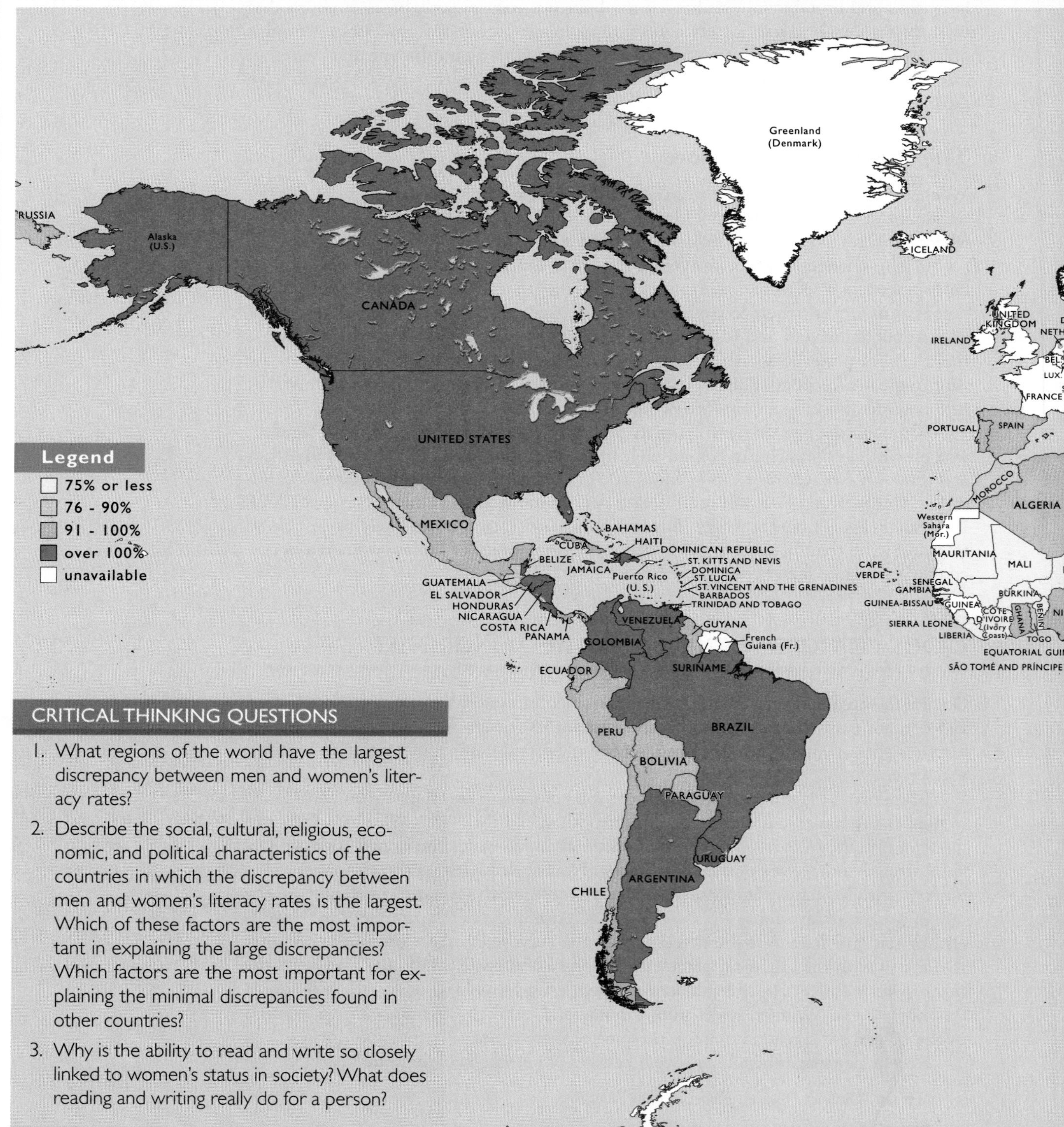

CRITICAL THINKING QUESTIONS

1. What regions of the world have the largest discrepancy between men and women's literacy rates?
2. Describe the social, cultural, religious, economic, and political characteristics of the countries in which the discrepancy between men and women's literacy rates is the largest. Which of these factors are the most important in explaining the large discrepancies? Which factors are the most important for explaining the minimal discrepancies found in other countries?
3. Why is the ability to read and write so closely linked to women's status in society? What does reading and writing really do for a person?

Sources: Ashford and Clifton 2005; Finnie and Meng 2006; National Center for Education Statistics 2006.

TABLE 4.1 Gender Expectations in Cross-National Perspective (% Agreeing)

Being a Housewife Is Fulfilling		Job Best Way for Women to be Independent		The Husband Should Work and the Wife Stay Home		Women Really Want a Home and Children	
Russia	95	East Germany	80	Philippines	91	Hungary	93
Japan	85	Philippines	77	Hungary	82	Philippines	88
Philippines	84	West Germany	76	Russia	82	Bulgaria	87
Hungary	83	Spain	75	Bulgaria	80	Poland	80
United States	**78**	Italy	73	Poland	79	Czech Republic	80
Poland	75	Bulgaria	71	Czech Republic	75	Slovenia	80
Ireland	75	Poland	69	Austria	61	Russia	76
Bulgaria	75	Ireland	68	Japan	60	Japan	72
Northern Ireland	73	Slovenia	65	Slovenia	57	Ireland	67
Australia	71	Israel	65	West Germany	52	Italy	64
New Zealand	69	Russia	64	Italy	52	Sweden	64
Netherlands	67	Sweden	63	Ireland	47	Australia	62
Great Britain	66	Great Britain	61	Spain	46	Spain	60
Sweden	65	Northern Ireland	60	Australia	45	Israel	60
Canada	65	**United States**	**56**	Northern Ireland	43	Austria	59
Austria	63	Japan	54	Great Britain	41	Netherlands	57
Slovenia	63	Norway	52	**United States**	**41**	**United States**	**57**
West Germany	62	Czech Republic	51	New Zealand	41	Norway	55
Spain	58	Netherlands	51	Israel	39	Northern Ireland	54
Norway	58	Australia	50	Netherlands	36	West Germany	52
Czech Republic	52	Canada	47	Norway	30	Great Britain	50
Italy	43	New Zealand	45	Sweden	29	New Zealand	46
Israel	37	Hungary	37	Canada	25	Canada	43
East Germany	31	Austria	37	East Germany	21	East Germany	29

Source: Smith 1999.

Not only do attitudes change slowly, so do social policies. Headlines like these remind us that patriarchy and sex discrimination continue to flourish even in western nations, including the United States. Policies enacted to end sex discrimination have not eradicated the practice.

However, not all examples of patriarchy reflect outright discrimination, subject to policy changes. Many examples of patriarchy are woven into the fabric of U.S. culture and go largely undetected. Described here are two everyday examples of patriarchy that many Americans fail to notice, but are important nonetheless.

What's in a Name?

Have you noticed that most women routinely change their last name when they marry, whereas men virtually never do (Scheuble and Johnson 1993)? When Melissa Smith marries John Brown, she usually goes by the new name of Melissa Brown, or she may be called Mrs. John Brown, taking on both his first and last name. Fueled by famous movie stars such as Farrah Fawcett-Majors and sports stars such as Chris Evert-Lloyd, a small number of married women in the 1970s and 1980s began hyphenating their last name at marriage or keeping their own name (Jayson 2005). However, in more recent years that trend has reversed. Based on almost 7,000 wedding announcements in the *New York Times* published from 1975 to 2000, women who kept their own names declined from 23 percent in 1990 to 17 percent in 2000 (Jayson 2005). Why is this? Moreover, what does it reflect?

Some people may answer,

"I never really thought about it."
"I didn't care and he did."
"It's easier this way."
"It helps make us a family to have the same name."
"Why burden children with parents who have different last names from one another, or a long hyphenated name?"
"I didn't really like my last name anyway."
"I gave my children my last name as a middle name."

There are many reasons why it may be easier to have only one last name in a family. However, one could also say that changing a last name on all pertinent legal documents is time-consuming, confusing, and interferes with one's career trajectory or makes tracking family history more difficult.

The changing of wives' names is a carryover from older patriarchal and patrilineal customs where, upon marriage, a woman became the legal property of her husband. It was important to name the child after the father so that he could identify and establish "ownership" of his heirs. According to Jackie Stevens, a political theorist who wrote *Reproducing the State* (1999), surnames (last names) were created to codify inheritance rules and thereby bolster tax revenues. "Inheritance laws, political bodies, surnames— it's all about compensating for men's inability to give birth," she contends. "The surname remains the only way of showing legitimacy. Without it, there's no certainty that the kid has a father" (Stevens 1999).

Traditions take many years to die. Until the 1970s, many state bureaucracies still prohibited women from keeping their own names after marriage and giving their children their last names. However the laws have since changed. So why is the tradition continued today? Historian Hendrik Hartog, author of *Man and Wife in America* (2000), suggests that much of what people do in marriage is simply done out of habit, even when the tradition has no legal or financial basis. There is a powerful pull toward reproducing tradition. Stevens (1999) also suggests that it remains important to women to demonstrate that they have found a husband. Women who keep their own last names are often assumed to be unmarried and they could face considerable stigma as they grow older. A 45-year-old "unmarried" woman is still an anomaly.

The Double Standard

A second example of patriarchy can be seen in sexual attitudes and behaviors. **Sexual scripts** are the norms or rules regarding sexual behavior, including number and type of sexual partners, activities, attitudes, and even purposes for engaging in sexual relationships. They inform us about what is expected and appropriate, and what is considered inappropriate or taboo. For example, U.S. culture prohibits sex with animals, children, or with

There is a double standard in sexual scripts; men are allowed far more permissiveness in sexual behavior and are expected to be sexually assertive, whereas women are more likely to be punished socially for their sexual experiences.

someone with whom you have paid money, although this is not the case in all societies (Fracher and Kimmel 1997).

We learn our sexual scripts from at least three different sources (Michael et al. 1994). First, we learn from the culture in which we live, including our parents, friends, and from the mass media. Second, scripts are learned from the interpersonal communication between two individuals as they begin, and attend to, their personal relationship. Third, sexual scripts also reflect personal views of sex, based on unique personal feelings, desires, and fantasies.

Gender and Sexual Scripts Traditionally, men have been allowed far more permissiveness in sexual behavior, whereas women are more likely to be socially punished for their sexual experiences. Men are expected to be assertive in seeking sexual behavior, always ready for sex, with the goal being orgasm rather than intimacy. Women, in contrast, are to walk a fine line by being sexy, yet not too sexy. They must make themselves desirable and attractive to the attentions of men, but by becoming too desirable or attractive they risk being labeled as easy or cheap. They must be careful not to appear to be too interested in sex. Men may be complimented as "studs" for their participation in nonmarital sex with a large number of partners, whereas the words "slut" or "whore" are derogatory terms commonly used to describe sexually active women. This has been referred to as the **double standard**. Gendered expectations are a critical component in sexual scripts because the sexual norms for males and females are socially constructed and remain highly differentiated in U.S. culture (Fracher and Kimmel 1997).

An analysis of the double standard is crucial because it contributes to a lack of knowledge about women's sexual needs, it fosters the mistaken idea that women have less important sexual needs, and it perpetuates the notion that male sexuality should be the normative baseline for eroticism and sexual activity. It objectifies women by keeping them as the "objects of desire" rather than recognizing their own human sexual needs. Furthermore, it inhibits communication between partners, can increase the likelihood of relationship violence, and it prevents individuals from seeking help when a sexual problem does occur.

Does the double standard exist today? Researchers have found that people are still more tolerant of nonmarital sexual activity among men than among women, particularly on the first date (Hatfield and Rapson 1996), in uncommitted relationships (Hynie et al. 1997), or with a large number of partners over time (Rubin 1990). Both men and women hold the double standard (Hynie et al. 1997). Using harsh sexual terms to refer to sexually active girls is common among people of all ages, including preadolescent boys and girls, middle and high schoolers, college students, and other adults (Hatfield and Rapson 1996; Rubin 1990).

Peggy Orenstein, in her book *School Girls* (1994), found that the fear of being labeled a slut in middle school acutely affects how girls see themselves, and directly influences how they relate to both other girls and to boys. In the book she describes one interview with Evie, a typical middle-school girl who is keenly obsessed with pointing out the girls at school who are "sluts." Evie is learning the rules, or scripts, about sexuality. She explains to Orenstein, that sex "ruins" girls but it enhances boys; that boys have far fewer constraints than do girls; that sexual behavior for girls is containable, but for boys it is inevitable and excusable: "Boys only think with their dicks" (Orenstein 1994). Girls who fail to follow the scripts, who dare to complain about them, or who confront a boy who is pressuring them for sex, learn quickly that it is *their* reputations that are on the line. "The thing is, we don't have control," Evie explains. "He could just say that we were asking for it or that we wanted it. Then everyone will think we're sluts" (Orenstein 1994).

Given the strong gendered sexual scripts in U.S. society, it is not surprising that the study of human sexuality by the National Opinion Research Center (1994) and the University of Chicago found significant differences between men and women in their sexual behavior, as shown in Figure 4.1. In their national survey with a representative sample of 3,432 adults, men reported thinking about sex more often and having more sexual partners than did women. Men and women also reported different motivations for sexual behavior. With respect to sexual intercourse, men reported the desire for sexual pleasure, conquest, and the relief of sexual tension more often than women, who were more likely than men to emphasize emotional closeness and affection (Michael et al. 1994).

It is possible, however, that differences in self-reported sexual behavior are exaggerated. One study conducted at Ohio State University found that women do not always answer surveys about sex honestly, but give answers they believe are expected of them. Men and women were asked about their sexual attitudes and behaviors under several different testing conditions, including being connected to a lie detector. Women's answers

FIGURE 4.1 **Number of Sexual Partners Since Age 18 Reported by Males (left) and Females (right) Aged 18–59 (Percent)**

Source: Adapted from Michael et al. 1994.

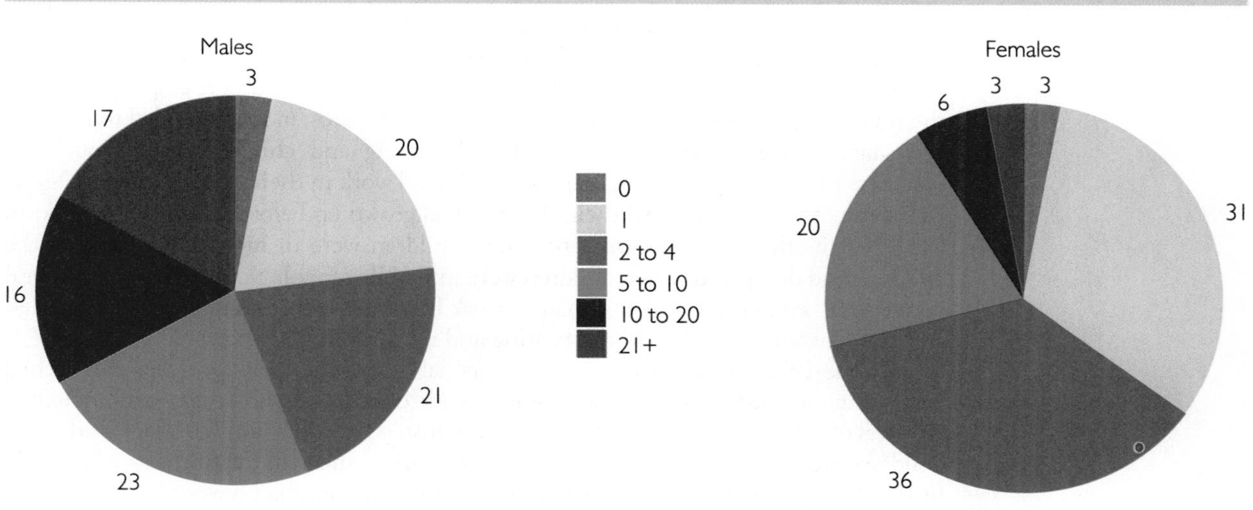

were similar to men's when they thought their lies could be detected by the machine (Science Daily 2003).

Implications for Families

While gender is forged into all aspects of social life, it is particularly evident within families and close relationships. Generally, who initiates a date, pays for it, chooses the activity, and drives? Who proposes marriage? Who earns the most money in a relationship, and interrelatedly, who does the most housework and childrearing? Who initiates sex? Who has the most power?

Jesse Bernard, the late sociologist who continued to be a prolific writer into her 90s, first introduced the idea of *his-and-her marriage* (Bernard 1972). She suggests that husbands and wives often have very different perceptions of their marriage, and they experience marriage and intimacy differently. Family scholars have come to acknowledge that the family is a gendered institution, meaning that gender organizes the way that families are organized, the way in which members interact, their practices, and the distributions of power. Most facets of daily family living, including taking care of the children, the division of household labor, decisions about where the family will reside, and employment practices, are not the same for women and for men. Feminists point out that families are structured toward male privilege, referring to the advantages, prerogatives, and benefits that systematically accrue to men.

The chapters throughout this text will highlight the gendered aspects of family relationships, and reveal how such macro issues as patriarchal customs and interpersonal power function to shape the microstructure of personal relationships. The text will examine seemingly everyday issues of dating and mate selection, the dynamics in marriage, childrearing, juggling work and family, and aging, as well as crises such as domestic violence, divorce, and repartnering. The following is an example that examines gender dynamics associated with labor market participation and earnings.

How Sex and Gender Matter: Income and Earnings

Women's position in the U.S. labor market also reflects the patriarchal nature of society. As discussed in depth in Chapter 11, since the late nineteenth century when records began to be kept, women's participation in the labor market has increased markedly while men's participation has remained roughly even at 75 percent.

Much of this increase is due to the rise in the number of mothers employed outside the home for pay. During the 1940s through the mid-1970s, mothers tended to organize their labor force participation around childbearing and childrearing, although researchers can see the increasing importance of paid work in their lives. In the 1940s and 1950s they tried to wait until their children had grown up before returning to work; in the 1960s mothers tried to wait until their children were in high school; and by the 1970s, it had dropped to when children were in middle school. Nonetheless, the general convention was, unless a mother had to work because of dire economic circumstances, employment was secondary to the bearing and rearing of children.

By the 1970s, a new pattern of mothers' labor force participation was entrenched and has continued. Today, most mothers work outside the home for pay, including mothers of infants and preschoolers. However, instead of continuing to adapt work to fit childbearing, the reverse has occurred. Childbearing and childrearing was adapted to fit the demands of work. Families delayed having children, had fewer of them, and an increasing number of women and men chose not to have children at all. Thus, a macro condition of changing norms surrounding womens' employment led to microlevel changes in the structure of families.

During this period Americans also witnessed a dramatic restructuring of the U.S. economy. We moved from a family-based economy, with the household as the primary unit of economic production, to an developed society in which we primarily rely on wages from work done outside the home. While once the country was heavily dependent on raw materials and manufacturing, today the U.S. economy is heavily geared toward the provision of a wide range of services from medical care to the food and entertainment industries. Wages have declined, and families increasingly rely on two paychecks to make ends meet. Today, about 59 percent of women aged 16 and older are employed for pay, as are 73 percent of men (U.S. Department of Labor 2006c).

How do female workers fare compared to their male counterparts? Figure 4.2 reports women's earnings as a percentage of men's earnings between 1951 and 2005, among persons who work full-time, over an entire year (Bureau of Labor Statistics 2006a). The data reveal that overall, employed women earn 81 percent of what men earn, at $585 per week, on average, as compared to $722 for men. The trend is moving toward equality, but the same statistics show it is an increase of only 17 percentage points since 1951. The bureau's numbers show the pay gap is somewhat higher for older workers, because the wages of men tend to increase as they age more quickly than do women's. The pay gap is also higher for white than minority women.

What accounts for the pay differentials? Realistically, differentials could be due to several factors, including **labor market segmentation**, which is that men and women often work in different types of jobs with distinct working conditions and pay. Women tend to work in less prestigious, nonunionized, and lower-paying jobs than men (Bureau of Labor Statistics 2006a). They are likely to be found working as secretaries and in other administrative support occupations, elementary school teachers, or service workers. To

FIGURE 4.2 **Women's Earnings as a Percentage of Men's, 1951–2005 (full-time)**

Source: Bureau of Labor Statistics, 2006a.

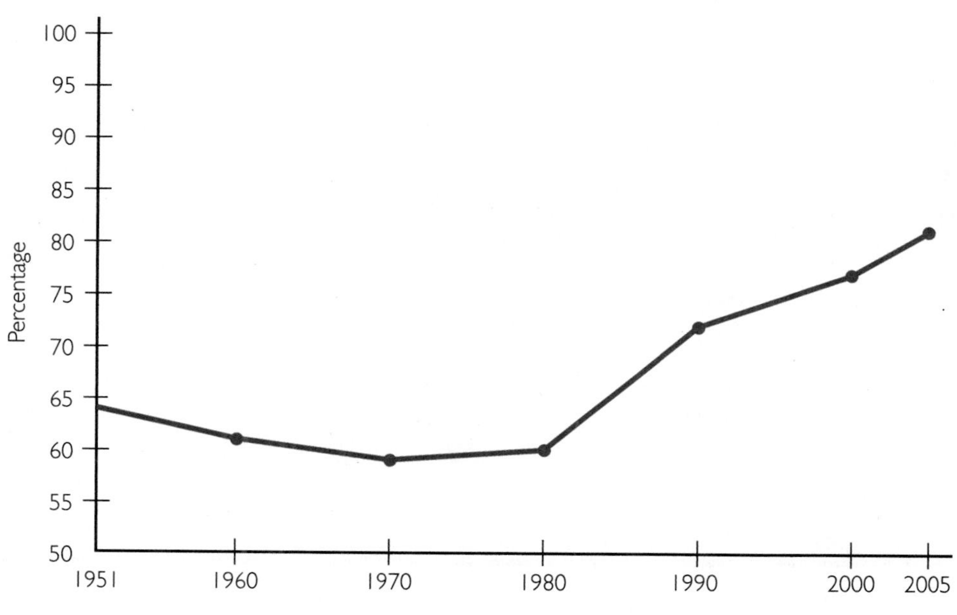

eliminate sex-segregated jobs in the United States, about half of male (or female) workers would have to change occupations.

Table 4.2 examines the 20 most popular occupations of employed women in the United States, reporting the median weekly earnings and comparing these to men's earnings in these same selected occupations. The table reveals that, even in these top 20 occupations, pay differential persists. In fact, pay differentials exist in almost all categories provided by the U.S. Bureau of Labor Statistics (2006f), including among such female-dominated occupations as registered nurses, elementary school teachers, and social workers, where women earn 92, 89, and 88 percent of men's income, respectively. One notable exception is among computer support specialists, where women earn 105 percent of men's earnings. Thus, there is more than just labor market segmentation going on.

TABLE 4.2 **Leading Occupations of U.S. Employed Women, 2005 annual averages**

Occupations	Women (%)	Women's Median Usual Weekly Earnings[1] ($)	Ratio of Women's Earnings to Men's Earnings (%)
Total	46	585	81
Secretaries and administrative assistants	97	559	85
Cashiers	76	322	83
Registered nurses	92	930	92
Elementary and middle school teachers	82	813	90
Retail salespersons	52	401	66
Nursing, psychiatric, and home health aides	89	385	95
First-line supervisors/managers or retail sales workers	41	525	73
Waiters and waitresses	72	332	86
Bookkeeping, accounting, and auditing clerks	91	551	95
Receptionists and information clerks	92	463	92
Childcare workers	95	330	—
Customer service representatives	69	505	81
Maids and housekeeping cleaners	89	328	84
First-line supervisors/managers of office and administrative support workers	70	656	82
Accountants and auditors	62	784	73
Teacher assistants	91	398	100
Office clerks, general	84	509	86
Cooks	42	314	90
Preschool and kindergarten teachers	99	520	—
Janitors and building cleaners	33	363	82

Note: Ranked by total number of women per occupation. Data not shown where base is less than 50,000.
[1]Wage and salary for full-time workers.

Source: U.S. Department of Labor 2006f.

What do these findings mean? Despite the fact that women comprise nearly half of the labor market, their share of earnings continues to lag behind men's. Although there has been some improvement over the past 50 years, many women continue to make significantly less than their male counterparts. Occupations dominated by women tend to be low paying, indicating that "women's work" is undervalued. Even when working in identical occupations, it appears that women are less successful in negotiating higher salaries or in securing pay raises or promotions that would allow for parity with men. Moreover, the income differential does not go away with increased education: While men with doctorates averaged $1,544 per week in 2004, women with doctorates averaged only $1,188 (U.S. Department of Labor 2006a).

The Equal Pay Act was signed in 1963, making it illegal for employers to pay unequal wages to men and women who hold the same job and do the same work. Nonetheless, employers manage to circumvent the intent of the law. Women workers make important contributions to the livelihood of their families. However, if working women earned the same as men (controlling for the same number of hours, education level, age, union status, and living in the same region of the country), their annual incomes would rise by about $4,000, and poverty rates would be cut in half.

Social Policy and Family Resilience

Attitudes about sex and gender permeate all aspects of family relationships. Can policies that pertain to sex and gender—and in particular focus on reducing disparities—help to build stronger families? The following is a discussion of how family planning programs strengthen families by delaying the age at which young girls become mothers; yet these critical programs are often politicized, and therefore are currently in jeopardy.

Family Planning Can Make a World of Difference

Family planning efforts have a tremendous and direct impact on the quality of women's lives throughout the world. Many women and girls in developing nations are pulled out of school at very young ages to marry and give birth. It is not uncommon for girls to marry at age 12 and have a baby soon thereafter. These young children are poorly equipped physically, socially, psychologically, and economically to raise the next generation of children and, with little education, their opportunities for work, independence, and self-determination are crushed.

Postponing childbirth among young women increases their chances of receiving a good education, which is vital to their social, political, and economic empowerment. Family planning information and availability are crucial for women to improve their status in society and to receive better health care, nutrition equal to men, and enable them to participate fully in their country's economic and political processes.

Moreover, each year more than 585,000 women die due to pregnancy-related causes. Family planning can reduce maternal mortality by 25 percent by reducing the number of high-risk pregnancies, by allowing women to space pregnancies further apart, or by eliminating pregnancies too early in a woman's life. This will promote child survival by reducing the risks associated with childhood malnutrition and disease. Family planning programs also have been found to reduce the need for abortion. For example, the introduction of modern contraception in Hungary coincided with a 60 percent reduction in abortions. Similar results can be seen in Chile, Colombia, Mexico, South Korea, Kazakhstan, Ukraine, and Russia (USAID 1999).

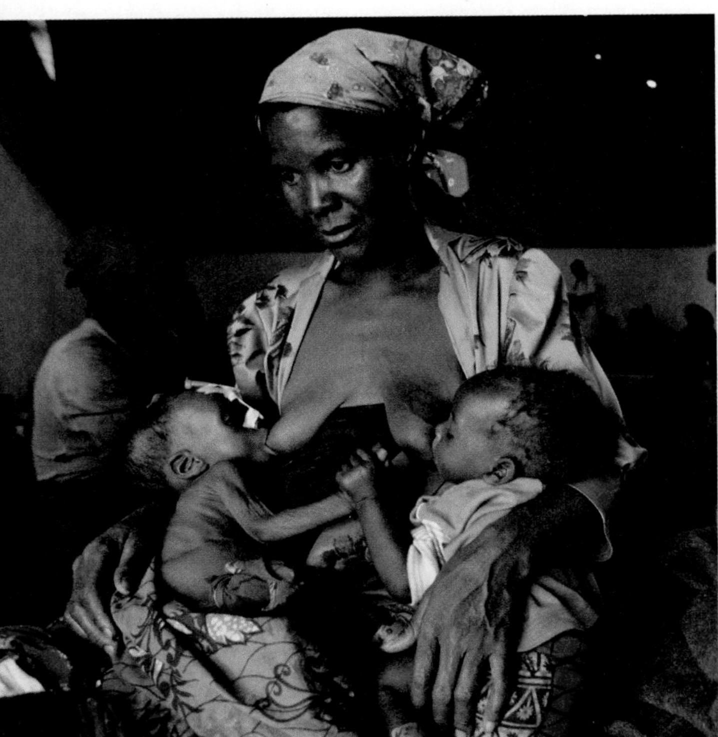

Family planning services for women around the world can dramatically increase their chance of receiving an education, which is vital to their social, political, and economic empowerment. Yet, rather than using U.S. resources to help, the "global gag rule" blocks family planning funds from going to any organization that may include abortion as a part of its program, no matter how small a component it is.

International family planning efforts limit the spread of HIV/AIDS diseases, which affected 39.5 million people living with HIV in 2006, to which young people are particularly susceptible (UNAIDS 2006a, b). Half of all new infections are among 15- to 24-year-olds. Worldwide, women are considerably more susceptible to the virus than men due to a combination of biological, social, and economic factors. In sub-Saharan Africa the overall rate of infection among girls and young women was 3 times that of boys their age (UNAIDS 2006a). The prime minister of Mozambique commented that (Abaid 2003):

> This is not because the girls are promiscuous, but because nearly three out of five are married by age 18, 40 percent of them to much older, sexually experienced men, who may expose their wives to HIV/AIDS. Abstinence is not an option for these child brides. Those who try to negotiate condom use commonly face violence or rejection.

For more than 30 years, the United States has supported international family planning programs that provide crucial family planning information, technology, and reproductive health services to 60 countries in some of the poorest regions of the world. U.S. involvement has empowered many women and girls to significantly improve their life options and allowed them to take better care of themselves and their families. Former Secretary of State Madeleine Albright said (USAID 1999):

> International family planning . . . serves important U.S. foreign policy interests: elevating the status of women, reducing the flow of refugees, protecting the global environment, and promoting sustainable development which leads to greater economic growth and trade opportunities for our businesses.

Despite the significant positive effects on millions of women and girls worldwide, family planning assistance has been reduced in recent years. On his first day in office, President George W. Bush reinstated a rule that denied U.S. assistance to all organizations that provide abortion services, counsel their patients on their options for abortions, refer their patients for abortion services, or educate their communities about or lobby their governments for safe abortion with their own, non-U.S. funding. This has been nicknamed "the **global gag rule**," and it has effectively eliminated millions of dollars targeted toward family planning programs that have nothing to do with abortion, but instead focus on abstinence, condom use, or other methods of birth control. In addition, President Bush blocked a congressionally approved $34 million contribution to the United Nations Population Fund (UNFPA) in July 2005 on the grounds that the agency was providing assistance to China's health ministry, which has indirectly supported coercive abortions in some countries (Lobe 2003).

The concern is that taxpayer funds should not be used to pay for abortions in other countries. However, since 1973 the Helms Amendment has banned the use of U.S. taxpayer money for abortion overseas, rendering this concern unnecessary (Planned Parenthood Federation of America 2003). The Bush administration takes this policy further by stating that money will not go to agencies that present abortion as an option or that use their own money for abortion services, even if U.S. money is actually spent on one of the many nonabortion-related programs offered. Planned Parenthood (2003) opposes this policy, and suggests:

> What's at the heart of the global gag rule is the attempt by U.S. anti-choice policymakers to attach strings to international family planning funds in order to stifle family planning and abortion-related activities in other countries, even if the activities are legal. As a result, countless individuals will suffer. Currently, more than 150 million couples would like to plan their families but lack the tools to do so. Penalizing family planning organizations because they use their own money to provide legal abortion services exacerbates this shortfall, leading to more unintended pregnancies, and in turn, more abortions.

What are some of the consequences of the global gag rule? It is impossible to precisely quantify the social, economic, and health costs; however, several examples include:

- In Nepal, over $700,000 has been lost for family planning, safe motherhood education, and contraceptive services.
- In Cambodia, over $3 million has been lost for HIV prevention, adolescent sex education, and counseling.
- In Albania, $242,000 for improving the reproductive health of women in Kosovo and counseling for young people has been lost.
- The Kenya Family Planning Association, which operates 14 health clinics that provide family planning positions, breast cancer screening, and annual pap smears to low-income women, has had its funding cut by 20 percent and has closed three clinics, which served 56,000 clients.
- In Ghana, nearly 700,000 clients lost access, not only to family planning services, but also to voluntary counseling and testing and HIV/AIDS prevention education.
- The St. Lucia Planned Parenthood Association was forced to cancel plans to train 218 "peer helpers" from eight secondary schools and one primary school. This program would have reached 12,000 school-age children with information about HIV prevention and sexual and reproductive health. (Feminist Majority Foundation 2002; Held to Ransom 2003; Planned Parenthood 2003).

Family planning programs and reproductive rights can improve the quality of women's lives in innumerable ways. Having access to reproductive health and family planning services can elevate women's social, economic, and political status throughout the world. Reproductive rights are far more than a personal issue; they are intertwined with historical, cultural, economic, and political forces, and have important ramifications for these as well.

Conclusion

Virtually all social institutions, whether political, religious, economic, educational, or familial, distinguish between men and women in fundamental ways that extend far beyond biological sex differences. However, gender is largely a social construction, and a comparative approach reveals that expected masculine and feminine behaviors are not uniform historically and cross-culturally. Several key agents of socialization are responsible for teaching gender norms, such as families, toys, schools, peer groups, and the mass media. Throughout the world people are obsessed with perceived differences between men and women, and these perceptions often become the basis for how power is distributed. Patriarchy is manifested in different forms around the world, and, despite thinking to the contrary, it persists in western nations, including the United States. The ways in which sex and gender are rooted in the U.S. social structure have critical implications for how families are constructed and how family members interact, and will be revealed in the upcoming chapters.

Key Terms

Clitoridectomy: A form of genital cutting or mutilation in which the clitoris is cut out of the body. (p. 113)

Double standard: Men are allowed more permissiveness in sexual behavior whereas women are more likely to be socially punished for their sexual experiences. (p. 120)

Gender: The culturally and socially constructed differences between males and females found in the meanings, beliefs, and practices associated with femininity and masculinity. (p. 99)

Gender socialization: Teaching the cultural norms associated with being male or female. (p. 102)

Global gag rule: Denies U.S. assistance to all organizations that provide abortion services, counsel their patients on their options for abortions, refer their patients for abortion services, or educate their communities about or lobby their governments for safe abortion with their own, non-U.S. funding. (p. 126)

Hermaphrodites: Persons born with both male and female genitals. (p. 99)

Hidden curriculum: Informal school curriculum that teaches gender socialization. (p. 106)

Infibulation: The most extreme form of genital cutting or mutilation in which the clitoris and vaginal lips are cut or scraped away, and the outer portion of the vagina is stitched together. (p. 113)

Intersexed: A person whose anatomical categories are not easily identifiable. (p. 99)

Labor market segmentation: Men and women often work in different types of jobs with distinct working conditions and pay. (p. 123)

Sex: Biological differences and one's role in reproduction. (p. 99)

Sexual scripts: A social construction that provides the norms or rules regarding sexual behavior. (p. 119)

Sharia: Radical interpretations of Islamic law being used to establish extreme and punitive rules by which Muslims are governed. (p. 114)

Socially constructed: Values or norms that are invented or "constructed" in a culture; people learn these and follow the conventional rules. (p. 99)

Transgendered: Persons who feel comfortable expressing gendered traits associated with the other sex. (p. 101)

Transsexual: Persons who undergo sex reassignment surgery and hormone treatments, either male to female, or female to male. (p. 101)

Resources on the Internet

Human Rights Watch
www.hrw.org
Human Rights Watch is an independent, nongovernmental organization, supported by contributions from private individuals and foundations worldwide. It works to prevent discrimination, to uphold political freedom, to protect people from inhumane conduct in wartime, and to bring offenders to justice. They investigate and expose human rights violations and hold abusers accountable and challenge governments and those who hold power to end abusive practices and respect international human rights law.

Planned Parenthood Federation of America, Inc
www.plannedparenthood.org
Planned Parenthood Federation of America, Inc., is the world's largest and most well-known voluntary reproductive health care organization. Founded by Margaret Sanger in 1916 as the United States' first birth control clinic, Planned Parenthood believes in everyone's right to choose when or whether to have a child, that every child should be wanted and loved, and that women should be in charge of their own destinies.

Institute for Women's Policy Research
www.iwpr.org
The Institute for Women's Policy Research (IWPR) is a public policy research organization dedicated to informing and stimulating the debate on issues of critical importance to women and their families. IWPR focuses on issues of poverty and welfare, employment and earnings, work and family issues, health and safety, and women's civic and political participation.

National Organization for Women
www.now.org
The National Organization for Women (NOW) is the largest organization of feminist activists in the United States. NOW has 500,000 contributing members and 550 chapters in all 50 states and the District of Columbia. Since its founding in 1966, NOW's goal has been to take action to bring about equality for all women. NOW works to eliminate discrimination and harassment in the workplace, schools, the justice system, and all other sectors of society; secure abortion, birth control, and reproductive rights for all women; end all forms of violence against women; eradicate racism, sexism, and homophobia; and promote equality and justice in our society.

Further Reading

Andersen, M. L., and P. H. Collins. 2006. *Race, Class and Gender: An Anthology*, 6th ed. Belmont, CA: Wadsworth.

Clayton, O., R. B. Mincy, and D. Blankenhorn. (Eds.) 2003. *Black Fathers in Contemporary American Society*. New York: Russell Sage Foundation.

De Beauvoir, S. 1989. *The Second Sex*. New York: Vintage.

Friedan, B. 2001. *The Feminine Mystique*. New York: W. W. Norton & Co.

Hertz, R., and N. L. Marshall. (Eds.). 2001. *Working Families: The Transformation of the American Home*. Berkeley: University of California Press.

hooks, B. 1984. *Feminist Theory: From Margin to Center*. Boston: South End Press.

Inglehart, R., and P. Norris. 2003. *Rising Tide: Gender Equality and Cultural Change Around the World*. New York: Cambridge University Press.

Messner, M. 2002. *Taking the Field: Women, Men, and Sports*. Minneapolis: University of Minnesota Press.

Roth, L. M. 2006. *Selling Women Short: Gender and Money on Wall Street*. Princeton, NJ: Princeton University Press..

Rothchild, J. 2006. *Gender Trouble Makers: Education and Empowerment in Nepal*. New York: Routledge.

Sax, L. 2006. *Why Gender Matters: What Parents and Teachers Need to Know About the Emerging Science of Sex Differences*. New York: Broadway.

Weitz, R. 2004. *Rapunzel's Daughter: What Women's Hair Tells Us About Women's Lives*. New York: Farrer Straus & Giroux.

Wharton, A. 2004. *The Sociology of Gender: An Introduction to Theory and Research*. New York: Blackwell.

Williams, C., and A. Stein. 2002. *Sexuality and Gender*. Oxford, UK: Blackwell.

CHAPTER 5

Social Stratification, Social Class, and Families

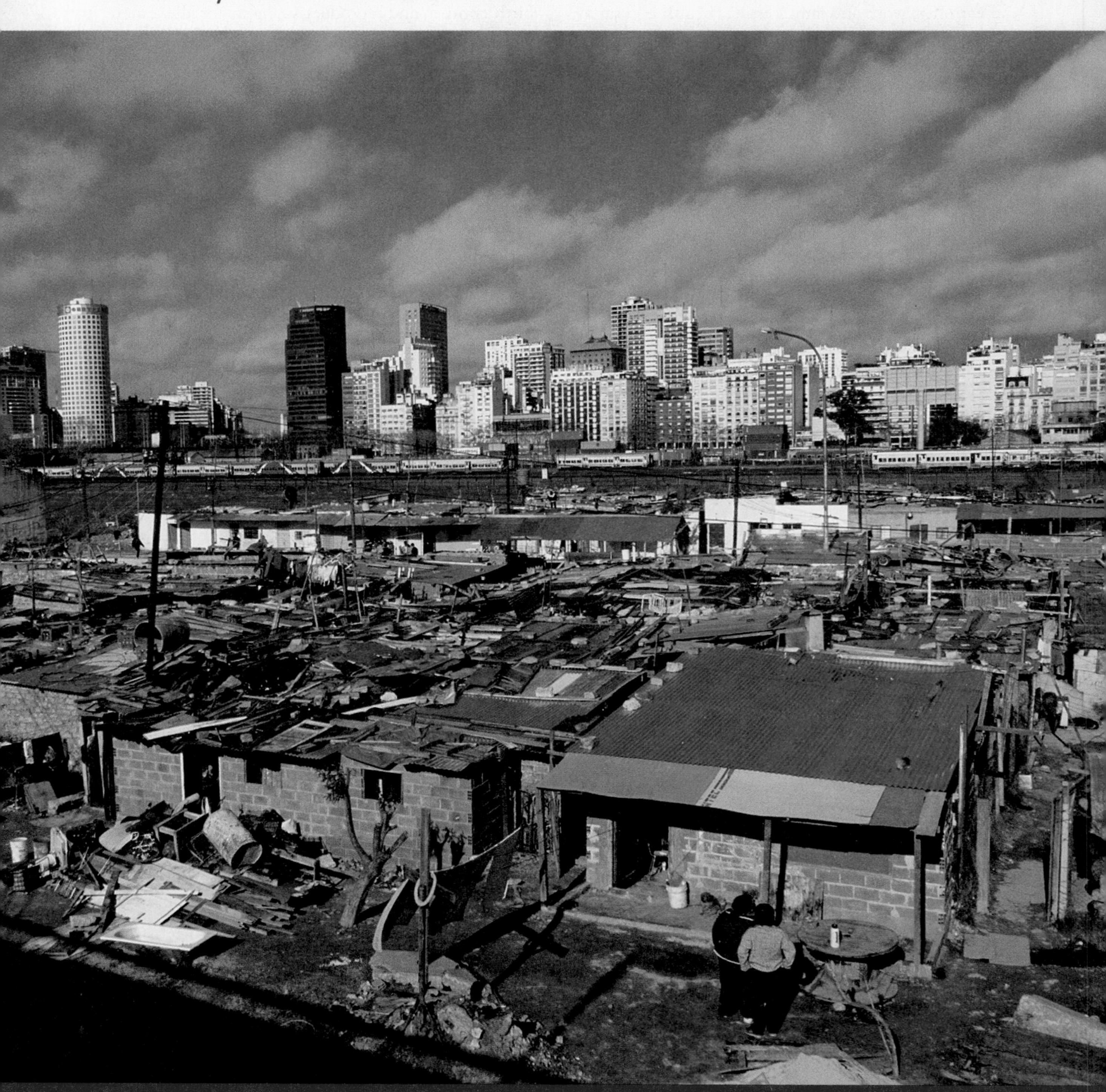

Chapter Outline

Chapter Preview

How does your social class position shape your family and intimate relationships? This chapter introduces the concepts of social stratification and social class and explores the many ways that class is interwoven with families. How would your life be different if you had been born among the richest of families or among the poorest? In this chapter you will learn:

- How social class influences your family relationships
- The difference between caste and social class, and a theoretical understanding of these systems
- Features of the social class system in the United States, from the upper class to the underclass
- How health and health insurance are class-related
- How poverty is defined and measured in the United States, and how this compares to other countries
- Differing perspectives on the causes of poverty
- The consequences of poverty for adults and children
- How building and improving social policy can build family resilience
- How the earned income tax credit is an important antipoverty strategy

Is it really possible to live and survive on minimum-wage work? Many adults work in jobs that service the rest of us and earn less than $7.00 an hour for their efforts. Barbara Ehrenreich, with a doctorate in biology and the author of several books, decided to answer this question. She went undercover as an uneducated, inexperienced, job-seeking housewife to see if it is really possible to live on minimum-wage work. Her plan was to visit three different cities (Florida, Maine, and Minnesota) with some money (around $1,000) plus a car to see if it would be possible to get a job and make enough money to live on. The jobs she took included waitress, house cleaner, hotel maid, and Wal-Mart clerk. In most cases, she made around $6 or $7 per hour and had no benefits. Ehrenreich takes us on an incredible journey inside a desperate world where few middle-class persons have ventured, except for perhaps a brief stint while in college. Although she maintains some advantages (she doesn't start out totally broke, she rents a car, she always has an ATM card to fall back on if she runs out of money for food or housing, she has no children, and she can walk away anytime she wants), she vividly describes the debasing and dangerous work that millions of women and men do every day. For example, while working for the Merry Maid company, she experiences firsthand the toll on the body: she learns to scrub all floors on her hands and knees and to strap vacuum cleaners on her back. Merry Maids spend their day bending, squatting, reaching, lifting, and scrubbing away grime, dirt, and feces. Nonetheless, little attention is paid to germs. The maids' focus is on mere cosmetics, and so maids may use the same wet rag on the toilet as they do on the kitchen countertops. The work is demeaning. Maids are not allowed to eat, drink, or use the bathroom for hours. When a fellow maid sprains her ankle, the boss demands, "Work through the pain!" Homeowners treat the maids no better. Ehrenreich learns to keep a steady supply of aspirin available to combat the pain and muscle fatigue.

What does her 2-year journey into the lives of the working poor reveal? She itemizes the wages she made at each job, along with her living expenses. With each job, her take-home pay minus expenses left her with less than $10 a week for savings or miscellaneous spending. Housing costs consumed most of her pay. There was virtually no money left for the investment needed to "pull herself up by her bootstraps." Many people who work in these jobs must take a second low-paying and demeaning job if they have any realistic hope of improving their circumstances even slightly. Ehrenreich's main reason for carrying out the experiment was to see if her income could match her expenses "as the truly poor attempt to do each day" (Ehrenreich 2001, 6). She demonstrates that it cannot be done and shows the economic, physical, and emotional vulnerability experienced by low-wage workers.

It is really an accident of birth that determines many things about a person's life. **Ascribed statuses** that a person is born with, such as his or her sex, race, ethnic background, and social class, are important because they lay the groundwork for a wide array of opportunities, privileges, and constraints.

This chapter introduces the concepts of social stratification and social class. It explores how, like gender, one's social class position is interwoven with families and touches virtually all aspects of our lives. How would your values, opportunities, and family life be different if you had been born among the richest of families? Conversely, what if you were born among the poorest—for example, to a single woman on welfare? While the effects of social class on family structure and family dynamics are discussed in depth throughout the remainder of this book, it is important here to introduce these signature concepts and the ways in which they influence our most intimate of relationships.

Social Class and Family Relationships

From cradle to grave, social class standing has a significant impact on our lives. Briefly, class standing influences:

- **Health status, health insurance, and access to health care.** Persons in lower social classes have higher infant mortality rates and lower life expectancy, rate their health as poorer, and suffer more mental distress than do those who are more affluent (Adams et al. 2007). This is due to a variety of factors, including more dangerous working conditions, more stressful living environments, poorer diet, and a lack of health insurance that limits access to health care (Nord et al. 2005; Seccombe 2007b).
- **Gender expectations for boys and girls and men and women within the family.** More egalitarian roles are more likely to be found in the middle- and upper-middle-class groups, while both upper and lower classes tend to emphasize and exaggerate the differences between males and females. Parents in lower social classes tend to have a more traditional division of household labor, and socialize their children for more traditional family and work roles (Rubin 1994).
- **The values that parents socialize in their children.** Working-class parents are more likely to value conformity and obedience to authority in their children, whereas middle- and upper-middle-class parents tend to value creativity and self-direction (Kohn 1977). Sociologist Melvin Kohn suggests that these values reflect the kinds of jobs parents hold and assume that their children will hold as well. Working-class jobs are those that tend to involve working with one's hands or machinery. They generally do not reward or expect creativity and self-direction; rather, workers are expected to follow orders and not challenge authority. In contrast, middle- and upper-class parents tend to work at jobs that focus on people or ideas (and assume that their children will as well) and thus, creativity, problem solving, and critical thinking are more highly valued.
- **How parents interact with their children.** The **home observation of the measurement of the environment (HOME)** is a widely used tool to measure maternal warmth and learning experiences provided to the child and is associated with a variety of child outcomes. Poverty has a significant negative effect on the quality and stimulation of the home environment, even after controlling for the effects of other variables (Yeung et al. 2002). Impoverished parents are less nurturing, more author-

itarian, and use more inconsistent and harsh physical discipline as a family's economic situation worsens (McLoyd 1990). Parents with low and unstable incomes experience more emotional distress and see themselves as less effective parents than do parents with higher incomes. Moreover, although child abuse can occur in any type of household, poor children have a higher probability of being abused, neglected, and injured more severely by the abuse than do their more affluent peers.

- **The likelihood of attending and graduating from college.** Persons growing up in the middle or upper class are more likely to attend college than are individuals growing up in working-class or poor families. Families earning $75,000 a year or more are about three times more likely to have a child between the ages of 18 and 24 attend college than are families earning $10,000 a year. Although some of the difference is due simply to economics, much of the difference is due to dissimilar values regarding college, poorer preparation because of overcrowded and underfunded schools, and the different structural constraints associated with being able to devote oneself full-time to such pursuits. Persons from the lower classes may know few people, if any, who have gone to college, and therefore may not value a college education or see that it is worth the time and expense.
- **Dating and premarital sexual expectations and behavior.** On average, teenage girls and boys from lower social classes begin dating at earlier ages than their middle- and upper-middle-class counterparts. Moreover, they are more likely to have a child outside of marriage (Alan Guttmacher Institute 2004). Once pregnant, they are less likely to have an abortion than are girls from middle- and upper-income families.
- **The likelihood of marriage and age at first marriage.** The relationship between class and the likelihood of marriage is complex. Although most people do marry, upper-middle-class women are less likely to marry than other groups, and when they do marry, they do so at later ages. However, a significant number of poor women also do not marry or marry late because of the limited availability of men they consider to be "good prospects" (Edin and Kefalas 2005). Poor women value marriage and have a desire to marry, but they have low marriage rates because the men they are likely to encounter are also poor and often do not have steady jobs (Wilson 1987).
- **Income and how money is spent in the family.** Consumption patterns vary by social class. Poor and working-class families spend virtually all of their money on food, shelter, and basic necessities. Most of their income is spent trying to make ends meet; therefore, they have little disposable income (Edin and Lein 1997; Hays 2003). Even holidays such as birthdays or Christmas can strain the family budget. Families in middle and upper classes have more disposable income for family outings, vacations, and holiday spending. These types of events can add spontaneity and fun to an otherwise repetitive daily routine (Seccombe 2007a).
- **Hobbies and pastimes within families.** How do you spend your free time—bowling or playing golf? Should we have Sunday dinner at my brother's house or at a restaurant? Social class influences the way in which we view leisure, the time and opportunities we have to participate in leisure activities, and with whom we share time. Working-class and poor families often spend more time together than do families in higher social classes and rely on each other for material and social support (Rubin 1994; Seccombe 2007a).
- **The types of stresses experienced and coping mechanisms employed.** Families in lower social classes face additional economic and social stresses because their jobs are less stable, offer less pay, and fewer benefits. Finances and budgeting are a common family stressor. Poor families worry about the most basic of needs, including an inadequate food supply (Siefert et al. 2004). Families in higher social classes have a wider range of coping strategies available to them such as travel, shopping, or working off stress physically in athletic clubs, whereas lower-income individuals may resort to

coping mechanisms that provide a more immediate gratification, such as smoking or overeating.

It is important to recognize that social class interacts with other statuses and dimensions of stratification. A person is not simply rich, poor, or somewhere in the middle. Social class interacts with sex, and with race and ethnic background to shape one's experience. A person is not simply working-class, but a working-class Hispanic woman; a Chinese American upper-class man; a black middle-class boy; or a poor white girl.

The social class in which we are born has an enormous impact on our life. How do you think the privileges and opportunities for the children in these two families differ, simply because of the social class of their parents?

What Is Social Stratification?

Social class differences can be perplexing because most Americans believe that the United States provides nearly equal opportunities for everyone. Nonetheless, it is clear that U.S. society is highly stratified and is becoming more so (Economist.com 2004). Some people earn extremely high wages or have amassed great wealth, while other families are struggling to meet their basic needs for food, shelter, and clothing. Ameri-cans like to think of themselves as a **meritocracy**, where financial and social rewards are based on their abilities, education, and skill sets, but the United States is turning its back on these ideals. For example, 30 years ago, the average real annual compensation of the top 100 chief executives was $1.3 million dollars: 39 times the pay of the average worker. Today it is $37.5 million, over 1,000 times the pay of the average worker (Economist.com 2004). Are top executives really a thousand times more able, more educated, and more skillful than the people they work with?

Money is one dimension of inequality, but so are power and occupational prestige. **Social stratification** refers to the hierarchical ranking of people within society on the basis of coveted resources. Some people have more or less of these resources than do others.

Caste and Class Systems in a Comparative Perspective

Generally speaking, there are two distinct types of stratification systems found throughout the world. In a **caste system**, social stratification is based on ascribed characteristics that one is born with, such as race, ethnicity, or family lineage. There is little or no opportunity for **social mobility** or movement in the stratification system based on individual effort or achievement. For example, in traditional rural Indian villages, caste members generally stay with their "own kind"; they work, marry, and socialize only with other members of their caste. Caste membership is handed down from parent to child, regardless of the child's talent, skill, beauty, or education.

Social class, in contrast, is a system of social stratification that is based on ascribed statuses from both birth and individual achievement. Social class segments the population into groups that broadly share similar types of resources, similar lifestyles, similar values, and a generally shared perception of their collective condition.

Social class is an obscure concept because there is no universally agreed-upon division, and we cannot immediately identify which people belong to which class. Boundaries are theoretically open so that people who gain schooling, skills, or income may experience a change in their social class position. Nonetheless, we know that social classes exist in a hierarchy and are generally based on some combination of income, wealth, occupational prestige, and educational level, although schools of thought, and particular societies, may emphasize one resource over another.

Conceptualizations of Class: Marx and Weber For Karl Marx, a nineteenth century German economist and philosopher, social classes are social structures formed by an historical and dynamic social process that resulted from one's relationship to the means of production. All groups in society must engage in the collective endeavor of economic production to stay alive. However, it is an endeavor fraught with conflict. The capitalist class, or the **bourgeoisie**, owns the means of production. They own the land and money needed to operate factories and businesses. Meanwhile, the **proletariat** represents those individuals who must sell their labor to the owners to earn enough money to survive. The conflict can be either open or covert, but it is always inherent in the production process, according to Marx.

Max Weber, in contrast, did not conceptualize social class as rooted in the production process. He took a multidimensional approach, emphasizing (1) **wealth**, which is the value of all of a person's or a family's economic assets, including income, real estate, stocks, bonds, and other items of economic worth, minus debt; (2) **prestige**, which is the esteem or respect a person is afforded; and (3) **power**, defined as the ability to achieve goals, wishes, and desires even in the face of opposition from others. Class is a combination of these subjective factors. In other words, noneconomic factors, such as the status that comes from educational attainment or family background, are also important causal factors in the determination of class standing.

Example: Social Class in Great Britain

A concept such as "social class" can be conceptualized differently across cultures. For example, in Great Britain social class refers to a well-known and long-established official classification scheme based on *occupation*. Beginning in 1911, and revised somewhat since then, the British government, health researchers, academics, and others routinely divide the population into broad, hierarchical groups to examine the variation in social and health issues within the population. A quick look at a governmental census document may include a breakdown of the population by social class. Unlike most class systems that tend to be implicit, such as in the United States, the British system is a sanctioned social class scheme in which the government finds value in making explicit gradients in the population.

The architect of the social class system in Great Britain was T. H. C. Stevenson, a medical statistician in the country's General Register Office who was interested in mortality and fertility. Stevenson argued that occupation was more important than income or wealth in explaining the lower mortality of the wealthier classes. He suggested that one's occupation develops and reflects an approach to culture, which in this case includes attention to health and hygiene. *Culture* includes a broad array of attitudes, behavior, lifestyles, personal choices, and values—in sum, an entire worldview. This worldview is associated with the type of job held more so than how much money or wealth the individual accumulates (although they may be highly correlated) (Rose 1995).

While individual occupations have been reallocated to different classes over the years, the overall shape of the model has changed very little since Stevenson's early work. The British population, based on data from the population census, is classified according to their occupation and occupational industry into six ordinal categories, or social grades:

- I Professional (e.g., accountants, engineers, doctors, professors)
- II Managerial and Technical/Intermediate (e.g., marketing and sales managers, teachers, journalists, nurses)
- IIIN Nonmanual Skilled (e.g., clerks, shop assistants, cashiers)
- IIIM Manual Skilled (e.g., carpenters, goods van drivers, cooks)
- IV Partly Skilled (e.g., security guards, machine tool operators, farmworkers)
- V Unskilled (e.g., building and civil engineering laborers, other laborers, cleaners)

The British social class system is a strategic way that the government (and therefore Britons) conceptualizes the population. Individual Britons are generally quite clear about where they fall in the system: "I'm a two," a schoolteacher would say.

Although there have been many attempts to modify the social class scheme, the scheme has changed little because there does appear to be evidence that occupation reflects a wide range of factors that influence health and social well-being. For example, Table 5.1 shows British social class differences in mortality, coronary heart disease, suicide and undetermined injury, lung cancer, and asthma, with persons in lower

TABLE 5.1 Rates of Selected Health Problems, Per 100,000 People, Great Britain

	Social Class[1]					
	I	II	IIIN	IIIM	IV	V
Mortality rates	280	300	426	493	492	806
Coronary heart disease	81	92	136	159	156	235
Suicide and undetermined injury	13	14	20	21	23	47
Lung cancer	17	24	34	54	52	82
Wheeze in the past 12 months, 1996	18[2]	—	20	22	23[3]	—

Notes:
[1] I Professional; II Managerial & Technical; IIIN Skilled, Nonmanual; IIIM Skilled, Manual; IV Partly Skilled; V Unskilled
[2] Classes I and II combined
[3] Classes IV and V combined

Source: Lung and Asthma Information Agency 2000.

social classes having a much greater incidence of these problems than do persons in the higher social classes.

What is particularly striking about the British system of classification is how explicit and sanctioned it is. This is contrary to the way Americans view social class. Americans try to ignore class differences, although everyone knows that they exist on some level. There are pros and cons to making social class gradients explicit or keeping them implicit, but the result is the same; some people are considerably better off, and it is not always due to merit.

Social Class in the United States

Unlike Great Britain, it is less clear how many social classes exist in the United States. Politicians in the 2004 presidential and 2006 midterm elections spoke of the middle class as though it were one very large and homogeneous group.

Although it might be most correct to think of class as a continuum, for practical purposes most people think of classes as ordinal categories. What makes up a class? Americans tend to think of social class as some vague combination of education, occupation, and income, and we sometimes call this **socioeconomic status (SES)**. No single measure of social class exists, nor is there agreement on how many social classes actually exist. Moreover, clear-cut class boundaries have eroded over the past 50 years as institutional footings have been loosened by social changes, such as the shift from an industrial to a service economy that relies heavily on higher education. When Americans are asked what class they belong to, most reply that they are in the middle class. Interestingly, both poor people and rich people may respond this way. One U.S. congressman, making over $200,000 a year, told a reporter that he was in the "lower middle class." The idea that we are all middle class reflects our historical roots—many settlers from Europe were fleeing the rigid stratification systems in their home countries. In the 1780s, Hector St. John De Crevecour wrote in *Letters of An American Farmer*, that "the rich and the poor are not so far recovered from each other as they are in Europe" (Vance-Granville Community College 2003).

Dennis Gilbert and Joseph A. Kahl have developed one model of social class based on SES that I will draw upon here (Gilbert and Kahl 1993). Their model includes six categories: (1) the upper class; (2) the upper middle class; (3) the middle class; (4) the working class; (5) the working poor; and (6) the underclass. However, the U.S. government rarely, if ever, uses these categories. Unlike Great Britain, virtually the only standardized measure is the federal government's poverty line, which is discussed later in the chapter. The estimates here are drawn from data from the July 2006 Congressional Budget Office, reported by the Center on Budget and Policy Priorities (Sherman and Avon-Dine 2007).

The Upper Class

This is the wealthiest and most powerful social class in the United States, and consists of only about 1 percent of the population. Although this class is small in number, its members have a tremendous influence upon the economy and the rest of society (Domhoff 2005). Their members may have very high incomes (averaging nearly $900,000 in 2004 [Sherman and Avon-Dine 2007]), but more importantly, they own substantial wealth. They may be entrepreneurs, sit on the boards of major corporations, or may get involved in politics by either running for office or by serving in key policy positions. The income of the upper class varies tremendously. Some have virtually no income, because the money is inherited rather than earned. Others earn millions of dollars each year in salaries or stock options. However, despite the influence of the upper class, less is known about their private lives because they have been able to insulate themselves from others (Kendall 2002).

Socialite Paris Hilton exposes the excesses of the very rich. Her privileged upbringing as heiress to the $300 million Hilton hotel fortune and her frenzied partying make her seem like a perfect subject for *Lifestyles of the Rich and Famous.*

Some families have been wealthy for generations. Names like Rockefeller, Kennedy, or Hilton come to mind. These individuals and their families have been nicknamed "upper-upper class," "old money" or "bluebloods." As described in Box 5.1, they may belong to the exclusive *Social Register*, an annual listing of elites that has been published since the late 1800s. The book advertises itself as ". . . the definitive listing of America's most prominent families, serving as an exclusive and trusted medium for learning about and communicating with their peers." Members, including recent political figures John Kerry and George Bush, have significant wealth, belong to exclusive clubs, are involved in philanthropy, and have considerable corporate, military, and political power (Domhoff 2005). Their children attend private prep schools and Ivy League colleges, where applicants are carefully screened. As sociologist G. William Domhoff (2005) writes:

> From infancy through young adulthood, members of the upper class receive a distinctive education. This education begins early in life in preschools that frequently are attached to a neighborhood church of high social status. Schooling continues during the elementary years at a local private school called a day school. The adolescent years may see the student remain at day school, but there is a strong chance that at least one or two years will be spent away from home at a boarding school in a quiet rural setting. Higher education will be obtained at one of a small number of heavily endowed private universities. Harvard, Yale, Princeton, and Stanford head the list. . . . The system of formal schooling is so insulated that many upper-class students never see the inside of a public school in all their years of education. This separate educational system is important evidence for the distinctiveness of the mentality and lifestyle that exists within the upper class, for schools play a large role in transmitting the class structure to their students.

There is very little mixing with other social classes. For example, the Debutante Ball, which brings together unmarried young men and women to meet and socialize in a series of elegant parties, teas, and dances, carefully controls even dating and mate selection so that it is almost castelike. Researcher Susan Ostrander interviewed members of the upper class, and asked them how they perceived their class position. One respondent told her, "I hate to use the word 'class.' We are responsible, fortunate people, old families, the people who have something." Another respondent revealed, "I hate 'upper class.' It's so non-upper class to use it. I just call it 'all of us,' those who are wellborn" (Ostrander 1980).

Other members of the upper class, sometimes nicknamed the "lower-upper class" or "new money," have acquired their great wealth within one generation. They often earned their money in business, entertainment, or sports. Despite their vast material positions, which may be ostentatiously displayed, they lack the prestige of bluebloods. Microsoft founder Bill Gates, entertainer Oprah Winfrey, and homemaker extraordinaire Martha Stewart are examples of persons who have amassed great wealth within one generation; they may not be completely accepted by those with old-time wealth. Nonetheless, Americans tend to look upon these persons favorably. They are seen as successfully fulfilling the American Dream and they reinforce the idea that the United States is a land of opportunity.

BOX 5.1 Using the Sociological Imagination

The *Social Register*, Class or Caste?

Is the United States really an open class system or is it more of a caste? Read the following discussion and decide.

Many middle-class people think of themselves as dominating the political and social landscape—they are, after all, the largest social class group. The middle class seems to receive the most attention at election time from politicians clamoring for votes. However, size is not to be confused with power.

The upper-upper class, the true "bluebloods," is a close-knit group that wields considerable power in society. Some even suggest that they form more of a caste than a social class because membership is based on ascription—being born into the right family—rather than achievement. As presidential candidates George W. Bush and John F. Kerry reveal, being born to families of certain means enabled them to attend the most prestigious schools that are virtually training grounds for the elite.

To illustrate their tight and cohesive bonds there is even a book listing fellow members of this privileged group. The *Social Register* has been published since 1887, and today lists about 40,000 families (*Social Register* 2003). Some may dismiss the book as nothing more than a glorified phone book—"a group of pals, really" says one entrant; others use it as an important resource to ensure that their children are socializing with others who share their economic and political interests. The *Social Register* is a powerful reminder that, for the upper class at least, ascription rather than achievement is fundamental to membership in the upper echelons of the upper class.

The *Social Register* describes families, not simply individuals. This is because most members are not known for their individual accomplishments, but are listed because of their family connections. Names include Kennedy, Roosevelt, Rockefeller, and Forbes. The families are mostly white. Listings describe the exclusive prep schools and colleges that family members have attended, the social clubs to which the family belongs, and women's maiden names so that their family lineage can be identified.

Noticeably absent are the occupations of its members. This is because individual achievements are largely irrelevant to membership. The "new rich"—people who have earned their wealth—are generally excluded. Instead, they may be listed in *Who's Who*—a book that focuses on achievement rather than ascription. The *Social Register* does not celebrate the rags-to-riches stories, but rather concentrates on those elite families who have amassed great fortunes that are passed down from generation to generation and who seem to have all the trappings of true pedigree. Old money and ancestry is what it takes to be considered for the *Social Register*.

Source: Hastings 2000.

CRITICAL THINKING QUESTIONS

1. Do you think that the upper-upper class is really a class or is it a caste?
2. How does the *Social Register* help these families insulate themselves from the rest of society?
3. Should wealth, power, and prestige come from ascription or achievement? How would you ensure that it comes from one rather than the other?

The Upper Middle Class

Approximately 15–20 percent of the U.S. population is categorized as upper middle class. Persons in this group are often highly educated professionals who work as physicians, dentists, lawyers, college professors, or business executives. They see their work as a career, not simply a job, and resulting from years of college and professional schooling. Careers are often central features of their lives, and distinctions between work and leisure may become blurred. Household income may be in the rough range of $100,000 to

$200,000, and perhaps more if both husband and wife are employed, which is increasingly the case. Part of the reason for the increasing gap between the upper middle class and the lower social classes is the greater likelihood that both husband and wife are employed in well-paying careers. They tend to have accumulated some degree of wealth through their jobs. Individuals in the upper middle class get married later and are more likely to delay (or forgo) having children because of education, careers, or leisure pursuits. They tend to have nice homes in well-respected neighborhoods within the community and play important roles in local political affairs. Education is strongly valued for their children: The vast majority of upper-middle-class children go on to college, and many continue into graduate education or professional programs as their parents did.

The Middle Class

Despite the rhetoric of being a middle-class society only about 40 percent of Americans fall into the middle class, with annual incomes of roughly $40,000 to even $100,000, if two adults are employed. The median annual household income in the United States was approximately $46,000 in 2005 for all households, and $66,000 for all married-couple households (DeNavas-Walt et al. 2006). Members of the middle class work in occupations that often require a college degree. Some occupations are classified as white-collar jobs such as nurses, teachers, lower- and mid-level managers, and many positions in sales or business. Some middle-class occupations include highly skilled blue-collar jobs, such as in electronics or building construction. Traditionally, middle-class jobs have been secure and provided avenues for advancement; however, with corporate downsizing, escalating housing costs, and a generally rising cost of living, many middle-class families find their lives considerably more tenuous than in the past. Thus, politicians respond to the concerns that middle-class families face. Young middle-class families may find it difficult to purchase their first home in many cities around the country, and older middle-class families find that saving for both retirement and their children's college bills stretches their budget beyond its means. However, they value home ownership and college educations for their children and hope for a secure retirement for themselves. Middle-class parents may make considerable effort and sacrifice to provide mobility resources for their children, such as limiting family size or having both parents working outside the home.

The Working Class

The title working class is misleading because most persons in other social classes work too. Other names for this group include blue collar, but that name is also misleading because some individuals in the working class hold white-collar jobs. Working class families earn less than do middle-class families, earning approximately $20,000 to $40,000 per year. About 20 percent of the U.S. population falls into this group. Some of these occupations may include those that require a short period of on-the-job training. Specific jobs may include salesclerks, factory workers, custodians, or semiskilled or unskilled laborers. Members of the working class report less satisfaction in their jobs than do those in higher social classes and experience less social mobility. Their jobs are often routinized and require conformity to external authority. Their work helps to form the basis for their childrearing values. They are more likely to place importance on traits such as conformity and obedience in their children rather than creativity or self-direction. Working-class individuals are often distrustful of or feel threatened by diversity. They are some of the fiercest opponents of gay and lesbian rights, affirmative action, and women's rights. Generally, working-class families live in modest neighborhoods and have some difficulty sending their children to college, although many would like to do so. Their lives are vulnerable, and family members often live from paycheck to paycheck, with little opportunity to amass savings. Families must budget carefully to pay their monthly bills, because unexpected doctor or car repair bills can wreak havoc on the family budget.

The Working Poor

The working poor account for about 15 percent of the U.S. population. Their wages hover around or slightly above minimum wage and may come up to about $20,000 per year. Jobs include service workers in the fast food, retail, or tourist industry, lower-paid factory jobs, or seasonal migrant labor. The opening vignette profiled a researcher going undercover to work in these types of jobs. Many of the working poor receive no fringe benefits such as health insurance or sick pay. Unemployment is common. A large component of the working poor include single mothers and their children. Some of these women intersperse work with bouts of welfare (Seccombe 2007a). It is a vicious cycle: They work in a variety of low-wage jobs with hopes for a better life, but the low wages and lack of benefits leave their families exceedingly vulnerable. They then seek the safety of welfare where at least they can get their families' basic needs taken care of, such as food, shelter, and medical care. Faced with the stigma and hardship of daily living on welfare they again obtain work, but soon find that their health and welfare benefits have been reduced or eliminated, and their families are vulnerable once more. There are many stresses in the lives of the working poor, because they live paycheck to paycheck in a constant struggle to make ends meet. Consequently, rates of domestic violence and child abuse are somewhat higher than for the middle or upper middle classes.

The Underclass

Gilbert and Kahl (1993) have defined this group, perhaps 3–5 percent of the population, as extremely poor and often unemployed. They suffer from chronic poverty, homelessness, and live outside the margins of society. Some cannot work because of disability or mental illness. Others face difficult employment prospects because they lack education and job skills. Many reside in the inner cities, where job prospects are few because factories and businesses have moved across town or overseas. Their circumstances are bleak, particularly those who suffer from mental illness. Their situations may be exacerbated by racial or ethnic discrimination.

The working poor, accounting for about 15 percent of the U.S. population, struggle to pay for food, shelter, and clothing on wages at or hovering only slightly above minimum wage. Many of the working poor must put up with the insecurity of shift work, minimal benefits, and impoverishing wages.

Some members of the underclass receive assistance from governmental welfare programs, perhaps drawing upon them for extended periods of time to live and survive. Others are ineligible for programs or do not know how to access them. Some beg for spare change during the day as people walk by and return to homeless shelters or sleep in parks at night. Children comprise 25 percent of the homeless population, and they and their parents are the fastest-growing segment of the homeless population, according to a study of homeless children in shelters in Los Angeles County. One study found that few homeless children escaped emotional, behavioral, and academic problems, and few received help for them (cited in Honberg 2003).

Social Mobility: Fact or Fiction?

Theoretically, Americans can be anything they want to be. Most Americans see nothing wrong with inequality of income because they believe there are opportunities for social mobility. Eight in 10 believe that although you may begin life poor, if you work hard, you can become rich (*Economist* 2006). This has been labeled *The American Dream.*

However, in reality there is little substantial upward social mobility. A study that compared the incomes of nearly 3,000 father-and-son pairs from 1979 to 1998 found that few sons moved up the social class ladder. Instead, nearly 70 percent of the sons remained either at the same level or were actually doing worse than their fathers. Upward mobility was primarily found at the highest income levels, with affluent sons moving even upwards from their fathers (Wysong 2003). Other researchers tend to find similar results: People usually live out their lives in the same social class from which they come. Moreover, a relatively large number of people today are worse off than their parents, while those who do better than their parents are disproportionately from the highest social classes to begin with. Why do you think this is? There is also growing evidence that the United States is less socially mobile than many other industrialized countries, including Germany, Sweden, Finland, and Canada (Beller and Hout 2006; Economist.com 2004; *Economist* 2006). Americans are mistaken if they believe they live in the world's most mobile society, where meritocracy rules.

One reason for so little social mobility is that the tools used for upward mobility are no longer as effective as they once were. For example, while education level is an important factor in social mobility, the education system is increasingly stratified by social class, and rich children have a distinct advantage. The elite colleges hold the keys to the best jobs, but getting into these colleges depends on far more than just grades. Most elite colleges have *legacy preferences*—a program for children of alumni—that far outstrip affirmative action programs for minority or poor applicants. In the most selective eight universities in the northeast, legacies make up between 10 and 15 percent of every class (Economist.com 2004). Meanwhile, federal Pell grants, which go to the poorest students, have been drying up. Is it any wonder that only the rich can attend expensive elite colleges? The median family income at Harvard, for example, is over $150,000, nearly three times the national average.

A second reason for so little upward mobility is that the U.S. tax structure increasingly favors rich families passing on their wealth to their heirs. This has not always been the case. Originally, one of the main purposes of taxes was to redistribute wealth so that it would not be concentrated into a few hands, be passed down through the generations, and erode the concept of meritocracy. Many early millionaires, such as Andrew Carnegie or the Rockefellers donated huge portions of their wealth to projects serving the public. Now, however, over 70 percent of Americans oppose the estate tax, which would tax extremely large inheritances after the death of the estate-holder, even though only 1 household in 100 pays it (*Economist* 2006). Repealing this tax would increase the federal deficit by over three-quarters of a trillion over its first decade (Center on Budget and Policy Priorities 2006). Although most Europeans would flatly oppose allowing the rich to transfer mass wealth to their heirs, Americans see this more favorably. "Americans want to join the rich, not soak them," reports an article in the *Economist* magazine (2006, 29).

The data are clear and unequivocal: The U.S. economy became pronouncedly more unequal over the past several decades, with the rich receiving a far greater share of the gains than those in the middle or lower incomes (Sherman and Avon-Dine 2007). Regardless of whether one looks at wages, household income, or spending, the benefits are skewed toward the wealthiest individuals and families. As shown in Figure 5.1, those with incomes in the highest fifth had an average after-tax increase of 69 percent in their incomes between 1979 and 2004. This increase is three times that of the middle fifth and over 11 times that of the poorest fifth. According to Sherman and Avon-Dine (2007), even more telling, those with the highest 1 percent of incomes had an increase of 176 percent between 1979 and 2004.

Nonetheless, most Americans tend to blame their financial problems not on the rich, but on the poor, and increasingly on illegal immigrants. Interestingly, despite Americans' positive attitude toward policies favoring amassed wealth, two of the world's wealthiest entrepreneurs, Bill Gates and Warren Buffett, have donated billions of dollars from their personal fortunes to public projects, similar in spirit to Carnegie and Rockefeller.

FIGURE 5.1 **Change in Real Average After-Tax Income: 1979–2004 (Percent)**

Source: Sherman and Avon-Dine 2007.

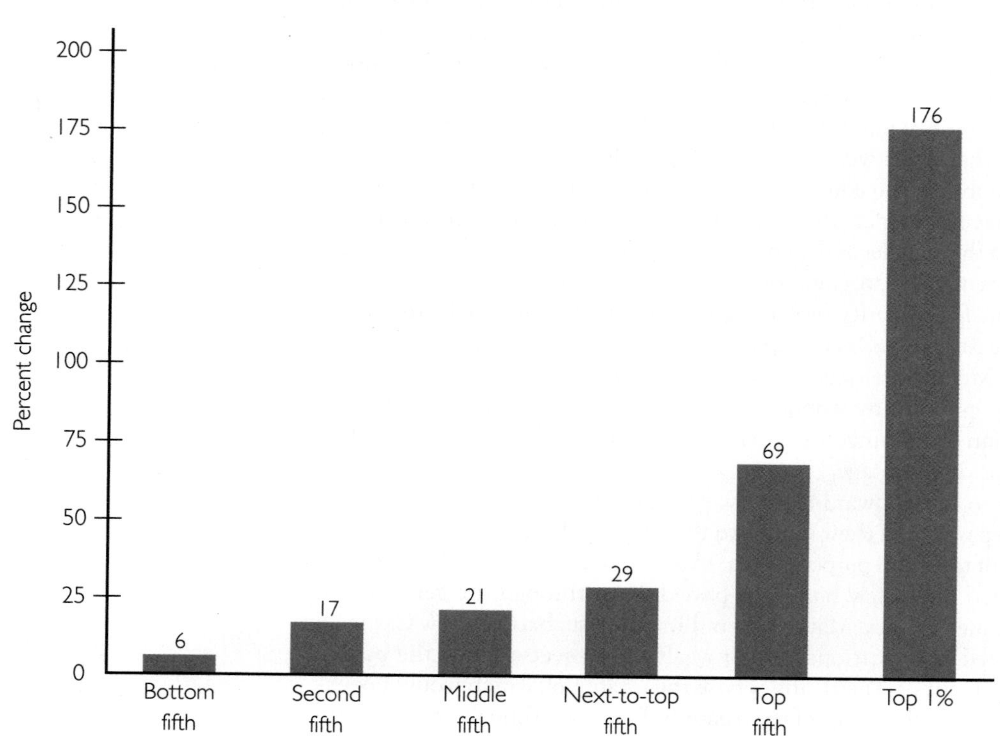

We have introduced many ways in which social class shapes values and opportunities. Let us examine one example in depth here: how social class affects health, access to health care, and ultimately family well-being.

Family Focus, How Class Matters: Health, Health Insurance, and Family Well-Being

The lack of health insurance is a serious and disturbing social problem in the United States because it is a primary mechanism for accessing health care services. About 47 million Americans, or nearly 16 percent of the population, had no health insurance at the time they were interviewed in 2005, and millions more were uninsured for part of the year (DeNavas-Walt et al. 2006). This does not include the many people who are *underinsured*—their high deductibles or copayments render their insurance virtually useless except in the most catastrophic conditions.

Although statistics point to the number or percentage of *individuals* without insurance, health insurance is a family matter, according to a report by the Institute of Medicine (Committee on the Consequences of Uninsurance 2002). If even one person within a family is uninsured, it can have dire financial, physical, and emotional consequences for the entire family. An uninsured mother may forgo expensive medical tests until she finds that her cancer has spread throughout her body and is now terminal. An uninsured father who has an emergency appendectomy may have to pay the costs himself, thereby exhausting all of the family savings. An uninsured child may not receive the routine immunizations and other well-child care needed to stay healthy, and therefore will be more susceptible to serious childhood diseases, causing unnecessary pain and suffering. Alternatively, these families may seek care, but join the other 20 million families who have problems paying off their medical debts, difficulty which then interferes with their ability to purchase food or pay their rent (May and Cunningham 2004; Seccombe and Hoffman 2007). About 60 million Americans are either uninsured themselves or live with at least one family member who is uninsured. The situation has become acute in recent years. Low-income families are particularly vulnerable, as shown in Figure 5.2, although it is becoming a serious problem at middle-income levels as well (DeNavas-Walt et al. 2006). Minorities also have higher than expected rates of being uninsured, with one-third of Hispanics lacking coverage.

Why is health insurance of such concern? Families without health insurance:

- Are more likely to delay or forgo seeking needed medical care. They are twice as likely to postpone seeking medical care, over four times as likely to forgo needed care, and are more than twice as likely to have a needed prescription go unfilled. They experience unnecessary pain and suffering (Dey and Bloom 2005).
- Have large **out-of-pocket costs**, meaning that they have to pay large sums of their own money for health care. For example, uninsured families pay 88 percent of their prescription costs and 47 percent of their costs for ambulatory care. Because of the limited income of most uninsured families, paying medical bills reduces money for other family necessities.
- Borrow to pay medical bills and risk bankruptcy. Medical bills are a factor in nearly half of all personal bankruptcy filings (Committee on the Consequences of Uninsurance 2002; Kaiser Commission on Medicaid and the Uninsured 2003).

In the United States, about 60 percent of Americans under 65 receive their health insurance through an employer (DeNavas-Walt et al. 2006). It is considered a fringe benefit of their employment and a supplement to their wages. However, employers are not

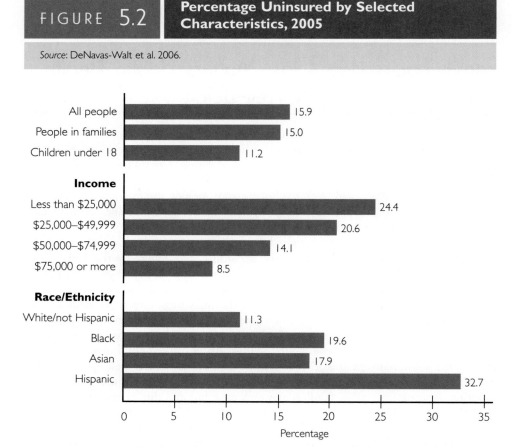

FIGURE 5.2 Percentage Uninsured by Selected Characteristics, 2005

Source: DeNavas-Walt et al. 2006.

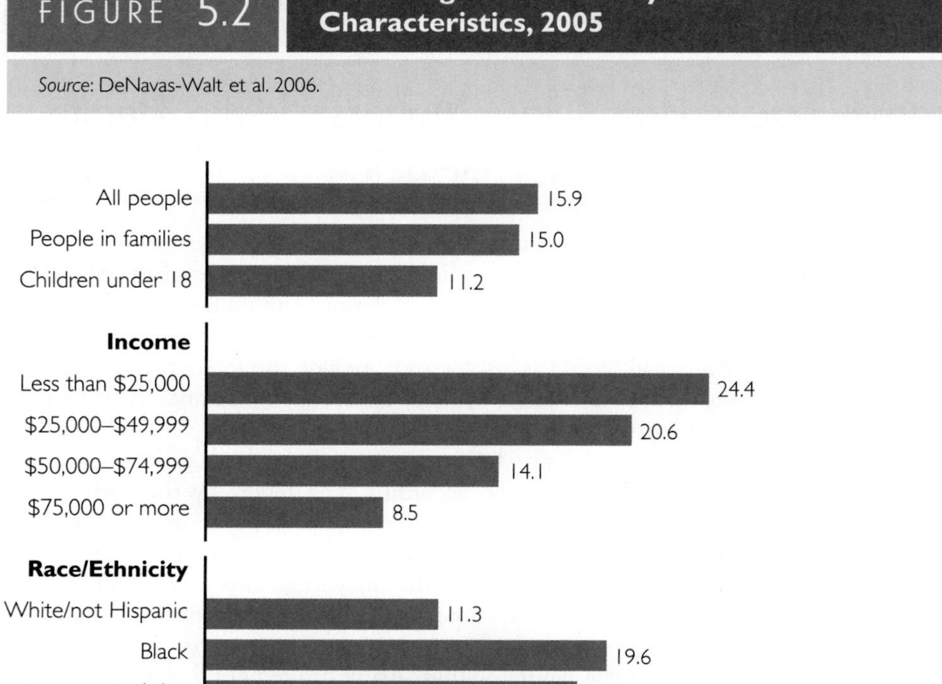

required to offer health insurance to their workers, and an increasing number are choosing not to do so because of rising costs. Low-income workers are at particular risk, as only 41 percent of workers earning less than $10 an hour have access to employer-sponsored insurance (Collins et al. 2004). Moreover, by virtue of their employment, they may not qualify for federal government programs, such as **Medicaid**, which is designed for the financially indigent who meet specific qualifications. Changing jobs or marital status can also put employer coverage at risk.

Asking employers to pay for the health insurance of their employees is virtually unheard of in other industrialized nations, as well as in many nonindustrialized ones. Instead, they have **national health insurance**. This means that access to health care is considered a public right of all citizens. It is viewed as a public good, like schools, police protection, and parks, and is therefore funded out of taxes and general revenues. Health care coverage is universal in these countries; virtually no one is uninsured. One consequence of the difference in coverage can be seen in that the United States has one of the highest maternal **mortality rates** (death rates) of any developed nation. This is because many uninsured women cannot get prenatal care—no doctor will see them (Population Reference Bureau 2006).

Ironically, universal coverage tends to be much less expensive than the U.S. system. For example, while the United States spends about 15 percent of its gross domestic product (GDP) on health care, Germany spends about 11 percent, Canada and France spend about 10 percent, and the United Kingdom, Japan, and Italy spend even less (Canada NewsWire 2004). Moreover, in each of these countries people are healthier; they live longer, and infant mortality is lower, on average.

Providing health insurance coverage to all family members can significantly improve the health, well-being, and financial security of families by:

- Increasing access to care for their children
- Improving children's access to routine well-child care
- Providing continued access to care for teens
- Fostering early intervention, which leads to better health outcomes for children with certain treatable conditions
- Leading to better access to care and better health outcomes for children with serious illnesses and disabilities
- Improving access to prenatal care and newborn care

Being without insurance is extremely stressful to families. They know that without insurance, they may not be able to get needed care. In in-depth interviews with mothers on welfare or families who have recently left welfare, I found that they commonly rated Medicaid as their most important benefit, more important than food stamps, subsidized housing, or even the welfare check itself (Seccombe 2007a; Seccombe and Hoffman 2007).

Families in Poverty

Conjure up a picture of a poor person and you will likely visualize someone who is on the fringes of society: inner-city unemployed black men, women on welfare raising numerous children, or mentally ill homeless persons begging for change on the street. If these are the images that come to mind, you are in for an awakening. Although inner-city black men, women on welfare, the homeless, and other stereotypically vulnerable groups comprise a significant portion of those in poverty, a surprising finding is that *most Americans will experience poverty and will turn to public assistance at some point during their lives*. As sociologist Mark Rank reveals, "rather than poverty and welfare use being an issue of *them*, it is more of an issue of *us*" (Rank 2003). Along with colleague Tom Hirschl, Rank used national longitudinal data to estimate the percentage of the American population that will experience poverty at some point during adulthood and the percentage that will use a safety net program, such as food stamps or cash welfare. They used an approach frequently used by health researchers who want to assess the risk of a particular disease such as breast cancer. They found that by the time Americans have reached age 75, 59 percent would have spent at least a year below the poverty line during their adulthood (Rank 2003). Moreover, approximately two-thirds will have received public assistance as adults for at least 1 year (Rank 2003). If poverty spells are this common, then why do we have so little understanding of poverty, its causes, and its consequences? Part of the reason is that poverty is generally examined by using **cross-sectional data**, which look at only one moment in time rather than looking at trends over time.

What Do We Mean by "Poor"?

Terms like poor, poverty, and impoverished are used a great deal in everyday conversation, but exactly what do they mean? How do we define these terms?

The Social Security Administration established the official **poverty line** in 1964 (Orshansky 1965) as a way to measure the number of people living in poverty and to assess how it changed from year to year. Survey data in the early 1960s indicated that families spent approximately one-third of their income on food. Therefore, the poverty line was calculated from the estimated annual costs of a minimal food budget designed by the U.S. Department of Agriculture (USDA), and then multiplied by three, a method that continues today. This food budget parallels the current Thrifty Food Plan, which forms the basis of Food Stamp benefits and is the least expensive food plan developed by the USDA (USDA 2006). It is far below the amount most middle-class families spend on food. Individuals or families with annual incomes below this established threshold are counted as poor. The poverty line varies by family size and the number of related children under age 18 living in the household. It is revised yearly based on inflationary changes in the Consumer Price Index. Thresholds are also different in Alaska and Hawaii to account for the increased cost of living (Cohen and Bloom 2005). The weighted average poverty line in 2005 was $19,971 for a family of four or $15,577 for a family of three (DeNavas-Walt et al. 2006).

Who Is Poor?

In 2005, 12.6 percent of the population, or 37 million people, lived below the poverty line, an increase of over 5 million people since 2000. Table 5.2 reports the degree of

TABLE 5.2 People and Families in Poverty by Selected Characteristics, 2005 (Percent)

Total U.S. Population		**12.6**
Age		
	Children Under 18	17.6
	18–64	11.1
	Elderly 65 and Over	10.1
Race		
	White (Non-Hispanic)	8.3
	Black	24.9
	Asian and Pacific Islander	11.1
	Hispanic	21.8
Region		
	Northeast	11.3
	Midwest	11.4
	South	14.0
	West	12.6
Family Type		
	Married Couple	5.1
	Female-Headed	28.7
	Male-Headed	13.0

Source: DeNavas-Walt et al. 2006.

poverty in the United States by age, race, region of residence, and family type. As shown, children are the age group most likely to be impoverished, at nearly 18 percent, a figure much higher than that for the elderly. Nearly one-quarter of African Americans are poor, with Hispanics close behind. Geographically, the south has the highest rates of poverty as compared to other regions in the United States. Finally, over one-quarter of female-headed families are impoverished, compared to about 5 percent of married-couple families.

What are the trends over time? Poverty declined significantly during the 1990s. Low-income workers benefited from a strong economy. Figures 5.3 and 5.4 reveal that poverty rates began increasing in 2000 among most age groups and across several racial and ethnic groups.

Can a family really make ends meet on a poverty-level budget? A budgeting exercise in Box 5.2 on page 151 illustrates the challenge.

Comparative Studies

Another means of addressing the scope of poverty is to compare the rates of poverty in the United States to those of other countries (Brandolini and Smeeding 2006; Rainwater and Smeeding 2003; Smeeding et al. 2000). Historically, precise comparisons have not been easy or straightforward, because measures of poverty vary from one country to another.

A comparison of poverty in the United States with poverty in other countries reveals that the United States is one of about 40 countries considered to be high income. Demographers use a *purchasing power parity conversion* that allows us to compare not only income differences, but also the purchasing power of that income (Taylor and Taylor 2004). Demographers convert a country's average annual income to *international dollars* that can indicate the amount of goods and services a person could buy in the United

FIGURE 5.3 **Poverty Status by Age: 1970–2005**

Source: DeNavas-Walt et al. 2006.

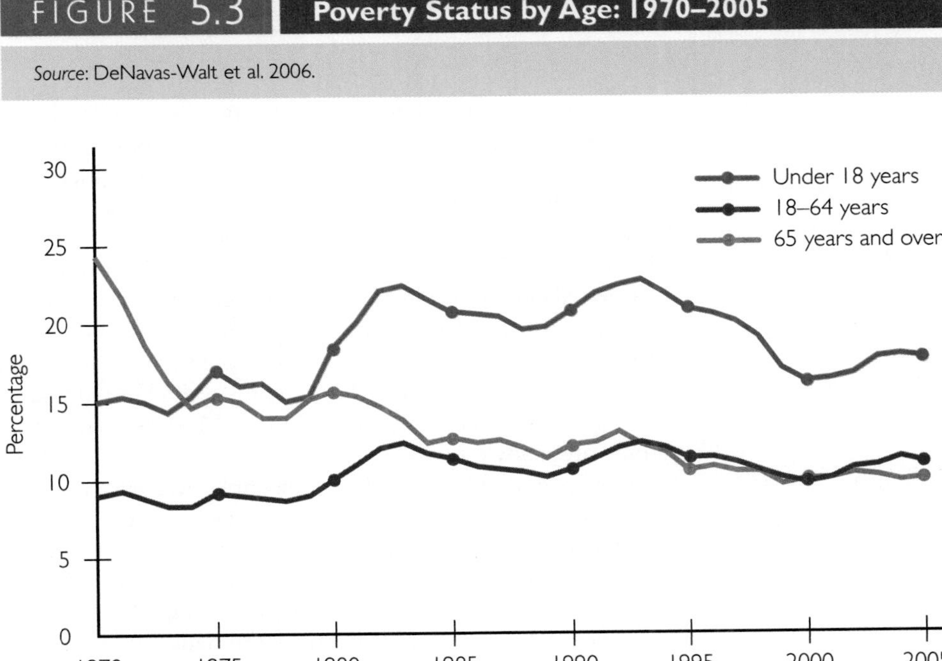

FIGURE 5.4 **Poverty Status of People by Race and Hispanic Origin: 1970–2005**

Source: DeNavas-Walt et al. 2006.

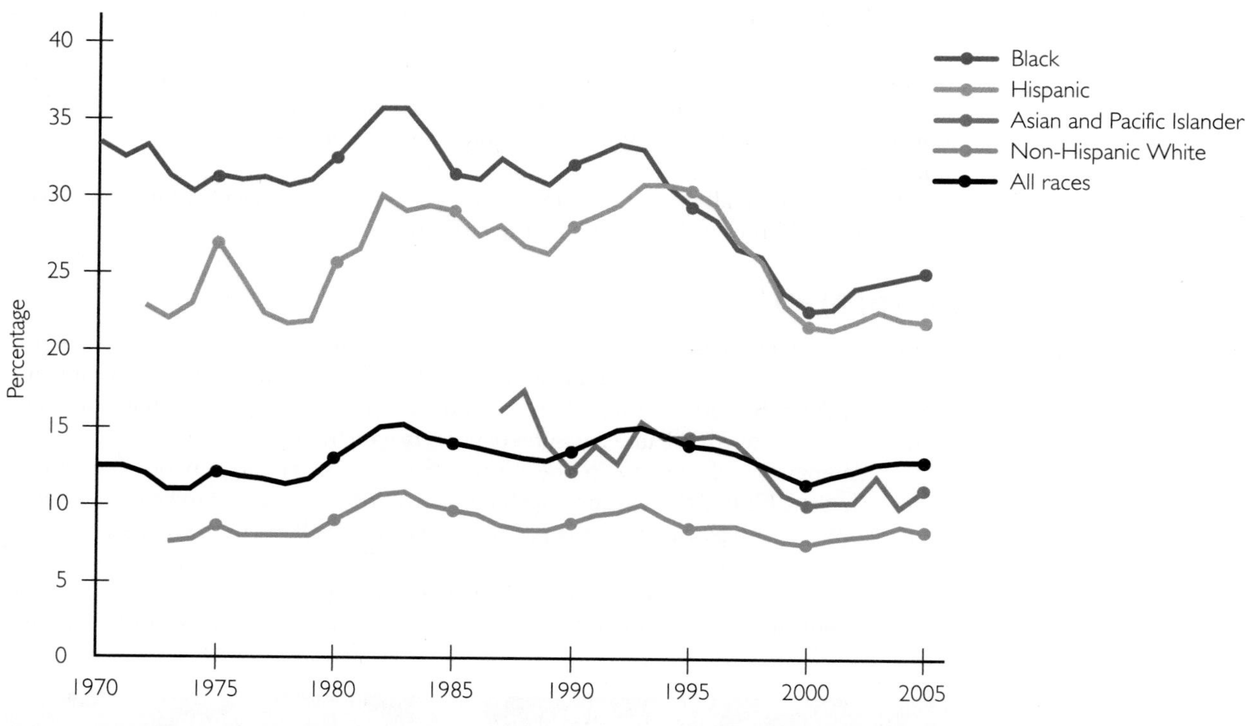

States. In more developed countries, such as Canada, the United States, Australia, and western Europe, this income comes to an average of $26,320 per person. People living in these countries tend to focus on **relative poverty**, which refers to the fact that some people lack basic resources relative to others in society. In contrast, **absolute poverty**, defined as the lack of resources such as food, housing, and clothing that is life-threatening, is characteristic of at least 60 low-income countries that are the home to roughly half of the world's people. In less-developed countries (excluding China), purchasing power parity averages only $4,100 per person. This means that, a person living in a country like India, Bolivia, Cambodia, or Nepal, would have, on average, an income equivalent to the purchasing power of $4,100 if living in the United States. (It does *not* mean that persons in these countries actually have $4,100 to spend.) Given that this is an average, there are many countries with a considerably lower purchasing power, as shown in Map 5.1 on pages 152 and 153. For example, the purchasing power of a person living in Tanzania, Africa, is only $660 dollars—meaning that he or she has the purchasing power for goods and services equivalent to someone in the United States living on only $660 per year. This clearly represents abject poverty. In stark contrast to this, the purchasing parity of a person in the United States is $39,710.

Box 5.3 on page 154 describes the daily life of a poor woman in Bhutan, a small country in Asia, and illustrates the toll absolute poverty can take; yet, while poverty painfully touches all aspects of life, the poor are not necessarily unhappy.

BOX 5.2 Social Policies for Families

Making Ends Meet on a Poverty Budget

The 2005 poverty line for a family of three averages $15,577 a year, which comes to about $1,300 a month (DeNavas-Walt et al. 2006). This means that a family with three people in it—a single mother and two children or two parents and one child—are only counted as poor if they live on less than $1,300 a month. If they live on more than this amount they are not counted as poor. Is this poverty line reasonable?

Could your family of three live on a poverty budget of $15,577 a year or $1,300 per month? Let's find out by examining a sample budget. These costs are from reports by the U.S. Department of Agriculture, the Center on Budget and Policy Priorities, and other consumer expenditure reports estimating the price of a "low-cost" food plan, the fair market rent for a two-bedroom apartment, the cost estimate for child care, and other expenditures. The cost of living varies somewhat from one community to another, so you may quibble over specific items in this budget. For example, maybe rents are higher (or lower) where you live than the estimate provided here. These are just sample estimates. Plug in figures that better represent costs in your own community if you feel that these are inadequate. The question is: Is it reasonable to assume that a family of three in the United States can live on $1,300 a month? Keep in mind that someone who works full-time, year round, at about $7.50 an hour would earn this amount. Many full-time workers earn considerably less, because the minimum wage in early 2007 remained $5.15 per hour.

Sample Expenses

Housing: (2 bedroom apartment and utilities)	$800
Food	$425
Child Care	$620
Health Care	$65
Clothing	$60
Transportation	$416
Miscellaneous	$100

TOTAL: $2,486/month or $29,832/year before taxes

Already we have gone way overbudget. What can we cut back on?

- A cheaper apartment or one in a less-desirable part of town? Don't forget that two children live here.
- Lower the utility bill by keeping the house colder? This is one reason why poor children are sick more often.
- Eliminate the telephone? This could be dangerous in times of an emergency.
- Cut back on toiletries? Toilet paper, shampoo, and tampons are basic needs.
- Eliminate car maintenance? How will the family get to work, school, or run errands? A bus system may not be available or feasible with children.

We are overbudgeted and we haven't yet included other basic needs for this family:

School Supplies	$25
Health Insurance	$300
Entertainment	$100
Laundry	$25

NEW TOTAL: $2,936/month or $35,232/year before taxes

Assumption: Even this revised budget assumes that the family already has a household set up. There is no money included to buy furniture, a car, or household items like towels or dishes. In other words, even $2,936 a month is unrealistically low.

As you can see, the poverty line is an inadequate measure of poverty. For all practical purposes, a family of three living on $1,300, or even $2,000 a month, is extremely vulnerable.

Source: Adapted from Seccombe 2007b.

CRITICAL THINKING QUESTIONS

1. What should the poverty line be based on? Should it be based on something other than the price of food? Should it remain three times the cost of a thrifty budget? What are the political implications of changing it?
2. How does a family make ends meet if a parent earns poverty-level wages?

MAP 5.1 Eye on the World: A Comparative Look at Purchasing Power Parity, in U.S. Dollars (2004)

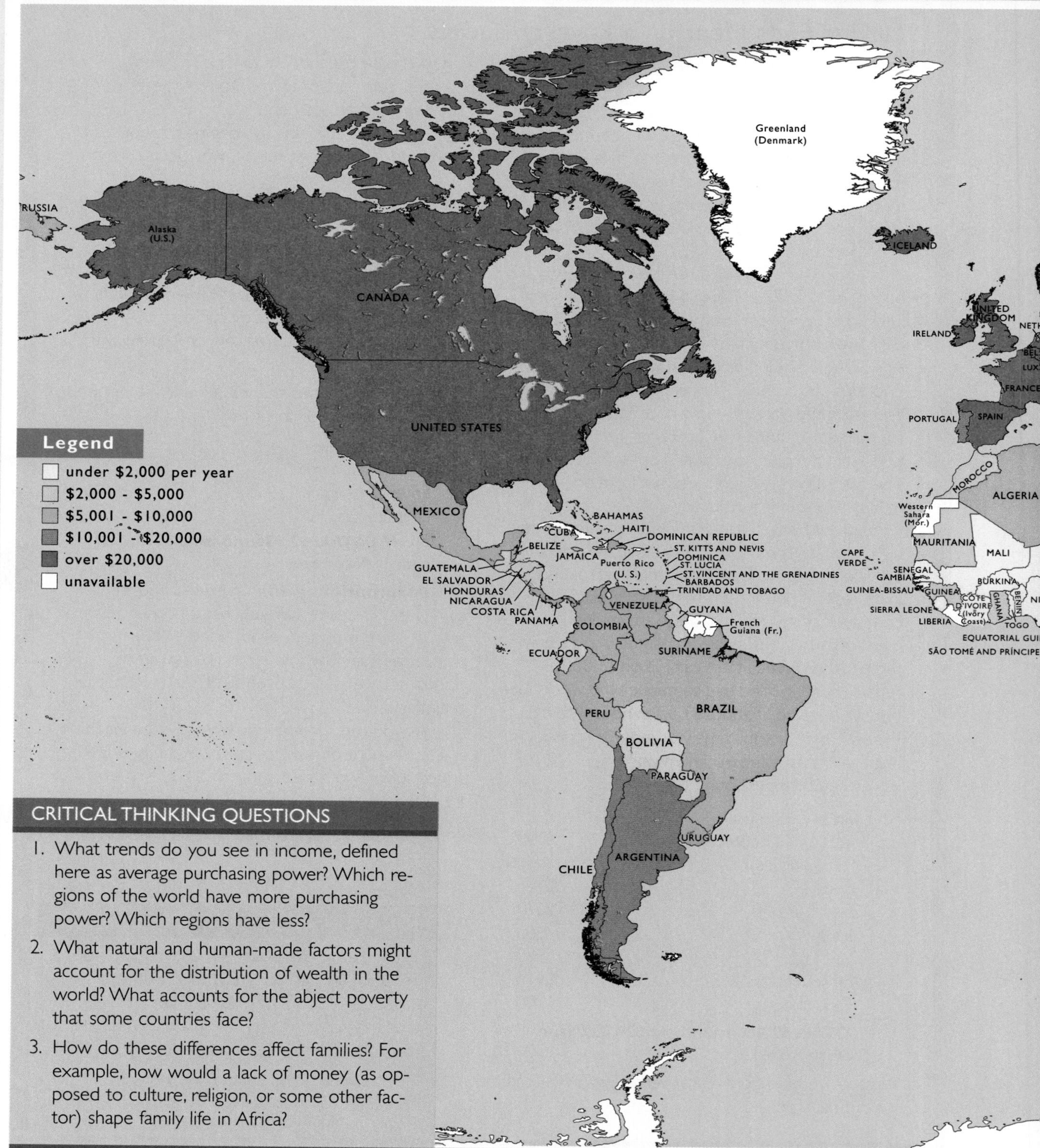

CRITICAL THINKING QUESTIONS

1. What trends do you see in income, defined here as average purchasing power? Which regions of the world have more purchasing power? Which regions have less?
2. What natural and human-made factors might account for the distribution of wealth in the world? What accounts for the abject poverty that some countries face?
3. How do these differences affect families? For example, how would a lack of money (as opposed to culture, religion, or some other factor) shape family life in Africa?

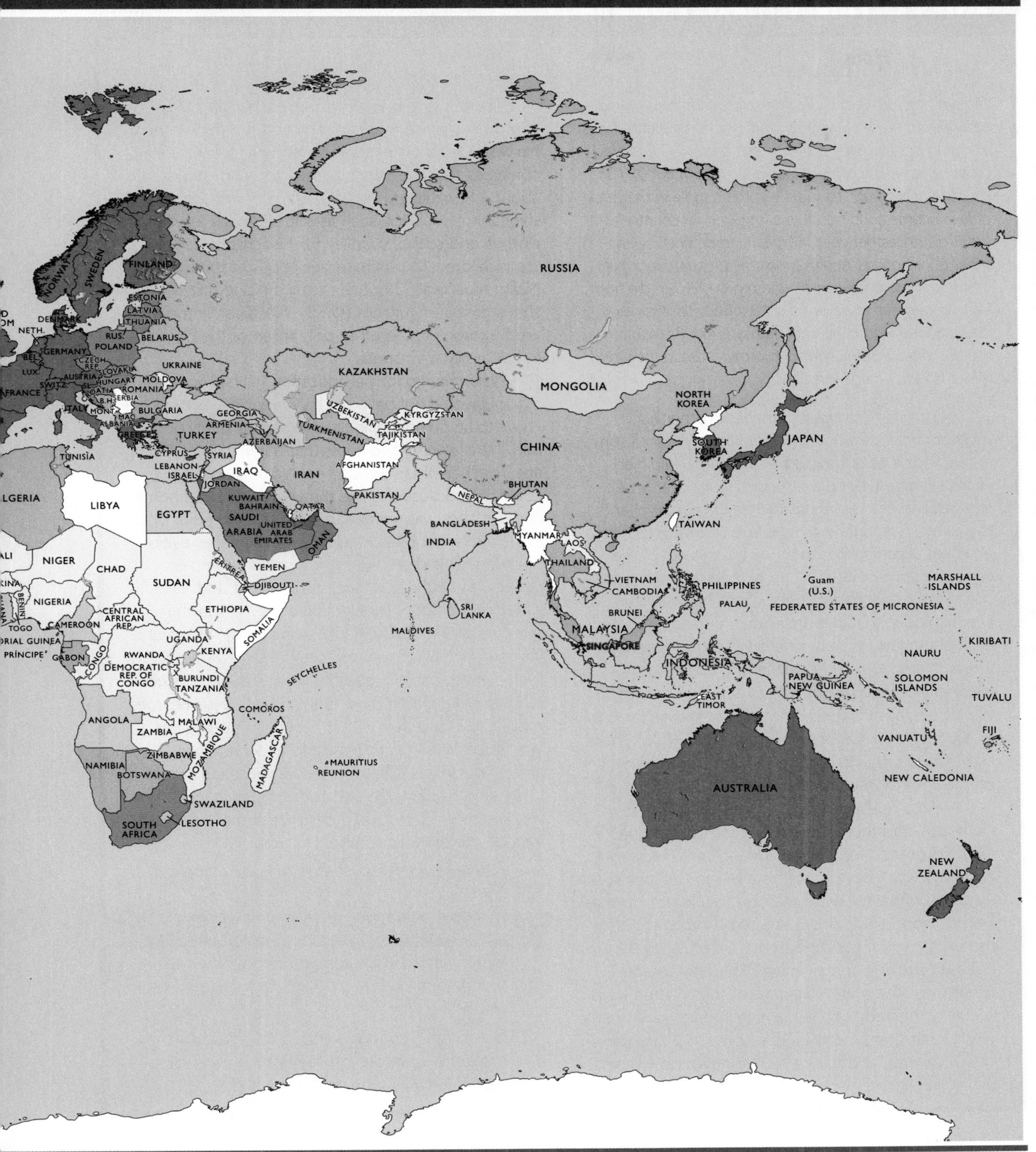
RUSSIA
FINLAND
SWEDEN
NORWAY
ESTONIA
LATVIA
LITHUANIA
DENMARK
NETH.
RUS.
BELARUS
POLAND
GERMANY
BEL.
LUX.
CZECH REP.
SLOVAKIA
AUSTRIA
UKRAINE
SWITZ.
HUNGARY
MOLDOVA
FRANCE
ROMANIA
SERBIA
B.H.
ITALY
MONT.
BULGARIA
MAC.
ALBANIA
GREECE
GEORGIA
ARMENIA
AZERBAIJAN
TURKEY
CYPRUS
SYRIA
LEBANON
ISRAEL
IRAQ
JORDAN
IRAN
KAZAKHSTAN
UZBEKISTAN
KYRGYZSTAN
TURKMENISTAN
TAJIKISTAN
AFGHANISTAN
PAKISTAN
MONGOLIA
CHINA
NORTH KOREA
SOUTH KOREA
JAPAN
TUNISIA
LIBYA
EGYPT
KUWAIT
BAHRAIN
QATAR
SAUDI ARABIA
UNITED ARAB EMIRATES
OMAN
YEMEN
NEPAL
BHUTAN
BANGLADESH
INDIA
MYANMAR
LAOS
TAIWAN
THAILAND
VIETNAM
CAMBODIA
PHILIPPINES
Guam (U.S.)
MARSHALL ISLANDS
PALAU
FEDERATED STATES OF MICRONESIA
SRI LANKA
MALDIVES
BRUNEI
MALAYSIA
SINGAPORE
KIRIBATI
NAURU
INDONESIA
PAPUA NEW GUINEA
SOLOMON ISLANDS
TUVALU
EAST TIMOR
FIJI
VANUATU
NEW CALEDONIA
AUSTRALIA
NEW ZEALAND
NIGER
CHAD
SUDAN
ERITREA
DJIBOUTI
NIGERIA
BENIN
TOGO
CENTRAL AFRICAN REP.
CAMEROON
ETHIOPIA
SOMALIA
UGANDA
KENYA
PRINCIPE
GABON
CONGO
RWANDA
DEMOCRATIC REP. OF CONGO
BURUNDI
TANZANIA
SEYCHELLES
COMOROS
ANGOLA
MALAWI
ZAMBIA
MOZAMBIQUE
MADAGASCAR
ZIMBABWE
NAMIBIA
BOTSWANA
MAURITIUS
REUNION
SWAZILAND
LESOTHO
SOUTH AFRICA

Source: Population Reference Bureau 2005

BOX 5.3 Our Global Community

"Nalim" in Bhutan

"Nalim" is a 49-year-old farmer, wife, and mother who struggles to feed a family of 13 in her home located in a village in the Himalayas of western Bhutan. The United Nations ranks Bhutan's affluence as 146th out of 185 countries. That puts it squarely in the middle in the pack of low-income countries. It is a largely rural country with great distances between villages. Characteristic with other poor nations, health problems plague the population. Infant mortality is high, and many children die from dehydration due to severe diarrhea from drinking dirty and polluted water. Life expectancy is low. Bhutan has the second-highest maternal mortality rate in the world. What is Nalim's daily life like?

Nalim shares a house with her brother, her mother, uncle, aunt, husband, her four children, a son-in-law, and three grandchildren. Her fifth child died years ago. She lives on the second story of a three-story house. The grain is stored on the top level, and the animals live on the ground floor. Although the government urges families to move animals out of the house because of disease, Nalim lacks the money for a barn. Flies and dung are everywhere. Nalim claims that she would like to move the animals outside because each of her children has suffered at least one serious illness related to their presence. Her house has no electricity or indoor plumbing. Only 70 percent of Bhutan's population used adequate sanitation facilities in 2004 (United Nations Children's Fund 2006). There is little furniture in the house and family members sit on the floor for their meals.

Nalim's husband has a physical disability—a clubfoot—and therefore the bulk of the farming tasks fall on her and her adult daughter. "He cannot do heavy work because of his leg—he is crippled—so even before we were married he did not do that kind of work." In addition, she also is responsible for the other typical gender-based tasks of caring for children, cooking, and cleaning. "The only season when they [the men] take care of the children a lot is during the paddy time. Planting paddies is women's work, so at that time they stay home and take care of the children and cook. . . . Men never do women's things, like harvest wheat or plant paddies."

The family grows almost all of the food they consume. She worries regularly about whether the harvest will be big enough to feed her family. She confesses that she needs money too and spends about 344 ngultrum (U.S.$11.50) a month on things she cannot produce, such as salt, sugar, tea leaves, clothes, and school supplies for her children and grandchildren. To purchase her goods at the market Nalim must walk 3 hours each way. One pair of shoes cost 50 ngultrum (U.S.$1.70), a cost considered exorbitant, therefore only three of the children in her family own shoes.

Nalim has no formal education. "If I had gone to school, I would not be living this kind of life—where I have to be out in the fields whether it is sunny or rainy," she laments. She notes that other children her age from her village were able to go to school, but she could not because she was the only daughter at home and her labor was needed to run the household.

Poverty touches all aspects of their lives every single day. This day-to-day existence is an endless struggle to cultivate enough food to eat and keep all family members healthy and alive—yet, in the midst of all this hardship is a loving family with real warmth. Family meals are lengthy affairs with much lively conversation. The adults are keenly interested in what the children have to say, a feature sometimes missing in U.S. culture. Nalim believes that she has a very good family, "with trust and understanding among ourselves." She married her husband out of love—and her love persists today more than 20 years later. Is it possible to describe someone who lives on the brink of survival as "happy?"

Sources: D'Aluisio and Menzel 1996; United Nations Children's Fund 2006.

CRITICAL THINKING QUESTIONS

1. What factors in Bhutan and throughout the world contribute to Bhutan's high rate of poverty?
2. Do you think that it is possible to describe someone who lives on the brink of survival as happy? Why or why not?

The Luxembourg Income Study (LIS), initiated in the 1980s and continuing today, has standardized variables across 70 data sets to allow for some comparisons of poverty across a limited number of countries. Using several different measures of poverty across 17 developed nations, researchers are now able to make relatively valid cross-national comparisons within these countries.

All measures of poverty show a similar pattern: The U.S. poverty rate exceeds those of 15 comparable countries with the exception of Ireland, as shown in Table 5.3. For example, using one method that defines poverty as the percentage of persons living with incomes below 50 percent of the median income, 17 percent of Americans lived under half the median income, far exceeding the average for the other countries. The percentage of U.S. children who live below 50 percent of the median income is greater than any of the other countries. Among the aged, only Ireland and Australia have a higher proportion of seniors living below the median income. Comparative data such as these indicate that high rates of poverty in a wealthy industrialized nation such as the United States are not inevitable (Mishel et al. 2007).

TABLE 5.3 Extent of Poverty Across 17 Developed Countries

	Percent of Population Below 50% of Median Income		
Country	**Overall**	**Children**	**Elderly**
United States	**17**	**22**	**25**
Ireland	17	17	36
Australia	14	16	30
Spain	14	16	23
Italy	13	17	14
United Kingdom	12	15	21
Canada	11	15	6
Denmark	9	9	7
Germany	8	9	10
France	8	8	10
Switzerland	8	7	18
Austria	8	8	14
Belgium	8	7	16
Netherlands	7	10	2
Sweden	7	4	8
Norway	6	3	12
Finland	5	3	9

Source: Luxembourg Income Study 2006. Cited in Mishel et al. 2007.

Causes of Poverty

A number of theories have been offered to explain the nature of poverty and account for why so many individuals are impoverished in the United States. Four major explanations are described here.

Individualism Tales of Horatio Alger–types abound—the "rags-to-riches" stories—with the moral that anyone can pull themselves up by their bootstraps with hard work, sweat, and motivation. The poor, and particularly welfare recipients, are blatant examples of those who have failed to "make it." An individualistic perspective argues that poverty is primarily a result of personal failings, and the poor generally have only themselves to blame for their predicament. This perspective suggests that the United States is still a land of meritocracy, and that hard work will reap financial and social rewards.

The following letter to the editor was published in *USA Today* (August 15, 2003, p. 11A) in response to an article on the homeless:

> Most people become homeless not as the result of one or two unforeseen happenings, but rather because of a long-term failing of lifestyle discipline. I must ask: How many $6 packs of cigarettes, $15 cases of beer, three-year new-car leases, trips to the mall for the latest merchandise and prepared foods instead of home-cooked meals have these people had during the years leading up to their becoming homeless? Homelessness is the end result of years of actions, most of which are under a person's control. People must be more moderate in their lifestyles. Spending less and saving more means that you will have more to spend, especially in an emergency. It is your personal responsibility to meet your obligations to your children, yourself, your credit card company, your bank, etc.—not mine.
>
> D.L.
> New Jersey

Proponents of individualism argue that because everyone theoretically has an equal chance to succeed, those who fail to make it have largely themselves to blame. The popular rags-to-riches stories promote the idea that virtually anyone can pull themselves up by their bootstraps with hard work and motivation.

There is great ambivalence toward the poor (Hancock 2004; Mann 1998; NPR Online 2001; Wolfe 1998). Many poor persons are assumed to be lazy, unmotivated, and living off the public dole. Attitudes toward the poor and government aid reflect the social and economic conditions of the rest of the country. As the economy strengthened in the 1990s, surveys report greater support for the individual perspective and less support of government assistance programs (Mann 1998; NPR Online 2001). Although the discrepancy in wealth and income between the richest and poorest Americans rose dramatically during the 1990s and early 2000s, most Americans were relatively unconcerned about it and did not see it as bad for the country (60 percent). In fact, one in five Americans thought that there were too *few* rich people (Zimmerman 2001) (probably because they hadn't yet become rich).

A study of middle-class Americans across the country found that 50 percent claimed that the biggest cause of poverty is that people are not doing enough to help themselves (NPR Online 2001). Another study found that more middle-class people opposed reductions in welfare benefits for people living in poverty (48 percent) than favored reductions (31 percent) (Wolfe 1998)—but Wolfe has also noted that the government was viewed as a last resort. The middle class believed that government aid should be temporary and limited, yet reliably there for people experiencing hard times (Zimmerman 2001).

Persons who are more likely to espouse individualistic explanations are white, live in the southern and north-central regions of the United States, are older than 50, and have moderate levels of education. Perhaps surprisingly, welfare recipients also tend to denigrate the poor. They distance themselves from other people on welfare, despite the fact that their circumstances are not altogether different (Seccombe 2007a). As "Sheri," a 27-year-old mother of 3 who had received welfare for 7 years, revealed:

> I think a lot of them are on it just to be on it. Lazy. Don't want to do nothing. A lot of them are on it because a lot of them are on drugs. Keep having kids to get more money, more food stamps. Now that's abusing the system. And a lot of women are abusing the system (Seccombe 2007a, 67).

Americans are more likely to prefer individual explanations of poverty than are those in many other industrialized nations. As shown in Figure 5.5, when people are asked, "Why are there persons in this country who live in need? ," Americans tend to attribute it to personal laziness over societal injustice, unlike in Canada, Great Britain, Sweden, and France (World Values Survey 1994).

Social Structuralism In contrast to individualism, a social structural approach assumes that poverty is a result of economic or social imbalances within the social structure that serve to restrict opportunities for some people. Drawing from a conflict perspective, the focus is on inequalities that are rooted in the social structure. For example, the U.S. economy has been changing over the last several decades, resulting in an erosion in the purchasing power of the minimum wage, a growth in low-paying service jobs, and job relocation from inner cities to the suburbs. As shown in the opening vignette, Barbara Ehrenreich found that it is virtually impossible to live on a minimum or near-minimum wage, let alone support a family. Yet nearly 2 million

FIGURE 5.5 Comparing Individual and Structural Causes of Poverty

Percentages for each country do not sum to 100 because less frequent causes of poverty were omitted from this figure.
Source: World Values Survey 1994.

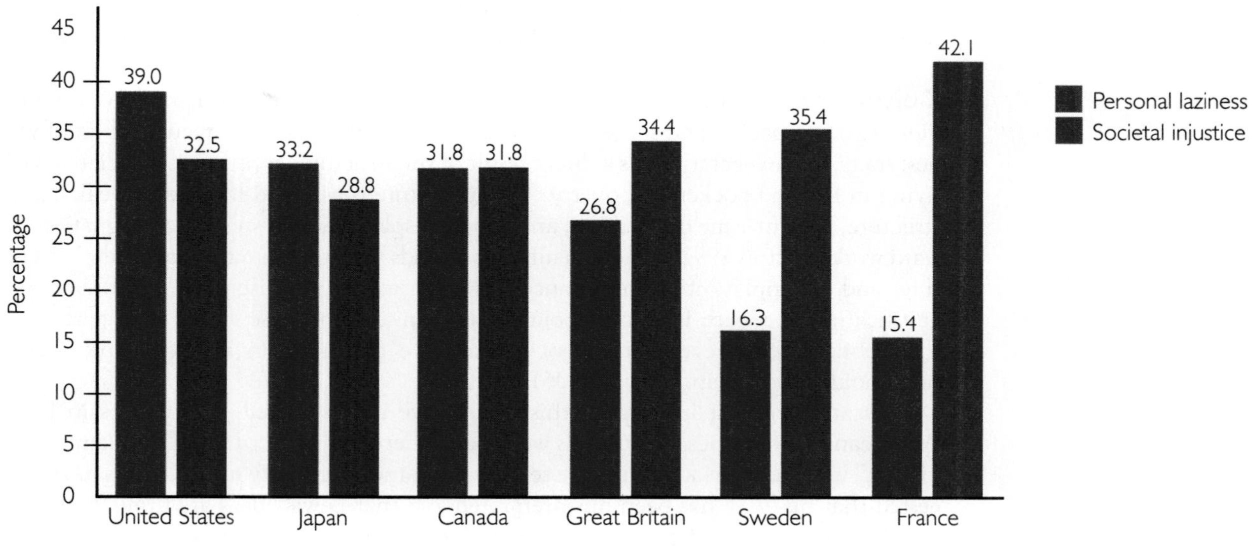

workers in 2005 earned $5.15 an hour or less (Bureau of Labor Statistics 2006). Former welfare recipients average only $7.15 in their jobs after leaving welfare (Loprest 2002). In the books *Flat Broke with Children* (Hays 2003) and "*So You Think I Drive a Cadillac?*" (Seccombe 2007a), sociologists document the struggle that women experience after leaving welfare for work. Although low wages may be enough to support a single person, a family trying to make ends meet would be living near or below the poverty threshold. Moreover, as noted, low-wage jobs often fail to provide families with health insurance.

These are social problems, not simply personal ones. People may find themselves vulnerable because of their social location and relationship to the social structure: a changing economy, a drive for profit inherent in capitalism, racism, patriarchal norms, and an eroding safety net have greater deleterious effects on some than on others. One woman highlights the value of these benefits as she compares what is available to families in Hungary to those in the United States. She writes in a letter to the editor of a magazine (Strong-Jekely 2006, 2):

> . . . I live in Hungary, where the benefits for families surpass those of any other country I've heard about. Maternity leave is three years. Daycare and preschool are free. Elementary school starts at eight a.m. and runs until two p.m., with optional aftercare. Most schools also offer ballet, music lessons, computer clubs, soccer, etc., in the afternoon. We all receive a monthly family supplement grant, which increases with each child and lasts until the child turns eighteen. When the child hits school age, we get an additional lump sum at the beginning of each school year amounting to about $100 per child to cover school supplies. All children have medical coverage through the age of eighteen—longer if they are in college—and pediatricians make house calls. If you have a child with a disability, you may stay home with the child for the rest of his/her life and receive the minimum wage. . . . There is no question that the United States needs more generous benefits for families. I am an American (my husband is Hungarian) and our choice to move to Hungary to have kids was a very conscious one. When I feel pangs of homesickness, I think of my overworked, stressed-out friends with kids back home and think: No way. I feel like I've got a balance in my life I would have a difficult time achieving in the States. I wish that all American parents had the same opportunities we've got here in Hungary to make life easier for families.

Her point is that families need programs and policies in place to remain socially and economically healthy. Families without these benefits are more likely to slip into poverty.

Culture of Poverty The culture of poverty perspective blends features of the previous two approaches and suggests that the poor have developed a subcultural set of values, traits, and expectations as a direct result of the structural constraints associated with living in isolated pockets of poverty. The subculture is assumed to foster a weak family structure, present-time orientation, and people display a helplessness and resignation toward work (Burton 1992). The subculture is at odds with the dominant middle-class culture and downplays the importance of hard work, self-discipline, and deferring gratification. Concern is voiced about the transmission of these values from parents to their children. However, most poor adults have grown up in nonpoor, "pro-social" households (Ludwig and Mayer 2006).

Oscar Lewis first introduced this perspective as he studied poor barrios in Latin American communities (1966). His work has sometimes been criticized as "blaming the victim," in which deviant values are seen as the causes of poverty itself. Others have suggested that his work has been misinterpreted and that Lewis' ideas are firmly grounded in a Marxist critique of capitalism. A *subculture* is a positive adaptation constructed to ease the pain associated with being part of a reserve and discarded labor force, "a process by which the poor pragmatically winnow what works from what does not, and pass it on to their children" (Harvey and Reed 1996).

Fatalism Finally, some people believe that poverty is attributable to quirks, chance, luck, inevitable human nature, illness, low intelligence, or other forces over which people have little control, a theoretical perspective referred to here as *fatalism*. Fate does not necessarily imply destiny, but rather a form of victimization that is rooted in complex events beyond one's immediate control. Poverty is not anyone's fault, per se, but rather is a potential consequence of unplanned, random, or natural human events or chain of events. For example, Herrnstein and Murray (1994) suggest that low intelligence is a primary cause of poverty. Arguing that intelligence is largely genetic, they argue that poor people with low intelligence quotients (IQs) give birth to another cohort with low IQs, and therefore their children are likely to remain impoverished. Seccombe and Hoffman (2007) found in their detailed in-person interviews that health problems were a primary reason why families leaving welfare for work remained poor.

Consequences of Poverty

Economically insecure and poor families experience more stress, disorganization, and other problems in their lives. Figure 5.6 summarizes the deleterious multidimensional and complex pathways through which poverty hurts children, integrating models from the Children's Defense Fund (1994) and Brooks-Gunn and Duncan (1997). Poverty is not simply a financial issue, but contributes to (a) poorer health and nutrition; (b) lower-quality home environment; (c) parental stress; (d) fewer resources for learning; (e) housing problems; and (f) poor-quality neighborhoods. These, in turn, can lead to significant negative consequences.

Consequences for Children Nearly one in five children grow up in the vice of poverty. Children's lives are particularly vulnerable, because their bodies and spirits need special nourishment to thrive. What do these conditions do to children?

Physical Health First, compared to others, children reared in poverty have significantly poorer health and are more likely to suffer from many chronic and acute health problems. The large-scale National Health Interview Survey reports that only 71 percent of children in families below the poverty line were reported to be in very good or excellent health compared with 87 percent of families at or above the poverty line (Cohen and Bloom 2005).

Poverty puts the health of children at risk by increasing the frequency of low birthweight babies and undernutrition. This increases their likelihood of serious chronic and acute illness during their first year and throughout their lives (Breslau et al. 2004; Children's Defense Fund 2005; Isaacs and Schroeder 2004; Seccombe 2007b).

Poor children continue to suffer from a variety of ailments at higher rates than do more affluent children, often because of an inadequate diet or dangerous social environment. For example, they are over three times more likely to be iron deficient; 1.5 times more likely to have frequent diarrhea or colitis; twice as likely to suffer from severe asthma; 1.5 times more likely to suffer partial or complete blindness or deafness; and three times more likely to have lead levels in their bloodstream of at least 10 micrograms of lead per deciliter of blood. This is dangerous because it is at this level that harmful effects to the brain and nervous system have been noted, causing lower intelligence, reduced physical stature, impaired hearing, and behavior issues. At least 300,000 children

FIGURE 5.6 **Pathways from Poverty to Adverse Child Outcomes**

Sources: From Seccombe, Karen. *Families in Poverty*, 1e. Published by Allyn and Bacon, Boston, MA. Copyright © 2007 by Pearson Education, by permission of the publisher; adapted from Children's Defense Fund 1994; Brooks-Gunn and Duncan 1997.

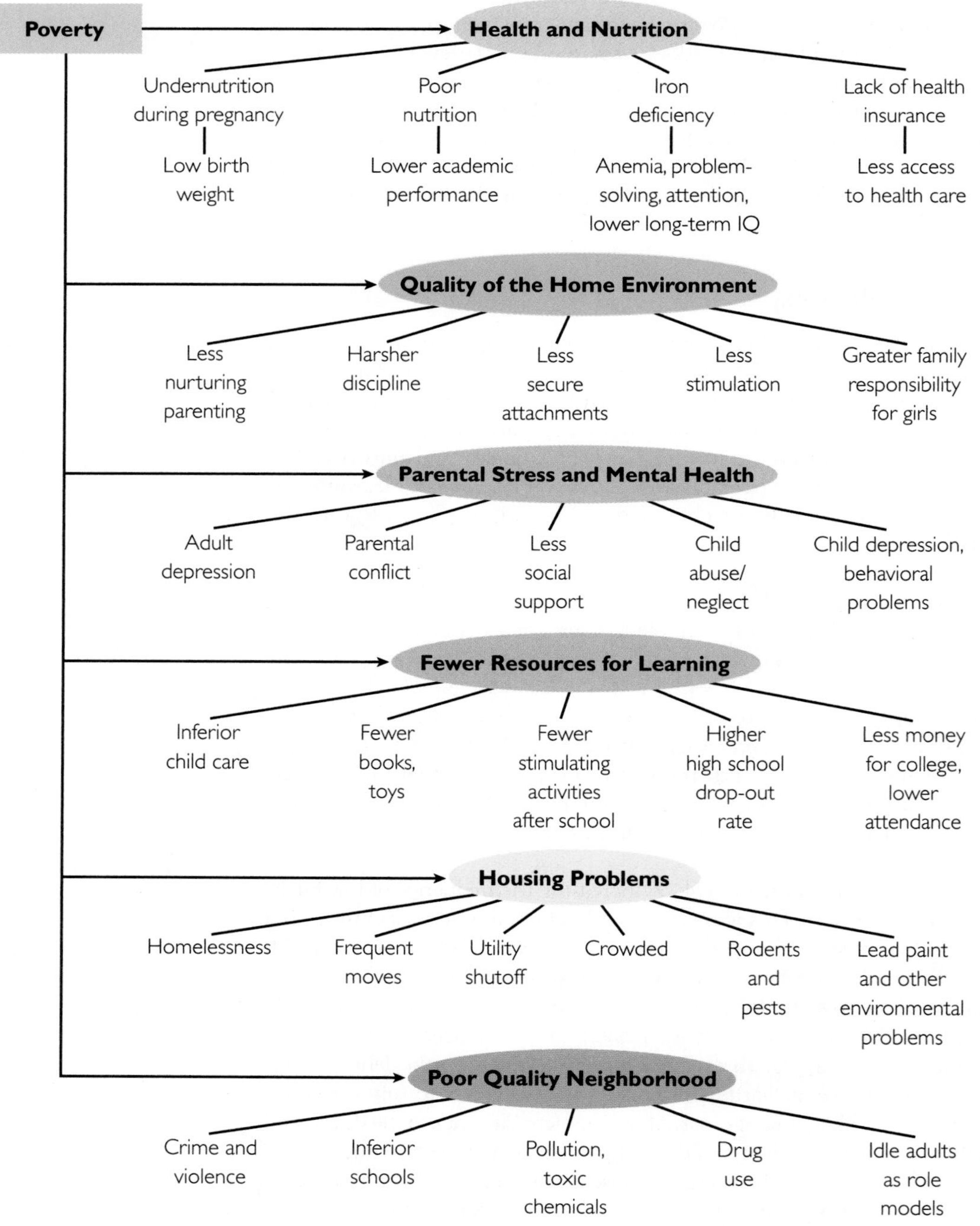

in the United States have blood levels that are high enough to cause serious impairment (CDC 2006).

Moreover, as many as 12.4 million children live in households with limited or uncertain access to sufficient food (USDA 2006). Without enough food and proper nutrition, children run the risk of anemia, more frequent colds, ear infections and other infectious diseases, impaired brain function, stunted growth, and are more vulnerable to lead and other environmental toxins. Data from multistate studies revealed that chronically hungry children were more likely to experience fatigue, irritability, anxiety, hyperactivity, and aggressive behaviors compared to other children. Not surprisingly, these children do more poorly in school, are tardy or absent more often, are more likely to repeat grades, and are more likely to be suspended from school (Center on Hunger and Poverty 2002; Children's Defense Fund 2005).

Children's Mental Health, Adjustment, and Well-Being Children living in poverty have more socioemotional and behavioral problems than do other children. They are more likely to suffer from depression, social withdrawal, to have peer relationship difficulties, low self-esteem, to have behavioral and conduct disorders, and to do poorly in school (Duncan and Brooks-Gunn 1997; Evans et al. 2005). Certainly not all poor children have these outcomes, but a study based on in-depth interviews found that poor children have a difficult time holding on to positive self-images (Weinger 1998). They know the deprivation associated with poverty and recognize that society is highly critical of their parents. Poor children internalize many of these negative messages.

Academic and School Achievement On average, children living in poverty perform lower academically than other children (Federal Interagency Forum 2005). Poor children tend to receive lower grades, receive lower scores on standardized tests, are less likely to finish high school, and are less likely to attend or graduate from college than are nonpoor youth, on average (NICHD Early Child Care Research Network 2005). There are many reasons for this, including that poor families have fewer resources to commit to

Children and adults living in poverty suffer many deleterious consequences, including food insecurity and hunger, which can then exacerbate other problems such as difficulty learning. To help feed hungry families, some communities offer food pantries from which families can receive a box of staples to help their food stretch through the month.

educationally relevant tools such as computers, books, and calculators. This type of impoverishment is associated with academic failure, which, in turn, may prompt or sustain misbehavior or emotional distress in school (Downey 1994; Gerard and Buehler 1999).

Specifically, Smith et al. (1997) found that children in families with incomes less than one-half of the poverty line scored between 6 and 13 points lower on various standardized tests than did children in families with incomes between 1.5 and 2.0 times the poverty line. Using three different types of assessment—IQ, verbal ability, and achievement tests—they also found that the longer the poverty spell and the more severe the poverty, the lower the score. Does this finding support the fatalistic explanation that somehow poor people are just not smart? Or might it reflect greater risk for inadequate diets, exposure to lead paint, inadequate health care, and a host of other structural factors that lead to poor school performance and lower levels of learning?

Consequences for Adults There are many potentially harmful health effects of poverty on adults, including higher morbidity (sickness) and a lower life expectancy than other adults. This is because the poor are more likely to work in dangerous occupations, to live in unsafe neighborhoods, and their homes are more likely to be located near toxic sites. These causes of poor health are structural in nature. The poor suffer from many chronic and acute illnesses and are less likely to have health insurance to cover the costs of seeing a doctor.

Poverty affects adults in other ways as well. One issue with far-reaching consequences for families is that poor men and women are less likely to marry (White and Rogers 2000). Poverty undermines economic security and makes men less attractive marriage partners (Edin and Kefalas 2005). For example, sociologist William Julius Wilson suggests that key factors in explaining the falling marriage rate among inner-city African Americans are their declining employment opportunities as jobs move to the suburbs or overseas (Wilson 1987, 1996). Unemployed or underemployed men are not deemed to be good marriage prospects.

Poverty and other forms of economic hardship also undermine marital stability (Conger et al. 1999; Vinokur et al. 1996). They are associated with lower levels of marital happiness and greater marital conflict because of the higher degree of stress involved in such a situation. Poverty and economic hardship can lead to greater levels of stress and depression, which can then lead to hostile marital interactions such as anger, resentment, hostility, and violence among partners (Conger et al. 1999; Gelles and Straus 1988). Poverty also contributes to parents' health problems, further undermining their ability to parent their children adequately (Adams et al. 2007).

Family Resiliency

Despite the toll that poverty can take, many children are resilient and overcome this adversity to lead successful and well-adjusted lives. **Resiliency** is the capacity to rebound from adversity, misfortune, trauma, or other transitional crises and become strengthened and more resourceful (McCubbin et al. 1997; Walsh 1998, 2002).

The well-cited Kauai Longitudinal Study provides an early and important look into resiliency (Werner 1994, 1995; Werner and Smith 1989, 1992). Based on a sample of 698 children born in 1955 on the island of Kauai in Hawaii, and following them for nearly 40 years, this study examined the long-term effects of growing up in high-risk environments. Most of the children were born to unskilled sugar plantation workers of Japanese, Filipino, Hawaiian, Portuguese, Polynesian, and mixed racial descent. More than half of the children lived in poverty. The survey found approximately one-third were considered high risk because of exposure to a combination of at least four individual, parental, or household risk factors such as having a serious health problem, familial alcoholism, violence, divorce, or mental illness in the family. The children were assessed from the perinatal period to ages 1, 2, 10, 18, and 32 years.

The research team found that two-thirds of high-risk 2-year-olds who experienced four or more risk factors by age 2 developed learning or behavior problems by age 18. One-third did not have any behavior problems, and instead developed into stable, competent, confident, and productive adults. In a later follow-up, at age 40, all but two of these individuals were still successful. In fact, many of them had outperformed the children from low-risk families.

Moreover, among the two-thirds of the surveyed high-risk children who had learning or behavioral problems at age 18, one-half did not exhibit these problems at age 30. As adults, they had satisfying jobs, stable marriages, and in other measures were deemed successful by the research team. Consequently, it appears that resiliency can be developed at any point in the life course. Conversely, a few individuals identified as resilient at age 18 had developed significant problems by age 30.

The evidence shows us that many adults and children reared in poverty do overcome their adversities. Why is this?

Individual, Family, and Community Factors

Most research on resilience has focused on three types of factors to improve resiliency in the face of adverse conditions: (1) individual-level protective factors; (2) family protective and recovery factors; and (3) community strengths.

Individual-level protective factors include individual personality traits and dispositions that enhance a person's ability to be successful. In their review of research and clinic experience, Wolin and Wolin (1993) identified seven traits of adults who survived a troubled childhood: insight (awareness of dysfunction); independence (distancing self from troubles); supportive relationships; initiative; creativity; humor (reframing the situation in a less-threatening way); and morality (justice and compassion rather than revenge). For example, the resilient high-risk adolescents in the Longitudinal Kauai Study developed a sense that obstacles were not insurmountable, and they believed that they had control over their fate. They had a high degree of self-esteem and self-efficacy, and many developed a special skill or hobby that was a source of pride.

Family protective and recovery factors are central features of the resiliency literature. **Family protective factors (FPF)** are those characteristics or dynamics that shape the family's ability to endure in the face of risk factors; **family recovery factors (FRF)** assist families in "bouncing back" from a crisis situation (McCubbin et al. 1997). Key characteristics of resilient families include warmth, affection, cohesion, commitment, clear expectations, shared goals, and emotional support for one another. Resilient families participate in family celebrations, share spiritual connections, have specific traditions, and predictable routines (Silliman 1998; Walsh 1998).

There are also factors in the **community**—geographic space, social networks, religious and faith-based fellowships—that affect resilience (Silliman 1998; Miller 2000). Community institutions are important aspects of developing resilient youth and fostering resiliency among adults. Blyth and Roelkepartian (1993) indicate several types of community strengths. First, opportunities for participation in community life, such as extracurricular activities in school, religious youth groups, scouting, or other activities can bond youth to their school, churches, or communities. In these settings, they can learn important skills such as teamwork, group pride, or leadership. Second, strong communities provide avenues for contributing to the welfare of others, which can foster a sense of inner strength and self-esteem. Third, there should be opportunities to connect with peers and other adults, such as with a role model, a friend, or a confidant. Teachers may play a critical role in providing this type of social support. Finally, a strong community provides specific community facilities and events for youth. Programs for youth should be a funding priority.

What Is Missing? Structural Conditions Although there is a growing recognition that strengthening families requires the interaction of individual, familial, and community contingencies, noticeably absent is an emphasis on *structural-level* conditions such as national and statewide policies that can strengthen families (Seccombe 2002). Referring back to Figure 5.6 we saw that poverty contributes to poorer nutrition, lower-quality home environment, parental stress, fewer resources for learning, housing problems, and poor-quality neighborhoods, which in turn lead to further negative consequences. Can we expect families to be resilient without supportive family policies? For example, how do we best help an impoverished child who lives with his single mother? Is it enough to surround this child with a loving extended family, church, and community groups? These may be important components of resiliency, but they are insufficient.

One study examined the gap in math and science achievement of third- and fourth-graders who lived with a single parent versus those who lived with two parents in 11 different countries (Pong et al. 2003). The researchers found that the United States (along with New Zealand) had the largest achievement gap between children in single versus two-parent families. An in-depth analysis revealed that those countries with family policies specifically designed to equalize resources between single and two-parent families are far more successful in decreasing the achievement gap. Other countries like the United States, which has few family supports for single-parent families, show large and persistent differences in academic scores. The authors conclude that national family policies are an important mechanism for offsetting poor academic outcomes of vulnerable children (Pong et al. 2003).

Social Policy and Family Resilience

One example of a sound social policy that has the potential to offset poverty is the earned income tax credit. As structured, it has increased the standard of living for millions of families and pulled many out of poverty. It has been applauded as an important incentive and reward for work. However, others argue that it is not as effective as it could be.

Example: Earned Income Tax Credit

The **earned income tax credit (EITC)** is a refundable federal tax credit for low-income workers and their families. The credit can reduce the amount of taxes owed and result in a tax refund to those who claim and qualify for the credit. It has been hailed as a boon to low-income workers, in effect raising their pay by up to several dollars per hour.

To qualify for the credit, the adjusted gross income for 2006 was less than $38,348 for a married couple with more than one child, $34,001 for a married couple with one child, and $14,120 for a married couple without children (IRS 2007). If the credit is larger than any taxes owed, the worker will receive a cash refund from the Internal Revenue Service (IRS) after filing a tax return. In essence, the government is providing low-income workers additional money beyond what they get paid at their jobs to encourage work and to reduce poverty.

The EITC is applauded for lifting millions of adults and children out of poverty each year. In the United States, where family allowances, health insurance, and worker benefits are largely excluded from national policy, the EITC is considered one of the country's largest sources of assistance for poor and low-income families. It is a cash subsidy that applies to low-income workers. Enacted in 1975 and expanded in the 1990s, about 21 million taxpayers receive more than $41 billion in EITC payments (Kuney and Levitis 2007). However, 15–20 percent of eligible persons fail to claim their credit, usually because they are unaware of it or need help with filling out their tax forms (Greenstein 2005).

Not surprisingly, the EITC has had a positive effect on employment because it offers a real supplement to wages for those low-income workers who qualify. The EITC has been credited with making it easier for families to transition from welfare into work (Ellwood 1999; Grogger 2003). Ellwood's research on the employment of single mothers in the 1990s suggests that welfare reform accounted for only one-half of the changing employment of female-headed households (1999). The EITC and other work accounts for roughly 30 percent of the change and the relatively robust economy during that period accounts for the remainder (Ellwood 1999). The 2000 recession has altered these findings somewhat because jobs are less plentiful; nonetheless, the EITC is a strong inducement to work, if a job is available.

More than three-quarters of all payments go to working families who earn below $20,000 per year. It provides a critical element of security for poor families, and contributes to basic necessities, enables families to make needed purchases, and can be used as a savings cushion to offset a future job loss, illness, or other situation that can leave families vulnerable.

Conclusion

This chapter has introduced the importance of social class to understanding families and close relationships, and subsequent chapters will examine specific aspects of this relationship more fully. Social stratification and social class are important components of C. Wright Mills' claim that personal experiences are in large part shaped by broad social, historical, and cultural forces. Social class in the United States is more vague than in Great Britain. Nonetheless, one's social class position influences family lifestyle, goals, opportunities, values, choices, and constraints. Persons living in poverty are particularly vulnerable in terms of their health and social well-being. Strong family policies, such as the EITC or national health insurance, can go a long way in assisting families as they struggle to make ends meet.

Key Terms

Absolute poverty: The lack of resources such as food, housing, and clothing that is life-threatening. (p. 150)

Ascribed statuses: The statuses a person is born with, such as his or her sex, race and ethnic background, and social class. (p. 133)

Bourgeoisie: According to Karl Marx, the capitalist class that owns the means of production. (p. 136)

Caste system: A system of social stratification that is based on ascribed characteristics one is born with, such as race, ethnicity, or family lineage. (p. 135)

Community: Can include geographic space, social networks, and religious and faith-based fellowships that affect resiliency. (p. 163)

Cross-sectional data: Data collected at only one point in time rather than following trends over time. (p. 147)

Earned income tax credit (EITC): A federal tax credit for low-income working families. (p. 164)

Family protective factors (FPF): Characteristics or dynamics that shape the family's ability to endure in the face of risk factors. (p. 163)

Family recovery factors (FRF): Assist families in "bouncing back" from a crisis situation. (p. 163)

Home observation of the measurement of the environment (HOME): A widely used tool that measures maternal warmth and learning experiences provided to the child; is associated with a variety of child outcomes. (p. 133)

Individual-level protective factors: Individual personality traits and dispositions that enhance resiliency. (p. 163)

Medicaid: A federally mandated health care financing program for the financially indigent who meet certain qualifications. (p. 146)

Meritocracy: A system in which economic and social rewards such as income, occupation, or prestige are obtained on individual merit rather than inheritance. (p. 135)

Mortality rates: Death rates. (p. 146)

National health insurance: Insurance is viewed as a public good, like schools, police protection, and parks, available to all, and funded out of taxes and general revenues. (p. 146)

Out-of-pocket costs: The amount that individuals pay of their own money to receive health care. (p. 145)

Poverty line: The official U.S. government method of calculating how many people are poor and assessing how that number changes from year to year. (p. 147)

Power: The ability to achieve goals, wishes, and desires even in the face of opposition from others. (p. 136)

Prestige: The esteem or respect a person is afforded. (p. 136)

Proletariat: According to Karl Marx, individuals who must sell their labor to the owners in order to earn enough money to survive. (p. 136)

Relative poverty: The lack of basic resources relative to others in society. (p. 150)

Resiliency: The capacity to rebound from adversity, misfortune, trauma, or other transitional crises and be strengthened and more resourceful. (p. 162)

Social class: A system of social stratification that is based both on ascribed statuses and individual achievement. (p. 136)

Social mobility: Movement in the stratification system based on individual effort or achievement. (p. 136)

Social stratification: The hierarchical ranking of people within society on the basis of specific coveted resources, such as income and wealth. (p. 135)

Socioeconomic status (SES): A vague combination of education, occupation, and income. (p. 138)

Wealth: The value of all of a person's or a family's economic assets, including income, real estate, stocks, bonds, and other items of economic worth, minus debt. (p. 136)

Resources on the Internet

Joint Center for Poverty Research
www.jcpr.org
The Northwestern University/University of Chicago Joint Center for Poverty Research (JCPR) supports academic research that examines what it means to be poor and live in the United States. JCPR concentrates on the causes and consequences of poverty in this country and the effectiveness of policies aimed at reducing poverty.

National Coalition for the Homeless
http://nch.ari.net
This site provides extensive information about homelessness, including the nature of homelessness

in the United States. It also offers a lengthy bibliography for those seeking further information.

The Urban Institute
www.urban.org
The Urban Institute is a research organization focusing on a wide spectrum of social problems and efforts to solve them. It focuses particularly on issues related to the poor and disadvantaged, including health insurance, welfare reform, poverty, and the working poor. You can access many of their working papers or full documents from their website.

United Nations
www.un.org
The United Nations website provides a wealth of information about global poverty, economic and social development, and human rights. Their website provides access to research reports and press releases.

Further Reading

Chang, G. 2000. *Disposable Domestics: Immigrant Women Workers in the Global Economy*. Cambridge, MA: South End Press.

Deparle, J. 2004. *American Dream: Three Women, Ten Kids, and a Nation's Drive to End Welfare*. New York: Viking Books.

Edin, K., and M. Kefalas. 2005. *Promises I Can Keep: Why Poor Women Put Motherhood Before Marriage*. Berkeley: University of California Press.

Ehrenreich, B. 2001. *Nickel and Dimed: On (Not) Getting by in America*. New York: Metropolitan Books.

Hays, S. 2003. *Flat Broke with Children: Women in the Age of Welfare Reform*. New York: Oxford University Press.

Kendall, D. 2002. *The Power of Good Deeds: Privileged Women and the Social Reproduction of the Upper Class*. Lanham, MD: Rowman and Littlefield.

McLeod, J. 1995. *Ain't No Makin' It: Aspirations and Attainment in a Low Income Neighborhood*. Boulder, CO: Westview Press.

Mishel, L., J. Bernstein, and S. Allegretto. 2007. *The State of Working America 2006/2007*. Washington, DC: Economic Policy Institute.

Moynihan, D. P., T. M. Smeeding, and L. Rainwater, 2006. *The Future of the Family*. New York: Russell Sage Foundation.

Pattillo-McCoy, M. 1999. *Black Picket Fences: Privilege and Peril Among the Black Middle Class*. Chicago: University of Chicago Press.

Rank, M. R. 2004. *One Nation, Underprivileged: Why American Poverty Affects Us All*. New York: Oxford University Press.

Reese, E. 2005. *Backlash Against Welfare Mothers: Past and Present*. Berkeley: University of California Press.

Seccombe, K. 2007. *Families in Poverty*. Boston: Allyn and Bacon.

Wilson, W. J. 1996. *When Work Disappears: The World of the New Urban Poor*. New York: Alfred A. Knopf.

Wolfe, A. 1998. *One Nation, After All*. New York: Penguin.

CHAPTER 6

Race, Ethnicity, and Families

CHAPTER PREVIEW

What is the significance of race and ethnicity to our understanding of families and intimate relationships? This chapter provides an important foundation to upcoming chapters by introducing basic facts about race, ethnicity, and the changing demographic landscape of the United States. We will explore general issues and then look at the demographic trends and social characteristics of several specific racial and ethnic groups. In this chapter you will learn:

- The United States is becoming increasingly diverse
- The history and current social issues surrounding legal and illegal immigration
- How to define basic concepts, including race, ethnicity, minority group, and racism
- Important and distinguishing characteristics of Hispanic, black, Asian American, Native American, and Alaska Native families, and how these affect those families
- The tremendous growth in interracial and interethnic families is changing the way we think about and conceptualize racial and ethnic categories
- Affirmative action programs can have real implications for improving the economic and social well-being of families

CHAPTER OUTLINE

Children's perceptions of occupational status and their own vocational interests are affected by the racial makeup of the workforce, according to a study involving first and sixth grade black children (Bigler et al. 2003). For both real and made-up jobs, children ascribed higher status to those occupations that are or were depicted as having all or mostly white workers (and no or low numbers of black workers) than to those jobs with no or low numbers of white workers (and all or high numbers of black workers).

Ninety-two black children (47 girls and 45 boys) from a racially mixed elementary school in the Midwest took part in the study (Bigler et al. 2003); about half of the children were from lower socioeconomic status (SES) backgrounds and the other half were from upper-middle SES backgrounds. The children were interviewed individually by one of four black experimenters. In the first session, children were asked about their perceptions of occupational status and their occupational aspirations. In the second session, the children were asked questions designed to assess their knowledge of racial stereotypes in occupations.

Each interview session involved 39 occupations, 27 of which were familiar occupations (like airline pilot or janitor). The remaining 12 were novel occupations that the children would not have known about previously, including newly coined job titles. For example, one made-up job was a "tenic"—a person who is in charge of creating handicapped parking places for city buildings and stores. The children were randomly assigned to conditions in which the workers shown in a drawing were either (a) four blacks; (b) four whites; or (c) two blacks and two whites.

Results of the study show that although the jobs themselves were identical, children's rating of the status of both familiar and novel jobs differed in relation to whether the jobs were depicted with only whites, only blacks, or both, according to study authors. The most compelling evidence of the role played by race in children's assessment of occupational status comes from the results of the novel occupation part of the study, according to the authors. Black children rated occupations that had been depicted with only white workers as being higher in status than the identical occupations depicted with only black workers. More specifically, black children in first grade and from lower SES backgrounds rated jobs performed solely by blacks as lower in status than jobs performed solely by white workers.

"The results clearly indicate that race has an independent effect on occupational judgments and thus that it cannot be only the qualities inherent in occupations themselves that affect children's judgments about job status," said Dr. Bigler. Despite this finding, the children's occupational interests did not appear to be affected by stereotyped beliefs concerning the appropriateness of various occupations for the two racial groups. "When children were asked which racial group 'should' perform the familiar occupations, the children responded in a highly unbi-

ased manner, almost always answering that both whites and blacks should perform all occupations," added Dr. Bigler.

The relations between race of workers and the status assigned to the jobs may lead to two types of vicious cycles, according to the researchers. "African American children, especially those from disadvantaged backgrounds, may preferentially seek out low-status jobs in which minorities are well represented and thereby ensure that such jobs remain overpopulated by minorities, leading a new generation of poor African American children to select low-status jobs," said Dr. Bigler. "Second, those medium- and high-status jobs that do attract an increasing proportion of African American workers (perhaps from more advantaged households) may, across time, be viewed as lower in status simply as a function of the race of the worker, and consequently show decreasing levels of pay and prestige." (Bigler et al. 2003; Partenheimer 2003) ■

Why a separate chapter on the influence of race and ethnicity on family life? Shouldn't coverage in the subsequent chapters—marriage, children, divorce—suffice? Although every chapter in this text focuses on many different families and their experiences, family scholars are developing a greater sensitivity to the specific social meanings associated with race and ethnicity, and how these shape the structure of and interactions within families (González et al. 2006; Umana-Taylor et al. 2006). For example, how does racial discrimination affect stress and psychological well-being? How do minority parents socialize children about race and racism?

This chapter introduces the importance of race and ethnicity and makes explicit the racial context in which we live. Whites have the privilege of rarely thinking about race or ethnicity; yet, the color of our skin, physical features, country of origin, culture, and dominant language also have a tremendous impact on family structure, role relationships, and family interaction. We will see many examples throughout this text, including:

- Blacks are more likely than whites to live in extended families.
- Native Americans have higher infant mortality rates than do other groups.
- Hispanics are less likely to cohabit outside of marriage than are other groups.
- Blacks are less likely than other groups to marry.
- Asian American families are more likely to emphasize the value of a college education than are other groups.
- Hispanics, particularly Mexican Americans, are less likely to have health insurance to cover family medical bills, which results in a variety of negative health outcomes for their families.
- Native American, black, Hispanic, and Asian American grandmothers play a more significant role in the lives of their grandchildren than do white grandmothers.
- Asian Americans are least likely to divorce and blacks are most likely to divorce.
- Teen pregnancy rates are declining most rapidly among blacks compared to other groups.
- Asian Americans are most likely to be child free, while Hispanics are least likely.

- Hispanic women and men have the lowest median annual income among full-time workers, and Asian American men and women have the highest.
- Whites remarry most quickly after a divorce, compared to other racial or ethnic groups.

There are positive attributes and specific challenges within each racial and ethnic group. The goal of this chapter is to better understand the ways in which race and ethnicity (alone, and in conjunction with other statuses such as sex and social class) operate in society, so that in subsequent chapters we can see how they specifically frame family lives.

Increasing Diversity in the United States

Anyone who takes a quick look at the United States cannot help but notice a diverse nation. There is an assortment of ethnic restaurants from which to choose, within schools many languages may be spoken, and a trip to the mall reveals people of different dress. The United States is quickly becoming even more diverse due to immigration patterns and birth rates among specific groups. In 2005, 69 percent of the U.S. population was non-Hispanic white, as shown in Figure 6.1. Their share of the population will steadily decrease due to the growth of minority groups; whites are expected to comprise only about 53 percent of the population in 2050. The percentage of blacks is expected

FIGURE 6.1 **Resident Population by Race and Hispanic Origin Status—Projections: 2005 to 2050**

Source: U.S. Census Bureau 2006.

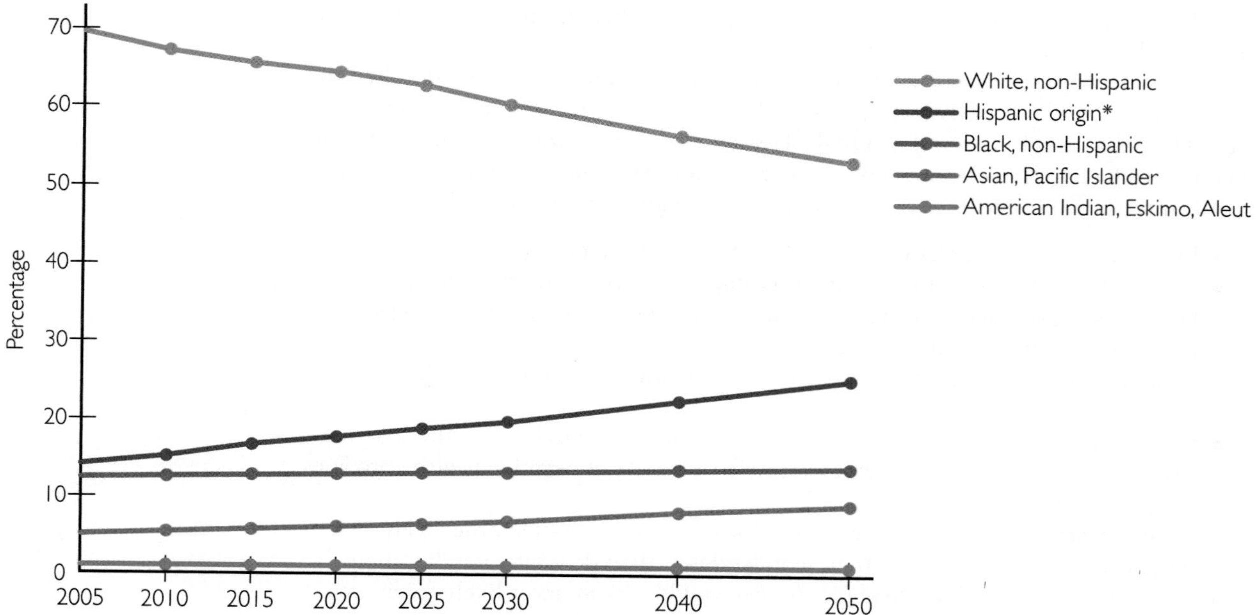

*Persons of Hispanic origin may be of any race.

to increase only slightly during this period, to 13 percent. Native Americans and Alaska Natives will remain at less than 1 percent. The largest increases will be found among Asian Americans and Hispanics. The proportion of Asian Americans is expected to more than double, from 4 percent to 9 percent, while Hispanics are expected to increase to 24 percent of the population (U.S. Census Bureau 2006). Minority used to be virtually synonymous with black in the minds of most people. This is quickly changing.

Immigration

Yue Lin Wang. *Jose Gonzalez*. *Min Nguyen*. What do these three people have in common? They have all immigrated to the United States. Their circumstances vary. Yue Lin Wang was orphaned in China because of the one-child policy and adopted by a loving American family when she was 9 months old. Jose Gonzalez, a journalist from Cuba, came to the United States seeking political asylum. Min Nguyen and her family escaped the ravages of the Vietnam War, after surviving for a year in a refugee camp in Laos. Over the past century, there has been a significant change in the country of origin among immigrants. In 1900, the majority of persons immigrating to the United States came from Europe. However, by 1980 four times as many Hispanics and Asians migrated to the United States as did Europeans as they fled persecution in their war-torn countries.

Today, about 35 million people, or 12 percent of the U.S. population, were not born in the United States but migrated. The largest number of immigrants came from Central America and Asia, although immigration from Asia has slowed somewhat as political strife has abated. The percentage of Europeans immigrating to the United States is a relatively small component of the total, as shown in Figure 6.2 (Pew Hispanic Center 2006a).

Characteristics of immigrants vary by their country of origin and length of time in the United States (as well as personal circumstances surrounding their immigration). For example, many Asians arriving from Cambodia and Vietnam in the 1980s came as young children. They were exposed to U.S. culture early on and are now attending college in large numbers. Their experiences in the United States may be vastly different from migrant farmworkers from Mexico. Nonetheless, some generalizations can be made:

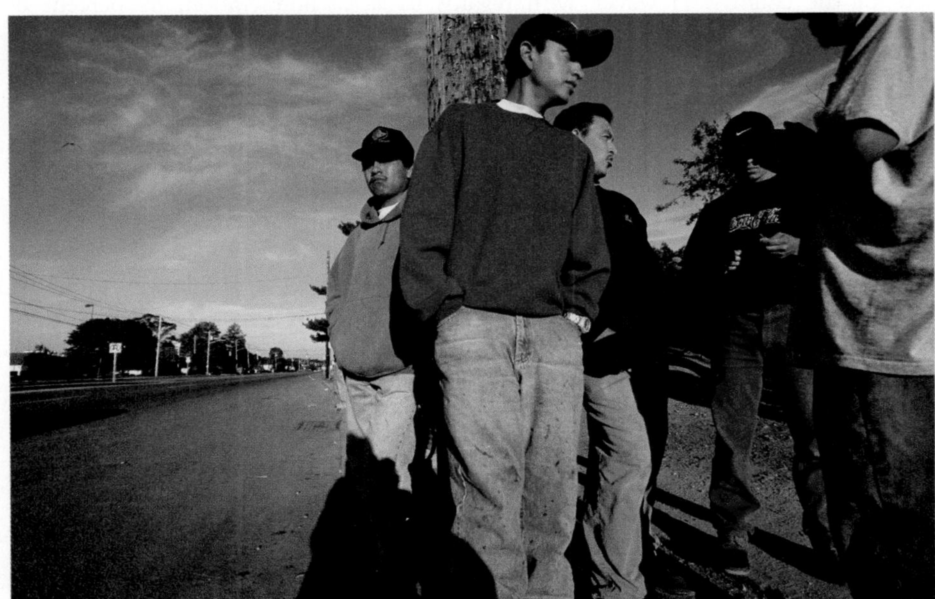

An estimated 11 to 12 million unauthorized migrants are in the United States. Most are eager to work, as are these men hoping for a day's labor, because jobs in their home countries are scarce and wages are extremely low.

FIGURE 6.2 U.S. Immigrants by Region of Birth (Percent) (2005)

Source: Pew Hispanic Center 2006a.

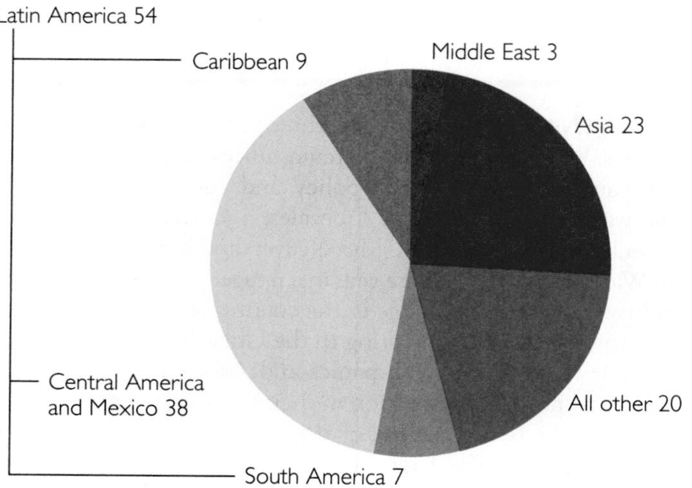

Immigrants are more likely than native-born residents to be in their childbearing years; they live in larger family households; they earn less money in their jobs; they are more likely to live in poverty; and they tend to reside in central cities within a metropolitan area (Kochhar 2005; Passel 2006).

Illegal Immigration

Citizens of the United States are nearly equally divided over whether immigration is good for the country. However, with regards to *illegal* immigration, 89 percent of Americans in a May 2006 New York Times/CBS survey said it was a "very serious" or "somewhat serious" problem. At the same time, most believe that illegal immigrants are taking jobs that Americans do not want, rather than taking jobs away from U.S. workers (Pew Hispanic Center 2006b).

Who are these illegal immigrants, "unauthorized workers" or "unauthorized migrants"? There were between 11 and 12 million illegal immigrants in the United States in 2006 (Passel 2006). Since 2000, the number of illegal immigrants has been growing by about 500,000 per year. Fifty-six percent come from Mexico and another 22 percent come from the rest of Latin America, where they face extreme poverty and limited job prospects in their countries. About half of illegal immigrants are adult males; the remainder are women and children, although two-thirds of the children living in unauthorized families are actually U.S. citizens by birth (amounting to over 3 million children in 2005) (Passel 2006).

Nearly half of illegal immigrants entered the country with visas that allowed them to visit or reside in the United States for a limited time, but who have now overstayed. More than half entered the United States illegally, by hiding in vehicles such as cargo trucks, trekking through the desert, wading across the Rio Grande, or otherwise eluding the U.S. Border Patrols (Pew Hispanic Center 2006c). Illegal immigrants face many horrific and dangerous situations in their trek to the United States to find work, and many do not make it. They are robbed and otherwise taken advantage of by guides, they are discovered by the border patrol, or they are killed or injured on the journey. As two men who were detected trying to come into the United States from Mexico emotionally explained in their native Spanish: "The Border Patrol treats us like animals, like dirt, like we don't matter. We know we are doing something wrong but it is not to hurt anyone but to feed our families. We have nothing to eat [at our homes]" (Arditti 2006). Those who do make it to the United States find jobs in a variety of occupations; nearly one-third work in low-paying service industries or in construction or agriculture (Passel 2006).

Defining Basic Concepts

What are the implications of the changing composition of the United States? The answers to this question will be hotly debated in the coming years. Before addressing this issue from the perspective of families, it is appropriate to define some basic concepts. The terms race, ethnicity, and minority group are used frequently, but not always correctly.

Race

Theoretically, the term **race** refers to a category composed of people who share real or alleged physical traits that members of a society deem as socially significant, such as skin color or hair texture. Nineteenth-century biologists created a three-part classification of races: **Caucasian**, comprised of those individuals with relatively light skin; **Negroid**, comprised of people with darker skin and other characteristics such as coarse curly hair; and **Mongoloid**, representing those individuals who have characteristics such as yellow or brown skin and folds on their eyelids (Simpson and Yinger 1985). However, this classification is considered woefully inadequate because people throughout the world display an array of racial traits. At least 75 percent of African Americans have white ancestry, in part because many female African slaves were raped and impregnated by their white owners. It is also estimated that between 1 and 5 percent of the genes carried by American whites are from African ancestors (Davis 1991). From a biological point of view, then, blacks and whites comprise a continuum rather than a dichotomy.

Most social scientists today suggest that such narrow conceptions of race are not accurate or useful for understanding the diversity in society. For example, narrow classifications lump together all Hispanic groups, including Mexican Americans, Cuban Americans, Central Americans, and Puerto Ricans, despite their significant cultural and linguistic differences. After all, how much do Mexican Americans and Cuban Americans really have in common?

Ethnicity

Ethnicity is generally thought to be a more useful way to understand diversity because it focuses on shared cultural characteristics such as place of origin, dress, food, religion, language, and values. Ethnicity represents culture, whereas race attempts to represent biological heritage. Thus, a black woman who recently moved to the United States, but who grew up in Jamaica, is not an African American. Her race may be the same as that of an African American (i.e., Negroid), but her cultural heritage is likely to be vastly different. This distinction causes some confusion. For example, the U.S. Census Bureau classifies black people according to their race, black, not by their ethnicity. Some scholars, however, use the term African American rather than black because they are interested in the uniquely African American experience. Likewise, the U.S. Census Bureau often classifies all Hispanics by race—separating white Hispanics from black Hispanics—but generally ignores ethnicity—Mexican American, Puerto Rican, Cuban

American—which masks the rich diversity found among Hispanic groups that may have little or nothing to do with skin color. Other times the U.S. Census Bureau will single out Hispanics as one ethnic group, combining black and white Hispanics and masking the diversity within these groups.

People who share specific cultural features are referred to as members of an **ethnic group**. There are many different ethnic groups in the United States, and hundreds throughout the world. Even Caucasians may identify themselves as members of ethnic groups such as Polish, German, or Italian, if they share interrelated cultural characteristics with others.

Minority Group

The term **minority group** refers to a category of people who have less power than the dominant group and who are subject to unequal treatment. A minority group may categorically earn less money, have less representation in politics, be disvalued, be subject to prejudice or discrimination, or be denied opportunities in society. In some cases, minority groups may actually represent the statistical majority, as is the case for blacks in South Africa, or women in most societies around the world. Generally, a minority group has the following characteristics:

- It possesses characteristics that are popularly regarded as different from the dominant group.
- It suffers prejudice and discrimination by the dominant group.
- Membership is usually ascribed (rather than achieved).
- Members feel a sense of group solidarity—a "we" feeling—that grows from shared cultural heritage and the shared experience of prejudice and discrimination.
- Marriages are typically among members of the same group (Simpson and Yinger 1985).

Racial discrimination remains a fact of life for many Americans of color, and this discrimination contributes to disparities in health and higher death rates from cancer, heart disease, diabetes, and HIV infection.

Racism: A Pervasive Problem That Affects Families

The late tennis star Arthur Ashe, a black man, was interviewed a few months prior to his death from AIDS. When a reporter queried that the battle with AIDS, which Ashe contracted through a blood transfusion, must have been the heaviest burden he ever had to bear, Ashe was quick to correct the reporter (Ashe 1994):

> . . . . being black is the greatest burden I've had to bear. Having to live as a minority in America. Even now it continues to feel like an extra weight tied around me. . . . Race is for me a more onerous burden than AIDS.

He is speaking of **racism**, the belief that one racial group is superior or inferior to others. The resulting prejudice and discrimination can hurt its victims in many ways, including health, stress, psychological functioning, depression, job and educational opportunities, family relationships, and coping strategies (Feagin and McKinney 2003; Gore and Aseltine 2003; Martin et al. 2003; Vernellia 2006; Viramontez Anguiano et al. 2004; Whitbeck et al. 2002). Many whites believe that significant numbers of blacks and Hispanics are unintelligent, lazy, prefer welfare to self-support, and are prone to violence (see Figure 6.3) (Rubio and Williams 2004). White Americans' attitudes toward Asian Americans are somewhat more positive, but remain far more negative than how whites evaluate themselves.

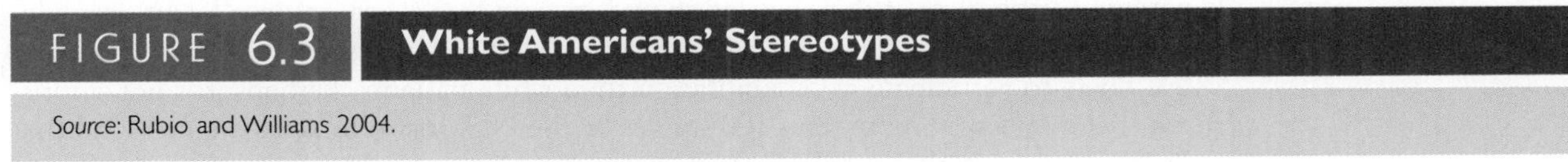

FIGURE 6.3 White Americans' Stereotypes

Source: Rubio and Williams 2004.

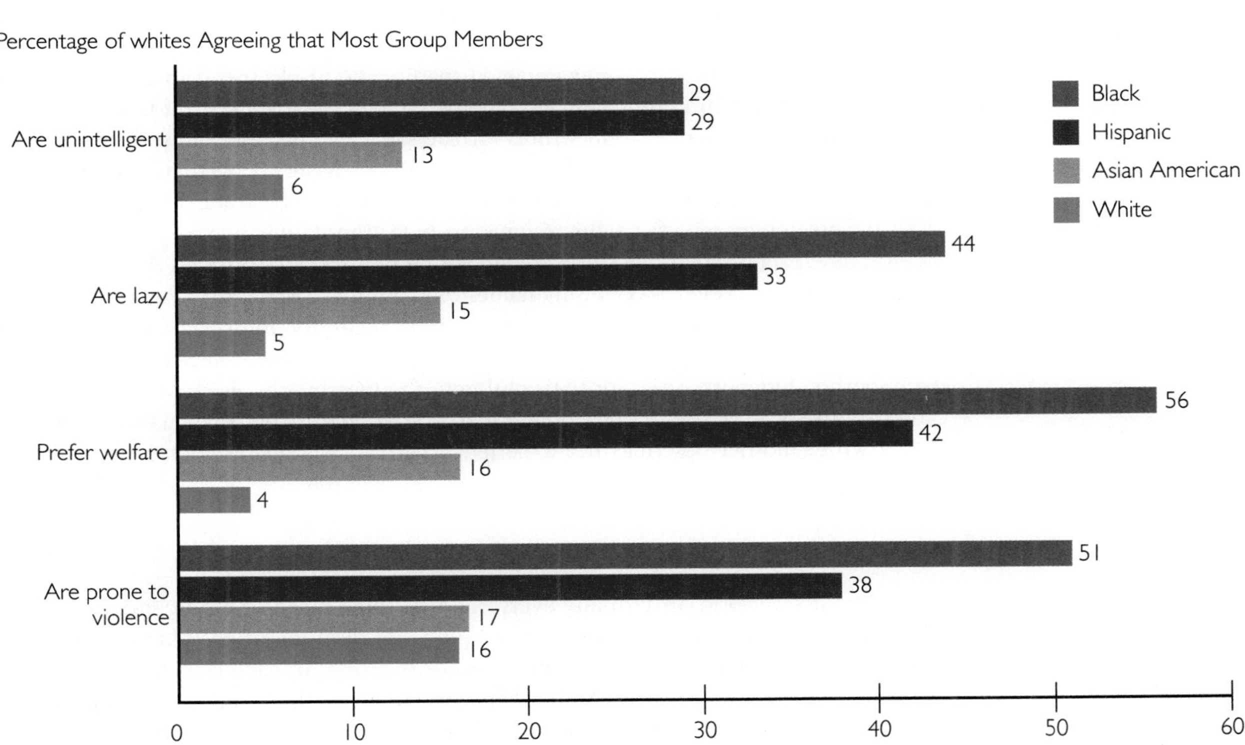

A study of working-class men elicited racism even when no direct questions were asked about race (Lamont 2003). One white electronics technician summarized his feelings (Lamont 2003):

> I work side by side constantly with blacks, and I have no problem with it. I am prejudiced to a point. What is a nice way to say it? I know this is a generality and it does not go for all, it goes for a portion. It is this whole unemployment and welfare gig. What you see mostly on there is blacks. I see it from working with some of them and the conversations I hear. A lot of the blacks on welfare have no desire to get off it. Why should they? It's free money. I cannot stand to see my hard-earned money going to pay for someone who wants to sit on his or her ass all day long and get free money. That is bull, and it may be white thinking, but hey, I feel it is true to a point. You hear it on TV all the time: "We don't have to do this because we were slaves 400 years ago. You owe it to us." I don't owe you, period. I had nothing to do with that and I am not going to pay for it. Also, I don't like the deal where a black person can say anything about a white, and that is not considered prejudice. But let a white person say even the tiniest little thing about a black person, and bang, get up in front of Reverend Al Sharpton and all the other schmucks. That is bull. That is a double standard all the way along the line.

According to the Southern Poverty Law Center, in 2005 there were 803 active hate groups and 179 active chapters of the Ku Klux Klan (*The Journal of Blacks in Higher Education* 2006a).

Even highly educated persons exhibit racism. Physicians have described black patients—regardless of their education and income levels—as less intelligent, less educated, more likely to abuse alcohol and drugs, less likely to follow medical advice, and less likely to participate in rehabilitation than white patients. Perhaps it is not surprising that a review of more than 100 studies by the U.S. Institute of Medicine found that discrimination itself contributes to racial disparities in health care and higher death rates among minorities from cancer, heart disease, diabetes, and HIV infection (Smedley et al. 2002).

Racism affects families. For example, Hispanics and blacks spend an average of over $3,000 more than whites to locate and buy the same house (Yinger 1995), often receive harsher criminal sentences than whites for the same offense, especially if their skin is dark (*The Journal of Blacks in Higher Education* 2006a; Mauer 1999), and are generally less likely to be hired than comparable white job applicants (Bertrand and Mullainathan 2004). Researchers sent fictitious résumés to help wanted ads placed in Chicago and Boston newspapers, and randomly assigned names that sounded African American (e.g., Latoya or Tyrone) or white-sounding names (e.g., Emily or Brendan). The résumés with white-sounding names received 50 percent more calls for interviews (Bertrand and Mullainathan 2004). Racism affects their purchasing power, their place of residence and neighborhood, opportunities for their children, the type of schools children attend, the way parents socialize their children, and many other factors that shape families. In Box 6.1, a white mother describes her experience with racism against her young adopted black daughter.

Who Counts as "Them"?

Throughout the world, in virtually every country, some racial or ethnic groups are singled out and subjected to negative stereotyping and discrimination. Map 6.1 on pages 180 and 181 illustrates the prevalence of minority groups in each country. Often there is severe tension and outright conflict between groups, perhaps related to religious differences, disagreement over territory, or a desire to change the power imbalance among peoples. **Ethnic cleansing** is the systematic killing, torturing, or removal of persons with the intention of eliminating a specific racial or ethnic group. We are familiar with his-

BOX 6.1 Families as Lived Experience

Loving Across the Color Line: A White Adoptive Mother Learns About Race

What would a liberal, white, civil rights law professor have to learn about race? When Sharon Rush adopted a black girl, she quickly learned that she had to throw out old assumptions and face deep questions about race. By living with her daughter, she learned about the harsh encounters blacks face regularly, and, below, describes one example of the everyday racism levied at her daughter (Rush 2000, 77–79).

My daughter was six years old and we were on our way to New Hampshire to climb her first mountain. As we were waiting for our connecting flight, she was off exploring the waiting lounge and getting drinks of water—all within my sight, of course. A white woman sat down next to me and placed her luggage in front of her chair. She hadn't been sitting long when her connecting flight was called. As she gathered her belongings, she noticed her purse was missing. I helped her look around the immediate area for it but did not see it. We looked around perhaps ten seconds; it did not take long to see it was not there, when she loudly announced, "I bet that black kid took it." She was pointing directly at my daughter, the only child and the only black person in the waiting area.

If the woman had reflected for a moment before making her accusation, she would have realized how silly her conclusion was. My daughter certainly was not trying to make a getaway; she was doing ballet turns in the waiting area, oblivious to everyone around her, and clearly did not have possession of a purse. I was so stunned and offended by the woman's accusation that I could not point this out to her. Instead, I responded, "I'm sorry, but you are talking about my daughter and I can assure you she is not a thief. Perhaps you left your purse at the ticket counter." Sure enough, she returned from the counter with her purse and flew out the door, remarking as she went, "Well, it's Friday the 13th. What do you expect?"

I was momentarily dumbstruck. I wasn't sure what I expected. Clearly, I did not expect an adult white woman to be suspicious of a six-year-old child—black or white, girl or boy—doing ballet twirls in the waiting area of an airport. I did not expect my daughter to pose a threat to her.

My daughter did not hear the woman's accusation, but she will learn about it when she reads this book. I hope when that day comes that she will be sufficiently older and will be able to situate the racist thinking behind the accusation in the white woman and not internalize it as a message about black inferiority. The woman's accusation was outrageous, but it was only one of many ways in which my daughter is rebuffed by white society every day.

Source: Rush 2000.

CRITICAL THINKING QUESTIONS

1. How do you think whites, blacks, and other minority groups would respond to this story? Do you think their responses would be similar or different? Why?
2. What special strategies do minority groups use to avoid internalizing the racism that they encounter? Do these strategies work? How do whites respond to these strategies?

torical accounts of the extermination of six million Jews (and others) in the Nazi regime, but ethnic cleansing has also occurred in recent years in Rwanda and Serbia.

Sociologists have noted that although prejudice and discrimination against minorities are widespread, the justifications for prejudice and discrimination may be radically different from one country to another. Sociologist Michele Lamont (2003) compared racism in the United States and France, two highly developed nations and asked the question, "Who counts as 'them'?" Lamont interviewed 150 white working-class men living in the suburbs of Paris and New York. Instead of asking directly about racism, respondents were asked to describe the kinds of people they like and dislike, the kinds of people they

MAP 6.1 Eye on the World: Comparative Ethnic and Racial Diversity

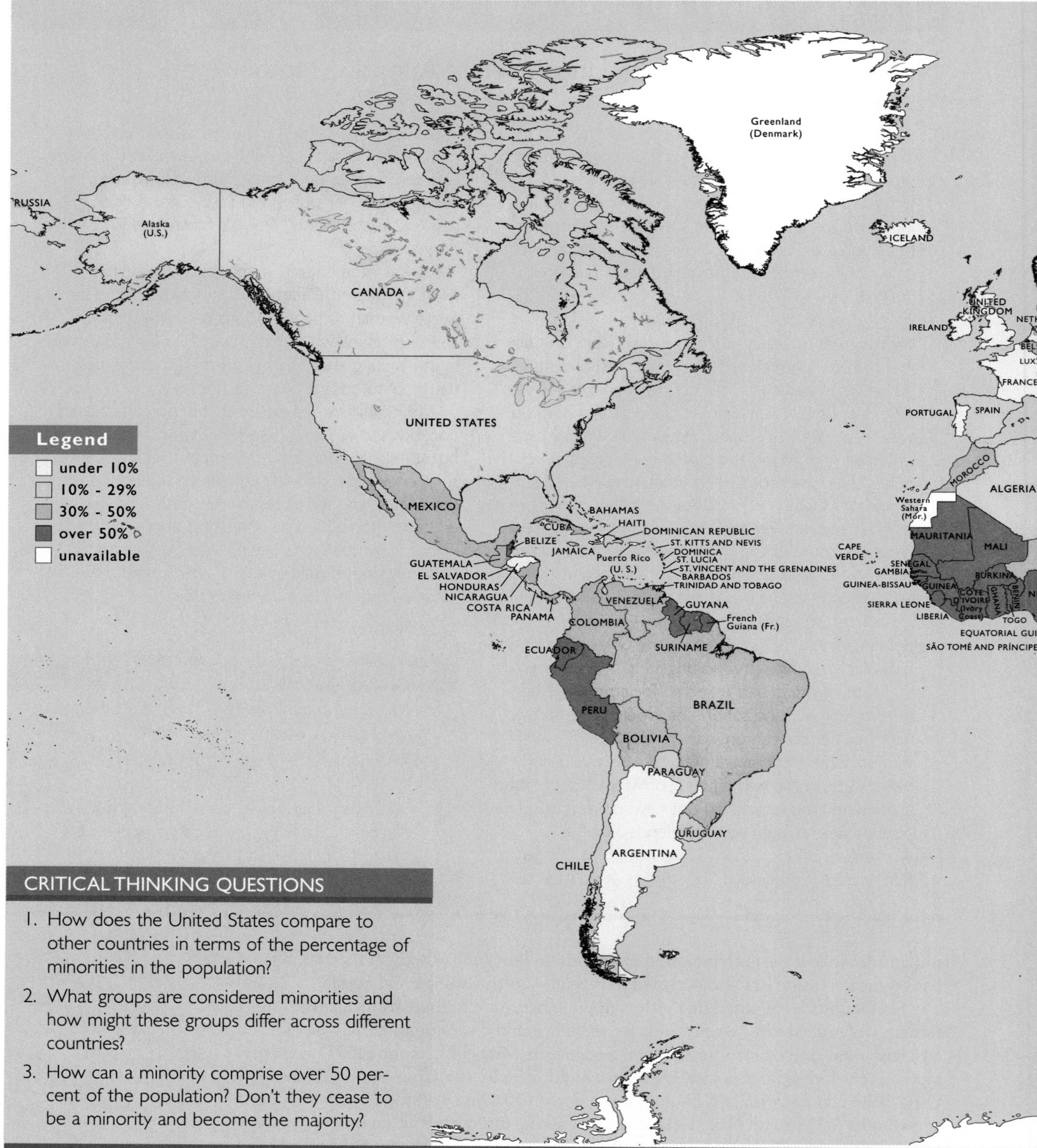

CRITICAL THINKING QUESTIONS

1. How does the United States compare to other countries in terms of the percentage of minorities in the population?
2. What groups are considered minorities and how might these groups differ across different countries?
3. How can a minority comprise over 50 percent of the population? Don't they cease to be a minority and become the majority?

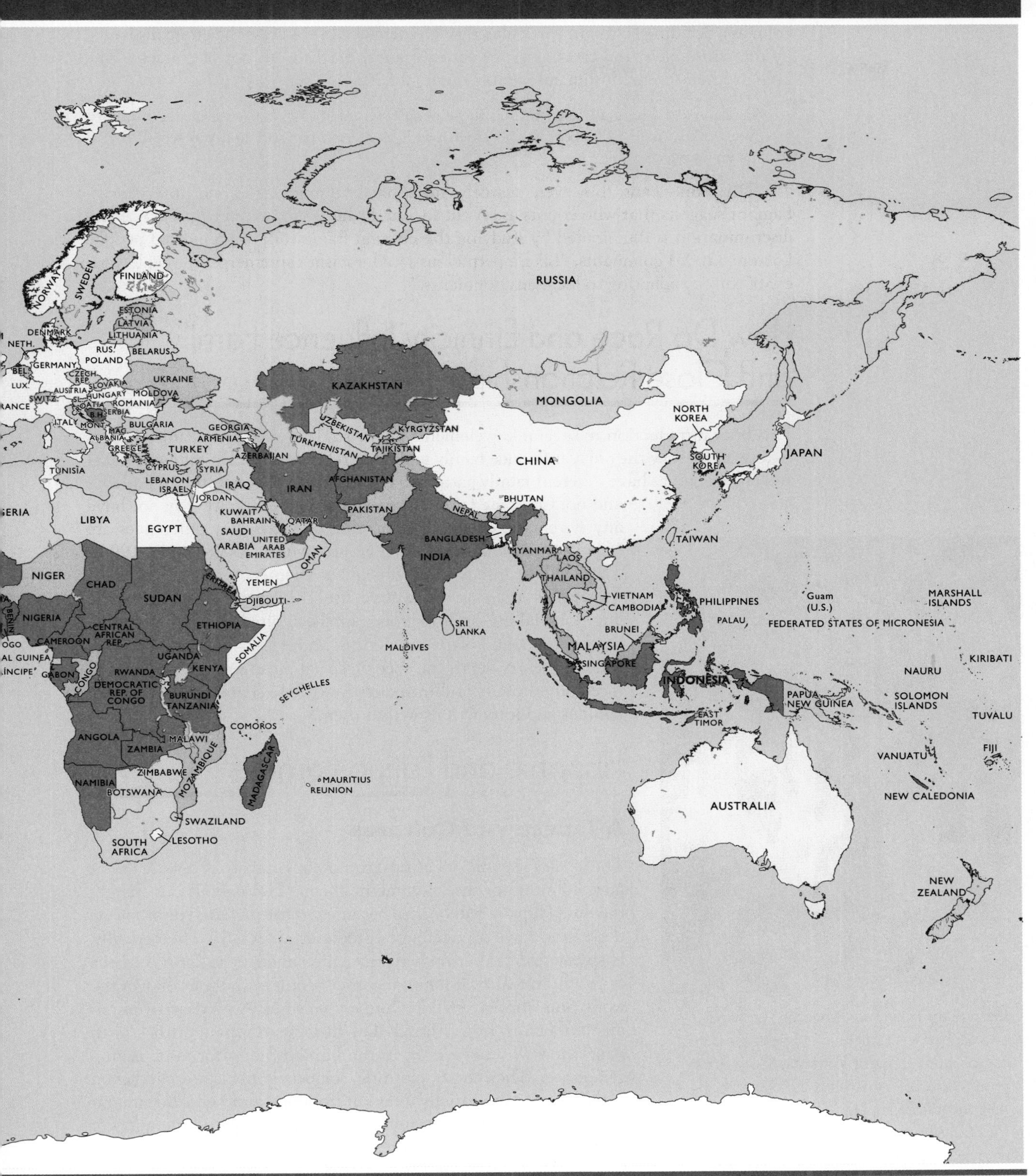

Source: Smith 1997.

feel similar to and different from, and the types of people to whom they feel inferior and superior to. The Americans were much more likely than the French to mention race or skin color as a deciding factor. In particular, blacks emerged most often as the group disdained by the white New Yorkers as "them"; yet in France, blacks were not of concern. The French "them" were Muslim immigrants (Lamont 2003):

> Parasites . . . I hate all of them. All those people who don't have a sense of responsibility. We work so hard to support them. When you look at your pay stub and you see all that is taken away!

The Americans, however, scarcely mentioned immigrants when interviewed. Lamont suggests that who counts as an outsider and who is victimized by prejudice and discrimination is illuminated by studying the cultural framework of prejudiced people. Lamont (2003) comments, "Like a pernicious weed, racism can emerge in a wide variety of soils by adapting to local environments."

How Do Race and Ethnicity Influence Family and Close Relationships?

This brief introduction to several key elements in the study of race and ethnicity leads us to wonder how they may influence family and close relationships. Do different racial and ethnic groups have different family patterns? The answer to that question is both yes and no. On some familial issues, race and ethnicity may not have any systematic effects, but in other contexts, key differences are noted across racial and ethnic groups (Murry 2000; Staples 1994). These will be discussed in subsequent chapters.

Rather than an exhaustive list, this chapter highlights the largest racial and ethnic groups in the United States—Hispanic, black, Asian, and Native American and Alaska Natives—to illustrate in greater depth the specific social meanings associated with race and ethnicity and introduce how these shape the structure of families and interactions within them.

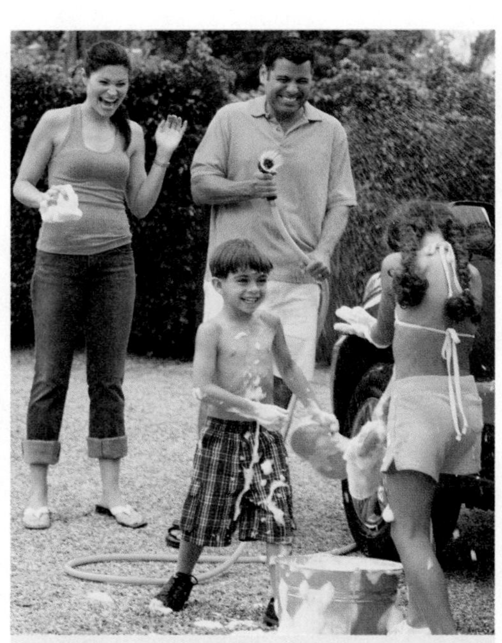

Despite their common language, the social and economic situations of Hispanic groups can be vastly different from one another; for example, Cuban Americans, as shown here, have incomes comparable to whites, while Mexican Americans are overrepresented among the poor.

Hispanic and Latino Families

A Tapestry of Cultures

The labels Hispanic or Latino cover groups that are so diverse that it makes almost no sense to combine them. (Throughout this chapter the term *Hispanic* will be used because it is the preferred term among those who have a preference [Brodie et al. 2002].) Theoretically, Hispanic refers to persons who trace their ancestry to Latin America or Spain. In reality, it lumps together people with roots all over the world and who have wildly different cultures. A newly arrived immigrant family from Mexico has little in common with Cuban Americans who have been in the United States for more than a generation. Their foods, clothing, socioeconomic status, and even language are substantially different from one another. The circumstances surrounding their immigration may be quite different. For example, affluent Cubans were welcomed during the early regime of Castro. Many were professionals in their home country. Their strong use of social capital has helped subsequent generations of Cuban immigrants to succeed. The average income of Cuban Americans is comparable to that of whites. In contrast, most Mexican Americans arriving in the United States are poor; many come illegally. They work in the lowest-paid jobs, sometimes seasonally. Many live in poverty and do not have basic resources such as health insurance. They do not have the financial resources or social capital to help others. In contrast to these two groups, Puerto Ricans are American citizens with no barriers to living in the United States, but who remain an impoverished group. Despite these vast differences, the U.S. Census Bureau and other research centers generally combine these groups together under the umbrella term Hispanic, only occasionally distinguishing by country of origin. Most data are still aggregated into one large group, and therefore potentially important variations in experience cannot be assessed.

The Hispanic population in the United States is growing and changing quickly. At 14.5 percent of the population, or 42 million people, Hispanics now comprise the largest minority group in the United States, increasing more than 50 percent since 1990 (Pew Research Center 2006d). Figure 6.4 shows the distribution of Hispanic population by country of origin. Nearly two-thirds of Hispanics in the United States are Mexican Americans; Puerto Ricans constitute the second largest group at 9 percent. Nearly half of Hispanics live in the western United States, and a third live in the south (Pew Research Center 2006d).

Hispanic Families Today

In the past, the growth in the Hispanic population was primarily due to immigration. Large numbers of Hispanics migrated to the United States from Mexico, Central America, Cuba, and other regions. Now, however, the growth is fueled more by a high fertility rate. Data from the U.S. Census Bureau, shown in Figure 6.5, indicate that Hispanic women have the highest fertility rate among all racial and ethnic groups shown (85 births per 1,000 women aged 15 to 44) (Dye 2005). To look at it another way,

FIGURE 6.4 **Percent Distribution of the Hispanic Population by Place of Origin: 2005**

Source: Pew Research Center 2006d.

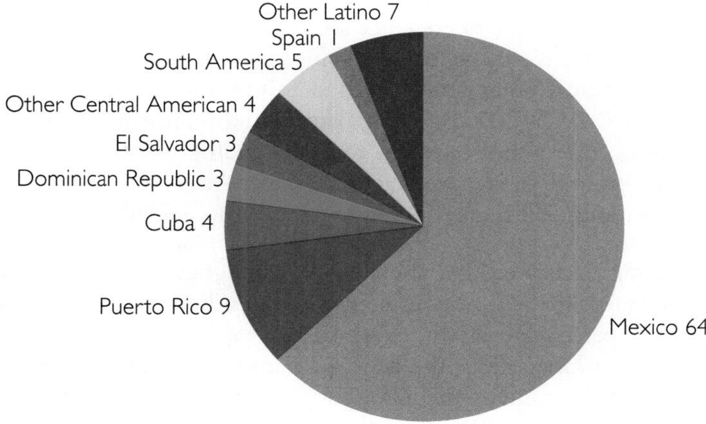

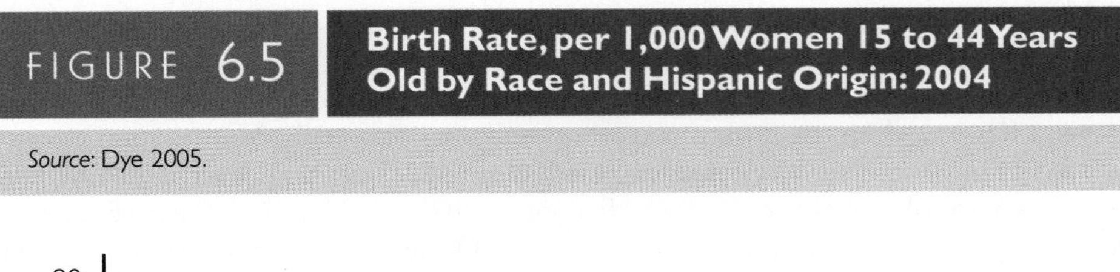

FIGURE 6.5 Birth Rate, per 1,000 Women 15 to 44 Years Old by Race and Hispanic Origin: 2004

Source: Dye 2005.

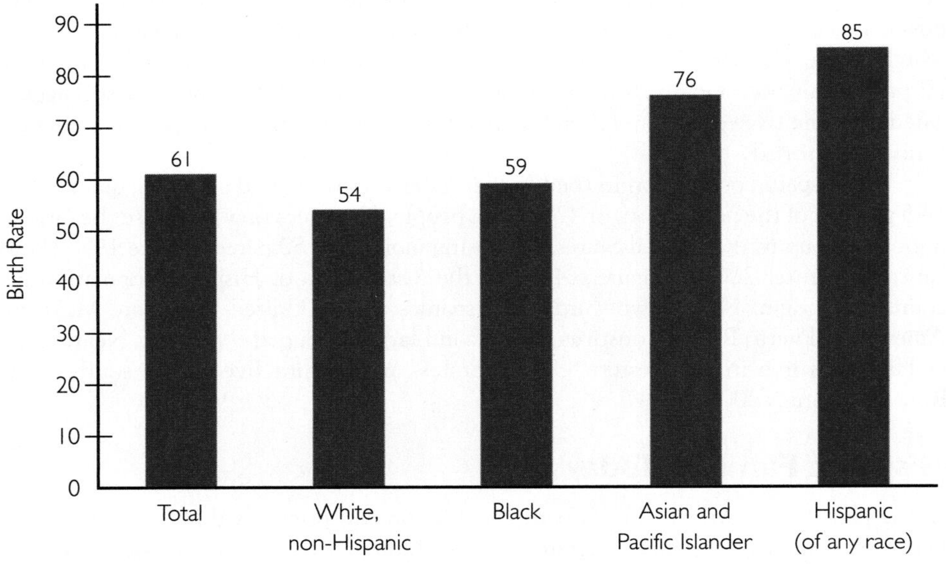

although Hispanic women aged 15 to 44 comprise only 15 percent of all women in that age group, they gave birth to 21 percent of all children in 2005. Foreign-born Hispanic women have particularly high fertility rates (Pew Hispanic Center 2006d). In other words, the population is now expanding not solely because of immigration, but because of children born to those immigrants.

This change poses many new and intriguing questions. How will the lives of the second generation be different from the first? Will the second generation do better economically? How much advantage comes from being raised and educated in the United States? Will the second generation speak English fluently? Will they retain their native language and Hispanic culture? What type of prejudice and discrimination do Hispanics face? How might the dynamics of this change in the coming years?

Studies by the Pew Hispanic Center attempt to address many questions about the Hispanic population (2002, 2005, 2006d). Using data from a representative sample of nearly 3,000 Hispanics, the authors covered topics including identity and assimilation, family relationships and gender expectations, experiences with prejudice and discrimination, finances, and health care. Some key highlights include:

- Overall, 9 in 10 Hispanics indicated that they believe immigrants need to learn to speak English to succeed in the United States, which, perhaps surprisingly, is slightly higher than the percentage of whites who feel this way. Spanish, however, remains the dominant language in the adult Hispanic population, although the second generation of Hispanics—the U.S.-born children of immigrants—predominantly speak English or are bilingual. Hispanic parents, even those who are immigrants, report that English is the language their children generally use when speaking with their friends.

- Hispanics tend to be more conservative on social and family issues than whites. For example, they are more likely to oppose divorce, homosexual relationships, and abortion. However, Hispanics that are more assimilated—that is, those who primarily speak English, who are native born, or who are from the second or third generation—tend to have social values that are more characteristic of mainstream Americans.
- Hispanics tend to express views that emphasize the importance of family ties. The majority (78 percent) believe that children should live with their parents until they are married, that elderly parents should live with their children (73 percent), and that relatives are more important than friends (87 percent). However, attitudes vary by assimilation. For example, while 91 percent of foreign-born Hispanics believe that children should live in their parents' home until they marry, only 57 percent of native-born Hispanics believe this.
- Hispanics tend to be more traditional in their orientation toward sex and gender than are whites, although again, this tends to vary by degree of assimilation into mainstream culture. For example, 43 percent of Hispanics who claim that Spanish is their dominant language agree with the statement, "In general the husband should have the final say in family matters," as compared to 27 percent of those Hispanics who speak English predominantly.
- Hispanics overwhelmingly (82 percent) say that discrimination against Hispanics is a problem in places such as schools (75 percent) and the workplace (78 percent). Many also believe that they are treated with less respect or receive poorer service than whites. Persons who are less assimilated—they speak Spanish as their dominant language or are foreign-born or first-generation Hispanics—are more likely to report that these are major problems. Interestingly, those persons who are *most assimilated* are more likely to report direct personal experience with discrimination. For example, 40 percent of English-dominant Hispanics have reported personal experience with discrimination, compared to 23 percent of those who predominantly speak Spanish.
- Overall, Hispanics have a weaker financial situation than whites. They report having lower household incomes, they are less likely to own the home they live in, and they are more likely to report having had financial difficulties in the past year. However, this does not mean that all Hispanics are struggling financially. Hispanics who were born in the United States and those who speak English are much more likely to have a higher income and less likely to experience financial hardship than those Hispanics who were born outside the United States or who primarily speak Spanish. Moreover, Hispanics tend to be more optimistic than whites or blacks that their children will have better jobs and make more money than they do.

These important data highlight two important facts: (1) there remain distinct differences in personal experience, values, opportunities, and constraints among Hispanic groups in the United States; and (2) there are also differences based on degree of assimilation. For example, the experiences and values of the second generation are often in marked contrast to those of the first (Fry and Lowell 2002; Pew Research Center 2006d). There are strong indications that the majority of U.S.-born children of Hispanic immigrants will move beyond the working-class jobs or impoverished circumstances that are typical of their parents. Although the second generation is still largely young (4 in 10 are between 16 and 24 years), the early analyses indicate substantial economic gains from the first generation to the second. They will likely receive more education, take jobs that demand greater skills, and be paid higher wages. However, the movement forward will not be enough to bring the second generation to equality with non-Hispanic whites. Consequently, rather than lumping Hispanic groups together, it is critical that we recognize that this is a diverse and rapidly changing ethnic group.

Family Focus: Health Insurance and Mexican American Families

Mexican culture is deeply rooted in families. Mexican families are characterized by close extended relationships with cousins, aunts, uncles, and grandparents. Strong families provide a critical support network that includes social, financial, and emotional support, which are important because Mexican families face risk factors such as poverty or fear of deportation (Pew Hispanic Center 2006d; Ramirez and de la Cruz 2003; Viramontez Anguiano et al. 2004).

One of those risk factors is the lack of health insurance. As discussed in Chapter 5, health insurance is an important mechanism by which individuals and families in the United States access the health care system when they are sick or injured. Without insurance, many people are turned away at hospitals, doctors' offices, and clinics all over the country.

Hispanic groups are particularly disadvantaged with respect to having health insurance. Approximately one-third of Hispanics were uninsured in 2005, which is three times the rate for whites and 50 percent higher than for blacks. Thirty-seven percent of Hispanics report that they had been uninsured for at least part of the year, and over one-quarter had been uninsured for more than 1 year (Cohen and Ni 2004; DeNavas-Walt et al. 2006).

Researchers have found that of all Hispanic groups, Mexican Americans are the least likely to have health insurance (Pew Hispanic Center 2004). About 40 percent of persons listing Mexico as their country of origin are uninsured, compared to 20 percent listing Cuba, or 18 percent listing Puerto Rico. This is likely due to several factors, including higher rates of unemployment; overrepresentation in jobs where health insurance is not provided, such as agricultural or other seasonal work; and a larger number of undocumented workers (Pew Hispanic Center 2004, 2006d).

What does this mean for Mexican American families? Economic security is tenuous for any family when even one member is uninsured. One medical event can exhaust financial resources and pull a family into poverty or near poverty. Mexican American families are particularly vulnerable to these conditions, and their family members suffer as a result. Children and adults are likely to go without needed health care and immunizations. Pregnant women are likely to forgo prenatal care, possibly resulting in a variety of negative health outcomes for themselves and their babies. To get the medical care they require may exhaust or seriously tax their financial resources. It is not a coincidence that Mexican American families, the group least likely to have insurance, are also more likely to live below the poverty line than are other Hispanic groups. Income and health insurance status are interrelated. It is likely that the family's poverty is both a cause and a consequence of the vulnerability of living without health insurance.

Illegal immigrants are in a particular bind because they may have no access to care except in dire emergencies. Box 6.2 reveals the struggle that one undocumented family faces trying to secure the health care they need.

BOX 6.2 SOCIAL POLICIES FOR FAMILIES

"Guadalupe"

How do illegal immigrants and their children find health care when they become ill or injured? Guadalupe is the mother of eight children and describes her struggles in accessing the health care system. This interview is part of a larger project based on a statewide study of families leaving welfare for work in Oregon.

•

"Guadalupe" is a hearty Mexican woman with soft round features and her smile is warm and welcoming. Originally from Durango, Mexico, she has been living in the sparsely populated, rural, dry climate of eastern Oregon with her husband and eight children for the past ten years. Only three of her eight children were born in the U.S., leaving the oldest five, along with Guadalupe and her husband, undocumented.

Her town has a population of about 1,700 people, and the closest town with any range of services is about 30 minutes away by car. The Hispanic population in this area reaches up to 25 percent, which is significantly higher than the state average of 9 percent, owing in large part to employment opportunities in the agricultural sector.

The first time we visited Guadalupe she answered the door and humbly welcomed us into her trailer. We passed through the entryway, which also served as a small laundry room, and into the kitchen where we saw a molcajete (a handmade stone mortar and pestle) with fresh salsa on the small kitchen table and a sack of apples overflowing on the floor. It was apple-picking season. The trailer was dark and quiet. As we walked past the kitchen counter my gaze fell underneath it only to find four children, hands folded on their laps, quietly and eagerly catching our stare. They introduced themselves one-by-one, each of their names beginning with the letter "G," just like their mother's. Guadalupe proceeded into the living room, and we sat on the worn couch and began chatting.

Guadalupe is a farmworker who gauges time by the harvest; her work comes in bits and spurts, and can be unconscionably demanding. The interview was nearly impossible to set up because Guadalupe would leave her house for the fields between 3 AM and 4 AM and wouldn't get home until after 10 PM, every single day of the week. She will do that during the harvest for about a month and then not have any work until the next harvest comes around. In the wintertime, multiple months without work are strung together to compound the difficulty of feeding eight growing children.

We talked in Spanish about other employment opportunities, but they are extremely limited because she doesn't have a "good" social security card. Her eldest daughter, who at 16 has lived three-quarters of her life in the United States, is also undocumented and has just started working in the fields during the summers. Her husband also works in the fields, but year-round, which provides some degree of stability for the family. When we asked if the farm labor was hard, she replied in her native language, "*A little, but, yeah. You have to endure it.*"

Because Guadalupe is undocumented, she is only eligible for minimal social services from the state and federal government. In fact, the only reason she is eligible at all is because three of her eight children were born in the U.S. and, as U.S. citizens, are eligible to apply for services like the Oregon Health Plan (OHP), Oregon's version of Medicaid. When Guadalupe applies for OHP, her three youngest get full coverage, but she, her husband, and other five children only qualify for emergency coverage, and they find that it covers very little:

> But it didn't cover anything. More than a year ago, I went to the clinic and asked if it would cover me, and they said that it wouldn't. [Interviewer: What was it for?] Oh, it's that I had a pain here, I was always carrying it here, so I went but it didn't cover me. It wasn't worth anything. They said only if it was something really bad, really serious. That was all it would cover.

When asked if she worried, Guadalupe replied,

> Yes, yes, I worry, I worry about that because it's hard, I mean. Because without insurance, without

(continued)

> medical, well, what do we have to pay with? It's hard.

On the whole, Guadalupe has had very few interactions with medical providers, clinics, and the emergency room. In the first interview with her she told us of an occasion when she went to the local doctor's office in her small town and was turned away because she didn't have insurance.

> One of my sons had a fever, a cough, and I gave him remedies and he needed medicine, and they said that they couldn't because I didn't belong there, I didn't have, what is it? The application. I didn't have it, and that is why I have never gone back.

She told us of a time when she went to the emergency room with one of her documented children who had OHP at the time. He had a twig lodged in his leg and received care without any problems. The hospital is about 30 minutes away by car. Sometimes she and her husband have a car, and sometimes they don't, "*because sometimes it breaks and takes a while to fix it.*" During times when they don't have a car, they have to ask around to see if anyone can give them a ride.

Fortunately, she and her husband and her kids are all very healthy. When asked about her health, she said, "*In that way I'm lucky,*" as if in contrast to all the other ways in which she is unlucky. She worries though that something will happen to her or one of her children and they won't be able to afford to go to the hospital.

> Like, at the hospital, if I took them to the emergency room, right then they don't charge you, but then you get the bill later. But if you bring in your check stubs, and tell them how much you make, then they give you a discount. . . . It takes, it's like an hour or two before they see you. You have to wait. And then after they see you, they give you medicine, and that's if you are sick, and then you get a bill.

Guadalupe is one of millions of people who live on the margins. She, her husband, and most of her children were undocumented, rendering her and her family ineligible for full health coverage from the state. Her undocumented status also severely limited her employment opportunities. As an apple or potato picker she made $6.90/hour, did not have benefits, and had no guarantee of work for any extended period of time. When she did have work, it was 18-hour days, 7 days a week. In addition to these considerable obstacles, she had little education and didn't speak any English. In terms of health care, she and her family lived so on the margins of the health care system that she had managed to live her life as if health care, except in the case of a life or death emergency situation, was simply not a viable option. While Guadalupe did express concerns about the costs associated with health care, she said,

> Well, you see there are necessities, but more than anything I would like work. That they give work to people even though they didn't have a good [social] security [number], to work, that is what I would like, work.

Source: Adapted from Seccombe and Hoffman 2007.

CRITICAL THINKING QUESTIONS

1. Do you think Guadalupe's problems are unique to her and her family? Why or why not?
2. What are the personal and structural factors that inhibit Guadalupe and her family from getting the health care that they may need?
3. How should state or federal policy respond to people like Guadalupe? Whose responsibility is it, if anyone's, to help her and her family?

Black Families

Racial and ethnic titles and categories are everchanging. Although few people today use the term Negro to describe blacks as they did in the past, what is the difference between the terms *African American* and *black*? Often we use the terms interchangeably, but it is not technically correct to do so. Black is a broad racial category, whereas African American is an ethnic group. Most blacks in the United States are indeed African Americans, but there are some who are not; for example, those of Haitian descent. Throughout this text the term black generally will be used to conform to Census Bureau definitions; however, the term African American will be used when it seems to be a more accurate description or when citing research by others who use that term.

Until recently blacks were the largest minority group in the United States and were generally considered synonymous with the term minority. This is no longer the case because the number and growth of Hispanic groups now exceed those of blacks. The U.S. Census Bureau (2006b) estimates that that there are a little over 36 million black Americans, comprising nearly 13 percent of the population; the majority lives in the south (54 percent) and in a central city (52 percent).

Overall, black families have historically had different family patterns than white families (Hill 2005). They are less likely to be married, have more children, are more likely to have close extended family relationships, and more likely to be poor. Family scholars have often interpreted these to be problematic. Daniel Patrick Moynihan crystallized the discussion in 1965 when he released the so-called *Moynihan Report* (more formally known as *The Negro Family: The Case for National Action*). In it, he suggested that the repercussions of slavery continued to be a destructive and destabilizing force to black families, resulting in a "tangle of pathology" (Moynihan 1965). One of his primary concerns was the dismal economic plight of blacks, which caused men to leave their families, mothers to become "matriarchs," and high rates of delinquency, illegitimacy, alcoholism, and school dropout (Moynihan 1965). He described these as by-products of urban structural conditions of society, failing social institutions, and racism; nonetheless, his book has sometimes been mistakenly used as criticism of black families.

Family scholars note that black families have many strengths (Hill 2005; Ladner 1998). Billingsley (1968) pointed out that the structure of black families was not the cause of social problems, but was actually an adaptive response to a racist culture. He suggested that rather than considering the black family as deteriorating, it is showing resilience in the face of economic and social difficulties. Likewise, Hill (1972) contended that strength and stability, not weakness and instability, are characteristics of black families. Another scholar, Charles Willie, claims that the notion of a black matriarchy is a myth and suggests that it was really an egalitarian relationship. He believes one of the greatest gifts of blacks to the culture of the nation has been the egalitarian family model in which neither the husband nor the wife is always in charge (Willie 1983; Willie and Reddick 2003).

Sociologist Shirley Hill (2005) suggests that the successes of the civil rights movement diversified blacks and created new class, race, and gender divisions. Increasing numbers of blacks are joining the middle class, and a larger number of women, in particular, are attending and completing college (*The Journal of Blacks in Higher Education* 2006a, b). Therefore, to really understand black families, scholars today are expanding their focus of racial inequality to also include a broader range of intersections: how do race, sex, and social class interact to shape lived experience in families? For example, although many studies note that black parents racially socialize their children, few look at how this racial socialization varies across social class. Likewise, while most scholars suggest that black parents are less rigid in the gender socialization of their children, rarely is this examined across social class lines. Hill (2005), for example, found that there is significant support for sex and gender equality if one looks at the educational and career aspirations parents have for their children, but beyond these overt measures, views of sex and gender are sharply divided on class lines, with lower-income blacks retaining traditional ideologies.

Black Families Today

Black families tend to live in larger families and households than do whites. For example, 18 percent of married couple black families contain five or more members, compared to only 12 percent of similar white families. Moreover, among female-headed households, 13 percent of blacks live in families with five or more members, compared to less than 5 percent of whites (U.S. Census Bureau 2006b). What accounts for the difference? One factor is birth rates; blacks average a greater number of children than do whites. However, another important factor is the greater likelihood of blacks who live in extended families (Cole 2003).

Economic Conditions One of the most pervasive stereotypes associated with blacks is that they are impoverished. As shown in Figure 6.6, this is a tremendous overgeneralization (DeNavas-Walt et al. 2006). In fact, nearly a third of blacks have household incomes of at least $50,000, a 20 percent increase since 1990. Income data for married couples show particular promise: Well over half of married black couples earn at least $50,000 per year, including 30 percent who earn at least $75,000 (U.S. Census Bureau 2006b). Similar trends can be found in educational attainment. Blacks now graduate from high school at nearly the same rate as whites, around 85 percent. Eighteen percent of blacks age 25 and over have a bachelor's degree or higher, while over 5 percent have an advanced graduate or professional degree (U.S. Census Bureau 2006b).

This means that many blacks are entering the world of the middle class, having worked themselves up from the working or lower classes. Most of these younger blacks did not have parents from whom they could inherit money or receive extensive finan-

FIGURE 6.6 **Income for White, Black, Asian, Hispanic: 2005 (Percent)**

Source: U.S. Census Bureau 2005.

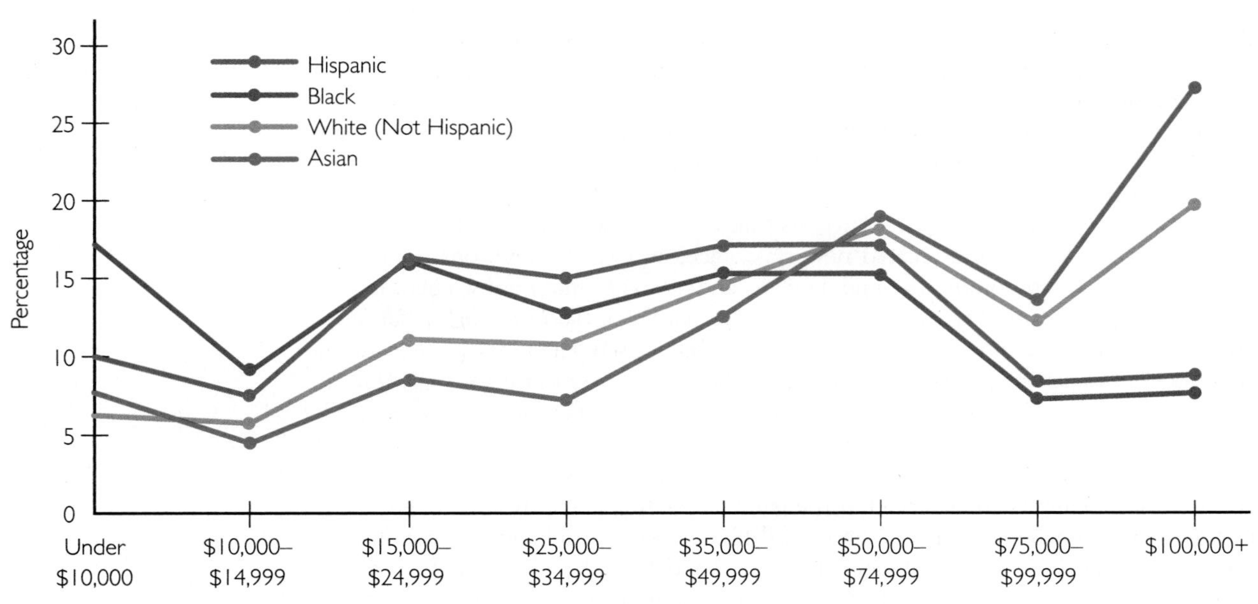

cial assistance and therefore, they have fewer assets than whites. Data from the U.S. Census Bureau reveal extensive differences in assets between blacks and whites, which have clear impacts on family consumptive patterns, family values, and family relationships. For example, only 48 percent of black adults own their own home, compared to 73 percent of whites. Moreover, blacks had average wealth worth 20 cents for every dollar of assets owned by their white counterparts (Mishel et al. 2007). The discrepancy is due to three factors: (1) whites are more likely to draw upon the assets of their parents through an inheritance or loan to be able to afford a home, car, or other high-ticket item; (2) whites have an easier time obtaining mortgage loans from banks; and (3) homes in predominantly white neighborhoods appreciate in value more rapidly than do homes in predominantly black neighborhoods (Oliver and Shapiro 1995). The Census Bureau reports that the gap in assets between blacks and whites has widened during the 1990s because of the economic recession leaving blacks further vulnerable (Armas 2004). Differences in assets affect patterns of social mobility. Black children born into the top quarter of the income distribution have only a 15 percent chance of remaining there, as compared to 45 percent of whites (Hertz 2004).

Family Focus: Blacks and Extended Families

Nearly one in five black children under the age of 15 lives in an extended family, more than three times the rate for whites and nearly double the rate for Hispanics (Glick and Van Hook 2002; Saluter 1996). **Extended families** include not only parents and children, but also other family members such as grandparents, uncles, aunts, or cousins. Extended families can provide critical resources to family members, yet they have sometimes been denigrated as a characteristic of only poor families. However, blacks are more likely than whites to live in extended families regardless of income level. Even upper-middle-class or wealthy black Americans are more likely to co-reside with other family members (Hatchett and Jackson 1993).

Blacks are more likely than whites to live in extended families, regardless of their income. What types of benefits accrue to people living in extended families?

Why are extended families more common among blacks than whites? Black families have a rich cultural heritage of drawing upon and sharing aid with other family members. One study of 487 black parents aged 18 to 34, drawn from the *National Survey of Black Americans*, found that parents most often nominated their own parents as the persons they could count on for child care assistance and parental guidance (Hunter 1997).

This rich family and cultural heritage of blacks is grounded in rural folkways (Wilkinson 1997). Important family rites, rituals, and ceremonies maintained the strong intergenerational ties within families. Historians have shown that extended families were highly valued during times of slavery. A review of 2,200 ex-slave narratives collected in the 1930s highlight the important role that grandparents played in the black community, including in raising children. Although some families were cruelly broken up by the slave trade, blacks nonetheless keenly appreciated older relatives, real and fictive, and coresided whenever possible (Covey and Lockman 1996). Herbert Gutman's book, *The Black Family in Slavery and Freedom* (1976), examines plantation records and census data for a number of cities between 1880 and 1925, and documents that two-parent households prevailed during slavery and after emancipation. Even when slavery destroyed biological families, kinship networks were rewoven so that unrelated slaves could join in and be part of a family (Gutman 1976).

Researchers have found that black families maintain a high degree of geographical closeness and maintain a strong sense of family and familial obligation. They note that household boundaries are often more fluid than among white families, with a greater willingness to take in relatives, both children and adults, if the need arises. Black families are characterized by frequent interaction with relatives and an established system of mutual aid. Extended families can provide closeness and intimacy, help with the day-to-day routines of raising children, reduce delinquency, and transmit cultural values to children (Hatchett and Jackson 1993; St. Jean and Feagin 1998).

Grandmothers play a crucial role in black families, especially among lower-income families. They often have a central place in the rearing of their grandchildren. One study that involved in-depth interviews with 19 grandmothers who were the biological mother of a teenage mother, found that the grandmothers were involved in seven key functions in their roles as grandmother (Flaherty et al. 1994):

1. *Managing:* Arranging of resources and activities so that they synchronize with each to meet family needs: "I didn't have nowhere to put the crib up . . . and I thought it would look kind of odd sitting in the front room. So I told Terri I'd try to get her one of those little playpen cribs which could fit out here in the front room."
2. *Caretaking:* Direct involvement in providing primary infant activities: ". . . in the morning after I get all the other kids out to go to school, I'll go ahead and feed Cecelia, give her a bath, brush her hair and read, and she'll go to sleep, as long as she's full . . . ."
3. *Coaching:* Role modeling or guidance about primary infant care activities or maternal role: ". . . little thing—I always tell her though, if the baby's full, make sure she's burped, or don't lay her down on her back . . . ."
4. *Assessing:* The evaluation of the mother's attitude about or competency in the maternal role: "She's doing better than I really expected that she would do. She really surprised me . . . giving the baby a bath. The baby's very clean. You know, some girls have babies and they don't really keep 'em . . . the way that she does it."
5. *Nurturing:* Emotional support and love of the mother and grandchild: ". . . the main thing is, that's my daughter, and the second important thing is this is my first grandbaby, and I love 'em both, and I wouldn't take nothing for either one of 'em."

6. *Assigning:* Expressions that suggest ownership of the baby: "Because I figure, like if I do it . . . make it too easy on her, she'll go out here again. So I told her, I said well, this is your body and your life and your baby."
7. *Patrolling:* Overseeing and evaluating the mother's lifestyle and personal life goals: "I took 'em to the doctor . . . and she is going on the pill though. She's going on something."

Despite the many benefits that an extended family can offer to poor or rich families, the dominant ideology in the United States suggests that extended families are dysfunctional in some way (Smith 1993). Too much interdependence is often characterized as a weakness rather than as a family strength. This is reflective of the uniquely American ideal of independence as a virtue, and that all families should be able to "go it alone" without help from family, friends, or the government. Many other cultures would disagree vehemently with this approach.

Asian American Families

An estimated 12 million U.S. residents report being Asian American or Asian in combination with one or more other races, comprising about 4 percent of the total population (U.S. Census Bureau 2006a). The term *Asian* is a catchall for many different groups of people who had origins with the early peoples of the Far East, Southeast Asia, or the Indian subcontinent. Often lumped in with these diverse groups are Pacific Islanders who have origins in Hawai'i, Guam, Samoa, or other Pacific islands. Some, like Japanese and Chinese Americans, may have been in the United States for generations. Others, such as the Hmong, Laotians, Cambodians, and Vietnamese are relative newcomers (Reeves and Bennett 2003). As is the case with Hispanics, these groups represent great diversity in culture, language, socioeconomic characteristics, and timing and reasons for migrating to the United States. Nonetheless, for statistical purposes, most government agencies combine these groups into one large category named "Asian American," and unfortunately, important nuances are lost. Much of what is discussed here is from government sources, and therefore, groups are most often combined.

Asian American Families Today

Asian Americans tend to live in metropolitan areas in the west. Nearly two-thirds were born in Asia, most commonly China, the Philippines, India, Vietnam, and Korea, and migrated to the United States at some point in their lives. The majority of the others are children, grandchildren, or other descendants of immigrants who came to the United States many years ago. Chinese girls orphaned because of China's one-child policy and adopted by U.S. families are another growing group, now numbering about 8,000 per year and increasing. These girls are receiving widespread attention, and an essay describing one such family's adoption is provided in Box 6.3.

Asian Americans have faced considerable prejudice and discrimination in the past; for example, Japanese Americans are the only racial or ethnic group rounded up against their will and put into internment camps with their property confiscated. Asian Americans continue to experience a great deal of prejudice today, for example, the assumption that someone named Zhou doesn't speak English or isn't really an American. Nonetheless, many Asian Americans have had remarkable success; indeed, they have sometimes been nicknamed a *model minority*.

BOX 6.3 Our Global Community

One Child's Very Special First Fourth of July

Many families are choosing to adopt children from other countries for infertility or humanitarian reasons. "Cloe" is a recent adoptee from the People's Republic of China. The following is a tribute by a grandmother, famous newspaper columnist Ellen Goodman, that reveals the love and pride she has in her new granddaughter.

It will be her very first parade, her very first Fourth of July. Our granddaughter will be both the newest citizen at the picnic and the newest member of our family.

Cloe, this little girl with shiny black hair and a quiet, curious stare, has come to America and to us. We have embraced her with a loyalty that is all the more tenacious for having not been preordained by biology. We have the sort of attachment that the word "adoption" cannot begin to describe.

Just six weeks ago, Cloe was halfway around the world in an orphanage in China. Six weeks before that, my stepdaughter and her husband got her photograph in the mail. It put a face—her face—on what had been a stack of papers, a mound of red tape, and of course, a hope.

Psychologists, neurologists, "ologists" of every variety may say it's impossible to bond to a photograph. But we connected to Cloe before she was named Cloe. We connected to her before she had any idea we existed or that there was a world outside the orphanage, outside the province, the country, the continent.

Before the travel papers arrived, we waited anxiously, tracking the reports of SARS, worried that Beijing would close down the border before our children became parents, before this child of China could become a child of America. But when the moment came to gather Cloe, it seemed as sudden as the wait had seemed interminable.

After all that time, she was just a plane trip away. In a single moment, a year-old child was transferred from one set of hands to another, and from one fate to another. The entire arc of her short life was transformed from being abandoned to being treasured.

Now we will take her to watch the parade of homemade flats come down the road and cheer the scramble up the greased pole. We will bring a newcomer to the American birthday party, but she has brought us to the wider world. We have made her an American and she has made us a part of the global village.

Our Cloe is one of about 20,000 international adoptions within the last year, one of the 5,000 girls from China. Over many months, we learned to spot them in the grocery store or the street. We learned to wonder what this wave of girls will make of their experience, of the great economic and political winds that changed the course of their lives.

"Model Minority" As a group, Asian Americans are considered an immigration success story. Asian Americans have the highest family incomes of any group, surpassing whites. They have the highest percentage of its workforce in white-collar positions and are more likely to graduate from college. They have the lowest rates of divorce, and their children are more likely to reside in married-couple households than are any other race or ethnic group (U.S. Census Bureau 2006a). How did diverse Asian American groups produce such successes?

There are many important factors that help to explain why Asian Americans are often heralded as a model minority. One major factor is the differences surrounding their immigration experience. People who have recently come from most Asian countries are generally from more privileged social classes in their countries. Many had considerable wealth to invest in their employment or educational opportunities in the United States. They also had a strong orientation to education; many were professionals with college degrees. Certainly this is not the case for all Asian Americans;

In China, an ancient culture that still sets a higher value on the head of a boy has collided with a government policy that pressures families to have only one child. As a result, hundreds of thousands of girls are growing up in orphanages. As a very different result, thousands of girls are growing up in America, more privileged than brothers left behind.

As for Cloe, we know the joy her story brings to our family. But we can only guess at the loss to the woman who left her day-old daughter on fortune's doorstep.

My stepdaughter tells me about the final medical exam Cloe was given on the way out of China. The pediatrician carefully examined the little patient. Then looking evenly at the new parents, she said directly, "You have a very beautiful, healthy daughter. You are very lucky."

What, we still wonder, did this accomplished, modern Chinese woman make of her own country that gives away so many of its daughters? What did she feel about a culture in which this "beautiful healthy daughter" faced the options of either an orphanage or America? For that matter, what did she think of Americans? Does she think we regard the world's children as a product—made in China—to import because we can afford to?

America is continually made and remade by newcomers. But this daughter of China has reminded us how small our world is and how vast: a village you can traverse in a day and a place of stunning disconnects and differences, haves and have-nots.

Ours was already a global family, brought together with luck of the draw and the pluck of ancestors who came from places as far away as Italy and England, Russia and Germany. On this Fourth of July, we add another continent to our heritage and another child to our list of supreme good fortune. Welcome, Cloe, to America.

Source: "Cloe's First Fourth" by Ellen Goodman, as appeared in *The Boston Globe*, July 3, 2003, p. A13. © 2003, The Washington Post Writers Group. Reprinted with Permission.

CRITICAL THINKING QUESTIONS

1. Why are international adoptions increasing in popularity?
2. Will children adopted from other countries—China, Guatemala, Korea, Russia—retain their own race or ethnic identity if white families raise them? What are the pros and cons of parents promoting a child's race or ethnic identity?
3. Following up on Goodman's questions, what do you think the female physician thinks of China? Of the one-child policy? Of the United States?

immigrants fleeing Vietnam, Cambodia, and Laos, for example, were often from rural villages and had little schooling or few employment skills.

Perhaps even more important is the long-standing emphasis on education, learning, and family that characterizes Asian culture. Individuality is deemphasized; the well-being of the family or greater community is of primary concern. In particular, families believe that the route to success in this country is through education and hard work. Parents may undergo great sacrifice to further their children's education, which is seen as the parents' most important mission. Children take their responsibility to succeed seriously as well. A child's actions, including their successes (or failures), reflect upon the entire family. Children are not only encouraged to do well in school for themselves, but also to bestow honor on the larger family. They share the status and monetary returns with their families.

As is the case with other minority groups, Asians often pool their resources to increase their upward mobility. However, in general, Asians have been more successful than other groups in quickly moving upward. One reason for this is that the pooling of resources often extends beyond family members; some Asian groups have created self-help organizations to provide loans and other financial aid to their members for starting up new businesses. Once a family achieves success, they are expected to do more than simply repay the loan. They are also expected to help out another family if possible.

Some of these cultural values are diluted the longer a person is exposed to the U.S. values of individualism and independence. Nonetheless, the strong emphasis on family and education, coupled with the generally greater resources of Asian immigrants compared to their counterparts from other regions of the world, have allowed marked success in the United States. Despite this, or perhaps *because* of their record of achievement, whites and other groups are sometimes prejudiced against them and resent their success.

Ignored is the fact that not all Asian Americans fit the image of the highly educated and high-earning professional. It is important to recognize that not all Asians are doing fabulously on these social indicators. Many of the more recent immigrants from Vietnam, Cambodia, and Laos lack the financial resources and social capital of other Asian American immigrants, and therefore have lower incomes and higher rates of poverty. For example, although Asians are more likely than whites to have earned a college degree, they are also more likely to have less than a ninth-grade education (Reeves and Bennett 2003). Likewise, 10 percent of Asian Americans live in poverty (U.S. Census Bureau Public Information Office 2003). Immigrants from Southeast Asia—Vietnam, Cambodia, and Laos—have some of the highest rates of welfare use in the United States.

Family Focus: Generational Tension

Children who are born and raised in the United States by parents who were born elsewhere, such as Mexico or Vietnam, are referred to as the *second generation*. These children often struggle with balancing their parents' culture with that found in the United States. Parents may hold on to their own cultural traditions about raising children even though these are at odds with mainstream traditions, such as dress or the close supervision of girls. Second-generation children may serve as linguistic and cultural brokers for their parents (who may not be bilingual) explaining to their parents how the U.S. culture operates. Children who are born in another country, but raised in the United States, are considered the *1.5 generation* and face similar challenges.

The large number of immigrants from Asian countries, particularly Southeast Asia, is a relatively new phenomenon in U.S. history. While immigrant children (and children of immigrants) may quickly adapt to U.S. culture, their parents are far less likely to assimilate, preferring to retain critical elements of their own culture and language (Kibria 1993, 1997; Pyke 2000a, b; Zhou and Bankston 1998). Key features of traditional Asian culture contrast sharply with U.S. culture. For example, traditionally, Asian parents are less apt to express emotion to one another or to their children; they emphasize the needs of the family over the individual; and they allow their children fewer freedoms and choices than do American parents. These cultural differences have the potential to lead to considerable tension between generations. Asian American children who were born here or who immigrated at young ages often invoke a monolithic image of U.S. family life, seeing themselves as outsiders, believing that their family doesn't measure up to an Americanized ideal (Pyke 2000a, b). In in-depth interviews with 73 grown children of Korean and Vietnamese immigrants, Pyke found that her respondents often viewed their parents as overly strict, emotionally distant, and deficient in comparison to what they saw as a typical American family. Being bombarded with a singular image of family life can lead children of Asian immigrants (and presumably children of other immigrants as well) to believe that their families are somehow inferior and are outside the realm of what is truly "American." As one of her Korean respondents, born in the United States, said (Pyke 2000a, b):

> I think there is somewhat of a culture clash between myself and my parents. They are very set on rules—at least my father is. He is very strict and demanding and very much falls into that typical Asian father standard. I don't like that too much and I think it is because . . . as a child, I was always watching television and watching other friends' fathers. All the relationships seemed so much different from me and my father's relationship. . . . I guess it's pretty cheesy but I can remember watching *The Brady Bunch* reruns and thinking Mike Brady would be a wonderful dad to have. He was always so supportive. He always knew when something was wrong with one of his boys. Whenever one of his sons had a problem, they would have no problem telling their dad anything and the dad would always be nice and give them advice and stuff. Basically I used what I saw on television as a picture of what a typical family should be like in the U.S.
>
> I only wished that my family could be like that. And friends too—I used to see how my friends in school would be in Little League Baseball and their dad would be like their coaches or go to their games to cheer their sons on and give them support. I could not picture my father to be like that kind of man I saw on TV, or like my friends' fathers.

Native American and Alaska Native Families

About 4.3 million people, or about 1.5 percent of the population, are American Indians or Alaska Natives, alone or in combination with another racial or ethnic category (Ogunwole 2006). The term *Native American* or *Alaska Native* refers to people having origins in any of the early peoples of North, Central, and South America who maintain tribal affiliation or community attachment. Three-quarters identify themselves as belonging to a specific tribe, such as Cherokee, Navajo, Choctaw, Blackfeet, Chippewa, Muscogee, Apache, or Lumbee. Cherokee is largest, with nearly 900,000 people reporting Cherokee alone or in combination with another race, ethnicity, or tribe. Eskimo is the most populous Alaska Native tribe, with nearly 50,000 members. Nineteen percent of Alaskans are Alaska Natives or Native Americans, Oklahoma (11 percent) and New Mexico (10 percent) have the second and third highest concentration of Alaska Natives or Native Americans in their populations.

Of the 4.3 million Native Americans or Alaska Natives, many live in substandard housing. About 10 to 20 percent live in homes without indoor plumbing and many do not even have kitchen facilities.

Most Native Americans live in the community and do not live on reservations or other trust lands. About one-third live on designated American Indian Areas (AIAs), which include reservations and off-reservation land trusts; 2 percent live in Alaska Native Village Statistical Areas (ANVSAs); and nearly two-thirds live outside tribal areas (Ogunwole 2006). The largest and most populous is the Navajo Nation reservation and trust lands, which span portions of Arizona, New Mexico, and Utah. Native Americans who reside off the reservation run the gamut; many return to the reservation regularly for meetings and events, and others do not return at all.

Native American Families Today

Nearly three-quarters of Native American and Alaska Native households are family households—significantly *higher* than for the general population. However, only 4 percent live in married-couple households, significantly *lower* than for the general population. Instead, female-headed households are nearly twice as prevalent among Native American families as they are for the general population. Most households contain children under age 18. The average age of Native Americans is only 28 years, 7 years younger than for the rest of the population, revealing larger-than-average family size and lower life expectancy.

Extended families are the cornerstone of Native American family life, with close parallels to black and Hispanic families in many ways. Fifty-six percent of Native Americans and Alaska Natives age 30 and over live with their grandchildren (U.S. Census Bureau 2006b). There is a strong cultural ethic of social, emotional, and financial support among relatives. Indeed, aunts and uncles often refer to their nieces and nephews as "daughter" or "son" (MacPhee et al. 1996).

However, the role of kinship networks extends beyond the roles found in other racial and ethnic groups. Prior to the twentieth century, kinship was an important component of political organization and provided the primary basis for tribe governance. Although some groups were matrilineal and others were patrilineal, kinship was the basis for political power and status unknown to other U.S. racial and ethnic groups. While this has waned considerably in recent years, kinship networks among Native Americans and Alaska Natives retain considerable importance because of the ties they establish to a specific tribe.

Within families, elders are of considerable importance not only for the status and family and cultural identity that they provide, but also because of the hands-on care that they offer to younger family members. Although some of the *cultural conservator* function that the elderly provide has been disvalued in recent years by younger generations as they move off the reservation and attempt to assimilate, there has been a resurgence in recognizing the importance of Native American spirituality, language, values, and cultural traditions.

Nonetheless, Native American families face difficulties that affect their family in many ways. Infant mortality rates are high, and life expectancy is low, particularly on reservations. Poverty rates are nearly triple those of other Americans and unemployment is even higher. Many Native Americans live in substandard housing. For example, approximately 10 percent of housing on reservations lacks indoor plumbing, and among some reservations the figure approaches 20 percent. Likewise, many do not have kitchen facilities. Suicide rates are far higher than the national average, especially among young men. Alcoholism is common, with up to 190 per 1,000 children born with fetal alcohol syndrome in some communities. Rates of accidents, violence, and domestic abuse are high, many of which involve alcohol (Bonnette 1995a, b; Hamilton 1997). Despite these obstacles, tribal leaders have implemented numerous strategies to improve economic and social conditions, sometimes developing profitable gambling establishments to raise money for critical services; opening tribally controlled colleges, creating alcohol education programs, and strengthening core Native American values held by youth through the rebound of traditional language programs. The census bureau reports that 18 percent of Native Americans age 5 and over speak a language in addition to English "very well" compared to only 10 percent of the general U.S. population (Ogunwole 2006).

Alaska Natives

Native Alaskans have been undergoing change since contact with Europeans in the mid-1700s, but the most dramatic changes have occurred in rapid succession during the past century. Alaska Natives are in a period of social, cultural, economic, and political transitions, many of which are sudden and traumatic. Many Alaska Natives live off the road system in isolated and remote communities separated from one another by vast regions of tundra or glaciers and have only recently been introduced to western ways. Cable television now broadcasts CNN 24 hours a day, The Disney Channel brings new ideas to children, and thousands of commercials fuel new desires for material goods. The result for many communities has been upheaval.

Traditional Alaska Native cultures, like most aboriginal cultures, are tied directly to nature and the bounty it provides. The practices of hunting, fishing, and gathering constitute a direct link between the old and the new. Subsistence is quite clearly an Alaska Native cultural imperative. A recent study of Alaska Natives found that 85 percent of Natives report that subsistence is "very important" or "important" to the respondents' household, and only 7 percent said it is "unimportant" or very "unimportant" (McDowell Group 2003).

Nonetheless, most Native villages now have what researchers describe as "mixed" economies, in which small to moderate amounts of earned cash are available on, most frequently, a seasonal basis. This has led to a substantial cultural shift, particularly among the young, yet the jobs generally do not pull families out of poverty.

With their way of life being drastically altered, their continued fight for subsistence rights threatened, and nearly third-world living conditions in many isolated rural villages off the road system, Alaska Native communities have been under increasing stress. This stress permeates all aspects of their lives from the physical to the spiritual and has caused severe damage to Native cultures. It has resulted in extremely high rates of suicide, particularly among young males, high levels of domestic violence and other forms of violence, and an incidence of alcohol abuse among Alaska Natives characterized as both a "plague" and an "epidemic" (Goldsmith et al. 2004).

These concerns have not gone unnoticed. Alaska Natives, along with federal and state governments, have attempted to improve living conditions, support people through the cultural transitions, and reduce the epidemics of violence and alcoholism, while paying tribute to the rich Native cultural heritage. With improving schools, health care, social services, and employment opportunities, culturally sensitive solutions are favored. For example, young people are increasingly taught the traditions and language of their elders; meanwhile, the importation, purchasing, and use of alcohol are banned in many rural communities.

Interracial and Interethnic Families

So far we have discussed race and ethnicity as though they are discrete categories, but for a growing number of people, especially children, this is not the case. The number of persons of different races or ethnic background who marry is increasing, as will be revealed in depth in Chapter 8 (Lee and Edmonston 2005). Their children are challenging traditional U.S. Census Bureau definitions.

To what extent do parents of different races identify their children as multiracial? Recent Census Bureau data help us to answer this question, because the 2000 census allowed respondents to mark more than one race for the first time. It is important because racial and ethnic identity is first established within the contexts of families. However, the 2000 census revealed that most interracial couples (66 percent) do not report their children as multiracial. Moreover, the likelihood of reporting a child as multiracial depends on the specific racial combination of the parents. For example, children of Asian-white or black-white interracial couples are far more likely to report their child as multiracial than American Indian-white or Hispanic-white (Tafoya et al. 2004). Low levels of multiracial reporting among American Indian-white couples may be due to the fact that the

Although we often think of race and ethnicity as discrete categories, in reality an increasing number of people are multiracial or multiethnic, including U.S. Senator and presidential contender Barack Obama.

American Indian population includes a large number of people with mixed ancestry and with varying degrees of American Indian identity. The low levels of multiracial reporting among Hispanic-white couples may be due to the prominence of ethnic Hispanic identity rather than racial identity. For many Latinos, the racial categories on the census forms are not particularly meaningful (Tafoya et al. 2004).

Parents of multiracial children face issues that same-race couples do not experience. For example, when both parents are white, they may know very little about how prejudice and discrimination operate, having the privilege of rarely being victims themselves. Multiracial couples do experience a great deal of prejudice and discrimination because many Americans are uncomfortable with whites and minorities dating, marrying, and having children (Childs 2005; Root 2001). Therefore, although the white parent of multiracial children may not completely understand the experiences of a biracial child, they likely do have some firsthand experience of racism. They now must face new tasks of socializing and preparing their children for the racism that they are someday likely to experience, and parents report a great deal of stress associated with trying to protect their children from prejudice and discrimination (Rockquemore and Laszloffy 2005).

In the 2006 book *Mixed: My Life in Black and White*, Angela Nissel recounts with both sadness and humor her experience growing up biracial in Philadelphia, daughter of a black mother and white father. She describes her anxiety as she moved back and forth between black inner-city schools and white prep schools, and her many attempts to find out where she best fit in. Her journey leads her to the discovery that being multiracial has its challenges in U.S. society, especially in terms of dating and romance. She reveals how she maintained her own sense of self, despite the racism in American society. U.S. Senator (and presidential contender) Barack Obama has also discussed the challenges of growing up biracial in his best-selling book, *Dreams From My Father: A Story of Race and Inheritance* (Obama 2007).

Social Policy and Family Resilience

As we have seen, racism can have disturbing effects on families. In the opening vignette, even young children make assessments on the basis of race or ethnicity, yet, policies designed to increase and strengthen minority families have sometimes been met with resistance. One important and well-known policy is called affirmative action.

Example: Affirmative Action

Affirmative action is a set of social policies designed to increase opportunities for minority groups, and one of the most misunderstood strategies of our time. Proponents see it as proactive measures to remedy inequality, fight discrimination, and have an integrated society with equal opportunities for all members (Ezorsky 1991; Orentlicher 2005). Opponents believe that it is misguided social engineering that uses quotas and preference to replace qualified males with unqualified minorities and women. They claim it promotes reverse discrimination (Cohen and Sterba 2003).

In what ways is affirmative action a *family policy*? As a tool to promote diversity and remedy inequalities in the workplace, higher education, or government contracting, it can have real implications for improving the economic and social well-being of families. It has improved the lives of countless minority families by providing educational training, job opportunities, and pay on par with their white counterparts. It has done the same for women, expanding opportunities that were previously reserved for men.

Until the mid-1960s, minorities were barred from certain jobs, some universities would not admit them, and many employers would not hire them. The Civil Rights Act of 1964 made discrimination illegal in the workplace, in federally funded programs, and in privately owned facilities open to the public. The original goal of the civil rights movement had been "color blind" laws; however, many people were concerned that simply ending a long-standing policy of discrimination did not go far enough. One year later, Congress passed the Voting Rights Act, which gave the U.S. Department of Justice the power to take "affirmative" steps to eliminate discrimination. President Lyndon B. Johnson gave the U.S. Department of Labor the responsibility to enforce affirmative action. In that role they began requiring government contractors to analyze the demographics of their workforce and to take proactive measures to remedy inequalities. Johnson stated in a 1965 speech at Howard University (Microsoft Encarta Online Encyclopedia 2004):

> You do not take a person who, for years, has been hobbled by chains and liberate him, bring him up to the starting line of a race and say, "you are free to compete with all the others," and still justly believe that you have been completely fair.

Perhaps the most controversial issue about affirmative action is whether it should use "quotas" to reach its goals. For example, if an employer knows he or she has a large disparity in the proportion of Hispanics in its workforce compared to the general population, it might use affirmative action to target its recruiting effort toward the Hispanic population in hopes of increasing the number of Hispanic new hires. The employer may identify a goal of how many Hispanics it wants to hire, at what levels, and in what time frame. Some argue that this is a quota system (Ethnicmajority.com 2006).

The U.S. Supreme Court has defined the scope of affirmative action policy through a series of legislative initiatives and decisions. Overall, the Court has upheld the constitutionality of affirmative action in principle, but has placed restrictions on how it is implemented. In the early case of *Regents of the University of California v. Bakke* (1978), Bakke claimed that he was denied entrance to medical school while "less qualified" minorities were admitted. The Court declared that it was unconstitutional for the medical school to establish a rigid quota system by reserving a certain number of places in each class for minorities, but upheld the right of schools to consider a variety of factors when evaluating applicants, including race, ethnicity, sex, and economic status.

In a 2003 case at the University of Michigan, the Supreme Court ruled that the school's point system that gave minority applicants a better chance of acceptance was unconstitutional. The justices affirmed the law school's more individualized method of reviewing applicants, which allows race to be one of many factors in deciding whom to admit. The point system was considered by the majority of the Supreme Court justices to be too "mechanistic" and was considered tantamount to a quota system.

Despite the legislative changes, the value of affirmative action programs in schools and work settings has been established by the Supreme Court. The need is not expected to last forever: "We expect that 25 years from now, the use of racial preferences will no longer be necessary to further the interest approved today," Justice O'Connor wrote in 2003. However, as for today, affirmative action policies have been a boon to minority families in their quest to break through into the middle and upper classes.

Conclusion

We all have a race and an ethnicity. Although whites have the privilege of rarely thinking about them, it remains that skin color, physical features, country of origin, culture, and dominant language shape family structure and family interaction. Each race or ethnic group has a rich history and culture associated with it, and draws upon its heritage in meaningful ways to create relevant family structures. These family structures need not be denigrated simply because they differ from others. The purpose of this chapter is to introduce the ideas that there is more than one model of family life, and that race and ethnicity (alone, and in conjunction with other statuses such as gender and class) provide unique opportunities and challenges, and are important statuses that frame our family lives. We will see specific examples of these throughout the remainder of the book.

Key Terms

Affirmative action: A set of social policies designed to increase opportunities for minority groups and one of the most misunderstood strategies of our time. (p. 200)

Caucasian: A theoretical racial category comprised of those individuals with relatively light skin. (p. 175)

Ethnic cleansing: The systematic killing, torturing, or removal of persons with the intention of eliminating a specific racial or ethnic group. (p. 178)

Ethnic group: People who share specific cultural features. (p. 176)

Ethnicity: Representing culture, including language, place of origin, dress, food, religion, and other values. (p. 175)

Extended families: Families that include other family members such as grandparents, uncles, aunts, or cousins, in addition to parents and their children. (p. 191)

Minority group: A category of people who have less power than the dominant group and who are subject to unequal treatment (p. 176)

Mongoloid: A theoretical racial category representing those individuals who have characteristics such as yellow or brown skin and folds on their eyelids. (p. 175)

Negroid: A theoretical racial category comprised of people with darker skin and other characteristics such as coarse curly hair. (p. 175)

Race: A category composed of people who share real or alleged physical traits that members of a society deem as socially significant. (p. 175)

Racism: The belief that one racial group is superior or inferior to others. (p. 177)

Resources on the Internet

Anti Defamation League (ADL)
www.adl.org
The primary purpose of the ADL is to stop the defamation of the Jewish people. Their website contains newspaper articles and other national and international educational materials.

Asian-Nation
www.asian-nation.org
Asian-Nation is a one-stop information source on the historical, political, demographic, and cultural issues that make up today's diverse Asian American community. The website says, "You can almost think of Asian-Nation as an online version of 'Asian Americans 101.'"

Families with Children from China (FWCC)
www.fwcc.org
The purpose of FWCC is to provide a network of support for families who have adopted in China and to provide information to prospective parents. The purpose of this site is to consolidate the information that has been put together by the families of FWCC, in order to make it easier for future parents to consider adopting from China.

First Alaskans Institute
www.firstalaskans.org
The First Alaskans Institute was founded by the Alaska Federation of Natives in 1989 as the AFN Foundation,

a 501(c)(3) organization. In 2000, the foundation became independent from AFN. The First Alaskans Institute helps develop the capacities of Alaska Native peoples and their communities to meet social, economic, and educational challenges, while fostering positive relationships among all segments of society. It focuses on policy, leadership, and education to improve the lives of Native Alaskans. Their motto is "Progress for the *next* ten thousand years."

National Association for the Advancement of Colored People (NAACP)
www.naacp.org
The primary focus of the NAACP is to protect and enhance the civil rights of blacks and other minorities. The NAACP works at the national, regional, and local levels to secure civil rights. They advocate for specific legislation and initiatives.

National Congress of American Indians (NCAI)
www.ncai.org
NCAI's mission is to inform the public and the federal government on tribal self-government, treaty rights, and a broad range of federal policy issues affecting tribal governments.

National Immigration Forum
www.immigrationforum.org
The purpose of the National Immigration Forum is to embrace and uphold the United States' tradition as a nation of immigrants. The forum advocates and builds public support for public policies that welcome immigrants and refugees and that are fair and supportive to newcomers in the United States.

Pew Hispanic Center
www.pewhispanic.org
The goal of the Pew Hispanic Center is to disseminate its research about the diverse Hispanic population in the United States to policy makers, business leaders, the media, and academic institutions. Their website contains many recent studies on all aspects of Hispanics' lives.

Further Reading

Ashe, A., and A. Ramperstad. 1994. *Days of Grace: A Memoir*. New York: Ballantine.

Bonaichich, E., and R. Applebaum. 2000. *Behind the Label: Exploitation in the Los Angeles Apparel Industry*. Berkeley: University of California Press.

Brown, E. 1992. *A Taste of Power: A Black Woman's Story*. New York: Pantheon Books.

Childs, E. C. 2005. *Navigating Interracial Borders: Black-White Couples and Their Social Worlds*. Piscataway, NJ: Rutgers University Press.

Espiritu, Y. L. 1997. *Asian American Women and Men*. Thousand Oaks, CA: Sage.

Feagin, J., and K. D. McKinney. 2003. *The Many Costs of Racism*. Lanham, MD: Rowman and Littlefield.

Hill, S. A. 2005. *Black Intimacies: A Gender Perspective on Families and Relationships*. Walnut Creek, CA: AltaMira Press.

Malcomson, S. L. 2000. *The American Misadventure of Race*. New York: Farrar, Straus, and Giroux.

McDermott, M. 2006. *Working-Class White: The Making and Unmaking of Race Relations*. Berkeley: University of California Press.

Obama, B. 2007. *Dreams From My Father: A Story of Race and Inheritance*. New York: Crown.

Omi, M., and H. Winant. 1994. *Racial Formation in the U.S.*, 2nd ed. New York: Routledge.

Rodriguez, C. E. 2000. *Changing Race: Latinos, the Census, and the History of Ethnicity in the U.S.* New York: New York University Press.

Rush, S. E. 2000. *Loving Across the Color Line: A White Adoptive Mother Learns About Race*. Lanham, MD: Rowman & Littlefield.

Taylor, R. L. 2001. *Minority Families in the U.S.: A Multicultural Perspective*, 3rd ed. Upper Saddle River, NJ: Prentice Hall.

Wu, F. H. 2002. *Yellow: Race in America Beyond B & W*. New York: Basic Books.

Zhou, M. and C. L. Bankston, III. 1998. *Growing Up American: How Vietnamese Children Adapt to Life in the U.S.* New York: Russell Sage Foundation.

CHAPTER 7

Courtship, Intimacy, and Partnering

Chapter Outline

CHAPTER PREVIEW

How do people become life partners? This seems like such a personal question that no amount of social research could answer it. However, personal choices are patterned and are surprisingly shaped by many intriguing social, cultural, and historical forces. This chapter explores how these forces shape courtship patterns, sexuality, and the mate selection processes. Specifically, in this chapter you will learn:

- What love has to do with courtship and mate selection
- Gender difference in the emotion of loving
- General cultural principles guiding sexuality and intimacy
- Sexual orientation and its causes
- How we learn sexual scripts as rules for sexual behavior and how scripts may differ by race, ethnicity, social class, and sex
- Sexually transmitted diseases are hidden epidemics that have enormous health and economic consequences in the United States and throughout the world
- Important issues surrounding heterosexual cohabitation, including children in cohabiting relationships
- About gay and lesbian relationships and social policy issues surrounding same-sex marriage

Trinidad

"When I was 17 years old and still in school, my father told me that he had chosen a wife for me. I realized that I did not have a choice and decided to go along with his decision. My father made all the arrangements for the wedding. We were poor, and I remember that I wore shoes for the first time on my wedding day. During the ceremony, I saw my bride's fingers were of a fair complexion, which assured me that she was a good woman. So, my love life began by seeing my wife's fingers. I saw my wife for the first time after our wedding ceremony. She was 14 years old." (Seegobin and Tarquin 2003)

Kenya

"As my sisters and I went about doing our daily chores, we choked on the dust stirred up by the herd of cattle and goats that had just arrived in our compound. I was surprised when I found out that these animals were my bride wealth, negotiated by my parents and the family of the man who had been chosen as my husband. His name is Simayia ole Mootian, and he is 27 years old. I have never met him. Because I have recently been circumcised, I am considered to be a woman. So, I am ready to marry, have children, and assume adult privileges and responsibilities. My name is Telelia ole Mariani. I am 14 years old. Here, life is difficult, and I wonder how this will change my life. I wonder whether he already has other wives. I wonder how we will live. Will we live together, or will he live away from the family to work in the city? Does he have a job? I probably will not continue in school or have a job. Instead, I will be having and taking care of children. Many people are infected with HIV/AIDS. That is changing the way children, parents, and grandparents take care of each other. I wonder whether he could have HIV/AIDS. If I become infected, who will care for our children? Will they have it? My mind is in a whirl of questions; I am excited, happy, nervous, and concerned." (Wilson et al. 2003)

Spain

"Two friends in their late 20s met at a café in downtown Madrid one morning. One of them asked the other whether he was happy with his current living arrangement or whether he desired to live by himself, independent from his parents. To this, the young man replied, 'Why should I leave my parents? I have it all where I am. My mother washes and irons my clothes, she cooks for me, and I don't have to pay rent. Plus, I don't believe that I earn enough to make it on my own. I have been trying to find a job in my field of study, and I haven't been able to find anything. Things are really hard at the moment.' To this, the other man responded, 'But what about your girlfriend? What does she think about all this?' 'She agrees with me,' the young man replied. 'I know that she would like to get married soon, but we recognize that we need to be more financially established before we can get married. For instance, we both believe that we should wait until we have enough money to buy and furnish our own apartment. And as it is, we are still able to get away and spend time together as a couple. As a matter of fact, next weekend we will be spending the weekend in Seville. So, I am content with the way things are." (Reyes 2003)

The Netherlands

"Karel and Muriel meet each other at a party when they both are in their early 20s. They have seen each other at times in college classrooms but do not know each other well. A few days after the party, Karel invites Muriel for dinner at his apartment. Over the course of a year, their relationship becomes closer and they decide to move in together. Their friends approve and congratulate them on the next step in their lives. They hold a housewarming party to celebrate. After living together for several years, Karel and Muriel decide that they are ready for the next step: a home. They have their attorney draft a cohabitation contract

so that they can legally organize their living arrangements. Within a few weeks, they move out of their apartment into their newly purchased home." (van Dulmen 2003)

These four scenarios from Trinidad, Kenya, Spain, and the Netherlands illustrate that the process by which people find partners, the ceremony or rite of passage that signifies commitment or marriage, and the expectations for partners afterwards could not be more different. People become intimate, form partnerships, or marry to improve their economic conditions, for sheer survival, to increase their social standing, or to please their parents and build family alliances.

This chapter explores the development of intimacy and mate selection, including courtship, love, sexuality, and cohabitation. Cultural traditions, the environment, social norms, and religious customs have as much to do with mate selection as love and affection, sexual convenience, or compatibility. In many cultures they are even more important.

Courtship and Mate Selection

A lot is at stake when two people marry. They make a lifelong commitment to one another and agree to conduct themselves in a manner befitting a married couple in that culture. Marriage is a legal contract, and the contract, shaped by cultural norms,

In many parts of the world parents choose the mate for their adult children, and the adult children would not have it any other way. Sometimes the mate selection choice, and even the marriage itself, occurs when the children are prepubescent.

defines the couple's living arrangements, their specific domestic responsibilities, sexual expectations, and other social roles, rights, and responsibilities. More is at stake in marriage than the interests of two individual people. Families, communities, and the state have an interest in marriage as well because marriage serves political, social, and economic functions. As discussed in Chapter 1, marriage is a social institution as well as a personal relationship. Marriage is a way to consolidate wealth, transfer property, construct alliances, and organize the division of labor. These important functions are not simply left to individuals to negotiate, but rather are embedded in a legal contract.

What's Love Got to Do with It?

Since families, communities, and the state all have an interest in marriage, they also have a hand in controlling the mate selection process. Sociologist William J. Goode suggests that this is done by controlling or channeling **love**, which he defines as a strong emo-

BOX 7.1 Using the Sociological Imagination

The Historical Relationship Between Love and Marriage

As the saying goes, ". . . first comes love, then comes marriage . . ." or does it? The following discussion by social historian Stephanie Coontz reveals that for most of history, love would have been a very poor reason to marry.

For thousands of years, marriage organized people's places in the economic and political hierarchy of society. Marriage was a way of raising capital, constructing political alliances, organizing the division of labor by age and gender, and deciding what claim, if any, children had on their parents, and what rights parents had in their children. Marriage served so many political, social, and economic functions that individual needs and desires were secondary considerations. In fact, for most people, whether rich or poor, marriage was as much about getting in-laws as about finding a mate and having a child.

For the propertied classes, marriage was the main way of consolidating wealth, transferring property, laying claim to political power, and even concluding peace treaties. When upper-class men and women married, dowry, bride wealth, or tribute changed hands, making the match a major economic investment by the parents and other kin of the couple. Even middle-class families had a huge economic stake in who married whom. Until the late eighteenth century marriage was the primary method of transferring property, occupational status, personal contacts, money, tools, and possessions across generations and kin groups. For most men, the dowry that a wife brought was the biggest infusion of cash, goods, or land that they would ever acquire. For most women, finding a husband was the most important investment they could make in their economic future.

In the lower classes, marriage was also an economic and political transaction, but on a different scale. The concerns of commoners were more immediate: "Do I marry someone with fields near my fields?" "Will my prospective mate meet the approval of the neighbors and relatives on whom I depend?" And because few farms or businesses could be run by a single person, the skills, resources, and tools prospective partners brought to the marriage were at least as important as their personality or attractiveness.

For all socioeconomic groups, marriage was the most important marker of adulthood and respectability. It was the primary way of organizing work along lines of age and sex. It was the main vehicle for redistributing resources to old and young—and also, contrary to contemporary romanticization of family life in the past, the main vehicle for extracting labor *from* the young.

For all of these reasons, love was considered a very poor reason to get married. It was desirable

tional attachment with at least the components of sex, desire, and tenderness (Goode 1959). Goode argues that all societies try to control or channel love to some degree because as a basis for marriage, love could be disruptive to families, communities, and to the state if not controlled. The connection between love and marriage that is found in many countries is a relatively recent phenomenon, as illustrated in Box 7.1—and the connection is not without risks, according to historian Stephanie Coontz (2004).

What are the various ways that families, communities, and the state try to control love?

1. Child marriage—One common method of controlling love is to have the child married or betrothed prior to puberty before feelings of love for another person can even develop. A child has no social or financial resources to oppose such a marriage.
2. Kinship rules—Some cultures clearly define the pool of eligible future spouses, such as a cousin. The major decision then is primarily *when*, rather than with *whom*, the marriage is to occur.

for love, or at least affection, to develop after marriage, and many parents allowed their children to veto a match with a partner who repelled them—but love was not the main thing that people took into account in deciding when and whom to marry. When divorce occurred, it was more often to get a better set of in-laws or because of childlessness rather than because of a lack of love.

In the seventeenth century, a series of interrelated political, economic, and cultural changes began to erode the older functions of marriage and throw into question the rights of parents, local elites, and government officials to limit individual autonomy in personal life, including marriage. In the eighteenth century, the revolutionary new ideal of the love match triumphed in most of Western Europe and North America. Suddenly, couples were supposed to invest more of their emotional energy in each other and their children than in their natal families, their kin, their friends, and their patrons. There was a new stress on marital companionship, intimacy, and privacy. Love became the primary motivation for marriage.

This new idea threatened to radically destabilize personal life and relations between men and women. No sooner was the ideal of the love match and lifelong intimacy invented than people who took it seriously began to demand the right to divorce. Even in stable marriages, conservatives complained, the new values caused the couple "to be constantly taken up with each other" instead of carrying out their duties to society. In other words, the very values that we have come to think of as traditional, the very values that invested marriage with such emotional weight in people's lives, had the inherent tendency to undermine the stability of marriage as an institution even as they increased the satisfaction of marriage as a relationship.

Source: Adapted from Coontz 2004.

CRITICAL THINKING QUESTIONS

1. How is it possible that marriage as an institution has become less stable, while marriage as a personal relationship has become more satisfying?
2. Even today some cultures do not believe that love should be a primary basis for marriage. What arguments would they make to defend their position? What grounds do you have to suggest that love should be a critical basis for marriage?

3. Isolation of young people—Socially segregating young people from one another can be a very effective means of controlling love. The goal is to eliminate opportunities for formal or informal interaction.
4. Close supervision—Short of isolation, some cultures watch their young people, especially young women, very carefully. A high value is placed on female chastity, and therefore, they are highly supervised whenever they are in the company of men.
5. Formally free—Love is encouraged and it is an expected element of mate selection. However, love remains controlled and channeled by the social contacts available to young people. Because people fall in love with those with whom they associate, love can be controlled by managing the social environment such as sending a child to particular schools, living in a certain neighborhood, involving the family in church or other civic associations, and channeling children toward a specific set of peers.

How do these rules play out across cultures? An interesting contrast in mate selection can be seen between India and the United States.

India

In other cultures, people find their mates through mechanisms that differ from those in the United States. India provides an example (Leeder 2004; Medora 2003). Most Indians would find the U.S. belief in dating and romance as odd as we might find their idea of arranged marriage. They would suggest that we are too focused on passionate love and on fun and games, to the detriment of building a solid lasting relationship. "I want an arranged marriage," said a 22-year-old Indian college student who considers himself a connoisseur of western fashions, "but I fear that Fashion Television, MTV, and [music] channel V are distorting the desires of the younger generation" (Derne 2003). He is not alone. A recent survey of 15- to 34-year-olds living in Delhi, Mumbai, Kanpur, and Lucknow found that 65 percent said that they would obey their elders "even if it hurts." Over two-thirds of urban college students in the mid-1990s preferred to have their parents arrange their marriage, "Any girl I could find for myself would not be as good as the one my parents will find," says a 19-year-old college student (Derne 2003).

Love is not a foreign concept to Indians. They simply have a different conception of it, influenced heavily by Hinduism, the caste system, and other norms in Indian culture. They see that much of a person's life is predetermined by his or her karma. Marriage is something that is out of the hands of the couple, and few would attempt to change fate. About 85 percent of marriages in India are arranged (Griffith 2006). Some educated professionals prefer to choose their own mates, but for the most part, Indians anticipate that their parents will select their marriage partner for them.

Commonly, before two Indians can consider marriage, both sets of parents consult an astrologer to examine their zodiac signs to determine the couple's compatibility. The astrologer helps to determine whether this is a proper match. If it is deemed to be a good match, then families can begin to discuss issues surrounding the dowry.

Despite their lower status in a patriarchal society, women are important because of their fertility; large families and large numbers of sons are highly desirable by most Indians. Therefore families spend considerable time negotiating a **dowry** or the financial gift given to a woman's prospective in-laws by her parents. The woman is generally not involved in the negotiations. Parents will spend large amounts on the dowry, depending on their caste or class standing, and may be left impoverished or in substantial debt as a result.

Child marriage was outlawed in 1978 in India; however, it still is a widespread practice in many parts of the country. In one province, Rajasthan, a 1996 survey of 5,000 women revealed that over half of them were married prior to their eighteenth birthday; some girls were married off as early as age 4 or 5 (Burns 1998). Child marriages free a family from the obligations of supporting a girl, who is destined to leave the family anyway. In the eyes of the parents, it also decreases her likelihood of engaging in premarital sex or being exploited sexually, which would reduce her status.

United States

Even in the United States we can see the influence of culture, the economy, changing norms, historical period, and geography in shaping the ways that marriage partners are found. Although today, the United States is best viewed as having a *formally free* mate selection process, in colonial America parental influence was relatively heavy. Unmarried women were highly supervised, and an unmarried couple was tightly chaperoned. Social interaction between young men and women tended to occur within their own homes under the watchful eye of other family members or at social or church gatherings. However, as discussed in Chapter 3, a young man would sometimes spend the night at the young woman's house, and because of the tight quarters in most houses, couples may have slept together, a practice called bundling. Historians have estimated that a third of women were pregnant at the time of their marriage in colonial America, obviously circumventing their parents' supervision (Demos 1970).

The Origins of Dating The late nineteenth and early twentieth centuries brought industrialization, urbanization, and a higher standard of living and disposable income for many people. In addition, there were many new freedoms stemming from a prolonged period of adolescence, greater interaction between males and females in schools and elsewhere, and the creation of and widespread purchasing of the private automobile. These changes led to the development of a social situation known as *dating*. As we saw in Chapter 3, the movement away from parental control and supervision brought a change of power and roles in the couple relationship. Dating was now done away from home and away from parents and family members. The young couple usually went somewhere: to a dance, a party, or dinner, or later, to a movie theater. Young men were expected to initiate and pay for dates. Men decided where the couple would go, they would make arrangements for the needed transportation, and they made the decision about what the couple would do on the date. Women largely waited to be chosen, yet frowned on last-minute invitations (saying yes indicated that no one else had chosen them). Women had little say-so in where the couple would go or what they would do. They expected men to make virtually all arrangements and anticipated that men

"Dating" began during the late nineteenth and early twentieth centuries due to many new freedoms stemming from an increased standard of living, prolonged period of adolescence, greater interaction between males and females in schools and elsewhere, and the availability of the automobile.

would pay all costs. Their only realm of control was related to the degree of intimacy and sexuality within the date.

During this time, social scientists began to conduct research on dating. In 1937, Willard Waller published a study conducted at Pennsylvania State University on the dating values of college men and women. Dating was a competitive game and success was defined as having the most dates and with the right kind of person, a process nicknamed *rating and dating*. In the late 1940s, anthropologist Margaret Mead was a harsh critic of the manner in which dating had evolved (Mead 1949). First, she complained that men and women defined their relationships in situational, rather than ongoing, terms; for example, "you have a 'date'"—a formal event with an appointed time and place. This kept men and women from truly getting to know one another. Second, she argued that sexual relationships were depersonalized. Men were encouraged to "score" and the focus was on keeping tabs on who in your social circle was "going all the way" (Mead 1949).

The Changing Nature of Courtship Margaret Mead may be pleased that today partner selection has evolved into something much less formal. Groups of young men and women often spend time together socializing, referring to the process as "getting together" or "hanging out" rather than "dating." In a group situation, young people feel more relaxed and informal. They may pair off more slowly, as traditional dating signifies something more serious. Norms have also changed so that women feel more comfortable initiating getting together. The age at first marriage has increased considerably for both men and women, which eases some pressure among young people.

One study examined the evolution of dating and mate selection values over a period of nearly 60 years (Buss et al. 2001). The authors compared data from 1939, 1956, 1967, 1977, 1984/1985, and 1996 at several locations around the country with respect to what traits men and women value in a mate. Several changes were noted, as shown in Table 7.1. First, the largest change is the value placed on chastity in a potential mate. In 1939, chastity emerged as the 10th most important trait out of a list of 18 traits. By 1967, it was ranked 15th, and by 1996, it was ranked 16th. Second, there has been an increased value associated with physical attractiveness in a mate among both men and women. For men, it jumped from 14th in 1939 to 8th in 1996. For women, it climbed from 17th to 13th during this period. A third clear trend is the increasing importance of good financial prospects in a partner, particularly among male respondents. Men ranked women's financial prospects as 17th in importance in 1939, jumping to 13th in the mid-1990s. Women reported a smaller change, increasing in importance from 13th to 11th. Fourth, men are less likely today to rate domestic skills as important in a mate, dropping from 8th in 1939 to 14th in 1996. Interestingly, the trend toward more equitable sharing of housework appear to have had no impact on women's ranking of domestic skills in a marriage partner, which remains ranked 16th over the 57-year period. The final significant shift in values focuses on the importance of mutual attraction and love. Although it was ranked 4th for men and 5th for women in 1939, by 1996 it was ranked first in importance. Americans believe that attraction and love are the center of marriage.

Why have these values shifted? Changes in values accompany structural changes in society. For example, urbanization and job mobility have contributed to a decline in the extended family. Likewise, changes in the economy and increased job opportunities for women result in a delay of childbirth. These structural changes may increase the importance of marriage as the primary source of intimacy (Buss et al. 2001).

Nonetheless, many traditions and values are slow to change. Research suggests that both men and women still feel comfortable with many traditionally gendered scripts

TABLE 7.1 Rank Ordering of Mate Preferences Across Six Decades by Gender

	Men			Women		
	1939	**1967**	**1996**	**1939**	**1967**	**1996**
Characteristics						
Dependable character	1	1	2	2	2	2
Emotional stability, maturity	2	3	3	1	1	3
Pleasing disposition	3	4	4	4	4	4
Mutual attraction, love	4	2	1*	5	3	1*
Good health	5	9	6	6	10	9
Desire for home, children	6	5	9	7	5	6
Refinement, neatness	7	7	11*	8	8	12*
Good cook, housekeeper	8	6	14*	16	16	16
Ambition, industriousness	9	8	10	3	6	7*
Chastity	10	15	16*	10	15	17*
Education, intelligence	11	10	5*	9	7	5*
Sociability	12	12	7*	11	13	8*
Similar religious background	13	13	12	14	11	14
Good looks	14	11	8*	17	17	13*
Similar education background	15	13	12*	12	9	10
Favorable social status	16	16	17	15	14	15
Good financial prospect	17	18	13*	13	12	11
Similar political background	18	17	18	18	18	18

Note: Asterisks highlight a preference change of at least three ranks from the first to the last assessment period.

Source: Buss et al. 2001.

(Bailey 1989; Ingraham 1999). Other longstanding social norms continue to define the field of eligible mates. These rules or customs indicate who is an appropriate mate, and include:

- **Endogamy**—mate selection is expected to occur with someone inside a particular social group, such as religious group, a member of a particular social class, racial or ethnic category, or in other cultures, a member of a specific clan
- **Exogamy**—mate selection is expected to occur with someone outside of a particular social group, such as your immediate family, or your sex

Violating these social norms brings varying degrees of societal concern. For example, miscegenation laws attempted to bar interracial marriage until as late as 1967. Gay and lesbian marriage continues to be controversial today and is barred in most states around the country. Although not illegal in any state, many parents would disapprove if their child married someone of a different religious faith. Not surprisingly then, most people look for **homogeneous relationships**, or partners similar to themselves. They tend to be about the same age and are of the same race, religion, or social class. **Heterogeneous relationships** are those in which the partners are significantly different from one another on some important characteristic, such as age.

Love

Love is a critical foundation for developing intimate relationships in the United States. How can a "feeling" be the subject of so many rules, regulations, and norms? What power does this emotion hold that parents, religions, or cultures will try to control and channel it? Everyone wants to experience love. We want to receive love (from parents, friends, our children, and our partners) and we want to love others. In the United States today, love is a primary basis for marriage—but exactly what is love? Can we find a useful definition that would include the love between a mother and child, as well as the love shared by married or cohabiting partners? The dictionary defines love as: (1) a strong affection for one another arising out of kinship or personal ties; (2) attraction based on sexual desire; (3) affection based on admiration, benevolence, or common interests (Merriam-Webster Online, accessed November 25, 2006).

Many sociologists, social psychologists, and anthropologists have studied attraction and love, attempting to describe and explain this deeply profound feeling. Anthropologist Helen Fisher studies the brain chemistry of people in love and argues that much of our romantic behavior is hard wired. Using a functional magnetic resonance imaging (MRI) machine on her subjects, she suggests that our brains create dramatic surges of energy and chemicals including norepinephrine, dopamine, and seratonin that fuel such feelings as passion, obsessiveness, joy, and jealousy (Fisher 2004). Using an evolutionary perspective, Fisher views love as a drive so powerful that it can override other drives, such as hunger and thirst (Fisher 2004).

Other researchers take a more process approach and look at the stages that love may pass through to fully develop (Kerchoff and Davis 1962; Reiss 1960), or look at the different dimensions of love and try to categorize different styles of loving (Sternberg 1986). Others look at the factors that predict falling in love. Research has found that people are drawn to those who are similar in attitudes and values, but there is no real connection either way with respect to personality styles.

Sex Differences in Loving

It may come as no surprise to you to read that men and women, on average, experience love differently. Differences are well touted, including in popular books such as *Men Are from Mars, Women Are from Venus*. Persons interested in better understanding the opposite sex have spent millions of dollars. The assumption held by most people is that women are more interested in love than are men. In the nineteenth century love became more "feminized" and was associated with the caregiving that women do in the home; it became a private feeling, separated from the outside world of work or politics (Cancian 1987). Hence, it is often viewed as the domain of women, and a cursory look at women's magazines at the supermarket checkout stand will confirm this:

"How to Make Him Fall Crazy in Love"
"The Sex Tips that Will Make Him Fall Head Over Heels"
"Don't Take No for an Answer: How to Land Your Man"
"Five New Recipes that He Is Guaranteed to Love"

"Where to Meet the Man of Your Dreams? We'll Tell You"
"Stand by Your Man Twenty-First Century Style"

Nonetheless, the commonly held belief that women are more interested in love than are men is far too simplistic. In fact, research shows that it is men, not women, who report falling in love sooner, are more resistant to a relationship breaking up, and are more upset when a breakup does occur (Hill 1976; Kephart 1967; Montgomery and Sorell 1998). It appears that women are more pragmatic or practical about falling in love and choosing a mate. They are more likely to evaluate a man's potential as a future spouse or partner, particularly his earning potential or social status (Buss et al. 2001; Hochschild 1983). Historically, women have been financially and socially dependent on their husbands in marriage. Although women are increasingly working full-time and their earnings and job status are on the rise, women are still less likely than men to see their primary family role as that of breadwinner. Thus, it makes pragmatic sense for many women, especially those who are not career oriented or who would like to take significant time away from work to raise children, to scrutinize the financial prospects of potential partners.

In contrast, men in heterosexual relationships are less likely to evaluate potential partners in terms of their earning capacity, although as the 60-year study revealed, this tendency is increasing (Buss et al. 2001). Men, at least initially, tend to focus on personal attractiveness. A study of dating classified advertisements found that male advertisers were twice as likely as women to mention the physical appearance or attractiveness of the person they hoped to meet (Dunbar 1995): "Single white 30-year-old non-smoking professional male looking for attractive and trim 19–30-year-old non-smoking woman who loves hiking and the out-of-doors. Blonds preferred." According to Dunbar (1995), women advertisers tended to seek a partner with high financial or occupational status or high levels of education and were four times as likely as men to use these types of terms in their advertisement: "Single, white, pretty, 30-year-old woman, seeking responsible, professional, and financially stable partner close to my age. No smoking, social drinking okay. Likes books and classical music. Homeowner a plus."

Nonetheless, once partners move beyond the initial attraction and focus on what characteristics they would like in a mate, women's and men's ratings are more alike than different (Regan et al. 2000). Internal characteristics such as personality or intelligence were evaluated as more important than external characteristics such as wealth or attractiveness. The previously mentioned study by Buss and colleagues that compared mate selection preferences over the years between 1939 and 1996 showed that the characteristics desired in a mate have somewhat converged among men and women. Both placed greater importance on physical attractiveness, love, and mutual attraction. Men's interest in a mate with domestic skills is declining, while their interest in a mate with good financial prospects is on the rise (Buss et al. 2001).

As couples fall in love, they share increasing intimacy. Sexuality may be one way of expressing this intimacy.

Sexuality

Sexuality is a universal human experience. Even young children are keenly interested in their genitals and in feelings of arousal. Among adults, sexuality is used as an expression of many different, even competing emotions. It can express love and tenderness or exploitation and revenge. Despite the universal nature of this biological phenomenon, sexual attitudes and behaviors vary remarkably by sex, across subpopulations in the United States, and across cultures throughout the world. How can something as personal and private (as well as so biologically driven) as sexuality be rooted in social and cultural norms? Anderson and Taylor (2006) remind us of the following principles:

1. *Sexual attitudes and behaviors are substantially different across cultures*. For example, in many cultures it is expected that a woman will be a virgin on the wedding day. A husband, in-laws, or other kin may demand proof that this is indeed the case; they may require the woman to undergo a physical examination by a physician who will verify her virginity, they may oversee a surgical procedure to remove the stitching that has closed off her vagina, or they may want a bloody sheet as evidence that the hymen was ruptured on the wedding night (although not all women bleed when their hymen is ruptured).
2. *Sexual attitudes and behaviors change over time*. We may have overestimated the "prim and proper" stereotype of the colonial and Victorian eras, because birth records indicate many women and men were indeed sexually active prior to marriage. However, sexuality was valued primarily in the confines of marriage and most religious and medical authorities generally did not believe that women experienced true sexual desires. Women who sought out sex were viewed as dangerous or evil (Ehrenreich and English 1989). Today things have changed a great deal. Sex outside of marriage is no longer taboo under many circumstances, and women are generally considered to be full sexual beings.
3. *Sexual identity is learned*. As you recall from Chapter 4, in contrast to sex, which is rooted in biology, gender refers to the culturally and socially constructed differences between males and females found in the meanings, beliefs, and practices associated with femininity and masculinity. These are learned attitudes and behaviors, not biological or physical qualities. We may be born male or female, but we learn the culturally and socially prescribed traits associated with masculine or feminine patterns of behavior, including ones related to sexuality. What are some attitudes or expectations surrounding sexual behavior that are different for men and women in U.S. culture?
4. *Social institutions channel and direct sexuality*. As we learned in Chapter 2, every culture regulates sexual behavior. Cultural norms make it clear who can have a sexual relationship with whom and under what circumstances. However, even within a culture, social institutions channel and direct sexual behavior. Institutions such as the family, religion, and government dictate with whom we can have sex and under what circumstances. For example, in U.S. culture these social institutions channel adults away from sex with children or with animals. They even influence consenting adults who exchange sex for money or have a sexual relationship with someone other than their spouse.

Sexual Orientation

Although much of our sexual behavior is rooted in our social and cultural norms rather than biology per se, research now strongly suggests that **sexual orientation**, the sex that one is attracted to, is the result of a complex set of factors that may have a strong root in biology. A **heterosexual** orientation refers to an attraction and preference for sexual and romantic relationships with members of the other sex (e.g., a man and a woman), and a **homosexual** orientation refers to a preference for same-sex sexual and romantic relationships. The term **gay** usually refers to homosexual men, whereas **lesbian** refers to homosexual women. **Bisexual** refers to an orientation in which a person is attracted to both males and females and engages in both heterosexual and homosexual relationships.

Early researcher Alfred Kinsey was instrumental in showing sexual orientation as a continuum rather than as a pair of polar opposites (Kinsey et al. 1953). He found that around one-quarter to one-third of survey respondents reportedly had at least some homosexual experience, although most still thought of themselves as heterosexual; he estimated that at least 3 percent of females were almost or exclusively homosexual as were at least 8 percent of males (Kinsey et al. 1953).

Exact numbers of gays and lesbians in the population are difficult to pinpoint, although the U.S. Census Bureau made the job easier. For the first time, the 1990 questionnaire allowed heads of households to mark "unmarried partner" in describing their relationship to another adult of the same sex living in the same house. With the processing of the 2000 questionnaire, the U.S. Census Bureau went one step further, recoding any same-sex "spouse" responses as "unmarried partner" responses (instead of recoding their sex). From these figures, it is estimated that at least 2 to 5 percent of the general population are gay and from 1 to 3.5 percent are lesbian. Likewise, in a study of human sexuality conducted in the 1990s by Michael, Gagnon, Laumann, and Kolata (1994) 6 percent of males and 4 percent of females reported being sexually attracted to individuals of the same sex, although only about 3 percent of males and a little over 1 percent of females reported having a self-concept as a homosexual or bisexual. This study was based on a random sample of 3,432 people between the ages of 18 and 59. These percentages represent millions of individuals.

What Causes Sexual Orientation? How do we come to have a specific sexual orientation? There has been a longstanding debate regarding choice versus biology, but the current research seems to be supporting the biological argument. One study examined different sets of siblings—identical twins, fraternal twins, and adopted siblings—one of which was known to be gay or lesbian. The purpose of the study was to determine if a homosexual orientation was more likely to occur in the other sibling in one type of sibling pair over another. The researchers found that 52 percent of the male identical twins, and 48 percent of the female identical twins (who share genetic material) were both homosexual. In contrast, in only 11 percent of the adopted siblings (who do not share any genetic material) were both homosexual. The likelihood of fraternal twins (who share only half of their genetic material) both being homosexual was between these two groups (22 percent and 16 percent for fraternal male and female twins, respectively) (Bailey and Pillard 1991; Bailey et al. 1993).

Other research also points to the conclusion that biology plays an important role in sexual orientation. For example, a study published in the *Proceedings of the National Academy of Sciences* found that gay men's brains respond differently from those of heterosexual males and are more like women's brains when exposed to chemicals derived from male and female sex hormones.

Attitudes Toward Gays and Lesbians Societal attitudes toward gays and lesbians vary greatly in different historical periods and in different cultures today. All cultures have their own attitudes toward sexual desire and may try to regulate sexual activity accordingly. For example, homosexual acts may be illegal, especially under sodomy laws, and where they are legal, the age of consent may vary across countries. Only as late as 2003 did the U.S. Supreme Court, by a 6–3 decision, strike down a Texas state law banning private consensual sex between adults of the same sex (CNN.com 2003). At that time, four states—Texas, Kansas, Oklahoma, and Missouri—prohibited oral and anal sex between same-sex couples, and nine other states—Alabama, Florida, Idaho, Louisiana, Mississippi, North Carolina, South Carolina, Utah, and Virginia banned consensual sodomy for everyone.

Table 7.2 reports the results of a 2002 Global Attitudes research survey that surveyed residents in many countries around the world about their attitudes with the following question: "Should homosexuality be accepted by society?" As the results show, Europe is the most permissive, with most countries in Asia and Africa the least permissive.

Sexual Scripts

Our sexual attitudes and behaviors are organized around **sexual scripts** that provide the norms or rules regarding sexual behavior. These scripts are socially constructed and govern who, what, where, when, and why—*who* is an appropriate sexual partner, *what* is appropriate sexual behavior, *where* sexual activity should take place, *when* sexual behavior is appropriate, and *why* or under what conditions sexual activity should occur. For example, Americans believe that a spouse is an appropriate sexual partner for a married person, but sex with a lover outside the marriage is not appropriate. Americans believe that sex should take place in private rather than out in the open in a public area.

TABLE 7.2 **The 2002 Pew Global Attitudes Project: "Should Homosexuality Be Accepted by Society?"**

Country	Percent Who Said Yes	Country	Percent Who Said Yes
North America		**Asia**	
United States	51	Philippines	64
Canada	69	Japan	54
Mexico	54	South Korea	25
Guatemala	44	Lebanon	21
Honduras	41	Vietnam	13
Europe		Jordan	12
Germany	83	Uzbekistan	10
Czech Republic	83	Pakistan	9
France	77	India	7
United Kingdom	74	Bangladesh	7
Italy	72	Indonesia	5
Slovak Republic	68	**Africa**	
Poland	40	South Africa	33
Bulgaria	37	Angola	30
Russia	22	Cote d'Ivoire	15
Turkey	22	Uganda	4
Ukraine	17	Nigeria	4
South America		Ghana	4
Argentina	66	Mali	3
Bolivia	55	Senegal	2
Brazil	54	Kenya	1
Venezuela	46		
Peru	45		

Source: Pew Research Center 2006.

Americans also believe that sexual behavior is appropriate beyond simply the need to reproduce and can be enjoyed for the sake of its own pleasurable experience. Not all cultures would agree with these views.

We learn our sexual scripts from the culture in which we live, including our parents, our friends, and the mass media (Miracle et al. 2003). We take these important messages and combine them with our personal feelings and desires and the desires of our partners. Together, these scripts become a blueprint and inform us what is appropriate behavior and what is taboo (Michael et al. 1994).

Race, Ethnicity, Social Class, and Sex Sexual scripts differ by race and ethnicity, social class, and sex. For example, whites are far more likely to engage in and receive oral sex (both cunnilingus and fellatio) than are blacks or Hispanics. Sex, race and ethnicity, and social class also interact in important ways to shape our sexual scripts. A study based on in-depth interviews with Mexican fathers who immigrated to the United States illustrates that the emphasis placed on girls' virginity is somewhat misunderstood (Gonzalez-Lopez 2004). The study found that virginity per se in a daughter's life was not a priority for any of the fathers born and raised in urban areas. These fathers have been exposed to more nontraditional values and experiences and are more likely to have attended college themselves or know someone who has. Instead of focusing on virginity for its own sake, they expressed an interest in helping their daughters postpone premarital sex so that their daughters could finish their education without being exposed to disease, an unintended pregnancy, or exploitation by a suitor. Along with their wives, these fathers advocate more egalitarian values for a new generation of women. They hope that their daughters will attend college and go on to have careers. Therefore, virginity itself is no longer an important source of social capital, but will help them obtain other forms of social capital, such as education (Gonzalez-Lopez 2003, 2004). As one father said:

> I am worried about her having a child, that she would not be able to take care of herself and leave the family home. I would not like it. I would love her to have a formal life, that is, that she goes to school, and that she is studying. Because for me . . . my preoccupation is that she makes it all the way to a university and graduates from college. That is my preoccupation and I will always fight for it. (Gonzalez-Lopez 2004)

Unlike their urban counterparts, Mexican immigrant fathers who came from rural areas were more likely to expect their daughters to refrain from premarital sexual activity for the sake of traditional symbolism. Virginity remains highly valued, is seen as a badge of honor and integrity, and is a source of power in an exchange relationship for a potential high-status husband. As one father said:

> . . . tell me, who would not wish for his daughter to possess integrity while wearing white on her wedding day? Do you think that would not be my wish? (Gonzalez-Lopez 2004)

However, even among these fathers from rural regions in Mexico, the primary factor that shaped their views of virginity was fear for their daughters living in the immigrant-filled barrios. Regardless of their place of origin, fear was the central emotion involved in constructing fathers' views of their daughters' sexuality—fear about pregnancy, of violence, of disease, and of a daughter's romantic involvement with men who were perceived as undesirable, such as gang members, drug dealers, or the chronically unemployed. The emphasis on virginity should not be oversimplified as elements of machismo that emphasize male dominance. Instead, these values are part of a complex set of social and cultural ideals that are intertwined with social class, race, ethnicity, and sex.

This intersection can also be seen vividly in black relationships (Hill 2005). The study of intimate relationships among blacks is often conducted in low-income communities with men and women who have been economically marginalized. Hill describes

Male and female sexual scripts are so much a part of a culture's norms that they are even used in advertising, as shown in this advertisement.

that low-income black women "are especially vulnerable when it comes to hanging all their hopes for a better life on finding the right man" (Hill 2005, 101). She notes that father absence and the paucity of fatherly love in their lives, along with their own dismal economic prospects, heighten their search for a boyfriend or husband who will provide them with a home, family, and adult status. They use their sexuality to try to secure these dreams, but rarely are they successful. The low-income males in their neighborhoods see little appeal in an exclusive relationship, and in fact are rewarded by their peers for having sexual relationships with a large number of women. Meanwhile the pursuit of intimacy among middle-class blacks is also shaped by class and gender dynamics, albeit different ones. The traditional norms of women "marrying up" hold little meaning in the black community where women have made tremendous gains in education and occupational status relative to men. Significantly more black women than men have college and graduate degrees, and more women work at jobs described as managerial/professional. In a culture where marrying up is valued for women, who is a bright, well-educated, professional black woman to marry? Over half of black women end up marrying down, compared to only 30 percent of white women who marry men with less education and income (Hill 2005).

Components of the Male and Female Sexual Scripts

Traditionally, men have been allowed far more permissiveness in sexual behavior than have women. Men are expected to be assertive in seeking sexual relationships, whereas women are expected to be more reticent and not appear too interested. What are some of the components of the *male* sexual script? Naturally these components may be modified somewhat or significantly in a long-term loving relationship where a man is able to break free from cultural stereotypes and experience true intimacy. Nonetheless, here we will present the cultural images that comprise the male script—whether you personally abide by them or not, chances are they will be very familiar.

- *A man's looks are relatively unimportant, but his status is enhanced if he is with a beautiful woman.* A woman is a trophy, and the more attractive the trophy, the more of a man he is perceived as being.
- *The man always wants sex and is ready for it.* It doesn't matter much what else is going on or what his feelings are toward a potential partner. A man is like a machine and can be "turned on" immediately.
- *A man is in charge.* He is the initiator, the leader, and knows more about sex than his partner does. He would not feel comfortable asking his partner what she really likes.
- *All physical contact leads to sex.* Ideally any physical contact should lead to sexual intercourse. Touching, caressing, and kissing are not pleasurable ends in themselves.
- *A man cannot easily stop himself once he gets turned on.* Biologically, a man has great sexual needs, and he may not be able to stop once he is aroused, regardless of whether his partner asks him to stop.
- *Sex equals intercourse.* The focus of sex is on stimulating the penis. Hopefully this will be satisfactory to his partner, and if not, she is the one with a problem.

- *Sexual intercourse always leads to orgasm.* The purpose of intercourse is for the male to have an orgasm. If one does not occur, the act is incomplete or a failure. It is less important that a female has an orgasm.

What are some components of the *female* sexual script? Again, these may be modified when in an exclusive or long-term committed relationship because people can truly be themselves and move away from rigid scripts. Nonetheless, the components of the female sexual script permeate all aspects of society and illustrate critical ideas about her sexual role. We can see that it emphasizes feelings over sex.

- *Women should make themselves attractive to men to get their attention, but they should not make themselves too sexually attractive.* Women should dress "a certain way," so that they will gain the attention of men, but they also run the risk of gaining too much attention. It is up to women to sort out the appropriate type of dress, makeup, and demeanor to attract the right amount of male attention.
- *Women's genitals are mysterious.* Many girls and women know little about their bodies. They have been taught not to touch them or explore them, and many have never even used a mirror to look at them. What they do know comes from media images that tell them that their genitals have odor, which must be controlled. Consequently, many women are very uncomfortable and unknowledgeable about their bodies.
- *Women should not know too much about sex or be too experienced.* Women walk a fine line today; they must not appear too uptight about sex, but they must not feel too comfortable with it either. Women should not be too experienced because they run the risk of being labeled a slut or a whore.
- *Good girls do not plan in advance to have sex or initiate it.* To plan in advance (and take appropriate birth control precautions) may indicate that she is too experienced or likes sex too much. She cannot take the lead or she may risk her reputation.
- *Women should not talk about sex.* Many women cannot talk about sex because they are not expected to be very knowledgeable or to feel very comfortable with it. Women may feel more comfortable *having* sex than having a simple conversation about it with their partner.
- *Men should know how to please a woman.* Although he may be primarily focused on his penis and his own orgasm, a woman feels it is his job to know how to arouse her. He is supposed to know what she wants, even if she does not want to tell him (or does not know how to have an orgasm).
- *Sexual intercourse is supposed to lead to orgasm and other stimulation should be unnecessary.* Studies indicate that at least one-third of women and possibly many more do not have an orgasm in sexual intercourse; they need additional oral or manual stimulation of the clitoris (Ross 2005; Sterk-Elifson 1994). Nonetheless, many women believe that there is something wrong with them if sexual intercourse by itself does not produce an orgasm.

Sexually Transmitted Disease

Sexually transmitted diseases (STDs) are hidden epidemics that have enormous health and economic consequences in the United States and throughout the world. They are hidden because many people are reluctant to address sexual health issues in an open way. People should have a significant interest in STD prevention because all communities are affected by STDs and all individuals directly or indirectly pay for the costs of these diseases. STDs are public health problems that lack easy solutions because they are rooted in human behavior and fundamental societal problems. Indeed,

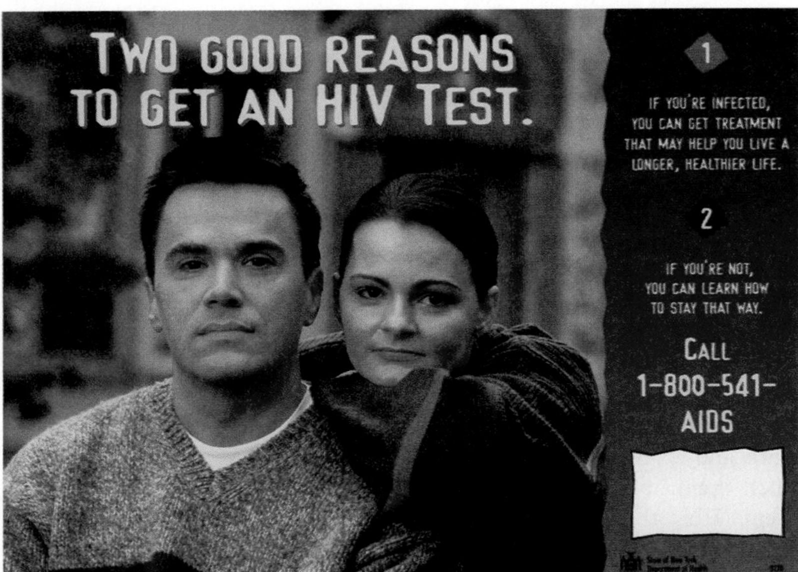

TWO GOOD REASONS TO GET AN HIV TEST.
1
IF YOU'RE INFECTED, YOU CAN GET TREATMENT THAT MAY HELP YOU LIVE A LONGER, HEALTHIER LIFE.
2
IF YOU'RE NOT, YOU CAN LEARN HOW TO STAY THAT WAY.
CALL 1-800-541-AIDS

Over one million Americans alive today have HIV or AIDS, and over one-half million have died from the disease. Although HIV and AIDS are most common among men who have sex with other men, heterosexual couples are far from immune to the deadly disease, and should always practice safe sex.

there are many obstacles to effective prevention efforts. The first hurdle is to address the reluctance of societies, including our own, to openly confront issues surrounding sexuality and STDs. Despite the barriers, there are existing individual- and community-based interventions that are effective and can be implemented (CDC 2004).

In the United States, millions of people have an incurable STD; an additional 19 million people become infected with STDs each year, and half of these are to young people aged 15 to 24 (Weinstock et al. 2004). Chlamydia is the most commonly *reported* infectious disease in the United States, with nearly a million diagnoses each year (CDC 2006a). Even so, most chlamydia cases go undiagnosed. It is estimated that there are approximately 2.8 million new cases of chlamydia in the United States each year. Many other STDs are likely far more prevalent, such as human papillomavirus or genital herpes, but are often not reported and therefore accurate data are missing. Nonetheless, it is estimated that genital herpes is the most common STD in the United States, affecting one in five adolescents and adults. Because it is so widespread, easily transmitted, and yet rarely discussed, it is the focus of Box 7.2. Although people might be inclined to dismiss STDs as personal problems, they affect large numbers of people and are, indeed, *social problems*, rather than merely personal ones. Ideas about family privacy and personal shame tend to exacerbate the misunderstanding of STDs, allowing them to spread at alarming rates and inhibiting effective treatment.

Although STDs like genital herpes and chlamydia are widespread across all racial and ethnic groups, average STD rates tend to be higher among blacks and Hispanics than among whites. Some of this can be attributed to differences in risk behaviors (e.g., beginning sexual intercourse at an early age, multiple partners, unprotected intercourse, level of drug use). Rates also reflect social conditions like poverty, access to health care, and language barriers. Part of the disparity is also because blacks and Hispanics are more likely to seek health care in public clinics that report STDs more thoroughly than do private providers (CDC 2001). Consequently, the statistics could possibly be underreporting the rates among whites.

HIV and AIDS HIV and AIDS receive more media attention than any other STD because the disease is so deadly and because of the social and political implications surrounding its discovery and treatment (i.e., stigmatized as a "gay" disease). AIDS is caused by infection with HIV passed from one person to another through blood-to-blood, sexual contact, and through pregnancy, delivery, or breastfeeding. Most people with HIV will develop full-blown AIDS. The CDC reports that scientists have different theories about the origin of HIV, but none have been proven (CDC 2001).

BOX 7.2 Families as Lived Experience

What Is Genital Herpes?

The Centers for Disease Control and Prevention has found that genital herpes infection is the most common sexually transmitted disease (STD) in the United States. They have developed a fact sheet to inform the public about this highly contagious STD and how it can be prevented.

What Is Genital Herpes?

Genital herpes is a sexually transmitted disease cased by the herpes simplex virus type 1 (HSV-1) and type 2 (HSV-2). HSV-2 is more common. Most individuals have no or only minimal signs or symptoms. When signs do occur, they typically appear as one or more blisters on or around the genitals or rectum. The blisters break, leaving tender ulcers (sores) that may take 2 to 4 weeks to heal the first time they occur. Typically, another outbreak can appear weeks or months after the first, but it almost always is less severe and shorter than the first outbreak. Although the infection can stay in the body indefinitely, the number of outbreaks tends to decrease over a period of years.

How Common Is Genital Herpes?

Nationwide, at least 45 million people age 12 and older, or one in five adolescents and adults, have had genital HSV infection. Between the late 1970s and the early 1990s, the number of Americans with genital herpes increased 30 percent. Genital HSV-2 is more common in women (about one in four women) than in men (almost one in five). This may be due to male-to-female transmissions being more likely than female-to-male transmission.

How Do People Get Genital Herpes?

HSV-1 and HSV-2 can be found in and released from the sores that the viruses cause, but they also are released between outbreaks from skin that does not appear to be broken or to have a sore. Transmission can occur from an infected partner who does not have a visible sore and may not know that he or she is infected. HSV-1 can cause genital herpes, but it more commonly causes infections of the mouths and lips, so-called fever blisters. HSV-1 infection of the genitals can be caused by oral-genital or genital-genital contact with a person who has HSV-1 infection.

What Are the Signs and Symptoms of Genital Herpes?

Most people infected with HSV-2 are not aware of their infection. However, if signs and symptoms occur during the first outbreak, about 2 weeks after the virus is transmitted, they can be quite pronounced. The sores typically heal within 2 to 4 weeks. Other signs and symptoms during the primary episode may include a second crop of sores and flu-like symptoms. However, most individuals with HSV-2 infection may have only mild sores or none at all.

What Are the Complications of Genital Herpes?

They can cause recurrent painful genital sores in many adults, and herpes infection can be severe in people with suppressed immune systems. Regardless of severity of symptoms, genital herpes frequently causes psychological distress in people who know they are infected. In addition, genital herpes can cause potentially fatal infections in babies. It is important that women avoid contracting herpes during pregnancy because a first episode during pregnancy causes a greater risk of transmission to the baby. If a woman has an active outbreak at delivery, a cesarean delivery is usually performed.

Is There a Treatment for Genital Herpes?

There is no treatment that can cure it, but antiviral medications can shorten and prevent outbreaks during the period of time the person takes the medication. In addition, daily suppressive therapy for symptomatic genital herpes can reduce transmission to partners.

How Can Genital Herpes Be Prevented?

The surest way to avoid transmission of genital herpes is to abstain from sexual contact or to be in a long-term mutually monogamous relationship

(continued)

with a partner who has been tested and is known to be uninfected. Correct and consistent use of latex condoms can reduce the risk of genital herpes only when the infected area or site of potential exposure is protected. Because a condom may not cover all infested areas, even correct and consistent use of latex condoms cannot guarantee protection from genital herpes.

Where Can I Get More Help?

National Herpes Hotline
(919) 361-8488

National Herpes Resource Center
www.ashastd.org/hrc
www.herpesnet@ashastd.org

Division of STD Prevention (DSTDP)
Centers for Disease Control and Prevention
www.cdc.gov/stds

Order Publications Online at
www.cdc.gov/std/pubs/

Source: Adapted from CDC 2006.

CRITICAL THINKING QUESTIONS

1. If genital herpes is so common and so easily transmitted, why is there so little discussion about it? Is herpes an individual problem or is it a social problem?
2. If you had genital herpes (or currently have it), how would it impact your life? What kinds of changes would you (do you) make? How would you tell a potential sexual partner—or would you?

History and Development In the early 1980s, physicians in a number of U.S. cities began to notice that numerous cases of rare diseases were occurring among otherwise strong and healthy men. Kaposi's sarcoma, a type of cancer of the blood vessels, and *Pneumocystis carinii* pneumonia, a usually mild lung infection, had become deadly diseases because of a breakdown in the immune system. The term AIDS was given even before the HIV virus was discovered.

At first AIDS seemed to be confined to few groups: gay men, people with hemophilia, and Haitians. Some argued that because the disease did not seem to run through the entire population, but among groups who had faced stigma and discrimination, the government was slow to act (Shilts 1987). It was labeled a "gay" disease and stigmatized. As Pat Buchanan, a conservative leader and former U.S. presidential hopeful said, "The poor homosexuals—they have declared war upon nature and now nature is exacting an awful retribution" (cited in Strong et al. 2002).

Current Status How many people have been affected by AIDS? The cumulative estimated number of diagnoses of full-blown AIDS through 2005 in the United States was 988,376, with about three-quarters of the cases occurring among men; there have been 550,394 deaths (CDC 2006c,e).

The CDC estimates over 1.1 million persons in the United States were alive and living with HIV or AIDS in 2005, with about one-quarter of these persons undiagnosed and unaware of their infection. It is likely that many, if not most of these persons will develop AIDS in the future if they have not already done so (CDC 2006e).

Some people believe that the threat of contacting AIDS is no longer a problem; however, according to the CDC, the number of new diagnoses has declined only slightly since 2001. It found in 2005 alone, there were roughly 41,000 *new* cases of AIDS. People still die from AIDS-related causes. In 2005, AIDS was implicated in the death of 16,000 Americans (CDC 2006e).

How did these people contact HIV/AIDS? Despite the continued stigma surrounding HIV/AIDS as a gay disease, one-third of men and all women contracted it through means other than homosexual sexual activity, as shown in Figure 7.1. In fact, 78 percent of women diagnosed with AIDS contracted it through heterosexual contact.

FIGURE 7.1 **How HIV/AIDS Is Contracted by Those Who Received a Diagnosis of HIV/AIDS—Males (top); Females (bottom)**

Source: Centers for Disease Control and Prevention 2006b.

MALES

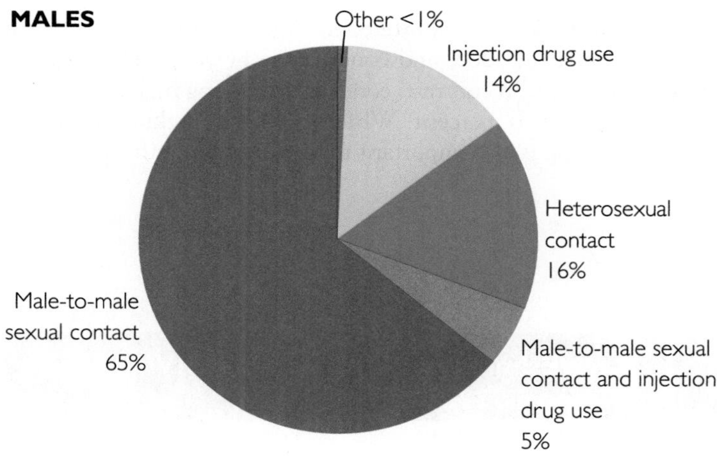

FEMALES

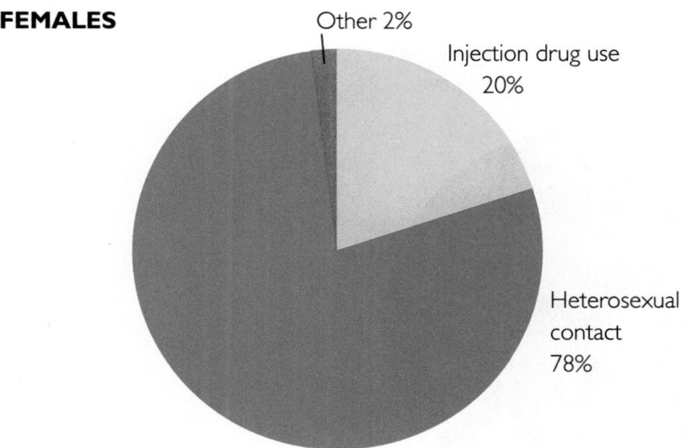

Note: Based on data from 33 areas with long-term confidential name-based HIV reporting.

As shown in Figure 7.2, blacks and Hispanics have been particularly hard hit by HIV/AIDS. Although blacks comprise about 13 percent of the U.S. population, they comprise 49 percent of new AIDS diagnoses. Likewise, Hispanics are also overrepresented in HIV/AIDS cases. The reasons for this are complex. These minority groups have higher than average rates of substance abuse, STDs, are more likely to live in poverty with all its deleterious consequences, and are more likely to engage in risky behaviors (CDC 2006b; Sharpe et al. 2004). Moreover, a significant number of black and Hispanic men are in denial; because black and Hispanic men who have sex with other men tend to identify themselves as heterosexual, they may not relate to prevention messages crafted for men who identify as homosexual. Cultural values of machismo ("manliness") in Hispanic communities may increase reluctance to identify risky behaviors (Suarez-Al-Adam et al. 2000).

To be effective in minority communities, the CDC recommends that prevention programs be culturally sensitive. Some evidence suggests that this approach is working. For example, studies of high school students indicate a significant increase in condom use by young blacks and Hispanics—a larger increase than was found among whites (CDC 2006e). Condom use "during last sexual intercourse" jumped from 48 percent of young blacks in 1991 to 69 percent in 2005, and condom use by young Hispanics increased from 37 percent to 58 percent. In contrast, condom use among high school-aged whites increased from 47 percent to 57 percent. While it is fair to acknowledge that more teens are practicing safer sex, it is also important to note that a significant number of teens do not.

FIGURE 7.2 **Race/Ethnicity of Persons with HIV/AIDS Diagnosis, 2005**

Source: Centers for Disease Control and Prevention 2006b.

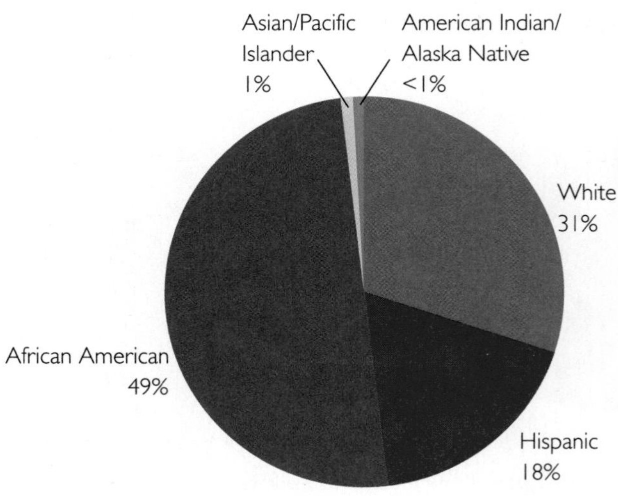

Heterosexual Cohabitation

One hundred years ago we spoke little of **cohabitation**. Although some unmarrieds did live together, it was usually considered a temporary state until the couple could marry, and therefore others in the community usually treated them as a married couple (Cott 2002). Perhaps a minister was unavailable or the couple was waiting until family could arrive for the wedding.

Today, with nearly 4.9 million U.S. households maintained by heterosexual cohabiting couples, virtually every adult knows someone who has, or is currently, cohabitating (Fields 2004, The National Marriage Project 2006). Unlike in the past, marriage may or may not be in the couple's future plans. Cohabitation may be an extension of dating (going "very steady") or it may be an alternative to marriage itself; however, in the United States cohabitation lacks the formal and informal support that marriage has (Seltzer 2004). People cohabit for many reasons including convenience, as a way to assess compatibility for marriage, economic considerations, or as an alternative to marriage. A primary challenge of characterizing cohabitations is that partners may have different motivations, their motivations may shift over time, or they may even disagree about whether or not they are in fact cohabiting (Seltzer 2004).

Who Cohabits?

Those who cohabit span all ages, race, and ethnic groups, and are found within all social classes. In fact, today the majority of people who marry begin their union by cohabitating (Bumpass and Lu 2000; Alternatives to Marriage Project 2006). Cohabitation is common in many countries and is as common as marriage among young adults in Sweden (Popenoe 2005). States that had the highest percentage of heterosexual cohabiting households were Alaska (12 percent), followed by Maine, Vermont, and Nevada (11 percent each); Utah had the lowest rate of cohabitation (4.4 percent), followed by Alabama (5.2 percent), according to Simmons and O'Connell (2003).

Although cohabitation is far more widespread than ever before in the United States, increasing 1,000 percent since 1960, it occurs most among certain groups. Cohabitors tend to be more politically liberal, have more nontraditional ideas about gender, and are more likely to share housework and breadwinning responsibilities than are married couples (Casper and Bianchi 2002; Hohmann-Marriott 2006; Seltzer 2004). Table 7.3 compares the characteristics of unmarried cohabiting men and women to their married counterparts. As you can see from the table, cohabiting men and women (Fields 2004):

1. are considerably younger than their married counterparts
2. have less education and are significantly less likely to have graduated from college
3. are more likely to be employed, but earn less money
4. are somewhat less likely to have children residing with them, although the differences are not large

Moreover, compared to their married counterparts, they are nearly three times as likely to have a female who is six or more years older than the male partner, who earns more, and who is more highly educated. In addition, they are nearly twice as likely as married couples to be interracial, particularly with one black and one white partner (Fields and Casper 2001; Fields 2004).

TABLE 7.3 Characteristics of Unmarried Cohabiting Partners and Married Spouses by Sex: March 2003 (Percent)

	Men		Women	
	Cohabiting Partners	**Married Spouses**	**Cohabiting Partners**	**Married Spouses**
Age				
15 to 24 years old	16	2	24	4
25 to 34 years old	34	16	32	19
35 to 44 years old	25	24	21	25
45 years old and over	25	58	22	51
Education				
Less than high school	18	15	16	13
High school graduate	39	31	35	35
Some college	25	25	30	27
College graduate	18	30	19	26
Labor Force Status				
Employed	80	74	72	59
Unemployed	8	3	5	2
Not in labor force	12	23	22	38
Personal Earnings				
Without earnings	11	20	17	36
With earnings	90	80	83	64
Under $9,999	12	7	20	19
$10,000 to $19,999	20	11	27	22
$20,000 to $29,999	23	14	24	20
$30,000 to $39,999	19	16	13	15
$40,000 to $49,999	10	12	7	9
$50,000 to $74,999	10	21	7	10
$75,000 and over	6	19	2	5
Presence of Children				
With children*	41	45	41	45

*May be own children of either or both partners; excludes ever-married children under 18 years

Source: Fields 2004.

Attitudes Toward Cohabitation

Along with the changing trend is a greater acceptance of cohabitation than ever before, particularly among women. As shown in Figure 7.3, 64 percent of male seniors in high school support cohabitation, up about 20 points from 25 years earlier, as do 57 percent of female seniors, up 25 points (National Marriage Project 2006).

Cohabitation has become nearly institutionalized. It is now routine for surveys to ask about cohabitation and to include it as a separate category rather than lumping it in with "never married" or "unmarried."

Demographer Judith Seltzer (2004) notes three important demographic trends that indicate that the meaning of cohabitation is changing. First, although the majority of marriages today begin by cohabitation, cohabiting unions are less likely to be a prelude to marriage now than they were in past decades. Second, cohabiting couples are more likely to be parents. One or both may have a child from a previous union or the couple may have a child together. Third, single women who become pregnant are nearly as likely to cohabit today as they are to marry the child's father.

Some voice grave concern over the rise in cohabitation. They may believe that it is wrong for people to engage in sexual relationships outside of marriage or they may be alarmed by the research that shows that cohabiting relationships are often unstable. In particular, they may voice concern for children in cohabiting relationships. For example, Barbara Dafoe Whitehead and David Popenoe, leaders in the National Marriage Project, argue (1999):

> Do not cohabit if children are involved. Children need and should have parents who are committed to staying together over the long term. Cohabiting parents break up at a much higher rate than married parents and the effects of breakup can be devastating and often long lasting. Moreover, children living in cohabiting unions are at higher risk of sexual abuse and physical violence, including lethal violence, than are children living with married parents.

Are these accusations correct? The next section examines the research on cohabitation, marriage, and children.

FIGURE 7.3 **Percentage of High School Seniors Who "Agreed" or "Mostly Agreed" with the Statement, "It's a Good Idea for a Couple to Live Together Before Getting Married in Order to Find Out if They Really Get Along."**

Source: National Marriage Project 2006.

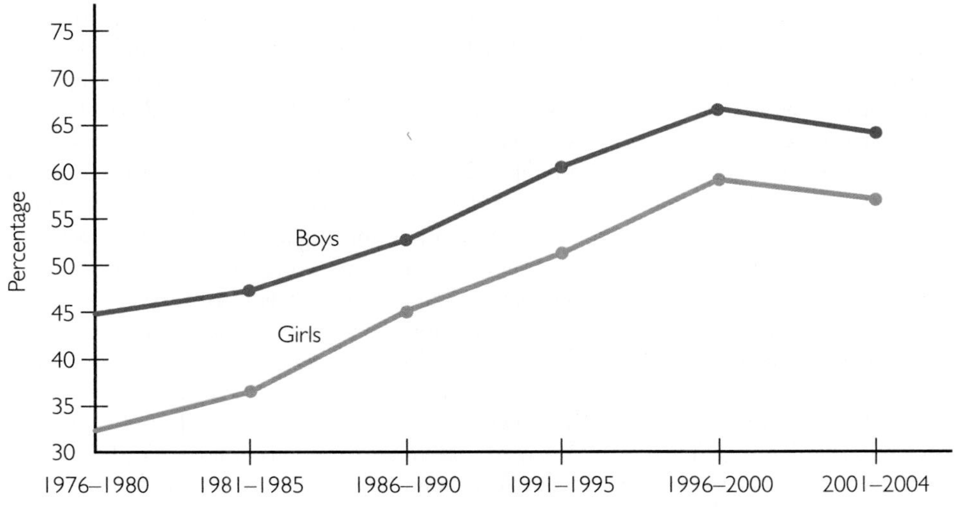

Cohabitation and Marriage

Cohabiting relationships generally do not last very long. About half of cohabiting relationships break up in less than a year and less than 10 percent last 5 years or more (Seltzer 2004). However, this is highly correlated with age. Older cohabitors report significantly higher levels of relationship quality and stability than do younger cohabitors, although they are less likely to have plans to marry their partners, according to a study of 966 cohabitors from the National Survey of Family and Households (King and Scott 2005). Older cohabitors are more likely to view their relationship as an alternative to marriage, whereas younger cohabitors are more likely to view their relationship as a prelude to it.

Despite the logic that suggests that living together prior to marriage would give partners the opportunity to test out the relationship and thus decrease their chances of divorce, it appears that cohabitation is positively correlated with divorce, particularly among whites, although less so among blacks or Mexican Americans (Phillips and Sweeney 2005). Cohabitation after a divorce is also associated with reduced marital satisfaction in a subsequent remarriage and a higher rate of divorce (Xu et al. 2006). This means that those who cohabit with their partners prior to marriage are *more*, not less, likely to eventually divorce. Why is this the case?

There are two possible reasons for the positive relationship between cohabitation and divorce. The first may simply be a **selection effect**—that the type of person who cohabits may be the same type of person who would willingly end an unhappy marriage. For example, someone who values personal freedom may be both more likely to cohabit and more likely to divorce, or a person who is religious may be less likely to cohabit and less likely to divorce. It is not the case that cohabitation *causes* the divorce per se; rather, the relationship between cohabitation and divorce is **spurious**, meaning that both cohabitation and divorce are really caused by a third factor—in this case, the high value placed on personal freedom, or looser religious values.

The second reason may be causal in nature—perhaps there is something about the cohabitation experience that weakens relationships. For example, couples who cohabit are more likely to maintain financial independence and keep separate checking accounts (Landale 2002; Seltzer 2002), possibly undermining a feeling of unity or creating tensions about differing contribution levels or how money is spent. However, Rindfuss and Van den Heuvel (1990) have suggested that because cohabiting couples are living more like singles, they therefore are not really "testing" the relationship as if it were marriage. Consequently, when they do marry, the social expectations that come along with being a husband, wife, son-in-law, and daughter-in-law remain new and uncharted territory. Another possibility is that the act of dissolving a cohabitation relationship generates a greater willingness to dissolve later relationships (DeMaris and MacDonald 1993). However, the causal links are unclear.

Why are there racial and ethnic differences in the relationship between cohabitation and divorce? Researchers Phillips and Sweeney (2005) speculate that it may be because whites are more likely to characterize their relationship as a trial marriage, whereas for blacks and Mexican Americans cohabitation is more likely to function as a substitute for marriage. They suggest, however, that more research is needed to truly understand the meanings of cohabitation across different racial and ethnic groups.

We do know that cohabiting relationships do not necessarily end easily and problem free. For example, after dissolution, formerly cohabiting women's economic standing declines precipitously compared to men's, leaving a substantial portion of women in poverty (Avellar and Smock 2005). This problem is particularly pronounced for black and Hispanic women. This may be due to women having custody of children (33 percent of formerly cohabiting women have children living with them, compared to 3 percent of men) and women's lower earnings. Women cannot maintain the same standard of living as men after their relationship ends, and nearly one-third become impoverished (Avellar and Smock 2005).

Cohabitation and Children

Forty-one percent of cohabiting couples have children under age 18 residing in the home, born to one or both partners, compared to 45 percent of married-couple households (Fields 2004). Most often, the children are from one partner's previous union, but today, about 15 percent of cohabiting couples have at least one child together. What effect does living in a cohabiting family have on children?

Whether cohabitation is good or bad for children largely depends on what alternatives exist. Alternatives include living with a single mother, living with a mother and her unmarried partner, living with a mother and her new spouse (stepfather), living with two cohabiting biological parents, or living with two married biological parents. Children can potentially benefit from living with a cohabiting partner when resources are shared with family members. For example, a study by sociologists Manning and Brown found that between 7 and 9 percent of children of cohabiting relationships faced high risk (defined as experiencing poverty, food insecurity, and housing insecurity) compared to only 2 percent of children in married biological or married stepparent families, but to 13 percent of children living with a single mother (Manning and Brown 2006). Likewise, Artis (2007) found that kindergarten-age children in cohabiting families average lower reading, math, and general knowledge skills than do similar children in married two-parent biological families, but many of the differences disappear when we account for differences in income, maternal depression, and parenting practices.

It seems that, in general, children receive the most support and do the best when they are reared in households with two married biological parents (Brown 2002; DeLeire and Kalil 2005; Hofferth and Anderson 2003). However, this is not the case for all families; some married-couple households are fraught with violence or conflict. Moreover, not all families can be constructed with two married parents anyway. Rather than embrace only one type of family structure as "best" and others as "less than," let us examine the research that summarizes the possible strengths and challenges of a variety of family forms. This information can then be used to help support those in need.

Much of the research contains problems associated with small sample sizes or cross-sectional designs that make it difficult to assess causality (Seltzer 2004). Longitudinal studies with large, nationally representative samples of children in different household forms are necessary to accurately determine the ways in which household structure shapes child well-being, Nonetheless, the following trends have been noted in the research literature:

- Cohabiting biological fathers spend less time in activities with their children than do married fathers, although they tend to spend more time with and be more supportive of their children than do unmarried fathers who do not live with their children (even when still romantically involved with the children's mother).
- Male cohabiting partners spend less time in children's organized activities, such as school and community activities, than do married stepfathers or biological fathers.
- Children who live with their mother and her male cohabiting partner have poorer school performance and exhibit more behavioral problems than do children who live solely with a single mother, with a mother and stepfather, or with two biological parents.
- Cohabiting families spend their money differently than do married-parent families, divorced single-parent families, or never-married single-parent families. For example,

compared to married families, cohabiting families spend a greater amount of money on alcohol and tobacco and a smaller amount of money on education.

Some of these differences may be due to the vagueness of the cohabiting partner's role in childrearing. For example, is a male cohabiting partner supposed to be a father-surrogate, a special adult male in the life of the child, or simply the mother's boyfriend? Few norms surround the role of cohabiting partner, and families are largely left on their own to negotiate this social terrain.

Gay and Lesbian Intimate Relationships

A look at other countries reveals differing opinions and policies surrounding gay and lesbian intimate relationships. For example, in 2001 a law went into effect in the Netherlands that gave gays and lesbians the right to marry and adopt children. Dutch civil servants wed nearly 2,000 gay and lesbian couples in the first 6 months after gay marriage was legalized, yet, in Ecuador until 1997, consensual sex between adults of the same sex could land them in prison for up to 8 years. In 1996, the U.S. Congress passed a federal law, the Defense of Marriage Act, which had two main goals: (1) to allow each state to deny constitutional marital rights between persons of the same sex that have been recognized in another state; and (2) defined marriage as a "legal union of one man and one woman as husband and wife" and by stating that the term "spouse" only refers to a person of the opposite sex who is a husband or a wife. This act therefore undermines the laws in states like Massachusetts. President George W. Bush emphasized, "I strongly believe that marriage should be defined as between a man and a woman. I am troubled by activist judges who are defining marriage." In contrast, the Supreme Court of Canada handed gay and lesbian civil rights advocates a hugely significant win in 2005 when it agreed to allow same-sex marriage. Even Cuba's Fidel Castro said that homosexuality was "a natural human tendency that simply must be respected" (Data Lounge 2004).

Gay and Lesbian Cohabitation

Despite popular stereotypes that homosexuals, particularly gay men, have frequent sex with multiple partners, in reality many gays and lesbians lead quiet and unassuming lives in committed monogamous relationships (Peplau and Beals 2004; Weston 1991). Estimating the number of gay and lesbian couples is difficult; many fear identification because of discrimination or abuse (Kaiser Family Foundation 2001), therefore, any current estimates are likely to be below the actual number. With this caveat in mind, some survey data suggest that 40–60 percent of gay men and 45–80 percent of lesbians are currently involved in steady romantic relationships (Patterson 2000; Peplau et al. 1996). Moreover, several studies report that perhaps up to one-fourth of gays and lesbians have lived together 10 years or more, obviously signifying a deep commitment (Kurdek 2004). The U.S. Census Bureau recently began to compile data on unmarried households as a way to measure the number of cohabiting gays and lesbians.

Differences Between Homosexual and Heterosexual Couples Do gay and lesbian couples differ significantly from heterosexual couples? To address this question, family scholar Lawrence Kurdek collected data over time from gay, lesbian, and heterosexual married couples and compared many aspects of their relationships (Kurdek 2001, 2004, 2006). He looked at such things as relationship quality, level of commitment, level of satisfaction with the relationship, social support from family and friends, conflict and its resolution, and equality. He controlled for important sociodemographic variables (e.g., age, months living together, or whether the couple had children) so that any findings could be attributed to sexual orientation rather than to other factors. Kurdek found that there were very few differences between homosexual and heterosexual couples, and most differences he did find were very small. For example, his research found that both gay and lesbian couples were more open with their partner, and were more autonomous in the relationship, compared to their married counterparts. Lesbians, in particular, reported greater levels of equality in their relationship and higher satisfaction. Gays and lesbians also reported receiving less support from family members than did the married couples, although lesbians reported greater support from friends. Yet, overall, on three-quarters of the indicators, there were no significant differences between gays and lesbians and heterosexual married couples. It would seem that heterosexual and homosexual couples are more alike than they are different (Kurdek 2001, 2004, 2006). These findings support the view that "despite variability in structure, close dyadic relationships work in similar ways" (Kurdek 2006, 509).

Many gay men, such as the couple here, live together happily in supportive and loving monogamous partnerships, despite the public image of swinging single bars and bathhouses.

Differences Between Gay and Lesbian Couples Kurdek then assessed how gay and lesbian couples differ from one another (Kurdek 2003). He found even fewer differences between gay and lesbian couples than he did when he compared them to married couples. There were virtually no differences between the two groups in the predictors of relationship quality, social support, and the likelihood of dissolution. The most significant results emerged in the relationship-related attitudinal questions, where there were differences in three of the eight variables: Lesbian couples reported stronger liking, trust, and equality than did gay couples. Again, it appears that differences among committed couples are generally minimal, whether gay, lesbian, or married heterosexual.

Social Policy and Family Resilience

One of the most compelling family policies on the table today is whether to allow same-sex couples to marry. Why do gays and lesbians want to be able to marry, and what specific benefits would they receive under marriage that they do not otherwise receive? What are the concerns surrounding same-sex marriage, and how might allowing gays or lesbians to wed strengthen or weaken marriage overall? This next section will explore the policy controversy surrounding same-sex marriage.

Example: Civil Unions versus Same-Sex Marriage

Ask just about anyone, and they will tell you that marital status matters. There are at least 1,400 documented legal rights associated with marriage that are not granted to cohabiting couples. These vary from joint parenting and adoption, to immigration and residency for spouses, to veterans' discounts, to crime victims' recovery benefits. *Spousal privilege* is common in U.S. legal, economic, and social institutions. As one heterosexual woman put it:

Marriage supports families, and it also supports married people. It is not always easy being married, but on life's hardest days—if you're in the hospital, if you are in a funeral home, if you are in court—being married matters. It's even truer on some of the best days in life: the birth or adoption of a child, the purchase of your first home, the celebration of your vows. On good days and on bad days, I'm glad I'm wearing a wedding ring.

Multnomah County Commissioner Serena Cruz (March 5, 2004).

Gays and lesbians also know that marital status matters. Table 7.4 outlines the rights and obligations that married couples receive versus couples who are unmarried or in **civil unions**, a public recognition that is more restrictive than marriage.

TABLE 7.4 **The Benefits of Marriage versus Civil Unions**

	Married Couples	Unmarried Couples	Civil Unions
Portability of Rights	Union automatically recognized in all 50 states.	Can register as domestic partners in some states.	Usually only recognized in the state that approves them; recently in New York, a civil union from Vermont was recognized in a wrongful-death suit.
Gifts and Property Transfers	May make unlimited transfers and gifts to each other.	Any gift or transfer worth more than $10,000 in a year requires filing a federal gift tax return.	Same as unmarried couples; larger gifts and transfers are subject to federal tax.
Income Tax Status	"Married filing jointly" generally works to the advantage of couples when one earns much more than the other, but creates a penalty when their incomes are similar.	Unmarried couples cannot file jointly, although an adult with custody of a child can file as head of household.	A couple can file only state tax returns jointly; federal returns are filed individually.
Child or Spousal Support	Criminal penalties are imposed on spouses who abandon a child or a spouse.	Unmarried partners have no legal obligation to support their partner or partner's children.	In states where the union is granted, the courts can impose penalties on a partner who abandons a child or a spouse.
Medical Decisions	A spouse or family member may make decisions for an incompetent or disabled person unless contrary written instructions exist.	A healthcare proxy, prepared before a problem occurs, can designate anyone, including a partner, to make decisions.	Partners in the state where the union was granted can make health decisions, but in other states that authority may not be recognized.
Immigration	U.S. citizens and legal permanent residents can sponsor their spouses and other immediate family members for immigration purposes.	Not allowed to sponsor a partner or other immediate family members.	Not allowed to sponsor a partner or other immediate family members.

Source: "The Benefits of Marriage Versus Civil Unions." From Gay & Lesbian Advocates & Defenders. www.glad.org/marriage/. Reprinted with permission.

The Canadian Parliament voted to allow same-sex marriage legislation throughout the country by a vote of 155 to 138 in June 2005. Canada becomes the third country after Belgium and the Netherlands to allow gays and lesbians to marry.

The battle to give gays and lesbians the right to wed is far more controversial in the United States. President George W. Bush supports a constitutional amendment prohibiting same-sex marriage. To date, Massachusetts is the only state that allows same-sex marriage, and only for citizens residing in that state. At least half of those living in Massachusetts support same-sex marriage, state polls reveal (Fox News.com 2003). However, Massachusetts is somewhat of an anomaly. Most states have passed explicit laws banning marriage among gays and lesbians. Nationally, a poll taken in June 2005 revealed that 36 percent supported allowing same-sex marriages, up from 29 percent 1 year earlier. An even larger number in June 2005, 53 percent (up from 48 percent in 2004), approved of gay civil unions that allow gays and lesbians to enter into legal arrangements that would provide many of the same rights as married couples (Pew Forum 2005). As shown in Table 7.5 on page 236, the United States is highly polarized. Although only 14 percent of self-labeled conservatives support gay marriage, 40 percent of moderates and 69 percent of those calling themselves liberals do so. Likewise only 31 percent of conservatives support civil unions, in contrast to 60 percent of moderates, and 80 percent of liberals. Dramatic differences are also noted across religious groups and political parties.

What is the history behind civil unions and same-sex marriage? Vermont led the country with the adoption of a civil union bill in 2000. By a vote of 79–68, Vermont moved the national debate to a new phase. Afterwards, the civil union law was challenged, but in 2002 the Vermont Supreme Court upheld their decision and refused to repeal the law.

TABLE 7.5 Opinions Toward Gay Marriage and Civil Unions (July 2005)

	Favor Gay Marriage (%)	Favor Civil Unions (%)
Total	36	53
White Protestant	25	46
Evangelical	14	35
Mainline	39	60
White Catholic	39	62
Black Protestant	25	31
Secular	61	75
Conservative	14	31
Moderate	40	60
Liberal	69	80
Republican	19	41
Democrat	45	59
Independent	46	61

Source: Pew Forum 2005.

Since then, several regions of the country have tested the waters, and pushed further for same-sex marriage. For example, the Massachusetts high court ruled in February 2004 that only full, equal marriage rights for gay couples, rather than civil unions, are constitutional. In the advisory opinion requested by the Senate, the four justices who ruled in favor of gay marriage wrote, "The history of our nation has demonstrated that separate is seldom, if ever, equal" (Peter 2004). Later that month San Francisco filed suit against the state of California claiming that laws barring the city from marrying gays and lesbians were invalid. The city granted more than 3,000 same-sex couples marriage licenses in a 2-week period (Data Lounge 2004). In Portland, Oregon, county commissioners, in conjunction with state attorneys, decided that not allowing same-sex marriages violated the Oregon state constitution, and on March 3, 2004, began offering marriage licenses to gays and lesbians. As in San Francisco, people lined up in front of the courthouse for hours, and hundreds of same-sex couples received marriage licenses within days. As one woman put it:

> There was a grand and somewhat unexpected leap in Portland. It was a leap of joy. My partner and I have waited 26 years to establish a legally binding commitment of our love. What we found on March 3, 2004 was not just a marriage license to receive our family's rights. We found a community that understands that love and commitment are rare and treasured gifts. (Tinker 2004, 1)

However, the weddings performed in San Francisco and Portland were later deemed to be invalid by the courts.

Advocates see same-sex marriage as a civil rights issue. Gays and lesbians should not be discriminated against and forbidding them to legally wed is an overt form of discrimination. Because they generally do not see homosexuality as a choice, they equate restrictions on same-sex marriage with the restrictions on interracial marriage that were strictly enforced in some states and repealed only a generation ago. Advocates believe that allowing same-sex couples to marry does not harm or diminish heterosexual marriage or hurt society in any way. Pointing to the few countries that do allow gays and lesbians to wed, they note no ill effects. No-fault divorce laws have had the greatest negative impact on the institution. Next to it, gay marriage as a legal reform is trivial. Love and public commitment should be encouraged, rather than squelched. Others suggest that this is an issue that should be left up to individual states to decide.

Opponents' views vary, but many invoke religion, suggesting that same-sex marriage is immoral and is in violation of God's teaching. For example, the Catholic church decries homosexual acts because they do not lead to procreation. Early American antisodomy laws discouraged all forms of nonprocreative sex (including heterosexual oral and anal sex). Islam shares a similar view. Others simply suggest that marriage has *always* been defined as between a man and a woman and see no need to change it. In particular, concern is voiced that allowing gays and lesbians to wed elevates the status of their relationship to that of a heterosexual couple and legitimizes their right to have and raise children. Some opponents support civil unions or domestic partnerships for gays and lesbians, but draw the line on legal marriage. President George W. Bush may be the most outspoken opponent and has discussed a constitutional ban of same-sex marriage. He says (White House 2004):

> After more than two centuries of American jurisprudence and millennia of human experience, a few judges and local authorities are presuming to change the most fundamental institution of civilization. Their actions have created confusion on an issue that requires clarity. On a matter of such importance, the voice of the people must be heard. Activist courts have left the people with one recourse. If we're to prevent the meaning of marriage from being

changed forever, our nation must enact a constitutional amendment to protect marriage in America. Decisive and democratic action is needed because attempts to redefine marriage in a single state or city could have serious consequences throughout the country.

The issue of whether to allow same-sex couples to legally marry is complex. There are a multitude of opinions on the subject, steeped in deeply held values. Perhaps the most vexing question is: How would allowing gays and lesbians who are in loving and devoted relationships to wed weaken the social institutions of marriage and family? The answer to that question has never been fully answered.

Conclusion

This chapter introduces several key concepts surrounding the development of intimacy, including mate selection, love, sexual orientation and sexuality, and cohabitation. People become intimate, form partnerships, or marry to improve their economic conditions, for sheer survival, to increase their social standing, or to please their parents and build family alliances. Many cultures do not necessarily equate love with marriage, and in fact may see love as dangerous to a good marital relationship. However, in the United States love and intimacy are increasingly valued. Changes are taking place in dating and mate selection in the United States. Today it is becoming increasingly common for unmarried couples to engage in sexual relationships and to cohabit. However, same-sex marriage continues to be steeped in controversy, with wider support for civil unions.

Key Terms

Bisexual: An attraction to both males and females. One who engages in both heterosexual and homosexual relationships. (p. 216)

Civil unions: A public recognition of a relationship that is more restrictive than marriage and offers fewer rights and privileges. (p. 234)

Cohabitation: Unmarried partners living together. (p. 227)

Dowry: The financial gift given to a woman's prospective in-laws by her parents. (p. 210)

Endogamy: Norms that encourage marriage between people of the same social category. (p. 213)

Exogamy: Norms that encourage marriage between people of different social categories. (p. 213)

Gay: Usually refers to homosexual men. (p. 216)

Heterogeneous relationships: Those in which the partners are significantly different from one another on some important characteristic. (p. 214)

Heterosexual: An attraction and preference for sexual relationships with members of the other sex (e.g., a man and a woman). (p. 216)

Homogeneous relationships: Those in which partners are similar to one another. (p. 213)

Homosexual: Refers to a preference for same-sex sexual and romantic relationships. (p. 216)

Lesbian: Homosexual woman. (p. 216)

Love: An enduring bond based on affection and emotion, including a sense of obligation toward one another. (p. 208)

Selection effect: People who engage in some behavior; e.g., cohabitation, are different from those who do not. (p. 230)

Sexual orientation: The sex that one is attracted to. (p. 216)

Sexual scripts: A social construction that provides the norms or rules regarding sexual behavior. (p. 218)

Spurious: An apparent relationship between two variables that is really caused by a third factor. (p. 230)

Resources on the Internet

Alternative to Marriage Project
www.unmarried.org
The Alternatives to Marriage Project (ATMP) is a national nonprofit organization advocating for equality and fairness for unmarried people, including people who choose not to marry, cannot marry, or live together without marriage. They provide support and information, fight discrimination on the basis of marital status, and educate the public and policymakers about relevant social and economic issues.

American Social Health Association
www.ashastd.org
The American Social Health Association (ASHA) is a nongovernmental agency recognized by the public, patients, providers, and policymakers for developing and delivering accurate, medically reliable information about STDs. It provides educational pamphlets, referrals, help groups and shares access to in-depth information about sexually transmitted diseases.

Division of STD Prevention
www.cdc.gov/std
The Division of STD Prevention, at the Centers for Disease Control and Prevention, provides national leadership through research, policy development, and support of effective services to prevent sexually transmitted diseases (including HIV infection) and their complications such as enhanced HIV transmission, infertility, adverse outcomes of pregnancy, and reproductive tract cancer.

National Gay and Lesbian Task Force (NGLTF)
www.ngltf.org
The NGLTF is the national progressive organization working for the civil rights of gay, lesbian, bisexual, and transgender people, with the vision and commitment to building a powerful political movement. They work in advocacy, grassroots training, informing policy, organizing, and partnering with other organizations. One of their current issues of interest is same-sex marriage.

Further Reading

Booth, A., and A. C. Crouter. (Eds.). 2002. *Just Living Together*. Mahwah, NJ: Lawrence Erlbaum.

Cahn, S. K. 2007. *Sexual Reckonings*. Cambridge, MA: Harvard University Press.

D'Augelli, A. R., and C. J. Patterson. (Eds.). 2001. *Lesbian, Gay, and Bisexual Identities and Youths*. New York: Oxford University Press.

D'Criz, P. 2004. *Family Care in HIV/AIDS: Exploring Lived Experience*. New Delhi, India: Sage.

Hamon, R. R., and B. B. Ingoldsby. (Eds.). 2003. *Mate Selection Across Cultures*. Thousand Oaks, CA: Sage.

Ingraham, C. 1999. *White Weddings: Romancing Heterosexuality in Popular Culture*. New York: Routledge.

Laumann, E., O. Gagnon, R. T. Michael, and S. Michaels. 1994. *The Social Organization of Sexuality: Sexual Practices in the United States*. Chicago: University of Chicago Press.

Otnes, C. C., and E. H. Pleck. 2003. *Cinderella Dreams: The Allure of the Lavish Wedding*. Berkeley: University of California Press.

Pascoe, C. J. 2007. *Dude, You're a Fag*. Berkeley: University of California Press.

Seidman, S., N. Fischer, and C. Meeks. 2006. *Handbook of the New Sexuality Studies*. New York Routledge.

Sullivan, M. 2004. *The Family of Women: Lesbian Mothers, Their Children, and the Undoing of Gender*. Berkeley: University of California Press.

Weston, K. 1999. *Love Makes a Family: Portraits of Lesbian, Gay, Bisexual and Transgender Parents and Their Families*. Amherst: University of Massachusetts Press.

Weston, K. 1991. *Families We Choose: Lesbians, Gays, and Kinship*. New York: Columbia University Press.

CHAPTER 8

Marriage: A Personal Relationship and Social Institution

Chapter Outline

CHAPTER PREVIEW

Marriage is a relationship that is found around the world. It is both a deep personal relationship and a social institution in society. This chapter reveals contrasting conceptions of marriage, explores the consequences of marriage for health and well-being, and describes current controversies and social policies surrounding marriage. In this chapter you will learn:

- Marriage is universal and the importance of such rituals as the wedding ceremony
- Marriage is changing rapidly in both structure and meaning, including declining marriage rates, delayed marriage, racial and ethnic intermarriage, and same-sex marriage
- Current attitudes and expectations about marriage, including nonmarital sex, dual jobs and dual career marriages, division of household labor, and nonmarital childbearing
- The debate over whether marriage as an institution is declining or is resilient
- The benefits of marriage according to research, including physical and mental health, economic advantages, sexuality, social capital, and social support
- The pros and cons of the movement to strengthen traditional marriage, including the marriage movement, covenant marriage, and statewide marriage initiatives

Women who are in satisfying marriages or long-term cohabiting relationships have a health advantage over unmarried women or those in unsatisfying marriages, according to a study involving 493 middle-aged women over a 13-year period. The researchers—Gallo, Troxel, Matthews, and Kuller—found that women in good marriages were less likely to develop risk factors that lead to cardiovascular diseases compared with other middle-aged women. Participants who were married or cohabiting completed a seven-item marital quality questionnaire that assessed satisfaction with amount of time spent together, communication, sexual activity, agreement on financial matters, and similarity of interests, lifestyle, and temperament. The questionnaire was completed at the beginning of the study and at the 3-year follow-up assessments over 13 years. Health risk factors included a blood draw to measure cholesterol and glucose levels, blood pressure evaluation, body-size measurement, assessment of health behaviors such as diet, smoking, and exercise, and psychosocial characteristics, such as depression, anxiety, anger, and stress. Results indicate that women in marriages characterized by high levels of satisfaction show a health advantage when compared with participants in marriages characterized by low levels of satisfaction and with unmarried participants (single, widowed, or divorced). This includes lower levels of biological and lifestyle risk factors—such as blood pressure, cholesterol levels, and body mass index—and lower levels of psychosocial cardiovascular risk factors, such as depression, anxiety, and anger. How might being in a good marriage influence health? Previous research indicates several direct and indirect factors may be at work. Marriage itself may offer a health advantage by providing social support and protecting against the risks associated with social isolation. Also, spousal influence and involvement may encourage health-promoting behaviors and deter unhealthy behaviors. Married people may also be at a health advantage relative to their unmarried counterparts through the increased availability of socioeconomic resources. However, poor marital quality may erase these health advantages. Marital stress is associated with lifestyle risk factors and nonadherence to medical regimens. Poor marital quality is also linked to more depression, hostility, and anger, all risk factors for coronary heart disease. Thus, marital status and quality could influence metabolic risk factors and acute stress responses, which in turn predict cardiovascular death and illness.
(Adapted from Partenheimer 2003) ■

What is there to marriage that can apparently keep people well—or make them sick? Why is marriage considered to be so important around the world? This chapter will explore some central tenets about marriage as both a social institution and a personal relationship. It will examine similarities and differences in marriage across countries, show

how marriage is changing, explore the consequences of marriage for the health and well-being of each partner, and describe the controversy surrounding the growing movement toward preserving and strengthening traditional marriage.

The Universality of Marriage

Marriage is recognized in some form worldwide. As a social institution there are rules, rights, and responsibilities surrounding marriage with significant state involvement. Only certain people qualify for marriage. For example, in the United States with few exceptions, gays and lesbians cannot legally marry, children cannot marry, and in many parts of the country, first cousins are prohibited from marrying as well. Why is the government so concerned about something as seemingly private as marriage? Because as a social institution, marriage is seen as a stabilizing force within societies (for example, by serving as the mechanism through which to socialize children) and the government sees this as its business. However, the rules, rights, and responsibilities surrounding marriage vary across social, historical, and cultural contexts. For example, interracial marriage was illegal in some states as recently as a few decades ago, and it remains illegal in certain parts of the world today.

As a personal relationship, marriage is deeply meaningful to the individuals involved, although "meaningful" is conceptualized differently within social, historical, and cultural contexts. Feelings of love and sexual intensity may be the core experience in one social location, but these feelings may be totally irrelevant to the meanings associated with marriage elsewhere. Indians think Americans do not take marriage seriously enough. They believe that the U.S. concepts of dating and romance are irresponsible because when the fun ends, a divorce ensues (Leeder 2004). In China, most parents no longer arrange their children's marriages; however, they continue to play a central role in marital relations. Marital quality is strongly influenced by the quality of the relationship with the extended family (Leeder 2004). Iraqi marriages may seem highly unusual to Americans, as shown in Box 8.1. In a world that is dichotomized into kin and strangers, it is not surprising to hear an Iraqi woman say, "It is safer to marry a cousin than a stranger." Norms surrounding marriage have a ripple effect on other aspects of the social structure.

What do Americans want from marriage? They want a relationship full of passion, sexual energy, tenderness, and love. They want a spouse who is a best friend, who is compassionate, understanding, and nurturing. They expect marriage to ward off loneliness and to be an oasis from the hustle and stress of their daily lives. Couples who have children seek a connection to the past and a bridge to the future. Americans want a complex set of relationships and emotions from marriage, and they want it for their entire lives (Blakeslee and Wallerstein 1995).

One universal feature of marriage is that its beginning is marked in some way by a ceremony. The ceremonial procedures differ in important ways. In some cultures they are festive; in others they are somber. Many have a lavish party or reception with food and drink. Some parties include both sexes; others are segregated. For example, an Islamic marriage ceremony is a private affair, and the lavish party afterwards is strictly segregated by sex.

Wedding Ceremony

Think about the last wedding you attended. What color was the bride's dress? Without knowing anything about the specific couple or about the wedding itself, most people

BOX 8.1 Our Global Community

Iraqi Marriages: "It's Safer to Marry a Cousin Than a Stranger"

Americans would shudder at the thought of an arranged marriage; not so, in many parts of the world. An understanding of different mate selection processes can teach Americans a lot about a culture, as shown in the following Iraqi example.

Iqbal Muhammad does not recall her first glimpse of her future husband, because they were both newborns at the time, but she remembers precisely when she knew he was the one. It was the afternoon her uncle walked over from his house next door and proposed that she marry his son Muhammad. "I was a little surprised, but I knew right away it was a wise choice," she said, recalling that afternoon 9 years ago, when she and Muhammad were both 22. "It is safer to marry a cousin than a stranger."

Her reaction was typical in a country where nearly half of marriages are between first or second cousins, a statistic that is one of the most important and least understood differences between Iraq and the United States. The extraordinarily strong family bonds complicate virtually everything Americans have done and are trying to do in Iraq, from punishing Saddam Hussein to changing women's status to creating a liberal democracy.

"Americans just don't understand what a different world Iraq is because of these highly unusual cousin marriages," said Robin Fox of Rutgers University, the author of *Kinship and Marriage*, a widely used anthropology textbook. "Liberal democracy is based on the Western idea of autonomous individuals committed to a public good, but that's not how members of these tight and bounded kin groups see the world. Their world is divided into two groups: kin and strangers."

Iraqis frequently describe nepotism not as a civic problem but as a moral duty. The notion that Iraq's next leader would put public service ahead of family obligations drew a smile from Iqbal's uncle and father-in-law, Sheik Yousif Sayel, the patriarch in charge of the clan's farm on the Tigris River south of Baghdad. "In this country, whoever is in power will bring his relatives in from the village and give them important positions," Yousif said, sitting in the garden surrounded by some of his 21 children and 83 grandchildren. "That is what Saddam did. . . ."

Saddam married a first cousin who grew up in the same house as he did, and he ordered most of his children to marry their cousins. Yousif said he never forced any of his children to marry anyone, but more than half of the ones to marry have wed cousins. The patriarch was often the one who first suggested the match, as he did with his son Muhammad 9 years ago. "My father said that I was old enough to get married, and I agreed," Muhammad recalled. "He and my mother recommended Iqbal. I respected their wishes. It was my desire, too. We knew each other. It was much simpler to marry within the family."

would venture a guess that the bride's dress was white. Other features about the wedding itself are probably also relatively routine. It most likely occurred in a church, there were people in attendance to watch, and afterwards there was a celebration of some sort with cake being served. If marriage is such a personal experience, why is the ceremony to mark it so routine? What is the true meaning or purpose of the wedding ceremony?

Elaborate weddings have become an important symbol of achievement on the part of the couple and a statement to guests that the couple has "made it" (Bulcroft et al. 2000; Otnes and Pleck 2003). Weddings are big business, and families can easily spend $20,000 on this single event (Ingraham 1999; Otnes and Pleck 2003). Even families of modest means will spend large sums on an elaborate wedding with traditional rituals. The wedding industry makes more than $32 billion a year; Ingraham (1999) suggests that "the wedding industrial complex" is not unlike the "military industrial complex"—a huge multibillion dollar entity that is dominated by many intertwined social institu-

A month later, after the wedding, Iqbal moved next door to the home of Yousif. Moving in with the in-laws might be an American bride's nightmare, but Iqbal said her toughest adjustment occurred 5 years later, when Yousif decided that she and Muhammad were ready to live by themselves in a new home he provided just behind his own. "I felt a little lonely at first when we moved into the house by ourselves," Iqbal said. Muhammad said he too felt lonely in the new house, and he expressed pity for American parents and children living thousands of miles from each other. "Families are supposed to be together," he said. "It's cruel to keep children and parents apart."

Yousif, who is 82, said he could not imagine how the elderly in the United States cope in their homes alone. "I could not bear to go a week without seeing my children," he said. Some of his daughters have married outsiders and moved into other patriarchal clans, but the rest of the children are never far away.

Muhammad and three other sons live on the farm with him, helping to supervise the harvesting of barley, wheat, and oranges and the dates from the palm trees on their land. The other six sons have moved 15 miles away to Baghdad, but they come back often for meals and in hard times. During the war in the spring, almost the whole clan took refuge at the farm, returning to the only institution they had been able to trust through the worst of Saddam's rule.

Cousin marriage was once the norm throughout the world, but it became taboo in Europe after a long campaign by the Roman Catholic Church. Theologians such as St. Augustine and St. Thomas argued that the practice promoted family loyalties at the expense of universal love and social harmony. Eliminating it was seen as a way to reduce clan warfare and promote loyalty to larger social institutions—such as the church.

The practice became rare in the west, especially after evidence emerged of genetic risks to offspring, but it has persisted in some places, notably the Middle East, which is exceptional because of both the high prevalence and the restrictive form it takes. In other societies, a woman typically weds a cousin outside her social group, like a maternal cousin living in a clan led by a different patriarch. However, in Iraq the ideal is for the woman to remain within the clan by marrying the son of her father's brother, as Iqbal did.

Source: Tierney 2003.

CRITICAL THINKING QUESTIONS

1. Why does Iraq prefer that the woman remain in the clan by marrying the son of her father's brother, rather than marrying a cousin in a different clan? In other words, is the purpose of cousin marriage simply to ensure that children find a suitable spouse or is there more involved that that?
2. How do American ideals of romance and love fit in with the Iraqi scheme? What would they think of our ideals?

tions. The cultural rituals associated with weddings involve exploitive practices: "Retailers are aware that the public regards the wedding gown as a sacred item and have sought to combine profit making with the redesign of the bridal store as a quasi-sacred space" (Otnes and Pleck 2003).

The romantic aura of weddings leads us to believe that it is simply a party to celebrate a new marriage. However, weddings serve a much greater purpose than what is seen on the surface. Weddings codify dominant social arrangements in society and legitimate power relationships. They give privileged status to heterosexual couples and exclude gays and lesbians. Weddings also codify patriarchal norms and legitimize men's power over women's. The custom of fathers walking their daughters down the aisle and "giving them away" debases women's status, as does the custom of throwing the bride's garter to a pack of eager men or tossing the bouquet to see who the next "lucky" bride will be. These examples of patriarchy are so entrenched in U.S. customs that we rarely notice

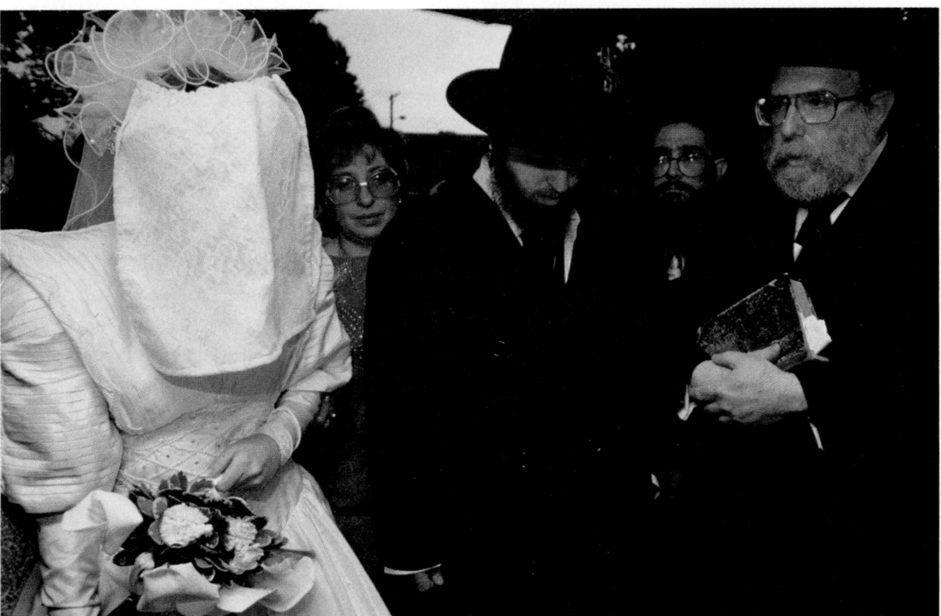

Although marriage may have different norms and social expectations historically and cross-culturally, one universal feature of marriage is that its beginning is marked in some way by a publicly recorded ceremony.

them, but critical thinking requires that we examine the issues we take for granted to see what hidden values are represented.

Many nonwestern countries are amending their wedding ceremonies so that they will look more like those found in the west (Leeder 2004). Women may now wear white wedding dressing instead of their traditional clothing. Families, even poor ones, may feel obligated to spend a handsome sum on the party, unlike in the past. As sociologist Elaine Leeder (2004) witnessed on her trip to Zambia:

> The brides were in fantastic white wedding dresses. They had long trains, flowers, tiaras, the whole works. Near them were the future husbands, some of them in suits, tuxedos, or the traditional African garb of their ethnic group. . . . I spoke with some people who were waiting and learned that this was the first of at least two ceremonies that each couple would have. This was the state-sanctioned event, which looked more western, with white gowns and government officials. Later the couple would return to their village, and another ceremony would take place, one that followed the traditions of the couple's ancestors. Sometimes, among those families that were more urbanized and educated—the "white weddings" would include some element of the traditional, tribal weddings. But for the most part, the state and the tribal ceremonies were very different events. (pp. 175–176)

The Changing Nature of Marriage

In what ways is marriage in the United States changing?

Marriage Rates

In the United States, most people want to marry and eventually do so. Although the practical necessity of marriage has declined as more women have become self-supporting and men have become more comfortable in the domestic arena, the symbolic importance of marriage has remained high. Marriage is now a sign of prestige rather than

conformity, because it often comes *after* a certain level of attainment (after a job, a career, savings, or children) rather than before.

Among the roughly 230 million Americans aged 15 and over, 53 percent are married (U.S. Census Bureau 2006d). This represents a significant decline in recent years. As shown in Figure 8.1 white, Hispanic, and Asian have the highest percentages married, while blacks have the lowest; only 34 percent of blacks aged 15 and over are married.

Sometimes these findings are misinterpreted to mean that blacks do not value marriage; however, research reveals that this is not the case (Edin and Kefalas 2005; Fragile Families Research Brief 2004). Blacks have a strong desire to marry, but many do not because they have set very high standards for marriage and they cannot meet the criteria that they have established. They want stable employment, a secure home, and an expensive wedding. As one young man revealed: "I'd like to do things right [when it comes to marriage], instead of cutting corners and doing everything half-assed. I'd rather get engaged for two years, save money, get a house, and make sure the baby's got a bedroom [than get married right now]"; his girlfriend added, "and I get a yard with grass, plus, I want a nice wedding" (Edin and Kefalas 2005). Given unstable employment and minimum-wage jobs, many of these goals are virtually unattainable.

Figure 8.2 on page 249 compares the marital status of men and women aged 15 and older between 1970 and 2005 (U.S. Census Bureau 2006d). The figure reveals that the percentage of both men and women who were currently married has declined, and the percentage who were separated or divorced has more than doubled. However, it is likely that most of these divorced and separated men and women will marry again. Americans are infatuated with marriage. Compared to many other industrialized nations Americans marry sooner, and if they divorce, remarry more quickly. The figure also reveals that the percentage of persons aged 15 and over who were widowed has changed very little since 1970. The small rise in the percentage of never-marrieds in the population, especially among men, is primarily due to postponing the age at which marriage occurs, rather than foregoing marriage altogether.

FIGURE 8.1 **Marital Status of the Total U.S. Population 15 Years and Over, 2005 (Percent)**

Source: U.S. Census Bureau 2006d.

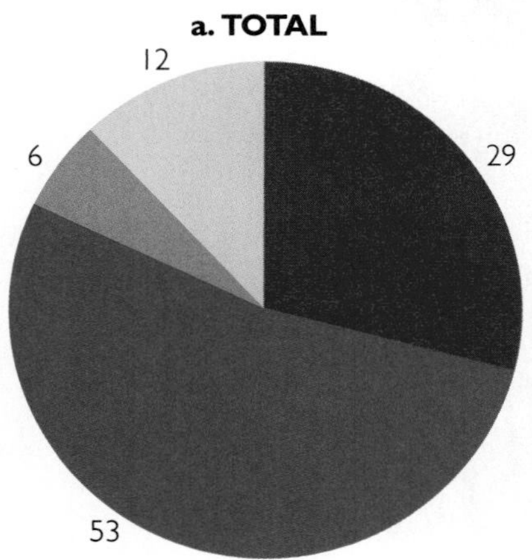

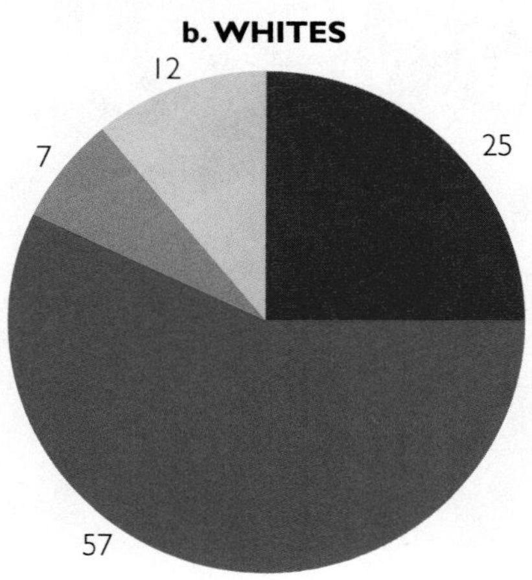

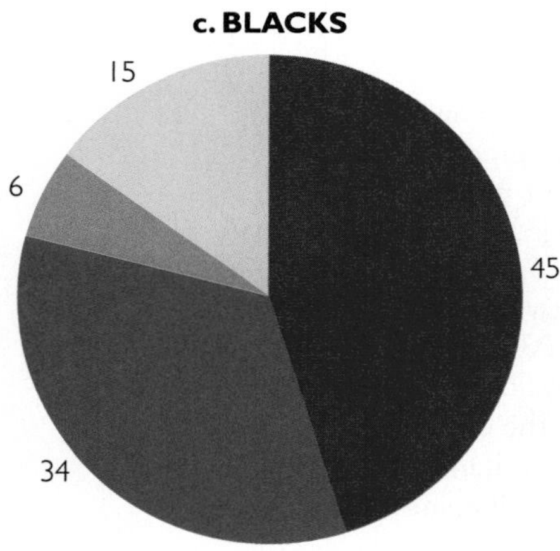

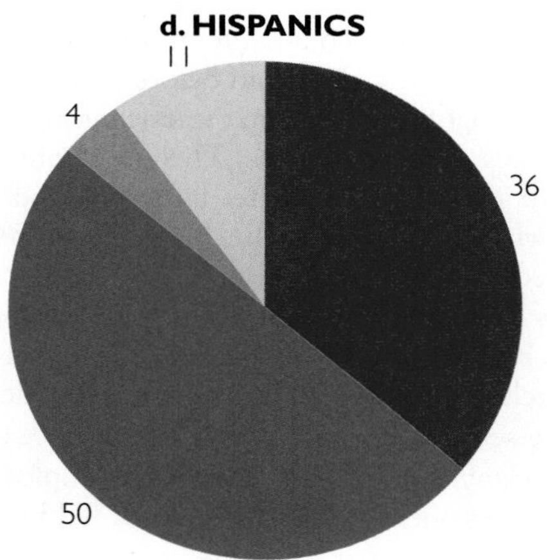

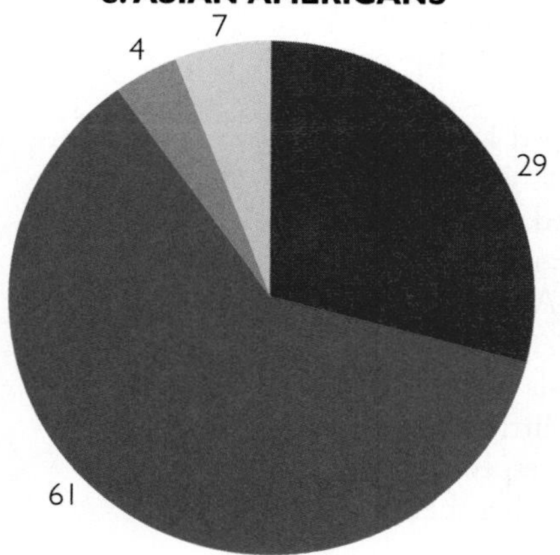

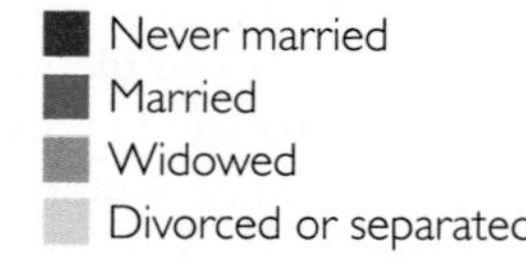

FIGURE 8.2 **Marital Status of the U.S. Population 15 Years and Over by Sex: 1970 and 2005 (Percent)**

Source: Fields and Casper 2001; U.S. Census Bureau 2006d.

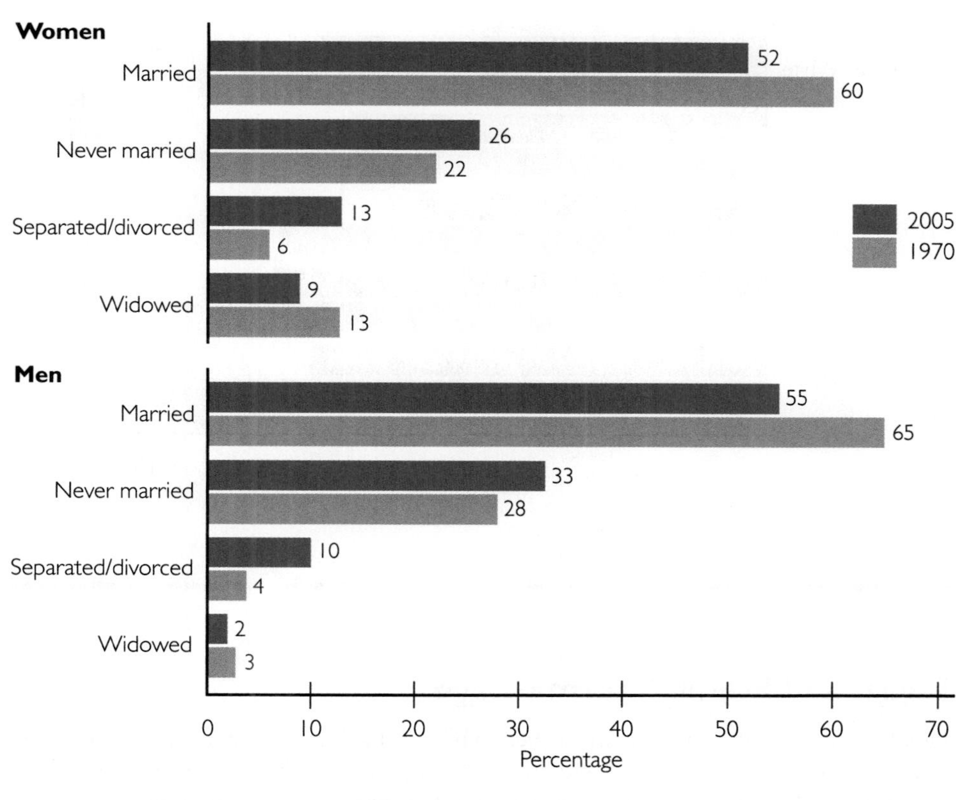

Delaying Marriage

Men and women are now older when they marry. For example, in 1970 the median age at first marriage was 21 for women and 23 for men; today these ages have risen to 25 and 27 years, for women and men respectively, increasing by 4 years in just a generation (Kreider 2005).

The delay of marriage is occurring among all racial and ethnic groups, as shown in Figure 8.3. The percentage of women aged 30–34 who were ever married in 2005, compared to 1980, declined 23 points for whites, 42 points for blacks, 23 points for Hispanics, 10 points for Asians, and 17 points for Native Americans between 1980 and 2005. Without a doubt, people tend to marry significantly later today than in the recent past. This is likely due to greater educational and economic opportunities, especially for women. Close to half of high school seniors expect to wait more than 5 years to get married (Thornton and Young-DeMarco 2001). As increasing numbers of women go to college, graduate school, or begin careers, they are more likely to postpone getting married and having children.

FIGURE 8.3 **Percentage of Women Age 30–34 Ever Married by Race/Ethnicity, 1980 and 2005**

Source: Lichter and Qian 2004; U.S. Census Bureau 2006d.

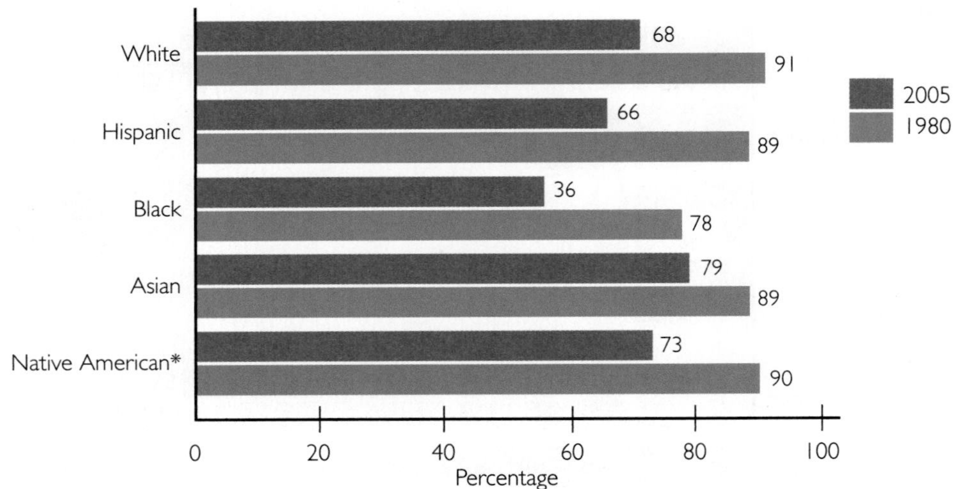

*Data for Native Americans are from 1980 and 2000 only.

Racial and Ethnic Intermarriage

People have a tendency to marry others who are like them, a concept described in Chapter 7 as homogamy. Racial and ethnic boundaries have been a key element of homogamy because race and ethnicity are master statuses that bestow a wide variety of privileges and constraints upon groups of people. As we learned in Chapter 6, most social scientists believe that race and ethnic groups represent social constructions rather than biological distinctiveness, yet racial and ethnic categories have become the basis for stratification and inequality. Norms governing marriage can influence this stratification and inequality by either maintaining boundaries between groups (thereby perpetuating privileges and constraints) or by breaking down the boundaries and encouraging assimilation between groups.

Interracial marriage may have always been part of the U.S. landscape; however, it was considered a dark and sinister feature. As early as colonial America, children were born of unions between American Indians, Europeans, and blacks; the early U.S. censuses included a category called *mulatto* to describe persons of multiple races. Nonetheless, laws banning marriage between whites and other races, referred to as **antimiscegenation laws**, were common well into the twentieth century, as revealed in Box 8.2. The U.S. Supreme Court struck down such laws in 1967; however, Alabama was the last state to formally repeal its antimiscegenation law through a state constitutional amendment as late as 2000.

Today many people continue to oppose people of different racial or ethnic backgrounds marrying, as the 2005 book, *Navigating Interracial Borders: Black-White Couples and Their Social Worlds* by Erica Chito Childs reveals. Drawing on personal accounts, in-depth interviews, and focus group responses, Childs provides compelling evidence

BOX 8.2 Social Policies for Families

Antimiscegenation Laws

In the United States, states define laws governing marriage. Today marriages can be freely contracted between people of different races in all states, but laws banning marriage between whites and other races—or antimiscegenation laws—were common from the colonial times into the twentieth century.

The first antimiscegenation law was passed in Maryland in 1661 and prohibited marriage between blacks and whites. By the end of the nineteenth century, most states had similar laws. In 1880, California prohibited the issuance of licenses for marriage between whites and Negroes, mulattos, and Mongolians (a term mainly applied to Chinese at that time). A Missouri judge prevented white and black intermarriage in 1883, reasoning that such marriages cannot lead to offspring, thereby justifying the ban on such marriages. In 1909 California added Japanese to its list of races forbidden from marrying whites, and in 1945, the California governor signed an expanded bill that prohibited marriage between whites and Negroes, mulattos, Mongolians (which included Chinese and Japanese), and Malays.

The end of World War II led to a gradual erosion of antimiscegenation laws. Between 1946 and 1957, large numbers of foreign-born wives and children of U.S. military personnel were permitted to enter the United States under the GI Fiancees Act or War Brides Act of 1946. Although most of those admitted were from Europe, some foreign-born Japanese and Korean wives and children were also admitted, as the occupation of Japan after World War II and the Korean War led to substantial numbers of U.S. armed services personnel being stationed in both Japan and Korea. The War Brides Act specified requirements for marriages when they occurred overseas, including extensive background checks on both individuals and the prohibition of marriages with women who had worked as prostitutes or bar hostesses. The rigorous requirements and checks were not relaxed until 1957.

Meanwhile, antimiscegenation laws were being challenged in the courts. The years following World War II brought the greatest changes to these laws, although there were some early exceptions (e.g., Pennsylvania repealed its antimiscegenation law in 1780, as did Ohio in 1887). In 1948 the California Supreme Court ruled the state's antimiscegenation law unconstitutional, Oregon repealed its law in 1951, and 13 other states followed suit over the next 16 years.

The most well-known and celebrated victory in the struggle against antimiscegenation laws was the 1967 U.S. Supreme Court ruling in the case of *Loving v. Virginia*. Richard Loving, a white man, married Mildred Jeter, a black woman, in Washington D.C. When the couple returned home to Virginia, they were arrested and convicted of violating Virginia's antimiscegenation law. The couple was sentenced to a year's imprisonment or a 25-year exile from Virginia. Rather than risk imprisonment, the couple moved to Washington, D.C. and sued the state of Virginia in 1963. The Virginia Supreme Court of Appeals upheld the law in 1966. The case was then appealed to the U.S. Supreme Court, which declared in 1967 that Virginia's antimiscegenation law and similar laws in 15 other states were unconstitutional. However, several states had bans on interracial marriage in their constitutions for many years, even though the laws were not enforceable. Alabama was the last state to repeal its antimiscegenation law through a state constitutional amendment in 2000.

The main purpose of the antimiscegenation laws was to prevent marriage between whites and individuals considered nonwhite. Marriages between different nonwhite races generally were not prohibited. Thus, these laws were clearly meant to maintain the power and privilege of whites and to uphold widely held beliefs in those days about racial separation, difference, and purity.

Source: Adapted from *New Marriages, New Families* 2005; Sickels 1972.

CRITICAL THINKING QUESTIONS

1. How do you feel about interracial dating and marriage? Do you distinguish between groups (e.g., it is okay between some groups but not others)? How were your attitudes formed?
2. How would antimiscegenation laws maintain the power and privilege of whites? Can you provide some examples?

that sizable opposition still exists toward black-white unions. Her analysis of media sources shows that popular films, Internet images, and pornography also continue to reinforce the idea that sexual relations between blacks and whites are deviant (Childs 2005).

Nonetheless, attitudes toward interracial and interethnic relationships have become more favorable in the last 30 to 40 years. According to a Gallup Poll conducted at the end of 2003, 86 percent of black, 79 percent of Hispanic, and 66 percent of white respondents revealed that they would accept a child or a grandchild marrying someone of a different race. Thus, while a third of whites still oppose interracial and interethnic marriages, most of these people do not necessarily go as far as to want such unions made illegal. The percentage of whites who supported laws barring marriages between whites and blacks declined from 35 percent in the 1970s to 10 percent today (*New Marriages, New Families* 2005). Persons who are least supportive of interracial marriage tend to be older and less educated (Heaton and Jacobson 2000; Qian et al. 2001). However, Childs makes us question these data because she frequently found that people who attest in surveys that they approve of interracial dating will also list various reasons why they and their families would not, should not, and could not marry someone of another race. Even many college students, who are heralded as more racially tolerant and open-minded, do not view interracial couples as acceptable when those partnerships move beyond the point of casual dating.

As described in Chapter 6, interracial marriage is increasing, but is still relatively rare, up to 5 percent of married couples in 2000 compared to only 1 percent in 1970. The typical interracial couple is a white person with a nonwhite spouse, as shown in Figure 8.4. Marriage between minorities (between Hispanics and Asians, for example) remains uncommon. Interracial couples tend to be disproportionately young, highly educated, foreign born (although this varies by race and gender), more likely to reside in urban areas, and live in the west. Over 29 percent of married Hawaiians are interracial couples, compared to less than 2 percent in West Virginia (*New Marriages, New Families* 2005).

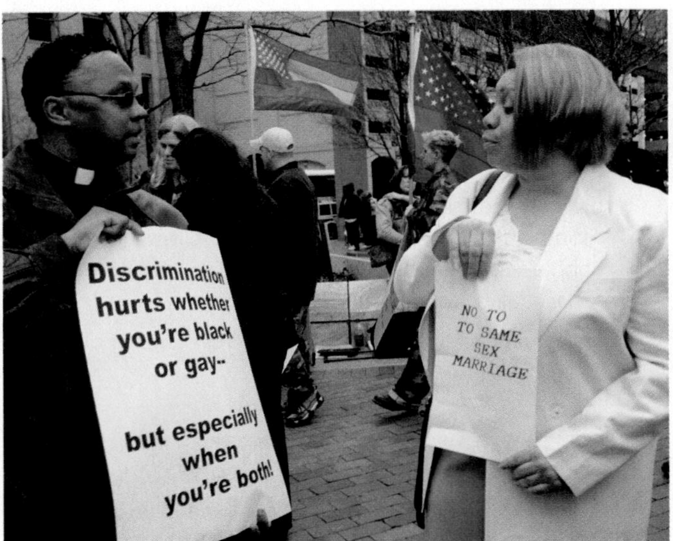

One of the most contentious current public policy debates is whether gays and lesbians should have the right to marry. Only Massachusetts now allows same-sex marriages among state residents.

Interethnic marriage (partners come from different countries or have different cultural, religious, or ethnic backgrounds) is more common than interracial marriage; however, it also challenges homogamy norms. These marriages require that partners be sensitive to cultural differences and the social and political forces that have created or perpetuated these differences. A study about intermarriages between western women and Palestinian men found that patriarchy and east-west power relations affect the women. They face marginalization as women and as "foreigners" (Roer-Strier and Ben Ezra 2006). One man described the pressure he felt from his mother and sisters about his American wife, "My mother and sister told me, 'Poor you, you will eat only fast food . . . foreigners want to be the same as men . . . with an Arab you might be happier.' You know, it's like brain washing. If you are not convinced in your ideas and you don't have confidence in your thinking it is very difficult" (Roer-Strier and Ben Ezra 2006, 50).

FIGURE 8.4 **Main Interracial Couple Types as Percentage of All Interracial Couples, 1970 and 2000**

Source: Lee and Edmonston 2005.

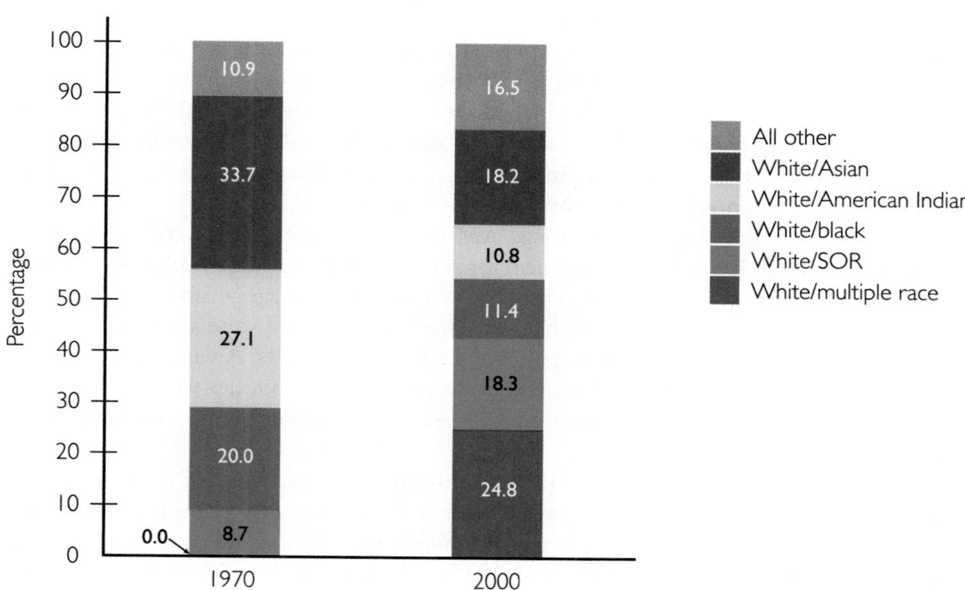

Note: SOR = Some other race. Nearly all SORs also identified as Hispanic, but not all Hispanics identified as SOR. Multiple race is available only for the 2000 Census.

Same-Sex Marriage

Another way that marriage is changing is the increased focus on same-sex marriage. As described in Chapter 7, in November 2003 the Massachusetts Supreme Judicial Court ignited a nationwide debate over same-sex marriage when it declared the state's ban on gay marriage unconstitutional. The ensuing battle has included fights in Congress over a federal marriage amendment that would define marriage as the union of a man and a woman; a flurry of same-sex wedding ceremonies (in some cases in violation of state laws); and the passage of numerous state constitutional amendments banning gay marriage (Pew Forum on Religion and Public Life 2005). Obviously, the United States is in a state of flux over this important social policy and human rights issue. Attitudes are shifting, and more people are agreeing that gays and lesbians should be granted the right to marry, although poll results vary depending on the exact wording of the questions asked.

Attitudes Toward Marriage

Most Americans, regardless of race, ethnicity, or income have very positive views toward marriage and rate a good marriage as one of the most important aspects of life (Axinn and Thornton 2000; Karney et al. 2003; National Marriage Project 2006; Thornton and Young-DeMarco 2001; Whitehead and Popenoe 2004). Using data from multiple national sources, sociologists Thornton and Young-DeMarco examined the degree of commitment Americans have toward marriage and family life. They found that Americans of all ages view marriage and parenthood as highly fulfilling and devote or plan to devote much of their lives to their spouses and children. They believe that marriage is a lifetime commitment and it should not be terminated except under extreme conditions (Thornton and Young-DeMarco 2001). These views have not weakened over the past several decades. Likewise, the percentage of high school seniors who believe that "having a good marriage and family life is extremely important" has remained stable over the past 25 years for girls, with 82 percent of girls and 70 percent of boys agreeing with this statement (National Marriage Project 2006). This is shown in Figure 8.5. However, what constitutes a "good" marriage? Looking at historical patterns, personal definitions of a good marriage have evolved to keep up with social, economic, and technological changes.

During colonial America, marriage was largely an instrumental relationship, as shown in Chapter 3. Marriage was critical for personal and community survival. As such, the community played an important role in regulating marriage as an institution and regulating roles within the relationship. The husband and wife were seen as "one" and the husband represented their legal, political, and social interests. A wife could not vote, hold property, or enter legal agreements on her own accord. Families were largely based on a model of male headship, monogamy (especially for women), and teamwork in an agriculture-based economy.

During the late nineteenth and early twentieth centuries, marriage began to evolve into a more companionship model, where love and affection were expected dimensions of the relationship. The couple's privacy was highly valued, and the community's influence took a backseat (Burgess and Locke 1945). The Industrial Revolution moved work away from the home, and many middle-class men and women found themselves in sep-

FIGURE 8.5 **Percentage of U.S. High School Seniors Who Said Having a Good Marriage and Family Life Is "Extremely Important," by Period, 1976–2004**

Source: National Marriage Project 2006.

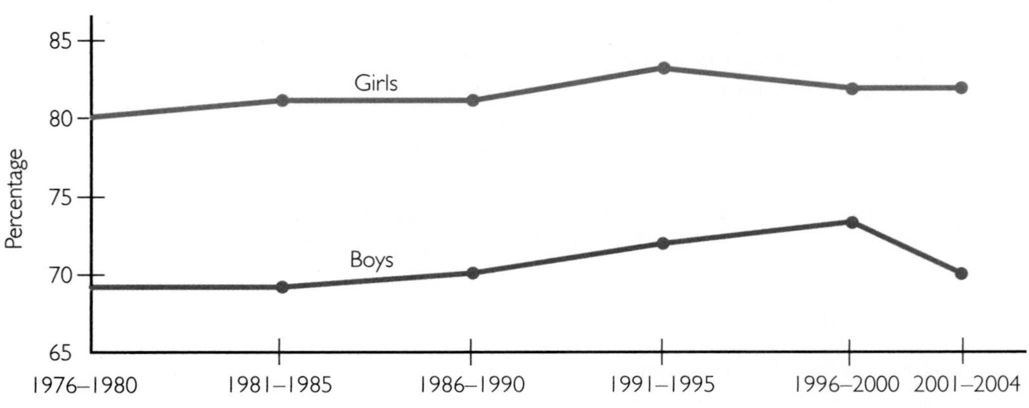

arate spheres doing different but complementary tasks for the family. In the idealized family, men worked outside the home for pay, while women stayed in the home to care for the children. The segregated roles deemed appropriate for men and women were a strong cultural norm, despite the fact that most poor and immigrant families needed the labor of both husband and wife to make ends meet.

The technological changes, world wars, and social problems of the early twentieth century contributed to increased privacy and a movement away from community involvement in marriage. New residential patterns included a growth of secluded suburbs, private automobiles made commutes more isolating, and the movement of women out of the labor market following the world wars and the Great Depression detached women from others in their communities.

Veroff, Douvan, and Kulka (1981) noted that beginning in the 1960s, the place of marriage in the lives of many Americans began to shift. People began to question the institution of marriage, voice negative attitudes about it, and raise concerns that it was too restrictive. Nonetheless, during this period people continued to marry, and there were only modest increases in the number of young people wanting to remain single (National Marriage Project 2005; Thornton and Young-DeMarco 2001). It appears that people did not really want to discard marriage, but rather they wanted to mold it to the changing nature of the times so that it could be of better benefit. What are some of the changes occurring in U.S. culture since the 1960s? How might these changes affect marriage? How might marriage be amended to accommodate them?

Nonmarital Sex Another way in which marriage is changing is that it is no longer seen as the sole way to fulfill sexual needs. Sexual relations among unmarried persons had been strongly frowned upon in the past, although occurring with surprising frequency. Attitudes began to shift in the 1960s, ushering in major changes in the sexual freedoms given to unmarried persons. Most people now believe that sexual relations between unmarried adults are not wrong, and most have engaged in nonmarital relations. Therefore, people no longer need to turn exclusively to marriage to fulfill their sexual needs. However, there are large differences in opinion by age. Persons in their 20s are more than twice as likely to approve of nonmarital sexual relations than are people in their 50s (Carter 2006).

Dual Jobs or Dual Careers An important change occurred during the 1960s and 1970s involving women and work. It became normative for middle-class women to work outside the home for pay, regardless of their marital or parental status. This trend likely reflected increasing job and educational opportunities for women, the ideas of the women's movement becoming more commonplace, and changes in the economy and consumption patterns that require two breadwinners. Today women comprise nearly one-half of all employed persons; 58 percent of Americans believe that both spouses *should* work, although this is considerably less than in many other industrialized nations, as shown in Table 8.1.

Women work for many reasons—as extra money for the family, as the sole provider, or for the joy work provides. Regardless of the reasons for their employment, and whether wives think of their employment as a "job" or a "career," their work has profoundly shaped marriage, including the distribution of power, decision making, and household labor (Perry Jenkins and Turner 2003). Blacks and Mexican Americans are more supportive of working wives than are whites; however, ironically, they are also more likely to suggest that the man should be the main breadwinner (Blee and Tickamyer 1995; Kamo and Cohen 1998).

TABLE 8.1 Gender Expectations in Cross-National Perspective (Percent Agreeing)

	Both Spouses Should Work		Both Spouses Should Work
East Germany	94	Northern Ireland	71
Bulgaria	93	West Germany	67
Slovenia	93	Austria	63
Philippines	90	Great Britain	62
Israel	87	Norway	60
Spain	84	Poland	58
Sweden	82	**United States**	**58**
Czech Republic	81	Canada	56
Italy	81	Japan	54
Ireland	77	Australia	45
Russia	74	New Zealand	39
Hungary	73	Netherlands	29

Source: Smith 1999.

Division of Household Labor Today more people are thinking about and questioning the division of household labor. Studies using several different methods to collect data show that the average married woman does two to three times more housework than the average married man (Coltrane 2000; Lee and Waite 2005). Even when both work full-time outside the home, wives' contributions to housework generally far exceed their husbands'. The term *second shift* refers to the idea that after women return home from work, they in essence have a second shift of work consisting of household labor and child care (Hochschild 1989). This is a carryover from earlier times in which housework was defined normatively as "women's work." Attitudes toward the division of household labor are in a state of flux, and these changes have enormous consequences for the marital relationship. Changing norms require that behaviors be negotiated (and renegotiated) within the context of the individual relationship. Men's time in housework is on the rise, and women's time is declining. It appears that younger men and women are more likely than older adults to believe that housework should be shared although it remains that the work is disproportionately done by women, young and old (Coltrane 2000; Thornton and Young-DeMarco 2001).

Nonmarital Childbearing Some people no longer believe that marriage is a prerequisite for having a child. Younger adults are likely to be more permissive in their views than are older adults. One study asked respondents to state their level of agreement with the statement "people who want children ought to get married"; over one-quarter of the respondents either had no opinion or disagreed with the statement (Thornton and Young-DeMarco 2001). Another study asked high school students about whether "having a child without being married is a worthwhile lifestyle;" 56 percent of these young men and women agreed with that statement (Whitehead and Popenoe 2006).

It appears that attitudes about marriage—its purpose, its structure, and what makes a marriage "good"—have changed significantly over the past several decades. People are more accepting of nonmarital sex and nonmarital childbearing. They are increasingly likely to cohabit with a partner. Couples hold high expectations that the relationship should meet their needs for companionship and intimacy. Traditional gender expectations regarding employment and household labor are being redefined and are subject to negotiation. Views about marriage are less rigid than in the past, and people are marrying at later ages, but overall the literature shows that, Americans remain enthusiastic about marriage.

Regardless of employment status, research findings are clear: women do considerably more household labor than do their partners.

Marital Decline versus Marital Resilience Perspectives

Given all of these changes, is marriage in the United States in a state of decline or is it strong and viable? Family scholars, as well as the popular media, debate the state of marriage today (National Marriage Project 2006; Stanton 2005). According to the **marital decline perspective**, the institution of marriage is increasingly being threatened by hedonistic pursuits of personal happiness at the expense of a long-term commitment. People are no longer willing to remain married through "better or worse" because the U.S. culture has become increasingly individualistic. Proponents of this perspective argue that the decline in marriage rates causes a host of other social problems from poverty to the erosion of neighborhoods. Their goal is to create a culture that is more supportive of marriage (Amato 2004; Whitehead and Popenoe 2004).

In contrast, others reject the idea that U.S. culture has become more individualistic, resulting in a decline of marriage and a host of other social ills. The **marital resilience perspective** notes that many marriages in the past were also highly troubled or unfulfilling, but were held together because of stigma, economics, or fear. For example, 100 years ago a woman who was physically abused by her husband may have had little recourse but to endure it. She had few economic opportunities, she likely had no credit in her name and no property or assets, and she faced a hostile social environment that may have blamed her for the abuse. Today, women and men can more easily end a poor marriage. Those supporting this perspective say divorce is not necessarily cause for alarm because it gives adults another chance at happiness and provides the opportunity to end a dysfunctional home life for children. They suggest that the real threats to marriage and families are social problems such as poverty, poor schools, discrimination, or a lack of social services that families need to remain strong and healthy (Amato 2004). They conclude that family disorganization is a result of these types of problems, not necessarily the cause of them.

Benefits of Marriage

Regardless of your perspective, Americans are ardent believers in marriage. Most Americans marry—less than 4 percent of persons aged 75 and over have never married, a figure that has remained relatively constant over time (U.S. Census Bureau 2006d). If marriage ends in divorce, most remarry again (sometimes several times). Why the intrigue with marriage? What specific benefits accrue to married persons?

Psychological Well-Being and Happiness

Research suggests that married people are happier than those who are single, cohabiting, separated, or divorced (Axinn and Thornton 2000; Bierman et al. 2006; Waite and Gallagher 2000). This is the case not only in the United States, but in other countries as well (Stack and Eshleman 1998). Stack and Eshleman examined the relationship between personal happiness and marital status in 17 industrialized nations that had "diverse social and institutional frameworks." They concluded (1998):

> Married persons have a significantly higher level of happiness than persons who are not married. This effect was independent of financial and health-oriented protections offered by marriage and was also independent of other control variables including ones for sociodemographic conditions and national character.

Married persons also score higher on other measures of psychological well-being and are less likely to be depressed (Partenheimer 2003; Waite and Gallagher 2000), although differences may be minimal among the married and long-term cohabitors (Willetts 2006). However, does marriage *cause* happiness, or are happier people more likely to marry in the first place? The latter is referred to as a **selection effect**. Research suggests that both issues are likely; yes, people who are happy are more likely to marry, but it is also true that marriage (particularly a good one) brings happiness and psychological well-being to partners.

The relationship between marriage and psychological well-being seems to be particularly strong for men; they seem to derive greater benefit from marriage than do women (Bernard 1972; Mirowsky and Ross 1995; Waite and Gallagher 2000). As Whitehead and Popenoe (2004) explain:

> One key reason is wives. Married women provide emotional support and physical care to their spouses. They monitor their husband's health habits, encourage them to seek medical treatment, when necessary, and often find a doctor or health professional to provide such treatment. In addition to TLC, wives commonly provide SDRs (stable domestic routines). Along with better health practices, stable routines help to reduce job absenteeism, quit rates and sick days and thus to strengthen men's workforce attachment. Moreover, since the majority of married women today work outside the home, including over half of wives with young children, men gain financial advantages from their wives' workforce participation. Wage-earning wives reduce pressure on husbands to be the sole breadwinner while, at the same time, increasing family income and assets, the traditional measure of a husband's contribution to the family. (p. 8)

Physical Health

On average, married persons live longer and are less likely to die from the leading causes of death, including heart disease, many types of cancers, or stroke. Married persons also engage in less risky behaviors, resulting in fewer car accidents, and lower murder and suicide rates. They drink less alcohol and are therefore less likely to suffer alcohol-related complications such as cirrhosis of the liver. Married persons have better health habits than their unmarried counterparts, they are more likely to have health insurance, and they receive more regular health care (Nock 1998; Waite and Gallagher 2000).

However, as the opening vignette illustrated, it is important to distinguish between types of marriages when examining health (and possibly other) data. It is not simply marriage that improves health outcomes, but rather, a *good* marriage that entails love, support, and personal fulfillment (Partenheimer 2003).

We have shown that marriage is correlated with better health for both men and women. However, is marriage the *cause* of better health? Possibly, yet there is a competing explanation as well; it could simply be that healthy people are more likely to marry, another selection effect. Perhaps healthy people are more likely to come into contact with prospective marriage partners, have more stable employment, or have higher self-esteem—all considerable pluses toward attracting a spouse. Which explanation makes the most sense? The answer is, again, that both are likely operating: Although healthy people are more likely to marry, there is also something about marriage itself that directly contributes to health and well-being. The health advantages associated with marriage are clear; again, husbands seem to derive greater benefit than do wives (Nock 1998). Mortality rates for unmarried men are twice that for married men, whereas the difference between married and unmarried women is considerably smaller.

Economic Advantages

People who are married earn more money and accumulate greater assets than those who are single or divorced, regardless of race or ethnic background (Nock 1998; Thomas and Sawhill 2002; Waite and Gallagher 2000; Wilmoth and Koso 2002). A study by sociologists at Purdue University noted that, among elders on the verge of retirement, those who were not continuously married had 63 percent less wealth than those who had remained married (Wilmoth and Koso 2002). Another study reported that even after controlling for age, education, job characteristics, work experience, and other background factors, married men averaged over 12 percent more per hour than single men. Married men whose wives stay at home earn over 30 percent more than their single counterparts (Chun and Lee 2001). It is possible that their wives are doing most of the child care and housework, thus freeing up husbands to focus on their jobs. Nock (1998) found that the difference between married and single men's earnings grew wider the longer the men were married.

Women receive financial gains from marriage as well (DeNavas-Walt et al. 2006; Lerman 2002; Waite and Gallagher 2000). Although married women do not earn more than their single counterparts, they benefit indirectly because of their husbands' income and greater earning power. Married women are able to pool their resources with a spouse; they have greater household income and assets; they have increased access to health insurance and retirement benefits; and are more likely to receive financial assistance (e.g., gifts or loans) from extended family members.

Once again we must closely examine the meaning behind the correlation between marital status and economic well-being. Is it fair to say that marriage is the *cause* of the higher income and assets among the married? Or is it possible that those with higher income-earning potential are more likely to marry in the first place? After all, researchers have found that men with poor economic prospects are often not deemed to be good marriage partners (Edin and Kafalas 2005; Wilson 1987, 1996). Again it is likely that the relationship is reciprocal and runs in both directions, as is the case with health and psychological well-being. Stronger economic conditions are both a cause and a consequence of marriage.

Marriage and Sex

Despite stereotypes that suggest that married sex is an oxymoron, married people are sexually active and report enjoying sex more than their cohabiting counterparts, according to a comprehensive study of adults aged 18–59 (Michael et al. 1994; Waite and Joyner 2001). Forty-two percent of wives said that they found sex extremely emotionally and physically satisfying, compared to 31 percent of cohabiting women; 48 percent of husbands were extremely satisfied, compared to 37 percent of cohabiting men. Even among married adults aged 60 and older, over half indicated that they had sexual intercourse at least once during the previous month, and among those who were sexually active, one-half reported having intercourse once a week or more (Marsiglio and Donnelly 1991).

Social Capital and Social Support

Social capital refers to the goods and services that are byproducts of social relationships among people. It differs from human capital (e.g., job skills, education level, competencies) because social capital is not acquired in the same way as one might acquire a bachelor's degree. Rather, it includes the connections, the social support, the information, and other important benefits that are produced through relationships among people. Marriage is an important source of social capital because it creates obligations and social bonds that can provide support in times of need between spouses; between parents and children; between the married couple and their extended families; and between the couple and the community (Whitehead 2004). These obligations are a part of the social norm of "being married." Consequently, marriage generates higher levels of help, support, and care than other kinds of personal relationships. For example, although single parents receive significant family support, they generally do not receive sustained help and support from the absent biological parent's side of the family. Close to 17 percent of married parents report support from the father's kin, whereas just 2 percent of single mothers and no unwed mothers received financial support from relatives of the father (Hao 1996).

With all these benefits, it could lead us to believe that all marriages must be happy and successful. This is not necessarily the case.

Marital Happiness, Satisfaction, and Success

Researchers have attempted to study marital quality since the pioneering work of Burgess and colleagues in the mid-1940s. The undertaking is complex because there are a multitude of ways to define happiness, satisfaction, and success, and little agreement on the best way to do so. For example, does the absence of divorce measure marital success? Can a single-item question such as "How satisfied with your marriage are you?" really measure something as complex as marital quality or satisfaction with marriage? Do "happy," "satisfying," and "successful" marriages always occur together or, for example, can a marriage be unhappy, but successful—meaning the couple did not divorce? Moreover, can a cross-sectional study, which collects data at only one point in time, really measure the deep and profound feelings associated with the concepts of marital happiness, satisfaction, and success? Longitudinal studies that follow couples over time are much preferred over cross-sectional ones. Nonetheless, despite these real caveats with measurement or data collection, researchers note that about 62 percent of married Americans report that they are "very happy" with their marriages and another 34 percent say that they are "pretty happy." Several variables are associated with happier, more satisfying, and successful marriages.

The Quality and Stability of the Couple's Parents' Marriages

Individuals whose parents have happy and stable marriages are more likely to have happier and long-lasting marriages themselves (Amato 1996; Amato and Deboer 2001;

Teachman 2002, 2004; Wolfinger 2000). One study found that when the wife alone experienced a parental divorce, the odds of divorce increased by 59 percent, but when both experienced parental divorce, the odds of divorce increased by 189 percent. One reason that people who experience a parental divorce have a higher divorce rate themselves may be because they tend to have a weaker commitment to the expectation of lifelong marriage (Amato and Deboer 2001). Adult children model their own parents' behavior, both positive and negative. Parents who have strong communication skills or who value commitment in their relationship model these types of behaviors for their own children. Conversely, parents who have a conflict-ridden relationship or who divorce place their children at greater risk for an unhappy marriage in the future.

Shared Values, Goals, and Characteristics of the Couple

Do "opposites attract" or do "birds of a feather flock together?" In other words, do people tend to marry others who are very different from—or similar—to themselves? We hear in the news about persons with widely divergent backgrounds marrying. Perhaps one partner is 25 years older than the other—or one partner is rich, while the other came from a very modest background—or one partner is black and the other is white.

Unfortunately, couples with very different backgrounds face more challenging odds of achieving a happy marriage. These relationships may violate social norms and carry a degree of stigma in some circles. The couple may be perpetually identified as "that old man who married a younger woman" or "the woman who snagged that rich guy" or "that white lady who married a black guy." Heterogamous relationships also are less likely to have a shared set of values, history, or culture corresponding to their social backgrounds and characteristics. The white woman who married a black man probably has little real conception of the ways that race and racism have touched her husband's life, and despite her love and good intentions, will always remain somewhat of an outsider. Many heterogamous marriages overcome these challenges, but overall, couples with more similar backgrounds and characteristics have a greater chance of success.

As for similar personalities, attitudes, and values, the research is somewhat mixed. Generally, the more similar people are in their values and life goals, the more likely they are to have a happy and lasting marriage (Alford-Cooper 1998; Larson and Holman 1994; Wallerstein and Blakeslee 1995). However, as revealed in Box 8.3, it appears that while people are drawn to those who are similar in attitudes and values, it may be similarity in personality styles, not in attitudes or values, that is more highly associated with having a happy marriage.

Age at Marriage

Some people suggest that couples who wait until they are older to marry generally have more happy, satisfying, and successful marriages (Heaton 2002; Waite and Lillard 1991). The reasoning is that older couples are more prepared for marriage and its responsibilities, they have greater financial resources, and may have their jobs or careers underway. However, a large-scale study of over 2,000 adults living in Oklahoma found that people who married below age 20 reported greater happiness with their marriage than did those persons who married later. Yet the research also reveals that youthful marriages are more prone to divorce; persons who marry in their teenage years are at particularly high risk of divorce. One government study found that 59 percent of marriages for women under age 18 ended in divorce or separation within 15 years, compared with 36 percent of those married at age 20 or older (National Center for Health Statistics 2002). These marriages are often associated with an unplanned pregnancy, and therefore couples may

BOX 8.3 Using the Sociological Imagination

Do Opposites Attract or Do Birds of a Feather Flock Together?

Is it possible to actually study something as personal as dating and mate selection? Yes, it is. Researchers have found some interesting patterns regarding how we choose mates.

Do people tend to select romantic partners that are similar to them or their opposite? Does spouse similarity lead to marital happiness? In one of the most comprehensive studies ever undertaken on these questions, researchers at the University of Iowa found that people tend to marry those who are similar in attitudes, religion, and values. However, it is similarity in personality that appears to be more important in having a happy marriage.

Psychologist Eva C. Klohnen and her graduate student Shanhong Luo looked at mating based on similar or opposite characteristics among 291 newlyweds who participated in the Iowa Marital Assessment Project. The newlyweds had been married less than a year at the time the study began and had dated each other for an average of three and a half years. The couples were assessed on a broad range of personality characteristics, attitudes, and relationship quality indicators.

Results show that couples were highly similar on attitudes and values; however, they had little similarity on personality-related domains such as attachment, extraversion, conscientiousness, and positive or negative emotions. There is no evidence that opposites attract. What is most intriguing is that when the researchers assessed marital quality and happiness, they found that personality similarity was related to marital satisfaction, but having similar attitudes was not.

"People may be attracted to those who have similar attitudes, values, and beliefs and even marry them—at least in part—on the basis of this similarity because attitudes are highly visible and salient characteristics and they are fundamental to the way people lead their lives," explain the authors. Personality-related characteristics, on the other hand, take much longer to be known and to be accurately perceived and are not likely to play a more substantial role until later in the relationship, they add. "However, once people are in a committed relationship, it is primarily personality similarity that influences marital happiness because being in a committed relationship entails regular interaction and requires extensive coordination in dealing with tasks, issues, and problems of daily living. Whereas personality similarity is likely to facilitate this process, personality differences may result in more friction and conflict in daily life," say the authors. "As far as attitudes are concerned, people who choose to marry each other should be well aware of how similar or different they are on these domains because attitudes are very visible and salient. This suggests that attitudinal and value differences, when they exist, are part of a conscious decision to stay together on the basis of other important considerations."

Source: Adapted from APA press release by David Partenheimer, Feb. 13, 2005. "Do Opposites Attract or Do Birds of a Feather Flock Together?" Online at apa.org/releases/attraction/html. Reprinted with permission of the American Psychological Association.

CRITICAL THINKING QUESTIONS

1. Do you think the results from this study based on people living in Iowa can be generalized to the rest of the U.S. population? Why or why not?
2. Do these findings confirm or conflict with your own experiences?

stop their education, which puts them at a greater risk of poverty and other stresses. It appears that people who marry young are more likely to divorce, but among those who beat the odds and remain married, their marriages may be as satisfying or more so than couples that marry later. However, a first marriage occurring after age 35 also shows relatively high rates of marital instability. The reasons for this are unknown, but could be related to a smaller pool of eligible people from which to choose, less value placed on marriage, or being more set in one's ways and unwillingness to compromise.

The Presence of Children

Couples with children are less likely to divorce than are couples without children (Heaton 2002; Larson and Holman 1994; Waite and Lillard 1991). Families who have young preschool-aged children in particular, or families with many children, are least likely to divorce. However, are their marriages happier or more satisfying? Apparently the answer is not necessarily, because people may stay in unfulfilling marriages because they feel that it is the appropriate thing to do for their children's sake. Most research shows that marital satisfaction begins to decline somewhat immediately after marriage, declines even further with the birth of children, and then either rises somewhat at around 20 or 25 years of marriage as the children leave home or remains relatively flat (Glenn 1998; VanLaningham et al. 2001). The amount of work involved in raising young children may strain the marriage.

Couples with boys are also less likely to divorce or consider divorce than couples with girls (Morgan et al. 1988; Katzev et al. 1994). The birth of a son also speeds up the rate at which an unmarried couple will marry (Lundberg and Rose 2003). Why does child sex matter? Researchers suggest that fathers of sons may be more involved in their children's lives and more vested in keeping the family together.

One of the factors associated with successful, high-quality marriages is religion. One study found that people who are more religious and attend church more frequently, regardless of their age, sex, the age at which they married, or income, report higher levels of commitment to their partners, higher levels of marital satisfaction, less thinking and talking about divorce, and lower levels of negative interactions.

Religious Faith and Practice

A study of over 2,000 adults in Oklahoma suggests that religious faith and practice are strongly associated with marital quality (Johnson et al. 2002). In this survey, respondents were first asked about their general religiousness: "All things considered, how religious would you say that you are?" Then they were asked about their involvement in religious services: "How often do you attend religious services?" The data revealed that people who were more religious, regardless of their age, sex, the age at which they married, or income, reported higher levels of commitment to their partners, higher levels of marital satisfaction, less thinking and talking about divorce, and lower levels of negative interactions. The patterns are particularly strong when looking at the frequency of church attendance, as shown in Table 8.2. The connection between shared religiosity and marital quality has declined somewhat, especially among the younger generation; however, it still remains that those who share a religious faith with a spouse report higher marital satisfaction than those who do not (Myers 2006).

TABLE 8.2 Ratings of Marital Happiness, By Frequency of Attendance at Religious Services (Percent)

Would You Say Your Marriage Is Very Happy, Pretty Happy, or Not Too Happy?	How Often Do You Attend Religious Services?			
	Never or Almost Never	Occasionally, But Less Than Once Per Month	One to Three Times Per Month	One or More Times Per Week
Very happy	52	66	72	73
Pretty happy	44	30	25	25
Not too happy	5	4	3	2

Source: Johnson et al. 2002.

Shared Interests

Couples who spend greater amounts of time together doing things that they both enjoy are more likely to have happy, satisfying, and successful marriages. The activities can be varied: hiking, visiting with relatives or friends, bowling, skiing, or simply walking the dog. The desire to spend time together and the specific activities the couple engages in are likely to be class-based. Lillian Rubin found that working-class couples generally spend less leisure time together because they are more content to live in separate worlds. They see men and women as generally having different interests, and therefore often prefer to spend free time with members of their own sex. When couples did engage in leisure activities together, their time was more likely spent visiting relatives, neighbors, or mutual friends (Rubin 1994).

Frequency and Satisfaction with Sexual Relationship

For most married couples sex remains a vital part of their lives. Couples who report having regular or frequent sex, and who report enjoying their sex life, are also more likely to evaluate their marriages favorably (Donnelly 1993; Haavio-Mannila and Kontula 1997; Lawrence and Byers 1995). The quality and quantity of sex are associated with feelings of love. Sexual satisfaction also contributes to marital stability. In a longitudinal study of married couples, a measure of sexual problems or dissatisfaction at the time of the first interview was associated with the likelihood of divorce by the second interview, even when marital happiness and other variables were controlled (White and Keith 1990). Other researchers found that couples who report a decline in sexual satisfaction over time are more likely to divorce (Edwards and Booth 1994).

Satisfaction with Gender Relations and the Division of Labor

Adults who subscribe to more egalitarian attitudes about gender tend to have higher levels of marital happiness, and this is particularly the case for men (Kaufman and

Taniguchi 2006). For example, marital satisfaction is higher among couples who share the housework (Erickson 1993; Orbuch and Eyster 1997). The fit between expectations of husbands and wives is particularly important; those couples who share views about housework and child care, regardless of what those views are, tend to evaluate their marriages more positively than do couples who have different opinions about who should shoulder the workload. In particular, when women perceive that the division of household labor is unfair (i.e., that they are doing the bulk of the work and do not want to), marital conflict increases, depression increases, and satisfaction with their marriage plummets (Frisco and Williams 2003; Perry-Jenkins and Folk 1994; Weigel et al. 2006).

The Marriage Movement

Some Americans are uncomfortable with changes witnessed in families over the past few decades and yearn for a more traditional marital structure and set of social roles. Armed with information to suggest that "marriage is an important social good, associated with an impressively broad array of positive outcomes for children and adults alike . . ." a group of family scholars, therapists, and civic leaders have come together in what is called the **marriage movement** in hopes of influencing public policy to promote and strengthen traditional two-parent marriage. A report called *The Marriage Movement: A Statement of Principles, 2000* (Marriage Movement 2000) outlines a broad political agenda in the following areas: reduce unmarried pregnancy; increase the likelihood that unmarried couples expecting a baby will marry before the child's birth; reduce unnecessary divorce; reduce or prevent excessive conflict in married couples; do not discourage married couples from having children if they want them; protect the boundaries of marriage by distinguishing it from other family and friendship units including cohabiting ones; treat the married couple as a social, legal, and financial unit; transmit and reinforce shared norms of responsible marital behavior, such as encouraging permanence, fidelity, financial responsibility, and mutual support; and communicate the preference for marriage as the ideal family form, particularly to young people of reproductive age (Marriage Movement 2004). Drawing upon the "family decline" perspective outlined previously, the marriage movement suggests that the decline of traditional marriage is responsible for a host of social problems, at considerable expense to the taxpayer (Marriage Movement 2000):

> Divorce and unwed childbearing create substantial public costs paid by taxpayers. Higher rates of crime, drug use, education failure, chronic illness, child abuse, domestic violence and poverty among both adults and children bring with them higher taxpayer costs in diverse forms: more welfare expenditure, increased remedial and special education expenses; higher day-care subsidies; additional child-support collections. . . . While no study has yet attempted precisely to measure these sweeping and diverse taxpayer costs stemming from the decline of marriage, current research suggests that these costs are likely to be quite extensive. (p. 11)

Members of the movement suggest that marriage makes an important and positive difference in the lives of children and adults, and therefore public policy should be used to support traditional marriage and reduce unmarried childbearing, cohabitation, and divorce. The marriage movement was further advanced by President George W. Bush, who pledged $1.5 billion to a "Healthy Marriage Initiative" during his presidency.

What are some of the criticisms of the marriage movement? The following are quotes from leading scholars who suggest that various social problems are a result of insufficient support of families in their multiple forms, rather than the result of a decline in marriage per se:

- "Too often, Americans blame all of society's ills on the breakdown of the traditional family. Poverty, crime, violence, teenage aimlessness—all are blamed on the purported breakdown of the family. . . . [However] family change is not new. Nor is family diversity. America's families have always been in flux—and Americans have always been anxious about the family's fate." (Council on Contemporary Families)
- "Treat [unmarried parents with new babies] as a couple, and give them the job training and economic support that will enable them to implement what they say they want to do. You have to do a lot more than issue them marriage licenses to bring them up to the married norm." (Sara McLanahan, Princeton University researcher, making policy recommendations regarding the unmarried families she studies)
- "We can encourage, pressure, preach, and give incentives to get people to marry. But we still have to deal with the reality that kids are going to be raised in a variety of ways, and we have to support all kinds of families with kids." (Stephanie Coontz, a family historian at Evergreen State College, in *Newsweek*, May 28, 2001)
- "My strong objection is to the notion that there's one kind of relationship that's best for everyone, that it's a moral failing if you don't achieve it, and that it will irreparably harm your children if you don't marry or if your marriage doesn't last." (Judith Stacey, University of Southern California sociologist, in *The Bergen Record*, August 13, 2000)
- "Paradoxically, more people today value marriage. They take it seriously. That's why they're more likely to cohabit. They want to make sure before they take the ultimate step." (Frank Furstenberg, University of Pennsylvania sociologist, in *Newsweek*, May 28, 2001)

Critics of the marriage movement suggest that, unfortunately, some marriages are not good matches, do not benefit children and spouses, cannot be fixed, and that the decline of marriage is not the primary cause of poverty, delinquency, abuse, illness, or drug use (Amato 2004; Huston and Melz 2004). They claim that problems facing families are complex and have roots stemming from changes in U.S. social structure rather than simply as a result of declining rates of marriage (Mintz 2003).

One problem that affects the strength and viability of all families is economic instability. Stable employment at a livable wage is a prerequisite for establishing secure, lifelong relationships. Yet, many poor women have difficulty finding partners who hold steady, fairly well-paid jobs. The poor are less likely to marry and more likely to divorce than the more affluent, yet the marriage movement minimizes structural concerns, and instead views poverty as a result, not a cause of family disorganization: "Job training programs, or earnings broadly distributed regardless of family status, are not by themselves likely to have a significant impact on marriage rates" (Marriage Movement 2004).

Structural changes in the economy mean that many families need two earners to support a middle-class standard of living. A result is severe stress as families attempt to balance work and family needs, such as housework, child care, and quality time together for the married couple. This stress can contribute to many negative family outcomes, including marital conflict, parent-child alienation, child abuse and neglect, and other tensions that adversely affect children's functioning and well-being. Moreover, with weakened extended family networks that offer social support and assistance, many families, regardless of their type, face difficult obstacles (Mintz 2003). Thus, social problems are the result of economic instability and the lack of support for struggling families.

Covenant Marriage

In the quest to elevate the status of marriage and restrict access to divorce, there is a small but passionate movement toward developing **covenant marriage**. This is a relatively new and optional form of marriage in which couples can sign a document in which they pledge to follow certain rules, including (1) some marriage preparation; (2) full disclosure of all information that could reasonably affect the decision to marry; (3) an oath of lifelong commitment to marriage; (4) acceptance of limited grounds for divorce (e.g., abuse, adultery, addiction, felony imprisonment, separation for 2 years); and (5) marital counseling if problems threaten the marriage (Hawkins et al. 2002).

Covenant marriage options now exist in three states—Arizona, Arkansas, and Louisiana—although only a small fraction of persons in those states choose it (Nock et al. 1999; Spaht 2002). Court clerks who issue marriage licenses are supposed to tell couples about the option of covenant marriage, but sometimes they fail to do so. Those couples who have chosen covenant marriage are more religious and more politically conservative than average couples (Nock et al. 1999).

Social Policy and Family Resilience

The marriage movement has brought the institution of marriage into the national spotlight. Although research notes many positive effects of marriage on couples and children, it is also a highly contested political issue: Can, and should, government be involved in promoting traditional marriage at the exclusion of other types of relationships? Oklahoma has begun a large experiment designed to promote marriage and reduce divorce, and it has received widespread support from residents of that state.

Example: The Oklahoma Marriage Initiative

In 1998, the University of Oklahoma and Oklahoma State University economists conducted a study on what Oklahomans needed to do to become a more prosperous state. They concluded that factors such as the high divorce rate, high rates of child deaths due to abuse, and high rates of nonmarital childbirths were contributing to Oklahoma's weak economy. The study prompted the development of a series of programs and policies now known as the *Oklahoma Marriage Initiative*. The primary goal of the initiative is to reduce the divorce rate by one-third by 2010. Other related goals include increasing the number of children who live in "healthy two-parent households" (Oklahoma Marriage Initiative 2005). These goals are to be achieved by collaboration between the department of human services and many social service programs to provide couples with the skills and tools needed to form and sustain healthy marriages.

Although then-governor Keating recognized that the program could be controversial, a baseline study conducted in 2001–2002 in Oklahoma indicated significant support for the initiative. Eighty-five percent of adults in a representative sample indicated that they felt "very good" or "good" about "a statewide initiative to promote marriage and reduce divorce." Sixty-six percent of those who were married or romantically involved indicated that they would consider attending relationship education courses. Support was found across racial and ethnic groups, with blacks offering the highest degree of support (Johnson and Stanley 2001). The next governor, Brad Henry, continued the program.

The marriage initiative is funded with $10 million that was originally targeted for the cash welfare program, Temporary Assistance for Needy Families (TANF). Because one of the goals of TANF is to strengthen marriage, funds could be diverted from TANF to the marriage initiative that serves all income groups as long as some of the services remained targeted to the poor.

The initiative includes free skill-based marriage and relationship courses to couples and individuals across the state. Courses are led by pastors and lay leaders in the faith community, social service providers, business leaders, community volunteers, tribal groups, mental health groups, and minority group specialists. They are not designed to be marriage counseling, but to provide some skills to help navigate the problems that are inevitable in relationships and marriages. Skills-based marriage education includes practical information to help partners connect, communicate actively, and process anger effectively. Other programs are designed to inspire and motivate rather than teach specific skills. Regardless of the type of program, the overall theme of the workshops and related media efforts is to encourage, strengthen, and preserve traditional two-parent marriage. Other types of family constellations are seen as inferior.

Opponents are outraged that money intended to help poor women and children on welfare is being diverted to promote a traditional marriage program. They believe the money would be better spent on providing meaningful job training or educational opportunities for the poor.

Conclusion

Marriage is both a social institution and a personal relationship and is recognized in some form around the world. As a social institution there are rules, rights, and responsibilities surrounding marriage because it is seen as a stabilizing force within societies and therefore the government sees marriage as its business. Cross-cultural research shows that feelings of love and sexual intensity may be the core experience in marriage or these feelings may be totally irrelevant to it. Americans are highly committed to marriage. Most claim that they want to marry and consider marriage important to their personal happiness. Nonetheless, many changes in marriage are underway. People tend to marry later, and many cohabit prior to marriage or in the place of marriage. Some propose to legalize same-sex marriages, and spouses are renegotiating terrain such as the division of household labor and other roles. These changes have also inspired a growing marriage movement designed to preserve, strengthen, and promote traditional marriage. Despite the changes in marriage, it remains as popular as ever and is associated with many benefits.

Key Terms

Antimiscegenation laws: The banning of marriage between whites and other races. (p. 250)

Covenant marriage: A type of marriage that restricts access to divorce, requires premarital counseling, and other rules and regulations. (p. 267)

Interethnic marriage: Partners coming from different countries or having different cultural, religious, or ethnic backgrounds. (p. 252)

Marital decline perspective: Suggests the institution of marriage is increasingly being threatened by hedonistic pursuits of personal happiness at the expense of a long-term commitment. (p. 257)

Marital resilience perspective: Suggests ending an unhappy marriage is not necessarily cause for alarm because it gives adults another chance at happiness and provides the opportunity to end a child's dysfunctional home life. (p. 257)

Marriage movement: A group of family scholars, therapists, and civic leaders who have come together in hopes of influencing public policy to promote and strengthen traditional marriage. (p. 265)

Selection effect: People who marry may be different from those who do not marry. (p. 258)

Social capital: The goods and services that are byproducts of social relationships, such as social support or personal connections. (p. 260)

Resources on the Internet

Marriage Support
www.couples-place.com
An online learning community for solving marriage problems, improving relationship skills, celebrating marriage, and achieving happiness with a partner. The goal is to promote success in marriage and other committed relationships by offering practical, how-to articles, and skills-training programs.

National Marriage Project
http://marriage.rutgers.edu
The mission of the National Marriage Project is to strengthen the institution of marriage by providing research and analysis that inform public policy, educate the American public, and focus attention on the consequences of marriage decline for millions of American children. They publish an annual report, *The State of Our Unions: The Social Health of Marriage in America.*

WeddingChannel.com
www.weddingchannel.com
This website is devoted to showing you "everything you need to plan the perfect wedding." Illustrates the big business associated with traditional weddings, including "30,000 photos to find the perfect wedding dress, hairstyle, cake, bouquet and more."

Further Reading

Alford-Cooper, F. 1998. *For Keeps: Marriages that Last a Lifetime*. Armonk, NY: M. E. Sharpe.

Blakeslee, S., and J. Wallerstein, 1995. *The Good Marriage: How and Why Love Lasts*. Boston: Houghton Mifflin.

Browning, D. S. 2003. *Marriage and Modernization: How Globalization Threatens Marriage and What to Do About It*. Grand Rapids, MI: William B. Eerdmans Publishing Co.

Coontz, S. 2006. *Marriage, A History: How Love Conquered Marriage*. New York: Penguin.

Edin, K., and M. Kefalas. 2005. *Why Poor Women Put Motherhood Before Marriage*. Berkeley: University of California Press.

Gallagher, S. K. 2003. *Evangelical Identity and Gendered Family Life*. New Brunswick, NJ: Rutgers University Press.

Grossbard-Schectman, S. A. (Ed.). 2003. *Marriage and the Economy*. Cambridge, UK: Cambridge University Press.

Harris, S. R. 2006. *The Meanings of Marital Equality*. Albany: State University of New York Press.

Nock, S. L. 1998. *Marriage in Men's Lives*. New York: Oxford University Press.

Noller, P., and J. A. Feeney. 2002. *Understanding Marriage: Developments in the Study of Couple Interaction*. Cambridge, UK: Cambridge University Press.

Popenoe, D. 1996. *Life Without Father*. New York: Free Press.

Root, Maria. 2001. *Love's Revolution: Interracial Marriage*. Philadelphia: Temple University Press.

Waite, L. J., C. Bachrach, M. Hindin, E. Thomas, and A. Thornton. (Eds.). 2000. *The Ties that Bind*. New York: Aldine de Gruyter.

CHAPTER 9

Becoming a Parent

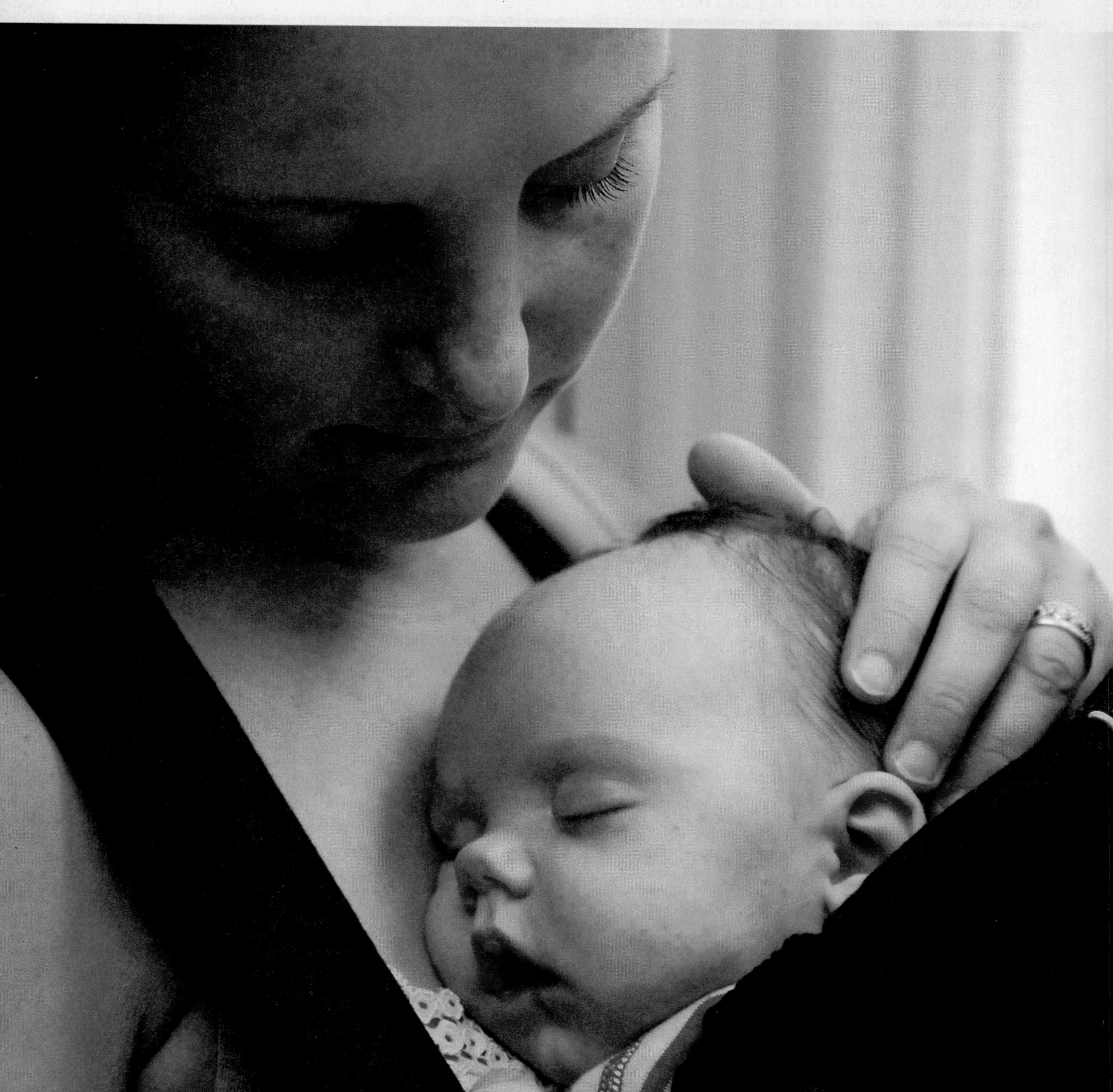

Chapter Outline

Chapter Preview

Most, but not all, adults become parents. How does the process of deciding if, when, and how we will be parents unfold? What types of changes does parenting bring? This chapter focuses on the process of becoming a parent. The transition to parenthood can be surprisingly challenging, yet tremendously rewarding. In this chapter you will learn:

- Population and fertility trends worldwide, and the ways in which some countries, such as China, try to limit their population growth, while other countries, such as Japan, try to increase theirs
- Fertility rates in the United States are changing, with more families delaying or forgoing parenthood
- The rewards and costs associated with children
- Large numbers of couples are remaining child free, often by choice, but sometimes because of infertility problems
- There are many types of adoptions—including open, closed, transracial, and international—and many nontraditional families are adopting, including single parents, and same-sex couples
- The natural process of childbirth has been vastly medicalized in the United States
- The transitions to parenthood can be challenging and men and women often face differences in these transitions
- Other industrialized nations offer extensive paid maternity and family leaves to help new parents

How do parents differ from their child-free counterparts in social and psychological resources, daily strains, and psychological well-being? Two convincing pictures of how children affect adults' lives can be painted: one with bright textures of joy, personal growth, and social benefits that children provide, and one that represents the costs and problems they create. Becoming a parent fundamentally changes one's life, making it more complex—not only through increasing demands, conflicts, and frustrations, but also by deepening joys, activating social ties, and enriching parents' self-concepts. Although virtually all young adults have some family members, such as spouses, siblings, or parents with whom they maintain contact, the birth or adoption of a first child creates a new family.

Sociologists Kei Nomaguchi and Melissa Milkie examine indicators that capture both costs and rewards of childrearing when adults become parents. These include (1) social resources, such as social integration; (2) psychological resources, such as self-concept; (3) daily strains, such as housework and disagreements with one's spouse; and (4) psychological well-being, such as depression. Moreover, the researchers pay explicit attention to how costs and rewards of becoming a parent are moderated by gender and marital status.

Using a nationally representative sample of 1,933 adults between the ages of 18 and 44 who were child free at the first interview, the authors compare several indicators of adults' lives for those who became parents and those remaining child free several years later. The results indicate that the effect of becoming a parent on adults' lives is multifaceted: New parents, regardless of sex and marital status, (1) report higher levels of social integration compared to their childless counterparts and (2) show no difference in self-esteem. For other indicators, the effects of becoming a parent vary by sex and marital status: (3) Mothers (regardless of marital status) report more daily strains such as hours spent doing housework and disagreements with their spouse, compared to those adults who did not have children; (4) married mothers report better psychological well-being and less depression than do those without children; and (5) unmarried mothers and fathers report lower levels of self-efficacy than adults who do not have children. (Nomaguchi and Milkie 2003) ■

There is reason to believe that fundamental changes are occurring in many parts of the world today in the values associated with having children. As educational and economic opportunities for young women continue to expand in both developed and less-developed nations, a wider range of lifestyle options becomes available. Coupled with the increasing availability of relatively effective birth control (and a growing acceptance of singlehood, cohabitation, and divorce in developing nations), many women are having far fewer children than ever before. Nonetheless, the world's population continues to expand.

This chapter focuses on issues surrounding fertility and parenthood. Although the likelihood of having children has declined alongside family size, most adults do become parents through either birth or adoption. Table 9.1 indicates that **pronatalism**, a cultural value that encourages childbearing, is a prevailing ideology in many parts of the world (Smith 1999). Pronatalist sentiment suggests that having children is a normal, natural part of a happy life and that those who voluntarily remain childfree are selfish, immature, lonely, unfulfilled, insensitive, and more likely to have mental problems than parents (Callan 1985). Pronatalism is supported by social institutions and social policies. For example, religious institutions often encourage large families. Pronatalism is interrelated with government family planning policies and women's rights. For example, the Japanese government took only 6 months to approve the impotence-treatment drug Viagra, but birth control pills designed to prevent pregnancy were reviewed for nearly a decade and have only recently been approved. In the United States many insurance companies cover the costs of Viagra but do not cover the costs of birth

TABLE 9.1 Pronatalist Attitudes with Percent Agreeing

"Children Are Life's Greatest Joy."		"People Without Children Lead Empty Lives."	
New Zealand	94	Netherlands	35
Australia	94	Ireland	36
Japan	94	New Zealand	40
Netherlands	94	Canada	41
Great Britain	94	Great Britain	41
Czech Republic	95	Northern Ireland	46
Canada	95	**United States**	**47**
Ireland	95	Norway	50
Israel	95	Australia	52
United States	**96**	Spain	52
Northern Ireland	96	Poland	63
West Germany	96	Czech Republic	67
Philippines	97	Sweden	67
Spain	97	West Germany	68
Norway	98	Philippines	70
Poland	98	Austria	72
Austria	98	Italy	72
Russia	98	Russia	73
Slovenia	98	Israel	79
Sweden	99	Japan	80
Bulgaria	99	East Germany	81
Italy	99	Slovenia	83
East Germany	99	Bulgaria	87
Hungary	100	Hungary	93

Source: Smith 1999.

control which some suggest is blatant sex discrimination (Colb 2001, Kageyama 1999; NARAL 2006; Parker 1999).

Population and Fertility Trends Worldwide

The world's population is currently growing at a rapid rate, but this has not always been the case. The population did not reach 1 billion people until about the year 1800. Then it increased to 1.6 billion only 100 years later. Today, after another century, the world's population is over 6 billion, and depending on the projection used, could reach nearly 11 billion by 2050. If the concept of a billion is difficult to comprehend, consider the following:

- If you were a billion seconds old, you would be 31.7 years of age.
- The circumference of the earth is 25,000 miles. If you circled the earth 40,000 times, you would have traveled 1 billion miles.

Population growth occurs unevenly. Less-developed countries contain about 81 percent of the world's population. In some countries, such as Mexico, the size of the population could double in less than 35 years (Population Reference Bureau 2006). In other countries, such as Japan, the population is not expected to double for nearly 500 years. Why such a difference? Population change is linked to many important issues for families, including health threats, infant mortality and life expectancy, the status of women, and overall quality of life.

Population statistics such as these reflect two important trends that occur at opposite ends of the lifespan. First, they represent **fertility rates**. There are several different ways to report fertility: (1) average number of children born to a woman during her lifetime; (2) number of children born per 1,000 women aged 15–49 (Many countries use age 49 as the cutoff; however, the United States normally uses age 44); and (3) number of children born per 1,000 population.

Map 9.1 (pages 276 and 277) shows the fertility rates throughout the world in 2005. Using the method calculating the average number of children born to a woman during her lifetime, we can see in Map 9.1 that South Korea, China, Taiwan, and much of western and eastern Europe have fertility rates below 1.5, well below replacement level. Countries with fertility rates this low must rely on immigration to maintain their population (Population Reference Bureau 2006).

Generally speaking, the fertility rate in developing nations (i.e., "third-world" countries) far exceeds the rate in developed nations—currently an average of 228 babies are born in less-developed countries every minute, compared to an average of 25 in more developed nations. In developing nations only about 20 percent of married women aged 15–49 use some sort of family-planning method. Part of this is due to obstacles such as inadequate funds for supplies and the lack of comprehensive programs to educate couples on their options. Moreover, large families are often valued as a means of social security. With few government aid programs, large numbers of children are seen as important social, economic, and political resources that can help maintain and provide for families. In reality, large numbers of children are likely to keep families impoverished, but as William Ogburn's cultural lag theory notes, nonmaterial culture (norms, values) changes more slowly than material culture (Ogburn 1964).

In addition to fertility rates, population statistics also reflect a country's **death rates**. Countries with a high death rate (i.e., a greater number of people dying) should take longer to double their populations than countries with a low death rate, if fertility rates are equal. However, we find that fertility rates and death rates are often positively related to one another; that is, those countries that have the most births also tend to have high death rates due to a lack of medical care and family planning services (e.g., most of Africa). Conversely, those countries with the lowest fertility rates tend to have lower death rates (e.g., the United States, Canada). However, there are some interesting exceptions. There are some countries with low fertility rates that also have high death rates, reflecting an aging population (e.g., much of Europe). Moreover, there are some countries with high fertility rates but also surprisingly low death rates, reflecting the youthfulness within a relatively healthy population (e.g., much of Central America).

In recent years many countries with traditionally high death rates have begun to lower them, which sounds like very good news, but it is also exacerbating population growth. More people have been exposed to improved vaccinations, sanitation, and modern medicines and have learned new ways to combat the spread of disease. Therefore, the population explosion that is occurring in these countries is not necessarily the result of increasing fertility rates (and in fact many of these countries have actually reduced their fertility rates), but rather is the result of rapidly declining death rates. The declining death rates pose significant challenges, including for food production. Many nations are struggling to feed their rapidly growing population, and therefore rely on the aid of wealthier nations such as the United States. With increasing globalization, some countries are in enormous debt to other nations, and it is highly unlikely that they will ever be able to repay what is owed. Attempts to repay the debt are virtually crippling their economies and making it even more difficult to feed their people, a basic tenet of the world systems theory, introduced in Chapter 2.

As an outsider looking at the plight of poorer countries, it is easy to suggest that they reduce their fertility rates further to offset their declines in death rates. Family-planning programs have been introduced, but often meet with limited success, particularly in rural regions where traditions remain strong. China is a notable exception. It provides an interesting example of the extent to which a nation will go to reduce its fertility rate. Through incentives and deterrents, China strongly encourages families in urban areas to have only one child. Families in the rural countryside can have two children under some circumstances. China's current fertility rate is 1.7, and its population is expected to grow only minimally between now and 2025 (Population Reference Bureau 2006).

To combat population growth the Chinese government implemented what is known as the one-child policy; however, the cultural preference for boys has resulted in a severe sex-ratio imbalance.

China's One-Child Policy

> The grandmother wrestled the baby girl from the mother's arms, after hours of arguments that were going nowhere. The decision had been made. Both women were sobbing, but the baby girl slept peacefully, not knowing what was in store for her. The grandmother put several layers of clothing on her granddaughter, despite the warmth on this June night. She then laid the 1-week-old girl in a box lined with blankets, a bottle, and an extra package of formula, and carried her off into the night. The grandmother could hear the wails of the baby's mother, her own daughter, as she headed down the road to a nearby village. "My baby, my baby, bring back my baby . . . ," the mother cried, although she felt too, deep in her heart, that this must be done. The grandmother quickly scurried with her bundle toward the park, which was eerily deserted in the late night. In the light of the moon she kissed her granddaughter for the very last time, propped up the bottle next to

MAP 9.1 Eye on the World: Comparative Total Fertility Rates, 2005

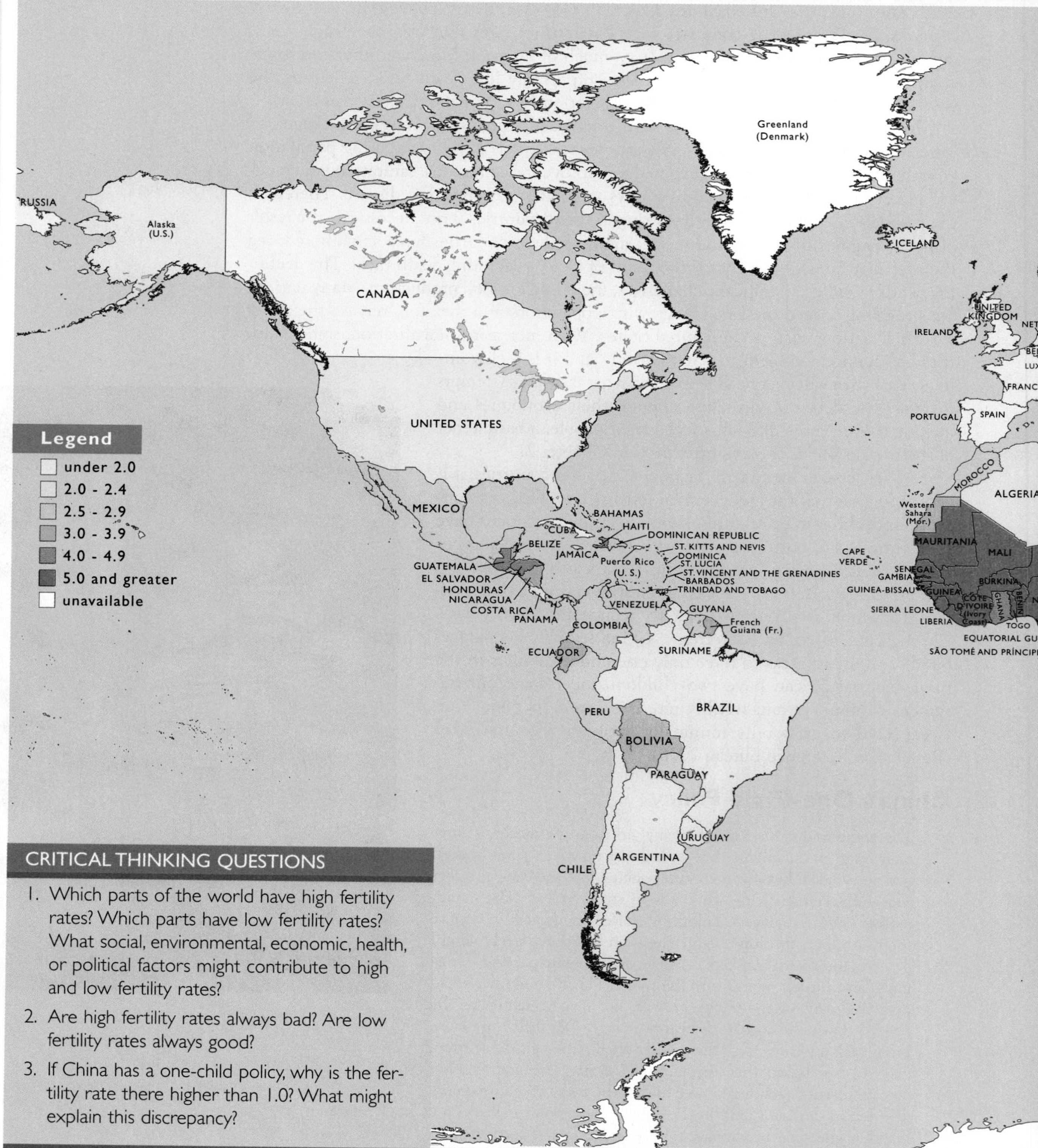

CRITICAL THINKING QUESTIONS

1. Which parts of the world have high fertility rates? Which parts have low fertility rates? What social, environmental, economic, health, or political factors might contribute to high and low fertility rates?
2. Are high fertility rates always bad? Are low fertility rates always good?
3. If China has a one-child policy, why is the fertility rate there higher than 1.0? What might explain this discrepancy?

There are several different ways to measure fertility rates. The total fertility rate is the average number of children born to a woman during her lifetime.

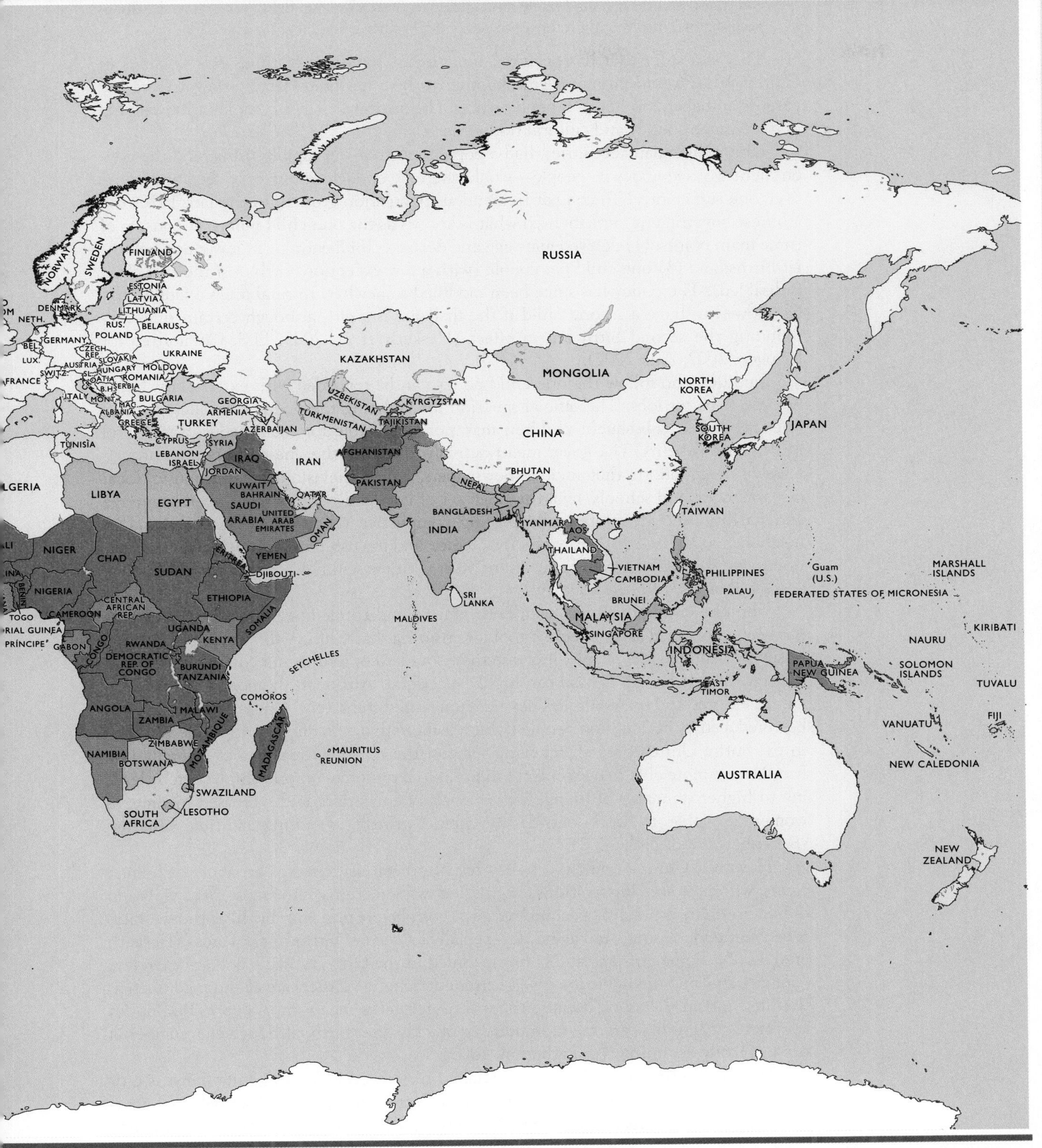

Source: Population Reference Bureau 2005.

the sleeping baby, and set the baby and her makeshift bed on a bench located in a popular area of the park. The grandmother looked up above with tears in her eyes and prayed to her god that the child be found safely and quickly in the early dawn light. With that, she disappeared alone into the night, never to see or hear of her granddaughter again.

This is a story that has occurred tens, if not hundreds of thousands of times in China. What would prompt a grandmother to take her granddaughter away from her parents and abandon her in a public place? The answer lies in a complex interweaving of government policy and cultural traditions.

China, like many countries, had a population that was rapidly rising, and the government worried about its people—would there be enough resources to feed and house everyone sufficiently? To combat tremendous population growth, in the late 1970s the Chinese government implemented what is known as the **one-child policy**. It consists of three main points: (1) delayed marriage and delayed childbearing; (2) fewer and healthier births; and (3) one child per couple (with a few exceptions such as if the first child is disabled). The policy has since been modified somewhat. In rural areas a family may be allowed to have a second child if the first one is a girl, although certain rules surrounding the second birth are in effect (Hesketh et al. 2005; U.S. Committee for Refugees 2002; Zink 2002).

Families who follow the one-child policy can be rewarded with extra salary, larger houses, or better jobs. The official sanction for violating the one-child policy is a stiff fine. Second or subsequent children may not be eligible for social, educational, and health care benefits. The government actively promotes the one-child policy through massive media efforts that include newspapers, radio, television, theater, music, local performances, and schools; by a thorough set of laws and policies that govern marriage and fertility; and by strategically placing compliance officers in workplaces and in neighborhoods. For example, each city, county, and township has a family-planning station focused on publicity and education. Most Chinese willingly comply with the policy and see it as good for the country.

The one-child policy has been both praised and condemned around the world. It has been applauded as an effective tool for ensuring that China will be able to continue to support and feed its people, increase their standard of living, and combat widespread poverty. In this regard, it has been highly successful. Although the policy can be difficult to enforce and some families have circumvented the intent, China's population has been reduced by 300 million people (which is more than the number of people who live in the entire United States), relieving some of the obvious stresses of overpopulation. Families are more able to concentrate their limited resources on one child, thereby leading to higher standards of living, higher levels of education, and increased income, as women are able to work outside the home instead of raising multiple children (Rosenberg 2006; Zink 2002).

However, China's one-child policy has also been criticized as an abuse of human rights, with profound implications for girls and women. Perhaps the most vivid violation of human rights is the disappearance of girls, both before and after birth, as the sex ratio is becoming increasingly imbalanced, especially for second births in rural areas (Hesketh et al. 2005). Some girls are simply not recorded in the birth statistics, and are therefore "noncitizens" and ineligible for any government benefits. Others are abandoned, such as the little girl in the story, because there is no formal mechanism to put a child up for adoption. Still, others are killed in utero or quickly after birth, although the number of these is likely declining (Hesketh et al. 2005).

No one knows exactly how many females have been killed in China but it is estimated that thousands have died from gross neglect, infanticide, and sex-selected abortion. Many researchers and policy makers around the world, including those in China itself, are alarmed. For example, Chinese officials have banned elective amniocentesis and have attempted to restrict the use of ultrasound scanners to determine the sex of the fetus to stop the selective abortion of female fetuses. In addition, a report by the State Family Planning Commission is promoting the idea that the birth of a girl is "just as good" as the birth of a boy and is calling for efforts to "eliminate the phenomenon of abandoning or drowning baby girls" (Herbert 1997).

Despite the promotion, in the year 2000, 900,000 fewer female births were recorded than what would be expected, given the number of male births, up from a shortfall of 500,000 in 1990 (Beech 2002). In some rural regions, boys outnumber girls by ten to one. If current trends continue, by 2020, the surplus of Chinese males will exceed the entire female population of Taiwan (Economist 1998).

Why have all the girls disappeared? In China, where generally only one child is allowed, girls are viewed as an economic liability and parents see boys as a better investment. Sons are expected to carry on the family lineage and take care of their aging parents. When a woman marries, she turns her focus to her husband's family. Traditionally women care for their husbands' parents, but they are not responsible for caring for their own. Customs like these reinforce the preference for sons—daughters are seen as expensive, as wasting precious resources, and provide little or no security for parents in old age. Although the Chinese government has expanded women's opportunities, rights, and obligations in recent decades, and women's work-family roles have similarly expanded, longstanding patriarchal attitudes change slowly.

Japan

In contrast to China, which is trying to limit births, the Japanese government is trying to increase the Japanese birth rate. In 2004, 163 hospital maternity wards, or 10 percent of the national total, closed, in part due to a low birth rate, one of the lowest in the world, and still declining (IOL 2005; Liberty Belles 2006). One of the reasons that women in Japan have so few children is because they have the primary or even exclusive responsibility of taking care of them rather than sharing the workload with their partners (BBC News 2005). According to a 1994 Family Life Education International Survey, 19 percent of Japanese fathers reportedly *never* spend time with their children on weekdays, compared to less than 1 percent of fathers in the United States (Makino and Nakano 1996). The government reasoned that if they can encourage fathers to become more involved in the lives of their children, families might choose to have more births. Consequently, the Japanese Ministry of Health and Social Welfare began a campaign in 1999 to emphasize the importance of fathers' participation in child care, profiling a well-known Japanese celebrity playing with his son, with a slogan claiming "A man who doesn't raise his children can't be called a father" (Ishii-Kuntz 2003; Ishii-Kuntz et al. 2004). It is not yet known if the campaign will be successful. The Japanese government may also need to address the lopsided division of labor more generally as well. In their review of 13 countries, Davis and Greenstein (2004) found that in Japan both husbands and wives were most likely to say that the wife always does the housework.

Fertility Rates in the United States

Historical Fluctuation

There are interesting patterns in the U.S. fertility rate. One of these is its degree of fluctuation, as shown in Figure 9.1 (Hamilton et al. 2006; Martin et al. 2006). The birth rate shows remarkable highs and lows, often occurring in quick succession. In 1920, a period of relative affluence and limited birth control, the U.S. fertility rate

FIGURE 9.1 **Fertility Rates: Live Births per 1,000 Women Aged 15–44, 1920–2004, by Race**

Source: Hamilton et al. 2006; Martin et al. 2006.

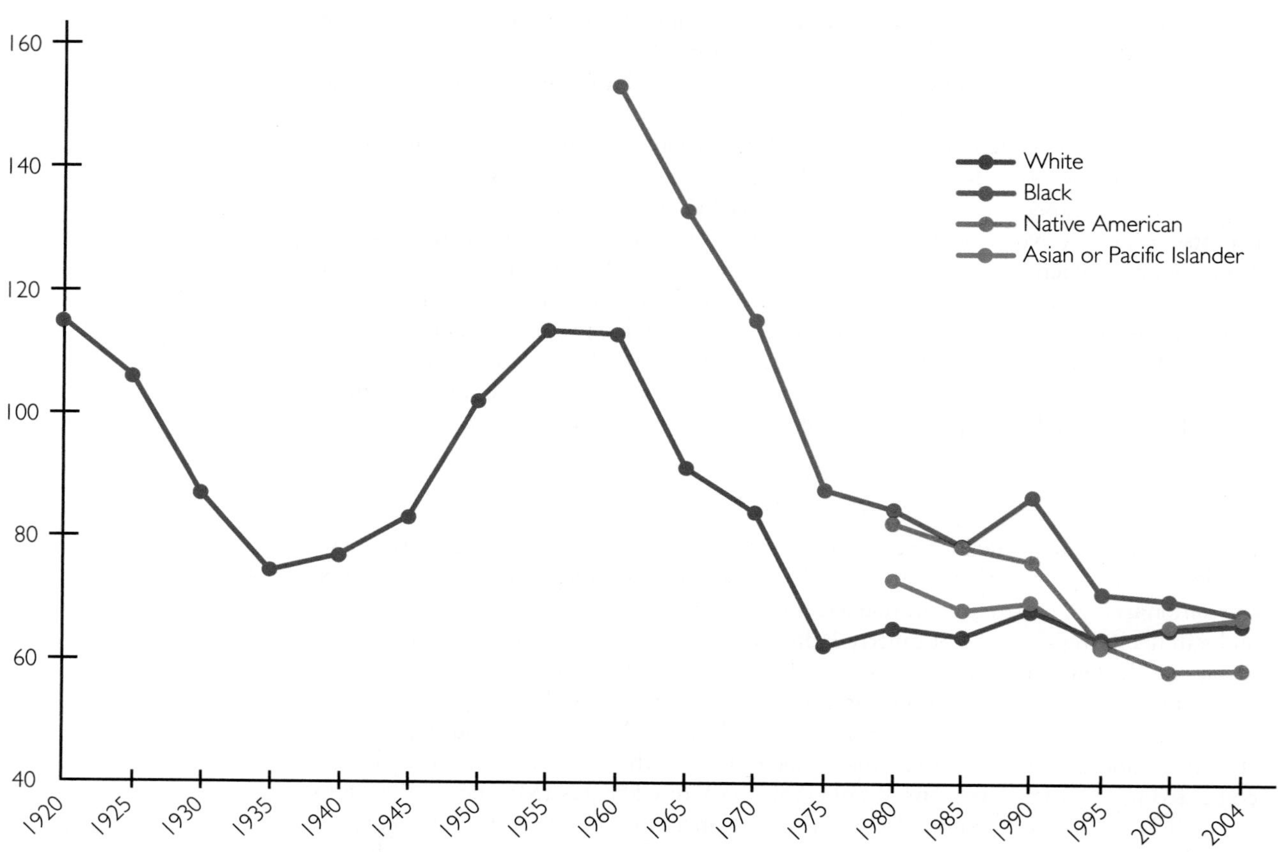

(defined here as live births per 1,000 women aged 15–44) hovered around 118 per 1,000 women—yet only 15 years later the fertility rate plummeted, bottoming out in 1935 to 77 per 1,000 women. Why would such a steep decline occur in such a short amount of time? Birth control measures were still fairly limited in the 1930s, so that could not be the primary factor.

A sharp decline such as this suggests that fertility rates are far more than simply biological phenomena. Personal choices are influenced by macro-level structural conditions and social trends. During the 1930s the United States fell into a deep economic depression. Because of the dire consequences of the Great Depression, fewer people were marrying, others were marrying later, and many families split up to pursue employment. Not surprisingly, the birth rate declined accordingly.

However, a decade later, as the depression was ending and the United States moved into and out of World War II, the birth rate rose to a level not seen for decades. By 1950, the fertility rate rose to 106 per 1,000 women aged 15–44, a period that has since been described as the "baby boom." The United States experienced a degree of affluence after the war, couples married younger, and the number of employed married women working outside the home declined. Women were encouraged to find fulfillment as a wife, mother, and homemaker, as a survey of the articles and advertisements in "women's magazines" reveals (Friedan 1963). Family, particularly motherhood, became a primary cultural goal.

By the early 1960s the fertility rate began to drop significantly. This period through the 1970s is sometimes referred to as the "baby bust," and rates continued on a downward trend to 66.3 births per 1,000 married women today (Hamilton et al. 2006). There are a number of reasons for the rapid decline in fertility rates. One demographic explanation is that the sheer number of women of childbearing age was lower in the 1970s, which generally translates into fewer children being born. Also, birth control pills became readily available. Other reasons for the decline in fertility rates are more social in origin and represent changing attitudes about women's social and family roles. More women began going to college, including graduate and professional schools, and gained employment in new fields. Likewise, the number of married women employed outside the home increased. Women saw that additional options were available to them, so many chose to delay childbearing, or not to have children at all.

Another interesting pattern is that U.S. fertility rates are higher than virtually any other industrialized nation (Population Reference Bureau 2006). The United States is one of the few industrialized nations whose birth rate approaches replacement level. Other countries must rely on immigration to maintain their population size.

Fertility rates vary across race and ethnic groups in the United States. Some are likely to have more children than others, as revealed in Figure 9.2. Data from the U.S.

FIGURE 9.2 Births per 1,000 Women 15–44 Years, by Race and Hispanic Origin, 2004

Source: Dye 2005.

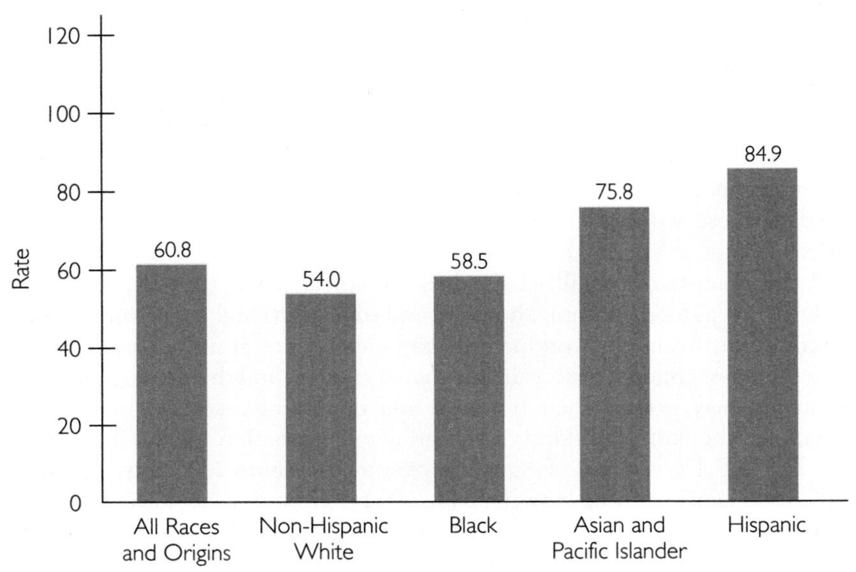

Many women are delaying the age at which they have their first child because of new educational or career opportunities.

Census Bureau reveal that non-Hispanic whites and blacks have the fewest children on average (54 and 59 births per 1,000 women aged 15–44, respectively). Hispanics have the highest fertility rate at 85 births per 1,000 women (Dye 2005).

Delayed Parenthood

Another interesting new pattern is the delay in having children. Because of women's increasing educational and employment opportunities, coupled with advances in birth control, women are delaying the age at which they have their first child. In 2004, 28 percent of women aged 30 to 34 did not have children, compared to only 16 percent of women of that age in 1976 (Downs 2003; Dye 2005). It is likely that some of these women will have one or more children eventually; they are simply postponing the age at which they have them. Delayed parenthood is, again, more than simply a biological phenomenon. The reasons for later parenthood are often social in nature (women wanting to pursue education or careers; the rise in the number of second marriages), and the response to persons having a child in their 40s or 50s, or even 60s takes on an interesting twist depending on the sex of the parent, as shown in Box 9.1. Although most people hardly bat an eye if a man becomes a father at age 50, the sentiment is quite different if a woman wants to become a mother at 50.

Deciding to Parent

The Rewards and Costs of Children

As the opening vignette illustrates, there are two contrasting pictures of how children affect adults' lives. One is bright and rosy, emphasizing the emotional rewards. The other is dark and gloomy, more likely emphasizing the emotional or financial costs. For many people, the realities involve merging these contrasting views.

The bulk of social science research has focused on the emotional costs, suggesting explicitly or implicitly that having children today is more costly than rewarding in terms of added stresses and strains. Some researchers have found that parents report being less happy, experiencing more stress, and experiencing a decline in intimacy with their partner, compared to those without children (Evenson and Simon 2005; Knoester and Eggebeen 2006; Twenge et al. 2003).

Moreover, economists often talk about **direct financial costs** (out-of-pocket expenses for things such as food, clothing, housing, and education) and **opportunity costs** (lost opportunities for income by working only part-time or not at all because of children). In rural societies, children are a valuable source of labor, and their economic benefits to the family may exceed their financial and opportunity costs. However, in developing nations, the cost of children is the primary explanation for the decline in fertility rates. The U.S. Department of Agriculture estimates that in 2005, a typical two-parent, middle-class family earning between $43,200 and $72,600 spent $190,980 (pretax) raising a child to the age of 18; families earning over $70,600 a year spent $279, 450 (pretax) on average (Lino 2006). Expenses include housing, food, transportation,

BOX 9.1 Using the Sociological Imagination

Having a Baby at 50 or 60

There is a lot of public concern about teenagers being too young to have a baby, but when is a person too old to have a baby? Biology used to answer that question, at least for women. With the onset of perimenopause, few women conceive naturally after their early 40s. However, modern technology has changed this, and with the help of donor eggs, women can now have children considerably later in life. The following summarizes some of the controversies surrounding having a baby at age 50 or even 60.

At first glance, Judith Cates' life seems the picture of ordinary as she brushes the hair of her 5-year-old twins, picks up their toys, and takes them to pizza parties. However, a closer look at their family reveals something highly unusual. Judith is 63 years old and gave birth to her girls when she was 57. "They keep us laughing with everything they do and say," said Cates. "If I wasn't so old, we'd try for two more."

Judith is a leader in a growing trend. A study by the Centers for Disease Control found that there were 6,546 first-time mothers between ages 45 and 54 in 2005. The number of births to women over 40 exceeded 110,000 for the first time.

Women in their 50s or even 60s can get pregnant with relative ease using eggs from younger women and can expect reasonably normal pregnancies and healthy babies. Older women's eggs, not their wombs, decline at menopause, leading to age-related fertility problems. Researchers tracked the fates of 77 postmenopausal women, aged 50 to 63 who underwent in-vitro fertilization with donor eggs at the University of Southern California (USC) from 1991 to 2001. Each woman had to pass a thorough medical exam, including a cardiac stress test and a uterine lining biopsy to ensure that the womb could still respond to the hormones that would be given to support the pregnancy. The women had, on average, three to four embryos transferred into their wombs. All told, 42 of the 77 women had live births—including three who each had two consecutive births—for a total of 45 births producing 61 babies (31 single children, 12 sets of twins, and two of triplets), all of them healthy. Some complications such as pregnancy-related high blood pressure do increase with age, but there was not any definitive medical reason for excluding these older women from becoming pregnant on the basis of age alone.

Helping women in their 50s and 60s become pregnant has been controversial. The ethics committee of the American Society of Reproductive Medicine concluded that the practice is not unethical but should be discouraged. Others echoed that view, warning against widely promoting the practice. "Just because you can do something doesn't mean you should," said Robert Stillman, medical director of the Shady Grove Fertility Reproductive Science Center in Rockville, Maryland. The center refused to treat women older than 50, the average age of menopause. There are no restrictions on men's ages for fertility treatment.

Even Judith Cates' niece Traci Wells says she is not sure she would recommend other women in their late 50s having children: "I'm concerned about when they get older, having to deal with the loss of their parents at an early age," she said. The Cates prefer to leave that in God's hands. "My mom lived to be 83. It was a wonderful life. I pray to God I will live to her age and have that much time with my girls and my husband. That's something nobody knows," Cates replied (Weiss 2002).

Yet, researchers have found that older parents often make excellent parents. A study of 30,000 households showed that people who had children in their 40s were better off financially, spent more time with their children, and had a closer connection to their children's friends than younger parents, according to Brian Powell, a sociology

(continued)

professor at Indiana University. His research can be summarized: The older the parent, the better off the child. He was not able to analyze the results of parents who had children in their 50s and 60s because statistically there are so few of them, but the presumption is that the findings would be consistent.

The medical, psychological, and social effects of late motherhood deserve careful consideration. However, for women who want to go down that path, the odds of success are remarkably good when they use donor eggs from women in their 20s and 30s.

Source: Hamilton 2006; Hefling 2004; Weiss 2002.

CRITICAL THINKING QUESTIONS

1. What arguments can you make for and against helping a 50- to 60-year-old woman to have a successful pregnancy by allowing her to use donor eggs?
2. Some people claim that it is unethical or inappropriate to help women in their 50s or 60s have babies. Do you think that these people would make the same argument against men who are in their 50s or 60s fathering babies? Why or why not?
3. A number of older men in recent years have fathered children while in their 50s and 60s, including Paul McCartney, Michael Douglas, and Larry King. Have they (or their younger wives) experienced stigma because of it? What if the reverse occurred—a 55-year-old woman had a baby with her 35-year-old husband? Is there a double standard?

clothing, health care, education/child care, and other miscellaneous expenses (personal care items, recreation expenses, etc.) and were based on the Consumer Expenditure Survey. They estimate what was actually spent, rather than some standard of what should be spent. However, costs do not include college expenses or opportunity costs (i.e., a parent taking work leave to raise the child).

With a financial picture such as this, one might wonder why anyone would want children at all. What are the rewards of being a parent?

Perhaps one reason that studies bleakly focus on the financial or emotional costs of parenthood is that the rewards are more difficult to measure. The emotional feelings of love and devotion are harder to quantify. However, as shown in Box 9.2, children can bring tremendous joy and purpose into people's lives (Groat et al. 1997; Hansen 2002). A nationwide Gallup poll asked parents about the things they gained most from having children. Common responses included "children bring love and affection"; "it is a pleasure to watch them grow"; "they bring joy, happiness, and fun"; "they create a sense of family"; and "they bring fulfillment and a sense of satisfaction." Other benefits include having an adult child to take care of a parent as he or she ages (Seccombe 1991). As will be discussed in Chapter 12, adult children often provide care to a frail elderly parent, preventing or postponing nursing home placement.

One area that has received considerable attention is the degree to which children connect parents socially with others. Research overwhelmingly shows that parents are more socially integrated than are adults without children (Gallagher and Gerstel 2001;

BOX 9.2 Families as Lived Experience

The "Costs" of Raising a Child

Without a doubt, raising children is expensive! So, what do you get for your money?

The government calculated the cost of raising a child from birth to age 18 and came up with $190,980 [numbers updated by author] for a middle-income family. Talk about sticker shock! That doesn't touch college tuition. For those with children, that figure leads to wild fantasies about all the money we could have banked if not for _____________ (insert your child's name here). For others, that number might confirm the decision to remain child free. However, $190,980 isn't so bad if you break it down: It translates into $10,610 a year, $884 a month, or $204 a week. That's a mere $29 a day—just over a dollar an hour. Still, you might think the best financial advice says don't have children if you want to be "rich." What do you get for your $190,980?

1. Naming rights; first, middle, and last
2. Glimpses of God every day
3. Giggles under the covers every night
4. More love than your heart can hold
5. Butterfly kisses and Velcro hugs
6. Endless wonder over rocks, ants, clouds, and warm cookies
7. A hand to hold, usually covered with jam
8. A partner for blowing bubbles, flying kites, building sandcastles, and skipping down the sidewalk in the pouring rain
9. Someone to laugh yourself silly with no matter what the boss said or how your stocks performed that day
10. You never have to grow up.
11. You get to finger-paint, carve pumpkins, play hide-and-seek, catch lightning bugs, and never stop believing in Santa Claus.
12. You have an excuse to keep reading the *Adventures of Piglet and Pooh*, watching Saturday morning cartoons, going to Disney movies, and wishing on stars.
13. You get to frame rainbows, hearts, and flowers under refrigerator magnets and collect spray-painted noodle wreaths for Christmas, hand prints set in clay for Mother's Day, and cards with backward letters for Father's Day.
14. There is no greater bang for your buck.
15. You get to be a hero just for retrieving a Frisbee off the garage roof, taking the training wheels off the bike, removing a splinter, filling the wading pool, coaxing a wad of gum out of bangs, and coaching a baseball team that never wins but always gets treated to ice cream regardless.
16. You get a front row seat to history to witness the first step, first word, first bra, first date, and first time behind the wheel.
17. You get to be immortal.
18. You get another branch added to your family tree, and if you're lucky, a long list of limbs in your obituary called grandchildren.
19. You get an education in psychology, nursing, criminal justice, communications, and human sexuality that no college can match.
20. In the eyes of a child, you rank right up there with God, Santa Claus, the Easter Bunny, and the Tooth Fairy.
21. You have all the power to heal a boo-boo, scare away the monsters under the bed, patch a broken heart, police a slumber party, ground them forever, and love them without limits, so one day they will, like you, love without counting the cost.

Source: Adapted from Hansen 2002.

CRITICAL THINKING QUESTIONS

1. If it costs middle-income families approximately $190,980 to raise a child to age 18, but wealthy families pay more and lower-income families less, what additional or fewer items are these other children receiving? Are the items extras? Are they necessities?
2. What do you see as the emotional rewards of parenting? How do you factor these against the financial costs, particularly if you want more than one child? Is it possible, or fair, to compare emotional and financial issues?

Ishii-Kuntz and Seccombe 1989; Nomaguchi and Milkie 2003). Children provide parents with opportunities to interact in new ways with relatives, neighbors, and friends. Children provide links for parents with social institutions such as churches or schools, thereby providing further opportunities to develop relationships.

Having children is also a symbol that a person has reached adulthood. Parents are assumed to be more stable than child-free adults. This works to men's advantage in the workforce, where they are seen as more reliable and dedicated to the job, as the term "family man" implies (Seccombe 1991). However, notice that there is no semantic equivalent for employed women who have families.

Remaining Child Free

According to census bureau data, in 2004, 19.3 percent of women between the ages of 40 and 44 did not have children, up from 10.3 percent in 1976 (Dye 2005). It is possible that a small number of these women may have children after age 44, but it is likely that the vast majority will not. This represents a rapid rise in the proportion of women without children over the past three decades. However, a look through U.S. history reveals a number of time periods with similar or even higher rates of being child free. For example, during the Great Depression of the 1930s, about 25 percent of women in their childbearing years did not have children as shown in Figure 9.3.

Although being child free is increasingly accepted (Thornton and Young-DeMarco 2001), cultural images of femininity include reproduction and mothering (Gillespie 2000). Many Americans still disapprove of or look oddly at those who opt to forgo parenthood (Smith 1999). It is assumed that all individuals, especially women, need children to fulfill their desire for love, companionship, and intimacy.

Who is most likely to be child free? Women aged 40 to 44 who do not have children are a diverse group; however, overall, they tend to have completed college or graduate school, are native born, and live in central cities and metropolitan areas. Blacks and whites are most likely to be child free (21 percent and 20 percent, respectively), and Hispanics are least likely (14 percent) (Dye 2005).

People have different reasons for remaining child free (Koropeckyj-Cox 2002). Some are child free because of longstanding physiological infertility; others postponed

FIGURE 9.3 Percentage of Women Aged 40–44 Who Do Not Have Children, 1976–2004

Source: Downs 2003; Dye 2005.

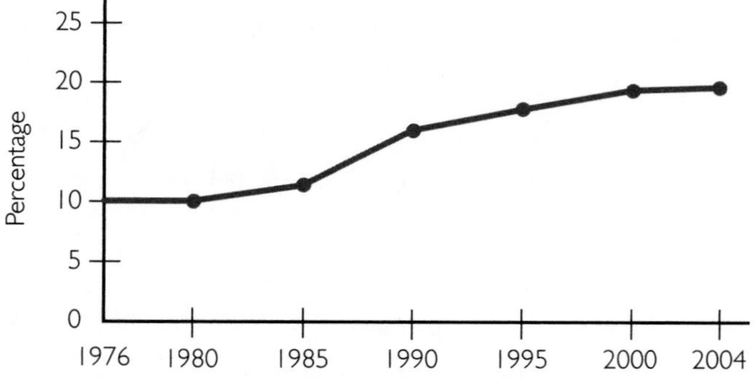

childbearing until age-related infertility prohibited it; and others voluntarily chose to remain child free. For example, during the Great Depression it is estimated that one-third to one-half of child-free couples were without children by choice (Graybill et al. 1958). However, there is also an important structural explanation for remaining child free: If we examine historical trends in childbirth alongside historical trends for marriage, we can see that the two are related to one another. Marriage is the strongest predictor of having (or not having) children (Bachu and O'Connell 2001). In other words, when rates of marriage decline, the proportion of child-free women in society goes up (Heaton et al. 1999).

Infertility Not all individuals without children are child free by choice. **Infertility** is the inability to conceive a child. It is a condition of the reproductive system that often goes undiagnosed until a couple has had at least 1 year of unprotected intercourse or until a woman has suffered from multiple miscarriages. About 12 percent of women of childbearing age in the United States have received an infertility service (CDC 2006f). Infertility affects men and women equally; 40 percent of infertility is due to a female factor, 40 percent to a male factor, and in the remaining cases, it results from problems in both partners or indeterminate causes (Resolve 2004).

Medical technology offers treatment options to women and men trying to conceive a child, including hormone treatments, intrauterine insemination, and more advanced technologies like in vitro fertilization (IVF), surrogacy, egg/sperm donation, and even embryo donation. **Assisted reproductive technology (ART)** includes all fertility treatments in which both egg and sperm are handled. For example, during IVF, a woman will use ovulation-stimulating drugs to produce an excess number of eggs. These eggs are then surgically removed and fertilized in a dish with sperm. If fertilization takes place, the physician implants the embryo(s) into the woman's uterus.

Many of these issues are controversial. For example, how many embryos can be implanted at one time? What happens to embryos that are not used? The procedures follow the guidelines of the American Society of Reproductive Medicine and the Society for Assisted Reproductive Technology. There were 128,000 ART cycles conducted in 2004, resulting in 36,700 births; in other words, it averages more than three attempts to have a successful birth (CDC 2006f). This can be extremely expensive, because most insurance companies do not cover all of the costs, and many insurance companies will not cover ART at all. It can also be emotionally and physically exhausting.

Voluntarily Child Free The decision to forgo children is usually not made once, but many times, because people undergo a *process* of deciding about children. Using data from a nationally representative sample of child-free women under 40 and men who were married to women under 40, and drawing upon exchange theory, Seccombe (1991) examined gender differences in the costs and benefits people calculated in their decision to have children. She found that *men* rather than women were more likely to report "it is better for a person to have a child than to go through life childless," and that *men* were more likely than women to personally want to have children (Seccombe 1991).

A common concern that child-free people express is "Will I regret my decision? Will I be lonely in my old age?" Research studies have examined the plight of the child-free elderly to answer these questions. Most studies report that the elderly without children are not disadvantaged in most ways. Some researchers have found that the child free have fewer relationships with friends or extended family, but have strong ties to their partners (Connidis and McMullin 1994, 1999; Ishii-Kuntz and Seccombe 1989; Zhang and Hayward 2001). Some, but not all, research indicates that they may be a bit more isolated than couples with children, but their finances are generally better, and they report being happy (or unhappy) as frequently as do those with children. However,

Koropeckyj-Cox (2002) reminds us that it is important to distinguish between those individuals who are voluntarily and involuntarily without children, because their experiences and perceptions greatly differ.

Adoption

Adoption touches the lives of many people. Although only about 4 percent of Americans are adopted, one survey based on a representative nationwide sample of 1,416 adults found that 64 percent reported a direct personal experience with adoption; they, a family member, or a close friend was adopted, had adopted a child, or had relinquished a child for adoption (National Adoption Information Clearinghouse 2002).

Despite its prevalence, Fisher (2003) reports that little attention is paid to adoption in current college textbooks that focus on family issues. Fisher conducted a content analysis of 21 family textbooks and 16 undergraduate readers that were published between 1998 and 2001. He found that 4 of the 21 texts reviewed (19 percent) and 3 of the 16 readers reviewed (19 percent) offered no coverage of adoption at all. Among those books that did discuss adoption, the texts devoted an average of 2.4 pages and the readers devoted little more. Moreover, as shown in Table 9.2, Fisher found that the negative points made about adoption far outnumbered the positive points. Books tended to comment on potential problems, such as the behavioral and psychological problems among adoptees; the unavailability of healthy children; the high costs of adoption; legal problems; the stigma surrounding adoption; ideological or ethical problems associated with adoption; long waits; or the unknowns about the child's genetic background or physical or emotional treatment. Although these problems may exist, Fisher notes that the multitude of positive points about adoption were far less likely to be discussed in these scholarly books, including the fact that despite the risks, most adoptions work out well; changes in public policy that have made adoption less difficult and less expensive; the benefits for adopted children and adoptive parents; the decline in stigma toward adoption; the benefits of a more open, less secretive process of adoption; and the humanitarian reasons that many adoptive parents offer for adopting.

Once stigmatized, and often kept secret, adoption is now more open and socially supported than ever (Fein 1998). Adoptions can occur through licensed public agencies that specialize in placing children in adoptive families, known as **public adoptions**. Adoptions can also be arranged directly between adoptive parents and the biological birth mother, usually through the assistance of an attorney. These are referred to as **private adoptions**. In a private adoption, the attorney may contact social workers, other attorneys, doctors, or place a notice in a newspaper looking for a woman who intends to relinquish her child. Although baby "selling" is prohibited, the adopting couple likely will pay the birth

TABLE 9.2 Number of Positive and Negative Points Made About Adoption, By Type of Book

Type of Book	Positive Points	Negative Points
Texts (n = 21)	38	57
Readers (n = 16)	10	37
All books (n = 37)	48	94

Source: Fisher 2003.

mother's medical fees and often her living expenses and other miscellaneous expenses. Private adoptions tend to be more expensive than public adoptions, although they are more common because they are likely to result in the adoptive family obtaining an infant. The children in public adoptions are often older or have special needs.

Whether public or private, most adoptions in the past were conducted under a cloak of secrecy. Unless the adoption was occurring among kin, chances are it was a **closed adoption**, with all identifying information sealed and unavailable to all parties. Adopted children knew nothing about their birth parents or their genetic makeup. Much has changed in the last two decades. Adoptions are far more likely to be **semi-open adoptions**, in which biological and adoptive families exchange personal information through a social worker or attorney, but have no direct contact, or **open adoptions**, which involve direct contact between the biological and adoptive parents. The contact can run the gamut from a one-time meeting to a lifelong relationship. Semi-open and open adoptions can have many advantages for the child, birth mother, and adoptive parents (Miall and March 2005).

Most adoptive parents are married, highly educated, and have higher-than-average incomes. Compared to other mothers, adoptive mothers are less likely to work full-time outside the home.

Transracial Adoptions Most adoptive parents are white, yet 40 percent of children in the United States available for adoption are black. This raises a controversial issue: Is it appropriate to place minority children with white families? In the 1970s the Association of Black Social Workers and Native American activists strongly objected to placing black and Native American children with white families, suggesting that transracial adoptions amounted to cultural genocide. Afterwards, the number of transracial adoptions declined sharply. However, a longitudinal study conducted over 20 years found that minority children placed in white homes generally develop positive racial and ethnic identities and are knowledgeable of their history and culture (Simon and

Forty percent of children in the United States available for adoption are black. Should they be placed with white families?

Alstein 2000). Today, the majority of transracial adoptions are Asian children—most often abandoned girls from China—who are adopted by white parents, in contrast to black children being adopted by whites.

Single Parent Adoptions A generation ago, if a single woman presented herself to an adoption agency to apply for a child, she may have been turned away. It was highly unusual for a single person to adopt a child, and in a number of states, it was illegal. Much has changed in 30 years. Today single women are actively involved in adoption, particularly with children who are older, are racial or ethnic minorities, or are from other countries. However, single men still experience bias. Despite growing recognition of men as nurturers, there is still suspicion that, "a single man could not be sensitive to a child's needs"; or "I wonder what kind of man wants to raise a child alone" (Marindin 1987).

Adoption by Gays and Lesbians Lesbians and gay men have always adopted, though in the past they usually hid their sexual orientation. Today, just as gays and lesbians are becoming more visible in all other aspects of American society, they are being considered more seriously as potential adoptive parents. As of 2006, only Florida specifically banned the adoption of children by gay and lesbian adults, although a few others threaten to do so. Only nine states allow for openly gay and lesbian adoptions: California, Massachusetts, New Jersey, New Mexico, New York, Ohio, Vermont, Washington, and Wisconsin, as well as Washington, D.C. In other states, the only real recourse is for one partner to adopt and then for the other partner to apply as the second parent or co-parent. Second-parent adoptions create a second legally recognized parent for the adoptive child, and is a common way for gay and lesbian couples to both become legal parents of their children (Craft 2006). Likewise, some countries, such as China, refuse to allow openly gay or lesbian couples to adopt.

There are many concerns surrounding gay and lesbian adoption, many of which are based on stereotypes or myths about sexual orientation or homosexuality. What are these concerns, and what do the research findings suggest?

- *Homosexual parents will molest their children.* There is no scientific research that indicates a significant link between homosexuality and pedophilia. One study looked at 269 cases of child sexual abuse and found only two cases where the offenders were gay or lesbian. Indeed, the author found that a child's risk of being molested by his or her parent's (or other relative's) *heterosexual* partner was over 100 times greater than being molested by someone identified as homosexual (Carole 1994).
- *Children raised in homosexual households will become gay.* Research findings suggest that children raised by gay and lesbian parents are no more likely to become homosexual than children raised by heterosexuals. An assessment of more than 300 children born to gay or lesbian parents in 12 different samples indicates the proportion of homosexual offspring similar to that of a random sample of the population (Patterson 1992).
- *Children raised in gay or lesbian households will have mental health problems.* Courts have expressed concern that children raised by gay and lesbian parents may have psychological difficulties or problems with self-esteem and peer relationships. Consequently researchers have focused on children's development in gay and lesbian families. Studies find virtually no difference between children of gay or lesbian parents and those raised by heterosexual parents (Patterson 1992). Children raised by a gay parent or parents have shown no difference in developmental outcomes as compared with children raised by heterosexual parents. For example, researchers Judith Stacey and Timothy Biblarz of the University of Southern California reported the results of their examination of 21 different studies on gay and lesbian par-

enting (2001). They found that the children of homosexual parents show no difference in levels of self-esteem, anxiety, depression, behavior problems, or social performance, but do show a higher level of affection, responsiveness, and concern for younger children. The children of gay and lesbian parents demonstrate some differences in gender behavior and preferences. Lesbian mothers reported their children, especially daughters, are less likely to conform to cultural gender norms in dress, play, and behavior, and are more likely to aspire to nontraditional gender occupations, such as doctors, lawyers, or engineers. They also discovered that although the children of gay and lesbian parents are no more likely to identify themselves as gay, lesbian, or bisexual than the children of heterosexual parents, they are more likely to consider or experiment with same-sex relationships during young adulthood. In sum, the study authors suggest that sexual orientation only matters because homophobia and discrimination say it matters.

- *Children will be teased and harassed.* Children of gay and lesbian parents may be vulnerable to teasing and harassment, particularly as they approach adolescence. Courts have often viewed the stigma surrounding gay and lesbian parenting as possibly damaging to a child's self-esteem, and therefore side with the heterosexual parent in custody disputes. However, gay and lesbian parents are generally aware of stigma and its effects and go to great lengths to prepare and support their children. Research has found that although children of gays and lesbians do report experiencing teasing because of their parents' sexual orientation, their self-esteem levels are no lower than those of children of heterosexual parents (Huggins 1989).

A consultant and adoption trainer prefers to focus on issues that extend beyond superficial stereotypes about sexual orientation when thinking about who would or would not make a good adoptive parent.

> I council workers to ask homosexual applicants where they are in their individual development. Have they recently come out? Are they comfortable with their self-image and with being gay? Having a positive self-image will provide a model for an adopted child. I want to know about family support and how those who are important in their lives view them and their idea of adopting. I ask questions about the stability of their relationship and try to see how committed they are to each other. Do they have wills? Have they bought a home? Do they share finances? Once you know more about their situation, you can help them access appropriate resources and connect them with other gay or lesbian adoptive parents. (National Adoption Information Clearinghouse 2000)

The leading medical society of pediatricians, the 65,000-member American Academy of Pediatrics, endorses the legal rights of homosexuals to adopt a partner's child, saying "children deserve to know their relationships with both parents are stable and legally recognized" (Hall 2002, 1).

Families in the United States adopted nearly 23,000 foreign-born children in 2005, more than any other country. Most children thrive when placed with a loving adoptive family.

International Adoption The number of Americans who are adopting children from other countries has increased sharply. In fact, the United States adopts more children from abroad than any other country (although Norway, Sweden, Denmark, Switzerland, and Canada adopt more children in relation to their annual births) (Selman 2002). American parents adopted nearly 23,000 foreign-born children in 2005, more than double the number of such adoptions a decade earlier. Figure 9.4 shows that almost three-quarters of all foreign-born children adopted by American parents in 2005 came from China (35 percent), Russia (20 percent), and Guatemala (17 percent) (U.S. Department of State 2006), a trend that has held steady for years. Figure 9.5 shows the growth in the number of adoptions from these three regions over the past decade. Political decisions or conflicts often produce orphans who need families. For example, adoptions from China are in response to the strict one-child policy enforced by the Chinese government; adoptions in Russia are in response to the extreme poverty following the transition to a market economy (Tarmann 2003). Nearly two-thirds of international adoptions are girls, and among adoptions from China virtually all are girls.

The rise in international adoptions is in large part due to the declining availability of U.S.-born babies available for adoption. There are several reasons for fewer available children, including (1) a declining teenage pregnancy rate; (2) increasing use of contraceptives; (3) declining numbers of women placing their children up for adoption; (4) the availability of legal abortion; and (5) the declining stigma of unwed motherhood. Prospective parents are also looking internationally for children because adopting within the United States is slow, costly, and often has stricter guidelines such as age restrictions. Moreover, there is usually a more clear-cut termination of birth parents' rights in international adoptions that appeals to many people. Finally, some people adopt internationally for humanitarian reasons or because they have a personal interest or stake in that part of the world.

Children adopted internationally are generally not available for adoption until they are at least 6 months to 1 year old, and in the case of Eastern Europe, sometimes considerably older. They are likely to have spent all or most of their infancy in orphanages, and therefore may have been exposed to a number of biological and social risks (Frank et al. 1996; Judge 2003). These risks vary by country, but may include infectious diseases such as parasites, and other deficits in cognitive, social, physical, and medical well-being.

FIGURE 9.4 Birth Country of International Adoptions by U.S. Parents, 2005

Source: U.S. Department of State 2006.

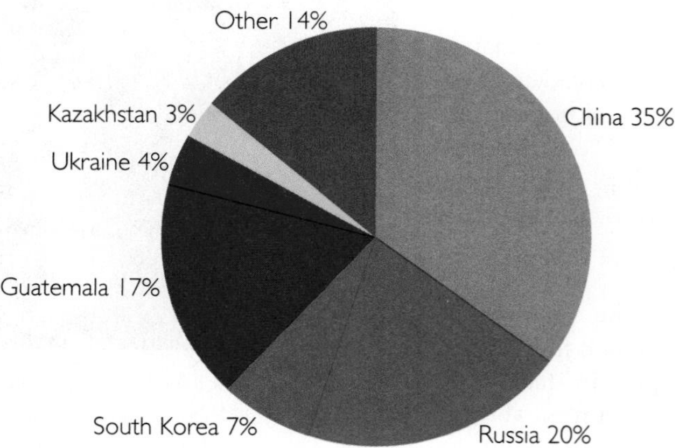

FIGURE 9.5 **Trends in International Adoption 1995–2005**

Source: U.S. Department of State 2006.

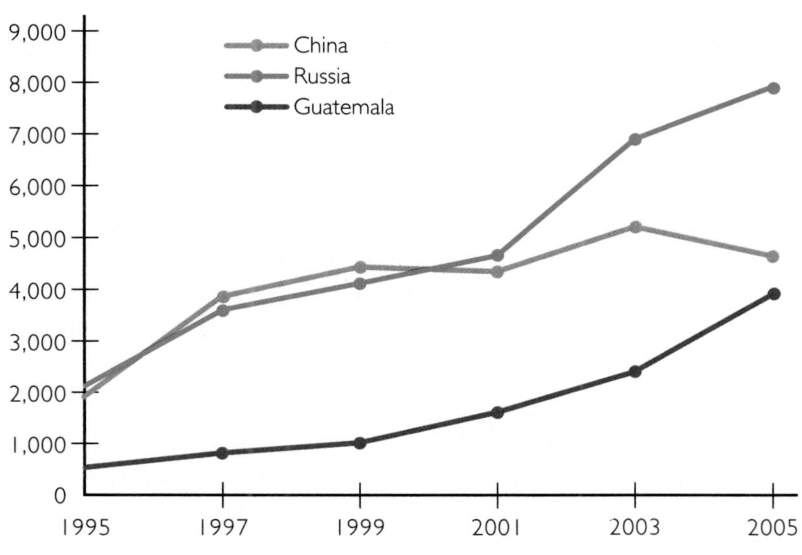

Research shows that international adoptees have a higher-than-average rate of developmental delays or behavior problems, depending on the length of time in the orphanage (Albers et al. 1997; Nelson and Camras 2000; O'Connor et al. 2000). To combat these problems, many babies in Guatemala are now in foster care instead of orphanages. Although foster care is still relatively rare in China, many orphanages have improved considerably because of the infusion of foreign money from previous adoptions.

Most children do well when placed with an adoptive family, and within a year, few children continue to display atypical behavior or socioemotional problems, especially if adopted young (Nelson and Camras 2000; Tan and Yang 2005). Organizations for adoptive families, such as Families with Children from China (FCC) offer education, support, play groups, and celebration of the children's birth heritage.

The Social Construction of Pregnancy and Childbirth

Although infertility and voluntarily choosing to forgo parenthood are on the rise, most women do become pregnant and have a child. These are normal conditions for most sexually active adult women; that is, a woman must actually do something extra (for example, use birth control or have an abortion) to prevent pregnancy and childbirth from happening. The biological processes involved in these events are universal. Women get pregnant the same way in Bangladesh as they do in England.

Nonetheless, it would be a mistake to assume that pregnancy and childbirth are simply biological processes. Many social factors are intertwined with biological processes, including how a baby is conceived, the experience of pregnancy, the process of giving birth, and the transition to parenthood. For example, historical, cultural, and social norms, which can vary remarkably, influence who should or should not get pregnant (ideal age or importance of marital status); who should impregnate a woman (the qualifications necessary for a spouse or partner); conditions and habits of the pregnant woman (what foods or beverages she should or should not consume); the degree of medical intervention appropriate to deliver a baby (whether a baby is born in a hospital or at home); and what a baby is fed (breast milk or formula). How we conceive children, give birth to them, and care for them are highly influenced by social contexts. The following is an illustration.

Childbirth

Children are born every minute in all parts of the world. However, what may be considered normal, healthy, and appropriate childbirth practices in one time or place may be viewed as dangerous or barbaric in another. Even something as routine as the position a woman gives birth in—laying down on her back or squatting—reflects the relationship between social norms and social structure. As feminist theorists point out, the medical establishment, the economic system, the political culture, and the degree of technological sophistication all play a part in defining something as intimate as a woman giving birth. The beliefs and practices of providers, insurers, hospital administrators, and medical staff play a role in influencing childbirth choices (Davis-Floyd 2004; McCool and Simeone 2002).

The Medicalization of Childbirth Until the nineteenth century childbirth was considered largely "women's business," attended to by mothers, sisters, friends, and a midwife, if one was available. **Midwives** are attendants who are trained to help women give birth (Litoff 1978). Doctors were generally absent because childbirth was not considered a medical event. Midwives believe that for most women childbirth is a normal part of life and their job is to help women do what they innately already know how to do.

By the middle of the nineteenth century, obstetricians seeking to develop the medical specialization of obstetrics worked to eliminate midwives (Dawley 2003; Marland and Rafferty 2005). To achieve their professional dominance, physicians began claiming that childbirth was inherently dangerous, required medical assistance, and that midwives were inadequately trained to deal with the complex nature of delivering babies (Borst 1995; Sullivan and Weitz 1988). Their desire to eliminate midwives had little to do with the safety of birth itself, but was due to professional turf battles. Midwives, particularly those who were immigrant, poor, or black were accused of being ignorant, dirty, and dangerous, despite data from the early 1900s indicating that maternal mortality rates were two to three times higher among women who were attended by physicians than among women attended by midwives.

As social class and race were drawn into the debate, one's choice in birth attendant was considered an element of social prestige—having a white upper-class male attendant was considered far more prestigious than being attended to by a minority or working-class female attendant. In her book *In Labor: Women and Power in the Birthplace*, Barbara Katz Rothman (1991) suggests that with the rise of the medical model, male physicians gained tremendous status, all but eliminating other health care providers, including midwives. In 1915, the *Boston Medical and Surgical Journal* reported that midwives were "inconsistent with the methods and ideals of civilization and of medical science in this country" (p. 785).

As providers shifted, so did the role of women in childbirth. Instead of being largely in control, women surrendered to the power and authority of doctors. Wealthy women were the first to flock to male doctors for childbirth, lured in large part by the promise of new technology and painkillers. In the early 1900s the German method of "twilight sleep" was introduced in the United States; a combination of morphine for pain relief and scopolamine and amnesiac that caused women to have no memories of giving birth (Rooks 1997). Because it was difficult to apply technology to childbirth in the home, births were moved to a hospital. By 1900, physicians in hospital settings were attending approximately one-half of births in the United States, largely along social class lines (Dawley 2003; Germano and Bernstein 1997; Rooks 1997). By 1970 virtually all births occurred in hospitals, usually attended by physicians. With this change of venue, birth shifted from being a normal, home-based event to a hospital-based and sickness-oriented experience (McCool and Simeone 2002). As Barbara Katz Rothman (1991) reminds us:

> The first thing to remember is that obstetrics is a surgical specialty. The management of childbirth within hospitals is essentially the same as the management of any other surgical event. . . . In surgery, the ideology of technology is dominant. Perhaps more clearly than anywhere else in medicine, the body is a machine, the doctor a mechanic.

In hospitals, women routinely had their pubic areas shaved, were strapped down to cold metal labor and delivery tables, were given enemas to empty the bowels, were hooked up to IVs and external fetal heart monitors that limit a laboring woman's mobility, and were given episiotomies (cutting through the perineum toward the anus to enlarge the vaginal opening).

Childbirth Today Childbirth in the United States is at a crossroads today (Davis-Floyd 2004; McCool and Simeone 2002). Americans are taking a new look at midwifery, in part fueled by the decline in the number of physicians who will deliver babies. Today about 8 percent of births are attended by a midwife, up from only 1 percent in 1975 (Martin et al. 2006). One study of 88 pregnant women found that those women who selected a midwife for a birth attendant reported feeling more knowledgeable about birth attendants, more in control over the attendant decision, more satisfied about their delivery decisions, more in control of and satisfied with pain medication decisions, more autonomous in their pregnancy decision making, more in agreement with "alternative birth" philosophies, and less in agreement with "conventional birth" philosophies (Galotti et al. 2000).

Like many European nations, some Americans are also questioning whether technological intervention is always needed to deliver healthy babies. Medical technology can indeed save lives; however, it is not without emotional, financial, and physical costs. Millions of Americans die or are seriously injured because of unnecessary surgeries and medical procedures. Research suggests that a low-technology approach can have more favorable results for both mother and baby than a high-technology approach for low-risk women (women who are not diabetic, having twins, or other identified fetal or maternal health problems) (Chamberlain et al. 1997; Davidson 2002). A *New England Journal of Medicine* study of 15 cases in which physicians sought court orders to force cesarean deliveries on mothers who disagreed with their diagnosis, found that six mothers delivered healthy babies vaginally. The remaining nine women were forced to have cesareans, so researchers cannot tell whether these operations were unnecessary as well (Kolder et al. 1987).

At the same time, elements of the medicalization of childbirth may be as fierce as ever. Today, 92 percent of U.S. births still occur in hospitals attended to by physicians (Martin et al. 2006). Some medical interventions remain routine, depending on hospital policy. Forty percent of women have an episiotomy (Robinson et al. 2000) and most women are hooked up to IVs, fetal heart monitors, and receive drugs to relieve some

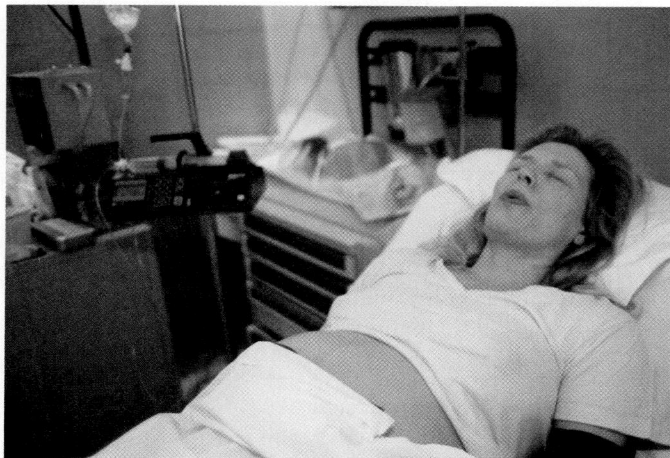

Most women have babies in a hospital (*above*). Few American women have their babies at home, but those that do are pleased with the more personal approach, the less invasive procedures, and the impressive safety record (*below*).

element of pain (which also numb the body). The rate of cesarean delivery increased to over 30 percent of all births in the United States in 2005, the highest rate ever reported, and the highest in the world (Hamilton et al. 2006). An increasing number of cesareans are elective surgery, arranged for the convenience of the mother or the physician (see Chapter 15). The World Health Organization (WHO) and the National Institutes of Health argue that many of these are medically unnecessary and do not improve infant or maternal mortality statistics (Martin 2006).

In recent years families have demanded that hospital policies and the hospital environment change so that a mother's needs take on a greater focus. Many hospitals have responded to requests to make their birthing rooms more personal and homelike and less sterile and cold. A woman can write her own birth plan, she may be able to labor in water, she may no longer be transferred to a different room between labor and delivery, and she may be able to have more free use of alternative positions for delivery. However, the medical approach is still apparent compared with birth in western Europe or other industrial nations: IVs, episiotomies, and fetal heart monitoring are the norm in the United States (Davis-Floyd 2004; Marland and Rafferty 2005).

Some families are seeking an approach further removed from the medical model. **Birth centers** are freestanding facilities, usually with close access to, but not affiliated with a hospital. Childbirth can be attended to by midwives, physicians, or naturopathic doctors. Birth centers usually present a homelike setting and offer clients a greater degree of autonomy to decide the conditions surrounding the birth, while at the same time offering a degree of medical security that many couples find appealing. However, insurance companies are less likely to cover births within a birthing center, as compared to a hospital.

A small segment of the population is opting for home births, attended to by midwives or naturopath physicians. One study found that 91 percent of women who had their last baby at home said that they would prefer to have their next baby at home. Among those who had experienced both a home birth and a hospital birth, 76 percent preferred the home birth. With skilled attendants present, women with low-risk pregnancies have outcomes at least as safe at home as in hospitals (England and Horowitz 1998; Johnson and Daviss 2005; Sullivan and Beeman 1983). One study, which matched 1,046 hospital births with 1,046 home births, found that women giving birth in a hospital were five times more likely to have high blood pressure in labor, nine times more likely to have a severe perineal tear, three times more likely to have a postpartum hemorrhage, and three times more likely to have had a cesarean section. Serious repercussions arose for the babies as well. Babies born in a hospital were six times more likely to have had fetal distress before birth, four times more likely to have needed assistance to start breathing, and four times more likely to have developed an infection. There were no birth injuries at home, but 30 infants in the hospital suffered injuries from their birth (cited in England and Horowitz 1998).

The Transition to Parenthood

The birth of a child is one of the most significant life events. People plan in anticipation, yet the transition to parenthood can be surprisingly difficult. In the past when extended families were more common, grandparents, aunts, and uncles all could help teach new parents how to parent a child. For example, they could help a woman learn to breastfeed, which can also be surprisingly challenging. They could offer sage advice about dealing with a colicky baby, and they could teach a parent how to hold or swaddle his or her child, how to get the baby to sleep through the night, or even how to correctly change a diaper. These things are not innate; they must be learned. How do new parents learn these things today, when extended family may not be around? Many new and expecting parents turn to advice books, such as the best-selling books, *What to Expect When You're Expecting* (Murkoff et al. 2002) or *What to Expect the First Year* (Murkoff et al. 2003), the series of advice books by Dr. Sears that emphasize attachment parenting (Sears and Sears 2001), or the book by La Leche League International advocating breastfeeding, *The Womanly Art of Breastfeeding* (La Leche League International 2004). These books have helped calm the nerves of many new parents, but the books are not without their critics. Some believe that they do more harm than good by promoting their own opinions as a gold standard; in other words, a woman *must* breastfeed, a baby *must* co-sleep with parents, babies *must* not be allowed to cry else the child will grow up emotionally disadvantaged in some critical way. The truth most likely is that there are multiple ways of raising healthy, happy, and well-adjusted children.

New parents are often shocked with the amount of "work" involved in taking care of an infant (Fox et al. 2000; Walzer 1998). As one new father said, "I mean, if I'm watching him during the day—she's at work—forget about doing anything. It's constant attention. You can't read, you can't study, you can't paint, you can't do anything. You really got to sit there and watch him" (Walzer 1998; 24).

The "pop" literature is full of survival "how-to" books, such as *Life After Birth: What Even Your Friends Won't Tell You about Motherhood* (Figes and Zimmerman 2001), *Mother Shock: Loving Every (Other) Minute of It* (Buchanan 2003), *Sippy Cups Are Not for Chardonnay: And Other Things I Had To Learn As a New Mom* (Wilder and Taylor 2006), and *PopCulture: The Sane Man's Guide to the Insane World of New Fatherhood* (Healy 2006).

Sociologist Alice Rossi suggested why the transition to parenthood can be so challenging, comparing the adoption of the parent role to that of other adult roles, such as becoming a spouse. She explains (Rossi 1968):

- Pronatalist sentiment may pressure people to become parents even though they may not really want to or be ready to parent. However, once a baby is born, there is little or no chance to change one's mind about parenthood.
- Most parents have little or no previous experience in child care. They must quickly learn how to care for a completely dependent human being.
- Becoming a parent is abrupt, unlike other adult roles. Expecting a baby is not the same thing as having one. New parents are suddenly on duty 24 hours a day, 7 days a week.

- The transition to parenthood necessitates complex changes in the couple's relationship. Activities become more instrumental, and the division of labor becomes more sex based. The brunt of the workload and lifestyle changes falls on the woman.

However, it is important to recognize differences among groups and situations. Several factors mediate the challenges faced by new parents. These factors include the child's temperament, the parents' expectations about their child and the assistance they would receive from kin, their marital adjustment and communication skills, the father's parenting behavior, whether the baby was planned, and the sex of the child (Bouchard et al. 2006; Cox et al. 1999; Knoester and Eggebeen 2006; Mulsow et al. 2002). For most parents, after the initial disruption, satisfaction and happiness resume, and couples generally do well (Demo and Cox 2000).

Sex Differences in the Transition to Parenthood

Few would disagree that women and men have different experiences as they transition into parenthood. Nonetheless, we know far more about how women are changed by becoming parents than we know about men.

In most families, babies spend considerably more time with their mothers than their fathers, even when both parents work outside the home. As will be shown in Chapter 10, women retain the bulk of child care responsibilities, and this is particularly true when a child is an infant and may be nursing. With half of mothers with children under the age of 1 in the labor force, work-family stress is a serious problem for many women.

However, as sociologist Susan Walzer explains, the transition to parenthood is far more than just a matter of the logistics of juggling work and family. Her study with 25 couples who recently had a baby revealed that the images of what it takes to be a "good" mother or "good" father are socially constructed and inextricably linked with views about gender. Parenthood is a vivid example of "doing gender." She writes (1998):

> "Mother" and "father" are social categories that existed before the individuals I interviewed became parents—or were born. These social categories have particular meanings attached to them—meanings that are socializing influences on new parents and that are institutionalized in cultural imagery associated with motherhood and fatherhood. . . . New parents are channeled toward differentiation by social arrangements, and especially by cultural imagery that constructs what it means to be a "good" mother or father, wife or husband, woman or man. (p. 7)

These images set up a difficult situation for women because the image of a *good mother* is one who is always there and available for her child, yet the image of a *good woman* is to work and have a career. Balancing these two cultural images that are at odds with each other is exceedingly difficult to do. Men do not face this contradiction in roles. An employed father who does minimal caregiving tasks may still be perceived as a devoted, involved, and good father. If a mother works outside the home, she and her husband usually frame her employment as something that should only minimally interfere with her mothering.

Walzer suggests that mothers and fathers think about babies in different ways, and they analyze their thoughts so that they fit the culturally appropriate image of "good" mothers and fathers. Mothers are expected to expend considerably more mental energy on their babies than do men. For examples, mothers worry more about their babies (and they worry about the way they are perceived by others), they buy and read the self-help books, they process the information and then translate it to instruct their husbands or partners, and they manage and orchestrate child care and the division of household labor.

Social Policy and Family Resilience

The transition to parenthood is a challenge for most families, and the challenge is exacerbated by family policies that seemingly fail to recognize the structural pressures associated with a new baby. One of these pressures involves time, including the ability to take time off from work when having a baby.

Author Judith Warner, in her book, *Perfect Madness: Motherhood in the Age of Anxiety* (2005) describes the assistance available to her as a new mother living in France[1]:

> I was living in France, a country that has an astounding array of benefits for families—and for mothers in particular. When my children were born, I stayed in the hospital for five comfortable days. I found a nanny through a free, community-based referral service, then employed her, legally and full-time, for a cost to me of about $10,500 a year, after tax breaks. My elder daughter, from the time she was eighteen months, attended excellent part-time preschools, where she painted and played with modeling clay and ate cookies and napped for about $150 per month—the top end of the fee scale. She could have started public school at age three, and could have opted to stay until 5 P.M. daily. My friends who were covered by the French social security system (which I did not pay into), had even greater benefits: at least four months of paid maternity leave, the right to stop working for up to three years and have jobs held for them, cash grants, after their second children were born, starting at about $105 per month.
>
> And that was just the beginning. There was more: a culture. An atmosphere. A set of deeply held attitudes toward motherhood—toward adult womanhood—that had the effect of allowing me to have two children, work in an office, work out in a gym, and go out to dinner at night and away for a short vacation with my husband without ever hearing, without ever thinking, the word "guilt." (pp. 9–10)

She later presents a jolting contrast after she returns to the United States:

> I knew what had worked for me in France. It wasn't just that I had access to a slew of government-run or subsidized support services; it was also that I'd had a whole unofficial network of people to help and support me—materially and emotionally—as I navigated the new world of motherhood. There was the midwife who'd appeared as if by magic on day four in the hospital to offer tissues as I succumbed to the tears of the "baby blues," and who'd said matter-of-factly, "Everything is coming out now. Blood, milk, tears. You have to let it flow."
>
> There was my local pharmacist who, unasked, filled my shopping bag with breast pads. The pediatrician who answered his own phone. The network of on-call doctors who made house calls at any time of the day or night. The public elementary school principal who gave us a personal tour of her school and encouraged us to call her if we had any questions. In short, an extended community of people who'd guaranteed that I was never, from the moment I became a mother onward, left to fend for myself alone. (pp. 30–31)

What is the impact of this collectivist orientation? The French receive a great deal of government assistance when they have a baby. This assistance begins early in the child's life, made possible by the existence of three kinds of parent leaves: 16 weeks of paid maternity leave for the mother; 11 days of paid paternity leave for the father; up to 3 years of unpaid leave for either parent with their job guaranteed (provided they have been on the job for at least 1 year) (Embassy of France 2006).

Example: Maternity and Family Leaves

The United States has by far the least generous maternity and family leave policy of any nation. Other countries have long recognized that working families also need to tend to their children and other family members. Rather than seeing work-family balance in a

[1]From *Perfect Madness: Motherhood in the Age of Anxiety* by Judith Warner, copyright © 2005 by Judith Warner. Used by permission of Riverhead Books, an imprint of Penguin Group (USA) Inc.

BOX 9.3 Social Policies for Families

Family and Medical Leave Act

The Family and Medical Leave Act is the closest thing the United States has to the extensive family leave policies found in other industrialized nations.

1. *What is the Family and Medical Leave Act?* The Family and Medical Leave Act (FMLA) is a federal law that provides unpaid, job-protected leave to eligible employees, both male and female, to care for their families or themselves for specified family and medical conditions. FMLA provides eligible employees with up to 12 work weeks of unpaid leave in a 12-month period for the birth, adoption, or foster care placement of a child; care of a spouse, son, daughter, or parent with a serious health condition; or their own serious health condition that causes an inability to work. If you qualify and have unused FMLA leave time, your employer cannot deny you FMLA leave.
2. *Which employers are covered by FMLA?* FMLA covers private sector employers with 50 or more employees. Part-time employees are counted toward the 50-employee minimum. Public employers are covered regardless of the number of workers they employ.
3. *Which employees are eligible for FMLA?* To be eligible, an employee must have worked for the employer at least 12 months and at least 1,250 hours within a 12-month period before the leave begins. The employer must employ at least 50 workers at or within 75 miles of the worksite.
4. *What is a "serious health condition" under FMLA?* A "serious health condition" under FMLA includes illness, injury, impairment, or physical or mental condition that involves in-patient care (defined as an overnight stay in a medical facility) and any related incapacity, and continuing treatment by a health care provider that includes at least one of the following:
   a. More than 3 consecutive days of incapacity and any subsequent treatment or period of incapacity related to the same condition that also involves two or more treatments (including examinations) by a health care provider; or one treatment that results in a regimen of continuing treatment using prescription medicine or special equipment under the provider's supervision
   b. Any period of incapacity due to pregnancy even if the treatment is not received during the absence
   c, Any period of incapacity or treatment for a chronic serious health condition requiring periodic treatment even if treatment is not received during the absence
   d. A long-term or permanent period of incapacity
   e. Any period of absence for multiple treatments and recovery from the treatments by a health care provider for restorative sur-

negative light, their policies promote integration of work and family. Strong families are viewed as an important resource. As Canada's former Prime Minister Jean Chretien said

> There is now overwhelming scientific evidence that success in a child's early years is the key to long-term healthy development. Nothing is more important than for parents to be able to spend the maximum amount of time with newborn children in the critical early months of a child's life. Therefore, I am proud to announce today that the government will introduce legislation in this parliament to extend employment insurance maternity and parental benefits from the current maximum of six months to one full year. (cited in Center for Families 2001)

The prime minister is referring to a growing body of research on the benefits that family leaves have for children, their parents, and their parents' employers (Center for Families, Work, and Well-Being 2001; Galtry and Callister 2005; Glass and Riley 1998;

gery or for a condition that would likely result in more than a 3-day period of incapacity if left untreated

If an employee's or family member's illness occurs over a weekend, holiday, or vacation, the "more than 3-consecutive-day period of incapacity" may require only a day or two of FMLA leave from work.

5. *How does an employer confirm a serious health condition?* An employer may require a medical certification that gives medical facts confirming the type of serious health condition. If the certification is for the employee's own serious health condition, it may require information on the employee's inability to perform essential job functions. An employer may require additional medical opinions at the employer's expense.
6. *How much leave can be taken at one time?* FMLA leave can be taken all at once (12 work weeks); 1 week; or 1 day at a time; on an intermittent basis in small blocks of time for a single qualifying condition; or on a reduced schedule of usual hours. Intermittent and reduced schedule leave can be used for the birth, adoption, or foster care placement of a child only if the employer agrees to it.
7. *What benefits does an employee receive during FMLA leave?* Benefits such as group health insurance coverage must be maintained during FMLA leave under the same terms and conditions as if the employer was working. Copayments normally paid by the employee when working can be required. A worker has a right to all benefits as provided during other forms of paid or unpaid leave and to benefit changes.
8. *What are an employee's rights upon returning from FMLA leave?* An employee must be returned to the same job or an equivalent job held before leave began with the same pay, benefits, and other terms and conditions of employment. All benefits such as group health coverage must be maintained upon return to work as if the employee had not taken leave. On return from leave, vacation based on hours of work can be affected.

Source: ChicagoLegalNet.com 2003.

CRITICAL THINKING QUESTIONS

1. It took the United States until 1993 to pass the FMLA, which provides only unpaid leave to certain qualified workers. Why did it take this long? Why is the FMLA less generous than the leave available in other countries? Who would oppose the FMLA—and why? Who would support it? Why?
2. Why did working families have difficulty mobilizing for an expanded or more generous leave policy?

Ruhm 1998). Long leaves are associated with better maternal health, vitality and role function, and lower rates of infant mortality. Moreover, women are likely to breast feed for longer periods if they have extended leave benefits. The benefits of longer parental leaves also extend to employers. Women are more likely to return to work after childbirth in those countries that have more lengthy leaves. It is more cost-effective to develop a well-planned parental leave policy than it is to rehire and retrain new employees.

What type of family leave policy exists in the United States? Despite the benefits of family leaves for all involved, the United States has been relatively slow to act (Wisensale 2001). Congress passed the **Family Medical Leave Act (FMLA)** in 1993. It requires employers with over 50 employees working for them (within a 75-mile radius) to provide 12 weeks of *unpaid* leave to eligible employees (both men and women) to care for themselves or their immediate families with specified medical conditions. Conditions include childbirth or

TABLE 9.3 **Maternity Leave Benefits, 2004**

	Length of Maternity Leave	Percentage of Wages Paid in Covered Period	Source
Developing Nations			
Bangladesh	12 weeks	100	Employer
Bulgaria	135 days	90	Social Security
Bolivia	60 days	100 of min wages + 70 of wages	Social Security
China	90 days	100	Employer
Cuba	18 weeks	100	Social Security
Egypt	50 days	100	Employer
India	12 weeks	100	Social Security/ Employer
Iran	90 days	67	Social Security
Iraq	62 days	100	Social Security
Mexico	12 weeks	100	Social Security
Morocco	14 weeks	100	Social Security
Nigeria	12 weeks	50	Employer
Vietnam	4–6 months	100	Social Security
Developed Nations			
Canada	17–18 weeks	55 for 15 weeks	Employment Ins
Denmark	18 weeks	90	State
Finland	105 days	70	Social Security
France	16 weeks	100 up to a ceiling	Social Security
Ireland	14 weeks	70 or fixed rate	Social Security
Italy	5 months	80	Social Security
Japan	14 weeks	60	Health Ins/Social Security
Netherlands	16 weeks	100	Unemployment Fund
New Zealand	14 weeks	100 up to a ceiling	State
Spain	16 weeks	100	Social Security
Sweden	14 weeks	390 days—80; 90 days—flat rate	Social Security
Switzerland	8 weeks	80	Social Security
United Kingdom	14–18 weeks	6 weeks—90; flat rate after	Employer
United States	**12 weeks[(1)]**	**0**	**—**

[1]Applies only to workers in companies with 50 or more workers.

Source: Adapted from United Nations Statistical Division 2005.

adoption; care of child, spouse, or parent with a serious health condition; or their own serious condition that renders them unable to work. Employees must have worked for the employer at least 1 year or 1,250 hours to be eligible for FMLA. Employers in small firms are not required to offer leaves at all. Details about FMLA are outlined in Box 9.3 (pages 300 and 301).

However, in reality, few people can afford to take unpaid leave. Therefore many come back to work shortly after their short-term disability, vacation, or sick pay has been exhausted. In a survey about the use and impact of family and medical leave, 34 percent of workers said they needed, but did not take leave (Commission on Family and Medical Leave 1996). Lower-educated and minority women are least likely to take leave after giving birth, probably because they cannot afford to (U.S. Census Bureau 2006).

In contrast to the United States:

- Japan offers 14 weeks of paid leave at 60 percent of a worker's salary.
- Denmark offers 18 weeks of paid maternity leave at 90 percent of a worker's salary.
- Spain offers 16 weeks of leave at 100 percent of a worker's salary.
- Switzerland provides 8 weeks at 80 percent of salary. (United Nations Statistics Division 2005)

Parental leave is also far more generous in poor or developing nations than it is in the United States, as shown in Table 9.3. Even in Bangladesh, one of the poorest nations on earth, women who work in *qualifying jobs* receive 12 weeks of maternity leave, paid at 100 percent of salary. Mexico offers 12 weeks of maternity leave at 100 percent of salary. In Iran, women receive 67 percent of their salary for 90 days. Granted, many women—perhaps most women—in poor nations do not work in qualifying jobs because they work as maids, in the fields, or in the underground economy. However, the United States is the only country in the world that does not guarantee any paid leave at all for any of its workers. Families may have vacation or sick pay that they can take, and if lucky, they have paid for short-term disability insurance that may cover 6 weeks of leave after a vaginal birth and 8 weeks of leave following a birth by cesarean section. However, because the leave is "disability" related, it would not provide any leave time for men or for mothers of children who are adopted and is only available to those who paid for this special insurance coverage in advance.

California is an example of a state taking matters into their own hands because of federal inaction (Hunsberger 2007). Families can have up to 6 weeks of paid leave at 55 percent of a worker's pay—up to $882 a week—while they care for family needs. Since the program was created, about 400,000 Californians have received claims averaging $465 a week. This is fewer than expected, perhaps because few people can live on only 55 percent of their pay. Nonetheless, California's program is a start, and other states, including Oregon and Washington, are following it closely (Hunsberger 2007).

Conclusion

This chapter introduced issues surrounding fertility in the United States and beyond. It also revealed that seemingly personal issues such as whether, when, who, and how to have a baby represent a complex intertwining of biological and social forces. Values, such as pronatalism, shape attitudes and behaviors. Political, religious, economic, health care, and other social institutions also shape family life, including fertility, pregnancy, adoption, childbirth, and transitioning to parenthood—dimensions of family life that many see as exceedingly personal. China, as the most extreme case, accepts a level of governmental policy that many around the world deem highly intrusive. Nonetheless, all countries have family policies, and those in the United States often minimize the connection between social structure (macro) and the lived experience (micro) of individual families. Compared to other nations, Americans are often expected to fend for themselves, as is the case with maternity and family leaves.

Key Terms

Assisted reproductive technology (ART): All fertility treatments in which both egg and sperm are handled. (p. 287)

Birth centers: Freestanding facilities, usually with close access to, but not affiliated with a hospital; childbirth is approached as a normal, healthy process. (p. 296)

Closed adoption: All identifying information is sealed and unavailable to all parties. (p. 289)

Death rates: Measures of the number of deaths for a given population. (p. 274)

Direct financial costs: Out-of-pocket expenses for things such as food, clothing, housing, and education. (p. 282)

Family Medical Leave Act (FMLA): Governmental act that requires employers with over 50 employees working for them (within a 75-mile radius) to provide 12 weeks of unpaid leave to eligible employees (both men and women) to care for themselves or their immediate families with specified medical conditions. (p. 301)

Fertility rates: Average number of children born to a woman during her lifetime (total); number of children born per 1,000 women aged 15–49 (refined); or number of children born per 1,000 population (crude). (p. 274)

Infertility: The inability to conceive a child. (p. 287)

Midwives: Attendants trained to help women give birth and who believe that childbirth is a normal part of life. (p. 294)

One-child policy: (1) Advocating delayed marriage and delayed childbearing; (2) advocating fewer and healthier births; and (3) advocating one child per couple, with a few exceptions for special circumstances. (p. 278)

Open adoptions: Involves direct contact between the biological and adoptive parents. (p. 289)

Opportunity costs: Lost opportunities for income by working only part-time or not at all because of children. (p. 282)

Private adoptions: Arranged directly between adoptive parents and the biological birth mother, usually through the assistance of an attorney. (p. 288)

Pronatalism: A cultural value that encourages childbearing. (p. 273)

Public adoptions: Occur through licensed public agencies. (p. 288)

Semi-open adoptions: Biological and adoptive families exchange personal information through a social worker or attorney, but have no direct contact. (p. 289)

Resources on the Internet

Alan Guttmacher Institute
www.guttmacher.org
This website offers information on reproductive issues, family planning, teenage pregnancy, and other issues in fertility. The Alan Guttmacher Institute publishes a bimonthly periodical called *Family Planning Perspectives*, a scholarly review of research and policy.

Resolve: The National Infertility Association
www.resolve.org
Resolve is an organization dedicated to providing information and support to people who are experiencing infertility, and general public education and advocacy. It provides information about medical treatment, adoption, and child-free living.

National Adoption Information Clearinghouse
www.calib.com/naic/index.cfm
Congress established the National Adoption Information Clearinghouse (NAIC) in 1987 to provide free information on all aspects of adoption. The mission of the clearinghouse is to connect professionals and concerned citizens to timely and well-balanced information on programs, research, legislation, and statis-

tics regarding the safety, permanency, and well-being of children and families.

Population Reference Bureau
www.prb.org
The Population Reference Bureau (PRB) offers timely information about world population statistics and trends. Topics include education, employment, fertility, family planning, health, income, marriage and family, youth, and aging.

Further Reading

Becker, G. 2000. *The Elusive Embryo: How Women and Men Approach Reproductive Technology*. Berkeley: University of California Press.

Carey, W. B. 1997. *Understanding Your Child's Temperament*. New York: Macmillan.

Cowen, C. P., and P. A. Cowen. 2000. *When Partners Become Parents: The Big Life Change for Couples*. Mahwah, NJ: Erlbaum.

Ehrlich, P. 1997. *The Population Explosion*. New York: Buccaneer Books.

England, P., and R. Horowitz. 1998. *Birthing from Within*. Albuquerque, NM: Partera Press.

Hertz, R. 2006. *Single by Chance, Mothers By Choice: How Single Women Are Choosing Parenthood Without Marriage and Creating the New American Family*. New York: Oxford University Press.

Hewlett, S., N. Rankin, and C. West. (Eds.). 2002. *Taking Parenting Public: The Case for a New Social Movement*. Lanham, MD: Rowman and Littlefield.

Luker, K. 1997. *Dubious Conceptions: The Politics of Teenage Pregnancy*. Cambridge, MA: Harvard University Press.

Martin, A. 1993. *The Lesbian and Gay Parenting Handbook: Creating and Raising Our Families*. New York: HarperPerennial.

Wagner, M. 2006. *Born in the USA: How a Broken Maternity System Must Be Fixed to Put Women and Children First*. Berkeley: University of California Press.

Walzer, S. 1998. *Thinking About the Baby: Gender and Transitions into Parenthood*. Philadelphia, PA: Temple University Press.

Wisensale, S. K. 2001. *Family Leave Policy: The Political Economy of Work and Family*. New York: M. E. Sharpe.

CHAPTER 10

Raising Children

Chapter Outline

Comparative Focus on Childhood and Parenting
Socialization
Parenting Styles and Practices
Parenting Contexts
Social Policy and Family Resilience
Conclusion
Key Terms
Resources on the Internet
Further Reading

CHAPTER PREVIEW

What does it mean to be a mother, a father, a parent? How are these roles different from one another? This chapter explains that mothering and fathering encompass the emotional, physical, and financial work involved with caring for children; however, these identities and the roles associated with mothering and fathering are in large part socially constructed. In this chapter you will learn:

- Differences and similarities across cultures with regard to parenting
- Three theoretical approaches regarding the socialization of children
- The importance of several agents of socialization
- How socialization occurs across social class, race, ethnicity, and gender
- "Mothering" and "fathering" concepts, roles, and expectations differ
- The unique characteristics of specific parenting contexts, including teenage parents, single parents, cohabiting parents, gay and lesbian parents, and grandparents raising grandchildren
- Parents in the United States receive less financial help from the government than is the case for parents in many other developed countries—for example, have you ever heard of a "family allowance"?

How does child rearing today differ from the past? As historian John Demos tells us, "Egalitarianism formed no part of seventeenth-century assumptions about the proper relationship between parents and children. But at Plymouth, Massachusetts, this relationship involved a set of reciprocal obligations. From the standpoint of the child, the Biblical commandment to honor thy father and mother was fundamental—and the force of law stood behind it. The relevant statute directed that 'If any Child or Children above sixteen years old, and of competent Understanding, shall Curse or Smite their Natural Father or Mother, he or they shall be put to Death, unless it can be sufficiently testified that the Parents have been very Unchristianly negligent in the Education of such Children, or so provoked them by extreme and cruel Correction, that they have been forced thereunto, to preserve themselves from Death or Maiming.' A corollary order prescribed similar punishment for behavior that was simply 'Stubborn or Rebellious'—or indeed, for any sort of habitual disobedience.

But if the child owed his parents an unceasing kind of obedience and respect, there were other obligations that applied in the reverse direction. The parent for his or her part must accept responsibility for certain basic needs of his or her children—for their physical health and welfare, for their education (understood in the broadest sense), and for the property they would require one day to 'be for themselves.' There were, moreover, legal provisions permitting the community to intervene in the case of parents who defaulted on these obligations. Parents who neglected any of these were subject to fines; and once again the ultimate recourse of transferring children into new families might be applied if the neglect were habitual." (Adapted from Demos 1970, 100–105)

Parenthood may be universal, but the act of *parenting* is highly variable. As discussed in Chapter 3, prior to the eighteenth century little attention was given to children's needs as we think of them today. Parenting was adult centered; if a child did not contribute to the parents' welfare, then he or she could simply be abandoned.

Today parents spend a great deal of time reflecting on what is in the best interest of children and are concerned about ways to enhance their social and emotional well-being. Many parents worry about the "right" type of child care, the "right" type of discipline, the "right" type of food. "Right" is now defined as not only what works for the parent, but also what is best for the child.

This chapter examines the empirical research and theoretical perspectives surrounding raising children. We will see that child-rearing values and behaviors are embedded in larger macro-level social structures.

Comparative Focus on Childhood and Parenting

Like historical events, culture also has important effects on parenting attitudes and practices (Parke and Buriel 1998). Levine suggests that there are three universal parenting goals: (1) ensuring physical health and survival; (2) developing behavioral capacities for economic maintenance; and (3) instilling behavioral capacities for maximizing cultural values such as morality, prestige, and achievement (1977, 1988). However, the emphasis placed on these three goals may differ cross-culturally, as well as how the goals are implemented. This may be due to divergent cultural values, but these goals also reflect larger macro structural forces operating in society, such as poverty or racism. Box 10.1 introduces a **transnational family**—defined as a family divided between two nations—who straddles the United States and Honduras because of the abject poverty in their home country (Schmalzbauer 2004). The need for survival wages forces many parents to live away from their children, with repercussions for both children and adults. Other women, such as grandmothers, aunts, sisters, or oldest daughters, must step in and care for the children while the parents live thousands of miles away. *Other-mothering* is central in the history of poor communities throughout the world (Aranda 2003; Schmalzbauer 2004).

Garcia-Coll (1990) surveyed the literature on the relationship between cultural beliefs and parenting and concluded that parenting attitudes and practices depend to a large extent on the type of tasks or competencies that members of society are expected to have. For example, if a culture expects adults to be economically self-supporting, parenting attitudes and tasks will likely involve fostering individual achievement in their children through school or sport; involve teaching children about handling money through an allowance or some similar means; and may encourage children to learn about the world of work through part-time jobs or in other ways contributing to the family economy. Other cultures that stress economic cooperation would approach parenting differently. Why would parents try to foster individual achievement in their children if a culture does not particularly value that trait? In fact, individual achievement could be detrimental to the group as a whole.

In some cultures, parents (particularly mothers) and their children sleep together on a regular basis for many years. An American woman visiting Yoruba West Africa describes her surprise at cultural differences in family sleep patterns:

> I quickly discovered there weren't any cribs in this compound. In fact, there weren't any cradles, bassinets, infant seats, or walkers. Babies (any child under three) were either being carried on their mother's back, playing at her feet, or sleeping with her on a mat. My questions concerning bedtime and night feedings were met with confusion. Babies slept when they were tired and rolled from their mother's back to her breast when they were hungry. Mothers hardly stirred in their sleep while babies fed. There weren't any issues about bedtime and night feeding. They were amazed when I explained that in our country babies were placed in cribs or cradles to sleep. When I clarified that the apparatus was frequently set in another room, away from the mother, they were horrified. They couldn't imagine banishing a baby to another room, away from its mother. . . . My life with the Yoruba taught me that many of our most firm child-rearing rules are based on cultural preferences rather than fact. Who is to say whether babies should sleep alone in cribs or on mats with their mothers? (Kurchinka 1998)

What do the U.S. preferences and beliefs in this example tell us about our culture? The United States values the separateness of children and parents to a larger degree than in other cultures; for instance, most young children spend significant time with paid caregivers; adolescent children's reference group is peer oriented rather than family oriented; young adult children choose their own mates; and adult children prefer to live separately

BOX 10.1 Our Global Community

Searching for Wages and Mothering from Afar: The Case of Honduran Transnational Families

Millions of mothers and fathers have made a dangerous trek to the United States in search of work, often forced to leave their own children behind in their home country. This is a story of Rosalie, a mother of five, and her struggle to keep her family "together" as they live thousands of miles apart.

Rosalia is a Honduran mother of five. She has been in the United States for 6 years and came to the United States on a tourist visa as part of a religious delegation. Her family's situation in Honduras was dire. She was working part-time managing the upkeep of a local church while her husband Ernesto worked as a bus driver. However, even with both of them working, they were barely scraping by, and the opportunities for mobility, especially for their children, appeared severely limited. They had talked for years about making the risky trip to the north to the United States to seek a better future. Rosalia's church trip proved the perfect opportunity. When the religious delegation was over, she slipped away to the house of a Honduran friend in Boston, with whom she stayed while working a patchwork of jobs to save money to bring her husband and children across the border.

Now, after 3 years of hard work, Rosalia has paid for her husband Ernesto and three youngest children's illegal journey to the United States. Her two oldest children, Magda and Franklin, remain in Honduras. They make do without their mother and father, for the most part understanding their parents' need to go north and the logic of bringing only the youngest children who could still benefit from a U.S. education. Franklin drives a taxi. He harbors some anger toward his parents for leaving, but remains committed to their family. On his slim income alone, Magda and Franklin would not be able to meet even their most basic needs, yet with the financial help they receive from their parents, they are able to get by. They have paid off the family's debts and they recently bought a refrigerator for the kitchen and a television, which, when they can get it to work, allows them to bond with their parents and siblings by watching the same *telenovelas*. Rosalia and Ernesto's family has not been together for 6 years, but they try to maintain closeness via weekly phone calls and a shared understanding that being apart is the only way for them to make ends meet.

The family of Rosalie is typical of many families who, because of severe financial hardship and limited opportunities, have transnationalized, negotiating the economic opportunities of two nations to sustain themselves and to pursue their hopes for a better future. Although divided by thousands of miles and by politics and culture, many transnational families maintain close ties across the distance. However, emotional struggle is a daily part of life. Parents express the greatest distress about trying to maintain connections with children who were very young when they left. Young children have difficulty understanding why their parent(s) had to leave, and they often do not remember the parent well. Going home to visit is a dangerous proposition, and visits can be confusing for children and painful for everyone upon departure.

Thousands of miles and a heavily guarded border prevent parents from taking care of their children, while the politics and legal mandates of immigration make it impossible for most families to know if their reunification will be possible. However, without transnationalizing, poor families often cannot secure their survival. Millions of families represent a new family form born out of the inequality in the global economy and reproduced by means of dependence on a transnational division of labor.

Source: Adapted from Schmalzbauer 2004.

CRITICAL THINKING QUESTIONS

1. What kinds of jobs do you think Rosalia was able to get when she came to the United States? How much did she earn? Do you think the jobs provided fringe benefits such as health insurance?
2. What should be the response of the United States to illegal immigrants? If they are doing labor that helps the United States or U.S. citizens, should they be allowed to stay? Should they be allowed to bring their families? Should they receive publicly funded services, such as education or health care?
3. How would world systems theory explain the structural circumstances surrounding the rise in transnational families? What additional insights would the feminist theory have to add?

from their aging parents. Other cultures value greater levels of interdependence throughout the life cycle, beginning in infancy.

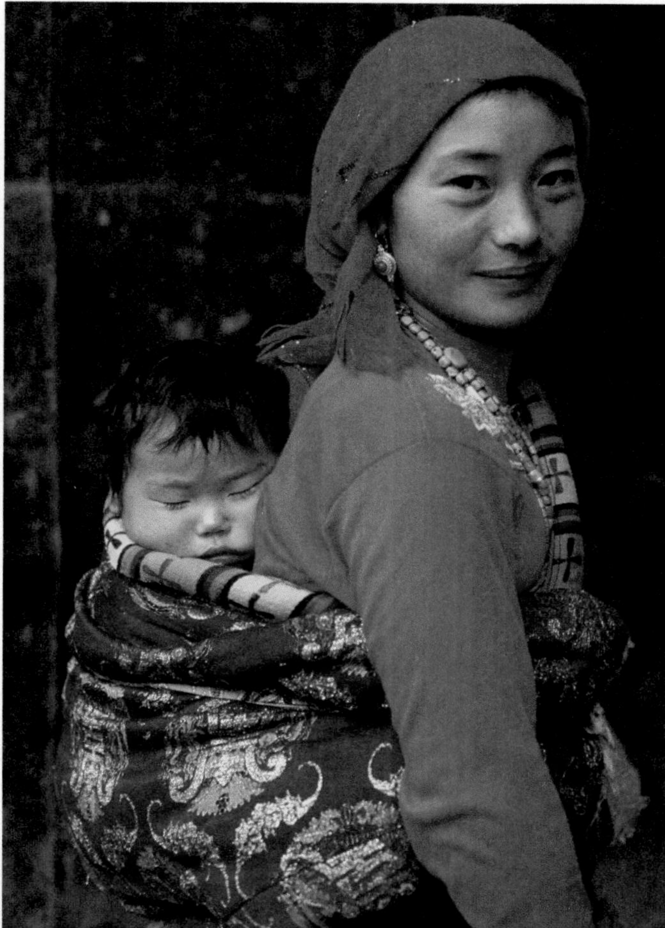

Parenting attitudes and practices reflect cultural expectations about the types of tasks or competencies that members of society are expected to have. Some cultures emphasize interdependence of family members much more than does the United States, and therefore mothers and babies may be inseparable for years.

Recent Trends

Despite these apparent differences, cross-cultural research shows that there are at least three trends with respect to child rearing that exist in both developed and developing countries, according to Bert Adams, a family scholar specializing in international families (Adams 2004; Adams and Trost 2004).

1. Although parents are central to child rearing, other people and social institutions are also involved in raising children, including grandparents and other relatives, day care settings, governmental agencies, schools, and factories. Related to this is the rising tide of women's employment outside the home. Even in historically poor and patriarchal countries such as Bangladesh, increases in women's employment are changing the nature of families, the distribution of spousal power, and the care of children in important ways (Ahmed and Bould 2004).
2. Parents around the world increasingly expect parental permissiveness and child independence. There is a decline in the value placed on obedience to parental authority, and more emphasis placed on independence and personal responsibility. Certainly not all cultures meet these changes with unabashed enthusiasm, but worldwide trends persist nonetheless.
3. A higher value is placed on boys than on girls in most societies in the world. The traditional preference for sons is based on family inheritance and the need for sons to care for aging parents. These values persist in several countries, such as China, Kenya, and India, but in many places the reasons for male preferences are more vague and are simply based on tradition rather than rational economics.

Socialization

Sociologists use the term **socialization** to refer to the lifelong process through which we acquire the cultural values and skills needed to function as human beings and participate in society. Socialization is unique to human beings because children are helpless at birth and have few instincts compared to other animals. Although the debate about how much of human nature is biological and how much is socially produced is not yet answered definitely and perhaps never will be, we do know that socialization is a powerfully complex process that imparts the qualities and cultural traits we think of as human.

Theoretical Approaches

Social psychologists have elaborated on many theories to explain child development and the process of socialization. Three of the more prominent ones are discussed here.

Sigmund Freud and the Psychoanalytic Perspective Sigmund Freud (1856–1939) lived in an era when biological explanations of human behavior were prevalent, as were male dominance and sexual repression. All of these historical and cultural factors influenced his proposition that human behavior and personality originate from unconscious forces within individuals. Freud suggested that human development occurs in three states that reflect different components of the personality. The **id** is the part of the personality that includes biological drives and needs for immediate gratification. The id is present at birth and readily visible in young children; however, this aspect of personality continues throughout our lives. The **ego** is the rational component of personality that attempts to balance the need for immediate gratification with the demands of society. It arises as we become aware that we cannot have all that we desire and that our needs must be balanced with the demands of society. The **superego** is our conscience, which draws upon cultural values and norms to help us understand why we cannot have everything we want.

Jean Piaget and Cognitive Development Jean Piaget (1896–1980) was a Swiss psychologist whose research focused on how people think and understand. He was particularly interested in how children come to understand the world and make meaning of their experiences. He identified four stages of cognitive development that are rooted in biology and based upon age. The first stage, which occurs in the first 18 to 24 months of life, is called the **sensorimotor intelligence**. The infant and toddler understand the world primarily through touch, sucking, listening, and looking. Children begin to organize and exercise some control over their lives. The second stage, **preoperational thought** occurs through age 5 or 6 as children learn language, symbolic play, and symbolic drawing. They do not grasp abstract concepts and their knowledge is tied to their own perceptions. The third stage, **concrete operational thought**, occurs between the ages of 6 and 11 or 12. During this period children begin to see the causal connections in their surroundings and can manipulate categories, classification systems, and hierarchies in groups. The final stage of cognitive development is **formal operational thought**, which begins in adolescence and continues through adulthood. During this stage, children develop capacities for abstract thought and can conceptualize more complex issues or rules that can be used for problem solving.

Charles Horton Cooley and George Herbert Mead: The Self Charles Horton Cooley (1864–1929) and George Herbert Mead (1863–1931) turned attention to a sociological perspective by arguing that a person cannot form a self-concept without social contact with others. A self-concept is not present at birth, but arises from social experience with others. Cooley and Mead minimize Freud's claim of biological drives or Piaget's assertion that humans develop chronologically as they age. Instead, they claim that human behavior and self-identity are shaped by interactions with others and the meanings attached to those interactions. Cooley suggested that we come to see ourselves as others perceive and respond to us, a process he described as the **looking-glass self**. For example, we will see ourselves as thin or heavy, intelligent or less intelligent, as attractive or unattractive, as trustworthy or irresponsible, based on the way that other people perceive and respond to us. Mead extended Cooley's insight in several ways, including the view that social experience includes **symbolic interaction**; we interact not just with words, but also with important symbols and meanings, such as eye contact or a wave of the hand. Mead also elaborated on Cooley's work by focusing on **role taking,** which is the process of mentally assuming the role of another person to understand the world from his or her point of view and to anticipate his or her response to us. This helps us to become self-reflective. Mead suggests that the self is divided into two components: the "I" and the "me." The "I" is the subjective element of the self and represents spontaneity and interaction that we initiate. The "me" is the objective element of self, reflecting the internalized perceptions of others toward us. Both the "I" and the "me" are needed to form the social self. In other words, the feedback loop is critical—we initiate behavior that is ultimately guided by the ways that others see us.

Agents of Socialization

Chapter 4 introduced the various ways persons, groups, or institutions collectively referred to as **agents of socialization**, teach children about the norms and values of their particular culture. These will be briefly recapped here:

- *Family members, particularly parents,* have the greatest impact in socializing children because they provide the first exposure to a particular culture. Parents provide children with a place to live, food to eat, clothes to wear, vocabulary to learn, medical care when sick, and introduce the child to values and customs (Bee and Boyd 2007; Favez et al. 2006. Harding et al. 2005; Loehlin 2005). They also pass on to the child his or her socioeconomic status and social position in terms of race, ethnicity, and religion. These can form a central feature of the child's identity because they affect so many dimensions of social life.
- *Schools and child care* enlarge children's worlds by introducing them to people and settings different from their immediate family. Schools organize and teach children a wide range of knowledge, skills, and customs, including the political ideology of the society. Schools also provide important lessons more covertly, which is sometimes referred to as a *hidden curriculum.* For example, children learn about the value of competition through spelling bees and games at recess (Rouse and Barrow 2006).
- By the time children enter school they are able to form *peer group* relationships without the direct supervision of family members and other adults. Peers usually reward conformity rather than deviations, so children learn to look, dress, talk, and act like others in their group. For example, young people learn which specific clothing styles are popular and which are not. Peers are a powerful agent of socialization and have tremendous influence, particularly during adolescence as young people begin to distance themselves from their parents (Cobb 2007; Garrod et al. 2008).
- *Toys and games* also reflect culture and teach children important messages about what it means to be a member of society. As revealed in Chapter 4, this is vividly seen in the ways in which toys and games inform children about what it means to

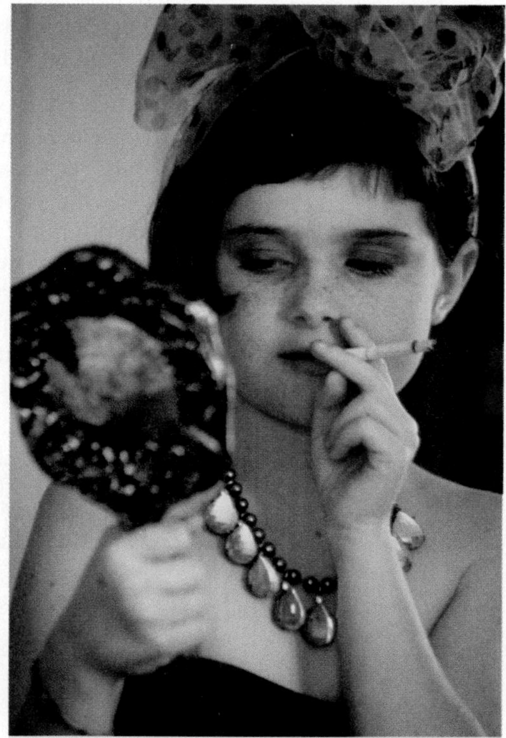

Children imitate those around them, including family, peers, and who they see in the mass media.

be a boy, girl, man, or woman in U.S. culture. Play tends to be sex typed, with toys, games, and peer group play styles differentiated on the basis of sex (Bee and Boyd 2007).

- *The mass media*, especially television, is an increasingly important mechanism for socializing children. Ninety-eight percent of households have at least one television set, a higher percentage than households with telephones. The United States has one of the highest rates of television ownership in the world, with 781 televisions per 1,000 people, compared to 582 per 1,000 people in France, or a worldwide average of 228 (*CIA World Factbook* 2002).

Socialization and Social Class

One of the primary tasks in socialization is to teach children about the culture in which they are growing up. Socioeconomic status greatly affects a child's cultural experiences. Social class position affects how much money parents have to spend on their children, which affects where they live, the quality of schools they will attend, the type of neighbors and friends they will have, the type of clothing they will wear, and the type and amount of toys, hobbies, and enrichment activities they are likely to have. Table 10.1 reveals a linear relationship between income and children's involvement in gifted classes, sports, clubs, and special lessons. The higher the family income, the more likely were children aged 6 to 17 to be involved in extracurricular activities (Lugaila 2003). Participation in these programs is expensive, may require parental involvement, and may necessitate significant preparation time, all of which low-income children may not have (or may have less of).

Social class, however, affects more than just material goods. It also affects the values, norms, and expectations that parents have for their children. It is possible that the lower participation rates of low-income families also represent a different set of core values. Research studies have generally noted the following differences:

- When parents are asked to choose from a list of childhood traits those that they consider most desirable for their children, lower-income parents tend to choose traits such as obedience, conforming, staying out of trouble, and keeping neat and clean. In contrast, higher-income parents tend to choose traits such as creativity, ambition, independence, curiosity, and good judgment.
- Lower-income parents tend to be more controlling, authoritarian, and arbitrary in their discipline and are more apt to use physical punishments, whereas higher-income parents tend to be more democratic and are more receptive to their children's opinions.
- Higher-income parents tend to show more warmth and affection toward their children, talk to them more, and use more complex language than do parents from

TABLE 10.1 Percentages of School-Age Children Enrolled in Extracurricular Activities, by Income

	Ages 6–11			Ages 12–17		
	Sports	Clubs	Lessons	Sports	Clubs	Lessons
Below Poverty Line	16	23	19	25	24	18
100%–199% of Poverty Line	24	27	24	31	30	21
200% or higher	39	41	40	42	40	31

Source: Lugaila 2003.

lower-income families. (Berns 2001; Children's Defense Fund 2005; Kohn et al. 1990; Seccombe 2007b).

Sociologist Melvin Kohn suggested that parents value traits in their children that reflect the parents' world, particularly their world of work (Kohn 1977). Lower-income parents tend to emphasize conformity and related traits because these are ones that will be useful in the working-class jobs that their children are likely to hold in the future. For example, success on an assembly line requires obedience and conformity, not creativity, ambition, or curiosity. Those characteristics could actually sabotage good job performance. In contrast, upper-income parents are likely to have jobs that entail working with people or ideas and involve self-direction and creativity. Upper-income parents value these characteristics and socialize their children to have them. Therefore, it is likely that class differences in socialization reflect not only simple economic resources, but also the core values that parents hold as they try to prepare their children for the roles in society that they will likely have.

Socialization, Race, and Ethnicity

As shown in Chapter 6, the United States is becoming more ethnically and racially diverse, creating a need for sensitivity and understanding that values and customs may differ among groups. The following story illustrates the importance of cultural values:

> One day a fifth-grade teacher noticed that Juanita, normally a tidy youngster, had a brown smear of dirt on one arm. That day and the next, the teacher said nothing. However, when Juanita came to class with the mark on her arm the third day, the teacher told her to go wash her dirty arm. When Juanita said it was not dirty, the teacher told her not to argue and to do as she was told. Juanita complied. Several days later, her parents took Juanita out of school to attend the funeral of her sister. Two weeks had passed and Juanita had still not returned to school, so the principal went to her home to find out why. Juanita's mother told the principal that when someone is ill, each family member places a spot of oil and soil somewhere on the body. "We are one with nature. When someone is ill, that person is out of balance with nature. We use the oil and soil of our Mother, the earth, to show her we wish our sick one to be back in balance with nature. When Juanita's teacher made her wash her arm, our oneness with nature was broken. That is why her sister died. The teacher caused her death; Juanita can never return to her class." (Berns 2001, 276)

Racial and ethnic families may differ from the majority culture in terms of how they practice religion or medicine, their degree of family ties and sense of family obligation, and their gendered patterns of behavior. They may have a different emphasis on time and promptness, how authority should be distributed in their relationships, and how strict or permissive parents should be with their children. Racial and ethnic families may differ on the importance placed on group cooperation or individual achievement. For example, the Japanese value conformity and loyalty to the group more than do Euro-Americans. Reflecting these values, Japanese parents encourage their children to be interdependent with others from early infancy. Japanese children are breast-fed longer, are carried or worn on the backs of their parents more frequently, and often sleep with their parents (Preston and Kono 1988).

One important difference between the socialization practices of white and minority parents is that minority parents must teach their children about their cultural heritage, prejudice, and discrimination and provide their children with the coping skills necessary to develop and maintain a strong and healthy self-image (Hughes and Chen 1999; Hughes and Johnson 2001; Johnson 2001; Murry et al. 2005). Referred to as **racial socialization**, parents' race-related communication is important in shaping children's attitudes, beliefs, and their own self-efficacy in dealing with race-related experiences. Moreover, when adults or peers treat children unfairly, parents become even more protective, and step up their cautions and warnings to children about intergroup relationships (Hughes and Johnson 2001). Perhaps, the most effective approach to racial socialization involves teaching children about the realities of racial oppression while remaining optimistic about the possibility of achieving success despite these obstacles (Stevenson et al. 1996). Parents who have a higher level of education, who are married, and who have warmer relationships with their children are more likely to have frequent discussions about their racial or ethnic heritage (Brown et al. 2007).

Socialization and Gender

Chapter 4 identified many ways in which gender is constructed by families, social institutions (e.g., schools), and cultural artifacts (e.g., toys). Although there is no definitive answer about precisely how much of our gendered selves is related to biology, most scientists suggest that gender differences probably are a result of biology and social environment (Kimmel 2000; Sax 2006). They maintain that social and cultural factors are very powerful and shape biological factors. Children learn about what it means to be a girl or a boy in a particular culture in a particular historical period first by the images, words, play, and rituals of their parents. Statements such as "big boys don't cry," "you throw like a girl," "let's play dress-up," "you're my little tomboy," "help your mother with the dishes," and "help your dad take the trash out" teach us about how masculinity and femininity are defined across time, culture, and social location. Parents are a major force in shaping the gendered attitudes of their children. For example, a longitudinal study that followed children for 30 years found that sons who grew up in a household where their mothers stayed home while their fathers worked outside the home held more traditional gendered views as adults than did sons with dual-earner parents (Cunningham-Burley 2001). Likewise, sons who saw their fathers doing stereotypical female labor in the home (e.g., washing dishes, cooking) were more likely to engage in these types of tasks as an adult than were other sons.

Parenting Styles and Practices

Over 40 years ago researchers studied parenting practices and developed a typology that is still used today. Baumrind noted that children who seemed the most competent and contented, who had the fewest behavioral problems, and who had the most academic successes were reared by parents who were demanding and maintained high levels of control over their children, but were also warm and receptive to their children (Baumrind 1966, 1968; Baumrind and Black 1967). She referred to this as an **authoritative parenting style**. Parents of withdrawn, fearful, or distrustful children often had an **authoritarian parenting style** that was strict, punitive, and less warm. Parents who adopted a **permissive parenting style**, put few controls or demands on their children, and often raised children who were aggressive and impulsive. Developmentalists indicate that the authoritative parenting style best predicts outcomes in children thought to be most desirable (Marsiglio et al. 2000; Parke and Buriel 1998).

Mothering

"Mothering" as an Identity What is a "mother"? What is "mothering"? Law defines the former as a relationship based on blood or adoption, although in some contexts the law may be inadequate. What word describes the relationship of a child to her lesbian mother's partner? Both adults may see themselves as mothers, although the law will only recognize one of them.

"Mothering" as a verb is even more complex. Most people will think of the emotional and physical work involved with caring for children, but it is important to keep in mind that mothering takes place within specific contexts and is framed by structures of sex, race, and class (Arendell 2000; Hays 1996; Roxburgh 1999, 2005; Warner 2005). The expectations associated with mothering are socially constructed—they are created by society and are never static, but forever changing. What is seen as "good" or "appropriate" mothering in one place and time may be perceived quite differently elsewhere. Anthropological literature provides many examples of the variability in mothering, suggesting that it is primarily western societies in which women (and their partners) raise children in isolation. Anthropologists illustrate other models that draw upon an extended circle of family, including older siblings, grandmothers and grandfathers, aunts, uncles, and cousins.

In the United States, motherhood is a powerful identity, more powerful than either marital status or occupation. Women with children report experiencing greater meaning in their lives than do child-free women (Ross and Van Willigen 1996).

Ironically, however, they also report greater distress and depression than do child-free women (Evenson and Simon 2005). This is because of the stresses associated with the extensive and ongoing emotional work; the increased household labor; the reduction in income (e.g., a mother quitting work or working only part-time) and the increased financial needs that accompany children; and the lack of social support and government assistance they receive for their mothering tasks.

Compared to other developed nations, U.S. mothering is more intense and fraught with anxiety (Warner 2005). In her book, *Perfect Madness: Motherhood in the Age of Anxiety*, author Judith Warner describes the "mess" that accompanies American motherhood—the unending anxiety over whether they are perfect mothers wreaks havoc on their emotional well-being. While American mothers fret about the pros and cons of combining work with employment or debate whether young children benefit from child care or should stay at home, women in other countries are more able to relax and feel confidence in their abilities as mothers. Much of this confidence comes from knowing that they are not mothering alone, but that they have a cadre of social and health professionals ready to help them and their children—midwives, physicians, nannies, and professional child care providers. For example, while many American mothers bear guilt over their child's time in child care, French mothers can relax knowing that their 3-year-olds are beginning their school career. With the benefits of early childhood education well documented, French children begin school at age 3, and the cost is subsidized by the government.

"Mothering" as an Activity Mothering can bring tremendous personal satisfaction, personal growth, and sheer love: "We have love bouncing off the walls at my house," one mother reveals in Box 10.2. Most women want to become mothers; however, mothering, especially in the United States, is not without personal and financial costs (Nichols et al. 2006).

Volumes of research show that mothers are more involved with their children than are fathers. Mothers do the majority of socialization, hands-on care, emotional work, discipline, transporting, and management (e.g., making the twice-yearly dental appointment). Mothers spend over twice the amount of time per day caring for children under the age of 6 as do fathers, including about three times the amount of time per day spent on actual physical care. Among children of all ages, mothers are far more involved than fathers, even when both work full-time outside the home (Lee and Waite 2005; Sandberg and Hofferth 2001; U.S. Department of Labor 2005a).

BOX 10.2 Families as Lived Experience

We Have Love Bouncing Off the Walls at Our House

The following story reveals the decision-making process of one woman to become a mother. It reveals some of the satisfaction, personal growth, and love that she experienced, but these are not without some personal and professional costs. With paltry maternity leaves, high child care costs, and minimal other supports, women often pay a price for having children.

I never thought I would have any children. I've often reflected on that decision, including the causes and consequences of it, and I now delightfully muse in the recent radical departure from that decision. I have an 18-month-old daughter who is the light of my life, and I am very happily pregnant again. This time, it looks like I'm having a son.

I was committed to never having children because I was extremely focused on my career. I am an attorney working in a well-respected firm in a city on the west coast and have been climbing the ladder toward becoming a partner. I worked long hours at a demanding job that I thoroughly enjoy and loved to spend whatever little free time I have camping and hiking with my husband, Chris, and our dog, Max. I just didn't see how a child would fit into this scenario.

But to be honest, I knew I didn't want children long before I established my career and hectic life. I was committed to never having children because I didn't have a very happy childhood. My parents were pretty detached from my life. I joyfully left home for college at 17.

After 5 years of college, 3 years of law school, and a couple of internship/clerking-type stints, I landed a dream job and have been here ever since. I met my husband while grocery shopping one day after work, believe it or not. We later met for lunch, and really hit it off, and married about a year later. We were both 28 years old.

Life was humming along nicely, when suddenly I had a few life-altering events occur all at once. First, my mother was diagnosed with breast cancer. It was a complete shock to me—although we are not particularly close, I always imagined that she would *be there*. Soon afterwards my friend's husband was seriously injured in a car accident. Watching her grieve and helping her through this was an extremely emotional experience for me. About 6 months later, another friend got divorced. As is often the case, she didn't even really reveal that she was having serious marital problems, until she could keep it a secret no longer.

These three events occurred within a year's time and I spent a lot of time thinking about the meaning of life. One important thing I learned is that I wanted to be a part of something larger than just Chris and me. I recognized that a sense of family, which I really never had much of, was actually very important. Motherhood began to intrigue me. "So, do you want to have a child?" I asked Chris. He gasped. Then he smiled. I knew that meant yes.

However, by this time I was 35 years old, and I read up on how fertility declines with age. I thought I

How does employment affect the time a woman has to spend mothering? Employed mothers spend about 27 hours per week engaged with or accessible to their children as compared to 32 hours a week for mothers who do not work outside the home (Sandberg and Hofferth 2001). They engage in virtually the same activities with their children as do mothers who do not work. One exception is that stay-at-home mothers tend to watch more television with their children (DeMeis and Perkins 1996).

Nonetheless, many employed mothers feel guilty about the time they spend away from home. There is a cultural contradiction: Even though most mothers work outside the home, they must deal with critical judgments for doing so. Yet if a mother stays at home, she pays the price of being treated as an outsider to the larger world. There does not seem to be any way to get it right. As one woman laments:

> I felt really torn between what I wanted to do. Like a gut-wrenching decision. Like, what's more important? Of course your kids are important, but you know, there's so many outside

might have missed the opportunity to be a mother—but, alas, I was pregnant within 6 months. Wow. Now what, Chris?

Little Katie was born in the early morning hours after 9 months of a relatively easy pregnancy. She is the light of our lives. However, after the initial euphoria diminished, we were faced with the daunting task of how to take care of her; more specifically, how do we combine our challenging work with the needs of family? My parents and I still don't get along well, and Chris's parents live a thousand miles away.

I took a 4-month maternity leave, but the latter half was unpaid because I had used up all my vacation pay. Things got a little tight financially. I went back to work, but finding child care for an infant proved to be a challenge. After what seemed like 50 telephone calls or visits to home-run day cares and day care centers, I finally found a good one that had an opening. Full-time care for Katie cost us about $900 per month.

During this time, I began a transformation. In the quest to balance work and family, I found that I preferred to have the scale tipped toward family rather than toward work. How could this be? I've always loved my job and didn't mind putting in 50- to 60-hour weeks—but no more. I tried to limit it to 40, then down to 30 hours. Fortunately my law firm was willing to let me go down to part time, although they made it clear that there would be career costs involved.

I met a group of stay-at-home moms at a library function. We get together regularly and I enjoy their camaraderie, yet I feel like I have a foot in two very different camps. On Monday, Wednesday, and Friday I don the dress-for-success outfit and play attorney. At work we rarely talk about children—even though most of my male colleagues have them. We are all business; I'm not even sure they know my daughter's name. Then on Tuesday and Thursday I don the mothering outfit—complete with food stains from my baby—and talk with other women about nothing but mothering. I'm not even sure these friends know what type of law I practice. They never ask, and to be honest, I don't ask them many questions about their "other" lives—but are mothers really *not* supposed to have any other life? I feel disjointed. Which hat am I wearing today?

Combining work and family is difficult psychologically and financially, yet this is also a very exciting time. As it turns out, we have love bouncing off the walls at our house.

Source: As told to Karen Seccombe, 2006.

CRITICAL THINKING QUESTIONS

1. How do childhood experiences shape our adult desires to have children? Do you think this woman's circumstances are unusual or typical? How have your experiences shaped your desires?
2. Why is combining work and family so difficult psychologically? Do you think it was equally difficult for her husband? Why or why not? Will it be (or is it) difficult for you?

pressures for women to work. Every ad you see in magazines or on television shows this working woman who's coming home with a briefcase and their kids are all dressed and clean. It's such a lie. I don't know of anybody who lives like that. (Hays 2001, 317)

Fathering

"Fathering" as an Identity Despite the stereotype of fathers as only "breadwinners," fathers have played other social roles throughout history, including moral overseer, nurturer, and a gender model for their sons (Coltrane 1996; LaRossa 1997; Marsiglio and Pleck 2005; Marsiglio et al. 2005). However, specific details about the hands-on role they have played with their children are sketchier. Sociologist Jessie Bernard (1973) traces the historical development and the changes in male roles in families in the United States. She observes that the Industrial Revolution in the mid-nineteenth century transformed men's roles into that of the "good provider," in which the focus shifted primarily to his

Most people want to have children; however, "mothering" and "fathering" are really quite different roles and identities. Mothers spend far more time than fathers do on their children's physical care, while a greater proportion of father's time is spent in play.

breadwinning capabilities. Instead of participating in the more nurturing and caretaking aspects of family life as they had done in the past, fathers were removed physically and emotionally from the work done at home. Being a good provider became the dominant concept of male identity. Moreover, having an employed wife was indicative of his failure to provide for his family and threatened to undermine his position as "head of the household."

This model continued until the 1970s and 1980s, when the women's movement and other social movements ushered in ideological changes about men's and women's positions and activities within the family. As more married women with children sought employment, families began to restructure themselves. Men are becoming more involved in domestic life, and many are relieved that they no longer have the economic burden of being the sole breadwinner.

During the past 20 to 30 years, there has been an explosion in research on fathering: What do fathers do with their children? What are the outcomes? What are the meanings associated with being a father? Male-only social movements, such as the Million Man March on Washington, D.C., illustrate that men in U.S. culture are wrestling with their role as fathers, and many hope to increase public awareness about the meaning and importance of fathers in their children's lives (Bulanda 2004; King et al. 2004).

"Fathering" as an Activity How involved are fathers in their children's lives? Comparative studies indicate that the results in other countries parallel findings in the United States: Mothers perform the vast majority of parenting tasks; however, paternal involvement appears to be increasing (Smith 2004). One study found that, on average, a child who lives with his or her biological or adopted father spends 1 hour and 13 minutes on a weekday and 3.3 hours on a weekend day interacting directly with his or her father. The amount of time spent with children tends to decline as the child ages (U.S. Department of Labor 2005a; Yeung et al. 2001). Fathers with children aged 2 and under spend most of their time playing with children. As the child ages, fathers spend a greater portion of time on caregiving activities such as personal care or making meals; however, caregiving tasks still consume 30 minutes or less on a weekday, and an hour or less on the weekend.

While most fathers do not provide extraordinary time with their children on a daily basis, most fathers who live with their children are involved in their lives. Fathers who have more egalitarian gender ideologies are more involved with their children, sons and daughters, than are fathers with more traditional gender ideologies

(Bulanda 2004). Figure 10.1 reports the degree to which fathers are involved in activities with their children on a weekly basis. Over two-thirds play sports, do outdoor activities, talk about their family, or go to the store with their children at least once a week (Brown et al. 2001). Involved fathers take pride and plea-sure in their participation, although they may try to justify why their participation is less than their wives', as these two men do (Gerson 2001, 335):

> I guess we both have to do some sacrificing; that's basically what it is to be a parent. It's probably not going to be fifty-fifty. . . . I think the mother would have a tendency to do a little more. But even sixty-forty is pretty good compared to the average.
>
> I wish I did more, but our time reference is quite different. I'll say, "Okay, I'll do that, but let me do this first." But she will frequently get frustrated and just not be able to stand the thought that it's not done, and then go ahead and do it.

How does involvement on the part of fathers affect their children's well-being? In their review of the research literature, Marsiglio and colleagues found that positive father involvement is beneficial to children (Marsiglio et al. 2000). These findings hold for whites and minorities (Amato and Rivera 1999). However, some suggest that the positive effects of father involvement are not very large, although they acknowledge this

FIGURE 10.1 **Fathers Are Likely to Be Engaged in a Variety of Activities with Their Children at Least Once a Week**

Source: Brown et al. 2001.

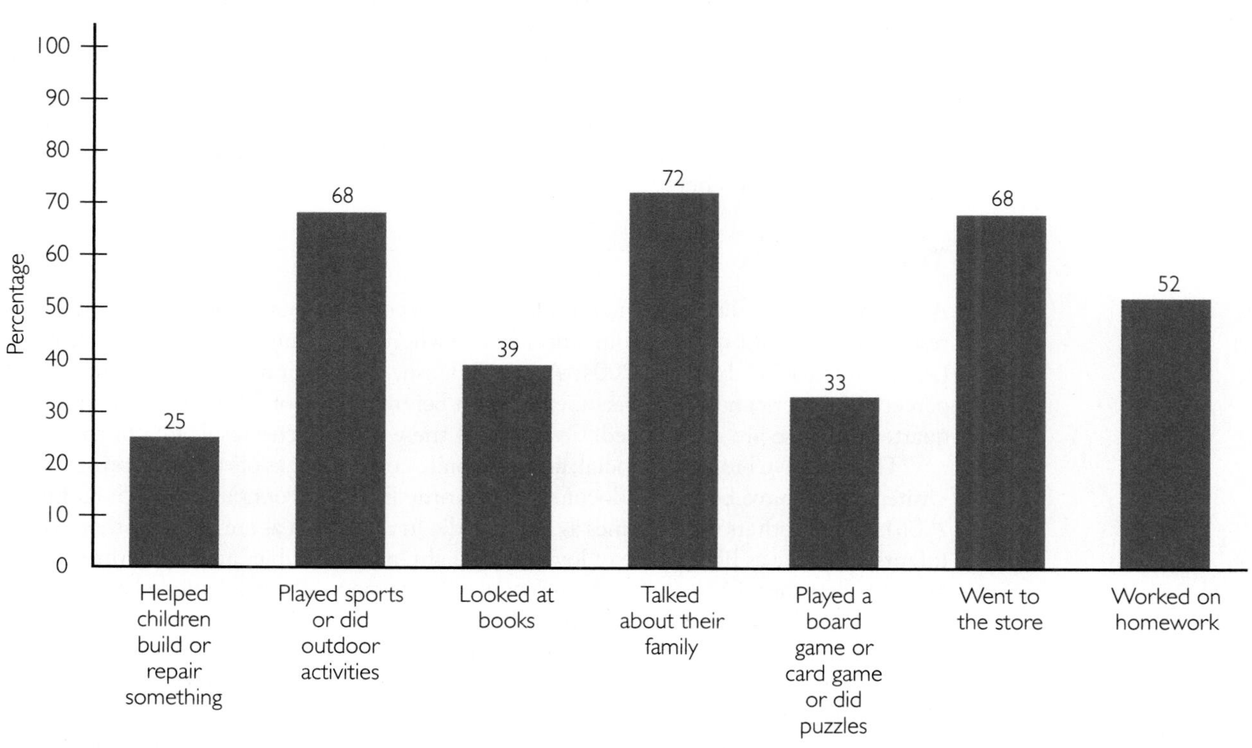

may be due to methodological problems in the research, such as failing to control for the quality of the mother-child relationship (Marsiglio et al. 2000). Others emphasize that father involvement is critically important to children's well-being. In an analysis of nearly 100 studies on parent-child relationships, father love (measured by children's perceptions of paternal acceptance/rejection, affection/indifference) was as important as mother love in predicting the social, emotional, and cognitive development and functioning of children and young adults (Horn and Sylvester 2006; Rohner and Veneziano 2001).

Many children do not live with their fathers because of death, divorce, separation, or because their parents never married. Nearly one half of U.S. children will experience living without a biological father for some period of their childhood. Some of these children see their fathers regularly, while others see their fathers sporadically or infrequently. Boys generally have more frequent contact with their nonresident biological father than do girls (King et al. 2004). Racial and ethnic differences exist as well in specific activities (staying overnight, playing sports, going to religious services, talking about dating) however, no one racial or ethnic group stands out as being significantly higher or lower on father involvement (King et al. 2004).

Research suggests that it is not just the amount of time that noncustodial fathers spend with their children that is important, but *how* fathers interact with their children. Noncustodial fathers who practice authoritative parenting seem to produce the best outcomes in their children, although this parenting style is more difficult to practice when the child lives elsewhere (Amato and Gilbreth 1999).

Parenting Contexts

Idealization of the traditional two-parent, heterosexual, biological family model is found in U.S. laws, policies, social institutions, and attitudes. Yet, changing family demographics have created new social contexts for raising children. The traditional family has given way to a variety of different family arrangements. Growing numbers of singles, gays and lesbians, grandparents, stepparents, cohabiting couples, and extended families have altered the social context of parenting and have fueled new legal debates over parental rights and responsibilities (Erera 2002; Skinner and Kohler 2002). We will explore several of these contexts here.

Teen Parents

About 840,000 American women under age 20 become pregnant each year, which represents a significant decline from a decade ago when about one million teens gave birth (Alan Guttmacher Institute 2004; Annie E. Casey Foundation 2005). Still, nearly 40 percent of American women become pregnant before the age of 20 and more than three-quarters of these are unintended. Over half of these pregnancies result in a birth.

The negative biological, social, and economic consequences of early parenting in the United States have been well documented (Annie E. Casey Foundation 2005; Hoffman 2006): Teen mothers are 2.5 times as likely to die in childbirth as are older mothers, their infants are twice as likely to be of low birth weight, and the babies are nearly three times more likely to die within the first month of life. Are teenagers poorly equipped biologically to be mothers? Not necessarily. Many of these biological problems have social roots; teen mothers are more likely to be poor and lack proper nutrition and prenatal care.

Other repercussions are more social and economic in nature. Teen mothers are more likely to drop out of school than are other teens, are considerably poorer, and more likely to receive welfare. Adolescent mothers are also less knowledgeable about child development than are other mothers, are less prepared for childrearing, and are more likely to be depressed (Annie E. Casey Foundation 2005; Fergusson and Woodward 2000). Children born to teen mothers have lower math and reading skills and increased behavioral problems, although many of these differences may be related to the background of the mother rather than her teen pregnancy, per se (Levine et al. 2007). It is therefore not surprising that social workers, health professionals, educators, researchers, and parents are alarmed at the relatively large number of teens—both young women and men—involved in adolescent pregnancies. It has been estimated that teen childbearing costs taxpayers at least $9.1 billion in 2004 for health care, child welfare, and in lost revenues (Hoffman 2006).

Despite this widespread concern, teenage pregnancy and birth rates have actually declined significantly in recent decades. The teenage birth rate stood at about 40 births per 1,000 women 15–19 years old in 2005 (Hamilton et al. 2006). This rate is significantly lower than the peak rate of 62 births per 1,000 teenage women reached in 1991.

The declines have occurred among teenagers of all ages and across racial and ethnic groups. Figure 10.2 illustrates the birth rates for white, black, Hispanic, Asian or Pacific Islander, and Native American teenage women in 1991 and in 2005. The birth rate among black teens has dropped more dramatically than in other groups; black teens between the ages of 15 and 19 experienced almost a 50 percent decline in the teenage birth rate between 1991 and 2005. In 2005 Hispanic women between the ages of 15 and 19 reported the highest birth rate at 82 births per 1,000 young women; Asian and Pacific Islander teens had the lowest birth rates, at 17 per 1,000 teen women (Hamilton et al. 2006).

What accounts for these trends? Obviously a decline in birth rates reflects changes in (a) the level of teenage pregnancies and (b) how these pregnancies are resolved. Since we know that the abortion rate among teens also declined during this period, it appears that the decline in teenage births is attributable to fewer pregnancies. The Alan Guttmacher Institute (2000) suggests that the pregnancy rate is declining, particularly

FIGURE 10.2 **Teenage Fertility Rates per 1,000 Women Aged 15–19 by Race and/or Ethnicity for 1991 and 2005**

Source: Hamilton et al. 2006.

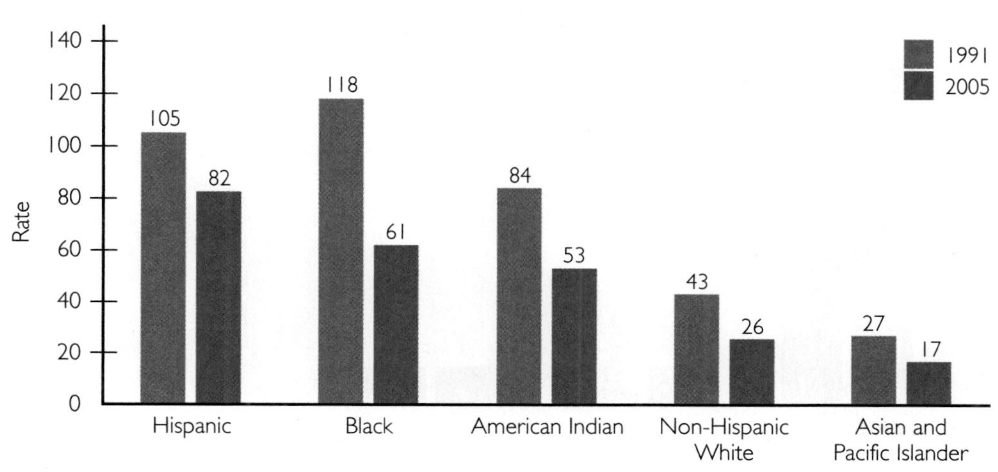

among blacks, because of (1) increased abstinence; (2) a decline in the frequency of sexual intercourse among the sexually active; and (3) teens are using more effective contraceptive methods.

Single Parents

Single-parent families are often seen as problematic and have been referred to as *broken homes*. The vast majority of single-parent families are single-mother families, and the terms are often used interchangeably. Single parents have been maligned for causing juvenile delinquency, poverty, and a host of social problems. The problem with such a generalization is that (1) there are different kinds of single-parent families with different kinds of circumstances (a teenager vs. a 40-year-old female executive); (2) there are different paths to becoming a single parent (never marrying, divorce, or widowhood); (3) the cause-and-effect relationship is unclear (e.g., Does poverty cause single parenthood or does single parenthood cause poverty?); and (4) single parenthood is less problematic in other industrialized nations because of a wide number of social supports that exist that are notably lacking in the United States (i.e., a higher minimum wage and nationalized health care) (Dowd 1997).

Nonetheless, the number of single parents is on the rise, and the likelihood of children living within a single-parent household for some or all of their childhood is increasing. Figure 10.3 reveals the percentage of children living in single-mother and single-father households. The rates of living with a single mother are highest among black children (48 percent) and lowest among Asian and Pacific Islander children (13 percent). Few children live with single fathers, and the differences across racial and ethnic groups are not large.

Much of the scrutiny and concern surrounding single-parent families is targeted toward teenagers. However, as we noted, the birth rate among unmarried teenagers has actually declined. The reason that the number of single-parent households has increased over the past several decades is the rise in unmarried women aged 30 and

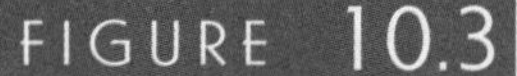
FIGURE 10.3 **Percentage of Children Living with Single Parents**

Source: Fields 2003, 2004.

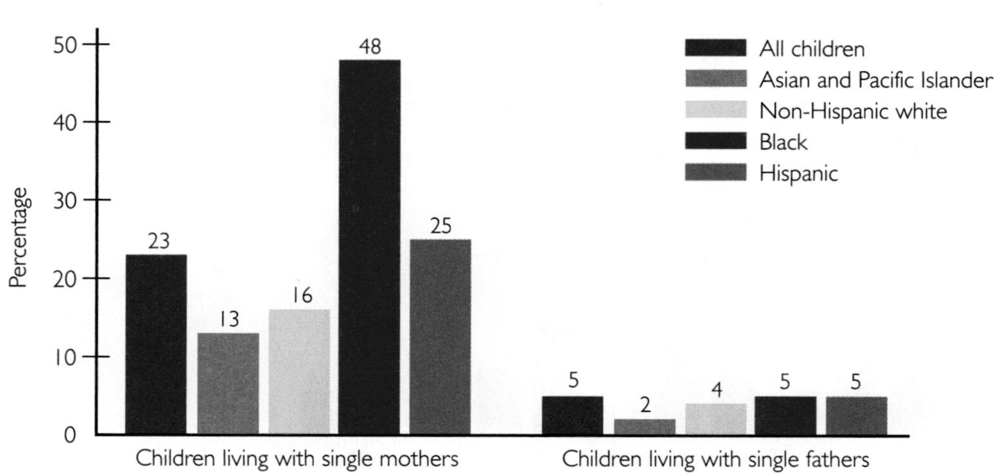

over who are having children. Older unmarried women represent a very different portrait of single parenthood than that conjured up by the image of an unmarried teen. Older women are likely to have completed their education and have jobs, perhaps even well-paying careers.

However, some people are still alarmed by the fact that so many children are being raised without a father present in the home (The National Marriage Project 2006). Children in single-mother families, in particular, are disadvantaged financially. For example, they are overrepresented among those living in poverty and receiving food stamps (DeNavas-Walt et al. 2006; Fields 2004).

Table 10.2 compares the poverty rate in 22 countries among children in single-parent versus other family types. Most of western Europe has significantly lower rates of poverty among single-parent households than does the United States, although single parents appear to be universally more vulnerable to poverty than two-parent families. Of the 22 selected countries, the rates of poverty among children in single-parent house-

TABLE 10.2 Child Poverty* in Single-Parent Families Relative to Other Family Types

	Poverty Rate of Children In:	
	Single-Parent Families (%)	Other Families (%)
Australia	36	9
Belgium	14	4
Canada	52	10
Czech Republic	31	4
Denmark	14	4
Finland	7	4
France	26	6
Germany	51	6
Greece	25	12
Hungary	10	10
Ireland	46	14
Italy	22	20
Luxembourg	30	3
Mexico	28	26
Netherlands	24	7
Norway	13	2
Poland	20	15
Spain	32	12
Sweden	7	2
Turkey	29	20
United Kingdom	46	13
United States	**55**	**16**

*Poverty defined as 50% of median national income.

Source: UNICEF Innocenti Research Centre 2000.

holds are highest in the United States, although Canada is a close second (UNICEF Innocenti Research Centre 2000).

Why is poverty so much less likely in other countries? Most industrialized countries offer universal family or child cash allowances and an assortment of other cash programs and social policies such as child care and health insurance specifically designed to help families with children. These programs and policies lift the income of families so that they are not impoverished.

Despite the concern over single-parent families, not all the news is depressing. For example, one study based on a representative sample in the United States found that children from single-parent families report that they talk to their mothers more often than do children in two-parent families (McLanahan and Sandefur 1994). Relationships between mothers and their children can be characterized by greater equality, intimacy, and companionship (Arditti and Madden-Derdich 1997; Guttman 1993). However, problems can also arise because single parents are generally challenged by a sheer lack of time as they juggle multiple roles and the lack of a back-up parent.

Cohabiting Families In some cases, what might first be viewed as a "single-parent" household is not really a single household at all. The single parent may be cohabiting with another adult. As cohabitation has increased, perhaps between 40 to 50 percent of nonmarital births are to mothers living with their child's father (Fields 2004; Osborne 2005). Of children living with a single mother, about 11 percent actually lived in a household with their mother and her unmarried partner. White children were more likely to live with their cohabiting mother and her partner than were blacks, Asians, or Hispanic children (Fields 2004). Of children living with a single father, a third of them were actually living with their single father and his partner. Hispanic children were more likely to live with their cohabiting father and his partner than were white, black, or Asian children. The parents' partner in these families plays varying roles. Some have close, near parent-like relationships with the children, while others are more distant.

About 7 million gays and lesbians are parents, perhaps through adoption, artificial insemination, or as stepparents to a partner's children. They have a great deal in common with other families, but also face some unique challenges given the prejudice and discrimination surrounding same-sex relationships.

Lesbian and Gay Families

Lesbians and gay men are still fighting for a basic human right: to be recognized and accepted as families. Although reliable data are lacking, it is estimated that up to 80 percent of lesbians and 60 percent of gay men in the United States live in couples and families and possibly up to 7 million are parents (Kurdek 1995; Patterson and Freil 2000). For the most part, they have a great deal in common with heterosexual couples and heterosexual parents (Kurdek 2004, 2005), yet because lesbians and gay men cannot legally marry in the United States (except for Massachusetts), they are often perceived as not "real" families. Even the courts have vastly different rulings on the rights of lesbian and gay parents (Connolly 1996; Skinner and Kohler 2002). The small amount of research on homosexual families tends to focus on lesbian families rather than families formed by gay males, furthering the stereotype that gay men are not interested in committed relationships with partners and nurturing relationships with children. These stereotypes are untrue (Bigner 1999; Spock 2004; Weston 1997).

There are many ways that lesbians and gay men can become parents. Chapter 8 discussed the route of adoption. Lesbians may also become parents through artificial insemination with a known or unknown sperm donor or from sexual intercourse with a male partner. However, most lesbian and gay families are formed as stepfamilies, in which the children were conceived in an earlier heterosexual relationship (Allen 1997). Although most aspects of raising children differ little (the daily tasks of getting children to school on time, taking children to soccer practice, or getting involved in the PTA), several specific features significantly affect the dynamics of lesbians and gays raising children (Erera 2002; Spock 2004; Stacey and Biblarz 2001):

- *Because lesbians and gay men are stigmatized for having children, the decision to parent is generally a deliberate choice that reflects a strong commitment to raising children*. Studies tend to show either no difference among homosexuals and heterosexuals in their fitness to parent, or that lesbian mothers and gay fathers may have an edge (Stacey and Biblarz 2001). For example, lesbian mothers exhibit more parenting skills and awareness of child development than heterosexual couples, and there is greater similarity between partners' parenting skills (Flaks et al. 1995). Likewise, compared to heterosexual fathers, gay fathers go to greater lengths to promote their children's cognitive skills, are more responsive to their children's needs, and more involved in activities with children (Bigner and Jacobson 1989). Lesbian and gay couples also tend to have a more egalitarian division of household labor than do heterosexual couples, and this is reflected in their joint division of child care (Dunne 2000).
- *Lesbian and gay families are more likely to be affected by loss*. Lacking institutional constraints and support such as legalized marriage, lesbian and gay relationships are somewhat more likely to dissolve than are heterosexual ones. However, because lesbians and gay men cannot legally marry, their trauma may not be publicly recognized or as easily supported. U.S. society acknowledges the tremendous disruption caused by a divorce; however, a "breakup" may be trivialized. Lesbian and gay families may experience other losses as well. Lesbian and gay stepfamilies are created following a divorce (as are heterosexual stepfamilies), and children experience a loss of family members (Kurdek 1997). Likewise, the HIV/AIDS epidemic has touched many lives. The CDC estimates that over a million U.S. residents are living with HIV infection, one-quarter of whom are unaware of it (CDC 2006d). Although the estimated annual number of AIDS-related deaths has fallen dramatically since 1995, it remains that about 16,000 men and women died in the United States from AIDS-related causes in 2005 (CDC 2006d).
- *Lesbian and gay families must cope with homophobia and discrimination*. Homosexuality is stigmatized, and living openly as a family leaves them vulnerable to ridicule or discrimination. Some people worry that children raised by lesbians or gay men are more apt to suffer confusion over their gender and sexual identity, are more likely to suffer depression and have other emotional difficulties, and are more likely to engage in deviant sexual behavior (Wardle 1997). However, these concerns have largely proved unfounded (Stacey and Biblarz 2001). Most studies find no difference (or the evidence is mixed and therefore inconclusive) that boys or girls depart from traditional gendered expectations and behaviors, that the child wishes she or he were the opposite sex, or that the child firmly self-identifies as gay or lesbian as a young adult when raised by lesbians or gay men. Nor do children growing up in gay or lesbian households experience lower self-esteem, depression, impaired cognitive functioning, or problems gaining employment in young adulthood. Furthermore, boys' level of aggressiveness and domineering disposition (a presumed precursor to molestation) is actually lower among children raised by lesbian and gay households

than among children raised in heterosexual households. Research does suggest that children raised by lesbian or gay parents are more tolerant of homosexuality. They are more likely to have either considered or have had same-sex sexual relationships, and they are more likely to have friends who are gay or lesbian. Moreover, girls raised by lesbian or gay parents have had a greater number of sexual partners from puberty to young adulthood, compared to their counterparts raised by heterosexual parents, while boys have had fewer.

- *Lesbians and gay men often have a close network of friends whom they regard as an extended family who provide emotional and social support.* Social support is crucial from family and friends as a way to ward off oppression and to create a safe and supportive environment for lesbians, gay men, and their children (Oswald and Culton 2003). They often have developed a close network of fellow lesbians and gays whom they regard as a sort of extended family (Hunter and Mallon 1998). These meaningful relationships, called fictive kin, stand in for biological family; they are there to celebrate birthdays, participate in commitment ceremonies, babysit when needed, and in countless ways offer the love and support that are needed to keep a household and a family running smoothly. In fact, fictive kin are often more reliable and consistent in their support than biological families (Demo and Allen 1996). Parents and families respond in a variety of ways and organizations such as Parents, Families, and Friends of Lesbians and Gays (PFLAG) provide education, advocacy, and support to those who need it.

Grandparents Raising Grandchildren

Some children live with, and are under the custodial care, of their grandparents. The U.S. Census Bureau estimates that about 8 percent, or 5.6 million children, live with their grandparents (Fields 2003). Sometimes one or both of the child's parents also live with the grandparent. The greatest growth has occurred among grandchildren living with one or both grandparents on their own without a parent present.

Where are these children's parents? Mothers and fathers are absent for many reasons, including death, desertion, incarceration, substance abuse, physical or mental illness, employment problems, HIV/AIDS, and child abuse. Among whites, alcohol and drug abuse were major reasons, whereas among Hispanics and blacks, financial need was commonly cited (Goodman and Silverstein 2006). One study of 129 grandparents raising their grandchildren examined the situations that precipitated this relationship (Sands and Goldberg-Glen 2000). There were multiple problems in the homes of the grandchildren's parents that led the grandparents to take over their grandchildren's care. The most commonly reported problem was substance abuse, but the parent's inability to care for the child, neglect, and psychological and financial problems were also cited as factors. Many of these problems are long-term issues for families. When the grandparents in this study first began to care for their grandchildren, only one-third expected to be the caregiver until the grandchild grew up, but by the time of the interview, over 75 percent of grandparents assumed that they would care for their grandchild until adulthood.

What are some of the characteristics of these intergenerational families that are maintained by the grandparents (Fields 2003; U.S. Census Bureau 2006d)?

- Coresident grandmothers outnumber coresident grandfathers five to three. One reason is that women live longer, and therefore are more likely to reach an age where they have grandchildren. Another reason is that women are more likely than men to assume a caregiving role, and therefore grandmothers may feel more obliged to take in grandchildren. Grandmothers are also more likely to be widowed and have lower incomes and may therefore want to live with their children or grandchildren for companionship or support.

- The majority of grandparents raising their grandchildren are younger than age 65. One-third are younger than age 50, and nearly half are between the ages of 50 and 64. Only one in five is aged 65 or older.
- Grandchildren in grandparent-maintained families are more likely to be black, younger, and living in the south, compared with grandchildren who live in intergenerational households maintained by their parents.
- Grandchildren in grandparent-maintained families are more likely to be poor than other children, as shown in Figure 10.4. They are also less likely to receive health insurance and more likely to receive public assistance.

Most grandparents have reservations about taking on their grandchildren's care, but feel that they have little choice in the matter because they are a last resort (Hayslip Jr. et al. 1998; Sands and Goldberg-Glen 2000). Taking care of their grandchildren is an act of love, but can lead to financial difficulties and feelings of emotional strain, helplessness, isolation, and depression (Bowers and Myers 1999; Goodman and Silverstein 2006; Ross and Aday 2006). Grandparents may neglect their own physical and emotional health because they give priority to their grandchildren's needs. They sometimes encounter problems that can require legal assistance to make decisions regarding their grandchild's medical care, school enrollment, immunizations, and other support services. They also express concern about their grandchild's emotional well-being, recognizing that they often became caregivers because of some traumatic event or abusive behavior. One study with 42 grandparents who were primary caregivers to their grandchildren found that they were in high agreement that their grandchildren would benefit from a specially designed support group geared to address the child's feelings of anger, guilt, and depression, adjusting to the loss of a parent, and helping them to understand the parents' substance abuse or other problems (Smith et al. 2002).

FIGURE 10.4 Percentage of Grandchildren in Poverty, Receiving Welfare, and Not Covered by Health Insurance, by Living Arrangement

Source: Fields 2003.

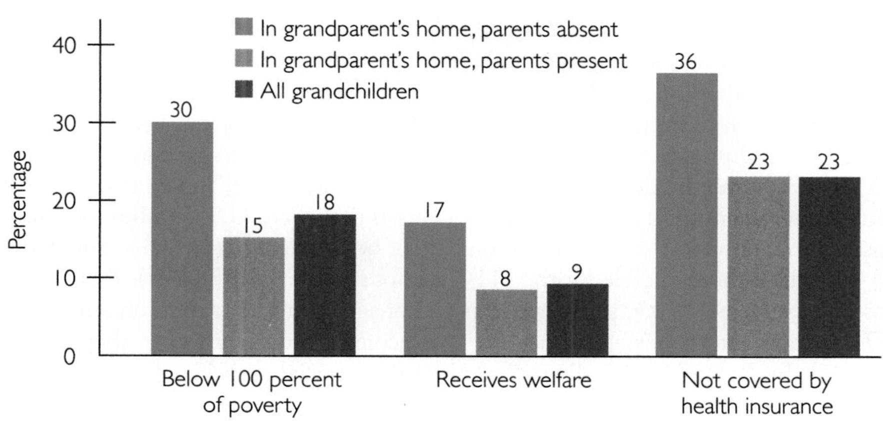

Social Policy and Family Resilience

As April 15 approaches and American families with children fill out their tax returns, they will find some relief in the form of the expanded child tax credits ($600 per child). These credits will reach $1,000 per child in 2010. Although many families are delighted to have these expanded credits, we cannot ignore the fact that Americans still receive considerably less support with regard to the costs of rearing children than families in many other countries.

Example: Family Allowances

The United States is one of the few industrialized nations that does not provide families with child or **family allowances**. These are cash benefits given to families with children by the government with the amount dependent upon the number or age of children (Centre des Liaisons Europeennes et Internationales de Securite Sociale 2006). The purpose of this cash grant is to help offset some of the costs associated with raising children. These are universal benefits, available to all families, regardless of income. A family's income has nothing to do with whether they receive a family allowance. For the most part, family allowances are modest benefits worth a little less than 10 percent of average wages for *each child*, but they can contribute a significant component of family income to large or low-income families. They are paid by government, business, or a combination of both. Many European countries began offering family allowances as early as the beginning of the twentieth century (Kamerman and Gatenio 2002; Ministere des Affaires Etrangeres 2005). In Canada, family allowances were considered the first real social welfare program (Canadian Encyclopedia 2005).

Does the United States provide any similar program? Not exactly; however, the United States does provide several tax benefits to families with children, particularly to low-income families. For example, low-income working families could apply for the refundable earned income tax credit (EITC) as long as their income was under $34,001 in 2006 (married, filing jointly, with one qualifying child) (IRS 2007). The EITC is designed to offset some of the taxes that low-income persons would otherwise pay, thereby serving as an inducement to work.

There is also the child tax credit given for each child. The government helps offset child care costs by offering a tax credit for up to 30 percent of some of these expenses for working families. For the family living on average earnings, the value of these tax credits is likely to equal about 6 percent of their income (Kamerman and Gatenio 2002). There are also tax credits or deductions for families adopting a child, paying for a child's education, and for the costs of a child in eligible child care. All of these are designed to help low- and middle-income families and phase out as a family's income rises.

Unlike most other industrialized countries, family benefits for Americans with children are not universal, but are usually means-tested. Applying for tax benefits can be confusing in the United States because it requires that a family be aggressive and savvy enough to understand the tax system, what programs are available, and be familiar with eligibility requirements and ceilings. The net effect is that those U.S. families who most need assistance are often the least likely to apply or be aware of the benefits. For example, 25 percent of those eligible for the EITC do not receive it (IRS 2005). Even when persons do receive assistance, it likely comes just once a year rather than on a monthly basis. These tax concessions are critical to low-income families; however, they do not make up for the lack of family allowances and other special cash benefits targeted to children in many other countries.

Currently 88 countries worldwide provide family allowances (Kamerman and Gatenio 2002). In some countries, family allowances may be supplemented by many other cash programs or tax credits, including birth grants, school grants, child-rearing or childcare allowances, adoption benefits, special supplements for single parents, guaranteed minimum child support benefits, and allowances for adult dependents and disabled children. By providing these cash benefits, governments are directly helping families with the costs associated with raising children and indirectly helping to lower the rate of child poverty.

Typically, family allowances have one or more of the following objectives (Kamerman and Gatenio 2002):

- *Horizontal equity*—the redistribution of income from childless households to families with children, in recognition of the heavier financial burden incurred by child rearing.
- *Vertical equity or redistribution*—supplementing the incomes of poor and modest income families with children as a means of reducing or preventing poverty.
- *Strengthening labor force attachments*—in some countries, benefits are only available to families with children who have at least one parent in the work force, or higher benefit levels are offered to families attached to the labor force.
- *Social inclusion/exclusion*—particularly as the European Union moves toward greater unity among its member states, family allowances are viewed as an instrument that can foster societal cohesion and progress.

Family allowance benefit levels are structured in different ways among countries. Several countries provide a uniform rate per child, regardless of the number of children in the family (Australia, Spain, Norway, and Sweden), while in other countries, benefits increase with each additional child or are larger for the third, fourth, or fifth child (Italy, Belgium, France, Germany, and Luxembourg). In still others, such as the United Kingdom, the benefit is higher for the first child, while in France a family is only eligible for the allowance after the second child is born. Many countries provide higher benefits for older children (Austria, Belgium, France, Luxembourg, and the Netherlands). Some countries provide a higher or special benefit for families with very young children (Austria, France, Germany, and Portugal) to make it possible for a parent to remain at home during a child's early years (until the child is age 3; age 1 in Portugal). In Finland and Norway, parents have the option of a subsidized place in child care or a cash benefit of equivalent value making it possible for a parent of a very young child (under 3) to stop working and provide care. Benefit levels may also be reduced as income rises or by including the benefit in taxable income, as in Spain and Greece. In some countries, benefit levels vary by geographic region. Austria, Germany, and Spain offer national benefits that vary by region, due to differences in the cost of living. Norway, too, supplements the family allowances of families in the Arctic region. Despite these differences, an important similarity is that there is no stigma attached to receiving benefits. Receipt is considered a right of citizenship, and countries actively encourage their residents to apply for benefits.

Coverage is generally extended to children from the time of birth to the age of majority or completion of formal education, provided other eligibility criteria are met. In almost all the industrialized countries, the universal family allowance is awarded to the mother or to the person caring for the child. The income-related cash benefit is more likely to go to the wage-earning parent (or to either parent if both are employed).

In recent years, some countries have begun to experiment with a combination of strategies, including family allowances and targeted tax credits. In most countries the basic benefit is universal, though recent trends suggest that means-tested benefits are growing, targeting families with children whose income is below a certain level. Ultimately, the issue is how much money reaches families with children. Given that poverty rates are significantly higher in the United States than elsewhere, it might be worth taking a look at family allowances to determine how they could offset poverty for millions of Americans (Kamerman and Gatenio 2002).

Conclusion

This chapter has explored several dimensions of parenting. It suggests that although raising children may be universal, the act of *parenting* is highly variable. Parenting attitudes and practices depend to a large extent on the type of tasks or competencies that members of a society (or subgroup) are expected to have. Mothering and fathering bring to mind the emotional, physical, and financial work involved with caring for children, but it is important to recognize that these identities take place within specific historical and cultural contexts, and even in the United States today they are framed by structures of sex, race, and class. Families are becoming increasingly diverse with more children being raised by single parents, gays and lesbians, and grandparents, while teen birth rates are actually declining. These contexts raise new challenges and stresses and are of critical policy concern. Many countries directly assist parents with the financial costs associated with raising children. The United States also does so, but leans toward annual tax credits rather than monthly assistance, such as a family allowance.

Key Terms

Agents of socialization: The persons, groups, or institutions that teach children about the norms and values of their particular culture. (p. 313)

Authoritarian parenting style: Strict, punitive, and not very warm. (p. 316)

Authoritative parenting style: Demand and maintain high levels of control over their children, but also warm and receptive to their children. (p. 316)

Concrete operational thought: Piaget's third stage of cognitive development; occurs between the ages of 6 and 11 or 12 when children begin to see the causal connections in their surroundings and can manipulate categories, classification systems, and hierarchies in groups. (p. 312)

Ego: According to Sigmund Freud, the rational component of personality that attempts to balance the need for immediate gratification with the demands of society. (p. 312)

Family allowances: Cash benefits given to families by the government. (p. 330)

Formal operational thought: Piaget's fourth stage of cognitive development; children develop capacities for abstract thought and can conceptualize more complex issues or rules that can be used for problem solving (p. 312).

Id: According to Sigmund Freud, the part of the personality that includes biological drives and needs for immediate gratification. (p. 312)

Looking-glass self: According to Cooley, we come to see ourselves as others perceive and respond to us. (p. 312)

Permissive parenting style: Having few controls or demands on the child. (p. 316)

Preoperational thought: Piaget's second stage of cognitive development; occurs through age 5 or 6 as the child learns language, symbolic play and symbolic drawing, but does not grasp abstract concepts. (p. 312)

Racial socialization: Teaching minority children about prejudice and discrimination; the coping skills necessary to develop and maintain a strong and healthy self-image. (p. 315)

Role taking: According to Mead, it is the process of mentally assuming the role of another person to understand the world from his or her point of view and to anticipate his or her response to us. (p. 313)

Sensorimotor intelligence: Piaget's first stage of cognitive development; infants and toddlers understand the world primarily through touch, sucking, listening, and looking. (p. 312)

Socialization: The lifelong process through which we acquire the cultural values and skills needed to function as human beings and participate in society. (p. 311)

Superego: According to Freud, our conscience; draws upon our cultural values and norms to help us understand why we cannot have everything we want. (p. 312)

Symbolic interaction: Humans interact not just with words, but also with symbols and meanings. (p. 313)

Transnational family: A family living between two nations, often in search of work that pays a survivable wage. (p. 309)

Resources on the Internet

Administration for Children and Families (ACF)
www.acf.dhhs.gov/index.htm
This federal agency funds a variety of family assistance programs at the community level. They provide data on many issues relevant to children and parenthood. Particularly helpful are their fact sheets about important issues and programs (child abuse, the Head Start program, and child support enforcement).

Children's Defense Fund
www.childrensdefense.org
The mission of the Children's Defense Fund is to Leave No Child Behind and to ensure every child a good start in life and successful passage to adulthood with the help of caring families and communities. They provide useful data on the education, health, income, and well-being of vulnerable families and children.

ChildStats.gov
www.childstats.gov
This website offers access to federal and state statistics and reports on children and their families, including population and family characteristics, economic security, health, behavior and social environment, and education. Reports of the Federal Interagency Forum on Child and Family Statistics include *America's Children: Key National Indicators of Well-Being*, the annual federal monitoring report on the status of the nation's children.

The Clearinghouse on International Developments in Child, Youth, and Family Policies
www.childpolicyintl.org
The clearinghouse provides cross-national, comparative information about the policies, programs, benefits, and services available in the advanced industrialized countries to address child, youth, and family needs. Coverage focuses on 23 advanced industrialized countries. Expansion to other countries and other parts of the world is planned.

UNICEF
www.unicef.org
UNICEF, the United Nations Children's Fund, is part of the Global Movement for Children—a broad coalition dedicated to improving the life of every child. UNICEF's staff works in 157 countries around the world to assure equality for those who are discriminated against, girls and women in particular. The UNICEF website offers current information about the state of children's lives throughout the world.

Further Reading

Bee, H., and D. Boyd. 2007. *The Developing Child*, 4th ed. Boston: Allyn and Bacon.

Bowles, S., H. Gintis, and M. Osborne-Groves (Eds.). 2005. *Unequal Chances: Family Background and Economic Success*. Princeton, NJ: Princeton University Press.

Bryceson, D., and U. Vuorela. (Eds.). 2002. *The Transnational Family: New European Frontiers and Global Networks*. New York: Berg.

Crouter, A. C., and A. Booth. (Eds.). 2003. *Children's Influence on Family Dynamics: The Neglected Side of Family Relationships*. Mahwah, NJ: Erlbaum.

Degler, C. 1980. *At Odds: Women and the Family in America from the Revolution to the Present*. New York: Oxford University Press.

Deparle, J. 2004. *American Dream: Three Women, Ten Kids, and a Nation's Drive to End Welfare*. New York: Viking Books.

Edin, K., and M. Kefalas. 2005. *Promises I Can Keep: Why Poor Women Put Motherhood Before Marriage*. Chicago: University of Chicago Press.

Hays, S. 2003. *Flat Broke with Children: Women in the Age of Welfare Reform*. New York: Oxford University Press.

Hays, S. 1996. *The Cultural Contradictions of Motherhood*. New Haven, CT: Yale University Press.

LaRossa, R. 1997. *The Modernization of Fatherhood: A Social and Political History*. Chicago: University of Chicago Press.

Seccombe, K., and K. A. Hoffman, 2007. *Just Don't Get Sick: Access to Health Care in the Aftermath of Welfare Reform*. Piscataway, NJ: Rutgers University Press.

Townsend, N. W. 2002. *The Package Deal: Marriage, Work, and Fatherhood in Men's Lives*. Philadelphia: Temple University Press.

White, M. I. 2000. *Perfectly Japanese: Making Families in an Era of Upheaval*. Berkeley: University of California Press.

CHAPTER 11

Families and the Work They Do

Chapter Outline

Chapter Preview

This chapter examines the work that families do inside and outside of the home. It may have been true in the past that one's place of employment and one's home were two different domains with little overlap, but this is no longer the case. Issues such as work-family conflicts, feelings of time deficits with children, negotiations over the division of household labor, and struggles to find suitable child care are well known to most families today. In this chapter you will learn:

- Ways in which the economy and work have changed for families, including changes in child labor and women's labor force trends
- Changes in the occupational structure, such as the rise in part-time, nonstandard, and temporary work
- Juggling work and family life is stressful for many families, although there are policies that could help reduce the stress and time crunch many families feel
- How household labor is defined and measured and discover who does the bulk of the work in the home
- Who is taking care of children as most mothers and fathers now work outside the home for pay
- What the United States could learn from other countries about early childhood education and child care policies

It's 7:40 A.M. when Cassie Bell, 4, arrives at the Spotted Deer Child-Care Center, her hair half-combed, a blanket in one hand, a fudge bar in the other. "I'm late," her mother, Gwen, a sturdy young woman whose short-cropped hair frames a pleasant face, explains to the child-care workers in charge. "Cassie wanted the fudge bar so bad, I gave it to her," she adds apologetically.

"Please, can't you take me with you?" Cassie pleads. "You know I can't take you to work," Gwen replies in a tone that suggests that she has been expecting this request. Cassie's shoulders droop. However, she has struck a hard bargain—the morning fudge bar—aware of her mother's anxiety about the long day that lies ahead at the center. As Gwen explains later, she continually feels that she owes Cassie more time than she gives her.

Arriving at her office just before 8:00, Gwen finds on her desk a cup of coffee in her personal mug, milk no sugar (exactly as she likes it), prepared by a coworker who managed to get in ahead of her. As the assistant to the head of public relations at a company called Amerco, Gwen handles responses to reports that may appear about the company in the press—a challenging job, but one that gives her satisfaction. As she prepares for her first meeting of the day, she misses her daughter, but she also feels relief. There is a lot to get done at Amerco.

Gwen used to work a straight 8-hour day. However, over the last 3 years, her workday has gradually stretched to 8.5 or 9 hours, not counting the e-mail messages and faxes she answers from home. She complains about her long hours to her coworkers and listens to their complaints—but she loves her job. Gwen picks up Cassie at 5:45 and gives her a long, affectionate hug.

At home, Gwen's husband, John, a computer programmer, plays with their daughter while Gwen prepares dinner. To protect the dinner "hour"—8:00 to 8:30—Gwen checks that the phone machine is on. After Cassie's bath, Gwen and Cassie have "quality time," or "Q.T." as John affectionately calls it. Half an hour later, at 9:30, Gwen tucks Cassie into bed.

There are, in a sense, two Bell households: the rushed family they actually are and the relaxed family they imagine they might be if only they had time. Gwen and John complain that they are in a time bind. What they say they want seems so modest—time to throw a ball, to read to Cassie, to witness the small dramas of her development, not to speak of having a little fun and romance themselves—yet even these modest wishes seem strangely out of reach. Before going to bed, Gwen has to e-mail messages to her colleagues in preparation for the next day's meeting: John goes to bed early, exhausted—he's out the door by 7 every morning.

This is an excerpt from the best-selling book, The Time Bind *(Hochschild 1997). Sociologist Arlie Hochschild reports that for many people, working hours have increased, and work has replaced home as the place of friendship, meaning, and even relaxation. Based on in-depth interviews with working families, she writes of a cultural reversal—as work has encroached on family time, the rewards of work have increased relative to those of family life. Home is where increasing numbers of people feel stressed by the demands of children and spouses, by household labor, and feelings of lack of control, and work is now where people obtain personal satisfaction.*

Sociologist K. Jill Kiecolt reexamined these ideas using data from the 1973–1994 General Social Surveys. Has there been a cultural reversal? Her conclusions do not support the assertions from The Time Bind. *Her analysis found that over a 20-year period, the percentage of individuals for whom work was more satisfying than family life actually shrank (Kiecolt 2003). More specifically, men's likelihood of finding work a haven did not change; however, women were less likely to find work a haven. She also found that respondents with preschool-aged children were particularly more likely to find a home a haven, which belies the idea in* The Time Bind *that individuals are less psychologically invested in their families than in the past. According to Kiecolt, a cultural reversal has not occurred; work has not become more satisfying than home, despite the stresses people face as they try to juggle work and family roles.* ■

Since the Industrial Revolution; we have considered "work" as an activity that was done outside the home. Home and work were separate spheres, generally unrelated to one another, and largely segregated by sex. Men went to work; women stayed at home. Today we recognize that work and family are not separate domains, but are highly interrelated with one another (Hill et al. 2004; Voydanoff 2004). First, a majority of mothers work outside the home whether married or not, including mothers with preschool-aged children. Women and men are no longer living in "separate spheres." Both are increasingly involved in work both inside and outside the home, and dual-worker or dual-career families are seen as normal rather than the exception.

Second, the organization of work done inside the home has an influence on the work done outside the home. Issues such as how child care, housework, or emotional labor is divided up between partners influence worker productivity, absenteeism, and retention. These so-called "family issues" influence the level of tension that many two-parent dual-worker or dual-career families experience as they combine work and family. For example, how do parents negotiate who leaves work early to pick up a sick child from school? Who will routinely arrive at work a few minutes late in order to drop a child off at school? Single working parents juggle this alone, while two-parent families are negotiating family labor.

Third, specific work policies have the ability to reduce work-family tensions and conflicts that parents experience through flex-time, part-time work options, health insurance, sick pay, parental leaves, and other important family-friendly fringe benefits

(Bond et al. 2002; Frone 2003; Hill et al. 2004). A study of IBM employees in 48 countries found that work-family conflicts are not unique to the United States, and that policies can greatly alleviate much of the tension that families feel (Hill et al. 2004). In sum, "it has become evident in recent years that paid work organized on the assumption that work and family are separate domains is no longer compatible with reality" (Voydanoff 2004, 398).

Today's families feel more pressure than ever. Work encroaches on family life for an increasing number of families as the number of single-parent households and dual-earner households continues to rise, hours on the job increase, and job benefits erode. Employment has not kept pace with the changing nature of the workforce by offering a family-friendly environment. Nonetheless, despite a "work speed-up," most adults want to have children; they are not willing to sacrifice children for the sake of work. They hope to find and maintain some semblance of balance in their lives. As we saw in Chapter 9, the rewards of parenthood are immense. Children can bring great joy to adults, enriching their lives in many ways. This chapter examines some key issues and challenges in the work that families do both inside and outside the home.

The Changing Economy and Work

The context of work and family life has changed dramatically over the past several hundred years. In early colonial America, most families worked closely with the land, as we learned in Chapter 2. Their lives revolved around the seasonal work necessary for farming and ranching. The labor of men, women, and children was needed and was considered invaluable to the success of the family enterprise. Men and women usually had different tasks, with men involved in the physical agricultural work while women and children did the cooking, cleaning, weaving, and tending to small animals. However, at several crucial times of the year associated with planting and harvesting, all family labor was needed in the fields. In other words, while sex may have been a central construct in dividing up labor, the line between men and women's work was mutable.

In the nineteenth century the U.S. economy was evolving from agriculture toward industrialization. During this period work transformed into something that was done away from home, and people were paid wages for their labor. There was considerable movement to urban areas in search of jobs, and over time many small family farms could not support themselves and folded. An urban middle class emerged, with men going off to work outside the home, and women doing the unpaid work inside it. More and more goods and services were produced for profit outside the home, and families purchased these with money from the wages they earned at outside jobs.

Meanwhile, an ideology emerged suggesting that a woman's proper role was in the home, serving as nurturer to her husband and family. Women and men increasingly inhabited "separate spheres." Her supposedly innate qualities of purity, submissiveness, and domesticity made her perfectly suited to make her home a refuge or a haven from the outside world of work. She was also now a consumer, no longer a producer of goods and services. Yet, the new industries needed large numbers of laborers so, in addition to recruiting men, they increasingly looked to young, poor, minority, and immigrant women and children. In 1890, 17 percent of women were in the labor force. Most of these women were unmarried and without children (Coontz 2000). Much of the work was dangerous and dirty, because there were minimal occupational safety standards compared to today. Thus, women's roles became increasingly intertwined with class and race: Poor or minority women *had* to work, whereas white middle-class women could bask in the glory of true womanhood far away from the world of work.

Trends in Child Labor

American children have often performed paid and unpaid labor, including indentured servitude. As industrialization took hold and families moved from farms into urban areas in search of work, poor children often toiled beside their parents in dangerous factories, textile mills, canneries, and mines (Child Labor Public Education Project 2006). Poor families needed the labor of all members in order to earn enough for even minimal food, shelter, and clothing. In fact, children were often preferred as laborers because they were seen as less expensive, less likely to strike, and more docile. Thousands of children were employed in dismal working conditions doing hard labor for only a fraction of the wages paid to men or women. Opposition to child labor began to grow in the northern states, such as the first state child labor law in Massachusetts in 1836 that required children under 15 working in factories to attend school at least 3 months per year, or the 1892 Democratic party platform that voted to ban factory employment for children under 15. Many factories moved south to avoid the growing protections of young workers. By the early decades of the twentieth century, the number of child laborers in the United States peaked and then began to decline as the labor and reform movements grew more outspoken about the horrendous plight of many young children. New protection laws were passed during this era, and by 1938, for the first time, a minimum age of employment and maximum hours of work for children were regulated by federal law (Child Labor Public Education Project 2006).

Recent Women's Labor Force Trends

The ideology of "separate spheres" for men and women persisted until well into the twentieth century. Even in 1970, only a generation ago, only 40 percent of married mothers worked. However, by 1980 we began to see an important cultural shift: The majority of mothers, whether married, single, or divorced, were employed outside the home

During the Industrial Revolution, child labor was commonplace in dangerous factories, textile mills, canneries, and mines. Parents needed the income of all family members to make ends meet and jobs for children were plentiful.

for pay. The jump in mothers' employment between 1970 and 1980 is by far the largest increase in any 10-year period. It likely reflects increasing job and educational opportunities for women, the ideas of the women's movement becoming commonplace, and changes in the economy. Mothers in the 1980s worked for a variety of reasons, as do mothers today, including for sheer economic need or personal fulfillment. Wives' earnings contribute 35 percent to the family income today, up from 27 percent in 1970 (U.S. Department of Labor, 2006a).

By the twenty-first century, employment became normative: 69 percent of married mothers, 73 percent of single mothers, and 82 percent of divorced, separated, or widowed mothers were employed for pay in 2005, as shown in Figure 11.1 (U.S. Census Bureau 2006a). The increase in mothers' employment has been linear (e.g., increasing every year) until recently. Beginning in 2000, the labor force participation rates of married and single mothers declined slightly, a trend that demographers are watching closely. The decline is most apparent among those with children under one year, declining from a high of 59 percent in 1998 to 53 percent in 2005 (U.S. Department of Labor 2006c).

Mothers with older children are more likely to work than are mothers with younger children, regardless of marital status, race, or ethnicity (U.S. Department of Labor

FIGURE 11.1 **Employment Status of Mothers by Marital Status: 1970–2005**

Source: U.S. Census Bureau 2006a.

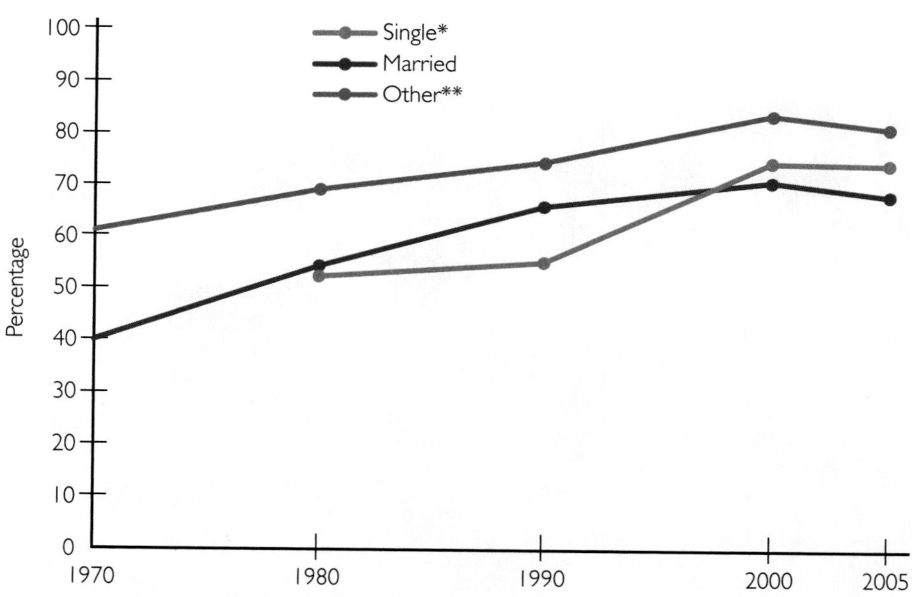

*Single data for 1970 not available.
**Widowed, divorced, or separated.

2006b). Figure 11.2 reports the rates of mothers' employment by age of children and her race/ethnicity. Black mothers have the highest labor force participation rates, and Hispanics have the lowest.

Despite the prevalence of families in which mothers are employed, *attitudes* toward working mothers are less positive than one might imagine. Table 11.1 compares the sentiment toward working mothers in 24 countries, by the age of the child, and whether mothers work full time or part time. As the table reveals, in only a few countries do the majority of respondents approve of a mother of a preschool-age child working outside the home for pay, either full-time or part-time (The Philippines, Israel, Canada, The Netherlands, the former East Germany, and Spain). Attitudes are more supportive of mothers working when the youngest child is in school. However, in no country surveyed did the majority of respondents support a mother working full time when her youngest child was in preschool or school-aged. Instead, respondents were more favorable toward part-time employment. Yet ironically, in many of these countries most women do indeed work full time outside the home for pay. These international data are 10 years old; have opinions changed?

The Changing Occupational Structure

U.S. industries have undergone rapid restructuring in the past few decades in response to technological changes and global competition. These changes have caused some striking changes for families, such as a decline in union membership and the various protections that unions provide; the rise in the number of dual-career families; and

FIGURE 11.2 **Mothers' Employment by Age of Children and Race/Ethnicity, 2005**

Source: U.S. Department of Labor 2006b.

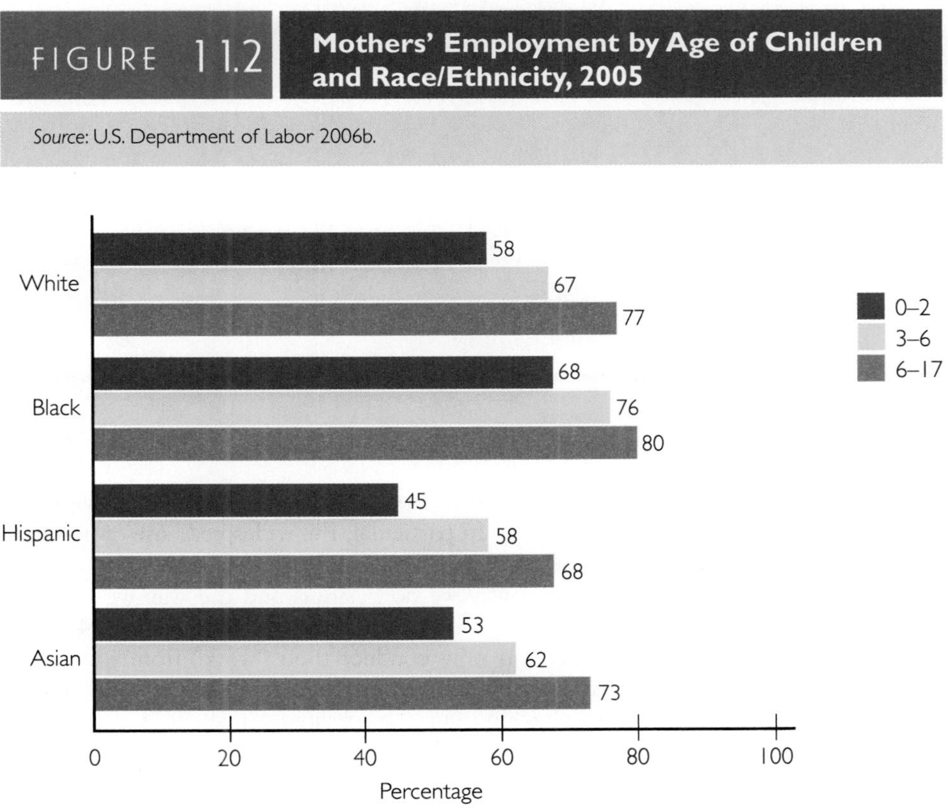

TABLE 11.1 **Percentage Approving of Woman Working Full Time/Part Time By Age of Children**

	Preschooler			Youngest in School	
	Full (%)	Part (%)		Full (%)	Part (%)
Philippines	25	35	Canada	46	43
Israel	18	63	Israel	38	54
Canada	18	37	**United States**	**38**	**54**
Netherlands	15	45	Slovenia	34	43
East Germany	15	65	Spain	33	45
Spain	14	39	Poland	30	30
Bulgaria	14	25	Netherlands	29	64
Ireland	12	39	Bulgaria	29	40
Poland	11	14	East Germany	27	67
United States	**11**	**34**	Ireland	26	50
Japan	11	26	Sweden	26	71
Slovenia	9	37	Norway	25	64
Sweden	8	62	Czech Republic	23	58
Northern Ireland	8	34	Northern Ireland	22	66
Norway	8	48	Philippines	21	37
Czech Republic	7	39	Hungary	20	50
Great Britain	6	32	Great Britain	18	73
Italy	5	56	Japan	17	57
Hungary	5	31	Italy	17	66
Russia	4	36	Australia	16	73
Australia	4	31	New Zealand	13	80
Austria	3	37	Russia	10	58
New Zealand	3	29	Austria	9	70
West Germany	1	30	West Germany	5	67

Source: Smith 1999.

the outsourcing of jobs to other countries as companies search for less-expensive labor costs and fewer governmental restrictions. In particular, the widespread use of personal notebook computers, virtually unheard of only 20 or 25 years ago, cell phones, fax machines, and pagers has changed the way we do business and the way we conduct our personal life. Many companies use this technology to conduct business 24 hours a day, 7 days a week. Many people can now conduct their "work" from just about anywhere, including the dining room table as their children romp in the living room. Likewise, when we are at "work" checking our work-related e-mail, it is easy to zap a quick letter off to mom. Thus, for many people the boundaries between work and family are becoming increasingly blurred.

Social scientists establish broad occupational categories by distinguishing between primary, secondary, and tertiary sectors in the labor market. The **primary sector** consists of jobs in which raw materials are harvested, such as in timber, agriculture, or mining. Jobs in the **secondary sector** transform raw materials into manufactured goods. The **tertiary sector**, or service sector, is the fastest-growing sector of the U.S. economy and provides a wide variety of jobs, such as salesclerk, attorney, cashier, and waitress. Within each sector we can also distinguish between tiers of workers. The **primary labor market** is characterized by having relatively high pay, benefits, and job security. Relatively low pay, few benefits, and little job security characterize the **secondary labor market**.

In recent years the number of workers needed in manufacturing has declined considerably. These disappearing jobs tended to pay relatively higher wages because of union protections. Instead, the U.S. economy is experiencing an explosion of jobs in the service sector—but compared to manufacturing jobs, those in the service sector, particularly within the secondary labor market, are generally without union protection and tend to be poorly paid, offering few fringe benefits to workers. The protections offered by unions are well established; for example, union workers receive higher pay than their nonunionized counterparts and are more likely to have retirement and health insurance benefits (United Auto Workers 2004).

What are some of the consequences of the changing economy?

Unemployment With the recession in the early 2000s, not everyone can find work easily. Although the U.S. unemployment rate averaged 4.4 percent overall in October 2006, it was double that for blacks (9.4 percent). The unemployment rate was more than triple the national average for white teens (13.5 percent), and significantly higher yet for black teens (26.8 percent) (U.S. Department of Labor 2006c).

Between 2001 and 2004, the economy had 8 percent fewer jobs because of a recession in the early 2000s. Employment was down in manufacturing by 15 percent, temporary help by 22 percent, accommodations by 11 percent, child day care by 7 percent, and retail trade by 7 percent (Boushey and Rosnick 2004). Moreover, the experiences of newer groups of workers within these sectors are likely to be worse because they are among those with the least seniority: "last hired, first fired." For example, research by the Urban Institute indicates that employment among recent welfare leavers fell from 50 percent to 42 percent between 1999 and 2002 (Loprest 2003).

Since then, the economy has recovered somewhat—a modest amount of jobs have been created, but pay has stagnated or declined for most workers. By December 2005, labor force participation rates were down for all workers except those 55 and over (U.S. Department of Labor 2006b).

What does it feel like to look for work week after week and turn up with nothing? When even jobs in the secondary labor market have stiff competition, many people feel psychologically wounded—wanting work, but not being able to find it, let alone maintain it (Elder et al. 1992). A study done during the Great Depression of the 1930s found that unemployed men experienced considerable distress, and they often took out their frustration and depression on their wives and families (Elder 1999). More recent work by William Julius Wilson found that the high unemployment experienced by inner-city blacks affects marriage rates. Black women are hesitant to marry a man without prospects for stable employment (Wilson 1987, 1996). It is clear that macro issues, such as unemployment, affect personal relationships.

Poverty-Level Wages Some families earn the minimum wage or wages only slightly above it. The federal minimum wage in the United States, at $5.15 per hour in early 2007, comes nowhere near to lifting even a small family out of poverty. At $5.15 an hour, working 40 hours per week yields less than $900 a month before taxes. Working 52 weeks a year, a full-time employee would average around $10,700 per year.

More than 7.5 million workers earn at or near the minimum wage. This includes 5.9 million adults (age 25 and older) and 1.8 million parents raising children. Most of these workers are employed full-time (U.S. Department of Labor 2006c).

For even the smallest families who have only one child, living and surviving on the minimum wage poses a serious challenge. Recognizing this, 18 states have set higher minimum-wage rates (U.S. Department of Labor 2006c). However, nationally the minimum wage has not been increased since 1997 and continues to lose value because of inflation. Its real value fell to around $4.50 by 2006 and continues to decline. It is not a living wage; even if increased to $6.65 an hour, full-time minimum-wage earnings would come to only $13,832 a year, or 20 percent less than the poverty guideline for a family of three in 2006 (U.S. Department of State 2006).

When discussions of raising the minimum wage surface, business leaders often cry "foul." They argue that increasing the minimum wage will harm poor families by raising prices and destroying entry-level job opportunities and that it will cost consumers and workers billions per year as the higher cost of entry-level jobs is passed on through higher prices and lower real wages.

However, these complaints have been used against all minimum wage increases, including the creation of the minimum wage itself. Instead, many economists and other social scientists argue that the income gains from a minimum wage hike would outweigh the job losses and price increases and would be an important component of reducing poverty (Economic Policy Institute 2005). A 1998 Economic Policy Institute (EPI) study did not find any systematic, significant job loss associated with the 1996–1997 minimum wage increase. In fact, following that most recent increase, the low-wage labor market performed better than it had in decades (lower unemployment rates, higher average hourly wages, higher family income, lower poverty rates). Economic models that look specifically at low-wage labor markets find that employers can absorb some of the costs of a wage increase through higher productivity, lower recruiting and training costs, decreased absenteeism, and increased worker morale. Moreover, a 2005 Fiscal Policy Institute (FPI) study of state minimum wages found no evidence of negative employment effects on small business (Economic Policy Institute 2005).

The concept of paying a **living wage** is taking hold. A living wage ordinance requires employers to pay wages that are above federal or state minimum wage levels, usually ranging from 100 to 130 percent of the poverty line. Only a specific set of workers is covered by living wage ordinances, usually those employed by businesses that have a contract with a city or county government or those that receive economic development subsidies from the locality. The rationale behind the ordinances is that city and county governments should not contract with or subsidize employers who pay poverty-level wages. Boston, Baltimore, Denver, Los Angeles, and Portland (Oregon) are among nearly 100 cities around the country that make particular companies pay their employees wages that are more in line with the cost of living in the area, usually $3.00 to $6.00 above minimum wage.

Part-Time, Nonstandard, and Temporary Work In addition to pay, another concern is that many of the new jobs associated with economic restructuring are part time, subcontracted, temporary in nature, or occur at night. Some offer irregular work schedules. Employees working in these types of jobs, called **nonstandard work schedules**, represent the fastest-growing category of workers in the United States (Presser 2003). Since 1982, temporary employment has increased several hundred percent. In other words, millions of women and men begin the workday not knowing if, and for how long, their jobs are likely to continue. There is also a growing trend toward jobs that require weekend, evening, or variable nonfixed schedules, particularly those found in the lower-paying service sector (Presser 2003; Presser and Cox 1997; U.S. Department of Labor 2006b).

Some part-time and contingency workers prefer this arrangement, especially highly paid professionals who value their freedom and independence on the job or mothers with young children who would prefer to work only sporadically, but most American families prefer the assurance of a steady job with prearranged hours, and an established pay scale with fringe benefits. Families with nonstandard work schedules may find it difficult to organize child care, because most child care centers normally are only open between 7 A.M. and 6 P.M. Furthermore, child care centers usually require a regular paid commitment to a particular schedule by the family, such as a Monday through Friday schedule or a Monday, Wednesday, Friday schedule. When a parent works full-time one week, 3 days the next week, and 4 half days the next, it wreaks havoc on child care arrangements, school schedules, parenting tasks and many other dimensions of family life (Strazdins et al. 2006).

On average, women contribute over one-third of a family's income, but many work in the low-paying tertiary service sector where their work schedule is part-time, nonstandard, and temporary.

Recent analyses of national data indicate that women with a high school diploma or less are most susceptible to nonstandardized work hours. Forty-three percent of women with a high school education or less work at least some weekend days or have varying shifts, compared with 36 percent of women who have more than a high school education. Most women with children do not want this arrangement and find it stressful (Joshi and Bogen 2007; Perry-Jenkins et al. 2007). Over half of women surveyed whose youngest child was between ages 5 and 13 reported that the main reason they worked these shifts was because it was a requirement of the job and that they could not get any other job (53 percent). Only 30 percent of women listed beneficial reasons for working these shifts, such as it allowed for better child care arrangements (18 percent); it allowed better arrangements for care of other family members (7 percent); it offered time for school (2 percent); or it provided better pay (3 percent) (Presser 2003).

Most women do not work these schedules out of personal inclination, but because these are the required working conditions of their jobs, such as cashiers, maids, nursing aides, cooks, and waiters. Moreover, these occupations are likely to grow in the future, which has important implications for the availability and costs of formal child care. It also affects the degree to which family, friends, and neighbors can provide child care.

Rhonda is a woman hoping to leave welfare, and she is one of many people who are looking for a good job with good pay (Seccombe 2007a). She would like to raise her young son Bobby without welfare, and recognizes the need for a permanent full-time job. Instead, however, she has been stymied by the tremendous growth in part-time, temporary positions (Seccombe 2007a, 205).

> Hopefully I can get me a job. A permanent job. My sister's trying to get me a job where she works. I put my application in last week. And it would be a permanent job. When you go through those agencies, it's just temporary work. It's just whenever they need you, and it's unfair too. Every job I've found is through this temporary agency, like Manpower, but it's only temporary. And they cut my check and my food stamps, and when my job ends, it's like you're stuck again. So I'm trying to find a permanent steady job. But it's hard around here. I've been out looking for work, and hoping that something comes through.

Rhonda may be surprised to learn that temporary agencies are booming. Manpower is one of the largest private employers in the United States, ranking 140 in the *Fortune* 500, employing over 2.5 million workers a year (Manpower 2005).

Disposable Workforce Turnover rates in many secondary labor market jobs are high, even those considered to be "permanent." Sometimes people quit work in hopes of finding something better. However, these jobholders are also considerably more likely to be laid off than are other workers; they are the expendable workforce. They work in the service industry, in clerical work, and on assembly lines performing routine tasks. To management, people in these largely unskilled or semiskilled jobs are interchangeable. A high turnover rate is not a problem for management, and in fact may even be considered desirable so that health insurance premiums and payments of other benefits can be avoided. These disposable workers generally earn less than those on the regular payroll and must live with the uncertainty that their jobs may permanently end today when they clock out at 5:00 P.M. Their anxiety is high, and for many, unemployment insurance is not an option.

Eliza, a single mother of four children, epitomizes the plight of many people who are looking for work, but find that they are at the mercy of employers who do not see as priorities providing stable employment, reliable and sufficient work hours, and benefits for their employees. Eager to work, Eliza was delighted to find a job in a fast-food restaurant. She told them up front that she was looking for 30 to 40 hours of employment per week. Knowing this, they hired her, but instead of meeting her needs, her boss routinely asks her to leave work early, unpaid, during the slow periods. She was hired to fill an organizational need and released as soon as the need for her labor abated. Because her income was so much less than she anticipated when being hired, Eliza found that the job did not pay her bills. In addition, she felt that the long commute was not worth her while, so she quit to return to welfare (Seccombe 2007a, 206):

> That's something I need is a job. I've been looking. I just can't find the right one. I used to work at <fast food industry>, but I wasn't making much money. By the time I caught the city bus, went out there, by the time I got to my kids, I spent all the money that they gave me. I liked the job, but it was just that I had to pay 75 cents to get to work, and paid 75 cents to get back. If I missed the bus I had to give somebody $3.00 or $4.00 to take me. And they wouldn't give me enough hours. I told them when they gave me this job that I needed at least 30–40 hours a week. I just can't afford to work less. But I was wasting my time going out there. I had to be at work by 11 o'clock, but they would send me home by 2 o'clock. I didn't even get 20 hours a week. You hear what I'm saying? Ten or 12, maybe. I think what they was doing was hiring you for the busy hour, and once the busy hour passed, you was sent out of there. I had to quit because it was costing me too much to go way over there.

Juggling Work and Family Life

Work-Family Interface

Because work and family are no longer separate domains, family researchers look at their interface (Bianchi et al. 2006; Chaudry 2006). They have found that combining work and family is not easy for most families, and there is a high degree of conflict. **Work-family conflict** has been defined as a form of inter-role conflict in which the role pressures from the work and family domains are mutually incompatible in some respect. There is a bidirectional relationship: Participation in the work role is made more difficult by virtue of participation in the family role, and participation in family roles is made more difficult by the work role (Frone 2003). The conflict is caused by many factors, including the level of responsibility and workload associated with paid work, inflexibility of when and where paid work is done, job dissatisfaction, minimal maternity and family leaves, the inflexibility of family demands (especially families with small children), and the lack of social and financial support for working families.

The relationship between work and family is highly gendered. Men receive pressure from their employers to fulfill work obligations and to ignore or minimize family obligations. The idea is to let someone else, presumably the wife, take off from work when a child is sick or has to go to the dentist. Women get more pressure from home to fulfill home obligations at the cost of work obligations (Spain and Bianchi 1996). Consequently, men are often not "penalized" at work for having children. As mentioned previously, the term *family man* implies that the employee is stable and hardworking, but there is no semantic equivalent for women, such as *family woman*.

Most research on the interface of work and family has been conducted in western countries; however, data from the IBM Corporation obtained in 48 countries revealed that significant work-family conflicts are experienced throughout much of the world (Hill et al. 2004). In particular, they found that the focus of concern is on how the conflict affects family life, not work. It was more likely that work was detrimental to family than family was thought to be detrimental to work. They found that having a spouse or intimate partner contributed to a reduced conflict for women in the east and west, but not for women in developing countries. They also found that responsibility for children contributed more than twice as much to conflict for women as it did for men, probably because women carry a larger load of child care responsibilities than do men.

Parents feel considerable pressures trying to balance work and family time. Many report that they do not spend as much time with their children as they would like; however, studies over the past 20 years indicate that parents today actually spend as much or even more time with their children, not less.

The Time Crunch

What is the largest challenge that parents report facing today? One study that asked parents to rate a list of challenges they might face found that 40 percent of full-time workers report balancing work and family is the biggest challenge they face as a parent, twice as many as those who voiced the number two concern of instilling moral values in their children (Rankin 2002). A study that used two different national samples found that nearly 50 percent of parents residing with their children feel that they spend too little time with them (Milkie et al. 2004). Another study found that 45 percent of workers report that work and family responsibilities interfere with each other "a lot" or "some" (Families and Work Institute 2004).

Finally, a qualitative study found that less than a quarter of respondents said they were satisfied with the time they spend with their spouse and children. Women felt that they wanted to improve the *quality* of their time together, whereas men were more likely to emphasize the *quantity* of time (Roxburgh 2006).

Parents find caring for their children, playing with them, and teaching them to be enjoyable activities. They also believe that spending time with their children is important for the children's sense of happiness and well-being and is necessary for their proper development (Bianchi 2000; Daly 2001; Kurz 2002).

Milkie and colleagues (2004) report that several factors are associated with feeling time deficits with children. These include amount of time in paid work, the age of the youngest child, and sex of parent—persons who work longer hours, who have a younger child, and fathers are more likely to report feeling a time strain. However, once the work hours are held constant, mothers actually feel more time strain than fathers. Interestingly, single parents did not report feeling more time strain than did married parents (Milkie et al. 2004).

Despite their feelings to the contrary, research suggests that parents actually spend as much time or even more time with children than they did in the past (Bianchi 2000; Sandberg and Hofferth 2001). Sandberg and Hofferth compared the amount of time mothers and fathers reportedly spent with their children in 1981 and 1997. *Employed mothers* averaged 27 hours per week with their children in 1997, an increase of 4 hours from 1981. *Nonemployed mothers* spent an average of 32 hours per week with their children in 1997, an increase of 6 hours. *Employed fathers* spent 23 hours per week with their children and *unemployed fathers* spent 22 hours in 1997, an increase of 5 and 3 hours, respectively, since 1981. Their study suggests (1) the amount of time both mothers and fathers spend with children is on the rise, regardless of employment status; (2) mothers continue to spend significantly more time with their children than do fathers; and (3) nonemployed mothers spend only slightly more time with their children than do employed mothers.

If the time parents spend with their children has actually increased rather than decreased, why do parents report feeling such a time squeeze? Daly (2001) speculates that parents are frustrated by their inability to respond spontaneously to their children because of encroaching demands placed on them by their employers. As parents work more hours per week, and as work conditions and hours become less standardized, parents may find it increasingly difficult to meet their children's needs. They apparently continue to spend time with them, but it may be at greater personal cost, such as lack of leisure activities, exercise, or sleep (Nomaguchi and Bianchi 2004; Rankin 2002).

Consequently, most parents report that they would prefer to stay home with their children when they are young (Farkas et al. 2000). If they would prefer to stay at home, then why do they work? There are many reasons; some are financial, others might be related to the fear they would be unable to enter the job market later or would reenter with a large disadvantage compared to other workers. Box 11.1 addresses some of these concerns, and offers a proposal to help families have a parent at home, if they prefer to do so. It is an innovative idea that would allow people to draw Social Security for a 3-year period while raising children.

Catch 22: Inflexible Full-Time Work or Part-Time Penalty

Despite the tensions associated with work and family, many workers have little control or flexibility over their working conditions—when they work, how long of a day they work, whether they can miss a day to take care of children, or whether they can take extended time off and reenter without penalty (Kornbluh et al. 2004). For example, one survey found that 43 percent of workers have no control over start and end times, and 54 percent of workers with children report that they have no time off to care for sick children without losing pay (Families and Work Institute 2004). Meanwhile, work is demanding more time of its employees: Dual-earner couples now work an average of 91 hours per week, up 10 hours since 1977 (Bond et al. 2002).

Because of the inflexibility of many workplaces, some parents have opted to reduce their work hours to part time. About 24 percent of workers are employed for less than 35 hours per week, classified as part-time by the U.S. Department of Labor (2006c). Most are women, and they generally pay a steep price for this added flexibility. Workers

BOX 11.1 Social Policies for Families

Fixing Social Insecurity

Most people want to be parents, yet most must work to provide for their children. Studies show that the majority would prefer to stay home while the children are young. What can we do to help strengthen our families? The following is an intriguing idea—let new families draw upon Social Security.

Ask parents, and many of them will tell you that they would like to be able to take some time out from their jobs so they can devote more attention and energy to their kids. A study by Public Agenda, a nonpartisan public policy research organization shows that most parents (68 percent) "would prefer to stay home with their children when they are young" (Farkas et al. 2000). Among parents with children under five, 80 percent of mothers and 52 percent of fathers say this (Farkas et al. 2000).

If so many parents are yearning to stay home with their children during their earliest years, what stops them? One factor is certainly well-founded anxieties about returning to the labor market and vision of lifetime career setbacks. Some want the continued rewards of work, but with scaled-down hours. For many parents, though, the biggest barrier is practical: They can't afford to.

Here's a proposal to help them. Why not allow working parents to draw Social Security benefits for up to 3 years during their prime child-rearing years? This would give moms and dads a real choice about how much time to spend working and how much time to spend with their kids. Those who elected to "borrow on their Social Security" would repay the system, at least in part. For example, they could increase the employee's share of the payroll taxes they pay in when they return to work, they could defer their age of retirement with full Social Security benefits on a year-for-year basis, or they could accept a reduced monthly benefit, as those who opt for early retirement do now.

How much of a difference would this make for parents trying to make ends meet? Plenty, it turns out. Taxes and child care costs take such a big bite out of parents' incomes that even modest Social Security benefits could largely replace the net income from an average job. For example, a parent earning a second salary of $30,000 (assuming the spouse also makes $30,000) would only net about $10,065 after taxes, child care, and work expenses (see below). That works out to about the same as the average annual Social Security income for retirees. It's enough to make a real difference for U.S. families.

Among mothers or fathers taking advantage of this option, most would probably stay at home during their children's earliest years—but we also know that kids' needs don't magically disappear at age 3. A struggling third-grader or a troubled teen can be just as demanding of parental attention. This proposal would let parents decide what makes sense for them and their families.

Net Income After Taxes, Child Care, and Work Expenses

Example: A two-earner couple, where each parent makes $30,000

The second salary:	$30,000
Subtract:	
Social Security and Medicare taxes	2,295
Additional state and local taxes	1,500
Estimated additional federal income tax	6,180
Additional child care (estimated at $120/week)*	6,240
Commuting cost ($25/week times 50)	1,250
Cost of work clothing and dry cleaning	870
Cost of restaurant meals on work days ($25/week times 50)	1,250
Other (nonreimbursed expenses, paid help, meals out, etc.)	350
Net Income	**$10,065**

*Based on U.S. Census figures for weekly total child care costs per family (for families including a preschooler), adjusted for inflation.

Source: U.S. Census Bureau 1995.

Note: Calculations used in this example are adopted from a model appearing online in offspringmag.com on April 13, 2000. Estimates are based on federal tax rates at that time.

(continued)

One issue that would need to be addressed is overcoming barriers to workforce reentry. It is unrealistic that employers be asked to guarantee someone's job after a leave of a year or more. Employers need to create more "on-ramps"; opportunities and recruitment strategies that give workers a path to accelerate back up to speed and full productivity. Continuation of health insurance would also need to be addressed, although for married workers with a covered spouse this would not be a problem. Others could buy into their former employees' group plan or perhaps into Medicare. More fundamentally, we need messages to change the national mindset, so that nurturing children is seen as a respectable addition to lifetime accomplishments, not discounted as a brain cell–diminishing resume gap.

The proposal offered here—allowing parents to actually draw Social Security at two points in their lives—would offer real relief from the time crunch to the millions of Americans struggling to meet the dual demands of job and family every day. In the last century we addressed old age. Today, compelling needs have emerged earlier in our lives when we are raising our families. A transformed labor force faces policies that have not adequately changed to compensate for the massive entry of women into paid employment. Our Social Security system has long been thought of as providing a measure of financial security in return for a lifetime of work. What could be a more vital contribution to the future of our country than raising children well?

Source: Adapted from Rankin 2002.

CRITICAL THINKING QUESTIONS

1. Do you think a program like this that would allow parents to draw upon social security as they raise their children would be popular among Americans? Why or why not? Would it be stigmatized as welfare?
2. What do you think might be some of the logistic barriers to adopting this type of program? Do you think the barriers (if any) are surmountable?
3. Do you think that most working parents have created a budget like the one listed to see just how much they are really ahead financially by working? Do you think the sample budget realistically reflects the budget of a spouse earning $30,000?

who go part-time or a nonstandard (temporary, contract) route earn nearly $4.00 per hour less than regular full-time workers. Moreover, only 14 percent of part-time or nonstandard workers receive health insurance from their employers, compared to 69 percent of their counterparts working full time in standard work arrangements, and only 16 percent receive a pension, compared to 66 percent of regular full-time workers (Wenger 2003). Only 7 percent are protected by unions, compared to 15 percent among full-time workers (U.S. Department of Labor 2006c).

The next section examines issues that affect the delicate balance of work and family life.

The Division of Household Labor

As sociologist Scott Coltrane reminds us, the family work that feeds, clothes, shelters, and cares for both adults and children is just as important to the maintenance of society as the work that occurs in the labor market (Coltrane 2000). However, household labor has been considered "women's work," trivialized, and not deemed worthy of scientific study until roughly 20 or 30 years ago. Since then, a tremendous amount of research has been done to examine who does what in the home, under what circumstances, why, and how housework is embedded in complex processes relating to the social construction of gender.

How Is Household Labor Defined and Measured?

How is **household labor** defined? This is an important question because it may be defined differently from one context to another. Generally, it refers to unpaid work that is done to maintain family members and/or a home (Knodel et al. 2004). It usually excludes child care and other types of emotional labor and caregiving. According to national surveys, the five most time-consuming major household tasks are (1) meal preparation or cooking; (2) housecleaning; (3) shopping for groceries and household goods; (4) washing dishes and cleaning up after meals; and (5) laundry, including washing, ironing, and mending clothes (Robinson and Godbey 1997). Coltrane (2000) refers to these as **routine household labor**, because they are repetitive and less able to be postponed than are other tasks. Although some people enjoy some or all of these activities, most people say that they do not enjoy routine household labor nor do they enjoy a significant number of specific tasks (Kroska 2003; Robinson and Milkie 1998). They are often referred to as boring, onerous, and mundane (Coltrane 2000). Other tasks, which are called **occasional labor**, occur less frequently and have more flexibility in timing such as gardening, paying bills, household repairs, or servicing the car.

Some people may wonder how something as private as housework can actually be a researchable topic, yet the number of studies on the topic has exploded over the past two decades. Household labor is researched many different ways, including self-reports made by one partner (usually the woman) or both partners, or by time diaries that are kept over a specific period of time. There is often a discrepancy between partners when assessing how much time each spends on housework (Kamo 2000; Lee and Waite 2005). Men and women report spending a greater number of hours on tasks than their partners say they do. Men are also more likely than women to claim that housework is shared equally. One study with over 350 couples found that 40 percent of men claimed that housework such as cooking, cleaning, and laundry was shared equally, compared to 31 percent of the women. Moreover, only 15 percent of men reported that the wife always does these tasks; however, 25 percent of women said that this was indeed the case (Davis and Greenstein 2004). In particular, partners tend to provide relatively similar estimates of women's time on household labor, but quite divergent estimates on the amount of time men spend. Some researchers suspect that men overestimate their time on household chores (Press and Townsley 1998), but both partners estimate the wife's time more accurately (Kamo 2000). Other researchers suggest that both partners overinflate wives' contribution, which results in a larger gap than really exists.

Who Does What?

Regardless of the way that housework is defined or measured, the research indicates that women do significantly more housework than men do. The size of men's and women's contributions vary across studies, but most find that women spend two to three times the amount of time on various household tasks than men do (Davis and Greenstein 2004; Hook 2004; Lee and Waite 2005). Table 11.2 estimates the number of hours spent on housework per week, showing the difference between husbands' and wives' self-reports and also between these and various E.S.M., or diary methods that include time spent on housework as a primary or secondary activity or include the mental labor associated with

TABLE 11.2 Estimated Number of Hours Spent on Housework per Week, by Two Different Measures

	Wives	Husbands	Difference	Proportion Done by Husband (%)
Survey				
Wives' report	26.0	12.8	13.2	33.0
Husbands' report	24.0	17.7	7.2	42.0
ESM*				
Primary	15.0	10.0	5.0	40.0
Primary + secondary	21.3	13.0	8.3	38.0
Primary + secondary + mental labor	24.4	15.3	9.1	39.0

*ESM: Experience Sampling Method is a diary-like method covering 1 week.

Source: Lee and Waite 2005.

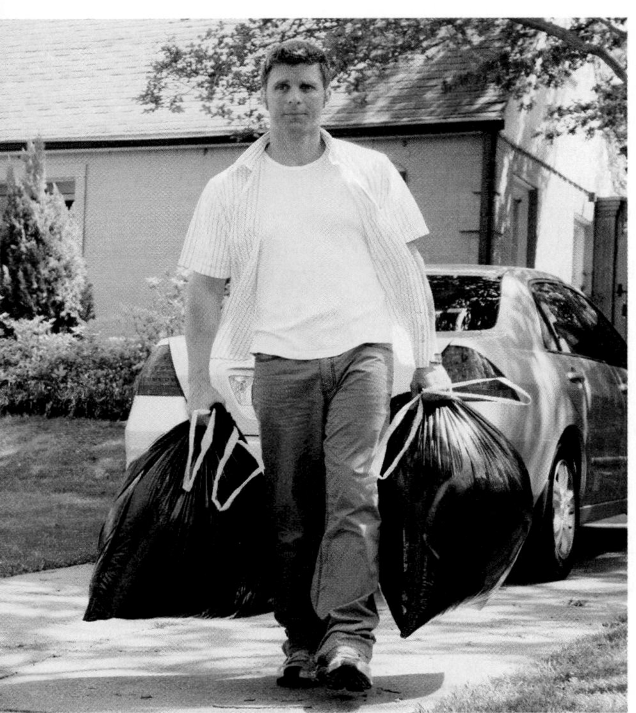

Men's share of housework is on the rise, but remains far short of that of their wives and partners. Housework is highly gendered, with men performing the outside tasks, such as taking out the garbage or working in the yard, which have greater flexibility on when they can be done.

housework. The results indicate that (1) women do significantly more housework than men; (2) the amount of time supposedly spent on housework varies tremendously by how it is measured; and (3) the proportion of housework done by husbands, on average, ranges from 33 to 42 percent.

Women's work tends to be routine housework, which tends to be nondiscretionary and repetitive. According to a study using the National Survey of Families and Households, which is based on a representative sample of Americans, the average married woman did about three times as much routine housework as the average married man (32 versus 10 hours per week). With respect to occasional care (which includes those tasks that tend to be more time flexible and discretionary), married men performed 10 hours per week while women performed about 6 hours. In total, women performed about twice as much household work as did men; other studies show an even greater imbalance (Coltrane 2000). Moreover, the tasks women do tend to be inflexible as to when they are performed. For example, women are more likely to be responsible for fixing dinner, which must be prepared in the next *hour*, whereas men are more likely to do the yard work, which could be done any time this *week*. This difference alone can add to family stress.

The typical pattern in dual-earner families is presented in the book *The Second Shift* by sociologist Arlie Hochschild (1989). In her sample of 50 dual-earner couples, 20 percent shared the housework equally. In 70 percent of families, men did somewhere between one-third and one-half of the housework, and in 10 percent of families, men did less than one-third. She found that at the end of a long workday women returned to do their "second shift"—their second job of housework and child care, which included arranging, supervising,

TABLE 11.3 Husbands' and Wives' Responses to Housework Question

	Who Does the Housework? (%)				
	Always Wife	**Usually Wife**	**About Equal**	**Usually Husband**	**Always Husband**
Bulgaria					
Husband	20	49	26	2	2
Wife	38	33	28	1	0
Czech Republic					
Husband	20	48	31	1	1
Wife	22	39	37	2	0
Estonia					
Husband	8	43	44	4	0
Wife	22	41	35	2	1
West Germany					
Husband	22	52	22	1	4
Wife	51	37	11	1	1
East Germany					
Husband	12	52	31	2	2
Wife	38	38	24	1	0
Hungary					
Husband	26	38	31	2	3
Wife	40	31	27	2	1
Japan					
Husband	63	30	5	0	2
Wife	79	19	2	0	0
Netherlands					
Husband	22	51	25	1	0
Wife	40	42	18	1	0
Poland					
Husband	33	43	19	2	3
Wife	52	30	14	3	1
Russia					
Husband	4	27	67	3	0
Wife	9	29	60	1	0
Slovenia					
Husband	29	47	18	3	3
Wife	46	36	18	0	0
United Kingdom					
Husband	22	43	30	4	2
Wife	41	35	22	1	1
United States					
Husband	**15**	**42**	**40**	**2**	**1**
Wife	**25**	**42**	**31**	**2**	**1**
All nations					
Husband	22	44	30	2	2
Wife	38	35	26	1	0

Note: Total working sample N = 10,153.

Source: Davis and Greenstein 2004.

and planning, in addition to accomplishing actual tasks. For the most part, men returned home to "help." She found that women, on average, work an extra 15 hours per week, compared to men.

The gender imbalance in the division of household labor is found throughout the world, although the extent of the imbalance varies, as shown in Table 11.3 (Davis and Greenstein 2004). Again, although men and women give somewhat different reports, Russia is the only country in which the housework—defined here as routine tasks of cooking, cleaning, and laundry—is reportedly shared equally by more than half the population. Sixty-seven percent of Russian husbands and 60 percent of Russian wives report that these tasks are shared equally, although another one-third report that they are usually or always done by the wife. These differences likely represent both the greater number of Russian women employed outside the home as well as cultural norms about men and women's roles in the family. In contrast to Russia, only 5 percent of Japanese men and 2 percent of Japanese women report that the cooking, cleaning, and laundry are equally shared. Instead, housework is highly segregated by sex in Japan, with 63 percent of husbands and 80 percent of wives reporting that the wife always does the cooking, cleaning, and laundry; the majority of the remaining Japanese respondents also report that they are usually done by the wife. Very few husbands or wives in any country reported that men always or usually did cooking, cleaning, or laundry.

Despite the imbalance, it appears that many families are renegotiating how household labor is performed. Studies reveal that men's time spent in housework is on the rise, and women's is on the decline (Evertsson and Nermo 2004). Black families, families in which the woman is employed, where the wife works longer hours and the husband works fewer hours, where the woman earns a higher income, where both man and woman have higher levels of education, where they have no or few children, and where both support gender equality are more likely to share housework to a greater degree than do other families (Coltrane 2000; Evertsson and Nermo 2004). Nonetheless, even these families do not come close to sharing housework equally. Therefore employed wives have less time for leisure and experience more stress and burnout than do their husbands in the "work-family balancing act" (Milkie and Peltola 1999, 476; Schor 2002).

One study conducted by the National Parenting Association reported that far more women than men claimed that they do not have enough time for themselves, as shown in Table 11.4. This stress and burnout is significant because it can lead to depression and marital instability. In particular, when women value equality in the home but end up doing the majority of household labor themselves, their sense of fairness is violated and their happiness with their marriage declines (Lavee and Katz 2002; Wilkie et al. 1998). Men may compare themselves to what their fathers did, and therefore believe "Wow, I am doing a lot," whereas many women compare their partners to what they are doing

TABLE 11.4 Who Feels the Time Crunch the Most?

Percentage of Parents Who Say . . .	Not Enough Time for Self	Not Enough Time for Kids
All parents	56	32
Working full-time		
Women	79	48
Men	53	36

Source: Rankin 2002.

and say, "This isn't fair." However, viewing something as *fair* is not the same as actually being *shared equally*. One study found that men see the division of labor as fair when they contribute 35 percent of the total time allocated to household tasks, and women consider the distribution fair when they contribute about 66 percent of the total time (Lennon and Rosenfeld 1994).

Explanations for the Division of Labor

Several theories have been used to analyze the relationship between sex and the division of household labor, including (1) the time availability perspective; (2) the relative resources perspective; and (3) the gender perspective.

Time Availability The **time availability perspective** suggests that the division of labor is largely determined by (1) the need for household labor, such as the number of children in the home; and (2) each partner's availability to perform household tasks, such as the number of hours spent in paid work (Shelton 1992). Both husband and wife are expected to perform domestic work to the extent that other demands on their lives allow them; simply put, the partner who has the most time available because of fewer other commitments will spend more time on housework. However, it is unclear whether women do the majority of the housework because they spend fewer hours in paid labor or whether they spend fewer hours in paid labor because they have to do most of the housework (Evertsson and Nermo 2004).

Relative Resources **Resource theory** is grounded in the premise of exchange theory (Becker 1981; Blood and Wolfe 1960). It posits that the greater the relative amount or value of resources contributed by a partner, the greater is his or her power within the relationship. This power can then be translated into bargaining to avoid tasks such as housework that offer no pay and minimal social prestige (Bittman et al. 2003). However, working-class partners often provide relatively similar resources to the family, yet their roles are often highly segregated (Rubin 1976). Resources are usually defined as monetary ones, but they can take other forms as well, such as occupational prestige, education level, or even good looks or an exceptionally charismatic personality.

Doing Gender The previous perspectives are largely gender neutral, but some scholars suggest that gender itself is the ultimate explanatory variable, not how much time a partner has available or how many resources he or she brings to the relationship. "**Doing gender**" suggests that housework is so ingrained as women's work that it functions as an area in which gender is symbolically created and reproduced (Fenstermaker Berk 1985; West and Zimmerman 1987). Wives do most of the housework because it is expected of them as women and they have heard these messages since childhood. Likewise, men do less because housework is not a part of their gendered identity. This is likely why many men and women feel that the division of household labor is fair even when it is not split equally between partners. Gendered norms exert a powerful influence on what we see as normative. When we remember the household tasks we may have done as children, most women will report that they were involved in "inside" domestic labor, such as helping with cooking, cleaning, or taking care of siblings, and men will remember that they were more involved in "outside" labor, such as mowing the lawn. In other words, even girls do more routine labor, while boys do occasional labor. Moreover, which is more highly valued? Typically we pay a lot more for someone to mow our lawn than babysit our children. These gendered values are so ingrained that we rarely question this logic.

Children's Labor in the Home

How much, and under what conditions, do sons and daughters provide housework or child care? What impact does their labor have on themselves and their families? There are many reasons that children perform household labor. Some parents are attempting

BOX 11.2 Families as Lived Experience

"Mini-Moms" Created as Low-Income Families Search for Affordable Day Care

Family researchers Lisa Dodson and Jillian Dickert examine how low-income families manage when mother goes off to work; teenage daughters are often called upon to do the household labor and child care. What are the consequences of this?

As parents in low-income and welfare-to-work families search for affordable day care and household help, they rely on "mini-moms" to take up the slack at home. Typically the oldest daughter acts as the mini-mom, helping to keep the family together by taking over the responsibilities of caring for younger children and substitution for the mom who is unavailable to do all the household work. "She has to make me do it because she hasn't got anyone else," said one 16-year-old.

Dr. Lisa Dodson, researcher at Boston College, and Dr. Jillian Dickert of Brandeis University examined how low-wage families survive and how youths in high schools prepare for economic survival. Their research, "Girls' Family Labor in Low-Income Households: A Decade of Qualitative Research" identifies the role of the daughter who, of necessity, takes on the role of child care provider and assistant housekeeper (Dodson and Dickert 2004). "An important, consistent, and unexpected finding in this research is the amount of girls' family labor," states Dr. Dodson. "The upside is that girls, mothers, and some teachers identified some strengths in children taking on family obligations. Low-income families with mini-moms may be more bonded and more loyal, and the girls much more mature about social responsibilities than adolescents in higher-income families."

However, Dodson and Dickert also found a downside to these girls' responsible family roles. Their commitments to their homes and to younger siblings undermine their education and social development outside the family and may even encourage early marriage and pregnancy. The heavy responsibilities at home impede the girls' chance to focus on their own development, and as a result they are more likely to carry poverty into the next generation.

Dodson concludes:

> While mothers and families are now entirely dependent on the labor market because welfare is largely obsolete for them, the big hidden cost is that children are in a sense making up for the inadequate wages by taking over all the work. Simply put, low wages and lack of social support for families in the U.S. affect the children's current and future life course. Family members put their loved ones first. In a society that does not invest in families and children adequately, that costs them and it costs their children's future.

Source: Adapted from National Council on Family Relations 2004. "Mini-moms Created As Low-Income Families Search for Affordable Daycare." Press Release; Dodson & Dickert 2004.

CRITICAL THINKING QUESTIONS

1. This research article reports that older daughters become mother-surrogates in the family, responsible for taking care of household chores and child care. Do you think that older sons are responsible for chores and child care in the same way? How might it be the same or different and why?
2. There appear to be pros and cons to the arrangement of mini-moms. How can the pros be enhanced and the cons minimized?
3. Do you think there is any upper-middle-class bias on the part of the researchers as they frame girls' home involvement as problematic? Why or why not?

to socialize their children to future adult or parental roles by teaching a child how to use the vacuum or washing machine. Other parents simply need the extra assistance to keep up with housework and child care demands and require a child to babysit a younger sibling after school (Blair 1992, 2000; Gill 1998). One study, based on a large nationally representative sample, found that in families with school-aged children, 5.9 hours of routine housework are performed by the children each week, which is almost as much labor as is contributed by fathers (Blair 1992). Young children's housework is less gendered than adults or teens and may include things such as picking up toys or making one's bed. Studies of teenage girls indicate that girls do about twice the amount of housework as boys. The work performed by girls tends to be routine inside chores, such as cleaning or cooking or caring for siblings, whereas boys do occasional outside chores, such as yard work (Antill et al. 1996; Blair 1992).

Children in two-parent, dual-earner families, and children of highly educated families tend to do less housework and child care than do children in other family types (Benin and Edwards 1990). Lower-income families and single-parent families rely on children, especially daughters, to a considerable extent to help with numerous household tasks and to take care of younger siblings. Box 11.2 describes this phenomenon of using "mini-moms," and examines some of the consequences of giving young girls so much responsibility (Dodson and Dickert 2004).

Child Care

With increasing numbers of mothers turning to employment over the past several decades, many children are spending substantial amounts of time in the care of someone other than their parents (Capizzano and Main 2005). Forty-two percent of children under age 5 with employed mothers spend at least 35 hours a week in child care. Among families in which the mother works full-time, 50 percent of children are in full-time care. Given these figures, are the quality of child care and its high costs private matters or public concerns?

Preschool-Aged Children

According to the National Survey of America's Families, 72 percent of children under age 3 with employed mothers, and 86 percent of children aged 3 and 4 with employed mothers spend time being cared for by a nonparent on a regular basis (Capizzano and Main 2005). Figure 11.3 shows the amount of time young children (age 0–2; age 3–4) spend in nonparental care. Some dual-earner families may arrange working different shifts so that one parent can always be home with the children, but these families are small in number. Most dual-earner or single-parent households with children turn to relatives and more formal arrangements, such as **day care centers**, where care is provided in nonresidential facilities, **family child-care providers**, where care is provided in a private home other than the child's home, or **nannies/babysitters**, where the child is cared for in the home by a nonrelative. In fact, many parents have multiple arrangements (e.g., with grandmother on Tuesday and Thursday and day care center on Monday, Wednesday, Friday), to ensure that their children are well cared for and to minimize costs.

Figure 11.4 on page 359 illustrates who cared for these young children. For children up to 2 years old, the most common form of nonparental care was in the home by another relative (e.g., other parent, grandmother, or aunt). For children aged 3 and over, the most common type of nonparental care was from a day care center (Capizzano and Adams 2004).

FIGURE 11.3 **Time Spent in Nonparental Care, Children of Employed Mothers, Part Time and Full Time (Percent)**

Source: Capizzano and Main 2005.

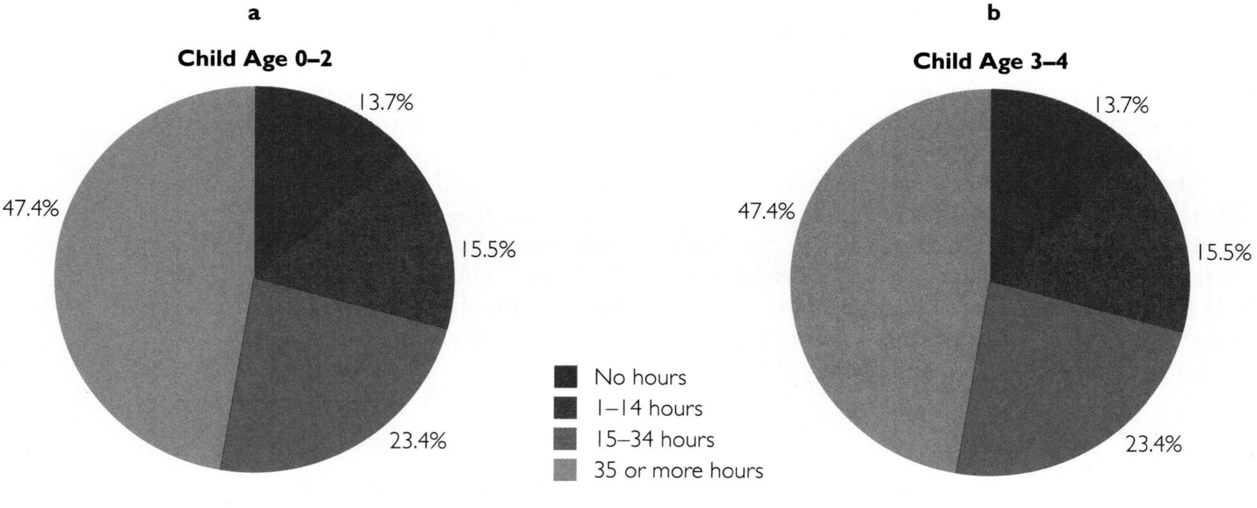

The type of child care that parents use varies across ethnicity and income. Hispanics are less likely to use day care centers than are other race groups and more likely to use care by a relative. When looking at three income groups: poor families (incomes less than 100 percent of the federal poverty level), low-income families (incomes between 100 and 200 percent of the poverty level), and higher-income families (incomes above 200 percent of poverty), center care is used more commonly for the children of higher-income families. Relative care is most common for low-income families (Capizzano and Adams 2004; Ehrle et al. 2001; Sonenstein et al. 2002).

These differences, in part, reflect the costs of child care. Relative care and care provided by other families are usually the least expensive child care options. Full-day child care costs in a day care facility can easily cost over $10,000 a year per child, which is higher than the costs of college tuition. Nannies and babysitters may cost even more; a perusal of the want ads in a newspaper and several nanny agencies in Portland, Oregon, revealed that most adult nannies/babysitters charge $10–$15 per hour. However, more than one in four families with young children earns less than $25,000 per year (Children's Defense Fund 2005); therefore, most forms of formal child care remain out of their reach without some sort of public subsidy.

School-Aged Children

As children begin school, the costs of child care may be reduced, but parents who work full time must look for child care arrangements to supplement the school day. Most school-aged children (6–12 years old) with employed parents are supervised before and after school. They are attended to by family, nanny/babysitters, and before- and after-school programs. However, largely because of cost, some school-aged children are left

FIGURE 11.4 **Primary Child Care Arrangements of Children with Employed Mothers**

Source: Capizzano and Adams 2004.

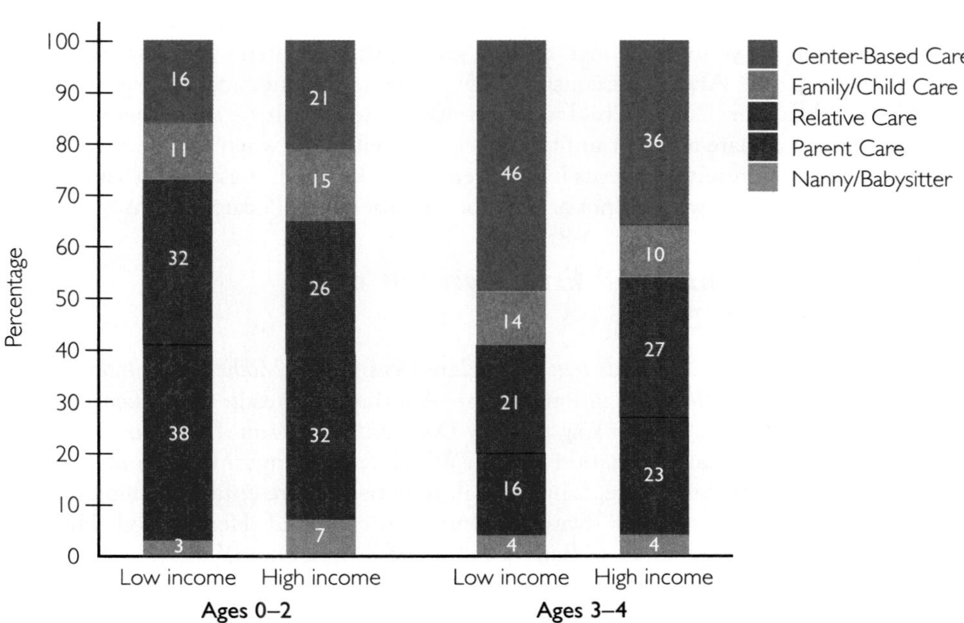

virtually unsupervised, called **self-care**. According to U.S. Census Bureau reports, about 7 percent of elementary-school children aged 5–11, and 33 percent of middle-school children aged 12–14 take care of themselves after school on a regular basis, according to a nationwide survey of parents (Johnson 2005). The percent of self-care among children ranged from 1 percent among 5- and 6-year-olds to 39 percent of 14-year-olds.

Higher-income children are more likely to be unsupervised than are low-income children, likely because both parents (in two-parent families) may be employed. Elementary and middle-school-aged children are also more likely to be left unsupervised if their parents are separated, divorced, or widowed (Johnson 2005).

While self-care is certainly not always harmful (it may make a child more independent), there are also potential problems with unsupervised children. When children under 13 are regularly left to spend time alone or to be cared for by young siblings, they may be at risk for accidents and injuries, social and behavior problems, lower academic achievement, and school adjustment problems (Vandivere et al. 2003). Most states do not have legal age limits of when it is appropriate to leave a child alone (U.S. Department of Health and Human Services 2006). Exceptions include Illinois and Maryland. Illinois law defines a neglected minor, in part, as "any minor under the age of 14 years whose parent or other person responsible for the minor's welfare leaves the minor without supervision for an unreasonable period of time without regard for the mental or physical health, safety or welfare of that minor." According to the Maryland statute, "a person who is charged with the care of a child under the age of 8 years may not allow the child to be locked or confined in a dwelling, building, enclosure, or motor vehicle while the person charged is absent and the dwelling, building, enclosure, or motor vehicle is out of the sight of the person charged unless the person charged provides a reliable person at least 13 years old to remain with the child to protect the child" (U.S. Department of Health and Human Services 2006). Other states may have guidelines that are distributed to child protective services and enforced at the county level; they often suggest that a child should be at least 12 before being left alone and at least 15 before caring for younger siblings, but recognizing that children's maturity levels differ (Prevent Child Abuse Wisconsin 2005; State of Connecticut Department of Children and Families 2003). Child welfare workers therefore have some degree of discretion but can declare a parent unfit if the child is left alone when it is deemed inappropriate. This can result in parents losing their children, which is a concern sometimes voiced by poor parents who cannot afford more traditional child care options.

The Effect of Mothers' Employment on Children's Well-Being

One headline reads: "*Study Finds that Child Care Does Impact Mother-Child Interaction*" (American Psychological Association 1999b). Another one reads: "*New Longitudinal Study Finds that Having a Working Mother Does No Significant Harm to Children*" (American Psychological Association 1999a). Which one is correct? Both studies report findings from studies using large, longitudinal, nationally representative samples. The first one uses data from the National Institute of Child Health and Human Development (NICHD) Study of Early Child Care, a longitudinal study of approximately 1,300 children. The second one uses data from the National Longitudinal Survey of Youth (NLSY), a survey of approximately 12,600 individuals. How can two good data sources yield opposite conclusions?

Determining the effects of mothers' employment and child care on children's well-being is a challenging task. It is made more difficult by the use of different measures of well-being, different types of child care settings and their varying quality, different types of relationships that mothers and children have (regardless of employment or child care), the role of the father and other family members in child care, the mother's physical and emotional health, the child's temperament, the age of the child, the mother's hours of work and other working conditions, and many other factors that may not yet even be identified. Because of all the confounding variables, it is not surprising that some studies report a negative association between mother's employment and cognitive and social outcomes such as less attachment or a child's greater level of aggression (Belsky et al. 2001), while others find positive outcomes such as daughters having higher academic achievement, greater career success, more nontraditional career choices, and greater occupational commitment (Hoffman 1998; Vandell and Ramanan 1992). Yet others report no overall effect (Blau and Grossberg 1990). Using NLSY data, Harvey (1999) reviewed the diverse ways that variables are measured or samples are constructed. In her reanalysis she found that neither maternal (nor paternal) employment, nor the timing and continuity of employment was significantly related to a child's cognitive or social outcomes (Harvey 1999). However, it appeared that employment during the first year of a child's life might be slightly beneficial for children in single-parent households and children from low-income households.

Another study that caught tremendous media attention was led by Jay Belsky. His team found that children who were in child care for more than 30 hours per week during the first 4 years of life were somewhat more likely to behave aggressively as compared to those who had been in child care for less than 10 hours a week (Belsky et al. 2001). However, both groups of children exhibited levels of aggression that were well within the normal range.

Using a large and nationally representative sample, Hickman (2006) compared the effects of day care centers of children's math and reading skills after they entered school. Using a cross-sectional research design—which is a snapshot in time—she found that kindergarteners who attended day care the year before did exhibit higher skills. However, when she used a longitudinal design—following children over several years—she found the difference did not persist, and that some social skills deteriorated.

It appears that the relationship between mother's employment and child well-being is somewhat mixed and contradictory because the results are relatively minor and dependent on many confounding variables. Perhaps the most important factor is the quality of care that the child experiences (Perry-Jenkins et al. 2000). Children in poor-quality child care have been found to be delayed in language and reading skills, display more aggression, demonstrate lower mathematical ability, have poorer attention skills, and have more behavioral problems than children in higher-quality care (Children's Defense Fund 2001).

Social Policy and Family Resilience

Child care is a necessity for most families, but it remains largely a private matter. Families are left on their own to find the highest-quality care that they can afford. However, quality controls are limited and vary by state. For example, first aid requirements differ and are nonexistent in some states. Pay for child care workers is low (average of $8.50 an hour in 2005), few workers receive fringe benefits such as health insurance, sick pay, or vacation time, and turnover is high (U.S. Department of Labor 2006c, f). Not all developed countries think of child care as a private matter. Some see it as a public concern, as a social good that can ultimately benefit everyone. What can other countries teach the United States about how to structure quality child care and early education to the benefit of everyone?

Example: A Comparative Look at Early Childhood Education and Child Care Policies

Early childhood education and care (ECEC) has become an important issue in many parts of the world because of the dramatic rise in labor force participation of mothers, the push for single mothers to work rather than receive public aid, and a growing interest in ensuring that all children begin elementary school with basic skills and ready to learn (Organization for Economic Co-operation and Development 2006). ECEC programs enhance and support children's cognitive, social, and emotional development. A 3-year study of 12 industrialized nations compared the availability and structure of ECEC programs. As Sheila B. Kamerman, director of the Columbia University Institute for Child and Family Policy, states: "If school readiness is a key goal, if meeting the needs of working mothers is an essential response, and if maximizing the health and well-being of children is a desirable outcome, Americans should take a look at this report of what is occurring in other industrialized countries. The contrast is dramatic" (Clearinghouse on International Developments in Child, Youth, and Family Practices 2001, 1).

What is dramatically different in these countries? To begin with, access to ECEC is a statutory right. Although compulsory school begins at age 6 or 7, ECEC avail-

In the United States, working parents are primarily on their own to pay for the costs of child care. However, in many other industrialized nations, access to high-quality child care is seen as a public good, and therefore the government subsidizes the costs.

ability begins at 1 year in Denmark, Finland, and Sweden (after generous maternity and family leave benefits are exhausted); at $2\frac{1}{2}$ years in Belgium; at 3 years in Italy and Germany; and at 4 years in Britain. Most countries have full coverage of 3- to 6-year-olds. In contrast, in the United States there is no statutory entitlement until age 5–7, depending on the state. Access to publicly funded ECEC programs is generally restricted to at-risk children (usually defined as poor or near-poor—such as the Head Start Program). The demand for these programs among vulnerable groups far outstrips their availability. Only New York and Georgia have developed universal prekindergarten programs for all 4-year-olds regardless of family income (Clearinghouse on International Developments in Child, Youth, and Family Practices 2001).

In most of the 12 countries reviewed, governments pay the largest share of the costs, with parents covering only 25–30 percent. Countries may also make arrangements for sliding-scale payments for low-income families to help make programs affordable. Most countries require staff to complete at least 3 years of training at universities or other institutes of higher education. Their earnings are in accordance. In contrast, U.S. parents pay an average of 60–80 percent of ECEC costs. Some of these costs can be recouped through tax benefits, but many low-income families find the tax system confusing and therefore end up using informal or unregulated child care. In the United States there is also no agreed-upon set of qualifications for staff. Their status and pay are low and turnover is high. Other countries make a clear investment in their ECEC. Denmark devotes 2 percent of its gross domestic product (GDP), with Sweden and Norway close behind. In contrast, the United States devotes less than one-half of 1 percent of its GDP to early childhood services (Organization for Economic Co-operation and Development 2006).

Ironically, the United States is a leader in research on child development, but has not developed the programs that research suggests are needed and are increasingly available in other developed nations. Dr. Kamerman suggests (Clearinghouse on International Developments in Child, Youth, and Family Policies 2001, 5):

> Most countries are giving major attention to ECEC. But the U.S. has not yet made the critical political commitment. The U.S. leads in child development research, I think it is time for us to catch up in practice.

Conclusion

This chapter examines the empirical research surrounding the topic of working families. All families do meaningful work inside or outside the home, but the overall trend has been an increase in mothers working outside the home for pay. The changing nature of the economy has altered the context and meaning of work. Employment is becoming increasingly temporary, with nonstandardized work schedules, and fewer union protections such as job fringe benefits. This has tremendous implications for how families combine work and family. Many families now need two paychecks to make ends meet. No longer are work and family domains separate; instead, they interact and influence each other in many ways. Issues such as work-family conflicts, feelings of time deficits with children, negotiations over the division of household labor, and struggles to find suitable child care are issues that most employed families face today. Family-friendly workplace policies, such as flexible work hours, and national family policies, such as assistance with child care, can help alleviate the stress that many employed families experience.

Key Terms

Day care centers: Child care provided in nonresidential facilities. (p. 357)

"Doing gender": Housework is so ingrained as women's work that it functions as an area in which gender is symbolically created and reproduced. (p. 355)

Early childhood education and care (ECEC): An international term for day care, preschool, and other programs to ensure that all children begin elementary school with basic skills and ready to learn. (p. 361)

Family child-care providers: Child care provided in a private home other than the child's home. (p. 357)

Household labor: Generally refers to the unpaid work done to maintain family members and/or a home. (p. 351)

Living wage: Ordinances that require employers to pay wages that are above federal or state minimum wage levels, usually ranging from 100 to 130 percent of the poverty line. (p. 344)

Nannies/babysitters: Child care provided in the home by a nonrelative. (p. 357)

Nonstandard work schedules: Jobs that are part time, subcontracted, temporary in nature, occur at night, or offer irregular work schedules. (p. 344)

Occasional labor: Household tasks that are more time-flexible and more discretionary, such as household repairs, yard care, or paying bills. (p. 351)

Primary labor market: Jobs that are characterized by having relatively high pay, benefits, and job security. (p. 343)

Primary sector: Consists of jobs in which raw materials are harvested, such as in timber, agriculture, or mining. (p. 342)

Resource theory: The greater the relative amount or value of resources contributed by a partner, the greater is his or her power within the relationship; can then be translated into bargaining to avoid tasks such as housework that offer no pay and minimal social prestige. (p. 355)

Routine household labor: Nondiscretionary, routine tasks that are less able to be postponed, such as cooking, washing dishes, or cleaning. (p. 351)

Secondary labor market: Jobs that have relatively low pay, few benefits, and little job security. (p. 343)

Secondary sector: Transforms raw materials into manufactured goods. (p. 343)

Self-care: School-age children who are unsupervised and taking care of themselves. (p. 359)

Tertiary sector: Also called the service sector; the fastest-growing sector of the U.S. economy; focuses on providing a wide variety of positions, such as salesclerk, attorney, cashier, and waitress. (p. 343)

Time availability perspective: Suggests that the division of labor is largely determined by (1) the need for household labor, such as the number of children in the home; and (2) each partner's availability to perform household tasks, such as the number of hours spent in paid work. (p. 355)

Work-family conflict: Inter-role conflict in which the role pressures from the work and family domains are mutually incompatible in some respect (p. 346).

Resources on the Internet

Bureau of Labor Statistics
www.bls.gov/
A component of the U.S. Department of Labor, this website provides detailed data on all aspects of employment, including occupational classifications, wages, benefits, health, and safety. Information is provided on women and minority workers.

Economic Policy Institute
www.epi.org/
The mission of the Economic Policy Institute is to provide research and education in order to promote a prosperous, fair, and sustainable economy. The Institute stresses real-world analysis and a concern for the living standards of working people, and it makes its findings accessible to the general public, the media, and policy makers.

Families and Work Institute
www.familiesandwork.org/
Families and Work Institute (FWI) is a nonprofit center for research that provides data to inform decision-making on the changing workforce, changing family and changing community. They also offer a speaker's series and lectures.

Institute for Women's Policy Research (IWPR)
www.iwpr.org/index.cfm
The IWPR conducts research and disseminates its findings to address the needs of women, promote public dialogue, and strengthen families, communities, and societies. IWPR focuses on issues of poverty and welfare, employment and earnings, work and family issues, health and safety, and women's civic and political participation.

Mothers and More
www.mothersandmore.org/
Mothers and More is a nonprofit organization dedicated to improving the lives of mothers through support, education, and advocacy. They have chapters throughout the United States. They see themselves as a part of an extended community of individuals and organizations talking about and working on the issues that impact mothers' lives.

Further Reading

Bianchi, S. M., J. P. Robinson, and M. A. Milkie. 2006. *Changing Rhythms of American Family Life*. New York: Russell Sage Foundation.

Blair-Loy, M. 2003. *Competing Devotions: Career and Family Among Women Executives*. Cambridge, MA: Harvard University Press.

Epstein, C. F., and A. L. Kallebreg. (Eds.). 2004. *Fighting for Time: Shifting Boundaries of Work and Social Life*. New York: Russell Sage Foundation.

Gerstel, N., D. Clawson, and R. Zussman. (Eds.). 2002. *Families at Work: Expanding the Bounds*. Nashville, TN: Vanderbilt University Press.

Gornick, J. C., and M. K. Meyers. 2005. *Families That Work: Policies for Reconciling Parenthood and Employment*. New York: Russell Sage Foundation.

Hareven, T. K. 2002. *The Silk Weavers of Kyoto: Family and Work in a Changing Traditional Industry*. Berkeley: University of California Press.

Heymann, J. 2007. *Forgotten Families: Ending the Growing Crisis Confronting Children and Working Parents in the Global Economy*. New York: Oxford University Press.

Hochschild, A. R., with A. MacHung. 1989. *The Second Shift: Working Parents and the Revolution at Home*. New York: Viking.

Jacobs, J. A., and K. Gerson. 2004. *The Time Divide: Work, Family, and Gender Inequality*. Cambridge, MA: Harvard University Press.

Moen, P. 2003. *It's About Time: Couples and Careers*. Ithaca, NY: ILR Press.

Mortimer, J. T. 2003. *Working and Growing Up in America*. Cambridge, MA: Harvard University Press.

Presser, H. B. 2005. *Working in a 24/7 Economy: Challenges for American Families*. New York: Russell Sage Foundation.

Shipler, D. K. 2004. *The Working Poor: Invisible in America*. New York: Knopf.

Thistle, S. 2006. *From Marriage to the Market: The Transformation of Women's Lives and Work*. Berkeley: University of California Press.

CHAPTER 12

Aging Families

Chapter Outline

CHAPTER PREVIEW

The United States, along with many other countries around the world, has a radically shifting population. Instead of a focus on children, as has been the case for most of history, we are increasingly becoming nations of older people. This chapter reports what it means to have increasing numbers of older persons in the population and examines issues such as retirement, Social Security, widowhood, and health, which are rapidly becoming concerns for all of society. In this chapter you will learn:

- Patterns of changing demographics in the United States and around the world
- The prevailing theories of aging
- Economic issues, including income, assets, and poverty
- The history and social philosophy of Social Security
- How aging couples fare, including aspects of marital satisfaction, division of household labor, sexuality, and widowhood
- Relationships with adult children and grandchildren
- Retirement as a socially constructed status that is increasingly important to U.S. men and women
- The health status of elders declines with age, and the United States faces many critical policy issues surrounding Medicare and long-term care for frail elders

For older adults, it really is better to give than to receive, a University of Michigan study suggests. The study finds that older people who are helpful to others reduce their risk of dying by nearly 60 percent compared to peers who provide neither practical help nor emotional support to relatives, neighbors, or friends. "Making a contribution to the lives of other people may help to extend our own lives," said the paper's lead author, Stephanie Brown, a psychologist at the University of Michigan Institute for Social Research (ISR), the world's largest academic and survey research organization.

For the study, funded in part by the National Institutes of Health, Brown analyzed data on 423 older couples, part of the ISR Changing Lives of Older Couples Study. This study was a random community-based sample of people who were first interviewed in 1987, then followed for 5 years to see how they coped with the inevitable changes in later life.

During the first set of interviews, the husbands and wives were asked a series of questions about whether they provided any practical support to friends, neighbors, or relatives, including help with housework, child care, errands, or transportation. They were also asked how much they could count on help from friends or family members if they needed it. Finally, they were asked about giving and receiving emotional support to or from their spouse, including being willing to listen if their spouse needed to talk.

Over the 5-year period of the study, 134 people died. In her analysis of the link between giving and receiving help and mortality, Brown controlled for a variety of factors, including age, sex, and physical and emotional health. "I wanted to rule out the possibilities that older people give less and are more likely to die, that females give more and are less likely to die, and that people who are depressed or in poor health are both less likely to be able to help others and more likely to die," said Brown.

She found that people who reported providing no help to others were more than twice as likely to die as people who did give some help to others. Overall, Brown found that 75 percent of men and 72 percent of women reported providing some help without pay to friends, relatives, or neighbors in the year before they were surveyed.

Receiving help from others was not linked to a reduced risk of mortality, however. "If giving, rather than receiving, promotes longevity, then interventions that are designed to help people feel supported may need to be redesigned so the emphasis is on what people can do to help others," said Brown. "In other words, these findings suggest that it isn't what we get from relationships that makes contact with others so beneficial; it's what we give."

The results, she notes, are consistent with the possibility that the benefits of social contact are shaped, in part, by the evolutionary advantages of helping others. "Older adults may still be able to increase their fitness (defined as the reproductive success of individuals who share their genes) by becoming motivated to stay alive and prolonging the amount of time they can contribute to family members," she noted. "Of course, this possibility relies on the assumption that a motivation for self-preservation can influence mortality. And in fact, there is evidence to suggest that individuals with a 'fighting spirit' survive longer with cancer than individuals who feel helpless or less optimistic about their chances for survival. Now it seems that the same may be true of a 'giving spirit.'" (University of Michigan News Service 2002)[1] ■

One hundred years ago our understanding of the physical and social aspects of aging was negligible. The elderly made up a small portion of the population and their numbers were small. We assumed that old age meant deterioration. Few people worried about dementia or Alzheimer's disease; instead the person was simply called "old," as though senility and old age were synonymous. Today we know far more about aging than we did in the past, and yet, we also recognize that we still have far to go. The demographics in the United States and worldwide are rapidly changing, and the proportion of elderly within the population is increasing faster than any other age group. They are a force to be reckoned with, as political clout often accompanies size. The AARP (formerly known as the American Association of Retired Persons) is the second largest social organization in the United States after the Roman Catholic Church (Farrell 1999). In many ways, aging is a social construction, not simply a biological phenomenon. Yes, we all grow older, but how aging is defined, how it is perceived by other members of the culture, and the policy implications that come from these definitions and perceptions can vary quite a lot from one social location to another.

This chapter examines the demographic changes underway and explores what it means to have increasing numbers of older persons in the population. The issues that aging families face and how we choose to address these issues—retirement, social security, widowhood, health, and family caregiving—are bound to become concerns for all members of society.

Changing Demographics

Aging Around the World

The world population is aging at a dramatic and unprecedented rate. Between now and 2015, the world's elderly population will grow by over 850,000 people each *month* (Kinsella and Phillips 2005).

Many people incorrectly assume that this growth occurs only in developed nations. It is true that most developed nations have a high and growing proportion of elderly; in fact some may have more grandparents than children before the middle of the twenty-first century. European countries lead the way. Italy is the "oldest" country, with over 19 percent of the population age 65 or older; Greece, Sweden, Japan, Spain, and Belgium are close behind (Kinsella and Phillips 2005).

However, what is less known is that the absolute numbers of elderly in poor, less developed nations are also quite large, and they are increasing at a staggering rate that far

[1]From "People Who Give, Live Longer, U-M Study Shows." November 2002. University of Michigan News Service. Reprinted with permission.

Between now and 2015, the world's elderly population will grow by over 850,000 people each month, and most of these elders will be in poor developing nations that have few, if any, provisions for taking care of elders.

exceeds the rate in developed nations. Fifty-nine percent of the world's elderly population (249 million people) lived in developing nations in 2000, and will increase to 71 percent (686 million elders) in 2030. Maps 12.1 and 12.2 (pages 372–375) reveal that the change between 2000 and 2030 will be explosive in many parts of the world. In many countries, the elderly population is expected to double or even triple, including Singapore, Malaysia, Colombia, Costa Rica, the Philippines, Indonesia, Mexico, South Korea, Egypt, Bangladesh, and Peru. These countries tend to be poorer and often are without economic or health care provisions for their elderly. The question of how to take care of these elders will become one of the most vexing policy issues in the coming decades. The effects will be felt far beyond the borders of individual nations; they will spread throughout the global economy.

To complicate these issues even further, the largest increase around the world is in the oldest cohorts. Adopting the often-used international cutoff of age 80 and over, this group constitutes 17 percent of the elderly population on average today, but will grow quickly in many countries, as shown in Figure 12.1. The oldest age groups are more likely to be found in developed nations. For example, in the United States, persons age 80 and over comprise 27 percent of all elders, while in Pakistan the oldest group remains at only 13 percent of all elders. Despite this difference, most countries will see a rapid increase in both the sheer numbers of this age group, and their proportion of the elderly overall. For example, by 2030, nearly 40 percent of all elderly in Japan will be age 80 and over.

As more people live to the oldest ages, we will see more chronic conditions such as arthritis, osteoporosis, and senile dementia. These types of conditions require more medical care and more personal help with cooking, cleaning, bathing, and home repair. Who will provide this care to an increasing number of elderly? Most countries have few government agencies or even private nursing homes. The vast majority of elderly around the world will be cared for by their adult children, often in their 60s or 70s themselves.

The growth among the oldest-old is so phenomenal that many government agencies are redefining their definitions of elderly. For example, the U.N. Population Division and the U.S. Census Bureau's International Programs have expanded their age categories, with the final category now being "age 100 and over," called **centenarians.** Box 12.1 on page 378 pays tribute to one such centenarian on her birthday.

Reasons for the Rapid Growth Why is the world's population aging so quickly? There are two reasons: (1) people are living longer and (2) fewer babies are being born.

Obviously the first reason for a rapid growth in the elderly population is that more people are living longer. **Life expectancy** (how long a person can expect to live) can be calculated at any age. However, usually data representing life expectancy *at birth* are reported; for a girl or boy born today, how long on average can she or he be expected to

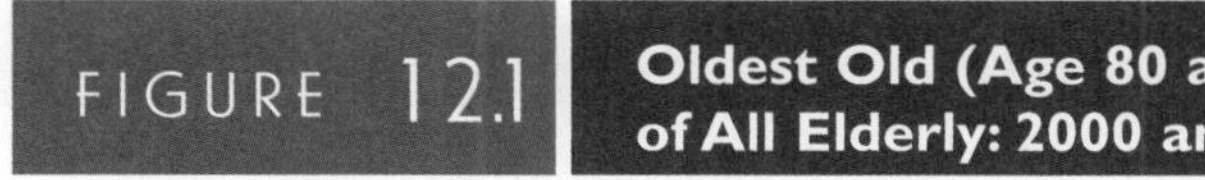

FIGURE 12.1 Oldest Old (Age 80 and Over) as a Percent of All Elderly: 2000 and 2030

Source: U.S. Census Bureau 2000.

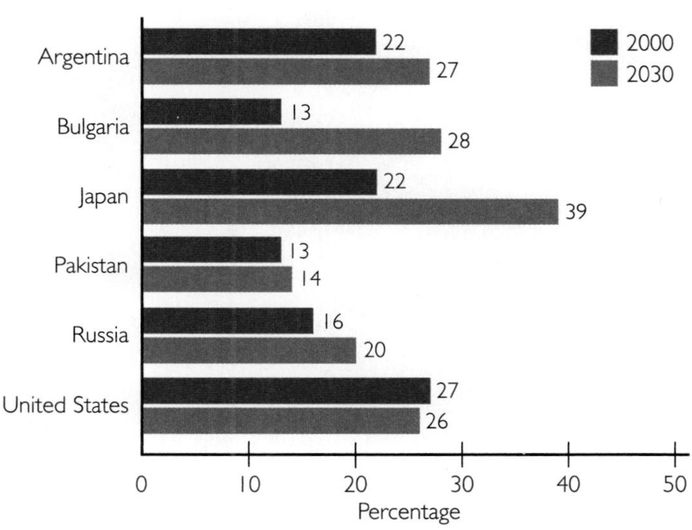

live? Extraordinary strides have been made in extending life expectancy in much of the world. In 1900, U.S. life expectancy was 48 years for males and 51 years for females. Today it has increased to 75 for males and 80 for females (National Center for Health Statistics 2005). Other countries have made even larger advances because of improved nutrition, sanitation, health care, and other scientific discoveries. Infectious diseases such as influenza, smallpox, or measles that killed many people in the past have been controlled in many parts of the world. However, a few countries have experienced no substantial gains in life expectancy. For example, life expectancy in Uganda has increased by only a few years since 1950. Why is this? The HIV/AIDS epidemic has had a horrific impact on life expectancy, particularly in parts of Africa. So many people are dying at young ages from HIV/AIDS that, on average, it is radically lowering the age of death. It is projected that by 2010, AIDS may actually reduce life expectancy in parts of Africa by up to 30 years from what it would otherwise be if there were no epidemic (Kinsella and Phillips 2005).

A second reason for the tremendous growth in the elderly population around the world is a decline in fertility rates; fewer babies are being born. Countries with low fertility rates such as Japan and Western Europe tend to have high proportions of the elderly and vice versa. With fewer births over an extended period of time, cohorts of older persons make up an increasing proportion of the population. Demographers use the term **demographic transition** to refer to the process in which a society moves from a situation of high fertility rates and low life expectancy, to one of low fertility rates and high life expectancy.

Figure 12.2 on page 376 shows three population pyramids from 1950, 1990, and the projections for 2030. Each pyramid shows the population by age, sex, and how they differ

MAP 12.1 Eye on the World: Comparative Aging—Percent of Population over Age 65, 2000

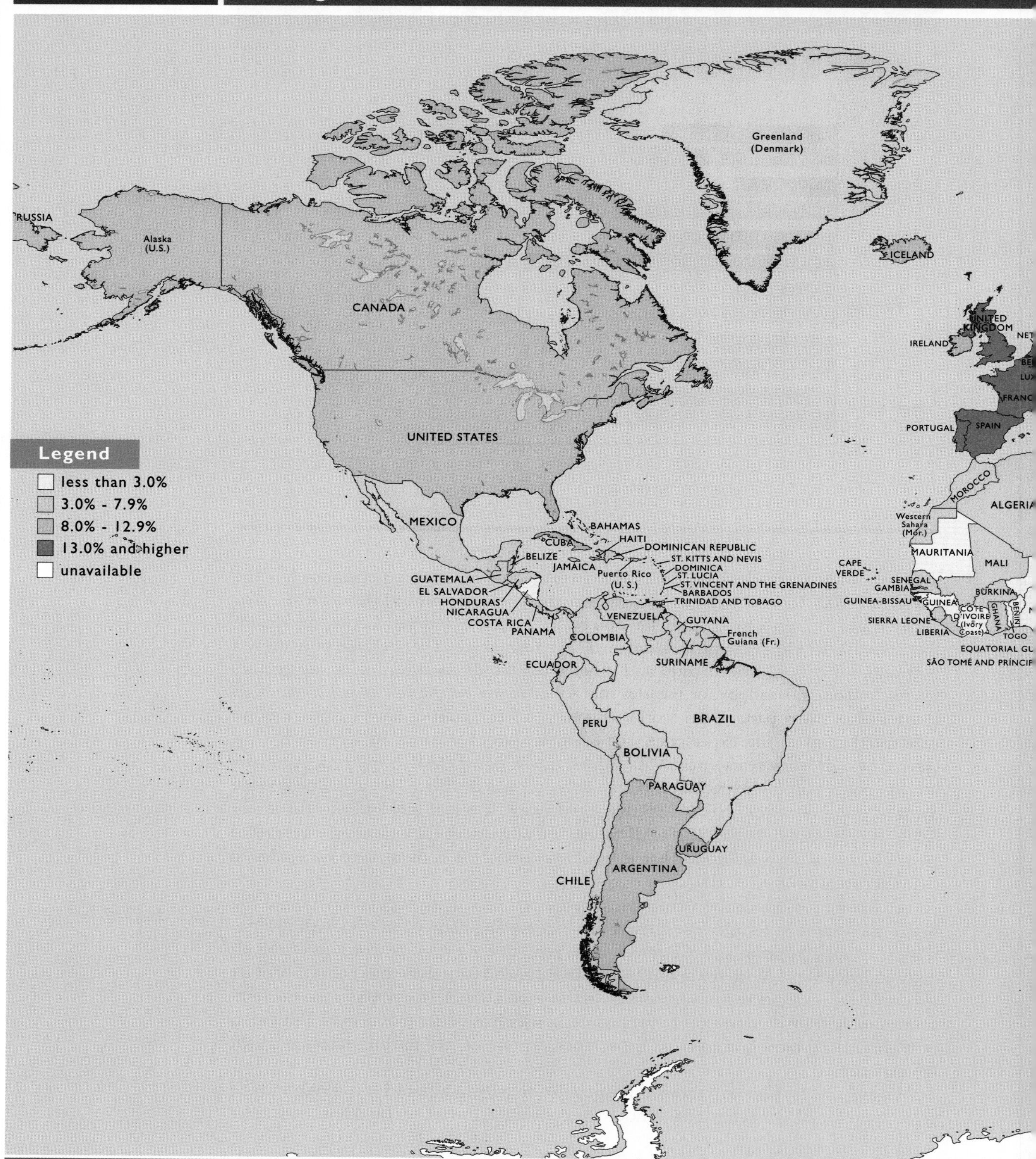

Greenland
(Denmark)
RUSSIA
Alaska
(U.S.)
ICELAND
CANADA
UNITED KINGDOM
IRELAND
FRANC
PORTUGAL
SPAIN
UNITED STATES
Legend
less than 3.0%
3.0% - 7.9%
8.0% - 12.9%
13.0% and higher
unavailable
MOROCCO
ALGERIA
Western Sahara (Mor.)
MAURITANIA
MALI
MEXICO
BAHAMAS
CUBA
HAITI
DOMINICAN REPUBLIC
BELIZE
ST. KITTS AND NEVIS
JAMAICA
DOMINICA
Puerto Rico (U. S.)
ST. LUCIA
ST. VINCENT AND THE GRENADINES
BARBADOS
TRINIDAD AND TOBAGO
GUATEMALA
EL SALVADOR
HONDURAS
NICARAGUA
COSTA RICA
PANAMA
CAPE VERDE
SENEGAL
GAMBIA
GUINEA-BISSAU
GUINEA
SIERRA LEONE
LIBERIA
CÔTE D'IVOIRE (Ivory Coast)
GHANA
BENIN
TOGO
BURKINA
EQUATORIAL GU
SÃO TOMÉ AND PRÍNCIP
VENEZUELA
GUYANA
French Guiana (Fr.)
SURINAME
COLOMBIA
ECUADOR
PERU
BRAZIL
BOLIVIA
PARAGUAY
URUGUAY
ARGENTINA
CHILE

The demographics of the world are changing quickly, as shown in these two maps—one from 2000 and another one, which estimates the population in 2030.

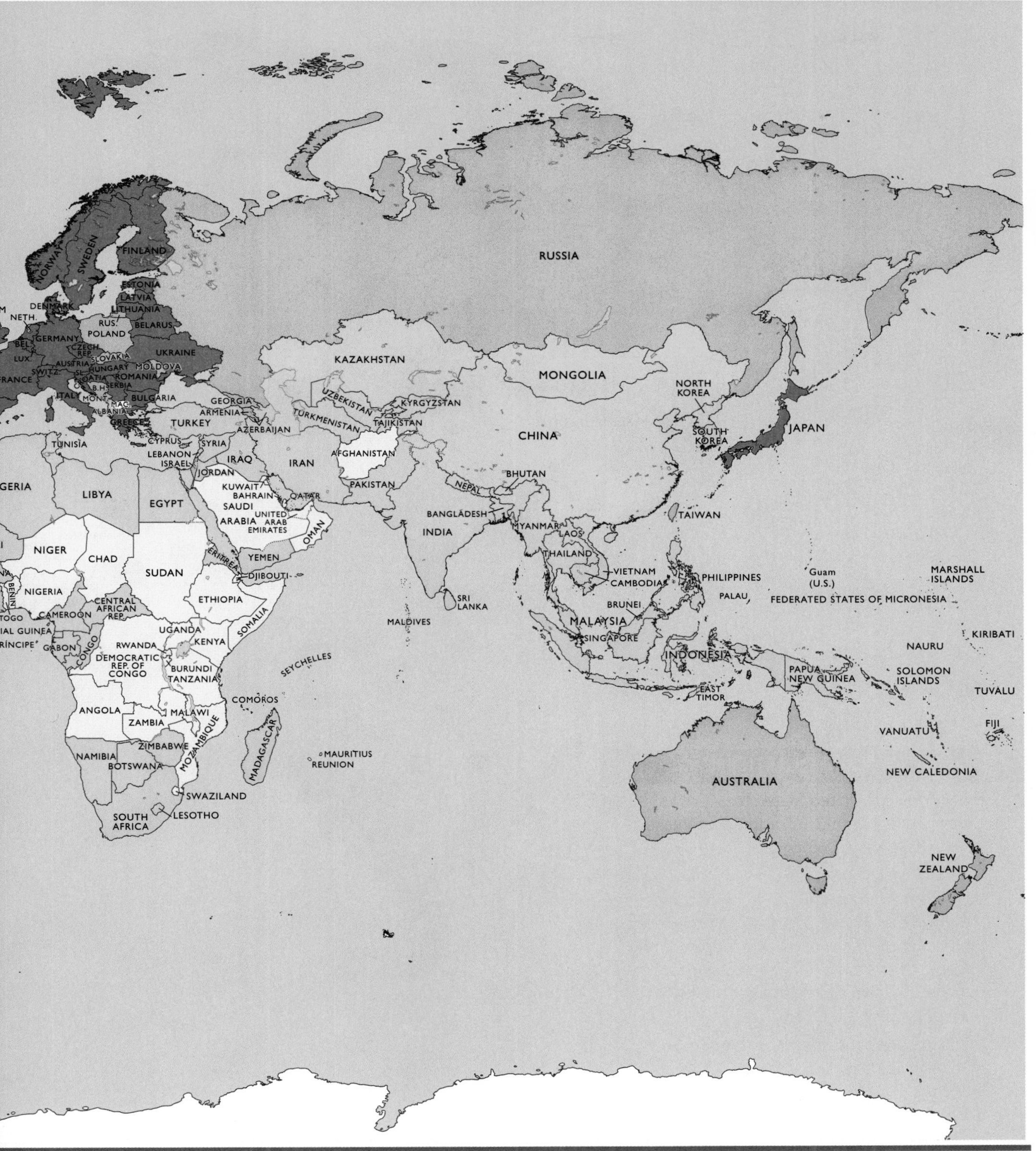

(continues)

MAP 12.2 Eye on the World: Comparative Aging—Percent of Population over Age 65, 2030

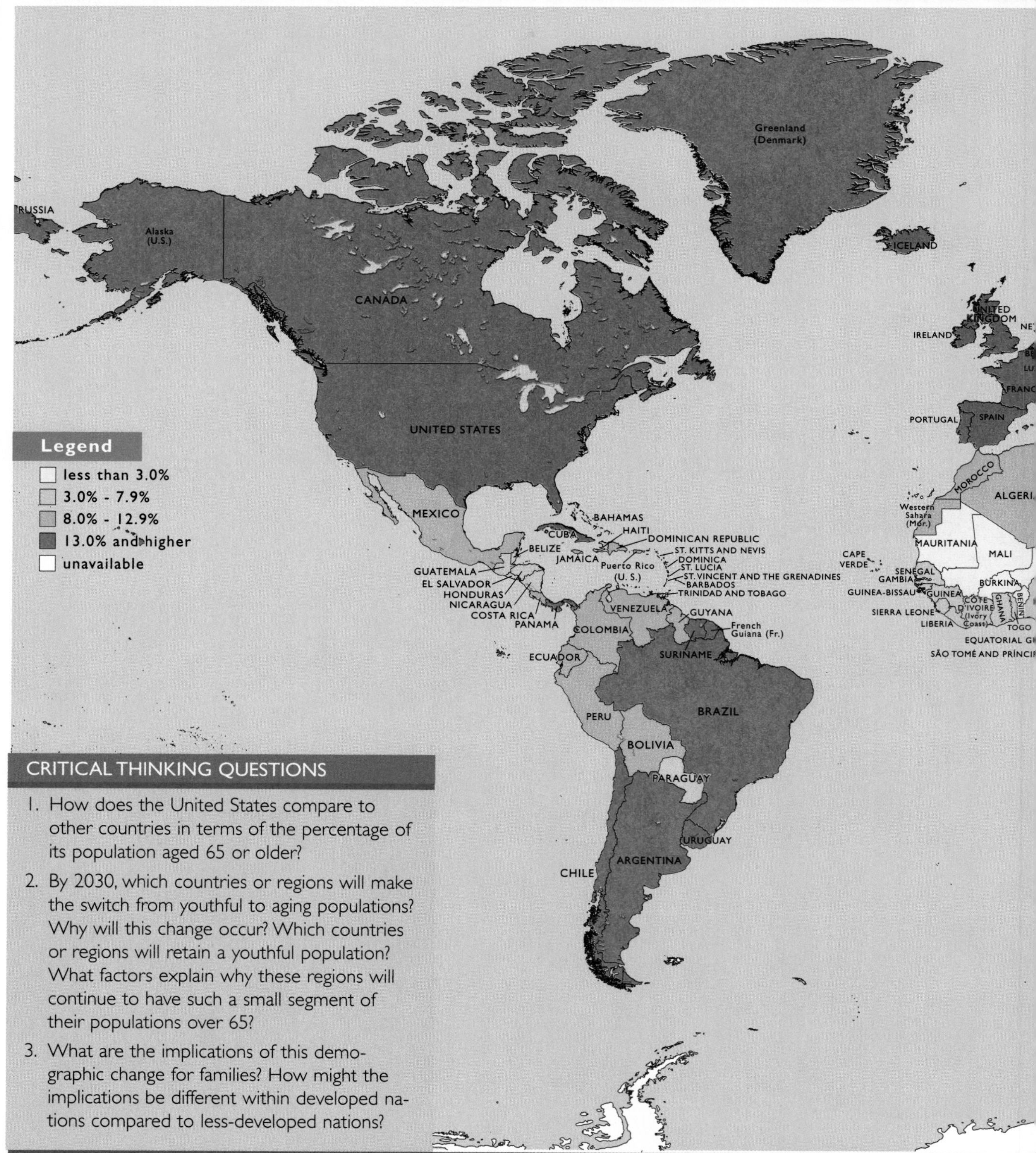

CRITICAL THINKING QUESTIONS

1. How does the United States compare to other countries in terms of the percentage of its population aged 65 or older?
2. By 2030, which countries or regions will make the switch from youthful to aging populations? Why will this change occur? Which countries or regions will retain a youthful population? What factors explain why these regions will continue to have such a small segment of their populations over 65?
3. What are the implications of this demographic change for families? How might the implications be different within developed nations compared to less-developed nations?

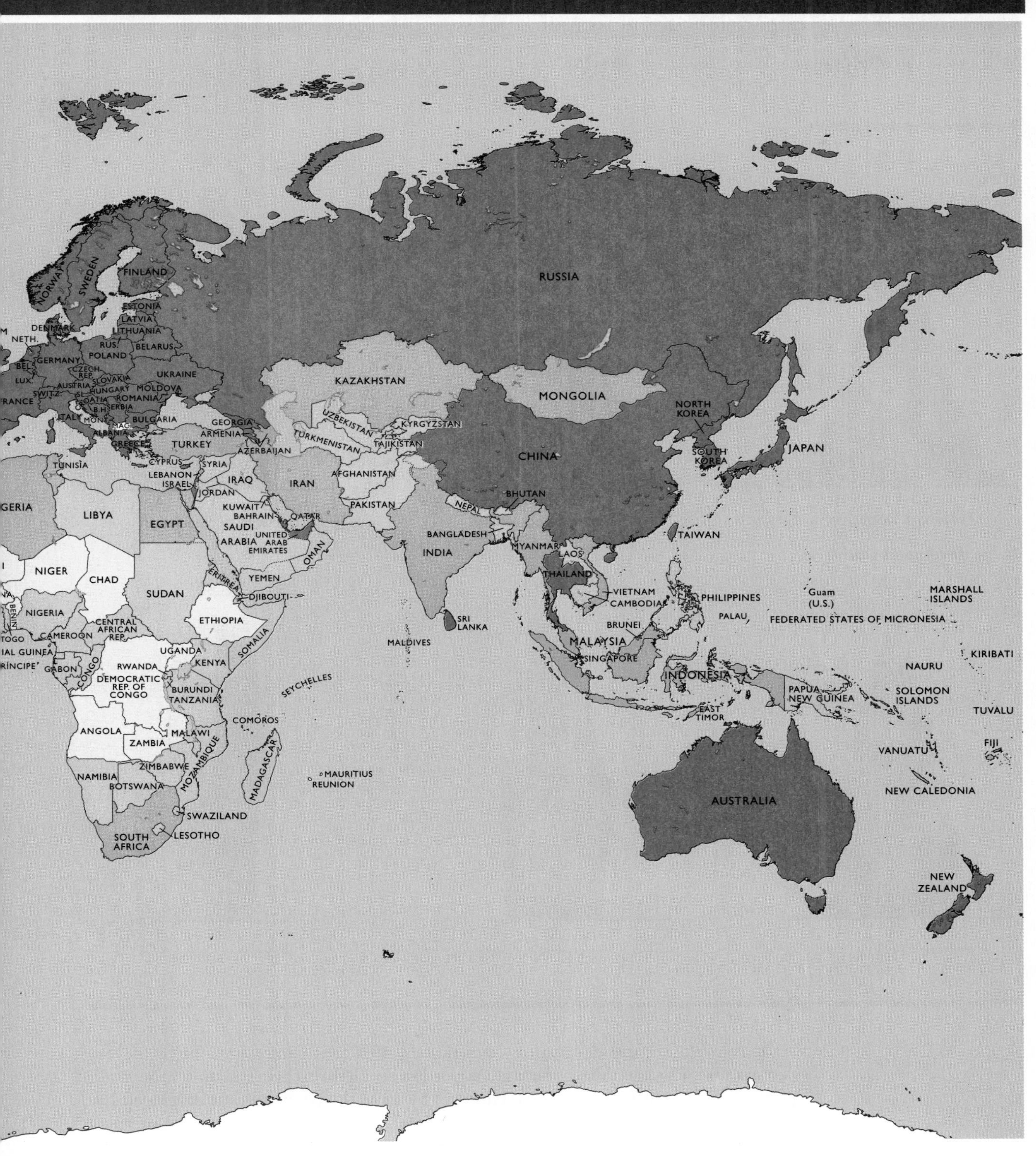

RUSSIA
FINLAND
SWEDEN
NORWAY
ESTONIA
LATVIA
LITHUANIA
DENMARK
NETH.
RUS.
BELARUS
POLAND
GERMANY
BEL.
LUX.
CZECH REP.
SLOVAKIA
UKRAINE
AUSTRIA
HUNGARY
MOLDOVA
SWITZ.
ROMANIA
SERBIA
B.H.
ITALY
MONT.
MAC.
BULGARIA
ALBANIA
GREECE
GEORGIA
ARMENIA
AZERBAIJAN
TURKEY
KAZAKHSTAN
MONGOLIA
UZBEKISTAN
KYRGYZSTAN
TURKMENISTAN
TAJIKISTAN
NORTH KOREA
SOUTH KOREA
JAPAN
CHINA
TUNISIA
CYPRUS
SYRIA
LEBANON
ISRAEL
IRAQ
IRAN
AFGHANISTAN
JORDAN
KUWAIT
BAHRAIN
QATAR
SAUDI ARABIA
UNITED ARAB EMIRATES
PAKISTAN
NEPAL
BHUTAN
BANGLADESH
INDIA
OMAN
LIBYA
EGYPT
TAIWAN
MYANMAR
LAOS
THAILAND
NIGER
CHAD
SUDAN
YEMEN
ERITREA
DJIBOUTI
VIETNAM
CAMBODIA
PHILIPPINES
Guam (U.S.)
MARSHALL ISLANDS
NIGERIA
ETHIOPIA
CENTRAL AFRICAN REP.
SRI LANKA
PALAU
FEDERATED STATES OF MICRONESIA
BRUNEI
BENIN
TOGO
CAMEROON
MALDIVES
MALAYSIA
UGANDA
SOMALIA
SINGAPORE
KENYA
GABON
CONGO
RWANDA
KIRIBATI
NAURU
DEMOCRATIC REP. OF CONGO
SEYCHELLES
INDONESIA
PAPUA NEW GUINEA
SOLOMON ISLANDS
BURUNDI
TANZANIA
EAST TIMOR
TUVALU
COMOROS
ANGOLA
MALAWI
ZAMBIA
MOZAMBIQUE
MADAGASCAR
FIJI
VANUATU
ZIMBABWE
NAMIBIA
MAURITIUS
REUNION
BOTSWANA
NEW CALEDONIA
AUSTRALIA
SWAZILAND
SOUTH AFRICA
LESOTHO
NEW ZEALAND

Source: Kinsella and Velkoff 2001.

FIGURE 12.2 **Population Age-Sex Structure in Less Developed and More Developed Countries, 1950, 1990, and 2030**

Source: UN Population Division, *World Population Prospects: The 2002 Revision.*

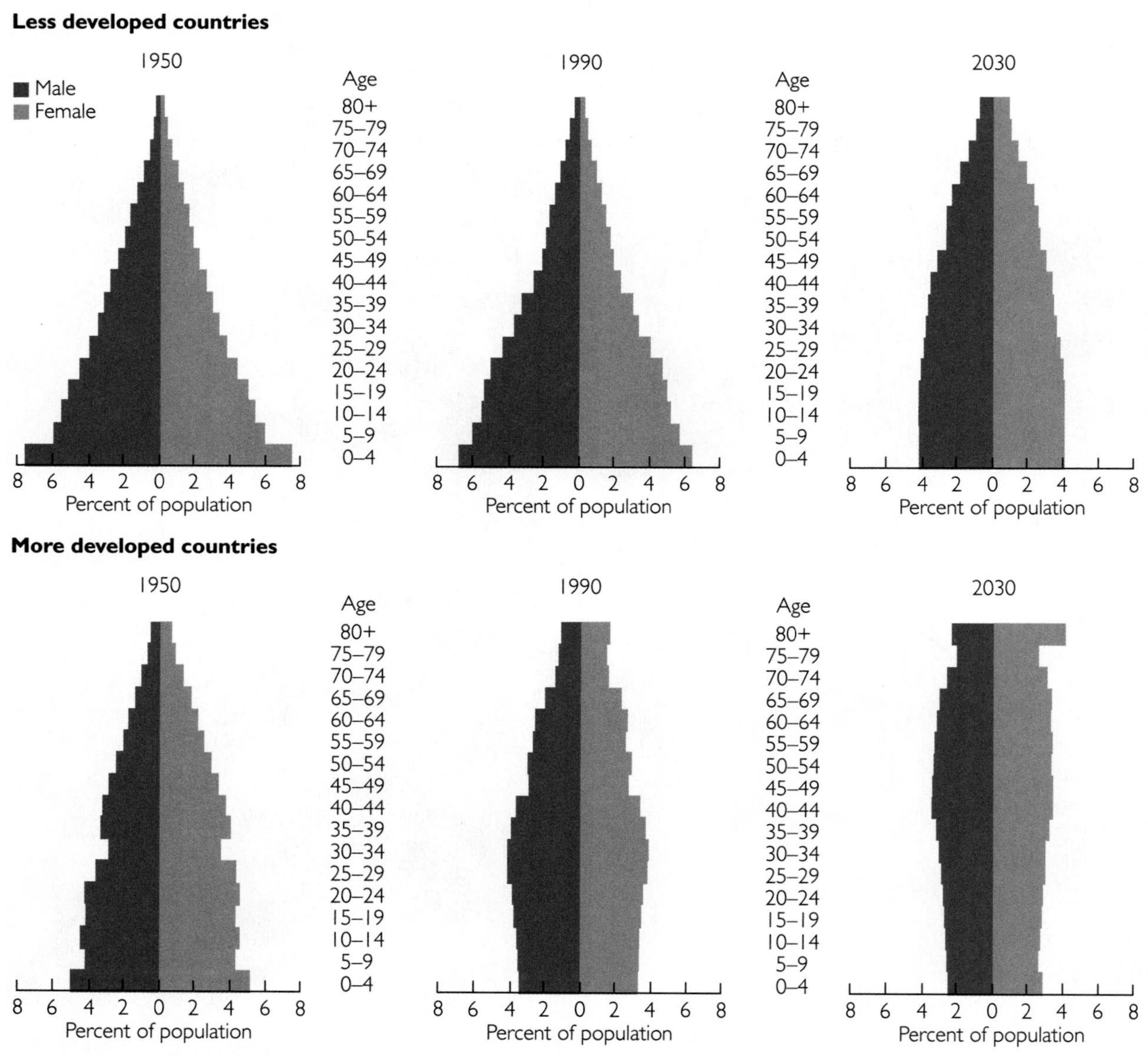

among developed and developing countries. In 1950 birth rates were high, life expectancy was low, and the number and proportion of elderly in the population were small, particularly in developing nations. However by 1990 the population in developed nations had changed. Birth rates were lower in 1990, and therefore there was a noticeably large "bulge" in the pyramid among those aged 25 to 45. This age group is known as the post-WWII **baby-boom generation**. By 2030, patterns are expected to shift in both developed and developing nations, as birth rates continue to decline and life expectancy increases (Kinsella and Phillips 2005). The "pyramids" are no longer pyramids!

Patterns of Aging in the United States

The United States is also in the midst of a demographic revolution, as shown in Figure 12.3. In 1900, few Americans were elderly. Roughly 3.1 million people were age 65 and older, about 1 in 25 people. It is likely that many Americans never saw or interacted with an elderly person. Most people did not live in three-generational families because life expectancy was low. People simply did not live long enough to live with their adult children and their offspring.

Today, because of lower birth rates, improved life expectancy, and the burgeoning baby-boom population, the number of elders has grown at a rate almost four times as fast as the population as a whole. Today, there are 35 million elders in the United States, outnumbering teenagers. One of every eight people is age 65 or older, and this is likely to increase to one of every five people by the middle of the twenty-first century (Gist and Hetzel 2004; He et al. 2005).

However, the likelihood of reaching old age is not the same across the subgroups in the population. Minorities are underrepresented in the aging population, given their size in the population overall. About 17 percent of elderly are minorities: 8 percent black, 6 percent Hispanic, 2 percent Asian, and less than 1 percent American Indian or Alaska

FIGURE 12.3 **Number of Persons 65+ in United States, 1900–2050**

Source: He et al. 2005.

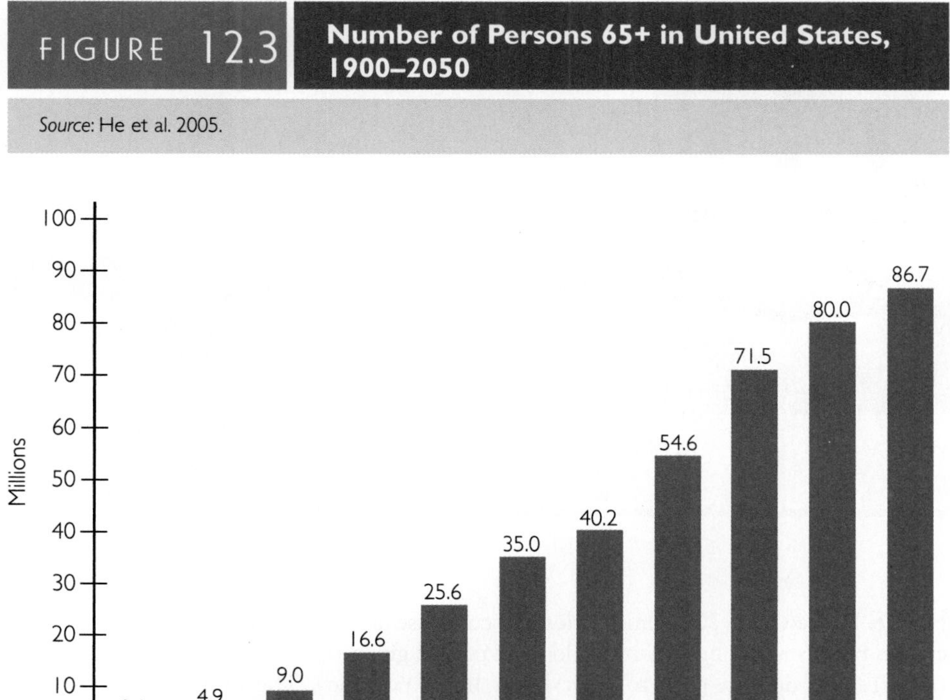

BOX 12.1 Families as Lived Experience

Celebrating My Grandmother's Birthday

As more adults are living past 100, many families now are celebrating birthdays that would have been unfathomed a generation or two ago. The essay below asks you to ponder what such a birthday could mean.

My grandmother just turned 105. Yes, you read that correctly—105! Our extended family gathered together in Montana to celebrate the marvelous and very long life of this amazing woman. She was born in 1901, and just imagine the changes she has witnessed:

- William McKinley was President of the United States when she was born
- Henry Ford showcased the first model T for $950 when she was 7 years old
- World War I began when she was 13
- Women did not receive the vote until she was 19
- The Roaring Twenties occurred when she was in her twenties
- World War II, the deadliest war in history, began when she was 38
- The case of *Brown v. the Board of Education*, which decided that separate schools for black children were inherently unequal, did not occur until she was in her fifties
- Medicare, the health insurance program for the elderly, was created when she was 64—just in time!
- Personal computers were not readily available until she was in her eighties
- Cell phones were not commonplace until she was well into her nineties
- Her youngest great-grandchild, Olivia, was born when she was 102; her youngest great-great-grandchild (to date), Colton, was born when she was 105.

Happy 105 Grandma!

Love,
Karen

Happy 105th birthday, Grandma!

CRITICAL THINKING QUESTIONS

1. If you live to be 105, what type of social and political changes do you think could occur during your lifetime?
2. How should my grandma plan to celebrate her 106th birthday?

Native. However, by 2030, minorities will comprise about 28 percent of all elders, an increase, but a smaller one than would be expected given their size in the overall population. This is due, in part, to their lower life expectancy. The number of Asian and Hispanic elders will grow more quickly than blacks (He et al. 2005).

Whites have significantly longer life expectancies than most other racial or ethnic groups in the United States. For example, a white girl born in 2006 can anticipate living an average of 81 years, 4 years longer than a black girl born the same year. A white boy born in 2006 may live an average of 75 years versus 70 years for his black counterpart. Females average considerably longer lives than do males, regardless of race. Consequently they face a far greater likelihood than do males of being widowed, of living alone, and of being poor (Gist and Hetzel 2004; He et al. 2005).

Historical Perspectives

Many people relish the thought that elders in the United States were highly respected in the past. However, historians have largely debunked the myth of the "golden age" when all seniors supposedly commanded respect, power, and prestige. Instead, we now realize that many elderly persons in early America were quite marginalized. For example, the elderly poor were despised and treated as outcasts. Likewise, elderly black slaves continued to be bought and sold at the mercy of their owners. Elderly women were largely dependent on their spouses for financial and social standing because they were not allowed to own property themselves, and when their spouses died, often so went their livelihood. Many elders never experienced "retirement"; they continued to work in dangerous or dirty jobs to put food on the table and have a roof over their head. Only a small segment of the elderly population—property-owning white males—experienced the status and prestige that we generally associate with old age (Farrell 1999).

Ideally, early American households were nuclear, with adult children located nearby, often on the same land. This family style has been called a "modified extended family system" (Greven 1970). Adult sons often lived at home until their fathers passed away or until they received land as a wedding gift (Demos 1986). Only 12–18 percent of households in the late nineteenth century contained extended family members outside the immediate nuclear family (Hareven 1977).

Early census takers found that people commonly reported that they were older than they actually were. People exaggerated their age because being older was considered a privileged status, at least in the idealized culture of white property owners. Today it would be difficult to imagine most adults inflating their age. This illustrates that ideas about aging are both socially constructed and continually changing.

Historians begin to see some evidence of changing cultural ideals about aging in the nineteenth century. This is likely due to cultural and structural changes that occurred in the process of moving from an agrarian to an industrial economy. Patriarchal power began to wane as more and more sons moved away from their fathers' farms to the city in search for manufacturing work. Family members became more independent of each other because of the distance between the cities and farms.

Over time, as this new breed of workers grew older in their manufacturing jobs, they often found that they could not keep up with younger workers and were displaced by them. Old age ceased to be an asset and was considered an economic liability (Farrell 1999). With geographic mobility, aging parents could not always rely on their children to take care of them when they became ill or frail. Americans began to shift from viewing aging as a natural process to seeing it as a period of life characterized by physical and mental decline, dependence, and weakness. During this period, geriatrics emerged as a branch of medicine focusing on medical symptoms of mental and physical decline (Hareven 2000). Social reformers, policymakers, and early researchers began to take a keen interest in the social problems associated with aging: poverty, poor health, and isolation. It is against this backdrop that early social scientists began to theorize about aging and the factors associated with successful aging.

Prevailing Theories of Aging

Since the 1940s, the field of **gerontology** has evolved into an interdisciplinary science of aging that draws upon biology, medicine, and the social sciences, including sociology, psychology, and family studies. There are multiple perspectives, and the interdisciplinary approach may be viewed as either complementary or fragmented, depending on your perspective (Estes et al. 1992). Some theories focus on micro issues, emphasizing the individual and his or her adaptation to aging. Others focus on macro issues, looking at the structure of society and how it facilitates or inhibits successful aging. The following are some of the more common theories found in the gerontological literature (Estes 2001).

Disengagement Theory

The disengagement theory explores the process by which elders and society simultaneously disengage from one another. This process of mutual separation is seen as a natural and universal part of the aging process and has laid the foundation for retirement policies and separate housing for seniors. It is a theory that was particularly popular in the 1950s and 1960s in the heyday of the broader functionalist paradigm. The withdrawal from society was viewed as beneficial or functional because it allowed an orderly transition from one generation to the next. Disengagement theory has since fallen somewhat out of fashion in academic communities, but is still a foundation for much of U.S. social policy.

Activity Theory

Adopting an opposite premise from disengagement theory, activity theory is interested in discovering the ways that the elderly continue the roles and activities they have developed over the life course or develop new ones to substitute for other losses. It is also a theory developed and popularized in the 1950s. A primary assumption behind this perspective is that aging is more successful and people are happiest when they remain active and stay involved in hobbies, interests, or social roles. Older people have the same social and psychological needs as do younger people and generally do not withdraw unless confined by poor health or a physical limitation (Havighurst et al. 1968).

Continuity Theory

The continuity theory was developed to explain a common research finding: Aging does not bring a radical departure from earlier years (Atchley 1999). Although there may be important changes in health and social circumstances, a large proportion of older adults show considerable consistency over time in their patterns of thinking, activity profiles, living arrangements, and social relationships. The continuity theory suggests that most people learn continuously from their life experiences and draw upon these experiences as they continue to grow and evolve.

Life Course Perspective

While these earlier theories focused on micro issues, the life course perspective broadens this to view the aging process as one phase of an entire lifetime (Dannefer and Uhlenberg 1999; George 1993). This perspective bridges micro- and macro-level perspectives. Individuals and larger cohorts have been shaped by historical, economic, and social factors that may have arisen at any time in the life course. For example, many current elderly were teenagers or young adults during World War II with all the harrowing experiences that a war of that magnitude entails. Whether they fought directly in the war itself, or resided at home in the United States, virtually no one was untouched by the war. Food rationing, labor shortages, the fear of a loved one being sent overseas to fight, the collapse of governments around the world, the distrust toward Japanese Americans, shotgun marriages as people rushed off to war, and the burgeoning divorce rate afterward had an effect on everyone.

Critical Theory

Critical theorists lament that many theories about aging reinforce ageist attitudes about the elderly and legitimize policies that reinforce dependency at the expense of empowerment (Estes 2001). Aging is a social process, not simply a biological one, and many experiences of the elderly are shaped by the inequalities they have encountered throughout the life course, such as racism, sex discrimination, or economic inequality. Without acknowledging this crucial fact, it is likely that society will reproduce rather than alter the conditions of the elderly. To understand aging, we must move beyond focusing on the individual. We must critically evaluate the social arrangements in society and see how these arrangements foster or inhibit successful aging. These arrangements include social institutions, statuses, roles, and the distribution of power that runs across them.

Political Economy of Aging

The political economy perspective is a component of critical theory. In particular, it describes the role of capitalism and the state in contributing to systems of power, domination, and marginalization of the elderly (Phillipson 1999; Quadagno and Reid 1999). It examines the role of the economic system, government, the military, the criminal justice system, business, labor, social welfare institutions, and other social structures in shaping, legitimizing, and reproducing power (Estes 2001). Social policies for the elderly, including those that focus on health, income, work and retirement, or social services likely reflect the power relations and tensions found in society. Policy decisions (and the financial allocations that accompany them) are subject to constant struggle over scarce resources. These struggles are related to interlocking systems of oppression, such as sex, race, class, and age.

Feminist Perspectives

The feminist theory, broadly defined, is an analysis of women's experience, the identification of gender oppression, and is emancipatory in nature (Osmond and Thorne 1993). It suggests that women's experiences may be different from men's, and these differences are often ignored or disvalued in the knowledge base. It acknowledges that women come from different cultures, places, historical times, racial and ethnic groups, and social classes, which further shape their gendered experiences (White and Klein 2002). However, as a class of people, women are routinely disvalued, ignored, or oppressed around the globe. With respect to aging, feminist theorists suggest that it is particularly important to bring women's experiences into greater focus. The vast majority of elderly people, particularly among the rapidly increasing oldest-old cohort, are women. Issues related to social security changes, pensions, antipoverty programs, housing assistance, family caregiving, intergenerational relationships, and health care, to name just a few, are indeed largely "women's issues."

The Economics of Aging

How the Elderly Fare: Income and Assets

Two contrasting images emerge in discussions of the economic conditions and well-being of the elderly. One projects an image of great wealth. The elderly are portrayed as retired tycoons, with expensive second homes in Palm Springs, California, or on the Florida coasts, and driving large, well-outfitted motorhomes. The other image is in stark contrast. The elderly are portrayed as poor, alone, living in ramshackle housing, and eating dog food to stay alive. Although there are elderly who fit each of these stereotypes, the reality is that most elderly are somewhere in the middle of these extremes. The median household income of a person age 65 or older in the United States is about $26,000, according to data from the Census Bureau (DeNavas-Walt et al. 2006). This income comes from a number of sources, as shown in Figure 12.4. The largest segment, 39 percent, comes from Social Security. Earnings comprise 24 percent of the average income of elders, and pensions account for 18 percent. Assets such as stocks, bonds, or income from rented real estate, and other unknown sources make up the remainder. Three percent of elders' income comes from government programs or other income transfers, including public assistance, workers' compensation, veteran's benefits, child support, and regular financial assistance from friends or relatives. These figures represent overall averages; however, there are some critical differences, such as the income differences between men and women, between whites and racial/ethnic minorities, or between different age groups. For example, elderly men who work full time earn about $32,000 per year, compared with only $23,000 by their female counterparts (Gist and Hetzel

FIGURE 12.4 **Average Median Income of the Elderly by Source**

Source: He et al. 2005.

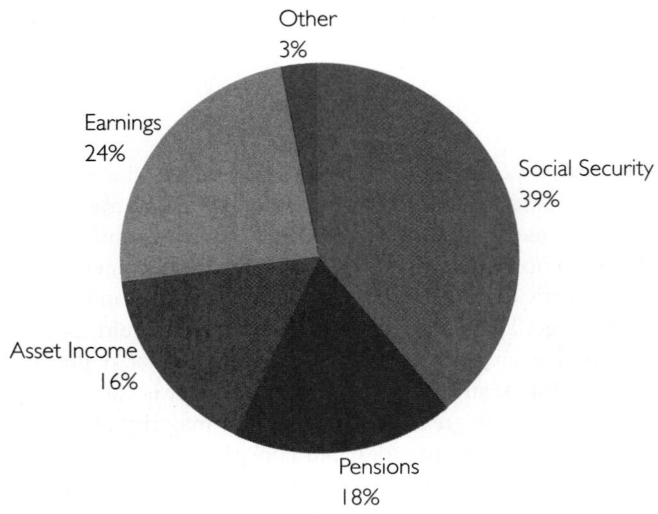

2004). Likewise, income, pensions, and annuities are a much larger component of the portfolios of white males, whereas elderly women and minorities derive a greater share of their income from Social Security.

Poverty and the Triple Jeopardy: Aging, Sex, and Race Overall, el-ders are no more likely to live in poverty than are younger working-age adults and they are 50 percent less likely to live in poverty than are children largely because of income programs like Social Security (DeNavas-Walt et al. 2006). Nonetheless, certain segments of the U.S. aging population are vulnerable to becoming impoverished, including the oldest-old, women, and minorities. For example, only 8 percent of elderly non-Hispanic whites are impoverished compared to 24 percent of blacks, 20 percent of Hispanics, and 14 percent of Asian/Pacific Islander elders. When age, sex, and minority statuses are combined—say an 85-year-old Hispanic woman—this is called a **triple jeopardy**, and her chances of being impoverished increase to over 50 percent (He et al. 2005). This is because of the cumulative disadvantages minorities and women have experienced throughout their lives. Structural barriers to employment during adulthood result in their greater economic vulnerability in old age. In addition, an older woman is more likely to be widowed and to live alone, increasing her likelihood of poverty.

Social Security

The United States is one of approximately 155 countries that have some sort of financial program for elders. Each program operates somewhat differently, but provides at least some minimal benefit to help the elderly survive. In the United States, the program to help elders is called Social Security, and its history is described in Box 12.2. The Social Security Act created many different kinds of assistance programs; the **Old Age Insurance** component that we have come to think of as "Social Security" is simply one of many programs.

The Old Age Insurance component of the Social Security Act has been significantly expanded since its inception in 1935. Benefits have been extended to widows, called Survivor's Insurance (SI), and the two components are linked together under a program called **Old Age and Survivor Insurance (OASI)**. Workers can now collect benefits at about age 62 or 65, although the age at payout will rise in the coming years to offset shortfalls in the budget due to growing numbers of elderly. Eligibility has been expanded to include, among others, farm and domestic workers, farmers, and federal employees hired after 1986, inching toward virtually 100 percent coverage among the elderly. Benefits from OASI are determined by applying a legislated formula to a person's earnings history (Clark 1990). It provides an extra boost to the lowest-income workers so that benefits will be more equitable and adequate.

OASI retirement benefits are financed by a tax on earnings covered by Social Security up to a legislated level. For the year 2006, that earnings level was $94,200. Any earnings over that amount are not taxed. The tax is paid by both the employee and the employer, at a rate of 6.2 percent each (Social Security Administration 2005). This tax has been called **regressive** because it taxes low earners at a higher rate than high earners. For example, let's say "Bob" earned $94,200 in 2006; he therefore paid 6.2 percent of his income or $5,840 in social security taxes. Meanwhile "Jordan" earned nearly twice that amount, or $190,000, and also paid 6.2 percent on the first $94,200 earned, or $5,840, the same amount as Bob. The rest of Jordan's income is tax free. Therefore, in reality while Bob paid 6.2 percent of his income in Social Security tax, Jordan paid out only 3.1 percent of her income. Therefore, as a higher wage earner, Jordan is, in effect, taxed at a lower rate.

BOX 12.2 Social Policies for Families

The Roots of Social Security

Everyone has heard of "Social Security" but what is the history of the program and the philosophy behind it? What historical and cultural forces converged to create this important program?

Social Security speaks to a universal human need; the need to be cared for if faced with uncertainty brought on by old age, illness, and disability. For most of human history, this care was provided primarily by feudal lords or family members. As societies grew in economic and social complexity and as individuals began to migrate away from their family farms to cities, some European communities began to see the emergence of organizations that sometimes took up the task of providing life insurance for their members. However, for the most part, public aid such as this was stigmatized and avoided. The **English Poor Laws of 1601**, which was the first systematic codification of English ideas about the responsibility of the state to provide for its citizens, was largely harsh and punitive. These ideas were brought to the United States as the English began to colonize the new world (Social Security Administration 2002).

Even up to the early part of the twentieth century, the government generally did not provide public pensions, and few companies had private pensions for seniors. There were a few notable exceptions, such as the teachers' pension plan of New Jersey, established in 1896, and a few municipalities enacted retirement plans for police officers and firefighters (Social Security Administration 2002). However, by and large, few people were eligible for pensions, and therefore, elderly persons continued to work if they were able. In 1900, two-thirds of men over the age of 65 were employed, compared to less than one-fifth today.

Meanwhile, many other industrialized nations had created publicly funded programs that provided pensions for the elderly. Germany implemented such a program in 1889, Great Britain in 1908, Sweden in 1913, Canada in 1927, and France in 1930 (Cockerham 1997). In the United States, bills for public pensions were introduced many times between 1900 and 1935 with no success.

During the Great Depression, it became obvious that the elderly could not rely on jobs, private pensions, savings, or families for financial support. While people of all ages were vulnerable during these hard times, the elderly were particularly hard hit. By 1935 unemployment rates among those 65 and older were well above 50 percent (Hardy and Shuey 2000). Moreover, pension plans were still relatively rare. A federal commission determined that nearly half of all seniors in the United States could not realistically support themselves (Achenbaum 1978).

The Social Security program is facing an impending challenge that causes many younger people to wonder if it will be around to help them in old age. Related to the demographic revolution, we have an increasing number of people living longer (drawing upon Social Security) and have had a decline in birth rates (people paying into the system). Thus, in 20 years, as the baby boomers retire, how can Social Security remain solvent? President George W. Bush proposed privatizing Social Security, removing much of the government's role, but this proposal was not well received by the public. Instead, the problem can be resolved with some sacrifices on the part of the public, such as increasing the retirement age (perhaps to age 70), increasing the tax rate above the current 6.2 percent, eliminating the regressive cap so that all income is taxed instead of just the first \$94,200, or changing Social Security to a means-tested rather than universal program.

The **Social Security Act** was signed on August 14, 1935, as a response to the austere poverty that enveloped many people. The act created many programs under one umbrella, including unemployment compensation, health programs, cash welfare assistance, food stamps, school lunch programs, and cash assistance for the blind, survivors, and for seniors. The timeline below outlines the development of Social Security programs in the United States. Nonetheless, despite the diversity of programs the term "Social Security" has become synonymous with Old Age Insurance (OAI), a cash assistance entitlement program for seniors. Moreover, it is seen as an earned right for seniors, not a stigmatized form of welfare as are so many of the other programs under Social Security (Trattner 1999).

Development of U.S. Social Security Programs

1935 Social Security Old-Age Insurance; Unemployment Insurance; and Public Assistance programs for needy aged, and blind (replaced by the SSI program in 1972); and Aid to Families with Dependent Children (replaced with block grants for Temporary Assistance for Needy Families in 1996)
1934 Railroad Retirement System
1937 Public Housing
1939 Social Security Old-Age and Survivors Insurance
1946 National School Lunch Program
1950 Aid to the Permanently and Totally Disabled (replaced by the SSI program in 1972)
1956 Social Security Disability Insurance
1960 Medical Assistance for the Aged (replaced by Medicaid in 1965)
1964 Food Stamp Program
1965 Medicare and Medicaid Programs
1966 School Breakfast Program
1969 Black Lung Benefits Program
1972 Supplemental Security Income Program (SSI)
1974 Special Supplemental Food Program for Women, Infants, and Children (WIC)
1975 Earned Income Tax Credit
1981 Low-Income Home Energy Assistance
1996 Temporary Assistance for Needy Families (TANF)

Source: Social Security Administration 2002.

CRITICAL THINKING QUESTIONS

1. Why did the bills to create public pensions in the early part of the 1900s fail? What changed between 1900 and 1935?
2. If welfare programs are also a part of the Social Security Act, why are they stigmatized, but Social Security for seniors is not?

The Aging Couple

The majority of men and women are married as they enter late adulthood. For example, over three-quarters of men age 65 to 74 are married, as are more than half of women. However, as we age, the likelihood of being married begins to decline, particularly for women (U.S. Census Bureau 2006c). Among those age 85 and over, 60 percent of men remain married, compared to only 17 percent of women, as shown in Figure 12.5.

This next section examines several important dimensions of the couple relationship: marital satisfaction, the division of household labor, sexuality, and widowhood.

FIGURE 12.5 Marital Status of the Population 65 Years and Over by Age and Sex, 2005

Sources: U.S. Census Bureau 2003; U.S. Census Bureau 2006.

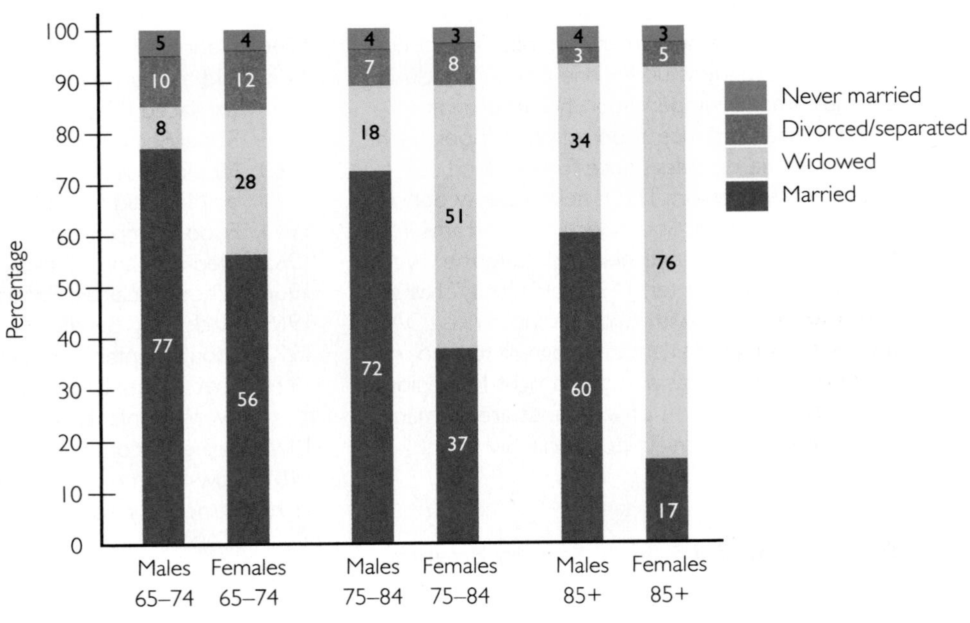

Marital Satisfaction

Most married older couples have a relationship that has endured many years. Many unhappy marriages may have already ended in divorce; therefore, those who remain married tend to rate their marriages as happy or very happy (Bookwala and Jacobs 2004). They have faced life and its transitions with a partner: the birth of a child, the raising of children, employment opportunities, finding the balance between work and family, the departure of their children from the home, and becoming a couple once again. Experiences such as traveling, expanded leisure, grandparenthood, and daily living can be enhanced by sharing them with a spouse.

How does the degree to which couples are satisfied with their spouses and their relationship change over the life course? One early study of 400 couples married in the 1930s involved a longitudinal comparison of marital satisfaction over 20 years. Each member of the couple was evaluated soon after their marriage, and then again 20 years later. Using a number of different measures, the study found that marital satisfaction diminished over time (Pineo 1961).

More recent studies have usually been cross-sectional, because it is extremely difficult to track couples for 20, 30, or 40 years to conduct a longitudinal study. Cross-sectional studies generally report that the marital satisfaction of couples may instead be curvilinear or "U-shaped." This means that a marriage begins with a high level of satisfaction, but it begins to drop as couples have children, and then rises again when the children leave home (Aldous 1996; Morgan and Kunkel 1998).

Sociologist Norval Glenn (1998) examined several cohorts of families over a 10-year period (marriages in the 1930s through the 1980s), and his work casts doubt on whether marital satisfaction actually rises after the children leave home. He found no evidence of the upturn; he suggested instead that variation in marital quality may simply be due to cohort differences; people of different cohorts have different expectations about marriage. A couple who married many years ago may be more likely to emphasize duty and responsibility in marriage and focus less on how the relationship can be personally fulfilling. Therefore it would not be surprising to see that their marriage is self-rated as happier than someone younger who has expectations about marriage that primarily focus on what the relationship can do for them personally.

The Division of Household Labor

As children leave the home and with changes brought on by retirement, the aging couple has opportunities to alter certain dimensions of their lives. One area that has been studied is the division of household labor (Coltrane and Ishii-Kuntz 1992; Szinovacz 2000). As couples spend more time at home, does the distribution of domestic tasks change?

Most studies show that the division of household labor changes little as a couple ages (Brubaker and Kinsel 1985; Price 2003; Szinovacz and Harpster 1994). As the continuity theory would suggest, for the most part, long-established patterns continue. Using a large, nationally representative longitudinal sample of seniors in which one spouse was employed at least 10 hours a week at the first interview, Szinovacz examined how retirement changed a couple's allocation of domestic labor (Szinovacz 2000). She found that retirees spend more time in housework than their employed counterparts, including in tasks that were considered to be in their partner's domain. Retiring husbands whose wives continue to work outside the home take on more responsibility; however, when the wife retires she appears to take on more domestic duties again.

Sexuality

A very common misperception about the elderly is that they are no longer sexually active. However, ask yourself, at what age do you plan to give up sex?

As the following data reveal, if an elderly person is married or partnered, it is quite likely that he or she is still sexually active. One national study asked *married* adults aged 60 and older, "About how often did you and your husband/wife have sex during the last month?" Fifty-three percent indicated that they had sexual intercourse at least once during the previous month. In fact, among those who said that they were sexually active, one-half claimed to have intercourse once a week or more (Marsiglio and Donnelly 1991). A study conducted by a senior center in California considered the sexual interests, desires, and performance of adults 56 to 85. The results indicate that while 92 percent of men and women said they would like to have sex once a week, only 55 percent reported that they met that goal. Participants of all ages tended to wish they could return to the sexual habits they enjoyed 10 years ago (Fleming and Curti 1994).

Although frequency of sexual activity declines with age, studies like these reveal that many older persons are still sexually active. Marsiglio and Donnelly (1991) also found that, among those married respondents age 66 and older, 44 percent reported having sex in the previous month. Among the oldest cohort of individuals age 76 and over, 24 percent were sexually active. Data such as these take many people by surprise.

Laumann and associates in their 2004 book, *The Social Organization of Sexuality*, report national data indicating that elderly men are more likely to be sexually active

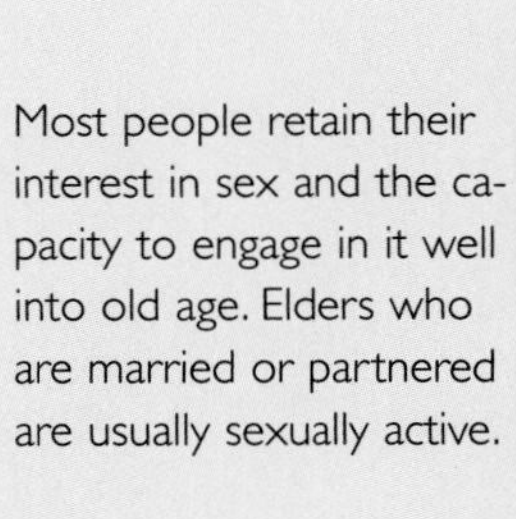

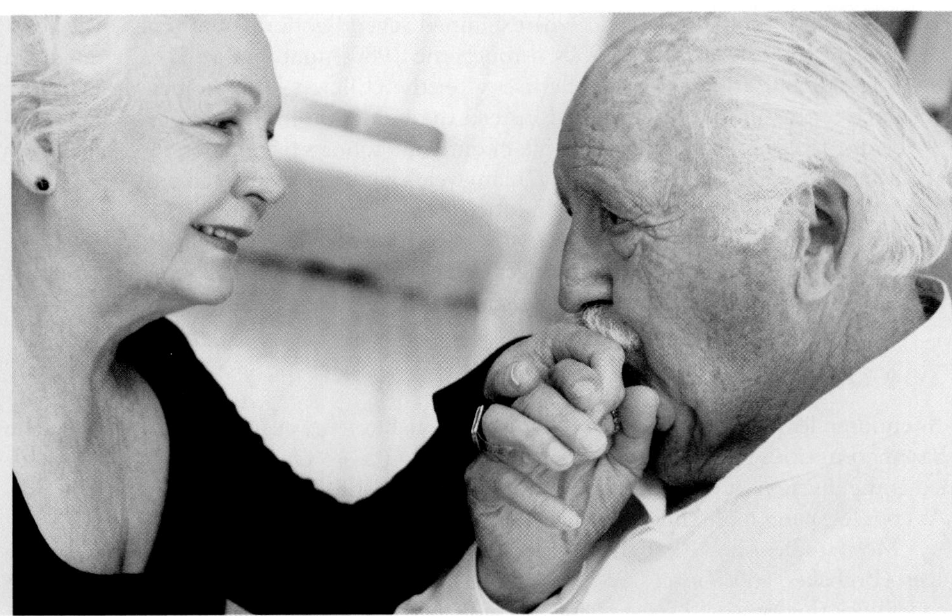

Most people retain their interest in sex and the capacity to engage in it well into old age. Elders who are married or partnered are usually sexually active.

than women. For example, among those aged 65 to 69, 75 percent of men report they are sexually active, as do about 40 percent of women. By age 85 to 89, about 45 percent of men report they are sexually active, compared to only 5 percent of women. The large sex differences are due to the fact that many more women are widowed and thus less likely to have available sexual partners than are men. When a partner is available, many couples continue to engage in sexual relations, but the lack of a sexual partner should not be taken as proof that interest in sexuality disappears in later life. Studies have noted that about one-third of women and slightly less than one-half of men over age 70 report masturbating (Marsiglio et al. 2000). It appears to be time to debunk the myth that the elderly are asexual. Most people retain their interest in sex and the capacity to engage in it well into old age. The continuity theory can help us understand that the elderly were young once, and just as young adults today do not plan to give up their sexual lives as they age, neither do today's elderly.

Gay and Lesbian Elders

Mention the word "lesbian" and chances are that you do not picture a 72-year-old woman. Nonetheless, it is likely that somewhere between 1 and 3 million elderly Americans are lesbian, gay, bisexual, or transgendered, perhaps increasing to 4 million by 2030. These elders are among the most invisible of all Americans. Little is known about them because of the neglect by governmental and academic researchers to include questions about sexual orientation or gender identity in their studies of the aged (National Gay and Lesbian Task Force 2005–2006).

They face many of the same transitions that heterosexual elderly couples and singles face, but they also have some unique concerns. For example, Social Security pays spousal benefits to married couples and survivor benefits to widows or widowers, but same-sex life partners do not have the same protections. Medicaid regulations protect the assets and homes of married spouses when the other spouse enters a nursing home or long-term care facility, but no such protections are offered to same-sex partners.

Seemingly basic rights such as hospital visitation or the right to die in the same nursing home are regularly denied same-sex partners (National Gay and Lesbian Task Force 2005–2006). They often hide their sexual orientation from health professionals and social service providers out of fear of being ostracized or harassed. The legal frameworks that excluded homosexuals produce social and economic consequences that deny them access to financial resources and community support networks.

Widowhood

The death of a spouse stands as one of life's most stressful events. It means the loss of a companion and friend, perhaps the loss of income, and the ending of a familiar way of life. Widowhood can occur at any point in the life cycle, but because it is most likely to occur among the elderly, research tends to focus on that population.

Approximately 13.5 million persons are classified as widowed in the United States; 85 percent of them are women. The number of persons who have *experienced* widowhood, however, is much larger than that, because some have remarried. There are three primary reasons for the significantly higher rates of widowhood among women than men. First, mortality rates among females are lower than for males, and therefore they live to older ages. The life expectancy of females at age 65 exceeds that of males by nearly 7 years. Second, wives are typically 2 to 3 years younger than their husbands and consequently have a greater chance of outliving them. Third, widowed women are less likely to remarry than are widowed men. There is a lack of eligible men because cultural norms encourage older men to date and marry younger women, but not the reverse (Berardo and Berardo 2000; He et al. 2005).

How do widows and widowers cope with such a traumatic loss? Sociologist Deborah Carr (2004) analyzed data from a large longitudinal study of 1,532 married men and women age 65 and older, a sample that was interviewed at regular intervals over a period of several years. The deaths of respondents were monitored, and follow-up interviews were conducted with the surviving spouses at 6 months, 18 months, and 4 years after being widowed. She found that sudden death was more emotionally distressing to women than to men. "Men cope best if their wives' deaths are quick and unexpected," she says, "while women cope best if their husband's deaths come after some period of warning. I think it is because, for this cohort anyway—the parents of baby boomers—women are used to the role of caregivers and do not find it stressful. But men do" (reported in University of Michigan News and Information Services 2001).

Is Widowhood More Difficult for Men or Women? Some studies report that men and women experience similar physical and emotional difficulties over time (see Brubaker 1991 for a review). Most studies suggest, however, that males who lose their spouse have a more difficult time because they are less likely to have same-sex widowed friends, are more likely to be older, may have poorer health themselves, have fewer family ties, and are not particularly proficient in domestic tasks (Berardo 1970; Carr 2006; Umberson et al. 1992).

On the other hand, older women have largely been dependent on their husbands, and when widowed, they may find two substantial difficulties. First, their incomes are profoundly reduced. Not all widows have life insurance policies, investments such as stocks and bonds, or employer pension plans. Second, widows may find that they face the daunting practical problems of maintaining a house alone. A study of 201 widows drawn from public death records in a Midwestern metropolitan area found that home repair needs caused greater stress than financial problems. Practical support such as help with home repairs significantly decreased widows' stress (Miller et al. 1998).

The U.S. Census classifies 13.5 million people as widowed, 85 percent of whom are women. Women and men face different types of adjustment after widowhood. Men are likely to experience greater loneliness and isolation, while women suffer greater financial problems.

A study of 200 older individuals found that widowed men are more likely than their female counterparts to want to find another romantic partner. Carr found that 6 months after a spouse had died, 15 percent of men, compared to less than 1 percent of women, were dating, and 30 percent of men, compared to 16 percent of women, claimed that they wanted to remarry (Carr 2004). Men's higher likelihood of remarriage can be attributed to at least two factors: (1) they have a greater pool of eligibles, and (2) they may be more motivated to find someone to take care of them and share their lives (Carr 2006).

Social Class, Race, Ethnicity, and Widowhood Social class is related to different experiences in widowhood. Lopata (1973, 1979) found that working-class couples are more likely to live in sex-segregated worlds, and consequently they may experience less disorganization in their lives immediately after the death of a spouse (Lopata 1973, 1979). However, finances are more vulnerable than is the case among the middle class. Less educated widows are more dependent on their adult children for financial and legal advice than are those with more education (Ha et al. 2006). Researchers have noted that whites have fewer children, are less likely to live in extended families, are more likely to live alone, and have fewer active support systems following widowhood than do minority elders. Therefore, in many ways they are more prone to loneliness and isolation.

Relationships with Children and Grandchildren

The Elderly and Their Adult Children

Relationships between older parents and their adult children tend to be strong and enduring as children leave home, cohabit, marry, and are employed (Aquilino 1997; Greenfield and Marks 2004; Umberson 2006). Both generations report strong feelings of connection to each other, although parents often have stronger feelings of attachment to their children than their children have to them (Lynott and Roberts 1997).

Generally, adult children and their parents want to get along, and therefore try to avoid those topics that cause tension in the relationship. Few adults report overt hostility or conflict with their aging parents. One study found that only 5 percent of adults reported frequent conflict with their aging mothers and 6 percent reported frequent conflict with their aging fathers (Cicirelli 1983).

Most elderly help out their adult children financially, emotionally, and with tasks such as child care assistance. Until parents are very old and frail, they give out far more assistance to their children than they receive from them. They may lend money to their adult children for a down payment on a new car or new house, they may set up a fund for their grandchildren's college costs, or they may be an important safety net in times of illness, divorce, or other family crisis (Gallagher 1994). A study comparing extended family ties of Mexican Americans, Puerto Ricans, and whites found that adult Mexican Americans and Puerto Ricans were more likely to live near or with their aging parents than were whites. Mexican Americans were also more likely than the two other groups to receive instrumental assistance with such things as transportation, housework, yard work, car repairs, or other work around the house. In contrast, whites were more likely to receive financial assistance from their parents (Sarkisian et al. 2006).

As older parents continue to age and eventually need assistance in caring for themselves, their children—particularly their daughters—often step in to help (Allen 2000). However, given the complexity in their lives combining work and family, the great geographical distances among family members, and their cultural values of independence, many adult children in the United States provide their assistance with a great deal of difficulty and ambivalence (Willson 2003).

Coresidence Elderly persons' living arrangements are of interest to family scholars and gerontologists. Particularly at issue has been whether the elderly live in extended families, nuclear families, live alone, or in an institutional setting. In the United States, most elderly live with a spouse or live alone. Cultural values stress individualism and personal freedom, and these often endure into a person's later years. Few elderly coreside with their adult children, although the likelihood varies considerably by race and ethnic groups (Kamo and Zhou 1994). For example, Asian American elderly and their adult children are far more likely to coreside than are their white counterparts.

Sociologists Lynn White and Stacy Rogers (1997) analyzed data from a sample of 435 young adults aged 19 to 40 to examine the effects of coresidence on parent-child solidarity. Their results indicate that young adults who coreside with an aging parent provide more assistance to each other and perceive more support from their parents than do families who do not coreside. However, their relationships are not necessarily more intimate or affectionate and may in fact be even less so. This may be because coresidence is uncommon for most Americans, at least among whites, and is generally reserved for when there is some sort of predicament (e.g., financial instability or poor health).

Unlike the United States, in many countries coresiding with adult children is commonplace. In the Philippines, Singapore, Thailand, and Vietnam, about three-quarters of adults aged 60 and over reside with their children (Kinsella and Velkoff 2001). Coresidence is deeply rooted in the tradition of filial responsibility and respect toward elders. Adult children feel a moral obligation to take care of their parents. Japan is a country undergoing rapid social change. In 1960 nearly 90 percent of elders coresided with their children. By 1995 that figure had been reduced to approximately 55 percent (Kinsella and Velkoff 2001). Kamo (1988) suggests that the impact of industrialization has undermined the indigenous culture of Japan, and has begun to erode elders' traditional high status.

Grandfathers are now more likely to recognize the importance of having direct emotional involvement with young children and have opportunities to participate in ways that seemed unavailable to them as fathers.

Grandparenthood

Most parents eventually become grandparents. On average, first grandchildren are born to adults who are in their late 40s or early 50s although the age is increasing as young couples wait longer to have children. Some people may not become grandparents until they are in their 70s. Children today are more likely to have all four grandparents alive when they are born, and most will continue to have at least two grandparents alive when they reach adulthood (Szinovacz 1998; Uhlenberg and Kirby 1998).

Grandparent roles are relatively new in society. Increasing longevity and falling fertility has meant that the grandparent generation is no longer still raising their own younger children when their oldest marries and has children. Until the twentieth century, grandparents did not generally have the time or resources to be intimately involved in the lives of their grandchildren.

Grandparenting Today The role of grandparent has changed over the past century (Cherlin and Furstenberg 1986). First, being a grandparent has become a role distinct from parenting itself because grandparents are now unlikely to have their own children still living in the home. Second, it has changed because the elderly are healthier, better educated, and have greater economic security than in the past. Third, grandparents, grandfathers in particular, are now more likely to recognize the importance of having direct emotional involvement with young children. Grandfathers have opportunities to participate in nurturing children that seemed unavailable to them as fathers or to grandfathers in the past (Cunningham-Burley 2001). Finally, families can more easily travel long distances and communicate by way of telephone or computer.

Most grandparents report that their relationships with their grandchildren are meaningful and report that fun and pleasure are key components of their relationships (Reitzes and Mutran 2004). In their national study of grandparents, Cherlin and Furstenberg (1986) found that 55 percent of grandparents reported having a *companionate* relationship with their grandchildren. This means that they enjoy recreational activities, occasional overnight stays, and even babysitting. The relationship is intimate, fun, and friendly. About 30 percent had *remote*, or emotionally distant, relationships with their grandchildren, often because they lived far away. Another 15 percent of grandparents were more *involved*, with more frequent interaction or possibly even living together. Figure 12.6 shows the percentage of grandparents engaging in various activities with their children during the previous 12 months.

Cherlin and Furstenberg (1986) also point to a marked change in the balance between respect and affection among grandparents and their grandchildren. They asked all grandparents in a national survey, "Are you and the [study child] more friendly, less friendly, or about the same as your grandparents were with you?" Forty-eight percent reported that they were "more friendly," while only 9 percent said "less friendly." Similarly,

FIGURE 12.6 **Percentage of Grandparents Engaging in Activities with Grandchild over Past 12 Months**

Source: Cherlin and Fuerstenberg 1986.

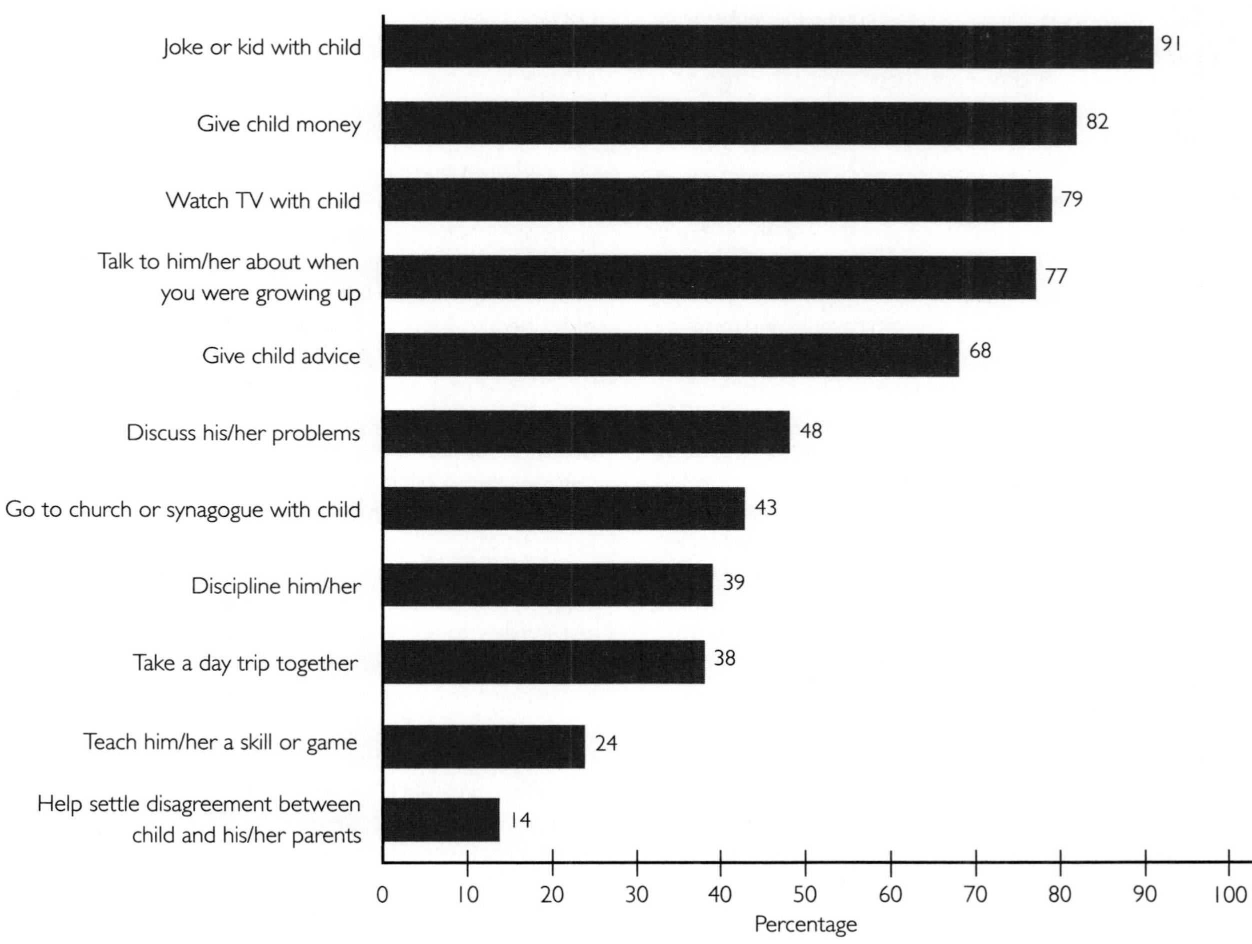

most claimed that their relationship with the child was "closer" than their own relationship with their grandparents. For one man's personal essay on what grandparenthood means to him, see Box 12.3.

Sex Differences in Grandparenting Styles Grandmothers and grandfathers often have different styles of interaction with their grandchildren. Grandmothers are more likely to be involved in planning and orchestrating family activities, nurturing their grandchildren, and assuming caregiving responsibilities (Walker et al. 2001). This is consistent with their role as family **kinkeeper** (having the primary responsibility for maintaining family relationships). For example, it is usually the women in the family who are responsible for sending greeting cards on holidays and birthdays. In contrast,

BOX 12.3 Families as Lived Experience

What Is It Like to Be a Grandparent?

Most students reading this book have experience being a grandchild, but what is it like to be a grandparent? While grandparenthood can mean different things to different people, the following story reveals the joy and happiness grandparenthood can bring.

A seven-year-old girl said about her grandmother: "She's old on the outside, but she acts like she's young on the inside." She hit the nail on the head! Living longer means that more of us now lead three lives: first as children, second as adults with careers and most likely as parents, and third as retirees from careers—and for most of us as grandparents. During each of these lives we continually discover and learn new things. We find sides of ourselves that we did not know existed. Our third life is a time for discovering new talents and creative possibilities in our inner worlds. It is a time for applying the wisdom of the ages to ourselves.

Being a grandparent means different things. Although grandparenting is not the dominant aspect of most of our lives, it is an aspect that is more important than most of us realize. For some of us who are actively raising our grandchildren, it is the most important part of our lives. Some of us are estranged from our children and from our grandchildren because of strife in our families. But most of us live at some distance from our grandchildren and manage to maintain an active role in their lives through the mail, the telephone, and visits.

As grandparents we have important symbolic and practical functions in our cultures. We are important simply for what we mean as the oldest living representatives of our families. We can be a matriarch or a patriarch for our families. Our roles as family historians, mentors, and role models can confer status and respect on us.

Without grandparents, there is no tangible family line. Children who have had no contact with grandparents miss knowledge of their ancestry. They may not be able to muster a confident sense of the future as concretely represented by the fact that older people have seen their futures become the present and the past. As grandparents we are the links to the past in our families. We are the repositories of information about our genealogies. That information often becomes useful material for themes that our grandchildren write in school, and sometimes it flowers into full-fledged writing about our family trees.

As grandparents we can provide advice to our children that is hopefully appreciated. We can bring our families together and foster and maintain communication between them. We can play healing roles in assuaging the challenges, hurts, and disappointments in our families. We are the conveyors of traditions in our families and in our cultures.

We have much to offer our families and our communities. We are the people who have been there. Whatever wisdom is should lie in us. We can see through the posturing of our everyday world. We can identify with the life stream and the cycles of human existence. We know that dis-

grandfathers are more likely to focus on practical issues and spend more time together exchanging help and services, particularly with their grandsons. One consequence of this difference in style is that family members generally feel more obligation and are closer to their grandmothers than to their grandfathers (Rossi and Rossi 1990; Dubas 2001). This may be the reason that grandmothers report greater satisfaction and overall meaning in grandparenthood than do grandfathers (Somary and Stricker 1998).

Racial and Ethnic Differences in Grandparenting Styles In racial and ethnic minority families, grandmothers frequently have important and influential roles in child rearing, often mimicking parent-like behavior (Dilworth-Anderson 2001; Hunter 1997; Morgan and Kunkel 1998; Uttal 1999). A 1997 study by psychologist Andrea

appointments, heartaches, and pain are natural parts of life. We know that life goes on without us. We have had enough dreams and life experiences to know that the mystical may be more real than the rational.

We also have the luxury of living our lives more or less as we wish. We have more control over our schedules because of the relinquishing of the responsibilities of the workplace. We have time to reflect and to enjoy the simple things in life. We can take time to appreciate the pleasures of simply being alive. We can enjoy the clouds, the trees, the flowers, and the smell of the air. We also can devote our time and energies to helping those who are less fortunate. Most importantly, we can relieve and resolve the past in our memories.

We gain profound meaning in life from the love and respect of our juniors. The attachment between grandparent and grandchild is second in emotional power only to the bond between parent and child. The arrival of a grandchild usually triggers a dormant instinct to nurture in us. This is accompanied by joy in the birth or adoption of our grandchild; by recalling our own experiences as a parent and as a grandchild; and by thoughts about continuity of our own lives in the next generation.

Our grandchildren have as much to offer us as we have to offer them. We can enjoy our pleasures with them without the responsibility of rearing them. The love and attention we give them builds their self-esteem. Their interest in our company and in our stories reminds us of our importance to our families. We offer each other the sense of belonging not only to our families but also to the human family.

As grandparents and as senior citizens, we are gaining an increasing amount of power in our society not only in the political arena but also in the moral leadership of our society. We really do have much to offer even though there is a tendency to disparage the elderly. We can advocate for the interests of the elderly, not only of our own but also of those of us who are subjected to elder ageism and abuse. But most importantly, we are aware of the interests and needs of future generations. We are in a position to be powerful advocates for children and parents.

As grandparents, we are crucial resources for our families. But the art of grandparenting requires commitment, understanding, practice, and perseverance. We can offer approval, loving delight of our grandchildren, and reliable support for our own offspring. We are the link between the past and the present and even the future! It is through our grandchildren that we and humanity itself flow in the stream of life.

Source: Westman 1998.

CRITICAL THINKING QUESTIONS

1. How do the esteem, power, and importance of grandparents differ cross culturally?
2. How does it differ in the United States across social class, race, or ethnicity?

Hunter examined black mothers' and fathers' reliance on grandmothers for parenting support. She used a sample of 487 parents aged 18 to 34 years old from the National Survey of Black Americans and examined their responses to the following questions: (a) "Do you have anyone who gives you advice about child rearing or helps you with problems having to do with children? If yes, what is this advisor's relationship to you?" and (b) "Do you have someone to count on to take care of the children? If yes, what is this person's relationship to you?" She found that 57 percent of the mothers and 56 percent of the fathers reported that they relied on grandmothers for parenting support, relying on them more frequently than anyone else. The majority of these persons said that they receive both advice and child care from the grandparent.

Three theories are often used to explain why racial and ethnic minority families are more likely than white families to use grandparents (and other kin) as caregivers for their grandchildren (Uttal 1999). The *cultural* explanation suggests that these practices are the product of different cultural experiences and adaptations. The *structural* explanation conceives of child care arrangements as an adaptation to structural constraints, such as racism or poverty. The *integrative* explanation combines these and suggests that these arrangements are due to the intersection of cultural values with structural constraints, operating alongside gendered expectations. In interviews with seven black mothers, seven Mexican American mothers, and 17 Anglo-American mothers, Uttal found that the major difference among the groups was how the mothers *felt* about using kin for care. White Anglos tended to feel that relying on grandparents and other kin was inappropriate or problematic, whereas black and Mexican American mothers willingly accepted this help because they felt that it was appropriate and acceptable.

Retirement

Employment provides us with more than an income. It also is an important part of our identity. We say, "I *am* a nurse . . ." "I *am* a teacher . . ." "I *am* a firefighter . . ." as though we *are* the occupation. Consequently, retirement is an important event because it alters a major identity as well as reduces our income.

The median age at retirement in the United States has fallen from 68 years in 1950 to 59 today, during a time when life expectancy has increased. This indicates that retirement is viewed as an earned privilege (O'Rand 1990). It also reflects a convergence of public and private employment policies. People now retire earlier because of publicly funded Social Security, because employer-sponsored pension or savings plans are more common, and because with an increasing amount of surplus labor many employers are inducing older persons to exit the labor force (Hardy and Shuey 2000).

The Social Construction of Retirement: Retirement Around the World

Historically speaking, retirement is an anomaly. Throughout most of history, families needed its members to work to support themselves. This is the case in many countries today, as seen in Figure 12.7. Unlike in more developed nations, elders in less-developed countries often remained employed well into old age. For example, in Bangladesh, over 70 percent of men aged 65 and over are in the labor market, as are 27 percent of the women (Kinsella and Velkoff 2001). It is important to remember that life expectancy in less-developed countries is significantly lower as well; therefore it is likely that many individuals work their entire life. There is no such thing as retirement at any age.

For significant numbers of elderly to be able to withdraw from the labor force, four conditions must exist in a society (Morgan and Kunkel 1998). First, a society must produce an economic surplus that is large enough to support its nonemployed members. Second, there must be a mechanism in place to divert some of that surplus to the nonemployed members such as through a pension or government transfer program. Third, nonemployed members should be viewed positively by the rest of society, and their activities or leisure must be seen as legitimate. Finally, the nonemployed members must have accumulated an acceptable number of years of productivity to warrant support by the other members of society. These conditions materialized in the United States after industrialization during the nineteenth and twentieth centuries.

FIGURE 12.7 **Labor Force Participation Rates for Men and Women Aged 65+ (Percent)**

Sources: U.S. Census Bureau 2000; Kinsella and Velkoff 2001.

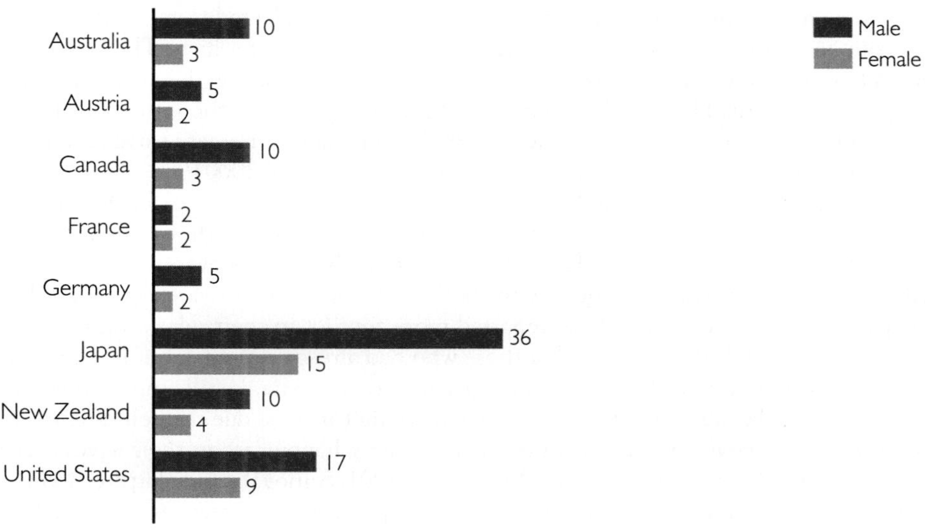

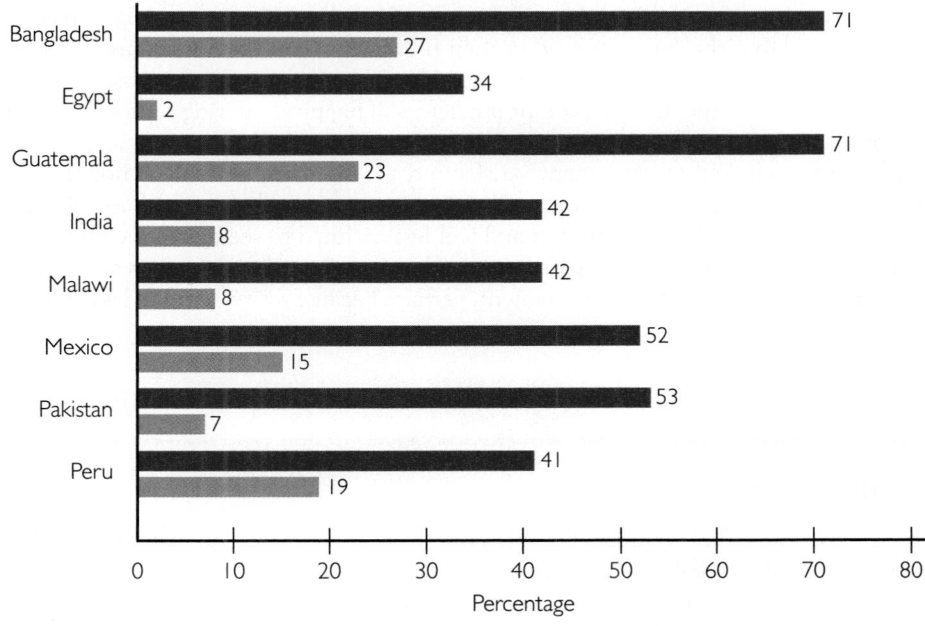

Sex Differences in Retirement

People often associate retirement with men, but as more women enter the labor force, retirement is relevant for them as well. Today, with almost half of the workforce comprised of women, and with the majority of workers married to other workers, couples are forging new retirement paths. Couples face not only two retirements, but also, they must coordinate their retirements and address whether to take up other paid work after they retire.

Researchers at Cornell University conducted a 5-year study of retirement with 762 men and women between the ages of 50 and 72 who were selected from six large employers in New York. Respondents were interviewed three separate times. The key questions addressed were: How do sex and career pathways influence the planning and timing of retirement? How do the timing of retirement, stresses of the retirement transition, and reemployment decisions affect marital quality and retirement satisfaction for both women and men (Cornell Gerontology Research Institute 2000)?

The team of researchers found that men in the sample began to plan for retirement earlier than did the women (ages 49 and 54, respectively), although they retired at similar ages (Han and Moen 1999). They also found that the process of retiring is associated with a decrease in marital quality for both men and women (Moen et al. 2001). Newly retired men and women both reported more conflict in their relationship, compared to couples who had not retired or those who had already retired. Conflicts arise in these families more often when one spouse, particularly the wife, is still employed while the other spouse begins to retire. This escalated conflict may be due to their difference in role status and power, with men in this cohort being happier when their wives conform to more traditional gender norms (Moen et al. 2001; Szinovacz and Harpster 1993).

Given the differences in men and women's employment experiences over the life course in terms of continuity, occupations, pay, and expectations, it is possible that they would have different experiences associated with retirement as well. Overall, men are more satisfied with retirement than are women; 71 percent of men and 56 percent of women report that they are better off in their retirement than the 5 years just before retirement (Quick and Moen 1998). While good health and a comfortable postretirement income are some of the most important predictors of happiness during retirement, there are some interesting differences among men and women as well. For example, part-time employment is linked to retirement satisfaction among men, but this is not the case among women. Researchers speculate that women are more likely to be busy with volunteer work or other family activities and feel less inclined to seek further employment for pay. Women who had more year-long employment gaps during their working years are more likely to be satisfied in retirement, perhaps because retirement is a less dramatic transition for them.

Health

Health Status

Cross-sectional studies conducted at one point in time find that the majority of elderly people report their health as good or excellent. Only 27 percent of elders assess their health as fair or poor. Elderly men and women report little difference in health. However, older blacks (42 percent) and older Hispanics (35 percent) are more likely to describe their health as only fair or poor than are whites (26 percent) (Administration on Aging 2002; National Center for Health Statistics 2005).

As one would expect, however, age is the most important predictor of illness and mortality. For example, while only 8 percent of persons between the ages of 65 and 69 report needing assistance, the figure jumps to 35 percent among those 80 and over. As we age we are increasingly likely to need someone to help us with many things that we used to do for ourselves.

Medicare

Health care is a rapidly growing segment of the U.S. economy, and the elderly use a significant portion of health care services. How do they pay for their health care costs? Although some elders have private insurance, most elders draw primarily or exclusively upon the **Medicare** program. Created in 1965, Medicare is a federal health insurance program for people age 65 and older (and some people with disabilities under 65, including people with permanent kidney failure requiring dialysis or a transplant). It has kept millions of elderly from impoverishing themselves to pay for their health care costs by making health insurance far more affordable and available to them. Because it is a universal rather than means-tested program, it has no stigma attached to it. Virtually all elderly qualify, so administrative costs are significantly lower than other programs that have stringent income requirements.

Medicare, however, is not without its critics. Given high deductibles, copayments, and payments for things not covered under Medicare, most elderly persons spend thousands of additional dollars each year on medical care. The elderly spend about $3,500 in annual out-of-pocket health care expenditures, an increase of more than 50 percent since 1990 (National Center for Policy Analysis 2001). Moreover, this is expected to rise to over $5,000 (in today's dollars), by 2025 (National Center for Policy Analysis 2001). Consequently, over 70 percent of elders have some form of additional insurance, a "medigap" policy. The poorest elderly may qualify for **Medicaid**, the health care program that is designed to serve poor persons, regardless of age, and also covers long-term care.

The changing U.S. demographic structure has some potentially distressing repercussions for the Medicare program. Medicare is primarily funded through Social Security taxes; working people pay taxes today for programs used by the elderly today. In the future, as the U.S. population ages, there will be fewer working adults paying taxes relative to the number of elderly persons needing Medicare services. There were about five workers for each beneficiary in 1960, and three in 2000, but there will be only 1.9 by 2040 (De Lew et al. 1992). Couple this with rising health care costs, and the country could be facing a serious challenge. To deal with this problem, Congress could modify the program in several ways, such as increasing the amount that elders pay out of their own pockets by raising deductibles and copayments, and covering fewer services. The goal is to keep Medicare solvent well into the future because society recognizes that the health of seniors is a social concern, not merely an individual problem.

However, this philosophy raises interesting questions about other age groups. Why do elders have a health care program on their behalf and children do not? This question is legitimate and has caused some tension among advocates of different generations. Without detracting from the serious needs many elders face and the lives that Medicare has saved or improved, extending coverage to one vulnerable age group while withholding coverage from another is a uniquely American inconsistency found in no other developed nation. Instead, all developed nations (and many developing ones) have some sort of national health insurance program designed for all citizens, regardless of age. An inconsistency such as this illustrates the lack of coherent family policy in the United States.

Social Policy and Family Resilience

Researchers have measured the degree of physical impairment by using a common set of **activities of daily living (ADLs)** such as bathing, dressing, eating, getting into and out of bed, walking indoors, and using the toilet. **Instrumental activities of daily living**

(IADLs) include meal preparation, shopping, managing money, and taking medication. By using a common set of measures, gerontologists can track elders' degree of impairment and can make some comparisons across different samples. Nearly four million older Americans are unable to perform at least one ADL by themselves, and seven million elders, or one in five, are unable to perform at least one IADL (Administration on Aging 2002). As people age, they likely become more disabled (Wolff and Kasper 2006). Gerontologists estimate that the number of older persons needing significant and long-term care will increase over the next 50 years as the oldest-old cohort expands: 14 million elders may need significant care by 2020 and 24 million by 2060.

Example: Long-Term Care

Who provides long-term care to the needy elderly? Given the sheer numbers of frail elders, we might find it perplexing that the United States has no formal long-term care policy (Olson 2003). Some elderly persons in the United States rely on **formal care** provided by social service agencies on a paid or volunteer basis. This could include a variety of types of care: paid visiting nurses, meals or housecleaning programs, a paid personal attendant, or nursing home care. These services are used far less than informal care and are far less available to the average-income person than is the case in many European countries. Some communities do not offer these programs at all. Various components of formal care rise and fall according to politically motivated funding streams. For example, when the 1980 Omnibus Reconciliation Act expanded coverage of home care, the number of home care providers rapidly expanded. However, when the 1997 Balanced Budget Amendment cut back funding, the number of agencies providing home care services dropped by 20 percent in just 5 years, despite a growing number of frail elderly needing services. Services have little to do with actual demand (Olson 2003).

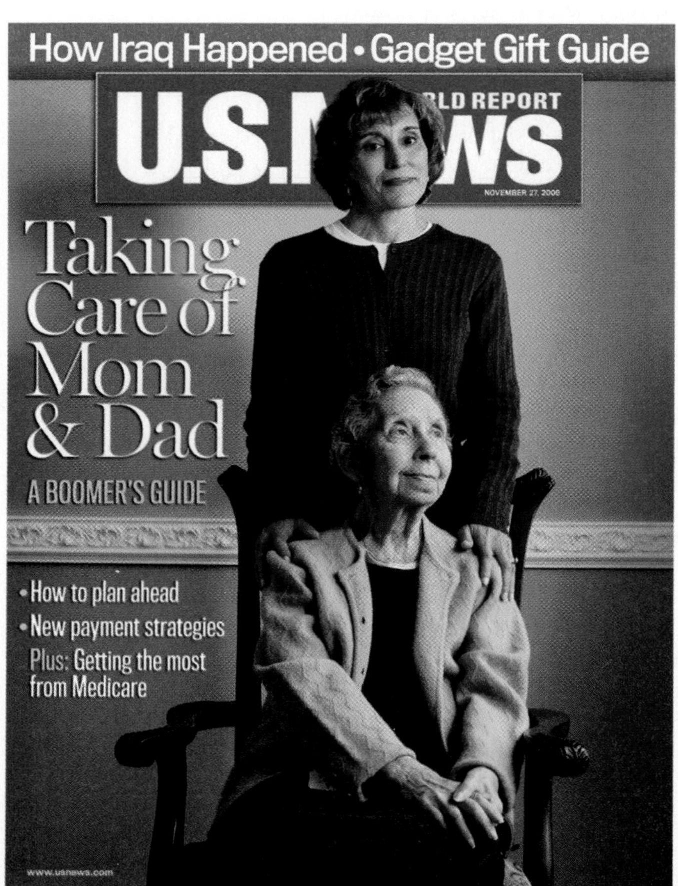

As the number of elderly continues to spiral upward, a pressing public policy question is who will care for them. A spouse is generally the first person in line to provide care, and if he or she is unavailable, an adult daughter or daughter-in-law usually helps. However, as more women are employed, it is increasingly difficult for them to provide the long-term care that many elders need.

One type of formal care is the nursing home, designed to provide custodial care. Few elderly persons live in nursing homes, although that number rises with age. Most people do not need that intense level of care, cannot afford such care, and would rather be cared for within their communities outside of institutions. However, 22 percent of persons 85 years and older live in nursing homes, and 40 percent of elders are likely to spend some time in a nursing home at one point or another in their lifetime (AARP and Administration on Aging 1997; Soldo and Agree 1988).

The majority of elders in the United States rely primarily on **informal care** (unpaid care by someone close to the care recipient). Eighty to 85 percent of informal care is provided by family members, usually a wife, daughter, husband, or son. About 41 percent of caregivers are children of the care recipient, 38 percent are spouses (usually the wife), and 20 percent are other family members (e.g., niece, siblings, grandchildren) or friends (Wolff and Kasper 2006). Most caregivers report working alone. They provide a wide variety of hands-on care and continue to do so even after an elder is institutionalized (Keefe and Fancey 2000).

A spouse is generally the first person in line to provide care if she or he is able, and among spouses, wives tend to care for their husbands rather than the reverse. Men have shorter life expectancies and so may need care earlier than women do. When a spouse is unavailable or is unable to provide this level of care, adult children, usually daughters, step in (Lee et al. 1993). This is particularly true for black and Latino families, where adult children (daughters and daughters-in-law) comprise about 75 percent of caregivers compared to 40 to 60 percent in white families (Montgomery 1996). Some of these adult daughters have children under age 18 to care for in addition to their disabled parent, and are referred to as the **sandwich generation**. One study of 273 married respondents who provided care found that having their own children, particularly daughters, seems to increase rather than decrease the amount of time spent in caregiving to frail relatives. The researchers found that children are more likely to connect the generations, rather than constrain the help that both mothers and fathers provide (Gallagher and Gerstel 2001).

A study of 341 lesbian, gay, bisexual, or transgendered adults aged 50 and over living in New York reported that 46 percent of the respondents were providing or had provided caregiving assistance to a family member, partner, or close friend within the past 5 years (Cantor et al. 2004). Nearly half of these provided care for a member of their family or origin, usually a parent, and two-thirds reported that they were the sole or primary caregiver. One-third believed that more was expected of them than from other family members because they were not heterosexual; it was assumed that they had fewer obligations or other personal responsibilities because they were unmarried. The remaining half who reported having provided care within the past 5 years were caring for a partner who was ill, disabled, or suffering from an age-related disability (e.g., Alzheimer's disease) or close friend, most often a male friend suffering from HIV/AIDS.

There are differences in caregiving across racial and ethnic lines. Studies, overall, report that minorities tend to provide more care and hold stronger beliefs about filial obligation (Pinquart and Sorenson 2005). Minority caregivers were more likely than whites to be adult children (rather than spouses), and tended to be younger.

There are also cross-cultural differences in caregiving. One study, which used data from 12,166 adult children from 2,527 Taiwanese families, found that sons generally carry the major responsibility for taking care of their older parents (Lin et al. 2003). Daughters fulfill the son's roles primarily when a son is not available, reflecting the patriarchal customs of Taiwanese society in which sons bear the primary responsibility for the continuation of the family line.

Caring for elderly parents or a spouse can be a labor of love, but it is also time intensive, potentially expensive, and often stressful (Cantor et al. 2004; Pinquart and Silverson 2005; Raschick and Ingersoll-Dayton 2004). Most caregivers provide assistance seven days a week, with nearly half reporting 21 hours or more of care per week, with little help from formal services (AARP and Travelers Foundation 1988). Adult daughters and sons are also likely to be employed outside the home, so they provide care to their relative on top of an already tight schedule. Furthermore, 40 percent of caregivers report spending their own money for care-related products, services, or activities. Sometimes these sums are substantial to people on a fixed income or to people who are caring for their children as well as a parent.

Given these challenges, most caregivers report experiencing emotional strain and nearly half are clinically depressed. Caregivers use prescription drugs for depression, anxiety and insomnia two to three times as often as the rest of the population (Gallagher et al. 1989; Scharlach 1991).

As society continues to age, the United States could benefit from an explicit plan for caring for frail elders. If caregiving is indeed a personal responsibility to be provided by family members, then families can be strengthened by a variety of financial and policy benefits, such as tax credits, paid family leave, free or low-cost senior day care, or respite care. Moreover, while the Family Medical Leave Act allows for 12 weeks of unpaid leave from employment to allow a person to care for a sick or disabled relative (in qualifying workplaces), same-sex partners do not have these same privileges.

Conclusion

The population around the world is aging rapidly with great implications for families and other social institutions. A comparative perspective is important for understanding these implications because the most rapid growth in the aging population is occurring in developing nations, which are often poor, and therefore less equipped to handle the strain on the economic and health care resources that this change will bring. To complicate these issues even further, the most striking increase around the world is among those aged 80 and over. The pronounced effects of these demographic changes will be felt throughout the global economy. In the United States, the elderly have achieved great success in actively promoting the concerns of an aging population. Given their size, their concerns become the concerns of everyone. Their agenda includes promoting social and economic well-being; supporting intimate relationships; fostering positive bonds with adult children and grandchildren; assessing concerns around retirement, widowhood, and caregiving; and looking at ways to improve health, access to health care, and health policy.

Key Terms

Activities of daily living (ADL): A common set of measures that gerontologists use to track elders' degree of impairment, such as bathing, dressing, eating, getting into and out of bed, walking indoors, and using the toilet. (p. 399)

Baby-boom generation: Persons born after WWII. (p. 376)

Centenarians: Persons age 100 and older. (p. 370)

Demographic transition: The process in which a society moves from a situation of high fertility rates and low life expectancy, to one of low fertility rates and high life expectancy. (p. 371)

English Poor Laws of 1601: The first systematic codification of English ideas about the responsibility of the state to provide for its citizens. (p. 384)

Formal care: Care for the elderly that is provided by social service agencies on a paid or volunteer basis. (p. 400)

Gerontology: An interdisciplinary science of aging that draws upon biology, medicine, and the social sciences, including sociology, psychology, and family studies. (p. 380)

Informal care: Care for the elderly that is unpaid, usually done by someone close to the elder. (p. 400)

Instrumental activities of daily living (IADL): Includes activities such as preparing meals, shopping, managing money, using the telephone, doing housework, and taking medications. (p. 399)

Kinkeeper: The person who has the primary responsibility for maintaining family relationships. (p. 393)

Life expectancy: How long a person can expect to live, usually calculated from birth. (p. 370)

Medicaid: A federally mandated health care financing program for the financially indigent who meet certain qualifications. (p. 399)

Medicare: A federal health insurance program primarily for people age 65 and older. (p. 399)

Old Age and Survivor Insurance (OASI): A cash assistance entitlement program for seniors that has also been extended to their widows. (p. 383)

Old Age Insurance (OAI): A cash assistance entitlement program for seniors. (p. 383)

Regressive tax: Lower-income persons pay a higher tax rate than do higher-income persons. (p. 383)

Sandwich generation: Adult children, usually daughters, who are caring for both their parents and their own children. (p. 401)

Social Security Act: Many programs under one umbrella, including unemployment compensation, health programs, cash welfare assistance, food stamps and school lunch programs, and cash assistance for the blind, survivors, and for seniors. (p. 385)

Triple jeopardy: People who face multiple disadvantages in society, e.g., old, female, and minority. (p. 383)

Resources on the Internet

AARP
www.aarp.org
Formerly known as the American Association of Retired Persons, this organization now represents over 34 million members aged 50 and over, whether they have retired or not. The goal is to increase the quality of life for older Americans, and AARP does this through advocacy, education, volunteer, and social opportunities.

Association for Gerontology in Higher Education (AGHE)
www.aghe.org/site/aghewebsite
This national organization is devoted primarily to gerontological education. The purpose of AGHE is to foster the commitment of higher education to the field of aging through education, research, and public service. The website contains information about careers in gerontology.

Gerontological Society of America
www.geron.org
The Gerontological Society of America is a nonprofit professional organization with more than 5,000 members in the field of aging. GSA provides researchers, educators, practitioners, and policymakers with opportunities to understand, advance, integrate, and use basic and applied research on aging to improve the quality of life as one ages.

National Institute on Aging
www.nih.gov.nia
This government agency provides extensive data on its website on the aging population in the United States. There are also many links to other relevant sites.

The Foster Grandparent Program
www.seniorcorps.org/research/overview_fgp.html
The Foster Grandparent Program offers seniors age 60 and older opportunities to serve as mentors, tutors, and loving caregivers for children and youth with special needs. They serve in community organizations such as schools, hospitals, Head Start, and youth centers.

Further Reading

Abraham, L. K. 1993. *Mama Might Be Better Off Dead.* Chicago: University of Chicago Press.

Baars, J., and D. Dannefer (Eds.). 2006. *Aging, Globalization, and Inequality: The New Critical Gerontology*. Amityville, NY: Baywood.

Connidis, I. A. 2001. *Family Ties and Aging*. Thousand Oaks, CA: Sage.

Cruikshank, M. 2003. *Learning to Be Old: Gender, Culture, and Aging*. Lanham, MD: Rowman and Littlefield.

Hatch, L. R. 2000. *Beyond Gender Differences: Adaptation to Aging in Life Course Perspective*. Amityville, NY: Baywood.

Hooyman, N., and A. Kiyak. 2008. *Social Gerontology: A Multidisciplinary Perspective* (8th ed.). Boston: Allyn and Bacon.

Myerhoff, B. 1980. *Number Our Days*. New York: Simon and Schuster.

Rossi, A. S. 2001. *Caring and Doing for Others*. Chicago: University of Chicago Press.

Umberson, D. 2006. *Death of a Parent: Transition to a New Adult Identity*. New York: Cambridge University Press.

Vissing, Y. 2002. *Women Without Children: Nurturing Lives*. New Brunswick, NJ: Rutgers University Press.

Walker, A. J., M. Manoogian-O'Dell, L. A. McGraw, and D. L. G. White. (Eds.). 2001. *Families in Later Life*. Thousand Oaks, CA: Pine Forge Press.

Walter, C. A. 2003. *The Loss of a Life Partner: Narratives of the Bereaved*. New York: Columbia University Press.

CHAPTER 13

Violence and Abuse

Chapter Outline

Chapter Preview

Many family problems are really *social problems*. Domestic violence is one of these. Abuse is rooted in complex and longstanding traditions promoting violence, and male privilege and authority within the family and other social institutions. In this chapter you will learn:

- Gender-based violence as a national human rights issue
- How violence is defined and measured
- The results of the National Violence Against Women Survey that revealed the commonality of violence and abuse
- About dating violence, sexual aggression, and rape
- Features of spouse/partner abuse, including its frequency, the factors associated with abuse, and how victims cope
- The types of child abuse, factors that contribute to child abuse, and the consequences of abuse
- The perpetrators and the victims of elder abuse
- Theoretical explanations for violence and abuse among intimates
- Ways in which legal and criminal justice systems are speaking out in favor of zero tolerance

What is the connection between violence to animals and various forms of family violence? Children's cruelty to animals deserves serious attention for several reasons. First, clinical studies of troubled youth and studies of sexual predators and violent criminals have revealed a link between abusing animals as children and violence toward others. Second, cruelty toward animals may indicate serious developmental problems or potential psychopathology, such as a lack of empathy for others, which could result in future violent or antisocial behavior. Third, children who are violent toward animals may also be currently living in violent and abusive families. Finally, countless animals suffer or die because of deliberate cruelty.

Research has demonstrated that there is a link between harsh physical punishment and a child's involvement in animal cruelty, particularly among boys. Males who committed cruelty to animals during their youth often reported experiencing family violence as they were growing up. But does this relationship hold when the domestic violence experienced is ordinary spanking?

Sociologist Clifton Flynn surveyed 267 college undergraduates attending a university in the southern United States to address this question. He defined animal cruelty as "socially unacceptable behavior that intentionally causes unnecessary pain, suffering, or distress to and/or death of an animal."

He found significant sex differences in the likelihood of abusing animals. Thirty-five percent of the males had inflicted abuse on animals, compared with 9 percent of females. Males were six times more likely to have killed a stray animal, three times more likely to have hurt or tortured an animal, and nearly six times more likely to have killed a pet than females. Flynn also found that males who were hit as teenagers were considerably more likely to abuse animals, particularly if the father did the hitting. Respondents who were hit as teenagers by their fathers were nearly three times more likely than those who were not hit to have committed animal cruelty. Further analysis of animal abuse by males showed that the relationship between being hit by fathers and inflicting cruelty persisted even after statistically controlling for whether the sons had suffered other abuse during childhood, whether they had witnessed their father hit their mother, and the level of the father's education. These results are important because they suggest that the link between spanking and animal cruelty cannot be explained simply by pointing to other forms of violence in the family or to socioeconomic status. Instead, it appears that some boys who have been spanked by those who are in positions of power—particularly fathers—may model this behavior in the abusive treatment of those who are less powerful—e.g., animals. (Flynn 1999) ■

This chapter will explore the issue of domestic violence and abuse, describing how these are related to the social context in which a person lives. We like to idealize families and our intimate relationships as safe havens—yet, for many people—this is not the case.

Although violence among intimates is experienced on a personal level, it is a social problem interwoven with cultural values, norms, social institutions, and gendered expectations. The chapter will explore the causes and consequences of violence and abuse among intimates. It begins with an international perspective on violence and abuse. The chapter then turns to the United States, and examines how Americans define and measure violence among intimates. It looks at violence in dating relationships, spouse/partner abuse, child abuse including the sexual abuse of children, and the abuse of the elderly. Many so-called personal problems experienced in families, whether they be violence among intimates, poverty, substance abuse, unemployment, or poor health are really problems deeply rooted in the broader social structure. This is illustrated in this chapter with the example of violence.

Gender-Based Violence: An International Human Rights Issue

Family violence is a widespread problem around the world, and women and girls are overwhelmingly its victims. Because violence against women and girls is so widespread, it is often referred to as **gender-based violence**, defined by the U.N. General Assembly as:

> Any act of gender violence that results in or is likely to result in physical, sexual or psychological harm and suffering to women, including threats of such acts, coercion, or arbitrary deprivations of liberty, whether occurring in public or private life. (Senanayake 1999)

This would include:

- Violence among intimates
- Sexual abuse
- Forced prostitution
- Female genital mutilation
- Rape
- Honor killings
- Selective malnourishing of female children

Gender-based violence occurs in both developed and developing nations, and it is estimated to be at epidemic levels in many countries. It causes more death and disability in women between the ages of 15 and 44 years than cancer, malaria, traffic accidents, and war *combined* (Senanayake 1999). Human Rights Watch, an international organization dedicated to protecting the human rights of people around the world, reports that many countries have horrendous records on addressing domestic violence. The organization explains, for example, that in Uganda, many women are infected with HIV and will eventually die because the government has failed in any meaningful way to condemn, criminalize, or prosecute violence against women in the home. In Pakistan, officials at all levels of the criminal justice system believe domestic violence is not a matter for criminal courts. Moreover, women who have been sexually assaulted and attempt to file charges face police harassment and disbelief and may themselves face arrest and prosecution for engaging in extramarital sex. In South Africa, the police and courts treat complaints by battered women as less serious than other assault complaints, and there are persistent problems with the provision of medical expertise to courts when women have been abused. In Jordan, "honor killings" occur when families deem women's behavior improper, and despite some legislative reforms, the perpetrators receive lenient sentences from the courts. In Russia and Uzbekistan, police scoff at reports of domestic violence and harass women who report such violence to stop them from filing complaints (Human Rights Watch 2006a).

Abuse of women and girls is often tolerated by the legal system. Discriminatory attitudes of law enforcement officials, prosecutors, and judges, who often consider domestic violence a private matter beyond the reach of the law, reinforce the batterer's attempts to demean and control his victim. Women's low social status and a long-established pattern of active suppression of women's rights by successive governments have contributed to the escalation in violence. Government often fails to acknowledge the scale and severity of the problem, much less take action to end the violence against women. As a result of such dismissive official attitudes, crimes of violence against women continue to be perpetrated with virtual impunity.

Trafficking of Women and Girls

Trafficking in persons (the illegal and highly profitable business of recruitment, transport, or sale of human beings into all forms of forced labor and servitude) is a tragic human rights issue (Farr 2005). The U.S. State Department estimates that anywhere from 600,000 to 800,000 persons, mostly women and girls, are trafficked across international borders annually and there may be as many as 27 million people in forced labor, bonded labor, forced child labor, and sexual servitude. Often they are sold into virtual sexual slavery and forced prostitution. The State Department estimates that

Desperate for money, some families sell their daughters to traffickers who force them into prostitution. Husbands, who have virtually complete control over their wives, may sell or "rent" them out for money.

18,000–20,000 persons are trafficked annually into the United States alone (U.S. Department of State 2006).

Child prostitution involves offering the sexual services of a child or inducing a child to perform sexual acts for any form of compensation (Willis and Levy 2002). Worldwide, an estimated 1 million children are forced into prostitution every year, and the total number of girls and boys working as prostitutes could be as high as 10 million. Many are coerced, kidnapped, sold, deceived, or otherwise trafficked into sexual encounters, as illustrated in the story of Maya and Parvati in Box 13.1. Increasingly around the world, girls are sought out in the mistaken belief that they are less likely to be HIV-positive. In reality, they are most vulnerable to HIV infections because their bodies are physically unready for sex and may tear more easily.

Sexual trafficking results from a broad range of factors. There has been increasing poverty, inequality, and economic crises in the last few decades in many countries. Globalization has triggered an influx of money and goods, further aggravating disparities between rich and poor, and promoting new levels of consumerism. Coupled with patriarchal norms in which women and girls are disvalued, some families sell their daughters to traffickers or put them in vulnerable positions as domestic workers in far-off urban locations. Husbands, who have virtually complete control over their wives, may sell or "rent" them out for money.

Women and children who are trafficked into prostitution face a multitude of dangers. In addition to injuries and disease associated with multiple sexual encounters, they become dangerously attached to pimps and brothel operators and become financially indebted to them. Moreover, they may become addicted to drugs that have been given to subdue them. If women and children do manage to escape and return to their families, they may be rejected because of the stigma associated with prostitution.

How Americans Define and Measure Family Violence

Although trafficking of women and children also occurs in the United States, the type of violence that directly touches more families is generally referred to as domestic or family violence. These are commonly used terms, but exactly what do they mean? How are they measured? Although definitions vary somewhat, it can encompass physical, economic, sexual, or psychological abuse, and many abusive situations involve more than one type (Hamby and Sugarman 1999). It also extends beyond the walls of a private home and can occur in dating or other intimate relationships as well. In fact, the term **violence among intimates** may be a more appropriate term than domestic violence because the former term encompasses a broader range of relationships.

Murray Straus and his colleagues conducted some of the earliest nationwide studies of family violence in the United States beginning in the mid-1970s. They conducted interviews with over 2,000 married or cohabiting adults with children between the ages of 3 and 17. They developed an important conflict assessment tool known as the **Conflict Tactics Scale (CTS)** that is commonly used today. In the CTS, people are asked about how they deal with disagreements in relationships. The following list is used in part or in its entirety in a variety of studies:

Nonaggressive responses:

Discussed an issue calmly
Got information to back up your side of things
Brought in or tried to bring in someone to help settle things
Cried

BOX 13.1 Our Global Community

Maya and Parvati: The End of a Dream

The sale of women for sexual purposes—trafficking—is, unfortunately, big business in many parts of the world. This moving account describes what happened to two teenage girls leaving Nepal for what they hoped would be a better life in India.

For millions of people in India, Bombay is a city of dreams. They are attracted to Bombay for many reasons, and they dream of making their future in this illusive city. Among them were Maya and Parvati for whom the city seemed a Promised Land of prosperity, a heavenly escape from their hard work at home. But these dreams were shattered. The horror stories of the shadier side of Bombay have not yet reached as far and wide as its jittering and well-publicized successes.

Maya and Parvati were two teenage mountain girls from a small village about 105 kilometers northwest of the capital, Kathmandu. Life was intolerable in their mountainous village where utter poverty and lack of opportunity have made hardship, starvation, and scarcity the villager's daily way of life. The girls wanted to escape. Finally, one spring day, the two girls left their village along with a group of other young girls and two men. Their journey brought them to Boudhanath. It is regarded as one of the largest market centers for hand-made woolen carpets. Maya and Parvati were employed by one of these factories, and joined the huge number of carpet weavers. Like the two girls, most of these workers had come from the mountain regions to start a new life.

After they had worked there for about six months, an old woman from their home village, who had lived in Bombay, offered to take them there. For the girls, it was as if their dreams had come true; they had always dreamed of going to Bombay, which was to them the ultimate city of joy. The tin-roofed house of that old woman and of others who had returned from Bombay, their silk sarees and golden ornaments, and most of all, their social prestige, had made a deep impression on the minds of these deprived girls. This image of affluence helped to nurture their dreams and desires to become just like these "successful" women.

So they eagerly agreed to go with the woman on the trip, which ended in them being sold to an infamous brothel in Sonagachhi, Calcutta. Their trafficker disappeared with the Rs. 25,000 that she made from the sale. The girls were not taken to Bombay. Maya and Parvati were imprisoned, and cruelly and violently treated: they had become sex slaves in a foreign country. The starry-eyed mountain girls lost their identities and became a part of the filth that surrounds Sonagachhi, one of the largest red-light areas in the world, where dozens of young girls are brought every day to start a life of hell. The majority of the 40,000-plus prostitutes in Sonagachhi are from Nepal.

After two years of being professional prostitutes in Calcutta, a seemingly magical change happened in the lives of Maya and Parvati. Two of their regular customers from Bengal, rescued and married them in Bow Bazar, Calcutta. Unfortunately this was not

Psychologically aggressive responses:
Insulted him/her or swore at him/her
Sulked or refused to talk about the issue
Stomped out of the room or house
Did or said something to spite him/her

Physically aggressive responses:
Threatened to hit him/her or throw something at him/her
Threw or smashed or hit or kicked something

the end of their suffering; their husbands began bringing "customers" home, filling their pockets by selling the flesh of their wives. There was no escape from this situation either.

One day Maya's husband took her to Bombay. This trip to Bombay meant big changes in her life; it separated her from her best friend, Parvati, and gave her another terrible shock. In spite of his deceit and cruelty, Maya had decided to live with her Bengali husband; she was so desperate that she clung to the hope that one day he would eventually come to love her. But Maya's husband sold her in Kamathipura, otherwise known as Falkland Road of Bombay, which is probably the biggest red-light area in Asia, harboring around 200,000 prostitutes. It is believed that the Kamathipura red light area is the oldest prostitution ring which was started by the British Army with the abduction of women from Germany at the time of the East India Company rule. Maya learned later that she had been sold for Rs. 15,000 and her husband had disappeared, just like the old village woman in Sonagachhi, Calcutta. Although she was deeply shocked by her abandonment, Maya was not new to the trade now. The brothel to which she had been sold was one of a thousand in the red-light area where thousands of Nepali women like herself were forced to be prostitutes. Maya met several other Nepali women in the brothel where she lived, and learned that all of them had a more or less similar story to tell.

She spent about 28 months in a dark room of this Kamathipura brothel receiving, on the average, four or five customers daily. She had no choice: Maya had to entertain all types of customers, from school boys and sick old men to men with venereal diseases and sexual perverts. She had to accept the maltreatment of the customers and the cruelty of the brothel owner as a part of her everyday life. For her services, she received nothing but two meals a day, and occasionally, small tips given to her by kind customers. She stayed inside her dark room waiting for customers, so that her Gharwali (brothel owner) would make money; she was never allowed to go out. Bombay, once her land of dreams, was now nothing more than the dark room and filth of the brothel area.

She became infected with several sexually transmitted diseases, and was admitted to a hospital where she was treated for more than three months. A sympathetic doctor in the hospital released her from the brothel. Three years after leaving her village, Maya returned, where many of her relatives and neighbors sympathized with her and her tragic situation. She died soon after. As for Parvati, who knows what happened to her?

Source: Adapted from ABC/Nepal 2003.

CRITICAL THINKING QUESTIONS

1. Why didn't Maya and Parvati simply leave the brothel in Calcutta if they were unhappy there? What would you have done differently, if anything?
2. If it is illegal to sell human beings, why do people do it? How do they get away with it?

Threw something at him/her
Pushed, grabbed, or shoved him/her
Slapped him/her
Kicked, bit, or hit him/her with a fist
Hit or tried to hit him/her with something
Beat him/her up
Choked him/her
Threatened him/her with a knife
Used a knife

Is There a Twist?

Some studies using the CTS have found that women tend to show *higher* rates of physical aggression than men (Felson 2006; Sugarman and Hotaling 1989). For example, one study of college students reports that women were more likely than men to be physically aggressive (43 percent versus 23 percent), and women were less likely to be a victim of physical aggression (34 percent versus 40 percent). This apparent gender twist may seem surprising.

Indeed, these counterintuitive findings have been questioned because the CTS does not take into account the meaning of violence/aggression in U.S. culture and the context in which it takes place. One potential problem with concluding that women are more physically aggressive than men is that there may be underreporting of physical violence perpetrated by men (Browning and Dutton 1986; Edleson and Brygger 1986). Men are less likely than women to remember their own acts of violence, and they may not perceive their acts as abusive. It is also true that for most acts of physical violence, the consequences are more serious for women than for men (Miller and Simpson 1991). Another problem is that the CTS is framed as a scale of *conflict resolution*; respondents are asked to tell the researcher how he or she has responded to a situation of conflict or disagreement. Some have argued that violence and abuse can take place without a preceding disagreement, and therefore the CTS may underreport some violence. Finally, the CTS does not include acts of sexual violence or aggression, which are far more likely to be perpetrated by men.

A New Typology of Violence

Michael Johnson and Kathleen Ferraro (2000) present a different typology of violence and abuse. They make critical distinctions among types of violence, motives of perpetrators, the social location of both partners, and the cultural context in which violence occurs. They have identified four patterns of violence (Johnson 2000; Johnson and Ferraro 2000; Johnson and Leone 2005):

1. **Common couple violence (CCV)** (or situational couple violence) arises out of a specific argument in which at least one partner lashes out physically. It is less frequent than other types of abuse and is less likely to escalate or involve severe injury, yet, it is this type of violence that is usually captured in research studies.
2. **Intimate terrorism (IT)** is motivated by a desire to control the other partner. It is more likely than CCV to escalate over time and to cause serious injury, although some cases of IT involve relatively little injury. The primary feature of this type of abuse is the general desire of control.
3. **Violent resistance (VR)** is the nonlegal term associated with self-defense. (Research on VR is scarce, and it is conducted almost entirely by women. Engaging in violent resistance may be an indicator that a person will soon leave the abusive partner.)
4. **Mutual violent control (MVC)** refers to a pattern of behavior in which both partners are controlling and violent; they are battling for control. Again, this is an understudied phenomenon.

Johnson and colleagues suggest that if we want to understand the true nature of domestic violence, we must distinguish between these different types. For example, victims of intimate terrorism are more likely to be injured, to experience post-traumatic stress syndrome, to use painkillers, and to miss work than are other types (Johnson and Leon 2005). Yet common-couple/situational violence dominates the general surveys, while intimate terrorism and violent resistance dominate agency caseloads, which may lead to different conclusions (Johnson 2006).

Recent Research: National Violence Against Women Survey (NVAW)

To better understand the prevalence, incidence, and consequences of violence among intimates, the National Institute of Justice (NIJ) and the Centers for Disease Control and Prevention (CDC) jointly sponsored a landmark telephone survey from 1995 to 1996 with a large and nationally representative sample of adult women and men, the **National Violence Against Women (NVAW) Survey**. The survey included questions about rape, physical assault, and stalking, both over the past year and throughout one's life. The sample included both men and women so that comparisons could be made on violent victimization. Detailed information about the characteristics and consequences of victimization was gathered, including injuries sustained and use of medical services (NIJ and CDC 1998).

The sample was drawn from random-digit dialing among all households with a telephone across the 50 states and the District of Columbia. Only female interviewers surveyed female respondents, and both male and female interviewers surveyed the male respondents. State-of-the-art techniques protected confidentiality and minimized the potential for retraumatizing victims. The telephone interview was conducted in Spanish when needed. Eight thousand women and 8,000 men completed the survey.

Several critical features of the NVAW survey set it apart from many victimization surveys. For example, information about both the prevalence and incidence of violence was gathered. Therefore, estimates could be compared with other surveys. Data were also gathered from male victims, which can provide important insights into similarities or differences in violence and victimization patterns between men and women. Moreover, information was gathered in a way that allowed tracking of victimizations by the same perpetrator.

This innovative study revealed many critical insights about domestic violence and abuse. First, it showed that violence is much more common than previously thought. Second, it revealed that violence against women is far more common than violence against men. Third, it revealed that violence against women is predominately *partner* violence. In other words, most victims know, and perhaps even are in love with, their attacker.

The results from this study will be presented throughout this chapter.

Dating Violence

> I didn't want to tell anybody what happened to me because I was too ashamed and embarrassed that I let it happen. I figured everybody would be like, "we told you so," because nobody liked my boyfriend. But I loved him, and I never expected him to hit me or force things during, like, sex. I don't say I was a victim, because I want to think on some level that he did love me. Karan, age 18 (Phillips 1998)

> Lynn began dating 17-year-old Garry when she was 15; he "regularly slapped and punched her, called her 'fat' and once flung her across the room." Once, he beat her so severely that she ended up in a hospital "with a smashed nose, black eyes, and bites, and blood and bruises all over her body." (Wolfe 1994)

Violence against women is typically cast as a problem facing adults, but many girls or young women also endure sexual violence or battering. According to the U.S.

Violence against teenage women is a hidden epidemic. Studies reveal that 13 percent of teenage girls who have been in a relationship report being physically hurt or hit, and 30 to 40 percent of teenage girls aged 14–17 know a peer who has been hit or beaten by a boyfriend.

Department of Justice, young women between the ages of 16 and 24 experience the highest rates of violence by a current or former boyfriend (Bureau of Justice Statistics 2001). Thirteen percent of teenage girls who have been in a relationship report being physically hurt or hit (Liz Claiborne Inc. 2005). Likewise, 30 to 40 percent of teenage girls aged 14–17 know a peer who has been hit or beaten by a boyfriend. Yet, violence against girls and young women is often not given the attention needed to address the problem and make them safe. The results of this silence are severe. A Harvard School of Public Health study (2001) found that female teenagers who experienced dating violence are significantly more likely to engage in substance abuse, risky sexual behaviors, and suicide.

Particularly alarming is that girls and young women often do not report the abuse and suffer in silence. One reason may be that young people fear parents' and friends' reactions to their poor choice of dating partners. Young women report feeling vulnerable and overly dependent on their partner and fear that they may never meet anyone better. "I think near the end, one of the reasons I was scared to let go was: 'Oh, my God, I'm 27.' I was worried that I was going to be like some lonely old maid. . . ." (Few and Rosen 2005). Particularly problematic with respect to underreporting is the incidence of sexual violence. Only about a third of rapes and sexual assaults are reported to the police (Bureau of Justice Statistics 2006). College students are even less likely to report assaults to the police, and often tell no one about the attack (Koss and Cook 1993; Koss et al. 1987).

Sexual Aggression and Rape in Dating Relationships

A commonly used measure of sexual aggression in dating relationships comes from the work of Mary Koss and her colleagues, work known as the Sexual Experiences Survey (SES) (Koss and Cook 1993; Koss et al. 1987). This survey asks about a variety of behaviors related to sex, including items about the use of threats, force, or alcohol to obtain sex from another. Using a large sample across the United States, they found that over half of college women had experienced some form of sexual aggression. Fifteen percent had been raped, 12 percent had experienced attempted rape, 12 percent had experienced sexual coercion, and 14 percent had experienced unwanted sexual contact (short of rape). Ironically, only 4 percent of men reported "committing rape" and another 3 percent acknowledged that they had "attempted rape," although a larger number of men admitted "forcing sexual relations." What is rape then, if not forced sexual relations? Semantics appear to be very important here.

Another nationwide study on sexual attitudes and behavior found that 22 percent of women in their sample reported being forced to do something sexual by a man. The vast majority of victims knew their attacker (96 percent), and interestingly, nearly half (46 percent) said they were in love with him (Michael et al. 1994). Other studies come to similar conclusions; for example, a study of nearly 200 college students found that 23 percent reported one (or more) case of rape (Daubman et al. 2007).

Violence occurs in adolescent same-sex couples as well, including female couples. A national study found that one-quarter of adolescents with same-sex romantic or sexual partners reported some type of victimization; 10 percent of these were physical assaults (Halpern et al. 2004).

Spouse/Partner Abuse

The "dark side" of families, including spouse and partner abuse, was not widely discussed among family scientists or researched systematically until the 1970s. What we did know about abuse was obtained from small, nonrepresentative samples in isolated case files of social workers, psychologists, or the police. These data had the potential to be very biased because only certain types of abuse, and certain types of abusers, come to the attention of professionals.

However, since the 1970s, with the help of the women's liberation movement and a spotlight on women's issues, family and social scientists have been trying to piece together a more accurate depiction of spouse and partner. Researchers have been trying, with some success, to amass large and representative samples to understand how often spouse and partner violence occurs; who is likely to be a victim; and its causes and consequences.

Frequency of Violence and Abuse

The results from the early surveys by Straus, Gelles, and Steinmetz (1980) show an alarming rate of spouse and partner abuse in the United States. These results have been confirmed in more recent studies such as the NVAW survey. This survey found that among all women who reported being victims of rape or physical assault, the perpetrator in 76 percent of the cases was an intimate partner (defined as current and former spouses, opposite and same-sex cohabiting partners, dates, boyfriends, and girlfriends). This is not the case for men. Among male victims, most rapes or assaults were perpetrated by strangers (60 percent), with only 18 percent of perpetrators being an intimate partner (NIJ and CDC 1998).

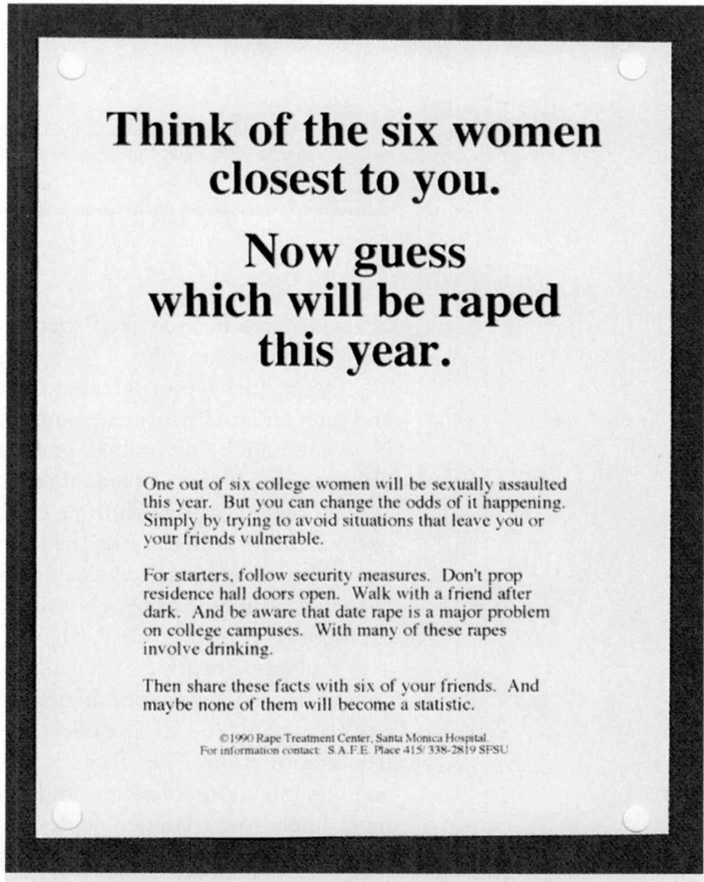

Unlike the case with men, most women who are raped or beaten know their attackers, often intimately.

Figure 13.1 shows the percentage of women and men who have been raped, physically assaulted, or stalked by an intimate partner over the course of the respondents' lifetime. We see that especially for women, violence by an intimate partner is a relatively common occurrence. Nearly 8 percent of women have been raped, 22 percent have been physically assaulted by someone close to them, and 25 percent have experienced either one or the other. The corresponding figures for men are 0.3 percent, 7.4 percent, and 7.6 percent, respectively. Women are also 8 times more

FIGURE 13.1 **Type of Victimization over a Lifetime by Intimate Partner**

Source: National Institute of Justice and Centers for Disease Control and Prevention 1998.

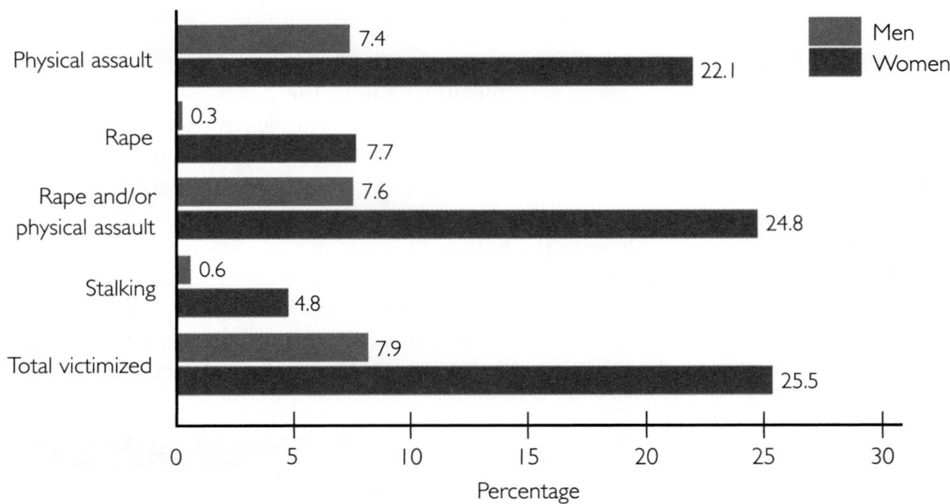

Definitions: Rape includes completed/attempted forced vaginal, oral, or anal sex. Physical assault ranges from slapping/hitting to using a gun. Stalking involves repeated harassment/intimidation inducing high fear levels.

likely to have been stalked than men. Overall, women are more than three times as likely to be victimized.

Figure 13.2 reports gender differences in the types of physical assaults that women and men endure by intimate partners. The most common types of violence experienced by women are being pushed, grabbed, or shoved (18 percent) and being slapped or hit (16 percent). Nearly 1 percent of women have had a gun or knife used on them.

Women were two to three times more likely than men to report that an intimate partner threw something at them, pushed, grabbed, or shoved them. However, in looking at the more dangerous assaults, women were 7 to 14 times more likely to report that they had been beaten up, choked, tied down, threatened with a gun, or had a gun used on them (NIJ and CDC 1998).

Violence sometimes occurs in pregnancy; it is estimated that between 4 and 8 percent of women experience domestic violence during their pregnancy (Gazamarian 2000; Saltzman et al. 2003). The effects of this violence can be devastating to the mother and her unborn child. They face a variety of potential pregnancy complications, including anemia, infections, bleeding, and low weight gain. Pregnant women who suffer abuse are more likely to experience depression and attempt suicide. They are also more likely to use tobacco, alcohol, and illegal drugs during pregnancy, possibly harming the fetus (Datner et al. 2007).

FIGURE 13.2 **Percentage of Persons Physically Assaulted by an Intimate Partner in a Lifetime by Type of Assault and Sex of Victim**

Source: National Institute of Justice and Centers for Disease Control and Prevention 1998.

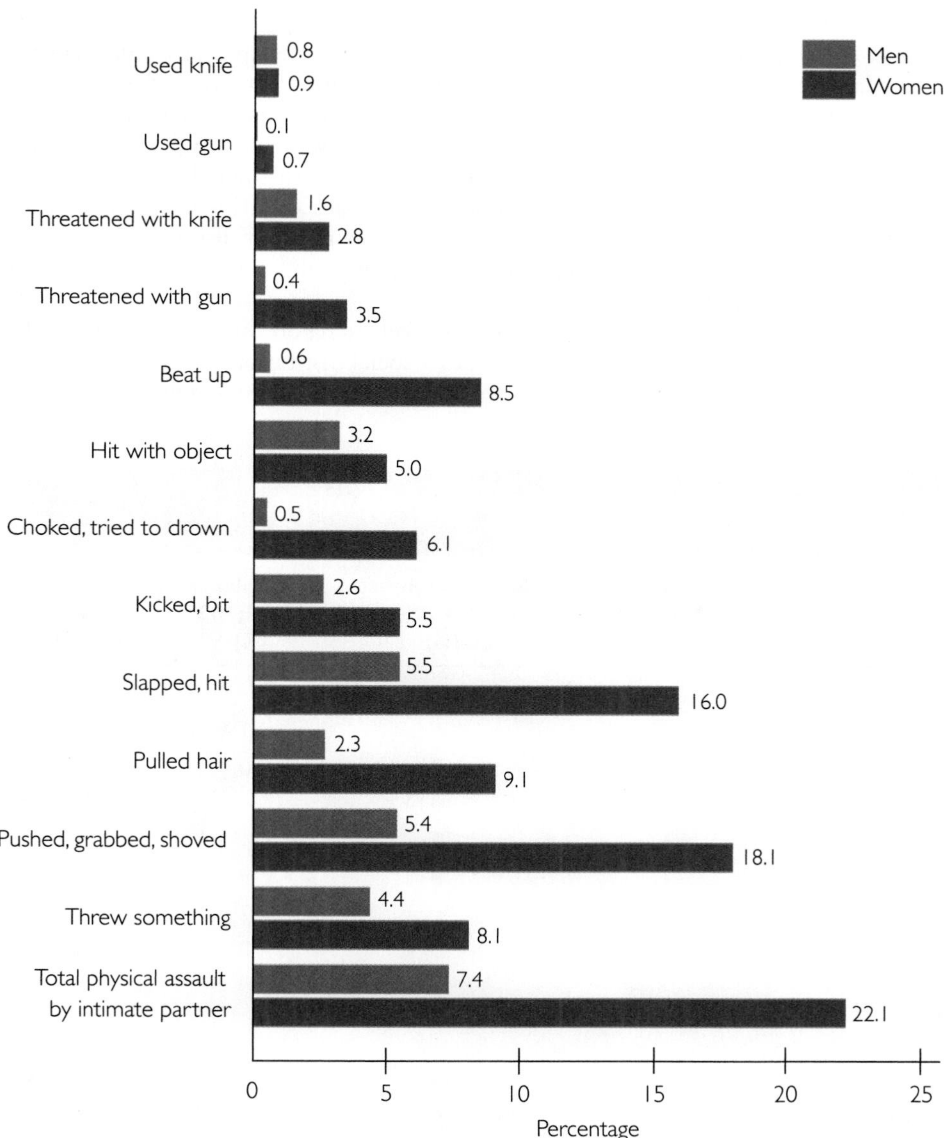

Intimate partner includes current or former spouses, opposite-sex cohabiting partners, same-sex cohabiting partners, dates, and boyfriends/girlfriends.

Race and Ethnic Differences

Violence among intimates may be experienced differently across racial and ethnic groups (Few and Bell-Scott 2002; Few and Rosen 2005; Johnson and Ferraro 2000; West 2003). Surveys indicate that minority women are more likely than whites to experience violence. This may be due to socioeconomic constraints and their lack of resources, racism, cultural values, or immigration status. One study of 2,400 low-income blacks, whites, and Hispanic women found that 30 percent of low-income blacks experienced spouse or partner violence, as did 24 percent of Hispanic women and 19 percent of whites (Frias and Angel 2005). Importantly, they discovered that the difference across Hispanic groups was quite large, as shown in Table 13.1; 29 percent of Hispanics of Mexican descent had experienced moderate or severe violence, compared to only 21 percent of Puerto Ricans, and 13 percent of Dominicans. Likewise, Hispanics who were born in the United States, U.S. citizens, and those who were proficient in English were all more likely to have experienced violence than their Hispanic counterparts. Although this is a sample of low-income groups only, these differences highlight the importance of distinguishing between different Hispanic groups and their experiences, rather than lumping Hispanics into one homogeneous group (Frias and Angel 2005).

Furthermore, minority women may be less likely to report the abuse because of their distrust of the criminal justice system and other social institutions born by their experiences with prejudice and discrimination. For example, black women are more likely to

TABLE 13.1 Race and Ethnic Differences in Violence Among a Low-Income Sample

	Moderate Violence N = 370 (%)	Severe Violence N = 223 (%)	No Violence N = 1,703 (%)	Total N=2,296
Race or ethnicity				
White and other	11	8	81	243
Black	20	10	70	965
Hispanic	14	10	76	1,088
Mexican	17	12	71	542
Puerto Rican	13	8	79	287
Dominican	7	6	87	146
Other	14	8	78	113
Hispanic characteristics				
Migration experience				
Born in the U.S. mainland	17	14	69	561
Less than 15 years old when migrated	17	8	74	147
More than 15 years old when migrated	8	4	88	380
U.S. citizenship				
Yes	15	12	73	788
No	11	5	84	300
English proficiency	10	11	9	

Source: Frias and Angel 2005.

turn to friends or family for help in an abusive situation, rather than rely on law enforcement or shelters for assistance (Few and Bell-Scott 2002).

Gay and Lesbian Relationships

The NVAW survey compared rates of violence among gay, lesbian, and heterosexual relationships. The researchers found further evidence that violence among intimates is perpetuated primarily by men, whether it is against female or other male intimate partners. Consequently, in lesbian relationships, violence among intimates is far less common than in either heterosexual or gay relationships. Slightly more than 11 percent of women in lesbian cohabiting relationships reported being raped, physically assaulted or stalked by a female partner, compared to nearly 22 percent of women in heterosexual relationships, and 23 percent of gay men who had lived with a male partner (NIJ and CDC 1998).

Welfare, Welfare Reform, and Abuse

Violence and abuse among intimates is more common than many people think; however, the rate of victimization among women receiving welfare is particularly high, possibly two to three times the national average (Goodwin et al. 2003; Lawrence 2002; Tolman et al. 2002). Many women who want to flee this violence have few resources and few avenues of support, and they therefore turn to Temporary Assistance for Needy Families (TANF), the cash welfare program, for help. The 1996 welfare reforms dictate that women on TANF must find jobs quickly. Yet the personal, social, and financial effects of abuse can be profound for the victims and their children and impede the ability to easily find and maintain employment (Staggs et al. 2007). There was a real concern among many people that victims of domestic violence would lose their TANF benefits before they were ready for stable employment, thereby becoming unemployed, uninsured, and possibly homeless and destitute. Consequently, the welfare reform legislation was amended to give states the option of providing exemptions to the time limits and work requirements for women who had been victims of domestic violence to allow them a little more time to ready themselves for employment. However, only 17 states have chosen to provide exemptions to victims, and among those states that do, they vary in how many exemptions will be provided per year and the duration of the exemptions (Rowe and Russell 2004).

Factors Associated with Abuse

The NVAW survey reveals that most women who are raped and assaulted are done so by intimate partners rather than by strangers, yet, it is also important to recognize that most men do not abuse their partners. What specific factors are associated with spouse/partner abuse? Several characteristics increase the odds of abuse (Delsol et al. 2003; DeMaris et al. 2003; Lawrence 2002; National Coalition Against Domestic Violence and Abuse 2006a, b):

- Youth. In most violent relationships, the partners are under the age of 30.
- Low levels of education. Often the husband/male partner has a high school diploma or less.
- Low income or employment problems. The family income may be below or near the poverty line, or the man may be unemployed. They may live in an economically disadvantaged neighborhood.
- Drug or alcohol use. Often one or both partners uses drugs or alcohol frequently and may use it as an excuse for conflict and violence.
- Abuse in family of orientation. One or both partners may have witnessed or experienced abuse as children.

- Personal traits. These may include extreme jealousy, possessiveness, a bad temper, low self-esteem, unpredictability, verbal abuse, aggressive tendencies such as fighting with others, and cruelty toward animals.

Researchers have rarely studied the effects of occupations on violence, other than to use broad categories, such as between white-collar and blue-collar jobs. Sociologist Scott Melzer (2002) looked carefully at the relationship between a man's job and his likelihood of committing violence. Because theory and previous research note a reciprocal relationship between work and family life in other areas, does the same relationship hold true for violence among intimates? Do violent jobs produce violent partners? Melzer used data from the National Survey of Families and Households, a large and nationally representative sample of adults to answer these questions. The key violent occupational categories are (1) supervisors of police and detectives; (2) supervisors of guards; (3) police and detectives (public service); (4) sheriffs and bailiffs; (5) correctional institution officers; (6) guards and police (excluding public service); (7) protective service occupations; and (8) current members of the armed forces. Persons in these violent occupations were compared with those holding managerial jobs to see if they were more likely to commit violence. Other important variables were controlled statistically so that the specific independent effects of occupation on violence could be seen. These variables included men's age, education, children in the home, whether he had an alcohol or drug problem, unemployment, and the proportion of the couple's income earned by the woman. The study found that men who work in physically violent occupations were 1.43 times more likely to commit violence against a spouse or intimate partner than were those in managerial jobs (Melzer 2000). These, however, were not the only occupational categories significantly more likely to commit violence. Those in clerical jobs (a traditionally female occupation) and those in professional positions were also far more likely to be violent compared to those holding managerial jobs. Men who were unemployed or who earned less than a third of the couple's income were also at a greater likelihood of committing violence. Age was also noted as a strong predictor of male violence; an 18-year-old man is twice as likely as a 38-year-old man to be violent. However, the single strongest predictor of violence is a man having an alcohol or drug problem. These men are 4.6 times as likely to commit violence as are men without such a problem (Melzer 2002).

Coping with Violence and Abuse: Reporting, Leaving, and Staying

Perhaps one of the primary ways of coping with violence and abuse is to report it to authorities. Nonetheless, analysis of the NAVW survey reveals that three-quarters of violent acts go unreported to law enforcement. When violence is reported to authorities it is most often reported by the victim herself, rather than a third party, such as a family member, friend, coworker, or someone who witnessed the abuse (Felson and Pare 2005). Women who have been victimized are less likely to report the violence if they know the offender, if they are of the same sex, or if they are sexually assaulted. The reasons for not reporting the violence are many—from believing that the violence was "too minor," feelings of "embarrassment," having a "fear of reprisal," feeling that the "police could not do anything," or worry that she "would not be believed." In particular, if the offender was a spouse or partner, victims were likely to fear reprisal and to think that the police could not do anything to help (Felson and Pare 2005).

A common question is why do women stay in an abusive situation? The truth is, however, that most do not stay. A recent longitudinal study revealed that by 2.5 years, three-quarters of battered women had either left the relationship or the abuse had ended (Campbell et al. 1998).

Leaving is often a *process* rather than a single event. It may be difficult for some women to garner the courage or coordinate the logistics to leave immediately. This is where the typology discussed by Johnson (2006) comes into play. The diverse types of spouse/partner abuse have repercussions for one's ability to leave the situation. For example, men engaged in IT use on their victims a wide range of control tactics that can cripple a victim's sense of command over her own life. This is generally less true with couples engaging in situational violence. What are some of these control tactics that may make it difficult for victims to leave an abusive and violent relationship?

- *Blaming the victim:* The perpetrator may blame the victim for the abuse: "If you weren't so stupid, I wouldn't have to hit you." After hearing blaming comments often enough, some women believe them. Their self-esteem is eroded, and they begin to believe that they must deserve the abuse and be unworthy of a positive, loving relationship.
- *Shame:* Feelings of embarrassment and shame are common among abused women because they know that many other women are not abused. They worry that other people will look down on them for either provoking the abuse or for tolerating it. Likewise, they may be embarrassed at how their spouse/partner will be perceived by others. Abused women may therefore try to hide their bruises when they go out in public by applying makeup or wearing certain types of clothing (such as scarves or hats).
- *Financial dependency:* Some women are particularly vulnerable because they are financially dependent on men; perhaps they have children and do not have specific job skills or recent employment experience. Some perpetrators foster this economic dependence by not letting their wives/partners establish credit in their own name, and refusing to put their wives' or partners' names on checking, savings, or other accounts.
- *Isolation:* Abused women are often isolated. The abuser may initiate the isolation as a control tactic, or the woman may initiate it out of shame. In either case, abused women are often cut off from family and friends. They may cease going to church, to work, or to school. They have little social support and no one to turn to for a "reality check."
- *Fear of retaliation:* Fear is an important reason why some women linger in abusive relationships. The perpetrator may have threatened the woman, her children, or even her pets. Because he has been abusive before, the threats are real and many victims live in fear.
- *Love and hope:* Many abused women harbor fantasies that their abuser will somehow miraculously change. They do not want the relationship to end; they just want the abuse to stop. They love their spouse/partner and believe that if they just work harder in the relationship, or if external forces change, the abuse will somehow stop.
- *Commitment to the relationship:* When we marry, we agree to take our partner "for better or worse, until death do we part." Although we take these vows seriously, most people would probably leave an out for particularly harsh circumstances that would include violence. However, not everyone feels this way. Some people, perhaps based on religious grounds, believe that they must endure their marriage regardless of the costs.
- *Fear of being alone:* Many people are afraid of being without a spouse or partner. They have low self-esteem and are unsure whether they can live alone and take care of themselves. Women have been socialized to derive a great deal of their social status through their affiliations with men. When this is coupled with possible financial dependence, we can see why some women may be hesitant to leave an abusive situation.

Other difficulties may exist as well, including having no place to go, no access to checking or savings accounts, or limited support from the legal system. Despite a

BOX 13.2 Social Policies for Families

History of the Battered Women's Shelter Movement

Shelters designed exclusively for women and their children fleeing violence are a relatively new phenomenon. The following essay reveals how the issue of domestic violence became defined as a social problem, and how shelters—originally marginalized—began to take root in many communities.

Domestic violence, or violence among intimates, as it is often called today, may have existed since the beginning of man, but for most of human history has not been viewed as a social problem. In fact, it was not recognized as a pervasive social problem in the United States until the mid-1970s, when research was published revealing its high frequency. Soon after, a grassroots battered women's movement gained momentum. The movement was inspired by the feminist analysis of rape as a social and political issue. Battered women began to speak out about the physical abuse they were suffering in their marriages and intimate relationships.

At first, battered women helped one another individually by setting up informal safe homes and apartments where they could hide from their abusers and have a brief respite while they reorganized their lives. In an environment free from intimidation of their abusers, battered women began to speak openly and soon discovered the commonality of their experience. Their bond with other women and their children lay in their sense of isolation and their need for safety. Moreover, the women realized that society was largely indifferent to their plight, and they found support lacking from social and justice systems. As these issues began to be publicized, women of all races, cultures, ages, abilities, and walks of life began to expose the violence they suffered. It quickly became clear that battering was a pervasive problem, and a nationwide movement started to take shape.

Initially the movement focused on the acute need for safe shelter for battered women and their children. Unless a woman was safe, she could not effectively evaluate her situation and make clear decisions about her future. Operating on extremely low budgets bolstered by volunteers, shelters began to open up around the country. Although only a handful of such programs existed

restraining order, it is possible for an abuser to repeat the assault (National Coalition Against Domestic Violence and Abuse 2003). Box 13.2 describes the development of battered women's shelters as safe havens.

Child Abuse

"He never listens to me. I try to tell him things, and he just doesn't seem to hear me unless I give him a good wallop."

A mother hits her child. Is this child abuse? Does it matter if the mother uses an open hand or a *fist*? How about if she uses an *object* to hit her child? Does it matter if her hitting leaves a *welt*? Does the *reason* for hitting the child make a difference? How about the *age* of the child? Does it matter *where* the child was hit? Does it matter how *often* the child is hit? Let's amend the story a bit.

"My 15-year-old son never listens to me. I try to tell him things, and he just doesn't seem to hear me, unless I give him a good wallop across his bare back with my belt."

Not all forms of child abuse are clearcut and obvious. For example, three-quarters of adults believe that it is appropriate to use corporal punishment on children, and over

in the mid-1970s, today there are more than 1,400 shelters, hotlines, and safe-home networks nationwide. The growth in the number of battered women's programs and their level of funding has been remarkable; nonetheless, many of the 3,000 counties in the United States still do not have services available to battered women. Moreover, among those counties that do have shelters, most remain inadequately funded and must turn away as many women as they accept. Most continue to rely heavily on donations and volunteers.

Shelter programs may differ somewhat in size, scope of services, and sources and level of funding; however, all share the premise that no one deserves to be beaten, and that battered women and their children need special resources to end the violence in their lives. The most critical functions include crisis intervention and safety provision for battered women and their children, and operation of a 24-hour hotlines. Women and their children may stay at the shelter only one night, or they may stay for several weeks or even months, depending on the demand for and supply of space. Typical shelter services include legal, economic, housing, and medical advocacy; court accompaniment; employment and job training assistance; support groups for residents and non-residents; and child care and counseling programs for children. This array of programs is designed to help women muster the confidence to leave an abusive situation, and to provide the initial resources to make it happen.

Source: Adapted from Florida Coalition Against Domestic Violence 2003.

CRITICAL THINKING QUESTIONS

1. If violence among intimates is an age-old problem, why was it not recognized as a pervasive social problem in the United States until the mid-1970s?
2. If the need is so great, why are battered women's shelters inadequately funded, and dependent on volunteer time and donations rather than funded at adequate levels by state or local governments?

90 percent of parents with 3- or 4-year-old children report having spanked them over the past year (Day et al. 1998; Straus and Donnelly 2001; Vandivere et al. 2003). In the second National Family Violence Survey, 56 percent of parents reportedly slapped or spanked a child; 31 percent pushed, shoved, or grabbed a child; 10 percent hit a child with an object; and 3 percent threw something at a child during the preceding 12 months. Parents used corporal punishment an average of nine times during that period (Straus and Donnelly 2001).

Using data from parents with a child between the ages of 1 and 11 from the National Survey of Families and Households, another study reported that mothers are more likely to spank their children than are fathers (44 percent versus 31 percent, respectively); and boys are more likely to be spanked than girls (Day et al. 1998). One study with nearly 1,000 mothers of children between the ages of 2 and 14 found that 36 percent spanked a child at least once in the last 6 months. Mothers were more inclined to spank when they had younger children, were of lower socioeconomic status, and perceived more intense messages to spank from such sources as newspapers, magazines, books, pediatricians, workshops, relatives, and friends (Vandivere et al. 2003; Walsh 2002).

Black women, closely followed by white women, are more likely to agree or strongly agree that spanking a child is sometimes necessary. One study found that 80 percent of black women, 74 percent of white women, and 56 percent of Hispanic women agreed that a child sometimes needs a "good hard spanking." Differences among men were not statistically significant.

Murray Straus, a leading researcher in domestic violence, argues that corporal punishment is detrimental to children and teaches them violent and abusive behavior because it legitimizes violence (Straus 2003). For example, adults who were hit as adolescents are more likely to abuse animals, as the opening vignette reported (Flynn 1999). In a review of 88 studies, with more than 36,000 children, corporal punishment was significantly associated with 11 negative outcomes in childhood, including poorer mental health, lower quality relationships with parents, and even criminal behavior (Gershoff 2002). Interestingly, states in which teachers are allowed to hit children have a higher rate of student violence and a higher murder rate, and nations where teachers favor corporal punishment have a higher infant murder rate. Yet, many parents continue to believe that the context of the spanking, slapping, shoving, hitting with or throwing an object may, in some cases, justify it. But exactly what is that context? There is a wide range of opinion about when, how, and under what conditions it is appropriate to use corporal punishment.

Nonetheless, some acts against children are unambiguously abusive. Physical abuse is an attack that results in injury and violates social norms (Straus 2003). According to the U.S. Department of Health and Human Services (2006), about 872,000 children were found to be victims of child abuse or neglect in calendar year 2004. Of these children, 62 percent suffered neglect, 18 percent were physically abused, 10 percent were sexually abused, 7 percent were psychologically maltreated, and 2 percent were medically ne-glected. The true rate is probably considerably higher than this. An estimated 1,500 children died in 2004 as a result of abuse and neglect; most were under age 4. Annually, more children under the age of 4 die from abuse and neglect than from falls, choking, drowning, fires, or motor vehicle accidents (U.S. Department of Health and Human Services 2006b).

Abuse occurs in all income, racial, religious, and ethnic groups, and in all types of communities. Female victims outnumber male victims, especially in cases of sexual abuse. Black children have the highest rates of victimization, followed by Pacific Islanders, American Indians/Alaska Natives, whites, Hispanics, and Asians as shown in Figure 13.3. Most perpetrators (79 percent) are biological parents, most often the mother.

FIGURE 13.3 **Race and Ethnicity of Child Abuse Victims, 2004 (rate per 1,000)**

Source: U.S. Department of Health and Human Services 2006.

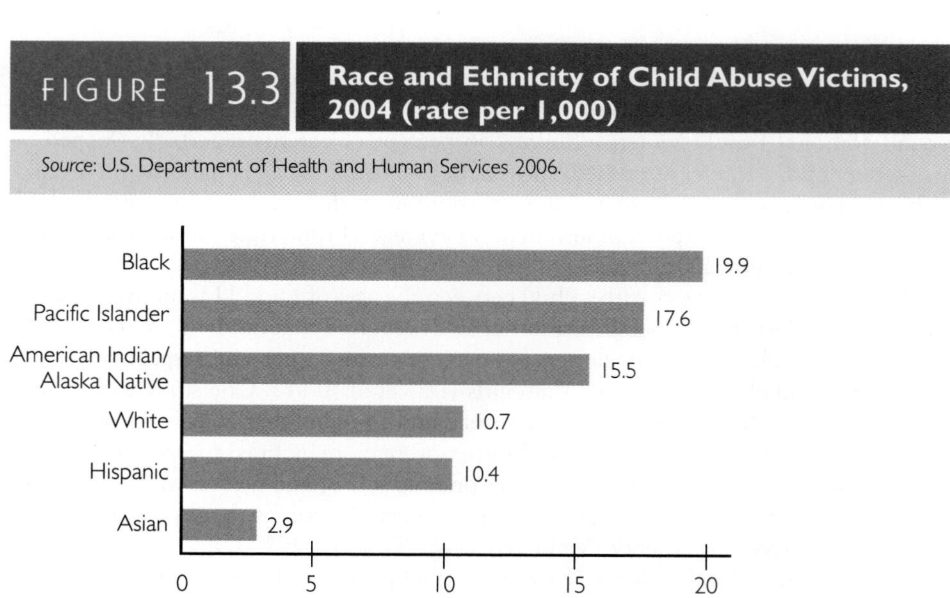

Types of Child Abuse

There are several different types of child abuse (Child Welfare Information Gateway 2006).

- **Physical abuse** involves inflicting physical injury and harm upon a child. This may include hitting, shaking, burning, kicking, or in other ways physically harming a child. Among substantiated child abuse cases, nearly one in five involved physical abuse. The most extreme cases may result in the death of a child. One study based on abused children admitted to a pediatric intensive care unit found that the most common forms of death were skull fracture and internal bleeding (Irazuzta et al. 1997).
- **Neglect** is the most common form of abuse and involves the failure to provide for the child's basic needs. Two-thirds of substantiated cases of abuse were based on neglect, which can be physical, such as failing to provide adequate food, clothing, shelter, a safe environment, or medical care to a dependent child. Emotional or psychological neglect occurs when a parent (or caretaker) fails to meet a child's most basic need for love and affection. This could involve chronically cold and distant behavior toward a child or allowing a child to witness spousal abuse or some other dysfunctional behavior in the family. An extreme form of neglect is outright abandonment.
- **Emotional abuse** involves about 7 percent of substantiated cases of child abuse and includes verbal, mental, or psychological maltreatment that destroys a child's self-esteem. Abuse of this nature often includes threatening, degrading, or humiliating the child, and extreme or bizarre forms of punishment, such as confinement to a dark room or being tied to a chair for long periods of time. It is likely that emotional abuse occurs far more frequently than what can be substantiated. The scars are not as visible as with other types of abuse.
- **Sexual abuse** involves inappropriate sexual behavior with a child for sexual gratification. It occurs in about 10 percent of substantiated child abuse cases. It could include fondling a child's genitals, making the child fondle the perpetrator's genitals, and progressing to more intrusive sexual acts such as oral sex and vaginal or anal penetration. Sexual abuse also includes acts such as exhibition or in other ways exploiting the child for sexual purposes.

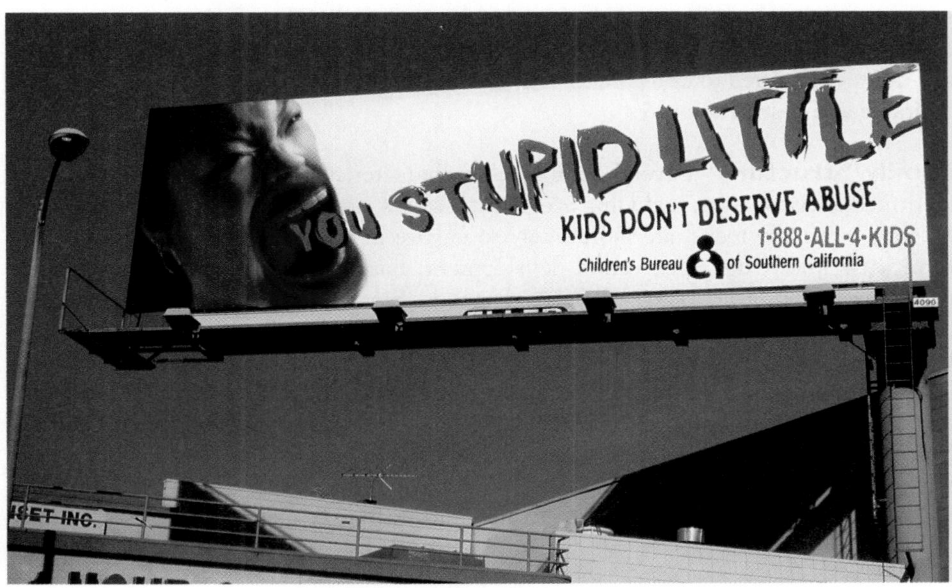

When does discipline become child abuse? Is spanking abuse? Is name calling? There is a wide range of opinion about what constitutes child abuse, and definitions vary across time and place. Nonetheless, some physical or emotional acts are clearly reprehensible—about 1,500 children die every year in the United States from abuse.

Factors Contributing to Child Abuse

There are complex combinations of social, cultural, and personal factors that explain child abuse, but perhaps surprisingly, fewer than 10 percent of abusers are considered mentally ill. The following are potential risk factors (Gelles 1979; Goldman et al. 2003).

Stress Parents that experience a great deal of stress are more likely to abuse their children. The stress could be brought on by many factors, including illness, unemployment, marital conflict, or financial problems. Sometimes specific traits of the child are associated with stress. For example, premature infants who require special care and who may cry harder and more frequently have an increased risk of abuse. Likewise, children with physical or developmental difficulties are more likely to be abused. Alcohol and drug use are key risk factors for abuse. They can aggravate stress, decrease coping skills, and impair judgment.

Social Isolation Parents (and other caretakers) who abuse children tend to be socially isolated. They may have little contact with other family members, have few friends, and belong to few community organizations. Sometimes this isolation predates the abuse (they abuse because they are so isolated) and in other families the abuse may predate the isolation (they isolate themselves to hide the abuse from others). Regardless, these families lack social support to help them with their stress, anger, and the challenges of raising children.

Learned Behavior A parent is more likely to abuse his or her child if the parent was abused as a child. This is dubbed the **intergenerational transmission of violence**. It has been estimated that about 30 percent of abused children become abusive parents themselves, 10 times the rate of all parents (Kaufman and Zigler 1987). Parents who are able to break the cycle of abuse realize, perhaps through therapy or a supportive partner, that the abuse was wrong, and they learn other ways to deal with their frustrations.

Unrealistic Parental Expectations Some adults have unrealistic expectations about parenthood. Very little in life prepares us for the challenges associated with being a parent. While we require a test to verify fitness to drive an automobile, virtually anyone can become a parent. There is no required course or formal certificate to verify that we have mastered a certain level of knowledge and skills. Therefore, some people become parents with little information regarding child development, and little sense of the self-sacrifice required to be a parent. This ignorance can translate into lashing out in undesirable and destructive ways.

Family Structure Several demographic characteristics of the parents have been identified as risk factors, including age, marital status, and socioeconomic status. Young parents, especially teens, are more likely to engage in abusive behaviors because they have little knowledge about child development, have unrealistic expectations about parenthood, and are unprepared for its demands. Single parents are twice as likely as married parents to abuse their children. Low socioeconomic status is another risk factor. Parents who earned less than $15,000 or $20,000 per year were 12 to 16 times more likely to physically abuse their children, 18 times more likely to sexually abuse them, and 44 times more likely to neglect them. It has been argued that this social class difference arose because abuse in low-income households was simply more likely to be detected by social workers, but researchers now believe that child abuse is indeed more frequent among low-income households. The most common explanation for this difference is that low-income parents are under a great deal of stress, have lower levels of education, have inadequate support systems, and higher rates of substance abuse. They are also more likely to be young and unmarried—other factors associated with child abuse.

Consequences of Child Abuse

Child abuse has numerous physical, cognitive, and emotional consequences for children. Abuse leaves approximately 18,000 children permanently disabled each year. Negative health consequences continue into adulthood for many victims, including increased rates of gynecological problems, migraine headaches, digestive problems, asthma, and a host of other disorders (Child Welfare Information Gateway 2006; Goldman et al. 2003; Hyman 2000).

Perhaps even more insidious are the emotional scars left behind. Child abuse often has devastating and long-term emotional consequences. For example, physically abused children tend to be more aggressive and more likely to get involved in delinquent activities, are more likely to have difficulty in school, and are more likely to be involved in early sexual activity, including a teen pregnancy. Even as adults, children who have been abused are more likely to suffer from nightmares, depression, panic disorders, and suicide ideation.

As shown in Table 13.2, the annual *direct* costs of child abuse in the U.S. are estimated at $24.4 billion in 2000 taking into account increased rates of hospitalization,

TABLE 13.2 Total Annual Cost of Child Abuse and Neglect in the United States

Direct and Indirect Costs	Statistical Justification Data
Direct Costs	**Estimated Annual Cost**
Hospitalization Rationale: 565,000 children were reported as suffering serious harm from abuse in 1993. One of the less severe injuries is a broken or fractured bone. Cost of treating a fracture or dislocation of the radius or ulna per incident is $10,983. Calculations: 565,000 × $10,983	$6,205,395,000
Chronic Health Problems Rationale: 30% of maltreated children suffer chronic medical problems. The cost of treating a child with asthma per incident in the hospital is $6,410. Calculations: .30 × 1,553, 800 = 446,140; 446,140 × $6,410	2,987,957,400
Mental Health Care System Rationale: 743,200 children were abused in 1993. For purposes of obtaining a conservative estimate, neglected children are not included. One of the costs to the mental health care system is counseling. Estimated costs per family for counseling is $2,860. One in five abused children is estimated to receive the services. Calculations: 743,200/5 = 148,640; 148,640 × $2,860	425,110,400
Child Welfare System Rationale: The Urban Institute published a paper in 1999 reporting on the results of a study it conducted estimating child welfare costs associated with child abuse and neglect to be $14.4 billion.	14,400,000,000

(continued)

TABLE 13.2 *(continued)*

Direct and Indirect Costs	Statistical Justification Data
Direct Costs	**Estimated Annual Cost**
Law Enforcement	24,709,800
Rationale: The National Institute of Justice estimates the following costs of police services for each of the following interventions: child sexual abuse ($56); physical abuse ($20); emotional abuse ($20) and child educational neglect ($2). Cross referenced against DHHS statistics on number of each incidents occurring annually.	
Calculations: Physical Abuse—381,700 × $20 = $7,634,000; Sexual Abuse—217,700 × $56 = $12,191,200; Emotional Abuse—204,500 × $20 = $4,090,000; and Educational Neglect—397,300 × $2 = $794,600	
Judicial System	341,174,702
Rationale: The Dallas Commission on Children and Youth determined the cost per initiated court action for each case of child maltreatment was $1,372.34. Approximately 16% of child abuse victims have court action taken on their behalf.	
Calculations: 1,553,800 cases nationwide × .16 = 248,608 victims with court action; 248,608 × $1,372.34	
Total Direct Costs	**$24,384,347,302**
Indirect Costs	
Special Education	$223,607,830
Rationale: Over 22% of abused children have a learning disorder requiring special education. Total annual cost per child for learning disorders is $655.	
Calculations: 1,553,800 × .22 = 341,386; 341,386 × $655	
Mental Health and Health Care	4,627,636,025
The health care cost per woman related to child abuse and neglect is $8,175,816/163,844 = $50. If the costs were similar for men, we could estimate that $50 × 185,105,441 adults in the United States cost the nation $9,255,272,050. However, the costs for men are likely to be very different and a more conservative estimate would be half of that amount.	
Juvenile Delinquency	8,805,291,372
Rationale: 26% of abused or neglected children become delinquents, compared to 17% of children as a whole, for a difference of 9%. Annual cost per child for incarceration is $62,966. Average length of incarceration in Michigan is 15 months.	
Calculations: 0.09 × 1,553,800 = 139,842; 139,842 × $62,966 = $8,805,291,372	
Lost Productivity to Society	656,000,000
Rationale: Abused and neglected children grow up to be disproportionately affected by unemployment and underemployment. Lost productivity has been estimated at $656 million to $1.3 billion. Conservative estimate is used.	
Adult Criminality	55,380,000,000
Rationale: Violent crime in the United States costs $426 billion per year. According to the National Institute of Justice, 13% of all violence can be linked to earlier child maltreatment.	
Calculations: $426 billion × .13	
Total Indirect Costs	**$69,692,535,227**
Total Costs	**$94,076,882,529**

Source: "Total Estimated Cost of Child Abuse and Neglect in the United States: Statistical Evidence." From: Prevent Child Abuse America 2001. Available online: www.preventchildabuse.org. Reprinted with permission..

chronic health problems, use of the mental health care and child welfare systems, law enforcement costs, and use of the judicial system. *Indirect* costs equal $69.7 billion for a *total cost* of $94.1 billion (Prevent Child Abuse America 2001). The physical, emotional, and financial costs of child abuse are far too great to ignore.

Elder Abuse

Each year an estimated 2.1 million elderly Americans are victims of physical, psychological, and other types of abuse and neglect yet most of these cases go unreported (American Psychological Association 2005; National Committee for the Prevention of Elder Abuse 2005). Many of these elders are frail and vulnerable, and are dependent on others to meet their basic needs. They face unique barriers to reporting violence, including mobility limitations, fear of being institutionalized, and fear of not being believed.

Elder abuse includes many forms, including physical abuse; sexual abuse; emotional abuse; **financial or material exploitation** (improperly using the resources of an older person, without his or her consent, for someone else's benefit); and neglect.

The 2004 Survey of State Adult Protective Services (APS), which is the most rigorous national study of state-level APS data, found 565,000 reported and substantiated cases of abuse among persons aged 60 in 2003 (National Center on Elder Abuse 2006). Ninety percent of these cases occurred in a domestic setting, not in an institution such as a nursing home or hospital. Reports of elder abuse to adult protective services are on the rise, increasing 20 percent over recent years. Because only about one-quarter of abuse cases are reported and substantiated by adult protective service agencies, it is likely that the true extent of elders who are abused each year may even exceed 2 million. Like other forms of violence among intimates, elder abuse often goes unreported because the elderly are reluctant or unable to talk about it to others. The report also found that persons aged 80 and over are particularly vulnerable. Neglect is the most common source of abuse (55 percent), followed by physical abuse (15 percent), and financial/material exploitation (12 percent).

Who Are the Perpetrators and Victims?

Elder abuse is extremely complex. Generally a combination of psychological, social, and economic factors, along with the mental and physical conditions of the victim and the perpetrator, contribute to abuse. Ninety percent of known perpetrators are family members; two-thirds of perpetrators are adult children or spouses, and they are often serving in a caregiving role (National Center on Elder Abuse 2006). The majority of victims are frail elders, dependent on family members to meet their basic needs. Data from Virginia Adult Protective Services with case files of 95 elderly abused women revealed that most had functional limitations and were dependent on their families for care. Few cases were prosecuted and the majority of the elderly women remained vulnerable to further abuses (Roberto et al. 2004).

Caring for frail older people can be difficult and stress-provoking (see Chapter 12). This is particularly true when older people are mentally or physically impaired, when the caregiver is ill-prepared for the task, or when the needed resources are lacking. Under these circumstances, the increased stress and frustration of a caregiver may lead to abuse or willful neglect. Researchers have found that abusers of the elderly (typically adult children) tend to have more personal problems than do nonabusers. Adult children who abuse their parents frequently suffer from such problems as mental and emotional disorders, alcoholism, drug addiction, and financial difficulty.

Explanations for Violence and Abuse Among Intimates

Virtually everyone claims to abhor domestic violence and abuse, so why then is it so widespread? One explanation draws attention to the societal and cultural causes of violence. Another focuses on the individual-level causes. It is likely that both factors are operating.

Societal and Cultural Causes

There are several perspectives that are rooted in cultural norms and values.

Patriarchy This perspective focuses on male domination and the overall cultural climate that tolerates or even promotes gender-based violence. It argues that violence is more likely to occur in those societies and households in which men are dominant and exert tight control over women and children. Men have the power and authority in their families (and in society at large), and see women as their "sexual property." Women have been socialized not to challenge men's authority over them.

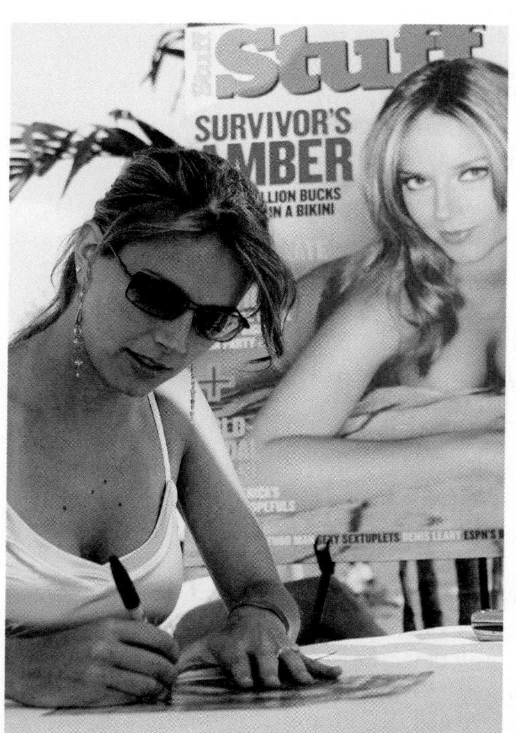

Why is abuse against women so prevalent? One theory is patriarchy. When women are not valued, viewed as sexual property, or have little social and economic status, violence against them may be woven into the cultural fabric of society. This woman proudly signs autographs, oblivious to the fact that she is a victim of patriarchy, yet also perpetuating it.

Being a victim of spousal assault has been considered a woman's lot for thousands of years across many different cultures. In fact the "rule of thumb" expression comes from an old common-law statute that imposed a limitation on men's disciplinary authority over "their" women by prohibiting husbands from hitting wives with a stick wider than their thumbs.

Because women are socialized in the same patriarchical culture as men, they often support and even perpetuate the patriarchy that can lead to violence. A large study of over 2,500 married women conducted in Minya, Egypt, found that 27 percent had experienced at least one beating since adulthood, and 4 percent had been beaten so severely that a doctor was needed. Only 27 percent of the surveyed women believed that a husband is "never justified" in beating his wife, whereas 52 percent believe that a husband is "seldom or sometimes justified," and 21 percent believe that a husband is "often justified" in beating her. The authors found that the more dependent a woman was on her husband (because of having sons, little education, and living with his kin) and the more socially isolated she was, the more likely she was to be abused and support that abuse (Yount 2005).

Anthropologist Peggy Sanday (1981) demonstrated the importance that patriarchy plays in promoting gender-based violence. In an extensive review of different types of societies, she found that rape is not a universal phenomenon. It is clearly absent in some cultures. Other cultures are more rape prone, occurring in places where women hold relatively low political and economic status, have rigid rules about the relationships between men and women, and encourage boys to be tough, aggressive, and competitive.

Although patriarchy is more evident in countries where women cannot drive, vote, or be seen in public without extensive covering of their face and bodies, patriarchy is observed in U.S. society as well, as noted in Chapter 4. Men establish their dominance by eschewing any semblance of femininity and often take more aggressive posturing. "You throw like a girl," "you're a sissy," "quit acting like a woman" all show contempt for the feminine. Men are taught that toughness, competitiveness, and controlling behavior are masculine attributes, and many adopt these attributes with a vengeance.

Cultural Norms Support Violence Some cultures are more tolerant of violence than others. In the United States, many types of violence are condoned, including in sporting events. Football, hockey, rugby, wrestling, and race car driving are notoriously violent sports, and the millions of fans who watch these events expect nothing less, all in the name of fun. Violence is very public, readily seen on television screens or at the theaters.

Violence among intimates is also supported by cultural norms in many regions of the world. The question becomes: How much violence among family members is "okay" and when does it turn into abuse? For example, many adults hit their children. However, are we talking about slapping, shoving, hitting, or beating? Is the child 2 or 12 years old? If corporal punishment is allowed under some circumstances, it is not surprising that in the heat of passion the boundaries of when it is and is not appropriate are sometimes blurred.

Corporal punishment of children is fully prohibited in the following 15 countries: Austria, Bulgaria, Croatia, Cyprus, Denmark, Finland, Germany, Hungary, Iceland, Israel, Latvia, Norway, Romania, Sweden, and Ukraine. The United Nations Committee on the Rights of Children has recommended that all countries prohibit spanking in the family and other institutions (Vandivere et al. 2003).

Family Privacy What goes on in U.S. families is generally a private matter (Berardo 1998). Sayings such as "a man's home is his castle" indicate that the man is not only dominant in his home, but what occurs there is no one else's business. Extended families are rare, and families often move hundreds or even thousands of miles away from other kin. In urban areas families commonly know few, if any, of their neighbors well, and therefore are increasingly isolated (Nock 1998).

Moreover, many people believe violence is a private matter between family members. Neighbors, coworkers, or even friends and other kin can be hesitant to get involved. "I didn't want to say anything because it's really none of my business" is a common sentiment in western society. Nicole Brown was repeatedly battered by her husband O. J. Simpson, yet no one spoke up about it until after her death.

As violence occurs, families can become even more isolated from friends, neighbors, and family because of embarrassment or stigma. Victims may be reluctant to seek help and may instead try to keep the abuse hidden.

Individual-Level Causes

Other reasons for violence among intimate partners focus more on the individuals involved.

The Intergenerational Transmission of Violence Drawing upon Bandura's social learning theory (1962), the intergenerational transmission of violence perspective (sometimes called the *cycle of violence*) suggests that we learn norms and behaviors by observing others, including violence. Families of orientation are the primary source of early learning. Therefore, it is likely that many adults who abuse their spouses, partners, or children are modeling the behavior they witnessed growing up. Perhaps they witnessed abusive or violent behavior between their own parents, or perhaps they were abused as young children. When we observe people to whom we are close engage in certain types of behavior, we learn scripts for our futures. In this case, the script includes an acceptance of aggressive behavior between family members or intimate partners.

Research suggests an intergenerational link; children, particularly boys, who witness or experience abuse are more likely to be in abusive relationships as an adult than are other children (Foshee et al. 1999; Heyman and Slep 2002; Lackey 2003; Straus 1990). Using a nationally representative sample of over 6,000 adults, Heyman and Slep (2002) found that the frequency of violence experienced as a child predicted adult abuse. They also found that children who lived with two abusive adults were more likely to abuse than those who lived with only one.

This perspective is controversial (Kaufman and Zigler 1987). It is also true that most people who witness or experience abuse as children do *not* abuse others. This is an important fact that can be easily overlooked. A 1980 study by Straus, Gelles, and Steinmetz reports a startling statistic from their research; sons of the most violent parents are 1,000 times more likely to abuse their spouses than the sons of nonviolent parents, but this still only translates into a rate of 20 percent. That means that 80 percent of those sons witnessing the most extreme forms of violence do *not* abuse their own wives. Therefore, it is very important to note that the intergenerational transmission of violence is referring to a greater *likelihood* of engaging in violence; it is not referring to determinism. Many persons who witnessed or experienced abuse as children grow up to be loving, supportive partners and parents without a hint of perpetuating violence and abuse. Likewise, some who are violent did not grow up with violence in the home. Therefore, researchers are examining many different parenting factors that could be associated with children behaving violently later in life (Schwartz et al. 2006).

Stress Many families today face considerable stress or tensions that test a family's emotional resources. Stressors can include such things as unemployment or chronic underemployment, poverty, being uninsured, having health problems, or struggling to manage the competing demands of work and family.

Sometimes the stress results from a specific crisis, which is a critical change of events that disrupts the functioning of a person's life. We tend to think of crises as negative events that serve as turning points; the death of a child, loss of a job, or a divorce. However, the birth or adoption of a baby or sending a child off to college may also bring a critical change that disrupts family relationships and functions and leads to considerable stress. Most often, families are expected to learn how to manage and effectively deal with the stressors on their own. Few families overall seek outside support, such as counseling or working with community agencies in dealing with the problems they face. If a family cannot cope adequately with the stress or crisis that occurs, the tension created can push them toward violence (Child Welfare Information Gateway 2006; Goldman et al. 2003).

While some stressors are unrelated to income level, many are highly correlated with income. For example, lower-income groups are more likely to face unemployment or underemployment, are less likely to be insured, and are more likely to have health problems in their families. Moreover, lower-income families have fewer coping mechanisms to help them ward off the emotional impact of the stressors. They have fewer savings and other assets to tide them over during a period of unemployment or underemployment, they do not have the resources to purchase health insurance privately, and they are more likely to engage in unhealthy coping mechanisms that jeopardize their health, such as smoking or eating poorly nutritious foods (rather than taking a trip to Hawaii to ward off stress). Not surprisingly then, research in domestic violence indicates that violence is more likely to occur in lower-income households, although it does occur at all income levels.

Social Policy and Family Resilience

As our society becomes more aware of family violence, we would like to believe that we become less tolerant of it.

Example: Zero Tolerance in the Legal and Criminal Justice Systems

> Last fall, Governor Hunt appointed a Task Force on domestic violence—bringing together representatives of local shelter and victim service programs, state and local government agencies, law enforcement and court officials, and other experts on domestic violence issues—to develop an action plan for North Carolina. Based on the Task Force recommendations, Governor Hunt has proposed four new strategies to fight domestic violence in North Carolina. These include: coordinating all state efforts through a permanent commission on domestic violence; providing access for domestic violence victims in all 100 counties; developing a coordinated, consistent response to domestic violence within the criminal justice system; and supporting a zero tolerance atmosphere for domestic violence in the workplace. (North Carolina Office of the Governor 1999)

> The "Zero Tolerance for Domestic Violence" initiative is a multi-jurisdictional partnership, created to help eliminate domestic and family violence and elder abuse in Contra Costa County. County staff, local law enforcement, the courts and community service providers have banded together under the leadership of the Board of Supervisors to offer a comprehensive, coordinated, community-wide response to break the progressive cycle of domestic and family violence. (Zero Tolerance for Domestic Violence 2003)

Throughout the country, state and local governments are taking a tougher stance against violence. **Zero tolerance** is a growing movement that emphasizes tougher laws; more stringent enforcement of those laws; training programs for those who work with victims and offenders, such as physicians or police officers; and a well-coordinated effort to offer victims the protection and services that they need. Most programs contain two main features. First, interventions are often concentrated at the misdemeanor level, because these crimes have most often been neglected. By addressing violence at the misdemeanor stage, it is hopeful that more serious injury can be avoided. Second, zero tolerance emphasizes system-wide coordination. Law enforcement, the courts, and social and health services work together to reduce violence and trauma. Together they identify gaps or duplication in services, and work to better coordinate services in a more efficient and productive manner (Zero Tolerance for Domestic Violence 2003).

Zero tolerance groups are demanding change:

No More . . . Excuses!
No More . . . Tolerance for Domestic Violence!
No More . . . Minimal sentencing for domestic violence homicides!
No More . . . Restraining order violations going minimally punished!
No More . . . Slap on the hands for offenders!
No More . . . Non-educated domestic violence prosecutors and judges!
No More . . . Excuses for lack of funding! Find funding!
No More . . . Tolerating any excuses![1]

Begun as a grassroots effort, zero tolerance is taking hold throughout the nation and the world. The United Nations Population Fund, which is the world's largest multilateral source of population assistance, providing $4.3 billion in assistance to more than

[1]Excerpt from "No More . . . Excuses!" From www.project-no-more.20fr.com/index.html.

160 countries, has recently called for "zero tolerance of violence against women." As the executive director writes,

> It is time that every one of us, individually and collectively, takes a stand to eradicate violence against women in all its manifestations. We must break the culture of violence against women. We must promote zero tolerance of violence against women everywhere. (U.N. Population Fund 1999)

Movements like this are having some effect. Between 1986 and 2000, the number of shelters, hotlines, and counseling programs specifically serving victims of domestic and partner violence in the United States increased by 50 percent, and the number of legal services programs increased over 300 percent (Tiefenthaler et al. 2005). However, because resources tend to be generated at the local rather than federal level, many low-income communities still have few resources, or none at all. We can do better.

Conclusion

This chapter attempts to illustrate that family problems often have a basis in social structure and cultural norms. The focus of this chapter is violence and abuse among intimates and gender-based violence. It examined dating violence, spouse/partner abuse, child abuse, and elder abuse. Drawing upon social science research and a comparative perspective, we see that many family problems, including violence and abuse, are really *social problems*, not merely personal ones, and therefore require that we examine them in their social, political, and cultural context. Violence among intimates and gender-based abuse have their roots in complex and longstanding traditions of accepting norms promoting violence and male privilege and authority within the family and other social institutions. Violence can also be exacerbated by individual factors such as stress or growing up in and witnessing a violent household.

Key Terms

Common couple violence (CCV): Violence that arises out of a specific argument in which at least one partner lashes out physically. (p. 412)

Conflict Tactics Scale (CTS): A violence scale based on people's responses about how they deal with disagreements in relationships. (p. 409)

Elder abuse: Abuse, neglect, and exploitation of the elderly, often by family members and others close to them. (p. 429)

Emotional abuse: Includes verbal, mental, or psychological maltreatment that destroys a person's self-esteem. (p. 425)

Financial or material exploitation: Improperly using the resources of another person, without his or her consent, for someone else's benefit. (p. 429)

Gender-based violence: Any act of gender violence that results in or is likely to result in physical, sexual, or psychological harm and suffering to women, including threats of such acts, coercion, or arbitrary deprivations of liberty, whether occurring in public or private life. (p. 407)

Intergenerational transmission of violence: Learning norms and behaviors, including violence, by observing others. (p. 426)

Intimate terrorism: Violence that is motivated by a desire to control the other partner. (p. 412)

Mutual violent control: A violent pattern of behavior in which both partners are controlling and violent. (p. 412)

National Violence Against Women Survey: The National Institute of Justice and the Centers for Disease Control and Prevention jointly sponsored a landmark telephone survey from 1995 to 1996 with a large and nationally representative sample of adult women and men about violence. (p. 413)

Neglect: The failure to provide for basic needs for someone who is dependent on you. (p. 425)

Physical abuse: Inflicting physical injury and harm on another person. (p. 425)

Sexual abuse: Inappropriate sexual behavior with someone (e.g., a child) for sexual gratification. (p. 425)

Trafficking: The illegal recruitment, transport, or sale of human beings into all forms of forced labor and servitude. (p. 408)

Violence among intimates: Physical, economic, sexual, or psychological abuse covering a broad range of relationships. (p. 409)

Violent resistance: Violence associated with self-defense. (p. 412)

Zero tolerance: A growing movement that emphasizes tougher laws; more stringent enforcement of those laws; training programs for those who work with victims and offenders, such as physicians or police officers; and a well-coordinated effort to offer victims the protection and services they need. (p. 433)

Resources on the Internet

National Coalition Against Domestic Violence
www.ncadv.org
Information and referral center for the public, media, battered women and their children, agencies and organizations.

National Clearinghouse on Child Abuse and Neglect Information
www.calib.com/nccanch
This website provides information on the prevention, identification, and treatment of child abuse and neglect; offers statistics and trends on all aspects of child abuse and neglect.

National Institute of Justice
www.ojp.usdoj.gov/nij
NIJ is the research and development agency of the U.S. Department of Justice and is the only federal agency solely dedicated to researching crime control and justice issues. NIJ provides objective, independent, nonpartisan, evidence-based knowledge and tools to meet the challenges of crime and justice, particularly at the state and local levels.

U.S. Department of Health and Human Services
www.os/dhhs.gov
The U.S. Department of Health and Human Services (DHHS) is the U.S. government's principal agency for protecting the health of all Americans and providing essential human services, especially for those who are least able to help themselves.

Further Reading

Bolen, R. M., and D. E. H. Russell. 2000. *The Epidemic of Rape and Child Sexual Abuse in the United States.* Thousand Oaks, CA: Sage.

Dobash, R. E., and R. P. Dobash. 1979. *Violence Against Wives: A Case Against the Patriarchy*. New York: Free Press.

Dugan, M. K., and R. R. Hock. 2000. *It's My Life: Starting Over After an Abusive Relationship or Domestic Violence*. New York: Routledge.

Farr, K. 2005. *Sex Trafficking: The Global Market in Women and Children*. London: Worth.

Fontes, L. A. (Ed.). 1995. *Sexual Abuse in Nine North American Cultures: Treatment and Prevention.* Thousand Oaks, CA: Sage.

Girshick, L. B. 2002. *Woman-to-Woman Sexual Violence: Does She Call It Rape?* Boston: Northeastern University Press.

Herek, G., and K. Berrill. (Eds.). 1991. *Hate Crimes: Confronting Violence Against Lesbians and Gay Men.* Newbury Park, CA: Sage.

Kempadoo, K., and J. Doezema. (Eds.). 1998. *Global Sex Workers: Rights, Resistance, and Redefinition.* New York: Routledge.

Parrot, A., and N. Cummings. 2007. *Forsaken Females.* Lanham, MD: Rowman and Littlefield.

Raine, N. V. 1999. *After Silence: Rape and My Journey Back*. New York: Three Rivers Press/Crown.

Richie, B. E., N. J. Skoloff, and C. Pratt. 2005. *Domestic Violence at the Margins: Readings on Race, Class, Gender, and Culture*. Piscataway, NJ: Rutgers University Press.

Straus, M. A., and D. A. Donnelly. 2001. *Beating the Devil Out of Them: Corporal Punishment in American Families and Its Effect on Children.* Piscataway, NJ: Transaction Publishers.

CHAPTER 14

Divorce and Repartnering

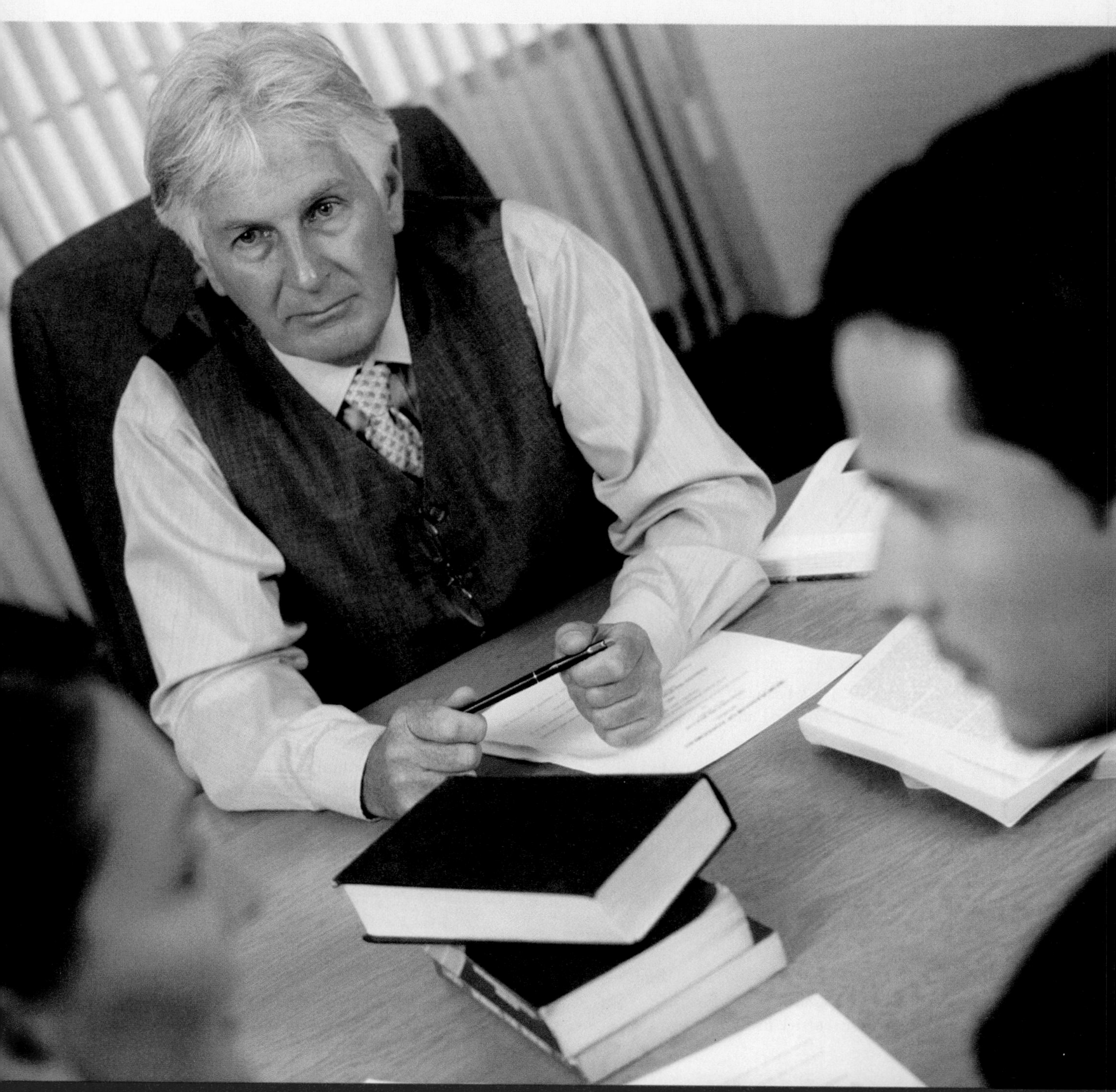

Chapter Outline

CHAPTER PREVIEW

Many people are unaware that divorce rates have declined significantly over the past 25 years. Nonetheless, the United States still has the highest rate of divorce in the world. This chapter examines why this is the case, and looks at the factors associated with divorce and the implications of divorce. While it is easy to talk about divorce rates, we must remember that ending a marriage is a difficult and highly emotional process that affects many people, not just the married couple. In this chapter you will learn:

- Divorce is measured in many different ways, but the most common way (e.g., "half of all marriages end in divorce") is not the best method
- Cross-cultural and historical trends in divorce
- The macro-level and micro-level factors that are associated with divorce
- Dimensions of the divorce experience and how these differ by sex
- Who has custody of children and who receives child support and alimony
- The short- and long-term consequences of divorce on children
- Issues surrounding repartnering and remarriage
- How stepfamilies are becoming more common and some of the rewards they receive and challenges they face

What are the effects of divorce on children? That is a complex question and one charged with emotion. When most people think of children and divorce, they imagine how the relationship between parent and child may be affected—but most children have a kin network that extends beyond simply their parents. They are part of an extended family of aunts, uncles, cousins, and grandparents.

The tie between grandparent and grandchild can be among the closest in this extended kin network. Grandparents can serve as storytellers, confidants, and mentors. Both grandchildren and grandparents themselves derive satisfaction and meaning from these roles. However, what happens when grandparents experience a divorce? How does their divorce affect their relationship with their grandchildren? These are important questions because about one-third of all individuals who had been married and reached age 65 in 2000 experienced a divorce at some point in their lives.

Sociologist Valerie King used data from a longitudinal study of 538 white rural grandparents living in Iowa to explore how a grandparent's divorce affects his or her relationship with grandchildren. Information was collected directly from grandparents through telephone interviews and mailed questionnaires. King addressed three questions:

1. Does the experience of divorce negatively influence the saliency of the grandparent role or involvements with grandchildren?
2. If so, what factors explain the negative influence of divorce on grandparenting?
3. What circumstances moderate the influence of divorce on the grandparent-grandchild relationship?

The results from her analyses indicate that many aspects of grandparenting are negatively associated with having experienced a divorce. Grandparents who had divorced report less contact, engage in fewer shared activities, report feeling less close to their grandchild, are less likely to see themselves as a friend, and report higher levels of conflict within the relationship, compared to grandparents who had not divorced. Most of these differences persisted even when the grandparent remarried.

Why are grandparents who have divorced less involved with their grandchildren? Some of this can be explained by distance. Divorced grandparents tend to live farther away from their grandchild, and therefore have less frequent contact. Divorced grandparents also report weaker bonds to their adult children, which may again affect visitation and make it more difficult to sustain strong grandparent-grandchild bonds.

Three factors were found to moderate these relationships. First, the negative effect of grandparental divorce was less for grandmothers than for grandfathers, reflecting their tendency to live closer to their adult child and grandchildren. Second, maternal grandparents tend to be closer than paternal grandparents. Third, a good grandparent-parent relationship can compensate for the negative effects of a grandparent's divorce on the relationship between grandparents and grandchildren. If grand-

parents and their adult children are close, it is likely that grandparents will have warm and enduring ties with their grandchildren.

King (2003) writes:

> *Understanding the significance of divorce for grandparent–grandchild relations is imperative given the vital role grandparenting plays in the well-being of both children and older adults. This study has advanced our knowledge about the way in which a grandparent's divorce affects the saliency of the grandparent role and involvements with grandchildren. The rising levels of divorce in the grandparent generation has and will continue to have negative consequences for grandparents, their children, and their grandchildren. (p. 181)* ■

A divorce decree may be granted in a matter of minutes by a judge. Family relationships, as just shown, can be irrevocably altered. However, behind those few tense minutes usually lies a long period in which a couple has analyzed, redefined, and reorganized virtually all aspects of their relationship and their lives (Ganong and Coleman 1994). A longitudinal study of roughly 1,000 people who were interviewed several times between 1980 and 1992 reports that couples who divorced in 1992 often expressed marital problems as early as 1980 (Amato and Rogers 1997). In another study based on in-depth interviews with 30 divorced persons, Hopper (1993) found that all respondents said that they were well aware of their marital problems for a long time, sometimes for 10 to 20 years. These studies reveal that couples who divorce tend to report problems in the marriage long before the actual divorce occurs.

Why do couples take years or even decades to move from an unhappy marriage to divorce? It is because most Americans take marriage very seriously and believe that divorce should not be considered a quick or easy reprieve (Hawkins et al. 2002; Martin and Parashar 2006).

This chapter examines the issue of divorce, how divorce affects children, and repartnering after divorce. It begins by explaining the various ways that divorce is measured.

Measuring Divorce

There is a paradox in the United States, although we place a high value on marriage, we also have one of the highest rates of divorce in the world. Other industrialized countries with which we have much in common pale in comparison.

We commonly hear that "half of all marriages end in divorce" in the United States. This phrase, however, is somewhat misleading. Some people interpret it to mean that if 100,000 couples married last year, 50,000 divorces were also granted; on the surface it looks as though 50 percent of marriages ended in divorce. This comparison is not appropriate because although these marriages took place in only 1 year, the divorces are from marriages that may have taken place many years ago. Therefore this is a misleading comparison and not very useful.

Others use the phrase "half of all marriages end in divorce" to mean that if the current rate of divorce continued over the next several decades, approximately half of all marriages would ultimately end in divorce at some time during that period. Although this may contain some truth, it is not an accurate way to present the frequency of divorce because divorce rates fluctuate. For most of history rates have climbed upward; however, since about 1980 the divorce rate has declined significantly. No one knows what the next 30 years will bring.

How then can we measure the frequency of divorce? What is meant by a divorce rate? One measure called the **crude divorce rate** examines the frequency of divorce per 1,000 people. In the United States, this amounted to about 3.6 divorces per 1,000 people in 2005 (Munson and Sutton 2006). This is a relatively common way of reporting divorce data (for example, by the Centers for Disease Control and Prevention) and can allow for comparisons over time or across countries, as shown in Map 14.1.

However, not all people have married; therefore, a more useful way to measure the frequency of divorce, one that also enables us to make comparisons, is to talk about the number of divorces that occur out of every 1,000 married women. This is called a **refined divorce rate**. It also allows us to make historical and international comparisons or to compare the divorce rate state by state. Using the refined divorce rate, there are 17.0 divorces per 1,000 married women in the United States each year (National Marriage Project 2006). This means that within a year, 17 out of 1,000 married women, or less than 2 percent, received a divorce.

These divorce rates are **cross sectional**, meaning that they reflect rates at only one point in time. However, even though a married woman had a less than 2 percent chance of divorcing last year, she has a far higher chance of divorcing over the *course* of her married life. It is unknown how high this chance is because the divorce rate fluctuates and some of the divorces are occurring to people married for a second or third time. If the current rate continues, which is unlikely according to family sociologists and demographers, her chances are about 50 percent.

Cross Cultural Comparisons

Map 14.1 on pages 442 and 443 shows the variation in the crude divorce rate around the world. What accounts for such large differences?

Divorce rates are related to several factors. First, the *level of socioeconomic development* within a country influences the frequency of divorce. Less-developed countries in Africa, Asia, or Central and South America have significantly lower divorce rates than do more developed industrialized countries in North America and Europe (Trent and South 1989).

China, which has undergone rapid socioeconomic development, has had a surge in the divorce rate, tripling between 1985 and 1997, and has continued to rise since then (Sommerville 2005). The increase is due to many factors, including new social and economic freedom, western influences, and the decline of political involvement in mate selection. Until recently separating couples needed their work unit's permission before a divorce could be granted, but that was rarely given. However, by the end of 2003, the rules had changed, and unhappy couples can now visit their local community center and—if both parties agree—the divorce can be issued in only 10 minutes. Ma Fengzhi, a sociology professor at Beijing University, suggests

> In the past, many marriages were political. Everyone from Army officers to bureaucrats to workers had to have their potential spouses approved by party bosses. Today people have the

freedom to choose their own partners, so it is natural that some want to discard their political matches. (Platt 1999, 1)

One factor associated with divorce rates is the level of patriarchy in a society. For example, in many Muslim cultures women cannot easily initiate a divorce.

A second factor that may influence how rarely or frequently divorce occurs is the *dominant religion* that is practiced. For example, much of Central and South America is dominated by Roman Catholicism, which strictly forbids divorce in all but the most extreme circumstances. In Italy, an industrialized but largely Catholic nation, divorce was illegal until the 1980s and remains rare today. Likewise, in Ireland, the Catholic Church was successful at forbidding divorce until 1997. Religious institutions play a strong role in defining cultural norms toward divorce and other moral issues.

Third, divorce tends to be more restrictive *in patriarchal societies* where women have few legal rights (Amato 1994; Chang 1993). In many countries men are allowed to divorce their wives for almost any reason, yet women are not allowed to initiate divorce except under the most extreme circumstances. In many Muslim countries, for example, husbands can unilaterally divorce their wives by repeating the phrase three times in front of witnesses, "I divorce thee." A wife seeking a divorce, in contrast, must go to a religious court and prove that her husband has failed to support his family or has otherwise had a harmful moral effect on the family (Neft and Levine 1997).

Women's low status, and particularly their economic dependence on men in patriarchal nations, is a critical factor in predicting divorce rates (Greenstein and Davis 2006; Seccombe and Lee 1986). For example, a study of 71 nations found that those countries in which women had greater access to economic resources had higher crude divorce rates than nations where women had less access to these resources (Greenstein and Davis 2006). Increased economic activity is one avenue through which women can be independent from their husbands, thereby possibly altering divorce law.

Moreover, the laws regarding child custody and spousal support are designed to perpetuate male dominance and control and discourage women from asking for a divorce. In Taiwan, custody of children goes automatically to the father, based on the tradition that children carry on the father's family name. In an exchange to obtain custody of children, some women pay their husbands large sums of money (Chang 1993). In Iran wives are only entitled to spousal support for 3 months, despite the very limited economic opportunities available for women. Most divorced women must therefore return to their families, often in shame. In India, a woman rarely receives any of the marital assets because these are assumed to belong to her husband and his family. Many Indian women do not even ask for child support out of fear that their husbands will also try to gain custody. Box 14.1 on page 444 reveals how Japanese laws disregard the rights of parents to see their children after a divorce. Custody laws are very restrictive.

Although cross-cultural divorce rates are related to socioeconomic development, dominant religious institutions, and level of patriarchy, other cultural factors also come into play. The United States has one of the highest rates of divorce in the world—nearly double that of Canada and Western Europe; yet, these countries are also highly developed and industrialized nations, have diverse religious institutions, and have relatively low levels of patriarchy. So why is the U.S. rate so much higher?

MAP 14.1 Eye on the World: Comparative Divorce Rates Per 1,000 People

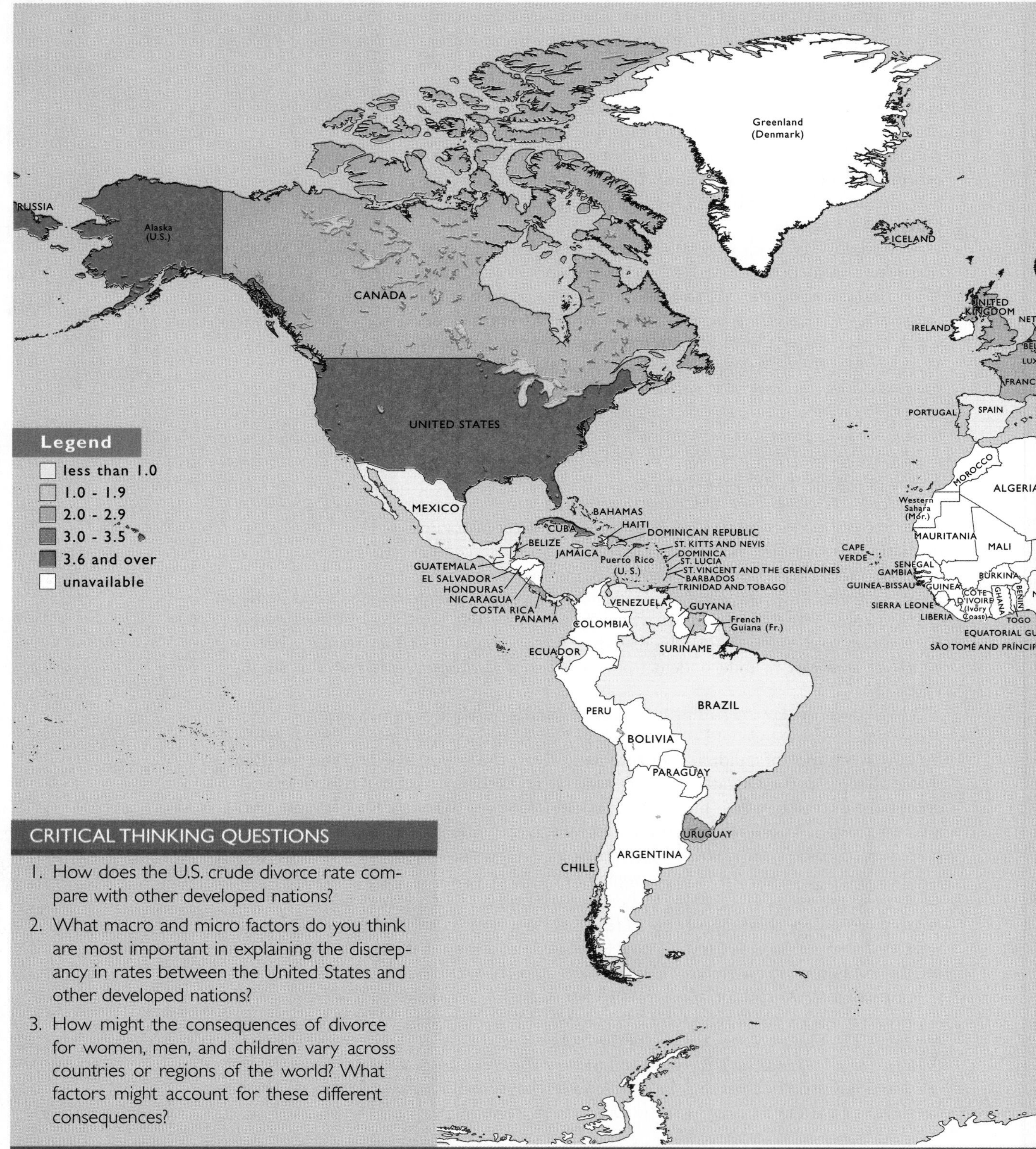

CRITICAL THINKING QUESTIONS

1. How does the U.S. crude divorce rate compare with other developed nations?
2. What macro and micro factors do you think are most important in explaining the discrepancy in rates between the United States and other developed nations?
3. How might the consequences of divorce for women, men, and children vary across countries or regions of the world? What factors might account for these different consequences?

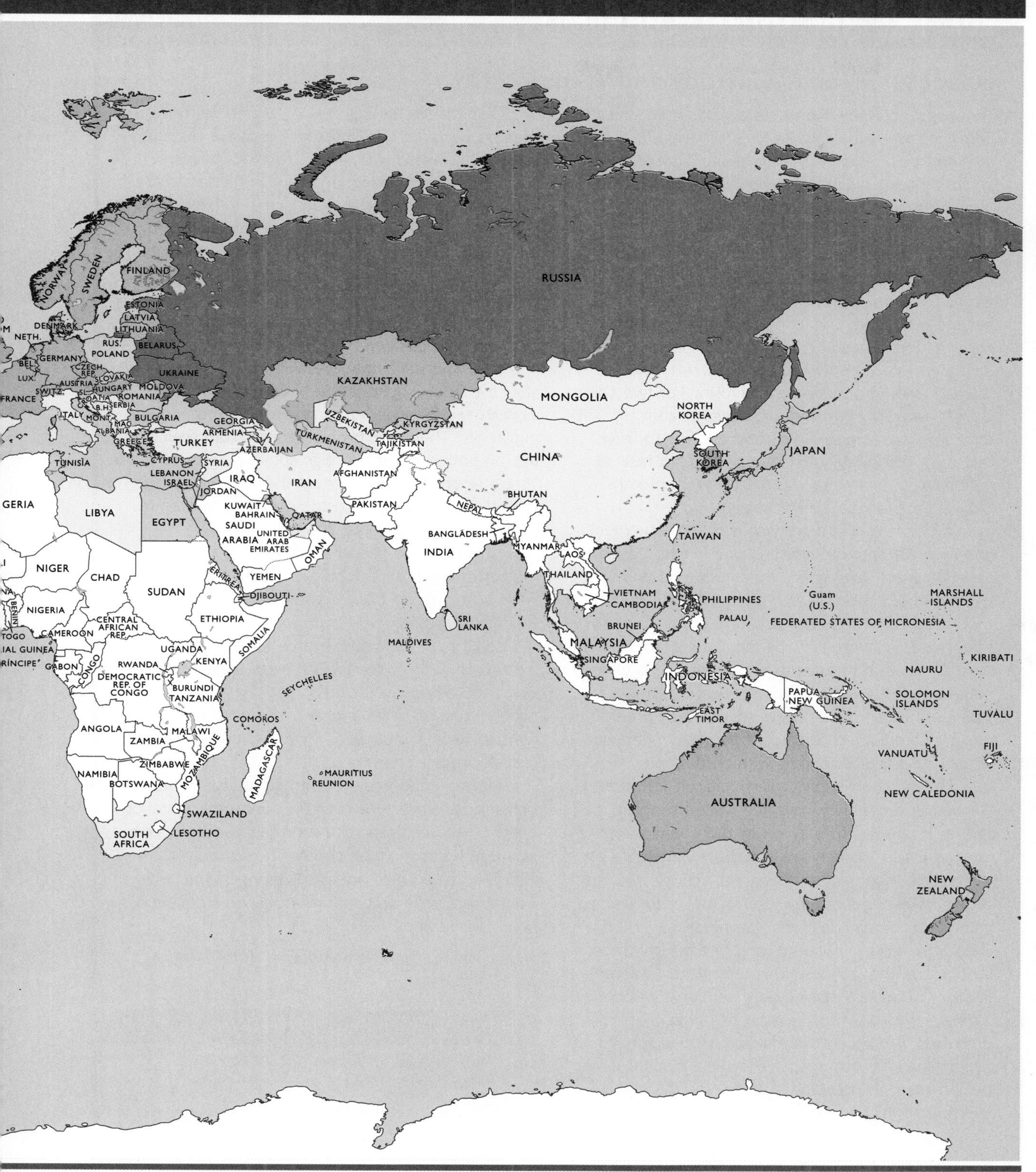

Source: Nugman 2002.

BOX 14.1 The Global Community

Japanese Divorce, Custody, and Visitation Laws

The laws surrounding divorce, custody, and visitation differ from one country to another and reflect deeply held cultural norms about families. The following illustrates how Japan, a modern industrialized nation, has approached divorce, custody, and visitation laws.

Divorce has constantly been on the mind of Imelda (not her real name), a 36-year-old Filipino woman who married a Japanese man 7 years ago, but the soft-spoken woman says that despite the nagging loneliness and physical abuse she sometimes has to endure from her husband, she will never leave the man she despises for fear of losing her two children. "I asked my husband for a divorce after my first child was born. He said okay, and told me to leave that night taking only my clothes. I couldn't bear to part from my son who was then only 10 months old," she explained—so she stayed on.

Imelda is one of a growing number of women and men who are locked in miserable marriages because Japanese laws ignore the individual rights of parents to see their children after a divorce. Joint custody is illegal, and child visitation is not a legal right under Japanese law. The right of children to have access to both parents is ignored. This is why in many cases women who want to leave their Japanese husbands do not do so, and their predicament is complicated by the fact that they often face economic difficulties coping with child rearing.

The situation is particularly difficult for foreign women because they have the added problem of getting legal visas to stay on in the country after a divorce. Asian women are especially vulnerable as a result of lingering discrimination, activists say. The problems experienced by foreign men and women with Japanese spouses with gaining access to children after separation or divorce were highlighted in 2006 by the Japanese chapter of the Children's Rights Council, a Washington-based organization. Saying the inability to maintain ties with their children was akin to child abduction, several foreign nationals spoke out against a system that they said denied their children the right to see them and the opportunity to develop closer ties with their biological parents.

Dale Martin, an Englishman, says he has not seen his 6-year-old daughter for the last 2 years because his Japanese wife refuses to allow it. This, he adds, is despite his telephone calls and letters and a hard-won visitation agreement signed in family courts. "I have no news about her even while living a few hours away from her home. I call this a violation of my daughter's rights to have access to her father," he told the press. Margaret Leyman, an American journalist living in Tokyo, says her Japanese former husband prohibits her son from meeting with her. "My son, who is 12 now, lives with my mother-in-law after the family court decided I was, as a working woman and foreigner, not a responsible mother," she explained. "They have prohibited him from seeing me." In both cases, the foreign spouses signed divorce papers that had, without their knowledge, included the awarding of custody of their children to their estranged husbands or wives.

Japanese laws recognize divorce, granted on mutual consent, on a form signed by both parties. Both Leyman and Martin assumed, in accordance with laws in many western countries, that custody is a separate issue from divorce and would be treated as such under the Japanese legal system. "I was shocked to realise that I had signed away my right to see my child and also denied my son's right to have a mother as well as enjoy a different culture," recalled Leyman.

In desperation, she tried to get at least visitation rights to her child. However, the concept of visitation rights is not deeply ingrained in the Japanese system. Japanese tradition views children not as individuals with their own rights but as belonging to the family. Even if successful, visitation may only be a couple of hours per month.

Sources: Children's Rights Network of Japan 2006; Kakuchi 2003.

CRITICAL THINKING QUESTIONS

1. Why do you think Japanese custody laws are so much different than those in the United States?
2. Do you think that the custody law is a gender issue? Why or why not?

Historical Trends in the United States

Although we might not like to think about it, divorce and desertion have been common throughout much of U.S. history (Degler 1980). Legal divorce was rare prior to the mid-nineteenth century; however, separation and desertion occurred in its place. The early colonies recognized adultery, desertion, and usually violence as grounds for divorce; however, because of patriarchal norms, few divorces were granted to wives at their initiation. An early study of marriage and divorce conducted in the mid-1800s examined 29 cases of divorce based on "cruelty" in which the wife was the defendant. In almost every case the "cruelty" committed was that the wife was attempting to break out of the traditional subordinate role in one way or another (Wright 1889). Half of these cases were based on her refusal to do domestic chores such as keeping her husband's clothes in repair or cooking his meals.

Early feminists spoke out in favor of making divorce more available to women as a way to improve women's rights and position in marriage (Degler 1980). They worried that women were locked into destructive marriages, further eroding their emancipation. The divorce rate steadily rose between 1860 and 1940. Then the divorce rate surged in the mid-1940s after World War II ended. It is possible that many couples rushed into marriages during wartime, and later faced difficulties they had not imagined in their hurry to marry.

Figure 14.1 illustrates the trends in the crude and refined divorce rates in the United States between 1940 and 2005. After the rush of divorces following World War II, the divorce rate fell to around 10 per 1,000 married women. During the 1950s, the divorce rate remained relatively low; however, by the 1960s the divorce rate began to rise again, peaking at approximately 23 divorces per 1,000 married women around 1980. Since 1980 the rate of divorce has declined to 17 per 1,000 married women, and 3.6 per 1,000 people.

FIGURE 14.1 Divorce Rates per 1,000 Population (Crude) and 1,000 Married Women (Refined) over the Years 1940–2005

Sources: Munson and Sutton 2006; Whitehead and Popenoe 2006; U.S. Census Bureau 2006a.

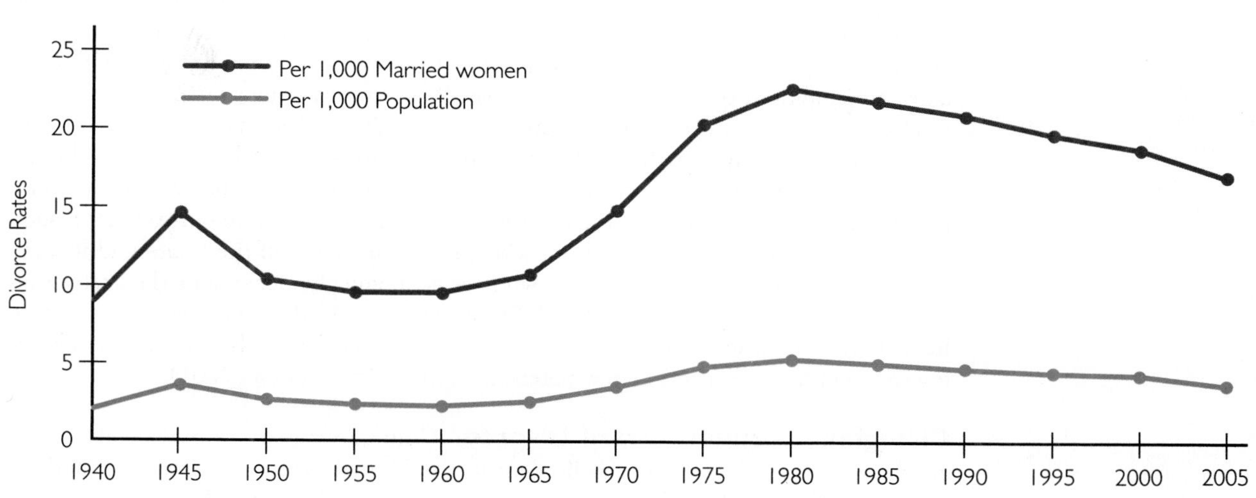

Factors Associated with Divorce

If we asked people why they divorced, we would likely get many different answers that primarily focus on individual attributes or personal problems: "We grew apart . . . ," "We are just too different . . . ," "She met someone new . . . ," "He doesn't listen to me. . . ." However, family scholars are interested in the *social patterns* associated with divorce. These patterns include structural factors as well as personal explanations to help us understand why people divorce.

Macro-Level Factors

Let us first examine the structural factors that contribute to divorce.

Changes in Divorce Laws The frequency of divorce reflects the laws of a particular culture. Until recently, to be granted a divorce in the United States one partner had to file suit against the other, blaming the partner for violating marriage vows, or making the marriage intolerable, such as mental cruelty, adultery, or desertion. Being found "at fault" could affect custody arrangements, property settlements, and alimony awards.

Beginning in 1953, states slowly began to amend their laws to support **no-fault divorce** as a way to make divorce less acrimonious, coercive, and restrictive. Instead, couples could simply say that they have irreconcilable differences and that they wished to divorce without assigning blame. Beginning in Oklahoma in 1953 and Alaska in 1962, no-fault divorce laws spread through the 50 states during the 1970s. Utah was the final holdout, but eventually enacted no-fault divorce legislation in 1987 (Nakonezny et al. 1995; Vlosky and Monroe 2002).

It is not clear how the passage of no-fault divorce laws affected the divorce rate because the rate was already rising rapidly prior to passage of legislation. However, there is some evidence that a high number of divorces occurred immediately after legislation was passed (Nakonezny et al. 1995; Rodgers et al. 1997). This may indicate that there was a backlog of unhappy couples waiting until the legislation went into effect so that they could divorce more easily and without blame.

Women's Employment Trends in women's employment also are correlated with divorce. As we have learned in previous chapters, throughout most of history, married couples were tightly bound together because they needed the labor of one another to survive and support their families. Today most married women, including those with children, are employed outside the home for pay. Women now comprise 46 percent of the total U.S. labor force (U.S. Department of Labor 2006b). This change in women's employment patterns has enabled women to more easily support themselves. Although their wages continue to lag behind men, women can more easily end an unhappy relationship because they can be a breadwinner. Women who are more self-sufficient, such as those who have higher incomes, or who earn more than half the household income are more likely to divorce than those who are economically dependent (Heckert et al. 1998; Heidemann et al. 1998; Ono 1998; Rogers 2004). Moreover, women are more likely to divorce when working in an occupation that has relatively many men, increasing the likelihood of meeting new potential partners (South et al. 2001).

Changing Attitudes Toward Divorce Cultural views about divorce also influence how frequently a divorce will occur in the United States. Divorce itself and divorced people faced heavy stigma even a generation ago. For example, the unflattering term *divorcee*, which was applied to women, had sexually suggestive connotations. Moreover, it was unlikely that any divorced woman or man would have been elected to a major political office, but in 1980 Ronald Reagan's divorce did not prevent him from being elected president of the United States. In the 1996 presidential election, candidate Bob Dole's divorce was barely mentioned. Attitudes toward divorce are changing as it becomes more common. The changing attitude toward divorce is probably both a consequence of an increasing divorce rate—and also a cause of it.

The stigma toward divorce, although reduced, has not been eliminated. Attitudes toward divorce are less disapproving than in the past, but disapproval of divorced *individuals* continues (Gerstel 1987). Family, friends, coworkers, and neighbors all want to know who is to blame, often in moralistic tones. Those who initiate divorce are viewed as the "bad guys," and they must deconstruct the relationship in a way that will define themselves to others as victims rather than the perpetrators of divorce. Moreover, women with 4-year college degrees, who previously had the most permissive attitudes toward divorce, have become more restrictive in their attitudes toward divorce than high school graduates and women with some college education, whereas women with no high school diplomas have increasingly permissive attitudes toward divorce (Martin and Parashar 2006).

Cultural Norms Other cultural norms may have indirect effects on the divorce rate. Immigrants to the United States often face new relationship stressors and increased rates of divorce. Some of these stressors revolve around gender expectations, which tend to be narrower in the country of origin. For example, immigrants from Latin America or the Middle East are more likely to believe that a man's primary responsibility is to earn a living and support the family, while a woman should tend to the home and children. However, after immigrating to the United States they find less support for these traditional expectations and it may take both spouses working to make ends meet financially. One study of Iranian immigrants to the United States found women tended to adopt views similar to mainstream America while men's views remained more traditional (Hojat et al. 2000). This difference, coupled with the need for two incomes and women's increased job opportunities, paved the way for potential conflict. "Americanized" women are criticized as poor mates. Therefore, divorce is six times more common among Iranian immigrants to the United States than it is among Iranians residing in their native country (Tohidi 1993).

Micro-Level Factors

In addition to these macro-level societal forces that influence divorce rates, specific individual characteristics may also influence the risk of couples divorcing.

Parental Divorce Individuals whose parents have divorced are also more likely to divorce themselves (Amato and Deboer 2001; National Marriage Project 2006; Teachman 2002). There are several possible explanations for this. First, adult children model their own parents' behavior and view divorce as a potential avenue out of an unpleasant situation, or they may model destructive behavior such as poor communication skills or family violence. Second, children of divorced parents also marry younger, generally have lower incomes, are more likely to be involved in a nonmarital pregnancy, and are less likely to go to college, which puts them in several higher risk categories. Third, parental divorce also has negative long-term consequences for children's mental health, such as emotional problems, anxiety, and depression, that can continue into their adulthood.

Age at Marriage Marrying young increases the likelihood of divorce (Kurdek 1993; National Marriage Project 2006; Waite and Lillard 1991). Teen marriages are at a particularly high risk because teenagers tend to be poorly prepared for marriage and its responsibilities. Moreover, teen marriages are often precipitated by a premarital pregnancy, which increases the likelihood of the marriage failing. Practically speaking, the couples are likely to have low incomes and have had their education interrupted, also putting them in a higher risk category.

Presence of Children Childfree couples are more likely to divorce (Waite and Lillard 1991). Families who have young preschool-aged children in particular, or families with many children, are least likely to divorce. This, of course, says nothing about the quality of these marriages; people may stay in unfulfilling marriages because they feel that it is the appropriate thing to do for their children's sake. The sex of the children seems to affect the likelihood of divorcing as well; families with only boys are less likely to divorce than are families with only girls.

Nonmarital Childbearing Couples who bear a child or conceive prior to marriage have higher divorce rates than other couples. Part of this may be explained by the fact that a nonmarital pregnancy may encourage people to marry when they may not otherwise have chosen to do so. It may also encourage them to marry before they are financially or emotionally ready. Pregnancy, caring for a newborn, and raising a child puts additional strains and stresses on a relationship. Couples who have not yet had the opportunity to truly get to know themselves and their partner as a couple may have a difficult time transitioning to their role as parents.

Race and Ethnicity The likelihood of divorce differs among racial or ethnic groups (U.S. Census Bureau 2006g). In 2005, 10.9 percent of blacks in the United States were currently divorced, according to the U.S. Census Bureau, as compared to 10 percent of whites, 7.4 percent of Hispanic groups, and 5 percent of Asians. These differences are likely a combination of structural and cultural factors. For example, the lack of jobs for urban black males and high rates of unemployment or poverty could make marriage and remarriage less attractive to black women (Wilson 1996). What might explain the relatively lower rate of divorce among most Hispanic and Asian groups? The most common explanation is a cultural one, focusing on the primacy of the family; the importance of Catholicism among Hispanics, which does not recognize divorce; and greater tolerance for patriarchal norms.

Education On average, persons with lower levels of education are more likely to divorce than are persons with higher levels of education (Heaton 2002; National Marriage Project 2006). A college degree reduces the risk of divorce, but the relationship is less clearcut for women than it is for men. Some studies suggest that women with very high levels of education are also more likely to divorce, especially later in the marriage, because it contributes to their ability to be economically independent (Heidemann et al. 1998).

Income Divorce is more common among persons with lower incomes than among those with higher incomes. Financial and job-related stresses can contribute to the deterioration of a marriage (Kurdek 1993; U.S. Census Bureau 2006). Unemployment, poverty, and financial strains increase the likelihood of family violence and disruption, and decrease displays of affection. In a study of separation and divorce conducted by Spanier and Thompson (1987), 56 percent of couples claimed that a major source of conflict was over the amount of money they had. *Who* earns the money is also of importance. Nontraditional couples in which wives earn between 50 percent and 75 percent of the household income are more likely to separate or divorce than are other couples (Heckert et al. 1998).

Degree of Similarity Between Spouses When spouses are similar to one another in socioeconomic characteristics, such as age, religion, race, or ethnic group, they are less likely to divorce. Couples who are very different on one or more of these dimensions face increased stresses and complications in their marriages because they may have different values and have less social support from friends and family. In a study of Chinese, Japanese, Filipino, Hawaiian, and Caucasian couples, it was found that interracial or interethnic marriages are more likely to end in divorce than are marriages between persons of the same racial or ethnic group (Jones 1996).

The Dimensions of the Divorce Experience

Divorce is not simply the ending of a relationship between two people; it alters or even severs many personal and legal ties. A divorce can end relationships with family members; with friends who find themselves taking sides; with neighbors if you have moved away; and with community groups of which you are no longer a member or can no longer afford to join.

The Emotional and Psychic Dimension

It is often thought that one spouse initiates the breakup of the marriage and therefore has the advantage of preparing emotionally for the separation or using its threat as a way to demand change. However, it is possible that who gets labeled as the initiator of the divorce is really accidental and random, according to in-depth interviews with divorcing couples (Hopper 1993). Hopper found that both spouses were generally aware of multiple marital problems, experienced discontent and contemplated divorce or separation, and were ambivalent about the best way to resolve the marital problems. However, he also noted that once their labels as either initiators or noninitiators emerged and took hold, these became the basis of distinct vocabularies used throughout the divorce.

As time passes, most people adjust to the separation and divorce. A study of nearly 800 divorced couples obtained from courthouse records from seven counties in one state reports that respondents have significantly better adjustment to divorce if they fit into one of two divergent categories: (1) high degree of friendship and low levels of preoccupation with the ex-spouse; and (2) high hostility toward the ex-spouse and low levels of preoccupation with them (Masheter 1997). Forgiveness is associated with many critical dimensions of well-being (Rye et al. 2004).

The Legal Dimension

There is a strong impetus to view family relationships as a private matter, but some aspects are governed by law. The state intervenes to mandate or restrict how family members act toward one another or to define rights or privileges, such as child support, visitation, or payment of alimony. The state is also involved in dividing up assets and property, including the home, cars, savings, and retirement accounts and dividing up debts, including credit cards or loans. Hiring attorneys to iron out the division of assets can cost each side thousands of dollars.

One study examined attorneys' views of several controversial issues in family law (Braver et al. 2002). One of these issues revolved around whether custody proceedings are gender biased. This is pertinent, because 45 states have established gender bias task forces in their state courts. Some suggest that the system is biased against women, pointing to their difficult financial status after a divorce or difficulty in contested custody decisions (Braver and O'Connell 1998). Others claim that men are the true victims of gender bias, suggesting that the system protects mothers at the fathers' expense (Pruett and Jackson 1999). Braver, Cookston, and Cohen (2002) surveyed 72 attorneys about their perceptions in the courts. These perceptions about bias are particularly important even if they are factually incorrect because the attorneys have an important advisory role. If they perceive the court as biased in some fashion, it could become a self-fulfilling prophecy. For example, if male clients are routinely told that the system is biased in favor of women (whether or not the courts really are), fathers may be less likely to seek custody or pursue other legal actions.

The researchers provided the following scenario to the attorneys, and the attorneys were asked to indicate what they would tell their client about his or her chances to prevail.

> Imagine that the financial issues of the case represent absolutely no special problems and appear readily resolvable. Imagine that there are no indications about lack of parental fitness, emotional or mental problems, drug or alcohol problems, domestic violence, or physical or sexual abuse on the part of either parent. Both parents have worked full-time (both M–F, 9–5) continuously except for a 3-month maternity leave taken by mother after the birth of each of the children. Father also took a lot of time off during those periods to help with the infants. Father earns $50,000, mother earns $35,000. The children currently stay in an after-school program until father picks them up, since he gets home 15 minutes earlier, while mother takes them to school in the morning. Mother has taken the children to most doctors' and dentist appointments; father is more involved than mother with each of the children's sports activities, soccer and T-ball. Mother and father are equally likely to stay home with an ill child, but this actually happens only rarely. (Braver et al. 2002, 330–331)

The study found that attorneys perceive that mothers were likely to prevail when seeking custody—even if in the above scenario they seek maximum parent time and offer their husbands very little time with the children. The only situation in which attorneys believed father's opinions equal the mother's is in cases where she seeks very little time with her children.

The Parental Dimension

When children are present, a couple must try to design and agree upon coparenting strategies. For example, there is the issue of custody.

Custody **Legal custody** refers to who has the legal authority to make important decisions concerning the children, such as where they will go to school, in what community or state they will reside, and who will be notified in case of a health emergency or school problem. In the past, legal custody was usually given solely to the parent with whom the child lived, but this is changing. Today **joint legal custody** is becoming more common, which refers to noncustodial parents (usually fathers) also retaining their legal rights with respect to their children (Cancian and Meyer 1998).

Physical custody refers to the place where the children actually reside. This seemingly simple concept can actually be difficult to measure. Mothers are more likely than fathers to report that children live with mother, while fathers are more likely than mothers to say that the children either live with the father or with both parents (Lin et al.

After a divorce, more than 80 percent of children reside with only one parent, usually the mother, an arrangement known as sole physical custody. They then may visit with the other parent.

2004). The court maintains that living arrangements should be based on the best interests of the child, which theoretically should not discriminate against men or women in any systematic way.

Most divorced families have sole physical custody arrangements, where the child formally resides with only one parent, and the other parent is awarded visitation. In about 8 of 10 divorces involving children, mothers have physical custody (U.S. Census Bureau 2005b). However, generally men do not seek physical custody. When men do ask for custody, they win either sole or joint custody more than 70 percent of the time (Mansnerus 1995).

In the past, fathers usually could not obtain custody of children unless the mother was proven to be unfit or there were other extenuating circumstances. Today, a small number of fathers seek and gain custody for a wide variety of reasons, often through mutual agreement with the mother. Their households tend to be better off financially than single-mother households, but they still have lower incomes and twice the poverty rate of families in which children live with both parents (Fields 2004).

Relative to white men, black men are less likely to have ever married the mothers of their children (Hamer and Marchioro 2002). Therefore, the circumstances of their custody arrangements are somewhat different. One study found that black fathers often became custodians of their children by default, often without any real discussion with the mothers. Most fathers were reluctant to accept their children at first but did so because of pressure or because they assumed the situation would be only temporary:

> I thought, "hey, she'll go in [into drug rehabilitation center], get cleaned up, and come and get these kids." But no! [laughing] it did not happen that way at all. These kids have been living with me; they are my pride and joy and have been since '94, that's when they came to live with Daddy. But in the beginning I tell you, I did not want any part of it and they [Child Service Workers] had to practically threaten me to do it—they made me realize there was no other place for my kids to go, and my kids had been through a lot of bad things with their mother. I didn't know the extent of it until they was living with me. (Hamer and Marchioro 2002, 121)

About 17 percent of families and courts are deciding on **joint physical custody**, meaning that children spend a near equal portion of time in the homes of both parents, perhaps alternating weeks or days within a week (U.S. Census Bureau 2005). It is far more common in dual earning families and those in which mothers have high levels of education or have failed to complete high school (Juby et al. 2005). This arrangement requires a tremendous amount of cooperation, and therefore tends to work best when both parents are willing to facilitate smooth transitions for the children. It is more difficult when there is conflict or tensions among parents or when one parent feels like the arrangement was thrust upon him or her (Arditti and Madden-Derdich 1997).

The results of joint physical custody are, for the most part, positive for children (Bauserman 2002; Fabricius 2003). Supporters of joint physical custody suggest that it lightens the economic and emotional responsibilities of single-parenthood and that it provides men with the opportunity to routinely care for and nurture their children, which, in turn, is in the child's best interests. It may also be in the fathers' interests (Bokker et al. 2006) because close relationships with biological children increase fathers' well-being as well. On the other hand, critics suggest that joint physical custody is disruptive to children's routines and school schedules. They claim that it can exacerbate conflict between parents because no two parenting strategies are identical and that it creates loyalty conflicts for children.

The Economic Dimension

There is reason to be concerned with the economic consequences of divorce, because divorce reduces the income of women and children considerably. One study reports that women's standard of living was reduced by 27 percent after a divorce, while that of men increased by 10 percent (Peterson 1996). A more recent study of 9,824 individuals approaching retirement found that those who divorced had considerably less wealth than those who had remained married throughout their lives (Wilmoth and Koso 2002).

Marital history is particularly important to women's wealth outcomes. Many divorced women are impoverished, or nearly so, by the divorce. Terry Arendell (1986) conducted in-depth interviews with 60 divorced women to see how they fared financially after their divorce. Most women initially assumed that after the divorce they would be able to maintain a middle-class lifestyle for themselves and their children. However, over time it became clear to virtually all women in the study that they had grossly underestimated the degree of financial hardship that they and their children would face. Ninety percent of them found that their incomes plummeted to the poverty line immediately after the divorce and remained very low for years. Most cut their expenses drastically or moved to cheaper housing so that they could pay their monthly bills. Few had any extra money left over after paying for the minimum necessities. Most felt trapped in their present situation and worried that their future would not improve. Women of all ages and at all income levels talked about the anxiety, depression, and despair that was associated with their financial difficulties—about trying to make ends meet after a divorce.

There are several reasons for the deleterious financial consequences of divorce for women. First, women generally retain custody of children. Eighty-three percent of single parents are mothers, and only 17 percent are fathers (Grall 2006). Therefore, childrearing responsibilities have a strong impact upon a single mother's lifestyle. For example, her employment opportunities may be more restricted than those of her ex-husband because the demands of children may force her to alter her work schedule, reduce her ability to work overtime, or limit opportunities for travel, relocation, and further training needed for advancement.

A second reason for divorced women's poor economic situation is the lower wages paid to women generally. Women who worked full time average about 81 percent of the wages paid to men. Women's median income is less than $30,000 a year among full-time year-round workers. Older women, women with less education, and minority women earn considerably less than this (U.S. Department of Labor 2006a).

Third, women are more likely to have intermittent work histories. Some couples had a mutual agreement that, at least while the children were young, the husbands would support the family while the mother stayed home to take care of their children. Not surprisingly, after several years of unemployment, some women are not able to reenter the labor force easily. Their skills might be outdated, and they cannot command high salaries. Yet, the legal system generally expects mothers to become self-supporting quickly.

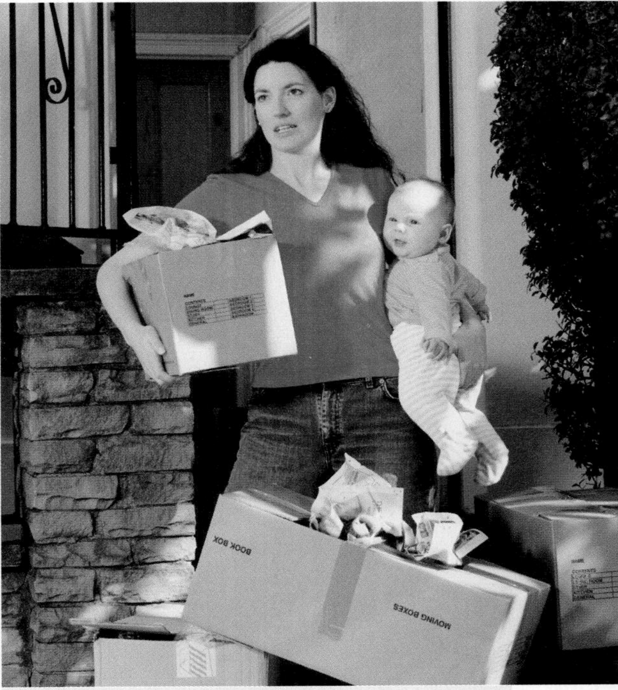

Two-thirds of divorced mothers move within the first year after a divorce, largely due to the significant drop in their income and financial resources. This can cause disruptions to children with respect to their schools or day care, friends, and social capital.

Child Support A fourth reason for divorced women's financial difficulties is that many noncustodial parents do not pay child support regularly or pay all that is owed (Grall 2006). Only 45 percent of families receive their full child support payment, as do only 35 percent of those families living in poverty (Grall 2006).

Why do so many parents fail to pay child support? One reason is that millions of families have no formal agreement about child support. Of about 14 million custodial parents, mostly mothers, only 8.4 million, or about 60 percent, have some type of legal child support agreement defined by the courts. Another 700,000 have a nonlegal, informal, support agreement, and 5.5 million have no child support agreement at all. It may seem odd that parents fail to have a child support agreement in place. Reasons for this are shown in Figure 14.2 and include sentiments such as "did not feel the need to make it legal" (32 percent), "other parent pays what they can" (29 percent), "other parent could not afford to pay" (27 percent), "did not want other parent to pay" (19 percent), or various other reasons (Grall 2006).

Moreover, of the 8.4 million who did have some sort of agreement, legal or nonlegal, one-quarter did not receive any payment at all, and less than half received their full payment, as shown in Figure 14.3. Mothers are even more likely to default on child support payments than are fathers, as are younger parents, those with less education, and blacks and Hispanics (Grall 2006). Moreover, only about one-third of parents paying child support provided health insurance for their children, paid their medical bills, or included health care costs in their child support payments, and thus custodial parents (usually mothers), end up paying these costs themselves (Grall 2006). Medical bills can easily pull families into poverty (Seccombe and Hoffman 2007).

Alimony One of the most contentious aspects of marital dissolutions may be the awarding of **alimony**, defined as post-divorce support for a former spouse (Shehan et al. 2002). Magazines and newspapers blare stories about extremely large alimony payments made by unfortunate fellows to greedy women. These stories fuel popular stereotypes

FIGURE 14.2 **Reasons No Legal Agreement Established for Custodial Parents, 2004 (Percent)**

Source: Grall 2006.

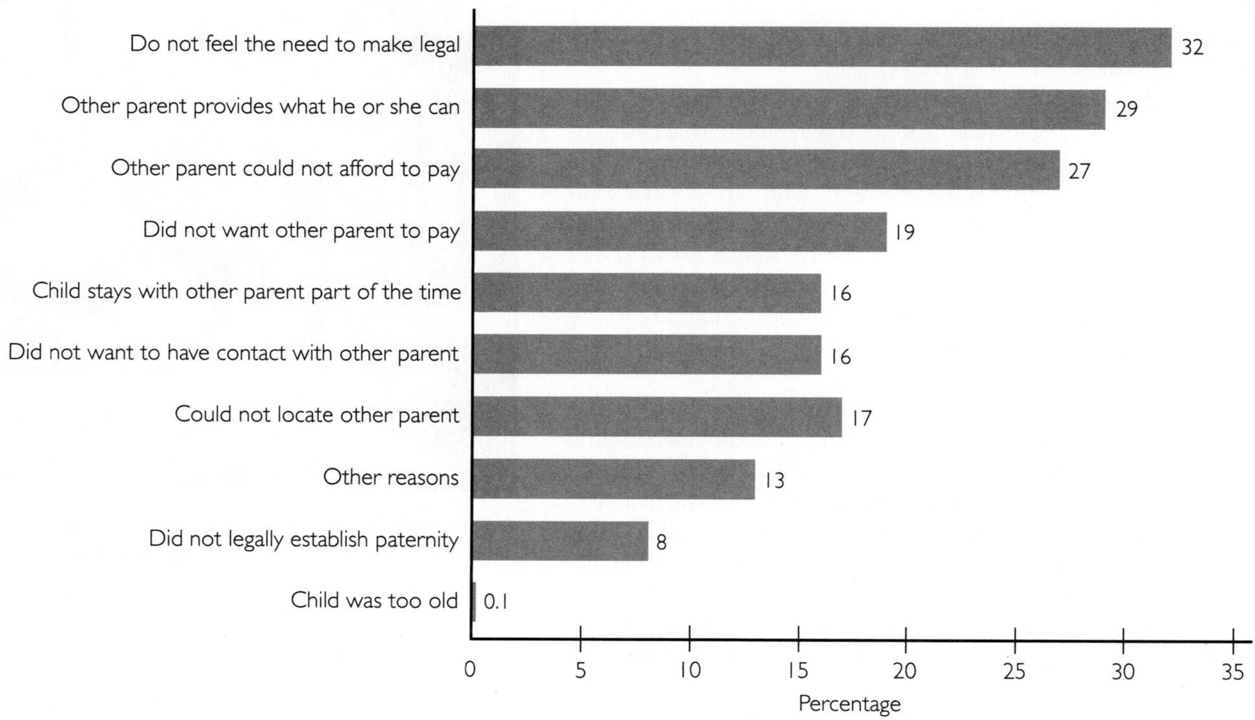

Note: Total of percentages exceeds 100 because respondents could list more than one reason.

about an alimony racket. In reality, alimony is awarded only rarely. A report by Kelly and Fox (1993) in the *Syracuse Law Review* showed that only about 15 percent of divorces include the provision of alimony. It can be awarded to either men or women, although usually the recipients are women because they are more likely to have been financially dependent within the marriage.

There are several factors a judge considers when deciding whether to grant alimony. These differ across states, but they usually involve things like the parties' relative ability to earn money, both now and in the future; their respective age and health; the length of the marriage; the age of any children; the amount of money and property involved; and the conduct of the parties. Generally, alimony is awarded if one spouse has been economically dependent on the other spouse for most of a lengthy marriage (Divorceinfo.com 2006).

The amount and duration of alimony payments can vary substantially. *Permanent alimony* provides payment for an indefinite or unlimited period of time and is designed to maintain a spouse's standard of living close to that which she or he had prior to the divorce. It may be awarded when the spouse is clearly unable to be self-supporting, such as

Custodial Parents Receiving Part or Full Child Support Payments Due (Percent)

Source: Grall 2006.

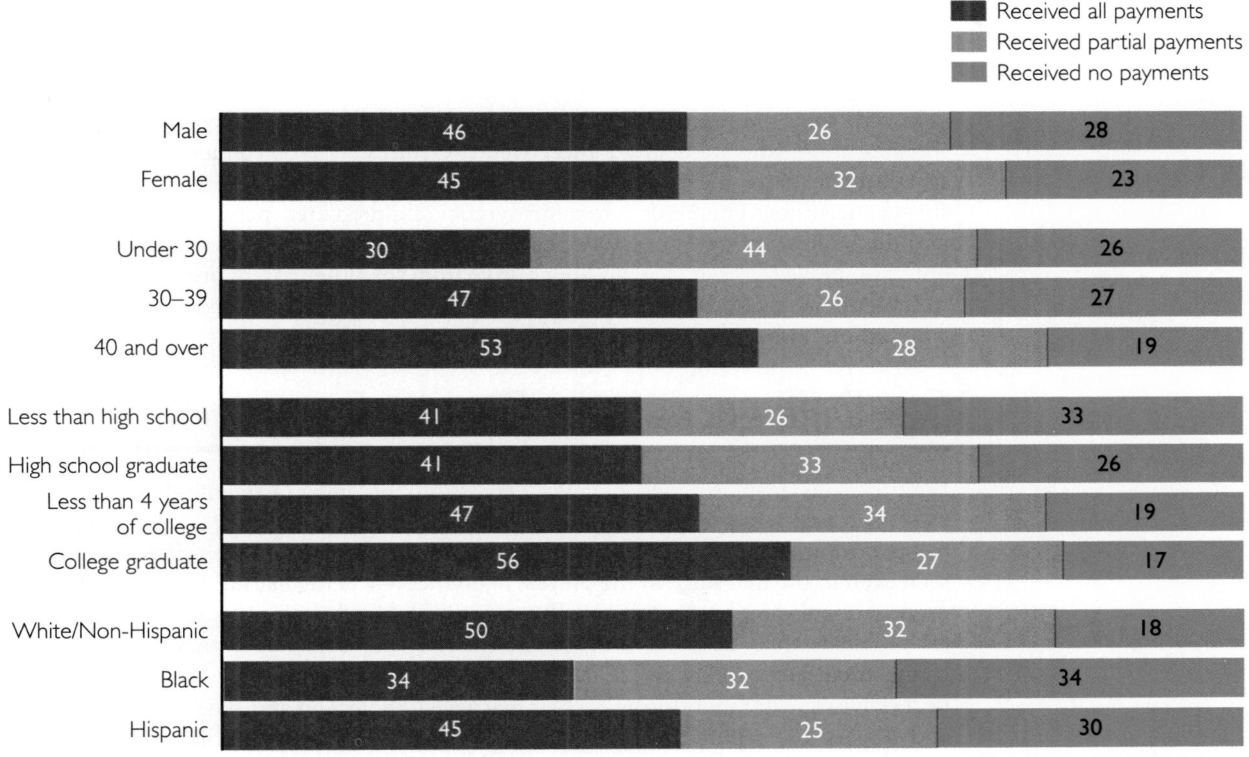

when she or he is elderly or in poor health. For example, a man who initiates a divorce from his 60-year-old wife who has been a full-time homemaker over the course of their marriage may be required to pay permanent alimony because it is unlikely that she will obtain employment sufficient to support herself. A woman in this situation may be referred to as a **displaced homemaker**.

Gross alimony is a fixed, lump-sum amount that can be paid in one, several, or monthly installments over a short period of time. It is designed to provide compensation for contributions made during the marriage. For example, a judge may require a man who has just completed medical school prior to the divorce to reimburse his wife for the financial costs she incurred putting him through school by paying her a lump sum of money.

Limited duration alimony involves payment over a fixed period of time, mandated by the judge or state statute. Its purpose is to help support the spouse during a period of transition and reorganization to become self-sufficient. For example, a judge may require a husband to pay a specific monthly sum for 1 year while the spouse secures work, or a few years until all the young children are in school.

Rehabilitative alimony is specifically targeted to improve the dependent spouse's employability. It may be awarded so the spouse can finish school or training. For example, a husband may be required to reimburse his former spouse for the costs associated with obtaining her college degree, including tuition, books, and partial or complete living expenses (Shehan et al. 2002).

The Community Dimension

Marriage joins families and friendship networks; divorce breaks them apart. Relationships can deteriorate or vanish altogether. Divorced people may feel uncomfortable with their old friends because of certain allegiances, or a newly single friend may threaten those who are married. Moreover, two-thirds of divorced mothers move in the first year after a divorce (McLanahan 1983). This may mean the severing of old ties with friends, neighbors, church or community groups, children's teachers, and their networks, and the building of new ones. One recent study reported that children of divorced parents who moved further than an hour's drive from the other parent are significantly less well off on many child mental and physical health measures compared to those children who did not move after divorce (Braver et al. 2003).

Sex Differences in the Divorce Experience

Both persons may experience guilt, depression, or embarrassment after a divorce. Husbands and wives experience divorce somewhat differently due to sex differences in opportunities and constraints deeply embedded in society. These differences can be seen even in the first stage in the process of divorce—voicing marital problems. Drawing on a national sample, Amato and Rogers (1997) found that wives report more marital problems than do their husbands, although they also found that wives tend to blame themselves for many of these problems. It is possible that this difference reflects wives' greater monitoring of their marriage (Thompson and Walker 1989). Amato and Rogers also report that husbands and wives see different problems affecting the relationship. Husbands were more likely than wives to say that their own hurt feelings, criticism, moodiness, and absence from home caused problems in the marriage. Wives claimed that it was their husband's jealousy and irritating habits that contributed to marital problems.

The process of divorce and its aftermath are generally stressful to both partners. Women, however, tend to show better emotional adjustment after a divorce (Arendell 1995). The stereotype of the carefree bachelor, free from the pressures of a wife and children, does not fit the reality of most men's lives. Men who are separated, widowed, or divorced have higher morbidity and mortality rates than do comparable women. This may have a variety of causes including that men tend to have a weaker network of supportive relationships and are more dependent on marriage (Hemstrom 1996).

One survey of over 400 divorced persons found that after 1 year, women tend to be more satisfied than men with a number of legal aspects of divorce, including custody of children, visitation, and property, and with financial settlements (medical insurance, school expenses, travel) with the notable exception of child support (Sheets and Braver 1996). Another study of 1,666 adults with household incomes of at least $100,000 found similar results: 37 percent of the men believed that the division of assets was equal compared to 52 percent of the women (Hammonds 1998). These findings are interesting given that women's standard of living declines more dramatically than that of men following a divorce.

Consequences of Divorce for Children

Approximately one-half of all divorce cases occur among families with children. While presumably at least one of the spouses *chooses* to divorce, children have little choice in the matter. Very few children want their parents to separate and divorce. In one study involving 28 children whose parents had separated, all the children wanted their parents to get back together (Holroyd and Sheppard 1997).

What are the social and psychological effects of divorce on children? It may be helpful to distinguish between short- and long-term effects.

Short-Term Effects

The process of divorce and the immediate aftermath can be very difficult for children (Sun and Li 2002). Using a large and nationally representative sample, the researchers examined the extent to which children's academic performance and psychological well-being before and after their parents' divorce compared with their peers whose parents did not divorce. They looked at four different points in time, from approximately 3 years before the divorce to 3 years after the divorce, and found significant differences between the two groups of children. It appears that exposure to marital conflict, not just the divorce per se, is associated with a wide range of problems in children (Buehler and Gerard 2002).

Before, during, and immediately after a divorce, parents may be less effective in their parental role because they are distracted and preoccupied with their own problems. Their distress may render them unable to offer the support, nurturance, and discipline that their children need (Buehler and Gerard 2002). Children often feel guilty and depressed. Young children in particular may feel that they are responsible for their parents' conflict and divorce; that if they had just behaved better, their parents would not have needed to divorce.

During this crisis period, children generally face many situations with which they must learn to cope. These may include (a) handling parental conflict; (b) weakened parental bonds; (c) coping with a reduced standard of living; and (d) adjusting to many transitions.

Handling Parental Conflict Sometimes parents involve children inappropriately in their disputes. They may try to use the children as a weapon to hurt the ex-spouse, get them to take sides in a dispute, or to use children as a way to pry out information. Parents may communicate their anger and hostility toward one another to their children and demean and ridicule their ex-spouse. During and after a breakup, children have fewer emotional and behavioral problems if their parents can cooperate or at least minimize overt conflict in front of the child.

Weakened Parental Bonds During a separation and after the divorce, children most often live with their mothers. How often do children see their fathers? For many children, the answer is "not very often." Frequency of visitation varies by many factors, including whether the child was born out of wedlock; the child's age, race, and ethnic background; mother's level of education; and family income (King 2006; King et al. 2004; Koball and Principe 2002; Schwartz and Finley 2005). Using data from the National Survey of American Families, Table 14.1 reveals several important findings. First, the marital status of parents at the child's birth influences the likelihood of frequent contact. Only two-thirds of children who were born out of wedlock report having seen their father at least once during the previous year, compared with about 80 percent of those children

TABLE 14.1 Proportion of Children Living with Single Mothers Who Visited Their Nonresident Fathers in the Previous Year, by Demographic Characteristics (Percent)

	Visited Father in Previous Year	
	Out of Wedlock	In Wedlock
Child's Age		
0 to 5	72	85
6 to 11	65	83
12 to 18	58	80
Child's Race/Ethnicity		
Hispanic	55	66
Black	73	83
White	63	86
Mother's Education		
Less than high school	63	70
High school or GED	67	83
More than high school	69	86
Family Income: % of Poverty Level		
Less than 100%	63	80
100% to 200%	70	78
More than 200%	72	88

Source: Koball and Principe 2002.

who were born to married parents. Second, black and white children were most likely to have seen their fathers and Hispanics were least likely. Third, children who have mothers with higher levels of education were more likely to have seen their fathers, and finally, children who live in families with higher incomes were more likely to have visited with their fathers during the previous year. Unfortunately, the quality of time spent with their fathers also tends to decline. Young adults from divorced families, as compared to intact families, received less mentoring and instrumental help from their fathers, and believed that their fathers were less nurturing and less expressive. These results were consistent across racial and ethnic groups, including native and foreign-born (Schwartz and Finley 2005). Other studies also indicate that relationships with fathers tend to decline after a divorce, although this may not be true of relationships with mothers (Boldac et al. 2006; Frank 2006). Divorce draws children closer to their mothers.

Why do so many noncustodial fathers fail to see their children regularly? The issue is more complicated than we might think at first. Certainly many fathers *choose* to ignore their children. They may remarry and begin new families, preferring to put their time, energy, and financial resources into their new family and spare themselves the conflict or emotional strains that come with seeing their children from a previous relationship. However, this is not the only reason that many fathers are absent. Sometimes mothers interfere with or discourage the relationship between father and children (Pearson and Thoennes 1998). A mother may see the visitation as a threat to her own relationships with the children or she cannot see past her own hurt and actually tries to sabotage any relationship between father and children.

Adjusting to Transitions A divorce forces children to go through many unsettling transitions. Some of these transitions include coping with a reduced standard of living; adapting to a visitation schedule with the noncustodial parent and adjusting to seeing the parent in unfamiliar surroundings; seeing their parents resume dating and meeting the new partners of their parents; if their parents cohabit, children's adapting to other adults moving in (and possibly back out of) the household; and experiencing stepfamily relationships as one or both of their parents remarry. Using data from a 17-year longitudinal study, Amato and Sobolewski (2001) found that children's psychological well-being generally declines with the number of family transitions.

Longer-Term Effects

Although most children adjust adequately over time to the transitions in their lives, some children continue to be plagued by depression, fear of commitment, or behavioral problems (Cartwright 2005). The impact of their parents' divorce continues to be felt for many years, even across generations. Amato and Booth (1991) compared the well-being of those adults who had experienced the divorce of their parents with those adults whose parents had not divorced. They found that the adults whose parents had divorced were more likely to be depressed and to have lower social, family, and psychological well-being, although the differences were not large.

Amato and Cheadle (2005) then examined links between divorce in a grandparent generation and outcomes in the grandchild generation, using a sample of nearly 700 adults. They found that divorce in the oldest generation was associated with lower education, more marital discord, weaker ties with mothers, and weaker ties with fathers in the grandchild generation. These associations were mediated by family characteristics in the middle generation, including lower education, more marital discord, more divorce, and greater tension in early parent-child relationships. In other words, divorce has consequences for subsequent generations, including individuals who were not even born at the time of the original divorce.

Other researchers have compared the achievements of children, adolescents, and adults who grew up in divorced and nondivorced households. They generally find that parental divorce is related to a variety of negative outcomes (McLanahan and Sandefur 1994; Sun and Li 2002; Wallerstein 2000; Wauterickx et al. 2006). Children whose parents divorce are more likely to become pregnant prior to marriage or impregnate someone, drop out of school and have lower academic achievement, experience more behavioral problems, use alcohol or drugs, have poorer health, are more likely to suffer from depression, and are more likely to be idle or unemployed. Certainly, not all children whose parents divorced have these outcomes. However, they are more *likely* to experience these problems, and the differences usually persist even after controlling for such factors as race, sex, and mother's level of education, year, and age. The significant drop in income seems to explain some of these differences, but often differences persist when income is controlled for as well.

Amato and Sobolewski (2001) examined the effect of divorce on adult children's psychological well-being. They found that marital conflict appears to erode children's emotional bonds with their mothers, whereas both divorce and marital conflict erode children's emotional bonds with their fathers. This places adult children at risk for distress, low self-esteem, and general unhappiness. Why does marital conflict potentially harm a child's relationship with both mother and father, but the actual divorce itself seems to have more negative repercussions for the child-father bond? It is probably related to the fact that many divorce children live with their mothers and see their fathers only sporadically.

These findings certainly do not mean that *all* children from divorced households experience these negative outcomes. Amato and Booth (1991) found that adults who grew up in conflict-ridden homes with parents who remained married to one another *also* experienced greater emotional problems. Moreover, they noted as well that adults who grew up in low-stress but divorced homes were about as happy as adults who grew up in low-stress homes with parents who remained married. Thus, Amato and Booth conclude that divorce does not always have harmful effects, especially if the parents' divorce causes minimum disruption in their children's lives.

Many children whose parents have divorced lead happy, well-adjusted, and successful lives; these studies simply mean that children of divorced parents are more likely to have these problems than are children from families in which parents have not divorced. In fact, many negative outcomes are related to the higher rates of poverty among children growing up in divorced households and are less apt to occur if the family has adequate financial resources.

The Million Dollar Question

Are children better off when their unhappily married parents remain married or are children better off when their parents divorce? Children do not fare well when there is tremendous conflict, violence, name-calling in the home, and when they are put in the middle of their parents' struggles. This is true regardless of whether parents divorce or remain married. In fact, many researchers suggest that it is the amount of conflict rather than a divorce per se that causes the most harm to children. For example, Jekielek (1998) examined data on families from the National Longitudinal Surveys of Youth. Looking at 1,640 children between the ages of 6 and 14, she found that children in high conflict but intact families had lower levels of well-being than did children whose highly conflicting parents divorced. A study by Amato and Booth (1997), which was based on telephone and in-person interviews conducted in 1980 and 1992 with a nationally representative sample, found that of the children who were in families with high marital conflict in 1980, they were actually doing *better* in 1992 if their parents had divorced than if they had stayed together. Likewise, Strohschein (2005) reported that antisocial behavior in highly dysfunctional families actually decreased once the parents divorced. Amato and Booth also found that children from relatively low-conflict families were *worse* off if their parents divorced than if their parents had remained together. These findings suggest that the worst situations for children are to be in either (1) a high-conflict marriage that does not end in divorce or (2) a low-conflict marriage that does end in divorce.

If a marriage contains severe conflict, a divorce may indeed be better for the children than to be subjected to a family in continued turmoil. However, it appears that most unhappy marriages do not display extreme forms of conflict. In the longitudinal study by Amato and Booth (1997), only one-quarter of parents who divorced between 1980 and 1992 reported any sort of domestic violence or even reported that they disagreed "often" or "very often" with their spouse. In fact, only 30 percent reported at least two serious quarrels during the previous month (Amato and Booth 1997). Consequently, the authors conclude that the majority of children whose parents divorce probably experienced relatively low conflict, and therefore would perhaps be better off if their parents had stayed together (1997).

Repartnering and Remarriage

When in the throes of a divorce, it can be difficult to think of it as a new beginning—yet for most people, it is exactly that; an opportunity to begin anew. The majority of divorced individuals do find another life partner. Generally, finding a new partner is the most important factor in improving life satisfaction for both men and women. Compared to divorced persons, remarried individuals have significantly lower rates of both economic and psychological distress and depression (Shapiro 1996).

As shown in Box 14.2, rebuilding relationships requires a critical level of introspection and analysis. Persons who are young and married only a short time may find it relatively easy to begin dating again. Dating may be more difficult for people who have been married for longer periods because they may feel awkward or be unaware of changing dating norms. Who should initiate a date? Who does the paying? Should I meet him/her at the restaurant or have them pick me up at my house? Who pays for the babysitter? What sexual expectations will there be? Am I supposed to like her children right away? Are my children supposed to like him right away?

One study asked remarried women to indicate the number of men that they had dated prior to meeting their future spouse. Most claimed that they dated between three and five men. One in 10 had dated only their future spouse, and one-third of the women indicated that they had dated more than 10 men prior to meeting their future spouse (Montgomery et al. 1992). Although "rebound" is cautioned among the newly divorced, there does not appear to be any evidence that waiting longer before repartnering results in a more stable relationship (Wolfinger 2006).

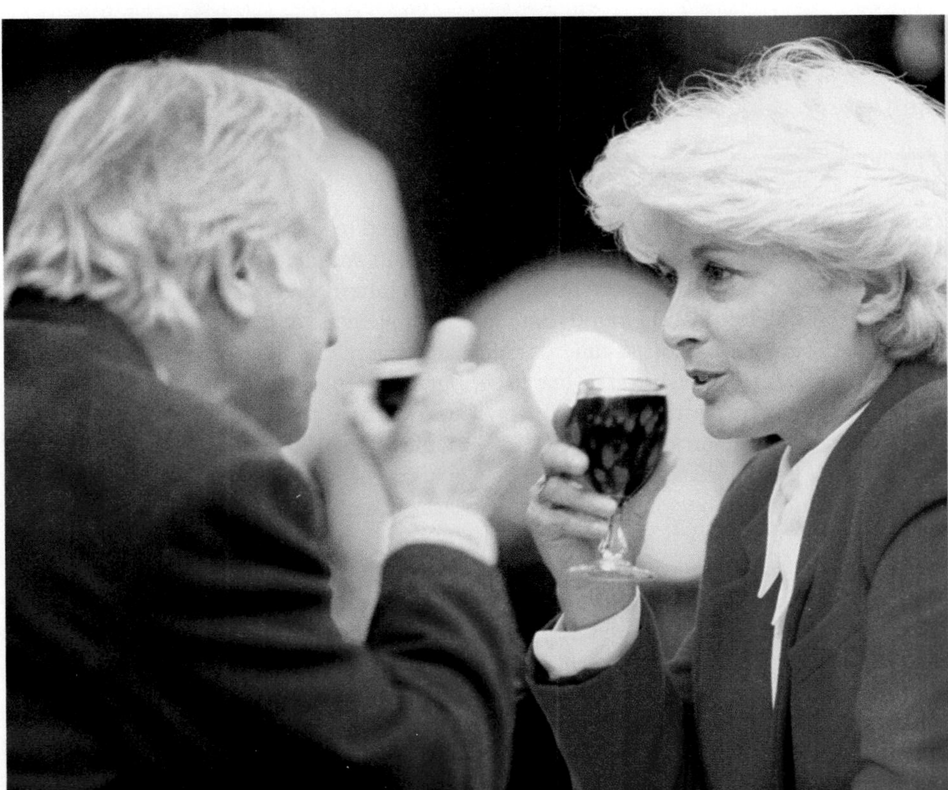

Approximately two-thirds of women and three-quarters of men remarry after a divorce. Why are men more likely to remarry than are women? The answer to this question is steeped in our gendered cultural norms.

BOX 14.2 Families as Lived Experience

Rebuilding When Your Relationship Ends

Divorce is a stressful and highly emotional experience. Here, nine divorcing individuals describe a wide range of emotions that they experienced during the process of ending their marriages.

Fear was my biggest obstacle. I was afraid of all the changes I had no control over, and at the same time, I was afraid nothing would ever change. My whole life was being influenced by my fears! I was afraid of being alone, and at the same time isolating myself, afraid of never really being loved again and yet pushing love away when it got too close. . . . I was completely stuck, paralyzed by my own fear. . . . It wasn't until I admitted my fears, listed them and talked about them openly that they lost their power over me.–Jere

In my first marriage I was the parent taking care of him. In my next love relationship I would like to have a parent to take care of me and nurture the little girl inside of me. And then in my third love relationship maybe I can become balanced and have a healthy relationship.–Janice

Maria and I had lots of friends and family around all the time. Most weekends we'd have a bar-b-que or go over to her sister's place or take a picnic with two or three other couples. Since we split up none of these people ever call me or drop by. How come married people don't seem to want us around when we're single?–Jose

I spent thirty-three years as a homemaker, raising a large family. I had the security and comfort of upper-middle-class living. When I became a single parent, with responsibility for our youngest child and faced with the task of becoming self-supporting, with few if any marketable skills, I was literally paralyzed with fear.–Joanne

I don't know what came over me. I saw his car in the parking lot and I knew he had met his girl friend and left in her car. I went over and let the air out of all four tires. Then I went behind the building and waited until they returned so I could watch them find his car with the tires flat. I watched them trying to solve their problem and I felt so good. I've never done anything like that before in my life. Guess I didn't know how angry I could get.–Jean

When I was a child, my father continually warned me about getting a "big head" and becoming "stuck

Cohabitation and Repartnering As reported in Chapter 7, cohabitation is increasingly common among previously married and middle-aged adults, and can be viewed as an extension of serious dating or an alternative to marriage altogether. Bulcroft and Bulcroft (1991) found that, among single persons over age 55 who date, cohabitation is favored almost as much as marriage. For many older persons, cohabitation may not simply be a precursor to marriage, but may replace it altogether. This is why some researchers interested in relationships after divorce prefer to focus on "repartnering" rather than "remarriage" per se (Lampard and Peggs 1999).

When a couple decides to remarry or cohabit, the decision usually occurs quickly after the relationship begins, unlike first marriages where dating may last for years before a commitment to marry. In their study of remarriage, Montgomery, Anderson, Hetherington and Clingempeel (1992) found that 80 percent of the women in their sample dated their future spouses for no more than a year before cohabiting together. Of these women, 38 percent dated for 3 months or less prior to cohabitation. Things progress more quickly, perhaps because divorced men and women are more focused about what they are looking for in a partner, have learned from previous mistakes, or are a better judge of character. Ganong and Coleman (1989), however, found that many couples who were preparing for remarriage failed to address critical issues such as financial matters.

on myself." Then I went to church and learned that I had been born sinful. At school it was the jocks and the brains that got all the attention. Finally I married so there would be someone who thought I was worthwhile. It made me feel good that someone cared. But then she became a pro at pointing out my faults. I finally reached a point where I began to believe that I was truly worthless. It was then that I decided to leave the marriage.–Carl

After my divorce, looking for ways to meet new people, I took a small part in a little theater production. One night at rehearsal I suddenly realized that's what I'd been doing in my marriage—reciting lines. I wasn't myself, I was a character in a romantic comedy-tragedy.–Scott

I felt many times in my marriage that I was trapped in a prison of love. It was hard to be myself when there were so many demands and expectations placed upon me. When I first separated I felt even worse. But now I have found that I can fly. I can be me. I feel as if I have left the chrysalis and have become a butterfly. I feel so free.–Alice

I've become aware that living as a single person is an affirmation of strength and self—not an embarrassing admission of failure. I'm more relaxed in the company of others—I'm no longer wasting emotional energy being a social chameleon. Post-marital guilt, self-doubt, and questions like "Will I ever love again?" are greatly diminished. I am happy as a single person—something I had not thought possible.–Larry

Source: From *REBUILDING: When Your Relationship Ends*, Third Edition © 2006 by Bruce Fisher and Robert E. Alberti. Reproduced for Karen Seccombe by permission of Impact Publishers, Inc., P.O. Box 6016, Atascadero, CA 93423 USA. Further reproduction prohibited.

CRITICAL THINKING QUESTIONS

1. How might these feelings associated with getting a divorce and rebuilding when the relationship ends differ between men and women?
2. Do you think the process of divorce and rebuilding is different for cohabiting couples or gay and lesbian couples compared to those couples who are legally married?

Remarriage

We often think of remarriage as a relatively new phenomenon that has accompanied a rising divorce rate yet it has always been a common feature of family life in the United States primarily because of high rates of widowhood (Phillips 1997). Today 9 in 10 remarriages occur following a divorce, rather than a death. A remarriage that occurs after a divorce has very different characteristics from a remarriage that occurs after death, primarily the fact that the ex-spouse may still have a commanding presence.

Demographic Trends: Who Remarries and When? Approximately two-thirds of women and three-quarters of men remarry after a divorce. On average, men remarry within 3 years, compared to 5 years for women; however, sex alone does not predict when or if a person will remarry. For women, the likelihood of remarriage is lower when they are older or have children (particularly children under age 6). For example, one nationwide study found that among persons under the age of 30, men and women were equally likely to remarry within 3 years (Lampard and Peggs 1999). However, among couples divorcing in their 30s, only 31 percent of women had remarried within 3 years, as compared to 42 percent of men. These differences are accentuated among couples divorcing in their 40s and 50s; less than 1 percent of women who divorce during their 50s will repartner in 3 years, while 41 percent of their male counterparts will do so. Why is the difference so large?

- Men are able to initiate contact more easily. They have a lifetime of experience as the initiator in social relationships. Moreover, men tend to have a larger circle of casual friends and acquaintances than do women, and these can be drawn upon to meet potential partners. Their incomes are considerably higher than those of women, and therefore men have more money to treat someone to a dinner, movie, or some other type of date.
- There is a double standard of aging. As men age, they are considered to be "distinguished" whereas women are considered to be less attractive as they grow older.
- The pool of eligible partners is larger for men than it is for women because of cultural norms that allow men to marry younger women. A 40-year-old male could easily marry a 40-year-old woman, or a 30-year-old woman, or even a 20-year-old woman without people giving it much thought, but older women are generally not granted the same latitude.
- Women are more likely than men to have children living with them. The presence of children tends to decrease one's chances of remarrying. Women may be cautious about bringing someone new into the family, and men may be hesitant to take on the financial and emotional responsibility that comes with a ready-made family.

Marital Satisfaction Second and subsequent remarriages are not necessarily happier than first marriages and are actually more likely to end in divorce (Ceglian and Gardner 1999; Hobart 1991). This may reflect a selection bias; people who remarry obviously consider divorce as an option to end an unhappy relationship. Remarried couples, however, are generally more prone to disagreements, and these are largely related to issues surrounding stepchildren. Stepchildren generally make the remarried relationship more tense because of arguments between stepchildren and stepparents or between parents and stepparents on issues related to child rearing or discipline (Brown and Booth 1996; Kurdek 1999).

Stepfamily Relationships

Stepfamilies are families in which one or both of the adult partners has at least one child, either residing with them or elsewhere. The majority of children first enter a stepfamily through their parent's cohabitation rather than through marriage, although often the parent later marries. Stepfamilies have an intricate weave of complex relationships. For example, children in stepfamilies can be referred to as (1) siblings (biologically related to same parents); (2) stepsiblings (not biologically related, but parents are married to each other); (3) half-siblings (share one parent biologically); (4) mutual child (a child born to the remarried couple); (5) residential stepchildren (live in the household with the remarried couple more than half of the time); and (6) nonresidential stepchildren (live in the household less than half of the time).

Stepfamily relationships receive a lot of bad press. They have been stigmatized as harmful environments for children and adolescents, a view that is shared in many different cultures (Ganong and Coleman 1997). For examples, views of the "wicked stepmother" are rampant, found from Shakespeare to Cinderella fairy tales, with connotations of cruelty, jealousy, and neglect.

Stepfamilies can also be an enriching experience (Crohn 2006; Michaels 2005). For example, children living in stepfamilies gain exposure to new behavior patterns and lifestyles. They also may profit from living with an adult who is possibly more objective than a biological parent. Children may also benefit from an increased standard of living made possible by two incomes and their parents' greater happiness at being involved in another relationship. Many children live in warm and loving stepfamilies. The 100,000 stepfamily adoptions conducted each year are a testament to this, indicating their love and commitment (Levine and Sallee 1990; Wolf and Mast 1987). Among minority groups, living in a stepfamily is often reported to have significantly positive effects on a child's well-being. Family researchers have found that high-quality relationships with stepfathers may have a positive effect on internalized problems such as depression or feelings of worth, and on externalizing problems, including impulsivity (White and Gilbreth 2001).

Nonetheless, stepfamilies face considerable challenges (Ganong and Coleman 2004). Despite their prevalence, society has really not acknowledged them in any systematic way. What formal rules and rights do stepfamily members have toward one another? Family scientist Jason Hans (2002) notes that stepparents are "legal strangers" to their stepchildren; the law does not protect the relationship during marriage or following a divorce.

Stepfamilies have been referred to as a **normless norm**; they are very common, yet the expectations, obligations, and rules within these families are vague and confusing (Lamanna and Riedmann 1997). Roles are ambiguous, and people do not know what is expected of them. There is no socially prescribed script for how family members are expected to relate to one another (Svare et al. 2004). Should a stepparent behave like a biological parent, like a friend, or like someone else entirely? To what extent can stepparents discipline their stepchildren? How are stepparents and stepchildren supposed to feel about one another? What names do children call their stepparent? Indeed, do stepparents and their stepchildren even include one another as part of their "family"? For example, if your father remarries when you are an adult and living away from home, would you consider his new wife your "stepmom"? Or would you think of her as "my dad's wife"? Would you think of her grown children, whom you may have never even met, as your "stepsiblings"? What type of relationship would you likely foster with them?

Stepfamilies are very common, but the rules and expectations for step-relationships are not very clear. This can create many challenges that stepfamilies must work to overcome.

How Do Children Fare in Stepfamilies?

How do children from stepfamilies fare? While there are many fantastic stories, on average, the news is not particularly encouraging. Just as children from single-parent households face an increased chance of certain negative outcomes, so do many children who live in stepfamilies. In other words, generally the well-being of children in stepfamilies is not significantly better than the well-being of children in divorced single-parent families.

Certainly not all stepchildren experience problems. Many stepchildren grow up feeling secure in happy, loving homes made possible by their parent's remarriage (Sample 1999). The longer a stepfamily has been together, the more positively children describe the relationship with their stepfathers.

Still despite these important exceptions, in general, stepchildren (and children living in single-parent households) earn lower grades in school, complete fewer grades, and score lower on achievement tests (Bogenschneider 1997; McLanahan and Sandefur 1994; Pong 1997; Teachman et al. 1997). They also have higher rates of depression and emotional problems, particularly when conflict between two households is present (Hanson et al. 1996; Zill et al. 1993). They are also more likely to exhibit behavioral problems such as involvement with alcohol and drugs, nonmarital childbearing, idleness, or being arrested.

In a small study of 15 adolescents, they were interviewed in depth about their experiences during their parents' divorce, remarriage, and stepfamilies. They responded to the divorce largely with resignation. Reactions to the single-parenting phase were divided, with about half expressing negative feelings about their parent's dating. Remarriage and stepfamilies were generally negative events. Adolescents expressed concern about their powerlessness, and the disruption resulting in living space, relationship expectations, and new rules. They felt excluded and resentful about sharing their parent with another person and about their reduced intimacy with their parent (Stoll et al. 2005).

Explanations for Added Risk Why do children living in stepfamilies face an increased chance for these outcomes? Several theoretical explanations have been proposed.

- *Stress*. Remarriage and repartnering involve many stressful changes and potential conflicts for both adults and their children (Crosbie-Burnett 1989). These include possibly moving to a new residence and adapting to new family members and new routines, all of which could contribute to poorer school performance, depression, and behavioral problems (Menaghan et al. 1997).
- *Economic and social capital deprivation*. Children living in stepfamilies and in single-parent families are disadvantaged because of their lower incomes and reduced levels of social capital (connections to other adults or institutions in the community) related to the divorce. Remarriage does not repair these deficits completely, perhaps because stepparents are expending resources on their children from a prior union, or because stepparents are not fully invested in their stepchildren (Bogenschneider 1997; McLanahan and Sandefur 1994). Children reared in stepfamilies created by marriage do seem to fare better than children living with parents in a cohabiting union, at least with respect to income and likelihood of poverty (Morrison and Ritualo 2000).
- *Parents may be investing time and energy into their new relationships rather than into child rearing*. For example, parents may not spend as much time talking with their children, helping them with their homework, or monitoring their friends and activities as they did prior to the remarriage because they are preoccupied with their new partner (Downey 1995; Pong 1997). Also, parents may become less involved in their children's lives when a new child is born into the family (Stewart 2005).

- *The lack of norms for stepfamily behavior*. Stepchildren fare worse on average than children in two-parent biological families because stepfamily members may be unsure how to relate to one another. They do not know how to express their feelings, and there is a lack of institutional support for helping them overcome difficulties.

Social Policy and Family Resilience

Children from divorcing families and stepfamilies are at special risk of behavioral and emotional problems, but they can gain remarkable strength from many sources, including neighbors, schools, and peers. Family scientists Kathleen Boyce Rodgers and Hilary Rose (2002) studied over 2,000 seventh-, ninth-, and eleventh-grade adolescents to examine the importance of these other relationships in time of divorce. They report that, although parents are of primary importance to the well-being of children, peers, schools, and neighbors are also critical in helping adolescents navigate risks and develop skills necessary to become productive and healthy adults. Youth clubs, organizations, sports, churches, or peer helper groups in schools may allow adolescents experiencing their parents' divorce to build supportive networks that can counterbalance the other stressors in their lives.

Example: Initiatives to Limit Divorce

There are divergent opinions throughout the world about the costs and benefits of divorce. Some countries believe that divorce is largely inappropriate if children are involved. Others see it as wrong regardless of whether the couple has children. Table 14.2 represents data from the International Social Survey Program (ISSP), a cross-national extension of the General Social Survey, which has monitored trends in U.S. society since 1972. The ISSP now covers 31 countries. It designs annual questions, uses probability samples, and sample sizes average about 1,200 to 1,400 per country. As shown in the table, the percentage of people agreeing with the statement "Parents ought to stay together if they have children," ranges from 26 percent in the Netherlands and 28 percent in Canada to 79 percent in Japan and 81 percent in Poland. In fact, the majority of respondents in the Philippines and Japan agree that the couple ought to stay together even if there are no children involved.

Many people in the United States are concerned about divorce and its consequences and believe that measures should be taken to lower the divorce rate (Maher 2006). What measures should be taken? A telephone survey was conducted with a representative sample of adults in Arizona, Louisiana, and Minnesota to assess the degree of support for a number of measures that could lower the divorce rate (Hawkins et al. 2002). The findings are reported in Table 14.3. Approximately two-thirds of adults in the Arizona and Louisiana samples and 56 percent of adults in the Minnesota sample believe that society would be better off if divorce were harder to get. Hawkins and associates (2002) also found that about 8 in 10 respondents in Arizona, Louisiana, and Minnesota believe that premarital counseling is important to making a marriage successful, and 9 in 10 support counseling if the couple is unable to resolve problems that come up in their marriage. About two-thirds of adults in Arizona and Louisiana and 58 percent of adults in Minnesota believe that long waiting periods would help a couple work out their problems. Finally, general attitudes about covenant marriage are either positive or mixed in all three states, with particular support in Arizona and Louisiana—both states that have covenant marriage statutes.

Given these attitudes, it is not surprising that many states are funding initiatives to strengthen marriage (as shown in Chapter 8) and passing legislation to make divorce

TABLE 14.2 Attitudes Toward Divorce in 23 Countries

Parents Ought to Stay Together if They Have Children (% Agreeing)		Couple Ought to Stay Together Even if No Children (% Agreeing)	
Netherlands	26	East Germany	10
Canada	28	Netherlands	10
Austria	28	New Zealand	12
East Germany	28	West Germany	13
New Zealand	30	Slovenia	13
United States	**33**	Czech Republic	14
West Germany	36	Austria	15
Slovenia	42	Great Britain	16
Israel	42	Israel	16
Great Britain	42	Australia	16
Spain	42	Canada	16
Australia	43	Russia	17
Russia	45	Norway	17
Northern Ireland	45	Hungary	17
Norway	48	Sweden	17
Ireland	49	**United States**	**18**
Sweden	49	Spain	19
Hungary	55	Ireland	20
Czech Republic	55	Italy	21
Italy	58	Northern Ireland	22
Philippines	62	Bulgaria	29
Japan	79	Poland	42
Poland	81	Philippines	51
Bulgaria	—	Japan	54

Note: Questions about divorce with children not asked in Bulgaria.

Source: Smith 1999.

more difficult to get. Although major changes may be difficult to enact, such as eliminating no-fault divorce, it has not kept some grassroots or religious groups from trying. There have been a number of successes (Hawkins et al. 2002; Maher 2006). For example, a Georgia law allows no-fault divorce only if both parties agree to the divorce and if no children are involved. Florida has implemented a 3-day waiting period for marriage licenses if couples do not seek premarital education. Florida also now requires high schools to offer a marriage education course parallel to driver education. Oklahoma committed $10 million in unspent welfare funds to an initiative to strengthen marriage and reduce divorce by 30 percent by 2010. As mentioned in Chapter 8, President George W. Bush targeted $1.5 billion toward a Healthy Marriage Initiative to not only encourage people to marry, but to stay married as well.

TABLE 14.3 Attitudes About Divorce and Covenant Marriage

	Total (%)	Arizona (%)	Louisiana (%)	Minnesota (%)
Society would be better off if divorce were harder to get				
Agree	62	66	63	56
Neither	7	7	5	11
Disagree	31	27	32	34
How important is it to making a marriage successful that the couple has counseling about marriage before the wedding?				
Very or somewhat important	80	77	81	80
Not very or not at all important	21	23	19	20
How important to making a marriage successful is it that the partners agree in advance to seek counseling if they are unable to resolve problems that come up in their marriage? (lower scores = disagree)				
Very or somewhat important	91	90	92	90
Not very or not at all important	9	10	8	10
Long waiting periods to get a divorce help people to get over their anger and work out their problems				
Agree	66	66	71	58
Neither	11	12	6	17
Disagree	23	22	24	25
General attitudes about covenant marriage				
Supportive	39	43	41	32
Mixed	47	44	48	49
Opposed	14	13	12	20

Source: Hawkins et al. 2002.

Covenant marriage options now exist in only three states—Louisiana, Arkansas, and Arizona—and allow couples the option of selecting a more rigid set of legal requirements surrounding their marriage (Maher 2006; Spaht 2002). Covenant marriage would require (Hawkins et al. 2002):

1. some marriage preparation
2. full disclosure of all information that could reasonably affect the decision to marry
3. an oath of lifelong commitment to marriage
4. acceptance of limited grounds for divorce (e.g., abuse, adultery, addiction, felony imprisonment, separation for two years)
5. marital counseling if problems threaten the marriage

So far, very few couples are choosing covenant marriage. Only about 2 percent of new marriages in Louisiana fall into the covenant category, and about 40 to 50 percent of spouses who chose the traditional marriage option had never heard of covenant marriage (Sanchez et al. 2002). In Arizona and Arkansas, less than one-half of 1 percent choose this option (Stritof and Stritof 2006).

Conclusion

The United States has one of the highest rates of divorce in the world, and to understand why this is the case, we must look at structural, historical, cultural, and personal factors. This chapter explored rising and falling divorce rates, divorce policy, and how families cope with a divorce and its aftermath. Children are particularly vulnerable to the hardships associated with divorce, including a greater likelihood of poverty and other behavioral and social problems. Most divorced persons remarry or repartner after the divorce. Stepfamilies, however, have many unique characteristics compared to two-parent biological families and face a number of specific challenges.

Key Terms

Alimony: Post-divorce support for a former spouse. (p. 453)

Cross-sectional divorce rate: A divorce rate at only one point in time. (p. 440)

Crude divorce rate: The number of divorces that occur out of 1,000 people in the population. (p. 440)

Displaced homemaker: A full-time homemaker who is divorced by her husband. (p. 455)

Joint legal custody: Both the custodial and noncustodial parents retain their legal rights with respect to their children. (p. 450)

Joint physical custody: Children spend substantial or nearly equal portions of time in the homes of each parent. (p. 452)

Legal custody: Refers to who has the legal authority to make important decisions concerning a child. (p. 450)

No-fault divorce: A divorce in which the couple can say they have irreconcilable differences and do not wish to assign blame. (p. 446)

Normless norm: Something common enough to be considered normative, but with vague and confusing expectations, obligations, and rules. (p. 465)

Physical custody: The child's legal residence. (p. 450)

Refined divorce rate: The number of divorces that occur out of every 1,000 married women. (p. 440)

Stepfamilies: One or both of the adult partners has at least one child, either residing with them or elsewhere. (p. 464)

Resources on the Internet

Parents Without Partners
http://parentswithoutpartners.org
Parents Without Partners (PWP) provides single parents and their children with an opportunity for enhancing personal growth, self-confidence, and sensitivity toward others by offering an environment for support, friendship, and the exchange of parenting techniques. PWP provides free referrals to local PWP chapters, which offer social and educational opportunities for single parents.

National Fatherhood Initiative
www.fatherhood.org
The National Fatherhood Initiative (NFI) was founded in 1994 to stimulate a society-wide movement to confront the growing problem of father absence. NFI's mission is to improve the well-being of children by increasing the number of children growing up with involved, committed, and responsible fathers in their lives. NFI offers a quarterly newsletter and a catalog of books and videos focusing on fatherhood issues.

Divorce Support
www.divorcesupport.com
This is a website devoted to connecting users to the most valuable and comprehensive divorce-related information on the Internet. They offer helpful and supportive information about divorce, child custody, child support, visitation, modifications, separation, alimony, spousal support, divorce laws, statutes, and much more.

Single Parent-Tips
www.singleparent-tips.com
This site offers advice on custody, visitation, dealing with ex-spouses, legal matters, and effective parenting for single parents.

Further Reading

Ahrons, C. 1994. *The Good Divorce: Keeping Your Family Together When Your Marriage Comes Apart*. New York: HarperCollins.

Amato, P. R., and A. Booth. 1997. *A Generation at Risk: Growing Up in an Era of Family Upheaval*. Cambridge, MA: Harvard University Press.

Basch, N. 2001. *Framing American Divorce*. Berkeley: University of California Press.

Ganong, L., and M. Coleman. 2004. *Stepfamily Relationships: Development, Dynamics, and Intervention*. New York: Springer.

Harvey, J. H., and M. A. Fine. 2004. *Children of Divorce: Stories of Loss and Growth*. Mahwah, NJ: Lawrence Erlbaum Associates.

Hetherington, M., and J. Kelly. 2003. *For Better or Worse: Divorce Reconsidered*. New York: W. W. Norton and Company.

Marsiglio, W. 2004. *Stepdads: Stories of Love, Hope, and Repair*. Lanham, MD: Rowman and Littlefield.

McLanahan, S., and G. Sandafer. 1994. *Growing Up with a Single Parent: What Hurts, What Helps*. Cambridge, MA: Harvard University Press.

Stacey, J. 1996. *In the Name of the Family*. Boston: Beacon Press.

Wallerstein, J. S., and S. B. Blakeslee. 2003. *What About the Kids? Raising Your Children Before, During, and After Divorce*. New York: Hyperion Books.

Wallerstein, J. S., J. M. Lewis, and S. B. Blakeslee. 2000. *The Unexpected Legacy of Divorce: A 25-Year Landmark Study*. New York: Hyperion Books.

Whitehead, B. D. 1998. *The Divorce Culture: Rethinking Our Commitments to Marriage and Family*. New York: Knopf.

CHAPTER 15

Summing It Up: Families and the Sociological Imagination

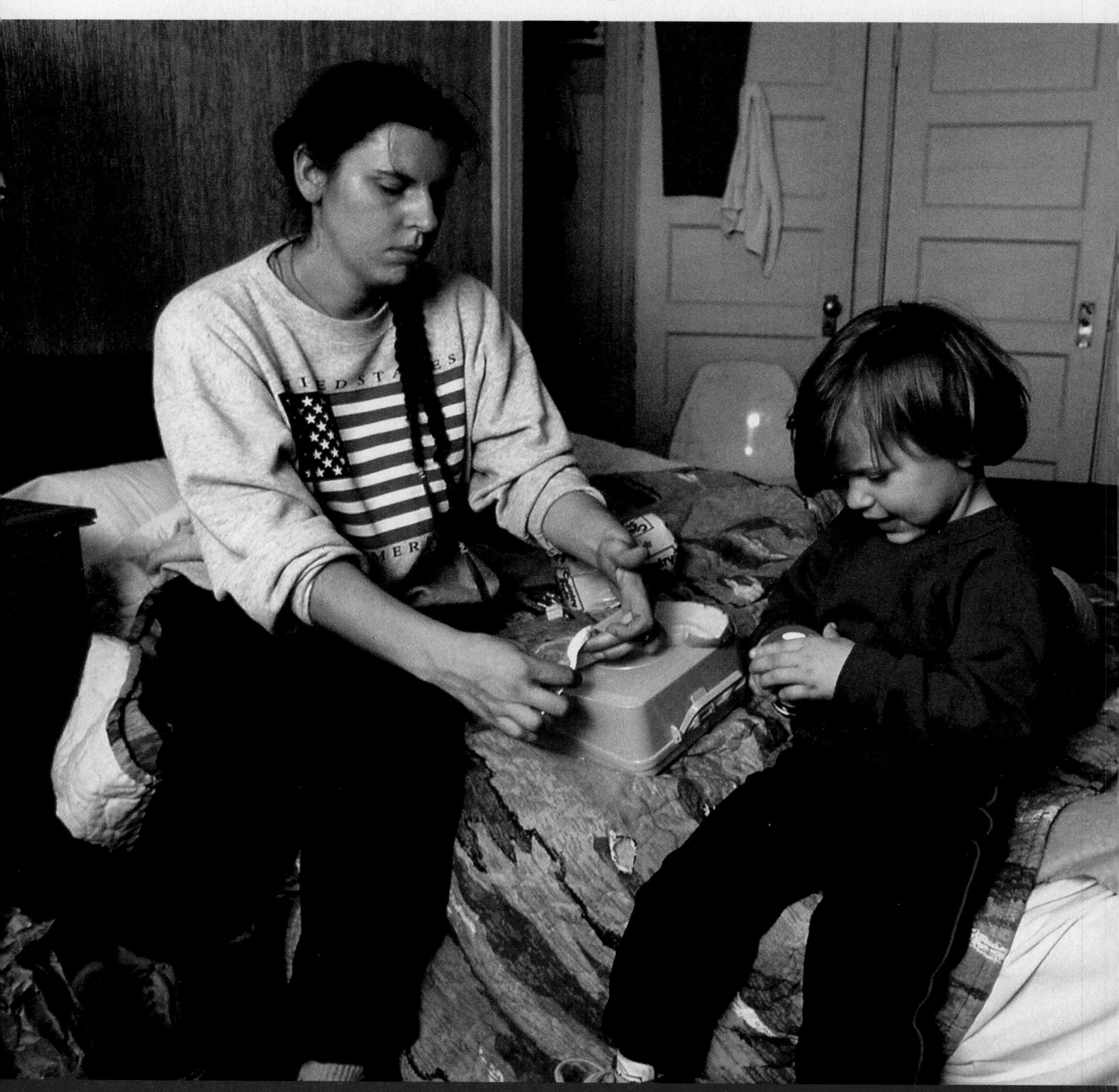

CHAPTER OUTLINE

CHAPTER PREVIEW

This chapter summarizes the contributions that the sociological imagination can make to our understanding of families. A family is far more than a personal relationship among related individuals; family is also a powerful social institution inextricably linked with other social institutions. In this chapter you will review:

- The sociological imagination, with its comparative and empirical approaches, as a powerful lens for understanding both the micro and macro aspects of families and personal relationships
- Families as both a social institution and a private personal relationship
- Social inequality with its powerful influence on family life
- Family policies as they reflect historical, cultural, political, and social factors
- Understanding families in the United States through a comparative perspective
- Trends for the future

John was born in a homeless shelter. His mother Susan was hardly a stereotypical candidate for homelessness. She was 25 years old, a receptionist at a corporation, and attending trade school. When the company suffered heavy losses, she was fired. Pregnant with John, she quickly headed down the slippery slope into homelessness. All the helping hands that should have been there let her down. The unemployment office refused to give her benefits unless she dropped her trade school classes to concentrate on finding work. Susan was trying hard to find work and believed a college degree would make her more employable. The welfare office caseworkers told her that she was ineligible for cash welfare because she was technically eligible for unemployment benefits, never mind that she wasn't collecting a penny of it. She had to go to soup kitchens for meals. Susan found a few temporary jobs that postponed her eviction, but for only 4 months. Homelessness is tough for anyone, but especially for a pregnant woman. Every 28 days she had to move from one shelter to another, dragging her belongings with her. She continued to look for work but was caught in the "catch-22" predicament of the homeless. She needed a job to secure a permanent address and phone number but without a permanent address and phone number, she couldn't land a job. When John was born, the job search was put on hold and she faced new child care demands that added obstacles to her path out of homelessness.

*It is suppertime and Marie, the mother of two young children and one handicapped adult daughter who contracted spinal meningitis as a toddler, surveys the nearly bare shelves in the kitchen—some beans, vegetables, and canned potato soup. The week's meat, which she buys when it is on sale, has been rationed and stretched as far as possible, and is gone. Marie always makes sure the children eat dinner first, although it might be just canned soup, and sometimes she goes hungry for the night. "As long as they get something," she says. Marie has been working for over a decade and a half; she is not on welfare. When she tried to apply for food stamps last year, she was told that she earned one dollar above the income requirement to be eligible. She is a child care provider. She works hard every day to make sure the toddlers in her care are safe and well fed, comforted when they cry, and given as much love and stimulation as possible. For her crucial work she brings home so little money she can barely feed and house her own children. The average child care worker makes about $18,000 [in 2005] and usually without health benefits. (*Children's Defense Fund 2002*)* ■

The stories of Susan, Marie, and their children portray accounts of struggle and hope. Are these just isolated stories? How can we interpret these circumstances? This chapter will synthesize the contributions that a sociological imagination can make to understanding something as common and yet as unique as families. It will review the importance of using a sociological perspective to understand families as a social institution and for understanding the everyday interactions that go on within families. The chapter will then review the basic themes of the text that were introduced in Chapter 1, providing examples from the previous chapters to illustrate and summarize these themes. Finally, the chapter concludes with a look forward. Given what we know about families today, what might we expect in the future?

The Sociological Imagination

Most people think they are experts in understanding the dynamics of the society in which they live. After all, when you experience something every day, what is there not to know? However, the text has asked us to move beyond personal experience to explore general patterns situated in a particular society, culture, or historical period. A sociological imagination reveals that many commonsense assumptions do not hold up when we look at the broader social trends, and it brings to light new insights about the way we live. These new insights expose both the opportunities and constraints in our lives.

As we have seen throughout this text, the social structure we live in and the social positions we hold shape our life experiences in many ways. Understanding social structures allows us to learn that many seemingly personal problems or isolated events are really social in nature and therefore often require broad policy changes for their solution. Moreover, the better we understand the ways in which social structures shape our personal lives, the better we may be able to adjust those social forces to pursue the life that we desire. A sociological imagination asks that we step back from our ordinary routines so that we may critically evaluate the strengths and weaknesses of different ways of organizing our lives (Mills 1959).

Susan, Marie, and Their Children

The quandaries of Susan, Marie, and their children described in the opening vignette are not simply personal problems or isolated events. These women and their children are poor or nearly so, but it is not because of laziness or inadequate parenting. On the contrary, Marie is doing socially productive work that millions of families depend on every day. It is not her fault that the pay for child care workers is notoriously low, roughly around $18,000 per year (U.S. Department of Labor 2006f) and fails to provide health care benefits. If she left the work she loves to get a higher-paying job with benefits, who then would care for the nation's children? Society depends on someone to do this work, yet balks at paying a living wage for it.

Likewise, Susan had an important and respectable, if low-paying, job as a receptionist. In addition, she was going to school to improve her employment prospects further. Through no fault of her own, she was laid off. She looked for assistance afterwards, but found none. The available programs thwarted her every effort to improve her circumstances. As structured, they virtually assured that she would stay in low-paying, dead-end jobs for the rest of her life. Given her ambition, Susan refused the benefits that would stifle her attempts at upward mobility. However, the result was that she lost her apartment and had to move into a homeless shelter, where she later gave birth to her son John.

Instead of placing the blame on individuals, let us look deeper within these two women's stories to see what particular insights a sociological imagination can provide.

Jobs, Income, and Poverty Both Susan and Marie are poor or nearly so. Are these women unique? Unfortunately, no. Poverty is a significant problem for many people, especially women (DeNavas-Walt et al. 2006). As shown in Chapters 4 and 11, the data reveal that women's incomes are significantly less than men's and have seen little improvement in recent years. The median weekly income of female full-time workers was under $600 in 2005, which is 81 percent of what men earn. The pay gap is even higher for older workers and for minority women (U.S. Department of Labor 2006b). Is this an individual problem or a social one?

The predicaments of women like Susan and Marie are rooted in the fact that the labor market is highly segregated into "men's" jobs and "women's" jobs (U.S. Department of Labor 2006b). Occupations dominated by women, such as child care worker or receptionist, tend to be low paying with little opportunity for advancement. Yet, there is nothing inherent in these occupations that warrants the low wages paid to them. The jobs are respectable and provide a valuable service. Thus, Susan and Marie's low incomes reflect far more than personal inadequacy; they reflect social inequalities that are embedded in the social structure.

Poverty is quickly becoming a women's problem, as the popular term *feminization of poverty* suggests. Women are far more likely than men to be impoverished, and single mothers are a particularly vulnerable group. About 30 percent of single mothers live below the poverty line (U.S. Department of Labor 2006a). If women earned the same pay as men (controlling for the same number of hours, education level, age, union status, and living in the same region of the country), their annual incomes would rise by about $4,000, and poverty rates would be cut in half.

Overall, 14.4 million families have critical housing needs because they cannot afford to pay rent. The demand for assisted housing overwhelms the supply: only about one-third of poor renter households receive any housing subsidy (Daskal 1998; National Coalition for the Homeless 2004). Not surprisingly, women and children make up the fastest-growing segment of the homeless population. Nationally, children make up nearly 40 percent of the homeless population. Unemployed women, without social and financial support, find themselves in a precarious situation, made even more difficult by the needs of their children. Nonetheless, it does not have to be this way in a country as wealthy as the United States.

Health Insurance It is unlikely that Susan, Marie, or their children have health insurance. They are part of the more than 47 million Americans who are without health insurance to meet their most basic health care needs (DeNavis-Walt et al. 2006). Millions more are underinsured; their high deductibles or copayments render their insurance virtually useless except in the most catastrophic conditions.

As shown in Chapter 5, living without health insurance can have serious financial, emotional, and health consequences for the entire family. If even one person within a family is uninsured, all share in the anguish of trying to pay medical bills and suffer the consequences when they cannot. Families without health insurance are more likely to delay or forgo seeking needed medical care. They are twice as likely to postpone seeking medical care, over four times as likely to forgo needed care, and are more than twice as likely to have a needed prescription go unfilled. Children may not get needed immunizations as preventative care.

Is the lack of health insurance a personal issue or a social problem? When nearly 16 percent of Americans (47 million) find themselves in the precarious situation of being uninsured, Americans must examine the social structure to best understand the problem and to seek solutions to it.

In the United States we rely heavily on workers to receive their health insurance from an employer as a fringe benefit to supplement their wages. However, about one in four persons employed full-time does not receive insurance on the job. Employers are not required to offer health insurance to their workers, and an increasing number are choosing not to do so because of rising costs. Low-income workers such as Marie and those who work in small firms are at particular risk. Only 41 percent of workers earning less than $10 an hour have access to employer-sponsored insurance (Collins et al. 2004). Moreover, by virtue of their employment, workers like Marie may not qualify for federal government programs such as Medicaid. Losing or changing jobs can also put employer coverage at risk, as Susan quickly found out.

Linking health insurance to employment is virtually unheard of in other developed nations and in many developing ones (Budrys 2005). What does employment have to do with health insurance, they ask? Instead, these countries have a national health insurance program that is funded by taxes, much the way education, parks, and police services are funded. This means that access to health care is considered a public right and available to all citizens, regardless of ability to pay. Virtually no one is left uninsured. As we might expect, countries with national health insurance programs tend to have much better health outcomes than does the United States. Their life expectancy is longer than ours, and their infant mortality rates are lower. Moreover, universal coverage tends to be much less expensive than the U.S. system (Budrys 2005).

Nonmarital Childbearing and Child Support Referring back to the cases of Susan and Marie, both are single mothers. Susan has never been married and had her child out of wedlock. It may be tempting to ask: Isn't Susan responsible for creating her own problem?

A simple answer might be "yes," if we take a cursory and dim view about out-of-wedlock births. However, a sociological analysis digs deeper to uncover the complexity of seemingly simple situations and their solutions. After all, Susan is hardly unique in having a baby outside of marriage. Today, over a third of all births occur outside of marriage, a significant increase from just a decade ago (Hamilton et al. 2005). Many women become pregnant and opt for an abortion rather than to carry the child to term. Susan did not want an abortion and chose to have her baby instead. Should we criticize her for that decision?

We tend to associate nonmarital births with teens, but the data in Chapter 10 reveal that the number of teenagers giving birth is on the decline. Instead, the largest increases in nonmarital childbearing are occurring among older women who have completed high school or have some college behind them. For most women the pregnancy was unplanned, but an increasing number of single women are becoming mothers by choice, many feeling that they have been unable to find a suitable partner but still long for the benefits associated with motherhood. In other words, having a child outside of marriage is becoming increasingly normative, following the trends in many other industrialized nations.

In other countries, having a child out of wedlock does not pose the great financial problem that it does in the United States (UNICEF Innocenti Research Centre 2000). Of 22 selected industrialized countries, the rates of poverty among children in single-parent households are highest in the United States. The reason children in other countries are better off is because they and their single mothers are eligible for many programs to help sustain them, including paid maternity leaves, child or family allowances, housing subsidies, health insurance, and free or low cost child care. The United States has a laissez-faire approach; parents are expected to assemble their own assistance. However, U.S. programs are limited, income thresholds are extremely low, and the social service maze can be daunting. The result is that many families, just like Susan and Marie's, fall through the cracks of the safety net.

Finally, it is easy to judge Susan for the choice she made (either to deliberately have a child outside of marriage or to be lax about using birth control), but let us remember that she did not impregnate herself—nor did Marie. Shouldn't we also pose questions for the fathers of their children, most notably, why aren't they paying child support?

Susan and Marie are among millions of women who fail to receive support from their children's fathers. As noted in Chapter 14, only 60 percent of custodial parents have some type of support agreement for their children (Grall 2006). Some of these are legal agreements and some are simply informal agreements between the parties. Among families who did have some sort of agreement, most received only a partial payment, or none at all. In 1988 and again in 1996 the federal government increased efforts to collect child support from absent parents, and there has been some improvement (Turetsky 2005); however, compliance is still woefully inadequate. Yet child-support dollars matter tremendously to families like Susan's, Marie's, and millions of others, and can prevent them from slipping into poverty.

A sociological imagination reveals that many seemingly private struggles are really large-scale social problems. When millions of women are paid poverty-level wages, when health insurance is a privilege dependent on the good will of employers rather than a right of citizenship, when critical safety nets are missing, and when children receive no or inadequate financial support from their noncustodial parents, these are much more than "Susan's" or "Marie's" problems. These are examples of social problems, requiring broad changes in U.S. social structure and policies.

A Comparative Perspective

As we learned in Chapter 1, the sociological imagination uses a comparative perspective to study families. If we want to understand contemporary patterns in the United States, we must compare ourselves to something else, such as other cultures or to other points in history. Is the U.S. divorce rate high or low? Is its rate of child poverty high or low? Answers to these questions are meaningless unless we ask, "Compared to what?" The U.S. divorce rate is indeed high compared to other countries, but it is much lower than it was 30 years ago. Likewise, the rate of child poverty is much higher than other countries that have universal programs specifically designed to enhance the lives of children, but again, it is much lower than it was 30 years ago.

In the past it was easier to ignore what was happening in the world, but this is no longer the case because societies are becoming increasingly interconnected. New technologies, immigration, commerce across borders, the outsourcing of jobs, and greater ease in world travel and communication have increased visibility. Societies are no longer isolated entities. What happens in one corner of the world affects us all. HIV/AIDS provides a vivid example of this interconnectedness.

HIV/AIDS Chapter 7 discussed the epidemic of HIV/AIDS in the United States, yet as common as this disease is in this country, its prevalence and incidence are dwarfed by what is happening around the globe. The effects of widespread HIV and AIDS ravage many millions of people around the world. A report by the United Nations reveals that the number of people living with HIV climbed to 39.5 million persons in 2006, with no signs of abatement. There were about 4.3 million new infections in 2006 alone, and nearly 3 million deaths. This brings the number of deaths since 1981—the year of the first documented case—to 25 million persons (UNAIDS 2006a). Over two-thirds of people living with HIV are men who most often contracted it through injecting drugs or from sex with other men. However, the number of women infected is increasing quickly in these countries, and they most often become infected from heterosexual intercourse.

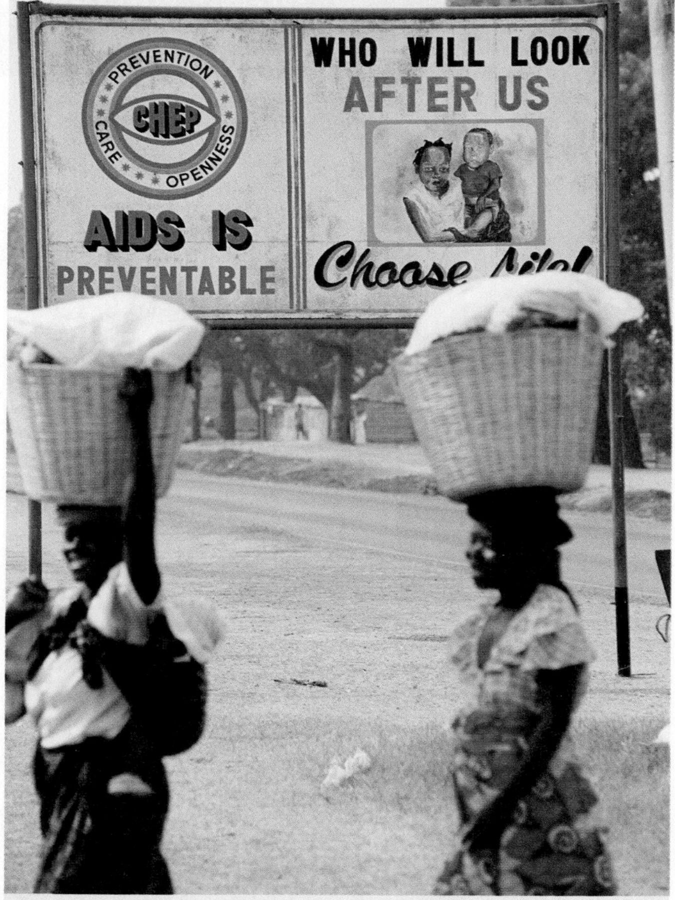

The HIV/AIDS epidemic is devastating families and the economies of many countries in sub-Saharan Africa. It is a widespread problem because countries have been slow to develop prevention and treatment programs, given the enormous stigma surrounding the disease.

The HIV/AIDS problem occurs everywhere, but it is particularly acute in sub-Saharan Africa, as shown in Map 15.1. Although the region has just over 10 percent of the world's population, it is home to more than 60 percent of all people living with HIV—25 million. In 2006 alone, nearly 3 million became newly infected, while 2.1 million died of AIDS.

The full impact of AIDS is not well understood. Its effects come in waves; first the infection, followed by opportunistic diseases, then later by a wave of AIDS-related illness, and then death. However, its effects are still accumulating across families and communities to the national and later, international levels. HIV/AIDS is ripping families apart. Millions of children are orphaned, living a life on the street in which they fight to survive (Guest 2003; UNAIDS 2006b). Food scarcities are exacerbated because families can no longer tend to their crops. Life expectancy has dropped because of the high number of AIDS-related deaths in many countries: In Zimbabwe the life expectancy at birth declined from 55 years in 1970 to 37 years in 2005. HIV and AIDS are shrouded in stigma, making effective prevention and treatment exceedingly difficult. Even governments are slow to acknowledge the epidemic because of its stigma.

In many parts of the world, especially sub-Saharan Africa, women suffer from HIV and AIDS at rates that outpace men. In sub-Saharan Africa, women make up almost 57 percent of adults living with HIV. On average in this region, there are now 13 women living with HIV for every 10 infected men, and the gap continues to grow. Most women are infected by their husbands. The patriarchal values embedded in the culture make it virtually impossible for these women to protect themselves from their husbands' sexual demands (UNAIDS 2006b).

HIV/AIDS is particularly devastating the young adult population. Nearly 12 million young people aged 15 to 24 around the world are living with HIV/AIDS, as shown in Map 15.1. Young people in this age group account for more than half of all new infections. As expected, the situation among young people is particularly acute in sub-Saharan Africa, especially among young women aged 15 to 24 who are 2 to 6 times more likely to be HIV-positive than are men of similar ages (UNAIDS 2006b). This highlights the vulnerability

MAP 15.1

Eye on the World: Adults and Children Estimated to Be Living with HIV in 2006

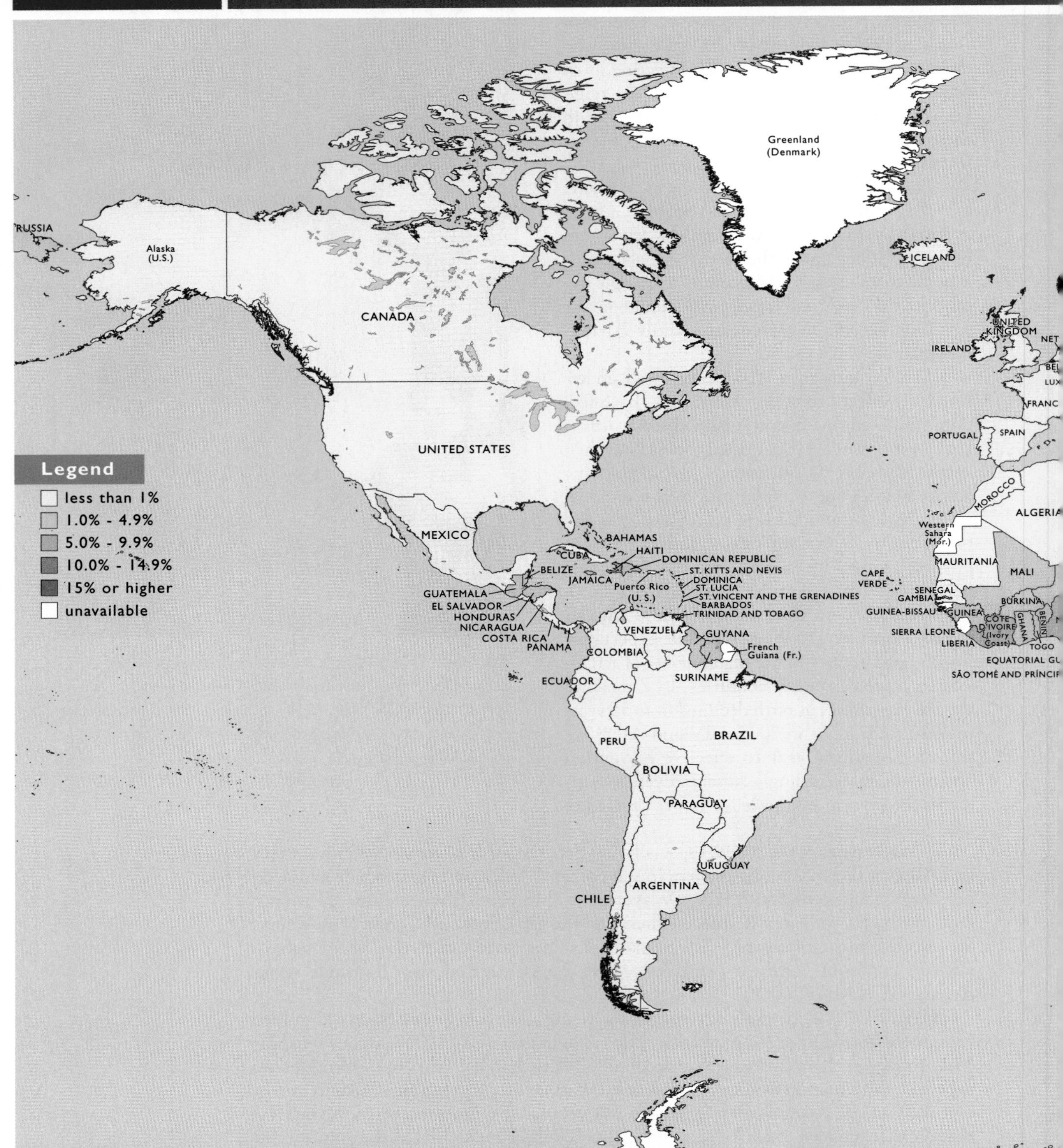

Source: UNAIDS 2006a

and exploitation of young girls, as reported in Box 15.1. There, young people lack solid information about HIV/AIDS, and misconceptions are rampant even in countries with HIV epidemics. In Somalia, only 26 percent of girls have heard of AIDS and only 1 percent know how to avoid infection. Young people are also likely to experiment sexually; boys avoid using condoms and girls are afraid to make them do so. Many young girls have sex with older and infected men, often under coercion or because he, in turn, has offered to feed her and her family. What does the United States have to offer other countries with respect to HIV/AIDS prevention and treatment?

Although HIV and AIDS remain significant problems in the United States, there have been widespread education efforts coupled with important breakthroughs in medical treatment. Fewer Americans are becoming infected, and those who are infected are living longer productive lives. If medical treatment is available in the United States, why is it not made available to those countries that need it the most? Decisions about public health measures are often rooted in politics or quests for profit. Tired of waiting for government action, many private organizations, such as the Bill and Melinda Gates Foundation (created by Microsoft billionaire Bill Gates) have poured many millions of dollars into HIV/AIDS prevention and cures.

An Empirical Approach

Most of us have opinions about how families are supposed to be structured, what they are supposed to do, or how they are supposed to behave. There are several universal functions for families, as revealed in Chapter 2. Families are associated with marriage, the regulation of sexual behavior, reproduction and socializing children, property and inheritance, economic cooperation, social placement, and intimacy.

Despite these universal expectations, precisely how these are implemented may differ based upon religious teachings, cultural customs, or societal laws. For example, how do we decide whom to marry? As we saw in Chapter 7, many cultures deem that parents will choose their children's mates, and the children would not want it any other way. Sometimes children are betrothed to each other. Different norms operate elsewhere; most young people raised in the United States would object strongly if their parents picked out their mate.

Likewise, as we learned in Chapter 13, views toward violence run the gamut. Some cultures condone violence against wives as a natural prerogative of husbands, whereas in other cultures violence is overtly frowned upon (although it may occur nonetheless). As another example, Chapter 14 revealed that one hundred years ago divorce in the United States was rare (although desertion was not). Today divorce is common, although declining the U.S. rate remains among the highest in the the world.

What can we depend on to help us understand family dynamics? Sociologists and other family scientists do not rely on common sense, personal experience, authority figures, or the sentiment "It's always been that way so it must be right." Instead, they use an empirical approach, in which they answer questions through a systematic collection and analysis of quantitative or qualitative data. The goals of empirical research can either be to describe some phenomena, to explain the cause-and-effect relationships, provide insight on why certain events do or do not occur, or to understand the meanings attached to behaviors. Empirical research findings often shatter popular ideas, and reveal their misconceptions.

Effects of Divorce on Children A compelling example of the importance of empirical research can be seen regarding the effects of divorce on children. For several decades the sentiment was that divorce did little harm to children. "Staying together for

BOX 15.1 Our Global Community

HIV/AIDS: Girls Are Very Vulnerable

In the United States, HIV/AIDS is far more common among men than among women. However, in other parts of the world, the most common victims of HIV/AIDS are heterosexual young women, as this report by UNICEF reveals.

Though as a global average there are slightly more men infected with HIV than women, adolescent girls are at a very high risk of getting infected. This pattern is especially clear in sub-Saharan Africa, the region most severely affected by HIV/AIDS. More than two-thirds of the newly infected 15- to 19-year-olds in this region are female. In Ethiopia, Malawi, the United Republic of Tanzania, Zambia, and Zimbabwe, for every 15- to 19-year-old boy who is infected, there are five to six girls infected in the same age group.

There are a number of reasons why girls in sub-Saharan Africa are becoming infected younger and dying earlier than boys are. In the major urban areas of eastern and southern Africa, epidemiological studies have shown that 17 to 22 percent of girls aged 15 to 19 are already HIV-infected compared with 3 to 7 percent of boys of similar age. This indicates a "sexual mixing" pattern whereby older men are having sex with young girls. In many countries where economic conditions make it difficult for girls to afford school fees, some seek favors of a *sugar daddy* (an older man who offers compensation in cash or in-kind exchange for sexual favors), engage in transactional sex (exchange sex for money or goods on an occasional basis), or enter sex work (willingly or forced) to pay for school, support their families, or take care of themselves.

The age-mixing is fueled by the dangerous myth among men in some places that having sex with a virgin can "cure" HIV. Many men also assume that younger girls are not yet infected. Cultural norms related to sexuality prevent many girls from taking active steps to protect themselves. In cultures where it is vital for girls to be virgins at marriage, some girls protect their virginity by engaging in unsafe sexual practices such as unprotected anal intercourse.

Biological factors also play an important role. The risk of getting infected during unprotected vaginal intercourse is always greater for women than men; the risk for girls is further heightened because their vaginal tracts are immature and the tissues tear easily. In Kisumu, Kenya, where over a quarter of girls said that they had had sex before age 15, one in 12 contracted the virus before her fifteenth birthday.

The danger of infection is highest among the poorest and least powerful. Young girls living in poverty are often enticed or coerced into having sex with someone older, wealthier, or in a position of authority, such as an employer, schoolteacher, or older sugar daddy, in order to stay in school or support themselves and their families. A study in Botswana found about one in five out-of-school adolescent girls reporting that it is difficult to refuse sex when money and gifts are offered; girls as young as 13 had engaged in sex with sugar daddies.

Marriage on its own offers no protection against HIV for young women, especially if their husband is much older. Another study in Kisumu, Kenya, reported that as many as half of the women with husbands at least a decade older were infected with HIV; by contrast, no women were infected whose husbands were only 3 years older or less. Another study of nearly 400 women attending the city's sexually transmitted disease clinic in Pune, India, found the vast majority were married and had never had sex with anyone but their husbands. Lacking the power to negotiate safe sex practices, many young brides may be even more vulnerable to HIV/AIDS and sexually transmitted diseases than unmarried girls.

Interventions to stem HIV must target boys as well as girls. A mutually respectful relationship can free both young men and young women from the dangers of coerced or unwanted sex and enable them to feel comfortable discussing sexual matters and negotiating safety and protection.

Source: Adapted from United Nations Children's Fund 2002.

CRITICAL THINKING QUESTIONS

1. How does patriarchy contribute to a woman's inability to negotiate safe sex and protect herself from HIV/AIDS?
2. How can the spread of HIV/AIDS be stopped in sub-Saharan Africa?

the sake of the children" became a meaningless phrase, because unhappily married adults argued that their children would be made better off by the divorce. However, as revealed in Chapter 14, a large and growing body of empirical research suggests that we may need to rethink this view; most children are not necessarily better off when their parents divorce. Many are decidedly worse off. Empirical studies reveal that children likely experience a significant drop in income and are subject to numerous transitions, such as moving or going to a new school. Although most children adjust adequately over time to the transitions in their lives, many are plagued by depression or other behavioral problems for many years. Adults whose parents had divorced are more likely to be depressed and to have lower social, family, and psychological well-being. These differences usually persist even after controlling for such factors as race, sex, mother's level of education, year, and age. The significant drop in income seems to explain some of these differences, but often differences persist when income is controlled for as well.

Are these problems related to divorce per se or are they a byproduct of witnessing parental conflict? We no longer need to guess at the answer. Using empirical data from large and representative samples, researchers have addressed these questions and found some interesting answers. If a marriage contains severe conflict, such as domestic violence, a divorce may indeed be better for the children. However, in cases of relatively low conflict, children benefit when their parents stay together. Therefore, empirical research has revealed that previous thinking may have been in error; it is likely that the majority of children whose parents divorce probably would be better off if their parents had stayed together.

Using the Sociological Imagination: Themes of the Text Revisited

Several themes have run throughout this look at families. We have witnessed how families are more than simply a private relationship; families are also a social institution and reflect and are reflective of other institutions in society. We have uncovered patterns of social inequality, noting their importance in fully understanding family structure and family dynamics. We have emphasized that family policies do not exist in isolation, but reflect historical, cultural, political, and social factors, and finally, we have found that understanding American families requires a comparative perspective.

Theme 1: Families Are Both a Public Social Institution and a Private Personal Relationship

Because families fulfill many of our own personal needs, it is easy to forget that families are a social institution with a set of beliefs and rules organized to meet basic human needs. In addition to talking about *your* specific family, we talk about *the* family. Families are a social institution, in much the same way our political, economic, religious, health care, and educational systems are social institutions.

Families can best be understood by examining how they interact with (and are influenced by) other social institutions within society. Families cannot merely be separated out as "havens" from the rest of society. Patterns of education, religious customs, economic systems, and political systems all shape family attitudes, behaviors, and the constraints and opportunities experienced by individual members. For example, education can determine the normative age at which young people marry in a society; religious customs can determine the degree of patriarchy; the economic system can determine the degree of struggle families are likely to experience meeting their basic needs for food, shelter, and clothing; and political systems can determine the degree to which a family experiences an open democracy or lives under tyranny.

In all likelihood, most people do not reflect very often on families as social institutions. Instead, most people focus on the lived day-to-day experiences and think about their families in very individualized terms, failing to see the interconnection to larger social structures.

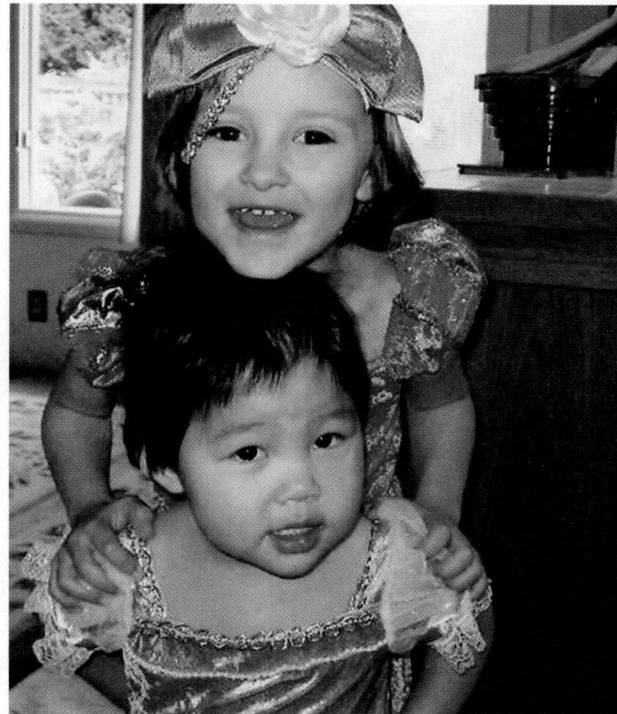

Chances are, these sisters do not spend a lot of time thinking about their family as a social institution.

Example: Childbirth and Cesarean Sections As discussed in Chapter 9, one certainly personal and private family experience is childbirth, yet it is shaped by the health care system and powerful special interest groups. Many expectant parents write personalized birth plans so that the experience will closely match their expectations. However, in reality, the birthing experience for most women is a highly medicalized impersonal event as witnessed in the growing rate of surgical births.

The rate of cesarean delivery increased to over 30 percent of all births in the United States in 2005, the highest rate ever reported. This rate reflects a nearly 40 percent increase from the mid-1990s, and cesareans are now the leading operation performed in the United States (Hamilton et al. 2005). The likelihood of having a surgical birth depends on far more than medical necessity; it varies by race and ethnicity, and it even varies by state. For example, Utah, Idaho, Alaska, and New Mexico all have cesarean rates below 20 percent; New Jersey and Louisiana have rates over 30 percent. Puerto Rico's rate is nearly 45 percent.

To put these numbers into perspective, leading health organizations, including UNICEF, the World Health Organization (WHO), and the United Nations Population Fund (UNFPA) agree that a cesarean section rate above 15 percent indicates improper use of the procedure (Maine and Bailey 2001; March of Dimes 2006). Births by cesarean section involve considerable risk, and thousands of women and babies are injured, maimed, or even die unnecessarily.

Why is the procedure increasing so remarkably in the wake of concerns by leading health organizations? The reasons can be divided into biological or sociocultural explanations, with most falling into the latter category. With respect to biology, increasing numbers of older women are giving birth, resulting in an increase in some complications including twins or other multiples. However, these factors alone do not account for the high rates of surgical births because most older women deliver their babies vaginally without any complications, as do many mothers of multiples. Moreover, other industrialized countries also have high numbers of older women giving birth, yet they have significantly lower rates of surgical births. Rather than biology, something else explains the United States' increasing reliance on a surgical procedure that continues to worry leading health officials.

While it is easy to blame doctors for the increase in surgical births (to ward off lawsuits, to speed up the birthing process, to make more money, to schedule their workload most efficiently), it appears that increasing numbers of women are, by themselves, *electing* to have surgical births. One study based on 157 pregnant women in a New Orleans hospital found that 14.7 percent requested cesarean sections. "I liked having a cesarean section because once you get in and have your epidural (anesthetic), it takes 20 minutes," reports one woman, despite the 6 weeks of recuperation needed (Pope 2004). Many women are becoming increasingly comfortable with the remedicalization of childbirth, in contrast to the move toward more natural methods that have been promoted since the 1980s. They want childbirth medicalized so that it can be quick, of minimal bother, painless, and coordinated with work or family schedules, something that ordinary childbirth itself is not (O'Neill 2005; Pope 2004).

> When Marilyn Hamilton learned she was pregnant, she was happy—then afraid. She would have no way of knowing when labor would start, how long it would last, how painful it would be and how much damage it might inflict on her and her child. So she plans to deliver by Caesarean section, even though, at 21, she might be considered healthy enough to withstand a conventional labor and delivery when she gives birth. "With the Caesarean section, you get a pretty good idea of when it's going to happen and how you're going to feel. . . ." (Pope 2004)

For years a cesarean section birth did not occur without a strong medical reason, but today many physicians are acquiescing to the wishes of their patients, recognizing significant convenience and profit from the procedure as well. Male physicians in particular are more likely than their female counterparts to agree to perform cesareans that were not medically needed but were requested by patients (O'Neill 2005). Moreover, insurance companies usually do not question physicians and will pay for this elective procedure even though it constitutes major abdominal surgery, is expensive, and carries significant health risks.

In all likelihood, most pregnant women do not reflect on the ways that childbirth is shaped by the medical institutions in society. They are generally unaware how something so seemingly private is intertwined with larger social structures. Instead, they focus on their daily personal experience—yet a sociological imagination asks that we be mindful of the social forces operating to shape our personal choices and experiences.

Theme 2: Social Inequality Has a Powerful Influence on Family Life

Social inequality is pervasive throughout the world. Wars have been fought, homes and communities have been ravaged, families have been torn apart, and ethnic groups have been obliterated in battles over valued resources. U.S. society is also highly stratified on the basis of valued resources; notably, economics, power, and social status. These patterns of social inequality shape all dimensions of family life.

Social class, sex, race, and ethnicity are key statuses that affect the distribution of economics, power, and social status. They also affect the way family members interact, and the way in which family members respond. For example, Chapter 6 revealed that multigenerational households are more common among minorities at all income levels than among whites, offering myriad opportunities for emotional and financial support and assistance with child rearing. Despite these benefits, extended families have been branded as deficient, rather than as a real source of strength. Instead, the model dominant among whites, the isolated nuclear family, is posited as the "ideal." Minority youth, in particular, are sensitive to the normative definitions of family and often feel frustrated or embarrassed that their family does not "measure up" to the idealized American family. This can become a form of internalized racism (Pyke 2000a, b).

Conversely, patterns of social inequality are also shaped *by* families. Americans fantasize that they can be anything they want to be, but in reality there is little substantial upward (or downward) social mobility. As revealed in Chapter 5, people usually live out their lives in generally the same social class in which they were born. Families pass on their wealth, educational opportunities, and social capital (or their lack of it) to their newest members, and this perpetuates social inequality. For example, President George W. Bush was accepted to college at Yale University despite having a C average in high school. Clearly, it was his family background that opened the doors to Yale, which then paved the way for many of his subsequent achievements. What if George W. Bush had been born to a middle-class or working-class family? What wealth, educational opportunities, or social capital would they have to pass on that would have helped him to become president of the United States?

Several theoretical perspectives help interpret the connections between inequality and families, as revealed in Chapter 1, and these have been used throughout this text. One particularly useful perspective for examining the influence that inequality has on family lives is conflict theory, which examines the assumptions, values, and ideologies that are used to justify or explain family dynamics and our understanding of society's role in shaping or helping families. The ideologies of the more powerful groups are presented as "normal" and persons with less power, status, and wealth come to accept the interests of the more powerful as their own. Box 15.2 reveals that even welfare recipients subscribe to the popular sentiment that women who receive welfare are lazy and unmotivated, although they vehemently deny that they are like that. A conflict perspective asks that we examine the assumptions, values, and ideologies that are used to define families, characterize family dynamics, and to create family policy.

Americans like to believe in social mobility, but, realistically, what are the odds that these children will grow up to be President of the United States?

Example: Sex and Gender as Dimensions of Social Inequality

Of all the issues shaping families, both as a social institution and the lived experiences within families, sex and gender are among the most influential. Regardless of social class, racial or ethnic identity, type of political or economic regime, or any other aspect of the U.S. social structure, there are cultural rules that govern the behavior of males and females in every society, as shown in Chapter 4. These rules begin virtually from the day girls are born. Although rigid expectations can be a burden on both men and women, clearly it is girls and women who suffer most acutely from unrelenting sex and gender rules in many parts of the world. From female infanticide at birth, through

BOX 15.2 Using the Sociological Imagination

Managing the Stigma of Welfare

The following looks at the ways that women who receive welfare manage the stigma associated with welfare programs.

Most Americans denigrate welfare recipients and accuse them of being lazy, unmotivated, irresponsible, and content to live off the public dole and take advantage of hardworking taxpayers. Famous author and welfare critic George Gilder wrote in the *American Spectator*, "On the whole, black or white, these women are slovenly, incompetent, and sexually promiscuous" (Gilder 1995, 25).

Are welfare recipients aware of the deep-rooted stigma surrounding welfare and those who receive it? Interviews with 49 women on welfare revealed that they are very aware of the hostilities. Rhonda, a 28-year-old woman with one child, summed up the sentiment:

> I heard one girl was going to quit working because all the taxes come to us. Plus, they downgrade us in every kind of way there is. They say we look like slobs, we keep our houses this way and that way. And our children, depending on the way they're dressed, we're like bad parents and all sorts of things like that.

Many respondents told me that the derogatory comments were very painful, discouraging, or humiliating to hear. Amy, a 23-year-old mother, revealed:

> It's a very humiliating experience—being on welfare and being involved in the system. You are treated as though you are the scum of the earth—a stupid, lazy, nasty person. How dare you take this money? It's a very unpleasant experience. I'd avoid it at all costs. But unfortunately, I can't avoid it right now.

How do women cope with, or manage, the stigma of being on welfare? Erving Goffman (1963) suggests that for someone with a known stigma, the basic issue is to manage the tension produced by the fact that people know of the problem. One can hide being on welfare in some contexts, but it is revealed in others such as grocery stores or in the welfare office.

During the interviews it became clear that women tend to rely on one or more of four primary strategies for coping with the stigma attached to using welfare: (1) denial that they were on welfare or that they had experienced any stigma; (2) distancing themselves from other recipients; (3) blaming external forces for their own need of welfare; and (4) extolling the importance of motherhood. Few women questioned the dominant views of welfare recipients, and instead, most women believe the stereotypes about welfare and welfare recipients. They denigrated welfare recipients, even referring to other recipients as "they." Virtually every woman then explained that she was different from all the others. For example, Janie sees her situation as unique because she bore a child as a result of a rape, and only intends to be on welfare for a short time, al-

female genital mutilation in childhood, to forced child marriages in adolescence, to the legal subjugation of women by their husbands, many women routinely face gross violations of their human rights. Why do these abuses continue? Why do women seemingly not object?

Of course many women do object. Millions of women are resisting their continued exploitation and are becoming increasingly empowered. They are creating grassroots organizations and joining established human rights organizations. They are sharing their skills with others, they are teaching girls and women how to read and write, and they are lobbying the police, courts, and legislatures for change.

Nonetheless, we also know that many women do not act in what would seem to be in their best interests. Some feel powerless to do so. Others believe in their subjugation.

though she has been on for 2 years already. She holds disdain for other recipients:

> There are some people on welfare who don't need to be on welfare. They can go out and get a job. They have nothing better to do than to live off welfare and to live off the system. I'm sorry. I have no sympathy. Look at all the signs on the road, "will work for food." Go down to Day Labor, for crying out loud. They'll pay you more money than you can make in a regular day. It's by choice. Either (1) they don't want to work; (2) they are being supported by others; or (3) they don't give a damn about themselves.

Despite the negative comments about other welfare recipients: "they're breeders . . . if they don't get themselves stopped they'll keep having babies," "I think a lot of them are on it just to be lazy." Virtually all the women told a story of their own personal hardship that they assumed was unique among women on welfare. Their situations were distinctly different from the others, they claimed. They were victims of unplanned and unfortunate circumstances. They fled intolerable domestic violence. They were victims of rape or incest. They were deserted by men after finding out they were pregnant. They left men who were having affairs or abused their children. They had serious health problems that interfered with their work, or their children were sick. They were on assistance only temporarily while they got on their feet, got a job, got their child into day care, found a job, or got their children's fathers to finally pay the child support owed. What was striking was how few women thought that other welfare recipients might have these problems too. Women perceived that their own use of welfare was caused by factors outside of their control, but welfare use by other women, in contrast, was attributed to laziness, personal shortcoming, or other inadequacies.

Given the strong negative messages about welfare and welfare recipients, perhaps it is not surprising that women who receive welfare blame other women for their circumstances. When the dominant ideology is repeated often enough, it becomes "common sense" and the poor and less powerful also internalize it. Poverty and welfare use become personal problems, rather than social ones.

Source: From Seccombe, Karen. *"So You Think I Drive a Cadillac?": Welfare Recipients' Perspectives on The System and Its Reform* © 2007. Published by Allyn and Bacon, Boston, MA. Copyright © 2007 by Pearson Education. Adapted by permission of the publisher.

CRITICAL THINKING QUESTIONS

1. How does the ideology of the prominent group become so powerful that even women on welfare will subscribe to negative stereotypes about women on welfare?
2. Do you think the ideological hegemony operates differently among minorities than it does for whites? Why or why not?
3. What would it take for the poor and powerless to see their collective interests?

Should we be surprised? Powerful agents socialize women into their culture, including family, friends, peers, schools, and the media. They spend a lifetime in their culture, and like many men, do not really know any other way of being. Cultural norms are powerful. Not surprisingly, women may believe in the religiously based or politically motivated justifications for inequality, and they often perpetuate it. To fail to do so means facing a terrible social risk. We saw this in Chapter 4, where 100 million women alive today have had their genitals mutilated. One study in Sudan found that 90 percent of women have had their daughter cut or infibulated or planned to do so (Williams and Sobieszczyk 1997). Despite the severe pain and health consequences, these women are willing to inflict the same procedure on their daughters to ensure her prospective husband that she is a virgin. To fail to cut or infibulate their daughters may make the young girls seem different, they will be ridiculed, it may eliminate virtually all marriage prospects, and it will subject the entire family to scorn. In other words, as Gramsci (1971) suggests, women, who certainly have little power, status, and wealth, come to accept the interests of the more powerful as their own. Women mutilate their daughters because their culture tells them that husbands should have all sexual privileges; over time they come to believe these messages and adopt them as their own.

Theme 3: Family Policies Reflect Historical, Cultural, Political, and Social Factors

Family policies do not exist in a vacuum. They reflect historical, cultural, political, and social factors in every society—values about personal responsibility versus collective good, the role of work in our lives, the expectations placed on mothers and fathers to manage the inherent conflicts between their work and family lives, and the level of concern over social inequality.

Countries that develop explicit family policies, such as Sweden, France, or Norway, see the family as the key unit of analysis. Their goal is to strengthen the entire family because they see that as good for all of society. It is in the best interest of all citizens to have well-cared-for and well-educated children. In contrast, countries such as the United States develop policies and programs that focus on individual needy members, such as the physically disabled, the juvenile delinquent, a qualifying poor child, or the aged (Bergmann 1996; Kamerman 2003; Kamerman and Kahn 1978). Moreover, the United States has a long history of "rugged individualism" and a distrust of government and governmental programs. Family policies in the United States reflect and promote the concepts of individualism and self-sufficiency. They tend to be selective, meaning that persons need to meet some eligibility requirement to qualify for benefits, but it is not always clear to the observer why some programs are available to everyone and others are not. Why is access to education a guaranteed "right," but not access to health care? Why does the federal government have a health care program for the elderly, Medicare, but none for children? Why does the government subsidize the cost of college attendance, but it does little to assist families to pay for preschool? We cannot turn simply to logic to answer these questions; the answers often reflect the success of special interest groups in having their agendas served.

The policies in the United States differ from those in other industrialized nations. Other countries lean toward universal programs that are available to all persons. As we have learned, not only is the United States the only industrialized country without universal health insurance coverage, but it is also virtually the only one without paid maternal/parental leave at childbirth, or a family allowance/child dependency grant. Americans think of these issues in individualistic terms and frown upon government assistance. There is the fear that assistance will make families weak and dependent on the system.

Example: Work and Family Many books have been written on the policies needed to reconcile parenthood and employment. As we learned in Chapter 11, not only are single parents employed, but most two-parent families in the United States have both parents employed outside the home for pay. Nonetheless, family policies have failed to keep up with the changing needs of families, and family and employment needs often collide with one another. Compared to other industrialized nations, American mothers and fathers work more hours per week; have less vacation time; and are more likely to report a preference for having more time with the family. Most European nations offer a minimum of 20 to 25 annual days of paid vacation, whereas the United

States offers none (Gornick and Meyers 2003). As revealed in Chapter 9, Americans receive even minimal maternity leaves.

Moreover, Chapter 11 showed that families in the United States have only a patchwork of child care and early childhood education arrangements, and these are plagued with limited access, variable quality, and high cost. Families' access to child care depends largely on their own private resources and what happens to be available in the community. Quality is uneven and often poor because there is little standardization or oversight. Pay is low, turnover is high, and working conditions are often deplorable. Early childhood education is not a valued occupation, despite its importance to the community, and workers have little incentive to upgrade their skills or provide the highest quality care. Yet, the cost is high because there is little government subsidization. For the most part, parents bear the full brunt of the costs. Head Start programs, or welfare-to-work day care subsidies, are an exception to this. Other industrial countries subsidize their early childhood education programs for all families far more than does the United States (Gornick and Meyers 2003).

Chapter 1 identified three approaches that can be used when family and work conflict with one another. The first approach establishes policies that create more family-friendly work environments, such as paid maternity and family leaves. A second approach mandates that workers themselves learn specific techniques for managing their conflicts, such as better managing their time. A third approach asks workers to modify the meanings of the situation, suggesting that people face family and work conflicts simply because they want to work more hours or want more money. Policies would focus on increasing personal responsibility and commitments. The second and third approaches can be commonly seen in social policies in the United States. Family concerns are generally viewed as personal issues or problems, in contrast to many other countries that take a more collective view, reflecting a diference in fundamental values.

Theme 4: Understanding Families in the United States Requires a Comparative Perspective

Because the world is so interconnected, societies are no longer isolated entities. They can see other ways of doing things and sometimes adopt pieces of another's culture as their own. This is the case for family life as well. Learning how other societies structure families, how they collectively think about families, how they encourage members to interact, and how they deal with the challenges families face can provide insight into our own concerns.

While many problems, such as poverty or HIV/AIDS, are considerably worse in other countries, other problems loom larger in the United States than elsewhere. For example, the U.S. infant mortality rate is among the highest in the developed world, and its life expectancy rate is among the lowest. Many minority babies have trouble surviving even their first year of life. How can a society as richly endowed as the United States have such poor health statistics? Poor health reflects both personal behavior, and an inadequate health care system. Likewise, the poverty rate is much higher in the U.S. compared to other developed nations. What can we learn from other countries to better understand our own? Chapter 10 introduced us to the concept of family allowances, a powerful tool that can elevate a family's standard of living and decrease impoverishment.

Example: Teenage Birth Rates Chapter 10 described the negative consequences of teen pregnancies and births. For example, teenage mothers are more than twice as likely to die in childbirth as are older mothers, their infants are twice as likely

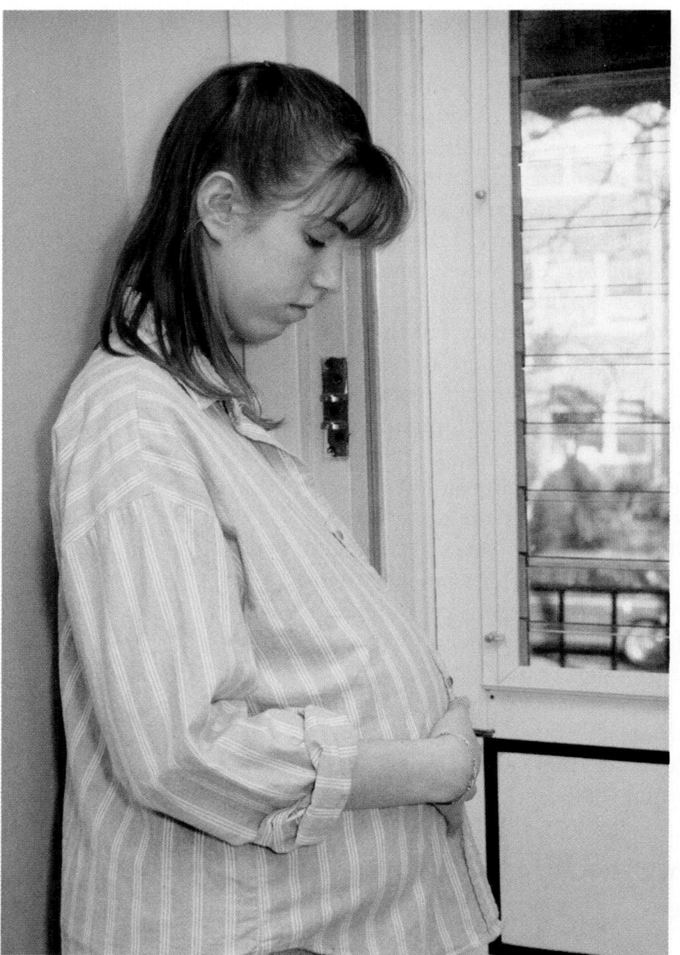

While the teenage birthrate has declined significantly since the 1990s, it remains higher than other industrialized nations. The United States should take note of other countries to find the most effective ways to reduce teen pregnancy even further.

to be of low birth weight, and nearly three times more likely to die within the first month of life. Teen mothers are also far more likely to be impoverished.

The teenage birth rate in the United States, although declining since the early 1990s, remains the highest among developed nations. The United States has a teenage birth rate almost twice as high as the country in the number two spot—the United Kingdom. The U.S. teen birth rate is over twice the rate as in Canada, our closest developed neighbor, and nearly 12 times the rate of Japan. It is three times as high as Australia's, four times as high as Germany's, six times as high as France's, and eight times as high as that of the Netherlands (Annie E. Casey Foundation 2005; Berne and Huberman 1999; Singh and Darroch 2000).

Why are rates so much lower in other countries? It is arguably due to policies in those countries that include mandatory, medically accurate sex education programs that provide comprehensive information and encourage teens to make responsible choices; easy access to contraceptives and other forms of reproductive health care; the social acceptance of adolescent sexual expression as normal and healthy; and other governmental and social programs that provide needed services such as medical care, education, or other social services (Berne and Huberman 1999). These countries are successful at curbing teenage pregnancies and births with a combination of education and medical technology, in contrast to the United States, which places a far greater emphasis on abstinence. The United States could learn better ways to curb the number of teens having babies by closely examining the values, policies, and practices of other countries.

A comparative perspective reveals that family practices are embedded in a social context. For example, in some societies teenage sexuality and pregnancy are considered normative. Among the Mangaia people of Polynesia, both girls and boys are expected to have a high level of sexual desire in early adolescence. At the age of 13 or 14, boys are given explicit instructions in how to please a girl through kissing, fondling, cunnilingus, and specific techniques for giving her multiple orgasms. Boys are taught these techniques through personal experience with an older female teacher. It is critical that a boy learn these techniques quickly. Soon he will begin sexual relationships with a girl his own age, and if he fails to satisfy her, she will likely publicly denounce him and his lack of sexual skill. This example can serve as a vivid reminder that social norms play important roles in characterizing seemingly biological phenomena. Pregnancy is a social status as well as a biological one, and it is socially constructed within a specific historical and cultural context.

A comparative perspective can enhance our understanding of families in many ways. Learning how other societies structure families, how they collectively think about families, and how they deal with the challenges families face can provide insight into our own concerns.

Future Trends: Where Are Families Heading?

Our study of families has revealed that they are dynamic and always changing rather than static. There is not one type of family that is inherently better (or worse) than others. Families are evolving and emerging to meet societies' needs.

Looking into the future is always a bit of a gamble, but given what we know about the social and demographic forces operating in the United States today and the changing nature of our social institutions, what might we anticipate with respect to the families of the future? The following are a few predictions.

1. *The age at marriage will continue to rise.* Today the average age of marriage is about 25 for women and 27 for men. However, I predict that the age of marriage will continue to rise somewhat for several reasons. First, greater educational and employment opportunities will continue for women, thus rendering a push toward early marriage less relevant. Second, as the population of unmarried persons increases (because of cohabitation, delayed marriage, or other reasons), there will be greater acceptance of nonmarital statuses.
2. *The rate of cohabitation will increase.* Disapproval of cohabitation is slowly vanishing, and is found largely among older persons today. I anticipate that cohabitation will

The number of Hispanics in the United States will continue to grow because of higher-than-average birth rates and immigration. Their presence will richly influence American culture.

increasingly become normative. As younger persons age, they will retain their support of cohabitation, and a new generation will see cohabitation as increasingly common and routine.

3. *The percentage of women and men without children will rise*. The percentage of women between the ages of 40 and 44 who do not have children has nearly doubled since 1980. I predict that this trend will continue. As U.S. society sees more child-free women and men, pronatalism may decline, and even greater numbers of individuals will see a child-free life as a legitimate and potentially positive option.
4. *The divorce rate will continue to decline moderately*. The divorce rate crested in 1980, and has since declined to about 17 per 1,000 married women. I anticipate that divorce will continue to decline as research becomes more public.
5. *The United States will become more diverse*. Demographers who study population trends predict that within a few decades, minorities will constitute nearly half of the U.S. population. Because racial and ethnic groups often have varying family structures and dynamics (the likelihood of extended families), we are likely to witness far more diversity in families than is the case today.
6. *The rapid growth in the Hispanic population will continue*. Hispanic groups now comprise the largest minority in the United States, eclipsing blacks. Because the birth rate of Hispanics is higher than average—and higher than other minority groups—coupled with immigration, I anticipate that their presence in the United States will continue to grow quickly. Hispanic culture will have a growing influence on U.S. culture and family life.
7. *The rate of mothers working outside the home will likely stabilize*. Today about two-thirds of married couples with children have both parents working outside the home for pay, either full- or part-time. Recent trends indicate a slight decline in the employment rate of mothers. However, because of the economic slump of the early 2000s, women's advancing education, and greater labor market opportunities, I anticipate that the employment of mothers will likely stabilize or rise again.
8. *The United States will remain highly stratified*. Since 1980, the income and wealth distribution in the United States has become more highly skewed in favor of the wealthy. The richest have made the greatest gains during this period, while the middle- and lower-income groups lost ground. Given the tax cuts and policies enacted in the early 2000s, it is likely that the income and wealth distribution will continue to be increasingly skewed.
9. *The elderly population will continue to rise quickly, changing the U.S. culture radically*. The elderly now constitute one of every eight people, increasing to about one of every five by the middle of this century as the baby-boomers age. This large aging cohort will have a significant effect on U.S. culture and social policies, just as they have throughout their lives. Moreover, the oldest-old cohort will continue to grow, and more people will need care and assistance than ever before.
10. *The United States will see some challenges to its piecemeal approach to family policy*. Historically no vocal and well-funded special interest group has taken on the plight of families, contributing to a lack of a national family policy. However, this may change, as people become more vocal about what they see as unfair or discriminatory programs or policies. For example, as more middle-income families are losing their health insurance, they are clamoring for change. Gays and lesbians are becoming increasingly vocal about marriage laws that they see as discriminatory. Families are increasingly voicing concern about the costs of child care. However, given U.S. values of rugged individualism, discussions of a more universal approach are bound to be controversial.

Conclusion

This chapter summarizes the contributions that the sociological imagination can make to our understanding of families. The four themes that run throughout the book are reviewed and specific examples from earlier chapters are provided: (1) families are both a public social institution and a private personal relationship; (2) social inequality has a powerful influence on family life; (3) family policies reflect historical, cultural, political, and social factors; and (4) understanding families in the United States requires a comparative perspective. A family is far more than a personal relationship among related individuals; family is also a powerful social institution inextricably linked with other social institutions. Despite important universals that are found in families throughout the world, family structures and the relationships embedded within families reflect historical, political, and cultural contexts. They also reflect power and social inequality. The goal is to understand family issues such as mate selection, marriage rituals, gendered expectations, division of household labor, fertility patterns, parent-child relationships, aging and the care of the elderly, family conflict and violence, and divorce and repartnering within these contexts. Only then can we reveal trends that illuminate both the past (where we've been) and the future (where we are going).

Resources on the Internet

Center for Law and Social Policy
www.clasp.org
The Center for Law and Social Policy is a national nonprofit organization that seeks to improve the economic security of low-income families with children and secure access for low-income persons to the civil justice system. Their work is concentrated on family policy and access to civil legal assistance for low-income families. Family policy projects include welfare reform, workforce development, child care, child support enforcement, child welfare, couples and marriage policy, and reproductive health and teen parents.

National Coalition for the Homeless
www.nationalhomeless.org
The mission of the National Coalition for the Homeless is to end homelessness. Toward this end, the organization engages in public education, policy advocacy, and grassroots organizing. They focus their work in the following four areas: housing justice, economic justice, health care justice, and civil rights.

UNAIDS
www.unaids.org
The Joint United Nations Programme on HIV/AIDS, UNAIDS, is the main advocate for global action on the epidemic. It leads, strengthens, and supports an expanded response aimed at preventing transmission of HIV, providing care and support, reducing the vulnerability of individuals and communities to HIV/AIDS, and alleviating the impact of the epidemic.

UNICEF
www.unicef.org
UNICEF works in 158 countries to overcome the obstacles that poverty, violence, disease, and discrimination place in a child's path. UNICEF is mandated by the United Nations General Assembly to advocate for the protection of children's rights, to help meet their basic needs, and to expand their opportunities to reach their full potential. Their website contains valuable information about children worldwide.

Further Reading

Beck-Gernsheim, E. 2002. *Reinventing the Family: In Search of New Lifestyles*. Malden, MA: Blackwell.

Carlson, A. 2003. *The American Way: Family and Community in the Shaping of American Identity*. Wilmington, DE: Intercollegiate Studies.

Children's Defense Fund. 2005. *The State of America's Children 2005*. Online: www.childrensdefense.org

Coltrane, S. (Ed.). 2004. *Families and Society: Classic and Contemporary Readings*. Belmont, CA: Wadsworth.

Driscoll, C. 2002. *Girls: Feminine Adolescence in Popular Culture and Cultural Theory*. New York: Columbia University Press.

Farmer, P. 2003. *Pathologies of Power: Health, Human Rights, and the New War on the Poor*. Berkeley: University of California Press. 2003.

Gornick, J. C., and M. K. Meyers. 2003. *Families that Work: Policies for Reconciling Parenthood and Employment*. New York: Russell Sage Foundation.

Mercier, J., S. Garasky, and M. Shelley II. (Eds.). 2000. *Redefining Family Policy: Implications for the 21st Century*. Ames: Iowa State University Press.

Pleck, E. H. 2000. *Celebrating the Family: Ethnicity, Consumer Culture, and Family Rituals*. Cambridge, MA: Harvard University Press.

Rainwater, L., and T. M. Smeeding. 2003. *Poor Kids in a Rich Country*. New York: Russell Sage Foundation.

Rothman, B. K. 2006. *Weaving a Family: Untangling Race and Adoption*. Boston: Beacon Press.

Sidel, R. 2006. *Unsung Heroines: Single Mothers and the American Dream*. Berkeley: University of California Press.

United Nations Children's Fund. December 2006. *The State of the World's Children, 2006: Excluded and Invisible*. Online: www.unicef.org/sowc06/fullreport/full_report.php

Glossary

Absolute poverty: The lack of resources such as food, housing, and clothing that is life-threatening. (p. 150)

Achieved statuses: Statuses achieved on our own. (p. 41)

Activities of daily living (ADL): A common set of measures that gerontologists use to track elders' degree of impairment, such as bathing, dressing, eating, getting into and out of bed, walking indoors, and using the toilet. (p. 399)

Affirmative action: A set of social policies designed to increase opportunities for minority groups and one of the most misunderstood strategies of our time. (p. 200)

Agents of socialization: The persons, groups, or institutions that teach children about the norms and values of their particular culture. (p. 313)

Alimony: Post-divorce support for a former spouse. (p. 453)

Antimiscegenation laws: The banning of marriage between whites and other races. (p. 250)

Ascribed statuses: The statuses a person is born with, such as his or her sex, race and ethnic background, and social class. (pp. 41, 133)

Assisted reproductive technology (ART): All fertility treatments in which both egg and sperm are handled. (p. 287)

Authoritarian parenting style: Strict, punitive, and not very warm. (p. 316)

Authoritative parenting style: Demand and maintain high levels of control over their children, but also warm and receptive to their children. (p. 316)

Baby-boom generation: Persons born after WWII. (p. 376)

Bilateral: Descent can be traced through both male and female sides of the family. (p. 52)

Birth centers: Freestanding facilities, usually with close access to, but not affiliated, with a hospital; childbirth is approached as a normal, healthy process. (p. 296)

Bisexual: An attraction to both males and females. One who engages in both heterosexual and homosexual relationships. (p. 216)

Bourgeoisie: According to Karl Marx, the capitalist class that owns the means of production. (p. 136)

Bundling: A dating practice in colonial America in which a young man and woman may continue their date by spending the night in a bed together separated by a wooden board. (p. 78)

Caste system: A system of social stratification that is based on ascribed characteristics one is born with, such as race, ethnicity, or family lineage. (p. 135)

Caucasian: A theoretical racial category comprised of those individuals with relatively light skin. (p. 175)

Centenarians: Persons age 100 and older. (p. 370)

Child allowance: A cash grant from the government for each child. (p. 62)

Civil unions: A public recognition of a relationship that is more restrictive than marriage and offers fewer rights and privileges. (p. 234)

Clitoridectomy: A form of genital cutting or mutilation in which the clitoris is cut out of the body. (p. 113)

Closed adoption: All identifying information is sealed and unavailable to all parties. (p. 289)

Cohabitation: Unmarried partners living together. (p. 227)

Common couple violence (CCV): Violence that arises out of a specific argument in which at least one partner lashes out physically. (p. 412)

Community: Can include geographic space, social networks, and religious and faith-based fellowships that affect resiliency. (p. 163)

Compadres: Godparents in the Mexican-American community who serve as coparents to children. (p. 83)

Companionate family: Built upon mutual affection, sexual attraction, compatibility, and personal happiness. (p. 88)

Comparative perspective: Looking at other societies around the world or looking at a culture historically to see how others organize their social life and respond to its challenges. (p. 9)

Concrete operational thought: Piaget's third stage of cognitive development; occurs between the ages of 6 and 11 or 12 when children begin to see the causal connections in their surroundings and can manipulate categories, classification systems, and hierarchies in groups. (p. 312)

Conflict Tactics Scale (CTS): A violence scale based on people's responses about how they deal with disagreements in relationships. (p. 409)

Conflict theory: This theoretical perspective emphasizes issues surrounding social inequality, power, conflict, and social change. (p. 15)

Covenant marriage: A type of marriage that restricts access to divorce, requires premarital counseling, and other rules and regulations. (p. 267)

Cross-sectional data: Data collected at only one point in time rather than following trends over time. (p. 147)

Cross-sectional divorce rate: A divorce rate at only one point in time. (p. 440)

Crude divorce rate: The number of divorces that occur out of 1,000 people in the population. (p. 440)

Cult of domesticity: The glorification of women's domestic role. (p. 85)

Day care centers: Child care provided in nonresidential facilities. (p. 357)

Death rates: Measures of the number of deaths for a given population. (p. 274)

Demographic transition: The process in which a society moves from a situation of high fertility rates and low life expectancy, to one of low fertility rates and high life expectancy. (p. 371)

Developmental theory: Family and family members go through distinct stages each with its own set of tasks, roles, and responsibilities. (p. 16)

Direct financial costs: Out-of-pocket expenses for things such as food, clothing, housing, and education. (p. 282)

Displaced homemaker: A full-time homemaker who is divorced by her husband. (p. 455)

"Doing gender": Housework is so ingrained as women's work that it functions as an area in which gender is symbolically created and reproduced. (p. 355)

Domestic partners: Heterosexual or homosexual unmarried couples in long-term committed relationships. (p. 7)

Double standard: Men are allowed more permissiveness in sexual behavior whereas women are more likely to be socially punished for their sexual experiences. (p. 120)

Dowry: The financial gift given to a woman's prospective in-laws by her parents. (p. 210)

Early childhood education and care (ECEC): An international term for day care, preschool, and other programs to ensure that all children begin elementary school with basic skills and ready to learn. (p. 361)

Earned income tax credit (EITC): A federal tax credit for low-income working families. (p. 164)

Egalitarian: The expectation that power and authority are equally vested in men and women. (p. 52)

Ego: According to Sigmund Freud, the rational component of personality that attempts to balance the need for immediate gratification with the demands of society. (p. 312)

Elder abuse: Abuse, neglect, and exploitation of the elderly, often by family members and others close to them. (p. 429)

Emotional abuse: Includes verbal, mental, or psychological maltreatment that destroys a person's self-esteem. (p. 425)

Empirical approach: Answers questions through a systematic collection and analysis of data. (p. 12)

Endogamy: Norms that encourage marriage between people of the same social category. (pp. 42, 213)

English Poor Laws of 1601: The first systematic codification of English ideas about the responsibility of the state to provide for its citizens. (p. 384)

Ethnic cleansing: The systematic killing, torturing, or removal of persons with the intention of eliminating a specific racial or ethnic group. (p. 178)

Ethnic group: People who share specific cultural features. (p. 176)

Ethnicity: Representing culture, including language, place of origin, dress, food, religion, and other values. (p. 175)

Ethnocentrism: The assumption that society's way of doing things is always the best way. (p. 9)

Ethnographies: Detailed accounts and interpretations of some aspect of culture. (p. 71)

Exogamy: Norms that encourage marriage between people of different social categories. (pp. 42, 213)

Extended families: Families that include other family members such as grandparents, uncles, aunts, or cousins, in addition to parents and their children. (p. 191)

Families: Relationships by blood, marriage, or affection, in which members may cooperate economically, may care for any children, and may consider their identity to be intimately connected to the larger group. (p. 5)

Familism: Family relationships are paramount and take precedence over individual needs or wants. (p. 82)

Family allowances: Cash benefits given to families by the government. (p. 330)

Family child-care providers: Child care provided in a private home other than the child's home. (p. 357)

Family Medical Leave Act (FMLA): Governmental act that requires employers with over 50 employees working for them (within a 75-mile radius) to provide 12 weeks of unpaid leave to eligible employees (both men and women) to care for themselves or their immediate families with specified medical conditions. (p. 301)

Family of orientation: The family into which you were born. (p. 27)

Family of procreation: The family you make through partnership, marriage, and/or with children. (p. 27)

Family protective factors (FPF): Characteristics or dynamics that shape the family's ability to endure in the face of risk factors. (p. 163)

Family reconstitution: Attempts are made to compile all available information about significant family events and everyday life within a particular family to piece together social history. (p. 71)

Family recovery factors (FRF): Assist families in "bouncing back" from a crisis situation. (p. 163)

Family systems theory: Family members, and the roles they play make up a system, and this system is larger than the sum of its individual members. (p. 17)

Feminist theory: Gender is the central concept for explaining family structure and dynamics. (p. 16)

Fertility rates: Average number of children born to a woman during her lifetime (total); number of children born per 1,000 women aged 15–49 (refined); or number of children born per 1,000 population (crude). (p. 274)

Fictive kin: Nonrelatives whose bonds are strong and intimate. (p. 5)

Financial or material exploitation: Improperly using the resources of another person, without his or her consent, for someone else's benefit. (p. 429)

Formal care: Care for the elderly that is provided by social service agencies on a paid or volunteer basis. (p. 400)

Formal operational thought: Piaget's fourth stage of cognitive development; children develop capacities for abstract thought and can conceptualize more complex issues or rules that can be used for problem solving. (p. 312)

Gay: Usually refers to homosexual men. (p. 216)

Gemeinschaft: A type of society that emphasizes the intimacy found in primary relationships. (p. 55)

Gender: The culturally and socially constructed differences between males and females found in the meanings, beliefs, and practices associated with femininity and masculinity. (p. 99)

Gender-based violence: Any act of gender violence that results in or is likely to result in physical, sexual, or psychological harm and suffering to women, including threats of such acts, coercion, or arbitrary deprivations of liberty, whether occurring in public or private life. (p. 407)

Gender socialization: Teaching the cultural norms associated with being male or female. (p. 102)

Gerontology: An interdisciplinary science of aging that draws upon biology, medicine, and the social sciences, including sociology, psychology, and family studies. (p. 380)

Gesellschaft: A type of society that is based on largely impersonal secondary relationships. (p. 55)

Global gag rule: Denies U.S. assistance to all organizations that provide abortion services, counsel their patients on their options for abortions, refer their patients for abortion services, or educate their communities about or lobby their governments for safe abortion with their own, non-U.S. funding. (p. 126)

Hermaphrodites: Persons born with both male and female genitals. (p. 99)

Heterogeneous relationships: Those in which the partners are significantly different from one another on some important characteristic. (p. 214)

Heterosexual: An attraction and preference for sexual relationships with members of the other sex (e.g., a man and a woman). (p. 216)

Hidden curriculum: Informal school curriculum that teaches gender socialization. (p. 106)

Home observation of the measurement of the environment (HOME): A widely used tool that measures maternal warmth and learning experiences provided to the child; is associated with a variety of child outcomes. (p. 133)

Homogeneous relationships: Those in which partners are similar to one another. (p. 213)

Homosexual: Refers to a preference for same-sex sexual and romantic relationships. (p. 216)

Household labor: Generally refers to the unpaid work done to maintain family members and/or a home. (p. 351)

Human agency: The ability of human beings to create viable lives even when they are constrained or limited by social forces. (p. 28)

Id: According to Sigmund Freud, the part of the personality that includes biological drives and needs for immediate gratification. (p. 312)

Immigration: People moving to the United States. (p. 84)

Incest taboo: A rule forbidding sexual activity (and marriage) among close family members. (p. 61)

Individual-level protective factors: Individual personality traits and dispositions that enhance resiliency. (p. 163)

Industrialization: Transforming an economy from a system based on small family-based agriculture to one of large industrial capital. (p. 83)

Infant mortality rate: The number of deaths within the first year of life per 1,000 births in the population. (p. 61)

Infertility: The inability to conceive a child. (p. 287)

Infibulation: The most extreme form of genital cutting or mutilation in which the clitoris and vaginal lips are cut or scraped away, and the outer portion of the vagina is stitched together. (p. 113)

Informal care: Care for the elderly that is unpaid, usually done by someone close to the elder. (p. 400)

Instrumental activities of daily living (IADL): Includes activities such as preparing meals, shopping, managing money, using the telephone, doing housework, and taking medications. (p. 399)

Interethnic marriage: Partners coming from different countries or having different cultural, religious, or ethnic backgrounds. (p. 252)

Intergenerational transmission of violence: Learning norms and behaviors, including violence, by observing others. (p. 426)

Intersexed: A person whose anatomical categories are not easily identifiable. (p. 99)

Intimate terrorism: Violence that is motivated by a desire to control the other partner. (p. 412)

Joint legal custody: Both the custodial and noncustodial parents retain their legal rights with respect to their children. (p. 450)

Joint physical custody: Children spend substantial or nearly equal portions of time in the homes of each parent. (p. 452)

Kinkeeper: The person who has the primary responsibility for maintaining family relationships. (p. 393)

Labor market segmentation: Men and women often work in different types of jobs with distinct working conditions and pay. (p. 123)

Legal custody: Refers to who has the legal authority to make important decisions concerning a child. (p. 450)

Lesbian: Homosexual woman. (p. 216)

Life course perspective: Examines how individuals' lives change as they pass through the events in their lives, recognizing that many changes are socially produced and shared among a cohort of people. (p. 17)

Life expectancy: How long a person can expect to live, usually calculated from birth. (p. 370)

Living wage: Ordinances that require employers to pay wages that are above federal or state minimum wage levels, usually ranging from 100 to 130 percent of the poverty line. (p. 344)

Looking-glass self: According to Cooley, we come to see ourselves as others perceive and respond to us. (p. 312)

Love: An enduring bond based on affection and emotion, including a sense of obligation toward one another. (p. 208)

Machismo: Mexican Americans have a long tradition of masculine authority, which is exercised in the home, in the work place, in sexual prowess, and in the raising of children. (p. 83)

Macro theories: A general framework that attempts to understand societal patterns, such as structural functionalism, conflict theory, and feminist theory. (p. 14)

Marital decline perspective: Suggests the institution of marriage is increasingly being threatened by hedonistic pursuits of personal happiness at the expense of a long-term commitment. (p. 257)

Marital resilience perspective: Suggests ending an unhappy marriage is not necessarily cause for alarm because it gives adults another chance at happiness and provides the opportunity to end a child's dysfunctional home life. (p. 257)

Marriage movement: A group of family scholars, therapists, and civic leaders who have come together in hopes of influencing public policy to promote and strengthen traditional marriage. (p. 265)

Matriarchy: A form of social organization in which the norm is that the power and authority in society would be vested in women. (p. 52)

Matrilineal: A descent pattern characterized as having the lineage more closely aligned with women's families rather than men's families. (p. 53)

Matrilocal: The married couple is expected to live with the family of the wife. (p. 54)

Means-tested: People have to be below a certain income to qualify for a social program. (pp. 22, 399)

Medicaid: A federally mandated health care financing program for the financially indigent who meet certain qualifications. (pp. 146, 399)

Medicare: A federal health insurance program primarily for people age 65 and older. (p. 399)

Meritocracy: A system in which economic and social rewards such as income, occupation, or prestige are obtained on individual merit rather than inheritance. (p. 135)

Micro theories: A general framework that focuses on personal dynamics and face-to-face interaction, including social exchange, symbolic interaction, developmental, and family systems theories. (p. 14)

Midwives: Attendants trained to help women give birth and who believe that childbirth is a normal part of life. (p. 294)

Minority group: A category of people who have less power than the dominant group and who are subject to unequal treatment. (p. 176)

Modernization: A process of social and cultural transformation from traditional societies to modern societies that influences all dimensions of social life. (p. 54)

Mongoloid: A theoretical racial category repre-senting those individuals who have characteristics such as yellow or brown skin and folds on their eyelids. (p. 175)

Monogamy: The law or custom that does not allow individuals to have multiple spouses. (p. 43)

Mortality rates: Death rates. (p. 146)

Mutual violent control: A violent pattern of behavior in which both partners are controlling and violent. (p. 412)

Nannies/babysitters: Child care provided in the home by a nonrelative. (p. 357)

National health insurance: Insurance is viewed as a public good, like schools, police protection, and parks, available to all, and funded out of taxes and general revenues. (p. 146)

National Violence Against Women Survey: The National Institute of Justice and the Centers for Disease Control and Prevention jointly sponsored a landmark telephone survey from 1995 to 1996 with a large and nationally representative sample of adult women and men about violence. (p. 413)

Neglect: The failure to provide for basic needs for someone who is dependent on you. (p. 425)

Negroid: A theoretical racial category comprised of people with darker skin and other characteristics such as coarse curly hair. (p. 175)

Neolocal: The married couple is expected to establish its own residence and live there independently. (p. 53)

No-fault divorce: A divorce in which the couple can say they have irreconcilable differences and do not wish to assign blame. (p. 446)

Nonstandard work schedules: Jobs that are part time, subcontracted, temporary in nature, occur at night, or offer irregular work schedules. (p. 344)

Normless norm: Something common enough to be considered normative, but with vague and confusing expectations, obligations, and rules. (p. 465)

Occasional labor: Household tasks that are more time-flexible and more discretionary, such as household repairs, yard care, or paying bills. (p. 351)

Old Age and Survivor Insurance (OASI): A cash assistance entitlement program for seniors that has also been extended to their widows. (p. 383)

Old Age Insurance (OAI): A cash assistance entitlement program for seniors. (p. 383)

One-child policy: (1) Advocating delayed marriage and delayed childbearing; (2) advocating fewer and healthier births; and (3) advocating one child per couple, with a few exceptions for special circumstances. (p. 278)

Open adoptions: Involves direct contact between the biological and adoptive parents. (p. 289)

Opportunity costs: Lost opportunities for income by working only part-time or not at all because of children. (p. 282)

Out-of-pocket costs: The amount that individuals pay of their own money to receive health care. (p. 145)

Patriarchy: A form of social organization in which the norm is that men have a natural right to be in positions of authority over women. (p. 51)

Patricians: During the Roman era, these were landowners, at the top of the stratification system. (p. 74)

Patrilineal: A descent pattern in which lineage is traced exclusively (or at least primarily) through the man's family line. (p. 53)

Patrilocal: A married couple will live with the husband's family. (p. 54)

Permissive parenting style: Having few controls or demands on the child. (p. 316)

Physical abuse: Inflicting physical injury and harm on another person. (p. 425)

Physical custody: The child's legal residence. (p. 450)

Polyandry: The marriage pattern that involves one woman and several husbands. (p. 48)

Polygamy: A law or custom that allows for more than one spouse at a time (gender unspecified). (p. 43)

Polygyny: The marriage pattern in which husbands can have more than one wife. (p. 43)

Poverty line: The official U.S. government method of calculating how many people are poor and assessing how that number changes from year to year. (p. 147)

Power: The ability to achieve goals, wishes, and desires even in the face of opposition from others. (p. 136)

Preoperational thought: Piaget's second stage of cognitive development; occurs through age 5 or 6 as the child learns language, symbolic play and symbolic drawing, but does not grasp abstract concepts. (p. 312)

Prestige: The esteem or respect a person is afforded. (p. 136)

Primary labor market: Jobs that are characterized by having relatively high pay, benefits, and job security. (p. 343)

Primary sector: Consists of jobs in which raw materials are harvested, such as in timber, agriculture, or mining. (p. 342)

Primogeniture: Families during the Middle Ages leaving their wealth or property to the eldest son. (p. 74)

Private adoptions: Arranged directly between adoptive parents and the biological birth mother, usually through the assistance of an attorney. (p. 288)

Progressive taxation: Those who earn more pay a higher percentage of their income in taxes. (p. 24)

Proletariat: According to Karl Marx, individuals who must sell their labor to the owners in order to earn enough money to survive. (p. 136)

Pronatalism: A cultural value that encourages childbearing. (p. 273)

Public adoptions: Occur through licensed public agencies. (p. 288)

Qualitative methods: The focus is on narrative description with words rather than numbers to analyze patterns and their underlying meanings. (p. 12)

Quantitative methods: The focus is on collecting data that can be measured numerically. (p. 12)

Race: A category composed of people who share real or alleged physical traits that members of a society deem as socially significant. (p. 175)

Racial socialization: Teaching minority children about prejudice and discrimination; the coping skills necessary to develop and maintain a strong and healthy self-image. (p. 315)

Racism: The belief that one racial group is superior or inferior to others. (p. 177)

Refined divorce rate: The number of divorces that occur out of every 1,000 married women. (p. 440)

Regressive tax: Lower-income persons pay a higher tax rate than do higher-income persons. (p. 383)

Relative poverty: The lack of basic resources relative to others in society. (p. 150)

Resiliency: The capacity to rebound from adversity, misfortune, trauma, or other transitional crises and be strengthened and more resourceful. (p. 162)

Resource theory: The greater the relative amount or value of resources contributed by a partner, the greater is his or her power within the relationship; can then be translated into bargaining to avoid tasks such as housework that offer no pay and minimal social prestige. (p. 355)

Role taking: According to Mead, it is the process of mentally assuming the role of another person to understand the world from his or her point of view and to anticipate his or her response to us. (p. 313)

Roles: Behaviors associated with social positions in society. (p. 40)

Routine household labor: Nondiscretionary, routine tasks that are less able to be postponed, such as cooking, washing dishes, or cleaning. (p. 351)

Sandwich generation: Adult children, usually daughters, who are caring for both their parents and their own children. (p. 401)

Secondary labor market: Jobs that have relatively low pay, few benefits, and little job security. (p. 343)

Secondary sector: Transforms raw materials into manufactured goods. (p. 343)

Selection effect: People who engage in some behavior; e.g., cohabitation, are different from those who do not. (pp. 230, 265)

Selective programs: Persons need to meet some eligibility requirement to qualify for benefits. (p. 22)

Self-care: School-age children who are unsupervised and taking care of themselves. (p. 359)

Semi-open adoptions: Biological and adoptive families exchange personal information through a social worker or attorney, but have no direct contact. (p. 289)

Sensorimotor intelligence: Piaget's first stage of cognitive development; infants and toddlers understand the world primarily through touch, sucking, listening, and looking. (p. 312)

Separate spheres: A dominant ideology within the nineteenth century middle and upper middle classes that suggested that women should stay home to rear the children and take care of the home while husbands should be the sole breadwinners. (p. 85)

Sex: Biological differences and one's role in reproduction. (p. 99)

Sexual abuse: Inappropriate sexual behavior with someone (e.g., a child) for sexual gratification. (p. 425)

Sexual orientation: The sex that one is attracted to. (p. 216)

Sexual scripts: A social construction that provides the norms or rules regarding sexual behavior. (pp. 119, 218)

Sharia: Radical interpretations of Islamic law being used to establish extreme and punitive rules by which Muslims are governed. (p. 114)

Social capital: The goods and services that are byproducts of social relationships, such as social support or personal connections. (p. 260)

Social class: A system of social stratification that is based both on ascribed statuses and individual achievement. (p. 136)

Social exchange theory: Individuals are rational and their behavior reflects an evaluation of costs and benefits. (p. 16)

Social institution: A major sphere of social life, with a set of beliefs and rules that is organized to meet basic human needs, such as the family, political, or educational systems. (p. 27)

Social mobility: Movement in the stratification system based on individual effort or achievement. (p. 136)

Social Security Act: Many programs under one umbrella, including unemployment compensation, health programs, cash welfare assistance, food stamps and school lunch programs, and cash assistance for the blind, survivors, and for seniors. (p. 385)

Social stratification: The hierarchical ranking of people within society on the basis of specific coveted resources, such as income and wealth. (p. 135)

Social structure: The organized pattern of social relationships and social institutions that together form the basis of society. (p. 8)

Socialization: The lifelong process through which we acquire the cultural values and skills needed to function as human beings and participate in society. (p. 311)

Socially constructed: Values or norms that are invented or "constructed" in a culture; people learn these and follow the conventional rules. (p. 99)

Socioeconomic status (SES): A vague combination of education, occupation, and income. (p. 138)

Sociological imagination: Reveals general patterns in what otherwise might be thought of as simple random events. (p. 8)

Spurious: An apparent relationship between two variables that is really caused by a third factor. (p. 230)

Statuses: Social positions in a group or society. (p. 40)

Stepfamilies: One or both of the adult partners has at least one child, either residing with them or elsewhere. (p. 464)

Structural functionalist theory: This theoretical perspective suggests that all social institutions, including the family, exist to fill a need in society. (p. 15)

Subsistence economies: Economies in which families use all of what they have, with virtually no surplus of food or other resources. (p. 71)

Superego: According to Freud, our conscience draws upon our cultural values and norms to help us understand why we cannot have everything we want. (p. 312)

Symbolic interaction: Humans interact not just with words, but also with symbols and meanings. (p. 313)

Symbolic interaction theory: This theoretical perspective focuses on the social interaction between family members and other groups, concerned with the meanings and interpretations that people have. (p. 16)

Temporary Assistance for Needy Families (TANF): The principal cash welfare program previously known as Aid to Families with Dependent Children (AFDC). (p. 24)

Tertiary sector: Also called the service sector; the fastest-growing sector of the U.S. economy; focuses on providing a wide variety of positions, such as salesclerk, attorney, cashier, and waitress. (p. 343)

Theory: A general framework, explanation, or tool to understand and describe the real-life world. (p. 14)

Time availability perspective: Suggests that the division of labor is largely determined by (1) the need for household labor, such as the number of children in the home; and (2) each partner's availability to perform household tasks, such as the number of hours spent in paid work. (p. 355)

Total fertility rates: The average number of births to women. (p. 90)

Trafficking: The illegal recruitment, transport, or sale of human beings into all forms of forced labor and servitude. (p. 408)

Transgendered: Persons who feel comfortable expressing gendered traits associated with the other sex. (p. 101)

Transnational family: A family living between two nations, often in search of work that pays a survivable wage. (p. 309)

Transsexual: Persons who undergo sex reassignment surgery and hormone treatments, either male to female, or female to male. (p. 101)

Triple jeopardy: People who face multiple disadvantages in society, e.g., old, female, and minority. (p. 383)

Universal programs: Social and economic programs that are available to all persons or families. (p. 22)

Violent resistance: Violence associated with self-defense. (p. 412)

Violence among intimates: Physical, economic, sexual, or psychological abuse covering a broad range of relationships. (p. 409)

Wealth: The value of all of a person's or a family's economic assets, including income, real estate, stocks, bonds, and other items of economic worth, minus debt. (p. 136)

Work-family conflict: Inter-role conflict in which the role pressures from the work and family domains are mutually incompatible in some respect. (p. 346)

World systems theory: A perspective that focuses on the economic and political interdependence and exploitation among nations. (p. 56)

Zero tolerance: A growing movement that emphasizes tougher laws; more stringent enforcement of those laws; training programs for those who work with victims and offenders, such as physicians or police officers; and a well-coordinated effort to offer victims the protection and services they need. (p. 433)

Bibliography

Abaid, Thoraya Ahmed. 2003. "Women and the United Nations: State of the World Population 2002—People, Poverty, and Possibilities." *Women's International Network* 29(1):7.

Abbott, Douglas A., and William Meredith. 1998. "Characteristics of Strong Families: Perceptions of Ethnic Parents." *Home Economics Research Journal* 17:140–147.

ABC/Nepal. 2003. "Red Light Traffic: The Trade in Nepali Girls." www.hsph.harvard.edu/Organizations/healthnet/SAsia/repro2/RED_LIGHT_TRAFFIC). Accessed March 19, 2003.

Abd el Salam, Seham. 1998. "Female Sexuality and the Discourse of Power: The Case of Egypt." Master's Thesis. Cairo, Egypt: American University in Cairo.

Abramovitz, Mimi. 1996. *Regulating the Lives of Women: Social Welfare Policy from Colonial Times to the Present* (rev. ed). Boston: South End Press.

Achenbaum, W. Andrew. 1978. *Old Age in the New Land: The American Experience Since 1790*. Baltimore, MD: Johns Hopkins University Press.

Acs, Gregory, and Pamela Loprest. 2001. *Synthesis Report of the Findings from ASPE's "Leavers' Grants."* Washington, DC: Office of the Assistant Secretary for Planning and Evaluation, U.S. Department of Health and Human Services.

Adams, Bert N. 2004. "Families and Family Study in International Perspective." *Journal of Marriage and Family* 66 (December):1076–1088.

Adams, Bert N., and Jan Trost (Eds.). 2004. *Handbook of World Families*. Thousand Oaks, CA: Sage.

Adams, Michele, and Scott Coltrane. 2003. "Boys and Men in Families." In Scott Coltrane (Ed.), *Families and Society: Classic and Contemporary Readings*, pp. 188–198. Belmont, CA: Wadsworth/Thomson Learning.

Adams, P. F., A. N. Dey, and J. L. Vickerie. 2007. "Summary Statistics for the U.S. Population: National Health Interview Survey 2005." National Center for Health Statistics. *Vital Health Statistics*, 10(233).

Administration on Aging. 2002. "A Profile of Older Americans." www.aoa.gov/prof/Statistics/profile/2002/profiles2002.asp. Accessed May 14, 2004.

Agnes, Flavia. 2001. *Law and Gender Inequality: The Politics of Women's Rights in India*. Oxford, England: Oxford University Press.

Ahmed, Sania Sultan, and Sally Bould. 2004. "One Able Daughter Is Worth 10 Illiterate Sons: Reframing the Patriarchal Family." *Journal of Marriage and Family* 66(5):1332–1341.

Alaimo, Katherine, Christine M. Olson, and Edward A. Frongillo, Jr. 2001. "Food Insufficiency and American School-Aged Children's Cognitive, Academic, and Psychosocial Development." *Pediatrics* 108(1): 44–53.

Alan Guttmacher Institute. 2004. *U.S. Teenage Pregnancy Statistics: Overall Trends, Trends by Race and Ethnicity and State-by-State Information*. New York: The Alan Guttmacher Institute.

______. 2000. "Why Is Teenage Pregnancy Declining? The Roles of Abstinence, Sexual Activity and Contraceptive Use." www.agi-usa.org/pubs/or_teen_preg_decline.html. Accessed June 14, 2000.

———. 1999. "Teenage Pregnancy: Overall Trends and State-by-State Information." www.agi-usa.org/pubs/teen_preg_stats.html. Accessed July 1, 2000.

Albers, L. H., D. E. Johnson, M. K. Hostetter, S. Iverson, and L. C. Miller. 1997. "Health of Children Adopted from the Former Soviet Union and Eastern Europe." *Journal of the American Medical Association* 278:922–924.

Aldous, Joan. 1996. *Family Careers: Rethinking the Developmental Perspective*. Thousand Oaks, CA: Sage.

Alford-Cooper, Finnegan. 1998. *For Keeps: Marriages that Last a Lifetime*. Armonk, NY: M. E. Sharpe.

Allen, Katherine R. 2000. "A Conscious and Inclusive Family Studies." *Journal of Marriage and the Family* 62:4–17.

Allen, Katherine R. 2004. "Feminist Visions for Transforming Families: Desire and Equality Then and Now." In Marilyn Coleman and Lawrence H. Ganong, (Eds.), *Handbook of Contemporary Families: Considering the Past, Contemplating the Future* (pp. 192–206). Thousand Oaks, CA: Sage.

———. 1997. "Lesbian and Gay Families." In T. Arendel (Ed.). *Contemporary Parenting*. Thousand Oaks, CA: Sage Publications.

Allen, Katherine R., Rosemary Blieszner, and Karen A. Roberto. 2000. "Families in the Middle and Later Years: A Review and Critique of Research in the 1990's." *Journal of Marriage and the Family* 62:911–926.

Alternatives to Marriage Project. 2006. "Frequently Asked Questions about Cohabitation." www.unmarried.org/cohabfaq.php. Accessed November 24, 2006.

———. 2004. "Marriage Movement." www.unmarried.org/marriagemovement.html. Accessed July 5, 2005.

Altman, Irwin, and Joseph Ginat. 1996. *Polygamous Families in Contemporary Society*. Cambridge, England: Cambridge University Press.

Amato, Paul R. 2004. "Tension Between Institutional and Individual Views of Marriage." *Journal of Marriage and Family* 66(November):959–965.

______. 1997. *A Generation at Risk: Growing Up in an Era of Family Upheaval*. Cambridge, MA: Harvard University Press.

———. 1996. "Explaining the Intergenerational Transmission of Divorce." *Journal of Marriage and the Family* 58(August):628–640.

———. 1994. "The Impact of Divorce on Men and Women in India and the United States." *Journal of Comparative Family Studies* 25:207–221.

Amato, Paul R., and Jacob Cheadle. 2005. "The Long Reach of Divorce: Tracking Marital Dissolution and Child Well-Being Across Three Generations." *Journal of Marriage and Family* 67:191–206.

Amato, Paul R., and Danelle D. Deboer. 2001. "The Transmission of Marital Instability Across Generations: Relationship Skills or Commitment to Marriage?" *Journal of Marriage and Family* 63:1038–1051.

Amato, Paul R., and Juliana M. Sobolewski. 2001. "The Effects of Divorce and Marital Discord on Adult Children's Psychological Well-Being." *American Sociological Review* 66:900–921.

Amato, Paul R., and Joan G. Gilbreth. 1999. "Nonresident Fathers and Children's Well-Being: A Meta-Analysis." *Journal of Marriage and the Family* 61:557–573.

Amato, Paul R., and Fernando Rivera. 1999. "Paternal Involvement and Children's Behavior Problems." *Journal of Marriage and the Family* 61:375–384.

Amato, Paul R., and Stacy J. Rogers. 1997. "A Longitudinal Study of Marital Problems and Subsequent Divorce." *Journal of Marriage and the Family* 59:612–624.

Amato, Paul R., and Alan Booth. 1991. "The Consequences of Parental Divorce and Marital Unhappiness for Adult Well-Being." *Social Forces* 69:895–914.

Amato, Paul R., and Bruce Keith. 1991. "Parental Divorce and Adult Well-Being: A Meta-Analysis." *Journal of Marriage and the Family* 53:43–58.

American Association of Retired Persons and Administration on Aging. 1997. *A Profile of Older Americans*. Washington DC: AARP.

American Association of Retired Persons and Travelers Foundation. 1988. *A National Study of Caregivers: Final Report*. Washington, DC: AARP.

American Association of University Women. 1992. *How Schools Shortchange Girls*. Washington, DC: AAUW Education Foundation.

American Psychological Association. 2005. "Elder Abuse and Neglect: In Search of Solutions." www.apa.org/pi/aging/eldabuse.html. Accessed January 7, 2006.

———. 1999a. "New Longitudinal Study Finds that Having a Working Mother Does No Significant Harm to Children." In press release for "Short-Term and Long-Term Effects of Early Parental Employment on Children of the National Longitudinal Survey of Youth." *Developmental Psychology* (35)2. www.apa.org/releases/wrkmom.html. Accessed July 27, 2003.

______. 1999b. "Study Finds that Child Care Does Impact Mother-Child Interaction." In press release for "Child Care and Mother-Child Interaction in the First 3 Years of Life," NICHD Early Child Care Research Network, *Developmental Psychology* 35(6). www.apa.org/releases/childcare.html. Accessed July 27, 2003.

AmeriStat. 2003. "U.S. Fertility Trends: Boom and Bust and Leveling Off." www.prb.org/AmeristatTemplate.cfm?Section=Fertility&template=/ContentManagement. Accessed June 23, 2003.

Amnesty International. 2003. "Amina Lawal: Sentenced to Death for Adultery." web.amnesty.org/pages/nga-010902-background-eng. Accessed December 20, 2003.

______. 2004. "What Is Female Genital Mutilation? Section One." In *Female Genital Mutilation—A Human Rights Information Pack*. www.amnesty.org/ailib/intcam/femgen/fgm1.htm. Accessed November 5, 2003.

Anderson, Margaret L., and Howard F. Taylor. 2004. *Sociology: Understanding a Diverse Society*, 3rd ed. Belmont, CA: Wadsworth.

Anderson, Margaret, and Howard F. Taylor. 2006. *Sociology: Understanding a Diverse Society*, 4th ed. Belmont CA: Wadsworth.

Annie E. Casey Foundation. 2005. *KIDS COUNT Data Book*. Baltimore, MD: The Annie E. Casey Foundation.

Antill, John K., Jacqueline Jarrett Goodnow, Graeme Russell, and Sandra Cotton. 1996. "The Influence of Parents and Family Context on Children's Involvement in Household Tasks." *Sex Roles* 34(3/4):215–236.

Aquilino, William S. 1997. "From Adolescent to Young Adult: A Prospective Study of Parent-Child Relations During the Transition to Adulthood." *Journal of Marriage and the Family* 59:670–686.

Aranda, Elizabeth. 2003. "Global Case Work and Gendered Constraints: The Case of Puerto Rican Transmigrants." *Gender and Society* 17:609–626.

Arditti, Joyce A. 2006. "Editor's Note." *Family Relations* 55(3):263–265.

Arditti, Joyce A., and Debra A. Madden-Derdich. 1997. "No Regrets: Custodial Mothers' Accounts of the Difficulties and Benefits of Divorce." *Contemporary Family Therapy* 25:61–81.

Arendell, Terry. 1986. *Mothers and Divorce: Legal, Economic, and Social Dilemmas*. Berkeley: University of California Press.

______. 2000. "Conceiving and Investigating Motherhood: The Decade's Scholarship." *Journal of Marriage and the Family* 62(4):1193–1207.

______. 1995. *Fathers and Divorce*. New York: Sage Publications.

Aries, Philippe. 1962. *Centuries of Childhood: A Social History of Family Life*. New York: Vintage Books.

Armas, Genaro C. 2004, 18 October. "Wealth Gaps Among Ethnicities Are Widening, According to Study." *The Oregonian*, p. A 5.

Artis, Julie E. 2007. "Maternal Cohabitation and Child Well-being Among Kindergarten Children." *Journal of Marriage and Family* 69:222–236.

Ashe, Arthur, and Arnold Rampersad. 1994. *Days of Grace*. New York: Ballantine Books.

Ashford, Lori, and Donna Clifton. 2005. *Women of Our World*. Population Reference Bureau. www.prb.org/pdf05/womenofourworld2005.pdf. Accessed January 7, 2006.

Atchley, Robert C. 1999. *Continuity and Adaptation in Aging: Creating Positive Experiences*. Baltimore, MD: Johns Hopkins University Press.

Atoh, Makoto. 1995. *The Recent Fertility Decline in Japan: Changes in Women's Role and Status and Their Policy Implications*. IPR Reprint Series No. 23. Tokyo, Japan: Institute of Population Problems, Ministry of Health and Welfare.

Avellar, Sarah, and Pamela J. Smock. 2005. "The Economic Consequences of the Dissolution of Cohabiting Unions." *Journal of Marriage and Family* 67(May):315–327.

AVERT.org. 2007. "Averting HIV and AIDS." http://avert.org/. Accessed July 23, 2007.

AVERT.org. 2005. "Children, HIV, and AIDS." www.avert.org/children.htm. Accessed July 7, 2005.

Axinn, William G., and Arland Thornton. 2000. "The Transformation in the Meaning of Marriage." In Linda J. Waite, Christine Bachrach, Michelle J. Hindin, Elizabeth Thompson, and Arland Thornton (Eds.), *The Ties That Bind: Perspectives on Marriage and Cohabitation*, pp. 147–165. New York: Aldine de Gruyter.

Baca Zinn, Maxine, and Bonnie Thornton Dill. 1994. "Difference and Domination." In Maxine Baca Zinn and Bonnie Thornton Dill (Eds.), *Women of Color in U.S. Society*, pp. 3–12. Philadelphia: Temple University Press.

Baca Zinn, Maxine, and D. Stanley Eitzen. 1996. *Diversity in Families*. New York: HarperCollins.

Bachu, Amara, and Martin O'Connell. 2001. "Fertility of American Women: June 2000." Current Population Reports No. P20-543RV. Washington, DC: U.S. Census Bureau.

Bailey, Beth. 1989. *From Front Porch to Back Seat: Courtship in Twentieth-Century America*. Baltimore, MD: Johns Hopkins University Press.

Bailey, J. Michael, and Richard C. Pillard. 1991. "A Genetic Study of Male Sexual Orientation." *Archives of General Psychiatry* 48:1089–1096.

Bailey, J. Michael, Richard C. Pillard, Michael C. Neale, and Yvonne Agyei. 1993. "Heritable Factors Influence Sexual Orientation in Women." *Archives of General Psychiatry* 50:217–223.

Baker, Joshua K. 2003. "Summary of Opinion Research on Same-Sex Marriage." IMAPP Policy Brief. www.imapp.org. Washington, DC: Institute for Marriage and Public Policy. Accessed June 30, 2005.

Bandura, Albert. 1962. *Social Learning through Imitation*. Lincoln: University of Nebraska Press.

Barcas, Francis Earle. 1983. *Images of Life on Children's Television: Sex Roles, Minorities, and Families*. New York: Praeger.

Bardwell, Jill R., Samuel W. Cochran, and Sharon Walker. 1986. "Relationship of Parental Education, Race, and Gender to Sex-Role Stereotyping in Five-Year-Old Kindergartners." *Sex Roles* 15:275–281.

Baumrind, Diana. 1968. "Authoritarian Versus Authoritative Parental Control." *Adolescence* 3:255–272.

———. 1966. "Effects of Authoritative Parental Control on Child Behavior." *Child Development* 37(4):887–907.

Baumrind, Diana, and Allen E. Black. 1967. "Socialization Practices Associated with Dimensions of Competence in Preschool Boys and Girls." *Child Development* 38(2):291–327.

Bauserman, Robert. 2002. "Child Adjustment in Joint-Custody Versus Sole-Custody Arrangements: A Meta-Analytic Review." *Journal of Family Psychology* 16(1):91–102.

Baxter, Janeen, and Emily K. Kane. 1995. "Dependence and Independence: A Cross-National Analysis of Gender Inequality and Gender Attitudes." *Gender and Society* 9(2):193–215.

BBC News. 2005. "Japan's Fertility Hits Record Low." Online: http://news.bbc.co.uk/2/hi/asia-pacific/4599071.stm. Accessed November 24, 2006.

Becker, Gary S. 1981. *A Treatise on the Family*. Cambridge, MA: Harvard University Press.

Bee, Helen, and Denise Boyd. 2007. *The Developing Child*, 11th ed. Boston: Allyn and Bacon.

Beech, Hannah. 2002. "With Women So Scarce, What Can Men Do?" *Time Magazine* 1(July):8.

Beecher, Catherine E., and Harriet B. Stowe. 1869. *The American Woman's Home*. Reprinted 2002 by Rutgers University Press, Piscataway, N.J.

Beller, Emily, and Michael Hout. 2006. "Intergenerational Social Mobility: The United States in Comparative Perspective." *The Future of Children*, 16:19–36.

Belsky, Jay, and Michael Rovine. 1990. "Patterns of Marital Change Across the Transition to Parenthood: Pregnancy to Three Years Postpartum." *Journal of Marriage and the Family* 52:5–19.

Belsky, Jay, Martha Weinraub, Margaret Owen, and Jean F. Kelly. 2001. "Quantity of Child Care and Problem Behavior." Presented at the Biennial Meeting of the

Society for Research on Child Development, Minneapolis, MN.

Bem, Sandra L. 1993. *The Lenses of Gender*. New Haven, CT: Yale University Press.

Benin, Mary H., and Debra A. Edwards. 1990. "Adolescents' Chores: The Difference Between Dual- and Single-Earner Families." *Journal of Marriage and the Family* 52:361–373.

Bennet, James. 1995. "Soaring New Car Prices: Will They Ever Stop?" *Denver Post*, 29 January, p. 3G.

Berardo, Felix M. 1970. "Survivorship and Social Isolation: The Case of the Aged Widower." *Family Coordinator* 19:11–25.

______. 1998. "Family Privacy: Issues and Concepts." *Journal of Family Issues* 19(1):4–19.

Berardo, Felix M., and Donna H. Berardo. 2000. "Widowhood." In E. F. Borgatta and R. J. Montgomery (Eds.), *Encyclopedia of Sociology*, 2nd ed., pp. 3255–3261. New York: Macmillan.

Berger, Peter. 1963. *Invitation to Sociology*. New York: Anchor Books.

______. 1977. *Facing Up to Modernity: Excursions in Society, Politics, and Religion*. New York: Basic Books.

Bergmann, Barbara R. 1996. *Saving Our Children from Poverty: What the United States Can Learn from France*. New York: Russell Sage Foundation.

Bernard, Jessie. 1972. *The Future of Marriage*. New York: World Pub.

Berne, Linda, and Barbara Huberman. 1999. *European Approaches to Adolescent Sexual Behavior and Responsibility*. Washington, DC: Advocates for Youth.

Berns, Roberta M. 2001. *Child, Family, School, Community: Socialization and Support*, 5th ed. New York: Thomson Learning.

Bernstein, Jared, and John Schmitt. 1998. "Making Work Pay: The Impact of the 1996–97 Minimum Wage Increase." No. 0-944826-80-6. Washington, DC: Economic Policy Institute.

Bertrand, Marianne, and Sandil Mullainathan. 2004. "Are Emily and Brendan More Employable than Latoya and Tyrone? Evidence on Racial Discrimination in the Labor Market From a Large Randomized Experiment." *American Economic Review* 94: 991–1013.

Bhutan Statistics. 2006. UNICEF. Available online: www.UNICEF.org/infobycountry/bhutan_bhutan_statistics.html

Bianchi, Suzanne M. 2000. "Maternal Employment and Time with Children: Dramatic Change or Surprising Continuity?" *Demography* 37:401–414.

———. 1990. "America's Children: Mixed Prospects." *Population Bulletin* 45(June):3–41.

Bianchi, Suzanne, John P. Robinson, and Melissa A. Milkie. 2006. *Changing Rhythms of American Family Life*. New York: Russell Sage Foundation.

Biblarz, Timothy J., and Greg Gottainer. 2000. "Family Structure and Children's Success: A Comparison of Widowed and Divorced Single-Mother Families." *Journal of Marriage and the Family* 62:533–548.

Bidwell, Lee D. Millar, and Brenda J. Vander Mey. 2000. *Sociology of the Family: Investigating Family Issues*. Boston: Allyn and Bacon.

Bierman, Alex, Elana Fazio, and Melissa Milkie. 2006. "A Multifaceted Approach to the Mental Health Advantage of Married Women: Assessing How Explanations Vary by Outcome Measures and Unmarried Group." *Journal of Family Issues* 27:554–582.

Bigler, Rebecca S., Cara J. Averhart, and Lynn S. Liben. 2003. "Race and the Workforce: Occupational Status, Aspirations, and Stereotyping Among African American Children." *Developmental Psychology* 39:572–580.

Bigner, Jerry J. 1999. "Raising Our Sons: Gay Men as Fathers." *Journal of Gay and Lesbian Social Services* 10(1):61–77.

Bigner, Jerry J., and R. Brooke Jacobsen. 1989. "The Value of Children to Gay and Heterosexual Fathers." *Journal of Homosexuality* 18:163–172.

Billingsley, Andrew. 1968. *Black Families in White America*. Upper Saddle River, NJ: Prentice-Hall, Inc.

Bittman, Michael, Paula England, Liana Sayer, Nancy Folbre, and George Matheson. 2003. "When Does Gender Trump Money? Bargaining and Time in Household Work." *American Journal of Sociology* 109:186–214.

Blackless, Melanie, Anthony Charuvastra, Amanda Derryck, Anne Fausto-Sterling, Karl Lauzanne, and Ellen Lee. 2000. "How Sexually Dimorphic Are We? Review and Synthesis." *American Journal of Human Biology* 12:151–166.

Blair, Sampson Lee. 1992. "Children's Participation in Household Labor: Child Socialization Versus the Need for Household Labor." *Journal of Youth and Adolescence* 21(2):241–258.

Blair, Sampson Lee, and Michael P. Johnson. 2000. "Parents and Family Structure: An Examination of Ethnic-Based Variations in Children's Household Labor." Paper presented at the 2000 American Sociological Association meeting in Washington, DC.

Blassingame, John W. 1972. *The Slave Community: Plantation Life on the Antebellum South*. New York: Oxford University Press.

Blau, Francine D., and Adam J. Grossberg. 1990. *Maternal Labor Supply and Children's Cognitive Development*. NBER Working Paper no. 3536. Cambridge, MA: National Bureau of Economic Research.

Blee, Kathleen, and Ann Tickamyer. 1995. "Racial Differences in Men's Attitudes About Women's Gender Roles." *Journal of Marriage and the Family* 57:21–30.

Blood, Robert O., and Donald M. Wolfe. 1960. *Husbands and Wives: The Dynamics of Married Living*. New York: Free Press.

Blyth, Dale A., and Eugene C. Roelkepartian. 1993. *Healthy Communities, Healthy Youth.* Minneapolis, MN: Search Institute.

Bogenschneider, Karen. 2000. "Has Family Policy Come of Age? A Decade Review of the State of U.S. Family Policy in the 1990s." *Journal of Marriage and the Family* 62:1136–1159.

———. 1997. "Parental Involvement in Adolescent Schooling: A Proximal Process with Transcontextual Validity." *Journal of Marriage and the Family* 59:718–733.

Bokker, Lon Paul, Roy C. Farley, and George Denny. 2006. "The Relationship Between Father/Child Contact and Emotional Well-Being Among Recently Divorced Fathers." *Journal of Divorce and Remarriage* 45: 63–77.

Bond, James T., Cindy Thompson, Ellen Galinsky, and David Prottas. 2002. *The National Study of the Changing Institute.* New York: The Families and Work Institute.

Bonnette, Robert. 1995a. *Housing of American Indians on Reservations—Equipment and Fuels.* U.S. Census Bureau No. Statistical Brief SB/95-11. Washington, DC: U.S. Government Printing Office.

______. 1995b. *Housing of American Indians on Reservations—Plumbing.* U.S. Census Bureau No. Statistical Brief SB/95-9. Washington, DC: U.S. Government Printing Office.

Bookwala, Jamila, and Jamie Jacobs. 2004. "Age, Marital Process, and Depressed Effect." *The Gerontologist*, 44:328–338.

Borst, Charlotte. 1995. *Catching Babies: The Professionalization of Childbirth.* Cambridge, MA: Harvard University Press.

Bose, Sunita, and Scott J. South. 2003. "Sex Composition of Children and Marital Disruption in India." *Journal of Marriage and Family* 65:996–1006.

Bouchard, Genevieve, Jolene Boudreau, and Renee Herbert. 2006. "Transition to Parenthood and Conjugal Life: Comparisons Between Planned and Unplanned Pregnancies." *Journal of Family Issues* 27:1512–1531.

Boushey, Heather, and David Rosnick. 2004. "For Welfare Reform to Work, Jobs Must Be Available." Center for Economic and Policy Research. www.cepr.net /labor_markets/welfarejobshit-2004april01.htm. Accessed December 8, 2005.

Bowers, Bonita F., and Barbara J. Myers. 1999. "Grandmothers Providing Care for Grandchildren: Consequences of Various Levels of Caregiving." *Family Relations* 48:303–311.

Braund, Kathleen E. H. 1990. "Guardians of Tradition and Handmaidens to Change: Women's Role in Creek Economic and Social Life During the Eighteenth Century." *American Indian Quarterly* 14(Summer): 239–258.

Brandolini, A., and Timothy M. Smeeding. 2006. "Patterns of Economic Inequality in Western Democracies: Some Facts on Levels and Trends." *PS: Political Science and Politics*, 39: 21–26.

Braver, Sanford L., and Diane O'Connell. 1998. *Divorced Dads: Shattering the Myths.* New York: Tarcher/ Putnam.

Braver, Sanford L., Ira M. Ellman, and William V. Fabricius. 2003. "Relocation of Children After Divorce and Children's Best Interests: New Evidence and Legal Considerations." *Journal of Family Psychology* 17:206–219.

Braver, Sanford L., Jeffrey T. Cookston, and Bruce R. Cohen. 2002. "Experiences of Family Law Attorneys with Current Issues in Divorce Practice." *Family Relations* 51:325–334.

Breslau, Naomi, Nigel S. Paneth, and Victoria C. Lucia. 2004. "The Lingering Academic Deficits of Low Birth Weight Children." *Pediatrics* 114(4):1035–1040.

Briere, John N. 1992. *Child Abuse Trauma: Theory and Treatment of Lasting Effects.* Newbury Park, CA: Sage Publications.

Brinton, Mary C. 1993. *Women and the Economic Miracle: Gender and Work in Postwar Japan.* Berkeley: University of California Press.

Broderick, Carlfred, and James Smith. 1979. "The General Systems Approach to the Family." In Wesley Burr, Reuben Hill, F. Ivan Nye, and Ira L. Reiss (Eds.), *Contemporary Theories About the Family*, vol. 2, pp. 112–129. Upper Saddle River, NJ: Prentice Hall.

Brodie, Mollyann, Annie Steffenson, Jaime Valdez, and Rebecca Levin. 2002. *2002 National Survey of Latinos: Summary of Findings.* Washington, DC: Pew Hispanic Center/Kaiser Family Foundation.

Brooks-Gunn, Jeanne, and Greg J. Duncan. 1997. "The Effects of Poverty on Children." *The Future of Children (Children and Poverty).* 7(2 Summer/Fall):55–71.

Brown, Brett V., Erik A. Michelsen, Tamara G. Halle, and Kristin A. Moore. 2001. "Fathers' Activities with Their Kids." *Child Trends Research Brief.* www.childtrends.org. Accessed November 14, 2003.

Brown, Susan L. 2002. "Child Well-Being in Cohabitating Families." In Alan Booth and Ann C. Crouter (Eds.), *Just Living Together*, pp. 173–187. Mahwah, NJ: Lawrence Erlbaum.

Brown, Susan L., and Alan Booth. 1996. "Cohabitation Versus Marriage: A Comparison of Relationship Quality." *Journal of Marriage and the Family* 58:668–678.

Brown, Tony N., Emily E. Tanner-Smith, Chase L. Lesane-Brown, and Michael E. Ezell. 2007. "Child, Parent, and Situational Correlates of Familial, Ethnic/Race Socialization." *Journal of Marriage and Family*, 69: 14–25.

Browning, James J., and Donald G. Dutton. 1986. "Assessment of Wife Assault with the Conflict Tactics Scale: Using Couple Data to Quantify the Differential Reporting Effect." *Journal of Marriage and the Family* 48:375–379.

Brubaker, Timothy H. 1991. "Families in Later Life: A Burgeoning Research Area." In Alan Booth (Ed.), *Contemporary Families: Looking Forward, Looking Back.*

Minneapolis, MN: National Council on Family Relations.

Brubaker, Timothy H., and Beth I. Kinsel. 1985. "Who Is Responsible for Household Tasks in Long Term Marriages of 'Young-Old' Elderly?" *Lifestyles: A Journal of Changing Patterns* 7:238–247.

Buchanan, Andrea A. 2003. *Mother Shock: Loving Every (Other) Minute of It*. Emeryville, CA: Seal Press.

Budrys, Grace. 2005. *Our Unsystematic Health Care System*, 2nd ed. New York: Rowman & Littlefield.

Buehler, Cheryl, and Jean M. Gerard. 2002. "Marital Conflict, Ineffective Parenting, and Children's and Adolescent's Maladjustment." *Journal of Marriage and Family* 64:78–92.

Bulanda, Ronald E. 2004. "Paternal Involvement with Children: The Influence of Gender Ideologies." *Journal of Marriage and the Family* 66:40–45.

Bulcroft, Kris A., and Richard A. Bulcroft. 1991. "The Nature and Functions of Dating in Later Life." *Research on Aging* 13:244–260.

Bulcroft, Richard, Kris Bulcroft, Karen Bradley, and Carl Simpson. 2000. "The Management and Production of Risk in Romantic Relationships: A Postmodern Paradox." *Journal of Family History* 25:63–92.

Buldac, Jessica L. Sandra L. Caron, and Mary Ellin Logue. 2006. "The Effects of Parental Divorce on College Students." *Journal of Divorce and Remarriage* 46:83–104.

Bumiller, Elisabeth. 1990. *May You Be the Mother of a Hundred Sons*. New York: Fawcett Columbine.

Bumpass, Larry L. 1998. "The Changing Significance of Marriage in the United States." In Karen O. Mason, Noriko O. Tsuya, and Minja K. Choe (Eds.), *The Changing Family in Comparative Perspective*, pp. 63–79. Honolulu, HI: East-West Center.

Bumpass, Larry, and Hsien-Hen Lu. 2000. "Trends in Cohabitation and Implications for Children's Family Contexts in the United States." *Population Studies* 54:29–41.

Bureau of Justice Statistics. 2001. *Special Report Intimate Partner Violence and Age of Victim, 1993–1999*. Washington, DC: U.S. Government Printing Office.

Bureau of Labor Statistics. 2006. "Employment Situation Summary." www.bls.gov/news/release/empsit.nro.htm. Accessed May 5, 2006.

Burgess, Ernest W., and Harvey J. Locke. 1945. *The Family: From Institution to Companionship*. New York: American Book Company.

Burns, John F. 1998. "Though Illegal, Child Marriage Is Popular in Parts of India." In J. Norton, *Global Studies: India & South Asia*, 4th ed., Guilford, CT: Pushkin.

Burton, C. Emory. 1992. *The Poverty Debate*. Westport, CT: Praeger.

Buss, David M., Todd K. Shackelford, and Gregory J. LeBlanc. 2000. "Number of Children Desired and Preferred Spousal Age Difference: Context-Specific Mate Preference Patterns Among 37 Cultures." *Evolution and Human Behavior* 21:323–331.

Buss, David M., Todd K. Shackelford, Lee A. Kirkpatrick, and Randy J. Larsen. 2001. "A Half Century of Mate Preferences: The Cultural Evolution of Values." *Journal of Marriage and Family* 63(May):491–503.

Callan, Victor J. 1985. "Perceptions of Parents, the Voluntarily and Involuntarily Childless: A Multidimensional Scaling Analysis." *Journal of Marriage and the Family* 47:1045–1050.

Campbell, Jacqueline C., Linda Rose, Joan Kub, and Daphne Nedd. 1998. "Voices of Strength and Resistance: A Contextual and Longitudinal Analysis of Women's Responses to Battering." *Journal of Interpersonal Violence* 13:743–762.

Canada NewsWire. 2004. "Health Care Spending to Reach $130 Billion this Year; Per Capita Spending to Hit $4,000." Press.arrivenet.com/business/article.php/533122.html. Accessed March 14, 2006.

Canadian Encyclopedia. 2005. "Family Allowance." www.thecanadianencyclopedia.com/index.cfm?PgNm=TCE&Params=A1ARTA0002718. Accessed June 26, 2005.

Cancian, Francesca M. 1989. "Love and the Rise of Capitalism." In Barbara J. Risman and Pepper Schwartz, *Gender in Intimate Relations: A Microstructural Approach*, pp. 12–25. Belmont, CA: Wadsworth.

———. 1987. *Love in America: Gender and Self-Development*. New York: Cambridge University Press.

Cancian, Maria, and Daniel R. Meyer. 1998. "Who Gets Custody?" *Demography* 35:147–157.

Cantor, Marjorie H., Mark Brennan, and R. Andrew Shippy. 2004. *Caregiving Among Older Lesbian, Gay, Bisexual, and Transgender New Yorkers*. New York: National Gay and Lesbian Task Force Policy Institute.

Capizzano, Jeffrey, and Gina Adams. 2004. "Children in Low-Income Families Are Less Likely to Be in Center-Based Child Care." No.16 in *Snapshots of America's Families III*. Urban Institute. www.urban.org/urlprint.cfm?ID=8701. Accessed July 11, 2005.

Capizzano, Jeffrey, and Regan Main. 2005. "Many Young Children Spend Long Hours in Child Care." No. 22 in *Snapshots of America's Families III*. The Urban Institute. www.urban.org/urlprint.cfm?ID=9232. Accessed July 11, 2005.

Capizzano, Jeffrey, Gina Adams, and Freya L. Sonenstein. 2000. "Child Care Arrangements for Children Under Five: Variation Across States." No. B-7 in *New Federalism: National Survey of America's Families*. Urban Institute. www.urban.org/url.cfm?ID=309438. Accessed July 15, 2003.

Carole, J. 1994. "Are Children at Risk for Sexual Abuse by Homosexuals?" *Pediatrics* 94(1).

Carr, Deborah. 2006. "Good Grief: Bouncing Back From a Spouse's Death in Later Life." *Contexts* 5:22–27.

———. 2004. "The Desire to Date and Remarry Among Older Widows and Widowers." *Journal of Marriage and the Family* 66:1051–1068.

Carter, Wendy Y. 2006. "Attitudes Toward Pre-Marital Sex, Non-Marital Childbearing, Cohabitation, and Marriage

Among Blacks and Whites." NSFH Working Paper No. 61. Center for Demography and Ecology, University of Wisconsin-Madison. Online: www.ssc.wisc.edu/cdc/nsfhwp/nsfh61.pdf. Accessed July 8, 2006.

Cartwright, Claire. 2005. "You Want to Know How It Affected Me? Young Adults' Perceptions of the Impact of Parental Divorce." *Journal of Divorce and Remarriage* 44:125–143.

Casper, Lynne M., and Suzanne M. Bianchi. 2002. "Cohabitation." In *Trends in the American Family*, pp. 39–68. Thousand Oaks, CA: Sage Publications, Inc.

Cassidy, Margaret, and Gary R. Lee. 1989. "The Study of Polyandry: A Critique and Synthesis." *Journal of Comparative Family Studies* 20:1–11.

Castro, Janice. 1993. "Disposable Workers." *Time Magazine*, March 29, pp. 43–47.

Cawthon, Laurie. 1996. *Planned Homebirths: Outcomes Among Medicaid Women in Washington State*. Olympia, WA: Department of Social and Health Services, Office of Research and Data Analysis.

Ceglian, Cindy Penor, and Scott Gardner. 1999. "Attachment Style: A Risk for Multiple Marriages." *Journal of Divorce and Remarriage* 31:125–139.

Center for Families, Work, and Well-Being. 2001. "Response to Extension of Parental Leaves." www.worklifecanada.ca/index.shtml. Accessed October 19, 2001.

Center on Budget and Policy Priorities. 2006. "New Estate Tax Compromise Even Costlier than Previous One." www.cbpp.org/policy-points6-23-06.htm. Accessed June 27, 2006.

———. 2003. "Facts About the Earned Income Credit: A Tax Credit for People Who Work." www.cbpp.org/eic2003/factseic-2003.pdf. Accessed August 26, 2003.

Center on Hunger and Poverty. 2002. *The Consequences of Hunger and Food Insecurity for Children: Evidence from Recent Scientific Studies*. Heller School for Social Policy and Management. Boston: Brandeis University.

Centers for Disease Control and Prevention, National Center for Environmental Health. 2006. "General Lead Information: Questions and Answers." www.cdc.gov/nceh/lead/faq/about.htm. Accessed March 19, 2006.

———. 2006a. "Chlamydia Fact Sheet." www.cdc.gov/std/chlamydia/STDFact-Chlamydia.htm. Accessed November 24, 2006.

———. 2006b. *HIV/AIDS Prevention. African Americans: Preventive Challenges*. www.cdc.gov/hiv/topics/aa/challenges.htm. Accessed August 18, 2006.

———. 2006c. "A Glance at the HIV/AIDS Epidemic: HIV/AIDS Diagnoses." www.cdc.gov/hiv/resources/factsheets/At-A-Glance.htm. Accessed May 5, 2006.

———. 2006d (April 5). "Healthy Youth! Youth Online: Comprehensive Results." apps.nccd.cdc.gov/yrbss/. Accessed July 15, 2006.

———. 2006e. HIV/AIDS Surveillance Report, 2005. Vol. 17. www.cdc.gov/hiv/topics/surveillance/resources/reports/. Accessed July 15, 2006.

———. 2006f. Assisted Reproductive Technology Success Rates: 2004. ftp.cdc.gov/pub/Publications/art/2004ART508.pdf Accessed August 18, 2006.

———. 2005. "Assisted Reproductive Technology Success Rates." www.cdc.gov/ART/ART2003/index.htm. Accessed October 29, 2006.

———. 2001. "A Glance at the HIV Epidemic." www.cdc.nchstp/od/news/At-a-Glance.pdf. Accessed June 7, 2005.

Central Intelligence Agency. 2006. "The World Handbook." www.odci.gov/cia/publications/factbook/index.html. Accessed March 7, 2006.

———. 2003. The World Factbook. www.cia.gov/cia/publications/factbook. Accessed July 23, 2003.

Centre des Liaisons Europeennes et Internationales de Securite Sociale. 2006. "The French Social Security System." www.cleiss.fr/docs/regimes/regime_france/an_3.html. Accessed January 15, 2006.

Chamberlain, Geoffrey, Ann Wraight, and Patricia Crowley. 1997. *Home Births: The Report of the 1994 Confidential Enquiry*. Nashville, TN: Parthenon Publishing.

Chang, Winnie. 1993. "Unequal Terms." *Free China Review* 43(11):26–31.

Chaudry, Ajay. 2006. *Putting Children First: How Low-Wage Working Mothers Manage Child Care*. New York: Russell Sage Foundation.

Cherlin, Andrew J., and Frank F. Furstenberg. 1986. *The New American Grandparent: A Place in the Family, A Life Apart*. New York: Basic Books.

ChicagoLegalNet.com. 2003. Family and Medical Leave Act. chicagolegalnet.com/FMLA.htm. Accessed November 14, 2005.

Child Labor Public Education Project. "Child Labor in U.S. History." www.continuetolearn.uiowa.edu/laborctr/child_labor/about/us_history.html. Accessed July 17, 2006.

Child Welfare Information Gateway. 2006. General Information Packet. www.childwelfare.gov/pubs/can_info_packet.cfm. Accessed December 5, 2006.

Children's Defense Fund. 2005. "Defining Poverty and Why It Matters for Children." www.childrensdefensefund.org. Accessed February 13, 2006.

______. 2002. *The State of Children in America's Union: A 2002 Action Guide to No Child Left Behind*. Washington, DC: Children's Defense Fund.

______. 2001a. *Child Care Basics*. www.childrensdefense.org/site/PageServer?pagename=research_national_data_child_care_basics. Accessed February 26, 2005.

______. 2001b. *The State of America's Children: Yearbook 2001*. Washington, DC: Children's Defense Fund.

———. 1994. *Wasting America's Future: The Children's Defense Fund Report on the Cost of Child Poverty*. Washington, DC: Children's Defense Fund.

Children's Rights Network of Japan. 2006. Child Custody. www.crnjapan.com/custody/en/. Accessed September 24, 2006.

Childs, Erica Chito. 2005. *Navigating Interracial Borders: Black-White Couples and Their Social Worlds*. New Brunswick, N.J.: Rutgers University Press.

Christopher, F. Scott, and Susan Sprecher. 2000. "Sexuality in Marriage, Dating, and Other Relationships: A Decade Review." *Journal of Marriage and the Family* 62(4):999–1017.

Chun, Hyunbae, and Injae Lee. 2001. "Why Do Married Men Earn More: Productivity of Marriage Selection?" *Economic Inquiry*. 39(2):307–319.

Cicirelli, Victor G. 1983. "Adult Children and Their Elderly Parents." In Timothy H. Brubaker (Ed.), *Family Relationships in Later Life*, pp. 31–46. Beverly Hills, CA: Sage Publications.

Clark, Robert L. 1990. "Income Maintenance Policies in the United States." In Robert H. Binstock and Linda K. George (Eds.), *Handbook of Aging and the Social Sciences*, 3rd ed. San Diego, CA: Academic Press, Inc.

Clearinghouse on International Developments in Child, Youth, and Family Policies. 2001. "New 12 Country Study Reveals Substantial Gaps in U.S. Early Childhood Education and Care Policies." www.childpolicyintl.org/issuebrief/issuebrief1.htm. Accessed July 28, 2003.

Cloud, John. 1998. "Trans Across America." *Time Magazine*, 20 July, pp. 48–49.

CNN.com. 2003. "Supreme Court Strikes Down Texas Sodomy Law." www.cnn.com/2003/LAW/06/26/scotus.sodomy/. Accessed July 5, 2006.

Coalition for Marriage, Family and Couples Education, the Religion, Culture, and Family Project of the University of Chicago Divinity School, and the Institute for American Values. 2000. "The Marriage Movement: A Statement of Principles, 2000." Press Release. www.smartmarriages.com/marriage.movement.html. Accessed July 5, 2003.

Cobb, Nancy J. 2007. *Adolescence: Continuity, Change, and Diversity*, 6th ed. New York: McGraw-Hill.

Cockerham, William C. 1997. *This Aging Society*. Upper Saddle River, NJ: Prentice Hall.

Cohen, Carl and James Sterba. 2003. *Affirmative Action and Racial Preference: A Debate*. Oxford, UK: Oxford University Press.

Cohen, Robin A., and Barbara Bloom. 2005. *Trends in Health Insurance and Access to Medical Care for Children Under Age 19 Years: United States, 1998–2003*. Advance Data from Vital and Health Statistics No. 355. Hyattsville, MD: National Center for Health Statistics.

Cohen, Robin A., and Hanyu Ni. 2004. "Health Insurance Coverage for the Civilian Noninstitutionalized Population: Early Release Estimates from the National Health Insurance Survey, January–June 2003." Centers for Disease Control and Prevention. www.cdc.gov/nchs/nhis.htm. Accessed January 20, 2004.

Colb, Sherry F. 2001. "Denial of Birth Control Insurance as a Form of Sex Discrimination: What 'Male' Drug Is Most Similar to Birth Control Pills?" Find Law. http://writ.news.findlaw.com/colb/20010103.html. January 3, 2001.

Cole, Kristen. 2003. "Census Study: Whites Less Likely than Blacks to Live with Extended Family." Brown University News Service. www.brown.edu/Administration/News_Bureau/2003-04/03-033.html. Accessed June 28, 2006.

Coley, Rebekah Levine, and P. Lindsay Chase-Lansdale. 1998. "Adolescent Pregnancy and Parenthood: Recent Evidence and Future Directions." *American Psychologist* 53:152–166.

Collins, Patricia Hill. 1999. "Will the Real Mother Please Stand Up." In Adele E. Clarke and Virginia L. Olesen (Eds.), *Revisioning Women, Health and Healing: Feminist, Cultural, and Technoscience Perspectives*. New York: Routledge.

———. 1994. "Shifting the Center: Race, Class, and Feminist Theorizing About Motherhood." In Evelyn N. Glenn, Grace Chang, and Linda R. Forcey (Eds.), *Mothering: Ideology, Experience, and Agency*. New York: Routledge.

Collins, Sara R., Karen Davis, Michelle Doty, and Alice Ho. 2004. *Wages, Health Benefits, and Workers' Health*. The Commonwealth Fund. www.cmwf.org/usr_doc/788_Collins_wageshltbenefits_workershlt_ib.pdf. Accessed March 17, 2005.

Coltrane, Scott. 1998. *Gender and Families*. Thousand Oaks, CA: Pine Forge Press.

———. 1996. *Family Man: Fatherhood, Housework, and Gender Equity*. New York: Oxford University Press.

______. 2000. "Research on Household Labor: Modeling and Measuring the Social Embeddedness of Routine Family Work." *Journal of Marriage and the Family* 62(November):1208–1233.

Coltrane, Scott, and Masako Ishii-Kuntz. 1992. "Men's Housework: A Life Course Perspective." *Journal of Marriage and the Family* 54:43–57.

Commission on Family and Medical Leave. 1996. "A Workable Balance: Report to Congress on Family and Medical Leave Policies." www.dol.gov/dol/esa/fmla.htm. Accessed February 17, 2000.

Committee on the Consequences of Uninsurance. 2002. "Health Insurance Is a Family Matter." Institute of Medicine. www.iom.edu/file.asp?id=4161. Accessed May 20, 2005.

Conger, Rand D., Katherine Conger, and Glen H. Elder Jr. 1997. "Family Economic Hardship and Adolescent Adjustment: Mediating and Moderating Processes." In Greg J. Duncan and Jeanne Brooks-Gunn, *Consequences of Growing Up Poor*, pp. 288–310. New York: Russell Sage Foundation.

Conger, Rand D., Martha A. Rueter, and Glen H. Elder Jr. 1999. "Couple Resilience to Economic Pressure." *Journal of Personality and Social Psychology* 76:54–71.

Congressional Budget Office. 2005. "Historical Effective Federal Tax Rates: 1979 to 2002." www.cbo.gov/showdoc.cfm?index=6133&sequence=0. Accessed October 25, 2005.

Connidis, Ingrid Arnet, and Julie Ann McMullin. 1999. "Permanent Childlessness: Perceived Advantages and Disadvantages Among Older Persons." *Canadian Journal on Aging* 18:447–465.

———. 1994. "Social Supports in Older Age: Assessing the Impact of Marital and Parent Status." *Canadian Journal on Aging* 13:510–527.

Connolly, Catherine. 1996. "An Analysis of Judicial Decisions in Same-Sex Visitation and Adoption Cases." *Behavioral Sciences and the Law* 14:187–203.

Contra Costa County (California) Board of Supervisors. 2003. "Zero Tolerance for Domestic Violence?" www.co.contra-costa.ca.us/depart/cao/DomViol/ztdv%20overview%20for%20website%202%2002.htm. Accessed March 23, 2003.

Coombs, Robert. 1991. "Marital Status and Personal Well-Being: A Literature Review." *Family Relations* 40:97–102.

Coontz, Stephanie. 2000. *The Way We Never Were: American Families and the Nostalgia Trap*. New York: Basic Books.

______. 2004. "The World Historical Transformation of Marriage." *Journal of Marriage and Family* 66(4):974–979.

______. 2005. *Marriage: A History*. New York: Viking Press.

———. 1997. *The Way We Really Are: Coming to Terms with America's Changing Families*. New York: Basic Books.

Cornell Gerontology Research Institute. 2000. "His and Her Retirement? The Role of Gender and Marriage in the Retirement Process." *The Edward R. Roybal Centers for Research on Applied Gerontology*.

Corsaro, William A. 1997. *A Sociology of Childhood*. Thousand Oaks, CA: Pine Forge Press.

Cott, Nancy F. 2002. *Public Vows: A History of Marriage and the Nation*. Cambridge, MA: Harvard University Press.

Cott, Nancy F. 1997. *The Bonds of Womanhood: "Woman's Sphere" in New England, 1780–1935*, 2nd ed. New Haven, CT: Yale University Press.

Coughlin, Chris, and Samuel Vuchinich. 1996. "Family Experience in Preadolescence and the Development of Male Delinquency." *Journal of Marriage and the Family* 58:491–501.

Coven, Martha. 2005. "An Introduction to TANF." Center on Budget and Policy Priorities. www.centeronbudget.org/1-22-02tanf2.htm. Accessed January 3, 2006.

Covey, Herbert C., and Paul T. Lockman. 1996. "Narrative References of Older African Americans Living Under Slavery." *Social Science Journal* 3:23–37.

Cox, Martha J., Blair Paley, Margaret Burchinal, and C. Chris Payne. 1999. "Marital Perceptions and Interactions Across the Transition to Parenthood." *Journal of Marriage and the Family* 61:611–625.

Crabb, Peter B., and Dawn Bielawski. 1994. "The Social Representation of Material Culture and Gender in Children's Books." *Sex Roles* 30:69–79.

Craft, Carrie. 2006. "Gay Adoption Basics." adoption.about.com/od/gaylesbian/a/gayadopt.htm. Accessed July 13, 2006.

Crohn, Helen. 2006. "Five Styles of Positive Stepmothering From the Perspective of Young Adult Stepdaughters." *Journal of Divorce and Remarriage* 46:119–134.

Crosbie-Burnett, Margaret. 1989. "Application of Family Stress Theory to Remarriage: A Model for Assessing and Helping Stepfamilies." *Family Relations* 38: 323–331.

Crum, Rosa M., John E. Helzer, and James C. Anthony. 1993. "Level of Education and Alcohol Abuse and Dependence in Adulthood: A Further Inquiry." *American Journal of Public Health* 83:830–837.

Cunningham, Jean, Thomas Pearce, and Patti Pearce. 1988. "Childhood Sexual Abuse and Medical Complaints in Adult Women." *Journal of Interpersonal Violence* 3:131–144.

Cunningham-Burley, Sarah. 2001. "The Experience of Grandfatherhood." In Alexis J. Walker, Margaret Manoogian-O'Dell, Lori A. McGraw, and Diana L. White, *Later Life: Connections and Transitions*, pp. 92–96. Thousand Oaks, CA: Pine Forge Press.

Curran, Dolores. 1987. *Stress and the Healthy Family: How Healthy Families Handle the 10 Most Common Stresses*. New York: Harper Collins.

D.L. 2003, 15 August. "Letter to the Editor." *USA Today*, p. 11A.

Dahl, Gordon, and Enrico Moretti. 2003. "The Demand for Sons: Evidence from Divorce, Fertility, and Shotgun Marriage." National Bureau of Economic Research, September. Unpublished draft.

Dalaker, Joe. 2005. *Alternative Poverty Estimates in the United States: 2003*. Current Population Reports P60-227. Washington, DC: U.S. Census Bureau. www.census.gov/prod/2005pubs/p60-227.pdf. Accessed June 6, 2006.

D'Aluisio, Faith, and Peter Menzel. 1996. *Women in the Material World*. Berkeley: University of California Press.

Daly, Kerry J. 2001. "Deconstructing Family Time: From Ideology to Lived Experience." *Journal of Marriage and Family* 63:283–294.

Dannefer, Dale, and Peter Uhlenberg. 1999. "Paths of the Life Course: A Typology." In Vern L. Bengtson and K. Warner Schaie (Eds.), *Handbook of Theories of Aging*, pp. 306–326. New York: Springer.

Daskal, Jennifer. 1998. *In Search of Shelter: The Growing Shortage of Affordable Rental Housing*. Washington, DC: Center on Budget and Policy Priorities.

Data Lounge. 2004. "City of San Francisco Sues California." www.datalounge.com/datalounge/news/record.html?record=21216. Accessed February 22, 2004.

Davidson, Michele R. 2002. "Outcomes of High-Risk Women Cared for by Certified Nurse-Midwives." *Journal of Midwifery and Women's Health* 47(1):46–49.

Davis, F. James. 1991. *Who Is Black? One Nation's Definition.* University Park, PA: The Pennsylvania State University Press.

Davis, Shannon N., and Theodore N. Greenstein. 2004. "Cross-National Variations in the Division of Household Labor." *Journal of Marriage and Family* 66(December):1260–1271.

Davis-Floyd, Robbie. 2004. *Birth as an American Rite of Passage.* Berkeley: University of California Press.

Dawley, Katy. 2003. "Origins of Nurse-Midwifery in the United States and Its Expansion in the 1940s." *Journal of Midwifery and Women's Health* 48(2):86–95.

Day, Randal D., Gary W. Peterson, and Colleen McCracken. 1998. "Predicting Spanking of Younger and Older Children by Mothers and Fathers." *Journal of Marriage and the Family* 60:79–94.

De Lew, Nancy, George Greenbery, and Kraig Kinchen. 1992. "A Layman's Guide to the U.S. Health Care System." *Health Care Financing Review* 14:151–165.

Deaux, Katherine. 1984. "From Individual Differences to Social Categories: Analysis of a Decade's Research on Gender." *American Psychologist* 39:105–116.

Degler, Carl N. 1980. *At Odds: Women and the Family in America from the Revolution to the Present.* New York: Oxford University Press.

______. 1983. *Out of Our Past.* London, England: Harper Perennial.

Del Castillo, Richard G. 1984. *La Familia: Chicano Families in the Urban Southwest, 1848 to the Present.* Notre Dame, IN: University of Notre Dame Press.

DeLeire, Thomas, and Ariel Kalil. 2005. "How Do Cohabiting Couples with Children Spend Their Money?" *Journal of Marriage and Family* 67(May): 286–295.

Delsol, Catherine, Gayla Margolin, and Richard S. John. 2003. "A Typology of Maritally Violent Men and Correlates of Violence in a Community Sample." *Journal of Marriage and Family* 65(3):635–651.

DeMaris, Alfred, and William MacDonald. 1993. "Premarital Cohabitation and Subsequent Marital Stability in the United States: A Reassessment." *Journal of Marriage and the Family* 55(May):399–407.

DeMaris, Alfred, Michael L. Benson, Greer L. Fox, Terrence Hill, and Judy Van Wyk. 2003. "Distal and Proximal Factors in Domestic Violence: A Test of an Integrated Model." *Journal of Marriage and Family* 65:652–667.

DeMeis, Debra K., and H. Wesley Perkins. 1996. "'Supermoms' of the Nineties: Homemaker and Employed Mothers' Performance and Perceptions of the Motherhood Role." *Journal of Family Issues* 17:777–792.

Demo, David H., and Katherine R. Allen. 1996. "Diversity Within Lesbian and Gay Families: Challenges and Implications for Family Theory and Research." *Journal of Social and Personal Relationships* 13(3):415–434.

Demo, David H., and Martha J. Cox. 2000. "Families with Young Children: A Review of Research in the 1990s." *Journal of Marriage and the Family* 62(November): 876–895.

Demo, David, Katherine Allen, and Mark A. Fine. 2000. *Handbook of Family Diversity.* New York: Oxford University Press.

Demos, John. 1970. *A Little Commonwealth: Family Life in Plymouth Colony.* New York: Oxford University Press.

______. 1986. *Past, Present and Personal: The Family and Life Course in American History.* New York: Oxford University Press.

DeNavas-Walt, Carmen, Bernadette D. Proctor, and Cheryl Hill Lee. 2006. "Income, Poverty, and Health Insurance Coverage in the United States: 2005." Current Population Reports No. P60-231. Washington, DC: U.S. Census Bureau.

Derne, Steve. 2006. "Arnold Schwarzenegger, Ally McBeal, and Arranged Marriages: Globalization's Effect on Ordinary People in India." In D. Stanley Eitzen and Maxine Baca Zinn (Eds.), *Globalization: The Transformation of Social Worlds*, pp. 146–153. Belmont, CA: Wadsworth Publishing Co.

Dey, Achintya N., and Barbara Bloom. 2005. "Summary Health Statistics for U.S. Children: National Health Interview Survey, 2003." National Center for Health Statistics: Vital Health Stat 10(223). Washington, DC: U.S. Government Printing Office.

Diekman, Amanda B., and Sarah K. Murnen. 2004. "Learning to Be Little Women and Little Men: The Inequitable Gender Equality of Nonsexist Children's Literature." *Sex Roles: A Journal of Research*, 50: 373–385.

Dilworth-Anderson, Peggye. 2001. "Extended Kin Networks in Black Families." In Alexis J. Walker, Margaret Manoogian-O'Dell, Lori A. McGraw, and Diana L. White (Eds.), *Families in Later Life: Connections and Transitions*, pp. 104–106. Thousand Oaks, CA: Pine Forge Press.

Dinh, Quang-Chi. 1995. "Projection de la Population Totale Pour la France Metropolitaine: Base RP90, Horizons 1990–2050." In *Demographie-Societe.* Paris, France: INSEE.

Divorceinfo.com. 2006. "Alimony in Divorce." www.divorceinfo.com/alimony.com. Accessed June 6, 2006.

Dodson, Lisa, and Jillian Dickert. 2004. "Girls' Family Labor in Low-Income Households: A Decade of Qualitative Research." *Journal of Marriage and Family* 66:318–332.

Doherty, William J., Edward F. Kouneski, and Martha F. Erickson. 1998. "Responsible Fathering: An Overview and Conceptual Framework." *Journal of Marriage and the Family* 60:277–292.

Domhoff, G. William. 2005. *Who Rules America: Power, Politics, and Social Change*. New York: McGraw-Hill.

Donnelly, Denise A. 1993. "Sexually Inactive Marriages." *The Journal of Sex Research* 30:171–179.

Dorr, Rheta C. 1970. *Susan B. Anthony: The Woman Who Changed the Mind of a Nation*. New York: AMS Press.

Dowd, Nancy E. 1997. *In Defense of Single-Parent Families*. New York: New York University Press.

Downey, Douglas B. 1995. "Understanding Academic Achievement Among Children in Stephouseholds: The Role of Parental Resources, Sex of Stepparent, and Sex of Child." *Social Forces* 73:875–894.

———. 1994. "The School Performance of Children from Single-Mother and Single-Father Families: Economics or Interpersonal Deprivation?" *Journal of Family Issues* 15:129–147.

Downs, Barbara. 2003. *Fertility of American Women: June 2002*. Current Population Reports No. P20-548. Washington, DC: U.S. Census Bureau.

Dubas, Judith Semon. 2001. "How Gender Modifies the Grandparent-Grandchild Relationship: A Comparison of Kin-Keeper and Kin-Selector Theories." *Journal of Family Issues* 22:478–492.

Dumka, Larry E., Mark W. Roosa, and Kristina M. Jackson. 1997. "Risk, Conflict, Mother's Parenting and Children's Adjustments in Low-Income Mexican Immigrant and Mexican-American Families." *Journal of Marriage and the Family* 59:309–323.

Dunbar, Robin. 1995. "Are You Lonesome Tonight?" *New Scientist*, February 11, pp. 26–31.

Duncan, Greg J., and Jeanne Brooks-Gunn. 1997. *Consequences of Growing Up Poor*. New York: Russell Sage Foundation.

Duncan, Greg J., Wei-Jun Yeung, Jeanne Brooks-Gunn, and Judith R. Smith. 1998. "How Much Does Childhood Poverty Affect the Life Chances of Children?" *American Sociological Review* 63:406–423.

Duncan, R. Paul, Karen Seccombe, and Cheryl Amey. 1995. "Changes in Health Insurance Coverage with Rural-Urban Environments." *Journal of Rural Health* 11:169–177.

Dunne, Gillian A. 2000. "Opting into Motherhood: Lesbians Blurring the Boundaries and Transforming the Meaning of Parenthood and Kinship." *Gender and Society* 14:11–35.

Durkheim, Emile. 1897 [reprinted 1967]. *Suicide*. New York: Houghton Mifflin.

Duvall, E. M., and Brent C. Miller. 1984. "Stage-Critical Family Development Tasks." In E. M. Duvall and Brent C. Miller (eds.) *Marriage and Family Development*, 6th ed. New York: HarperCollins.

Dye, Jane Lawler. 2005. *Fertility of American Women: June 2004*. Current Population Reports No. P20-555. Washington, DC: U.S. Census Bureau.

East, Patricia L. 1999. "The First Teenage Pregnancy in the Family: Does It Affect Mothers' Parenting, Attitudes, or Mother-Adolescent Communication?" *Journal of Marriage and the Family* 61(2):306–319.

Economic Policy Institute. 2005. "Minimum Wage." In *EPI Issue Guide*. www.epi.org/content.cfm/issueguides_minwage. Accessed December 19, 2005.

Economist. 2006. "The Rich, the Poor, and the Growing Gap Between Them." Special Report: Inequality in America. 17 June.

———. 1998. "6.3 Brides for Seven Brothers." www.economist.com/displayStory.cfm?story_ID=179826. Accessed July 7, 2002.

Economist.com. 2004. "Ever Higher Society, Ever Harder to Ascend." www.economist.com/world/na/PrinterFriendly.cfm?story_id=3518560. Accessed June 24, 2006.

Edin, Kathryn. 2000. "What Do Low-Income Single Mothers Say About Marriage?" *Social Problems* 47:112–133.

Edin, Kathryn, and Maria Kefalas. 2005. *Promises I Can Keep: Why Poor Women Put Motherhood Before Marriage*. Chicago: University of Chicago Press.

Edin, Kathryn, and Laura Lein. 1997. *Making Ends Meet*. New York: Russell Sage Foundation.

Edleson, Jeffrey L., and Mary Pat Brygger. 1986. "Gender Differences in Reporting of Battering Incidences." *Family Relations* 35:377–382.

Edwards, John N., and Alan Booth. 1994. "Sexuality, Marriage, and Well-Being: The Middle Years." In Alice Rossi (Ed.), *Sexuality Across the Life Course*, pp. 233–259. Chicago: University of Chicago Press.

Egeland, Byron. 1993. "A History of Abuse Is a Major Risk Factor for Abusing the Next Generation." In Richard J. Gelles and Donileen R. Loseke (Eds.), *Current Controversies on Family Violence*, pp. 197–208. Newbury Park, CA: Sage Publications.

Ehrenreich, Barbara. 2001. *Nickel and Dimed: On (Not) Getting By in America*. New York: Henry Holt and Co.

Ehrenreich, Barbara, and Deirdre English. 1989. *For Her Own Good: 150 Years of Experts' Advice to Women*. New York: Anchor Books/Doubleday.

Ehrle, Jennifer, Gina Adams, and Kathryn Tout. 2001. "Who's Caring for Our Youngest Children? Child Care Patterns of Infants and Toddlers." Urban Institute. www.urban.org/url.cfm?ID=310029. Accessed July 27, 2003.

Elder, Glen H., Jr. 1999. *Children of the Great Depression: Social Change in Life Experience*, 25th anniversary ed. Boulder, CO: Westview Press.

———. 1998. "The Life Course and Human Development." In Richard M. Lerner (Ed.), *Handbook of Child Psychology*, 5th ed., vol. 1, pp. 939–991. New York: Wiley.

Elder, Glen H., Jr., Rand D. Conger, E. Michael Foster, and Michael Ardelt. 1992. "Families Under Economic Pressure." *Journal of Family Issues* 13:5–37.

Ellis, Albert. 1963. *The Origins and Development of the Incest Taboo*. New York: Lyle Stewart.

Ellwood, David T. 1999. "The Impact of the EITC on Work and Social Policy Reforms on Work, Marriage, and Living Arrangements," Kennedy School of Government, Harvard University, Cambridge, MA. Unpublished manuscript.

Elrod, Linda. 1999. "Epilogue: Of Families, Federalism, and a Quest for Policy." *Family Law Quarterly* 33:843–863.

El-Zanaty, Fatma, Enas M. Hussein, Gihan A. Shawky, Ann A. Way, and Sunita Kishor. 1996. *Egypt Demographic and Health Survey 1995*. Calverton, MD: Macro International, Inc.

Embassy of France. 2006. "Childcare." Embassy of France in the United States. www.ambafrance-us.org/atoz/childcare.asp. Accessed January 15, 2006.

Ember, Carol R., and Melvin Ember. 2006. *Cultural Anthropology*, 12th ed. Englewood Cliffs, NJ: Prentice Hall.

Employee Benefit Research Group. 2004. www.ebri.org/publications/ib/index.cfm?fa=main&doc_type=1. Accessed April 2, 2005.

______. June 2002. *Facts from EBRI: Income of the Elderly, 2000*. Washington, DC: Employee Benefit Research Institute.

———. 2000. "Domestic Partner Benefits: Facts and Background (Updated June 2000)." www.ebri.org/publications/facts/dis_0600fact2.cfm. Accessed March 7, 2006.

Engels, F. 1902, original 1884. *The Origin of the Family*. Chicago: Charles H. Kerr and Company.

England, P., and S. Li. 2006. "Desegregation Stalled: The Changing Gender Composition of College Majors 1971–2002." *Gender and Society* 20:657–677.

England, Pam, and Rob Horowitz. 1998. *Birthing from Within*. Albuquerque, NM: Partera Press.

Erera, Pauline Irit. 2002. *Family Diversity: Continuity and Change in the Contemporary Family*. Thousand Oaks, CA: Sage Publications.

Erickson, Rebecca J. 1993. "Reconceptualizing Family Work: The Effect of Emotion Work on Perceptions of Marital Quality." *Journal of Marriage and the Family* 55:888–900.

Estes, Carroll L., and Associates. 2001. *Social Policy and Aging: A Critical Perspective*. Thousand Oaks, CA: Sage.

Estes, Carroll L., E. A. Binney, and R. A. Culbertson. 1992. "The Gerontological Imagination: Social Influences on the Development of Gerontology, 1945–Present." *International Journal of Aging and Human Development* 35(1):49–65.

Etaugh, Claire. 2003. "Witches, Mothers, and Others: Females in Children's Books." *Bradley University Hilltopics* (Winter):10–13.

Ethnicmajority.com. 2006. "African, Hispanic, and Asian American Demographics." www.ethnicmajority.com/demographics_home.htm. Accessed March 19, 2006.

Evans, Gary W., Carrie Gonnella, Lyscha A. Marcynyszyn, L. Gentile, and N. Salpekar. 2005. "The Role of Chaos in Poverty and Children's Socioemotional Adjustment." *Psychological Science* 16(7 July):560–565.

Evertsson, Marie, and Magnus Nermo. 2004. "Dependence Within Families and the Division of Labor: Comparing Sweden and the United States." *Journal of Marriage and Family* 66(December):1272–1286.

Ezorsky, Gertrude. 1991. *Racism and Justice: The Case for Affirmative Action*. Ithaca, NY: Cornell University Press.

Fabricius, William V. 2003. "Listening to Children of Divorce." *Family Relations* 52(4):385–396.

Family Economics and Nutrition Review. 1997. "Cost of Food at Home." 10(4):65.

Farkas, Steve, Ann Duffett, and Jean Johnson. 2000. *Necessary Compromises*. New York: Public Agenda, Carnegie Corporation.

Farr, Kathryn. 2005. *Sex Trafficking: The Global Market in Women and Children*. London: Worth.

Farrell, Betty G. 1999. *Family: The Making of an Idea, an Institution, and a Controversy in American Culture*. Boulder, CO: Westview Press.

Favez, Nicolas, F. Frascarolo, C. Carneiro, V. Montfort, A. Corboz-Warnery, and E. Fivaz-Depeursinge. 2006. "The Development of the Family Alliance From Pregnancy to Toddlerhood and Child Outcomes at 18 months." *Infant and Child Development*, 15:59–73.

Feagin, Joe R. 1975. *Subordinating the Poor: Welfare and American Beliefs*. Upper Saddle River, NJ: Prentice Hall.

Feagin, Joe R., and Karyn McKinney. 2003. *The Many Costs of Racism*. Lanham, MD: Rowman & Littlefield.

Federal Interagency Forum on Child and Family Statistics. 2005. "America's Children: Key National Indicators of Well-Being." www.childstats.gov/americaschildren/pdf/ac2005/econ.pdf. Accessed March 14, 2006.

Federal Writers Project. 1936. "Slave Narrative Collection." In Donald Scott and Bernard Wishy (Eds.), *America's Families: A Documentary History, 1982*, pp. 321–323. New York: Harper Collins.

Fein, Esther B. 1998, 25 October. "Secrecy and Stigma No Longer Clouding Adoptions." *New York Times National Sunday*, pp. 18–19.

Felson, Richard B. 2006. "Is Violence Against Women About Women or About Violence?" *Contexts* 5(2):21–25.

Felson, Richard B., and Paul-Philippe Pare. 2005. "The Reporting of Domestic Violence and Sexual Assault by Nonstrangers to the Police." *Journal of Marriage and Family* 67(3):597–610.

Feminist Majority Foundation. 2002. "Gag Rule Puts Family Planning Under Fire in Kenya." In *Feminist Daily News Wire*. www.feminist.org/news/newsbyte/uswirestory.asp?id=6382. Accessed December 20, 2003.

Fenstermaker Berk, Sarah. 1985. *The Gender Factory: The Apportionment of Work in American Households*. New York: Plenum Press.

Fergusson, David M., and Lianne J. Woodward. 2000. "Teenage Pregnancy and Female Educational

Underachievement: A Prospective Study of a New Zealand Birth Cohort." *Journal of Marriage and the Family* 62:147–161.

Few, April L., and Karen H. Rosen. 2005. "Victims of Chronic Dating Violence: How Women's Vulnerabilities Link to Their Decisions to Stay." *Family Relations* 54(April):265–279.

Few, April L., and Patricia Bell-Scott. 2002. "Grounding Our Feet and Hearts: Black Women's Coping Strategies and the Decision to Leave." *Women and Therapy, Special Edition: Violence in the Lives of Black Women* 25(3/4):59–77.

Fields, Jason. 2004. *America's Families and Living Arrangements: 2003*. Technical Report No. P20-553. Washington, DC: U.S. Census Bureau.

———. 2003. "Children's Living Arrangements and Characteristics: March 2002." In Current Population Reports P20-547. Washington, DC: U.S. Census Bureau.

Fields, Jason, and Lynne M. Casper. 2001. "America's Families and Living Arrangements: March 2000." In Current Population Reports, P20-537. Washington, DC: U.S. Census Bureau.

Figes, Kate and Jean Zimmerman. 2001. *Life After Birth: What Even Your Friends Won't Tell You About Motherhood.* New York: St. Martin's Griffin.

Finnie, R., and R. Meng. 2006. "The Importance of Functional Literacy: Reading and Math Skills and Labour Market Outcomes of High School Dropouts." 11F0019MIE no. 205. Ottawa, Ontario Statistics Canada.

Fisher, Allen P. 2003. "A Critique of the Portrayal of Adoption in College Textbooks and Readers on Families, 1998–2001." *Family Relations* 52:154–160.

Fisher, Bruce, and Robert Alberti. 2005. *Rebuilding: When Your Relationship Ends*. Dunedin, FL: Impacts Publishing.

Fisher, Helen. 2004. *Why We Love: The Nature and Chemistry of Romantic Love*. New York: Owl Books.

Flaherty, Mary Jean, L. Facteau, and P. Garver. 1994. "Grandmother Functions in Multi-Generational Families: Exploratory Study of Black Adolescent Mothers and Their Infants." In Robert Staples (Ed.), *The Black Family: Essays and Studies*, 5th ed., pp. 195–203. Belmont, CA: Wadsworth.

Flaks, D. K., I. Ficher, F. Masterpasqua, and G. Joseph. 1995. "Lesbians Choosing Motherhood: A Comparative Study of Lesbian and Heterosexual Parents and Their Children." *Developmental Psychology* 31(1):105–125.

Fleming & Curti, PLC. 1994. "Sex Among the Elderly." In *Elder Law Issues* 2(3). www.elder-law.com/1994/ISSUE203.HTML. Accessed July 21, 2006.

Flexner, Eleanor. 1959. *Century of Struggle*. Cambridge, MA: Harvard University Press.

Florida Coalition Against Domestic Violence. 2006. "FCADV History." www.fcadv.org/aboutHistory.html. Accessed March 20, 2006.

Flynn, Clifton P. 1999. "Exploring the Link Between Corporal Punishment and Children's Cruelty to Animals." *Journal of Marriage and the Family* 61:971–981.

Forger, Nancy G., Greta J. Rosen, Elizabeth M. Waters, Dana Jacob, Richard B. Simerly, and Geert J. de Vries. 2004. "Deletion of Bax Eliminates Sex Differences in the Mouse Forebrain." Proceedings of the National Academy of Sciences 101(37):13666–13671.

Foshee, Vangie A., Karl E. Bauman, and G. Fletcher Linder. 1999. "Family Violence and the Perpetration of Adolescent Dating Violence: Examining Social Learning and Social Control Processes." *Journal of Marriage and the Family* 61:331–342.

Fox News.com. 2003. "Polls Show Mass. Supports Gay Marriage." www.foxnews.com/story/0,2933,103871,00.html. Accessed July 5, 2006.

Fox, Greer L., Carol Bruce, and Terri Combs-Orme. 2000. "Parenting Expectations and Concerns of Fathers and Mothers of Newborn Infants." *Family Relations* 49(2):123–131.

Fracher, Jeffrey, and Michael S. Kimmel. 1997. "Hard Issues and Soft Spots: Counseling Men About Sexuality." In Michael S. Kimmel and Michael A. Messner, *Men's Lives*, 4th ed., pp. 455–466. Paramus, N.J.: Prentice Hall.

Fragile Families Research Brief. 2004. *Racial and Ethnic Differences in Marriage Among New Unwed Parents*. Technical Report No. 25. Bendheim-Thoman Center for Research on Child Wellbeing, Princeton University. crcw.princeton.edu/briefs/ResearchBrief25.pdf. Accessed June 17, 2006.

Frank, Deborah A., Perri E. Klass, Felton Earls, and Leon Eisenberg. 1996. "Infants and Young Children in Orphanages: One View from Pediatrics and Child Psychiatry." *Pediatrics* 97:569–578.

Frank, Hallie. 2006. "Young Adults' Relationships With Parents and Siblings: The Role of Marital Status, Conflict and Post-Divorce Predictors." *Journal of Divorce and Remarriage* 46:105–124.

Frias, Sonia M., and Ronald J. Angel. 2005. "The Risk of Partner Violence Among Low-Income Hispanic Subgroups." *Journal of Marriage and Family* 67(3):552–564.

Friedan, Betty. 1963. *The Feminine Mystique*. New York: Dell.

Friedlander Jr., Blaine P. 2004. "Supporters of Gay Marriage Tend to Be Young, Educated, Earn a Good Living and Watch CNN, Says Cornell Researchers' Survey." www.news.cornell.edu/releases/March04/GayMarriage.bpf.html. Accessed March 22, 2006.

Frisco, Michelle and Kristi Williams. 2003. "Perceived Housework Equity, Marital Happiness, and Divorce in Dual-Earner Households." *Journal of Family Issues* 24:51–73.

Fromm, Suzette. 2001. "Total Estimated Cost of Child Abuse and Neglect in the United States: Statistical Evidence."

Washington, DC: Prevent Child Abuse America. member.preventchildabuse.org/site/UserLogin?NEXTURL=. .%2Fsite%2FDocServer%2Fcost_analysis.pdf%3FdocID%3D144. Accessed November 17, 2005.

Frone, Michael R. 2003. "Work-Family Balance." In James C. Quick and Lois E. Tetrick (Eds.), *Handbook of Occupational Health Psychology*, pp. 143–162. Washington, DC: American Psychological Association.

Fry, Richard, and B. Lindsay Lowell. 2002. "Work or Study: Different Fortunes of U.S. Latino Generations." pewhispanic.org/files/reports/9.pdf. Washington, DC: Pew Charitable Trust.

Furstenberg, Frank F., and Kathleen E. Kiernan. 2001. "Delayed Parental Divorce: How Much Do Children Benefit?" *Journal of Marriage and Family* 63:446–457.

Galinsky, Ellen, James T. Bond, and E. Jeffrey Hill. *When Work Works: A Status Report on Workplace Flexibility. Who Has It? Who Wants It? Does It Make a Difference?* New York: Families and Work Institute.

Gallagher, Dolores, Jon Rose, P. Rivera, Steven Lovett, and Larry W. Thompson. 1989. "Prevalence of Depression in Family Caregivers." *The Gerontologist* 29:449–456.

Gallagher, Maggie. Marriage Movement. 2004. "Can Government Strengthen Marriage? Evidence from the Social Sciences." National Fatherhood Initiative, Institute for Marriage and Public Policy, and Institute for American Values. www.marriagedebate.com/pdf/Can%20Government%20Strengthen%20Marriage.pdf. Accessed July 5, 2005.

Gallagher, Sally K. 1994. "Doing Their Share: Comparing Patterns of Help Given by Older and Younger Adults." *Journal of Marriage and the Family* 56:567–578.

Gallagher, Sally K., and Naomi Gerstel. 2001. "Connections and Constraints: The Effects of Children on Caregiving." *Journal of Marriage and the Family* 63:265–275.

Gallo, Linda C., Wendy M. Troxel, Karen A. Matthews, and Lewis H. Kuller. 2003. "Marital Status and Quality in Middle-Aged Women: Associations With Levels and Trajectories of Cardiovascular Risk Factors." *Health Psychology* 22(5):453–463.

Gallup Poll. 2001. "What's the Best Arrangement for Today's Families?" www.gallup.com/tuesdaybriefing.asp. Accessed July 8, 2003.

Galotti, Kathleen M., Beverly Pierce, Rebecca L. Reimer, and Amy E. Luckner. 2000. "Midwife or Doctor: A Study of Pregnant Women Making Delivery Decisions." *Journal of Midwifery and Women's Health* 45(4):320–329.

Galtry, Judith. 1997. "Suckling and Silence in the USA: The Costs and Benefits of Breast Feeding." *Feminist Economics* 3(3):1–24 www.lawsocietyalberta.com/legalinfo/parental.htm. Accessed July 8, 2002.

Galtry, Judith, and Paul Callister. 2005. "Assessing the Optimal Length of Parental Leave for Child and Parental Well-being: How Can Research Inform Policy?" *Journal of Family Issues* 26:219–246.

Ganong, Larry, and Marilyn Coleman. 2004. *Stepfamily Relationships: Development, Dynamics, and Intervention.* New York: Springer.

Ganong, Lawrence H., and Marilyn Coleman. 1997. "How Society Views Stepfamilies." *Marriage and Family Review* 26:85–106.

______. 1994. *Remarried Family Relationships*. Newbury Park, CA: Sage Publications.

———. 1989. "Preparing for Remarriage: Anticipating the Issues, Seeking Solutions." *Family Relations* 38:28–33.

Garcia-Coll, Cynthia T. 1990. "Developmental Outcome of Minority Parents: A Process-Oriented Look into Our Beginnings." *Child Development* 61(2):270–289.

Garrod, Andrew C., Lisa Smulyan, Sally I. Powers, and Robert Kilkenny. 2008. *Adolescent Portraits: Identity, Relationships, and Challenges*, 6th ed. Boston: Allyn and Bacon.

Gazamarian, Julie A., Ruth Petersen, Alison M. Spitz, Mary M. Goodwin, Linda E. Saltzman, and James S. Marks. 2000. "Violence and Reproductive Health: Current Knowledge and Future Research Directions." *Maternal and Child Health Journal* 4(2):79–84.

Gelles, Richard J. 1979. *Family Violence*. Beverly Hills, CA: Sage Publications.

______. 1992. "Poverty and Violence Toward Children." *American Behavioral Scientist* 335:258–274.

Gelles, Richard J., and Murray A. Straus. 1988. *Intimate Violence*. New York: Simon and Schuster.

George, L. K. 1993. "Sociological Perspectives on Life Transitions." *Annual Review of Sociology* 19:353–373.

Gerard, Jean M., and Cheryl Buehler. 1999. "Multiple Risk Factors in the Family Environment and Youth Problem Behaviors." *Journal of Marriage and the Family* 61:343–361.

Germano, Elaine, and Judith Bernstein. 1997. "Home Births and Short-Stay Delivery: Lessons in Health Care Financing for Providers of Health Care for Women." *Journal of Nurse-Midwifery* 42:489–498.

Gershoff, Elizabeth Thompson. 2002. "Corporal Punishment by Parents and Associated Child Behaviors and Experiences: A Meta-analytic and Theoretical Review." *Psychological Bulletin* 128:539–579.

Gerson, Kathleen. 2001. "Dilemmas of Involved Fatherhood." In Susan J. Ferguson (Ed.), *Shifting the Center: Understanding Contemporary Families*, pp. 324–339. Mountain View, CA: Mayfield Publishing Company.

Gerstel, Naomi. 1987. "Divorce and Stigma." *Social Problems* 34:172–186.

Giele, Janet Z. 1996. "Decline of the Family: Conservative, Liberal, and Feminist Views." In David Popenoe, Jean B. Elshtain, and David Blankenhorn (Eds.), *Promises to Keep: Decline and Renewal of Marriage in America*, pp. 57–76. Lanham, MD: Rowman and Littlefield.

Gilbert, Dennis, and Joseph A. Kahl. 1993. *The American Class Structure: A New Synthesis*, 4th ed. Belmont, CA: Wadsworth.

Gilder, George. 1995. "Welfare Fraud Today." *The American Spectator* 5(September):B6.

Gill, Gurgeet K. 1998. "The Strategic Involvement of Children in Housework: An Australian Case of Two-Income Families." *International Journal of Comparative Sociology* 39(3):301–314.

Gillespie, Rosemary. 2000. "When No Means No: Disbelief, Disregard and Deviance as Discourses of Voluntary Childlessness." *Women's Studies International Forum* 23:223–234.

Gilman, Robert, and Diane Gilman. 1989. "Swedish Family Policy: An Interview with Inga Gustaffson." *Caring for Families* 32. Context Institute. www.context.org/ICLIB/IC21/Gstaffsn.htm. Accessed May 24, 2005.

Gist, Yvonne J., and Lisa Hetzel. 2004. *We the People: Aging in the United States*. Census 2000 Special Report No. CENSR-19. Washington, DC: U.S. Census Bureau.

Glass, Jennifer L., and Lisa Riley. 1998. "Family Responsive Policies and Employee Retention Following Childbirth." *Social Forces* 76(4):1401–1435.

Glenn, Norval D. 1998. "The Course of Marital Success and Failure in Five American 10-Year Marriage Cohorts." *Journal of Marriage and the Family* 60:569–576.

Glick, Jennifer E., and Jennifer Van Hook. 2002. "Parent's Coresidence with Adult Children: Can Immigration Explain Race and Ethnic Variation?" *Journal of Marriage and the Family* 64:240–253.

Glynn, M. Kathleen, and P. Rhodes. 2005. "Estimated HIV Prevalence in the United States at the End of 2003." Abstract T1-B1101. Presented at the 2005 National HIV Research Conference, June 14, 2005, in Atlanta, GA.

Goffman, Erving. 1963. *Stigma*. Upper Saddle River, NJ: Prentice Hall.

Goldman, Jill, Marsha K. Salus, Deborah Wolcott, and Kristie Y. Kennedy. 2003. "A Coordinated Response to Child Abuse and Neglect: The Foundation." www.childwelfare.gov.pubs/usermanuals/foundation/index.cfm. Accessed December 2, 2006.

Goldscheider, Frances, and Calvin Goldscheider. 1994. "Leaving and Returning Home in 20th Century America." *Population Bulletin* 48(4):1–35.

Goldsmith, Scott, Jane Angvik, Lance Howe, Alexandra Hill, and Linda Leask. 2004. "The Status of Alaska Natives Report 2004." Institute for Social and Economic Research. www.iser.uaa.alaska.edu/Home/ResearchAreas/AlaskaNativeStudies.htm. Accessed March 19, 2006.

Gonzales, Andrea G., Adriana J. Umana-Taylor, and Mira Y. Bamaca. 2006. "Familial Ethnic Socializations Among Adolescents of Latino and European Descent: Do Latina Mothers Exert the Most Influence?" *Journal of Family Issues* 27:184–207.

Gonzalez, Arturo. 2002. "The Impact of the 2001/2002 Economic Recession on Hispanic Workers: A Cross-Sectional Comparison of Three Generations." pewhispanic.org/reports/report.php?ReportID=4. Accessed July 27, 2004.

Gonzalez-Lopez, Gloria. 2004. "Fathering Latina Sexualities: Mexican Men and the Virginity of Their Daughters." *Journal of Marriage and the Family* 66:1118–1130.

———. 2003. "De Madres a Hijas: Gendered Lessons on Virginity Across Generations of Mexican Immigrant Women." In Pierrette Hondagneu-Sotelo (Ed.), *Gender and U.S. Immigration: Contemporary Trends*, pp. 217–240. Berkeley: University of California Press.

Goode, William J. 1993. *World Changes in Divorce Patterns*. New Haven, CT: Yale University Press.

———. 1963. *World Revolution and Family Patterns*. New York: Free Press.

———. 1959. "The Theoretical Importance of Love." *American Sociological Review* 24:38–47.

Goodman, Catherine Chase and Merril Silverstein. 2006. "Grandmothers Raising Grandchildren: Racial and Ethnic Differences in Well-Being Among Custodial and Coparenting Families." *Journal of Family Issues* 27:1605–1626.

Goodman, Ellen. 2003, 3 July. "Cloe's First Fourth." *Boston Globe*, p. A13.

Goodwin, Sandra Naylor, Daniel Chandler, and Joan Meisel. 2003. *Violence Against Women: The Role of Welfare Reform*. Final Report for National Institute of Justice Grant #98-WT-VX-0009. Sacramento, CA: California Institute for Mental Health.

Gordon, Linda. 1979. "The Struggle for Reproductive Freedom: Three Stages of Feminism." In Zillah Eisenstein (Ed.), *Capitalist Patriarchy and the Case for Socialist Feminism*, pp. 107–136. New York: Monthly Review Press.

Gordon, Tuula. 1994. *Single Women: On the Margins?* New York: New York University Press.

Gore, Susan, and Robert H. Aseltine Jr. 2003. "Race and Ethnic Differences in Depressed Mood Following the Transition from High School." *Journal of Health and Social Behavior* 44(3):370–389.

Gornick, Janet C., and Marcia K. Meyers. 2003. *Families that Work: Policies for Reconciling Parenthood and Employment*. New York: Russell Sage Foundation.

Graff, E. G. 2004. "Gay & Lesbian Advocates & Defenders." *The* [Portland] *Oregonian*, 14 February: A-5.

Grall, Timothy S. 2006. "Custodial Mothers and Fathers and Their Child Support: 2003." U.S. Census Bureau. www.census.gov/prod/2006pubs/p60-230.pdf. Accessed December 5, 2006.

______. 2005. "Support Providers: 2002." Current Population Reports: P70-99. Washington, DC: U.S. Census Bureau. www.census.gov/prod/2005pubs/p70-99.pdf. Accessed March 6, 2006.

———. 2003. "Custodial Mothers and Fathers and Their Child Support: 2001." Current Population Reports P60-225. Washington, DC: U.S. Census Bureau. www.census.gov/prod/2003pubs/p60-225.pdf. Accessed March 6, 2006.

Gramsci, Antonio. 1971. *Selected Readings from the Prison Notebooks of Antonio Gramsci*. Translated by

Q. Hoare and G. N. Smith. New York: International Publishers.

Graybill, Wilson H., Clyde V. Kiser, and Pascal K. Whelpton. 1958. *The Fertility of American Women*. New York: Wiley & Sons.

Greenfield, Emily A., and Nadine F. Marks. 2004. *Linked Lives: Adult Children's Distress and Their Parents' Well-Being*. Center for Democracy and Ecology CDF Working Paper No. 2004-27. Madison, WI: University of Wisconsin–Madison.

Greenstein, Robert. 2005. "The Earned Income Tax Credit: Boosting Employment, Aiding the Working Poor." Center on Budget and Policy Priorities. Available www.cbpp.org/7-19-05eic.htm. Accessed August 18, 2006.

Greenstein, Theodore N., and Shannon N. Davis. 2006. "Cross-National Variations in Divorce: Effects of Women's Power, Prestige and Dependence." *Journal of Comparative Family Studies* 37:253–273.

Greenwald, John. 1996. "Barbie Boots Up." *Time Magazine*. November 11: 48–50. www.time.com/time/magazine/article/0,9171,985509-2,00.html. Accessed April 7, 2006.

Greven, Philip. 1970. *Four Generations: Population, Land, and Family in Colonial Andover, Massachusetts*. Ithaca, NY: Cornell University Press.

Griffith, Wendy. 2006. "A Look at India's Arranged Marriages." CBN.com. www.cbn.com/cbnnews/news/050323c.aspx. Accessed July 24, 2006.

Groat, H. Theodore, Peggy C. Giordano, Stephen A. Cernkovich, M. D. Pugh, and Steven P. Swinford. 1997. "Attitudes Toward Childbearing Among Young Parents." *Journal of Marriage and Family* 59:568–581.

Grogger, Jeffrey. 2003. "The Effects of Time Limits, the EITC, and Other Policy Changes on Welfare Use, Work, and Income among Female-Head Families," *Review of Economics and Statistics*, 85:394–408.

Guest, Emma. 2003. *Children of AIDS: Africa's Orphan Crisis*, 2nd ed. London, England: Pluto Press.

Gunderson, Laura, and David Austin. 2004, 4 March. "Families Come to Embrace Women's Love." *The* [Portland] *Oregonian*, p. A11.

Gurian, Michael. 1999. *The Good Son: Shaping the Moral Development of Our Boys and Young Men*. New York: Putnam.

Gurko, Miriam. 1974. *The Ladies of Seneca Falls: The Birth of the Woman's Rights Movement*. New York: MacMillan Publishing Co., Inc.

Gustaffson, Siv, and Frank Stafford. 1994. "Three Regimes of Childcare: The United States, the Netherlands, and Sweden." In Rebecca M. Blank (Ed.), *Social Protection Versus Economic Flexibility*, 1st ed., pp. 333–361. Chicago: University of Chicago Press.

Gutman, Herbert. 1976. *The Black Family in Slavery and Freedom, 1750–1925*. New York: Pantheon.

Guttman, Josef. 1993. *Divorce in Psychosocial Perspective*. Hillsdale, NJ: Lawrence Erlbaum Associates.

Ha, Jung-Hwa, Deborah Carr, and Rebecca L. Utz. 2006. "Older Adults Perception of Intergenerational Support After Widowhood: How do Men and Women Differ?" *Journal of Family Issues* 27:3–30.

Haas, Linda. 1992. *Equal Parenthood and Social Policy: A Study of Parental Leave in Sweden*. Albany: State University of New York Press.

Haas, Linda, and Philip Hwang. 1995. "Company Culture and Men's Usage of Family Leave Benefits in Sweden." *Family Relations* 44:28–36.

Haavio-Mannila, E., and O. Kontula. 1997. "Correlates of Increased Sexual Satisfaction." *Archives of Sexual Behavior* 26:399–419.

Hale-Benson, Janice E. 1986. *Black Children: Their Roots, Culture, and Learning Styles*. Provo, UT: Brigham Young University Press.

Hall, Carl T. 2002. "Pediatricians Endorse Gay, Lesbian Adoption 'Children Deserve to Know Their Relationships with Both Parents Are Stable, Legally Recognized.' " *San Francisco Chronicle*. www.sfgate.com/cgi-bin/article.cgi?file=/chronicle/archive/2002/02/04/MN227427. Accessed July 13, 2006.

Halpern, Carolyn Tucker, Mary L. Young, Martha W. Waller, Sandra L. Martin, and Lawrence L. Kupper. 2004. "Prevalence of Partner Violence in Same-Sex Romantic and Sexual Relationships in a National Sample of Adolescents." *Journal of Adolescent Health* 35:124–131.

Hamby, Sherry L., and David B. Sugarman. 1999. "Acts of Psychological Aggression Against a Partner and Their Relation to Physical Assault and Gender." *Journal of Marriage and the Family* 61:959–970.

Hamer, Jennifer, and Kathleen Marchioro. 2002. "Becoming Custodial Dads: Exploring Parenting Among Low-Income and Working-Class African American Fathers." *Journal of Marriage and the Family* 64:116–129.

Hamilton, Brady E., Joyce A. Martin, and Stephanie J. Ventura. 2006. "Births: Preliminary Data for 2005." Health E-Stats. Released November 21, 2006. www.cdc.gov/nchs/products/pubs/pubd/hestats/prelimbirths05/prelimbirths05.htm. Accessed November 27, 2006.

______. 2006. "Final Births for 2004." National Center for Health Statistics. www.cdc.gov/nchs/products/pubs/pubd/hestats/finalbirths04/finalbirths04.htm. Accessed July 13, 2006.

Hamilton, C. 1997. "Indians to Tackle Housing Crisis—On Their Own." *Christian Science Monitor*, 8 August, pp. 4–5.

Hammonds, Keith H. 1998. "BuisnessWeek Harris Poll: He Said, She Said." www.businessweek.com/1998/31/b3589005.htm. Accessed June 26, 2006.

Han, Shin-Kap, and Phyllis Moen. 1999. "Work and Family over Time: A Life Course Approach." *The Annals of the American Academy of Political and Social Sciences* 562:98–110.

Hancock, Ange-Marie. 2004. *The Politics of Disgust: The Public Identity of the Welfare State*. New York: New York University Press.

Hans, Jason D. 2002. "Stepparenting After Divorce: Stepparents' Legal Position Regarding Custody, Access, and Support." *Family Relations* 51(4):301–307.

Hansen, Chris. 2002. "The Cost of Raising a Child." familyguardian.betterthanyours.com/Subjects/Parenting/Articles/CostofChild.htm. Accessed June 25, 2003.

Hanson, Thomas L., Sara S. McLanahan, and Elizabeth Thomson. 1996. "Double Jeopardy: Parental Conflict and Stepfamily Outcomes for Children." *Journal of Marriage and the Family* 58:141–154.

Hao, Lingxin. 1996. "Family Structure, Private Transfers, and the Economic Well-Being of Families with Children." *Social Forces* 75:269–292.

Harding, David J., Christopher Jencks, Leonard M. Lopoo, and Susan M. Mayer. 2005. "The Changing Effect of Family Background on the Incomes of American Adults." In Samuel Bowles, Herbert Gintis, and Melissa Osborne (Eds.), *Unequal Chances: Family Background and Economic Success*, pp. 100–144. Princeton, NJ: Princeton University Press.

Hardy, Melissa A., and Kim Shuey. 2000. "Retirement." In Edgar F. Borgatta and Rhonda J. V. Montgomery (Eds.), *Encyclopedia of Sociology*, 2nd ed., pp. 2401–2410. New York: Macmillan.

Hareven, Tamara K. 2000. *Families, History, and Social Change: Life Course; Cross-Cultural Perspectives.* Boulder, CO: Westview Press.

———. 1973. "Introduction: The Historical Study of the Family in Urban Society." *Journal of Urban History* 1:259–267.

Hartog, Hendrik. 2000. *Man and Wife in America: A History.* Cambridge, MA: Harvard University Press.

Harvey, David L., and Michael H. Reed. 1996. "The Culture of Poverty: An Ideological Analysis." *Sociological Perspectives* 39:465–495.

Harvey, Elizabeth. 1999. "Short-Term and Long-Term Effects of Parental Employment on Children of the National Longitudinal Survey of Youth." *Developmental Psychology* 35:445–459.

Hastings, Deborah. 2000. "Register Ranks Ultra Rich: Social Register Keeps Track of Who's Who in the Upper Crust." *The Detroit News.* www.detnews.com/2000/nation/0006/11/a07-72601.htm. Accessed March 25, 2003.

Hatchett, Shirley, and James J. Jackson. 1993. "African-American Extended Kin System: An Assessment." In Harriete Pipes McAdoo (Ed.), *Family Ethnicity: Strength in Diversity*, pp. 90–108. Newbury Park, CA: Sage.

Hatfield, Elaine, and Richard L. Rapson. 1996. *Love and Sex: Cross Cultural Perspectives.* Boston: Allyn and Bacon.

Havighurst, Robert J., Bernice L. Neugarten, and Sheldon S. Tobin. 1968. "Disengagement and Patterns of Aging." In Bernice L. Neugarten (Ed.), *Middle Age and Aging*, pp. 161–172. Chicago: University of Chicago Press.

Hawkins, Alan J., Steven L. Nock, Julia C. Wilson, Laura Sanchez, and James D. Wright. 2002. "Attitudes About Covenant Marriage and Divorce: Policy Implications from a Three-Stage Comparison." *Family Relations* 51:166–175.

Hays, Sharon. 2003. *Flat Broke with Children: Women in the Age of Welfare Reform.* New York: Oxford University Press.

______. 2001. "The Mommy Wars: Ambivalence, Ideological Work, and the Cultural Contradictions of Motherhood." In Susan J. Ferguson (Ed.), *Shifting the Center: Understanding Contemporary Families*, 2nd ed., pp. 305–323. Mountain View, CA: Mayfield Publishing Company.

———. 1996. *The Cultural Contradictions of Motherhood.* New Haven, CT: Yale University Press.

Hayslip Jr., Bert, R. Jerald Shore, Craig E. Henderson, and Paul L. Lambert. 1998. "Custodial Grandparenting and the Impact of Grandchildren with Problems on Role Satisfaction and Role Meaning." *Journal of Gerontology: Social Sciences* 53B:S164–173.

He, Wan, Manisha Sengupta, Victoria A. Velkoff, and Kimberly A. DeBarros. 2005. *65+ in the United States: 2005.* Current Population Reports: Special Studies, P23-209. Washington, DC: U.S. Census Bureau.

Healy, Christopher, 2006. *Pop Culture: The Sane Man's Guide to the Insane World of New Fatherhood.* New York: Penguin.

Heaton, Tim B. 2002. "Factors Contributing to Increasing Marital Stability in the United States." *Journal of Family Issues* 23-3 (April):392–409.

Heaton, Tim B., and Cardell K. Jacobson. 2000. "Intergroup Marriage: An Examination of Opportunity Structures." *Sociological Inquiry* 70(1):30–41.

Heaton, Tim B., Cardell K. Jacobson, and Kimberlee Holland. 1999. "Persistence and Change in Decisions to Remain Childless." *Journal of Marriage and the Family* 61:531–539.

Heckert, D. Alex, Thomas C. Nowak, and Kay A. Snyder. 1998. "The Impact of Husbands' and Wives' Relative Earnings on Marital Disruption." *Journal of Marriage and the Family* 60:690–703.

Hefling, Kimberly. 2004, 27 November. "Benefits Cited as More U.S. Women Over 40 Give Birth." The Associated Press. *The Oregonian*, p. A2.

Heidemann, Bridget, Olga Suhomlinova, and Angela O'Rand. 1998. "Economic Independence Economic Status, and Empty Nest in Midlife Marital Disruption." *Journal of Marriage and the Family* 60:219–231.

Held to Ransom. 2003. "Gag Rule." www.heldtoransom.org/gag.asp. Accessed December 20, 2003.

Hemstrom, Orjan. 1996. "Is Marriage Dissolution Linked to Difference in Mortality Risks for Men and Women?" *Journal of Marriage and the Family* 58:366–378.

Herbert, Bob. 1997, 20 November. "The Game Is Rigged." *New York Times.* www.nytimes.com/199711/20oped. Accessed March 7, 2003.

Herrnstein, Richard, and Charles Murray. 1994. *The Bell Curve: Intelligence and Class Structure in American Life.* New York: Free Press.

Hertz, Thomas. 2004. "Rags, Riches, and Race: The Intergenerational Economic Mobility of Black and White Families in the United States." In Samuel Bowles, Herbert Gintis, and Melissa Osborne Groves (Eds.), *Unequal Chances: Family Background and Economic Success*, pp. 165–191. New York: Russell Sage and Princeton University Press.

Hesketh, Therese, Li Lu, and Zhu Wei Xing. 2005. "The Effect of China's One-Child Family Policy After 25 Years." *New England Journal of Medicine* 353(11):1171–1176.

Hewitt, B., J. Baxter, and M. Western. 2005. "Marriage Breakdown in Australia: The Social Correlates of Separation and Divorce," *Journal of Sociology*, 41: 163–183.

Heyman, Richard E., and Amy M. Smith Slep. 2002. "Do Child Abuse and Interparental Violence Lead to Adulthood Family Violence?" *Journal of Marriage and Family* 64:864–870.

Hickman, Lisa. 2006. "Who Should Care for Our Children? The Effects of Home Versus Center Care on Child Cognition and Social Adjustment." *Journal of Family Issues* 26:652–684.

Hill, Charles T., Zick Rubin, and Letitia Anne Peplau. 1976. "Breakups Before Marriage: The End of 103 Affairs." *Journal of Social Issues* 32:147–168.

Hill, E. Jeffrey, Chongming Yang, Alan J. Hawkins, and Maria Ferris. 2004. "A Cross-Cultural Test of the Work/Family Interface in 48 Countries." *Journal of Marriage and Family* 17:1300–1316.

Hill, Robert B. 1972. *The Strengths of Black Families*. New York: Emerson Hall Publishers.

Hill, Shirley A. 2005. *Black Intimacies*. Lanham, MD: AltaMira Press.

Hines, Melissa. 2005. *Brain Gender*. New York: Oxford University Press.

Hirsch, Jennifer S. 2003. *A Courtship After Marriage: Sexuality and Love in Mexican Transnational Families*. Berkeley: University of California Press.

Hirschman, Charles, and Nguyen Huu Minh. 2002. "Tradition and Change in Vietnamese Family Structure in the Red River Delta." *Journal of Marriage and Family* 64:1063–1079.

Hobart, Charles. 1991. "Conflict in Remarriages." *Journal of Divorce and Remarriage* 15:69–86.

Hochschild, Arlie Russell. 1997. *The Time Bind: When Work Becomes Home and Home Becomes Work*. New York: Metropolitan Books.

______. 1989. *The Second Shift: Working Parents and the Revolution at Home*. New York: Viking.

———. 1983. *The Managed Heart: Commercialization of Human Feeling*. Berkeley: University of California Press.

Hofferth, Sandra L., and Kermyt G. Anderson. 2003. "Are All Dads Equal? Biology Versus Marriage as a Basis for Parental Investment." *Journal of Marriage and Family* 65:213–232.

Hofferth, Sandra, Lori Reid, and Frank L. Mott. 2001. "The Effects of Early Childbearing on Schooling Over Time." *Family Planning Perspectives* 33(6):259–267.

Hoffman, Saul D. 2006. "By the Numbers: The Public Costs of Teen Childbearing. "The National Campaign to End Teen Pregnancy. Washington DC. Online: www.teenpregnancy.org/costs/national.asp. Accessed November 27, 2006.

———. 1998. "Teenage Childbearing Is Not So Bad After All . . . or Is It? A Review of the New Literature." *Family Planning Perspectives* 30:236–239, 243.

Hoffmann, John P., and Robert A. Johnson. "A National Portrait of Family Structure and Adolescent Drug Use." *Journal of Marriage and the Family* 60:633–645.

Hohmann-Marriott, Bryndle E. 2006. "Shared Beliefs and the Union Stability of Married and Cohabiting Couples." *Journal of Marriage and Family*, 68: 1015–1028.

Hojat, Mohammadreza, Reza Shapurian, Danesh Foroughi, Habib Nayerahmadi, Mitra Farzneh, Mahmood Shafieyen, and Mohin Parsi. 2000. "Gender Differences in Traditional Attitudes Toward Marriage and the Family: An Empirical Study of Iranian Immigrants in the United States." *Journal of Family Issues* 21:419–434.

Holcomb, Pamela A., Karen Tumlin, Robin Koralek, Randy Capps, and Anita Zuberi. 2003. *The Application Process for TANF, Food Stamps, Medicaid and SCHIP: Issues for Agencies and Applicants, Including Immigrants and Limited English Speakers*. Washington, DC: U.S. Department of Health and Human Services.

Holroyd, R., and A. Sheppard. 1997. "Parental Separation: Effects on Children; Implications for Service." *Child: Care, Health and Development* 23:369–378.

Honberg, Ron. 2006. "Almost 25% Homeless Are Kids." NAMI: The Nation's Voice in Mental Illness. www.nami.org/Content/ContentGroups/Policy/Updates/Updates_andamp__What_s_New___NIMH__Homeless_Kids__Single_Housing.htm. Accessed December 3, 2006.

Hook, Jennifer L. 2004. "Reconsidering the Division of Household Labor: Incorporating Volunteer Work and Informal Support." *Journal of Marriage and Family* 66(February):101–117.

Hopper, Joseph. 1993. "The Rhetoric of Motives in Divorce." *Journal of Marriage and the Family* 55:801–813.

Horn, Wade F., and Tom Sylvester. 2006. "Father Facts: Research Notes." Gaithersburg, MD: National Fatherhood Initiative. www.fatherhood.org/fatherfacts_rsh.asp. Accessed July 16, 2006.

Hotz, V. Joseph, Charles H. Mullin, and John Karl Scholz. 2001. "The Earned Income Tax Credit and Labor Market Participation of Families on Welfare." *Poverty Research News*, May–June, pp. 13–15.

Huggins, Sharon L. 1989. "A Comparative Study of Self-Esteem of Adolescent Children of Divorced Lesbian Mothers and Divorced Heterosexual Mothers." *Journal of Homosexuality* 18(1/2):123–135.

Hughes, Diane, and Deborah Johnson. 2001. "Correlates in Children's Experiences of Parents' Racial Socialization Behaviors." *Journal of Marriage and Family* 63(4): 981–995.

Hughes, Diane, and L. Chen. 1999. "The Nature of Parents' Race-Related Communications to Children: A Developmental Perspective." In Lawrence Balter and Catherine S. Tamis-Lemonda (Eds.), *Child Psychology: A Handbook of Contemporary Issues*, pp. 467–490. Philadelphia: Psychology Press.

Hull, Jon D. 1995. "The State of the Union." *Time Magazine*, January 30, pp. 53–75.

Human Relations Area Files, Inc. New Haven, CT: Yale University. www.yale.edu/hraf/. Accessed November 27, 2004.

Human Rights Campaign Foundation. 2006. "Employers that Offer Domestic Partner Health Benefits." The Human Rights Campaign. www.hrc.org/Template.cfm?Section=Search_the_Database&Template=/CustomSource. Accessed March 7, 2006.

Human Rights Watch. 2006a. "Trafficking." www.state.gov/g/tip/rls/tiprpt/2006/65983.htm. Accessed December 3, 2006.

———. 2006b. "Swept Under the Rug: Abuses Against Domestic Workers Around the World." http://hrw.org/reports/2006/wrd0706/. Accessed December, 3, 2006.

______. 2004. "Domestic Violence." hrw.org/women/domesticviolence.html. Accessed July 19, 2005.

______. 2001. "Sacrificing Women to Save the Family? Domestic Violence in Uzbekistan." In *Women's Human Rights: Domestic Violence in Uzbekistan*. www.hrw.org/women/domesticviolence.php?country=Uzbekistan. Accessed March 19, 2003.

———. 1999. "Pakistan: Women Face Their Own Crisis." In *Women's Human Rights: Domestic Violence in Pakistan*. www.hrw.org/women/domesticviolence.php?country=Pakistan. Accessed March 19, 2003.

Hunsberger, Brent. 2007. "Oregon Edges Toward Paid Leave." *The Oregonian*. March 11, 2007. www.oregonlive.com/business/oregonian/index.ssf?/base/business/1173493507285220.xml&coll=7&thispage=1.

Hunter, Andrea G. 1997. "Counting on Grandmothers: Black Mothers' and Fathers' Reliance on Grandmothers for Parenting Support." *Journal of Family Issues* 18:251–269.

Hunter, Joyce, and Gerald P. Mallon. 1998. "Social Work Practice with Gay Men and Lesbians Within Communities." In Gerald P. Mallon (Ed.), *Foundations of Social Work Practice with Lesbian and Gay Persons*, pp. 229–248. New York: Haworth.

Huston, Ted L., and Heidi Melz. 2004. "The Case for (Promoting) Marriage: The Devil Is in the Details." *Journal of Marriage and Family* 66:943–958.

Hyde, Janet, and Marcia Linn. 1988. "Gender Differences in Verbal Ability: A Meta-Analysis." *Psychological Bulletin* 104:53–69.

Hyman, Batya. 2000. "The Economic Consequences of Child Sexual Abuse for Adult Lesbian Women." *Journal of Marriage and the Family* 62:199–211.

Hynie, Michaela J., John E. Lydon, and Ali Taradash. 1997. "Commitment, Intimacy, and Women's Perceptions of Premarital Sex and Contraceptive Readiness." *Psychology of Women Quarterly* 21:447–464.

Independent Online. 2005. "Japan Fertility Rate Drops to Record Low." www.iol.co.za/index.php?set_id=14&click_id=117&art_id=qw1135840144519B215. Accessed November 24, 2006.

Infoplease.com. 2004a. "African Americans by the Numbers from the U.S. Census Bureau." www.infoplease.com/spot/bhmcensus1.html. Accessed January 12, 2005.

———. 2004b. "Teen Birth Rates Continue to Decline." www.infoplease.com/ipa/A0193727.html. Accessed March 27, 2004.

———. 2003. "The Wage Gap." www.infoplease.com/ipa/A0763170.html. Accessed June 17, 2006.

Ingoldsby, Bron, Suzanne Smith, and J. Elizabeth Miller. 2004. *Exploring Family Theories*. Los Angeles: Roxbury Press.

Ingraham, Chrys. 1999. *White Weddings: Romancing Heterosexuality in Popular Culture*. New York: Routledge.

Institute for American Values. 2000. *The Marriage Movement: A Statement of Principles, 2000*. New York. marriagemovement.org. Accessed July 8, 2005.

Interfaith Worker Justice. 2005. *Why the U.S. Needs a Raise in the Federal Minimum Wage*. Chicago: Interfaith Worker Justice.

Internal Revenue Service. 2007. "Important EITC Changes for 2006." www.irs.gov/individuals/article/0,i.d.=164506,00.html.

______. 2006. "EITC Thresholds and Tax Law Updates: Current Tax Year 2005." www.irs.gov/individuals/article/0,id=150513,00.html. Accessed May 25, 2006.

———. 2005. "Earned Income Tax Credit (EITC) Questions and Answers." www.irs.gov/individuals/article/0,,id=96466,00.html. Accessed June 26, 2005.

International Institute for Population Sciences and ORC Macro. 2000. *India: National Family Health Survey (NFHS-2) 1998–99*. Mumbai, India: International Institute for Population Sciences.

Irazuzta, Jose E., James E. McJunkin, Kapriel Danadian, Forest Arnold, and Jianliang Zhang. 1997. "Outcome and Cost of Child Abuse." *Child Abuse and Neglect* 21:751–757.

Isaacs, Stephen L., and Steven Schroeder. 2004. "Class: The Ignored Determinant of the Nation's Health." *New England Journal of Medicine* 351:1137–1142.

Ishii-Kuntz, Masako. 2004. "Asian American Families: Diverse History, Contemporary Trends, and the Future," In Marilyn Coleman and Lawrence H. Ganong (Eds.), *Handbook of Contemporary Families: Considering the Past, Contemplating the Future* (pp. 369–384). Thousand Oaks, CA: Sage.

______. 2003. "Balancing Fatherhood and Work: Emergence of Diverse Masculinities in Contemporary Japan." In James Roberson and Nobue Suzuki (Eds.), *Men and Masculinities in Contemporary Japan: Dislocating the Salaryman Doxa*, pp. 198–216. New York: Rutledge.

———. 1998. "Fathers' Involvement and Children's Social Network: A Comparison Between Japan and the United States." *Journal of Family Education Research Institute* 20:5–16.

———. 1994. "Paternal Involvement and Perception Toward Fathers' Roles: A Comparison Between Japan and the United States." *Journal of Family Issues* 15:30–48.

Ishii-Kuntz, Masako, and Karen Seccombe. 1989. "The Impact of Children upon Social Support Networks Throughout the Life Course." *Journal of Marriage and the Family* 51:777–790.

Ishii-Kuntz, Masako, Katsuko Makino, Kuniko Kato, and Michiko Tsuchiya. 2004. "Japanese Fathers of Preschoolers and Their Involvement in Child Care." *Journal of Marriage and Family* 66(August):779–791.

Janssen, Patricia A., Victoria L. Holt, and Susan J. Myers. 1994. "Licensed Midwife-Attended, Out-of-Hospital Births in Washington State: Are They Safe?" *Birth* 21:141–148.

Jayson, Sharon. 2005, 30 May. "Hyphenated Names Less-and-Less Used." *USA Today*. www.usatoday.com/life/2005-05-30-name-change_x.htm. Accessed November 17, 2005.

Jean M. Twenge, W. Keith Campbell, and Craig A. Foster. 2003. "Parenthood and Marital Satisfaction: A Meta-Analytic Review," *Journal of Marriage and the Family* 65:574–583.

Jekielek, Susan M. 1998. "Parental Conflict, Marital Disruption, and Children's Emotional Well-Being." *Social Forces* 76:905–936.

Jenny, Carole, Thomas A. Roesler, and Kimberly L. Poyer. 1994. "Are Children at Risk for Sexual Abuse by Homosexuals?" *Pediatrics* 94(1):41–44.

Jerome, Richard, Silvia Sansoni, and Eileen Finan. 2003. "Will She Be Stoned to Death?" *People*, September 15.

Joe, Jennie, Shannon Sparks, and Lisa Tiger. 1999. "Changing American Indian Marriage Patterns: Some Examples from Contemporary Western Apaches." In Sandra Lee Browning and R. Robin Miller (Eds.), *Till Death Do Us Part: A Multicultural Anthology on Marriage*, pp. 5–21. Greenwich, CT: JAI Press.

John, Robert. 1988. "The Native American Family." In Charles H. Mindel, Robert W. Habenstein, and Roosevelt Wright Jr. (Eds.), *Ethnic Families in America: Patterns and Variations*, 3rd ed., pp. 325–366. New York: Elsevier.

Johnson, Christine A., and Scott M. Stanley (Eds.). 2001. *The Oklahoma Marriage Initiative Statewide Baseline Survey*. 306 HES. Stillwater, OK: Bureau for Social Research, Oklahoma State University.

Johnson, Christine A., Scott M. Stanley, Norval D. Glenn, Paul R. Amato, Steve L. Nock, Howard J. Markman, and M. Robin Dion. 2002. *Marriage in Oklahoma: 2001 Baseline Statewide Survey on Marriage and Divorce*. Stillwater, OK: Bureau for Social Research, Oklahoma State University.

Johnson, Colleen L., and Barbara M. Barer. 1997. *Life Beyond 85 Years: The Aura of Survivorship*. New York: Springer Publishing Co.

Johnson, Deborah J. 2001. "Parental Characteristics, Racial Stress, and Racial Socialization Processes as Predictors of Racial Coping in Middle Childhood." In Angela Neal Barnett (Ed.), *Forging Links: Clinical/Developmental Perspective of African American Children*, pp. 57–74. Westport, CT: Greenwood Press.

Johnson, Julia Overturf. 2005. "Who's Minding the Kids? Childcare Arrangements: Winter 2002." Current Population Reports. U.S. Census Bureau. www.census.gov/prod/2005pubs/p70-101.pdf. Accessed June 23, 2006.

Johnson, Kenneth C., and Betty-Anne Daviss. 2005. "Outcomes of Planned Home Births with Certified Professional Midwives: Large Prospective Study in North America." *British Medical Journal* 330(18):1416.

Johnson, Michael P. 2006. "Conflict and Control: Gender Symmetry and Asymmetry in Domestic Violence." *Journal of Family Issues* 27:1003–1018.

———. 2000. "Conflict and Control: Images of Symmetry and Asymmetry in Domestic Violence." In Alan Booth, Ann C. Crouter, and Mari Clements (Eds.), *Couples in Conflict*. Hillsdale, NJ: Lawrence Erlbaum.

Johnson, Michael P. and Janel M. Leone. 2005. "The Differential Effects of Intimate Terrorism and Situational Couple Violence: Findings From the National Violence Against Women Survey." *Journal of Family Issues* 26:322–349.

Johnson, Michael P., and Kathleen J. Ferraro. 2000. "Research on Domestic Violence in the 1990's: Making Distinctions." *Journal of Marriage and the Family* 62:948–963.

Joint United Nations Programme on HIV/AIDS (UNAIDS), UNICEF, and the U.S. Agency for International Development. 2004. "Children on the Brink, 2004." www.unicef.org/publications/index_22212.html. Accessed July 7, 2005.

Jolivet, Muriel. 1997. "The Ten Commandments of the Mother." In Muriel Jolivet (Ed.), *Japan: The Childless Society*, pp. 77–105 London: Routledge.

Jones, Frank L. 1996. "Convergence and Divergence in Ethnic Divorce Patterns: A Research Note." *Journal of Marriage and the Family* 58:213–218.

Joseph, Elizabeth. 1997. "Polygamy—The Ultimate Feminist Lifestyle." www.polygamy.com/articles/templates/?a=10&z=m. Accessed April 21, 2003.

Joshi, Pamela, and Karen Bogen. 2007. "Nonstandard Schedules and Young Children's Behavioral Outcomes

Among Working Low-Income Families." *Journal of Marriage and Family*, 69:139–156.

Journal of Blacks in Higher Education. 2006a. Issue No. 51 (Spring) "Vital Statistics." www.jbhe.com/vital/51_index.html. Accessed November 24, 2006.

———. 2006b. Issue No. 52 (Summer) "Vital Statistics." www.jbhe.com/vital/52_index.html. Accessed November 24, 2006.

Juby, H., C. Le Bourdais and N. Marcil-Gratton. 2005. "Sharing Roles—Sharing Custody? Couples' Characteristics and Children's Living Arrangements at Separation." *Journal of Marriage and Family* 67(1):157–172.

Judge, Sharon. 2003. "Determinants of Parental Stress in Families Adopting Children from Eastern Europe." *Family Relations* 52(3):241–248.

Kageyama, Y. 1999, 11 February. "A Tale of Two Drugs Irks Japan's Women." *The* [Portland] *Oregonian*, p. A6.

Kaiser Commission on Medicaid and the Uninsured. 2006. "The Medicaid Program at a Glance." Kaiser Family Foundation. www.kff.org/medicaid/upload/7235.pdf. Accessed December 3, 2006.

Kaiser Family Foundation. 2001. "Inside-OUT: A Report of the Experiences of Lesbians, Gays, and Bisexuals in America and the Public's Views on Issues and Policies Related to Sexual Orientation." www.kff.org/content/2001/3193/LGBChartpack.pdf. Accessed October 27, 2002.

Kakuchi, Suvendrini. 1998. "Women: Foreign Spouses in Japan Seek Easier Child Custody Laws." www.crnjapan.com/articles/pre2003/en/199803-oneworld.html. Accessed May 8, 2003.

Kamerman, Sheila. 2003. "Welfare States, Family Policies, and Early Childhood Education, Care and Family Support." Paper presented to the *Consultation Meeting on Family Support Policy in Central and Eastern Europe*. September 3. Budapest, Hungary: UNESCO and the Council of Europe.

Kamerman, Sheila B., and Alfred J. Kahn. 1978. "Families and the Idea of Family Policy." In Sheila B. Kamerman and Alfred J. Kahn (Eds.), *Family Policy: Government and Families in Fourteen Countries*, pp. 1–16. New York: Columbia University Press.

Kamerman, Sheila, and Shirley Gatenio. 2002. "Tax Day: How Do America's Child Benefits Compare?" www.childpolicyintl.org/issuebrief/issuebrief4.htm. Accessed July 15, 2002.

Kamo, Yoshinori, and Ellen E. Cohen. 1998. "Division of Household Work Between Partners: A Comparison of Black and White Couples." *Journal of Comparative Family Studies* 29(1):131–145.

Kamo, Yoshinori, and Min Zhou. 1994. "Living Arrangements of Elderly Chinese and Japanese in the United States." *Journal of Marriage and the Family* 56:544–558.

Kamo, Yoshinori. 2000. "'He Said, She Said': Assessing Discrepancies in Husbands' and Wives' Reports on the Division of Household Labor." *Social Science Research* 22:361–382.

______. 1994. "Division of Household Work in the United States and Japan." *Journal of Family Issues* 15:348–378.

———. 1988. "A Note of Elderly Living Arrangements in Japan and the United States." *Research on Aging* 10:297–305.

Kane, E. 2006. "No Way My Boys Are Going to Be Like That! Parents' Responses to Children's Gender Nonconformity." *Gender and Society* 20:149–176.

Kaplan, April. 1997. "Domestic Violence and Welfare Reform." Welfare Information Network. www.financereport.org/Publications/domesticissue.htm. Accessed July 22, 2006.

Karney, B. J., C. W. Garvan, and M. S. Thomas. 2003. "Family Formation in Florida: 2003 Baseline Survey of Attitudes, Beliefs, and Demographics Relating to Marriage and Family Formation." University of Florida, Department of Psychology. www.relationshipscience.net. Accessed February 17, 2004.

Kashiwase, Haruna. 2002. "Shotgun Weddings a Sign of the Times in Japan." Population Today, Population Reference Bureau. www.prb.org/Template.cfm?Section=PRB&template=/ContentManagement/ContentDisplay.cfm&ContentID=6480. Accessed April 21, 2003.

Katzev, Aphra R., Rebecca L. Warner, and Alan C. Acock. 1994. "Girls or Boys? Relationship of Child Gender to Marital Stability." *Journal of Marriage and the Family* 56:89–100.

Kaufman, Gayle. 1999. "The Portrayal of Men's Family Roles in Television Commercials." *Sex Roles* 313:439–451.

Kaufman, Gayle, and Hiromi Taniguchi. 2006. "Gender and Marital Happiness in Later Life." *Journal of Family Issues* 27:737–757.

Kaufman, Joan, and Edward Zigler. 1987. "Do Abused Children Become Abusive Parents?" *Journal of Orthopsychiatry* 57:186–192.

Keefe, Janice, and Pamela Fancey. 2000. "The Care Continues: Responsibility for Elderly Relatives Before and After Admission to a Long Term Care Facility." *Family Relations* 49:235–244.

Kelly, R. F., and Greer Litton Fox. 1993. "Determinants of Alimony Awards: An Empirical Test of Current Theories and a Reflection on Public Policy." *Syracuse Law Review* 44:641–722.

Kemp, Alan. 1998. *Abuse in the Family: An Introduction*. Pacific Grove, CA: Brooks/Cole.

Kendall, Diana. 2002. *The Power of Good Deeds: Privileged Women and the Social Reproduction of the Upper Class*. Lanham, MD: Rowman & Littlefield.

Kephart, William M. 1967. "Some Correlates of Romantic Love." *Journal of Marriage and the Family* 29:470–474.

Kerchoff, Alan C., and Keith E. Davis. 1962. "Value Consensus and Need Complementarity in Mate Selection." *American Sociological Review* 27:295–303.

Kestenbaum, Bert. 1992. "A Description of the Extreme Aged Population Based on Improved Medicare Enrollment Data." *Demography* 29(4):565–580.

Kibria, Nazli. 1997. "The Construction of 'Asian American': Reflections on Intermarriage and Ethnic Identity Among Second-Generation Chinese and Korean Americans." *Ethnic and Racial Studies* 20:523–544.

———. 1993. *The Family Tightrope: The Changing Lives of Vietnamese Americans*. Princeton, N.J.: Princeton University Press.

Kiecolt, K. Jill. 2003. "Satisfaction with Work and Family Life: No Evidence of a Cultural Reversal." *Journal of Marriage and Family* 65:23–35.

Kimball, Meredith M. 1986. "Television and Sex-Role Attitudes." In Tannis M. Williams (Ed.), *Impact of Television: A Natural Experiment in Three Communities*. Orlando, FL: Academic Press.

Kimmel, Michael S. 2000. *The Gendered Society*. New York: Oxford University Press.

Kimura, Doreen. 2002. "Sex Differences in the Brain." *Scientific American.Com*, www.sciam.com/print_version .cfm?articleID=00018E9D-879D-1D06-8E49809EC5. Accessed June 23, 2006.

King, Valerie. 2006. "The Antecedents and Consequences of Adolescents' Relationships with Stepfathers and Nonresident Fathers." *Journal of Marriage and Family* 68:910–928.

———. 2003. "The Legacy of a Grandparent's Divorce: Consequences for Ties Between Grandparents and Grandchildren." *Journal of Marriage and Family* 65:170–183.

King, Valerie, and Mindy E. Scott. 2005. "A Comparison of Cohabiting Relationships Among Older and Younger Adults." *Journal of Marriage and Family* 67(May):271–285.

King, Valerie, Kathleen Mullan Harris, and Holly E. Heard. 2004. "Racial and Ethnic Diversity in Nonresident Father Involvement." *Journal of Marriage and Family* 66(February):1–21.

Kinsella, Kevin, and David R. Phillips. 2005. *Global Aging: The Challenge of Success*. Population Bulletin No. 60(1). Washington, DC: Population Reference Bureau.

Kinsella, Kevin, and Victoria A. Velkoff. 2001. *An Aging World: 2001*. U.S. Census Bureau, No. P95-011. Washington, DC: U.S. Government Printing Office.

Kinsey, Alfred, Wardell B. Pomeroy, and Clyde E. Martin. 1953. *Sexual Behavior in the Human Female*. Philadelphia: W.B. Saunders.

Knodel, John, Vu Manh Loi, Rukmalie Jayakody, and Vu Tuan Huy. 2004. *Gender Roles in the Family: Change and Stability in Vietnam*. PSC Research Report 04-559. Ann Arbor, MI: Population Studies Center at the Institute for Social Research, University of Michigan.

Knoester, Chris, and David J. Eggebeen. 2006. "The Effects of the Transition to Parenthood and Subsequent Children on Men's Well-Being and Social Participation." *Journal of Family Issues* 27:1532–1560.

Koball, Heather, and Desiree Principe. 2002. *Do Nonresident Fathers Who Pay Child Support Visit Their Children More?* New Federalism: National Survey of America's Families Series B, No. B-44. Washington, DC: The Urban Institute. www.urban.org/UploadedPDF/310438.pdf. Accessed March 8, 2006.

Kochhar, Rakesh. 2005. "Survey of Mexican Migrants, Part Three: The Economic Transition to America." Pew Research Center. pewhispanic.org/files/execsum/58.pdf. Accessed June 28, 2006.

Kohn, Melvin L. 1977. *Class and Conformity: A Study in Values*, 2nd ed. Chicago: University of Chicago Press.

Kohn, Melvin L., Atsushi Naoi, Carrie Schoenbach, Carmi Schooler, and Kazimierz M. Slomczynski. 1990. "Position in the Class Structure and Psychological Functioning in the United States, Japan, and Poland." *American Journal of Sociology* 95(4):864–1008.

Kolder, Veronika E. B., Janet Gallagher, and Michael T. Parsons. 1987. "Court-Ordered Obstetrical Interventions." *New England Journal of Medicine* 316:1192–1196.

Kornbluh, Karen, Katelin Isaacs, and Shelley Waters Boots. 2004. *Workplace Flexibility: A Policy Problem*. Work and Family Program: Issue Brief #1. Washington, DC: New America Foundation. www.newamerica.net/files/archive /Pub_File_1584_1.pdf. Accessed December 8, 2005.

Koropeckyj-Cox, Tanya. 2002. "Beyond Parental Status: Psychological Well-Being in Middle and Old Age." *Journal of Marriage and Family* 64:957–971.

Koss, Mary P., and Sarah L. Cook. 1993. "Facing the Facts: Date and Acquaintance Rape Are Significant Problems for Women." In Richard J. Gelles and Donileen R. Loseke (Eds.), *Current Controversies in Family Violence*, pp. 104–119. Newbury Park, CA: Sage Publications.

Koss, Mary P., Christine Gidycz, and Nadine Wisniewski. 1987. "The Scope of Rape: Incidence and Prevalence in a National Sample of Higher Education Students." *Journal of Consulting and Clinical Psychology* 55:162–170.

Krach, Constance A., and Victoria A. Velkoff. 1999. *Centenarians in the United States*. Current Population Reports P23-199. Washington, DC: U.S. Census Bureau.

Kraditor, Aileen S. 1965. *The Ideas of the Woman Suffrage Movement: 1890–1920*. New York: Columbia University Press.

Kramer, Laura. 2004. *The Sociology of Gender*. Los Angeles: Roxbury Publishing Co.

Kreider, Rose M. 2005. "Number, Timing, and Duration of Marriages and Divorces: 2001." Current Population Reports, P70-97. Washington, DC: U.S. Census Bureau.

Kroska, Amy. 2003. "Investigating Gender Differences in the Meaning of Household Chores and Child Care." *Journal of Marriage and Family* 65:456–473.

Kulikoff, Allan. 2000. *From British Peasants to Colonial American Farmers*. Chapel Hill, NC: University of North Carolina Press.

Kuney, Sloan, and Jason Levitis. 2007. "How Much Would a State Earned Income Tax Credit Cost in 2008?" Center on Budget and Policy Priorities. www.cbpp.org/2-7-07sfp.pdf. Accessed January 14, 2007.

Kurchinka, Mary Sheedy. 1998. *Raising Your Spirited Child.* New York: Harper Perennial.

Kurdek, Lawrence A. 2006. "Differences Between Partners from Heterosexual, Gay, and Lesbian Cohabiting Couples." *Journal of Marriage and Family* 68(2):509–528.

______. 2005. "What Do We Know About Gay and Lesbian Couples?" *Current Directions in Psychological Science* 14(5):251–254.

______. 2004. "Are Gay and Lesbian Cohabiting Couples Really Different from Heterosexual Married Couples?" *Journal of Marriage and Family* 66:880–900.

______. 2003. "Differences Between Gay and Lesbian Cohabiting Couples." *Journal of Social Personal Relationships* 20:411–436.

______. 2001. "Differences Between Heterosexual-Nonparent Couples and Gay, Lesbian, and Heterosexual Parent Couples." *Journal of Family Issues* 22:727–754.

______. 1999. "The Nature and Predictions of the Trajectory of Change and Marital Quality for Husbands and Wives Over the First 10 Years of Marriage." *Developmental Psychology* 35:1283–1296.

______. 1997. "Adjustment to Relationship Dissolution in Gay, Lesbian, and Heterosexual Partners." *Personal Relationships* 11:109–124.

______. 1995. "Lesbian and Gay Couples." In Anthony R. D'Augelli and Charlotte J. Patterson (Eds.), *Lesbian and Gay Identities Over the Lifespan: Psychological Perspectives on Personal, Relational, and Community Processes*, pp. 243–261. New York: Oxford University Press.

———. 1993. "The Allocation of Household Labor in Gay, Lesbian, and Heterosexual Married Couples." *Journal of Social Issues* 49:127–134.

Kurz, Demie. 2002. "Caring for Teenage Children." *Journal of Family Issues* 23:748–767.

La Leche League International. 2004. *The Womanly Art of Breastfeeding*, 7th rev. ed. New York: Plume Publishing.

Lackey, Chad. 2003. "Violent Family Heritage, the Transition to Adulthood, and Later Partner Violence." *Journal of Family Issues* 24:74–98.

Ladner, Joyce A. 1998. *The Ties that Bind: Timeless Values for African American Families*. New York: John Wiley.

Lamanna, Mary Ann, and Agnes Riedmann. 1997. *Marriages and Families: Making Choices in a Diverse Society*, 6th ed. Belmont, CA: Wadsworth.

Lamont, Michele. 2003. "Who Counts as "Them?": Racism and Virtue in the United States and France." *Contexts* 2(4):36–41.

Lampard, Richard, and Kay Peggs. 1999. "Repartnering: The Relevance of Parenthood and Gender to Cohabitation and Remarriage Among the Formerly Married." *The British Journal of Sociology* 50:443–465.

Landale, Nancy S. 2002. "Contemporary Cohabitation: Food for Thought." In Alan Booth and Ann C. Crouter (Eds.), *Just Living Together*, pp. 33–40. Mahwah, NJ: Lawrence Erlbaum.

Landsburg, Steven E. 2003. "Oh, No: It's a Girl! Do Girls Cause Divorce?" *Slate*. www.slate.us/id/2089142/. Accessed October 2, 2003.

LaRossa, Ralph. 1997. *The Modernization of Fatherhood: A Social and Political History*. Chicago: University of Chicago Press.

LaRossa, Ralph, Charles Jaret, Malati Gadgil, and G. Robert Wynn. 2000. "The Changing Culture of Fatherhood in Comic-Strip Families: A Six-Decade Analysis." *Journal of Marriage and the Family* 62:375–387.

Larsen, Luke J. 2004. *The Foreign-Born Population in the United States: 2003*. Current Population Reports No. P20-551. Washington, DC: U.S. Census Bureau.

Larson, Jeffry H., and Thomas B. Holman. 1994. "Premarital Predictors of Marital Quality and Stability." *Family Relations* 43:228–237.

Laslett, P. 1984. *The World We Have Lost: England Before the Industrial Age*, 3rd ed. New York: Charles Scribner's Sons.

Laumann, Edward O., John H. Gagnon, Robert T. Michael, and Stuart Michaels. 1994. *The Social Organization of Sexuality: Sexual Practices in the United States*. Chicago: University of Chicago Press.

Lavee, Yoav, and Ruth Katz. 2002. "Division of Labor, Perceived Fairness, and Marital Quality: The Effect of Gender Ideology." *Journal of Marriage and Family* 64:27–39.

Lawrance, Kelli-An, and E. Sandra Byers. 1995. "Sexual Satisfaction in Long-Term Heterosexual Relationships: The Interpersonal Exchange Model of Sexual Satisfaction." *Personal Relationships* 2:267–285.

Lawrence, Sharmila. 2002. *Domestic Violence and Welfare Policy*. New York: National Center for Children in Poverty, Mailman School of Public Health, Columbia University.

Leaper, Campbell. 2002. "Parenting Girls and Boys." In Marc H. Bornstein (Ed.), *Handbook of Parenting*, vol. 3, pp. 189–225. Mahwah, NJ: Lawrence Erlbaum.

Lee, Gary R., Jeffrey W. Dwyer, and Raymond Coward. 1993. "Gender Differences in Parent Care: Demographic Factors and Same-Gender Preferences." *Journal of Gerontology: Social Sciences* 48:S9–S16.

Lee, John A. 1988. "Love-Styles." In Robert J. Sternberg and Michael L. Barnes (Eds.), *The Psychology of Love*, pp. 38–67. New Haven, CT: Yale University Press.

Lee, Sharon M., and Barry Edmonston. 2005. New Marriages, New Families: U.S. Racial and Hispanic Intermarriage. *Population Bulletin*, vol. 60, no. 2. Washington, DC: Population Reference Bureau. www.prb.org/pdf05/60.2NewMarriages.pdf. Accessed January 27, 2006.

Lee, Yun-Suk, and Linda J. Waite. 2005. "Husbands' and Wives' Time Spent on Housework: A Comparison of

Measures." *Journal of Marriage and Family* 67(May): 328–336.

Leeder, Elaine. 2004. *The Family in Global Perspective: A Gendered Perspective*. Thousand Oaks, CA: Sage Publications.

Lennon, Mary Clare, and Sarah Rosenfeld. 1994. "Relative Fairness and the Division of Housework: The Importance of Options." *American Journal of Sociology* 100(2):506–531.

Lenski, Gerhard. 1984. *Power and Privilege: A Theory of Social Stratification*. Chapel Hill, NC: University of North Carolina Press.

Leonard, Lori. 2000. "Interpreting Female Genital Cutting: Moving Beyond the Impasse." *Annual Review of Sex Research* 11:158–191.

Lerman, Robert I. 2002. "Married and Unmarried Parenthood and Economic Well-Being: A Dynamic Analysis of a Recent Cohort." www.urban.org/exoert.cfm?ID=RobertLerman. Accessed June 27, 2005.

"Letters Between Abigail Adams and Her Husband John Adams." www.thelizlibrary.org/suffrage/abigail.htm. Accessed December 20, 2003.

Levine, Elaine S., and Alvin L. Sallee. 1990. "Critical Phases Among Adoptees and Their Families: Implications for Therapy." *Child and Adolescent Social Work* 7:217–232.

Levine, Judith, Clifton R. Emery, and Harold Pollack. 2007. "The Well-being of Children Born to Teen Mothers." *Journal of Marriage and Family*, 69:105–122.

Levine, Robert A. 1977. "Child Rearing as a Cultural Adaptation." In P. Leiderman, S. Tulken, and A. Rosenfeld (Eds.), *Culture and Infancy*. New York: Academic Press.

Levine, Robert J. 1988. *Ethics and Regulation of Clinical Research*, 2nd ed. New Haven, CT: Yale University Press.

Lewis, Oscar. 1966. "The Culture of Poverty." *Scientific American* 215:19–25.

Liberty Belles. 2006. "Japan's Fertility Crisis." http://toughlove.catallarchy.net/blog/2006/05/01/japans-fertility-crisis/. Accessed November 24, 2006.

Lichter, Daniel T., and Zhenchao Qian. 2004. *Marriage and Family in a Multiracial Society*. Washington, DC: Population Reference Bureau. www.prb.org/Template.cfm?Section=PRB&template=/Content/ContentGroups/04_Articles/Marriage_and_Family_in_a_Multiracial_Society.htm. Accessed June 27, 2005.

Lin, I-Fen, Nora Cate Schaeffer, Judith A. Seltzer, and Kay L. Tuschen. 2004. "Divorced Parents' Qualitative and Quantitative Reports of Children's Living Arrangements." *Journal of Marriage and Family* 66(May):385–397.

Lin, I-Fen, Noreen Goldman, Maxine Weinstein, Yu-Hsuan Lin, Tristan Gorrindo, and Teresa Seeman. 2003. "Gender Differences in Adult Children's Provision of Support to Their Elderly Parents in Taiwan." *Journal of Marriage and the Family* 65(1):184–200.

Lino, Mark. 2006. "Expenditures on Children by Families, 2005." U.S. Department of Agriculture, Center on Nutrition, Policy, and Promotion. Miscellaneous publication Number 1528-2005. www.cnpp.usda.gov/Publications/CRC/crc2005.pdf. Accessed November 24, 2006.

Lips, Hilary. 1997. *Sex and Gender*, 3rd ed. Mountain View, CA: Mayfield.

Litoff, Judy. 1978. *American Midwives: 1860 to the Present*. Westport, CT: Greenwood.

Liz Claiborne Inc. 2005. "Study on Teen Dating Abuse." Teenage Research Unlimited. www.loveisnotabuse.com. Accessed November 8, 2005.

Lobe, Jim. 2003. "Bush Charged with Leading 'Secret War' Against Reproductive Freedom." Common Dreams Newscenter. www.commondreams.org/headlines03/0123-02.htm. Accessed December 20, 2003.

Loehlin, John C. 2005. "Resemblance in Personality and Attitudes Between Parents and Their Children: Genetic and Environmental Contributions." In Samuel Bowles, Herbert Gintis, and Melissa Osborne (Eds.), *Unequal Chances: Family Background and Economic Success*, pp. 192–207. Princeton, NJ: Princeton University Press.

Lopata, Helena Z. 1973. *Widowhood in an American City*. Cambridge, MA: Shenckman.

______. 1979. *Women as Widows: Support Systems*. New York: Elsevier.

Loprest, Pamela. 2003. *Fewer Welfare Leavers Employed in Weak Economy*. Washington, DC: The Urban Institute. www.urban.org/UploadedPDF/310837_snapshots3_no5.pdf. Accessed January 6, 2005.

______. 2002. "Making the Transition from Welfare to Work: Successes but Continuing Concerns." In Alan Weil and Kenneth Feingold (Eds.), *Welfare Reform: The Next Act*, pp. 17–31. Washington, DC: The Urban Institute Press.

———. 2001. *How Are Families that Left Welfare Doing? A Comparison of Early and Recent Welfare Leavers*. Technical Report No. Series B, No. B-36. Washington, DC: The Urban Institute.

Ludwig, Jens, and Susan Mayer. 2006. "Culture and the Intergenerational Transmission of Poverty: The Prevention Paradox." *The Future of Children*, 16:176–196.

Lugaila, Terry A. 2003. *A Child's Day: Home, School, and Play (Selected Indicators of Child Well-Being)*. Technical Report No. P70-89. Washington, DC: U.S. Census Bureau.

Lundberg, Shelly, and Elaina Rose. 2003. "Child Gender and the Transition to Marriage" (Economics Working Paper). Seattle: University of Washington. www.econ.washington.edu/user/lundberg/transmar.pdf. Accessed June 26, 2006.

Lung and Asthma Information Agency. 2000/3. "Asthma and Social Class." London, UK: Public Health Sciences

Dept., St. George's Hospital Medical School. www.sghms.ac.uk/depts/laia/laia.htm. Accessed August 28, 2003.

Lynott, Patricia Passuth, and E. L. Roberts. 1997. "The Developmental Stake Hypothesis and Changing Perceptions of Intergenerational Relations, 1971–1985." *The Gerontologist* 37:394–405.

Maccoby, Eleanor E. 1998. *The Two Sexes: Growing up Apart, Coming Together*. Cambridge, MA: Harvard University Press.

Maccoby, Eleanor E., and Carol N. Jacklin. 1974. *The Psychology of Sex Differences*. Stanford, CA: Stanford University Press.

Mackey, Richard A., Bernard A. O'Brien, and Eileen F. Mackey. 1997. *Gay and Lesbian Couples: Voices from Lasting Relationships*. Westport, CT: Praeger.

Mackie, Gerry. 2000. "Female Genital Cutting: The Beginning of the End." In Bettina Shell-Duncan and Ylva Hernlund (Eds.), *Female "Circumcision" in Africa: Culture, Controversy, and Change*, pp. 253–282. Boulder, CO: Lynne Reinner.

———. 1996. "Ending Footbinding and Infibulation: A Convention Account." *American Sociological Review* 61:999–1017.

MacPhee, David, Janet Fritz, and Jan Miller-Heyl. 1996. "Ethnic Variations in Personal Social Networks and Parenting." *Child Development* 67:3278–3295.

Maher, Bridget E. 2006. "Why Marriage Should Be Privileged in Public Policy." Family Research Council. www.frc.org/index.cfm?i=IS03D1. Accessed June 6, 2006.

Maine, Deborah, and Patsy Bailey. 2001. *Indicators for Design, Monitoring, and Evaluation of Maternal Morbidity Programs*. New York: Measure Project, AMDD Programme, Columbia University, Family Health International.

Makino, Katsuko, Y. Nakano, and K. Kashiwagi. 1996. *Kodomo No Hattatsu To Chichioya No Yakuwari* [*Child Development and Fathers' Roles*]. Kyoto, Japan: Minerva.

Mann, Thomas E. 1998. "Is the Era of Big Government Over?" *Public Perspective* 9(February–March):27–29.

Manning, Wendy D. 2002. "The Implications of Cohabitation for Children's Well-Being." In Alan Booth and Ann C. Crouter (Eds.), *Just Living Together*, pp. 121–152. Mahwah, NJ: Lawrence Erlbaum.

Manning, Wendy D., and Susan Brown. 2006. "Children's Economic Well-Being in Married and Cohabiting Parent Families." *Journal of Marriage and Family* 68(2):345–362.

Manning, Wendy D., and Kathleen Lamb. 2002. "Parental Cohabitation and Adolescent Well-Being." Working Paper No. 02-04. Bowling Green, OH: Bowling Green State University, Center for Family and Demographic Research.

Manpower. 2005. "Profile." www.us.manpower.com/uscom/contentSingle.jsp?articleid=297. Accessed October 3, 2005.

Mansnerus, Laura. 1995. "The Divorce Backlash." *Working Woman* 70(February):38–47.

March of Dimes. 2006. "C-Section: Medical Reasons." www.marchofdimes.com/pnhec/240_1031.asp. Accessed June 15, 2006.

Marindin, Hope. 1987. *The Handbook for Single Adoptive Parents*. Chevy Chase, MD: National Council for Single Adoptive Parents.

Marland, Hillary, and Anne Marie Rafferty. 2005. *Midwives, Society, and Childbirth*. Oxford, England: Taylor and Francis Publishers.

Marsiglio, William, and Joseph H. Pleck. 2005. "Fatherhood and Masculinities." In Robert W. Connell, Jeff R. Hearn, and Michael S. Kimmel (Eds.), *The Handbook of Studies on Men and Masculinities*, pp. 249–269. Thousand Oaks, CA: Sage Publications.

Marsiglio, William, and Denise Donnelly. 1991. "Sexual Relations in Later Life: A National Study of Married Persons." *Journal of Gerontology: Social Sciences* 46:S338–S344.

Marsiglio, William, Kevin Roy, and Greer Litton Fox (Eds.). 2005. *Situated Fathering: A Focus on Physical and Social Spaces*. Lanham, MD: Rowman and Littlefield Publishers.

Marsiglio, William, John H. Scanzoni, and Kendal L. Broad. 2000. "Sexual Behavior Patterns." In Edgar F. Borgatta and Rhonda V. J. Montgomery (Eds.), *Encyclopedia of Sociology*, 2nd ed., pp. 2549–2564. New York: Macmillan.

Martin, C., and Fabes, R. A. 2001. "The stability and consequences of young children's same-sex peer interactions." *Developmental Psychology* 37(3):431–446.

Martin, Jack K., Steven A. Tuch, and Paul Roman. 2003. "Problem Drinking Patterns Among African-Americans: The Impacts of Experiences with Discrimination, Perceptions of Prejudice, and 'Risky' Coping Strategies." *Journal of Health and Social Behavior* 44:408–425.

Martin, Joyce A., Brady E. Hamilton, Paul D. Sutton, Stephanie J. Ventura, Fay Menacker, and Martha L. Munson. 2005. *Births: Final Data for 2003*. Technical Report No. 54(2). National Vital Statistics Reports. Hyattsville, MD: National Center for Health Statistics.

Martin, Joyce, A., Bradley E. Hamilton, Paul D. Sutton, Stephanie J. Ventura, Fay Manaker, and Sharon Kirmeyer. 2006. "Births: Final Data for 2004." National Vital Statistics Report. Vol. 55, No. 1. Hyattsville, MD: National Center for Health Statistics.

Martin, K. A. 2005. "William Wants a Doll. Can He Have One? Feminists, Child Care Advisors, and Gender-Neutral Childrearing." *Gender and Society* 19:456–479.

Martin, Steven P., and Sangeeta Parashar. 2006. "Women's Changing Attitudes Toward Divorce, 1974–2002: Evidence for an Educational Crossover." *Journal of Marriage and Family* 68(1):29–40.

Marx, Karl, and Friedrich Engels. 1971. [Original work published 1867.] *Manifesto of the Communist Party*. New York: International Publishers.

Masheter, Carol. 1997. "Health and Unhealthy Friendship and Hostility Between Ex-Spouses." *Journal of Marriage and the Family* 59:463–475.

Mauer, Marc. 1999. *Race to Incarcerate*. New York: The New Press.

May, Jessica H., and Peter J. Cunningham. 2004. "Tough Trade-Offs: Medical Bills, Family Finances, and Access to Care." Electronic document. www.hs.change.org /CONTENT/689/.

Maza, Penelope L. 2002. "About Single Mother Adoption." www.clwl.org/programs/adoption/singlmother.htm. Accessed September 3, 2002.

McCabe, Kristen M. 1997. "Sex Differences in the Long-Term Effects of Divorce on Children: Depression and Heterosexual Relationship Difficulties in the Young Adult Years." *Journal of Divorce and Remarriage* 27:123–135.

McCool, William F., and Sara A. Simeone. 2002. "Birth in the United States: An Overview of Trends Past and Present." *Nursing Clinics of North America* 37(4): 735–746.

McCubbin, Hamilton I., Marilyn A. McCubbin, Anne I. Thompson, Sae-Young Han, and Chad T. Allen. 1997. "Families Under Stress: What Makes Them Resilient." Commemorative Lecture. Washington, DC: AAFCS.

McDowell Group. 2003. "Areas of Expertise." www .mcdowellgroup.net/pages/areaexpert/aknative.html. Accessed March 19, 2006.

McElvaine, Robert S. 1993. *The Great Depression: America, 1929–1941*. New York: Times Books.

McLanahan, Sara. 1983. "Family Structure and Stress: A Longitudinal Comparison of Two-Parent and Female-Headed Families." *Journal of Marriage and the Family* 45:347–357.

McLanahan, Sara, and Gary Sandefur. 1994. *Growing Up with a Single Parent: What Hurts, What Helps*. Cambridge, MA: Harvard University Press.

McLoyd, Vonnie C. 1990. "The Impact of Economic Hardship on Black Families and Children: Psychological Distress, Parenting, and Socioemotional Development." *Child Development* 61:311–346.

Mead, Margaret. 1935. *Sex and Temperament in Three Primitive Societies*. New York: Morrow.

______. 1949. *Male and Female: A Study of the Sexes in a Changing World*. New York: Morrow.

Medora, Nilufer P. 2003. "Mate Selection in Contemporary India." In Raeann R. Hamon and Bron B. Ingoldsby (Eds.), *Mate Selection Across Cultures*, pp. 209–230. Thousand Oaks, CA: Sage Publications.

Melzer, Scott A. 2002. "Gender, Work, and Intimate Violence: Men's Occupational Violence Spillover and Compensatory Violence." *Journal of Marriage and Family* 64(4):820–833.

Menaghan, Elizabeth G., Lori Kowalski-Jones, and Frank L. Mott. 1997. "The Intergenerational Costs of Parental Social Stressors: Academic and Social Difficulties in Early Adolescence for Children of Young Mothers." *Journal of Health and Social Behavior* 38:72–86.

Merriam-Webster Online. 2006. "Love." www.m-w.com /dictionary/love&. Accessed November 25, 2006.

Messner, Michael. 2002. *Taking the Field: Women, Men, and Sports*. Minneapolis: University of Minnesota Press.

Miall, Charlene E. and Karen March. 2005. "Open Adoption as a Family Form: Community Assessments and Social Support." *Journal of Family Issues* 26:380–410.

Michael, Robert T., John H. Gagnon, Edward O. Laumann, and Gina Kolata. 1994. *Sex in America: A Definitive Survey*. New York: Little, Brown and Company.

Michaels, Marsha. 2005. "Factors That Contribute to Stepfamilies' Success: A Qualitative Analysis." *Journal of Divorce and Remarriage* 44:53–66.

Microsoft Encarta Online Encyclopedia. 2004. "Affirmative Action." encarta.msn.com/encyclopedia_ 761580666/Affirmative_Action.html. Accessed January 17, 2004.

Milardo, Robert M., Ed. 2000. "The Decade in Review." *Journal of Marriage and Family* 62(4):873.

Milkie, Melissa, and Pia Peltola. 1999. "Playing All the Roles: Gender and the Work-Family Balancing Act." *Journal of Marriage and the Family* 61:476–490.

Milkie, Melissa A., Marybeth J. Mattingly, Kei M. Nomaguchi, Suzanne M. Bianchi, and John P. Robinson. 2004. "The Time Squeeze: Parental Statuses and Feelings About Time with Children." *Journal of Marriage and Family* 66(August):739–761.

Milkman, Ruth. 1976. "Women's Work and the Economic Crisis: Some Lessons from the Great Depression." *Review of Radical Political Economics* 8:73–97.

Miller, J. Elizabeth. 2000. "Religion and Families Over the Life Course." In Sharon Price, Patrick McHenry, and Megan J. Murphy (Eds.), *Families Across Time: A Life Course Perspective*, Sec. III, Ch. 13. Los Angeles: Roxbury Publishing Co.

Miller, Nancy B., Virginia L. Smerglia, D. Scott Gaudet, and Gay C. Kitson. 1998. "Stressful Life Events, Social Support, and the Distress of Widowed and Divorced Women." *Journal of Family Issues* 19:181–203.

Miller, Susan L., and Sally S. Simpson. 1991. "Courtship Violence and Social Control: Does Gender Matter?" *Law and Society Review* 25:335–365.

Mills, C. Wright. 1959. *The Sociological Imagination*. New York: Oxford University Press.

Mindel, Charles H. 1980. "Extended Familism Among Urban Mexican-Americans, Anglos, and Blacks." *Hispanic Journal of Behavioral Sciences* 2:21–34.

Ministere des Affaires Etrangeres. 2005. "France Society: Family Policy." www.france.diplomatic.fr/france/gb /societe/societe07.html. Accessed June 26, 2005.

Mintz, Steven. 2004. *Huck's Raft: A History of American Childhood*. Cambridge, MA: Belknap Press.

———. 2003. "Introduction: The Contemporary Crisis of the Family." Council on Contemporary Families.

www.contemporaryfamilies.org/public/fact1.php. Accessed July 5, 2005.

Mintz, Steven, and Susan Kellogg. 1989. *Domestic Revolution: A Social History of Family Life*. New York: Free Press.

Miracle, Tina S., Andrew W. Miracle, and Roy F. Baumeister. 2003. *Human Sexuality*. Upper Saddle River, NJ: Prentice Hall.

Mirandé, Alfredo. 1985. *The Chicano Experience: An Alternative Perspective*. Notre Dame, IN: University of Notre Dame Press.

Mirowsky, John, and Catherine E. Ross. 1995. "Sex Differences in Distress: Real or Artifact?" *American Sociological Review* 60:449–468.

Mishel, Lawrence, Jared Bernstein, and Sylvia Allegretto. 2007. *The State of Working America 2006/2007*. Washington, DC: Economic Policy Institute.

Moen, Phyllis, Jungmeen Kim, and Heather Hofmeister. 2001. "Couples' Work/Retirement Transitions, Gender, and Marital Quality." *Social Psychology Quarterly* 64:55–71.

Montgomery, Marilyn J., and Gwendolyn T. Sorell. 1998. "Love and Dating Experience in Early and Middle Adolescence: Grade and Gender Comparisons." *Journal of Adolescence* 21:677–689.

Montgomery, Marilyn J., Edward R. Anderson, E. Mavis Hetherington, and W. Glenn Clingempeel. 1992. "Patterns of Courtship for Remarriage: Implications for Child Adjustment and Parent-Child Relationships." *Journal of Marriage and the Family* 54:686–698.

Montgomery, Rhonda J. V. 1996. "The Influence of Social Context on the Caregiving Experience." In Zaven S. Khachaturian and Teresa S. Radenbaugh (Eds.), *Alzheimer's Disease: Causes, Diagnosis, Treatment, and Care*, pp. 313–321. New York: CRC Press.

Morgan, Leslie, and Suzanne Kunkel. 1998. *Aging: The Social Context*. Thousand Oaks, CA: Pine Forge Press.

Morgan, Lewis Henry. 1962. [1851]. *League of the Ho-de-No-Sau-Ne, or Iroquois*. New York: Corinth Press.

Morrison, Donna Ruane, and Amy Ritualo. 2000. "Routes to Children's Economic Recovery After Divorce: Are Cohabitation and Remarriage Equivalent?" *American Sociological Review* 65:560–580.

Moynihan, Daniel P. 1965. *The Negro Family: The Case for National Action*. Washington, DC: U.S. Government Printing Office.

Mulsow, Miriam, Yvonne M. Caldera, Marta Pursley, Alan Reifman, and Aletha C. Huston. 2002. "Multilevel Factors Influencing Maternal Stress During the First Three Years." *Journal of Marriage and Family* 64(November):944–956.

Munson, Martha L., and Paul D. Sutton. 2005. *Births, Marriages, Divorces, and Deaths: Provisional Data for May 2005*. National Vital Statistics Reports 54(7). Washington, DC: Centers for Disease Control and Prevention.

Munson, Martha L., and Paul D. Sutton. 2006. "Births, Marriages, Divorces, and Deaths: Provision data for 2005." National Vital Statistics Reports; vol. 54 no. 20. Hyattsville, MD: National Center for Health Statistics.

Murdock, George. 1967. *Ethnographic Atlas*. Pittsburgh, PA: University of Pittsburgh Press.

______. 1957. "World Ethnographic Sample." *American Anthropologist* 59:664–687.

———. 1949. *Social Structure*. New York: Macmillan.

Murkoff, Heidi, Arlene Eisenberg, and Sandee Hathaway. 2002. *What to Expect When You're Expecting*, 3rd ed. New York: Workman Publishing.

Murkoff, Heidi, Sandee Hathaway, and Arlene Eisenberg. 2003. *What to Expect the First Year*, 2nd ed. New York: Workman Publishing.

Murray, Charles. 1988. *In Pursuit of Happiness and Good Government*. New York: Simon and Schuster.

———. 1984. *Losing Ground: American Social Policy, 1950–1980*. New York: Basic Books.

Murry, Velma McBride. 2000. "Challenges and Experiences of Black American Families." In Patrick C. McKenry and Sharon J. Price (Eds.), *Families and Change: Coping with Stressful Events*, 2nd ed., pp. 333–358. Thousand Oaks, CA: Sage.

Murry, Velma McBride, Gene H. Brody, Lily D. McNair, Zupei Luo, Frederick X. Gibbons, Meg Gerrard, and Thomas Ashby Wills. 2005. "Parental Involvement Promotes Rural African American Youths' Self-Pride and Sexual Self-Concepts." *Journal of Marriage and Family* 67(3):627–642.

Myers, Scott M. 2006. "Religious Homogamy and Marital Quality: Historical and Generational Patterns, 1980–1997." *Journal of Marriage and Family* 68(2):292–304.

Nakonezny, Paul A., Robert D. Shull, and Joseph Lee Rodgers. 1995. "The Effect of No-Fault Divorce Law on the Divorce Rate Across the 50 States and Its Relation to Income, Education, and Religiosity." *Journal of Marriage and the Family* 57:477–488.

NARAL. 2006. Insurance Coverage for Contraception: A Proven Way to Protect and Promote Women's Health. www.prochoiceamerica.org/assets/files/Birth-Control-Insurance-Coverage.pdf

National Adoption Information Clearinghouse. 2002. "Single Parent Adoption: What You Need to Know." U.S. Department of Health and Human Services: Administration for Children and Families. www.calib .com/naic/pubs/factsheets.cfm. Accessed June 11, 2003.

———. 2000. "Gay and Lesbian Adoptive Parents: Resources for Professionals and Parents." U.S. Department of Health and Human Services: Administration for Children and Families. www.calib.cfm/naic/pubs/factsheets.cfm. Accessed June 11, 2003.

National Center for Education Statistics. 2006. "A First Look at the Literacy of America's Adults in the 21st Century." nces.gov/NAAL/PDF/2006470.PDF. Accessed July 8, 2006.

National Center for Health Statistics. 2005. *Health, United States, 2005 with Chartbook on Trends in the Health of Americans*. Hyattsville, MD: National Center for Health Statistics.

———. 2002. "Cohabitation, Marriage, Divorce, and Remarriage in the United States." U.S. Department of Health and Human Services. www.cdc.gov/nchs/data/series/sr_23/sr23_022.pdf. Accessed June 30, 2005.

National Center for Injury Prevention and Control. 2005. "Suicide: Fact Sheet." www.cdc.gov/ncipc/factsheets/suifacts.htm. Accessed March 7, 2006.

National Center for Policy Analysis. 2001. "Health Issues—Urban Institute Study: Out-of-Pocket Medicare Expenses Will Rise." *Idea House*. www.ncpa.org/pi/health/pd011201d.html. Accessed June 1, 2006.

National Center on Elder Abuse. 2006. *Fact Sheet: Abuse of Adults Aged 60+ 2004 Survey of Adult Protective Services*. Washington, DC: National Center on Elder Abuse. www.elderabusecenter.org/pdf/2-14-06%2060FACT%20SHEET.pdf. Accessed July 14, 2006.

National Coalition Against Domestic Violence. 2006a. "The Problem." www.ncadv.org/learn/TheProblem_100.html. Accessed June 1, 2006.

National Coalition Against Domestic Violence. 2006b. "Dating Violence Facts." www.ncadv.org/files/DatingViolence_.pdf. Accessed June 1, 2006.

National Coalition for the Homeless. 2004. "People Need Affordable Housing." www.nationalhomeless.org/facts/housing.html. Accessed March 28, 2004.

National Committee for the Prevention of Elder Abuse. 2005. "2005 White House Conference on Aging Post-Event Summary Report." www.preventelderabuse.org/whcoaging2005.html. Accessed April 8, 2005.

National Council on Family Relations. 2004. "Mini-moms Created As Low-Income Families Search for Affordable Day Care." Press Release. www.ncfr.org/pdf/May2004pressrelease.pdf. Accessed February 15, 2005.

National Gay and Lesbian Task Force. 2005–2006. "The Issues: Aging." www.thetaskforce.org/theissues/issue.cfm?issueID=24. Accessed July 21, 2006.

National Institute of Justice and Centers for Disease Control and Prevention. 2005. *The State of Our Unions: The Social Health of Marriage in America*. Piscataway, NJ: National Marriage Project. marriage.rutgers.edu/Publications/SOOU/TEXTSOOU2005.htm. Accessed January 17, 2006.

———. 1998. "Prevalence, Incidence, and Consequences of Violence Against Women: Findings from the National Violence Against Women Survey." www.ojp.usdoj.gov/nii/pubs-sum/172837.htm. Accessed November 14, 2002.

National Marriage Project. 2006. "The State of Our Unions 2006." http://marriage.rutgers.edu/Publications/SOOU/SOOU2006.pdf. Accessed November 30, 2006.

Nationmaster.com. 2004. "Top 100 Teenage Birth Rate." Factoid 33. www.nationmaster.com/graph-T/peo_tee_bir_rat. Accessed March 27, 2004.

Needleman, Herbert L., Alan Schell, David Bellinger, Alan Leviton, and Elizabeth L. Allred. 1990. "The Long-Term Effects of Exposure to Low Doses of Lead in Childhood." *New England Journal of Medicine* 322:83–88.

Neft, Naomi, and Ann D. Levine. 1997. *Where Women Stand: An International Report on the Status of Women in Over 140 Countries, 1997–1998*. New York: Random House.

Nelson, Rebecca, and Linda Camras. 2000. "Developmental Status of Adopted Chinese Children." *Holt International Magazine*. November/December.

Nemeth, Danielle. 2000. "The 19th Amendment Is Ratified." www.thenagain.info/WebChron/USA/19Amend.html. Accessed August 10, 2005.

NICHD Early Child Care Research Network. 2005. "Duration and Developmental Timing of Poverty and Children's Cognitive and Social Development From Birth Through Third Grade." *Child Development* 76 (4 July):795–810.

Nichols, Laura, Cheryl Elman, and Kathryn M. Feltey. 2006. "The Economic Resource Receipt of New Mothers." *Journal of Family Issues* 27:1305–1330.

Nissel, Angela. 2006. *Mixed: My Life in Black and White*. New York: Villard Publishing.

Nock, Steven L. 1998. *Marriage in Men's Lives*. New York: Oxford University Press.

Nock, Steven L., James D. Wright, and Laura Sanchez. 1999. "America's Divorce Problem." *Society* 36:43–52.

Nolan, Patrick, and Gerhard Lenski. 1999. *Human Societies: An Introduction to Macrosociology*. New York: McGraw-Hill.

Nomaguchi, Kei M., and Melissa A. Milkie. 2003. "Costs and Rewards of Children: The Effects of Becoming a Parent on Adults' Lives." *Journal of Marriage and Family* 65:356–374.

Nomaguchi, Kei M., and Suzanne M. Bianchi. 2004. "Exercise Time: Gender Differences in the Effects of Marriage, Parenthood, and Employment." *Journal of Marriage and Family* 66(May):413–430.

Nord, M. M. Andrews, and S. Carlson. 2005. "Household Food Security in the United States, 2004." Washington, DC: U.S. Department of Agriculture, Economic Research Service, Report No. 11.

North Carolina Office of the Governor. 1999. "Governor Jim Hunt's Domestic Violence Prevention Initiative." govhunt.gov.state.nc.us/news/speeches/domspeech.htm. Accessed March 23, 2003.

NPR Online. 2001. "Poverty in America." NPR/Kaiser/Kennedy School Poll. www.npr.org/programs/specials/poll/poverty. Accessed December 1, 2005.

Nugman, Gulnar. 2002. *World Divorce Rates*. Washington, DC: The Heritage Foundation. www.divorcereform.org/gul.html. Accessed June 6, 2006.

Nye, F. Ivan. 1979. "Choice, Exchange, and the Family." In Wesley Burr, Reuben Hill, F. Ivan Nye, and Ira L. Reiss (Eds.), *Contemporary Theories About the Family*, vol. 2, pp. 1–41. New York: Free Press.

O'Connor, Thomas G., Michael Rutter, Celia Beckett, Lisa Keaveney, Jana M. Kreppner, and the English and Romanian Adoptees Study Team. 2000. "The Effects of Global Severe Privation on Cognitive Competence: Extension and Longitudinal Follow-Up." *Child Development* 71:376–390.

Office of the Assistant Secretary for Planning and Evaluation, U.S. Department of Health and Human Services. 2005. *The 2005 HHS Poverty Guidelines*. Washington, DC: Federal Register. Vol. 70(33), pp. 8373–8375.

Ogawa, Naohiro, and Robert D. Retherford. 1993. "Care of Elderly in Japan: Changing Norms and Expectations." *Journal of Marriage and the Family* 55:585–597.

Ogburn, W. F. 1964. *On Cultural and Social Change: Selected Papers*. Chicago: University of Chicago Press.

Ogunwole, Stella U. 2006. *We the People: American Indians and Alaska Natives in the United States*. Technical Report No. CENSR-28. Washington, DC: U.S. Census Bureau.

Oklahoma Marriage Initiative. 2006. "Frequently Asked Questions." www.okmarriage.org/Marriage AdviseQuestionsDetail.asp?id=10. Accessed July 5, 2006.

Oláh, Livia Sz., Eva M. Bernhardt., and Frances K. Goldscheider. 2003. "Coresidential Paternal Roles in Three Countries: Sweden, Hungary, and the United States." www.sociology.su.se/cgs/Conference/1_olah.pdf. Accessed May 1, 2003.

Oliver, Melvin L., and Thomas M. Shapiro. 1995. *Black Wealth/White Wealth: A New Perspective on Racial Inequality*. New York: Routledge.

Olson, Laura Katz. 2003. *The Not-So-Golden Years: Caregiving, the Frail Elderly and the Long Term Care Establishment*. Lanham, MD: Rowman & Littlefield.

O'Neill, P. 2005, 2 January. "C-Sections a Growing Trend." *The Sunday* [Portland] *Oregonian*, pp. B1–B2.

Onion, Amanda. 2005. "Scientists Find Sex Differences in Brain." *ABC News: Technology and Science*. abcnews .go.com/Technology/Health/story?id=424260&page=1. Accessed June 23, 2006.

Ono, Hiromi. 1998. "Husbands' and Wives' Resources and Marital Dissolution." *Journal of Marriage and the Family* 60:674–689.

O'Rand, Angela M. 1990. "Stratification and the Life Course." In Robert H. Binstock and Linda K. George (Eds.), *Handbook of Aging and the Social Sciences*, 3rd ed., pp. 130–148. San Diego, CA: Academic Press.

Orbuch, Terri L., and Sandra L. Eyster. 1997. "Division of Household Labor Among Black Couples and White Couples." *Social Forces* 76:301–332.

Orenstein, Peggy. 1994. *School Girls*. New York: Anchor Books.

Orentlicher, David. 2005. "Diversity: A Fundamental American Principle." *Missouri Law Review* 70:777. ssrn.com/abstract=832724. Accessed 11/24/06.

Organisation for Economic Co-operation and Development. 2006. "Starting Strong II: Early Childhood Education and Care." www.childpolicyintl.org. Accessed November 28, 2006.

Orshansky, Mollie. 1965. "Counting the Poor: Another Look at Poverty." *Social Security Bulletin* 28:3–29.

Osborne, Cynthia. 2005. "Marriage Following the Birth of a Child Among Cohabiting and Visiting Parents." *Journal of Marriage and Family* 67(1):14–26.

Osmond, Marie Withers, and Barrie Thorne. 1993. "Feminist Theories: The Social Construction of Gender in Families and Society." In Pauline G. Boss, William J. Doherty, Ralph LaRossa, Walter R. Schumm, and Suzanne K. Steinmetz (Eds.), *Sourcebook of Family Theories and Methods: A Contextual Approach*, pp. 591–623. New York: Plenum Press.

Ostrander, Susan A. 1980. "Upper Class Women: The Feminine Side of Privilege." *Qualitative Sociology* 3:23–44.

Oswald, Ramona Faith, and Linda S. Culton. 2003. "Under the Rainbow: Rural Gay Life and Its Relevance for Family Providers." *Family Relations* 52(1):72–81.

Otnes, Cele, and Elizabeth H. Pleck. 2003. *Cinderella Dreams: The Allure of the Lavish Wedding*. Berkeley: University of California Press.

Pagani, Linda, Bernard Boulerice, Richard E. Tremblay, and Frank Vitaro. 1997. "Behavioral Development in Children of Divorce and Remarriage." *Journal of Divorce and Remarriage* 38:769–781.

Parasuraman, S., and J. Greenhaus. 1997. *Integrating Work and Family: Challenges and Choices for a Changing World*. Westport, CT: Quorum Books.

Parke, Ross D., and Raymond Buriel. 1998. "Socialization in the Family: Ethnic and Ecological Perspectives." In William Damon and Nancy Eisenberg (Eds.), *Handbook of Child Psychology*, vol. 3. *Social, Emotional, and Personality Development*, 5th ed., pp. 463–552. New York: Wiley.

Parker, Ginny. 1999. "Japan Approves Birth Control Pill." *Associated Press*. www.yorkweekly.com/1999news /6_2_w2.htm. Accessed June 2, 2003.

Parsons, Talcott. 1951. *The Social System*. Glencoe, IL: Free Press.

———. 1937. *The Structure of Social Action*. New York: McGraw-Hill.

Parsons, Talcott, and Robert F. Boles. 1955. *Family, Socialization, and Interaction Process*. New York: Free Press.

Partenheimer, David. 2005. "Do Opposites Attract or Do Birds of a Feather Flock Together?" American Psychological Association. www.apa.org/releases /attraction.html. Accessed June 21, 2005.

———. 2003. "Marriage Appears to Be Beneficial to Women's Health, but Only When Marital Satisfaction Is High, New Research Shows." American Psychological Association. www.apa.org/releases/maritalbenefits.html. Accessed June 21, 2005.

———. 2001. "Same-Sex Peers Reinforce Sex Role Behavior in Social Activities, Study Finds." American Psychological Association. www.apa.org/releases /peerplay.html. Accessed November 6, 2003.

Passel, Jeffrey S. 2006. *The Size and Characteristics of the Unauthorized Migrant Population in the U.S.: Estimates Based on the March 2005 Current Population Survey*. Washington, DC: Pew Hispanic Center.

Patterson, Charlotte J. 2000. "Family Relationships of Lesbians and Gay Men." *Journal of Marriage and the Family* 62:1052–1069.

———. 1992. "Children of Lesbian and Gay Parents." *Child Development*. 1025–1039.

Patterson, Charlotte J., and Lisa V. Freil. 2000. "Sexual Orientation and Fertility." In Gillian R. Bentley and C. G. Nicholas Mascie-Taylor (Eds.), *Infertility in the Modern World: Biosocial Perspectives*. Cambridge, England: Cambridge University Press.

Pearson, Jessica, and Nancy Thoennes. 1998. "Programs to Increase Fathers' Access to Their Children." In Irwin Garfinkel, Sara S. McLanahan, Daniel R. Meyer, and Judith A. Seltzer (Eds.), *Fathers Under Fire*, pp. 220–252. New York: Russell Sage Foundation.

Peplau, Letitia A., and Kristin P. Beals. 2004. "The Family Lives of Lesbians and Gay Men." In Anita L. Vangelisti (Ed.), *Handbook of Family Communication*, pp. 233–248. Mahwah, NJ: Lawrence Erlbaum Associates.

Peplau, Letitia A., Rosemary C. Veniegas, and Susan M. Campbell. 1996. "Gay and Lesbian Relationships." In Ritch C. Savin-Williams and Kenneth M. Cohen (Eds.), *The Lives of Lesbians, Gays, and Bisexuals*, pp. 250–273. New York: Harcourt Brace.

Perry-Jenkins, Maureen, Abbie E. Goldberg, Courtney P. Pierce, and Aline G. Sayer. 2007. "Shift Work, Role Overload, and the Transition to Parenthood." *Journal of Marriage and Family* 69:123–138.

Perry-Jenkins, Maureen, and Elizabeth Turner. 2003. "Jobs, Marriage, and Parenting: Working It Out in Dual-Earner Families." In Marilyn Coleman and Lawrence H. Ganong (Eds.), *Handbook of Contemporary Families*, Part III, Ch. 9. Thousand Oaks, CA: Sage Publications.

Perry-Jenkins, Maureen, and Karen Folk. 1994. "Class, Couples, and Conflict: Effects of the Division of Labor on Assessments of Marriage in Dual-Earner Families." *Journal of Marriage and the Family* 56:165–180.

Perry-Jenkins, Maureen, Rena L. Repetti, and Ann C. Crouter. 2000. "Work and Family in the 1990s." *Journal of Marriage and the Family* 62(4):981–998.

Peter, Jennifer. 2004. "Gay Marriage in MA." *Nitecrawler*. donfox.blogdns.org/archives/000531.html. Accessed March 9, 2004.

Peters World Atlas, 2001. Niagara Falls, NY: USA New International Publisher.

Pew Forum on Religion and Public Life. 2005. "Abortion and Rights of Terror Suspects Top Court Issues: Strong Support for Stem Cell Research." pewforum.org/docs/index.php?DocID=91. Accessed July 5, 2006.

Pew Hispanic Center. 2006a. "From 200 Million to 300 Million: The Numbers Behind the Population Growth (Fact Sheet)." Washington, DC: Author.

———. 2006b. "The State of American Public Opinion on Immigration in Spring 2006: A Review of Major Surveys (Fact Sheet)." Washington, DC: Author.

———. 2006c. "Modes of Entry for the Unauthorized Migrant Population (Fact Sheet)." Washington, DC: Author.

———. 2006d. "A Statistical Portrait of Hispanics at Mid Decade." Washington, DC: Author.

———. 2004. "Survey Brief: Health Care Experiences." Washington, DC: Pew Hispanic Center.

Pew Research Center. 2006. Global Attitudes: 44 Nation Major Survey, 2002. Available online: pewglobal.org/reports/pdf/185topline.pdf. Accessed March 25, 2006.

———. 2005. *Trends Ch. 5 Hispanics: A People in Motion*. pewresearch.org/assets/files/trends2005-hispanic.pdf. Accessed March 8, 2005.

Phillips, Julie A., and Megan M. Sweeney. 2005. "Premarital Cohabitation and Marital Disruption Among White, Black, and Mexican American Women." *Journal of Marriage and Family* 67(May):296–314.

Phillips, Lynn. 1998. *The Girls Report—What We Know and Need to Know About Growing Up Female*. New York: National Center for Research on Women.

Phillips, Roderick. 1997. "Stepfamilies from a Historical Perspective." In Irene Levin and Marvin B. Sussman (Eds.), *Stepfamilies: History, Research and Policy*, pp. 5–18. New York: Haworth.

Phillipson, Chris. 1999. "The Social Construction of Retirement." In Meredith Minkler and Carroll L. Estes (Eds.), *Critical Gerontology: Perspectives from Political and Moral Economy*, pp. 315–325. Amityville, NY: Baywood.

Pineo, Peter. 1961. "Disenchantment in the Later Years of Marriage." *Marriage and Family Living* 23:3–11.

Pinquart, Martin, and Silvia Sorenson. 2005. "Ethnic Differences in Stressors, Resources, and Psychological Outcomes of Family Giving: A Meta-Analysis." *The Gerontologist* 45:90–106.

Planned Parenthood Federation of America, Inc. 2003. *A Planned Parenthood Report on the Administration and Congress—The Bush Administration, the Global Gag Rule, and HIV/AIDS Funding*. Washington, DC. www.plannedparenthood.org/files/PPFA/news-030702_AIDS_report.pdf. Accessed July 17, 2004.

Platt, Kevin. 1999. "Item from the Smart Marriages Archive: Reproduced in the Divorce Statistics Collection." *Christian Science Monitor*. www.divorceform.org/mel/achina.html. Accessed May 8, 2003.

Pleck, Joseph H., Freya L. Sonenstein, and Leighton C. Ku. 1994. "Problem Behaviors and Masculinity Ideology in Adolescent Males." In Robert D. Ketterlinus and Michael E. Lamb (Eds.), *Adolescent Problem Behaviors: Issues and Research*, pp. 165–186. Hillsdale, NJ: Lawrence Erlbaum Associates.

Pollack, William. 1999. *Real Boys: Rescuing Our Sons from the Myths of Boyhood*. New York: Henry Holt.

Pollock, Linda A. 1987. *Lasting Relationship: Parents and Children Over Three Centuries*. Hanover, NH: University Press of New England.

———. 1983. *Forgotten Children: Parent-Child Relations from 1500 to 1900*. New York: Cambridge University Press.

Pong, Suet-Ling. 1997. "Family Structure, School Context, and Eighth-Grade Math and Reading Achievement." *Journal of Marriage and the Family* 59:734–746.

Pong, Suet-Ling, Jaap Dronkers, and Gillian Hampden-Thompson. 2003. "Family Policies and Children's School Achievement in Single- Versus Two-Parent Families." *Journal of Marriage and Family* 65(3):681–699.

Pope, John. 2004. "More Women Ask for Caesareans: Doctors Debate Procedure." Newhouse News Service. www.newhouse.com/archive/pope080904.html. Accessed June 15, 2006.

Popenoe, David. 2005. "Marriage and Family: What Does the Scandinavian Experience Tell Us?" In *The State of Our Unions 2006*. Piscataway, NJ: National Marriage Project.

______. 2001. "Marriage." In Don Eberly (Ed.), *Building a Healthy Culture: Strategies for an American Culture Renaissance*, Section III. Grand Rapids, MI: Wm. Eerdmans.

______. 1996. *Life Without Father*. New York: The Free Press.

______. 1993. "American Family Decline, 1960–1990: A Review and Appraisal." *Journal of Marriage and the Family* 55:527–555.

______. 1991. "Family Decline in the Swedish Welfare State." *The Public Interest* 102:65–77.

———. 1986. *Disturbing the Nest: Family Change and Decline in Modern Societies*. New York: Aldine de Grupter.

Popenoe, David, and Barbara Dafoe Whitehead. 2005. *The State of Our Unions: The Social Health of Marriage in America*. Piscataway, N.J.: The National Marriage Project.

———. 2002. *Should We Live Together? What Young Adults Need to Know About Cohabitation Before Marriage: A Comprehensive Review of Recent Research*, 2nd ed. Piscataway, NJ: The National Marriage Project.

Population Reference Bureau. 2006. "2006 World Population Data Sheet." Washington, DC: Population Reference Bureau.

______. 2005. "2005 World Population Data Sheet." www.prb.org/pdf05/05WorldDataSheet_Eng.pdf. Accessed March 4, 2006.

Porter, Kirk H. 1971. *A History of Suffrage in the United States*. New York: AMS Press.

Premi, Mahendra K. 2002. "The Girl Child: Some Issues for Consideration." Paper presented at the Symposium on Sex Ratio in Mumbai, India, on January 10.

Press, Julie E., and Eleanor Townsley. 1998. "Wives' and Husbands' Household Reporting: Gender, Class, and Social Desirability." *Gender and Society* 12:188–219.

Presser, Harriet B. 2003. *Working in a 24/7 Economy: Challenges for American Families*. New York: Russell Sage Foundation.

———. "Nonstandard Work Schedules and Marital Instability." *Journal of Marriage and the Family* 62:93–110.

Presser, Harriet B., and Amy G. Cox. 1997. "The Work Schedules of Low-Educated American Women and Welfare Reform." *Monthly Labor Review* 120:25–34.

Preston, Samuel H., and Shigemi Kono. 1988. "Trends in the Well-Being of Children and the Elderly in Japan." In John L. Palmer, Timothy M. Smeeding, and Barbara Boyle Torrey (Eds.), *The Vulnerable*, pp. 277–307. Washington, DC: The Urban Institute Press.

Prevent Child Abuse Wisconsin. 2005. "Snow Day: Can Your Child Stay Home Alone?" www.preventchild abusewi.org/$spindb.query.pressrelease2.pcawview .96. Accessed July 17, 2006.

Price, Christine A. 2003. *Marriage After Retirement*. The Ohio Department of Aging, The Aging Network. Columbus, OH: The Ohio State University.

Project No More! 1998. "Sign the Proclamation Against Domestic Violence." www.project-no-more.20fr.com/custom4.html. Accessed March 23, 2005.

Pruett, Marsha Kline, and Tamara D. Jackson. 1999. "The Lawyer's Role During the Divorce Process: Perceptions of Parents, Their Young Children, and Their Attorneys." *Family Law Quarterly* 33:283–310.

Pyke, Karen. 2000a. "Ideology of 'Family' Shapes Perception of Immigrant Children." Minneapolis, MN: National Council on Family Relations.

______. 2000b. " 'The Normal American Family' as an Interpretive Structure of Family Life Among Grown Children of Korean and Vietnamese Immigrants." *Journal of Marriage and the Family* 62:240–245.

Qian, Zhenchao, Sampson Lee Blair, and Stacey D. Ruf. 2001. "Asian American Interracial and Interethnic Marriages: Differences in Education and Nativity." *International Migration Review* 35(2):577–586.

Quadagno, Jill. 1982. *Aging in Early Industrial Society*. New York: Academic Press.

Quadagno, Jill, and Jennifer Reid. 1999. "The Political Economy Perspective in Aging." In Vern L. Bengtson and K. Warner Schaie (Eds.), *Handbook of Theories of Aging*, pp. 344–358. New York: Springer.

Quick, Heather E., and Phyllis Moen. 1998. "Gender, Employment, and Retirement Quality: A Lifecourse Approach to the Differential Experiences of Men and Women." *Journal of Occupational Health Psychology* 3:44–64.

Raabe, Phyllis H., and Chikako Usui. 1991. "Modernization and Marriage: Couple Relations in Japan and the U.S." Presented at the International Symposium on Families: East and West, Indianapolis, Indiana, on July 26.

Rainwater, Lee and Timothy M. Smeeding 2003. *Poor Kids in a Rich Country: America's Children in Comparative Perspective*. New York: Russell Sage Foundation.

Raley, R. Kelly. 2001. "Increasing Fertility in Cohabiting Unions: Evidence for the Second Demographic

Transition in the United States." *Demography* 38(1):59–66.

Ramirez, Roberto R., and G. Patricia de la Cruz. 2003. *The Hispanic Population in the United States: March 2002.* Current Population Reports No. P20-545. Washington, DC: U.S. Census Bureau.

Ranae, J. Evenson, and Robin W. Simon. 2006. "Clarifying the Relationship Between Parenthood and Depression," *Journal of Health and Social Behavior* 46:341–358.

Rank, Mark R. 2003. "As American as Apple Pie: Poverty and Welfare." *Contexts* 2(3):41–49.

Rankin, Nancy. 2002. "The Parent Vote." In Sylvia A. Hewlett, Nancy Rankin, and Cornel West (Eds.), *Taking Parenting Public*, pp. 251–264. Lanham, MD: Rowman & Littlefield.

Raschick, Michael, and Berit Ingersoll-Dayton. 2004. "The Costs and Rewards of Caregiving Among Aging Spouses and Adult Children." *Family Relations* 53:317–325.

Raymo, James M. 1998. "Later Marriages or Fewer? Changes in the Marital Behavior of Japanese Women." *Journal of Marriage and the Family* 60:1023–1034.

Reeves, Terrance, and Claudette Bennett. 2003. *The Asian and Pacific Islander Population in the United States: March 2002.* Current Population Reports No. P20-540. Washington, DC: U.S. Census Bureau.

Regan, Pamela C., Lauren Levin, Susan Sprecher, F. Scott Christopher, and Rodney Cate. 2000. "Partner Preferences: What Characteristics Do Men and Women Desire in Their Short-Term Sexual and Long-Term Romantic Partners?" *Journal of Psychology and Human Sexuality* 12:1–21.

Reid, Lori L. 2000. "The Consequences of Food Insecurity for Child Well-Being: An Analysis of Children's School Achievement, Psychological Well-Being, and Health." JCPR Working Paper 137. Chicago: Northwestern University/University of Chicago Joint Center for Poverty Research. www.jcpr.org/wpfiles/Reid_WP.pdf?CFID=4915378&CFTOKEN=61585925. Accessed December 17, 2005.

Reiss, Ira L. 1960. "Toward a Sociology of the Heterosexual Love Relationship." *Marriage and Family Living* 22:139–145.

Reitzes, Donald C., and Elizabeth J. Mutran. 2004. "Grandparent Identity, Intergenerational Family Identity, and Well-Being" *Journal of Gerontology: Psychological Sciences and Social Sciences* 59:S213–S219.

Rennison, Callie Marie. 2003. *Intimate Partner Violence, 1993–2001.* Washington, DC: U.S. Department of Justice, Bureau of Justice Statistics.

Resolve. 2004. "Frequently Asked Questions About Infertility." www.resolve.org/site/PageServer?pagename=lrn_wii_faq. Accessed June 10, 2003.

Reyes, J. Roberto. 2003. "Couple Formation Practices in Spain." In Raeann R. Hamon and Bron B. Ingoldsby (Eds.), *Mate Selection Across Cultures*, pp. 175–190. Thousand Oaks, CA: Sage Publications, Inc.

Rindfuss, Ronald R., and Audrey Van den Heuvel. 1990. "Cohabitation: A Precursor to Marriage or an Alternative to Being Single?" *Population and Development Review* 16:703–726.

Roberto, Karen A., Pamela B. Teaster, and Joy O. Duke. 2004. "Older Women Who Experience Mistreatment: Circumstances and Outcomes." *Journal of Women and Aging* 16:3–16.

Robinson, John P., and Melissa A. Milkie. 1998. "Back to the Basics: Trends in and Role Determinants of Women's Attitudes Toward Housework." *Journal of Marriage and the Family* 60:205–218.

Robinson, John P., and Geoffrey Godbey. 1997. *Time for Life: The Surprising Ways Americans Use Their Time.* University Park, PA: Penn State University Press.

Robinson, Julian N., Errol R. Norwitz, Amy P. Cohen, and Ellice Lieberman. 2000. "Predictors of Episiotomy Use at First Spontaneous Vaginal Delivery." *Obstetrics and Gynecology* 96(2):214–218.

Rockquemore, Kerry Ann, and Tracey Laszloffy. 2005. *Raising Biracial Children.* Lanham, MD: AltaMira Press.

Rodgers, Joseph Lee, Paul A. Nakonezny, and Robert D. Shull. 1997. "Feedback: The Effect of No-Fault Divorce Legislation on Divorce Rates: A Response to a Reconsideration." *Journal of Marriage and the Family* 59:1026–1030.

Rodgers, Kathleen Boyce, and Hilary A. Rose. 2002. "Risk and Resiliency Factors Among Adolescents Who Experience Marital Transitions." *Journal of Marriage and Family* 64(November):1024–1037.

Rodgers, Roy H., and James M. White. 1993. "Family Development Theory." In Pauline G. Boss, William J. Doherty, Ralph LaRossa, Walter R. Schumm, and Suzanne K. Steinmetz (Eds.), *Sourcebook of Family Theories and Methods: A Contextual Approach*, pp. 225–254. New York: Plenum Press.

Roer-Strier, Dorit, and Dina Ben Ezra. 2006. "Intermarriages Between Western Women and Palestinian Men: Multidirectional Adaptation Processes." *Journal of Marriage and Family* 68(1):41–55.

Rogers, Stacy J. 2004. "Dollars, Dependency, and Divorce: Four Perspectives on the Role of Wives' Income." *Journal of Marriage and Family* 66(February):59–74.

Rohner, Ronald P., and Robert A. Veneziano. 2001. "The Importance of Father Love: History and Contemporary Evidence." *Review of General Psychology* 5(4):382–405.

Ronfeldt, Heidi M., Rachel Kimerling, and Ileana Arias. 1998. "Satisfaction with Relationship Power and the Perpetration of Dating Violence." *Journal of Marriage and the Family* 60:70–78.

Rooks, Judith. 1997. *Midwifery and Childbirth in America.* Philadelphia: Temple University Press.

Root, Maria P. P. 2001. *Love's Revolution: Interracial Marriage.* Philadelphia: Temple University Press.

Rose, David. 1995. "Official Social Classifications in the UK." *Social Research Update*. www.soc.surrey.ac.uk/sru/SRU9.html. Accessed August 28, 2003.

Rosenberg, Matt. 2006. "China's One Child Policy." geography.about.com/od/populationgeography/a/onechild.htm. Accessed July 14, 2006.

Ross, Catherine E., and Marieke Van Willigen. 1996. "Gender, Parenthood, and Anger." *Journal of Marriage and the Family* 58:572–784.

Ross, Emma. 2005, 8 June. "Genes Affect Woman's Orgasm, Study Shows." *The* [Portland] *Oregonian*, p. A15.

Ross, Mary Ellen Trail, and Lu Ann Aday. 2006. "Stress and Coping in African American Grandparents Raising Their Grandchildren." *Journal of Family Issues* 27:912–932.

Rossi, Alice S. 1968. "Transition to Motherhood." *Journal of Marriage and the Family* 30:26–39.

Rossi, Alice S., and Peter H. Rossi. 1990. *Of Human Bonding: Parent-Child Relations Across the Life Course*. New York: Aldine de Gruyter.

Rothman, Barbara Katz. 1991. *In Labor: Women and Power in the Birthplace*. New York: W. W. Norton and Co.

Rothstein, B. 2002. "Martial Strife: Do the Voters Really Care?" *The Hill*. Available online: www.hillnewsw.om.041002/marital.aspx. Retrieved July 8, 2003.

Rouse, Cecilia Elena and Lisa Barrow. 2006. "U.S. Elementary and Secondary Schools: Equalizing Opportunity or Replicating the Status Quo?" *The Future of Children*, 16:99–124.

Rowe, Gretchen, and Victoria Russell. 2004. *The Welfare Rules Databook: State Policies as of July 2002*. Washington, DC: The Urban Institute.

Roxburgh, Susan. 2006. "I Wish We Had More Time Together: The Distribution and Predictors of Perceived Family Time Pressures Among Married Men and Women in the Paid Labor Force." *Journal of Family Issues* 27:529–553.

Rubin, Jeffrey, Frank Provenzano, and Zella Luria. 1974. "The Eye of the Beholder: Parents' Views on Sex of Newborns." *American Journal of Orthopsychiatry* 44:512–519.

Rubin, Lillian B. 1994. *Families on the Fault Line: America's Working Class Speaks About the Family, the Economy, and Ethnicity*. New York: Harper Collins.

______. 1990. *Erotic Wars: What Happened to the Sexual Revolution?* New York: Farrar, Straus and Giroux.

———. 1976. *Worlds of Pain*. New York: Basic Books.

Rubio, Mercedes, and David R. Williams. 2004. "The Social Dimension of Race." In Bettina M. Beech and Maurine Goodman (Eds.), *Race and Research*, pp. 1–26. Washington, DC: American Public Health Association.

Ruhm, Christopher J. 1998. "Parental Leave and Child Health." Working Paper 6554. National Bureau of Economic Research. papers.nber.org/papers/W6554.pdf. Accessed June 26, 2003.

Rush, Sharon E. 2000. *Loving Across the Color Line: A White Adoptive Mother Learns About Race*. Lanham, MD: Rowman & Littlefield.

Rye, Mark S., Chad D. Folck, Todd A. Heim, Brandon T. Olszewski, and Elizabeth Traina. 2004. "Forgiveness of an Ex-Spouse: How Does it Relate to Mental Health Following Divorce?" *Journal of Divorce and Remarriage* 41:31–51.

Sadker, Myra, and David Sadker. 1994. *Failing at Fairness: How America's Schools Cheat Girls*. New York: Scribner.

Saltzman, Linda E., Christopher H. Johnson, Brenda Colley Gilbert, and Mary M. Goodwin. 2003. "Physical Abuse Around the Time of Pregnancy: An Examination of Prevalence and Risk Factors in 16 States." *Maternal and Child Health Journal* 7:31–42.

Saluter, Arlene F. 1996. *Marital Status and Living Arrangements: March 1995*. Washington, DC: U.S. Census Bureau, Department of Commerce, Economics and Statistics Administration.

Sample, Neal. 1999. "What I Felt Like Being Adopted." www.stepfamilynetwork.net/Adoption.htm. Accessed April 4, 2001.

Sanchez, Laura, and Elizabeth Thomson. 1997. "Becoming Mothers and Fathers: Parenthood, Gender, and the Division of Labor." *Gender and Society* 11:747–772.

Sanchez, Laura, Steven Nock, and James D. Wright. 2002. "Social and Demographic Factors Associated with Couples' Choice Between Covenant and Standard Marriage in Louisiana." www.bgsu.edu/organizations/cfdr/research/pdf/2002/2002_06.pdf. Accessed November 28, 2004.

Sanday, Peggy Reeves. 1981. "The Socio-Cultural Context of Rape: A Cross-Cultural Study." *Journal of Social Issues* 37:5–27.

Sandberg, John F., and Sandra L. Hofferth. 2001. "Changes in Children's Time with Parents: United States, 1981–1997." *Demography* 38:423–436.

Sands, Roberta G., and Robin S. Goldberg-Glen. 2000. "Factors Associated with Stress Among Grandparents Raising Their Grandchildren." *Family Relations* 49:97–105.

Sarkisian, Natalia, Mariana Gerena, and Naomi Gerstel. 2006. "Extended Family Ties Among Mexicans, Puerto Ricans, and Whites: Superintegration or Disintegration?" *Family Relations* 55(3):331–344.

Savage, Howard Allan, and Peter J. Fronczek. 1993. *Who Can Afford to Buy a House in 1991?* Current Housing Reports H121/93-3. Washington, DC: U.S. Census Bureau.

Sax, Leonard. 2006. *Why Gender Matters: What Parents and Teachers Need to Know About the Emerging Science of Sex Differences*. New York: Doubleday.

Scanzoni, John. 2004. "Household Diversity: The Starting Point for Healthy Families in the New Century," In Marilyn Coleman and Lawrence H. Ganong (Eds.), *Handbook of Contemporary Families: Considering the Past,*

Contemplating the Future (pp. 3–22). Thousand Oaks, CA: Sage.

Schaie, K. Warner, and Glen H. Elder Jr. 2005. *Historical Influences on Lives and Aging*. New York: Springer Publishing Co.

Scharlach, Andrew E., Beverly F. Lowe, and Edward L. Schneider. 1991. *Elder Care and the Work Force: Blue Print for Action*. Lexington, MA: Lexington Books.

Scheuble, Laurie, and David R. Johnson. 1993. "Marital Name Change: Plans and Attitudes of College Students." *Journal of Marriage and the Family* 55:747–754.

Schiller, Bradley R. 2001. *The Economics of Poverty and Discrimination*. Upper Saddle River, NJ: Prentice Hall.

Schmalzbauer, Leah. 2004. "Searching for Wages and Mothering from Afar: The Case of Honduran Transnational Families." *Journal of Marriage and Family* 66(December):1317–1331.

Schmid, Randolph E. 2005, 10 May. "Scent Studies Find Gay, Straight Divide." *The* [Portland] *Oregonian*, p. A3.

Schor, Juliet B. 2002. "Time Crunch Among American Parents." In Sylvia Ann Hewlett, Nancy Rankin, and Cornel West (Eds.), *Taking Parenting Public*, pp. 83–102. Lanham, MD: Rowman & Littlefield.

Schulman, Karen. 2000. *The High Cost of Child Care Puts Quality Care Out of Reach for Many Families*. Washington, DC: Children's Defense Fund.

Schvaneveldt, Jay D., Robert S. Pickett, and Margaret H. Young. 1993. "Historical Methods in Family Research." In Pauline G. Boss, William J. Doherty, Ralph LaRossa, Walter R. Schumm, and Suzanne K. Steinmetz (Eds.), *Sourcebook of Family Theories and Methods: A Contextual Approach*, pp. 591–623. New York: Plenum.

Schwartz, Jonathan P., Sally M. Hage, Imelda Bush, and Lauren Key Burns. 2006. "Unhealthy Parenting and Potential Mediators As Contributing Factors to Future Intimate Violence: A Review of the Literature." *Trauma, Violence, and Abuse* 7:206–221.

Schwartz, Seth J. and Gordon E. Finley. 2005. "Fathering in Intact and Divorced Families: Ethnic Differences in Retrospective Reports." *Journal of Marriage and Family* 67:207–215.

ScienceDaily. 2006. "Transgender Experience led Stanford Scientist to Critique Gender Differences." www.sciencedaily.com/releases/2006/07/060714174545.htm. Accessed November 21, 2006.

———. "Women's Sexual Behaviors May Be Closer to Men's than Previously Thought," www.sciencedaily.com/releases/2003/07/03070122080.htm. Accessed November 21, 2006.

Scott, Donald M., and Bernard Wishy, eds. 1982. *America's Families: A Documentary History*. New York: Harper & Row Publishers.

Sears, William, and Martha Sears. 2001. *The Attachment Parenting Book: A Commonsense Guide to Understanding and Nurturing Your Baby*. New York: Little, Brown.

Seccombe, Karen. 2007a. *So You Think I Drive a Cadillac?: Welfare Recipients' Perspectives on the System and Its Reform*. 2nd ed. Boston: Allyn and Bacon.

———. 2007b. *Families in Poverty*. Boston: Allyn and Bacon.

———. 2005. Families as Lived Experience: "We Have Love Bouncing Off Our Walls." Personal communication with unidentified woman about family/work balance. June 15. Portland, Oregon.

———. 2002. " 'Beating the Odds' Versus 'Changing the Odds': Poverty, Resilience, and Family Policy." *Journal of Marriage and Family*, 64:384–394.

———. 1986. "The Effects of Occupational Conditions Upon the Division of Household Labor: An Application of Kohn's Theory." *Journal of Marriage and the Family* 48(November):839–848.

Seccombe, Karen, and Kim A. Hoffman. 2007. *Just Don't Get Sick: Access to Health Care in the Aftermath of Welfare Reform*. Piscataway, NJ: Rutgers University Press.

Seccombe, Karen, and Rebecca L. Warner. 2004. *Marriages and Families: Relationships in Social Context*. Belmont, CA: Wadsworth Publishing Co.

______. 1991. "Assessing the Costs and Benefits of Children: Gender Comparisons Among Childfree Husbands and Wives." *Journal of Marriage and the Family* 53:191–202.

Seccombe, Karen, and Gary R. Lee. 1986. "Female Status, Wives' Autonomy and Divorce: A Cross-Cultural Study." *Family Perspectives* 20:241–249.

Seccombe, Karen, Heather Hartley, Jason Newsom, Clyde Pope, and Kim Hoffman. 2005. *Final Report to the Agency for Healthcare Research and Quality: Access to Healthcare and Welfare Reform*. Center for Public Health Studies. Portland, OR: Portland State University.

Sedlak, Andrea J., and Diane D. Broadhurst. 1998. "Executive Summary of the Third National Incidence Study of Child Abuse and Neglect." www.casanet.org/library/abuse/stabuse.htm. Accessed March 4, 2003.

Seegobin, Winston, and Kristen M. Tarquin. 2003. "Mate Selection in Trinidad and Tobago." In Raeann R. Hamon and Bron B. Ingoldsby (Eds.), *Mate Selection Across Cultures*, pp. 61–75. Thousand Oaks, CA: Sage Publications.

Seiter, Ellen. 1993. *Sold Separately: Children and Parents in Consumer Culture*. New Brunswick, NJ: Rutgers University Press.

Selman, Peter. 2002. "Intercountry Adoption in the New Millennium: The 'Quiet Migration' Revisited." *Population Research and Policy Review* 21(3):205–225.

Seltzer, Judith A. 2004. "Cohabitation and Family Change." In Marilyn Coleman and Lawrence H. Ganong (Eds.), *Handbook of Contemporary Families*, pp. 57–78. Thousand Oaks, CA: Sage.

———. 2002. "Income Pooling and Individual and Family Mobility." Presented at the XV World Congress of Sociology, Brisbane, Australia, on July 11.

Senanayake, Pramilla. 1999. "Global Challenges in Ending Gender-Based Violence." International Planned

Parenthood Federation. www.ippf.org/resource/gbv/chogm99/global.htm. Accessed March 19, 2003.

Shapiro, Adam D. 1996. "Explaining Psychological Distress in a Sample of Remarried and Divorced Persons: The Influence of Economic Distress." *Journal of Family Issues* 17:186–203.

Shapiro, Isaac. 2005. *New IRS Data Show Income Inequality Is Again on the Rise*. Washington, DC: Center on Budget and Policy Priorities.

Sharpe, Tanya T., Lisa M. Lee, Allyn K. Nakashima, Laurie D. Elam-Evans, and Patricia L. Fleming. 2004. "Crack Cocaine Use and Adherence to Antiretroviral Treatment Among HIV-Infected Black Women." *Journal of Community Health* 29:117–127.

Sheets, Virgil L., and Sanford L. Braver. 1996. "Gender Differences in Satisfaction with Divorce Settlements." *Family Relations* 45:336–342.

Shehan, Constance L., Felix M. Berardo, Erica Owens, and Donna H. Berardo. 2002. "Alimony: An Anomaly in Family Social Science." *Family Relations* 51:308–316.

Sheldon, Jane P. 2004. "Gender Stereotypes in Educational Software for Young Children." *Sex Roles: A Journal of Research* 51:433–444.

Shelton, Beth Anne. 1992. *Women, Men and Time: Gender Differences in Paid Work, Housework, and Leisure*. Westport, CT: Greenwood.

Shelton, Beth Anne, and Daphne John. 1993. "Ethnicity, Race, and Difference: A Comparison of White, Black, and Hispanic Men's Household Labor Time." In Jane C. Hood (Ed.), *Men, Work, and Family*, pp. 131–150. Newbury Park, CA: Sage.

Sherman, Arloc, and Aviva Aron-Dine. 2007. "New CBO Data Show Income Inequality Continues to Widen: After-Tax Income for Top 1 Percent Rose By 146,000 in 2004." Center on Budget and Policy Priorities. www.cbpp.org/1-23-07inc.htm

Shilts, Randy. 1987. *And the Band Played On: Politics, People, and the AIDS Epidemic*. New York: St. Martins Press.

Sickels, Robert J. 1972. *Race, Marriage, and the Law*. Albuquerque: University of New Mexico Press.

Siefert, K., C. Heflin, M. Corcoran, and D. Williams. 2004. "Food Insufficiency and Physical and Mental Health in a Longitudinal Survey of Welfare Recipients." *Journal of Health and Social Behavior* 45:171–186.

Siegel, Judith M., and David H. Kuykendall. 1990. "Loss, Widowhood, and Psychological Distress Among the Elderly." *Journal of Consulting and Clinical Psychology* 58:519–524.

Silliman, Ben. 1998. "The Resiliency Paradigm: A Critical Tool for Practitioners." *Human Development and Family Life Bulletin*. Columbus, OH: The Ohio State University, College of Human Ecology.

Simon, Rita J., and Howard Alstein. 2000. *Adoption Across Borders: Serving the Children in Transracial and Intercountry Adoptions*. Lanham, MD: Rowman & Littlefield.

Simmons, Tayla, and Martin O'Connell. 2003. *Married-Couple and Unmarried-Partner Households: 2000*. Census 2000 Special Report No. CENSR-5. www.census.gov/prod/2004pubs/p20-553.pdf. Accessed May 24, 2004.

Simpson, George Eaton, and J. Milton Yinger. 1985. *Racial and Cultural Minorities: An Analysis of Prejudice and Discrimination*, 5th ed. New York: Plenum.

Sinclair, Upton. 1906, republished 1981. *The Jungle*.

Singh, Susheela, and Jacqueline E. Darroch. 2000. "Adolescent Pregnancy and Childbearing: Levels and Trends in Developed Countries." *Family Planning Perspectives* 32:14–23.

Skinner, Denise A., and Julie K. Kohler. 2002. "Parental Rights in Diverse Family Contexts: Current Legal Developments." *Family Relations* 51(4):293–300.

Smedley, Brian D., Adrienne Y. Stith, and Alan R. Nelson (Eds.). 2002. *Unequal Treatment: Confronting Racial and Ethnic Disparities in Health Care*. Washington, DC: National Academy Press.

Smeeding, Timothy A. 1997. *Financial Poverty in Developed Countries: The Evidence from LIS*. Luxembourg Income Study Working Paper Series No. 155. www.lisproject.org/publications/liswps/155.pdf. Accessed May 24, 2004.

Smeeding, Timothy A., Lee Rainwater, and Gary Burtless. 2000. *United States Poverty in a Cross-National Context*. Luxembourg Income Study Working Paper Series No. 244. www.lisproject.org/publications/liswps/244.pdf. Accessed May 24, 2004.

Smith, Alison J. 2004. *Who Cares? Fathers and the Time They Spend Looking After Children*. Department of Sociology Working Paper No. 2004-05. Oxford, UK: University of Oxford. www.nuff.ox.ac.uk/users/smith/2004-05. Accessed May 23, 2006.

Smith, Dan. 1997. *The State of War and Peace Atlas*. Brighton, UK: Myriad Editions Ltd.

Smith, Dorothy E. 1993. "The Standard North American Family: SNAF as an Ideological Code." *Journal of Family Issues* 14:50–65.

Smith, Gregory C., Susan E. Savage-Stevens, and Ellen S. Fabian. 2002. "How Caregiving Grandparents View Support Groups for Grandchildren in Their Care." *Family Relations* 51(3):274–281.

Smith, Judith, Jeanne Brooks-Gunn, and Pamela Klebanov. 1997. "Consequences of Living in Poverty for Young Children's Cognitive and Verbal Ability and Early School Achievement." In Greg J. Duncan and Jeanne Brooks-Dunn (Eds.), *Consequences of Growing Up Poor*, pp. 132–189. New York: Russell Sage Foundation.

Smith, William L. 1999. *Families and Communes: An Examination of Nontraditional Lifestyles*. Newbury Park, CA: Sage Publications.

Social Register. 2003. *Social Register*. New York: Social Register Association.

Social Security Administration. 2005. "2005 Social Security Changes." www.ssa.gov/pressoffice/factsheets/colafacts2005.htm. Accessed July 18, 2005.

———. 2002. "Historical Background and Development of Social Security." www.ssa.gov/history/briefhistory3.html. Accessed May 24, 2003.

Social Security Administration, Social Security Online, Office of Policy Data. 2004. "Social Security Programs Throughout the World: Europe, 2004." www.ssa.gov/policy/docs/progdesc/ssptw/2004–2005/europe/. Accessed March 7, 2006.

Soldo, Beth J., and Emily M. Agree. 1988. "America's Elderly." *Population Bulletin* 43(3).

Somary, Karen, and George Stricker. 1998. "Becoming a Grandparent: A Longitudinal Study of Expectations and Early Experiences as a Function of Sex and Lineage." *The Gerontologist* 38:53–61.

Sommerville, Quentin. 2005. "China Booms, So Does Divorce Rate." BBC News, International Version News.bbc.co.uk/2/hi/programmes/newsnight/4240988.stm. Accessed June 6, 2006.

Sonenstein, Freya L., Gary Gates, Stefanie R. Schmidt, and Natalya Bolshun. 2002. "Primary Child Care Arrangements of Employed Parents: Findings from the 1999 National Survey of America's Families." The Urban Institute. www.urban.org/url.cfm?ID=310487. Accessed July 27, 2003.

Sorensen, Elaine. 2003. "Child Support Gains Some Ground." The Urban Institute. www.urban.org/UploadedPDF/310860_snapshots3_no11.pdf. Accessed April 20, 2005.

South, Scott J., Katherine Trent, and Shen Yang. 2001. "Changing Partners: Toward a Macrostructural-Opportunity Theory of Marital Dissolution." *Journal of Marriage and the Family* 63:743–754.

Spaht, Katherine S. 2002. "Why Covenant Marriage May Prove Responsive to the Culture of Divorce." In Alan J. Hawkins, Lynn D. Wardle, and David O. Coolidge (Eds.), *Revitalizing the Institution of Marriage for the 21st Century: An Agenda for Strengthening Marriage*, pp. 59–67. New York: Praeger.

Spain, Daphne, and Suzanne Bianchi. 1996. *Balancing Act: Motherhood, Marriage, and Employment Among American Women*. New York: Russell Sage Foundation.

Spalter-Roth, Roberta, Heidi Hartmann, and Beverly Burr. 1994. "Income Inequality: The Failure of Unemployment Insurance to Reach Working AFDC Mothers." Paper presented at the Conference on Employment Law and Unemployment Compensation in Washington, DC, on March 20.

Spanier, Graham B., and Linda Thompson. 1987. *Parting: The Aftermath of Separation and Divorce*. Newbury Park, CA: Sage Publications.

Spicher, Cynthia Hart, and Mary A. Hudak. 1997. "Gender Role Portrayal on Saturday Morning Cartoons: An Update." Presented at the American Psychological Association in Chicago, Illinois, on August 18.

Spock, Benjamin. 2004. "Gay and Lesbian Parents." www.drspock.com/article/0,1510,4028,00.html. Accessed May 25, 2006.

Spraggins, Renee E. 2005. *We the People: Women and Men in the United States*. Technical Report No. CENSR-20. Washington, DC: U.S. Census Bureau.

St. Jean, Yanick, and Joe R. Feagin. 1998. *Double Burden: Black Women and Everyday Racism*. Armonk, NY: M. E. Sharpe.

Stacey, Judith, and Timothy J. Biblarz. 2001. "(How) Does the Sexual Orientation of Parents Matter?" *American Sociological Review* 66(2):159–183.

Stack, Peggy Fletcher. 1998. "Globally, Polygamy Is Commonplace." *Salt Lake Tribune*. polygamy.com/other-globally-polygamy-18-commonplace.htm. Accessed April 21, 2003.

Stack, Steven. 1992. "The Effect of Divorce on Suicide in Japan: A Time Series Analysis, 1950–1980." *Journal of Marriage and the Family* 54:327–334.

Stack, Steven, and J. Ross Eshleman. 1998. "Marital Status and Happiness: A 17-Nation Study." *Journal of Marriage and the Family* 60(2):527–536.

Stanton, Glenn T. 2005. "How Is Marriage Dying in Our Culture?" In *CitizenLink*, Focus on the Family. www.family.org/cforum/fosi/marriage/facts/a0028319.cfm. Accessed June 30, 2005.

Staples, Robert. 1994. *The Black Family*, 5th ed. Belmont, CA: Wadsworth.

State of Connecticut Department of Children and Families. 2003. "Useful Information: Leaving Your Child Home Alone." www.state.ct.us/def/Good_News/staying.htm. Accessed July 17, 2006.

Steinberg, Stephen. 1981. *The Ethnic Myth: Race, Ethnicity, and Class in America*. Boston: Beacon Press.

Stephens, William N. 1963. *The Family in Cross-Cultural Perspective*. New York: Holt, Rinehart, and Winston.

Sterk-Elifson, Claire. 1994. "Sexuality Among African American Women." In Alice Rossi (Ed.), *Sexuality Across the Life Course*, pp. 99–127. Chicago: University of Chicago Press.

Stern, Marilyn, and Katherine Hildebrandt Karraker. 1989. "Sex Stereotyping of Infants: A Review of Gender Labeling Studies." *Sex Roles* 20:501–522.

Sternberg, Robert J. 1986. "A Triangular Theory of Love." *Psychological Review* 93(2):119–135.

Stevens, Jacqueline. 1999. *Reproducing the State*. Princeton, NJ: Princeton University Press.

Stevenson, Howard C., Jocelyn Reed, and Preston Bodison. 1996. "Kinship Social Support and Adolescent Perceptions of Racial Socialization: Extending Self to Family." *Journal of Black Psychology* 22:498–508.

Stewart, Susan D. 2005. "How the Birth of a Child Affects Involvement with Stepchildren." *Journal of Marriage and Family* 67(2):461–473.

Stinnett, Nick, and John DeFrain. 1985. *Secrets of Strong Families*. Boston: Little, Brown and Company.

Stinnett, Nick, Linda M. Carter, and James E. Montgomery. 1972. "Older Persons' Perceptions of Their Marriages." *Journal of Marriage and the Family* 32:428–434.

Stockard, Janice E. 2002. *Marriage in Culture*. Orlando, FL: Harcourt Brace.

Stoll, Barre M., Genevieve L. Arnaut, Donald K. Fromme, and Jennifer A. Felker-Thayer. 2005. "Adolescents in

Stepfamilies: A Qualitative Analysis." *Journal of Divorce and Remarriage* 44:177–189.

Stone, Robyn, Gail L. Cafferata, and Judith Sangl. 1987. "Caregivers of the Frail Elderly: A National Profile." *The Gerontologist* 27:616–626.

Straus, Murray A. 2003. *The Primordial Violence: Corporal Punishment by Parents, Cognitive Development, and Crime*. Walnut Creek, CA: AltaMira Press.

______. 1990. "The Conflict Tactics Scales and Its Critics: An Evaluation and New Data on Validity and Reliability." In Murray A. Straus and Richard J. Gelles (Eds.), *Physical Violence in American Families: Risk Factors and Adaptations to Violence in 8,145 Families*, pp. 49–73. New Brunswick, NJ: Transaction Publishers.

———. 1979. "Measuring Intrafamily Conflict and Violence: The Conflict Tactics (CT) Scale." *Journal of Marriage and the Family* 41:75–88.

Straus, Murray A., and Denise A. Donnelly. 2001. *Beating the Devil Out of Them: Corporal Punishment in American Families and Its Effects on Children*, 2nd ed. New Brunswick, NJ: Transaction Publishers.

Straus, Murray, A., Richard J. Gelles, and Suzanne K. Steinmetz. 1980. *Behind Closed Doors: Violence in the American Family*. New York: Anchor Books.

Strazdins, Lyndall, Mark Clements, Rosemary J. Korda, Dorothy H. Broom, and Rennie M. D'Souza. 2006. "Unsociable Work? Nonstandard Work Schedules, Family Relationships, and Children's Well-being." *Journal of Marriage and Family* 68:394–410.

Stritof, Sheri, and Bob Stritof. 2006. "Covenant Marriage Statistics." marriage.about.com/cs/covenantmarriage /a/covenant_3.htm. Accessed June 6, 2006.

Strohschein, Lisa. 2005. "Parental Divorce and Child Mental Health Trajectories." *Journal of Marriage and Family* 67(5):1286–1300.

Strong, Bryan, Christine DeVault, Barbara W. Sayad, and William L. Yarber. 2002. *Human Sexuality: Diversity in Contemporary America*, 4th ed. Boston: McGraw Hill.

Strong-Jekely, Lara. 2006. Letter to the Editor. *Brain, Child*. Winter:2.

Struening, Karen. 2002. *New Family Values: Liberty, Equality, Diversity*. Lanham, MD: Rowman & Littlefield.

Strug, David L., and Susan E. Mason. 2002. "Social Service Needs of Hispanic Immigrants: An Exploratory Study of the Washington Heights Community." *Journal of Ethnic and Cultural Diversity in Social Work* 10(3):69–80.

Suarez-Al-Adam, Mariana, Marcela Raffaelli, and Ann O'Leary. 2000. "Influence of Abuse and Partner Hypermasculinity on the Sexual Behavior of Latinas." *AIDS Education and Prevention* 12:263–274.

Sudarkasa, Niara. 1999. "Interpreting the African Heritage in Afro-American Family Organization." In Stephanie Coontz, Maya Parson, and Gabrielle Raley (Eds.), *American Families: A Multicultural Reader*, pp. 59–73. New York: Routledge.

Sugarman, David B., and Gerald T. Hotaling. 1989. "Dating Violence: Prevalence, Context, and Risk Markers." In Maureen A. Pirog-Good and Jan E. Stets (Eds.), *Violence in Dating Relationships: Emerging Social Issues*, pp. 3–32. New York: Praeger.

Sullivan, Deborah A., and Rose Weitz. 1988. *Labor Pains: Modern Midwives and Home Birth*. New Haven, CT: Yale University Press.

Sullivan, Deborah A., and Ruth Beeman. 1983. "Four Years' Experience with Homebirth by Licensed Midwives in Arizona." *American Journal of Public Health* 73:641–645.

Sun, Yongmin, and Yuanzhang Li. 2002. "Child Well-Being During Parents' Marital Disruption Process: A Pooled Time-Series Analysis." *Journal of Marriage and the Family* 64:472–488.

Sundstrom, Marianne. 1996. "Determinants of the Use of Parental Benefits by Women in Sweden in the 1980s." *Scandinavian Journal of Social Welfare* 5(2):76–82.

Sussman, Marvin B. 1959. "The Isolated Nuclear Family: Fact or Fiction." *Social Problems* 6:333–340.

Sutton, P. D., and M. L. Munson. 2006. Births, Marriages, Divorces, and Deaths: Provisional Data for April 2006. National Vital Statistics Reports; vol. 55, no. 5. Hyattsville, MD: National Center for Health Statistics.

Svare, Gloria Messick, Sydney Jay, and Mary Ann Mason. 2004. "Stepparents on Stepparenting: An Exploratory Study of Stepparenting Approaches." *Journal of Divorce and Remarriage* 41:81–97.

Swanbrow, Diane. 2002. "Study Finds American Men Doing More Housework." www.umich.edu/~urecord /0102Mar25_02/16.htm. Accessed May 27, 2003.

Szasz, Margaret Connell. 1985. "Native American Children." In Joseph M. Hawes and N. Ray Hiner (Eds.), *American Childhood: A Research Guide and Historical Handbook*, pp. 311–342. Westport, CT: Greenwood Press.

Szinovacz, Maximiliane E. 2000. "Changes in Housework After Retirement: A Panel Analysis." *Journal of Marriage and the Family* 62:78–92.

———. 1998. "Grandparents Today: A Demographic Profile." *The Gerontologist* 38:37–52.

Szinovacz, Maximiliane E., and Paula Harpster. 1994. "Couples' Employment/Retirement Status and the Division of Household Tasks." *Journal of Gerontology: Social Sciences* 49(3):S125–S136.

———. 1993. "Employment Status, Gender Role Attitudes, and Marital Dependence in Later Life." *Journal of Marriage and the Family* 49:927–940.

Tafoya, Sonya M., Hans Johnson, and Laura E. Hill. 2004. *Who Chooses to Choose Two?* New York: Russell Sage Foundation and Population Reference Bureau.

Takaki, Ronald. 1989. *Strangers from a Different Shore: A History of Asian Americans*. Boston: Little, Brown and Company.

Tan, Tony Xing, and Yi Yang. 2005. "Language Development of Chinese Adoptees 18–35 Months Old." *Early Childhood Research Quarterly* 20:57–68.

Tapestry Against Polygamy. 2006. "Tapestry Concerned About HBO Disclaimer." www.polygamy.org/releases.shtml. Accessed March 7, 2006.

Tarmann, Allison. 2003. "International Adoption Rate in U.S. Doubled in the U.S." Population Reference Bureau. www.prb.org/Template.cfm?Section=PRB&template=/ContentManagement/Content. Accessed April 14, 2003.

Tatchell, Peter. 2002. "Gay Rights and Wrongs in Cuba." Gay and Lesbian Humanist. www.galha.org/glh/213/cuba.html. Accessed March 16, 2005.

Taylor, Alan M., and Mark P. Taylor. 2004. "The Purchasing Power Parity Debate." *Journal of Economic Perspectives*, 18:135–158.

Teachman, Jay D. 2002. "Childhood Living Arrangements and the Intergenerational Transmission of Divorce." *Journal of Marriage and Family* 64:717–729.

______. 2004. "The Childhood Living Arrangements of Children and the Characteristics of Their Marriages." *Journal of Family Issues* 25(1):86–111.

Teachman, Jay D., Kathleen M. Paasch, R. D. Day, and Karen P. Carver. 1997. "Poverty During Adolescence and Subsequent Educational Attainment." In Greg J. Duncan and Jeanne Brooks-Gunn (Eds.), *Consequences of Growing Up Poor*, pp. 382–418. New York: Russell Sage Foundation.

Terkel, S. 1970. *Hard Times—An Oral History of the Great Depression*. New York: Pantheon Books.

The Urban Institute. 2000. *A New Look at Homelessness*. Washington, DC: www.urban.org/url.cfm?ID=900366. Accessed June 4, 2004.

Thomas, Adam, and Isabel Sawhill. 2002. "For Richer or for Poorer: Marriage as an Antipoverty Strategy." *Journal of Policy Analysis and Management* 21:4.

Thompson, Dick. 2002. *Coordinates 2002: Charting Progress Against AIDS, Tuberculosis, and Malaria*. Geneva, Switzerland: World Health Organization.

Thompson, Linda, and Alexis J. Walker. 1989. "Gender in Families: Women and Men in Marriage, Work, and Parenthood." *Journal of Marriage and the Family* 51:845–871.

Thornton, Arland, and Linda Young-DeMarco. 2001. "Four Decades of Trends in Attitudes Toward Family Issues in the United States: The 1960s Through the 1990s." *Journal of Marriage and the Family* 63:1009–1037.

Tiefenthaler, Jill, Amy Farmer, and Amandine Sambira. 2005. "Services and Intimate Partner Violence in the United States: A County-Level Analysis." *Journal of Marriage and Family* 67(3):565–578.

Tierney, John. 2003, 28 September. "Iraqi Marriage Bedevils Americans." *The* [Portland] *Oregonian*, p. A2.

Tinker, Bonnie. 2004, 4 March. "A Day of Courage, Newlyweds, and Love." *The* [Portland] *Oregonian*, p. D9.

Tjaden, Patricia, and Nancy Thoennes. 2000. *Extent, Nature, and Consequences of Intimate Partner Violence: Research Report*. Washington, DC: U.S. Department of Justice, National Institute of Justice. www.ncjrs.gov/pdffiles1/nij/181867.pdf. Accessed: December 14, 2005.

Tohidi, Nayereh. 1993. "Iranian Women and Gender Relation in Los Angeles." In Ron Kelley, Jonathan Friedlander, and Anita Colby (Eds.), *Irangeles: Iranians in Los Angeles*, pp. 175–217. Berkeley: University of California Press.

Tolman, Richard M., Sandra K. Danziger, and Daniel Rosen. 2002. "Domestic Violence and Economic Well-Being of Current and Former Welfare Recipients." Joint Center for Poverty Research Working Paper 304. www.jcpr.org/wpfiles/tolman_danziger_rosen_SRI2001.pdf?CFID=1956522&CFTOKEN=81196971. Accessed July 24, 2006.

Tonnies, Ferdinand. 1963. *Community and Society*. New York: Harper and Row.

Trattner, Walter I. 1999. *From Poor Law to Welfare State: A History of Social Welfare in America*, 6th ed. New York: Free Press.

Trent, Katherine, and Scott J. South. 1989. "Structural Determinants of the Divorce Rate: A Cross-Societal Analysis." *Journal of Marriage and the Family* 51:391–404.

Tsuya, Noriko O., and Karen Oppenheim Mason. 1995. "Changing Gender Roles and Below Replacement Fertility in Japan." In Karen O. Mason and An-M. Jensen (Eds.), *Gender and Family Change in Industrialized Countries*, pp. 139–167. Oxford, England: Clarendon Press.

Turetsky, Vicki. 2005. "The Child Support Program: An Investment that Works." Washington, DC: Center for Law and Social Policy.

Turner, Margery A., Michael Fix, and Raymond J. Struyk. 1991. *Opportunities Denied, Opportunities Diminished: Racial Discrimination in Hiring*. Washington, DC: The Urban Institute Press.

U.S. Agency for International Development (USAID). 1999. *Overview of USAID Population Assistance, FY 1998*. Arlington, VA: Family Planning Logistics Management for USAID.

U.S. Census Bureau. 2006a. *Statistical Abstract of the United States*, 125th ed. Washington, DC: Government Printing Office.

______. 2006b. "The 2006 Statistical Abstract: Vital Statistics: Life Expectancy." In *Table 96, Expectation of Life at Birth, 1970 to 2003 and Projections, 2005 and 2010*.

______. 2006c. "The 2006 Statistical Abstract: Vital Statistics: Life Expectancy." In *Table 98, Expectation of Life and Expected Deaths by Race, Sex, and Age: 2002*.

______. 2006d. "America's Families and Living Arrangements: 2005." www.census.gov/population/www/socdemo/hh-fam/cps2005.html. Accessed June 28, 2006.

______. 2006e. "America's Families and Living Arrangements: 2005, Table A1." www.census.gov/population/www/socdemo/hh-fam/cps2005.html. Accessed June 6, 2006.

______. 2006f. "The Asian Alone Population in the United States: March 2004 (PPL-184) Tables 6, 7, 15." www.census.gov/population/www/socdemo/race/ppl-184.html. Accessed June 28, 2006.

______. 2006g. "The Black Population in the United States: March 2004 (PPL-186) Tables 6, 7, 15, 20." www.census.gov/population/www/socdemo/race/ppl-186.html. Accessed June 28, 2006.

______. 2005a. "America's Families and Living Arrangements: 2004, Table C-3." www.census.gov/population/www/socdemo/hh-fam/cps2004.html. Accessed July 16, 2006.

______. 2005b. "Child Custody Statistics 2004." In *America's Families and Living Arrangements 2004, Current Population Survey, Table FG-6*. www.gocrc.com/research/custody-stats.html. Accessed June 6, 2006.

______. 2005c. "Median Income for 4-Person Families, by State." www.census.gov/hhes/income/4person.html. Accessed October 25, 2005.

———. 2003. "Table 2: Marital Status of the Population 55 Years and Over by Age and Sex: March 2002." *Current Population Survey*. Special Populations Branch, Population Division. www.census.gov/population/socdemo/age/ppl-167/tab02.xls. Accessed July 8, 2005.

———. 2000. "Projections of the Total Resident Population by 5 Year Age Groups, Race, and Hispanic Origin with Special Age Categories: Middle Series, 1999 to 2000." Population Projections Program, Population Division. www.census.gov/population/projections/nation/summary/np-t4-a.pdf. Accessed July 8, 2005.

U.S. Census Bureau Public Information Office. 2003. "Facts for Features: Asian Pacific American Heritage Month: May 2003." www.census.gov/Press-Release/www/2003/cb03-ff05.html. Accessed January 9, 2004.

U.S. Committee for Refugees. 2002. "Worldwide Refugee Information: China's One-Child Policy." www.refugees.org/world/articles/women_rr99_8.htm. Accessed June 11, 2003.

U.S. Department of Agriculture. 2006a. "Food Security in the United States: Conditions and Trends." Online: www.ers.usda.gov/briefing/foodsecurity/trends/htm.

———. 2006b. "Official USDA Food Plans: Costs of Food at Home at Four Levels, U.S. Average, May, 2006." www.cnpp.usda.gov. Accessed June 23, 2006.

U.S. Department of Health and Human Services. 2006. Number of Adult Recipients: Total CY 2005. www.acf.hhs.gov/programs/ofa/caseload/2005/adult05ssp.htm

U.S. Department of Health and Human Services, Administration for Children and Families. 2006. "Children Home Alone and Babysitter Age Guidelines" www.nccic.org/poptopics/homealone.html. Accessed July 17, 2006.

———. 2005. "Welfare Rolls Continue to Fall." www.acf.hhs.gov/news/press/2005/TANFdeclineJune04.htm. Accessed December 14, 2005.

U.S. Department of Health and Human Services, Administration on Aging. 2001. "Grandparents Raising Grandchildren." www.aoa.gov/prof/notes/Docs/Grandparents_Raising_Grandchildren.pdf. Accessed May 4, 2004.

U.S. Department of Health and Human Services, Office of Child Support Enforcement. 2004. "Child Support Enforcement FY 2003 Preliminary Data Report, Table 6." www.acf.dhhs.gov/programs/cse/pubs/2004/reports/preliminary_data/table_6.html. Accessed April 20, 2005.

U.S. Department of Health and Human Service. 2006b. "Child Maltreatment 2004." www.acf.dhhs.gov/programs/cb/pubs/cm04. Accessed December 4, 2006.

______. 2006a. "TANF: Total Number of Families (Fiscal Year 2005)." www.acf.hhs.gov/programs/ofa/caseload/2005/family05tanf.htm. Accessed April 4, 2006.

U.S. Department of Justice, Bureau of Justice Statistics. 2006. Sourcebook of Criminal Justice Statistics Online. www.albany.edu/sourcebook/pdf/t3332004.pdf. Accessed November 10, 2006.

U.S. Department of Labor, Bureau of Labor Statistics. 2006a. "Women in the Labor Force: A Databook." www.bls.gov/cps/wlf-databook-2006.pdf. Accessed November 28, 2006.

———. 2006b. "Charting the U.S. Labor Market in 2005." www.bls.gov/cps/labor2005/chartbook.pdf. Accessed November 28, 2006.

———. 2006c. "Labor Force Statistics from the Current Population Survey." www.bls.gov/cps/. Accessed November, 29, 2006.

______. 2006d. "May 2005 National Occupational Employment and Wage Estimates." www.bls.gov/oes/current/oes_nat.htm. Accessed June 23, 2006.

______. 2006e. "Employment Situation Summary." www.bls.gov/news.release/empsit.nr0.htm. Accessed May 5, 2006.

______. 2006f. "Median Weekly Earnings of Full-Time Wage and Salary Workers by Selected Characteristics, Table 37." www.bls.gov/cps/cpsaat37.pdf. Accessed June 23, 2006.

———. 2006g. "Minimum Wage Laws in the States - April 3, 2006." www.dol.gov/esa/minwage/america.htm. Accessed August 17, 2006.

———. 2005. "American Time Use Survey Summary." www.bls.gov/news.release/atus.nr0.htm. Accessed May 25, 2006.

U.S. Department of State. 2006a. "2006 Poverty Guidelines." Online: http://travel.state.gov/visa/immigrants/info/info_1327.html. Accessed November, 28, 2006.

———. 2006b. "Immigrant Visas Issued to Orphans Coming to the U.S." Travel.state.gov/family/adoption /stats/stats_451.html. Accessed July 13, 2006.

———. 2006c. "Trafficking in Persons Report." Bureau of Public Affairs. www.state.gov/g/tip/rls/tiprpt/2006 /65983.htm. Accessed October 12, 2006.

Uhlenberg, Peter, and James B. Kirby. 1998. "Grandparenthood Over Time: Historical and Demographic Trends." In Maximiliane E. Szinovacz (Ed.), *Handbook on Grandparenthood*, pp. 23–39. Westport, CT: Greenwood.

Umana-Taylor, Adriana J., Ruchi Bhanot, and Nana Shin. 2006. "Ethnic Identity Socialization Among Adolescence: The Critical Role of Families." *Journal of Family Issues* 27:390–414.

Umberson, Debra. 2006. "Parents, Adult Children, and Immortality." *Contexts* 5:48–53.

Umberson, Debra, and Kristi Williams. 1999. "Family Status and Mental Health." In Carol S. Aneshensel and Jo C. Phelan (Eds.), *Handbook of the Sociology of Mental Health*, pp. 225–253. New York: Kluwer Academic/ Plenum.

Umberson, Debra, and Walter Gove. 1989. "Parenthood and Psychological Well-Being: Theory, Measurement, and Stage in the Family Life Course." *Journal of Family Issues* 10:440–462.

Umberson, Debra, Camille B. Wortman, and Ronald C. Kessler. 1992. "Widowhood and Depression: Explaining Long-Term Gender Differences in Vulnerability." *Journal of Health and Social Behavior* 33:10–24.

UNAIDS. 2006a. "2006 Report on the Global AIDS Epidemic." www.unaids.org/en/HIV_data /2006GlobalReport/default.asp. Accessed November 22, 2006.

———. 2006b. Report on the Global AIDS Epidemic. Online: www.unaids.org/en/HIV_data/2006GlobalReport /default.asp. Accessed December 8, 2006.

UNICEF Innocenti Research Centre. 2000. *A League Table of Child Poverty in Rich Nations Innocenti Report Card No. 1*. www.unicef-icdc.org/cgi-bin/unicef/main .sql?menu=/publications/menu.html&testo=download_ insert.sql?ProductID=226. Accessed December 5, 2005.

United Auto Workers. 2004. "The Union Advantage—for Workers and Their Families." In *Research Bulletin*. www.uaw.org/resrch/rbart.cfm?rbid=11. Accessed May 27, 2006.

United National Development Programme. 2006. *Human Development Report*. New York: United Nations.

United Nations Children's Fund. 2006. "The State of The Worlds Children: 2007." www.unicef.org/sowc07/report /full_report.php. Accessed February 15, 2007..

United Nations Children's Fund. 2003. "The State of the World's Children 2004: Girls, Education, and Development." www.unicef.org/sowc04/files /SOWC_O4_eng.pdf. Accessed November 10, 2005.

United Nations Development Programme. 1995. *Human Development Report*. New York: Oxford University Press.

United Nations General Assembly Special Session on AIDS. 2001. www.unaids.org/UNGASS/index.html. Accessed May 13, 2003.

United Nations Population Fund. 1999. "UNFPA Executive Director Dr. Nafis Sadik to Address Global Videoconference, Calls for 'Zero Tolerance of Violence Against Women'." www.unfpa.org/news/pressroom /1999/iwd99rel.htm. Accessed March 23, 2003.

United Nations Statistics Division. 2005. "Table 5c—Maternity Leave Benefits." In *Statistics and Indicators on Women and Men*. unstats.un.org/unsd/demographic /products/indwm/ww2005/tab5c.htm. Accessed January 14, 2006.

———. 2000. *The World's Women 2000: Trends and Statistics*. unstats.un.org/unsd/demographic/products/indwm /wwpub2000overview.htm. Accessed June 14, 2004.

United Nations, Department of Economic and Social Affairs, Population Division. 2005. "World Population Prospects: The 2004 Revision." www.un.org/esa /population/publications. Accessed December 14, 2005.

United States Agency for International Development. 1999. "Agency Performance Report." dec.usaid.gov/partners /1999_apr/pdf_docs/05phn_99apr.pdf. Accessed July 8, 2005.

University of Michigan News Service. 2002. "People Who Give, Live Longer: U-M Study Shows." www.umich.edu /4.7Enewsinfor/Release2002/Nov02/r11112026.html. Accessed May 4, 2004.

———. 2001. "Widowhood: Research Dispels Some Common Myths." www.umich.edu~newsinfo /Release/2001/Mar01/ro32701a.html. Accessed March 2, 2003.

Uttal, Lynet. 1999. "Using Kin for Child Care: Embedment in the Socioeconomic Networks of Extended Families." *Journal of Marriage and the Family* 61:845–857.

van Dulmen, Manfred H. M. 2003. "The Development of Intimate Relationships in the Netherlands." In Raeann R. Hamon and Bron B. Ingoldsby (Eds.), *Mate Selection Across Cultures*, pp. 191–206. Thousand Oaks, CA: Sage Publications.

Vance-Granville Community College. 2003. "HUM 122." oit.vgcc.edu/hum122/TOC2.htm. Accessed August 23, 2003.

Vandell, Deborah L., and Janaki Ramanan. 1992. "Effects of Early and Recent Maternal Employment on Children from Low-Income Families." *Child Development* 63:938–949.

Vandivere, Sharon, Kathryn Tout, Jeffrey Capizzano, and Martha Zaslow. 2003. "Left Unsupervised: A Look at the Most Vulnerable Children." *Research Brief*. Washington, DC: Child Trends. 12.109.133.224/ Files/UnsupervisedRB.pdf. Accessed July 27, 2003.

VanLaningham, J., David R. Johnson, and P. Amato. 2001. "Marital Happiness, Marital Duration, and the U-

Shaped Curve: Evidence from a Five-Wave Panel Study." *Social Forces* 78:1313–1341.

Vaupel, James W., and Bernard, Jeune. 1995. "The Emergence and Proliferation of Centenarians." In Bernard Jeune and James Vaupel (Eds.), *Exceptional Longevity: From Prehistory to the Present*, vol. 2, pp. 109–116. Odense, Denmark: Odense University Press.

Vedantam, S. 2006. "Male Scientist Writes Off Life as Female Scientist." Washingtonpost.com. www.washingtonpost.com. July 13. Accessed November 21, 2006.

Vernellia, Randal R. 2006. *Dying While Black*. Seven Principles Press. sevenprinciplespress.com/about.htm. Accessed November 24, 2006.

Veroff, Joseph, Elizabeth Douvan, and Richard A. Kulka. 1981. *The Inner American*. New York: Basic Books.

Vinokur, Amiram D., Richard H. Price, and Robert D. Caplan. 1996. "Hard Times and Hurtful Partners: How Financial Strain Affects Depression and Relationship Satisfaction of Unemployed Persons and Their Spouses." *Journal of Personality and Social Psychology* 71:166–179.

Viramontez Anguiano, Ruben P., C. Johnson, and T. E. Davis III. 2004. "The Education of Rural Latino Children: Rural Latino Families and Schools in Eastern North Carolina." *Journal of Early Education and Family Review* 11:33–48.

Visher, Emily B., and John S. Visher. 1979. *Stepfamilies: A Guide to Working with Stepparents and Stepchildren*. New York: Brunner/Mazel.

Vlosky, Denise Ashbaugh, and Pamela A. Monroe. 2002. "The Effective Dates of No-Fault Divorce Laws in the 50 States." *Family Relations* 51:317–324.

Voydanoff, Patricia. 2004. "Community as a Context for the Work-Family Interface." *Organizational Management Journal* 1(1):49–54.

Waite, Linda J., and Kara Joyner. 2001. "Emotional and Physical Satisfaction with Sex in Married, Cohabiting, and Dating Sexual Unions." In E. Laumann and R. Michael (Eds.), *Sex, Love, and Health in America*, pp. 239–269. Chicago: University of Chicago Press.

Waite, Linda J., and Lee A. Lillard. 1991. "Children and Marital Disruption." *American Journal of Sociology* 96:930–953.

Waite, Linda J., and Maggie Gallagher. 2000. *The Case for Marriage: Why Married People Are Happier, Healthier, and Better Off Financially*. New York: Doubleday.

Waite, Linda J., and Yun-Suk Lee. 2005. "Husbands' and Wives' Time Spent on Housework: A Comparison of Measures." *Journal of Marriage and Family* 67(May):328–336.

Walker, Alexis J., Margaret Manoogian-O'Dell, Lori A. McGraw, and Diana L. G. White. 2001. *Families in Later Life: Connections and Transitions*. Thousand Oaks, CA: Pine Forge Press.

Walker, Kathryn E. 1970. "Time Spent by Husbands in Household Work." *Family Economics Review* 4:8–11.

Wall, Helena M. 1990. *Fierce Communion: Family and Community in Early America*. Cambridge, MA: Harvard University Press.

Waller, Willard. 1937. "The Rating and Dating Complex." *American Sociological Review* 2:727–734.

Wallerstein, Immanuel. 1974. *The Modern World System: Capitalist Agriculture and the Origin of the European World Economy in the Sixteenth Century*. New York: Academic Press.

______. 1980. *The Modern World System II: Mercantilism and the Consolidation of the European World-Economy, 1600–1750*. New York: Academic Press.

Wallerstein, Judith S., and Sandra Blakeslee. 1989. *Second Chances: Men, Women and Children a Decade After Divorce*. New York: Ticknor & Fields.

———. 1995. *The Good Marriage: How and Why Love Lasts*. Boston: Houghton Mifflin.

Wallerstein, Judith S., Julia M. Lewis, and Sandra Blakeslee. 2000. *The Unexpected Legacy of Divorce. A 25-Year Landmark Study*. New York: Hyperion.

Wallis, Claudia. 2003. "The Thing About Thongs." *Time*, 6 October, p. 94.

Walsh, Froma. 1998. *Strengthening Family Resilience*. New York: Guilford.

______. 2002. "A Family Resilience Framework: Innovative Practice Applications." *Family Relations* 51:130–137.

Walzer, Susan. 1998. *Thinking About the Baby: Gender and Transitions into Parenthood*. Philadelphia: Temple University Press.

Wardle, Lynn D. 1997. "The Potential Impact of Homosexual Parenting on Children." University of Illinois Law Review 1997:833–919.

Ware, Helen. 1979. "Polygyny: Women's Views in a Transitional Society, Nigeria 1975." *Journal of Marriage and the Family* 41:185–195.

Warner, Judith. 2005. *Perfect Madness: Motherhood in the Age of Anxiety*. New York: Penguin Group USA.

Warner, Rebecca L. 1986. "Alternative Strategies for Measuring Household Division of Labor: A Comparison." *Journal of Family Issues* 7:179–195.

Watkins, Tom H. 1993. *The Great Depression: America in the 1930s*. New York: Little, Brown and Company.

Wauterickx, Naomi, Anneleen Gouwy, and Piet Bracke. 2006. "Parental Divorce and Depression Long-Term Effects on Adult Children." *Journal of Divorce and Remarriage* 45:43–68.

Weatherford, D. 1986. *Foreign and Female: Immigrant Women in America, 1840–1930*. New York: Schocken Books.

Weber, Max. 1925. *The Theory of Social and Economic Organization*. New York: Free Press.

Weigel, Daniel J., Kymberley K. Bennett, and Deborah Ballard-Reisch. 2006. "Roles and Influence in Marriage: Both Spouses' Perceptions Contribute to Marital Commitment." *Family and Consumer Sciences Research Journal* 35:74–92.

Weinger, Susan. 1998. "Poor Children "Know Their Place": Perceptions of Poverty, Class, and Public Messages." *Journal of Sociology and Social Welfare* 25:100–118.

Weinick, Robin M., Margaret E. Weigers, and Joel W. Cohen. 1998. "Children's Health Insurance, Access to Care, and Health Status: New Findings." *Health Affairs* 17:127–136.

Weinstock, Hillard, Stuart Berman, and Willard Cates, Jr. 2004. "Sexually Transmitted Diseases Among American Youth: Incidence and Prevalence Estimates, 2000." *Perspectives on Sexual and Reproductive Health* 36(1):6–10.

Weiss, R. 2002, 13 November. *The* [Portland] *Oregonian*, pp. A10.

Weitz, Rose. 2001. *The Sociology of Health, Illness, and Health Care: A Critical Approach*, 2nd ed. Belmont, CA: Wadsworth Publishing Co.

Welch, Charles E., and Paul C. Glick. 1981. "The Incidence of Polygamy in Contemporary Africa: A Research Note." *Journal of Marriage and the Family* 191–193.

Wellhousen, Karyn, and Zenong Yin. 1997. "Peter Pan Isn't a Girls' Part: An Investigation of Gender Bias in a Kindergarten Classroom." *Women and Language* 20:35–40.

Wells, Robert V. 1982. *Revolutions in Americans' Lives: A Demographic Perspective on the History of Americans, Their Families, and Their Society*. Westport, CT: Greenwood Press.

Welter, Barbara. 1966. "The Cult of True Womanhood: 1820–1860." *American Quarterly* Summer:151–174.

______. 1977. *Dimity Convictions: The American Woman in the Nineteenth Century*. Athens, OH: Ohio University Press.

______. 2002. *Women's Rights in the United States, 1619–1995*. Melbourne, FL: Krieger Publishing Company.

Wenger, J. 2003. *Share of Workers in "Nonstandard" Jobs Declines*. Washington, DC: Economic Policy Institute.

Werner, Emmy E. 1994. "Overcoming the Odds." *Developmental and Behavioral Pediatrics* 15:131–136.

______. 1995. "Resilience in Development." *American Psychological Society* 4:81–85.

Werner, Emmy E., and Ruth S. Smith. 1992. *Overcoming the Odds*. Ithaca, NY: Cornell University Press.

———. 1989. *Vulnerable but Invincible: A Longitudinal Study of Resilient Children and Youth*. New York: Adams, Bannister, Cox.

West, Candace, and Don H. Zimmerman. 1987. "Doing Gender." *Gender and Society* 1:125–151.

West, Carolyn M., Ed. 2003. *Violence in the Lives of Black Women: Battered, Black, and Blue*. New York: Haworth Press.

Westley, Sidney B. 2002. *Assessing Women's Well-Being in Asia*. Asia-Pacific Population and Policy No. 61. Honolulu, HI: East-West Center, Population and Health Studies.

Westman, Jack C. 1998. "Grandparenthood." In *Parenthood in America*. Proceedings of the Parenthood in America Conference held in Madison, Wisconsin, April 19–21. parenthood.library.wisc.edu/Westman/Westman-grandparenthood.html. Accessed May 4, 2004.

Weston, Kath. 1991. *Families We Choose: Lesbians, Gays, Kinship*. New York: Columbia University Press.

______. 1997. *Families We Choose: Lesbians, Gays, Kinship*, 2nd ed. New York: Columbia University Press.

Wharton, Amy. 2005. *The Sociology of Gender: An Introduction to Theory and Research*. Malden, MA: Blackwell Publishers.

Whitbeck, Les B., Barbara A. McMorris, Dan R. Hoyt, Jerry D. Stubben, and Teresa LaFramboise. 2002. "Perceived Discrimination, Traditional Practices, and Depressive Symptoms Among American Indians in the Upper Midwest." *Journal of Health and Social Behavior* 43:400–418.

White House. 2004. "President Calls for Constitutional Amendment Protecting Marriage." www.whitehouse.gov/news/releases/2004/02/20040224-2.html. Accessed October 7, 2005.

White, James M., and David M. Klein. 2002. *Family Theories*, 2nd ed. Thousand Oaks, CA: Sage.

White, Lynn, and Bruce Keith. 1990. "The Effect of Shift Work on the Quality and Stability of Marital Relations." *Journal of Marriage and the Family* 52:453–462.

White, Lynn, and Joan G. Gilbreth. 2001. "When Children Have Two Fathers: Effects of Relationships with Stepfathers and Noncustodial Fathers on Adolescent Outcomes." *Journal of Marriage and the Family* 63:155–167.

______. 2000. "Economic Circumstances and Family Outcomes: A Review of the 1990s." *Journal of Marriage and Family* 62:1035–1051.

———. 1997 "Strong Support but Uneasy Relationships: Coresidence and Adult Children's Relationships with Their Parents." *Journal of Marriage and the Family* 59:62–76.

Whitehead, Barbara Dafoe. 2004. "Testimony Before the Committee on Health, Education, Labor and Pensions Subcommittee on Children and Families." U.S. Senate. Piscataway, NJ: The National Marriage Project.

Whitehead, Barbara Dafoe, and David Popenoe. 2005. "Marriage and Family: What Does the Scandinavian Experience Tell Us?" In *The State of Our Unions: The Social Health of Marriage in America 2005*. marriage.rutgers.edu/Publications/Print/PrintSOOU2005.htm. Accessed August 9, 2005.

______. 2004. *The Marriage Kind: Which Men Marry and Why*. Piscataway, NJ: The National Marriage Project.

———. 2003a. Sidebar: "Did a Family Turnaround Begin in the 1990s?" Piscataway, NJ: The National Marriage

Project. Rutgers University. www.marriage.rutgers.edu /publications/print/familyturnaorund2003.htm. Accessed November 20 2006.

———. 2003b. *The State of Our Unions: The Social Health of Marriage in America*. Piscataway, NJ: National Marriage Project. marriage.rutgers.edu/Publications/SOOU/ TEXTSOOU2003.htm. Accessed July 8, 2005.

______. 2002. "Why Men Won't Commit." In *The State of Our Unions: The Social Health of Marriage in America*. Piscataway, NJ: The National Marriage Project.

———. 1999. *Why Wed?: Young Adults Talk About Sex, Love, and First Unions*. New Brunswick, NJ: The National Marriage Project.

Wikipedia.org. "Societal Attitudes Towards Homosexuality." En.wikipedia.org/wiki/Societal _attitudes_towards _homosexuality. Accessed June 22, 2006.

Wilder-Taylor, Stefanie. 2006. *Sippy Cups Are Not for Chardonnay: And Other Things I Had to Learn As a New Mom*. New York: Simon Spotlight Entertainment.

Wilkie, Jane R., Myra M. Ferree, and Kathryn S. Ratcliff. 1998. "Gender and Fairness: Marital Satisfaction in Two-Earner Families." *Journal of Marriage and the Family* 60:577–594.

Wilkinson, Doris Y. 1997. "American Families of African Descent." In Mary Kay DeGenova (Ed.), *Families in Cultural Context: Strength and Challenges in Diversity*, Ch. 3. Mountain View, CA: Mayfield Publishing Company.

Wilkinson, Emma. 2002. "Birth Weight and Social Class Linked to Educational Achievement." In *Press Release for Birth Weight, Childhood Socioeconomic Environment, and Cognitive Development in the 1958 British Birth Cohort Study*, vol. 325, pp. 305–308. www.eurekalert.org/ pub_releases/2002-08/bmj-bwa080702.php. Accessed August 28, 2003.

Willetts, Marion C. 2006. "Union Quality Comparisons Between Long-Term Heterosexual Cohabitation and Legal Marriage." *Journal of Family Issues* 27:110–127.

Williams, Kristi. 2003. "Has the Future of Marriage Arrived? A Contemporary Examination of Gender, Marriage, and Psychological Well-Being." *Journal of Health and Social Behavior* 44(4):470–487.

Williams, Lindy, and Teresa Sobieszczyk. 1997. "Attitudes Surrounding the Continuation of Female Circumcision in the Sudan: Passing the Tradition to the Next Generation." *Journal of Marriage and the Family* 59:966–981.

Williams, Norma. 1990. *The Mexican American Family: Tradition and Change*. Dix Hills, NY: General Hall.

Willie, Charles Vert. 1983. *Race, Ethnicity, and Socioeconomic Status: A Theoretical Analysis of Their Interrelationship*. Lanham, MD: Rowman and Littlefield.

Willie, Charles Vert, and Richard J. Reddick. 2003. *A New Look at Black Families*. Lanham, MD: AltaMira Press.

Willis, Brian M., and Barry S. Levy. 2002. "Child Prostitution: Global Health Burden, Research Needs, and Interventions." *Lancet* 359:1417–1422.

Willson, Andrea E., Kim Shuey, and Glen E. Elder. 2003. "Ambivalence in the Relationship of Adult Children to Aging Parents and In-Laws." *Journal of Marriage and Family* 18:1055–1072.

Wilmoth, Janet, and Gregor Koso. 2002. "Does Marital History Matter? Marital Status and Wealth Outcomes Among Preretirement Adults." *Journal of Marriage and the Family* 64:254–268.

Wilson, Stephan M., Lucy W. Ngige, and Linda J. Trollinger. 2003. "Connecting Generations: Kamba and Maasai Paths to Marriage in Kenya." In Raeann R. Hamon and Bron B. Ingoldsby (Eds.), *Male Selection Across Cultures*, pp. 95–118. Thousand Oaks, CA: Sage Publications.

Wilson, William J. 1996. *When Work Disappears: The World of the New Urban Poor*. New York: Alfred A. Knopf.

———. 1987. *The Truly Disadvantaged: The Inner City, the Underclass, and Public Policy*. Chicago: University of Chicago Press.

Wisensale, Steven K. 2001. *Family Leave Policy: The Political Economy of Work and Family in America*. New York: M. E. Sharpe.

Wolf, Patricia A., and Emily Mast. 1987. "Counseling Issues in Adoption by Stepparents." *Social Work* 32:69–74.

Wolfe, Alan. 1998. *One Nation, After All*. New York: Penguin.

Wolfe, Leslie R. 1994. "Girl Stabs Boy at School": Girls and the Cycle of Violence. *Women's Health Issues* 4(2):109–116.

Wolff, Jennifer L. and Judith D. Kasper. 2006. "Caregivers of Frail Elders: Updating a National Profile." *The Gerontologist* 46:344–356.

Wolfinger, Nicholas H. 2000. "Beyond the Intergenerational Transmission of Divorce: Do People Replicate the Pattern of Marital Instability They Grew Up With?" *Journal of Family Issues* 21:1061–1086.

Wolfinger, Nicholas H. 2006. "Does the Rebound Effect Exist? Time to Remarriage and Subsequent Union Stability." *Journal of Divorce and Remarriage* 46:9–20.

Wolin, Steven, and Sybil Wolin. 1993. *The Resilient Self*. New York: Villiard Books.

Wood, Julia. 1994. *Gendered Lives: Communication, Gender, and Culture*. Belmont, CA: Wadsworth.

World Values Survey. 1994. *World Values Survey, 1990–1993*. Ann Arbor, MI: Inter-University Consortium for Political and Social Research.

Wright, Carroll. 1889. *A Report on Marriage and Divorce in the United States 1867–1886*. Washington, DC: U.S. Bureau of Labor.

Wysong, Earl. 2003. *The New Class Society: Goodbye American Dream?* 2nd ed. Lanham, MD: Rowman and Littlefield Publishers.

Xu, Xiaohe, Clark D. Hudspeth, and John P. Bartkowski. 2006. "The Role of Cohabitation in Remarriage." *Journal of Marriage and Family* 68(2):261–274.

Yanowitz, Karen L. and Kevin J. Weathers. 2004. "Do Boys and Girls Act Differently in the Classroom? A Content Analysis of Student Characters in Educational Psychology Textbooks." *Sex Roles: A Journal of Research,* 51: 101–107.

Yeung, Wei-jun Jean, John F. Sandberg, Pamela E. Davis-Kean, and Sandra L. Hofferth. 2001. "Children's Time with Fathers in Intact Families." *Journal of Marriage and Family* 63(1):136–154.

Yeung, Wei-jun Jean, Miriam R. Linver, and Jeanne Brooks-Gunn. 2002. "How Money Matters for Young Children's Development: Parental Investment and Family Processes." *Child Development* 73:1861–1879.

Yinger, John. 1995. *Closed Doors, Opportunities Lost: The Continuing Costs of Housing Discrimination.* New York: Russell Sage Foundation.

Yorburg, Betty. 2002. *Family Realities: A Global View.* Upper Saddle River, NJ: Pearson Education.

Yount, Kathryn M. 2005. "Resources, Family Organization, and Domestic Violence Against Married Women in Minya, Egypt." *Journal of Marriage and Family* 67(3):579–596.

———. 2002. "Like Mother, Like Daughter? Female Genital Cutting in Minia, Egypt." *Journal of Health and Social Behavior* 43(September):336–358.

Zelizer, Vivian A. 1985. *Pricing the Priceless Child: The Changing Social Values of Children.* New York: Basic Books.

Zhang, Zhenmei, and Mark D. Hayward. 2001. "Childlessness and the Psychological Well-Being of Older Persons." *Journal of Gerontology: Social Sciences* 56B:S311–S320.

Zhou, Min, and Carl L. Bankston III. 1998. *Growing Up American: How Vietnamese Children Adapt to Life in the United States.* New York: Russell Sage Foundation.

Zill, Nicholas, Donna R. Morrison, and Mary J. Cioro. 1993. "Long-Term Effects of Parental Divorce on Parent-Child Relationships, Adjustment, and Achievement in Young Adulthood." *Journal of Family Psychology* 7:91–103.

Zimmerman, Shirley L. 2001. *Family Policy: Constructed Solutions to Family Problems.* Thousand Oaks, CA: Sage.

Zink, Jesse. 2002. "China's One Child Policy." axe.acadiau.ca /~043638z/one-child/. Accessed June 11, 2003.

Name Index

Subject Index

Credits

1: Yuan Lui; 2: © Kevin Dodge/CORBIS All Rights Reserved; 7L: © Royalty-Free/Corbis; 7R: © Michael Keller/CORBIS All Rights Reserved; 9: Courtesy of Karen Seccombe; 19: © Bill Aron/PhotoEdit; 25: © Shepard Sherbell/CORBIS SABA; 30: Reproduced with the permission of Her Majesty the Queen in Right of Canada 2007; 31: REUTERS/Edward Parsons/UNHCR/Landov; 36: Michael Newman/PhotoEdit; 44: © PCL/Alamy; 48: © SALT LAKE TRIBUNE/CORBIS SYGMA; 51: Getty Images, Inc.; 56: © Picture Contact/Alamy; 63: © Henrik Trygg/CORBIS All Rights Reserved; 66: North Wind Picture Archives; 76: Smithsonian American Art Museum, Washington, DC/Art Resource, NY; 77: "The Peale Family Group," by Charles Willson Peale, oil on canvas, 56–1/2 x 89–1/2 inches, ca. 1770–1773, 1808, neg. #34501, acc. #1867.298. Collection of The New-York Historical Society; 81: © Bettmann/CORBIS All Rights Reserved; 84: © CORBIS All Rights Reserved; 91: © H. Armstrong Roberts/CORBIS All Rights Reserved; 86: Courtesy of Brown Brothers; 96: Andy Sacks/Stone/Getty Images; 103L: Courtesy of Ben Barres; 103R: Courtesy of Timothy Archibald; 105L: Getty Images, Inc.; 105R: Getty Images, Inc. - Blend Images; 107: © Jeff Greenberg/PhotoEdit; 112: © Ulrike Kotermann/CORBIS All Rights Reserved; 120: © David Vintiner/zefa/Corbis; 126: © Louise Gubb/CORBIS SABA; 130: © Michael Brennan/CORBIS All Rights Reserved; 135T: © Lynne Fernandes/The Image Works; 135B: © Michael Newman/PhotoEdit; 139: Getty Images, Inc.; 142: © Bob Daemmrich/PhotoEdit; 161: © Alison Wright/CORBIS All Rights Reserved; 168: Getty Images, Inc.; 173: © Erik Freeland/CORBIS SABA; 176: Getty Images, Inc.; 182: Getty Images, Inc.; 191: Getty Images, Inc.; 197: Getty - National Geographic Society; 200: © Steve Pope/zefa/Corbis; 204: © Jutta Klee/CORBIS All Rights Reserved; 207: AFP/Getty Images; 211: © Bettmann/CORBIS All Rights Reserved; 220: © Bill Aron/PhotoEdit; 222: Reprinted with permission of the New York State Dept. of Health; 233: © Bob Daemmrich/CORBIS All Rights Reserved; 240: © Royalty-Free/Corbis; 246: © Annie Griffiths Belth/CORBIS All Rights Reserved; 247: © Dinodia Images/Alamy; 252: © REBECCA COOK/Reuters/Corbis; 257: © Michael Newman/PhotoEdit; 263: © Bob Daemmrich/PhotoEdit; 270: © Rune Hellestand/CORBIS All Rights Reserved; 275: Courtesy of Karen Seccombe; 282: © Serge Krouglikoff/zefa/Corbis; 289: © Dan Habib/The Concord Monitor/CORBIS All Rights Reserved; 291: Yuan Lui; 296T: © Owen Franken/CORBIS All Rights Reserved; 296B: Sally and Richard Greenhill/Alamy; 306: © Creasource/CORBIS All Rights Reserved; 311: © Alison Wright/CORBIS All Rights Reserved; 313: © Ariel Skelley/CORBIS All Rights Reserved; 320T: © Kate Mitchell/zefa/Corbis; 320B: © Mark Seelen/zefa/Corbis; 326: Justine Hunt/The Boston Globe/Redux, Republished with permission of Globe Newspaper

Company, Inc., from the May 31, 2006 issue of The Boston Globe, © 2006; 334: © Kim Eriksen/zefa/Corbis; © Bettmann/CORBIS All Rights Reserved; 345: © Michael Newman/PhotoEdit; 347: © Michael Newman/PhotoEdit; 352: © Royalty-Free/Corbis; 362: © Mike Abrahams/Alamy; 366: © Simon Marcus/CORBIS All Rights Reserved; 370: © Alan Gignoux/Alamy; 376: Courtesy of Karen Seccombe; 388: © Royalty-Free/Corbis; 390: © Michael Newman/PhotoEdit; 392: © Larry Hirshowitz/CORBIS All Rights Reserved; 400: Copyright 2006 U.S. News & World Report, L.P. Reprinted with permission. Photo courtesy of Timothy Archibald; 404: © Royalty-Free/Corbis; 408: © Kris Van Exel/CORBIS All Rights Reserved; 414: © Roy Morsch/CORBIS All Rights Reserved; 415: © Rachel Epstein/PhotoEdit; 425: © Patrick Olear/PhotoEdit; 430: © Katy Winn/CORBIS All Rights Reserved; 436: © Creasource/CORBIS All Rights Reserved; 441: AP Photo/Hasan Sarbakhshian; 451: © David Young-Wolff/PhotoEdit; 453: Getty Images, Inc.; 461: Getty Images, Inc.; 465: © Kayte M. Deioma/PhotoEdit; 472: © Mark Richards/PhotoEdit; 479: © Louise Gubb/CORBIS SABA; 485: Courtesy of Karen Seccombe; 487: © Janine Wiedel Photolibrary/Alamy; 492: © Robert Brenner/PhotoEdit; 493: © Royalty-Free/Corbis